Mark Hennings

Cambridge Pre-U
Mathematics
Coursebook

CAMBRIDGE
UNIVERSITY PRESS

University Printing House, Cambridge CB2 8BS, United Kingdom

One Liberty Plaza, 20th Floor, New York, NY 10006, USA

477 Williamstown Road, Port Melbourne, VIC 3207, Australia

4843/24, 2nd Floor, Ansari Road, Daryaganj, Delhi - 110002, India

79 Anson Road, #06-04/06, Singapore 079906

Cambridge University Press is part of the University of Cambridge.

It furthers the University's mission by disseminating knowledge in the pursuit of education, learning and research at the highest international levels of excellence.

www.cambridge.org
Information on this title: www.cambridge.org/9781316635759 (Paperback)

First published 2017

20 19 18 17 16 15 14 13 12 11 10 9 8 7 6 5 4 3

Printed in Great Britain by CPI Group (UK) Ltd, Croydon CR0 4YY

A catalogue record for this publication is available from the British Library

Cambridge University Press has no responsibility for the persistence or accuracy of URLs for external or third-party internet websites referred to in this publication, and does not guarantee that any content on such websites is, or will remain, accurate or appropriate. Information regarding prices, travel timetables, and other factual information given in this work is correct at the time of first printing but Cambridge University Press does not guarantee the accuracy of such information thereafter.

Past paper questions reproduced with kind permission from Cambridge International Examinations. The past paper questions are taken from exam papers prior to 2002, therefore specific citation for each question is not possible.

STEP questions taken from the specimen papers available on the Cambridge Assessment website (www.admissionstestingservice.org). Reprinted by permission of the University of Cambridge Local Examinations Syndicate.

....

To Susie, as always.

Contents

Introduction

This book has been designed to be a self-contained text which covers all the material, both Pure and Applied, required for the Cambridge Pre-U course in Mathematics (Principal) 9794. It includes the most recent adjustments to the specification, introduced for examination from 2016. Hitherto, no single text has fully covered all the required material in the desired manner.

This book has been prepared in four Parts, covering (in order) the Pure Mathematics, Mechanics and Probability aspects of the course, followed by Problem-solving. One of the important facets of a linear course, such as the Pre-U, is the interconnectivity of the material. This does lead to a design problem for a textbook, since there is no clear order in which the material must be presented; increasingly, different topics in the course rely on each other. The order of presentation of the Pure Mathematics material largely follows the order used in the Mathematics Department at Rugby School and develops the material progressively. The final three chapters in that Part, on Vectors, Complex Numbers and Numerical Methods are (to a larger extent) free-standing, and can be taught earlier in the course than their position in the Part might suggest, particularly the chapter on Numerical Methods. The Part on Mechanics does depend on the student having an understanding of vectors and a degree of sophistication with calculus, and so probably shouldn't be presented at the start of the course. The Part on Probability is self-contained to a large degree, and can be presented early on in a course of study, with the possible exception of the chapter on Permutations and Combinations. Experience shows that, while there are few facts in this topic, their application to problem-solving asks for a degree of sophistication from the student that is more likely to be found during the second half of the course.

At various stages in the book, attention is drawn to facts and information that are either crucial to an understanding of the topic, or else merely interesting, or in the nature of extension material. The different types of information is presented in boxes:

- **Key Facts** The information in these boxes is crucial, and students would be well-advised to learn them!

Key Fact 3.1 The Gauss Sum

The formula for the sum of the first n integers is

$$1 + 2 + 3 + \cdots + n = \sum_{r=1}^{n} r = \tfrac{1}{2}n(n+1)$$

- **Food for Thought** While not essential to the course, information provided in these boxes is related to the material at hand, and should be informative to the interested reader.

- **For Interest** The information in these boxes is provided as a matter of interest, and is not essential to an understanding of the course. The enthusiastic reader should find these boxes interesting, but they can be omitted if desired.

Finally, any section which is particularly difficult, or slightly beyond the syllabus, is indicated by a bar in the margin, as shown here. I make no apologies for adding extra and demanding material to this book. The aim of the Pre-U is to encourage mathematical thought and problem-solving, and the aim of these extra entries is to show the interested student 'what happens next'.

Problem-solving is a particular feature of the Pre-U — the 'D1 tie-breaker' questions currently at the end of each paper require a degree of mental flexibility. The fourth Part, and last chapter, of this book contains a number of problems, and discusses a variety of solution techniques for each. It is important that the student develops an awareness of the possibility of there being more than one solution to a problem, so that they have the ability to handle an unusual question which might require a different technique to solve than the more standard questions.

Exercises are given at all stages of the book, and each set of questions provides a range of difficulty to train all students and to challenge the more able. For summary purposes, Revision Exercise sections are included every three chapters, again summarising the techniques learnt in each set of three chapters at a variety of levels. At all stages, harder questions are marked with an asterisk ★. Answers to all questions (where an answer is appropriate) are provided in the Appendix.

The Cambridge Sixth Term Examination Paper, being used as it is for admission to Mathematics courses at a number of Universities — Cambridge in particular — provides an excellent set of problems which stretch the student beyond the usual level of difficulty required by Pre-U questions. A number of STEP questions are included in each set of Revision Exercises, roughly one question per chapter of the book. To help (and encourage!) the student, full solutions to these STEP questions are given in Chapter A2 in the Appendix.

The List of Formulae MF20 is the official list of formulae for both the Pre-U Mathematics and Further Mathematics courses. Since it covers both courses, it necessarily contains much information that is not needed for the Single Mathematics qualification, which is the target of this book. The final Appendix of this book contains a cut-down version of List MF20, and contains only those formulae which are relevant to the Single Mathematics Pre-U. The fact that this cut-down list is half the size of the full list reinforces the need for students to be familiar with these formulae; finding the correct formula amongst a list containing twice as many results as needed is a challenge made unnecessary if these formulae have already been learned!

Mark Hennings,
Rugby School,
June 2016.

Part 1

Pure Mathematics

Surds and Indices

In this chapter we will learn:

- how to manipulate expressions involving surds,

- how to manipulate expressions involving indices.

1.1 Types of Number

Modern Mathematics is built on the back of thousands of years of mathematical thought. Over the centuries, mathematicians saw the need for ever more complicated ideas of number. It is still important nowadays to be aware of the hierarchy of number types, since different mathematical ideas and argumchents can be applied at different levels. We start by setting out the fundamental different types of number that we will encounter:

- The most fundamental numbers are those used for counting: the positive whole numbers $1, 2, 3, 4, \ldots$ These are called the **natural numbers**. The set of all natural numbers is denoted by the special symbol $\mathbb{N}$, so that

$$\mathbb{N} = \left\{ 1, 2, 3, 4, \ldots \right\}$$

- The natural numbers are sufficient to count (sheep, coins, etc.), and can be used to add, but they are insufficient if we want to be able to subtract (as Alice told the Red Queen, 'nine from eight I can't, you know'). To be able to do subtraction neatly, the number zero and negative whole numbers were introduced, giving us the integers: $\ldots, -3, -1, 0, 1, 2, 3, \ldots$. The set of all the integers is denoted by the special symbol $\mathbb{Z}$ ('Z' for *Zahl*, the German for 'number'), so that

$$\mathbb{Z} = \left\{ \ldots, -4, -3, -2, -1, 0, 1, 2, 3, 4, \ldots \right\}$$

The integers are a very important set of numbers. As well as being able to add and subtract integers, multiplication is possible, as is factorisation into primes. Studying the properties of the integers has generated some of the richest areas of modern mathematics.

- The **rational** numbers are those which can be expressed as fractions of integers in the form $\frac{p}{q}$, where p and q are integers, and $q \neq 0$. The set of rational numbers is denoted by the special symbol $\mathbb{Q}$ ('Q' for *quotient*), so that

$$\mathbb{Q} = \left\{ \frac{p}{q} \,\middle|\, p, q \in \mathbb{Z}, q \neq 0 \right\}$$

> **For Interest**
>
> We are using a standard notation to describe sets here. A set can be written in the form
>
> $$\{x \,|\, A\}$$
>
> where x is an expression for a number in the set, and A is a condition, or set of conditions, that specify the types of number that are permitted. The vertical bar | (sometimes a colon is used) should be read as 'such that'. Thus the formula for $\mathbb{Q}$ given above can be read as 'the set of numbers $\frac{p}{q}$ such that p and q are integers where q is non-zero'.

- Not all numbers are rational, however. Important numbers, like $\sqrt{2}$ and π, cannot be written as fractions. Numbers that cannot be expressed as fractions are called **irrational** numbers, and the irrational and rational numbers together form the **real** numbers. The collection of all real numbers is denoted by $\mathbb{R}$. Actually what is meant by a number here is quite a difficult question: integers and rationals have a fairly concrete existence which is founded in our experience, but irrational numbers are more elusive. The Pythagorean schools of mathematics in Ancient Greece thought that all numbers should be fractions, and that numbers which were not fractions were irrational in both senses of the word! We will have to be content with thinking that numbers are quantities that can have a place found for them along a number line.

- Eventually, we will want to move off the number line and study numbers that do things that real numbers cannot. In particular, we will want to introduce the square root of -1, denoted i. Numbers of the form $a + ib$, where a, b are real, are called **complex** numbers, and the set of all complex numbers is denoted $\mathbb{C}$.

It is worth observing that:
$$\mathbb{N} \subseteq \mathbb{Z} \subseteq \mathbb{Q} \subseteq \mathbb{R} \subseteq \mathbb{C}.$$

Each of our special sets contains all the preceding special sets as a subset. A Venn diagram for these sets would be five concentric circles!

When we cannot express a number as a fraction, we try to express it in decimals. Rational numbers either have decimal expansions which terminate

$$\frac{7}{10} = 0.7 \qquad \frac{3}{16} = 0.1875 \qquad \frac{11}{20} = 0.55$$

or they have recurring decimal expansions, i.e. ones which eventually start repeating in a regular pattern:

$$\frac{3}{11} = 0.\dot{2}\dot{7} = 0.27272727\ldots \qquad \frac{8}{15} = 0.5\dot{3} = 0.533333\ldots$$

$$\frac{7}{17} = 0.\dot{4}117647058823529\dot{9} = 0.411764705882352941176\ldots$$

The converse is true: any terminating or recurring decimal describes a rational number. It is therefore easy to write down irrational numbers, by constructing decimals which definitely do not recur:

$$0.101001000100001000001000000100\ldots$$

but it is more interesting to be able to find out whether particular numbers are irrational or not.

Example 1.1.1. *Show that* $\sqrt{2}$ *i.e. the square root of 2 is irrational.*

Suppose that $\sqrt{2}$ was rational. Then we could write $\sqrt{2} = \frac{a}{b}$ as a fraction. We can assume that the fraction is in its lowest terms, so that the positive integers a, b have no common factor. Squaring the formula for $\sqrt{2}$ and multiplying by b^2 gives

$$a^2 = 2b^2,$$

and hence a^2 is an even integer. But this can only happen when a is even. Thus $a = 2c$ for some integer c. But then $2b^2 = (2c)^2 = 4c^2$, and hence

$$b^2 = 2c^2.$$

But this implies that b^2 is even, and so b is even.

We have come to the conclusion that a and b, which have no common factor, are both even, and hence both divisible by 2. The only way out of this impasse is to deduce that our original idea, that $\sqrt{2}$ was rational, is not true. Thus we deduce that $\sqrt{2}$ is irrational.

This is an example of an important method of argument: *Proof by Contradiction*. If assuming a fact leads to nonsense, we may deduce that our original assumption was incorrect.

EXERCISE 1A

1. It is easy to 'place' a fraction on the number line. For example, $4\frac{2}{3}$ is two-thirds of the way from 4 to 5. How can we be sure about where to place $\sqrt{2}$? Can we be sure it exists? Were the ancient Greeks right to be worried?

2. Do there exist real numbers which possess two or more different decimal expansions? If so, which?

3. Express $0.1\dot{2}\dot{3}$ and $0.2\dot{2}\dot{7}$ as fractions.

4. If a real number x has a recurring decimal expansion which comprises a sequence of n repeated digits (so that $n = 3$ for $x = 0.1\dot{2}8\dot{5}$), show that $(10^n - 1)x$ has a terminating decimal expansion, and hence that x is rational.

5*. How many remainders are possible when dividing an integer by 17? Show that any fraction with denominator equal to 17 has a recurring decimal expansion. Extend the argument to deal with all rational numbers.

1.2 Surds

Square roots, or surds, were the first examples of irrational numbers to be identified.

For Interest

Irrational numbers were considered *(ab)surd*.

It is important to work with surds without using a calculator. Except to a limited extent (the most common calculators can work with surds $\sqrt{n}$, provided that the integer n is not too big), calculators can only handle the decimal expansion of a surd, and then only to 9 or so decimal places. Using a calculator inevitably means, therefore, that answers obtained will be inexact. They may be very accurate, but they will not be perfect. It is important to be able to work without reference to a calculator when possible. The main properties of surds are these:

Key Fact 1.1 Properties of Surds

- For any $x \geq 0$, the number $\sqrt{x}$ is the **non-negative (positive or zero)** square root of x.

- $\sqrt{xy} = \sqrt{x} \times \sqrt{y}$ for any $x, y \geq 0$.

- $\sqrt{\frac{x}{y}} = \frac{\sqrt{x}}{\sqrt{y}}$ for any $x \geq 0, y > 0$.

The result for $\sqrt{xy}$ and $\sqrt{\frac{x}{y}}$ can be seen, because

$$\left(\sqrt{x}\times\sqrt{y}\right)\times\left(\sqrt{x}\times\sqrt{y}\right) = \left(\sqrt{x}\times\sqrt{x}\right)\times\left(\sqrt{y}\times\sqrt{y}\right) = x\times y = xy$$

and so $\sqrt{xy} = \sqrt{x}\times\sqrt{y}$. Moreover, since $\frac{x}{y}\times y = x$, we have

$$\sqrt{\frac{x}{y}}\times\sqrt{y} = \sqrt{x}$$

and hence $\sqrt{\frac{x}{y}} = \frac{\sqrt{x}}{\sqrt{y}}$.

These results can be used in a variety of ways to establish exact identities between surds.

Example 1.2.1. *Simplify the following expressions:*

a) $\sqrt{8}$, b) $\sqrt{75}$, c) $\sqrt{18}\times\sqrt{2}$, d) $\frac{\sqrt{27}}{\sqrt{3}}$,

e) $\sqrt{40}\times\sqrt{2}$, f) $\sqrt{28}+\sqrt{63}$, g) $\sqrt{5}\times\sqrt{10}$, h) $3\sqrt{2}\times4\sqrt{7}$.

(a) $\sqrt{8} = \sqrt{4\times2} = \sqrt{4}\times\sqrt{2} = 2\sqrt{2}$,

(b) $\sqrt{75} = \sqrt{25\times3} = \sqrt{25}\times\sqrt{3} = 5\sqrt{3}$,

(c) $\sqrt{18}\times\sqrt{2} = \sqrt{18\times2} = \sqrt{36} = 6$,

(d) $\frac{\sqrt{27}}{\sqrt{3}} = \sqrt{\frac{27}{3}} = \sqrt{9} = 3$,

(e) $\sqrt{40}\times\sqrt{2} = \sqrt{40\times2} = \sqrt{16\times5} = \sqrt{16}\times\sqrt{5} = 4\sqrt{5}$,

(f) $\sqrt{28}+\sqrt{63} = \sqrt{4}\times\sqrt{7}+\sqrt{9}\times\sqrt{7} = 2\sqrt{7}+3\sqrt{7} = 5\sqrt{7}$,

(g) $\sqrt{5}\times\sqrt{10} = \sqrt{5}\times\left(\sqrt{5}\times\sqrt{2}\right) = \left(\sqrt{5}\times\sqrt{5}\right)\times\sqrt{2} = 5\sqrt{2}$,

(h) $3\sqrt{2}\times4\sqrt{7} = 12\sqrt{2\times7} = 12\sqrt{14}$.

Surds can also be used to handle algebraic problems:

Example 1.2.2. *Simplify the following expressions:*

(a) $\sqrt{x^5y^2}$, (b) $\sqrt{x^3yz^2}\times\sqrt{xy^2}$, (c) $\frac{\sqrt{p^5q}}{\sqrt{p^2q^3}}$

(a) $\sqrt{x^5y^2} = \sqrt{x^4y^2\times x} = x^2y\sqrt{x}$.

(b) $\sqrt{x^3yz^2}\times\sqrt{xy^2} = \sqrt{x^3yz^2\times xy^2} = \sqrt{x^4y^3z^2} = x^2yz\sqrt{y}$.

(c) $\frac{\sqrt{p^5q}}{\sqrt{p^2q^3}} = \sqrt{\frac{p^5q}{p^2q^3}} = \sqrt{\frac{p^3}{q^2}} = \frac{\sqrt{p^3}}{\sqrt{q^2}} = \frac{p\sqrt{p}}{q}$.

Example 1.2.3. *Solve the simultaneous equations*

$$y = \sqrt{x} \qquad y^3 = 2x$$

We see that

$$2x = y^3 = \sqrt{x}\times\sqrt{x}\times\sqrt{x} = x\sqrt{x}$$
$$x\sqrt{x}-2x = 0$$
$$x(\sqrt{x}-2) = 0$$

and hence either $x = 0$ or $\sqrt{x} = 2$, so either $x = 0$ or $x = 4$.

Similar rules can be applied to cube and higher roots.

Example 1.2.4. *Simplify the following expressions:*
(a) $\sqrt[3]{16}$,   (b) $\sqrt[3]{12} \times \sqrt[3]{18}$,   (c) $\sqrt[5]{1215}$.

(a) $\sqrt[3]{16} = \sqrt[3]{8 \times 2} = \sqrt[3]{8} \times \sqrt[3]{2} = 2\sqrt[3]{2}$,

(b) $\sqrt[3]{12} \times \sqrt[3]{18} = \sqrt[3]{12 \times 18} = \sqrt[3]{216} = 6$,

(c) $\sqrt[5]{1215} = \sqrt[5]{243 \times 5} = \sqrt[5]{243} \times \sqrt[5]{5} = 3\sqrt[5]{5}$.

We frequently want to remove a surd from the denominator of a fraction. This is done either by cancelling the same surd in the numerator, or else by 'multiplying top and bottom' by a suitable expression. This process is called **rationalising the denominator**.

Key Fact 1.2 Rationalising the Denominator

- For any $x > 0$,

$$\frac{1}{\sqrt{x}} = \frac{1}{\sqrt{x}} \times \frac{\sqrt{x}}{\sqrt{x}} = \frac{\sqrt{x}}{x}$$

and so

$$\frac{x}{\sqrt{x}} = \sqrt{x}$$

- For any $y \geq 0$,

$$\frac{1}{x+\sqrt{y}} = \frac{1}{x+\sqrt{y}} \times \frac{x-\sqrt{y}}{x-\sqrt{y}} = \frac{x-\sqrt{y}}{x^2-y}$$

Note the use of the 'Difference of Two Squares' technique to rationalise the denominator when the denominator was $x + \sqrt{y}$. Multiplying by $\frac{x-\sqrt{y}}{x-\sqrt{y}}$ does not change the value of the expression, because this fraction is equal to 1.

Example 1.2.5. *Write in simplified surd form:*
(a) $\frac{1}{\sqrt{2}}$,   (b) $\frac{6}{\sqrt{2}}$,   (c) $\frac{3\sqrt{2}}{\sqrt{10}}$,   (d) $\frac{1}{3-\sqrt{2}}$

(a) $\frac{1}{\sqrt{2}} = \frac{1}{\sqrt{2}} \times \frac{\sqrt{2}}{\sqrt{2}} = \frac{\sqrt{2}}{2}$,

(b) $\frac{6}{\sqrt{2}} = \frac{3 \times 2}{\sqrt{2}} = 3\sqrt{2}$,

(c) $\frac{3\sqrt{2}}{\sqrt{10}} = \frac{3\sqrt{2}}{\sqrt{5} \times \sqrt{2}} = \frac{3}{\sqrt{5}} = \frac{3\sqrt{5}}{5}$,

(d) $\frac{1}{3-\sqrt{2}} = \frac{1}{3-\sqrt{2}} \times \frac{3+\sqrt{2}}{3+\sqrt{2}} = \frac{3+\sqrt{2}}{7}$

Using the 'Difference of Two Squares' method to rationalise the denominator, as shown in Example 1.2.5, is a surprisingly useful technique.

Example 1.2.6. *Find a positive integer n such that $\sqrt{n+1} - \sqrt{n} < 10^{-3}$.*

Note that
$$0 < \sqrt{n+1} - \sqrt{n} = \left(\sqrt{n+1} - \sqrt{n}\right) \times \frac{\sqrt{n+1}+\sqrt{n}}{\sqrt{n+1}+\sqrt{n}} = \frac{1}{\sqrt{n+1}+\sqrt{n}}.$$

Now $n + 1 > n$, and so $\sqrt{n+1} > \sqrt{n}$, and hence $\sqrt{n+1} + \sqrt{n} > 2\sqrt{n}$. This tells us that

$$0 < \sqrt{n+1} - \sqrt{n} < \frac{1}{2\sqrt{n}},$$

and we see that $\sqrt{n+1} - \sqrt{n} < 10^{-3}$ will be true if $2\sqrt{n} \geq 1000$, and so if $n \geq 500^2 (= 250000)$.

EXERCISE 1B

1. Simplify the following:

    a) $\sqrt{3} \times \sqrt{3}$ b) $\sqrt{8} \times \sqrt{2}$ c) $\sqrt{3} \times \sqrt{12}$ d) $2\sqrt{5} \times 3\sqrt{5}$

    e) $\left(2\sqrt{7}\right)^2$ f) $\sqrt[3]{x} \times \sqrt[3]{x^2 y}$ g) $\sqrt[4]{125} \times \sqrt[4]{5}$ h) $\left(2\sqrt[4]{x}\right)^4$

2. Simplify the following (assuming that $x, y > 0$):

    a) $\sqrt{18}$ b) $\sqrt{45}$ c) $\sqrt{675}$ d) $\sqrt{x^3 y^5}$

    e) $\sqrt{2000}$ f) $\sqrt[3]{250}$ g) $\sqrt[4]{32x^4 y^4}$ h) $\sqrt{x^3 + 2x^2 y + xy^2}$.

3. Simplify the following (assuming that $x, y > 0$):

    a) $\sqrt{8} + \sqrt{18}$ b) $\sqrt{20} - \sqrt{5}$ c) $2\sqrt{20} + 3\sqrt{45}$

    d) $\sqrt{x^3} + \sqrt{xy^2}$ e) $\sqrt{99} + \sqrt{44} - \sqrt{11}$ f) $\sqrt{52} - \sqrt{13}$

    g) $\sqrt{4x^2 + 4xy + y^2} - \sqrt{x^2 + 2xy + y^2}$

4. Simplify the following:

    a) $\frac{\sqrt{8}}{\sqrt{2}}$ b) $\frac{\sqrt{40}}{\sqrt{20}}$ c) $\frac{\sqrt{3}}{\sqrt{48}}$ d) $\frac{\sqrt{50}}{\sqrt{200}}$

    e) $\frac{1}{\sqrt{5}}$ f) $\frac{3\sqrt{5}}{\sqrt{3}}$ g) $\frac{4\sqrt{2}}{\sqrt{12}}$ h) $\frac{2\sqrt{18}}{9\sqrt{12}}$

    i) $\frac{1}{2 - \sqrt{3}}$ j) $\frac{1}{3\sqrt{5} - 5}$ k) $\frac{4\sqrt{3}}{2\sqrt{6} + 3\sqrt{2}}$ l) $\frac{12}{\sqrt{2} + \sqrt{3} + \sqrt{5}}$

5. You are given that, correct to 12 decimal places, $\sqrt{26} = 5.099019513593$. Find the value of $\sqrt{650}$ correct to 10 decimal places.

6. Solve the simultaneous equations:

$$7x - (3\sqrt{5})y = 9\sqrt{5} \qquad (2\sqrt{5})x + y = 34$$

7. Assuming that $x > 0$, show that $\frac{\sqrt{x}}{\sqrt{x^2 + x} + x} = \sqrt{x+1} - x\sqrt{x}$.

8*. Assuming that $x > 1$, evaluate

$$\frac{1}{\sqrt{x + \sqrt{x^2 - x}}} - \sqrt{1 - \sqrt{1 - x^{-1}}}$$

9*. Put the following numbers in ascending order: $7 - 4\sqrt{3}, 8 - 3\sqrt{7}, 9 - 4\sqrt{5}, 10 - 3\sqrt{11}$.

1.3 Indices

When mathematicians started solving quadratic, cubic and quartic equations, they wrote expressions like xx, xxx and $xxxx$ to denote the repeated product of a variable x with itself (just as abc is the product of a, b and c). It was found to be more economical to use the notations x^2, x^3 and x^4 instead, and so index notation was invented. However, index notation is not just a method of writing expressions conveniently; it introduces a new method of thought about number and algebra without which much of modern mathematics would be impossible.

1.3.1. POSITIVE INDICES

In general the symbol a^m stands for the result of multiplying m copies of a together:

$$a^m = \underbrace{a \times a \times \cdots \times a}_{m \text{ copies}}$$

This operation is described in words as 'a raised to the mth power', or 'a to the power m' or even just 'a to the m'. The number a is called the **base**, and the number m the **index**. For the present, while a can be any number, m must be a positive integer. We shall extend consideration to negative indices below.

Expressions in index notation can be simplified, subject to a few simple rules:

> **Key Fact 1.3** Rules for Positive Indices
>
> - $a^m \times a^n = a^{m+n}$,
> - $a^m \div a^n = a^{m-n}$, if $m > n$,
> - $(a^m)^n = a^{mn}$,
> - $(ab)^m = a^m b^m$.

- $a^m \times a^n = \underbrace{a \times a \times \cdots \times a}_{m \text{ copies}} \times \underbrace{a \times a \times \cdots \times a}_{n \text{ copies}} = \underbrace{a \times a \times \cdots \times a}_{m+n \text{ copies}} = a^{m+n}$

- $a^m \div a^n = \underbrace{a \times a \times \cdots \times a}_{m \text{ copies}} \div \underbrace{a \times a \times \cdots \times a}_{n \text{ copies}} = \underbrace{a \times a \times \cdots \times a}_{m-n \text{ copies}} = a^{m-n}$

- $(a^m)^n = \underbrace{\underbrace{a \times a \times \cdots \times a}_{m \text{ copies}} \times \cdots \times \underbrace{a \times a \times \cdots \times a}_{m \text{ copies}}}_{n \text{ brackets}} = \underbrace{a \times a \times \cdots \times a}_{mn \text{ copies}} = a^{mn}$

- $(ab)^m = \underbrace{ab \times ab \times \cdots \times ab}_{m \text{ copies}} = \underbrace{a \times a \times \cdots \times a}_{m \text{ copies}} \times \underbrace{b \times b \times \cdots \times b}_{m \text{ copies}} = a^m \times b^m$

It is important to remember that, until we meet logarithms, the last of these rules is the only rule that can be applied to powers of different bases.

Example 1.3.1. *Simplify* $(2a^2b)^3 \div 4a^4b$.

Applying the rules,

$$(2a^2b)^3 \div 4a^4b = 2^3(a^2)^3 b^3 \div 4a^4b = 8a^6b^3 \div 4a^4b = 2a^2b^2$$

> **For Interest**
>
> A common error is to write $2^3 \times 3^5 = 6^8$, multiplying the bases as well as adding the indices. Avoid it!

1.3.2. Zero and Negative Indices

The previous definition for a^m makes no sense if m is not a positive integer. Nevertheless it is possible to extend the definition of a^m to allow m to be any integer (provided that a is non-zero). If we look at the following table:

n	5	4	3	2	1
2^n	32	16	8	4	2
3^n	243	81	27	9	3

Every time the index n decreases by 1, the value of 2^n halves, and the value of 3^n is a third of its previous value. It is natural to extend the process

n	5	4	3	2	1	0	-1	-2	-3
2^n	32	16	8	4	2	1	$\frac{1}{2}$	$\frac{1}{4}$	$\frac{1}{8}$
3^n	243	81	27	9	3	1	$\frac{1}{3}$	$\frac{1}{9}$	$\frac{1}{27}$

It seems that 2^0 and 3^0 should both be defined to be 1, while 2^{-m} should be the same as $\frac{1}{2^m}$, and 3^{-m} should be the same as $\frac{1}{3^m}$. This observation can be extended to any non-zero base a, and the resulting extension enables the previous rules for positive integer indices to be extended to general integer indices (and non-zero base).

Key Fact 1.4 Rules for Integer Indices

- $a^m \times a^n = a^{m+n}$,
- $a^m \div a^n = a^{m-n}$,
- $(a^m)^n = a^{mn}$,

- $(ab)^m = a^m b^m$,
- $a^0 = 1$,
- $a^{-m} = \frac{1}{a^m}$

To show that the rules for positive integer indices can be extended (for non-zero base) to all integer indices, we need to check a number of cases. Here are two of them (m and n are positive integers):

$$a^m \times a^{-n} = a^m \times \frac{1}{a^n} = \frac{1}{a^n \div a^m} = \frac{1}{a^{n-m}} = a^{m-n} \qquad (m < n),$$

$$(a^m)^{-n} = \frac{1}{(a^m)^n} = \frac{1}{a^{mn}} = a^{-mn}.$$

Example 1.3.2. *Simplify the following:*
(a) $4a^2b \times (3ab^{-1})^{-2}$, (b) $4^3 \times 2^{-5}$, (c) $(2xy^2z^3)^2 \div (2x^2y^3z)$

(a) $4a^2b \times (3ab^{-1})^{-2} = 4a^2b \times 3^{-2}a^{-2}b^2 = \frac{4}{9}b^3$,

(b) $4^3 \times 2^{-5} = (2^2)^3 \times 2^{-5} = 2^6 \times 2^{-5} = 2^1 = 2$,

(c) $(2xy^2z^3)^2 \div (2x^2y^3z) = 4x^2y^4z^6 \div 2x^2y^3z = 2yz^5$.

EXERCISE 1C

1. Simplify the following, writing each answer as a power of 2:
   a) $2^{11} \times (2^5)^3$
   b) $(2^3)^2 \times (2^2)^3$
   c) 4^3
   d) 8^2
   e) $\frac{2^7 \times 2^8}{2^{13}}$
   f) $\frac{2^2 \times 2^3}{(2^2)^2}$
   g) $4^2 \div 2^4$
   h) $2 \times 4^4 \div 8^3$

2. Simplify the following:
   a) $a^2 \times a^3 \times a^7$
   b) $c^7 \div c^3$
   c) $(e^5)^4$
   d) $5g^5 \times 3g^3$
   e) $(2a^2)^3 \times (3a)^2$
   f) $(4x^2y)^2 \times (2xy^3)^3$
   g) $(6ac^3)^2 \div (9a^2c^5)$
   h) $(49r^3s^2)^2 \div (7rs)^3$
   i) $(3h^2)^{-2}$
   j) $(\frac{1}{2}j^{-2})^{-3}$
   k) $(3n^{-2})^4 \times (9n)^{-1}$
   l) $(2q^{-2})^{-2} \div (\frac{4}{q})^2$

3. Solve the following equations:
   a) $3^x = \frac{1}{9}$
   b) $5^y = 1$
   c) $2^z \times 2^{z-3} = 32$
   d) $7^{3x} \div 7^{x-2} = \frac{1}{49}$
   e) $4^y \times 2^y = 8^{120}$
   f) $3^t \times 9^{t+3} = 27^2$

4. Write $8^3 \times 4$ as a power of 2.

5. Simplify $\left(\frac{1}{\sqrt{3}}\right)^9$.

6. Solve the equation $\frac{3^{5x+2}}{9^{1-x}} = \frac{27^{4+3x}}{729}$.

7. Why do we not need brackets when considering powers of powers: in other words, why is a^{m^n} equal to $a^{(m^n)}$, and not to $(a^m)^n$?

8*. Which of 3^{4^3} and 4^{3^3} is bigger?

1.3.3. FRACTIONAL INDICES

Up to now, we have assumed that the rules for indices work for integer indices. What can we deduce if we were to assume that the rules were still true for fractional indices? It would follow that

$$(a^{\frac{1}{2}})^2 = a^{\frac{1}{2} \times 2} = a^1 = a$$

for any positive a. Since $a^{\frac{1}{2}}$ squares to a, we deduce that $a^{\frac{1}{2}}$ is either $\sqrt{a}$ or $-\sqrt{a}$. Just as with surds, we **define** $a^{\frac{1}{2}}$ to be positive, so that $a^{\frac{1}{2}} = \sqrt{a}$. More generally we can show that $(a^{\frac{1}{m}})^m = a$, so that $a^{\frac{1}{m}} = \sqrt[m]{a}$ for any positive integer m and $a > 0$ (while it is possible to take m^{th} roots of negative numbers when m is odd, it is simpler to restrict fractional indices to strictly positive bases). Thus we can define the fractional power of any positive real number.

Key Fact 1.5 Rules for Fractional Indices

- $a^{\frac{1}{m}} = \sqrt[m]{a},$

- $a^{\frac{m}{n}} = (\sqrt[n]{a})^m = \sqrt[n]{a^m}.$

With these definitions, it should be noted that the rules for integer indices now hold for all fractional indices (and positive bases).

Example 1.3.3. *Simplify the following:*

(a) $16^{-\frac{3}{4}}$,   (b) $(2\frac{1}{4})^{\frac{1}{2}}$,   (c) $\dfrac{(2x^2y^2)^{-\frac{1}{2}}}{(2xy^{-2})^{\frac{3}{2}}}$

(a) $16^{-\frac{3}{4}} = (2^4)^{-\frac{3}{4}} = 2^{-3} = \frac{1}{8}$,

(b) $(2\frac{1}{4})^{\frac{1}{2}} = (\frac{9}{4})^{\frac{1}{2}} = \frac{3}{2}$,

(c) $\dfrac{(2x^2y^2)^{-\frac{1}{2}}}{(2xy^{-2})^{\frac{3}{2}}} = \dfrac{2^{-\frac{1}{2}}x^{-1}y^{-1}}{2^{\frac{3}{2}}x^{\frac{3}{2}}y^{-3}} = 2^{-2}x^{-\frac{5}{2}}y^2 = \dfrac{y^2}{4x^{\frac{5}{2}}}$

EXERCISE 1D

1. Evaluate the following:

   a) $25^{\frac{1}{2}}$ b) $36^{\frac{1}{2}}$ c) $81^{\frac{1}{4}}$ d) $16^{-\frac{1}{4}}$

   e) $1000^{-\frac{1}{3}}$ f) $27^{\frac{1}{3}}$ g) $64^{\frac{2}{3}}$ h) $125^{-\frac{4}{3}}$

   i) $4^{\frac{3}{2}}$ j) $27^{\frac{4}{3}}$ k) $32^{\frac{3}{5}}$ l) $4^{2\frac{1}{2}}$

   m) $10000^{-\frac{3}{4}}$ n) $(\frac{1}{125})^{-\frac{4}{3}}$ o) $(3\frac{3}{8})^{\frac{2}{3}}$ p) $(2.25)^{-\frac{1}{2}}$

2. Simplify the following expressions:

   a) $a^{\frac{1}{3}} \times a^{\frac{5}{3}}$ b) $3b^{\frac{1}{2}} \times 4b^{-\frac{3}{2}}$ c) $6c^{\frac{1}{4}} \times (4c)^{\frac{1}{2}}$

   d) $(d^2)^{\frac{1}{3}} \div (d^{\frac{1}{3}})^2$ e) $(2x^{\frac{1}{2}})^6 \times (\frac{1}{2}x^{\frac{3}{4}})^4$ f) $(24e)^{\frac{1}{3}} \div (3e)^{\frac{1}{3}}$

   g) $\dfrac{(5p^2q^4)^{\frac{1}{3}}}{(25pq^2)^{-\frac{1}{3}}}$ h) $(m^3n)^{\frac{1}{4}} \times (8mn^3)^{\frac{1}{3}}$ i) $\dfrac{(2x^2y^{-1})^{-\frac{1}{4}}}{(8x^{-1}y^2)^{-\frac{1}{2}}}$

3. Solve the following equations:

   a) $x^{\frac{1}{2}} = 8$ b) $x^{\frac{1}{3}} = 3$ c) $x^{\frac{2}{3}} = 4$

   d) $x^{\frac{3}{2}} = 27$ e) $x^{-\frac{3}{2}} = 8$ f) $x^{-\frac{2}{3}} = 9$

   g) $x^{\frac{3}{2}} = x\sqrt{2}$ h) $x^{\frac{3}{2}} = 2\sqrt{x}$ i) $4^x = 32$

   j) $9^y = \frac{1}{27}$ k) $16^z = 2$ l) $100^x = 1000$

   m) $8^z = \frac{1}{128}$ n) $(2^t)^3 \times 4^{t-1} = 16$ o) $\dfrac{9^y}{27^{2y+1}} = 81$

4*. Which is bigger, $2^{\frac{1}{2}}$ or $3^{\frac{1}{3}}$?

Chapter 1: Summary

- If $x \geq 0$, the square root of x, denoted $\sqrt{x}$, is the non-negative square root of x. Another word for a number which is the square root of another number is surd.

- For $x, y \geq 0$, $\sqrt{xy} = \sqrt{x}\sqrt{y}$.

- In fractions involving surds, the denominator may be rationalised as follows:

$$\frac{1}{\sqrt{x}} = \frac{1}{x}\sqrt{x} \qquad\qquad \frac{1}{x + \sqrt{y}} = \frac{x - \sqrt{y}}{x^2 - y}$$

- The laws of indices state that

$$a^m \times a^n = a^{m+n} \qquad\qquad (a^m)^n = a^{mn}$$
$$a^m \div a^n = a^{m-n} \qquad\qquad (ab)^m = a^m b^m$$
$$a^0 = 1 \qquad\qquad a^{-n} = \frac{1}{a^n}$$

These identities hold:

  ★ for all $a, b > 0$ and any values of m and n, or

  ★ for all non-zero a, b any integer values of m and n.

Coordinate Geometry

In this chapter we will learn to:

- find the length, gradient and midpoint of a line segment, given the coordinates of its end points,

- find the equation of a straight line, given sufficient information,

- understand and use the relationships between the gradients of parallel and perpendicular lines,

- interpret and use linear equations in context.

2.1 Introducing a Coordinate System

We have already studied a fair amount of geometry. We will have studied properties of parallel lines, similar and right-angled triangles, meeting Pythagoras' Theorem along the way. We are also aware of a number of results (mostly about angles) concerning figures constructed inside circles (like 'the angle at the centre is twice the angle at the circumference'), and we are aware of a number of results concerning the angles in quadrilaterals and polygons.

Armed with these results, and a good diagram of a problem, we can answer a pleasing number of questions. At the same time, we have already seen some benefits of the interplay between algebra and geometry. We have seen that straight lines can be represented by linear equations, and that the intersection of two lines can be determined by solving simultaneous equations. These results are the starting point for our considerations in this chapter. We will see that it is possible to implement a large number of geometric ideas and constructions solely in algebraic terms, and geometric results are obtained by solving suitable equations.

To be able to work this algebraic approach to geometry, we need to be able to describe points in space in terms of numbers. We do this by introducing a **coordinate system**. Before we start, we need to decide what sort of space we want to describe.

- Much mathematics is performed in a two-dimensional world; we can imagine an infinite sheet of flat paper, or an infinite whiteboard; this space is colloquially called **the plane**.

- Alternatively, we could be interested in a fully three-dimensional space, and want to be able to describe the position of anywhere in an infinite three-dimensional world.

> **For Interest**
>
> Mathematicians are not content with stopping at three dimensions, and the geometry of higher dimensional spaces can be investigated. We will not need to go that far!

Restricting our attention to the two-dimensional plane, we need a system whereby we can describe the position of any point on the plane. There are many ways of doing this, but we will confine our attention to the **Cartesian coordinate system**, discovered by the 17th century French mathematician René Descartes (and also by Pierre de Fermat). To do so, we need to make a number of (basically arbitrary) choices:

- we need to identify one specific point in the plane, called the **origin**, and denoted by O,

- we need to choose two preferred directions, each perpendicular to the other,

- we need to choose a unit of length to be used for all measurements.

The position of a point P in the plane can be expressed by two numbers. It is possible to move from the origin O to the point P by moving a distance x parallel to the first direction, and then a distance y parallel to the second direction.

It is conventional to have the first preferred direction drawn horizontally on the page, and the second preferred direction drawn vertically. The distances x and y are signed; a negative value of x means that P is to the left of O, and a negative value of y means that P is below O. We call x and y the **coordinates** of P, and write them as a pair inside a set of brackets, (x, y).

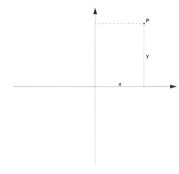

Figure 2.1

If we wanted to work three-dimensionally, a similar procedure would require us to define three mutually perpendicular directions as well as the origin, and we could describe the position of any point in this space by a triple of coordinates (x, y, z).

2.2 The Length of a Line Segment

Two points A and B have coordinates $(-2, 1)$ and $(4, 4)$ respectively. The straight line joining A to B is called the **line segment** AB. The length of the line segment AB is the distance between the points A and B.

A third point C is created by drawing lines from A and B parallel to the coordinate axes. Note that ABC is a right-angled triangle. It is clear that C has the same x-coordinate as B, namely 4, and the same y-coordinate as A, namely 1, so that C has coordinates $(4, 1)$. It is clear that AC has length $4 - (-2) = 6$, while BC has length $4 - 1 = 3$. Using Pythagoras' Theorem, we deduce that the length of $AB = \sqrt{6^2 + 3^2} = \sqrt{45} = 3\sqrt{5}$.

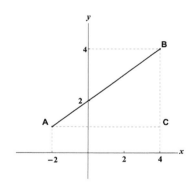

Figure 2.2

While we could use a calculator to write this length to a given accuracy, it is better to be exact and write the length as a surd.

The important thing to notice is that this method can be used wherever A and B are in the plane, and Pythagoras' Theorem will give us a formula to use for the length of AB, even though the diagram we might have to draw looks different every time.

If the points A and B have coordinates (x_1, y_1) and (x_2, y_2) respectively, then the horizontal and vertical sides of the right-angled triangle with AB as hypotenuse have lengths $|x_1 - x_2|$, $|y_1 - y_2|$ respectively. We can therefore use Pythagoras' Theorem, and obtain a general formula for the distance between two points on the plane:

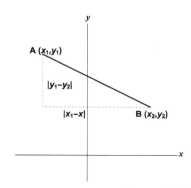

Figure 2.3

Key Fact 2.1 The Length of a Line Segment

If A and B have coordinates (x_1, y_1) and (x_2, y_2), then the distance between A and B is

$$\sqrt{(x_1 - x_2)^2 + (y_1 - y_2)^2}$$

The key point to remember is that we can use this formula without drawing any diagram. The distance between two points can be found by purely algebraic manipulations.

Example 2.2.1. *Show that the triangle ABC is isosceles, where A, B and C have coordinates* $(1, 3), (6, -1)$ *and* $(5, 8)$ *respectively.*

We see that $AB = \sqrt{(1-6)^2 + (3--1)^2} = \sqrt{5^2 + 4^2} = \sqrt{41}$, while $AC = \sqrt{(1-5)^2 + (3-8)^2} = \sqrt{4^2 + 5^2} = \sqrt{41}$, and so $AB = AC$.

Example 2.2.2. *The triangle PQR is right-angled, where P, Q and R have coordinates* $(1, 4), (3, 1)$ *and* $(k, 8)$. *Find the possible values of k.*

We calculate $PQ = \sqrt{2^2 + 3^2} = \sqrt{13}$, $PR = \sqrt{(k-1)^2 + 4^2} = \sqrt{k^2 - 2k + 17}$, and $QR = \sqrt{(k-3)^2 + 7^2} = \sqrt{k^2 - 6k + 58}$. There are three cases to consider, depending on where the right angle is.

- If the right angle is at P, then

$$
\begin{aligned}
PQ^2 + PR^2 &= QR^2 \\
13 + k^2 - 2k + 17 &= k^2 - 6k + 58 \\
4k &= 28 \\
k &= 7.
\end{aligned}
$$

- If the right angle is at Q, then

$$
\begin{aligned}
PQ^2 + QR^2 &= PR^2 \\
13 + k^2 - 6k + 58 &= k^2 - 2k + 17 \\
54 &= 4k \\
k &= \tfrac{27}{2}.
\end{aligned}
$$

- If the right angle is at R, then

$$
\begin{aligned}
PR^2 + QR^2 &= PQ^2 \\
k^2 - 2k + 17 + k^2 - 6k + 58 &= 13 \\
2k^2 - 8k + 62 &= 0 \\
k^2 - 4k + 31 &= 0
\end{aligned}
$$

Since this quadratic has discriminant $-100 < 0$, there are no solutions for k.

Thus the only possible values for k are 7 and $\tfrac{27}{2}$.

2.3 The Midpoint of a Line Segment

Consider a line segment AB, where the end-points A and B have coordinates (x_1, y_1) and (x_2, y_2) respectively. Let M be the midpoint of the line segment AB, and construct the points C and D by drawing lines parallel to the coordinate axes as shown.

It is clear that C has coordinates (x_1, y_2). Moreover the triangles ACB and MDB are similar, and hence the lengths CD and DB are equal. Thus D is the midpoint of CB, and hence it is clear that D has coordinates $\left(\frac{1}{2}(x_1 + x_2), y_2\right)$. Moreover AC is twice the length of MD, and hence the y-coordinate of D is $y_2 + \frac{1}{2}(y_1 - y_2) = \frac{1}{2}(y_1 + y_2)$.

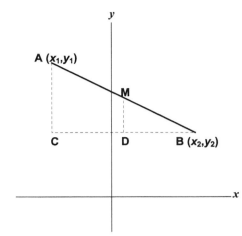

Figure 2.4

Key Fact 2.2 The Midpoint of a Line Segment

If A and B have coordinates (x_1, y_1) and (x_2, y_2), then the midpoint of AB has coordinates

$$\left(\tfrac{1}{2}(x_1 + x_2), \tfrac{1}{2}(y_1 + y_2)\right)$$

Where coordinate geometry comes into its own is when it is coupled with standard geometry, and we use our standard geometrical knowledge and insight to understand what calculations to perform.

Example 2.3.1. *The parallelogram $ABCD$ has coordinates $A(1,4)$, $B(5,7)$ and $D(3,5)$. What are the coordinates of C?*

We know that the diagonals of a parallelogram bisect each other. The midpoint of BD has coordinates $(4,6)$, and is also the midpoint of AC. Thus C must have coordinates (u, v), where $\left(\frac{1}{2}(1+u), \frac{1}{2}(4+v)\right) = (4,6)$, and hence $u = 7$ and $v = 8$. The coordinates of C are $(7,8)$.

2.4 The Gradient of a Line Segment

The gradient of a line is its slope. The steeper the line, the larger the gradient. Unlike coordinates, the gradient of a line is a property of the whole line, and not of just one point on it. The gradient is colloquially defined as the ratio

$$\frac{\text{RISE}}{\text{RUN}}$$

where the RISE is the amount that the line has increased by between two points on that line, and the RUN is the amount that has been travelled from left to right between those two points. Although the rise and the run will differ, depending on the two points on the line that are chosen, their ratio does not.

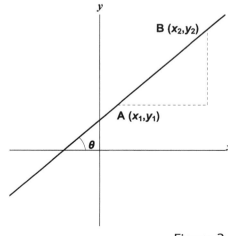

Figure 2.5

Again, the convenience of coordinate geometry is that this calculation can be performed very neatly in coordinates, without the need to draw a diagram. If A has coordinates (x_1, y_1), and B has coordinates (x_2, y_2), then the line segment has risen by $y_2 - y_1$ between A and B, and hence the rise is $y_2 - y_1$. Similarly, the run between these two points is $x_2 - x_1$.

Key Fact 2.3 The Gradient of a Line Segment

The gradient of the line segment AB, where A and B have coordinates (x_1, y_1) and (x_2, y_2), is
$$\frac{y_2 - y_1}{x_2 - x_1}$$
The gradient is the tangent $\tan\theta$ of the angle that the line segment makes with the x-axis.

This formula works whether the coordinates of A and B are positive or negative.

Example 2.4.1. *Find the gradient of the line segment AB, where A and B have coordinates:*

$$a)\ A(3,5),\ B(7,12) \qquad\qquad b)\ A(-4,5),\ B(6,-4)$$

The gradient in the first case is $\frac{12-5}{7-3} = \frac{7}{4}$. In the second case it is $\frac{-4-5}{6-(-4)} = -\frac{9}{10}$.

For Interest

The formula fails to work if $x_1 = x_2$, because we are trying to divide by 0. In this case, the two points have the same x-coordinate, and the line segment is vertical. In this case, we say that the gradient of the line is infinite, written ∞.

Even more importantly, we do not have to know that A is 'to the left of' B. In other words, we do not need to know that the rise is positive. Since

$$\frac{y_2 - y_1}{x_2 - x_1} = \frac{y_1 - y_2}{x_1 - x_2}$$

the formula for the gradient tells us that the gradient of AB is the same as the gradient of BA. They are, after all, the same line. This is particularly important when we are performing algebraic calculations, and we might not know (at least initially) whether $x_1 < x_2$ or the reverse.

Example 2.4.2. *The lines AB and CD have the same gradient, where $A(3,1)$, $B(p,p)$, $C(5,3)$ and $D(2p,2p)$. What is the value of p?*

Since the two gradients are the same, we see that

$$\begin{aligned}
\frac{p-1}{p-3} &= \frac{2p-3}{2p-5} \\
(p-1)(2p-5) &= (p-3)(2p-3) \\
2p^2 - 7p + 5 &= 2p^2 - 9p + 9 \\
2p &= 4
\end{aligned}$$

and hence we deduce that $p = 2$.

Recall that lines with the same gradient are called **parallel**.

Example 2.4.3. *Prove that the points $A(1,1)$, $B(5,3)$, $C(3,0)$ and $D(-1,-2)$ form a parallelogram.*

There are two ways in which this can be done. We can calculate the lengths of the four sides:

$$AB = \sqrt{(5-1)^2 + (3-1)^2} = \sqrt{20}$$

$$CD = \sqrt{(-1-3)^2 + (-2-0)^2} = \sqrt{20}$$

$$BC = \sqrt{(3-5)^2 + (0-3)^2} = \sqrt{13}$$

$$AD = \sqrt{(-1-1)^2 + (-2-1)^2} = \sqrt{13}$$

Since opposite pairs of sides have the same length, we have a parallelogram.

Alternatively, we could calculate the gradients of the sides. The sides AB, BC, CD and DA have respective gradients

$$\frac{3-1}{5-1} = \frac{1}{2} \qquad \frac{0-3}{3-5} = \frac{3}{2} \qquad \frac{-2-0}{-1-3} = \frac{1}{2} \qquad \frac{1-(-2)}{1-(-1)} = \frac{3}{2}$$

Since opposite pairs of sides are parallel, $ABCD$ is a parallelogram.

EXERCISE 2A

Do not use a calculator. Where appropriate, leave square roots in your answers.

1. Find the lengths of the line segments joining these pairs of points. Where necessary assume that $a > 0$ and $p > q > 0$.
   a) $(2, 5)$ and $(7, 17)$
   b) $(-3, 2)$ and $(1, -1)$
   c) $(4, -5)$ and $(-1, 0)$
   d) $(-3, -3)$ and $(-7, 3)$
   e) $(2a, a)$ and $(10a, -14a)$
   f) $(a + 1, 2a + 3)$ and $(a - 1, 2a - 1)$
   g) $(2, 9)$ and $(2, -14)$
   h) $(12a, 5b)$ and $(3a, 5b)$
   i) (p, q) and (q, p)
   j) $(p + 4q, p - q)$ and $(p - 3q, p)$

2. Show that the points $(1, -2)$, $(6, -1)$, $(9, 3)$ and $(4, 2)$ are vertices of a parallelogram.

3. Show that the triangle formed by the points $(-3, -2)$, $(2, -7)$ and $(-2, 5)$ is isosceles.

4. Show that the points $(7, 12)$, $(-3, -12)$ and $(14, -5)$ lie on a circle with centre $(2, 0)$.

5. Find the coordinates of the midpoints of the line segments joining these pairs of points.
   a) $(2, 11), (6, 15)$
   b) $(5, 7), (-3, 9)$
   c) $(-2, -3), (1, -6)$
   d) $(-3, 4), (-8, 5)$
   e) $(p + 2, 3p - 1), (3p + 4, p - 5)$
   f) $(p + 3, q - 7), (p + 5, 3 - q)$
   g) $(p + 2q, 2p + 13q), (5p - 2q, -2p - 7q)$
   h) $(a + 3, b - 5), (a + 3, b + 7)$

6. $A(-2, 1)$ and $B(6, 5)$ are the opposite ends of the diameter of a circle. Find the coordinates of its centre.

7. $M(5, 7)$ is the midpoint of the line segment joining $A(3, 4)$ to B. Find the coordinates of B.

8. $A(1, -2)$, $B(6, -1)$, $C(9, 3)$ and $D(4, 2)$ are the vertices of a parallelogram. Verify that the midpoints of the diagonals AC and BD coincide.

9. Which one of the points $A(5, 2)$, $B(6, -3)$ and $C(4, 7)$ is the midpoint of the other two? Check your answer by calculating two distances.

10. Find the gradients of the lines joining the following pairs of points.
    a) $(3, 8), (5, 12)$
    b) $(1, -3), (-2, 6)$
    c) $(-4, -3), (0, -1)$
    d) $(-5, -3), (3, -9)$
    e) $(p + 3, p - 3), (2p + 4, -p - 5)$
    f) $(p + 3, q - 5), (q - 5, p + 3)$
    g) $(p + q - 1, q + p - 3), (p - q + 1, q - p + 3)$
    h) $(7, p), (11, p)$

11. Find the gradients of the lines AB and BC where A is $(3, 4)$, B is $(7, 6)$ and C is $(-3, 1)$. What can you deduce about the points A, B and C?

12. The point $P(x,y)$ lies on the straight line joining $A(3,0)$ and $B(5,6)$. Find expressions for the gradients of AP and PB. Hence show that $y = 3x - 9$.

13. A line joining a vertex of a triangle to the midpoint of the opposite side is called a median. Find the length of the median AM in the triangle $A(-1,1)$, $B(0,3)$, $C(4,7)$.

14. A triangle has vertices $A(a,b)$, $B(p,q)$ and $C(u,v)$.

    a) Find the coordinates of M, the midpoint of AB, and N, the midpoint of AC.

    b) Show that MN is parallel to BC.

15. The points $A(2,1)$, $B(2,7)$ and $C(-4,-1)$ form a triangle. M is the midpoint of AB and N is the midpoint of AC.

    a) Find the lengths of MN and BC.   b) Show that $BC = 2MN$.

16. The vertices of a quadrilateral $ABCD$ are $A(1,1)$, $B(7,3)$, $C(9,-7)$ and $D(-3,-3)$. The points P, Q, R and S are the midpoints of AB, BC, CD and DA respectively.

    a) Find the gradient of each side of $PQRS$.   b) What type of quadrilateral is $PQRS$?

17. The origin O and the points $P(4,1)$, $Q(5,5)$ and $R(1,4)$ form a quadrilateral.

    a) Show that OR is parallel to PQ.   c) Show that $OP = OR$.

    b) Show that OP is parallel to RQ.   d) What shape is $OPQR$?

18. The origin O and the points L(-2, 3), M(4, 7) and N(6, 4) form a quadrilateral.

    a) Show that $ON = LM$.   b) Show that ON is parallel to LM.

    c) Show that $OM = LN$.   d) What shape is $OLMN$?

19. The vertices of a quadrilateral $PQRS$ are $P(1,2)$, $Q(7,0)$, $R(6,-4)$ and $S(-3,-1)$.

    a) Find the gradient of each side of the quadrilateral.

    b) What type of quadrilateral is $PQRS$?

20. The vertices of a quadrilateral are $T(3,2)$, $U(2,5)$, $V(8,7)$ and $W(6,1)$. The midpoints of UV and VW are M and N respectively. Show that the triangle TMN is isosceles.

21. The vertices of a quadrilateral $DEFG$ are $D(3,-2)$, $E(0,-3)$, $F(-2,3)$ and $G(4,1)$.

    a) Find the length of each side of the quadrilateral.

    b) What type of quadrilateral is $DEFG$?

22. The points $A(2,3)$, $B(4,x)$ and $C = (2x,-3)$ are such that $BC = AC$. What are the possible values of x?

23*. The triangle ABC has vertices $A(a,b)$, $B(p,q)$ and $C(u,v)$. The points L, M and N are the midpoints of BC, AC and AB respectively.

    a) Write down the coordinates of L, M and N.

    b) If G is the point $\left(\frac{1}{3}(a+p+u), \frac{1}{3}(b+q+v)\right)$, show that G lies on the line AL.

    c) Explain why the three medians of the triangle all pass through one point (we say that the medians are **concurrent**).

24*. The quadrilateral $ABCD$ has perpendicular diagonals. Let O be the point of intersection of the two diagonals. Suppose that $OA = a$, $OB = b$, $OC = c$, and $OD = d$.

    a) Write down expressions for AB and CD

    b) Prove that $AB^2 + CD^2 = AD^2 + BC^2$.

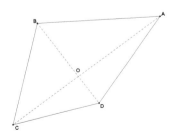

25*. We know that the diagonals of a parallelogram bisect each other. Prove now that any quadrilateral $ABCD$ whose diagonals bisect each other is a parallelogram (Hint: Define coordinate axes so that AC lies on the x-axis, with O being the midpoint of the diagonal.).

2.5 The Equation of a Line

There are various ways by which we can specify a line. We might, for instance, know the line's gradient and one of the points it passes through. Suppose then that a straight line has gradient m, and crosses the y-axis at the point $(0, c)$. In this case, c is called the y-**intercept**. If we consider a point (x, y) on the line, then we calculate the line's gradient to be

$$m = \frac{y-c}{x-0}$$

and hence we deduce that $y = mx + c$.

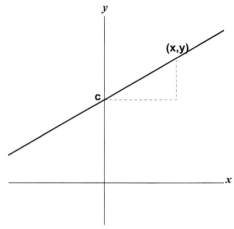

Figure 2.6

Key Fact 2.4 The Equation of a Line 1

The equation of the line with gradient m with y-intercept c is

$$y = mx + c$$

More generally, we might know the gradient of the line, but instead of knowing the y-intercept, we might have the coordinates of a point through which the line passes (to know the y-intercept is, of course, to know the point on the y-axis through which the line passes). Suppose that a straight line has gradient m, and passes through the point (x_1, y_1). If (x, y) is any point on the line, we calculate the gradient of the line to be

$$m = \frac{y - y_1}{x - x_1}$$

so the line has equation $y - y_1 = m(x - x_1)$.

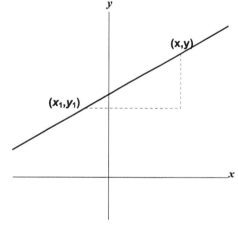

Figure 2.7

Key Fact 2.5 The Equation of a Line 2

The equation of the line with gradient m passing through the point (x_1, y_1) is

$$y - y_1 = m(x - x_1)$$

This formula clearly sets up the equation of a line with gradient m. Since both sides of the equation are equal to 0 when $x = x_1$ and $y = y_1$, it is clear that this line passes through the point (x_1, y_1). Note that a line with y-intercept c is a line passing through $(0, c)$, and so the $y = mx + c$ formula is a special case of this one.

What can we do if we do not know the gradient of the line? All that it takes to define a straight line is to know two points on that line. Suppose now that a line passes through the points (x_1, y_1) and (x_2, y_2). Then this line has gradient

$$\frac{y_2 - y_1}{x_2 - x_1}$$

and hence its equation is

$$y - y_1 = \frac{y_2 - y_1}{x_2 - x_1}(x - x_1)$$

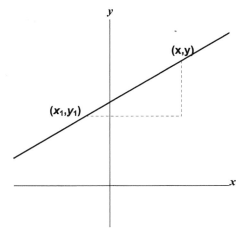

Figure 2.8

For Interest

When drawing straight line graphs in previous years, you were probably taught to plot three points before drawing the line. Three points were not necessary to define the line, but the third point was useful as a means of detecting calculation error in determining the coordinates of those points, or identifying if one of those points had been plotted incorrectly.

Key Fact 2.6 The Equation of a Line 3

The equation of the line passing through the points (x_1, y_1) and (x_2, y_2) is

$$\frac{y - y_1}{y_2 - y_1} = \frac{x - x_1}{x_2 - x_1}$$

It is worth noting that both sides of this equation are equal to 0 at the point (x_1, y_1), and both sides are equal to 1 at (x_2, y_2). This is a useful point to remember, since it helps us to substitute the right values into the formulae correctly.

Example 2.5.1. *Find the equation of the line with gradient -1 passing through the point $(-2, 3)$.*

The equation is $y - 3 = -1\big(x - (-2)\big) = -x - 2$, or $y = 1 - x$.

Example 2.5.2. *Find the equation of the line passing through the points $(3, 4)$ and $(-1, 2)$.*

There are two possible approaches here. We could start by finding the gradient $\frac{4-2}{3-(-1)} = \frac{1}{2}$, so that the equation is $y - 4 = \frac{1}{2}(x - 3)$, or $y = \frac{1}{2}x + \frac{5}{2}$. Alternatively we could use the last formula, so that the equation is

$$\tfrac{1}{2}(y - 2) = \frac{y - 2}{4 - 2} = \frac{x - (-1)}{3 - (-1)} = \tfrac{1}{4}(x + 1)$$

which gives $y = \frac{1}{2}x + \frac{5}{2}$

We note that none of these methods for obtaining the equations of lines work if the line is 'vertical' (has infinite gradient). Lines of this type have equations of the form $x = k$ for some constant k. This means that the first two formulae fail to work, because we have no value for the gradient m that we can use, and the third formula fails because two points on the line will have the same x-coordinate, and hence the formula asks us to divide by 0. There should be little difficulty in recognising such lines, and finding their equations without reference to any of the three formulae above.

2.6   The equation $ax + by + c = 0$

It is untidy that we do not currently have a method of writing equations of lines which can represent **all** lines: the $y = mx + c$ shape is not good enough, since it does not handle vertical lines. It is easy to see that an equation of the form $y = mx + c$ can be written as $mx - y + c = 0$, while a vertical line, with equation $x = k$, can be written in the form $x - k = 0$.

Food For Thought 2.1

For any straight line, constants a, b and c can be found such that the equation of the line is
$$ax + by + c = 0$$

Example 2.6.1. *Find the equation of the line passing through the points $(2, 4)$ and $(5, -3)$ in the form $ax + by + c = 0$, where a, b and c are integers.*

Using the third formula, the equation is
$$\begin{aligned}
\frac{y - 4}{-3 - 4} &= \frac{x - 2}{5 - 2} \\
-\tfrac{1}{7}(y - 4) &= \tfrac{1}{3}(x - 2) \\
-3(y - 4) &= 7(x - 2) \\
7x + 3y - 26 &= 0
\end{aligned}$$

Example 2.6.2. *What is the equation of the line passing through A and the midpoint of BC, where A, B and C have coordinates $(1, 4)$, $(-2, 7)$ and $(4, 11)$? Write the equation in the form $ax + by + c = 0$.*

The midpoint of BC has coordinates $(1, 9)$. The desired line is a vertical one, with equation $x = 1$, or $x - 1 = 0$.

Example 2.6.3. *What is the gradient of the line $3x + 11y - 6 = 0$?*

This equation can be written as $y = -\tfrac{3}{11}x + \tfrac{6}{11}$, and hence its gradient is $-\tfrac{3}{11}$.

The last example shows another benefit of this new way of writing equations of lines. The $y = mx + c$ formulation might involve complicated fractions, whereas the new format only needs integers to describe the line.

Example 2.6.4. *One side of a parallelogram lies on the straight line with equation $3x - 4y - 7 = 0$. The point $(2, 3)$ is a vertex of the parallelogram. Find the equation of one other side.*

The line $3x - 4y - 7 = 0$ can be written $y = \tfrac{3}{4}x - \tfrac{7}{4}$, and hence has gradient $\tfrac{3}{4}$. The point $(2, 3)$ does not lie on this line. Hence another side of the parallelogram (the only other side we can be certain about) passes through $(2, 3)$ with gradient $\tfrac{3}{4}$, and so has equation $y - 3 = \tfrac{3}{4}(x - 2)$, or $3x - 4y + 6 = 0$.

What this method of describing lines gains in elegance and convenience, however, it loses in uniqueness. There is no longer exactly one equation of a line. The equations
$$x + 3y - 1 = 0 \qquad 3x + 9y - 3 = 0 \qquad -2x - 6y + 2 = 0$$

all describe the same equation (each can be obtained from the other by multiplying through by some constant). However, the benefits of being able to describe all lines in a single manner outweigh this disadvantage.

2.7   The Point of Intersection of Two Lines

Where do the two lines $2x - y = 4$ and $3x + 2y + 1 = 0$ meet? How do we find the coordinates of the point of intersection of these two lines.

We want the point (x, y) that lies on both lines, and hence the values (x, y) must satisfy both equations. To find these values, then, we need to solve the two equations simultaneously. These particular equations have simultaneous solution $x = 1$, $y = -2$, so the point of intersection is $(1, -2)$.

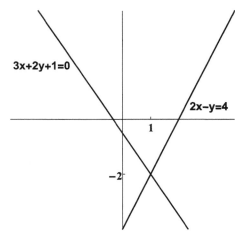

Figure 2.9

This technique will find the point of intersection of any pair of nonparallel lines. Solving simultaneous equations will also enable us to find the points of intersection of more complicated curves.

EXERCISE 2B

1. Test whether the given point lies on the straight line (or curve) with the given equation.

   a) $(1, 2)$ on $y = 5x - 3$,
   b) $(3, -2)$ on $y = 3x - 7$,
   c) $(3, -4)$ on $x^2 + y^2 = 25$,
   d) $(2, 2)$ on $3x^2 + y^2 = 40$,
   e) $\left(1, 1\frac{1}{2}\right)$ on $y = \frac{x+2}{3x-1}$,
   f) $\left(5p, \frac{5}{p}\right)$ on $y = \frac{5}{x}$,
   g) $(p, (p-1)^2 + 1)$ on $y = x^2 - 2x + 2$,
   h) $(t^2, 2t)$ on $y^2 = 4x$.

2. Find the equations of the straight lines through the given points with the gradients shown. Your final answers should not contain any fractions.

   a) $(2, 3)$, gradient 5,
   b) $(1, -2)$, gradient -3,
   c) $(0, 4)$, gradient $\frac{1}{2}$,
   d) $(-2, 1)$, gradient $-\frac{3}{8}$,
   e) $(0, 0)$, gradient -3,
   f) $(3, 8)$, gradient 0,
   g) $(-5, -1)$, gradient $-\frac{3}{4}$,
   h) $(-3, 0)$, gradient $\frac{1}{2}$,
   i) $(-3, -1)$, gradient $\frac{3}{8}$,
   j) $(3, 4)$, gradient $-\frac{1}{2}$,
   k) $(2, -1)$, gradient -2,
   l) $(-2, -5)$, gradient 3,
   m) $(0, -4)$, gradient 7,
   n) $(0, 2)$, gradient -1,
   o) $(3, -2)$, gradient $-\frac{5}{8}$,
   p) $(3, 0)$, gradient $-\frac{3}{5}$,
   q) $(d, 0)$, gradient 7,
   r) $(0, 4)$, gradient m,
   s) $(0, c)$, gradient 3,
   t) $(c, 0)$, gradient m.

3. Find the equations of the lines joining the following pairs of points. Leave your final answer without fractions and in one of the forms $y = mx + c$ or $ax + by + c = 0$.

   a) $(1, 4)$ and $(3, 10)$,
   b) $(4, 5)$ and $(-2, -7)$,
   c) $(3, 2)$ and $(0, 4)$,
   d) $(3, 7)$ and $(3, 12)$,
   e) $(10, -3)$ and $(-5, -12)$,
   f) $(3, -1)$ and $(-4, 20)$,
   g) $(2, -3)$ and $(11, -3)$,
   h) $(2, 0)$ and $(5, -1)$,
   i) $(-4, 2)$ and $(-1, -3)$,
   j) $(-2, -1)$ and $(5, -3)$,
   k) $(-3, 4)$ and $(-3, 9)$,
   l) $(-1, 0)$ and $(0, -1)$,
   m) $(2, 7)$ and $(3, 10)$,
   n) $(-5, 4)$ and $(-2, -1)$,
   o) $(0, 0)$ and $(5, -3)$,
   p) $(0, 0)$ and (p, q),
   q) (p, q) and $(p + 3, q - 1)$,
   r) $(p, -q)$ and (p, q),
   s) (p, q) and $(p + 2, q + 2)$,
   t) $(p, 0)$ and $(0, q)$.

4. Find the gradients of the following lines.

a) $2x + y = 7$,   b) $3x - 4y = 8$,   c) $5x + 2y = -3$,
d) $y = 5$,   e) $3x - 2y = -4$,   f) $5x = 7$,
g) $x + y = -3$,   h) $y = 3(x + 4)$,   i) $7 - x = 2y$,
j) $3(y - 4) = 7x$,   k) $y = m(x - d)$,   l) $px + qy = pq$.

5. Find the equation of the line through $(-2, 1)$ parallel to $y = \frac{1}{2}x - 3$.

6. Find the equation of the line through $(4, -3)$ parallel to $y + 2x = 7$.

7. Find the equation of the line through $(1, 2)$ parallel to the line joining $(3, -1)$ and $(-5, 2)$.

8. Find the equation of the line through $(3, 9)$ parallel to the line joining $(-3, 2)$ and $(2, -3)$.

9. Find the equation of the line through $(1, 7)$ parallel to the x-axis.

10. Find the equation of the line through $(d, 0)$ parallel to $y = mx + c$.

11. Find the points of intersection of the following pairs of straight lines.
    a) $3x + 4y = 33$, $2y = x - 1$,   b) $y = 3x + 1$, $y = 4x - 1$,
    c) $2y = 7x$, $3x - 2y = 1$,   d) $y = 3x + 8$, $y = -2x - 7$,
    e) $x + 5y = 22$, $3x + 2y = 14$,   f) $2x + 7y = 47$, $5x + 4y = 50$,
    g) $2x + 3y = 7$, $6x + 9y = 11$,   h) $3x + y = 5$, $x + 3y = -1$,
    i) $y = 2x + 3$, $4x - 2y = -6$,   j) $ax + by = c$, $y = 2ax$,
    k) $y = mx + c$, $y = -mx + d$,   l) $ax - by = 1$, $y = x$,

12. $ABCD$ is a rectangle, where A, B and C have coordinates $(0, 0)$, $(6, 0)$ and $(6, 3)$ respectively. Let P be the midpoint of AB, and let Q be the midpoint of CD. The lines DP and QB meet the diagonal AC at the points M and N respectively. Show that $AM = MN = NC$.

13. Let P, with coordinates (p, q), be a fixed point on the line with equation $y = mx + c$, and let Q, with coordinates (r, s), be any other point on that line. Show that the gradient of PQ is m for all positions of Q.

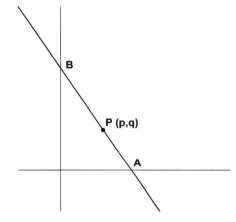

14. There are some values of a, b and c for which the equation $ax + by + c = 0$ does not represent a straight line. What are they?

15*. The point P has coordinates (p, q). The line ℓ passes through P, and has negative gradient $-m$, where $m > 0$. The line ℓ meets the x-axis and y-axis at A and B respectively. Find an expression for the area of the triangle OAB. What happens when $q = -mp$?

16*. The points A and B have coordinates $(-a, 0)$ and $(a, 0)$ respectively. The line ℓ_1 passes through A with gradient m, while the line ℓ_2 passes through B with gradient $-m^{-1}$. Find the coordinates (u, v) of the point of intersection C of the lines ℓ_1 and ℓ_2, and show that $u^2 + v^2 = a^2$.

17*. The triangle ABC has coordinates $A(a_1, a_2)$, $B(b_1, b_2)$ and $C(c_1, c_2)$. A **median** of a triangle is the line passing through one vertex and the midpoint of the opposite edge (so that median through A passes through A and the midpoint of BC).

    a) Write down the equation of the median through A.

    b) Show that the point G with coordinates $\left(\frac{1}{3}(a_1 + b_1 + c_1), \frac{1}{3}(a_2 + b_2 + c_2)\right)$ lies on this median.

    c) Why does this show that all three medians of a triangle meet at a point (such lines are called **concurrent**)? The point where all three medians meet is called the **centroid**, or **centre of gravity**, of the triangle.

2.8   Perpendicular Lines

If two lines are parallel, then they have the same gradient. What can we say about the gradients of two lines which are perpendicular?

Certainly, if a line has a positive gradient, then the perpendicular line has a negative gradient, and vice versa. But we can be more precise than this.

If we have a line with positive gradient m, then we can pick points P and B on the line so that the run from P to B is 1, and so the rise from P to B is m. We have the 'gradient triangle'

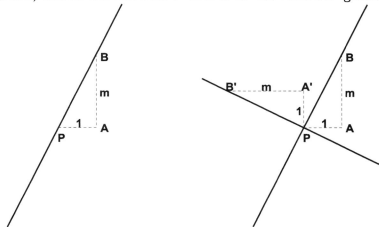

PAB.
Figure 2.10

If we consider a second line which is perpendicular to the first, and which meets the first line at P, then this line can be obtained from the first by rotating it through $90°$ about the point P. The gradient triangle PAB is then rotated to the gradient triangle $PA'B'$. Thus, between B' and P, the new line has run m and rise -1, and hence the gradient of the second line is

$$\frac{-1}{m} = -m^{-1}.$$

Key Fact 2.7 Perpendicular Lines

If two lines are perpendicular, then their gradients m_1 and m_2 are such that

$$m_1 m_2 = -1 \qquad \text{or} \qquad m_1 = -\frac{1}{m_2}$$

For Interest

This formula is not true if the lines are parallel to the two coordinate axes, when their gradients are 0 and ∞. There is no difficulty, however, in identifying such perpendicular lines!

It is also true that if two lines have gradients m_1 and m_2 such that $m_1 m_2 = -1$, then these lines are perpendicular. Showing this is a question to be found in Miscellaneous Exercises 1.

Example 2.8.1. *Show that the points $A(0,-5)$, $B(-1,2)$, $C(4,7)$ and $D(5,0)$ form a rhombus.*

We could show this by calculating the four side lengths, but here is an alternative approach. The midpoint of AC is $\left(\frac{1}{2}(0+4), \frac{1}{2}(-5+7)\right) = (2,1)$, while the midpoint of BD is $\left(\frac{1}{2}(-1+5), \frac{1}{2}(2+0)\right) = (2,1)$. Since the midpoints of the two diagonals coincide, the quadrilateral is a parallelogram.

The gradient of AC is $\frac{7-(-5)}{4-0} = 3$, while the gradient of BD is $\frac{0-2}{5-(-1)} = -\frac{1}{3}$. Since $3 \times -\frac{1}{3} = -1$, the two diagonals are perpendicular, and hence $ABCD$ is a rhombus.

Example 2.8.2. *Find the coordinates of the foot of the perpendicular from $A(-2,-4)$ to the line joining $B(0,2)$ and $C(-1,4)$.*

It is often worth drawing a sketch of the problem. It makes it easier to be clear about what needs to be done. The perpendicular from A to the line BC is the line through A that is perpendicular to BC, and its foot is the point where it meets the line BC. The question is asking for the coordinates of P.

First, we calculate that the gradient of BC is $\frac{2-4}{0-(-1)} = -2$. Since its y-intercept is 2, the equation of BC is $y = -2x + 2$.

Thus the perpendicular from A has gradient $\frac{1}{2}$ (since $\frac{1}{2} \times -2 = -1$), and so has equation

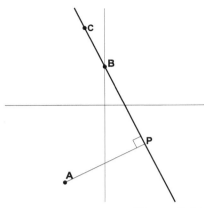

Figure 2.11

$$\begin{aligned} y + 4 &= \tfrac{1}{2}(x + 2) \\ x - 2y &= 6 \end{aligned}$$

Solving the simultaneous equations $2x + y = 2$ and $x - 2y = 6$, we deduce that the coordinates of P are $(2, -2)$.

Example 2.8.3. *Find the equation of the perpendicular bisector of the line AB, where A and B have coordinates $(-2, 5)$ and $(3, 2)$.*

The perpendicular bisector of AB is the line which is perpendicular to AB that passes through the midpoint M of AB.

The midpoint M has coordinates $\left(\frac{1}{2}(-2 + 3), \frac{1}{2}(5 + 2)\right) = (\frac{1}{2}, \frac{7}{2})$, and the line AB has gradient $\frac{2-5}{3-(-2)} = -\frac{3}{5}$. Thus the perpendicular bisector of AB has gradient $\frac{5}{3}$, and so has equation

$$\begin{aligned} y - \tfrac{7}{2} &= \tfrac{5}{3}\left(x - \tfrac{1}{2}\right) \\ 5x - 3y + 8 &= 0 \end{aligned}$$

2.9   The Angle Between Two Lines

Using easy trigonometric ideas, the following is clear:

> **Food For Thought 2.2**
>
> The tangent of a straight line is the tangent of the angle that the line makes with the x-axis.

In the diagram on the right, the two lines have gradients $\tan\theta$ and $\tan\phi$ respectively.

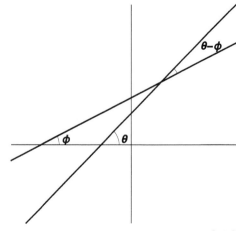

Figure 2.12

The angle between the two lines is $\theta - \phi$, and this can be calculated by elementary means.

Example 2.9.1. *Find the angle between the lines $y = 3x + 1$ and $y = x + 7$.*

These lines make the angles $\tan^{-1} 3 = 71.6°$ and $\tan^{-1} 1 = 45°$ with the x-axis, and so the angle between them is $71.6° - 45° = 26.6°$.

Although we will need a little more trigonometry to understand why it works, there is a useful formula which can be used to calculate the angle between two lines more directly.

> **Key Fact 2.8** The Angle Between Two Lines
>
> If two lines have gradients m_1 and m_2, where $m_1 > m_2$, then the angle between these lines is
> $$\tan^{-1} \frac{m_1 - m_2}{1 + m_1 m_2}$$

Considering the previous example again, since the lines $y = 3x + 1$ and $y = x + 7$ have gradients 3 and 1 respectively, the angle between them is

$$\tan^{-1} \frac{3 - 1}{1 + 3 \times 1} = \tan^{-1} \tfrac{1}{2} = 26.6°$$

Note that this formula for the angle between two lines is not properly defined when $m_1 m_2 = -1$, since we are then trying to divide by 0. However, in this case the two lines are perpendicular, and the lack of definition in this formula matches the lack of definition of the tangent of $90°$.

2.10 The Distance from a Point to a Line

If P is the foot of the perpendicular from the point A to the line ℓ, and if Q is any other point on the line ℓ, then the distance AQ is the hypotenuse of a right-angled triangle, one of whose other sides is AP. Thus $AQ \geq AP$, and we see that the perpendicular distance AP is the shortest distance from A to any point on the line ℓ. This distance is called, simply, the **distance from the point A to the line ℓ**.

In principle, we know how to calculate this distance. If we know the equation of ℓ and the coordinates of A, then we can find the equation of AP and solve to find the coordinates of P, finally calculating the distance AP. What is interesting is that there is an elegant formula which enables us to avoid all this work!

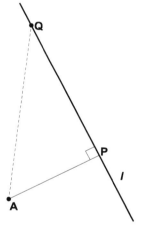

Figure 2.13

Suppose that the line ℓ has equation $ax + by + c = 0$, and that A has coordinates (u, v). Then ℓ has gradient $-\frac{a}{b}$, and so the perpendicular through A has gradient $\frac{b}{a}$, and hence has equation

$$bx - ay = bu - av$$

Solving the equations

$$ax + by + c = 0$$
$$bx - ay = bu - av$$

simultaneously, we obtain

$$(a^2 + b^2)x + ac = a(ax + by + c) + b(bx - ay) = b^2 u - abv$$
$$(a^2 + b^2)y + bc = b(ax + by + c) - a(bx - ay) = a^2 v - abu$$

and so the coordinates of P are

$$\left(\frac{b^2 u - abv - ac}{a^2 + b^2}, \frac{a^2 v - abu - bc}{a^2 + b^2} \right)$$

Thus the perpendicular distance d is given by the formula

$$
\begin{aligned}
d^2 &= \left(u - \frac{b^2 u - abv - ac}{a^2 + b^2}\right)^2 + \left(v - \frac{a^2 v - abu - bc}{a^2 + b^2}\right)^2 \\
&= \frac{1}{(a^2 + b^2)^2}\left[(a^2 u + abv + ac)^2 + (b^2 v + abu + bc)^2\right] \\
&= \frac{1}{(a^2 + b^2)^2}\left[a^2(au + bv + c)^2 + b^2(au + bv + c)^2\right] \\
&= \frac{(au + bv + c)^2}{a^2 + b^2}
\end{aligned}
$$

To calculate d, we need to take the positive square root of the right-hand side.

Key Fact 2.9 Perpendicular Distance to a Line

The perpendicular distance from a point (u, v) to the line $ax + by + c = 0$ is

$$
\frac{au + bv + c}{\sqrt{a^2 + b^2}}
$$

(or minus the above if this expression is negative).

Looking ahead to Chapter 4, we use the modulus function to write this expression as

$$
\frac{|au + bv + c|}{\sqrt{a^2 + b^2}}
$$

EXERCISE 2C

1. In each part write down the gradient of a line which is perpendicular to one with the given gradient.

   a) 2 b) -3 c) 4 d) $-\frac{5}{6}$

   e) -1 f) $1\frac{3}{4}$ g) $-\frac{1}{m}$ h) m

   i) $\frac{p}{q}$ j) 0 k) $-m$ l) $\frac{a}{b-c}$

2. In each part find the equation of the line through the given point which is perpendicular to the given line. Write your final answer so that it doesn't contain fractions.

   a) $(2, 3),\ y = 4x + 3$ b) $(-3, 1),\ y = -\frac{1}{2}x + 3$

   c) $(2, -5),\ y = -5x - 2$ d) $(7, -4),\ y = 2\frac{1}{2}$

   e) $(-1, 4),\ 2x + 3y = 8$ f) $(4, 3),\ 3x - 5y = 8$

   g) $(5, -3),\ 2x = 3$ h) $(0, 3),\ y = 2x - 1$

   i) $(0, 0),\ y = mx + c$ j) $(a, b),\ y = mx + c$

   k) $(c, d),\ ny - x = p$ l) $(-1, -2),\ ax + by = c$

3. Find the equation of the line through the point $(-2, 5)$ which is perpendicular to the line $y = 3x + 1$. Find also the point of intersection of the two lines.

4. Find the equation of the line through the point $(1, 1)$ which is perpendicular to the line $2x - 3y = 12$. Find also the point of intersection of the two lines.

5. Find the angle between the lines $y = 2x - 1$ and $y = \frac{1}{2}x + 7$ to 2 decimal places.

6. A line through a vertex of a triangle which is perpendicular to the opposite side is called an **altitude**. Find the equation of the altitude through the vertex A of the triangle ABC where A is the point $(2, 3)$, B is $(1, -7)$ and C is $(4, -1)$.

7. $P(2, 5),\ Q(12, 5)$ and $R(8, -7)$ form a triangle.

    a) Find the equations of the altitudes (see Question 6) through R and Q.

    b) Find the point of intersection of these altitudes.

    c) Show that the altitude through P also passes through this point.

8. The vertices of the triangle PQR are $P(1,5)$, $Q(2,-2)$ and $R(-2,6)$.

    a) Write down the equations of the perpendicular bisectors of PQ and QR. Find the point X where these two lines meet.

    b) Show that $XP = XQ = XR$.

    c) Does X lie on the perpendicular bisector of PR as well?

9*. The vertices of the triangle ABC are $A(a_1,a_2)$, $B(b_1,b_2)$ and $C(c_1,c_2)$, where $a_1^2 + a_2^2 = b_1^2 + b_2^2 = c_1^2 + c_2^2$.

    a) Find the equation of the perpendicular bisector of BC. Does this line pass through the origin?

    b) Show that the perpendicular bisectors of the three sides of ABC are concurrent.

10*. The vertices of the triangle ABC are $A(a_1,a_2)$, $B(b_1,b_2)$ and $C(c_1,c_2)$, where $a_1^2 + a_2^2 = b_1^2 + b_2^2 = c_1^2 + c_2^2$.

    a) Find the equation of the altitude from A.

    b) Show that the point $H(a_1 + b_1 + c_1, a_2 + b_2 + c_2)$ lies on this altitude.

    c) Explain why this shows in general that the three altitudes of a triangle are concurrent. The common point is called the **orthocentre** of the triangle.

    d) Show that the origin O, the orthocentre H of the triangle and the centroid G of the triangle (see Question 17 of Exercise 2B) lie in a straight line (are **collinear**).

Chapter 2: Summary

- The length of the line segment AB, where A and B have coordinates (x_1,y_1) and (x_2,y_2) respectively, is

$$\sqrt{(x_1 - x_2)^2 + (y_1 - y_2)^2}\,.$$

  The gradient of the line segment is

$$\frac{y_2 - y_1}{x_2 - x_1}$$

  and the midpoint of AB has coordinates

$$\left(\tfrac{1}{2}(x_1 + x_2), \tfrac{1}{2}(y_1 + y_2)\right).$$

- The line with gradient m and y-intercept c has equation

$$y = mx + c\,.$$

  The line with gradient m passing through the point (x_1,y_1) has equation

$$y - y_1 = m(x - x_1)\,.$$

  The line passing through the two points (x_1,y_1) and (x_2,y_2) has equation

$$\frac{y - y_1}{y_2 - y_1} = \frac{x - x_1}{x_2 - x_1}\,.$$

- Any line can have its equation written in the form $ax + by + c = 0$ for constants a, b and c. This form is not unique.

- Parallel lines have identical gradients. Lines with gradients m_1 and m_2 are perpendicular when $m_1 m_2 = -1$.

- The distance from the point (u,v) to the straight line with equation $ax + by + c = 0$ is

$$\pm \frac{au + bv + c}{\sqrt{a^2 + b^2}}$$

Quadratics and Inequalities

In this Chapter we will learn:

- how to complete the square of a quadratic expression, and understand the relationship between the resulting expression and the shape of the graph of the quadratic,

- how to find the discriminant of a quadratic, and understand its relationship to the number of zeros of the quadratic,

- how to solve quadratic equations, and quadratic and linear inequalities,

- how to solve simultaneous equations involving one quadratic equation and one linear one,

- to recognise and solve equations which are quadratic in some function.

3.1 Quadratic Expressions

An equation of the form $bx + c$, where b, c are constants, is called **linear**. Its graph $y = bx + c$ is a straight line. If we add a term in x^2, the resulting expression $ax^2 + bx + c$ is called a **quadratic**, and the corresponding graph $y = ax^2 + bx + c$ is a **parabola**.

Thus a quadratic is an expression of the form $ax^2 + bx + c$, where a, b, c are constants (of course, a must be non-zero: otherwise the expression is linear). Examples of quadratics are $2x^2 - 7x + 3$, $x^2 + 29x$ and $4 - 3x^2$. The constants a, b, c are called **coefficients**: a is the coefficient of x^2, b the coefficient of x, and c is called the constant coefficient.

The graph of a quadratic is always either a 'smile' or a 'frown', with a line of symmetry parallel to the y-axis: the graph is a 'smile' if the coefficient a of x^2 is positive, and a 'frown' otherwise.

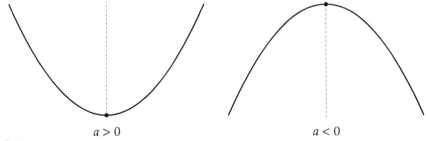

$a > 0$ $\qquad\qquad\qquad$ $a < 0$

Figure 3.1

The minimum value of a 'smile', and the maximum value of a 'frown' quadratic occurs where the quadratic meets the line of symmetry. Knowing where the line of symmetry is, and knowing the **vertex** of the quadratic (the point where the quadratic meets the line of symmetry) is important, if we are to know the shape of the curve. This can be done by elementary trial-and-error methods.

Example 3.1.1. *Find the line of symmetry and vertex of the quadratic* $y = x^2 + 4x - 9$.

> Since $y = -4$ when $x = 1$ and also when $x = -5$, the line of symmetry occurs midway between these two values, so that the line of symmetry has equation $x = -2$.

x	−6	−5	−4	−3	−2	−1	0	1	2
y	3	−4	−9	−12	−13	−12	−9	−4	3

When $x = -2$, $y = -13$, and hence the coordinates of the vertex are $(-2, -13)$.

3.2 Completing The Square

Finding the line of symmetry and the vertex can be done much more effectively by writing the quadratic in an equivalent form. Considering the case of $y = x^2 + 4x - 9$ discussed above, we note that we can write

$$y = x^2 + 4x - 9 = (x+2)^2 - 4 - 9 = (x+2)^2 - 13$$

Since $(x+2)^2$ is a perfect square, it is always at least zero, and it is only zero when $x + 2 = 0$. Thus $y \geq -13$ everywhere, and $y = -13$ precisely when $x = -2$. Thus it is clear that the vertex is $(-2, -13)$, and the line of symmetry is $x = -2$.

Example 3.2.1. *Find the line of symmetry and the vertex of the quadratic* $y = 11 - 2(x+1)^2$.

Since $(x+1)^2$ is a perfect square, $(x+1)^2 \geq 0$, and so $y \leq 11$ for all x, and that $y = 11$ precisely when $x = -1$. Thus the line of symmetry is $x = -1$, and the vertex is $(-1, 11)$.

How do we put a quadratic into this new shape? Start with the simple case where $a = 1$, and consider the quadratic $x^2 + bx + c$. We note that x^2 and bx are the first two terms of the perfect square $\left(x + \frac{1}{2}b\right)^2$. Since $\left(x + \frac{1}{2}b\right)^2 = x^2 + bx + \frac{1}{4}b^2$, we have

$$x^2 + bx = \left(x + \tfrac{1}{2}b\right)^2 - \tfrac{1}{4}b^2$$

and hence

$$x^2 + bx + c = \left(x + \tfrac{1}{2}b\right)^2 + \left(c - \tfrac{1}{4}b^2\right)$$

This process is known as **completing the square**. It can be easily extended to deal with more complex quadratics.

Example 3.2.2. *Complete the square for these quadratics:*
(a) $x^2 + 10x + 32$,   (b) $2x^2 + 10x + 7$,   (c) $3 - 4x - 2x^2$

(a) $x^2 + 10x + 32 = (x+5)^2 - 25 + 32 = (x+5)^2 + 7$

(b) Start by taking out the factor of 2 in front of x^2, so that

$$\begin{aligned} 2x^2 + 10x + 7 &= 2(x^2 + 5x) + 7 = 2\left[\left(x + \tfrac{5}{2}\right)^2 - \tfrac{25}{4}\right] + 7 \\ &= 2\left(x + \tfrac{5}{2}\right)^2 - \tfrac{25}{2} + 7 = 2\left(x + \tfrac{5}{2}\right)^2 - \tfrac{11}{2} \end{aligned}$$

(c) Do the same with the factor of -2, so

$$\begin{aligned} 3 - 4x - 2x^2 &= 3 - 2(x^2 + 2x) = 3 - 2\left[(x+1)^2 - 1\right] \\ &= 3 - 2(x+1)^2 + 2 = 5 - (x+1)^2 \end{aligned}$$

where we have completed the square for $x^2 + 2x$ to obtain $(x+1)^2 - 1$.

Example 3.2.3. *Complete the square for* $x^2 - 3x + 1$; *use the result to solve the equation* $x^2 - 3x + 1 = 0$.

Since $x^2 - 3x + 1 = \left(x - \frac{3}{2}\right)^2 - \frac{9}{4} + 1 = \left(x - \frac{3}{2}\right)^2 - \frac{5}{4}$, we solve the equation

$$\begin{aligned} x^2 - 3x + 1 &= 0 \\ \left(x - \tfrac{3}{2}\right)^2 - \tfrac{9}{4} + 1 &= 0 \\ \left(x - \tfrac{3}{2}\right)^2 &= \tfrac{5}{4} \\ x - \tfrac{3}{2} &= \pm\tfrac{1}{2}\sqrt{5} \\ x &= \tfrac{1}{2}(3 \pm \sqrt{5}) \end{aligned}$$

Example 3.2.4. *Complete the square for* $12x^2 - 7x - 12$, *and use the result to factorise the quadratic.*

We have

$$
\begin{aligned}
12x^2 - 7x - 12 &= 12\left[x^2 - \tfrac{7}{12}x\right] - 12 = 12\left[\left(x - \tfrac{7}{24}\right)^2 - \tfrac{49}{576}\right] - 12 \\
&= 12\left(x - \tfrac{7}{24}\right)^2 - \tfrac{49}{48} - 12 = 12\left(x - \tfrac{7}{24}\right)^2 - \tfrac{625}{48}
\end{aligned}
$$

and so, using the 'Difference of Two Squares' technique,

$$
\begin{aligned}
12x^2 - 7x - 12 &= 12\left[\left(x - \tfrac{7}{24}\right)^2 - \tfrac{625}{576}\right] = 12\left[\left(x - \tfrac{7}{24}\right)^2 - \left(\tfrac{25}{24}\right)^2\right] \\
&= 12\left(x - \tfrac{7}{24} - \tfrac{25}{24}\right)\left(x - \tfrac{7}{24} + \tfrac{25}{24}\right) = 12\left(x - \tfrac{4}{3}\right)\left(x + \tfrac{3}{4}\right) \\
&= (3x - 4)(4x + 3)
\end{aligned}
$$

To sum up:

Key Fact 3.1 Completing the Square

$$
\begin{aligned}
x^2 + bx + c &= \left(x + \tfrac{1}{2}b\right)^2 + c - \tfrac{1}{4}b^2 \\
ax^2 + bx + c &= a\left(x + \tfrac{b}{2a}\right)^2 - \tfrac{b^2 - 4ac}{4a}
\end{aligned}
$$

It is probably just as easy to understand the process for completing the square in general, and to work out each case ' 'by hand', as to learn these formulae!

EXERCISE 3A

1. Find the vertex and the line of symmetry for each of the following:

   a) $y = (x - 2)^2 + 3$
   b) $y = (x - 5)^2 - 4$
   c) $y = (x + 3)^2 - 7$
   d) $y = (2x - 3)^2 + 1$
   e) $y = (5x + 3)^2 + 2$
   f) $y = (3x + 7)^2 - 4$
   g) $y = (x - 3)^2 + c$
   h) $y = (x - p)^2 + q$
   i) $y = (ax + b)^2 + c$

2. Find the least (or, if appropriate, the greatest) value of each of the following quadratic expressions, and the value of x for which this value occurs.

   a) $(x + 2)^2 - 1$
   b) $(x - 1)^2 + 2$
   c) $5 - (x + 3)^2$
   d) $(2x + 1)^2 - 7$
   e) $3 - 2(x - 4)^2$
   f) $(x + p)^2 + q$
   g) $(x - p)^2 - q$
   h) $r - (x - t)^2$
   i) $c - (ax + b)^2$

3. Solve the following quadratic equations, leaving surds in your answer.

   a) $(x - 3)^2 - 3 = 0$
   b) $(x + 2)^2 - 4 = 0$
   c) $2(x + 3)^2 = 5$
   d) $(3x - 7)^2 = 8$
   e) $(x + p)^2 - q = 0$
   f) $a(x + b)^2 - c = 0$

4. Complete the square for the following quadratic expressions:

   a) $x^2 + 2x + 2$
   b) $x^2 - 8x - 3$
   c) $x^2 + 3x - 7$
   d) $5 - 6x + x^2$
   e) $x^2 + 14x + 49$
   f) $2x^2 + 12x - 5$
   g) $3x^2 - 12x + 3$
   h) $7 - 8x - 4x^2$
   i) $2x^2 + 5x - 3$

5. By completing the square, factorise the following expressions:

   a) $x^2 - 2x - 35$
   b) $x^2 - 14x - 176$
   c) $x^2 + 6x - 432$
   d) $6x^2 - 5x - 6$
   e) $14 + 45x - 14x^2$
   f) $12x^2 + x - 6$

6. By completing the square, find (as appropriate) the least or greatest value of each of the following expressions, and the value of x for which this occurs.

   a) $x^2 - 4x + 7$
   b) $x^2 - 3x + 5$
   c) $4 + 6x - x^2$
   d) $2x^2 - 5x + 2$
   e) $3x^2 + 2x - 4$
   f) $3 - 7x - 3x^2$

3.3   Solving Quadratic Equations

We now have three methods that can be used to solve quadratic equations:

- Factorisation is often the simplest method. To solve $x^2 - 6x + 8 = 0$ we write $(x-2)(x-4) = 0$. Thus either $x - 2 = 0$ or $x - 4 = 0$, so that $x = 2$ or $x = 4$. The numbers 2 and 4 are the **roots** of the equation. This method might be impossible, or just difficult, to do: try finding the factors of $30x^2 - 11x - 30$, for example.

- We can use the so-called **Quadratic Formula**: the roots of the equation $ax^2 + bx + c = 0$ are

$$x = \frac{-b \pm \sqrt{b^2 - 4ac}}{2a}$$

- Quadratics can also be solved by completing the square. The equation $x^2 + 2x - 4 = 0$ becomes $(x+1)^2 - 5 = 0$, and hence $(x-1)^2 = 5$, so that $x - 1 = \pm\sqrt{5}$, and hence $x = 1 \pm \sqrt{5}$.

It is worth noting that the Quadratic Formula is actually derived by completing the square! We see that

$$
\begin{aligned}
ax^2 + bx + c &= 0 \\
a\left(x + \tfrac{b}{2a}\right)^2 - \tfrac{b^2 - 4ac}{4a} &= 0 \\
\left(x + \tfrac{b}{2a}\right)^2 &= \tfrac{b^2 - 4ac}{4a^2} \\
x + \tfrac{b}{2a} &= \pm \tfrac{\sqrt{b^2 - 4ac}}{2a} \\
x &= \tfrac{-b \pm \sqrt{b^2 - 4ac}}{2a}
\end{aligned}
$$

Of course, for the Quadratic Formula (or the general method of completing the square) to work we need $a \neq 0$. Since the quadratic equation becomes a linear one (and thus easy to solve) when $a = 0$, this is not a demanding restriction!

If a quadratic equation cannot be solved by simple factorisation, it is likely that the roots will involve surds. Always try to express solutions **exactly**, using surds. It is far better to say that the roots of an equation are $\frac{1}{2}(1 \pm \sqrt{2})$, instead of saying that the roots are 1.21 and -0.21 to 2 decimal places. Any result giving an answer to a fixed number of decimal places will be an approximation, and using that approximation in later calculations will probably produce errors. It is better to be exact whenever possible.

> **For Interest**
>
> There is a school of thought that says that if you can do a problem on a calculator, you are not doing mathematics, but just sums. While there are problems where calculators are necessary, try to adopt the strategy of not using your calculator as a first resort!

It is important to realise that there are some quadratics which we cannot (as yet) solve! It is quite possible to choose constants a, b and c such that $b^2 - 4ac$ is negative, in which case the Quadratic Formula cannot be implemented (or at least not until we have learned about Complex Numbers).

Example 3.3.1. *Solve the equations:*
(a) $2x^2 - 3x - 4 = 0$ (b) $2x^2 - 3x + 4 = 0$ (c) $30x^2 - 11x - 30 = 0$

(a) Using the formula

$$x = \frac{3 \pm \sqrt{(-3)^2 - 4 \times 2 \times (-4)}}{4} = \tfrac{1}{4}\left[3 \pm \sqrt{41}\right]$$

(b) Completing the square

$$
\begin{aligned}
2\left(x - \tfrac{3}{4}\right)^2 - \tfrac{9}{8} + 4 &= 0 \\
\left(x - \tfrac{3}{4}\right)^2 &= -\tfrac{23}{16}
\end{aligned}
$$

Since the right-hand side is negative, we cannot take its square root, and hence there are no solutions. Had we used the formula, we would have been asked to calculate $\sqrt{-23}$, which would indicate that there was no solution.

(c) Completing the square

$$30\left(x^2 - \tfrac{11}{30}x\right) = 30$$
$$x^2 - \tfrac{11}{30}x = 1$$
$$\left(x - \tfrac{11}{60}\right)^2 = 1 + \tfrac{121}{3600} = \tfrac{3721}{3600}$$
$$x - \tfrac{11}{60} = \pm\tfrac{61}{60}$$
$$x = \tfrac{72}{60} = \tfrac{6}{5}, \ -\tfrac{50}{60} = -\tfrac{5}{6}$$

Having found the solutions we observe that the equation **could** have been solved by finding the elusive factorisation $(5x - 6)(6x + 5) = 0$.

3.4 The Discriminant

Considering the quadratic formula, the expression $b^2 - 4ac$ inside the square root has a particular importance.

- If $b^2 - 4ac > 0$, then there is no problem evaluating both roots of the quadratic, and the quadratic equation $ax^2 + bx + c = 0$ has two distinct roots.

- If $b^2 - 4ac = 0$, then the formula tells us that $x = -\frac{b}{2a}$ is the single root of the equation. In a sense that will be made clear later, this root can be regarded as occurring twice, and is often called a **repeated root**.

- If $b^2 - 4ac < 0$, then the quadratic formula fails to give any solutions, and hence there are no solutions.

Key Fact 3.2 The Discriminant

The quantity $\Delta = b^2 - 4ac$ is called the **discriminant** of the quadratic $ax^2 + bx + c$, since it discriminates between the possible types of solution of the equation $ax^2 + bx + c = 0$: the equation $ax^2 + bx + c = 0$ has two distinct roots if $\Delta > 0$, has one (repeated) root if $\Delta = 0$, and has no real roots if $\Delta < 0$.
Moreover, if a, b, c are integers and $\Delta > 0$ is a perfect square, then the roots of the quadratic equation will be rational. In this case, a simple factorisation of the quadratic is possible.

Example 3.4.1. *What can be said about the roots of the following quadratic equations?*
a) $2x^2 - 3x - 4 = 0$
b) $2x^2 - 3x - 5 = 0$
c) $2x^2 - 4x + 5 = 0$
d) $2x^2 - 4x + 2 = 0$.

(a) Since $\Delta = (-3)^2 - 4 \times 2 \times (-4) = 41 > 0$ is not a perfect square, the equation has two irrational roots.

(b) This time $\Delta = (-3)^2 - 4 \times 2 \times (-5) = 49 = 7^2 > 0$, and hence the equation has two rational roots.

(c) This time $\Delta = (-4)^2 - 4 \times 2 \times 5 = -24 < 0$, and hence the equation has no roots.

(d) Finally $\Delta = (-4)^2 - 4 \times 2 \times 2 = 0$, so the equation has one (repeated) root.

Example 3.4.2. *The equation $kx^2 - 2x - 7 = 0$ has two real roots. What can be said about the value of k?*

The quadratic has discriminant $4 + 28k$. Since the equation has two real roots, $\Delta > 0$, and hence $k > -\frac{1}{7}$.

Example 3.4.3. *The equation $3x^2 + 2x + k = 0$ has a repeated root. Find the value of k.*

The quadratic has discriminant $4 - 12k$. Since this must be equal to 0, it follows that $k = \frac{1}{3}$.

Note that in none of these cases was it necessary to find the roots: determining the discriminant was enough.

EXERCISE 3B

1. Solve the following equations, where possible, giving exact answers.

   a) $x^2 + 3x - 5 = 0$ b) $x^2 - 4x - 7 = 0$ c) $x^2 + 6x + 9 = 0$
   d) $2x^2 + 7x + 3 = 0$ e) $8 - 3x - x^2 = 0$ f) $x^2 + x + 1 = 0$

2. Use the discriminant to determine whether the following equations have two roots, one root or no roots. The constants p and q are positive.

   a) $x^2 - 3x - 5 = 0$ b) $x^2 + 2x + 1 = 0$ c) $x^2 - 3x + 4 = 0$
   d) $3x^2 - 6x + 5 = 0$ e) $x^2 + px - q = 0$ f) $x^2 - px + p^2 = 0$

3. The following equations have the number of roots shown in brackets. Deduce as much as you can about the value of k.

   a) $x^2 + 3x + k = 0 \ (2)$ b) $x^2 - 7x + k = 0 \ (1)$ c) $kx^2 - 3x + 5 = 0 \ (0)$
   d) $3x^2 + 5x - k = 0 \ (2)$ e) $x^2 - 4x + 3k = 0 \ (1)$ f) $kx^2 - 5x + 7 = 0 \ (0)$
   g) $x^2 - kx + 4 = 0 \ (2)$ h) $x^2 + kx + 9 = 0 \ (0)$ i) $kx^2 + 7x + k = 0 \ (1)$.

4. If a and c are both positive, what can be said about the graph of $y = ax^2 + bx - c$?

5. If a is negative and c is positive, what can be said about the graph of $y = ax^2 + bx + c$?

6. If α and β are the roots of the quadratic equation $x^2 + bx + c = 0$, express $\alpha + \beta$ and $\alpha\beta$ in terms of b and c (Hint: Factorise the quadratic).

7. If α and β are the roots of the quadratic equation $ax^2 + bx + c = 0$, express $\alpha + \beta$ and $\alpha\beta$ in terms of a, b and c.

8. Show that the equation $\frac{x+1}{x-4} = \frac{x+7}{2x+5}$ has no real roots.

9. Show that there is no real value of p for which the equation

   $$(p+1)x^2 + (2p+1)x + 9 = 0$$

   has a repeated root. How many solutions does this equation have, for any value of p?

10*. Find the only values of p and q such that the equation $x^2 + px = q^2$ has a unique solution.

11*. Given that the roots of the equation $x^2 + ux + (u + 5) = 0$ differ by 1, find the possible values of u, and the roots of the equation for each value of u.

3.5   Simultaneous Equations

Suppose we want to solve the simultaneous equations

$$y = x^2 \qquad x + y = 6.$$

The standard technique is to use the linear expression to express either x or y in terms of the other variable, and substitute this expression into the quadratic equation.

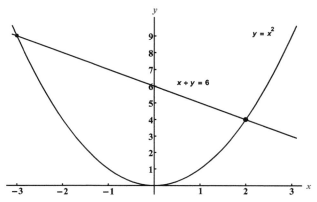

Figure 3.2

In this case we can write $y = 6 - x$, and substitution gives us

$$
\begin{aligned}
6 - x &= x^2 \\
x^2 + x - 6 &= 0 \\
(x + 3)(x - 2) &= 0
\end{aligned}
$$

so that $x = -3, 2$. Substituting these values for x into the linear expression gives the corresponding values of y. They are $y = 9, 4$. Thus there are two solutions: either $x = 2, y = 4$ or $x = -3, y = 9$. Note that the x and y values go together in pairs: $x = 2$ corresponds to $y = 4$ and not to $y = 9$. This correspondence can be seen in the graph, where the coordinates of the two points of intersection of the parabola $y = x^2$ and the line $x + y = 6$ are $(2, 4)$ and $(-3, 9)$.

Example 3.5.1. *Solve the simultaneous equations $x^2 - 2xy + 3y^2 = 11$ and $x - 3y = 1$.*

The linear expression can be written $x = 3y + 1$. We substitute:

$$
\begin{aligned}
x^2 - 2xy + 3y^2 &= 11 \\
(3y + 1)^2 - 2y(3y + 1) + 3y^2 &= 11 \\
9y^2 + 6y + 1 - 6y^2 - 2y + 3y^2 &= 11 \\
6y^2 + 4y - 10 &= 0 \\
3y^2 + 2y - 5 &= 0 \\
(3y + 5)(y - 1) &= 0
\end{aligned}
$$

so that $y = 1, -\frac{5}{3}$. The corresponding values of x are $4, -4$. Thus the solutions are $x = -4, y = -\frac{5}{3}$ and $x = 4, y = 1$.

Example 3.5.2. *At how many points does the line $x + 2y = 3$ meet the curve $2x^2 + y^2 = 4$?*

Substituting $x = 3 - 2y$ into the other equation, we obtain

$$
\begin{aligned}
2(3 - 2y)^2 + y^2 &= 4 \\
9y^2 - 24y + 14 &= 0
\end{aligned}
$$

Since this quadratic has discriminant $(-24)^2 - 4 \times 9 \times 14 = 72$, this quadratic has two solutions. Thus the line meets the curve at two points.

3.6 Disguised Quadratics

Sometimes you will meet equations which are not, at first sight, quadratics. However, these equations can be turned into quadratics by careful algebra and a sensible substitution.

Example 3.6.1. *Solve the equations*
(a) $x = 2 + 8x^{-1}$, (b) $t^4 - 13t^2 + 36 = 0$, (c) $\sqrt{x} = 6 - x$.

(a) Multiplying the equation by x yields $x^2 = 2x + 8$, or $x^2 - 2x - 8 = 0$. This factorises to read $(x - 4)(x + 2) = 0$, and hence $x = 4, -2$.

(b) Substituting $x = t^2$ yields $x^2 - 13x + 36 = 0$, or $(x-4)(x-9) = 0$, so that $x = 4, 9$. Thus $t^2 = 4, 9$ so that $t = \pm 2, \pm 3$.

(c) Substituting $\sqrt{x} = y$ yields $y = 6 - y^2$, so that $y^2 + y - 6 = 0$, and hence $(y+3)(y-2) = 0$, so that $y = -3, 2$. But since $y = \sqrt{x}$ **must** be positive we must have $y = 2$, so that $\sqrt{x} = 2$, and hence $x = 4$.

An alternative approach would be to square both sides, yielding $x = (6-x)^2 = 36 - 12x + x^2$, and hence $x^2 - 13x + 36 = 0$. Solving this as above, we deduce that $x = 4, 9$. Where has this (incorrect) 'solution' of $x = 9$ come from? The problem is that the squared equation $x = (6-x)^2$ is satisfied by solutions to the equation $-\sqrt{x} = 6 - x$, as well as by solutions to the original equation. Squaring frequently results in an equation which is satisfied by more than the solutions of the initial equation. The only case when this is not true is when both sides of the equation are known to be positive (or both negative); keeping this in mind is an added complication which can be avoided by adopting the first approach.

EXERCISE 3C

1. Solve the following pairs of simultaneous equations:

   a) $y = x + 1$, $\quad x^2 + y^2 = 25$
   c) $2x + y = 5$, $\quad x^2 + y^2 = 25$
   e) $y = 2x + 1$, $\quad y = x^2 - x + 3$
   g) $y = 2x - 12$, $x^2 + 4xy - 3y^2 = -27$

   b) $x + y = 7$, $\quad x^2 + y^2 = 25$
   d) $y = 1 - x$, $\quad y^2 - xy = 0$
   f) $y = 3x + 2$, $\quad x^2 + y^2 = 26$
   h) $2x - 5y = 6$, $2xy - 4x^2 - 3y = 1$

2. Find the number of points of intersection of the straight line with the curve in each case:

   a) $y = 1 - 2x$, $x^2 + y^2 = 1$
   c) $y = 3x - 1$, $\quad xy = 12$
   e) $3y - x = 15$, $4x^2 + 9y^2 = 36$

   b) $y = \frac{1}{2}x - 1$, $\quad y = 4x^2$
   d) $4y - x = 16$, $\quad y^2 = 4x$
   f) $4y = 12 - x$, $\quad xy = 9$

3*. Solve the simultaneous equations

$$x^2 + y^2 + 2x - 4y = 0 \qquad x^2 + y^2 + 5x - 3y = 6$$

4. Solve the following equations exactly:

   a) $x^4 - 5x^2 + 4 = 0$
   b) $x^4 - 10x^2 + 9 = 0$
   c) $x^6 - 7x^3 - 8 = 0$
   d) $x^6 + x^3 = 12$
   e) $x = 3 + 10x^{-1}$
   f) $2t + 5 = \frac{3}{t}$
   g) $x = \frac{12}{x+1}$
   h) $\sqrt{t}(\sqrt{t} - 6) = -9$
   i) $x - \frac{2}{x+2} = \frac{1}{3}$
   j) $\frac{12}{x+1} - \frac{10}{x-3} = -3$
   k) $\frac{15}{2x+1} + \frac{10}{x} = \frac{55}{2}$
   l) $\frac{1}{y^2} - \frac{1}{y^2+1} = \frac{1}{2}$
   m) $x - 8 = 2\sqrt{x}$
   n) $x + 15 = 8\sqrt{x}$
   o) $t - 5\sqrt{t} - 14 = 0$
   p) $\sqrt[3]{x^2} - \sqrt[3]{x} - 6 = 0$
   q) $\sqrt[3]{t^2} - 3\sqrt[3]{t} = 4$

5. Solve the equation $(x^2 + 2)^2 - 14(x^2 + 2) + 33 = 0$

6. Solve the equation $x(x+2) + \frac{24}{x(x+2)} = 11$.

7*. By substituting $y = x - x^{-1}$ show that the expression

$$6x^4 - 25x^3 + 12x^2 + 25x + 6$$

   can be written as $x^2(6y^2 - 25y + 24)$. Hence solve the quartic equation

$$6x^4 - 25x^3 + 12x^2 + 25x + 6 = 0$$

8*. Solve the equation $(7 + 4\sqrt{3})^x + (7 - 4\sqrt{3})^x = 4$.

3.7   Sketching Quadratics

We frequently want to know the shape of a curve. Drawing a graph inexactly, while showing enough information to indicate its key properties, is called **sketching** the graph. When sketching straight line graphs, it is generally enough to indicate the x- and y-intercepts (the points where the line meets the x- and y-axes, or perhaps (qualitatively) the gradient of the curve:

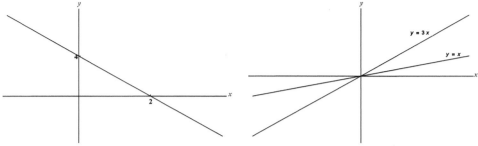

Figure 3.3

We certainly do not need to plot individual points on the curve, as if we were drawing the graph on graph paper! The same thing is true when we want to sketch a quadratic curve: we are not being asked to draw an accurate graph, and do not need to plot a large number of individual points:

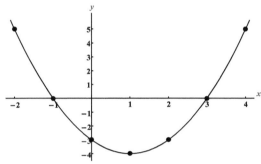

This is a plot, not a sketch!

Figure 3.4

A sketch of a quadratic should include the key essentials of the curve, which can be determined by factorisation or completing the square:

- Is it a 'smile' or a 'frown'?

- Where does it intercept the axes?

- Where is the vertex?

Example 3.7.1. *Sketch the quadratic $y = x^2 + 6x - 16$.*

Since $y = (x+8)(x-2) = (x+3)^2 - 25$, the quadratic is a 'smile' with x-intercepts 2 and -8 and a y-intercept -16, with vertex $(-3, -25)$.

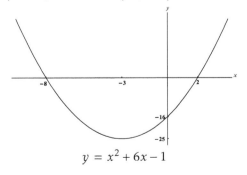

$$y = x^2 + 6x - 1$$

Figure 3.5

Sometimes it is not even necessary to provide this much information. We might only be interested in the sketch for the information about when the function is positive or negative, or we might only be interested in when the function has a positive gradient and when it has a negative one. You need to decide from context what information is needed in your sketch.

Example 3.7.2. *Sketch the curve* $y = 10 + x - 2x^2$, *and hence determine the range of values of* x *for which the curve is above the x-axis.*

We want to know the sign of y, so shall not include information about the vertex. Since $y = (5 - 2x)(2 + x)$, there are x-intercepts at -2 and $\frac{5}{2}$. An adequate sketch can omit the y-axis. The graph lies above the x-axis for $-2 < x < \frac{5}{2}$.

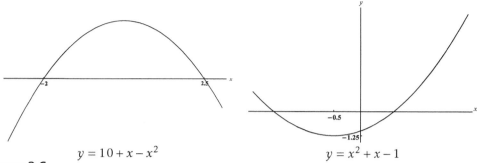

$$y = 10 + x - x^2 \qquad\qquad y = x^2 + x - 1$$

Figure 3.6

Example 3.7.3. *Sketch the curve* $y = x^2 + x - 1$.

Since $y = \left(x + \frac{1}{2}\right)^2 - \frac{5}{4}$, the vertex occurs at $\left(-\frac{1}{2}, -\frac{5}{4}\right)$. The intercepts at $\frac{1}{2}[-1 \pm \sqrt{5}]$ are a little too complicated to add to a small sketch (the question does not make it plain that they are needed!)

These ideas can be used in reverse to retrieve the quadratic from its key properties.

Example 3.7.4. *Write down the equation of the quadratic with vertex* $(1, 2)$ *which passes through* $(3, -6)$.

The quadratic must have equation $y = a(x - 1)^2 + 2$ for some a, since $-6 = a(3-1)^2 + 2 = 2 + 4a$, we deduce that $a = -2$, so that $y = -2(x-1)^2 + 2 = 4x - 2x^2$.

EXERCISE 3D

1. Sketch the following graphs, showing all intercepts with the axes and the vertex (the constants a and b are positive, with $b > a$):

   a) $y = x^2 - 6x + 8$ b) $y = 3 - 2x - x^2$ c) $y = x^2 - 2x$

   d) $y = 2x^2 - 5x - 3$ e) $y = -3(x - 4)^2$ f) $y = 12 + x - x^2$

   g) $y = x^2 + 2ax$ h) $y = (x - a)^2 - b^2$

2. By sketching the graphs, determine the range of values of x for which each graph is below the x-axis:

   a) $y = x^2 + 2x - 1$ b) $y = 7 - 6x - x^2$ c) $y = x^2 + 8x + 16$

3. Find the equation of the parabola which:

   a) crosses the x-axis at $(1, 0)$ and $(5, 0)$, and crosses the y-axis at $(0, 15)$,

   b) crosses the x-axis at $(-2, 0)$ and $(7, 0)$ and crosses the y-axis at $(0, -56)$,

   c) passes through the points $(-6, 0)$, $(-2, 0)$ and $(0, -6)$,

   d) has a minimum value at $(1, 3)$ and passes through $(4, 39)$,

   e) passes through the points $(1, 3)$, $(5, 3)$ and $(2, 6)$

4*. What is the equation of the quadratic passing through the points $(1, 0)$, $(2, 5)$ and $(6, 45)$?

5*. Use your sketch of $y = x^2 - 6x + 8$ from Question 1 to sketch $y = (x + k)^2 - 6(x + k) + 8$ for $2 < k < 4$.

3.8 Solving Inequalities

3.8.1. NOTATION AND ALGEBRA

We often want to compare one number with another and say which is the greater. This comparison is expressed by using the inequality symbols $>$, $<$, $\leq$ and $\geq$. These symbols should already be familiar.

- The symbol $a < b$ means that a is less than b,

- the symbol $a > b$ means that a is greater than b,

- the symbol $a \leq b$ means that a is less than or equal to b,

- the symbol $a \geq b$ means that a is greater than or equal to b.

Thus $a < b$ and $b > a$ mean the same thing. Similarly, $a \leq b$ and $b \geq a$ mean the same thing. The symbols $<$ and $>$ are called **strict** inequalities, while the symbols $\leq$ and $\geq$ are called **non-strict** inequalities.

We often wish to manipulate algebraic inequalities. When solving algebraic equations, we use a number of techniques, which boil down to 'do the same thing to both sides of the equation'. We have almost the same amount of freedom with inequalities.

The rules for handling inequalities are easy to write down, but since they differ subtly from those for equations, it is worth taking the time to see why they work. The simplest way to do this is to note that all inequality statements are equivalent to statements about positive numbers:

$$a < b \qquad \Leftrightarrow \qquad b - a > 0$$
$$a \leq b \qquad \Leftrightarrow \qquad b - a \geq 0$$

and the positive numbers have the property that they remain positive when added together or multiplied together:

$$c, d > 0 \qquad \Rightarrow \qquad c + d, cd > 0$$
$$c, d \geq 0 \qquad \Rightarrow \qquad c + d, cd \geq 0$$

From these observations we can deduce that following:

> **Key Fact 3.3** Operations on Inequalities
>
> $$a < b \quad \Rightarrow \quad a + c < b + c \qquad \text{for any real } c$$
> $$a \leq b \quad \Rightarrow \quad a + c \leq b + c \qquad \text{for any real } c$$
> $$a < b \quad \Rightarrow \quad ad < bd \qquad \text{for any } d > 0$$
> $$a \leq b \quad \Rightarrow \quad ad \leq bd \qquad \text{for any } d > 0$$
> $$a < b \quad \Rightarrow \quad ae > be \qquad \text{for any } e < 0$$
> $$a \leq b \quad \Rightarrow \quad ae \geq be \qquad \text{for any } e > 0$$

If $a < b$, then $(b + c) - (a + c) = b - a > 0$ and hence $a + c < b + c$. The second inequality follows similarly. If $a < b$, then $b - a > 0$, and hence (for $d > 0$) $bd - ad = (b - a)d > 0$, so that $ad < bd$. The fourth inequality follows similarly. The last two need care, since they state that when an inequality is multiplied by a **negative** number, the sense of the inequality needs to be reversed. To see why this is so, we note that $-e > 0$ when $e < 0$. Thus

$$a < b \quad \Rightarrow \quad -ae = (-e)a < (-e)b = -be \quad \Rightarrow \quad ae - be > 0 \quad \Rightarrow \quad ae > be$$

Thus we can manipulate inequalities in almost exactly the same way that we manipulate equations: we can add or subtract numbers to both sides, and can multiply both sides by positive numbers. We just have to remember that multiplying both sides of an inequality by a negative number reverses the sense of that inequality.

3.8.2. SOLVING LINEAR INEQUALITIES

Solving many inequalities is simply a matter of exploiting the above rules, and using standard algebra.

Example 3.8.1. *Solve the inequality $\frac{1}{3}(4x + 3) - 3(2x - 4) \geq 20$.*

We successively multiply both sides of the inequality by 3, subtract 39 from both sides, and divide both sides by -14 to obtain the answer.

$$
\begin{aligned}
\tfrac{1}{3}(4x+3) - 3(2x-4) &\geq 20 \\
4x + 3 - 9(2x-4) &\geq 60 \\
4x + 3 - 18x + 36 &\geq 60 \\
-14x + 39 &\geq 60 \\
-14x &\geq 60 - 39 = 21 \\
x &\leq \tfrac{21}{-14} = -\tfrac{3}{2}
\end{aligned}
$$

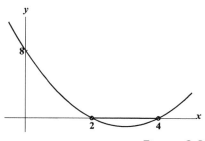

Figure 3.7

The series of operations performed is the same as would have been performed had we been asked to solve the equation $\tfrac{1}{3}(3x-4) - 3(2x-4) = 20$. The only time we need to take care is when multiplying by a number; the sign of that number has to be considered, since it affects the sense of the inequality.

Exercise 3E

Solve the following inequalities.

1. a) $x - 3 > 11$ b) $x + 7 < 11$ c) $2x + 3 \leq 8$ d) $3x - 5 \geq 16$
    e) $3x + 7 > -5$ f) $5x + 6 \leq -10$ g) $2x + 3 < -4$ h) $3x - 1 \leq -13$

2. a) $\frac{x+3}{2} > 5$ b) $\frac{x-4}{6} \leq 3$ c) $\frac{2x+3}{4} < -5$ d) $\frac{3x+2}{5} \leq 4$
    e) $\frac{4x-3}{2} \geq -7$ f) $\frac{5x+1}{3} > -3$ g) $\frac{3x-2}{8} < 1$ h) $\frac{4x-2}{3} \geq -6$

3. a) $x - 4 \leq 5 + 2x$ b) $x - 3 \geq 5 - x$ c) $2x + 5 < 4x - 7$
    d) $3x - 4 > 5 - x$ e) $4x \leq 3(2 - x)$ f) $3x \geq 5 - 2(3 - x)$
    g) $6x < 8 - 2(7 + x)$ h) $5x - 3 > x - 3(2 - x)$ i) $6 - 2(x + 1) \leq 3(1 - 2x)$

4. a) $\tfrac{1}{3}(8x + 1) - 2(x - 3) > 10$ b) $\tfrac{5}{2}(x + 1) - 2(x - 3) < 7$
    c) $\tfrac{1}{4}(x + 1) + \tfrac{1}{6} \geq \tfrac{1}{3}(2x - 5)$ d) $\tfrac{1}{2}x - \tfrac{1}{5}(3 - 2x) \leq 1$

3.8.3. Quadratic Inequalities

Solving inequalities involving quadratics requires us to determine where some quadratic expression is positive or negative. The easiest way of handling these inequalities involves factorisation.

Example 3.8.2. *Solve the inequality* $x^2 - 6x + 8 < 0$.

We sketch the curve of $y = x^2 - 6x + 8$. Since $y = (x - 2)(x - 4)$, we see that the graph crosses the x-axis at $x = 2$ and $x = 4$. Since the curve is a 'smile', the vertex of the curve lies below the x-axis, and we obtain the sketch.

We now need to find on the graph where $y < 0$. This occurs when x lies between 2 and 4, so when both $x > 2$ and $x < 4$.

Figure 3.8

Note that, since $2 < 4$, it is acceptable to put these two inequalities together and write the solution as $2 < x < 4$. A solution set of this type is called an **interval**.

Example 3.8.3. *Solve the inequality* $x^2 \leq 2x + 3$.

We sketch the curve of $y = x^2 - 2x - 3$. Since $y = (x+1)(x-3)$, we see that the graph crosses the x-axis at $x = -1$ and $x = 3$. Since the curve is a 'smile', the vertex of the curve lies below the x-axis, and we obtain the sketch.

We now need to find on the graph where $y \leq 0$. This occurs when either $x \leq -1$ or $x \geq 3$.

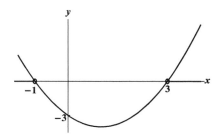

Figure 3.9

However, since it is not true that $3 \leq -1$, we cannot put these two inequalities together and write $3 \leq x \leq -1$. Another reason why we cannot do this is that the two inequalities cannot be true at the same time — either one is true or the other. Writing a single inequality implies that both inequalities are intended to be true at the same time, as was the case in the previous example.

An alternative approach can solve these problems without sketching a graph, by simply determining the sign of the function for key values of x. This method is not as important in this case, since we know the shapes of quadratic graphs, but will be very useful when we want to consider more complex inequalities, involving cubic or worse expressions.

Example 3.8.4. *Solve the inequality* $5 + 4x - x^2 \leq 0$.

Since $5 + 4x - x^2 = (5-x)(1+x)$, the function equals zero at $x = 5$ and $x = -1$. These values of 5 and -1 are called the **critical values** of the function. Make a table showing the signs of the factors in the product $(5-x)(1+x)$.

	$x < -1$	$x = -1$	$-1 < x < 5$	$x = 5$	$x > 5$
$5 - x$	$+$	$+$	$+$	0	$-$
$1 + x$	$-$	0	$+$	$+$	$+$
$5 + 4x - x^2$	$-$	0	$+$	0	$-$

We see that the solution is $x \leq -1$ or $x \geq 5$ (the critical values are included, due to the non-strict inequality).

Example 3.8.5. *If* $a > 0$, *solve the inequality* $x^2 \leq a^2$.

We need to solve $(x - a)(x + a) = x^2 - a^2 \leq 0$. The function $x^2 - a^2$ has critical values at $\pm a$. We calculate a sign table

	$x < -a$	$x = -a$	$-a < x < a$	$x = a$	$x > a$
$x - a$	$-$	$-$	$-$	0	$+$
$x + a$	$-$	0	$+$	$+$	$+$
$x^2 - a^2$	$+$	0	$-$	0	$+$

and so the solution is $-a \leq x \leq a$

This result is a precursor of discussions we shall have in the next chapter.

Key Fact 3.4 Square Roots of Inequalities

The following are equivalent (for $a > 0$):

$$x^2 \leq a^2 \quad \Leftrightarrow \quad -a \leq x \leq a$$
$$x^2 < a^2 \quad \Leftrightarrow \quad -a < x < a$$
$$x^2 \geq a^2 \quad \Leftrightarrow \quad x \leq -a \quad \text{or} \quad x \geq a$$
$$x^2 > a^2 \quad \Leftrightarrow \quad x < -a \quad \text{or} \quad x > a$$

Completing the square enables us to solve quadratic inequalities, even if the quadratics do not factorise neatly.

Example 3.8.6. *Solve the inequalities:* (a) $2x^2 - 8x + 11 \leq 0$, (b) $2x^2 - 10x + 7 \leq 0$.

(a) Completing the square tells us that $2x^2 - 8x + 11 = 2(x-2)^2 + 3$. Since it is a square, $(x-2)^2 \geq 0$ for all real x, and so $2x^2 - 8x + 11 \geq 3$ for all real x, so there are no solutions to the inequality $2x^2 - 8x + 11 \leq 0$.

(b) Completing the square gives

$$
\begin{aligned}
2x^2 - 10x + 7 &\leq 0 \\
2\left(x - \tfrac{5}{2}\right)^2 - \tfrac{11}{2} &\leq 0 \\
\left(x - \tfrac{5}{2}\right)^2 &\leq \tfrac{11}{4}
\end{aligned}
$$

and hence $-\tfrac{1}{2}\sqrt{11} \leq x - \tfrac{5}{2} \leq \tfrac{1}{2}\sqrt{11}$, and so the solution is the interval

$$\tfrac{1}{2}(5 - \sqrt{11}) \leq x \leq \tfrac{1}{2}(5 + \sqrt{11})$$

The properties of the discriminant can lead to solving quadratic inequalities.

Example 3.8.7. *The quadratic $2x^2 - kx + 50$ has 2 real roots. What does this tell us about the constant k?*

This quadratic must have positive discriminant, and so $k^2 - 400 > 0$, which tells us that either $k > 20$ or $k < -20$.

Example 3.8.8. *Solve the inequality $\frac{x+3}{5x-1} \leq \frac{1}{3}$.*

When solving equations of this type, our first instinct is to clear the denominators. This creates a problem, because we do not know whether $5x - 1$ is positive or not; multiplying this inequality by $5x - 1$ will change the direction of the inequality when $x < \tfrac{1}{5}$. We avoid this problem by multiplying by $(5x - 1)^2$, which is always nonnegative. Note that the original inequality only makes sense if $x \neq \tfrac{1}{5}$ (otherwise we are being asked to divide by 0), and so we may assume that $(5x - 1)^2 > 0$ for all relevant values of x.

Thus the inequality becomes, after multiplying by $3(5x - 1)^2$,

$$
\begin{aligned}
3(x+3)(5x-1) &\leq (5x-1)^2 \\
(5x-1)^2 - 3(x+3)(5x-1) &\geq 0 \\
2(5x-1)(x-5) &\geq 0
\end{aligned}
$$

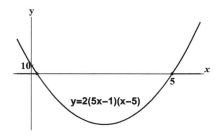

Figure 3.10

According to the sketch, we want the regions $x \leq \tfrac{1}{5}$ or $x \geq 5$. However, we need to remember that the original inequality excluded the possibility of $x = \tfrac{1}{5}$, and so we must exclude that point from our solution. Thus the solution to the original inequality is either $x < \tfrac{1}{5}$ or $x \geq 5$.

Note that this technique of multiplying by the square of the denominator automatically creates a factor of $5x - 1$ in what follows. Do not make the mistake of multiplying out both sides of the inequality, since you might lose track of the factor which this method gives us for free!

An alternative approach would be to consider this inequality in cases, allowing for the two possible signs of $5x - 1$. Thus

- If $x > \tfrac{1}{5}$, the inequality becomes $3(x + 3) \leq 5x - 1$, or $x \geq 5$.

- If $x < \tfrac{1}{5}$, the inequality becomes $3(x + 3) \geq 5x - 1$, or $x \leq 5$.

Putting these two cases together we determine that the set of solutions is $x < \tfrac{1}{5}$ or $x \geq 5$, as before.

Exercise 3F

Solve the following inequalities. Give exact answers. Where necessary, assume that a and b are positive, with $a < b$.

1. a) $(x - 2)(x - 3) < 0$
    d) $(x - 4)(x + 10) \geq 0$
    g) $(x + 2)(4x + 5) \geq 0$
    j) $(x - 5)(x + 5) < 0$

    b) $(x - 4)(x - 7) > 0$
    e) $(2x - 1)(x + 3) > 0$
    h) $(1 - x)(3 + x) < 0$
    k) $(3 - 4x)(3x + 4) > 0$

    c) $(x - 1)(x - 3) < 0$
    f) $(3x - 2)(3x + 5) \leq 0$
    i) $(3 - 2x)(5 - x) > 0$
    l) $(2 + 3x)(2 - 3x) \leq 0$

2. a) $x^2 + 3x - 5 > 0$
    d) $x^2 - x + 1 \geq 0$
    g) $2x^2 - 3x - 1 < 0$
    j) $x^2 - (a + b)x + ab > 0$

    b) $x^2 + 6x + 9 < 0$
    e) $x^2 - 9 > 0$
    h) $8 - 3x - x^2 > 0$
    k) $x^2 + (a - b)x - ab \leq 0$

    c) $x^2 - 5x + 2 < 0$
    f) $x^2 + 2x + 1 \leq 0$
    i) $2x^2 + 7x + 1 \geq 0$
    l) $x^2 - ab < 0$

3. a) $x^2 + 5x + 6 > 0$
    d) $2x^2 - 18 \geq 0$
    g) $x^2 + 5x + 2 > 0$
    j) $x^2 + ax - b < 0$

    b) $x^2 - 7x + 12 < 0$
    e) $2x^2 - 5x + 3 \geq 0$
    h) $7 - 3x^2 < 0$
    k) $12x^2 + 5x - 3 > 0$

    c) $x^2 - 2x - 15 \leq 0$
    f) $6x^2 - 5x - 6 < 0$
    i) $x^2 + ax + a^2 < 0$
    l) $3x^2 - 7x + 1 \leq 0$

4. a) $\frac{4}{x-7} \leq 1$
    d) $7 - \frac{x}{5-2x} \geq 0$

    b) $\frac{12}{x+4} > 2$
    e) $\frac{x+2}{7x+4} - 2 < 0$

    c) $3 + \frac{4}{2x-3} < 0$
    f) $7 + \frac{5-x}{x} < 0$

5. The quadratic equation $kx^2 + 6x + k = 0$ has two real roots. What range of values of k are possible?

6. The quadratic equation $kx^2 + (k + 1)x + 2 =$ has no real roots. What range of values of k are possible?

7. The quadratic equation $kx^2 + (k + 2)x + (2k + 1) = 0$ has no real roots. What range of values of k are possible?

8*. Solve the following inequalities, giving exact answers.

    a) $x^3 - 7x^2 + 10x < 0$
    b) $\frac{2+3x}{4-x} \geq 2x$
    c) $\frac{x+3}{x-3} + \frac{x+1}{(x-2)^2} \leq 0$

Chapter 3: Summary

- Every quadratic expression can be expressed in the form $p(x + q)^2 + r$ for some constants p, q and r. The vertex of the quadratic curve $y = p(x + q)^2 + r$ occurs at the point $(-q, r)$.

- If $p > 0$, then r is the minimum value of the quadratic $p(x + q)^2 + r$, and this value is achieved at $x = -q$. If $p < 0$, then r is the maximum value of the quadratic $p(x+q)^2 + r$, and this value is achieved at $x = -q$.

- The quadratic equation $ax^2 + bx + c = 0$ can be solved by factorisation, by use of the quadratic formula

$$x = \frac{-b \pm \sqrt{b^2 - 4ac}}{2a} \, ,$$

  or by completing the square.

- The discriminant of the quadratic $ax^2 + bx + c$ is the quantity $\Delta = b^2 - 4ac$. If $\Delta > 0$, the equation $ax^2 + bx + c = 0$ has two real roots; if $\Delta = 0$ this equation has one real root; if $\Delta < 0$ this equation has no real roots.

- Inequalities, both quadratic and linear and even simultaneous, are best solved by sketching the corresponding curves and considering their signs.

1. Express $\frac{5}{\sqrt{7}}$ in the form $k\sqrt{7}$ where k is rational. (OCR)

2. In the triangle PQR, Q is a right angle, $PQ = \left(6 - 2\sqrt{2}\right)$ cm and $QR = \left(6 + 2\sqrt{2}\right)$ cm. Find the area of the triangle, and show that $PR = 2\sqrt{22}$ cm.

3. Simplify $\sqrt[3]{36} \times \sqrt[6]{\frac{4}{3}} \times \sqrt{27}$.

4. Write $(\sqrt{3})^{-3} + (\sqrt{3})^{-2} + (\sqrt{3})^{-1} + (\sqrt{3})^{0} + (\sqrt{3})^{1} + (\sqrt{3})^{2} + (\sqrt{3})^{3}$ in the form $a + b\sqrt{3}$, where a, b are rational.

5. If $u = x - x^{-1}$ and $v = x^2 + x^{-2}$, find $u(v + 1)$ in terms of x, giving your answer in its simplest form.

6. Solve the simultaneous equations $5x - 3y = 41$ and $(7\sqrt{2})x + (4\sqrt{2})y = 82$.

7. Express $(9a^4)^{-\frac{1}{2}}$ as an algebraic fraction in simplified form. (OCR)

8. Show that the triangle formed by the points $(-2, 5)$, $(1, 3)$ and $(5, 9)$ is right-angled.

9. A triangle is formed by the points $A(-1, 3)$, $B(5, 7)$ and $C(0, 8)$.

    a) Show that the angle $\angle ACB$ is a right angle.
    b) Find the coordinates of the point where the line through B parallel to AC cuts the x-axis.

10. $A(7, 2)$ and $C(1, 4)$ are two vertices of a square $ABCD$.

    a) Find the equation of the diagonal BD.
    b) Find the coordinates of B and of D.

11. A quadrilateral $ABCD$ is formed by the points $A(-3, 2)$, $B(4, 3)$, $C(9, -2)$ and $D(2, -3)$.

    a) Show that all four sides are equal in length.
    b) Show that $ABCD$ is not a square.

12. P is the point $(7, 5)$ and ℓ_1 is the line with equation $3x + 4y = 16$.

    a) Find the equation of the line ℓ_2 which passes through P and is perpendicular to ℓ_1.
    b) Find the point of intersection of the lines ℓ_1 and ℓ_2.
    c) Find the perpendicular distance of P from the line ℓ_1.

13. Prove that the triangle with vertices $(-2, 8)$, $(3, 20)$ and $(11, 8)$ is isosceles. Find its area.

14. Find the equation of the perpendicular bisector of the line joining $(2, -5)$ and $(-4, 3)$.

15. The points $A(1, 2)$, $B(3, 5)$, $C(6, 6)$ and D form a parallelogram. Find the coordinates of the midpoint of AC. Use your answer to find the coordinates of D.

16. The point P is the foot of the perpendicular from the point $A(0,3)$ to the line $y = 3x$.

    a) Find the equation of the line AP.

    b) Find the coordinates of the point P.

    c) Find the perpendicular distance of A from the line $y = 3x$.

17. Points which lie on the same straight line are called **collinear**. Show that the points $(-1,3)$, $(4,7)$ and $(-11,-5)$ are collinear.

18. Find the equation of the straight line that passes through the points $(3,-1)$ and $(-2,2)$, giving your answer in the form $ax + by + c = 0$. Hence find the coordinates of the point of intersection of the line and the x-axis. (OCR)

19. The coordinates of the points A and B are $(3,2)$ and $(4,-5)$ respectively. Find the coordinates of the midpoint of AB, and the gradient of AB.

    Hence find the equation of the perpendicular bisector of AB, giving your answer in the form $ax + by + c = 0$, where a, b and c are integers. (OCR)

20. The curve $y = 1 + \frac{1}{2+x}$ crosses the x-axis at the point A and the y-axis at the point B.

    a) Calculate the coordinates of A and of B.

    b) Find the equation of the line AB.

    c) Calculate the coordinates of the point of intersection of the line AB and the line with equation $3y = 4x$. (OCR)

21. The straight line p passes through the point $(10,1)$ and is perpendicular to the line r with equation $2x + y = 1$. Find the equation of p.

    Find also the coordinates of the point of intersection of p and r, and deduce the perpendicular distance from the point $(10,1)$ to the line r. (OCR)

22. The line $3x - 4y = 8$ meets the y-axis at A. The point C has coordinates $(-2,9)$. The line through C perpendicular to $3x - 4y = 8$ meets it at B. Calculate the area of the triangle ABC.

23. The points $A(-3,-4)$ and $C(5,4)$ are the ends of the diagonal of a rhombus $ABCD$.

    a) Find the equation of the diagonal BD.

    b) Given that the side BC has gradient $\frac{5}{3}$, find the coordinates of B and hence of D.

24. Two lines have equations $y = m_1 x + c_1$ and $y = m_2 x + c_2$, where $m_1 m_2 = -1$. Prove that the lines are perpendicular.

25. Find the values of x for which $x^{\frac{1}{3}} - 2x^{-\frac{1}{3}} = 1$. (OCR)

26. Solve the equation $4^{2x} \times 8^{x-1} = 32$.

27. Given that $343^n = 49^{n+2}$, find the value of n.

28. Solve the equation $\frac{125^{3x}}{5^{x+4}} = \frac{25^{x-2}}{3125}$.

29. Solve the simultaneous equations $x + y = 2$ and $x^2 + 2y^2 = 11$. (OCR)

30. For what values of k does $2x^2 - kx + 8 = 0$ have a repeated root?

31. A rectangle has perimeter 16 cm and its area is at least 15 cm^2. If one side of the rectangle has length x cm, form a quadratic inequality in x, and find the set of possible values of x.

32. a) Solve the equation $x^2 - (6\sqrt{3})x + 24 = 0$ exactly.

     b) Find all four solutions of the equation $x^4 - (6\sqrt{3})x^2 + 24 = 0$, giving your answers correct to 2 decimal places. (OCR, adapt.)

33. Show that the line $y = 3x - 3$ and the curve $y = (3x + 1)(x + 2)$ do not meet.

34. Find, correct to 3 significant figures, all the roots of the equation $8x^4 - 8x^2 + 1 = \frac{1}{2}\sqrt{3}$. (OCR)

35. The constant k is real, and the equation $10x^2 + 8x + 1 = k(x^2 + 2x)$ has one real root. Find the range of values of k.

36. The equation of a curve is $y = ax^2 - 2bx + c$, where a, b, c are constants with $a > 0$.

    a) Find, in terms of a, b, c, the coordinates of the vertex of the curve.

    b) Given that the vertex of the curve lies on the line $y = x$, find an expression for c in terms of a and b. Show that, in this case, $4ac \geq -1$, irrespective of the value of b.   (OCR, adapt.)

37. Solve the inequality $x(x + 1) < 12$.   (OCR)

38. Solve the inequality $x - x^3 < 0$.

39. Solve the inequality $x^3 \geq 6x - x^2$.

40. Find the set of values of x for which $9x^2 + 12x + 7 > 19$.   (OCR)

41*. Let A and B have coordinates (p_1, q_1) and (p_2, q_2) respectively. Suppose that P is a point with coordinates (x, y). Find the condition that must be satisfied by x and y if $AP = PB$. Hence show that the locus of points equidistant from A and B is the perpendicular bisector of A and B.

42*. Find all real roots of the following equations:

    a) $x + 10\sqrt{x + 2} - 22 = 0$,

    b) $x^2 - 4x + \sqrt{2x^2 - 8x - 3} - 9 = 0$,

    giving exact answers.   (STEP)

43*. Given that
$$5x^2 + 2y^2 - 6xy + 4x - 4y = a(x - y + 2)^2 + b(cx + y)^2 + d$$
find the values of the constants a, b, c and d.

Solve the simultaneous equations   (STEP)

$$5x^2 + 2y^2 - 6xy + 4x - 4y = 9 \qquad 6x^2 + 3y^2 - 8xy + 8x - 8y = 14.$$

The Modulus Function

In this chapter we will learn:

- the meaning of the modulus function $|x|$,

- how to sketch the graph of $y = |f(x)|$ for linear functions f,

- algebraic properties of the modulus function,

- how to solve elementary equations and inequalities involving the modulus function.

Mathematics contains many functions. Functions are rules which take one or more numbers and assign a value to that number or numbers. We shall study functions in general in greater depth, but at this stage we simply note that we have already met a large number of what might be called **standard** functions, such as addition, subtraction, multiplication, division, and taking powers or roots. Addition is the function which takes two numbers and assigns to them their sum, the square root is the function that takes a non-negative number and extracts its square root. In addition we have met the trigonometric functions of sine, cosine and tangent. All these standard functions are distinguished by having their own buttons on calculators: they are used so often in day-to-day mathematics that they merit this convenience. The modulus function is another standard function.

4.1   The Modulus Function and its Graph

The modulus function is one which 'strips away' the sign from a number, giving an idea of its size but not caring whether it is positive or negative. In other words we want the modulus of 3 to be 3, and the modulus of -4 to be 4. The fact that the modulus function behaves differently for positive and negative numbers means that we need to define it in two stages: we write the modulus of x as $|x|$, and define it to be equal to x if $x \geq 0$, and to be equal to $-x$ if $x < 0$. This two-stage definition is written mathematically in the following manner:

Key Fact 4.1   The Modulus Function

The **modulus** of x, written $|x|$, is defined to be

$$|x| = \begin{cases} x & \text{if } x \geq 0, \\ -x & \text{if } x < 0. \end{cases}$$

The brace in the definition indicates that the formula for $|x|$ takes different forms according to the possible values of x indicated in the list of options ($x \geq 0$, $x < 0$). Mathematicians say that the formula for $|x|$ is defined **piecewise**.

The modulus $|x|$ of x is known as the **absolute value** of x: for this reason the modulus function on calculators is either labelled MOD or ABS.

The graph of $y = |x|$ consists of a 'V' shape; the line to the right of the origin has a gradient of 1, while the line to the left of the origin has a gradient of -1.

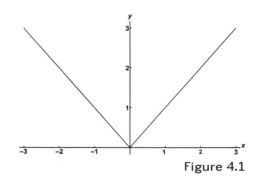

Figure 4.1

4.2 Graphs of Functions Involving the Modulus

Suppose that we want to sketch the graph of $y = |x - 2|$. Note that a sketch does not have to be an exact plot of the function. What is important is that key features of the graph (general shape, intercepts with axes etc.) are shown. There are two ways of thinking about this problem:

- When $x \geq 2$, the function $|x-2| = x-2$. Thus the graph of $y = |x - 2|$ coincides with the graph of $y = x - 2$ in this region. On the other hand, similar thinking tells us that the graph of $y = |x - 2|$ coincides with the graph of $y = 2 - x$ in the region $x < 2$.

- Another, more geometric approach is to see that the graph of $y = |x - 2|$ is obtained from the graph of $y = x - 2$ by reflecting all negative parts of that graph in the x-axis.

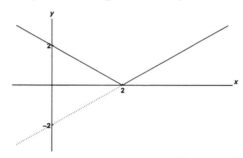

Figure 4.2

These methods can be used to sketch most graphs involving the modulus function.

Example 4.2.1. *Sketch the graphs of: (a)* $y = |2x - 3|$, *(b)* $y = |(x - 1)(x - 3)|$.

The portions of the functions $y = 2x - 3$ and $y = (x - 1)(x - 3)$ that lie below the axis drawn dotted to emphasise the reflection in the x-axis.

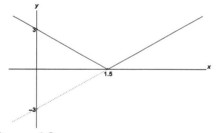 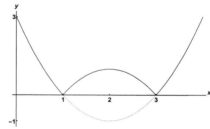

Figure 4.3

Example 4.2.2. *Sketch the graph of* $y = |x - 2| + |1 - x|$.

This problem is best handled using the definition of modulus, and finding a piecewise expression for y.

- When $x \geq 2$ we can remove the modulus signs, writing $|x - 2| = x - 2$ and $|1 - x| = x - 1$, so that $y = 2x - 3$,

- When $1 < x < 2$ we write $|x - 2| = 2 - x$ and $|1 - x| = x - 1$, so that $y = 1$,

- When $x \leq 1$ we write $|2 - x| = 2 - x$ and $|1 - x| = 1 - x$, so that $y = 3 - 2x$.

The sketch is now easy.

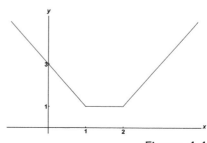

Figure 4.4

4.3 Algebraic Properties of the Modulus

It is clear that there are two square roots of x^2, namely x and $-x$. One of these is positive and the other negative, but which one? The answer is different, according to whether x is positive or negative. The modulus tidies this point up nicely, and this new insight into the modulus function helps us establish more of its properties.

Key Fact 4.2 The Modulus Function — Algebraic Properties

The **modulus** of x, written $|x|$, satisfies the identity:

$$|x| = \sqrt{x^2}$$

and hence

$$|ab| = |a||b| \qquad \left|\frac{a}{b}\right| = \frac{|a|}{|b|}$$

for all suitable a, b.

Since $(ab)^2 = a^2 b^2$ and $\left(\frac{a}{b}\right)^2 = \frac{a^2}{b^2}$, taking square roots proves these identities.

However addition and subtraction are not so simple. It is not true that $|a + b| = |a| + |b|$ for all a, b. For example, if $a = 3, b = -2$ then $a + b = 1$, and so $|a + b| = 1$, $|a| = 3$, $|b| = 2$, and hence $|a + b|$ is strictly less than $|a| + |b|$.

For Interest

It is a common mistake to assume that functions 'behave nicely' with respect to addition. Students frequently make errors by making statements like $(a + b)^2 = a^2 + b^2$ or $\sqrt{a + b} = \sqrt{a} + \sqrt{b}$, or $\sin(a + b) = \sin(a) + \sin(b)$. Try to avoid this error!

Example 4.3.1. *Show that $|a + b| \le |a| + |b|$ for all real a, b.*

It is clear that $ab \le |ab|$ at all times (either ab is negative, or else $ab = |ab|$). Since

$$(a + b)^2 = a^2 + 2ab + b^2 = |a|^2 + 2ab + |b|^2 \le |a|^2 + 2|a||b| + |b|^2 = (|a| + |b|)^2$$

the result follows by taking square roots.

The modulus function has another important use. When we calculate the difference between two numbers, we always subtract the smaller from the larger, to obtain a positive answer. Thus the difference between a and b is $a - b$ if $a \ge b$ (so that $a - b \ge 0$), and is $b - a$ if $b > a$ (so that $a - b \le 0$). This observation can be simplified by stating that the difference between two numbers a and b is the modulus $|a - b|$ of their difference. Thus $|a - b|$ can be interpreted as the distance between the two points a and b. Students will recall the modulus symbol used to denote the length of a vector, so that $|\overrightarrow{AB}|$, the modulus of the vector $\overrightarrow{AB}$, is the distance between the points A and B. The use of the modulus symbol in these cases is consistent.

Example 4.3.2. *What can we say about x if we know that: (a) $|x| = 5$, (b) $|x| \le 4$, (c) $|x - 2| < 3$?*

(a) Since $|x| = |x - 0|$, the difference between x and 0 is 5. Thus $x = 5$ or -5.

(b) The difference between x and 0 is less than or equal to 4, and hence $-4 \le x \le 4$.

(c) The difference between x and 2 is less than 3, so that x lies strictly between $2 - 3$ and $2 + 3$, and hence $-1 < x < 5$.

These arguments can go the other way. If $-1 < x < 5$, then $-3 < x - 2 < 3$, so the distance between $x - 2$ and 0 is less than 3, and hence $|x - 2| < 3$. Thus a number of multiple inequalities can be usefully expressed in terms of the modulus function.

Food For Thought 4.1

If $a > 0$ then

$$|x| \leq a \quad \Leftrightarrow \quad -a \leq x \leq a$$
$$|x| < a \quad \Leftrightarrow \quad -a < x < a$$
$$|x - k| \leq a \quad \Leftrightarrow \quad k - a \leq x \leq k + a$$
$$|x - k| < a \quad \Leftrightarrow \quad k - a < x < k + a$$

The symbol $\Leftrightarrow$ means 'is equivalent to'. Whenever it separates two statements, it means that the statement on the left-hand side means exactly the same thing as the statement on the right. Whenever we meet the left-hand statement in a mathematical argument we can, if we wish, replace it by the right-hand statement and vice versa. The symbol $\Leftrightarrow$ will be most commonly met in proofs of mathematical results.

It is interesting to note that the inequality $|x| > 2$ is equivalent to saying that either $x > 2$ or $x < -2$ (so that the distance of x from 0 is greater than 2). The modulus function is therefore useful in expressing the solution to quadratic inequalities.

Example 4.3.3. *Solve the inequality* $(x - 1)(x - 3) > 0$.

Using the sketch of $y = (x-1)(x-3)$ given in Example 4.2.1 we deduce that the solution is $x < 1$ or $x > 3$. This could be written as $|x - 2| > 1$.

EXERCISE 4A

---

1. Sketch the following graphs:

   a) $y = |x + 3|$ b) $y = |3x - 1|$ c) $y = |x - 5|$
   d) $y = |3 - 2x|$ e) $y = 2|x + 1|$ f) $y = 3|x - 2|$
   g) $y = -2|2x - 1|$ h) $y = 3|2 - 3x|$ i) $y = |x + 2| + |1 - x|$
   j) $y = |6 + x| + |4 - x|$ k) $y = |x - a| - |x - b|$ where   l) $y = 2|x - a| + |x + a|$ for
                                $a > b > 0$ $a > 0$

2. Sketch the following graphs:

   a) $y = |x^2 - 2|$ b) $y = |(x - 1)(x - 2)(x - 3)|$
   c) $y = \big||x| - 2\big|$ d) $y = \big||x - 2| - x\big|$

3. Write the given inequalities without using the modulus notation:

   a) $|x - 3| \leq 1$ b) $|x + 2| > \frac{1}{2}$ c) $|2x - 3| \leq 0.1$ d) $|4x - 3| \geq 8$

4. Solve the simultaneous inequalities:

$$|x - 2| \leq 4 \qquad |x + 4| > 3$$

5*. Find the smallest possible value of $|a - b|$, assuming that a and b are real and $a \neq b$.

4.4 Equations and Inequalities Involving Moduli

In the last section, we started to solve equations and inequalities of a fairly simple type. We used the idea of distance to solve inequalities like $|x| \leq 4$. To solve more complicated inequalities and equations, we need to use more sophisticated ideas. There are essentially two approaches to consider.

The first is in some ways the simplest, since it is purely algebraic. However, caution has to be exercised in its use, since it can only be used in particular circumstances. This method is based on the following consequences of the definition of $|x|$ as the positive square root of x^2:

> **Key Fact 4.3** Squaring The Modulus
>
> For any numbers a, b,
>
> $$|a| = |b| \iff a^2 = b^2$$
> $$|a| < |b| \iff a^2 < b^2$$
>
> and, for any **positive** a, b,
>
> $$a = b \iff a^2 = b^2$$
> $$a < b \iff a^2 < b^2$$

The first two results follow from the identity

$$b^2 - a^2 = |b|^2 - |a|^2 = (|b| - |a|)(|b| + |a|)$$

Thus, if $|a| = |b|$ it is clear that $a^2 = b^2$. On the other hand, if $a^2 = b^2$, then either $|a| - |b| = 0$ or $|a| + |b| = 0$. In the first case $|a| = |b|$, in the second case $|a| = |b| = 0$. On the other hand, if $|a| < |b|$ then $|a| + |b| > 0$ and hence $|b| - |a|$ and $|b| + |a|$ are both positive, so that $b^2 - a^2 > 0$, and hence $a^2 < b^2$. Conversely, if $a^2 < b^2$ then $(|b| - |a|)(|b| + |a|) > 0$. Moreover $b \neq 0$, and hence $|b| + |a| > 0$, so that $|b| - |a| > 0$, and hence $|a| < |b|$. The second two results are just special cases of the first results.

Example 4.4.1. *Solve the equation* $|x - 2| = |2x - 1|$.

$$
\begin{aligned}
|x - 2| = |2x - 1| &\iff (x - 2)^2 = (2x - 1)^2 \\
&\iff x^2 - 4x + 4 = 4x^2 - 4x + 1 \\
&\iff 3x^2 - 3 = 0 \\
&\iff 3(x - 1)(x + 1) = 0 \\
&\iff x = \pm 1
\end{aligned}
$$

Example 4.4.2. *Solve the inequality* $|x - 2| \geq |2x - 3|$.

$$
\begin{aligned}
|x - 2| \geq |2x - 3| &\iff (x - 2)^2 \geq (2x - 3)^2 \\
&\iff x^2 - 4x + 4 \geq 4x^2 - 12x + 9 \\
&\iff 3x^2 - 8x + 5 \leq 0 \\
&\iff (x - 1)(3x - 5) \leq 0 \\
&\iff 1 \leq x \leq \tfrac{5}{3}
\end{aligned}
$$

Example 4.4.3. *Solve the inequality* $x^2 + 1 \leq |x - 1|$.

$$
\begin{aligned}
x^2 + 1 \leq |x - 1| &\iff (x^2 + 1)^2 \leq (x - 1)^2 \\
&\iff x^4 + 2x^2 + 1 \leq x^2 - 2x + 1 \\
&\iff x^4 + x^2 + 2x \leq 0 \\
&\iff x(x + 1)(x^2 - x + 2) \leq 0
\end{aligned}
$$

Completing the square, $x^2 - x + 2 = \left(x - \tfrac{1}{2}\right)^2 - \tfrac{1}{4} + 2 = \left(x - \tfrac{1}{2}\right)^2 + \tfrac{7}{4}$. Since a square is always greater than or equal to 0, it follows that $x^2 - x + 2 \geq \tfrac{7}{4}$ for all real x, and so $x^2 - x + 2$ is always positive. Thus the above condition is equivalent to the simpler condition $x(x + 1) \leq 0$, which means that $-1 \leq x \leq 0$.

The deduction that $x^2 - x + 2$ is always positive could also be achieved by noting that this quadratic has discriminant -7, and hence has no real root. Hence it is either positive everywhere or negative everywhere. Since the quadratic is a 'smile', it is positive everywhere.

Equations and inequalities can be solved by squaring both sides, provided that both sides of the initial equation or inequality are positive. In the cases shown above, both sides were either explicitly positive through being the moduli of expressions, or else were positive for other algebraic reasons. Moreover, this method is only valuable so long as squaring both sides of the equation removes the modulus signs; this is not always the case.

Example 4.4.4. *Solve the equation* $|x + 2| = 2x + 1$.

First see why squaring both sides does not work well here. If we do so, we obtain $(x + 2)^2 = (2x + 1)^2$, or $3x^2 - 3 = 0$, yielding $x = \pm 1$. However, while 1 is a solution of the original equation, -1 is not. Where has this extra solution come from, and how can we avoid it? The squared equation $(x + 2)^2 = (2x + 1)^2$ is the same as the equation $|x + 2| = |2x + 1|$, which might (and in this case does) include solutions of the equation $|x + 2| = -(2x + 1)$. The way round this difficulty is to sketch the two graphs on the same set of axes.

It is clear from the sketch that the line $y = 2x + 1$ (with gradient 2) meets the right-hand half of the line $y = |x + 2|$ (with gradient 1), but that the line $y = 2x + 1$ (which is below the x-axis for $x \leq -2$) does not meet the left-hand half of the line $y = |x + 2|$ at all. Thus we simply need to solve the equation $x + 2 = 2x + 1$, and look for solutions that are bigger than -2. This gives us the single solution $x = 1$. Note that the line $y = -2x - 1$ meets the right-hand half of $y = |x + 2|$ once, and the left-hand half not at all, and that the solution of the equation $-2x - 1 = x + 2$ gives the 'rogue' solution $x = -1$ found above.

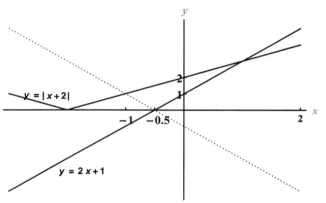

Figure 4.5

This graphical method can be used to solve problems that can be dealt with by purely algebraic means:

Example 4.4.5. *Solve the inequality* $|x - 2| \geq |2x - 1|$.

Example 4.4.2 handles a very similar inequality by algebraic means. The same method can be used to show that the solution is $-1 \leq x \leq 1$.

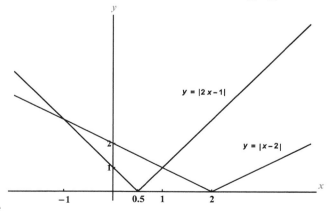

Figure 4.6

Inspecting the graph shows that the right-hand half of $y = |x - 2|$ never meets $y = |2x - 1|$, and that the left-hand half of $y = |x - 2|$ meets each half of $y = |2x - 1|$

once. Solving $2 - x = 2x - 1$ (for $\frac{1}{2} < x < 2$) yields $x = 1$. Solving $2 - x = 1 - 2x$ (for $x < \frac{1}{2}$) yields $x = -1$. Inspection of the graph shows that the required solution is $-1 \le x \le 1$, as expected.

Example 4.4.6. *Solve the inequality $|x - 3| \ge 1 + 2|x|$.*

Both sides of this inequality are positive, and so we could square both sides. The only problem is that doing so yields the inequality $x^2 - 6x + 9 \ge 1 + 4|x| + 4x^2$, or $4|x| \le 8 - 6x - 3x^2$. In other words we have not removed the modulus sign from the inequality, and squaring this last inequality would cause problems, since the right-hand side $8 - 6x - 3x^2$ is not always positive. Even if it were positive, squaring one more time would create an inequality involving terms including x^4, which is rather intimidating!

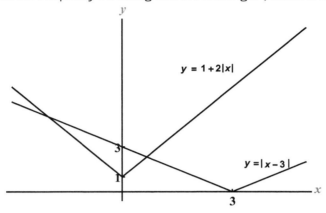

Figure 4.7

A sketch shows the right-hand half of the curve $y = |x - 3|$ (with gradient 1) misses the curve $y = 1 + 2|x|$ entirely, and the left-hand half of the curve $y = |x - 3|$ meets both halves of the curve $y = 1 + 2|x|$. Thus one intercept between these curves can be found by solving $3 - x = 1 + 2x$, giving $x = \frac{2}{3}$, and the other intercept can be found by solving $3 - x = 1 - 2x$, giving $x = -2$. Looking at the sketch, we deduce that the solution to the problem is $-2 \le x \le \frac{2}{3}$.

There is one final method which can be used with any type of equation: Considering cases.

Example 4.4.7. *Solve the equation $|x + 3| + 2|x| + 3x = 9$.*

The key values of x are -3 and 0, because these are the values where the two moduli functions 'change direction'. What happens between those values? If $x \ge 0$, the equation becomes $x + 3 + 2x + 3x = 9$, or $x = 1$. This value of x is in the range $x \ge 0$, and hence is a solution. If $-3 \le x < 0$, the equation becomes $x + 3 - 2x + 3x = 6$, or $x = \frac{3}{2}$. This value of x is not in the range $-3 \le x < 0$, and hence is not a solution. If $x < -3$, the equation becomes $-x - 3 - 2x + 3x = 9$, or $-3 = 9$. This equation has no solutions.

Thus the only solution to the equation is $x = 1$. In effect, we have found the piecewise form of the function $|x + 3| + 2|x| + 3x$:

$$|x + 3| + 2|x| + 3x = \begin{cases} 6x + 3, & x \ge 0, \\ 2x + 3, & -3 \le x < 0, \\ -3, & x \le -3. \end{cases}$$

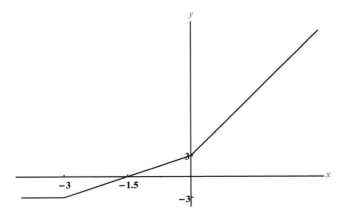

Figure 4.8

and checked to see whether each piece of the function can equal 9. The problem with this method is that it gives no insight into solving inequalities, something a sketch of the function could do.

EXERCISE 4B

1. Solve the following equations:

   a) $|x + 2| = 5$
   b) $|3x + 1| = 10$
   c) $|2x - 3| = 3$
   d) $|x + 1| = |2x - 3|$
   e) $|x - 3| = |3x + 1|$
   f) $|2x + 1| = |3x + 9|$
   g) $|x - 3| = 5x + 9$
   h) $|x| = 6 - x^2$
   i) $|x - 2| = x^2 - 8$

2. Solve the following inequalities:

   a) $|x + 2| < 1$
   b) $|2x + 7| < 3$
   c) $|3x + 2| \geq 8$
   d) $|x + 2| < |3x + 1|$
   e) $|2x + 5| > |x + 2|$
   f) $|x| > |2x - 3|$
   g) $2|x + 1| \geq x + 3$
   h) $|x + 4| < 2x - 1$
   i) $|x + 1| < 7 - x^2$

3. Solve the equations:

   a) $|x + 1| + |1 - x| = 2$
   b) $|x + 1| - |1 - x| = 2$
   c) $|1 - x| - |1 + x| = 2$

4. Solve the equation $|x - 3| = \sqrt{x} - 1$ ($x > 0$).

5*. Solve the equation $5||x| - 4| = x + 10$.

6*. Solve the inequality $|x^2 - a^2| < bx$, where $a, b > 0$.

Chapter 4: Summary

- The modulus function $|x|$ is defined by the formula

$$|x| = \begin{cases} x & x \geq 0 \\ -x & x < 0, \end{cases}$$

For any real x, the number $|x|$ is the non-negative square root of x^2.

- For real numbers x and y, $|xy| = |x||y|$. In addition, $x^2 = y^2$ precisely when $|x| = |y|$.

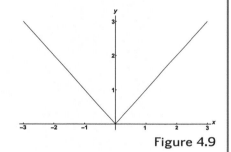

Figure 4.9

- For real numbers x and y, $|x| < |y|$ precisely when $x^2 < y^2$. In general these two statements are not, however, the same as the statement $x < y$.

- Sketching the graphs of the associated functions is a useful method for solving many equations or inequalities involving the modulus function.

Polynomials

In this chapter we will learn:

to add, subtract and multiply polynomials,

that two polynomials are identical precisely when they have the same coefficients,

how to divide one polynomial by another, using long division, identifying the quotient and the remainder,

how to use the Remainder Theorem and the Factor Theorem to simplify the process of dividing by linear polynomials,

how these techniques enable us to solve certain cubic and higher order equations.

5.1   What is a Polynomial?

We have already met a variety of polynomials, particularly linear, quadratic and cubic ones. Examples of these are

$$3x^3 - 2x^2 + 1 \qquad 3 \qquad 4 - 2x \qquad x^2 \qquad 1$$
$$2x^2 - 8x + 1001 \qquad (x-2)^2 \qquad x^3 + x^2 + x - 1 \qquad \sqrt{2}x^2 \qquad x$$

In this chapter we shall consider more general polynomials.

Key Fact 5.1 What is a Polynomial?

An expression of the form

$$a_n x^n + a_{n-1} x^{n-1} + a_{n-2} x^{n-2} + \cdots + a_2 x^2 + a_1 x + a_0 \,,$$

where $a_n, a_{n-1}, \ldots, a_0$ are real numbers with $a_n \neq 0$ and n is a non-negative integer, is called a **polynomial of degree n.**

Polynomials of degree 0 are called **constant,**

polynomials of degree 1 are called **linear,**

polynomials of degree 2 are called **quadratic,**

polynomials of degree 3 are called **cubic,**

polynomials of degree 4 are called **quartic,**

and polynomials of degree 5 are called **quintic.**

While Latin words exist to describe polynomials of degree higher than five, it is more usual simply to refer to such polynomials by their degree. For example, it is more usual to talk about polynomials of degree 6 than to refer to sextic polynomials.

The expressions $a_n x^n$, $a_{n-1} x^{n-1}$, ..., $a_1 x$ and a_0 which go together to form the polynomial are called the **terms** of the polynomial, while the numbers $a_n, a_{n-1}, \ldots, a_0$ are called the **coefficients** of the polynomial. The coefficient a_n of the highest power of x in the polynomial is called the **leading coefficient**, and the term $a_n x^n$ is called the **leading term**. Thus the degree of a polynomial is the index of x in the leading term of that polynomial.

Example 5.1.1. *Find the degrees and the leading coefficients of these polynomials:*

$$a) \quad 7x^8 - 19x^6 + 3x^4 + 5x^3 - 2x + 1 \qquad b) \quad x^4 - 3x^2 + 8x^{10} - 7x$$

The first polynomial has degree 8 and leading coefficient 7, while the second polynomial has degree 10 and leading coefficient 8. Note that the highest power of x in the second polynomial was not to be found in the first term written down; as a result we had to look at the polynomial carefully to identify the leading term. To avoid confusion and potential errors, it is normal to be systematic about the way we write down polynomials. We either write the terms of a polynomial with their powers of x in **ascending order** (for example, $1 + 2x - 3x^2 + 4x^7$) or else with their powers of x in **descending order** (for example, $4x^7 - 3x^2 + 2x + 1$).

Note, however, that $\frac{1}{x}$ and $\sqrt{x}$ are not polynomials. While both are powers of x, the indices of the powers are not non-negative integers.

What about 0? This constant expression does not satisfy the conditions given above to be a polynomial of degree 0, since it does not possess a non-zero leading coefficient (or any non-zero coefficients, for that matter). Nevertheless we will want to include 0 within the class of polynomials (in the next section, we will be performing algebra on polynomials, and any polynomial subtracted from itself will give 0 as a result). We shall therefore decide to call 0 a polynomial. Like any other polynomial, it ought to have a degree. As noticed above, however, it cannot have any non-negative integer degree. If we really must assign a degree to the zero polynomial, it needs to be $-\infty$, the negative infinity. This will be explained later.

5.2 Addition and Subtraction of Polynomials

Adding or subtracting polynomials is simply a matter of adding or subtracting the coefficients of the corresponding powers of x; in other words, collecting like terms. Care needs to be taken to ensure that the correct coefficients are collected together. This can be done by writing out the various polynomials in carefully aligned columns, one to each power of x, as below.

Example 5.2.1. *Given the polynomials* $f(x) = 3x^3 + 7x^2 - 5x + 8$, $g(x) = -x^5 + 6x^4 - 2x^3 + x - 3$, $h(x) = x^4 - x^2 - 1$, *find*

$$a) \quad f(x) + g(x) \qquad b) \quad f(x) - g(x) \qquad c) \quad 2g(x) + h(x)$$

(a) $f(x) + g(x) = $

$$\begin{array}{cccccc} & & 3x^3 & +7x^2 & -5x & +8 \\ -x^5 & +6x^4 & -2x^3 & & +x & -3 \end{array} = -x^5 + 6x^4 + x^3 + 7x^2 - 4x + 5,$$

(b) $f(x) - g(x) = $

$$\begin{array}{cccccc} & & 3x^3 & +7x^2 & -5x & +8 \\ x^5 & -6x^4 & +2x^3 & & -x & +3 \end{array} = x^5 - 6x^4 + 5x^3 + 7x^2 - 6x + 11,$$

(c) $2g(x) + h(x) = $

$$\begin{array}{cccccc} -2x^5 & +12x^4 & -4x^3 & & +2x & -6 \\ & +x^4 & & -x^2 & & -1 \end{array} = -2x^5 + 13x^4 - 4x^3 - x^2 + 2x - 7.$$

Note that $2g(x) = g(x) + g(x)$ is simply obtained by doubling all the coefficient of $g(x)$, as might be expected.

Suppose that $f(x)$ has degree m and $g(x)$ has degree n, and that $f(x)$ has leading term ax^m, while $g(x)$ has leading term bx^n.

- If $m > n$, then the highest power of x that appears in either $f(x)$ or $g(x)$ is x^m. Thus the leading term of $f(x) + g(x)$ is ax^m, and hence $f(x) + g(x)$ has degree m.

- If $m < n$, then the highest power of x that appears in either $f(x)$ or $g(x)$ is x^n. Thus the leading term of $f(x) + g(x)$ is bx^n, and hence $f(x) + g(x)$ has degree n.

- If $m = n$, then the highest power of x that occurs in either $f(x)$ or $g(x)$ is x^n, and this occurs in both $f(x)$ and $g(x)$. Thus $f(x) + g(x) = (a + b)x^n + h(x)$, where $h(x)$ is a polynomial involving powers of x no greater than x^{n-1}. Most of the time this will mean that $f(x) + g(x)$ will have degree n. However, it might happen that $a + b = 0$, in which case it will follow that $f(x) + g(x)$ will have degree smaller than n.

Food For Thought 5.1

Let $\deg(h)$ denote the degree of a polynomial $h(x)$. For any two polynomials $f(x)$ and $g(x)$, the degree of $f(x) + g(x)$ is at most the greater of the degrees of $f(x)$ and $g(x)$, so that

$$\deg(f + g) \leq \max\big(\deg(f), \deg(g)\big)$$

We note that the above inequality is in fact an equality when the degrees of $f(x)$ and $g(x)$ are distinct.

For Interest

Note that $-f(x)$ has the same degree as $f(x)$, and that $f(x) + -f(x) = f(x) - f(x) = 0$. If this result is to hold for all polynomials $f(x), g(x)$, the degree of 0 must be less than the degree of any non-zero polynomial. The convention that $\deg(0) = -\infty$ is compatible with this requirement.

5.3 Multiplying Polynomials

We have just seen that the sum or difference of two polynomials is still a polynomial. The same is true of the product of two polynomials, but determining the product is more complex.

The FOIL technique can be usefully used for multiplying out brackets, where each bracket contains two terms, like $(a + b)(c + d)$:

- The First numbers from each bracket are multiplied together, yielding ac,

- the product of the Outer pair of numbers is found, yielding ad,

- the product of the Inner pair of numbers is found, yielding bc,

- the Last numbers from each bracket are multiplied together, yielding bd,

and these four terms are added together, yielding

$$(a + b)(c + d) = ac + ad + bc + bd$$

The FOIL mnemonic is a way of ensuring that every term in the left-hand bracket gets multiplied by every term in the right-hand bracket. To handle the product of two brackets containing more than two terms, we need to extend the FOIL concept.

We do this by using a key property of algebra, which enables us to multiply out brackets:

$$(a_1 + a_2 + \cdots + a_n)b = a_1 b + a_2 b + \cdots + a_n b \qquad a(b_1 + b_2 + \cdots + b_m) = ab_1 + ab_2 + \cdots + ab_m$$

We say that **multiplication is distributive over addition**. These rules for multiplying out a single bracket can be used to multiply out a pair of brackets.

For example, to multiply $a + b + c$ by $d + e + f$, write $z = d + e + f$. Then

$$\begin{aligned}(a + b + c)(d + e + f) &= (a + b + c)z = az + bz + cz = a(d + e + f) + b(d + e + f) + c(d + e + f) \\ &= ad + ae + af + bd + be + bf + cd + ce + cf\end{aligned}$$

While a mnemonic like FOIL would not be practical in this context (particularly if one bracket had four terms and the other six, for example), the principle of multiplying out brackets is clear:

> **Food For Thought 5.2**
>
> The product of two brackets is obtained by first multiplying every term in the first bracket by every term in the second bracket, and then adding up all these products.

If we set out to multiply two polynomials together, then every term in both brackets is a number times a power of x, and so the product of any two terms (one from each bracket) is also a number times a power of x, and hence the sum of all such terms is a polynomial. Thus the product of two polynomials is itself a polynomial.

Example 5.3.1. *Given the polynomials $f(x) = x^4 + 3x - 1$, $g(x) = x^3 + 2x^2 - 5$ and $h(x) = x^2 - 3$, find the polynomials*

$$a) \quad f(x)g(x) \qquad\qquad b) \quad xf(x) + \big(g(x)\big)^2 \qquad\qquad c) \; \big(h(x)\big)^3$$

(a) We have

$$
\begin{aligned}
f(x)g(x) &= (x^4 + 3x - 1)(x^3 + 2x^2 - 5) \\
&= x^4(x^3 + 2x^2 - 5) + 3x(x^3 + 2x^2 - 5) - 1(x^3 + 2x^2 - 5) \\
&= \quad x^7 \quad +2x^6 \qquad -5x^4 \\
&\qquad\qquad\qquad\quad +3x^4 \quad +6x^3 \qquad\qquad -15x \\
&\qquad\qquad\qquad\qquad\qquad\quad -x^3 \quad -2x^2 \qquad\qquad +5 \\
&= x^7 + 2x^6 - 2x^4 + 5x^3 - 2x^2 - 15x + 5 \\[4pt]
xf(x) + \big(g(x)\big)^2 &= x(x^4 + 3x - 1) + (x^3 + 2x^2 - 5)(x^3 + 2x^2 - 5) \\
&= x^5 + 3x^2 - x + x^3(x^3 + 2x^2 - 5) + 2x^2(x^3 + 2x^2 - 5) - 5(x^3 + 2x^2 - 5) \\
&= \qquad\qquad\quad x^5 \qquad\qquad\qquad\quad +3x^2 \quad -x \\
&\qquad +x^6 \quad +2x^5 \qquad\qquad -5x^3 \\
&\qquad\qquad\quad +2x^5 \quad +4x^4 \qquad\qquad\quad -10x^2 \\
&\qquad\qquad\qquad\qquad\qquad -5x^3 \quad -10x^2 \qquad\qquad +25 \\
&= x^6 + 5x^5 + 4x^4 - 10x^3 - 17x^2 - x + 25 \\[4pt]
\big(h(x)\big)^3 &= (x^2 - 3)^3 = (x^2 - 3)(x^2 - 3)^2 = (x^2 - 3)(x^4 - 6x^2 + 9) \\
&= \quad x^6 \qquad -6x^4 \qquad +9x^2 \\
&\qquad\qquad\qquad -3x^4 \qquad +18x^2 \qquad -27 \\
&= x^6 - 9x^4 + 27x^2 - 27
\end{aligned}
$$

It is frequently useful to be able to identify the coefficients of various powers of x in a product, without having to calculate the entire product.

Example 5.3.2. *Find the coefficient of x^3 in the product $(x^2 + 3x - 1)(x^3 + 2x^2 + 4)$, and find the coefficient of x^4 in the product $(x^4 + x^3 + 2x^2 + 3x - 1)(x^4 + 2x^3 - 6x^2 + 5x - 2)$.*

The only ways that terms involving x^3 will be created in the first product are when $3x$ is multiplied by $2x^2$, and when -1 is multiplied by x^3 (all other pairs of terms generate different powers of x).

$$(x^2 + 3x - 1)(x^3 + 2x^2 + 4)$$

Thus the term in x^3 in the first product is

$$3x \times 2x^2 + (-1) \times x^3 = 5x^3$$

and hence the coefficient of x^3 in the first product is 5. Similar considerations for the second product

$$(x^4 + x^3 + 2x^2 + 3x - 1)(x^4 + 2x^3 - 6x^2 + 5x - 2)$$

show that the term in x^4 in the second product is

$$x^4 \times (-2) + x^3 \times 5x + 2x^2 \times (-6x^2) + 3x \times 2x^3 + (-1) \times x^4 = -4x^4 .$$

and so the coefficient of x^4 is -4.

Suppose that $f(x)$ is a polynomial of degree m, while $g(x)$ is a polynomial of degree n, and suppose that the leading term of $f(x)$ is ax^m while the leading term of $g(x)$ is bx^n. Then the product $ax^m \times bx^n = abx^{m+n}$ contributes towards $f(x)g(x)$, and every other product of terms which contributes towards $f(x)g(x)$ must involve a power of index of index smaller than $m+n$. Since $a, b \neq 0$, we deduce that the degree of $f(x)g(x)$ is $m+n$. In other words

---
Food For Thought 5.3

If $f(x)$ and $g(x)$ are polynomials, then

$$\deg(fg) = \deg(f) + \deg(g)$$

For Interest

Since $0 \times g(x) = 0$ for any polynomial $g(x)$, this result requires that $\deg(0) = \deg(0) + \deg(g)$ for any polynomial $g(x)$. This is why we chose $\deg(0)$ is defined to be $-\infty$.

EXERCISE 5A

1. State the degree of each of the following polynomials.

   a) $x^3 - 3x^2 + 2x - 7$ b) $5x + 1$ c) $8 + 5x - 3x^2 + 7x + 6x^4$

   d) 3 e) $3 - 5x$ f) x^0

2. In each part find $p(x) + q(x)$, and give your answer in descending order.

   a) $p(x) = 3x^2 + 4x - 1, q(x) = x^2 + 3x + 7$,

   b) $p(x) = 4x^3 + 5x^2 - 7x + 3, q(x) = x^3 - 2x^2 + x - 6$,

   c) $p(x) = 3x^4 - 2x^3 + 7x^2 - 1, q(x) = -3x - x^3 + 5x^4 + 2$,

   d) $p(x) = 2 - 3x^3 + 2x^5$, $q(x) = 2x^4 + 3x^3 - 5x^2 + 1$,

   e) $p(x) = 3 + 2x - 4x^2 - x^3, q(x) = 1 - 7x + 2x^2$.

3. For each of the pairs of polynomials given in Question 2 find $p(x) - q(x)$.

4. Let $p(x) = x^3 - 2x^2 + 5x - 3$ and $q(x) = x^2 - x + 4$. Express each of the following as a single polynomial.

   a) $2p(x) + q(x)$ b) $3p(x) - q(x)$ c) $p(x) - 2q(x)$ d) $3p(x) - 2q(x)$

5. Find the following polynomial products.

   a) $(2x - 3)(3x + 1)$ b) $(x^2 + 3x - 1)(x - 2)$

   c) $(x^2 + x - 3)(2x + 3)$ d) $(3x - 1)(4x^2 - 3x + 2)$

   e) $(x^2 + 2x - 3)(x^2 + 1)$ f) $(2x^2 - 3x + 1)(4x^2 + 3x - 5)$

   g) $(x^3 + 2x^2 - x + 6)(x + 3)$ h) $(x^3 - 3x^2 + 2x - 1)(x^2 - 2x - 5)$

   i) $(1 + 3x - x^2 + 2x^3)(3 - x + 2x^2)$ j) $(2 - 3x + x^2)(4 - 5x + x^3)$

   k) $(2x + 1)(3x - 2)(x + 5)$ l) $(x^2 + 1)(x - 3)(2x^2 - x + 1)$

6. In each of the following products find the coefficient of x and the coefficient of x^2.

   a) $(x + 2)(x^2 - 3x + 6)$ b) $(x - 3)(x^2 + 2x - 5)$

   c) $(2x + 1)(x^2 - 5x + 1)$ d) $(3x - 2)(x^2 - 2x + 7)$

   e) $(2x - 3)(3x^2 - 6x + 1)$ f) $(2x - 5)(3x^3 - x^2 + 4x + 2)$

   g) $(x^2 + 2x - 3)(x^2 + 3x - 4)$ h) $(3x^2 + 1)(2x^2 - 5x + 3)$

   i) $(x^2 + 3x - 1)(x^3 + x^2 - 2x + 1)$ j) $(3x^2 - x + 2)(4x^3 - 5x + 1)$

7. In each of the following the product of $Ax + B$ with another polynomial is given, where A and B are constants. Find A and B.

a) $(Ax + B)(x - 3) = 4x^2 - 11x - 3$

b) $(Ax + B)(x + 5) = 2x^2 + 7x - 15$

c) $(Ax + B)(3x - 2) = 6x^2 - x - 2$

d) $(Ax + B)(2x + 5) = 6x^2 + 11x - 10$

e) $(Ax + B)(x^2 - 1) = x^3 + 2x^2 - x - 2$

f) $(Ax + B)(x^2 + 4) = 2x^3 - 3x^2 + 8x - 12$

g) $(Ax + B)(2x^2 - 3x + 4) = 4x^3 - x + 12$

h) $(Ax + B)(3x^2 - 2x - 1) = 6x^3 - 7x^2 + 1$

5.4 Equations and Identities

Up to now, we have written expressions like

$$(2x + 3)(x^2 - 7x + 1) = 2x^3 - 11x^2 - 19x + 3$$

to record the process of multiplying out brackets. However, this is not an equation in the ordinary sense of the word, and so the use of the equals sign should be considered.

An **equation** for x is an algebraic expression of a condition involving x which might or might not be true for different values of x. Solving the equation involves determining the set of values of x for which the condition holds. Thus the expression

$$x^2 - 5x + 6 = 0$$

is an equation. It is true when $x = 2$ or $x = 3$, but not otherwise (and so the solution of this equation is $x = 2, 3$).

An **identity** in x is an algebraic expression which is true for all values of x. If we solved an identity as an equation, its solution would be the set $\mathbb{R}$ of all real numbers. We often indicate the fact that an identity has this very special solution set (being always true) by using the symbol $\equiv$ instead of the equals sign $=$. Thus the statement

$$(1 + x)(1 - x + x^2) \equiv 1 - x^3$$

is an identity: the use of the symbol $\equiv$ indicates that we know that both sides of the expression are identically equal to each other (and so there is no need to try to solve the corresponding equation).

For Interest

The practice of using the symbol $\equiv$ to indicate an identity is not universally observed, however. Some mathematicians just use the symbol $=$, and let context indicate which expressions are equations and which are identities.

Determining when two polynomials are identically equal is relatively straightforward.

Example 5.4.1. *In the identity*

$$(x^2 + 2x + a)(x^2 - bx + c) + d \equiv x^4 + x^3 - 2x^2 + x - 4$$

determine the numbers a, b, c, d.

If we multiply out the bracket on the left-hand side of this identity, we obtain

$$x^4 + (2 - b)x^3 + (a - 2b + c)x^2 + (2c - ab)x + (ac + d) \equiv x^4 + x^3 - 2x^2 + x - 4$$

and this will certainly be true if $2 - b = 1$, $a - 2b + c = -2$, $2c - ab = 1$ and $ac + d = -4$. Solving these equations tells us that $a = -\frac{1}{3}$, $b = 1$, $c = \frac{1}{3}$ and $d = -\frac{35}{9}$.

Certainly, two polynomials will be identical if they have the same constant coefficients, the same coefficient of x, the same coefficient of x^2 and so on. It turns out that having the same set of coefficients is precisely what characterises identically equal polynomials, and so identities between polynomials can be established by the process of **equating coefficients**.

Key Fact 5.2 Equating Coefficients

If $f(x) = a_m x^m + a_{m-1} x^{m-1} + \cdots + a_1 x + a_0$ is a polynomial, and $f(x) \equiv 0$, then

$$a_m = a_{m-1} = \cdots = a_1 = a_0 = 0.$$

If $f(x) = a_m x^m + a_{m-1} x^{m-1} + \cdots + a_1 x + a_0$ and $g(x) = b_n x^n + b_{n-1} x^{n-1} + \cdots + b_1 x + b_0$ are polynomials of degree m and n, and if $f(x) \equiv g(x)$, then

$$m = n \qquad \text{and} \qquad a_0 = b_0, \ a_1 = b_1, \ \ldots, \ a_{n-1} = b_{n-1}, \ a_n = b_n.$$

While it is obvious that polynomials with the same set of coefficients are identically equal, it is perhaps less obvious that identically equal polynomials must have the same set of coefficients. However, the two polynomials can be regarded as functions of x which take the same values at all points x (two identical functions), and methods of calculus can be used to deduce that the sets of coefficients must be the same.

Equating coefficients enables us to establish identities.

Example 5.4.2. *If $x^3 - 7x^2 + 4x + 2 \equiv (x-1)(x^2 + Ax + B)$, determine the coefficients A and B.*

Equating the coefficient of x^2 tells us that $-7 = A - 1$, so that $A = -6$. Equating the constant coefficients tells us that $2 = -B$, and so $B = -2$. Note that we did not need to consider the coefficients of x ($4 = B - A$) to solve the problem.

EXERCISE 5B

---

1. In each of the following identities find the values of A, B and R.

    a) $x^2 - 2x + 7 \equiv (x+3)(Ax+B) + R$ b) $x^2 + 9x - 3 \equiv (x+1)(Ax+B) + R$
    c) $15x^2 - 14x - 8 \equiv (5x+2)(Ax+B) + R$ d) $6x^2 + x - 5 \equiv (2x+1)(Ax+B) + R$
    e) $12x^2 - 5x + 2 \equiv (3x-2)(Ax+B) + R$ f) $21x^2 - 11x + 6 \equiv (3x-2)(Ax+B) + R$

2. In each of the following identities find the values of A, B, C and R.

    a) $x^3 - x^2 - x + 12 \equiv (x+2)(Ax^2 + Bx + C) + R$

    b) $x^3 - 5x^2 + 10x + 10 \equiv (x-3)(Ax^2 + Bx + C) + R$

    c) $2x^3 + x^2 - 3x + 4 \equiv (2x-1)(Ax^2 + Bx + C) + R$

    d) $12x^3 + 11x^2 - 7x + 5 \equiv (3x+2)(Ax^2 + Bx + C) + R$

    e) $4x^3 + 4x^2 - 37x + 5 = (2x-5)(Ax^2 + Bx + C) + R$

    f) $9x^3 + 12x^2 - 15x - 10 = (3x+4)(Ax^2 + Bx + C) + R$

3. In each of the following identities find the values of A, B, C, D and R.

    a) $2x^4 + 3x^3 - 5x^2 + 11x - 5 \equiv (x+3)(Ax^3 + Bx^2 + Cx + D) + R$

    b) $4x^4 - 7x^3 - 2x^2 - 2x + 7 \equiv (x-2)(Ax3 + Bx2 + Cx + D) + R$

    c) $6x^4 + 5x^3 - x^2 + 3x + 2 \equiv (2x+1)(Ax3 + Bx2 + Cx + D) + R$

    d) $3x^4 - 7x^3 + 17x^2 - 14x + 5 \equiv (3x-1)(Ax3 + Bx2 + Cx + D) + R$

4*. Why is that two identically equal polynomials must have identical sets of coefficients?

5.5   Division of Polynomials

When dividing integers by integers, long division would give an answer in terms of a quotient and a remainder. Thus 1254 divided by 17 gives a quotient of 73 and a remainder of 13.

$$
\begin{array}{r}
7\ \ 3 \\
17\ \overline{\smash{\big)}\ 1\ \ 2\ \ 5\ \ 4} \\
1\ \ 1\ \ 9 \\
\hline
6\ \ 4 \\
5\ \ 1 \\
\hline
1\ \ 3
\end{array}
$$

Note that the quotient/remainder formulation of division relates to the fractional expression of $\frac{1254}{17}$ as a mixed number, $\frac{1254}{17} = 73\frac{13}{17}$. The two equivalent statements

$$
a = qb + r \qquad\qquad \frac{a}{b} = q\frac{r}{b}
$$

describe the role of the quotient q and the remainder r when a is divided by b.

Long division can be used to divide one polynomial by another. We shall demonstrate the method by dividing $x^4 + 3x^3 + 2x^2 - 3x + 1$ by $x^2 + x - 1$.

- How many times does $x^2 + x - 1$ go into $x^4 + 3x^3 + 2x^2 - 3x + 1$? If we knew this straight away, we would not need to perform long division! Instead, ask a simpler question: how many times does x^2 (the first term of the divisor) go into x^4 (the first term of the dividend)? The answer is x^2. Multiply $x^2 + x - 1$ by x^2, and subtract that from the divisor, leaving a working remainder of $2x^3 + 3x^2 - 3x + 1$.

- Looking at the first terms of the divisor and the working remainder, we see that x^2 goes $2x$ times into $2x^3 + 3x^2 - 3x + 1$. Multiply $x^2 + x - 1$ by $2x$ and subtract, obtaining a new working remainder of $x^2 - x + 1$.

- Repeat the process, noting that x^2 goes once into x^2, yielding a final working remainder of $-2x + 2$.

- Since $-2x + 2$ has smaller degree than $x^2 + x - 1$, we cannot divide $-2x + 2$ by $x^2 + x - 1$, so the process of division stops. We obtain a quotient of $x^2 + 2x + 1$ and a remainder of $-2x + 2$.

$$
\begin{array}{r|lllll}
& x^2 & +2x & +1 & & \\
\hline
x^2 + x - 1 & x^4 & +3x^3 & +2x^2 & -3x & +1 \\
& x^4 & +x^3 & -x^2 & & \\
\hline
& & 2x^3 & +3x^2 & -3x & +1 \\
& & 2x^3 & +2x^2 & -2x & \\
\hline
& & & x^2 & -x & +1 \\
& & & x^2 & +x & -1 \\
\hline
& & & & -2x & +2
\end{array}
$$

This process works because, each time we divide the leading term of the divisor into the leading term of either the original dividend or else any of the working remainders, we obtain a new working remainder of smaller degree than the one before (at each stage, we have done enough to 'kill off' the leading term in the divisor). Thus this process gives us a sequence of working remainders, each of which has smaller degree than its predecessor. Eventually, we will reach a working remainder which either has degree smaller than the divisor, or else is sero (in this case, the working remainder has degree $-\infty$, which is also smaller than the degree of the divisor!). At this point the process must stop, and the current working remainder is the actual working remainder. This tells us that the remainder must always have smaller degree than the divisor. This important result is known in mathematics as the **Euclidean Division Algorithm**.

> **Food For Thought 5.4**
>
> When a polynomial $a(x)$, the **dividend**, is divided by a second polynomial $b(x)$, the **divisor**, we obtain a **quotient** polynomial $q(x)$ and **remainder** polynomial $r(x)$ such that
>
> $$a(x) = q(x)b(x) + r(x)$$
>
> and $r(x)$ is either sero or else has smaller degree than $b(x)$.

It is easy to use our previous observations about degrees and polynomial addition and multiplication to deduce the following about the degree of the quotient:

$$\deg(q) = \begin{cases} \deg(a) - \deg(b), & \deg(a) \ge \deg(b), \\ -\infty, & \deg(a) < \deg(b). \end{cases}$$

Note that, in the second case, $q = 0$ and $r = a$.

Care must be taken with this method, particularly when there are 'gaps' in the powers of x in dividend or divisor.

Example 5.5.1. *Divide $x^4 + x^3 + 3x - 1$ by $x^2 - 3$.*

$$
\begin{array}{r}
x^2 \quad +x \quad\quad +3 \\
x^2 - 3 \overline{\smash{\big)}\, x^4 \quad +x^3 \quad\quad\quad +3x \quad -1} \\
x^4 \quad\quad\quad -3x^2 \\
\hline
x^3 \quad +3x^2 \quad +3x \quad -1 \\
x^3 \quad\quad\quad\quad -3x \\
\hline
3x^2 \quad +6x \quad -1 \\
3x^2 \quad\quad\quad -9 \\
\hline
6x \quad +8
\end{array}
$$

Another approach to polynomial division equates coefficients to do the work.

Example 5.5.2. *Find the quotient and remainder when $x^4 + x + 2$ is divided by $x + 1$.*

Since the dividend is quartic and the divisor is linear, the quotient will be cubic and the remainder constant. If the quotient is $q(x) = ax^3 + bx^2 + cx + d$ and the remainder is $r(x) = r$, we have

$$x^4 + x + 2 = (x+1)(ax^3 + bx^2 + cx + d) + r$$

Comparing coefficients of x^4 tells us that $a = 1$.

Comparing coefficients of x^3 gives $a + b = 0$, so $b = -1$.

Comparing coefficients of x^2 gives $b + c = 0$, so $c = 1$.

Comparing coefficients of x gives $c + d = 1$, so $d = 0$.

Comparing constant coefficients gives $d + r = 2$, so $r = 2$.

Thus the quotient is $x^3 - x^2 + x$ and the remainder is 2.

With practice, this method can be achieved without writing down any working, since the calculations can be done mentally.

Example 5.5.3. *Find the quotient and remainder when $x^4 + 3x^3 - x + 1$ is divided by $x^2 + 2x - 1$.*

We shall go through the stages of the process. The quotient must be quadratic, and the divisor linear. To obtain the leading term x^4 in the dividend, it is clear that the leading term in the quotient must be x^2:

$$x^4 + 3x^3 - x + 1 = (x^2 + 2x - 1)(x^2 + \cdots) + \cdots$$

The remainder has no term in x^3, and the product of $x^2 + 2x - 1$ by the quotient (so far as we know it) currently contributes the cubic term $2x^3$. We need another x^3, and this will be achieved if the coefficient of x in the quotient is 1, so that

$$x^4 + 3x^3 - x + 1 = (x^2 + 2x - 1)(x^2 + x + \cdots) + \cdots$$

The remainder has no term in x^2, and the product of $x^2 + 2x - 1$ by the quotient (so far as we know it) currently contributes the quadratic term $2x^2 - x^2 = x^2$. We need another $-x^2$, and this will be achieved if the constant coefficient in the quotient is -1, so that

$$x^4 + 3x^3 - x + 1 = (x^2 + 2x - 1)(x^2 + x - 1) + \cdots$$

Thus the quotient is $x^2 + x - 1$. The right-hand side (so far as we know it) currently contributes the linear term $-2x - x = -3x$ and the constant term 1, so we deduce that the remainder must be $2x$.

$$x^4 + 3x^3 - x + 1 = (x^2 + 2x - 1)(x^2 + x - 1) + 2x$$

EXERCISE 5C

1. Find the quotient and the remainder when

   a) $x^2 - 5x + 2$ is divided by $x - 3$,
   b) $x^2 + 2x - 6$ is divided by $x + 1$,
   c) $2x^2 + 3x - 1$ is divided by $x - 2$,
   d) $2x^2 + 3x + 1$ is divided by $2x - 1$,
   e) $6x^2 - x - 2$ is divided by $3x + 1$,
   f) x^4 is divided by x^3.

2. Find the quotient and the remainder when the first polynomial is divided by the second.

   a) $x^3 + 2x^2 - 3x + 1,\ x + 2$,
   b) $x^3 - 3x^2 + 5x - 4,\ x - 5$,
   c) $2x^3 + 4x - 5,\ x + 3$,
   d) $5x^3 - 3x + 7,\ x - 4$,
   e) $2x^3 - x^2 - 3x - 7,\ 2x + 1$,
   f) $6x^3 + 17x^2 - 17x + 5,\ 3x - 2$.

3. Find the quotient and the remainder when

   a) $x^4 - 2x^3 - 7x^2 + 7x + 5$ is divided by $x^2 + 2x - 1$,

   b) $x^4 - x^3 + 7x + 2$ is divided by $x^2 + x - 1$,

   c) $2x^4 - 4x^3 + 3x^2 + 6x + 5$ is divided by $x^3 + x^2 + 1$,

   d) $6x^4 + x^3 + 13x + 10$ is divided by $2x^2 - x + 4$.

5.6   The Remainder and Factor Theorems

Whatever method is used, polynomial division is quite laborious. There are circumstances, however, when some of the calculations can be performed quickly and easily. This is particularly true when the divisor is a linear polynomial.

If we divide the polynomial $f(x)$ by the linear term $x - a$, we can find a quotient polynomial $q(x)$ and a constant remainder r such that

$$f(x) \equiv (x - a)q(x) + r$$

We want to calculate r without needing to know $q(x)$. The trick is to note that, since the above identity is true for all values of x, it is also true for any particular value of x that we might choose. Choosing $x = a$ is particularly useful, since $(x - a)q(x)$ evaluates to $0 \times q(0) = 0$, whatever the polynomial $q(x)$ might be. Thus

$$f(a) = (a - a)q(a) + r = r.$$

This important result is called the Remainder Theorem.

> **Key Fact 5.3** The Remainder Theorem
>
> The remainder when the polynomial $f(x)$ is divided by $x - a$ is the constant $f(a)$.
> The remainder when the polynomial $f(x)$ is divided by $ax - b$ is the constant $f\left(\frac{b}{a}\right)$.

The second half of the Remainder Theorem is obtained by substituting $x = \frac{b}{a}$ into the identity $f(x) \equiv (ax - b)q(x) + r$.

Example 5.6.1. *Find the remainder when $x^3 - 3x + 4$ is divided by $x + 3$. What is the remainder when the same polynomial is divided by $2x - 3$?*

Substituting $x = -3$ into $f(x) = x^3 - 3x + 4$, the first remainder is $f(-3) = (-3)^3 - 3(-3) + 4 = -14$. The second remainder is $f\left(\frac{3}{2}\right) = \left(\frac{3}{2}\right)^3 - 3 \times \frac{3}{2} + 4 = \frac{23}{8}$.

Example 5.6.2. *When the polynomial $f(x) = x^3 - 3x^2 + ax + b$ is divided by $x - 1$ the remainder is -4. When $f(x)$ is divided by $x - 2$ the remainder is also -4. What is the remainder when $f(x)$ is divided by $x - 3$?*

Applying the Remainder Theorem twice gives us the equations

$$-4 = f(1) = a + b - 2 \qquad -4 = f(2) = 2a + b - 4$$

Solving these simultaneous equations for a and b gives $a = 2$, $b = -4$, so that $f(x) = x^3 - 3x^2 + 2x - 4$. Thus the remainder on dividing $f(x)$ by $x - 3$ is $f(3) = 27 - 27 + 6 - 4 = 2$.

With a little care, the Remainder Theorem can be used to handle more than linear divisors.

Example 5.6.3. *Find the remainder when $x^4 - 3x^3 + 2x^2 + x - 1$ is divided by $x^2 - 4x + 3$.*

Since the divisor is quadratic, the remainder will be linear (courtesy of the Euclidean Division Algorithm), and so we can write

$$f(x) \equiv x^4 - 3x^3 + 2x^2 + x - 1 \equiv (x^2 - 4x + 3)q(x) + (ax + b) \equiv (x - 1)(x - 3)q(x) + (ax + b)$$

The remainder when $f(x)$ is divided by $x - 1$ is $f(1)$. Putting $x = 1$ into this identity gives the equation $a + b = 0$. Similarly, the remainder when $f(x)$ is divided by $x - 3$ is $f(3) = 3a + b = 20$. We have a pair of simultaneous equations for a, b, which solve to give $a = 10, b = -10$. Thus the remainder is $10x - 10$.

The Remainder Theorem can be used to determine whether linear polynomials are factors of a given polynomial. Although it is just a special case of the Remainder Theorem, this result is often referred to as the Factor Theorem.

> **Key Fact 5.4** The Factor Theorem
>
> Let $f(x)$ be a polynomial. Then $x - a$ is a factor of $f(x)$ precisely when $f(a) = 0$. Similarly $ax - b$ is a factor of $f(x)$ precisely when $f\left(\frac{b}{a}\right) = 0$.

We know that the remainder when $f(x)$ is divided by $x - a$ is $f(a)$, so that

$$f(x) = (x - a)q(x) + f(a)$$

for some polynomial $q(x)$. If $f(a) = 0$ it follows that $f(x) = (x - a)q(x)$, and hence $x - a$ divides $f(x)$. If, on the other hand, $x - a$ divides $f(x)$, then there is no remainder when $f(x)$ is divided by $x - a$, and hence $f(a) = 0$.

What we are seeing is that the condition that $x - a$ divides $f(x)$ is equivalent to the condition that $f(x)$ leaves remainder 0 when divided by $x - a$. Since that remainder is $f(a)$, a third equivalent condition is that $f(a) = 0$.

Similarly, $ax - b$ is a factor of $f(x)$ precisely when $f(x)$ leaves a remainder of 0 when divided by $ax - b$, which happens precisely when $f\left(\frac{b}{a}\right) = 0$.

Example 5.6.4. *Show that $x + 1$ is a factor of $x^3 - x^2 - 5x - 3$, and solve the equation $x^3 - x^2 - 5x - 3 = 0$.*

If we put $f(x) = x^3 - x^2 - 5x - 3$, we note that $f(-1) = -1 - 1 + 5 - 3 = 0$. By the Factor Theorem, $x + 1$ is a factor of $f(x)$. We now divide $f(x)$ by $x + 1$ (by any method we prefer) to deduce that $f(x) = (x + 1)(x^2 - 2x - 3)$. Factorising this quadratic gives $f(x) = (x+1)(x+1)(x-3)$, and so the roots of the equation $f(x) = 0$ are -1 (twice) and 3.

Example 5.6.5. *Solve the equation $x^4 + x^3 - x - 1 = 0$.*

We need to factorise the quartic $f(x) = x^4 + x^3 - x - 1$. Looking for linear factors, we see that $f(1) = 1 + 1 - 1 - 1 = 0$ and $f(-1) = 1 - 1 + 1 - 1 = 0$, so that both $x - 1$ and $x + 1$ are factors of $f(x)$. Thus $x^2 - 1$ is a factor of $f(x)$, so we factorise to obtain $f(x) = (x^2 - 1)(x^2 + x + 1)$. Thus we need to solve the equation

$$(x - 1)(x + 1)(x^2 + x + 1) = 0$$

Since the quadratic in the third term has discriminant $-3 < 0$, it has no real roots. Thus the only solutions of the equation are $x = 1, -1$.

Example 5.6.6. *Find a linear factor of $f(x) = x^3 - x^2 + x - 6$.*

A few tests tell us that

$$f(1) = 1 - 1 + 1 - 6 = -5 \qquad f(-1) = -1 - 1 + 1 - 6 = -7 \qquad f(2) = 8 - 4 + 2 - 6 = 0$$

and so, on the third attempt, we see that $x - 2$ is a factor.

It turns out that we are not forced to search blindly for our linear factor. A deep result of mathematics tells us that since $f(x)$ is a polynomial with integer coefficients and leading coefficient 1 (a polynomial with leading coefficient 1 is called **monic**), if $x - a$ is a factor of $f(x)$ then a is an integer. Indeed, any polynomial factor of $f(x)$ will have integer coefficients. Since we intend to be able to divide $f(x)$ by $x - a$ and have no reminder, we want to be able to write

$$f(x) \equiv (x - a)(x^2 + bx + c)$$

for some integers b and c. Comparing the constant coefficients of this identity tells us that $-ac = -6$, and so we deduce that a must be a factor of the constant coefficient -6. Thus the only possible linear factors were $x \pm 1$, $x \pm 2$, $x \pm 3$ and $x \pm 6$, and we only have a finite number of cases to check.

Example 5.6.7. *Find a linear factor of $f(x) = 3x^3 + 4x^2 + 5x - 6$.*

This is a little harder, since the polynomial is not monic. However, if we look for a factor of the form $ax - b$, and assume that a and b are integers, then a must be a factor of the leading coefficient 3 of $f(x)$, while b must be a factor of the constant coefficient -6 of $f(x)$. Thus $a \in \{-3, -1, 1, 3\}$ and $b \in \{-6, -3, -2, -1, 1, 2, 3, 6\}$, and hence $\frac{b}{a} \in \left\{ \pm 1, \pm 2, \pm 3, \pm 6, \pm \frac{1}{3}, \pm \frac{2}{3} \right\}$. Working through these options, we eventually reach the fact that

$$f\left(\tfrac{2}{3}\right) = 3\left(\tfrac{2}{3}\right)^3 + 4\left(\tfrac{2}{3}\right)^2 + 5 \times \tfrac{2}{3} - 6 = \tfrac{8}{9} + \tfrac{16}{9} + \tfrac{10}{3} - 6 = 0$$

and hence the linear factor is $2x - 3$.

EXERCISE 5D

1. Find the remainder when the polynomial $f(x)$ is divided by the polynomial $g(x)$.

   a) $f(x) = x^3 - 5x^2 + 2x - 3$, $g(x) = x - 1$
   b) $f(x) = x^3 + x^2 - 6x + 5$, $g(x) = x + 2$
   c) $f(x) = 2x^3 - 3x + 5$, $g(x) = x - 3$
   d) $f(x) = 4x^3 - 5x^2 + 3x - 7$, $g(x) = x + 4$
   e) $f(x) = x^3 + 3x^2 - 2x + 1$, $g(x) = 2x - 1$
   f) $f(x) = 2x^3 + 5x^2 - 3x + 6$, $g(x) = 3x + 1$
   g) $f(x) = x^4 - x^3 + 2x^2 - 7x - 2$, $g(x) = x - 2$
   h) $f(x) = 3x^4 + x^2 - 7x + 6$, $g(x) = x + 3$

2. When $x^3 + 2x^2 - px + 1$ is divided by $x - 1$ the remainder is 5 . Find the value of p.

3. When $2x^3 + x^2 - 3x + q$ is divided by $x - 2$ the remainder is 12. Find the value of q.

4. When $x^3 + 2x^2 + px - 3$ is divided by $x + 1$ the remainder is the same as when it is divided by $x - 2$. Find the value of p.

5. When $x^3 + px^2 - x - 4$ is divided by $x - 1$ the remainder is the same as when it is divided by $x + 3$. Find the value of p.

6. When $3x^3 - 2x^2 + ax + b$ is divided by $x - 1$ the remainder is 3. When divided by $x + 1$ the remainder is -13. Find the values of a and b.

7. When $x^3 + ax^2 + bx + 5$ is divided by $x - 2$ the remainder is 23. When divided by $x + 1$ the remainder is 11. Find the values of a and b.

8. When $x^3 + ax^2 + bx - 5$ is divided by $x - 1$ the remainder is -1. When divided by $x + 1$ the remainder is -5. Find the values of a and b.

9. When $2x^3 - x^2 + ax + b$ is divided by $x - 2$ the remainder is 25. When divided by $x + 1$ the remainder is -5. Find the values of a and b.

10. Use the factor theorem to factorise the following cubic polynomials $f(x)$. In each case write down the real roots of the equation $f(x) = 0$.

   a) $x^3 + 2x^2 - 5x - 6$ b) $x^3 - 3x^2 - x + 3$ c) $x^3 - 3x^2 - 13x + 15$
   d) $x^3 - 3x^2 - 9x - 5$ e) $x^3 + 3x^2 - 4x - 12$ f) $2x^3 + 7x^2 - 5x - 4$
   g) $3x^3 - x^2 - 12x + 4$ h) $6x^3 + 7x^2 - x - 2$ i) $x^3 + 2x^2 - 4x + 1$

11. Use the factor theorem to factorise the following quartic polynomials $f(x)$. In each case write down the real roots of the equation $f(x) = 0$.

   a) $x^4 - x^3 - 7x^2 + x + 6$ b) $x^4 + 4x^3 - x^2 - 16x - 12$
   c) $2x^4 - 3x^3 - 12x^2 + 7x + 6$ d) $6x^4 + x^3 - 17x^2 - 16x - 4$
   e) $x^4 - 2x^3 + 2x - 1$ f) $4x^4 - 12x^3 + x^2 + 12x + 4$

12. Factorise the following.

   a) $x^3 - 8$ b) $x^3 + 8$ c) $x^3 - a^3$
   d) $x^3 + a^3$ e) $x^4 - a^4$ f) $x^5 + a^5$

13.   a) Show that $x - a$ is a factor of $x^n - a^n$.

   b) Under what conditions is $x + a$ a factor of $x^n + a^n$? Under these conditions, find the other factor.

14*. The monic cubic polynomial $f(x)$ leaves the remainder 1 when divided by x, $x - 1$ and $x - 2$. What is $f(3)$?

15*. The cubic polynomial $f(x)$ gives the remainders 1, $\frac{1}{2}$, $\frac{1}{3}$ and $\frac{1}{4}$ when divided by $x - 1$, $x - 2$, $x - 3$, and $x - 4$ respectively. What is the leading coefficient of $f(x)$?

Chapter 5: Summary

1. A polynomial is an expression of the form $f(x) = a_n x^n + a_{n-1} x^{n-1} + \cdots + a_1 x + a_0$, where n is an integer and $a_0, a_1, \ldots, a_n$ are constants, called the coefficients of the polynomial. The degree, or order, or a polynomial is the largest index n for which a_n is non-sero.

2. Two polynomials are identical precisely when their degrees are the same and their coefficients are the same.

3. Polynomials can be added and subtracted by adding or subtracting corresponding components; polynomials can be multiplied by 'expanding out brackets' and collecting like terms.

4. One polynomial may be divided by another polynomial, using long division, obtaining a quotient and a remainder. The remainder polynomial always has smaller degree than does the divisor.

5. The Remainder Theorem states that the remainder obtained when the polynomial $f(x)$ is divided by $x - a$ is the number $f(a)$.

6. The Factor Theorem states that $x - a$ is a factor of the polynomial $f(x)$ precisely when $f(a) = 0$.

Algebraic Fractions

In this chapter we will learn:

- to add, subtract, multiply, divide and simplify algebraic fractions,

- use the technique of partial fractions to decompose algebraic fractions in cases where the denominator is at most cubic.

6.1 Simplifying Algebraic Fractions

An **algebraic fraction**, or **rational function**, is simply a fraction where both numerator and denominator are polynomials. Here are a couple of examples:

$$\frac{x^2 + 2x + 3}{x + 1} \qquad \frac{x + 7}{x^5 - 3x^2 + 1}$$

Just as the algebra of polynomials had much in common with the algebra of integers (dividing one by another yielded a quotient and a remainder, for example), the algebra of algebraic fractions has much in common with the algebra of ordinary fractions.

6.1.1. Cancelling Factors

Fractions can be simplified by cancelling common factors. For example, the fraction $\frac{12}{14}$ can be simplified to become $\frac{6}{7}$. Much the same can be done with rational functions, but care must be taken to be clear about what is a factor. Just because the same expression appears in both the numerator and the denominator, we cannot always cancel it. For example, we cannot cancel the x^2 terms in $\frac{x^2+x+1}{x^2+2}$, obtaining $\frac{x+1}{2}$ (putting $x = 2$, we see that $\frac{2^2+2+1}{2^2+2} = \frac{7}{6}$ is not equal to $\frac{2+1}{2} = \frac{3}{2}$, and so these two algebraic fractions are not identically equal), nor can we cancel the 2s in $\frac{2x+3}{2x^2+1}$, obtaining $\frac{x+3}{x^2+1}$ (again, these two algebraic fractions are not equal when $x = 2$).

The key point is that x^2 is not a factor of either $x^2 + x + 1$ or of $x^2 + 2$, since

$$x^2 + x + 1 \equiv x^2(1 + x^{-1} + x^{-2}) \qquad x^2 + 2 \equiv x^2(1 + 2x^{-2})$$

and so x^2 can only be regarded as being a factor of either the numerator or the denominator by involving non-polynomial factors.

> **For Interest**
>
> While it is true that
>
> $$2x + 3 \equiv 2(x + \tfrac{3}{2}) \qquad\qquad 2x^2 + 1 \equiv 2(x^2 + \tfrac{1}{2})$$
>
> so that we could write $\frac{2x+3}{2x^2+1} \equiv \frac{x+\frac{3}{2}}{x^2+\frac{1}{2}}$. Note that his sort of factor-cancelling is not a standard mathematical procedure; we tend to avoid fractions within fractions. This cancellation of the factor of 2 does not lead to an incorrect result because the 2 is outside both brackets.

Factors of polynomials are expressions that are normally multiplied together, surrounded by brackets (so that $x - 1$ and $x - 2$ are factors of $x^2 - 3x + 2$, with $x^2 - 3x + 2 \equiv (x-1)(x-2)$). A single term can always have brackets put round it without changing its meaning, so that $2x - 3 \equiv (2x - 3)$. When cancelling common factors in a rational function, the procedure is to factorise both numerator and denominator, and only cancel terms which occur as brackets in both the top and the bottom.

Example 6.1.1. *Simplify*   *a)* $\dfrac{2x - 3}{6x^2 - x - 12}$,   *b)* $\dfrac{x - 2}{2x - 4}$,   *c)* $\dfrac{3x^2 - 8x + 4}{6x^2 - 7x + 2}$.

(a) $\dfrac{2x - 3}{6x^2 - x - 12} \equiv \dfrac{(2x - 3)}{(2x - 3)(3x + 4)} \equiv \dfrac{1}{3x + 4}$

(b) $\dfrac{x - 2}{2x - 4} \equiv \dfrac{(x - 2)}{2(x - 2)} \equiv \dfrac{1}{2}$

(c) $\dfrac{3x^2 - 8x + 4}{6x^2 - 7x + 2} \equiv \dfrac{(x - 2)(3x - 2)}{(2x - 1)(3x - 2)} \equiv \dfrac{x - 2}{2x - 1}$

6.1.2. Addition and Subtraction

We want to extend our earlier study of polynomials to include what are called **algebraic fractions**, or **rational functions**. These are expressions that are fractions, where both numerator and denominator are polynomials.

To add or subtract ordinary fractions, the key technique is to put both fractions over the same common denominator, generally the lowest common multiple (LCM) of the two denominators. This same technique works for adding or subtracting algebraic fractions, but the matter of finding a common multiple of both denominators is slightly more complicated.

It is clear that $f(x)g(x)$ is a common multiple of the polynomials $f(x)$ and $g(x)$, but what is the LCM of the two polynomials? For that matter, do two polynomials have a LCM? The answer to that last question is 'yes', but the reason behind it is a delicate matter. Happily, we do not need to worry about this: we will be dealing with polynomials which are sufficiently straightforward for a pragmatic approach to work. Given a numerator and a denominator, factorise both as much as possible. Each polynomial will have been written as a product of

- (prime) numbers,

- linear polynomials that cannot be factorised,

- quadratic polynomials that cannot be factorised,

- cubic polynomials that cannot be factorised,

and so on. It is extremely unlikely that we will meet a polynomial containing more complicated terms than these (and cubic factors would be very rare). Then no two polynomials of these types have a common factor except ± 1. For the purposes of calculating the LCM of two polynomials, these terms can all be treated like prime factors for integers. Thus the lowest common multiple of $2x^5 - 4x^4 + 6x^3 - 8x^2 + 4x \equiv 2x(x - 1)^2(x^2 + 2)$ and $6x^5 + 36x^4 - 36x^3 - 6x^2 \equiv 6x^2(x-1)(x^2 + 7x + 1)$ is $6x^2(x - 1)^2(x^2 + 2)(x^2 + 7x + 1) \equiv 6x^8 + 30x^7 - 60x^6 + 90x^5 - 138x^4 + 60x^3 + 12$.

Example 6.1.2. *Find the LCM of*

(a) $2x - 4$ and $x^2 - 5x + 6$,

(b) $x + 2$ and $3x - 7$,

(c) $x^4 + 4$ and $(x^2 + 2x + 2)^2$.

(a) Since $2x - 4 \equiv 2(x - 2)$ and $x^2 - 5x + 6 \equiv (x - 2)(x - 3)$, the LCM is $2(x - 2)(x - 3) \equiv 2x^2 - 10x + 12$.

(b) The LCM is $(x + 2)(3x - 7) \equiv 3x^2 - x - 14$.

(c) Since $x^4 + 4 \equiv (x^2 + 2)^2 - 4x^2 \equiv (x^2 + 2x + 2)(x^2 - 2x + 2)$, the LCM is $(x^2 + 2x + 2)^2(x^2 - 2x + 2)$.

Now we can calculate the LCM of two polynomials, adding and subtracting algebraic fractions is now possible. Care needs to be taken when multiplying out and combining the numerators, to ensure that the correct signs are used. In view of the fact that we might well want to cancel factors at a later stage of the calculation, it is generally best to leave the common denominator in a factorised form right until the end.

Example 6.1.3. *Simplify the following algebraic fractions:*

$$a)\ \frac{1}{x} - \frac{2}{3}, \qquad b)\ \frac{3}{x + 2} - \frac{6}{2x - 1}, \qquad c)\ \frac{31x - 8}{2x^2 + 3x - 2} - \frac{14}{x + 2}.$$

(a) The LCM of x and 3 is $3x$, and so

$$\frac{1}{x} - \frac{2}{3} \equiv \frac{1 \times 3}{3x} - \frac{2 \times x}{3x} \equiv \frac{3}{3x} - \frac{2x}{3x} \equiv \frac{3 - 2x}{3x}$$

(b) The LCM of $x + 2$ and $2x - 1$ is $(x + 2)(2x - 1)$, and so

$$\frac{3}{x + 2} - \frac{6}{2x - 1} \equiv \frac{3(2x - 1)}{(x + 2)(2x - 1)} - \frac{6(x + 2)}{(x + 2)(2x - 1)} \equiv \frac{6x - 3 - 6x - 12}{(x + 2)(2x - 1)} \equiv \frac{-15}{(x + 2)(2x - 1)}$$

(c) The LCM of $2x^2 + 3x - 2 \equiv (x + 2)(2x - 1)$ and $x + 2$ is $(x + 2)(2x - 1)$, and so

$$\frac{31x - 8}{2x^2 + 3x - 2} - \frac{14}{x + 2} \equiv \frac{31x - 8}{(x + 2)(2x - 1)} - \frac{14(2x - 1)}{(x + 2)(2x - 1)} \equiv \frac{31x - 8 - 28x + 14}{(x + 2)(2x - 1)}$$
$$\equiv \frac{3x + 6}{(x + 2)(2x - 1)} \equiv \frac{3(x + 2)}{(x + 2)(2x - 1)} \equiv \frac{3}{2x - 1}$$

It is worth noting that, if we had not taken the time to determine the LCM of these two polynomials, we could still have derived the correct answer (at the expense of greater algebraic effort):

$$\frac{31x - 8}{2x^2 + 3x - 2} - \frac{14}{x + 2} \equiv \frac{(31x - 8)(x + 2) - 14(2x^2 + 3x - 2)}{(2x^2 + 3x - 2)(x + 2)}$$
$$\equiv \frac{(31x^2 + 54x - 16) - (28x^2 + 42x - 28)}{(2x^2 + 3x - 2)(x + 2)} \equiv \frac{3x^2 + 12x + 12}{(2x^2 + 3x - 2)(x + 2)}$$
$$\equiv \frac{3(x + 2)^2}{(2x^2 + 3x - 2)(x + 2)} \equiv \frac{3(x + 2)}{2x^2 + 3x - 2} \equiv \frac{3(x + 2)}{(x + 2)(2x - 1)} \equiv \frac{3}{2x - 1}$$

6.1.3. MULTIPLICATION AND DIVISION

Multiplication and division of algebraic fractions proceeds exactly as does multiplication and division of ordinary fractions. Notice that since

$$\frac{1}{b(x)} \times \frac{1}{d(x)} \times b(x)d(x) \equiv \frac{1}{b(x)} \times b(x) \times \frac{1}{d(x)} \times d(x) \equiv \frac{b(x)}{b(x)} \times \frac{d(x)}{d(x)} \equiv 1$$

we see that

$$\frac{1}{b(x)} \times \frac{1}{d(x)} \equiv \frac{1}{b(x)d(x)}$$

for any polynomials $b(x), d(x)$, and hence

$$\frac{a(x)}{b(x)} \times \frac{c(x)}{d(x)} \equiv a(x) \times \frac{1}{b(x)} \times c(x) \times \frac{1}{d(x)} \equiv a(x)c(x) \times \frac{1}{b(x)} \times \frac{1}{d(x)} \equiv a(x)c(x) \times \frac{1}{b(x)}d(x) \equiv \frac{a(x)c(x)}{b(x)d(x)}$$

for polynomials $a(x), b(x), c(x)$ and $d(x)$ (we have just used the result that the order in which polynomials are multiplied together does not affect the result). We also note that

$$F(x) \equiv \frac{a(x)}{b(x)} \div \frac{c(x)}{d(x)} \quad \Leftrightarrow \quad F(x) \times \frac{c(x)}{d(x)} \equiv \frac{a(x)}{b(x)}$$

$$\Leftrightarrow \quad F(x) \times c(x) \equiv \frac{a(x)}{b(x)} \times d(x) = \frac{a(x)d(x)}{b(x)}$$

$$\Leftrightarrow \quad F(x) \equiv \frac{a(x)d(x)}{b(x)} \times \frac{1}{c(x)} \equiv \frac{a(x)d(x)}{b(x)c(x)}$$

and hence

$$\frac{a(x)}{b(x)} \div \frac{c(x)}{d(x)} \equiv \frac{a(x)d(x)}{b(x)c(x)} \equiv \frac{a(x)}{b(x)} \times \frac{d(x)}{c(x)}$$

for polynomials $a(x), b(x), c(x)$ and $d(x)$, so that usual technique of 'when dividing by a fraction, turn it upside down and multiply' still works.

Example 6.1.4. *Simplify the algebraic fractions*

$$a) \frac{x-2}{x} \times \frac{x^2 - 3x}{x-2}, \qquad b) \frac{x-2}{x^2 - 4x + 3} \div \frac{x}{2x^2 - 7x + 3} \ .$$

(a) $\dfrac{x-2}{x} \times \dfrac{x^2 - 3x}{x-2} \equiv \dfrac{(x-2)(x^2 - 3x)}{x(x-2)} \equiv \dfrac{x(x-2)(x-3)}{x(x-2)} \equiv x - 3.$

(b)

$$\frac{x-2}{x^2 - 4x + 3} \div \frac{x}{2x^2 - 7x + 3} \equiv \frac{x-2}{x^2 - 4x + 3} \times \frac{2x^2 - 7x + 3}{x} \equiv \frac{(x-2)(2x^2 - 7x + 3)}{x(x^2 - 4x + 3)}$$

$$\equiv \frac{(x-2)(2x-1)(x-3)}{x(x-1)(x-3)} \equiv \frac{(x-2)(2x-1)}{x(x-1)}$$

EXERCISE 6A

1. Simplify

   a) $\dfrac{4x - 8}{2}$,

   b) $\dfrac{9x + 6}{3}$,

   c) $\dfrac{2x^2 - 6x + 12}{2}$,

   d) $\dfrac{6}{18x + 12}$,

   e) $\dfrac{(2x + 6)(2x - 4)}{4}$,

   f) $\dfrac{x}{x^3 + x^2 + x}$.

2. Simplify

   a) $\dfrac{5x + 15}{x + 3}$,

   b) $\dfrac{x + 1}{4x + 4}$,

   c) $\dfrac{2x + 5}{5 + 2x}$,

   d) $\dfrac{3x - 7}{7 - 3x}$,

   e) $\dfrac{(2x - 8)(3x + 6)}{(2x + 4)(3x + 12)}$,

   f) $\dfrac{2x^2 - 6x + 10}{3x^2 - 9x + 15}$.

3. Simplify

   a) $\dfrac{x^2 + 5x + 4}{x + 1}$,

   b) $\dfrac{x - 2}{x^2 + 5x - 14}$,

   c) $\dfrac{6x^2 + 4x}{4x^2 + 2x}$,

   d) $\dfrac{x^2 + 5x - 6}{x^2 - 4x + 3}$,

   e) $\dfrac{2x^2 + 5x - 12}{2x^2 - 11x + 12}$,

   f) $\dfrac{8x^2 - 6x - 20}{2 + 5x - 3x^2}$.

4. Simplify

   a) $\dfrac{2x}{3} - \dfrac{x}{4}$,

   b) $\dfrac{5x}{2} + \dfrac{x}{3} - \dfrac{3x}{4}$,

   c) $\dfrac{x + 2}{3} + \dfrac{x + 1}{4}$,

   d) $\dfrac{2x + 1}{5} - \dfrac{x + 2}{3}$,

   e) $\dfrac{(x + 1)(x + 3)}{2} - \dfrac{(x + 2)^2}{4}$,

   f) $3x + 4 - \dfrac{2(x + 3)}{5}$.

5. Simplify

   a) $\dfrac{2}{x} + \dfrac{3}{4}$,

   b) $\dfrac{1}{2x} + \dfrac{2}{x}$,

   c) $\dfrac{5}{4x} - \dfrac{2}{3x}$,

   d) $\dfrac{x+3}{2x} + \dfrac{x-4}{x}$,

   e) $\dfrac{3x-1}{x} - \dfrac{x+1}{2}$,

   f) $\dfrac{x+1}{x} + \dfrac{x+1}{x^2}$.

6. Simplify

   a) $\dfrac{2}{x+1} + \dfrac{4}{x+3}$,

   b) $\dfrac{5}{x-2} + \dfrac{3}{2x+1}$,

   c) $\dfrac{4}{x+3} - \dfrac{2}{x+4}$,

   d) $\dfrac{7}{x-3} - \dfrac{2}{x+1}$,

   e) $\dfrac{4}{2x+3} + \dfrac{5}{3x+1}$,

   f) $\dfrac{6}{2x+1} - \dfrac{2}{5x-3}$.

7. Simplify

   a) $\dfrac{5}{3x-1} - \dfrac{2}{2x+1}$,

   b) $\dfrac{6}{4x+1} - \dfrac{3}{2x}$,

   c) $\dfrac{3x}{x+2} + \dfrac{5x}{x+1}$,

   d) $\dfrac{8x}{2x-1} - \dfrac{x}{x+2}$,

   e) $\dfrac{x+1}{x+2} + \dfrac{x+2}{x+1}$,

   f) $\dfrac{2x+1}{x+4} - \dfrac{x-5}{x-2}$.

8. Simplify

   a) $\dfrac{2x+3}{(x+1)(x+3)} + \dfrac{2}{x+3}$,

   b) $\dfrac{5x}{x^2+x-2} + \dfrac{1}{x+2}$,

   c) $\dfrac{5}{x-3} + \dfrac{x+2}{x^2-3x}$,

   d) $\dfrac{8}{x^2-4} - \dfrac{4}{x-2}$,

   e) $\dfrac{13-3x}{x^2-2x-3} + \dfrac{4}{x+1}$,

   f) $\dfrac{11x+27}{2x^2+11x-6} - \dfrac{3}{x+6}$.

9. Simplify

   a) $\dfrac{4x+6}{x-4} \times \dfrac{3x-12}{2x+3}$,

   b) $\dfrac{x^2-4}{x+2} \times \dfrac{3x}{x-2}$,

   c) $\dfrac{x^2+9x+20}{x+3} \times \dfrac{3}{x+4}$,

   d) $\dfrac{x^2+3x+2}{x^2+4x+4} \times \dfrac{x^2+5x+6}{x^2+2x+1}$,

   e) $\dfrac{4x+12}{2x+2} \times \dfrac{x^2+2x+1}{x^2+6x+9}$,

   f) $\dfrac{4x^2-9}{9x^2-4} \times \dfrac{9x^2-12x+4}{4x^2-12x+9}$.

10. Simplify

   a) $\dfrac{x+2}{2x+3} \div \dfrac{2x+4}{8x+12}$,

   b) $\dfrac{x}{5-2x} \div \dfrac{3x}{2x-5}$,

   c) $\dfrac{1}{x^2+6x+8} \div \dfrac{1}{x^2+8x+16}$,

   d) $\dfrac{5x-1}{2x^2+x-3} \div \dfrac{1}{2x^2+7x+6}$,

   e) $\dfrac{x^2+5x-6}{x^2-5x+4} \div \dfrac{x^2+9x+18}{x^2-x-12}$,

   f) $\dfrac{-2x^2+7x-6}{8x^2-10x-3} \div \dfrac{7x-x^2-10}{5+19x-4x^2}$.

11. Given that $\dfrac{a}{x-2} + \dfrac{b}{x+c} \equiv \dfrac{15x}{x^2+2x-8}$, find the values of the constants a, b and c.

12. Given that $\dfrac{(x+2)f(x)}{(x+3)(x^2-x-6)} \equiv 1$ find $f(x)$ in its simplest form.

13. Given that $P(x) \equiv \dfrac{5}{x+4}$ and $Q(x) \equiv \dfrac{2}{x-3}$,

   a) find $2P(x) + 3Q(x)$ in simplified form,

   b) find $R(x)$, where $R(x) + 4Q(x) \equiv 3P(x)$.

14. Simplify

   a) $\dfrac{2}{x^3-3x^2+2x} + \dfrac{1}{x^3-6x^2+11x-6}$,

   b) $\dfrac{5}{2x+1} - \dfrac{4}{3x-1} - \dfrac{7x-10}{6x^2+x-1}$.

6.2 Partial Fractions

Sometimes we need to reverse the simplification processes outlined above! There will be a number of occasions when the expression

$$\frac{x^2 + 5x + 5}{(x + 1)(x + 2)}$$

will be easier to study when written in the expanded form

$$1 + \frac{1}{x + 1} + \frac{1}{x + 2}$$

for example. The process of splitting algebraic fractions in this manner is called **splitting into partial fractions**.

This technique can be applied to a variety of types of algebraic fraction. For the while, we shall always assume that the numerator of the algebraic fraction has smaller degree than does the denominator.

- **Denominators with Distinct Linear Factors**: It is possible, for example, to write the algebraic fraction $\frac{7x - 8}{(2x - 1)(x - 2)}$ in the form

$$\frac{7x - 8}{(2x - 1)(x - 2)} \equiv \frac{A}{2x - 1} + \frac{B}{x - 2}$$

for some constants A and B. The challenge is to find the values of the constants A and B. Multiplying through by $(2x - 1)(x - 2)$, the identity becomes

$$7x - 8 \equiv A(x - 2) + B(2x - 1)$$

Equating coefficients of x, we require $A + 2B = 7$. Equating constant coefficients, we require $-2A - B = -8$. Thus we have a pair of simultaneous equations for A and B, which can be solved to obtain $A = 3$ and $B = 2$, and hence

$$\frac{7x - 8}{(2x - 1)(x - 2)} \equiv \frac{3}{2x - 1} + \frac{2}{x - 2}$$

This result could be checked by using earlier methods of combining fractions to show that the right-hand side of this identity indeed simplifies to the left-hand side. We have exhibited a special case of a general result, whenever the algebraic fraction has a denominator which is a product of two distinct linear factors.

Key Fact 6.1 Partial Fractions: Template 1

If a, b, p, q, r, s are numbers, and if $px + q$ and $rx + s$ are distinct linear factors (so that one is not a constant multiple of the other) then there always exist numbers A, B such that

$$\frac{ax + b}{(px + q)(rx + s)} \equiv \frac{A}{px + q} + \frac{B}{rx + s}$$

The same technique as above shows that the result is possible provided that A and B are solutions of a pair of simultaneous equations. The condition on the linear terms $px + q$ and $rx + s$ is enough to ensure that those simultaneous equations are always soluble!

While this method can be used to show that the technique must work, once we accept that it does, there is a much faster way with which to identify the constants A, B.

Example 6.2.1. *Split* $\dfrac{13x - 6}{x^2 - 5x + 6}$ *into partial fractions.*

Since $x^2 - 5x + 6 = (x - 2)(x - 3)$, we look for the identity

$$\frac{13x - 6}{x^2 - 5x + 6} \equiv \frac{A}{x - 2} + \frac{B}{x - 3}$$

which identity is equivalent to

$$13x - 6 \equiv A(x - 3) + B(x - 2)$$

Since this is an identity, it is true for any value of x. A judicious choice of values for x gives us the constants A and B without the need to solve equations.

 ★ Putting $x = 2$ makes the $x - 2$ term vanish, so the identity tells us that $20 = -A$, so that $A = -20$.
 ★ Putting $x = 3$ makes the $x - 3$ term vanish, so the identity tells us that $B = 33$.

Thus we deduce that

$$\frac{13x - 6}{x^2 - 5x + 6} \equiv \frac{33}{x - 3} - \frac{20}{x - 2}$$

Example 6.2.2. *Split* $\dfrac{5x}{(x + 2)(2x - 1)}$ *into partial fractions.*

We are aiming for an expansion of the form

$$\frac{5x}{(x + 2)(2x - 1)} \equiv \frac{A}{x + 2} + \frac{B}{2x - 1}$$

Multiplying by $(x + 2)(2x - 1)$ gives the identity

$$5x \equiv A(2x - 1) + B(x + 2)$$

Putting $x = -2$ gives $-10 = -5A$, so that $A = 2$. Putting $x = \frac{1}{2}$ gives $\frac{5}{2} = \frac{5}{2}B$, so that $B = 1$. Thus

$$\frac{5x}{(x + 2)(2x - 1)} \equiv \frac{2}{x + 2} + \frac{1}{2x - 1}$$

There is no limit to the number of distinct linear factors we can handle in the denominator (although the syllabus only requires us to be able to handle cubic denominators).

Key Fact 6.2 Partial Fractions: Template 2

If $a, b, c, p, q, r, s, t, u$ are numbers, and $px + q$, $rx + s$, $tx + u$ are distinct linear factors, then there exist numbers A, B and C such that

$$\frac{ax^2 + bx + c}{(px + q)(rx + s)(tx + u)} \equiv \frac{A}{px + q} + \frac{B}{rx + s} + \frac{C}{tx + u}$$

Example 6.2.3. *Split* $\dfrac{2x^2 + 6x}{(x + 1)(2x + 3)(x - 3)}$ *into partial fractions.*

We are aiming for a decomposition of the form

$$\frac{2x^2 + 6x}{(x + 1)(2x + 3)(x - 3)} \equiv \frac{A}{x + 1} + \frac{B}{2x + 3} + \frac{C}{x - 3}$$

Multiplying through by $(x + 1)(2x + 3)(x - 3)$ gives the identity

$$2x^2 + 6x \equiv A(2x + 3)(x - 3) + B(x + 1)(x - 3) + C(x + 1)(2x + 3)$$

Putting $x = -1$ 'kills off' both the term involving B and the term involving C. We deduce that $-4 = -4A$, so that $A = 1$. Similarly putting $x = -\frac{3}{2}$ tells us that $-\frac{9}{2} = \frac{9}{4}B$, so that $B = -2$. Putting $x = 3$ gives $36 = 36C$, so $C = 1$. Thus

$$\frac{12x}{(x + 1)(2x + 3)(x - 3)} \equiv \frac{1}{x + 1} - \frac{2}{2x + 3} + \frac{1}{x - 3}$$

- **Denominators with a Repeated Linear Factor**: Suppose the algebraic fraction has quadratic denominator which involves a repeated linear factor. The algebraic fraction must be of the form

$$\frac{ax+b}{(px+q)^2}$$

Since

$$\frac{px}{(px+q)^2} \equiv \frac{px+q-q}{(px+q)^2} \equiv \frac{1}{px+q} - \frac{q}{(px+q)^2}$$

we deduce that

$$\frac{ax+b}{(px+q)^2} \equiv \frac{ax}{(px+q)^2} + \frac{b}{(px+q)^2} \equiv \frac{a}{p}\frac{px}{(px+q)^2} + \frac{b}{(px+q)^2}$$

$$\equiv \frac{a}{p}\left[\frac{1}{px+q} - \frac{q}{(px+q)^2}\right] + \frac{b}{(px+q)^2}$$

$$\equiv \left(b - \frac{aq}{p}\right)\frac{1}{(px+q)^2} + \frac{a}{p}\frac{1}{px+q}$$

so that the algebraic fraction can be written as a combination of $\frac{1}{px+q}$ and $\frac{1}{(px+q)^2}$.

Key Fact 6.3 Partial Fractions: Template 3

If a, b, p, q are numbers, then there exist numbers A and B such that

$$\frac{ax+b}{(px+q)^2} \equiv \frac{A}{px+q} + \frac{B}{(px+q)^2}$$

Let us consider an algebraic fraction of the form $\dfrac{ax^2+bx+c}{(px+q)^2(rx+s)}$, where $px+q$ and $rx+s$ are distinct linear factors. In the cases we have considered so far, algebraic fractions with quadratic denominators (that can be factorised) needed two constants A and B in their partial fraction form, while functions with cubic denominators that can be written as products of distinct linear factors needed three constants A, B and C, It seems reasonable, therefore, to expect that we will need three constants in this new case. In view of the way that we gave a partial fraction expansion for $\frac{ax+b}{(px+q)^2}$, it seems reasonable to try to establish an identity of the form

$$\frac{ax^2+bx+c}{(px+q)^2(rx+s)} \equiv \frac{A}{px+q} + \frac{B}{(px+q)^2} + \frac{C}{rx+s}$$

Multiplying through by $(px+q)^2(rx+s)$ yields the identity

$$ax^2+bx+c \equiv A(px+q)(rx+s) + B(rx+s) + C(px+q)^2$$

between quadratic polynomials. Matching the coefficients for x^2, x^1 and x^0 would give use three equations for A, B and C. Without going into the detail of the proof that these equations do indeed have a solution, we shall assume that everything works fine.

Key Fact 6.4 Partial Fractions: Template 4

If a, b, c, p, q, r, s are numbers, and if $px+q$ and $rx+s$ are distinct linear factors, then there exist numbers A, B and C such that

$$\frac{ax^2+bx+c}{(px+q)^2(rx+s)} \equiv \frac{A}{px+q} + \frac{B}{(px+q)^2} + \frac{C}{rx+s}$$

Example 6.2.4. *Split* $\dfrac{3x^2 + 6x + 2}{(2x+3)(x+1)^2}$ *and* $\dfrac{x^2 - 7x - 6}{x^2(x-3)}$ *into partial fractions.*

Look for an expansion of the form

$$\frac{3x^2 + 6x + 2}{(2x+3)(x+1)^2} \equiv \frac{A}{2x+3} + \frac{B}{x+1} + \frac{C}{(x+1)^2}$$

which yields, after multiplication by $(2x+3)(x+1)^2$, the identity

$$3x^2 + 6x + 2 \equiv A(x+1)^2 + B(2x+3)(x+1) + C(2x+3)$$

Two of these coefficients can be found quickly. Putting $x = -\frac{3}{2}$ gives $-\frac{1}{4} = \frac{1}{4}A$, or $A = -1$. Putting $x = -1$ gives $-1 = C$. There is no easy substitution for x which will isolate the number B directly, so we need a different approach. Comparing the coefficient of x^2 (for example) gives $3 = A + 2B$, and hence $B = 2$. Thus

$$\frac{3x^2 + 6x + 2}{(2x+3)(x+1)^2} \equiv -\frac{1}{2x+3} + \frac{2}{x+1} - \frac{1}{(x+1)^2}$$

For the second case, we try

$$\frac{x^2 - 7x - 6}{x^2(x-3)} \equiv \frac{A}{x} + \frac{B}{x^2} + \frac{C}{x-3}$$

and hence

$$x^2 - 7x - 6 \equiv Ax(x-3) + B(x-3) + Cx^2$$

Putting $x = 0$ gives $-6 = -3B$, or $B = 2$. Putting $x = 3$ gives $-18 = 9C$, or $C = -2$. Equating the coefficients of x^2 gives $1 = A + C$, so that $A = 3$. Thus

$$\frac{x^2 - 7x - 6}{x^2(x-3)} \equiv \frac{3}{x} + \frac{2}{x^2} - \frac{2}{x-3}$$

Note that it is not necessary to equate the coefficients of x^2, but it is frequently the case that the leading coefficient is the easiest to work with (its coefficient does not involve all three of A, B and C, for example).

It is worth noting that this method does not stop here, although the syllabus does! Higher degree denominators, and higher degrees of repetition of roots, can be dealt with analogously. For example, it is possible to write

$$\frac{6x^5 + 2x^4 - 36x^3 - 44x^2 + 37x + 31}{(x+1)^3(x-2)^2(x+3)} \equiv \frac{A}{x+1} + \frac{B}{(x+1)^2} + \frac{C}{(x+1)^3} + \frac{D}{x-2} + \frac{E}{(x-2)^2} + \frac{F}{x+3}$$

Clearing the denominators, and then a combination of choosing key values for x and equating coefficients could then enable use to evaluate A, B, C, D, E and F.

- **Denominators with an Irreducible Quadratic Factor**: To this stage, all denominators have been ones which can be written as a product of linear factors. We need to consider what options remain.

  If the denominator is quadratic, the only remaining possibility is that the denominator cannot be factorised (for example, the denominator could be $x^2 + 2x + 2$). Polynomials than cannot be factorised are called **irreducible**. There is nothing that the method of partial fractions can achieve here.

  If the denominator is cubic, there must be a linear factor, but it is possible that the denominator is a product of a linear term and an irreducible quadratic term.

For Interest

Just because it exists, it does not mean that it is easy to find a linear factor! For example, the cubic polynomial $x^3 + 3x + 3$ has a linear factor, but only the brave would attempt to factorise it. Its linear factor is $x + \left(\dfrac{2}{\sqrt{13}-3}\right)^{\frac{1}{3}} - \left(\dfrac{\sqrt{13}-3}{2}\right)^{\frac{1}{3}}$. Thus, for practical purposes, we will only apply this method to polynomials whose factorisation is 'easy'.

Suppose, for example, we wanted to split $\dfrac{4x+6}{(x-1)(x^2+9)}$ into partial fractions. We would expect to have to write

$$\frac{4x+6}{(x-1)(x^2+9)} \equiv \frac{A}{x-1} + \frac{f(x)}{x^2+9}$$

for some polynomial $f(x)$, but what sort of polynomial? To answer that question, clear the denominator:

$$4x+6 \equiv A(x^2+9)+(x-1)f(x)$$

and so, putting $x=1$, we see that $10=10A$, so that $A=1$. But then

$$(x-1)f(x) \equiv 4x+6-(x^2+9) \equiv -(x^2-4x+3) \equiv -(x-1)(x-3)$$

and hence $f(x) = 3-x$. We note that $f(x)$ is of the form $Bx+C$, which is the most general numerator for the quotient $\frac{f(x)}{x^2+9}$, if the numerator is to be of smaller degree than the denominator (and every algebraic fraction we have been considering for the partial fractions method has had that property).

These considerations give us the method that we shall use in this final case.

Key Fact 6.5 Partial Fractions: Template 5

Suppose that a, b, c, p, q are numbers, and that $g(x)$ is an irreducible quadratic polynomial. Then there exist numbers A, B and C such that

$$\frac{ax^2+bx+c}{(px+q)g(x)} \equiv \frac{A}{px+q} + \frac{Bx+C}{g(x)}$$

Example 6.2.5. *Split* $\dfrac{4x+6}{(x-1)(x^2+9)}$ *and* $\dfrac{x^2-1}{(x+2)(x^2+x+1)}$ *into partial fractions.*

In the first case we write

$$\frac{4x+6}{(x-1)(x^2+9)} \equiv \frac{A}{x-1} + \frac{Bx+C}{x^2+9}$$

which leads to

$$4x+6 \equiv A(x^2+9)+(Bx+C)(x-1)$$

Putting $x=1$ gives $10=10A$, so that $A=1$. In the absence (at least, until we have discovered complex numbers))of useful values of x to substitute for, we equate coefficients instead. Equating coefficients of x^2 tells us that $0=A+B$, so that $B=-1$. Equating constant coefficients (this is actually substituting in the value $x=0$) gives $6=9-C$, and so $C=3$. Hence

$$\frac{4x+6}{(x-1)(x^2+9)} \equiv \frac{1}{x-1} + \frac{3-x}{x^2+9}$$

as expected. In the second case we write

$$\frac{x^2-1}{(x+2)(x^2+x+1)} \equiv \frac{A}{x+2} + \frac{Bx+C}{x^2+x+1}$$

which leads to

$$x^2-1 \equiv A(x^2+x+1)+(Bx+C)(x+2)$$

Putting $x=-2$ gives $3=3A$, or $A=1$. Equating coefficients of x^2 gives $1=A+B$, or $B=0$. Equating constant coefficients gives $-1=A+2C$, or $C=-1$, and hence

$$\frac{x^2-1}{(x+2)(x^2+x+1)} \equiv \frac{1}{x+2} - \frac{1}{x^2+x+1}$$

EXERCISE 6B

1. Split the following into partial fractions.

   a) $\dfrac{2x+8}{(x+5)(x+3)}$
   b) $\dfrac{10x+8}{(x-1)(x+5)}$
   c) $\dfrac{x}{(x-4)(x-5)}$
   d) $\dfrac{28}{(2x-1)(x+3)}$

2. Split the following into partial fractions.

   a) $\dfrac{8x+1}{x^2+x-2}$
   b) $\dfrac{25}{x^2-3x-4}$
   c) $\dfrac{10x-6}{x^2-9}$
   d) $\dfrac{3}{2x^2+x}$

3. Split into partial fractions

   a) $\dfrac{35-5x}{(x+2)(x-1)(x-3)}$,
   b) $\dfrac{8x^2}{(x+1)(x-1)(x+3)}$,
   c) $\dfrac{15x^2-28x-72}{x^3-2x^2-24x}$.

4. Split into partial fractions

   a) $\dfrac{4ax-a^2}{x^2+ax-2a^2}$
   b) $\dfrac{2x}{x^2-a^2}$
   c) $\dfrac{ax+5a^2}{(x^2-a^2)(x+2a)}$

5. Split into partial fractions

   a) $\dfrac{4\sqrt5}{x^2-5}$
   b) $\dfrac{2x-2}{x^2+4x+1}$
   c) $\dfrac{1}{x^2+6x-1}$

6. Split into partial fractions

   a) $\dfrac{4}{(x-1)(x-3)^2}$,
   b) $\dfrac{6x^2+11x-8}{(x+2)^2(x-1)}$,
   c) $\dfrac{6}{x^3-4x^2+4x}$,
   d) $\dfrac{8-7x}{2x^3+3x^2-1}$,
   e) $\dfrac{6x^2+27x+25}{(x+2)^2(x+1)}$,
   f) $\dfrac{97x+35}{(2x-3)(5x+2)^2}$.

7. Express each of the following in partial fractions.

   a) $\dfrac{x^2+x}{(x-1)(x^2+1)}$
   b) $\dfrac{4-x}{(x+1)(x^2+4)}$
   c) $\dfrac{2x^2+x-2}{(x+3)(x^2+4)}$
   d) $\dfrac{2x^2+11x-8}{(2x-3)(x^2+1)}$
   e) $\dfrac{x^2-3x+14}{(3x+2)(x^2+16)}$
   f) $\dfrac{3+17x^2}{(1+4x)(4+x^2)}$
   g) $\dfrac{6-5x}{(1+2x)(4+x^2)}$
   h) $\dfrac{x^2+18}{x(x^2+9)}$
   i) $\dfrac{17-25x}{(x+4)(2x^2+7)}$

8. Express $\dfrac{1}{x^3-1}$ in partial fractions.

9. Express $\dfrac{1}{(x+1)(x+2)}$ in partial fractions, and hence show that

   $$\frac{1}{(x+1)^2(x+2)^2} \equiv \frac{1}{(x+1)^2} + \frac{1}{(x+2)^2} - \frac{2}{x+1} + \frac{2}{x+2}$$

10. Express $\dfrac{1}{(x+1)(x-6)}$ and $\dfrac{x}{(x+1)(x-6)}$ in partial fractions, and hence show that

    $$\frac{x^2}{(x+1)^2(x-6)^2} \equiv \frac{1}{343}\left[\frac{252}{(x-6)^2} + \frac{7}{(x+1)^2} + \frac{2}{x-6} + \frac{2}{x+1}\right]$$

11*. If a,b,c,d are numbers, with $c \neq d$, why must there exist numbers A and B such that

    $$\frac{ax+b}{(x+c)(x+d)} \equiv \frac{A}{x+c} + \frac{B}{x+d} \text{ ?}$$

12*. Show that

    $$\frac{1}{x^3(x+1)^3} \equiv \frac{6}{x} - \frac{3}{x^2} + \frac{1}{x^3} - \frac{6}{x+1} - \frac{3}{(x+1)^2} - \frac{1}{(x+1)^3}$$

13*. What are the constants A,B,C,D,E,F in the partial fraction expansion

    $$\frac{6x^5+2x^4-36x^3-44x^2+37x+31}{(x+1)^3(x-2)^2(x+3)} \equiv \frac{A}{x+1} + \frac{B}{(x+1)^2} + \frac{C}{(x+1)^3} + \frac{D}{x-2} + \frac{E}{(x-2)^2} + \frac{F}{x+3} \text{ ?}$$

6.3 Improper Fractions

Throughout this chapter we have restricted our attention to algebraic fractions with denominators that are at most cubic, and to numerators of smaller degree than the denominators. The restriction to no greater than cubic denominators means that there is only a fairly small range of possible types of algebraic fraction to split into partial fractions; however, this restriction could be overcome, extending the ideas of this chapter by analogy. The second restriction is more important, since the methods we have set out so far only work when the algebraic fractions we consider have their numerators restricted in this way.

However, it is relatively easy to handle algebraic fractions whose numerators have larger degrees. Recall the discussion in Section 5.5 of the previous Chapter concerning division of integers; the formulae

$$a = qb + r \qquad \frac{a}{b} = q\frac{r}{b}$$

relating the dividend a, divisor b, quotient q and remainder r enable us to view the process of integer division as the means whereby we convert improper fractions into mixed numbers.

When dividing integers, the remainder r was less than the divisor b, so that $\frac{r}{b}$ was a proper fraction. As we know, however, there is a similar formula describing the division of the polynomial $a(x)$ by $b(x)$:

$$a(x) \equiv q(x)b(x) + r(x)$$

where either the remainder $r(x) = 0$ or else $r(x)$ has smaller degree than does the divisor $b(x)$.

> **For Interest**
>
> If we accept the notion that the zero polynomial has degree $-\infty$, then it is enough to state that $\deg(r) < \deg(b)$.

But this identity is equivalent to the identity

$$\frac{a(x)}{b(x)} \equiv q(x) + \frac{r(x)}{b(x)}$$

concerning algebraic fractions. What we see is that any algebraic fraction can be written as the sum of a polynomial and another algebraic fraction whose numerator has smaller degree than its denominator. If we need to, therefore, we can expand this second algebraic fraction into partial fractions.

Example 6.3.1. *Split* $\dfrac{2x^2 + 4x - 3}{(x+1)(2x-3)}$ *into partial fractions.*

Dividing $2x^2 + 4x - 3$ by $(x+1)(2x-3) = 2x^2 - x - 3$, we have

$$2x^2 + 4x - 3 \equiv 1(x+1)(2x-3) + 5x$$

so that

$$\frac{2x^2 + 4x - 3}{(x+1)(2x-3)} \equiv 1 + \frac{5x}{(x+1)(2x-3)}$$

Applying standard partial fractions techniques to this second algebraic fraction, we look for

$$\frac{5x}{(x+1)(2x-3)} \equiv \frac{A}{x+1} + \frac{B}{2x-3}$$

which leads to

$$5x \equiv A(2x-3) + B(x+1)$$

Putting $x = -1$ gives $-5 = -5A$, or $A = 1$. Putting $x = \frac{3}{2}$ gives $\frac{15}{2} = \frac{5}{2}B$, or $B = 3$. Thus we deduce that

$$\frac{2x^2 + 4x - 3}{(x+1)(2x-3)} \equiv 1 + \frac{1}{x+1} + \frac{3}{2x-3}$$

Rather than solving this problem as a two-stage process, it is possible to perform the whole calculation in an extended partial fractions manner. All this single-stage approach requires is that we calculate in advance the degree of the quotient, and include a general polynomial of that degree in our calculations.

Example 6.3.2. *Split* $\dfrac{x^3 + x^2 + 3x - 3}{x(x-1)}$ *into partial fractions.*

When dividing $x^3 + x^2 + 3x - 3$ by $x^2 - x$, the quotient will have degree $3 - 2 = 1$, so it will be linear. Thus we look for an expansion of the form

$$\frac{x^3 + x^2 + 3x - 3}{x(x-1)} \equiv Ax + B + \frac{C}{x} + \frac{D}{x-1}$$

Multiplying out by $x(x-1)$, we obtain the identity

$$x^3 + x^2 + 3x - 3 \equiv x(x-1)(Ax + B) + C(x-1) + Dx$$

Putting $x = 0$ gives $-3 = -C$, or $C = 3$. Putting $x = 1$ gives $2 = D$. Equating the coefficients of x^3 gives $1 = A$. Finally, equating the coefficients of x^2 gives $1 = -A + B$, or $B = 2$. Thus

$$\frac{x^3 + x^2 + 3x - 3}{x(x-1)} \equiv x + 2 + \frac{3}{x} + \frac{2}{x-1}$$

The techniques of partial fractions still work in this extended manner when the denominator is cubic and/or contains repeated or quadratic factors.

Example 6.3.3. *Split* $\dfrac{4x^3 + 10x^2 + 8x - 1}{(2x+1)^2(x+2)}$ *into partial fractions.*

This time, the quotient will have degree $3 - 3 = 0$, so will be constant. We look for an expansion of the form

$$\frac{4x^3 + 10x^2 + 8x - 1}{(2x+1)^2(x+2)} \equiv A + \frac{B}{2x+1} + \frac{C}{(2x+1)^2} + \frac{D}{x+2}$$

which leads to

$$4x^3 + 10x^2 + 8x - 1 \equiv A(2x+1)^2(x+2) + B(2x+1)(x+2) + C(x+2) + D(2x+1)^2$$

Putting $x = -\frac{1}{2}$ gives $-3 = \frac{3}{2}C$, or $C = -2$. Putting $x = -2$ gives $-9 = 9D$, or $D = -1$. Equating coefficients of x^3 gives $4 = 4A$, or $A = 1$. Equating constant coefficients gives $-1 = 2A + 2B + 2C + D$, or $B = 1$. Thus

$$\frac{4x^3 + 10x^2 + 8x - 1}{(2x+1)^2(x+2)} \equiv 1 + \frac{1}{2x+1} - \frac{2}{(2x+1)^2} - \frac{1}{x+2}$$

EXERCISE 6C

1. Express each of the following in partial fractions.

   a) $\dfrac{x+1}{x}$

   b) $\dfrac{x}{x+1}$

   c) $\dfrac{x+1}{x-1}$

   d) $\dfrac{x^2+1}{x^2-1}$

   e) $\dfrac{6x^2 - 22x + 18}{(2x-3)(x-2)}$

   f) $\dfrac{24x^2 + 67x + 11}{(2x+5)(3x+1)}$

2. Express each of the following in partial fractions.

   a) $\dfrac{x^3 - 1}{x^2(x+1)}$

   b) $\dfrac{x^3 + 2x + 1}{x(x^2+1)}$

   c) $\dfrac{x^3 + 3x^2 + x - 14}{(x+4)(x^2+1)}$

   d) $\dfrac{2x^3 + 6x^2 - 3x - 2}{(x-2)(x+2)^2}$

   e) $\dfrac{6x^3 + x + 10}{(x-2)(x+2)(2x-1)}$

   f) $\dfrac{-4x^3 + 16x^2 + 15x - 50}{x(4x^2 - 25)}$

   g) $\dfrac{x^3 2x + 1}{x(x+1)(x-1)}$

   h) $\dfrac{x^3 - 2x^2 + 3x + 6}{x^2(2+x)}$

   i) $\dfrac{12x^3 - 20x^2 + 31x - 49}{(4x^2+9)(x-1)}$

3*. Express $\dfrac{x^4 + a^4}{x^3 + a^3}$ in partial fractions.

Chapter 6: Summary

- Algebraic fractions can be manipulated using the ideas behind ordinary fractions combined with the rules for manipulating polynomials.

- The method of partial fractions enables us to decompose algebraic fractions $\dfrac{f(x)}{g(x)}$, where $g(x)$ is at most cubic and $f(x)$ has smaller degree than does $g(x)$, according to one of the following templates:

$$\frac{ux + v}{(x + a)(x + b)} \equiv \frac{A}{x + a} + \frac{B}{x + b}$$

$$\frac{ux + v}{(x + a)^2} \equiv \frac{A}{x + a} \frac{B}{(x + a)^2}$$

$$\frac{ux^2 + vx + w}{(x + a)(x + b)(x + c)} \equiv \frac{A}{x + a} + \frac{B}{x + b} + \frac{C}{x + c}$$

$$\frac{ux^2 + vx + w}{(x + a)(x + b)^2} \equiv \frac{A}{x + a} + \frac{B}{x + b} + \frac{C}{(x + b)^2}$$

$$\frac{ux^2 + vx + w}{(x + a)q(x)} \equiv \frac{A}{x + a} + \frac{Bx + C}{q(x)}$$

where a, b, c are distinct and $q(x)$ is an irreducible quadratic, such as $x^2 + 1$.

---

1. Solve the inequality $|x + 1| < |x - 2|$. (OCR)

2. Find the greatest and smallest values of x satisfying the inequality (OCR)

$$|2x - 1| \leq 5.$$

3. Sketch the graphs $x + 2y = 6$ and $y = |x + 2|$ on the same set of axes, and hence solve the inequality $|x + 2| < \frac{1}{2}(6 - x)$. (OCR)

4. Solve the inequality $|x + 1| > 2x + 1$. (OCR)

5. Solve the inequality $4|x| > |x - 1|$.

6. Find the solution set of the equation $|x - a| + |x + a| = 2a$, where $a > 0$. (OCR, adapt.)

7*. On the same diagram, sketch the graphs of

$$y = 3 - x \qquad\qquad y = |2x + 3|$$

a) Find the coordinates of all the points of intersection of the two graphs with the axes.

b) Hence, or otherwise, find the set of values of x for which $|2x + 3| > 3 - x$.

8. It is given that
$$(x + a)(x^2 + bx + 2) = x^3 - 2x^2 - x - 6$$

where a and b are constants. Find the value of a and the value of b. (OCR)

9. Find the remainder when $(1 + x)^4$ is divided by $x + 2$.

10. Show that $x - 1$ is a factor of $6x^3 + 11x^2 - 5x - 12$, and find the other two linear factors of this expression. (OCR)

11. The cubic polynomial $x^3 + ax^2 + bx - 8$, where a and b are constants, has factors $x + 1$ and $x + 2$. Find the values of a and b. (OCR)

12. Find the value of a for which $x - 2$ is a factor of $3x^3 + ax^2 + x - 2$. Show that, for this value of a, the cubic equation $3x^3 + ax^2 + x - 2 = 0$ has only one real root. (OCR)

13. Solve the equation $4x^3 + 8x^2 + x - 3 = 0$ given that one of the roots is an integer. (OCR)

14. The cubic polynomial $x^3 - 2x^2 - 2x + 4$ has a factor $x - a$, where a is an integer.

a) Use the factor theorem to find the value of a.

b) Hence find exactly all three roots of the cubic equation $x^3 - 2x^2 - 2x + 4 = 0$. (OCR)

15. The cubic polynomial $x^3 - 2x^2 - x - 6$ is denoted by $f(x)$. Show that $x - 3$ is a factor of $f(x)$. Factorise $f(x)$. Hence find the number of real roots of the equation $f(x) = 0$, justifying your answer.

Hence write down the number of points of intersection of the graphs with equations

$$y = x^2 - 2x - 1 \qquad \text{and} \qquad y = \frac{6}{x},$$

justifying your answer. (OCR)

16. Given that $2x + 1$ is a factor of $2x^3 + ax^2 + 16x + 6$, show that $a = 9$.

Find the real quadratic factor of $2x^3 + 9x^2 + 16x + 6$. By completing the square, or otherwise, show that this quadratic factor is positive for all real values of x. (OCR)

17. Show that both $x - \sqrt{3}$ and $x + \sqrt{3}$ are factors of $x^4 + x^3 - x^2 - 3x - 6$.

Hence write down one quadratic factor of $x^4 + x^3 - x^2 - 3x - 6$, and find a second quadratic factor of this polynomial. (OCR)

18. The diagram shows the curve

$$y = -x^3 + 2x^2 + ax - 10.$$

The curve crosses the x-axis at $x = p$, $x = 2$ and $x = q$.

a) Show that $a = 5$.

b) Find the exact values of p and q.

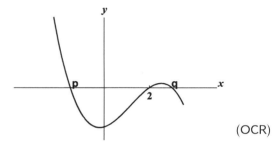

(OCR)

19. The polynomial $x^3 + 3x^2 + ax + b$ leaves a remainder of 3 when it is divided by $x + 1$ and a remainder of 15 when it is divided by $x - 2$. Find the remainder when it is divided by $(x - 2)(x + 1)$.

20. Find the quotient and the remainder when $x^4 + 4$ is divided by $x^2 - 2x + 2$.

21. Let $p(x) = 4x^3 + 12x^2 + 5x - 6$.

a) Calculate $p(2)$ and $p(-2)$, and state what you can deduce from your answers.

b) Solve the equation $4x^3 + 12x^2 + 5x - 6 = 0$.

22. It is given that $f(x) = x^4 - 3x^3 + ax^2 + 15x + 50$, where a is a constant, and that $x + 2$ is a factor of $f(x)$.

a) Find the value of a.

b) Show that $f(5) = 0$ and factorise $f(x)$ completely into exact linear factors.

c) Find the set of values of x for which $f(x) > 0$. (OCR)

23. The diagram shows the graph of $y = x^2 - 3$ and the part of the graph of $y = \frac{2}{x}$ for $x > 0$. The two graphs intersect at C, and A and B are the points of intersection of $y = x^2 - 3$ with the x-axis. Write down the exact coordinates of A and B.
Show that the x-coordinate of C is given by the equation $x^3 - 3x - 2 = 0$.
Factorise $x^3 - 3x - 2$ completely.
Hence

a) write down the x-coordinate of C,

b) describe briefly the geometrical relationship between the graph of $y = x^2 - 3$ and the part of the graph of $y = \frac{2}{x}$ for which $x < 0$. (OCR)

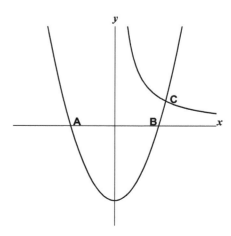

24. The polynomial $x^5 - 3x^4 + 2x^3 - 2x^2 + 3x + 1$ is denoted by $f(x)$.

    a) Show that neither $x - 1$ nor $x + 1$ is a factor of $f(x)$.

    b) Find the remainder when $f(x)$ is divided by $x^2 - 1$.

    c) Show that when $f(x)$ is divided by $x^2 + 1$, the remainder is $2x$.

    d) Find all the real roots of the equation $f(x) = 2x$. (OCR)

25. Express $\dfrac{4}{(x-3)(x+1)}$ in partial fractions. (OCR)

26. Express $\dfrac{2}{x(x-1)(x+1)}$ in partial fractions. (OCR)

27. Express $\dfrac{2x^2 + 1}{x(x-1)^2}$ in partial fractions. (OCR)

28. Express $\dfrac{x^2 - 11}{(x+2)^2(3x-1)}$ in partial fractions. (OCR)

29. Express $\dfrac{3 + 2x}{x^2(3-x)}$ in partial fractions.

30. Simplify $\sqrt{\dfrac{3x^2 + 5x - 2}{4x - 3} \div \dfrac{4x^3 + 13x^2 + 4x - 12}{2x(x+3) - (2-x)(1+x)}}$.

31. Simplify $\dfrac{x - 21}{x^2 - 9} - \dfrac{3}{x + 3} + \dfrac{4}{x - 3}$.

32. Express $\dfrac{8x^3 - 12x^2 - 18x + 15}{(4x^2 - 9)(2x - 3)}$ in partial fractions.

33. Express in partial fractions: a) $\dfrac{x^2 - x + 3}{x(2x^2 + 3)}$ b) $\dfrac{7x^2 - 2x + 5}{(x-1)(3x^2 + 2)}$.

34. Split $\dfrac{1}{x^4 - 13x^2 + 36}$ into partial fractions.

35. It is given that $g(x) = (2x - 1)(x + 2)(x - 3)$.

    a) Express $g(x)$ in the form $Ax^3 + Bx^2 + Cx + D$, giving the values of the constants A, B, C and D.

    b) Find the value of the constant a, given that $x + 3$ is a factor of $g(x) + ax$.

    c) Express $\frac{x-3}{g(x)}$ in partial fractions. (OCR)

36. Express $\frac{3}{(x-1)(x+2)}$ in partial fractions. Hence show that

$$\dfrac{27}{(x-1)^2(x+2)^2} \equiv \dfrac{3}{(x-1)^2} + \dfrac{3}{(x+2)^2} - \dfrac{2}{x-1} + \dfrac{2}{x+2}$$

37*. a) The number a is real and greater than 1. On the same diagram, sketch the graphs of

$$y = \dfrac{1}{x - a} \quad \text{and} \quad y = |x| - a$$

    Identify the coordinates of any points of intersection with the coordinate axes.

    b) Hence, or otherwise, find the set of values of x for which

$$\dfrac{1}{x - a} < |x| - a$$

    c) What is the set of values of x for which $1 < (x - a)(|x| - a)$?

38*. Solve the inequality $\frac{|x|}{x^2+1} \leq \frac{2}{5}$.

39*. Solve the following inequalities: (OCR)

   a) $\frac{x+1}{x-1} < 4$

   b) $\frac{|x|+1}{|x|-1} < 4$

   c) $\left|\frac{x+1}{x-1}\right| < 4$

40*. a) Show that $x - 3$ is a factor of

$$x^3 - 5x^2 + 2x^2 y + xy^2 - 8xy - 3y^2 + 6x + 6y .$$

Express this polynomial in x and y in the form $(x-3)(x+ay+b)(x+cy+d)$ where a, b, c, d are integers to be determined.

   b) Factorise $6y^3 - y^2 - 21y + 2x^2 + 12x - 4xy + x^2 y - 5xy^2 + 10$ into three linear factors. (STEP)

41*. Let

$$f(x) = x^n + a_1 x^{n-1} + \cdots + a_n ,$$

where $a_1, a_2, \ldots, a_n$ are given numbers. You are told that $f(x)$ can be written in the form

$$f(x) = (x + k_1)(x + k_2) \cdots (x + k_n) .$$

By considering $f(0)$, or otherwise, show that $k_1 k_2 \cdots k_n = a_n$. Show also that

$$(k_1 + 1)(k_2 + 1) \cdots (k_n + 1) = 1 + a_1 + a_2 + \cdots + a_n$$

and find a corresponding result for $(k_1 - 1)(k_2 - 1) \cdots (k_n - 1)$.

Find the roots of the equation

$$x^4 + 22x^3 + 172x^2 + 552x + 576 = 0 ,$$

given that they are all integers. (STEP)

Functions

In this chapter we will learn:

- to define a function by specifying both a rule and a domain, and identify the function's range as the set of images of elements in the domain,

- to use graphs to identify the range in simple cases,

- how translations, scalings and reflections of graphs are represented in the defining rules of the functions these graphs represent,

- to understand the terms function, domain, codomain, range, and one-to-one function,

- how to construct the composition of two suitable functions, and how to determine when a function is invertible, and to calculate the inverse function of such functions.

7.1 A Function Needs A Rule!

We already have a general notion of a function, since we have drawn straight line, quadratic and other curves.

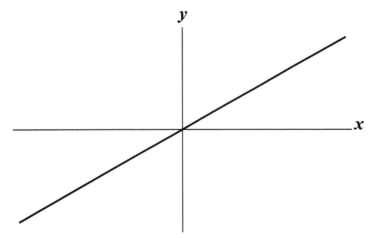

Figure 7.1

A graph is a diagram which represents a rule. To every value a, the rule assigns a new number, b, say. As a varies, so does the value of b. The graph is the collection of all points (a, b), where each b has been determined from a by the conversion rule. To indicate that b depends on a, we often write $b = f(a)$ to indicate that a conversion rule, which we are calling f, has acted on a to obtain b. The fact that this collection of points often forms a smooth curve is a reflection of the type of conversion rule; it is not always the case, since it possible to write down some pretty wild conversion rules!

If we know the specific form of the conversion rule, and have an explicit formula that tells us what $f(a)$ actually is, then the graph is unnecessary, since all the information contained in the graph is described by that formula. Thus, rather than consider the quadratic graph $y = x^2 - 3x + 1$, we could consider the rule f, where $f(x) = x^2 - 3x + 1$.

> **For Interest**
>
> Instead of writing $f(x) = x^2 - 3x + 1$, some authors write $f : x \mapsto x^2 - 3x + 1$, which can be read as 'the rule f such that x maps to $x^2 - 3x + 1$'. There is no difference in meaning between these two notations.

A rule can be thought of as a 'black box': if you put in an input value x, out comes a definite output value. If we decide to label this particular rule, or 'black box', by calling it f, then the output value is $f(x)$. The output value $f(x)$ is called the **image** of x under f.

Going back over the last two chapters, we observe that polynomials and rational functions are all rules, and we have been using the $f(x)$ notation to represent them. Here are some examples of rules. Some of them can be defined simply in algebra, others take more effort; the key thing is that each rule assigns a unique output value to each input value. Note that we are free to give rules any name we like: they don't all have to be called f.

$$
\begin{aligned}
f(x) &= \tfrac{4}{3}\pi x^3, \\
g(x) &= \tfrac{1}{2}(x + |x|), \\
a(x) &= \frac{1}{x-1}, \\
k(x) &= \frac{1}{\sqrt{x^2+1}}, \\
m(x) &= \begin{cases} 1, & x \in \mathbb{Q}, \\ 0, & x \notin \mathbb{Q}, \end{cases} \\
p(n) &= \text{the } n^{\text{th}} \text{ prime number, for any positive integer } n, \\
\pi(x) &= \text{the number of prime numbers} \le x, \\
q(x) &= \sqrt{x}, \\
d(n) &= \text{the number of positive integer divisors of the positive integer } n, \\
H(n) &= 1 + \tfrac{1}{2} + \tfrac{1}{3} + \tfrac{1}{4} + \cdots + \tfrac{1}{n}, \text{ for any positive integer } n.
\end{aligned}
$$

7.2   The Domain and the Range

Looking at the examples of rules given above, we note different rules have different properties. To begin with, not all rules can accept all inputs. For example, the rule a makes no sense when acting on 1, while the function q only makes sense for non-negative inputs. Even worse, p, d and H only accept inputs which are positive integers.

A function is a rule, together with a statement about what numbers the rule will accept as inputs.

> **Key Fact 7.1 Domain and Range**
>
> The set of all possible input x values for a function f is called the **domain** of f. The set of all possible images of f is called the **range** of the function.

In the figure shown on the right, the function f has domain $\{1,2,3,4,5,6\}$. A rule assigns a number to each member of the domain, namely

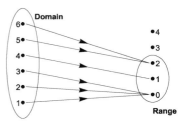

Figure 7.2

$$f(1) = f(2) = f(3) = 0, \quad f(4) = 1, \quad f(5) = f(6) = 2.$$

This makes the range of the function equal to the set $\{0,1,2\}$. The fact that the domain and range might or might not have numbers in common is unimportant; equally unimportant is the fact that there might be other numbers (like 3 and 4 in the figure) that do not appear in the range of f.

A function has not been properly defined until both its rule f and its domain have been specified. We shall meet a more formal notation for functions shortly, but the following shorthand notation is adequate for most purposes. Here are examples of functions:

$$f_1(x) = \tfrac{4}{3}\pi x^3, \qquad\qquad\qquad\qquad x \in \mathbb{R},$$
$$f_2(x) = \tfrac{4}{3}\pi x^3, \qquad\qquad\qquad\qquad x \in \mathbb{R}, x > 0,$$
$$a_1(x) = \tfrac{1}{x-1}, \qquad\qquad\qquad\qquad x \in \mathbb{R}, x \neq 0,$$
$$a_2(x) = \tfrac{1}{x-1}, \qquad\qquad\qquad\qquad x \in \mathbb{R}, x > 0,$$
$$q(x) = \sqrt{x}, \qquad\qquad\qquad\qquad\quad x \in \mathbb{R}, x \geq 0,$$
$$d(n) = \text{the number of positive integer divisors of } n, \qquad n \in \mathbb{N},$$
$$s(n) = \text{the sum of the digits in the decimal expansion of } n, \qquad n \in \mathbb{N}, n \geq 10.$$

For each function, both the rule and the domain have been specified. Note that it is possible for different functions to have the same rule applied to different domains. We have already met this idea when considering problems where physical considerations might lead us to accept certain solutions and discard others. Suppose that one side of a rectangle is 4 cm shorter than the other side, and that the area of the rectangle is 21 cm^2. Calling the two sides x cm and $x - 4$ cm, the area of the rectangle is $x(x-4)$ cm^2. Solving the equation $x(x-4) = 21$, we deduce that $x = 7$ or -3. Since we cannot have a rectangle of sides -3 cm and -7 cm, we discard the $x = -3$ solution and deduce that $x = 7$, so that the rectangle is 7 cm by 3 cm. Using the ideas of functions, we can say instead that the area function is given by

$$A(x) = x(x-4), \qquad\qquad x \in \mathbb{R}, x > 4,$$

and then the only value of x in the domain for which $A(x) = 21$ is $x = 7$. Defining the correct domain for the area function ruled out having to consider rectangles with negative edge lengths.

In short, a function is specified by first defining its rule, then adding a collection of conditions which are sufficient to specify the domain. Technically, the domains of a_2 and s are

$$\left\{ x \in \mathbb{R} \,\middle|\, x > 0 \right\} \qquad \text{and} \qquad \left\{ n \in \mathbb{N} \,\middle|\, n \geq 10 \right\}$$

since the domains are sets, not conditions, but this abuse of notation is convenient and easy to use. Thus a domain might be written down as a set (for example, $\mathbb{R}$ or $\mathbb{Q}$), or else as a collection of conditions (for example, $x \in \mathbb{R}, x > 0$ or $x \in \mathbb{N}, 1 \leq n \leq 100$).

Similarly, a range might be written as a set (such as $\mathbb{R}$), or else as a set of conditions (such as $x \in \mathbb{R}, x > 0$). If we know the name of the function, the conditions might be written down explicitly involving that name (such as $f(x) \in \mathbb{R}, f(x) \geq 2$).

Example 7.2.1. *If $f(x) = \sqrt{x+1}$,*

    (a) *what is the largest possible subset of the reals $\mathbb{R}$ that can be a domain for f, and what is its corresponding range,*

    (b) *what is the range when the domain is $x \in \mathbb{R}, 3 \leq x \leq 8$,*

    (c) *which integers are in the range of f if the domain is $\mathbb{N}$?*

    (a) We cannot take the square root of a negative number, and so the largest possible domain is $x \in \mathbb{R}, x \geq -1$ (to ensure that $x + 1 \geq 0$ throughout the domain). Clearly $f(x) \geq 0$ for all $x \geq -1$, and since $y^2 - 1$ is in the domain of f, with $f(y^2 - 1) = y$, for any $y \in \mathbb{R}, y \geq 0$, we see that any non-negative real number is in the range. The range of f is $f(x) \in \mathbb{R}, f(x) \geq 0$.

(b) If $x \in \mathbb{R}$ with $3 \le x \le 8$ then $2 \le f(x) \le 3$. On the other hand, if $y \in \mathbb{R}$ with $2 \le y \le 3$, then $y^2 - 1$ belongs to the domain of f and $f(y^2 - 1) = x$, and so x is in the range of f. Thus the range of f is $f(x) \in \mathbb{R}, 2 \le f(x) \le 3$.

(c) Since $f(n) = \sqrt{n+1}$ for any positive integer n, the range of f consists of all numbers of the form $\sqrt{n+1}$, where n is a positive integer. Thus the range is $\left\{ \sqrt{n+1} \mid n \in \mathbb{N} \right\}$. Another way of describing this set is $\left\{ \sqrt{n} \mid n \in \mathbb{N}, n \ge 2 \right\}$.

Since $n = \sqrt{n^2}$ for any $n \in \mathbb{N}$, and $n^2 \ge 2$ for any positive integer n except 1, we see that the range contains all positive integers except 1.

EXERCISE 7A

1. Given $f(x) = 2x + 5$, find the values of
   a) $f(3)$,
   b) $f(0)$,
   c) $f(-4)$,
   d) $f\left(-\frac{1}{2}\right)$.

2. Given $f(x) = 3x^2 + 2$, find the values of
   a) $f(4)$,
   b) $f(1)$,
   c) $f(3)$,
   d) $f(-3)$.

3. Given $f(x) = x^2 + 4x + 3$, find the values of
   a) $f(2)$,
   b) $f\left(\frac{1}{2}\right)$,
   c) $f(1)$,
   d) $f(3)$.

4. Given $g(x) = x^3$ and $h(x) = 4x + 1$,
   a) find the value of $g(2) + h(2)$;
   b) find the value of $3g(-1) - 4h(-1)$;
   c) show that $g(5) = h(31)$;
   d) find the value of $h(g(2))$.

5. Given $f(x) = x^n$ and $f(3) = 81$, determine the value of n.

6. Given that $f(x) = ax + b$ and that $f(2) = 7$ and $f(3) = 12$, find a and b.

7. Find the largest possible subset of $\mathbb{R}$ which can be a domain of each of the following functions.
   a) $\sqrt{x}$
   b) $\sqrt{-x}$
   c) $\sqrt{x-4}$
   d) $\sqrt{4-x}$
   e) $\sqrt{x(x-4)}$
   f) $\sqrt{2x(x-4)}$
   g) $\sqrt{x^2 - 7x + 12}$
   h) $\sqrt{x^3 - 8}$
   i) $\frac{1}{x-2}$
   j) $\frac{1}{\sqrt{x-2}}$
   k) $\frac{1}{1+\sqrt{x}}$
   l) $\frac{1}{(x-1)(x-2)}$

8. The domains of these functions are the set of all positive real numbers. Find their ranges.
   a) $f(x) = 2x + 7$
   b) $f(x) = -5x$
   c) $f(x) = 3x - 1$
   d) $f(x) = x^2 - 1$
   e) $f(x) = (x+2)^2 - 1$
   f) $f(x) = (x-1)^2 + 2$

9. Find the range of each of the following functions. All the functions are defined for all real values of x.
   a) $f(x) = x^2 + 4$
   b) $f(x) = 2(x^2 + 5)$
   c) $f(x) = (x-1)^2 + 6$
   d) $f(x) = -(1-x)^2 + 7$
   e) $f(x) = 3(x+5)^2 + 2$
   f) $f(x) = 2(x+2)^4 - 1$

10. These functions are each defined for the given domain. Find their ranges.
    a) $f(x) = 2x$ for $x \in \mathbb{R}, 0 \le x \le 8$
    b) $f(x) = 3 - 2x$ for $x \in \mathbb{R}, -2 \le x \le 2$
    c) $f(x) = x^2$ for $x \in \mathbb{R}, -1 \le x \le 4$
    d) $f(x) = x^2$ for $x \in \mathbb{R}, -5 \le x \le -2$

11. Find the range of each of the following functions. All the functions are defined for the largest possible domain of values of x.
    a) $f(x) = x^8$
    b) $f(x) = x^{11}$
    c) $f(x) = \frac{1}{x^3}$
    d) $f(x) = \frac{1}{x^4}$
    e) $f(x) = x^4 + 5$
    f) $f(x) = \frac{1}{4}x + \frac{1}{8}$
    g) $f(x) = \sqrt{4-x^2}$
    h) $f(x) = \sqrt{4-x}$

12. A piece of wire 24 cm long has the shape of a rectangle. Given that the width is w cm, show that the area, A cm^2, of the rectangle is the function given by $A = 36 - (6 - w)^2$. Find the greatest possible domain for the area function in this context.

13. Given that a cuboid has height x cm, length $(22 - 2x)$ cm and width $(8 - 2x)$ cm, state an appropriate domain for the function representing the volume of the cuboid.

7.3 Graph Transformations

The method shown above for determining the range of a function is precise, but laborious! In many cases, a graphical approach will suffice, and so it will be useful to add to the techniques we already know for graph-sketching.

There are a variety of curves whose shapes we already know, such as straight lines, quadratics, cubics. We also know the shape of reciprocal graphs, such as $y = \frac{1}{x}$, and the graph of the modulus function $y = |x|$.

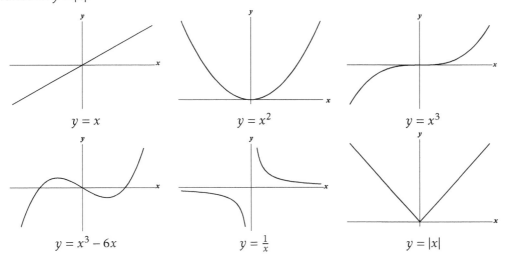

$$y = x \qquad y = x^2 \qquad y = x^3$$

$$y = x^3 - 6x \qquad y = \frac{1}{x} \qquad y = |x|$$

Figure 7.3

We have already discussed methods for sketching more general quadratic graphs, looking for intercepts with the axes and identifying the vertex, but similar methods for cubics are that much more complex. Factorising cubics is not straightforward, and identifying whether or not a particular cubic has local maxima or minima, as in the graph of $y = x^3 - 6x$, above, is not easy to do until we have studied more calculus. It is useful, therefore, to have an array of geometric techniques which enable us to sketch more curves than the standard six above relatively easily. This will be achieved by recognising how certain algebraic operations on the function are reflected by some standard geometric transformations to their graphs.

- **Translations:** Consider the three equations

$$y = x^2, \qquad y = x^2 + 3, \qquad y = x^2 - 2.$$

If we introduce the function f given by $f(x) = x^2$, $x \in \mathbb{R}$, then these three equations are

$$y = f(x), \qquad y = f(x) + 3, \qquad y = f(x) - 2.$$

and so the second and third equations have been derived from the first by adding or subtracting a constant to the function f. If we compare the graphs of these functions, then we see that the graph of the second function has been obtained by translating the graph of the first function a distance of 3 units parallel to the y-axis, while the graph of the third function has been obtained by translating the graph of the first function a distance of -2 units parallel to the y-axis. Here a negative translation is a translation 'down', in the direction of the negative y-axis.

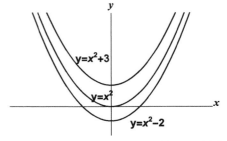

Figure 7.4

Key Fact 7.2 Graph Transformations: Vertical Translations

The graph of the equation $y = f(x) + a$ is obtained from the graph of the equation $y = f(x)$ by translating it through a distance of a units parallel to the y-axis.

How to perform a horizontal translation through a units is less clear. Consider the following graph of $y = x^2 + 1$ and $y = (x-a)^2 + 1$.

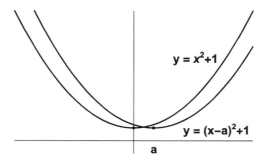

Figure 7.5

It certainly looks as if the graph of $y = (x-a)^2 + 1$ has been obtained from the graph of $y = x^2 + 1$ by translating it through a distance of a units parallel to the x-axis.

For Interest

Why does this work? Consider the equations $y = f(x)$ and $y = f(x-a)$. If we introduce a new coordinate $X = x - a$, then the second equation becomes $y = f(X)$, and hence the graph of $y = f(x-a)$ will look exactly the same, plotted on the Xy-axis system, as the graph of $y = f(x)$ when plotted on the xy-axis system. The question that remains is to find what the Xy-axis system looks like, compared to the xy-axis system.

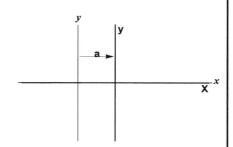

Figure 7.6

A point with coordinates (x, y) in the xy-axis system has coordinates $(x-a, y)$ in the Xy-axis system, and so the point $(a, 0)$ in the xy-axis system becomes the origin of the new Xy-coordinate system. It is clear that the Xy-axis system is obtained by translating the xy-axis system a distance of a units parallel to the x-axis.

Key Fact 7.3 Graph Transformations: Horizontal Translations

The graph of the equation $y = f(x-a)$ is obtained from the graph of the equation $y = f(x)$ by translating it through a distance of a units parallel to the x-axis.

Looking ahead to Chapter 19, we note that graph translation can be described in terms of vectors. The combination of a horizontal translation by a and vertical translation by b can be more simply described as a translation through the vector $\binom{a}{b}$: a vertical translation by b would be a translation through $\binom{0}{b}$, for example.

If we know that a particular equation $y = g(x)$ represents a translation of the curve $y = f(x)$ then there is another way of identifying the precise translation. This is done by identifying a particular point on the curve $y = f(x)$ and finding its corresponding point on $y = g(x)$.

Example 7.3.1. *What translation maps the curve $y = x^2$ onto the curve $y = (x - 2)^2 - 3$?*

A key (and easily identified) point on each quadratic is its vertex. The vertex of $y = x^2$ is the point $(0, 0)$, while the vertex of $y = (x - 2)^2 - 3$ is the point $(2, -3)$. Any translation of $y = x^2$ will map its vertex $(0, 0)$ onto the vertex of the image quadratic. We conclude that this translation maps the vertex $(0, 0)$ to the point $(2, -3)$. Thus $y = (x - 2)^2 - 3$ is obtained from $y = x^2$ by translating by the vector $\binom{2}{-3}$, namely a horizontal translation through 2 and a vertical translation through -3.

Example 7.3.2. *Sketch the curves of $y = x^3 + 3x^2 + 3x$ and $y = |x - 1|$.*

The graph of $y = x^3 + 3x^2 + 3x = (x + 1)^3 - 1$ is obtained from that of $y = x^3 - 1$ by a horizontal translation through -1, while the graph of $y = x^3 - 1$ is obtained from that of $y = x^3$ by a vertical translation through -1. Altogether, the graph of $y = x^3$ has been translated through a vector $\binom{-1}{-1}$. On the other hand, the graph of $y = |x|$ needs to be translated horizontally through a distance of 1 to obtain the graph of $y = |x - 1|$.

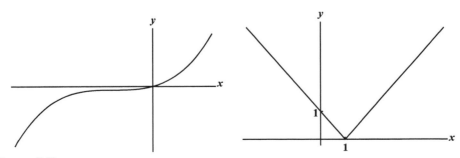

Figure 7.7

- **Stretches:** The following graphs compare the functions $y = |x - 1|$, $y = |3x - 1|$ and $y = 3|x - 1|$.

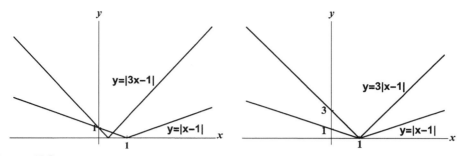

Figure 7.8

The first diagram indicates that the graph of $y = |3x - 1|$ has been obtained from the graph of $y = |x - 1|$ by stretching it parallel to the x-axis by a factor of $\frac{1}{3}$, so that the vertex of the new curve occurs at the point $\left(\frac{1}{3}, 0\right)$. The second diagram indicates that the graph of $y = 3|x - 1|$ has been obtained from the graph of $y = |x - 1|$ by stretching it parallel to the y-axis by a factor of 3. Note that, if we define $f(x) = |x - 1|$ for $x \in \mathbb{R}$, then $|3x - 1| = f(3x)$, while $3|x - 1| = 3f(x)$. These observations lead to the following ideas:

Key Fact 7.4 Graph Transformations: Stretches

The graph of the equation $y = f(ax)$ is obtained from that of the equation $y = f(x)$ by stretching it parallel to the x-axis by a factor of $\frac{1}{a}$.
The graph of the equation $y = af(x)$ is obtained from that of the equation $y = f(x)$ by stretching it parallel to the y-axis by a factor of a.

This tells is that a vertical stretch of scale factor a is achieved by the graph transformation

$$y = f\left(\frac{x}{a}\right).$$

As in the case of translations, the way that the stretches are implemented is different for horizontal and vertical stretches. A stretch by a factor of a is obtained in one case by dividing by a, and in the other by multiplying by a. This apparent confusion can be removed by noting that both can be written in terms of division

$$y = f\left(\frac{x}{a}\right) \qquad \frac{y}{a} = f(x)$$

with one or other of the coordinates being directly acted upon by a. Similar to the case of translations, these graph stretches can be seen in terms of alterations to one or other of the coordinate axes. In this case, the alteration is a stretch instead of a translation.

Example 7.3.3. *If $f(x) = x^2 + 3$, $g(x) = 4x^2 + 3$, $h(x) = 4x^2 + 12$ and $k(x) = 2x^2 + 4x + 8$ (for $x \in \mathbb{R}$), describe transformations that will change the graph of $y = f(x)$ into the graphs of $y = g(x)$, $y = h(x)$ and $y = k(x)$ respectively.*

Since $g(x) = f(2x)$, we see that the graph of $y = g(x)$ is obtained from that of $y = f(x)$ by a horizontal stretch of factor $\frac{1}{2}$. Since $h(x) = 4f(x)$ we see that the graph of $y = h(x)$ is obtained that of $y = f(x)$ by a vertical stretch of factor 4.

Finally, since $k(x) = 2\left(x^2 + 2x + 4\right) = 2\left((x+1)^2 + 3\right)$, we see that the graph of $y = k(x)$ is obtained from that of $y = f(x)$ by a horizontal translation through -1, followed by a vertical scale by factor 2.

A little care needs to be exercised when considering the effect or more than one transformation.

Example 7.3.4. *If $f(x) = x^2$, $g(x) = (2x + 1)^2$ and $h(x) = 2x^2 + 2$ (for $x \in \mathbb{R}$), describe transformations which convert the graph of $y = f(x)$ into the graphs of $y = g(x)$ and $y = h(x)$.*

Note that

$$g(x) = f(2x+1) = f\left(2(x+\tfrac{1}{2})\right)$$

and so there are two ways of obtaining the graph of $y = g(x)$ from that of $y = f(x)$:

- ★ the graph of $y = f(x)$ could be translated horizontally through -1 (obtaining the graph of $y = f_1(x) = f(x+1)$) and then scaled horizontally by a factor of $\tfrac{1}{2}$ (obtaining the graph of $y = f_1(2x) = f(2x+1) = g(x)$).
- ★ the graph of $y = f(x)$ could be scaled horizontally by a factor of $\tfrac{1}{2}$ (obtaining the graph of $y = f_2(x) = f(2x)$) and then translated horizontally through $-\tfrac{1}{2}$ (obtaining the graph of $y = f_2\left(x+\tfrac{1}{2}\right) = f\left(2(x+\tfrac{1}{2})\right) = f(2x+1) = g(x)$).

Similarly,

$$h(x) = 2\left(f(x)+1\right) = 2f(x)+2$$

and so there are two ways of obtaining the graph of $y = h(x)$ from that of $y = f(x)$:

- ★ the graph of $y = f(x)$ could be translated vertically through -1 (obtaining the graph of $y = f_3(x) = f(x)+1$) and then stretched vertically by a factor of 2 (obtaining the graph of $y = 2f_3(x) = h(x)$).
- ★ the graph of $y = f(x)$ could be stretched vertically by a factor of 2 (obtaining the graph of $y = f_4(x) = 2f(x)$) and then translated vertically through 2 (obtaining the graph of $y = f_4(x)+2 = h(x)$).

Thus the order in which a translation and a stretch in the same direction are applied makes a difference!

We could also observe that $h(x) = f\left(\sqrt{2}x\right)+2$, so that the graph of $y = h(x)$ can also be obtained from that of $y = f(x)$ by applying a horizontal stretch of factor $\tfrac{1}{\sqrt{2}}$, followed by a vertical translation through 2. That this third option exists is a consequence of the nature of the function f.

It is perfectly possible to have negative scale factors in stretches, just like we can have negative scale factor enlargements (an enlargement is, after all, the composition of a horizontal and a vertical stretch of the same scale factor). The stretches when $a = -1$ are particularly important.

Key Fact 7.5 Graph Transformations: Reflections

The graph of $y = f(-x)$ is obtained from the graph of $y = f(x)$ by reflection in the y-axis (which is the same as a horizontal stretch of scale factor -1).
The graph of $y = -f(x)$ is obtained from the graph of $y = f(x)$ by reflection in the x-axis (which is the same as a vertical stretch of scale factor -1).

Example 7.3.5. *Describe a sequence of transformations that will transform the graph of $y = x^2$ into that of $y = -x^2 + 4x + 1$, and hence identify the vertex of the second quadratic.*

Since $y = 5 - (x-2)^2$, the required sequence of transformations is:

- ★ a horizontal translation through 2 (obtaining $y = (x-2)^2$),
- ★ reflection in the x-axis (obtaining $y = -(x-2)^2$),
- ★ a vertical translation through 5 (obtaining $y = -x^2 + 4x + 1$).

Following the vertex $(0,0)$ of the original through these transformations $(0,0) \to (2,0) \to (2,0) \to (2,5)$, we deduce that the new vertex is at $(2,5)$.

- **Taking Moduli:** We have already seen in Chapter 3 how the modulus function can be used to adjust the shape of some functions. There are two cases to consider: given the graph of $y = f(x)$, transformation of this graph yields the graphs of the functions

$$y = |f(x)| \qquad y = f(|x|)$$

We have already seen the first of these.

Key Fact 7.6 Graph Transformations: Taking the Modulus 1

The graph of $y = |f(x)|$ is obtained from the graph of $y = f(x)$ by reflecting all parts of that graph that lie below the x-axis in the x-axis.

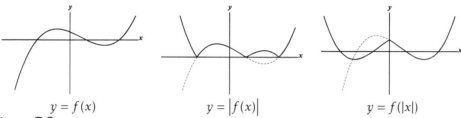

$$y = f(x) \qquad\qquad y = |f(x)| \qquad\qquad y = f(|x|)$$

Figure 7.9

What happens to $y = f(|x|)$? It is clear that $f(|x|) = f(x)$ for all $x \geq 0$, and so the graph of $y = f(x)$ is unchanged for non-negative x. However, since $f(|-2|) = f(2)$, for example, the graph for negative x is just the mirror image (in the y-axis) of the graph for positive x.

Key Fact 7.7 Graph Transformations: Taking the Modulus 2

The graph of $y = f(|x|)$ is obtained from the graph of $y = f(x)$ by taking the graph of $y = f(x)$ for $x \geq 0$ and reflecting this in the y-axis.

Example 7.3.6. *Sketch the graph of* $y = \big||x-1|-2\big|$ *for* $x \in \mathbb{R}$.

The graph of $y = |x|$ is translated horizontally by 1, then vertically by -2. This yields the graph of $y = |x-1|-2$. Then a further modulus is taken. We obtain the sketch:

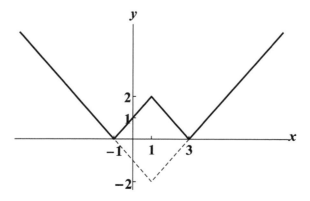

Figure 7.10

EXERCISE 7B

1. Given $f(x) = x^3$, $x \in \mathbb{R}$, sketch the graph of each of the following functions. Use the same set of axes for all four sketches. Mark any intercepts with the axes.

   a) $y = f(x)$ b) $y = f(-x)$ c) $y = f(x+3)$ d) $y = |f(x)| + 10$

2. Given $f(x) = x + 1$, $x \in \mathbb{R}$, sketch the graph of each of the following functions. Use the same set of axes for all four sketches. Mark any intercepts with the axes.

   a) $y = f(x)$ b) $y = f(2x)$ c) $y = f(|x|) + 3$ d) $y = -f(x)$

3. Given $f(x) = x^2$, $x \in \mathbb{R}$, sketch the graph of each of the following functions. Use the same set of axes for all four sketches. Mark any intercepts with the axes.

   a) $y = f(x)$ b) $y = 4 - 9f(x)$ c) $y = f(2x) - 4$ d) $y = f(|x - 2|)$

4. Given $f(x) = \frac{1}{x^2+1}$, $x \geq 0$, sketch the graph of each of the following functions. Use the same set of axes for all three sketches. Mark any intercepts with the axes.

   a) $y = f(x+2)$, $x \geq -2$ b) $y = f(x) + 4$, $x \geq 0$ c) $y = |2f(x) - 1|$

5. Show that $\frac{x}{x+1} = 1 - \frac{1}{x+1}$, and hence sketch the curve $y = \frac{x}{x+1}$ for $x \neq -1$.

6. The diagrams below show the graphs of four functions, each of which vanish for values of x outside the interval $-2 \leq x \leq 2$. Sketch the graphs of the following functions, using separate axes each time.

   a) $y = a(x) - 4$, $y = a(2x)$ and $y = \frac{1}{2}a(x)$,

   b) $y = |b(x) - 2|$, $y = b(|x|)$ and $y = |b(|x|) - 2|$,

   c) $y = c(x) + 3$, $y = c(x+3)$ and $y = c(|x|)$,

   d) $y = |d(x)|$, $y = d(|x|)$ and $y = |d(-|x|)|$.

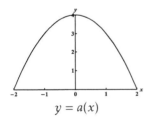
$y = a(x)$
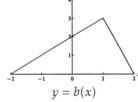
$y = b(x)$
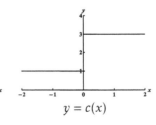
$y = c(x)$
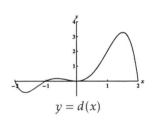
$y = d(x)$

7. a) What is the equation of the graph that is obtained from $y = f(x)$ by first translating horizontally through 1, then horizontally stretching by a factor of 2?

   b) What is the equation of the graph that is obtained from $y = f(x)$ by first stretching horizontally by a factor of 2, then translating horizontally through 1?

8*. Show how the graph of any quadratic $y = ax^2 + bx + c$ can be obtained from the graph of $y = x^2$ by a combination of translations and stretches.

9*. What sequence of transformations will transform the graph of $y = x^3 - 3x$ into the graph of $y = 8x^3 + 24x^2 + 18x$?

7.4 Graphs, Domains and Ranges

Now that we have a larger set of skills with which to sketch curves, it will be easier for us to use these sketches to determine properties of functions. In particular, determining the range becomes fairly straightforward.

Suppose we need to determine the range of the function g, where

$$g(x) = \sqrt{x}, \qquad x \in \mathbb{R}, 1 \le x \le 3.$$

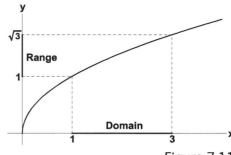

A sketch of $y = \sqrt{x}$ is given, and the section of the x-axis (between 1 and 3) has been marked as the range. The section of the curve which corresponds to x belonging to the domain has been shown. Since this is the graph of the equation $y = \sqrt{x}$, the range of the function is the values of y that we obtain as x runs through the domain $1 \le x \le 3$.

Figure 7.11

Thus the range of the function is $y \in \mathbb{R}, 1 \le y \le \sqrt{3}$. Note that it is fairly common to indicate the range by giving an inequality for y, confirming the relationship between the range and y-axis.

Key Fact 7.8 Domain and Range – Graphical Interpretation

Roughly speaking, while the **domain** of a function is that part of the x-axis which is needed to plot its graph, the **range** of a function is that part of the y-axis which the graph sweeps through.

Example 7.4.1. *Find the ranges of the functions a and b given by*

$$a)\, a(x) = x^2 + 4x + 5, \, x \in \mathbb{R}, -1 \le x \le 3 \qquad b)\, b(x) = x^2 + 5, \, x \in \mathbb{R}, -1 \le x \le 3$$

Sketches of the two functions are given in Figure 7.12 below. Since the vertex of $y = x^2 + 4x + 5$ occurs at $(-2, 1)$, it is clear that the range of a is the set of real values from 1, the value of the function at $x = -1$, to 26, the value of the function at $x = 3$. Thus the range of a is $y \in \mathbb{R}, 1 \le y \le 26$. On the other hand, while the largest possible value of $x^2 + 5$ is 14, occurring at $x = 3$, the smallest possible value of y does not occur at $x = -1$, but rather at $x = 0$. Thus the range of b is $y \in \mathbb{R}, 5 \le y \le 26$.

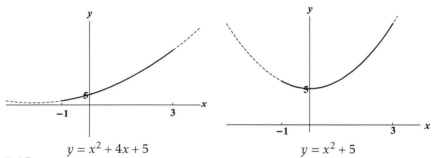

$$y = x^2 + 4x + 5 \qquad\qquad y = x^2 + 5$$

Figure 7.12

For Interest

The definition of a domain or range is often abbreviated. A variable such as x may be assumed to belong to the reals if it has not been explicitly defined differently. This is a space-saving convention that is useful in the definition or description of more complicated functions.

Example 7.4.2. *Find the range of the function f, where*

$$f(x) = \begin{cases} 2x + 3, & -1 \le x < 0, \\ -\sqrt{1 - x^2}, & 0 \le x \le 1. \end{cases}$$

If we sketch this piecewise function, we see that the straight line portion of the curve involves y values in the interval $1 \le y < 3$, while the curved portion of the curve involves y values in the interval $-1 \le y \le 0$. Thus the range of f is $y \in \mathbb{R}, -1 \le y \le 0$ or $1 \le y < 3$.

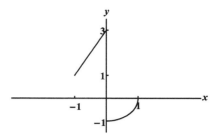

Figure 7.13

Sometimes the range of a function can be determined, even if sketching the graph is too challenging.

Example 7.4.3. *Find the range of the function f, where $f(x) = \frac{x+1}{x^2+2}$, $x \in \mathbb{R}$.*

If y belongs to the range of f, then there exists $x \in \mathbb{R}$ such that $y = f(x)$, and so

$$
\begin{aligned}
y &= \tfrac{x+1}{x^2+2} \\
y(x^2 + 2) &= x + 1 \\
yx^2 - x + (2y - 1) &= 0
\end{aligned}
$$

Thus we have a quadratic, with coefficients involving y, which has at least one real solution. Hence the discriminant of this quadratic cannot be negative. Thus

$$
\begin{aligned}
(-1)^2 - 4y(2y - 1) &\ge 0 \\
8y^2 - 4y - 1 &\le 0 \\
16y^2 - 8y - 2 &\le 0 \\
(4y - 1)^2 &\le 3 \\
|4y - 1| &\le \sqrt{3}
\end{aligned}
$$

and hence we deduce that $\tfrac{1}{4}(1 - \sqrt{3}) \le y \le \tfrac{1}{4}(1 + \sqrt{3})$. Thus the range of f must be contained in this interval. On the other hand, if y lies in this interval, then the quadratic $yx^2 - x + (2y - 1) = 0$ must have roots, and hence there exists x such that $y = f(x)$, so that y belongs to the range of f. Thus the range of f is the whole interval $y \in \mathbb{R}, \tfrac{1}{4}(1 - \sqrt{3}) \le y \le \tfrac{1}{4}(1 + \sqrt{3})$.

EXERCISE 7C

1. Find the range of the function $y = x^2 + 4x + 5$ if the domain is

   a) $\mathbb{R}$,
   b) $x \in \mathbb{R}, 0 \le x \le 5$,
   c) $x \in \mathbb{R}, -3 \le x \le 3$.

2. Find the range of the function $y = \frac{x}{x+2}$ if the domain is

   a) $x \in \mathbb{R}, x \ne -2$,
   b) $x \in \mathbb{R}, x > -2$,
   c) $x \in \mathbb{R}, 0 \le x \le 2$.

3. Find the range of the function

$$
f(x) = \begin{cases}
0, & x < 0 \\
x^2, & 0 \le x \le 1 \\
3 - 2x, & 1 < x < 3, \\
-4 & x = 3, \\
0 & x > 3.
\end{cases}
$$

4. If the function $f(x)$, defined on the domain $x \in \mathbb{R}, 0 \le x \le 1$, has range $y \in \mathbb{R}, -2 \le y \le 5$,

   a) what is the range of the function $f(x + 2)$, defined on the domain $x \in \mathbb{R}, -2 \le x \le -1$,

   b) what is the range of the function $3f(x)$, defined on the domain $x \in \mathbb{R}$, $0 \le x \le 1$,

   c) what is the range of the function $|f(x)|$, defined on the domain $x \in \mathbb{R}$, $0 \le x \le 1$,

   d) what is the range of the function $f(|x|)$, defined on the domain $x \in \mathbb{R}$, $-1 \le x \le 1$?

5. If π is the function

$$\pi(x) = \text{the number of positive primes integers less than } x$$

with domain $x \in \mathbb{R}$, $0 \le x \le 50$, what is the range of π?

6. What is the range of the function $f(x) = \frac{x+1}{(x+2)^2}$ for $x \in \mathbb{R}$, $x \ne -2$?

7*. Find the range of the function $f(x) = \frac{ax+b}{cx+d}$ for $x \in \mathbb{R}$, $x \ne -\frac{d}{c}$, where a,b,c,d are non-zero numbers.

8*. Find the range of the function $f(x) = ax^2 + bx + c$, with domain $\mathbb{R}$, where $a > 0$.

9*. What is the range of the function $f(x) = \big||x - 2a| - a\big|$ for $x \in \mathbb{R}$, $0 \le x \le 5a$, where $a > 0$?

7.5   Functions as Mappings

We have seen that a function is a rule which is applied to each element of a particular set, called its domain. This rule assigns a number to each number in the domain, but what sort of number? Is it always a real number, or is it always an integer? Consider the functions, both with $\mathbb{R}$ as domain,

$$\pi(x) = \text{the number of positive primes} \le x \qquad f(x) = \frac{1}{x^2+1}$$

We might find it useful to indicate that $\pi(x)$ will always be a non-negative integer, and that $f(x)$ is a real number between 0 and 1, without requiring the reader to infer these facts from the details of the rules defining the functions. This requirement of including some knowledge of the type of output provided by a function forces us to introduce a more formal way of expressing functions. It is worth the effort!

Suppose we have two non-empty sets U and V. A **mapping** from U to V is a rule which assigns a unique element of V to each element of U. Note that the elements of U and V do not have to be numbers; we could have

$$U = \{2000, 2001, 2002, \ldots, 2099\}$$

$$V = \{\text{Monday, Tuesday, Wednesday, Thursday, Friday, Saturday, Sunday}\}$$

while the mapping f assigns to each number in U the day of the week on which April 1st fell that year, so that $f(2015) =$ Wednesday, for example.

A **function** is simply a mapping between two sets of numbers.

> **Key Fact 7.9** Mappings: Domain, Codomain and Range
>
> A mapping f from the set U to the set V is denoted by $f : U \to V$ (to be read as 'the mapping f from U to V').
> The set U is called the **domain** of the mapping. The set V is called the **codomain** of the mapping. The set of all images of elements in the domain is called the **range** of the mapping.

For example, consider the function $f : \mathbb{R} \to \mathbb{R}$ given by the formula

$$f(x) = x^2, x \in \mathbb{R}.$$

This function has domain $\mathbb{R}$ and codomain $\mathbb{R}$. However, the range of f is $\{x \in \mathbb{R} \,|\, x \ge 0\}$, since every real number greater than or equal to 0 is the square of a real number. On the other hand, the similar function $g : \{x \in \mathbb{R} \,|\, x \ge 2\} \to \mathbb{R}$ given by the formula

$$g(x) = x^2, x \in \mathbb{R}, x \ge 2$$

has domain $\{x \in \mathbb{R} \mid x \geq 2\}$, codomain $\mathbb{R}$ and range $\{x \in \mathbb{R} \mid x \geq 4\}$.

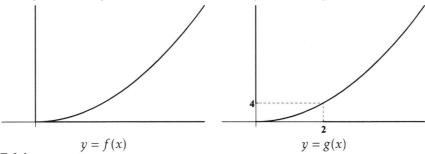

$$y = f(x) \qquad\qquad y = g(x)$$

Figure 7.14

If U only contains a finite number of elements, a mapping $f : U \to V$ can be represented by a diagram, where each element in U is linked to its image element in V by an arrow.

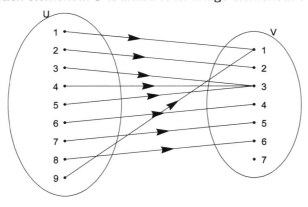

Figure 7.15

In the above example, $U = \{1, 2, 3, 4, 5, 6, 7, 8, 9\}$, $V = \{1, 2, 3, 4, 5, 6, 7\}$ and, for example $f(5) = 3$. Note that:

- a mapping can map more than one element of U to the same element of V (for example, $f(1) = f(9) = 1$),

- not every element of V has to be the image of some element of U (in this case, 7 is not).

This second point that not every element of V has to be mapped to by f is important. It tells us that the range of the function f, while always a subset of V, is not necessarily equal to V. For example, in the above example, the range of f is $\{1, 2, 3, 4, 5, 6\}$; a proper subset of V.

> **Food For Thought 7.1**
>
> The range of a function is always a subset of the codomain, but is not necessarily equal to the codomain.

There may be much more freedom available in choosing a codomain. For example, consider the function f with domain $\mathbb{R}$ given by the rule

$$f(x) = x^2, x \in \mathbb{R}.$$

Any set V which has $\{x \in \mathbb{R} \mid x \geq 0\}$ as a subset could be a codomain for f, but there is no choice for the range of f, which must be $\{x \in \mathbb{R} \mid x \geq 0\}$.

What, then, is the point of the codomain? The following functions:

$$
\begin{array}{ll}
f_1 : \mathbb{R} \to \mathbb{R} & f_1(x) = \frac{1}{x^2+1}, \ x \in \mathbb{R}, \\
f_2 : \mathbb{R} \to \{x \in \mathbb{R} : x > 0\} & f_2(x) = \frac{1}{x^2+1}, \ x \in \mathbb{R} \\
f_3 : \mathbb{R} \to \{x \in \mathbb{R} : 0 < x \leq 1\} & f_3(x) = \frac{1}{x^2+1}, \ x \in \mathbb{R}
\end{array}
$$

are basically the same, differing only in their choice of codomain. Graphically, we can represent the difference between the three functions by deciding how much of the y-axis to include in a sketch:

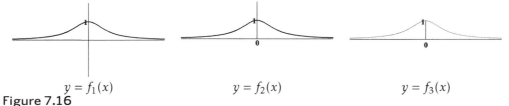

$$y = f_1(x) \qquad\qquad y = f_2(x) \qquad\qquad y = f_3(x)$$

Figure 7.16

To this extent, the codomain is unimportant. However, it is convenient. Firstly, it may not be obvious from the outset exactly what the range is, or the range may be a fairly complicated set. It is not at all clear what the range of the function

$$f(x) = \frac{x^3 + 7x^2 + 13x - 4}{x^4 + 12x^2 + 13}, x \in \mathbb{R}$$

is, but it is obvious that $f(x) \in \mathbb{R}$ for all x, and so it is convenient to define its codomain to be $\mathbb{R}$, and hence refer to it as the function $f : \mathbb{R} \to \mathbb{R}$: we can define this function quickly with this choice of codomain, and then move on (if we wish) to consider what its range is.

There are also times where a choice of codomain is natural. Consider the function p, with domain $\mathbb{N}$, where $p(n)$ is the probability that n identical unbiased 6-sided dice will together roll a total which is a multiple of 3. Since a fair amount of work will be required to determine the value of $p(n)$ for a general integer n, we certainly not know the range of p at the moment. However it makes sense to give p the codomain $\{x \in \mathbb{R} : 0 \le x \le 1\}$, since any probability must lie in that set! For a similar reason, a function all of whose outputs are positive integers might usefully be given the codomain $\mathbb{N}$ instead of $\mathbb{R}$.

Finally, it is a good habit to get used to the idea that the range and codomain of a function are not the same. This is an important issue, particularly when we move on to consider composing and inverting functions.

7.6 Composition of Functions

Calculators possess many buttons that apply functions to numbers. The square root button $\sqrt{x}$ takes an input value and outputs its square root (displaying an error message if the input value is negative, and so outside the domain of the square root function). The sin button will take any angle $x°$ and return its sine, $\sin x°$, while the inverse cosine button $\cos^{-1}$ button will produce the inverse cosine of any real number between -1 and 1 (once, again, producing an error message if the input is outside the domain).

We already know how to combine the function buttons on our calculators to obtain more complicated functions. If we want to calculate $\sqrt{x-3}$, for example, we first subtract 3 and then take the square root. If we want to calculate $\sin(2x - 1)°$, we first multiply by 2, then subtract 1, then finally take the sine of the result. We obtain more complicated functions by putting more than one of them together, applying first one, and then another.

If we have two functions f and g, consider the function we obtain by applying first f, and then g. If we start with the number x, applying f obtains the number $f(x)$. We then apply g to that number, obtaining the final number $g\big(f(x)\big)$. The result is a function, called the **composite** of f and g, written gf.

$$gf(x) = g\big(f(x)\big)$$

The notation makes sense, just removing one set of brackets for clarity. What is confusing is that gf looks like g comes before f, and it is easy to forget that f acts on x before g does; in an operational sense, f acts before g. The easiest way to remember the right way is to think that, in the expression $fg(x)$, g nearest to x, and so acts on x first. There is no way to avoid this point of confusion. We are writing functions using the convention of 'action from the left', in that the image of the point x under the function f is written as $f(x)$, with the symbol f to the left of x. Action from the left requires that the composite function fg means 'g first, then f'.

Example 7.6.1. *If $f : \mathbb{R} \to \mathbb{R}$ and $g : \mathbb{R} \to \mathbb{R}$ are the functions*

$$f(x) = x+3 \qquad g(x) = x^2$$

calculate fg and gf. Show that there is just one value of x for which $fg(x) = gf(x)$.

We see that $fg(x) = f(x^2) = x^2+3$, while $gf(x) = g(x+3) = (x+3)^2$. Thus $fg(x) = gf(x)$ precisely when $x^2 + 3 = x^2 + 6x + 9$, or when $x = -1$.

This is fine, but problems occur when we consider more complicated functions.

Example 7.6.2. *If f and g are given by $f(x) = \cos x°$ and $g(x) = \frac{1}{x}$, calculate $gf(60)$ and $gf(90)$.*

While $f(60) = \frac{1}{2}$, so that $gf(60) = 2$, the fact that $f(90) = 0$ means that we cannot calculate $gf(90)$, since $g(0)$ does not exist.

The easiest way around this problem is to require that the codomain of the first function is the same as the domain of the second function. Thus a function $f : U \to V$ and a function $g : V \to W$ can be composed to form the composite function $gf : U \to W$. The fact that the codomain of f and the domain of g are both V ensures that $f(x)$ becomes to the domain of g for all $x \in U$.

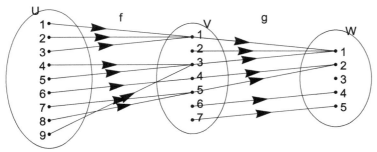

Figure 7.17
In this case the composite function gf sends $1, 2, 3, 3, 4, 5$ and 9 to 1, and $6, 7, 8$ to 2.
Requiring the codomain of f and the domain of g to be the same is the simplest method of ensuring that gf can be defined. However, a slightly weaker condition is good enough.

Food For Thought 7.2

A function f can be composed with a function g to form a function gf provided that the range of f is a subset of the domain of g.

Example 7.6.3. *If $f(x) = 3x + 2$ for $x \in \mathbb{R}$, $0 \le x \le 3$ and $g(x) = x^2$ for $x \in \mathbb{R}$, find the function gf and state its range.*
What is the largest possible domain that g could have which would make it possible to define fg?

It is clear that $gf(x) = (3x + 2)^2 = 9x^2 + 12x + 4$ for $x \in \mathbb{R}$, $0 \le x \le 3$. The simplest way to find the range of gf is to note that f maps the domain of f to $x \in \mathbb{R}$, $2 \le x \le 11$, and this interval is in turn mapped by g to $x \in \mathbb{R}$, $4 \le x \le 121$. Thus the range of gf is $x \in \mathbb{R}$, $4 \le x \le 121$.

To be able to define $fg(x)$, $x^2 = g(x)$ must belong to the domain of f, and hence $0 \le x^2 \le 3$. Thus we need $-\sqrt{3} \le x \le \sqrt{3}$. Thus the largest possible domain of g which would enable us to define fg is $x \in \mathbb{R}$, $-\sqrt{3} \le x \le \sqrt{3}$.

EXERCISE 7D

1. Given that $f(x) = 2x + 1$ and $g(x) = 3x - 5$, where $x \in \mathbb{R}$, find the value of the following:

   a) $gf(1)$ b) $gf(-2)$ c) $fg(0)$ d) $fg(7)$

   e) $ff(5)$ f) $ff(-5)$ g) $gg(4)$ h) $gg\left(2\tfrac{2}{9}\right)$.

2. Given that $f(x) = x^2$ and $g(x) = 4x - 1$, where $x \in \mathbb{R}$, find the value of the following:

   a) $fg(2)$ b) $gg(4)$ c) $gf(-3)$

   d) $ff\left(\tfrac{1}{2}\right)$ e) $fgf(-1)$ f) $gfgf(2)$

3. Given that $f(x) = 5 - x$ and $g(x) = \tfrac{4}{x}$, where $x \in \mathbb{R}$, $x \ne 0, 5$, find the value of the following:

   a) $ff(7)$ b) $ff(-19)$ c) $gg(1)$ d) $gg\left(\tfrac{1}{2}\right)$

   e) $gggg\left(\tfrac{1}{2}\right)$ f) $fffff(6)$ g) $fgfg(2)$ h) $fggf(2)$

4. Given that $f(x) = 2x + 5$, $g(x) = x^2$ and $h(x) = \tfrac{1}{x}$, where $x \in \mathbb{R}$, $x \ne 0, -\tfrac{5}{2}$, find the following composite functions:

   a) fg b) gf c) fh d) hf

   e) ff f) hh g) gfh h) hgf

5. Given that $f(x) = \sin x°$, $g(x) = x^3$ and $h(x) = x - 3$, where $x \in \mathbb{R}$, find the following functions:

   a) hf b) fh c) fhg

   d) fg e) hhh f) gf

6. Given that $f(x) = x + 4$, $g(x) = 3x$ and $h(x) = x^2$, where $x \in \mathbb{R}$, express each of the following in terms of f, g, and h:

   a) $x \mapsto x^2 + 4$ b) $x \mapsto 3x + 4$ c) $x \mapsto x^4$

   d) $x \mapsto 9x^2$ e) $x \mapsto 3x + 12$ f) $x \mapsto 3\left(x^2 + 8\right)$

   g) $x \mapsto 9x + 16$ h) $x \mapsto x^2 + 8x + 16$ i) $x \mapsto 9x^2 + 48x + 64$

7. Given that $f(x) = x^2$ and $g(x) = 3x - 2$, where $x \in \mathbb{R}$, find a, b and c such that

   a) $fg(a) = 100$ b) $gg(b) = 55$ c) $fg(c) = gf(c)$.

8. Given that $f(x) = ax + b$ and that $ff(x) = 9x - 28$, find the possible values of a and b.

9. For $f(x) = ax + b$, $f(2) = 19$ and $ff(0) = 55$. Find the possible values of a and b.

10. The functions $f(x) = 4x + 1$ and $g(x) = ax + b$ are such that $fg = gf$ for all real values of x. Show that $a = 3b + 1$.

11*. The two functions

$$f(x) = ax^2, \quad x \in \mathbb{R}, -1 \le x \le 4 \qquad g(x) = \begin{cases} x + b, & -1 \le x \le 0, \\ c - x, & 0 \le x \le 1, \end{cases}$$

where $a, b, c > 0$, have the same range. Show that either $b = 1$ or else $c = 1$. What is the largest possible value of a?

12*. If $f(x) = \tfrac{x-1}{x}$ for $x \in \mathbb{R}$, $x \ne 0, 1$, show that it is possible to define ff and fff. Write down a formula for the function $f^{(2015)}$. Here $f^{(n)}$ represents the composition of n copies of f, so that (for example) $f^{(3)} = fff$.

7.7 One-to-One and Monotonic Functions

We frequently want to solve equations of the form $f(x) = 0$ for some function f.

Example 7.7.1. *Solve the equations*

$$a)\ 2x + 1 = 19, \qquad b)\ \sin x° = \tfrac{1}{2}, \quad 0 \le x \le 90, \qquad c);\ x^2 + 3x - 1 = 0$$

$$a)\quad x = \tfrac{19-1}{2} = 9. \qquad b)\quad x = \sin^{-1}\tfrac{1}{2} = 30. \qquad c)\quad x = \tfrac{1}{2}\left[-3 \pm \sqrt{13}\right].$$

The third of these examples is different to the other two. In the first two cases there was a single solution, but the third equation had two different solutions. This reflects the fact that the first two of the three functions

$$f_1(x) = 2x - 1, \qquad f_2(x) = \sin x°, x \in \mathbb{R}, 0 \le x \le 90, \qquad f_3(x) = x^2 + 3x - 1$$

share a property which the third function does not possess: f_1 and f_2 map different elements of their domains to different numbers, but there are distinct elements of $\mathbb{R}$ which f_3 maps to the same point. For example $f_3(-5) = f_3(2) = 9$.

Key Fact 7.10 One-to-One Functions

A function $f : U \to V$ is called **one-to-one** if distinct elements of its domain map to distinct numbers. Thus a function is one-to-one if

$$x \ne y \qquad \Rightarrow \qquad f(x) \ne f(y).$$

Functions which are not one-to-one are called **many-to-one**.

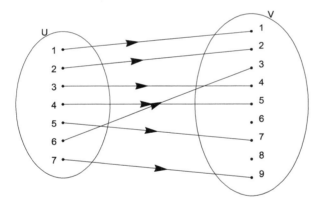

Figure 7.18

While it is quite easy to show that a function is not one-to-one algebraically, it is often easiest to show that a function is one-to-one by looking at its graph.

Example 7.7.2. *Decide whether the following functions are one-to-one or not:*

$$a)\ f_1(x) = x^2 + 4x + 3, \qquad b)\ f_2(x) = x^2 + 4x + 3, \quad x \in \mathbb{R}, x \ge -1, \qquad c)\ f_3(x) = \tfrac{x}{x^2+1}, \quad x \in \mathbb{R}, x \ge 1.$$

The function f_1 is not one-to-one, because $f_1(-1) = f(-3) = 0$. If we consider the graph of the second function, we see that the domain $x \in \mathbb{R}, x \ge -1$ is totally to the right of the vertex $(-2,-1)$ of the quadratic, and so there is clearly exactly one $x \ge -1$ such that $f_2(x) = y$ for any $y \ge 0$ (the other solution of the equation $f_1(x) = y$ would be less than -3). The function f_2 is one-to-one (and its range is $y \in \mathbb{R}, y \ge 0$).

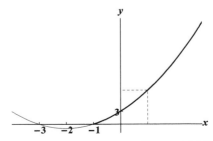

Figure 7.19

The third function is harder to handle, but only because sketching its curve is quite challenging at present. Suppose that $u, v \geq 1$ and that $f_3(u) = f_3(v)$. Then

$$
\begin{aligned}
\frac{u}{u^2+1} &= \frac{v}{v^2+1} \\
u(v^2 + 1) &= v(u^2 + 1) \\
uv^2 + u - u^2 v - v &= 0 \\
(u - v)(1 - uv) &= 0
\end{aligned}
$$

If $u = v = 1$, then $u = v$. If either u or v is greater than 1, then $uv - 1 > 0$, and hence $u = v$. Thus we have shown that $f_3(u) = f_3(v)$ for $u, v \geq 1$ implies that $u = v$, which tells us that f_3 is one-to-one.

Alternatively, if y belongs to the range of f_3 then (since $f_3(x) > 0$ for all $x \geq 1$) $y > 0$ and there exists $x \geq 1$ such that $y = f_3(x)$, so that $yx^2 - x + y = 0$. The discriminant $1 - 4y^2$ of this polynomial must be non-negative, and hence $0 < y \leq \frac{1}{2}$. For any $0 < y \leq \frac{1}{2}$ the solutions of $yx^2 - x + y = 0$ are

$$
x = x_\pm = \frac{1 \pm \sqrt{1 - 4y^2}}{2y}
$$

Since $0 < y \leq \frac{1}{2}$, $x_+ \geq \frac{1}{2y} \geq 1$, and so x_+ belongs to the domain of f_3. If $y = \frac{1}{2}$, then $x_- = x_+$. If $y < \frac{1}{2}$ then $x_- < 1$. Thus x_+ is the only solution of the equation $yx^2 - x + y = 0$ which belongs to the domain of f_3. This also shows that f_3 is one-to-one.

These arguments should encourage us to learn to be able to sketch this more complicated function as quickly as possible, since the fact that f_3 is one-to-one is clear from its graph.

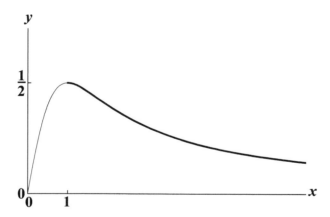

Figure 7.20

There is one particularly important class of functions to consider. They occur frequently in mathematics, and have a number of very useful properties.

Key Fact 7.11 Monotonic Functions

A function f is called **increasing** if $f(x) \leq f(y)$ whenever $x \leq y$; it is called **strictly increasing** if $f(x) < f(y)$ whenever $x < y$.
A function f is called **decreasing** if $f(x) \geq f(y)$ whenever $x \geq y$; it is called **strictly decreasing** if $f(x) > f(y)$ whenever $x < y$.
A function that is either increasing or decreasing is called **monotonic**.

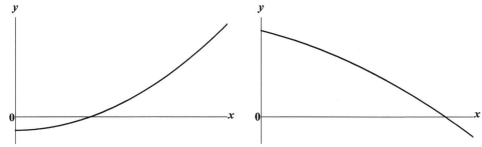

Figure 7.21

We shall mostly be concerned with strictly monotonic functions. Monotonic functions that are not strictly monotonic are ones where the function can be constant throughout some part of the domain.

A key property of monotonic functions is the following:

Food For Thought 7.3

Any strictly monotonic function is one-to-one.

To see this, suppose for example that f is strictly increasing. If $x \neq y$, without loss of generality we can assume that $x < y$. Then $f(x) < f(y)$, which certainly implies that $f(x) \neq f(y)$.

Example 7.7.3. *Show that the function $f(x) = \sqrt{x^2 + 1}$ for $x \in \mathbb{R}, x \geq 0$ is strictly increasing.*

Note that the functions $x \mapsto x^2 + 1$ and $x \mapsto \sqrt{x}$ are both strictly increasing on the common domain $x \in \mathbb{R}, x \geq 0$. If a and b are strictly increasing (and the composite ba can be defined) we see that

$$x < y \quad \Rightarrow \quad a(x) < a(y) \quad \Rightarrow \quad ba(x) < ba(y)$$

and so the composite ba is also strictly increasing. Hence the function f is strictly increasing.

Note that when we have studied further calculus, there will be a better method available to us to show that this function is strictly increasing.

All of the examples of one-to-one functions we have seen so far have been one-to-one by virtue of their being monotonic. There are, however, one-to-one functions that are not monotonic.

Example 7.7.4. *Show that the function $f(x)$ is one-to-one but not monotonic, where*

$$f(x) = \begin{cases} x + 4, & -1 \leq x \leq 0, \\ 2 - x, & 0 < x \leq 1, \end{cases}$$

The graph shows that f has range $y \in \mathbb{R}, 1 \leq y < 2$ or $3 \leq y \leq 4$, and it is clear that every point in this range is achieved by exactly one point in the domain. However, since $f(-1) > f(1)$, f is not increasing and, since $f(-1) < f(0)$, f is not decreasing either.

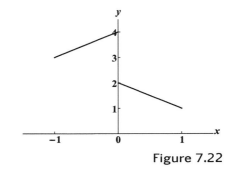

Figure 7.22

EXERCISE 7E

1. Each of the following functions has domain $\mathbb{R}$. Determine which are one-to-one functions.

   a) $x \mapsto 3x + 4$
   b) $x \mapsto x^2 + 1$
   c) $x \mapsto x^2 - 3x$
   d) $x \mapsto 5 - x$
   e) $x \mapsto \cos x°$
   f) $x \mapsto x^3 - 2$
   g) $x \mapsto \frac{1}{2}x - 7$
   h) $x \mapsto \sqrt{x^2}$
   i) $x \mapsto x(x - 4)$
   j) $x \mapsto x^3 - 3x$
   k) $x \mapsto x^9$
   l) $x \mapsto \sqrt{x^2 + 1}$

2. Determine which of the following functions, with the specified domains, are one-to-one.

   a) $f(x) = x^2, x > 0$
   b) $f(x) = \cos x°, -90 \le x \le 90$
   c) $f(x) = 1 - 2x, x < 0$
   d) $f(x) = x(x - 2), 0 < x < 2$
   e) $f(x) = x(x - 2) \ x > 2$
   f) $f(x) = x(x - 2), x < 1$
   g) $f(x) = \sqrt{x}, x > 0$
   h) $f(x) = x^2 + 6x - 5, x > 0$
   i) $f(x) = x^2 + 6x - 5, x < 0$
   j) $f(x) = x^2 + 6x - 5, x > -3.$

3. Each of the following functions has domain $x \in \mathbb{R}, x \ge k$. In each case, find the smallest possible value of k such that the function is one-to-one.

   a) $f(x) = x^2 - 4$
   b) $f(x) = (x + 1)^2$
   c) $f(x) = (3x - 2)^2$
   d) $f(x) = x^2 - 8x + 15$
   e) $f(x) = x^2 + 10x + 1$
   f) $f(x) = (x + 4)(x - 2)$
   g) $f(x) = x^2 - 3x$
   h) $f(x) = 6 + 2x - x^2$
   i) $f(x) = (x - 4)^4.$

4. Which of the following functions are monotonic, and which are one-to-one?

   a) $a : \mathbb{R} \to \mathbb{R}, a(x) = x^2 + x - 1,$

   b) $b : \mathbb{N} \to \mathbb{N}, b(n) = n^2 + n - 1,$

   c) $c(x) = \frac{1}{x-1}$ for $x \in \mathbb{R}, x \ne 1,$

   d) $d(x) = \frac{1}{x-1}$ for $x \in \mathbb{R}, x > 1,$

   e) $e : \{0, 1, 2, 3, 4\} \to \{0, 1, 2, 3, 4\}$, where $e(n)$ is the remainder obtained when $2n$ is divided by 5,

   f) $f : \{0, 1, 2, 3, 4, 5\} \to \{0, 1, 2, 3, 4, 5\}$, where $f(n)$ is the remainder obtained when $3n$ is divided by 6,

   g) $g(x) = \frac{1}{(x-2)^2}$ for $x \in \mathbb{R}, x \ne 2,$

   h) $h(x) = \frac{1}{(x-2)^2}$ for $x \in \mathbb{R}, x > 2,$

   i) $j(x) = x^3 - x^2$ for $x \in \mathbb{R}, x \ge 0,$

   j) $k(x) = x^3 - x^2$ for $x \in \mathbb{R}, 0 \le x \le \frac{2}{3},$

   k) $m(x) = |x|$ for $x \in \mathbb{R},$

   l) $n(x) = |x - a| - |x - b|$ for $x \in \mathbb{R}$, where $a < b.$

5. In Example 7.7.2 it was stated that $x_- < 1$ for $0 < y < \frac{1}{2}$. Why?

7.8 Inverse Functions

Consider the functions

$$
\begin{aligned}
f_1(x) &= 3x + 2, & x \in \mathbb{R}, & & g_1(x) &= \tfrac{1}{3}(x - 2), & x \in \mathbb{R}, \\
f_2(x) &= x^2, & x \in \mathbb{R}, x \ge 0, & & g_2(x) &= \sqrt{x}, & x \in \mathbb{R}, x \ge 0, \\
f_3(x) &= x^4, & x \in \mathbb{R}, & & g_3(x) &= \sqrt[4]{x}, & x \in \mathbb{R}, x \ge 0,
\end{aligned}
$$

It is easy to see that

$$
\begin{aligned}
f_1 g_1(x) &= x, & x \in \mathbb{R}, & & g_1 f_1(x) &= x, & x \in \mathbb{R}, \\
f_2 g_2(x) &= x, & x \in \mathbb{R}, x \ge 0, & & g_2 f_2(x) &= x, & x \in \mathbb{R}, x \ge 0
\end{aligned}
$$

but while $f_3 g_3(x) = x$ for all $x \in \mathbb{R}, x \ge 0$, it is not the case that $g_3 f_3(x) = x$ for all $x \in \mathbb{R}$: for instance, $g_3 f_3(-1) = 1$. Thus, while it is possible, sometimes, to 'unzip' a function, applying a second function to undo the work of the first, this is not always possible. What do f_1 and f_2 have which f_3 does not?

We have noted before that if a function f is one-to-one, then the equation $f(x) = y$ has a unique solution x for any y in the range of f. This means that we could find a uniquely defined function g, whose domain is the range of f, such that $g(y)$ is the solution of the equation $f(x) = y$ for any y in the range of f. In other words, we can find a function g, with domain equal to the range of f, such that $fg(y) = y$ for all y in the range of f. Actually we can say more than this. If x belongs to the domain of x, then x is the only element of the domain of f that is mapped by f to the number $f(x)$. Thus we deduce that $gf(x) = x$ as well.

Key Fact 7.12 Inverse Mappings

A mapping $f : U \to V$ is **invertible** if there exists a mapping, denoted $f^{-1} : V \to U$ such that

$$f^{-1}f(u) = u, u \in U, \qquad\qquad ff^{-1}(v) = v, v \in V.$$

The mapping f^{-1} is called the **inverse** of f.

Thinking pictorially, the diagram of the inverse $f^{-1} : V \to U$ of the mapping $f : U \to V$ is the same as the diagram of the function f, but with the direction of the arrows reversed.

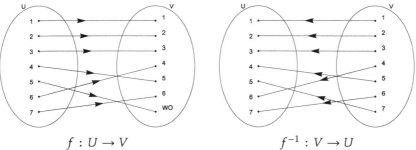

$$f : U \to V \qquad\qquad\qquad f^{-1} : V \to U$$

Figure 7.23

For this to be possible, every element in V must be at the end of an arrow in the diagram of f. This means that the range of f must be the whole of V. Since there has to be a unique value of $f^{-1}(v)$ for every v in V, there cannot be more than one arrow pointing to any element of V. In other words, f must be one-to-one.

Food For Thought 7.4

A function f is invertible precisely when it is one-to-one and its range equals its codomain.

Example 7.8.1. *Find the inverse of the function $f : \mathbb{R} \to \mathbb{R}$ given by $f(x) = 2x + 7$.*

Note that f is strictly increasing, so one-to-one, and its range is the whole of $\mathbb{R}$, and hence f is invertible. To find the inverse function, note that if $y = f(x)$, then $x = f^{-1}$. Thus the algebraic manipulations

$$
\begin{aligned}
y &= f(x) = 2x + 7 \\
y - 7 &= 2x \\
x &= \tfrac{1}{2}(y - 7)
\end{aligned}
$$

tell us that the inverse function is $f^{-1}(x) = \tfrac{1}{2}(x - 7)$ for $x \in \mathbb{R}$.

Key Fact 7.13 Inverting a Function

To find the inverse of a function f, write down the equation $y = f(x)$, and make x its subject. The result is a formula for $f^{-1}(y)$.

For practical purposes, we will often be working with a looser definition of the function that does not specify the codomain. Part of the process of defining the inverse function will be to specify its domain.

If we consider the function $f(x) = x^2 - 2x$ for $x \in \mathbb{R}$, $x \geq 1$, then the above approach leads us to try

$$
\begin{aligned}
y &= f(x) = x^2 - 2x \\
y + 1 &= (x - 1)^2 \\
x &= 1 \pm \sqrt{y + 1}
\end{aligned}
$$

This calculation raises two questions, that need to be answered before we can use this argument:

- which sign, $+$ or $-$, do we choose?

- for which values of y do we apply this calculation?

To answer this, we really need to specify the codomain of the function f properly. We know the domain of f is $U = \{x \in \mathbb{R} : x \geq 1\}$. Since $(1, -1)$ is the vertex of the quadratic $y = x^2 - 2x$, the function is strictly increasing, and so one-to-one, on this domain. For f to be invertible, its codomain V should be equal to its range, and so we need to define $V = \{x \in \mathbb{R} : x \geq -1\}$. Then the inverse will be a function $f^{-1} : V \to U$. Thus the domain of the inverse function will be the range of the original function f. This answers the second question. Since f^{-1} should take values in U, $f^{-1}(y) \geq 1$ for all $y \in V$. Thus we deduce that

$$
f^{-1}(y) = 1 + \sqrt{y + 1} \,, y \in \mathbb{R}, y \geq -1 \,.
$$

Key Fact 7.14 Inverse Functions

A function f is **invertible** if it is one-to-one and its codomain equals its range. The inverse function f^{-1} has domain equal to the range of f, and its range is equal to the domain of f:

Domain of f^{-1} = Range of f $\qquad$ Range of f^{-1} = Domain of f

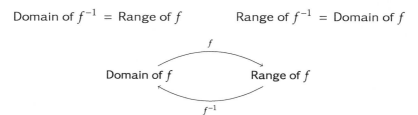

Example 7.8.2. *Find the inverse of the function $y = \frac{5x+6}{x+3}$ for $x \in \mathbb{R}$, $x \neq -3$.*

Since $y = 5 - \frac{9}{x+3}$, we can sketch the curve, and so we deduce that f is one-to-one and has range $y \in \mathbb{R}$, $y \neq 5$. Writing

$$
\begin{aligned}
y &= \frac{5x+6}{x+3} \\
y(x + 3) &= 5x + 6 \\
x &= \frac{6 - 3y}{y - 5}
\end{aligned}
$$

we deduce that

$$
f^{-1}(x) = \frac{6 - 3x}{x - 5} \,, \qquad x \in \mathbb{R}, x \neq 5 \,.
$$

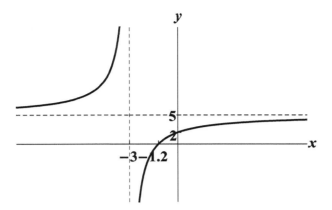

Figure 7.24

7.9   The Graph of the Inverse Function

If we consider the graph of an invertible function f, with domain D and range R, what relationship does it bear to the graph of the inverse function $y = f^{-1}(x)$?

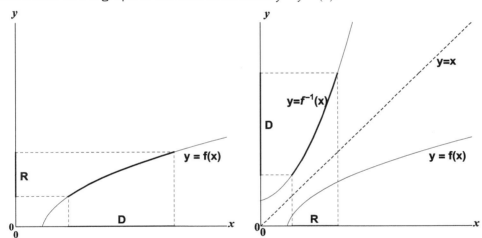

Figure 7.25

The equation $y = f^{-1}(x)$ is of course the same as the equation $x = f(y)$, which is what happens if you swap x and y in the equation $y = f(x)$. Thus the graph of $y = f^{-1}(x)$ is obtained by swapping the x and y values of the graph $y = f(x)$. The process of swapping x- and y-coordinates (so that the point $(3, 4)$ is replaced by the point $(4, 3)$) is achieved by the geometric operation of reflecting in the line $y = x$.

> **Key Fact 7.15 The Graphs of $y = f(x)$ and $y = f^{-1}(x)$**
>
> The graph of $y = f^{-1}(x)$ is obtained from the graph of $y = f(x)$ by reflecting it in the line $y = x$.

Note that this reflection suitably interchanges the roles of domain and range, with R becoming the domain of the inverse function, and D becoming its range.

EXERCISE 7F

1. Each of the following functions has domain $\mathbb{R}$. In each case use a graph to show that the function is one to one, and write down its inverse.

    a) $f(x) = x + 4$ b) $f(x) = x - 5$ c) $f(x) = 2x$

    d) $f(x) = \frac{1}{4}x$ e) $f(x) = x^3$ f) $f(x) = \sqrt[5]{x}$.

2. Given the function $f(x) = x - 6$, $x \in \mathbb{R}$, find the values of:

    a) $f^{-1}(4)$,   b) $f^{-1}(1)$,   c) $f^{-1}(-3)$,   d) $ff^{-1}(5)$,   e) $f^{-1}f(-4)$.

3. Given the function $f(x) = 5x$, $x \in \mathbb{R}$, find the values of:

    a) $f^{-1}(20)$,   b) $f^{-1}(100)$,   c) $f^{-1}(7)$,   d) $ff^{-1}(15)$,   e) $f^{-1}f(-6)$.

4. Given the function $f(x) = \sqrt[3]{x}$, $x \in \mathbb{R}$, find the values of:

    a) $f^{-1}(2)$,   b) $f^{-1}\left(\frac{1}{2}\right)$,   c) $f^{-1}(8)$,   d) $f^{-1}f(-27)$,   e) $ff^{-1}(5)$.

5. Find the inverse of each of the following functions.

    a) $f(x) = 3x - 1$, $x \in \mathbb{R}$ b) $f(x) = \frac{1}{2}x + 4$, $x \in \mathbb{R}$

    c) $f(x) = x^3 + 5$, $x \in \mathbb{R}$ d) $f(x) = \sqrt{x} - 3$, $x \geq 0$

    e) $f(x) = \frac{1}{2}(5x - 3)$, $x \in \mathbb{R}$ f) $f(x) = (x - 1)^2 + 6$, $x \geq 1$

6. For each of the following, find the inverse function and sketch the graphs of $y = f(x)$ and $y = f^{-1}(x)$.

    a) $f(x) = 4x$, $x \in \mathbb{R}$ b) $f(x) = x + 3$, $x \in \mathbb{R}$

    c) $f(x) = \sqrt{x}$, $x \in \mathbb{R}, x \geq 0$ d) $f(x) = 2x + 1$, $x \in \mathbb{R}$

    e) $f(x) = (x - 2)^2$, $x \in \mathbb{R}, x \geq 2$ f) $f(x) = 1 - 3x$, $x \in \mathbb{R}$

    g) $f(x) = \frac{3}{x}$, $x \in \mathbb{R}, x \neq 0$ h) $f(x) = 7 - x$, $x \in \mathbb{R}$

7. Show that $f^{-1} = f$ for all these functions. Such functions are called **self-inverse**.

    a) $f(x) = 5 - x$, $x \in \mathbb{R}$ b) $f(x) = -x$, $x \in \mathbb{R}$

    c) $f(x) = \frac{4}{x}$, $x \in \mathbb{R}, x \neq 0$ d) $f(x) = \frac{6}{5x}$, $x \in \mathbb{R}, x \neq 0$

    e) $f(x) = \frac{x+5}{x-1}$, $x \in \mathbb{R}, x \neq 1$ f) $f(x) = \frac{3x-1}{2x+3}$, $x \in \mathbb{R}, x \neq \frac{3}{4}$

8. Find the inverse of each of the following functions:

    a) $f(x) = \frac{x}{x-2}$, $x \in \mathbb{R}, x \neq 2$ b) $f(x) = \frac{2x+1}{x-4}$, $x \in \mathbb{R}, x \neq 4$

    c) $f(x) = \frac{x+2}{x-5}$, $x \in \mathbb{R}, x \neq 5$ d) $f(x) = \frac{3x-11}{4x-3}$, $x \in \mathbb{R}, x \neq \frac{3}{4}$

9. The function $f(x) = x^2 - 4x + 3$ has domain $x \in \mathbb{R}, x > 2$.

    a) Determine the range of f.

    b) Find the inverse function f^{-1} and state its domain and range.

    c) Sketch the graphs of $y = f(x)$ and $y = f^{-1}(x)$.

10. The function $f(x) = \sqrt{x - 2} + 3$ has domain $x \in \mathbb{R}, x > 2$.

    a) Determine the range of f.

    b) Find the inverse function f^{-1} and state its domain and range.

    c) Solve the equation $f(x) = f^{-1}(x)$.

11. The function $f(x) = x^2 + 2x + 6$ has domain $x \in \mathbb{R}, x \leq k$. Given that f is one-to-one, determine the greatest possible value of k. When k has this value,

    a) determine the range of f,

    b) find the inverse function f^{-1} and state its domain and range,

    c) sketch the graphs of $y = f(x)$ and $y = f^{-1}(x)$.

12. Given the functions $f(x) = 2x + 1$ and $g(x) = 4x - 3$, for $x \in \mathbb{R}$, calculate the functions f^{-1}, g^{-1}, gf and $(gf)^{-1}$. Verify that $(gf)^{-1} = f^{-1}g^{-1}$.

13. The function $f(x) = px + q$, $x \in \mathbb{R}$, is such that $f^{-1}(6) = 3$ and $f^{-1}(-29) = -2$. Find $f^{-1}(27)$.

14. The function $e : \{0,1,2,3,4\} \to \{0,1,2,3,4\}$ is such that $e(n)$ is the remainder obtained when $2n$ is divided by 5. Show that $e^{-1}(n)$ is the remainder when $3n$ is divided by 5.

15*. The functions $f : U \to V$ and $g : V \to W$ are invertible. Explain why $gf : U \to W$ must be invertible, and show that $(fg)^{-1} = g^{-1}f^{-1}$.

16*. The function f is defined by $f(x) = \frac{px+q}{rx+s}$, $\quad x \in \mathbb{R}, x \neq -\frac{s}{r}$ where p,q,r,s are non-zero numbers.

   a) What can we say about the function f if $ps - qr = 0$?

   b) We know that $ps - qr \neq 0$ and that f is self-inverse. Show that $p + s = 0$.

17*. The function f is defined by $f(x) = \frac{p}{x} + q$, $\quad x \in \mathbb{R}, x \neq 0$, where p,q are non-zero numbers. What condition on p and q ensures that the equation $f(x) = f^{-1}(x)$ has no solutions?

Chapter 7: Summary

- A function f is a rule defined on a domain; for any x in the domain, the rule assigns a value $f(x)$ to be the image of f under the function. The range of a function is the set of images of points in the domain.

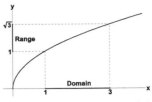

Figure 7.26

- If the graph $y = f(x)$ of a function f is drawn, then the domain of f is the set of x values for which the graph is drawn, and the range of f is the set of y values obtained.

- The graph $y = f(x)$ is affected by transformations as follows:

  ★ if the graph is translated through a horizontal distance of a units, the equation of the new graph is $y = f(x - a)$,

  ★ if the graph is translated through a vertical distance of a units, the equation of the new graph is $y = f(x) + a$,

  ★ if the graph is subjected to a horizontal scale of factor a, the equation of the new graph is $y = f\left(\frac{x}{a}\right)$,

  ★ if the graph is subjected to a vertical scale of factor a, the equation of the new graph is $y = af(x)$,

  ★ if the graph is reflected in the y-axis, the equation of the new graph is $y = f(-x)$,

  ★ if the graph is reflected in the x-axis, the equation of the new graph is $y = -f(x)$,

  ★ the graph of the equation $y = |f(x)|$ is obtained by reflecting all parts of the graph of $y = f(x)$ which lie below the x-axis in the x-axis,

  ★ the graph of the equation $y = f\left(|x|\right)$ is obtained by combining the portion of the graph of $y = f(x)$ for positive x with its reflection in the y-axis.

- A function can be regarded as a mapping $f : U \to V$ from its domain U to its codomain V; every element of the domain U is assigned to a unique element $f(u)$ in the codomain V. The range of f is a subset of V, which does not have to be equal to V.

- Provided that the domain of g contains the range of f, the composite function gf can be defined. Its domain is the same as the domain of f, and $(gf)(x) = g\left(f(x)\right)$ for all x in the domain of f.

- A function f is one-to-one when distinct elements of its domain are mapped to distinct elements of its codomain. If a function f is one-to-one, then every element of the range of f is the image of a unique element of the domain of f. Examples of one-to-one functions are strictly monotonic functions.

- The inverse of a function f is a function f^{-1} such that $\left(f^{-1}f\right)(x) = x$ for all x in the domain of f, and such that $\left(ff^{-1}\right)(y) = y$ for all y in the range of f. To be invertible, a function must be one-to-one, and its range must equal its codomain.

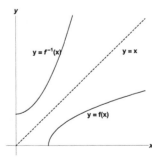

- If a function f is invertible, then the domain of f^{-1} is the range of f, and the range of f^{-1} is the domain of f. The graph of $y = f^{-1}(x)$ is obtained from the graph of $y = f(x)$ by reflecting it in the line $y = x$.

Figure 7.27

Circles, Radians & Elementary Trigonometry

In this chapter we will learn:

- to recognise and use the equation of a circle,

- to use the relationship between points of intersection of graphs and solutions of equations, including the relationship between tangents and repeated roots,

- about the definition of radian measure, and the relationship between radians and degrees,

- the formulae concerning the arc-length and sector area of a circle,

- review elementary properties of the trigonometric functions, and learn the exact values of sine, cosine and tangent for fundamental angles,

- to solve problems using the sine and cosine rules, and use the formula for the area of a triangle.

We shall look at the circle from two different points of view. Now that we have studied quadratics, we can learn the coordinate geometry of the circle. In addition, properties of the circle lead us to introduce a new system for measuring angles. This system is much more natural mathematically, and leads to simpler formulae and easier calculations.

8.1   The Equation of a Circle

A circle can be easily drawn with a pencil, a drawing pin and a piece of string or, to be more technological, using a pair of compasses. Both of these methods ensure that all the points drawn on the curve are a fixed distance (the length of the string or the spread of the compasses) from a fixed point.

Thus a circle is the locus of the set of points which are a fixed distance (called the **radius**) from some specified point (called the **centre**). Consider the circle which has radius r and centre C, where C has coordinates (p,q). Then the circle is the set of points P such that the distance CP is equal to r. If P has coordinates (x,y), then we know that the distance CP is equal to $\sqrt{(x-p)^2 + (y-q)^2}$. Thus:

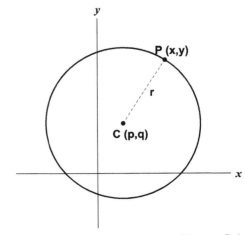

Figure 8.1

> **Key Fact 8.1** The Equation of a Circle
>
> The equation of a circle of radius r with centre $C(p, q)$ is
> $$(x - p)^2 + (y - q)^2 = r^2.$$

Example 8.1.1. *Find the equation of the circle with centre $(1, 2)$ and radius 3.*

Using the formula, the equation is
$$(x - 1)^2 + (y - 2)^2 = 9.$$

You could multiply out the brackets and collect terms to write this equation as
$$\begin{aligned} x^2 - 2x + 1 + y^2 - 4y + 4 &= 9 \\ x^2 + y^2 - 2x - 4y - 4 &= 0 \end{aligned}$$

Both the expanded and the unexpanded versions of the formula are equally acceptable as equations of the circle.

We can use the technique of completing the square to determine the centre and radius of a circle.

Example 8.1.2. *Find the centre and radius of the circle with equation $x^2 + y^2 + 2x - 3y - 17 = 0$.*

Completing the square in both x and y, we obtain
$$\begin{aligned} x^2 + y^2 + 2x - 3y - 17 &= 0 \\ (x + 1)^2 - 1 + \left(y - \tfrac{3}{2}\right)^2 - \tfrac{9}{4} - 17 &= 0 \\ (x + 1)^2 + \left(y - \tfrac{3}{2}\right)^2 &= \tfrac{81}{4} \end{aligned}$$

and hence the circle has centre $(-1, \tfrac{3}{2})$ and radius $\tfrac{9}{2}$.

Example 8.1.3. *The line segment AB is the diameter of a circle, where A and B have coordinates $(2, 3)$ and $(-6, 7)$. Find the equation of the circle.*

The centre of the circle is the midpoint of AB, so has coordinates $(-2, 5)$. The diameter of the circle is
$$\sqrt{(2 - (-6))^2 + (3 - 7)^2} = \sqrt{64 + 16} = 4\sqrt{5},$$

and so the radius is $2\sqrt{5}$, and the equation of the circle is
$$(x + 2)^2 + (y - 5)^2 = 20.$$

Example 8.1.4. *Find the equation of the circle that passes through the three points $A(5, -1)$, $B(-2, 6)$ and $C(-4, 2)$.*

There are two approaches to this problem. One is purely algebraic. We know that a circle must have an equation of the form
$$(x - u)^2 + (y - v)^2 = r^2$$

for some constants a, b and c; to pass through the points A, B and C means that a, b and c must satisfy the equations

$$\begin{aligned} (5 - u)^2 + (-1 - v)^2 &= r^2 \\ (-2 - u)^2 + (6 - v)^2 &= r^2 \qquad \text{or} \\ (-4 - u)^2 + (2 - v)^2 &= r^2 \end{aligned} \qquad \begin{aligned} u^2 + v^2 - 10u + 2v &= r^2 - 26 \\ u^2 + v^2 + 4u - 12v &= r^2 - 40 \\ u^2 + v^2 + 8u - 4v &= r^2 - 20 \end{aligned}$$

Subtracting the first equation from the second (in the right-hand set) gives $14u - 14v = -14$, or $u - v = -1$. Subtracting the second equation from the third gives

$4u + 8v = 20$, or $u + 2v = 5$. Hence we deduce that $u = 1$ and $v = 2$. Substituting these values into any of the above equations tells us that $r^2 = 25$, or $r = 5$. Thus the equation of the circle is $(x-1)^2 + (y-2)^2 = 25$, and the circle has radius 5 and centre $(1,2)$.

This approach is not very satisfying or instructive, since it does not use take advantage of our geometrical insight. As is well-known, for any triangle ABC it is possible to find a circle which passes through all three vertices of that triangle. The circle is called the **outcircle** or **circumcircle** of the triangle. Constructing the outcircle of a triangle is an elementary application of ruler-and-compass construction.

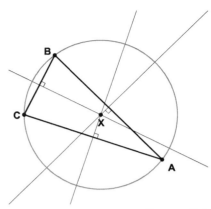

Figure 8.2

The perpendicular bisector of the line AB is the set of points equidistant from both A and B. The perpendicular bisector of the line BC is the set of points equidistant from both B and C. Where these two lines meet is a point X which is equidistant from A and B and also equidistant from B and C. Thus the distances from this point to A, B and C are all the same, and hence this point of intersection is the centre of a circle which can be drawn passing through all three points A, B and C. In addition, we deduce that the point X must also lie on the perpendicular bisector of the line AC, which shows that the three perpendicular bisectors of a triangle must be concurrent.

For our problem, we can find the outcentre of our triangle by mirroring this construction. The line AB has midpoint $(\frac{3}{2}, \frac{5}{2})$ and gradient $\frac{-1-6}{5-(-2)} = -1$, and so the perpendicular bisector of AB has equation $y - \frac{5}{2} = 1(x - \frac{3}{2})$, or $y = x+1$. The line BC has midpoint $(-3,4)$ and gradient $\frac{6-2}{-2-(-4)} = 2$, and so the perpendicular bisector of BC has equation $y - 4 = -\frac{1}{2}(x+3)$, or $x + 2y = 5$. Solving the equations $y = x+1$ and $x + 2y = 5$ simultaneously, we obtain $x = 1$ and $y = 2$. Thus the coordinates of X are $(1,2)$. It is easy to check that $AX = BX = CX = 5$, and hence the equation of the circle is indeed $(x-1)^2 + (y-2)^2 = 25$.

Example 8.1.5. *Find the points of intersection of the circle with equation $x^2 + y^2 + 2x + 4y = 15$ and the line $y = x+1$.*

This is just a matter of solving a quadratic equation and a linear equation simultaneously. Substituting the linear equation into the quadratic gives

$$\begin{aligned} x^2 + (x+1)^2 + 2x + 4(x+1) &= 15 \\ x^2 + x^2 + 2x + 1 + 2x + 4x + 4 &= 15 \\ 2x^2 + 8x - 10 &= 0 \\ 2(x+5)(x-1) &= 0 \end{aligned}$$

and hence $x = 1$, -5. The corresponding values of y are 2, -4 respectively, and so the points of intersection are $(1,2)$ and $(-5,-4)$.

8.2 Tangents

We need to remember key geometric properties of circles. For example, a tangent to a circle is perpendicular to its corresponding radius.

Example 8.2.1. *What is the equation of the tangent to the circle $x^2 + y^2 - 2x - 4y + 3 = 0$ at the point $(2,1)$?*

Since the equation of the circle can be written (after completing squares) $(x-1)^2 + (y-2)^2 = 2$, the centre of the circle is at $(1,2)$. Thus the radius at the point

$(2,1)$ has gradient $\frac{1-2}{2-1} = -1$, and so the tangent at that point has gradient 1 (since it is perpendicular to the radius). The equation of the tangent is $y - 1 = 1(x - 2)$, or $y = x + 1$.

Example 8.2.2. *The circle C has centre $(1,2)$ and is tangent to the line $3x + 2y = 1$. What is the radius of the circle?*

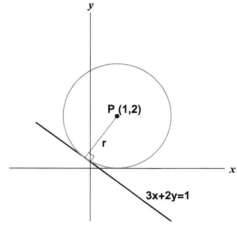

Figure 8.3

The perpendicular distance from the centre $(1,2)$ of the circle to the tangent line $3x + 4y = 1$ is the length of the radius of the circle. Thus the radius of the circle is

$$r = \frac{3 \times 1 + 4 \times 2 - 1}{\sqrt{3^2 + 4^2}} = \tfrac{10}{5} = 2$$

Since the problem of finding the points of intersection of a line and a circle involves solving a simultaneous quadratic/linear equation system, there are either 2, 1 or 0 solutions. Geometrically, the line can either intersect with, touch, or completely miss the circle:

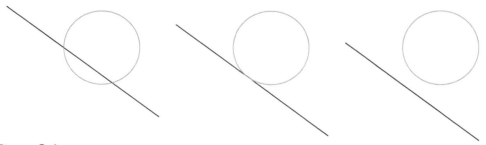

Figure 8.4

We can use this idea to determine whether a particular line is a tangent to a circle or not.

Example 8.2.3. *The line $x + 3y = k$ is a tangent to the circle $x^2 + y^2 - 4x - 8y = 20$. What are the possible values of k?*

Substituting the linear equation into the quadratic equation, we want the equation

$$\begin{aligned}
(k - 3y)^2 + y^2 - 4(k - 3y) - 8y &= 20 \\
9y^2 - 6ky + k^2 + y^2 - 4k + 12y - 8y &= 20 \\
10y^2 - (6k - 4)y + (k^2 - 4k - 20) &= 0
\end{aligned}$$

to have one real root. This quadratic in y must therefore have zero determinant, so we deduce that

$$\begin{aligned}
(6k - 4)^2 - 4 \times 10 \times (k^2 - 4k - 20) &= 0 \\
36k^2 - 48k + 16 - 40k^2 + 160k + 800 &= 0 \\
-4k^2 + 112k + 816 &= 0 \\
k^2 - 28k - 204 &= 0 \\
(k - 34)(k + 6) &= 0
\end{aligned}$$

and hence the possible values of k are 34 and -6.

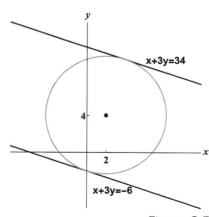

Figure 8.5

An alternative approach would be to note that the lines $x + 3y = k$ have gradient $-\frac{1}{3}$, and so the diameter defined by the possible points of tangency must have gradient 3 and pass through the centre $(2, 4)$, and hence has equation $y = 3x - 2$. The line $y = 3x - 2$ can be shown to meet the circle at the points $(0, -2)$ and $(4, 10)$. These points lie on the lines $x + 3y = -6$ and $x + 3y = 34$ respectively.

Example 8.2.4. *Show that the two circles*

$$x^2 + y^2 + 6x + 4y - 67 = 0 \quad \text{and} \quad x^2 + y^2 - 6x - 2y + 5 = 0$$

touch, with the second circle being inside the first, and find the equation of their common tangent.

The two circles have equations

$$(x + 3)^2 + (y + 2)^2 = 80 \qquad (x - 3)^2 + (y - 1)^2 = 5$$

so that the first has centre $(-3, -2)$ and radius $r_1 = 4\sqrt{5}$, while the second has centre $(3, 1)$ and radius $r_2 = \sqrt{5}$. The distance between the two centres is $\sqrt{6^2 + 3^2} = 3\sqrt{5}$. Since $3\sqrt{5} + r_2 = r_1$, it follows that the second circle is internally tangent to the first, and the point of contact of the two circles has coordinates $(5, 2)$. The line of centres has gradient $\frac{1 - (-2)}{3 - (-3)} = \frac{1}{2}$, and hence the common tangent has gradient -2, and hence has equation $y - 2 = -2(x - 5)$, or $2x + y = 12$.

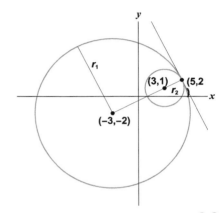

Figure 8.6

It is interesting to note that subtracting the two equations of the circles from each other yields

$$
\begin{aligned}
(x^2 + y^2 + 6x + 4y - 67) - (x^2 + y^2 - 6x - 2y + 5) &= 0 \\
12x + 6y - 72 &= 0 \\
2x + y &= 12
\end{aligned}
$$

We have obtained the equation of the common tangent straight away!

EXERCISE 8A

1. Write down the equation of the circles with the following centres and radii. Your answer should be in the form $x^2 + y^2 + ax + by + c = 0$.
   a) Centre $(1, -3)$, radius 10,
   b) Centre $(-2, -2)$, radius 1,
   c) Centre $(0, 2)$, radius 2,
   d) Centre $(-3, 0)$, radius 3,
   e) Centre $(a, 0)$, radius a,
   f) Centre (a, b) radius a.

2. What are the centres and radii of the following circles?
   a) $(x - 3)^2 + (y - 2)^2 = 16$,
   b) $(x - 7)^2 + y^2 = 4$,
   c) $x^2 + y^2 = 10$,
   d) $(x + 10)^2 + (y + 10)^2 = 200$,
   e) $x^2 + y^2 + 8x + 2y - 19 = 0$,
   f) $x^2 + y^2 + 3x - 7y + \frac{11}{2} = 0$,
   g) $x^2 + y^2 + 3x - 4y = 0$,
   h) $x^2 + y^2 - 2x - 3 = 0$,
   i) $x^2 + y^2 + 2by = 0$,
   j) $x^2 + y^2 + ax + by = 2a^2 + 2b^2$.

3. The following are equations of circles. What values of k are possible?
   a) $x^2 + y^2 + 4x + 8y + k = 0$,
   b) $x^2 + y^2 + ax + 2ay = k$,
   c) $x^2 + y^2 + 2kx + 2y + 1 = 0$,
   d) $x^2 + y^2 + 4kx - 2ky = k$.

4. What is the equation of the circle with centre $(2, -3)$ that passes through the point $(1, 5)$?

5. What is the equation of the circle with points $A(2, 5)$ and $B(8, -3)$ at the opposite ends of a diameter?

6. What is the equation of the circle with centre $(3, 5)$ which touches the y-axis?

7. What is the equation of the circle with centre $(2, 7)$ which touches the line $y = x$?

8. What standard circle theorem is being demonstrated in Question 16 of Exercise 2B (page 23)?

9. What is the equation of the circle passing through the points $(1, 4)$, $(1, 6)$ and $(13, 10)$?

10. Find the equation of the circle passing through the points $P(2, 3)$ and $Q(-1, 4)$, where the tangent at P has equation $y = x + 1$?

11. Show that the circles $x^2 + y^2 + 2x + 8y + 6 = 0$ and $x^2 + y^2 - 8x + 2y - 6 = 0$ intersect each other at right angles.

12*. a) The points A and B have coordinates $(-3, 0)$ and $(3, 0)$ respectively. The point P has coordinates (x, y), and is such that $AP = 2BP$. Find the equation satisfied by x and y. What is the locus of the set of points which are twice as far away from A as they are from B?

b) If you have access to graphing software, draw a graph of the locus of the point P such that $AP = k \times BP$ for various positive values of k. Do your results remind you of anything? You might want to consult your Physics teacher.

13*. Show that the circles $x^2 + y^2 - 2x - 5 = 0$ and $x^2 + y^2 - x + 3y - 12 = 0$ intersect each other in two points, and find the equation of the common chord.

14*. The points $A(-1, 0)$ and $B(1, 0)$ lie on the circle $x^2 + y^2 + ay = 1$, where $a > 0$. If $P(x, y)$ is another point on the circle, let ℓ_A be the line through A and P, and let ℓ_B be the line through B and P. Let m_A and m_B be the gradients of the line ℓ_A and ℓ_B respectively. Calculate

$$\frac{m_A - m_B}{1 + m_A m_B}$$

What standard theorem about circles has been demonstrated?

8.3 Radians

It is a historical curiosity that we measure angles in degrees. The fact that we have $360°$ in a circle, or indeed 60 minutes in an hour and 60 seconds in a minute (whether we are discussing units of time or subdivisions of degrees) is a consequence of the fact that the ancient Babylonians had a number system based on the number 60. The degree is not a natural unit of angle. It is not likely that someone with the chance to invent a unit of angle would choose the degree (if they did not already know it). If we are to work with angles as mathematicians, we need a better definition of angle; one which is natural mathematically. There will be many benefits to making the jump to this new method for measuring angles; many mathematical formulae will be much simplified and (when we meet it) particularly so when we investigate the calculus of trigonometric functions.

Consider the sector of a circle of radius r which subtends an angle θ at the centre of the circle. What is the (curved) arc length s of that portion of the circumference of the circle which is part of the sector? It is clear that the arc length s is proportional to the angle θ, and is also proportional to the radius of the circle. Thus there must be some constant k such that the formula

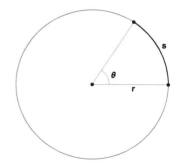

$$s = kr\theta$$

describes the relationship between s, r and θ, where k is the constant of proportionality.

Figure 8.7

What determines the value of the constant k? Provided that the distances r and s are measured in the same units (whether miles or millimetres), they will have no effect on the value of k. The only thing that determines the value of k is the choice of unit for angle.

Working in degrees, suppose that the angle subtended at the centre is $\theta°$. Then we can argue that s is $\frac{\theta}{360}$ of the circumference $2\pi r$ of the circle, and hence that

$$s = \tfrac{\theta}{360} \times 2\pi r = \tfrac{\pi}{180} r\theta$$

so that $k = \frac{\pi}{180}$.

The value $\frac{\pi}{180}$ is not a particularly 'nice' one, and it is certainly not the most natural one that could have been chosen. The 'nicest' possible constant of proportionality is 1, so is it possible to define a unit of angle so that 1 is the right constant?

The answer to all this is 'Yes'. The unit of angle we are looking for is the **radian.**

Key Fact 8.2 Definition of a Radian

An angle of 1 radian is the angle subtended by an arc length of 1 unit on a circle of radius 1 unit.

For a sector on a circle of radius r with arc length s, the angle subtended at the centre is the ratio

$$\theta = \tfrac{s}{r}$$

so that

$$s = r\theta .$$

It is worth noting that the angle in Figure 8.7 above is 1 radian.

A radian is a ratio of two lengths, and so is a dimensionless quantity. Therefore it needs no units (just as a scale factor needs no units). We can quite properly write an angle simply as a number. Thus we can describe an angle as just 2, although we might sometimes write '2 radians' for clarity. There is no need for a special symbol.

We need to be able to convert between degrees and radians. Since the circumference of a circle is $2\pi r$, it is clear that there are 2π radians in 360° (the fact that there is a strange number like 2π radians in a circle is probably the main reason why non-mathematicians prefer to work in degrees.

For Interest

There are those who want to decimalise degrees, and these people argue for a unit of degree called the **grad.** There are 100 grads in a right angle. We will not choose this approach.

Key Fact 8.3 Converting Degrees to Radians

We have the following identities:

$$360° = 2\pi \text{ radians}, \qquad 180° = \pi \text{ radians} \qquad 90° = \tfrac{1}{2}\pi \text{ radians} .$$

The general conversion rule between degrees and radians is the following:

$$\theta° = \tfrac{\pi}{180}\theta \text{ radians} .$$

It is important to be able to convert between degrees and radians when required, and to be able to perform calculations entirely in radians. Your calculators are able to do this (they have 'degrees' and 'radians' modes, and probably 'grads' mode as well. You must learn to recognise what angle mode your calculator is in, and how to change modes as necessary.

Note that many of the 'standard' angles can be written neatly as simple fractional multiples of π, and it is common to refer to angles in this manner, when it is sensible to do so.

Example 8.3.1. *Express the angles* $45°, 60°, 30°$ *and* $10°$ *in radians.*

$$45° = \tfrac{1}{4}\pi, 60° = \tfrac{1}{3}\pi, 30° = \tfrac{1}{6}\pi \text{ and } 10° = \tfrac{1}{18}\pi.$$

8.4 Radians and Trigonometric Functions

Mathematical calculations concerning angles regularly involve trigonometry. For the present we shall consider the trigonometric functions for acute and obtuse angles only. This will be sufficient to handle the issues raised in geometric problems. The behaviour of the standard trigonometric functions is well-known when angles are measured in degrees. Now angles will be presented in radians, so that we will be considering angles between 0 and π.

In a later chapter we will return to make a much more thorough study of the trigonometric functions; for the present we are simply recalling what is already familiar, but presenting the material in a new way.

The graph of $y = \sin x$ for $0 \le x \le \pi$, has its usual reflectional symmetry, with a starting value of 0, which rises to a maximum of 1 at $x = \frac{1}{2}\pi$ ($90°$) and then declines to 0 again. The symmetry in this graph is reflected in the formula

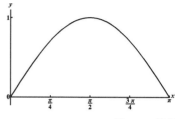

Food For Thought 8.1

$$\sin(\pi - x) = \sin x, \qquad 0 \le x \le \pi.$$

Figure 8.8

The graph of $y = \cos x$ for $0 \le x \le \pi$ has its usual rotational symmetry, starting at its maximum value of 1 and then decreasing continuously through the value of 0 at $x = \frac{1}{2}\pi$ to its minimum value of -1 at $x = \pi$. The symmetry in this graph is reflected in the formula

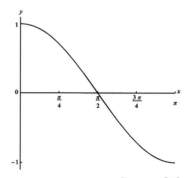

Food For Thought 8.2

$$\cos(\pi - x) = -\cos x, \qquad 0 \le x \le \pi.$$

Figure 8.9

The graph of $y = \tan x$ for $0 \le x \le \pi$ has its usual symmetry, starting at 0 an increasing without limit as x approaches $\frac{1}{2}\pi$ ($\tan\frac{1}{2}\pi$ is not defined), and then returning from negative infinity to reach the value of 0 again at $x = \pi$. The symmetry in this graph is reflected in the formula

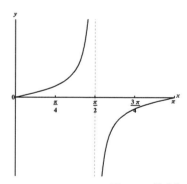

Food For Thought 8.3

$$\tan(\pi - x) = -\tan x, \qquad 0 \le x \le \pi, x \ne \frac{1}{2}\pi.$$

Figure 8.10

It is also important to remember the values of the trigonometric functions on special angles, when these angles are expressed in radians. The values for $\frac{1}{6}\pi$, $\frac{1}{4}\pi$ and $\frac{1}{3}\pi$ can be worked out by considering the sides of right-angled triangles that are either half of a square, or else half of an equilateral triangle.

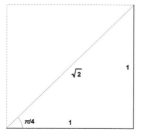
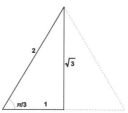

Figure 8.11

Key Fact 8.4 Trigonometric Functions for Special Angles

The trigonometric values of special angles are set out in the following table:

θ	$\sin\theta$	$\cos\theta$	$\tan\theta$
$\frac{1}{6}\pi = 30°$	$\frac{1}{2}$	$\frac{1}{2}\sqrt{3}$	$\frac{1}{\sqrt{3}}$
$\frac{1}{4}\pi = 45°$	$\frac{1}{\sqrt{2}}$	$\frac{1}{\sqrt{2}}$	1
$\frac{1}{3}\pi = 60°$	$\frac{1}{2}\sqrt{3}$	$\frac{1}{2}$	$\sqrt{3}$
$\frac{1}{2}\pi = 90°$	1	0	∞

EXERCISE 8B

---

1. Write each of the following angles in radians, leaving your answer as a multiple of π.

   a) $90°$ b) $135°$ c) $45°$ d) $30°$

   e) $72°$ f) $18°$ g) $120°$ h) $22\frac{1}{2}°$

   i) $20°$ j) $75°$ k) $100°$ l) $1°$

2. Each of the following is an angle in radians. Without using a calculator, change these to degrees.

   a) $\frac{1}{3}\pi$ b) $\frac{1}{20}\pi$ c) $\frac{1}{5}\pi$ d) $\frac{3}{8}\pi$

   e) $\frac{2}{9}\pi$ f) $\frac{4}{5}\pi$ g) $\frac{5}{8}\pi$ h) $\frac{3}{5}\pi$

   i) $\frac{1}{45}\pi$ j) $\frac{3}{2}\pi$ k) $\frac{1}{12}\pi$ l) $\frac{5}{18}\pi$

3. Without the use of a calculator write down the exact values of the following.

   a) $\sin\frac{1}{3}\pi$ b) $\cos\frac{1}{4}\pi$ c) $\tan\frac{1}{6}\pi$ d) $\cos\frac{2}{3}\pi$

   e) $\sin\frac{3}{4}\pi$ f) $\cos\frac{5}{6}\pi$ g) $\tan\frac{1}{3}\pi$ h) $\sin\frac{2}{3}\pi$

8.5   A Refresher in Key Trigonometric Results

The sine and cosine rules are key results in trigonometry. They are the first rules that we meet that can be applied to triangles which are not right-angled. Since the triangles that arise from considering sectors of circles are rarely right-angled, it is worthwhile adding a brief discussion of these rules now.

If we consider a triangle ABC, we shall adopt the standard convention of letting the angles at the vertices A, B and C also be denoted A, B and C respectively, and use lower case letters a, b and c to denote the length of the three sides of the triangle, where a is the side opposite angle A (so that $a = BC$) and so on.

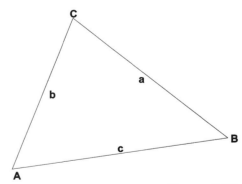

Figure 8.12

Of course, it is perfectly possible to perform calculations with the sine and cosine rules, working with angles in degrees. Performing such calculations is radians is, for the moment, good practice in learning about this new angle measurement system.

8.5.1. THE SINE RULE

Suppose that the triangle ABC has been inscribed in its circumcircle, and suppose that the radius of the circumcircle is R. Concentrate of the angle A. There are two lines of argument to consider, depending on whether the angle A is acute or obtuse. In either of these diagrams the triangle OBC is isosceles, so the line OM joining O to the midpoint of the line BC bisects the angle $\angle BOC$, and is also the perpendicular bisector of BC.

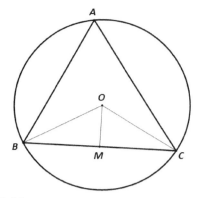

Figure 8.13

If the angle A is acute, then the angle $\angle BOC = 2A$ (the angle at the centre is twice the angle at the circumference). Thus $\angle BOM = A$, and so

$$BM = R\sin\angle BOM = R\sin A.$$

With A obtuse, the reflex angle $\angle BOC = 2A$, and so the obtuse angle $\angle BOC = 2\pi - 2A$. If follows that $\angle BOM = \pi - A$, and so

$$BM = R\sin\angle BOM = R\sin(\pi - A) = R\sin A.$$

Whether A is acute or obtuse, we deduce that $a = 2BM = 2R\sin A$. Since similar calculations can be made for the angles B and C, we obtain the sine rule:

Key Fact 8.5 The Sine Rule

$$\frac{a}{\sin A} = \frac{b}{\sin B} = \frac{c}{\sin C}$$

---

noting the interesting, and occasionally useful, fact that these three ratios are all equal to $2R$.

Example 8.5.1. *Suppose that the triangle ABC has sides $AC = 7$ cm and $BC = 9$ cm, and that angle A is equal to 1.2. Calculate the other two angles and the remaining side, giving all your answers to 3 significant figures.*

The sine rule tells us that

$$\frac{\sin B}{7} = \frac{\sin 1.2}{9} = \frac{\sin C}{c}$$

so that $\sin B = 0.7249$, giving $B = 0.8109$.

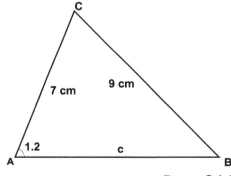

Figure 8.14

Note that it is clear from the diagram that B is acute. As the third angle in the triangle, $C = \pi - A - B = 1.1307$. Thus

$$c = \frac{9\sin C}{\sin 1.2} = 8.7360.$$

Results have all been calculated to 4 decimal places. To 3 significant figures, $B = 0.811$, $C = 1.13$ and $c = 8.74$ cm.

Food For Thought 8.4

It is important to perform all intermediate calculations to a higher degree of accuracy than the last required result, to ensure that rounding errors do not give the wrong final answer. For example, had we used the value of 1.13 for C in the final calculation, the calculated value for c would have been 8.73 cm, which is incorrect.

8.5.2. THE AMBIGUOUS CASE OF THE SINE RULE

In the preceding example, we used the diagram to deduce that angle B was acute. There is a difficulty with using the sine rule to calculate angles in triangles, since the Rule determines the sine of the angle, and that means that the angle could be either acute or obtuse. There are cases where both possibilities can occur, in which case we need to take care to find the solution we want.

Example 8.5.2. *The triangle ABC has $AB = 9$ cm, $BC = 7$cm and $\angle CAB = 0.8$. Find the possible values of $\angle C$, and the corresponding values of AC.*

The reason for the ambiguity is that the triangle ABC is not uniquely defined by the information in the question. To specify a triangle, we either need to know all three sides (this is the 'SSS' case) or two sides and the angle between them (this is the 'SAS' case). The triangle given here is an 'SSA' case: the known angle is not the angle in between the two sides. As the figure shows, there are two possible triangles, with vertices C_1 and C_2.

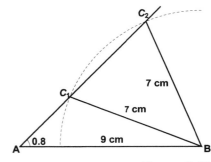

Figure 8.15

The sine rule tells us that

$$\frac{\sin C}{9} = \frac{\sin 0.8}{7} = \frac{\sin B}{AC}$$

and hence $\sin C = 0.9223$. There are two possible values for C, 1.1740 and $\pi - 1.1740 = 1.9676$. These give corresponding values of 1.1676 and 0.3740 for B as the third angle in the triangle, and so the sine rule enables us to calculate the length AC as being 8.9754 or 3.5653 respectively.

Looking at the diagram shows that, since BC_1C_2 is isosceles, the angles $\angle AC_1B$ and $\angle AC_2B$ are complementary (add to π), which confirms the calculations of the sine rule that they have the same sine value.

8.5.3. THE COSINE RULE

The sine rule is only usable when one angle and its opposing side are known (for example, A and a), so that the value of the common ratio can be calculated. There are circumstances where we are given information about triangles which cannot be processed by the use of the sine rule. In such cases, the cosine rule comes to the rescue.

When proving the cosine rule, there are three cases to consider, depending on which of B and C are acute. In all cases P is the foot of the perpendicular from A to the (extended) line BC; P may lie inside or outside the line segment BC itself.

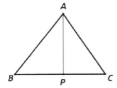 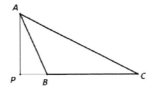

Figure 8.16

$$
\begin{aligned}
a &= BP + PC & a &= BP - PC & a &= -PB + PC \\
&= c\cos B + b\cos C & &= c\cos B - b\cos(\pi - C) & &= -c\cos(\pi - B) + b\cos C \\
& & &= c\cos B + b\cos C & &= c\cos B + b\cos C
\end{aligned}
$$

Thus $a = c\cos B + b\cos C$, and so $a^2 = ac\cos B + ab\cos C$. Similar arguments can be applied to calculate b^2 and c^2, and hence

$$a^2 - b^2 - c^2 = (ac\cos B + ab\cos C) - (bc\cos A + ab\cos C) - (bc\cos A + ac\cos B) = -2bc\cos A$$

We have thus proved:

Key Fact 8.6 The Cosine Rule

$$a^2 = b^2 + c^2 - 2bc\cos A$$

Example 8.5.3. *The triangle ABC has AB = 7 cm, AC = 4 cm and ∠BAC = 0.65. Find the length BC and the angle ∠ABC.*

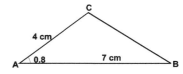

Figure 8.17

Using the cosine rule,

$$BC^2 = 4^2 + 7^2 - 2 \times 4 \times 7 \times \cos 0.65$$

and hence $BC = 4.5188 = 4.52$ cm. Now we have the length $a = BC$, we can calculate $\angle ABC$ using the sine rule,

$$\frac{\sin \angle ABC}{4} = \frac{\sin 0.65}{4.5188}$$

so that $\sin \angle ABC = 0.5357$, and hence (since $\angle ABC$ is acute) $\angle ABC = 0.5653 = 0.565$.

If we had not been clear that $\angle ABC$ was acute, we could have deduced that it was. The other possible value of $\angle ABC$ was $\pi - 0.5653 = 2.5762$, and since $2.5762 + 0.65 > \pi$, this is not possible, since two angles of a triangle cannot add to more than π.

The cosine rule can frequently be used to calculate angles, and it has the advantage over the sine that there is no ambiguous case to worry about. Acute angles have positive cosines, while obtuse angles have negative cosines, so there is no cause for confusion.

Example 8.5.4. *The triangle ABC has a = 6 cm, b = 4 cm and c = 8.5 cm. Find the angles A and C.*

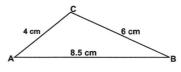

Figure 8.18

We have

$$\cos A = \frac{4^2 + 8.5^2 - 6^2}{2 \times 4 \times 8.5} = 0.7684 \qquad \cos C = \frac{6^2 + 4^2 - 8.5^2}{2 \times 6 \times 4} = -0.4219$$

and hence $A = 0.694$ and $C = 2.01$ to 3 significant figures.

8.5.4. THE AREA OF A TRIANGLE

Let M be the foot of the perpendicular from A to the side BC. Then the area of the triangle ABC ('half base times height') is equal to

$$\tfrac{1}{2} BC \times AM = \tfrac{1}{2} a \times AM .$$

Applying trigonometry to the right-angled triangle AMC tells us that

$$AM = AC \sin \angle ACB = b \sin C$$

Thus

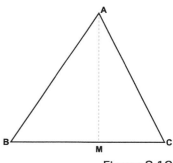

Figure 8.19

Key Fact 8.7 The Area of a Triangle

The area of a triangle is

$$\tfrac{1}{2} ab \sin C$$

Example 8.5.5. *Find the areas of the triangles in Examples 8.5.3 and 8.5.4*

The area of the triangle in Example 8.5.3 is

$$\tfrac{1}{2} \times 4 \times 7 \times \sin 0.8 \;=\; 10.0 \text{ cm}^2 \,,$$

while the triangle in Example 8.5.4 is

$$\tfrac{1}{2} \times 4 \times 8.5 \times \sin A \;=\; \tfrac{1}{2} \times 4 \times 8.5 \times 0.6400 \;=\; 10.9 \text{ cm}^2 \,.$$

Example 8.5.6. *An equilateral triangle has area 25 cm². What is the length of one of its sides?*

If the side's length is x cm, then

$$25 \;=\; \tfrac{1}{2} x^2 \sin \tfrac{1}{3}\pi \;=\; \tfrac{1}{4} x^2 \sqrt{3}$$

and hence $x = 7.60$ cm.

EXERCISE 8C

All numerical answers should be written to 3 significant figures.

1. Use the cosine rule to find the largest angle (in radians) of the triangle:
   a) $a = 6$ cm, $b = 7$ cm, $c = 8$ cm, b) $a = 3.5$ cm, $b = 4.5$ cm, $c = 7$ cm,
   c) $a = 2.5$ cm, $b = 19$ cm, $c = 17.5$ cm, d) $a = 1$ cm, $b = 5$ cm, $c = 5$ cm.

2. Find the remaining sides of the following triangles, using the sine rule:
   a) $a = 10$ cm, $B = 0.87$, $C = 1.25$, b) $a = 6$ cm, $A = 1.9$, $B = 0.5$,
   c) $b = 5.5$ cm, $A = 2$, $B = 0.17$, d) $c = 10$ cm, $B = 0.48$, $C = 2.4$.

3. Find the length of the side BC of a triangle if $AB = 8$ cm, $AC = 12$ cm and
   a) $\angle BAC = 1$, b) $\angle BAC = 0.2$, c) $\angle BAC = 2.9$.

4. Find the areas of the four triangles in Question 2.

5. Suppose that ABC is an isosceles triangle with $\angle BAC = 2\theta$ and equal sides $AB = AC = x$. The angle θ is acute. In the diagram, M is the midpoint of the side BC, so that $\angle CAM = \theta$ and AM is perpendicular to BC.

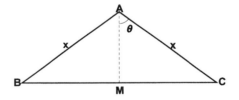

   a) By calculating the length BC in two different ways, show that $\cos 2\theta = 1 - 2\sin^2\theta$.

   b) By calculating the area of the triangle in two different ways, find an expression for $\sin 2\theta$ in terms of $\sin\theta$ and $\cos\theta$.

6. By calculating one of the triangle's angles, find the area of a triangle with sides 6 cm, 7 cm and 9 cm.

7*. Suppose that ABC is a triangle with $AB = 5$ cm, $BC = 8$ cm and $AC = 9$ cm. Let M be the midpoint of BC, and suppose that $\angle CMA = \theta$. Write down expressions for AC^2 and AB^2 in terms of AM and θ, and hence calculate AM.

8*. Let ABC be a triangle with $AB = 4$ cm and $AC = 7$ cm. Let AM be the angle bisector of $\angle BAC$, so that $\angle BAM = \angle MAC = \theta$. Find the exact value of the fraction $\frac{MC}{MB}$.

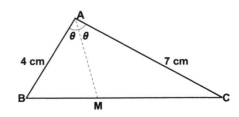

131

9*. a) Explain why, in any nontrivial triangle, $a < b + c$, $b < a + c$ and $c < a + b$.

   b) Use these inequalities to show that

$$-1 < \frac{b^2 + c^2 - a^2}{2bc} < 1$$

10*. Suppose that a triangle ABC has sides a, b and c.

   a) Show that $\cos A = \frac{b^2 + c^2 - a^2}{2bc}$.

   b) Deduce that

$$\sin^2 A = \frac{(a+b+c)(b+c-a)(a+c-b)(a+b-c)}{4b^2c^2}$$

   c) If we introduce the **semiperimeter** $s = \frac{1}{2}(a + b + c)$, show that the area of the triangle is equal to

$$\sqrt{s(s-a)(s-b)(s-c)}$$

   This result is known as **Heron's formula**.

   d) What geometric property of a triangle is reflected by the requirement that $s - a$, $s - b$ and $s - c$ are all positive (so that it is possible to take the square root)?

8.6 Sectors and Segments

Recall that if we consider a sector of a circle that subtends an angle θ at the centre of a circle of radius r, then the definition of radians means that the curved arc length of the sector is $r\theta$, and its perimeter is $r\theta + 2r$.

What can we say about the area A of this sector? Suppose that the sector is taken from a circle of radius r and with central angle θ. Since there are 2π radians in the circle, the sector is $\frac{\theta}{2\pi}$ of the whole circle, and hence the area A is $\frac{\theta}{2\pi}$ of the area πr^2 of the whole circle.

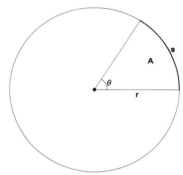

Figure 8.20

Key Fact 8.8 A Sector of a Circle

The curved arc length of a sector is given by the formula

$$s = r\theta$$

while its perimeter is

$$r(\theta + 2).$$

The area of a sector is

$$A = \tfrac{1}{2}r^2\theta.$$

A **segment** of a circle is the portion of a sector OPQ cut off by the chord PQ; it is obtained from the sector OPQ by removing the triangle (also labelled OPQ). It is easy to determine key properties of segments.

Since the triangle OPQ is isosceles, the length of PQ can be found by bisecting the angle at O, splitting the triangle OPQ into two congruent right-angled triangles (see Question 5 in Exercise 8C). Simple trigonometry tells us that $PQ = 2r\sin\frac{1}{2}\theta$. Moreover, the area of the triangle OPQ is $\frac{1}{2}r^2\sin\theta$.

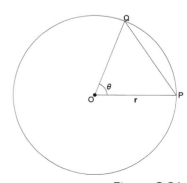

Figure 8.21

> **Key Fact 8.9** A Segment of a Circle
>
> If a segment subtends an angle θ at the centre of a circle of radius r, then its perimeter is
> $$r\theta + 2r\sin\tfrac{1}{2}\theta$$
> while its area is
> $$\tfrac{1}{2}r^2(\theta - \sin\theta)$$

It is interesting to note that the π in formulae concerning sectors has been 'absorbed' into the angle θ. Expressions for arc length and area, $r\theta$ and $\tfrac{1}{2}r^2\theta$, do not contain π explicitly.

Example 8.6.1. *Find the perimeter and area of the segment created by a chord PQ of length 8 cm in a circle of radius 6 cm.*

We need to calculate the angle θ that the chord subtends at the centre. Since $8 = 12\sin\tfrac{1}{2}\theta$, we have $\sin\tfrac{1}{2}\theta = \tfrac{2}{3}$, and so $\theta = 1.4595$.

Thus the perimeter is $8 + 6\theta = 16.8$ cm, while the area is $18(\theta - \sin\theta) = 8.38$ cm^2.

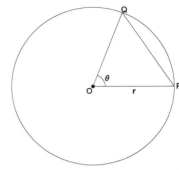

Figure 8.22

Example 8.6.2. *A chord of a circle which subtends an angle θ at the centre of the circle cuts off a segment whose area is equal to one third of the area of the whole circle. Show that $\theta = 2.61$, correct to 3 significant figures.*

If the circle has radius r cm, then the segment has area $\tfrac{1}{2}r^2(\theta - \sin\theta)$, so we deduce that
$$\tfrac{1}{2}r^2(\theta - \sin\theta) = \tfrac{1}{3}\pi r^2$$
which implies that $\theta - \sin\theta = \tfrac{2}{3}\pi$. If we consider the function $f(\phi) = \phi - \sin\phi$ then $f(2.61) = 2.103$, which is roughly equal to $\tfrac{2}{3}\pi = 2.094$.

This, while suggestive, is not enough to show that $\theta = 2.61$ to 3 significant figures. To do this, we need to show that θ lies between 2.605 and 2.615.

Since $\tfrac{1}{2}r^2 f(\phi)$ is the area of a segment subtending an angle ϕ at the centre, it is clear that $f(\phi)$ is an increasing function of ϕ for $0 < \phi < \pi$. Since $f(2.605) = 2.093$ is slightly less than $\tfrac{2}{3}\pi$, while $f(2.615) = 2.112$ is slightly more than $\tfrac{2}{3}\pi$, we deduce that the actual value of θ lies between 2.605 and 2.615, and hence that $\theta = 2.61$ to 3 significant figures.

EXERCISE 8D

1. The following questions refer to the diagram, where

   - r is the radius of circle (in cm),

   - s is the arc length (in cm),

   - A is the area of the sector (in cm^2),

   - θ is the angle subtended at centre (in radians).

   In each case you are given some of these values, and need to find some or all of the rest.

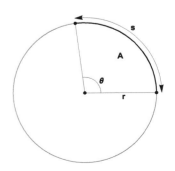

a) $r = 7, \theta = 1.2$. Find s and A.

b) $r = 3.5, \theta = 2.1$. Find s and A.

c) $s = 12, r = 8$. Find θ and A.

d) $s = 14, \theta = 0.7$. Find r and A.

e) $A = 30, r = 5$. Find θ and s.

f) $A = 64, s = 16$. Find r and θ.

g) $A = 24, r = 6$. Find s.

h) $A = 30, s = 10$. Find θ.

2. Find the area A of the shaded segment in each of the following cases:

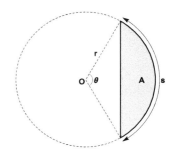

a) $r = 5$ cm, $\theta = \frac{1}{3}\pi$,

b) $r = 3.1$ cm, $\theta = \frac{2}{5}\pi$,

c) $r = 28$ cm, $\theta = \frac{5}{6}\pi$,

d) $r = 6$ cm, $s = 9$ cm,

e) $r = 9.5$ cm, $s = 4$ cm.

3. Find the area of a segment cut off by a chord of length 10 cm from a circle of radius 13 cm.

4. Find the perimeter of the segment cut off by a chord of length 14 cm from a circle of radius 25 cm.

5. The points A and B lie on a circle with centre O and radius 10 cm. If the minor (shorter) arc AB has length 5 cm find the area of the corresponding sector.

6. A chord of a circle which subtends an angle of θ at the centre cuts off a segment equal in area to $\frac{1}{4}$ of the area of the whole circle.

a) Show that $\theta - \sin\theta = \frac{1}{2}\pi$.

b) Verify that $\theta = 2.31$, correct to 2 decimal places.

7. Two circles of radii 5 cm and 12 cm are drawn, partly overlapping. Their centres are 13 cm apart. Find the area common to the two circles.

8. The diagram shows two intersecting circles of radius 6 cm and 4 cm with centres 7 cm apart. Find the perimeter and area of the shaded region common to both circles.

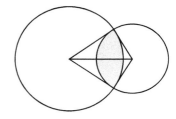

9. An eclipse of the sun is said to be 10% total when 10% of the area of the sun's disc is hidden behind the disc of the moon. A child models this with two discs, each of radius r cm, as shown.

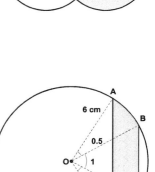

a) Calculate, in terms of r, the distance between the centres of the two discs.

b) Calculate also the distance between the centres when the eclipse is 80% total.

10. The shaded region $ABCD$ is inside the a circle with centre O and radius 6 cm, where $\angle AOB = \angle COD = 0.5$, and the angle $\angle BOC = 1$.

a) What is the perimeter of the shaded region?

b) What is the area of the shaded region?

11. Three circles of radius 5 cm are mutually tangent.

    a) Find the perimeter of the shaded region.

    b) Find the area of the shaded region.

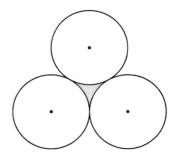

12*. Three circles of radius r are drawn so that the centre of each lies on the circumferences of the other two.

    a) Show that the area of the central, darker shaded, region is $\frac{1}{2}r^2(\pi - \sqrt{3})$.

    b) Find an expression for the area of the lighter shaded region.

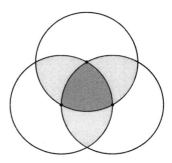

Chapter 8: Summary

- A circle with centre (a, b) and radius r has equation $(x - a)^2 + (y - b)^2 = r^2$. There is a unique circle passing through any three non-collinear points.

- A tangent to a circle can be identified by the fact that the solving the equation of the line and circle simultaneously leads to a repeated root.

- If we consider a sector of a circle, the measure of the angle of the sector in radians is equal to the ratio of the curved arc-length to the radius of the circle:

$$r = r\theta.$$

There are 2π radians in $360°$.

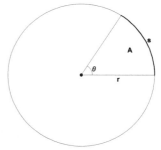

- The area A of a sector of a circle is given in terms of the angle θ and the radius r as follows:

$$A = \tfrac{1}{2}r^2\theta.$$

Figure 8.23

- The following formulae identify the basic trigonometric functions for key angles:

θ	$\sin\theta$	$\cos\theta$	$\tan\theta$
$\tfrac{1}{6}\pi = 30°$	$\tfrac{1}{2}\sqrt{3}$	$\tfrac{1}{2}$	$\tfrac{1}{\sqrt{3}}$
$\tfrac{1}{4}\pi = 45°$	$\tfrac{1}{\sqrt{2}}$	$\tfrac{1}{\sqrt{2}}$	1
$\tfrac{1}{3}\pi = 60°$	$\tfrac{1}{2}$	$\tfrac{1}{2}\sqrt{3}$	$\sqrt{3}$
$\tfrac{1}{2}\pi = 90°$	1	0	∞

- For angles θ between 0 and π (between $0°$ and $180°$), the basic trigonometric functions satisfy the following identities:

$$\sin(\pi - \theta) = \sin\theta \qquad \cos(\pi - \theta) = -\cos\theta \qquad \tan(\pi - \theta) = -\tan\theta.$$

- The Sine Rule states that, for a triangle,

$$\frac{a}{\sin A} = \frac{b}{\sin B} = \frac{c}{\sin C}.$$

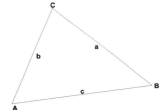

- The Cosine Rule states that, for a triangle,

$$a^2 = b^2 + c^2 - 2bc\cos A.$$

- The area of a triangle is $\tfrac{1}{2}bc\sin A$.

Figure 8.24

Sequences and Series

In this chapter we will learn:

- to use formulae for the nth term of a sequence, and for the sum of a finite series, using the sigma notation where necessary,

- understand the use of recurrence relations in defining some sequences, and recognise alternating, periodic, convergent and divergent sequences,

- to recognise arithmetic and geometric progressions, and use the formulae for the nth term and the sum of the first n terms to solve problems involving arithmetic and geometric progressions,

- to use the condition for the convergence of a geometric progression and the formula for the sum to infinity of a convergent geometric progression.

9.1 Constructing Sequences

Here are eight lists of numbers, each forming a pattern of some kind. What are the next three numbers in each list?

a) $1, 4, 9, 16, 25, \ldots$

b) $\frac{1}{2}, \frac{2}{3}, \frac{3}{4}, \frac{4}{5}, \frac{5}{6}, \ldots$

c) $99, 97, 95, 93, 91, \ldots$

d) $1, 1.1, 1.21, 1.331, 1.4641, \ldots$

e) $2, 4, 8, 14, 22, \ldots$

f) $3, 1, 4, 1, 5, \ldots$

g) $1, 1, 2, 3, 5, 8, \ldots$

h) $2, 3, 5, 7, 11, \ldots$

Lists of this kind are called **sequences**, and the separate numbers are called **terms** in the sequence. The implication of the ellipsis (...) at the end of each list is that the sequence carries on forever, following some pattern. In the examples above, we might guess:

(a) Continuing the pattern of squares suggests 36, 49 and 64 as the next three numbers.

(b) Both the numerator and the denominator go up by 1 each time; this suggests $\frac{6}{7}$, $\frac{7}{8}$ and $\frac{8}{9}$ as the next three numbers.

(c) Subtracting 2 each time, we obtain 89, 87 and 85.

(d) Multiplying each number by 1.1 each time, we obtain 1.61051, 1.771561 and 1.9487171.

(e) The differences between successive numbers in this sequence are 2, 4, 6, 8. We might presume that the next three differences are 10, 12 and 14, giving the next three numbers as 32, 44 and 58.

(f) We might guess 1, 6 and 1 as the next three numbers (every second number is 1, and the other numbers increase by 1 each time). Alternatively, we might guess 9, 2 and 6 as the next three numbers, if we decide that this sequence is listing the digits in the decimal expansion of π.

(g) These seem to be the **Fibonacci numbers**: each number in the sequence is the sum of the preceding two numbers. The next three numbers are 13, 21 and 34.

(h) Continuing the listing of primes, the next three numbers might be 13, 17 and 19.

The usual notation for the first, second, third, and so on terms of a sequence is u_1, u_2, u_3, and so on. There is nothing special about the choice of the letter u, and other letters such as v, x, t and I are often used instead, especially if the letter chosen might have a meaning in the question (t might be used if the numbers in the sequence are all times, for example). If r is a natural number, then the rth term will be u_r, v_r, x_r, t_r or I_r. Note that sometimes it is convenient to number the terms $u_0, u_1, u_2, \ldots$, starting with $r = 0$, but care then need to be taken when referring to 'the first term'; is it u_0 or u_1?

Most sequences in which we are interested follow a particular pattern, and there are a variety of ways in which patterns can be defined:

- A sequence can be thought of as a function $u : \mathbb{N} \to \mathbb{R}$, with u_r being a different notation for the value $u(r)$ that the function u takes on the natural number r. One very important way of describing a sequence is to write down an explicit formula for the function u. In other words, we would like to be able to write down a concrete expression for the rth term of the sequence.

- It might not always be possible, or even easy, to write down an explicit formula for u_r. However, it might be possible to express a rule for calculating u_r that can be expressed mathematically.

Returning to our examples

(a) This sequence might be defined by the formula $u_r = r^2$.

(b) This sequence might be defined by the formula $u_r = \frac{r}{r+1}$.

(c) This sequence might be defined by the formula $u_r = 101 - 2r$. Alternatively, however, we might be interested in simply expressing the idea that u_r is obtained from u_{r-1} by subtracting 2 mathematically. To do this we could write the formula

$$u_{r+1} = u_r - 2$$

to describe this property. With this rule, knowing u_1 gives us u_2, which in turn gives us u_3, and hence u_4 and so on. However, we need to specify u_1 to be clear about where we start. Thus this sequence can be defined by the rule:

$$u_{r+1} = u_2 - 2, \qquad u_1 = 99.$$

(d) Each term in this sequence is obtained by multiplying its predecessor by 1.1. Thus a rule for this sequence might be:
$$u_{r+1} = 1.1 u_r, \qquad u_1 = 1.$$

Alternatively, it is possible to give an explicit formula for this sequence as well: $u_r = 1.1^{r-1}$.

(e) The rule for this sequence is

$$u_{r+1} = u_r + 2r, \qquad u_1 = 2$$

(f) We found two different explanations of this sequence. The first explanation could be expressed by the piecewise formula

$$u_r = \begin{cases} \frac{1}{2}(r+5), & r \text{ odd,} \\ 1, & r \text{ even.} \end{cases}$$

Alternatively, 'u_r is the rth digit in the decimal expansion of π'.

(g) It is easy to encapsulate the defining property of the Fibonacci numbers in the rule

$$F_{r+1} = F_r + F_{r-1}, \qquad F_1 = F_2 = 1.$$

but an explicit formula for F_r is hard to find.

(h) There is no formula for this sequence: nor is there a rule which obtains the next term from the preceding terms. The best we can do is to state that 'u_r is the rth prime number'.

> **Key Fact 9.1** Definitions of Sequences
>
> There are three ways of defining a sequence:
>
> - An explicit **function** can be used to define all terms in the sequence. Examples are:
> $$u_r = r^2 + 3r - 1, \qquad u_r = \sqrt{r^4 + \sin r}.$$
>
> - A **rule** can be defined which defines how u_r is to be calculated from the preceding term or terms in the sequence. Examples are:
> $$u_r = 2u_{r-1} + 3r, \qquad u_r = u_{r-1} + u_{r-2}, \qquad u_r = u_{r-1}^2 + r^3.$$
>
> Rules such as these are called **inductive definitions**, or **recurrence relations. A recurrence relation is not complete unless the value of u_1 is also given.**
>
> - A **rule** can be defined which describes what each term in the sequence is, without giving an explicit formula or method for determining it. An example of this might be:
>
> u_r is the number of prime numbers that are less than or equal to r.

The fact that there was more than one plausible answer to example (f) illustrates a key point: a sequence can never be uniquely defined by its first few terms. If we consider the sequence

$$u_r = r^2 + (r-1)(r-2)(r-3)(r-4)(r-5),$$

then this sequence has the first five terms equal to 1, 4, 9, 16, 25, but its next three terms are not 36, 49, 64. Thus we have found another possible answer to example (a).

It is always possible to check that a formula satisfies a recurrence relation!

Example 9.1.1. *Show that the sequence $u_r = r^2 - r + 2$ satisfies the recurrence relation*

$$u_{r+1} = u_r + 2r, \qquad u_1 = 2.$$

Since

$$\left(r^2 - r + 2\right) + 2r = r^2 + r + 2 = r^2 + 2r + 1 - r - 1 + 2 = (r+1)^2 - (r+1) + 2$$

we see that the sequence with formula $u_r = r^2 - r + 2$ does satisfy the recurrence relation, since we obtain an identity when we replace u_{r+1} and u_r by the correct expressions determined by the formula; moreover $1^2 - 1 + 2 = 2$, and so the formula gives the right result for $r = 1$.

We note that this has shown us the explicit formula for our example sequence (e).

EXERCISE 9A

1. Write down the first five terms of the sequences with the following definitions.

   a) $u_1 = 7$, $u_{r+1} = u_r + 7$,
   b) $u_1 = 13$, $u_{r+1} = u_r - 5$,
   c) $u_1 = 4$, $u_{r+1} = 3u_r$,
   d) $u_1 = 6$, $u_{r+1} = \frac{1}{2}u_r$,
   e) $u_1 = 2$, $u_{r+1} = 3u_r + 1$,
   f) $u_1 = 1$, $u_{r+1} = u_r^2 + 3$.

2. Suggest inductive definitions which would produce the following sequences.

   a) $2, 4, 6, 8, 10, \ldots$
   b) $11, 9, 7, 5, 3, \ldots$
   c) $2, 6, 10, 14, 18, \ldots$
   d) $2, 6, 18, 54, 164, \ldots$
   e) $\frac{1}{3}, \frac{1}{9}, \frac{1}{27}, \frac{1}{81}, \ldots$
   f) $\frac{1}{2}a, \frac{1}{4}a, \frac{1}{8}a, \frac{1}{16}a, \ldots$
   g) $b - 2c, b - c, b, b + c, \ldots$
   h) $1, -1, 1, -1, 1, \ldots$
   i) $\frac{p}{q^3}, \frac{p}{q^2}, \frac{p}{q}, p, \ldots$
   j) $\frac{a^3}{b^2}, \frac{a^2}{b}, a, b, \ldots$
   k) $x^3, 5x^2, 25x, \ldots$
   l) $1, 1 + x, (1 + x)^2, (1 + x)^3, \ldots$

3. Write down the first five terms of each sequence and give an inductive definition for it.

   a) $u_r = 2r + 3$,

   b) $u_r = r^2$,

   c) $u_r = \frac{1}{2}r(r+1)$,

   d) $u_r = \frac{1}{6}r(r+1)(2r+1)$,

   e) $u_r = 2 \times 3^r$,

   f) $u_r = 3 \times 5^{r-1}$.

4. For each of the following sequences give a possible formula for the rth term.

   a) $9, 8, 7, 6, \ldots$

   b) $6, 18, 54, 162, \ldots$

   c) $4, 7, 12, 19, \ldots$

   d) $4, 12, 24, 40, 60, \ldots$

   e) $\frac{1}{4}, \frac{3}{5}, \frac{5}{6}, \frac{7}{7}, \ldots$

   f) $\frac{2}{2}, \frac{5}{4}, \frac{10}{8}, \frac{17}{16}, \ldots$

5. Find the first five terms of the following sequences:

   a) $u_r = u_{r-1}^2 - 2, u_1 = 3$,

   b) $u_r = u_{r-1}^2 - 2, u_1 = 2$,

   c) $u_r = 2|u_{r-1} - 3|, u_1 = 0$,

   d) $u_r = 3u_{r-1} - 2u_{r-2}, u_1 = 1, u_2 = 2$,

   e) $u_r = u_{r-1} + u_{r-2}, u_1 = 2, u_2 = 4$,

   f) $u_r = \frac{u_{r-1}}{u_{r-2}}, u_1 = 2, u_2 = 8$,

   g) $u_r = u_{r-1}u_{r-2}, u_1 = 2, u_2 = 4$,

   h) $u_r = 2u_{r-1}(1 - u_{r-1}), u_1 = 2$.

6. The sequence u_r is defined by the recurrence relation

$$u_r = 2u_{r-1} - 3u_{r-2}$$

   If $u_4 = -3$ and $u_5 = -15$, what are u_1, u_2 and u_3?

7. The sequence u_r is defined by the recurrence relation

$$u_r = 3u_{r-1} + 6u_{r-2}.$$

   If $u_3 = 0$ and $u_6 = 180$, what are the values of u_1, u_2 and u_7?

8. The sequence u_r is defined by the recurrence relation

$$u_r = 2u_{r-1} - 2u_{r-2}$$

   If $u_4 = 2$ and $u_8 = -8$, what are u_5, u_6 and u_7?

9. The Fibonacci numbers F_r satisfy the recurrence relation

$$F_r = F_{r-1} + F_{r-2}, \qquad F_1 = F_2 = 1.$$

   Show that the Fibonacci numbers also satisfy the recurrence relation

$$F_r = 3F_{r-2} - F_{r-4}$$

10. Show that the Fibonacci numbers satisfy the formula

$$F_r^2 - F_{r-1}F_{r+1} = -\left(F_{r-1}^2 - F_{r-2}F_r\right).$$

11. The sequence u_r satisfies the recurrence relation

$$u_r = au_{r-1} + bu_{r-2}$$

   for some numbers a and b. Determine the values of a and b in the following cases:

   a) $u_1 = 1, u_2 = 2, u_3 = 3, u_4 = 4$,

   b) $u_1 = 1, u_2 = 2, u_3 = 7, u_4 = 29$,

   c) $u_1 = 1, u_2 = 2, u_3 = 4, u_4 = 8$,

   d) $u_1 = 2, u_2 = 7, u_3 = 2, u_4 = 7$,

   e) $u_1 = 2, u_2 = -4, u_3 = 18, u_4 = -46$,

   f) $u_1 = 2, u_2 = 6, u_3 = 16, u_4 = 40$.

12. The sequence u_r satisfies the recurrence relation

$$u_r = au_{r-1} + bu_{r-2}$$

   for some numbers a and b. We know that $u_1 = 1$, $u_2 = 2$, $u_3 = 7$ and $u_5 = 76$.

   a) Show that $b = 7 - 2a$ and find a quadratic equation satisfied by a.

   b) Hence write down the two possible recurrence relations that can be satisfied by u_r.

13. Show that the formula $u_r = 3^r$ satisfies the recurrence relation

$$u_r = 4u_{r-1} - 3u_{r-2}, \qquad u_1 = 3.$$

14. Show that the formula $u_r = (r+1)5^r$ satisfies the recurrence relation

$$u_r = 10u_{r-1} - 25u_{r-2}, \qquad u_1 = 10.$$

15. Consider the sequence defined by the recurrence relation

$$u_r = \frac{1 + u_{r-1}}{1 - u_{r-1}}, \qquad u_1 = 2.$$

Calculate u_2, u_3 and u_4. What is u_{2015}?

What would happen if we replaced the statement $u_1 = 2$ with the statement that $u_1 = -1$?

16*. Using the result of Question 10, what is the value of $F_r^2 - F_{r+1}F_{r-1}$?

17*. Suppose that a and b are distinct numbers, and consider the recurrence relation

$$u_r = (a+b)u_{r-1} - ab u_{r-2}.$$

a) Show that $u_r = Aa^r + Bb^r$ satisfies this recurrence relation for any values of the constants A and B.

b) Hence find a formula for the rth term of the sequence defined by the recurrence relation

$$u_r = 7u_{r-1} - 12u_{r-2}, \qquad u_1 = 1, u_2 = 7.$$

c) Derive the rth term formula for the Fibonacci numbers:

$$F_r = \frac{1}{\sqrt{5}}\left[\left(\frac{1+\sqrt{5}}{2}\right)^r - \left(\frac{1-\sqrt{5}}{2}\right)^r\right]$$

9.2   Special Types of Sequence

There are a number of important properties that a sequence can possess:

- **Periodic Sequences**: Consider the sequence defined by the recurrence relation

$$u_r = 10 - u_{r-1}, \qquad u_1 = 3.$$

It is clear that successive terms of this sequence are $3, 7, 3, 7, \ldots$. The sequence consists of a continually repeating pattern of 3 followed by 7, followed by 3, and so on. A sequence which is made up of a continually repeating pattern of numbers is called **periodic**. The length of the repeated pattern is called the **period** of the sequence. In the example above, u_r is periodic of period 2. The periodicity of this sequence can be summarised by noting that $u_{r+2} = u_r$ for all values of r.

Food For Thought 9.1

A sequence u_r is **periodic**, with **period** k (a positive integer), if the sequence satisfies the equation

$$u_{r+k} = u_r$$

for all r.

Periodic sequences of period 1 are such that $u_{r+1} = u_r$ for all r, and so all terms in the sequence are the same. They are simply called **constant** sequences.

- **Monotonic Sequences**: Recall that functions can be monotonic, namely either increasing or decreasing. Since sequences can be regarded as functions with domain $\mathbb{N}$, they can be monotonic.

> **Food For Thought 9.2**
>
> A sequence u_r is:
>
> ★ **increasing** if $u_r \leq u_{r+1}$ for all r,
>
> ★ **decreasing** if $u_r \geq u_{r+1}$ for all r,
>
> Sequences can also be **strictly** monotonic.

- **Convergent Sequences:** The sequences $u_r = \frac{1}{r}$, $u_r = 1 + \frac{(-1)^r}{r}$, $u_r = \sqrt{\frac{2^r - r - 1}{2^{r+1} + r}}$ and $u_r = \frac{\sin r}{r^2 + 1}$ all share an important property:

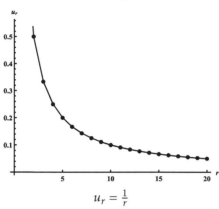

$$u_r = \frac{1}{r}$$

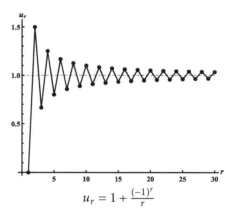

$$u_r = 1 + \frac{(-1)^r}{r}$$

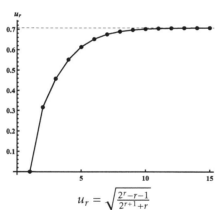

$$u_r = \sqrt{\frac{2^r - r - 1}{2^{r+1} + r}}$$

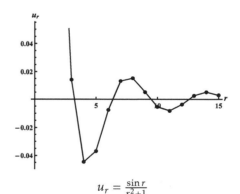

$$u_r = \frac{\sin r}{r^2 + 1}$$

Figure 9.1

As r increases, the value of terms of the sequence approaches a definite value.

★ The values of the sequence $u_r = \frac{1}{r}$ approach 0 as r gets large,

★ $u_r = 1 + \frac{(-1)^r}{r}$ approaches 1 as r gets large,

★ $u_r = \sqrt{\frac{2^r - r - 1}{2^{r+1} + r}}$ approaches $\frac{1}{\sqrt{2}}$ as r gets large,

★ $u_r = \frac{\sin r}{r^2 + 1}$ approaches 0 as r gets large.

> **Food For Thought 9.3**
>
> If there exists a value λ such that the values of u_r approach λ as r gets large, we say that the sequence u_r **converges** to λ. We also say that λ is the **limit** of u_r.

The exact nature of what it means for a sequence to be convergent is a very delicate matter, and a proper study of convergence is not within the range of a school-level course; we shall, however, only meet sequences for which convergence is immediately obvious, and we shall avoid all detailed technical discussion of the matter.

A sequence that is not convergent is called **divergent**. A sequence like $u_r = 2^r$ is said to diverge to ∞; no matter how large we want to be, the sequence u_r is that large for big enough r.

- **Oscillating and Alternating Sequences**: Often, when sequences are not monotonic, they have the property of being alternately greater and smaller than a particular value: such sequences are called **oscillating**. Sequences can be oscillating and converge, but oscillating sequences can be divergent too, as the examples below show:

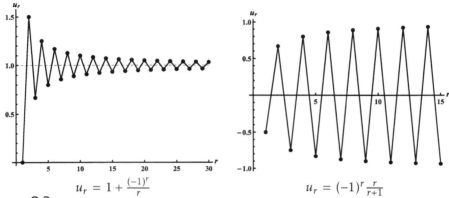

$$u_r = 1 + \frac{(-1)^r}{r} \qquad\qquad u_r = (-1)^r \frac{r}{r+1}$$

Figure 9.2

A sequence whose values oscillate about 0, so that terms are alternately positive and negative, are called **alternating**; the second of the two examples above is alternating.

- **'Eventually' Sequences**: Sometimes a sequence 'takes some time' to settle down to its true behaviour:

  ★ Apart from the first two terms, the sequence $1, 4, 0, 0, 0, 0, 0, \ldots$ is constant.

  ★ Apart from the first three terms, the sequence $0, 4, -1, 1, \frac{1}{2}, \frac{1}{3}, \frac{1}{4}, \frac{1}{5}, \ldots$ is decreasing.

  ★ Apart from the first two terms, the sequence $7, 2, 1, 2, 3, 1, 2.\,3, \ldots$ is periodic of period 3.

In such circumstances, it is convenient to describe such sequences as **eventually constant, eventually increasing** or **eventually periodic**. There is no such thing as an **eventually convergent** sequence.

EXERCISE 9B

1. Which of the following sequences are convergent, and which are convergent? What are the limits of the convergent sequences?

   a) $u_r = 7r - 5$, b) $u_r = \frac{1}{3r+2}$, c) $u_r = \frac{r}{r+7}$, d) $u_r = \frac{r^2}{r+1}$,

   e) $u_r = 2 + \frac{(-1)^r}{r}$, f) $u_r = r(r+3)$, g) $u_r = \frac{r(r+3)}{(r+2)^3}$, h) $u_r = \frac{\sin r}{r^3}$,

   i) $u_r = \frac{1}{2^r}$, j) $u_r = \frac{2^r}{3^r+1}$, k) $u_r = \frac{2^r}{2^r+1}$, l) $u_r = \frac{2^r}{2^r+r}$.

2. In the text above, it was stated that the following sequences are convergent. Prove it!

   a) $u_r = \frac{1}{r}$, b) $u_r = 1 + \frac{(-1)^r}{r}$,

   c) $u_r = \sqrt{\frac{2^r - r - 1}{2^{r+1} + r}}$, d) $u_r = \frac{\sin r}{r^2 + 1}$.

3. Which of the following sequences are convergent, and which are divergent? What are the limits of the convergent sequences?

143

a) $u_r = u_{r-1} + 11$, $u_1 = -7$,

b) $u_r = \frac{4}{u_{r-1}}$, $u_1 = 3$,

c) $u_r = 2(5 - u_r^2)$, $u_1 = 2$,

d) $u_r = 2u_{r-1} - u_{r-2}$, $u_1 = 1$, $u_2 = 2$,

e) $u_r = u_{r-1}u_{r-2}$, $u_1 = 1$, $u_2 = -1$,

f) $u_r = \frac{u_{r-1}^2}{u_{r-2}}$, $u_1 = 2$, $u_2 = 1$.

4. Which of the sequences in Question 2 are periodic, and what are the periods of the periodic sequences?

5. The sequence u_r is given by the recurrence relation

$$u_r = \begin{cases} 3u_{r-1} + 1, & u_{r-1} \text{ odd}, \\ \frac{1}{2}u_{r-1}, & u_{r-1} \text{ even}. \end{cases}$$

where u_1 is some positive integer. Show that the sequence u_r is eventually periodic when:

a) $u_1 = 32$,   b) $u_1 = 3$,   c) $u_1 = 7$,   d) $u_1 = 19$.

The Collatz Conjecture (at the time of writing, this is still unproved) claims that this sequence is eventually periodic, whatever the value of the initial integer u_1.

6. Use the formula for the Fibonacci numbers F_r found in Question 17 of Exercise 9A to show that the sequence of ratios $\frac{F_{r+1}}{F_r}$ converges to the number $\frac{1}{2}(1 + \sqrt{5})$. This famous number is known as the Golden Section, and this result is one of the celebrated properties of the Fibonacci sequence.

7*. Consider the sequence u_r defined inductively as follows:

$$u_r = \frac{1}{2}u_{r-1} + u_{r-1}^{-1}, \qquad u_1 = 1.$$

a) Show that $u_r - \sqrt{2} = \frac{1}{2u_{r-1}}\left(u_{r-1} - \sqrt{2}\right)^2$.

b) Explain why the sequence u_r converges to $\sqrt{2}$.

8*. The sequence u_r is defined inductively as follows:

$$u_r = 2 + u_{r-1}^{-1}, \qquad u_1 = 1.$$

a) If this sequence converges to some limit α, explain why α must satisfy the quadratic equation $\alpha^2 - 2\alpha - 1 = 0$, and hence determine the only possible value of the limit α.

b) Does this sequence converge to this value?

9.3 Series and the Sigma Notation

We frequently do not just want to consider sequences of numbers. We might also want to add these numbers together. When we add the terms of a sequence, we obtain what is called a **series**.

- **Triangular numbers** are numbers that can be arranged into triangular arrays, like red snooker balls before the break.

Figure 9.3

The nth triangular number is equal to the sum of the first n positive integers, so that

$$
\begin{aligned}
1 &= 1 \\
3 &= 1 + 2 \\
6 &= 1 + 2 + 3 \\
10 &= 1 + 2 + 3 + 4 \\
15 &= 1 + 2 + 3 + 4 + 5 \\
21 &= 1 + 2 + 3 + 4 + 5 + 6
\end{aligned}
$$

are the first six terms.

- The sequence of squares can be obtained through summation. Note that each square can be obtained from the preceding one by adding an odd number.

Figure 9.4

This means that the nth square can be written as the sum of the first n odd positive integers, as seen in the first six cases:

$$
\begin{aligned}
1^2 &= 1 \\
2^2 &= 1+3 \\
3^2 &= 1+3+5 \\
4^2 &= 1+3+5+7 \\
5^2 &= 1+3+5+7+9 \\
6^2 &= 1+3+5+7+9+11
\end{aligned}
$$

- The **harmonic series** is obtained by adding the reciprocals of positive integers. The first few terms in this series are

$$
\begin{aligned}
1 &= 1 \\
\tfrac{3}{2} &= 1+\tfrac{1}{2} \\
\tfrac{11}{6} &= 1+\tfrac{1}{2}+\tfrac{1}{3} \\
\tfrac{25}{12} &= 1+\tfrac{1}{2}+\tfrac{1}{3}+\tfrac{1}{4} \\
\tfrac{137}{60} &= 1+\tfrac{1}{2}+\tfrac{1}{3}+\tfrac{1}{4}+\tfrac{1}{5} \\
\tfrac{49}{20} &= 1+\tfrac{1}{2}+\tfrac{1}{3}+\tfrac{1}{4}+\tfrac{1}{5}+\tfrac{1}{6}
\end{aligned}
$$

> **Key Fact 9.2 What is a Series?**
>
> A **series** is the sum of the terms of a sequence. If u_r is a sequence, we denote the sum of the first r terms of the sequence as S_n, so that
>
> $$ S_n = u_1 + u_2 + u_3 + \cdots + u_n $$

We need a new notation to cope with the business of adding an indeterminate (like n) number of terms together. At the moment we can only indicate this sum using dots, so the expression

$$ n^2 = 1+3+5+\cdots+(2n-1) $$

should be read as saying that n^2 is the nth term in the series of the sums of the odd positive integers. This is not particularly elegant or precise, in particular since it presumes that the pattern that the sequence follows is obvious from the first few and the last terms (the only ones written down). We would like to have a way of describing series that 'did not use the dots'; it needs to be explicit about exactly which terms are being added, and how many. The notation we are looking for is the so-called **sigma notation**. Sigma (Σ) is the Greek capital 'S', and the 'S' is used to denote 'sum'.

If I have a sequence u_r, and I want to express in mathematics a formula representing the sum of the first n terms of this sequence. I do this as follows:

$$ \sum_{r=1}^{n} u_r $$

This notation has four key elements, each of which need explaining:

- u_r This part represents an expression for what is actually being added. It is a general formula of the rth term of the series that is being added is given.

- $\sum$ This symbol tells us that we are adding terms in a series.

- $r = 1$ This section starts to tell us how to decide which terms to add. Since this part of the expression starts '$r = \ldots$', we are going to be varying the value of r as we add terms. Since this part of the expression states '$r = 1$', we know that 1 is the smallest value of r as we perform the sum.

- n This tells us when to stop adding terms. We started adding (in this case) with $r = 1$. We must add together u_1, u_2, u_3, ... (note that the value of r always increases by 1), stopping when we reach this upper value of n.

Thus the expression above can be read in words as 'add up the terms u_r for r between 1 and n inclusive', or 'evaluate $u_1 + u_2 + u_3 + \cdots + u_n$'.

The great strength of this notation is that we always have a specific expression for the general, or r^{th} term in the series. This will be important when we want to perform algebra and analysis on series.

Example 9.3.1. *Write the following series in sigma notation:*

(a) $1 + 3 + 5 + \cdots + (2n - 1)$,   (b) $1 + 2 + 4 + \cdots + 2^n$,   (c) $1 + \frac{1}{2} + \frac{1}{3} + \cdots + \frac{1}{n}$

(a) The odd integers can be expressed by the series $u_r = 2r - 1$, where $r = 1$ gives the initial value of 1, $r = 2$ the second value of 3 and so on. The final value in the series of $2n - 1$ is given by $r = n$. Thus the series can be written as

$$\sum_{r=1}^{n} (2r - 1)$$

Note that if we had chosen a different formula to express the odd integers, we would have obtained a slightly different result. The required terms being added in the series can be expressed as $2r + 1$ where r now varies from 0 to $n - 1$, and so a different expression for the series is

$$\sum_{r=0}^{n-1} (2r - 1)$$

(b) All summands in the series are powers of 2, and so we are interested in adding the values 2^k together as k varies from 0 to n. The series is

$$\sum_{k=0}^{n} 2^k$$

Note that there is nothing sacred about the use of the letter r. Any other letter would do, and the meaning of the formula has not changed in doing so. Choosing a different letter in this way is called **changing the dummy variable**.

(c) The most natural expression for the harmonic series is

$$\sum_{r=1}^{n} \frac{1}{r}$$

Example 9.3.2. *Evaluate the following expressions:*

$$\text{(a) } \sum_{m=0}^{10} (3m + 1) \qquad \text{(b) } \sum_{j=3}^{7} j^2 \qquad \text{(c) } \sum_{r=0}^{100} (-1)^r$$

(a) $\displaystyle\sum_{m=0}^{10} (3m + 1) = 1 + 4 + 7 + \cdots + 31 = 176.$

(b) $\displaystyle\sum_{j=3}^{7} j^2 = 3^2 + 4^2 + 5^2 + 6^2 + 7^2 = 135.$

146

(c) $\displaystyle\sum_{r=0}^{100}(-1)^r = 1 - 1 + 1 - 1 + 1 - 1 + \cdots + 1 = 1.$

It is important to be able to retrieve the sequence from the series of sums.

Example 9.3.3. *The sum of the first n terms of a series is given by the formula*

$$S_n = \tfrac{1}{6}n(n+1)(2n+1).$$

Find an expression for the rth term of the series.

If u_r is the rth term of the series, then

$$S_n = \sum_{r=1}^{n} u_r, \qquad S_{n-1} = \sum_{r=1}^{n-1} u_r$$

and hence

$$
\begin{aligned}
u_n &= S_n - S_{n-1} = \tfrac{1}{6}n(n+1)(2n+1) - \tfrac{1}{6}(n-1)n(2n-1) \\
&= \tfrac{1}{6}n\big[(n+1)(2n+1) - (n-1)(2n-1)\big] = \tfrac{1}{6}n\big[(2n^2+3n+1) - (2n^2-3n+1)\big] \\
&= \tfrac{1}{6}n \times 6n = n^2
\end{aligned}
$$

and hence $u_r = r^2$.

EXERCISE 9C

1. Evaluate the following expressions:

a) $\displaystyle\sum_{r=1}^{4} r^3$

b) $\displaystyle\sum_{r=1}^{7}(-1)^r r^2$

c) $\displaystyle\sum_{r=1}^{7}\frac{1}{r}$

d) $\displaystyle\sum_{r=1}^{4} r(r+1)(r+2)$

e) $\displaystyle\sum_{r=2}^{5} 4^r$

f) $\displaystyle\sum_{r=0}^{9} 4$

g) $\displaystyle\sum_{r=0}^{15}(2r+1)$

h) $\displaystyle\sum_{r=1}^{4}\frac{1}{r(r+1)}$

i) $\displaystyle\sum_{r=0}^{7}\big[1+(-1)^r\big]r^2.$

2. Write down all the terms in each of these series:

a) $\displaystyle\sum_{r=1}^{5}(r^2 - r)$

b) $\displaystyle\sum_{r=2}^{5}(-1)^r 2^r$

c) $\displaystyle\sum_{r=0}^{5}\sqrt{r+1}$

d) $\displaystyle\sum_{r=7}^{10}|r-8|$

e) $\displaystyle\sum_{r=1}^{4}\sin\tfrac{1}{5}\pi r$

f) $\displaystyle\sum_{r=2}^{4}\frac{1}{r^2+1}$

3. Express these series using sigma notation:

a) $1 + 4 + 9 + 16 + 25$

b) $1 - 4 + 9 - 16 + 25 - 36$

c) $7^3 + 8^3 + 9^3 + 10^3 + 11^3 + 12^3$

d) $3 + 8 + 15 + \cdots + 10 \times 12$

e) $1 - 3 + 5 - 7 + \cdots - 23$

f) $1 + 2 + 4 + 8 + 16 + \cdots + 1024$

g) $\tfrac{1}{2} + \tfrac{2}{3} + \tfrac{3}{4} + \cdots + \tfrac{100}{101}$

h) $\tfrac{1}{2} - \tfrac{2}{4} + \tfrac{3}{8} - \tfrac{4}{16} + \cdots + \tfrac{7}{128}$

i) $3^2 + 4^2 + \cdots + n^2$

j) $0 + 3 + 8 + \cdots + (n^2 - 1)$

k) $\tfrac{1}{2} + \tfrac{2}{5} + \tfrac{3}{10} + \cdots + \tfrac{n}{n^2+1}$

l) $\tfrac{3}{4} + \tfrac{7}{8} + \tfrac{11}{16} + \cdots + \tfrac{27}{256}$

4. The sum of n terms of a series is equal to

$$S_n = \tfrac{1}{3}n(n+1)(n+8)$$

Find an expression for the rth term of the series.

5. The sum of n terms of a series is equal to

$$S_n = \tfrac{1}{30}n(n+1)(2n+1)(3n^2+3n-1)$$

Find an expression for the rth term of the series.

6. In this question you may assume the following formula for the nth triangular number:

$$T_n = \sum_{r=1}^{n} r = \tfrac{1}{2}n(n+1)$$

a) Explain why

$$\sum_{r=1}^{n}(3r+2) = 3\sum_{r=1}^{n} r + \sum_{r=1}^{n} 2$$

b) Find a formula for $\displaystyle\sum_{r=1}^{n}(3r+2)$.

c) Explain why

$$\sum_{r=1}^{2n}(-1)^r r = -\sum_{r=1}^{2n} r + 4\sum_{r=1}^{n} r$$

and hence show that

$$\sum_{r=1}^{2n}(-1)^r r = n.$$

d) Find an easier way of getting this answer.

7*. What is the value of

$$\sum_{r=1}^{10}\left(\sum_{s=1}^{n} \frac{(-1)^{r+s}}{s}\right) \quad ?$$

9.4 Arithmetic Sequences and Series

9.4.1. ARITHMETIC SEQUENCES

An **arithmetic sequence**, or **arithmetic progression**, or **AP** is a sequence whose terms go up or down by constant steps. Examples are:

$$1, 2, 3, 4, 5, \ldots \qquad 13, 11, 9, 7, 5, \ldots \qquad 1.2, 1.3, 1.4, 1.5, 1.6, \ldots$$

Traditionally, the first term of an arithmetic progression is denoted by a, and the amount by which terms change, called the **common difference**, is denoted by d. A general arithmetic sequence, whose r^{th} term is u_r, is defined by the inductive formula:

$$u_1 = a, \qquad u_{r+1} = u_r + d.$$

In the three examples given above, the values of a and d are 1 and 1, 13 and -2 and 1.2 and 0.1 respectively.

> **For Interest**
>
> Like all traditions, it is well not to get too attached to them. We might need to change the names we assign to the first term and common difference of an AP. In some problems the variables a and d might have a different meaning.

If we want to find a formula for the nth term of an arithmetic progression, we need to recall that this term is obtained from the first term by adding d to it $n-1$ times:

Key Fact 9.3 Arithmetic Progressions — The nth Term

An arithmetic progression with initial term a and common difference d has n^{th} term given by the formula
$$u_n = a + (n-1)d \, .$$

Example 9.4.1. *Adrienne would like to give a sum of money to a charity each year for 10 years. She decides to give £100 in the first year, and to increase her contribution by £20 each year. How much does she give in the last year?*

Adrienne's contribution in her tenth year is $£u_{10}$, where $u_{10} = 100 + 9 \times 20 = 280$. Thus Adrienne donates £280 in her final year.

9.4.2. ARITHMETIC SERIES

Suppose that, in the last Example, Adrienne wanted to know how much money she had donated to charity after those ten years. Instead of the arithmetic sequence of individual payments 100, 120, 140, ... 180, we are now interested in the value of the sum $100 + 120 + 140 + \cdots + 280 = 1900$. Adrienne gave £1900 to charity over the ten year period.

When the terms of an arithmetic progression are added together, we refer to the result as an **arithmetic series.**

Is there a formula for the sum of the terms of an arithmetic series? Karl Friedrich Gauss (1777 - 1855), one of the major figures in the history of Mathematics, famously discovered the solution to this problem while still at primary school. His teacher asked the class to find the sum of the integers from 1 to 100 inclusive, doubtless expecting to have some quiet time for a cup of coffee. Gauss noticed that, if the required sum was S, it could be written in two ways as follows:

$$S = 1 + 2 + 3 + \cdots + 99 + 100$$
$$S = 100 + 99 + 98 + \cdots + 2 + 1$$

Adding these two equations gives

$$2S = 101 + 101 + 101 + \cdots + 101 + 101$$

so that $S = \frac{1}{2} \times 100 \times 101 = 5050$.

The same argument works for a general arithmetic series. If S_n is the sum of the first n terms of an arithmetic series, with first term a and common difference d, then

$$S_n = \big[a\big] + \big[a+d\big] + \big[a+2d\big] + \cdots + \big[a+(n-2)d\big] + \big[a+(n-1)d\big]$$
$$S_n = \big[a+(n-1)d\big] + \big[a+(n-2)d\big] + \big[a+(n-3)d\big] + \cdots + \big[a+d\big] + \big[a\big]$$

Adding these two equations gives

$$2S_n = \big[2a+(n-1)d\big] + \big[2a+(n-1)d\big] + \big[2a+(n-1)d\big] + \cdots + \big[2a+(n-1)d\big] + \big[2a+(n-1)d\big]$$

and so

$$S_n = \tfrac{1}{2}n\big[2a+(n-1)d\big] \, .$$

Note that the last term in the arithmetic series that contributes to this sum is $\ell = a+(n-1)d$, and hence the sum can also be written as $\frac{1}{2}n(a+\ell)$.

Key Fact 9.4 The Sum of an Arithmetic Series

The sum S_n of the first n terms of an arithmetic series, whose first term is a and whose common difference is d, is given by the formula

$$S_n = \tfrac{1}{2}n\big[2a + (n-1)d\big].$$

If the last (i.e. the nth) term in this sum is ℓ, the sum of the series is

$$S_n = \tfrac{1}{2}n(a + \ell).$$

All of these results can be stated using the sigma notation. Gauss' insight can be summarised by the formula

$$\sum_{r=1}^{n} r = \tfrac{1}{2}n(n+1).$$

for the nth triangular number. The general result for the sum of the first n terms of a general arithmetic series can be derived from this result, since

$$\begin{aligned}
S_n &= \sum_{r=1}^{n} u_r = \sum_{r=1}^{n}\big[a + (r-1)d\big] = \sum_{r=1}^{n} a + \sum_{r=1}^{n}(r-1)d \\
&= na + d\sum_{r=1}^{n}(r-1) = na + d\sum_{r=0}^{n-1} r = na + d \times \tfrac{1}{2}(n-1)n \\
&= \tfrac{1}{2}n\big[2a + (n-1)d\big]
\end{aligned}$$

Note that this argument has used the fact that

$$\sum_{r=1}^{n}(r-1) = \sum_{r=1}^{n-1} r .$$

This sort of algebraic manipulation of dummy variables, to obtain a more convenient expression of a particular value, is a technique to which we shall revert frequently.

Example 9.4.2. *The third and seventh terms of an AP are* 17 *and* 41 *respectively. Find the first term and the sum of the first* 25 *terms of the series.*

If this series has starting term a and common difference d, then

$$a + 2d = 17 \qquad a + 6d = 41 .$$

Solving these equations simultaneously, we deduce that $a = 5, d = 6$. Thus the sum of the first 25 terms of the series is $\tfrac{1}{2} \times 25\big[2 \times 5 + 24 \times 6\big] = 1925$.

Example 9.4.3. *An AP has first term* 3 *and last term* 115. *If the sum of the series is* 1003, *how many terms are there in the series, and what is the common difference?*

If there are n terms in the series, then

$$1003 = \tfrac{1}{2}n(3 + 115)$$

and hence $n = 17$. Thus the last term is $115 = 3 + 16d$, and so the common difference is $d = 7$.

Example 9.4.4. *The three terms x,* $2x + 11$ *and* $x^2 - 6$ *are in arithmetic progression. Find the possible values of the common difference.*

The common difference is $d = (2x + 11) - x = (x^2 - 6) - (2x + 11)$, and hence

$$\begin{aligned}
x^2 - 2x - 17 &= x + 11 \\
x^2 - 3x - 28 &= 0 \\
(x - 7)(x + 4) &= 0
\end{aligned}$$

and so x can be either 7 or -4. The corresponding common differences are 18 or 7.

Example 9.4.5. *A student reading a 426 page book finds that he reads faster as he gets into the subject. He reads 19 pages on the first day, and his rate of reading then goes up by 3 pages each day. How long does he take to finish the book?*

We are told that $a = 19$, $d = 3$. We want to find n such that $S_n \geq 426$. This means we want

$$
\begin{aligned}
\tfrac{1}{2}n\big[38 + (n-1)3\big] &\geq 426 \\
n(3n + 35) &\geq 852 \\
3n^2 + 35n - 852 &\geq 0 \\
(3n + 71)(n - 12) &\geq 0
\end{aligned}
$$

Since n must be positive, we deduce that $n \geq 12$. The student finishes the book in 12 days.

EXERCISE 9D

1. Which of the following sequences are the first four terms of an AP? For those that are, write down the value of the common difference.

   a) $7, 10, 13, 16, \ldots$ b) $3, 5, 9, 15, \ldots$ c) $1, 0.1, 0.01, 0.001, \ldots$
   d) $4, 2, 0, -2 \ldots$ e) $2, -3, 4, -5, \ldots$ f) $p - 2q, p - q, p, p + q, \ldots$
   g) $\tfrac{1}{2}a, \tfrac{1}{3}a, \tfrac{1}{4}a, \tfrac{1}{5}a, \ldots$ h) $x, 2x, 3x, 4x, \ldots$

2. Write down the sixth term, and an expression for the rth term, of the arithmetic sequences which begin as follows.

   a) $2, 4, 6, \ldots$ b) $17, 20, 23, \ldots$ c) $5, 2, -1, \ldots$
   d) $1.3, 1.7, 2.1, \ldots$ e) $1, 1\tfrac{1}{2}, 2, \ldots$ f) $73, 67, 61, \ldots$
   g) $x, x + 2, x + 4, \ldots$ h) $1 - x, 1, 1 + x, \ldots$

3. In the following arithmetic progressions, the first three terms and the last term are given. Find the number of terms.

   a) $4, 5, 6, \ldots, 17$ b) $3, 9, 15, \ldots, 525$
   c) $8, 2, -4, \ldots, -202$ d) $2\tfrac{1}{8}, 3\tfrac{1}{4}, 4\tfrac{3}{8}, \ldots, 13\tfrac{3}{8}$
   e) $3x, 7x, 11x, \ldots, 43x$ f) $-3, -1\tfrac{1}{2}, 0, \ldots, 12$
   g) $\tfrac{1}{6}, \tfrac{1}{3}, \tfrac{1}{3}, \tfrac{1}{2}, 2\tfrac{2}{3}$ h) $1 - 2x, 1 - x, 1, \ldots, 1 + 25x$

4. Find the sum of the given number of terms of the following APs.

   a) $2 + 5 + 8 + \cdots$, (20 terms)   b) $4 + 11 + 18 + \cdots$, (15 terms)
   c) $8 + 5 + 2 + \cdots$, (12 terms)   d) $\tfrac{1}{2} + 1 + 1\tfrac{3}{2} + \cdots$, (58 terms)
   e) $7 + 3 + (-1) + \cdots$, (25 terms)   f) $1 + 3 + 5 + \cdots$, (999 terms)
   g) $a + 5a + 9a + \cdots$, (40 terms)   h) $-3p - 6p - 9p - \cdots$, (100 terms)

5. Find the number of terms and the sum of each of the following arithmetic series.

   a) $5 + 7 + 9 + \cdots + 111$ b) $8 + 12 + 16 + \cdots + 84$
   c) $7 + 13 + 19 + \cdots + 277$ d) $8 + 5 + 2 + \cdots + (-73)$
   e) $-14 - 10 - 6 - \cdots + 94$ f) $157 + 160 + 163 + \cdots + 529$
   g) $10 + 20 + 30 + \cdots + 10000$ h) $1.8 + 1.2 + 0.6 + \cdots + (-34.2)$

6. In each of the following APs you are given two terms. Find the first term and the common difference.

   a) 4th term $= 15$, 9th term $= 35$ b) 3rd term $= 12$, 10th term $= 47$
   c) 8th term $= 3.5$, 13th term $= 5.0$ d) 5th term $= 2$, 11th term $= -13$
   e) 12th term $= -8$, 20th term $= -32$ f) 3rd term $= -3$, 7th term $= 5$
   g) 2nd term $= 2x$, 11th term $= -7x$,   h) 3rd term $= 2p + 7$, 7th term $= 4p + 19$

7. Find how many terms of the given arithmetic series must be taken to reach the given sum.

   a) $3 + 7 + 11 + \cdots$, sum $= 820$ b) $8 + 9 + 10 + \cdots$, sum $= 162$
   c) $20 + 23 + 26 + \cdots$, sum $= 680$ d) $27 + 23 + 19 + \cdots$, sum $= -2040$
   e) $1.1 + 1.3 + 1.5 + \cdots$, sum $= 1017.6$ f) $-11 - 4 + 3 + \cdots$, sum $= 2338$

8. A squirrel is collecting nuts. It collects 5 nuts on the first day of the month, 8 nuts on the second, 11 on the third and so on in arithmetic progression.

    a) How many nuts will it collect on the 20th day?

    b) After how many days will it have collected more than 1000 nuts altogether?

9. Kulsum is given an interest-free loan to buy a car. She repays the loan in unequal monthly instalments; these start at £30 in the first month and increase by £2 each month after that. She makes 24 payments. Find the amount of her final payment and the total amount of her loan.

10. An employee starts work on 1 January 2000 on an annual salary of £30,000. His pay scale will give him an increase of £800 per annum on the first of January until 1 January 2015 inclusive. He remains on this salary until he retires on 31 December 2040. How much will he earn during his working life?

11. The numbers $1 + 4p$, $4 + p$ and $5 + 2p$ are successive terms in an AP. Find the value of p.

12. The numbers $3x - 1$, $5x - 3$ and $x^2 + 7$ are successive terms in an AP. Find the possible values of x.

13. The numbers $x + 6$, x and $-4 - 4x$ are the first, third and sixth terms in an arithmetic sequence. Find the value of x.

14. Evaluate the following arithmetic series:

    a) $\displaystyle\sum_{r=n+1}^{2n} r$ b) $\displaystyle\sum_{r=n}^{n^2} (2r + 3)$ c) $\displaystyle\sum_{r=1}^{2n-1} (3r - 2)$

15. Given that $10283 = 91 \times 113$, solve the equation

$$\sum_{r=n}^{n^2} (2r + 3) = 10283.$$

16. Five numbers are in arithmetic progression. The sum of the squares of the first, third and fifth terms is 54 more than the sum of the squares of the middle three terms. What is the value of the common difference?

17*. The first term, the last term and the sum of an AP are positive numbers which are themselves in an arithmetic progression. State the largest number of terms than can be in the original progression, and list the terms in the sequence in that case (as multiples of the first term).

18*. The non-zero numbers a, b and c are in arithmetic progression, with $a < b < c$. The numbers $\frac{1}{a}$, $\frac{1}{b}$, and $\frac{1}{c}$, are (in some order) in arithmetic progression. List the possible values of a, b and c.

19*. The positive numbers p, q, r are such that p^2, q^2 and r^2 are in arithmetic progression. Show that the numbers $\frac{1}{q+r}$, $\frac{1}{r+p}$ and $\frac{1}{p+q}$ are also in arithmetic progression.

9.5 Geometric Sequences and Series

9.5.1. GEOMETRIC SEQUENCES

An arithmetic sequence is one where each term is obtained from its predecessor by adding a constant. A sequence in which you obtain each term from its predecessor by multiplying by a constant ia called a geometric sequence.

We have met arithmetic sequences, in which you get from one term to the next by adding a constant. A sequence in which you get from one term to the next by multiplying by a constant is called a geometric sequence.

An **geometric sequence**, or **geometric progression**, or **GP**, is a sequence whose terms vary by the successive application of a common factor. A general geometric sequence, whose n^{th} term is u_n, is defined by the inductive formula:

$$u_1 = a, \qquad u_{n+1} = r u_n.$$

As for arithmetic sequences, the first term is usually denoted a, and the constant multiplied, called the **common ratio** is usually denoted r. Thus the nth term of a geometric progression is obtained by multiplying a by r a total of $n-1$ times:

Key Fact 9.5 Geometric Progressions — The nth Term

A geometric progression with initial term a and common difference d has n^{th} term given by the formula
$$u_n = ar^{n-1}.$$

For Interest

Note that flexibility is again required in our choice of variables. Since the symbol r often has a specific meaning for a GP, we can no longer talk about the rth term of the sequence.

Example 9.5.1. *A GP has first term $u_1 = 1$ and common ratio 1.1. Which is the first term greater than:* *(a) 2,* *(b) 5,* *(c) 10,* *(d) 1000?*

On many calculators you can keep multiplying by 1.1 by repeatedly pressing a single key. This makes it easy to display successive terms of a geometric sequence.

(a) Experimentation shows that $u_8 = 1.1^7 = 1.949$, while $u_9 = 1.1^8 = 2.144$. The first term greater than 2 in the sequence is u_9.

(b) Continued testing gives $u_{17} = 1.1^{16} = 4.594$ and $u_{18} = 1.1^{17} = 5.054$. The first term greater than 5 is u_{18}.

(c) Rather than just testing, let us think. Since $1.1^8 > 2$ and $1.1^{17} > 5$, it must be true that $1.1^{25} > 10$. Since $1.1^{24} = 9.850$, the first term greater than 10 is $u_{26} = 1.1^{25}$.

(d) Since $1.1^{24} < 10 < 1.1^{25}$, taking cubes tells us that $1.1^{72} < 1000 < 1.1^{75}$. Since $1.1^{73} = 1051.2$, the first term, greater than 1000 is $u_{74} = 1.1^{73}$.

You can see from this example that, even with a common ratio only slightly greater than 1, the terms of a geometric sequence get big quite quickly.

Example 9.5.2. *The third term of a GP is 18, and the sixth term is $\frac{243}{4}$. Find the common ratio and the first term of the progression.*

If the first term is a and the common ratio is r, then
$$ar^2 = 18 \qquad ar^5 = \tfrac{243}{4}$$

Dividing these two equations tells us that $r^3 = \frac{27}{8}$, and hence $r = \frac{3}{2}$. Thus $\frac{9}{4}a = 18$, so $a = 8$.

Example 9.5.3. *The second, fourth and fifth terms of an arithmetic progression form a geometric progression. Find the common ratio of the geometric progression.*

The second, fourth and fifth terms of a non-constant arithmetic progression can be written $a+d$, $a+3d$ and $a+4d$ (using the normal notation). If these three terms form a geometric progression with common ratio r, then
$$a+3d = r(a+d) \qquad a+4d = r^2(a+d)$$

and hence
$$(a+3d)^2 = r^2(a+d)^2 = (a+d)(a+4d)$$
$$a^2 + 6ad + 9d^2 = a^2 + 5ad + 4d^2$$
$$5d^2 = -ad$$

Since the arithmetic progression is not constant, $d \neq 0$, and so $d = -\frac{1}{5}a$. Thus
$$\tfrac{2}{5}a = a+3d = r(a+d) = \tfrac{4}{5}ar$$

and hence $r = \frac{1}{2}$ (since the arithmetic progression is non-constant, $a \neq 0$).

9.5.2. EXPONENTIAL GROWTH AND DECAY

Many everyday situations are described by geometric sequences. Of the next two examples, the first has a common ratio greater than 1, and the second has a common ratio between 0 and 1.

Example 9.5.4. *A person invests £1000 in a savings bank account which pays interest of 6% annually. Calculate the amount in the account over the next 8 years.*

This is a standard compound interest question. Adding 6% interest to a sum means that the money in the account at the end of a year is equal to the money in the account at the start of the year times 1.06. To the nearest pound, the amount in the account after n years is given by the following table:

Number of Years n	0	1	2	3	4	5	6	7	8
Account Balance (£)	1000	1060	1124	1191	1262	1338	1419	1504	1594

The amount in the account after n years is £u_n, where $u_n = 1000 \times 1.1^n$ (note that, in this case, the geometric progression starts with $n = 0$). Note that all points of the progression lie on the curve $y = 1000 \times 1.1^x$.

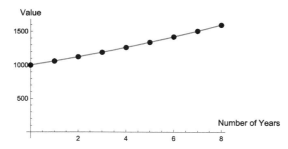

Figure 9.5

Example 9.5.5. *A car cost £15000 when new, and each year its value decreases by 20%. Find its value on the first five anniversaries of its purchase.*

The value at the end of each year is 0.8 times its value a year earlier.

Number of years	0	1	2	3	4	5
Value (£)	15000	12000	9600	7680	6144	4915

The value of the car after n years is £u_n, where $u_n = 15000 \times 0.8^n$. Note that all points in the geometric progression lie on the curve $y = 15000 \times 0.8^x$.

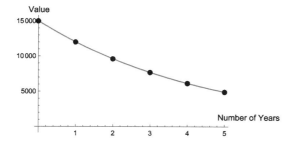

Figure 9.6

These are both examples of **exponential** sequences. The word 'exponential' comes from 'exponent', which is another word for index. The reason for the name is that the variable n in the formula for u_n occurs in the exponent, or index. Thus geometric sequences are exponential ones: if $u_n = ar^{n-1}$, then the sequence is one of **exponential growth** if $r > 1$, while the sequence is one of **exponential decay** if $0 < r < 1$.

154

9.5.3. GEOMETRIC SERIES

The story goes that a king wanted entertainment. A wise man appeared, and offered the king the game of chess. The king was so impressed with the game that he told the wise man to name any reward he wished. The wise man asked that the king place one grain of rice on the first square of the board, two grains of rice on the second square, four grains on the third square, and so on, doubling the number of grains of rice on each square until all the squares of the chessboard had been covered. The wise man would take that amount of rice as a reward

2^{56}	2^{57}	2^{58}	2^{59}	2^{60}	2^{61}	2^{62}	2^{63}
2^{48}	2^{49}	2^{50}	2^{51}	2^{52}	2^{53}	2^{54}	2^{55}
2^{40}	2^{41}	2^{42}	2^{43}	2^{44}	2^{45}	2^{46}	2^{47}
2^{32}	2^{33}	2^{34}	2^{35}	2^{36}	2^{37}	2^{38}	2^{39}
2^{24}	2^{25}	2^{26}	2^{27}	2^{28}	2^{29}	2^{30}	2^{31}
2^{16}	2^{17}	2^{18}	2^{19}	2^{20}	2^{21}	2^{22}	2^{23}
256	512	1024	2048	4096	8192	16384	32768
1	2	4	8	16	32	64	128

Figure 9.7

> **For Interest**
>
> This story exists in many forms. There are Persian stories using wheat instead of rice, stories about a Chinese emperor, and Indian ones about a king being tricked by the God Krishna.

The king was, we are told, minded to agree, until his advisors intervened. How much rice would the king have had to give? Suppose the king did as the wise man asked. The number of grains of rice on each square forms a GP, with the number of grains on the nth square being $u_n = 2^{n-1}$. If S_n is the number of grains of rice on the first n squares, then S_n satisfies the recurrence relation

$$S_{n+1} = S_n + 2^n, \qquad S_1 = 1 .$$

A little experimentation reveals a pattern in the numbers S_n:

The number of grains of rice on the first square is	$1 = 1 = 2^1 - 1$
The number of grains of rice on the first two squares is	$1 + 2 = 3 = 2^2 - 1$
The number of grains of rice on the first three squares is	$1 + 2 + 4 = 7 = 2^3 - 1$
The number of grains of rice on the first four squares is	$1 + 2 + 4 + 8 = 15 = 2^4 - 1$
The number of grains of rice on the first five squares is	$1 + 2 + 4 + 8 + 16 = 31 = 2^5 - 1$

It is reasonable to guess that the number of grains of rice on the first n squares is $S_n = 2^n - 1$. Since

$$2^{n+1} - 1 = \left(2^n - 1\right) + 2^n$$

we see that this is the correct formula for S_n, since it satisfies the defining recurrence relation.

The king would have agreed to give a total of $2^{64} - 1 = 18446744073709551615$ grains of rice. This is enough to cover all the land surface area of the Earth with 12 grains of rice for every square centimetre of land, or alternatively to cover the entire United Kingdom to a depth of 1.5 m!

> **For Interest**
>
> The story does not tell if the wise man became one of the king's advisors, or whether the king beheaded him!

Just like the king, we often need to sum the terms in a geometric progression. In this context it is usual to talk about a **geometric series**. The method used previously to calculate the sum of the first n terms of an arithmetic series cannot be used here. Instead we shall apply a different trick.

155

Consider any GP. We want to find the value of the sum of the first n terms:

$$S_n = a + ar + ar^2 + \cdots + ar^{n-2} + ar^{n-1}$$

This time, instead of simply rearranging the terms in the series, we multiply the whole expression by r:

$$\begin{array}{rcccccccccc}
S_n & = & a & + & ar & + & ar^2 & + & \cdots & + & ar^{n-2} & + & ar^{n-1} \\
rS_n & = & & & ar & + & ar^2 & + & \cdots & + & ar^{n-2} & + & ar^{n-1} & + & ar^n
\end{array}$$

If we subtract these two expressions, nearly all the terms on the right-hand side cancel out, and we are left with the result

$$\begin{aligned}
rS_n - S_n &= ar^n - a \\
(r-1)S_n &= a(r^n - 1) \\
S_n &= \frac{a(r^n-1)}{r-1}
\end{aligned}$$

It is good practice to use the sigma notation to prove this result. Since

$$S_n = \sum_{k=1}^{n} ar^{k-1}$$

we see that

$$(r-1)S_n = rS_n - S_n = \sum_{k=1}^{n} ar^k - \sum_{k=1}^{n} ar^{k-1} = \sum_{k=1}^{n} ar^k - \sum_{k=0}^{n-1} ar^k = ar^n - a = a(r^n - 1)$$

Note the key stages of the argument:

- Changing the value of the function being summed, and adjusting the range of summation, enabled us to replace $\sum_{k=1}^{n} ar^{k-1}$ by $\sum_{k=0}^{n-1} ar^k$.

- We are then subtracting sums of the same expression ar^k over different ranges of values of k. The contributions of the values of k which are common to both sums therefore cancel out, and we are just left with the two terms which are not common to both sums.

This technique of manipulating the dummy variable to be able to combine and compare sums is a key part of using the sigma notation.

> **Key Fact 9.6** The Sum of a Geometric Series
>
> The sum of the first n terms of a geometric series with first term a and common ratio r is
> $$S_n = \frac{a(r^n - 1)}{r - 1} = \frac{a(1 - r^n)}{1 - r}, \qquad r \neq 1.$$

There is no algebraic difference between the two expressions for S_n given here. The second one is simply convenient when the common ratio r is less than 1, since it means that the denominator is positive (with tends to make calculations easier).

Example 9.5.6. *A child lives 200 metres from school. He walks 60 metres in the first minute, and in each subsequent minute he walks 75% of the distance he walked in the previous minute. Show that he takes between 6 and 7 minutes to get to school.*

The distances walked in successive minutes form a geometric progression with common ratio $\frac{3}{4}$, and so the distance walked in the nth minute is given by the formula $u_n = 60 \times \left(\frac{3}{4}\right)n - 1$. The distance walked in the first n minutes is thus

$$S_n = \frac{60\left[1 - \left(\frac{3}{4}\right)^n\right]}{1 - \frac{3}{4}} = 240\left[1 - \left(\frac{3}{4}\right)^n\right]$$

Thus $S_6 = 197.3$, while $S_7 = 208.0$. Thus the child takes between 6 and 7 minutes to get to school.

Example 9.5.7. *Find a simple expression for the sum*

$$p^6 - p^5q + p^4q^2 - p^3q^3 + p^2q^4 - pq^5 + q^6 .$$

This is a GP with 7 terms, whose first term is p^6 and whose common ratio is $-\frac{q}{p}$. Thus the sum is

$$\frac{p^6\left[1 - \left(-\frac{q}{p}\right)^7\right]}{1 + \frac{q}{p}} = \frac{p^7 + q^7}{p + q}$$

Food For Thought 9.4

The formula for the sum of the first n terms of a geometric series requires that $r \neq 1$, since otherwise the formula asks us to divide by 0. This does not mean that we cannot have a geometric series with common ratio 1, or that we cannot find the sum of the first n terms of such a series; it simply means that the formula we have is not a good one in that case. Looking at the formula more carefully, when $r = 1$ both the numerator and the denominator are 0. Although no meaning can be attached to the bald expression $\frac{0}{0}$, there are plenty of circumstances in which mathematicians can assign meanings to it, depending on the context in which it arises. We shall see later how this is one of those cases.

Even without worrying about the $\frac{0}{0}$ problem, the value of S_n is clear when $r = 1$. If a geometric progression has common ratio $r = 1$, then it is a constant sequence, with $u_n = a$ for all n. Thus the sum of the first n terms of this series is $S_n = na$.

If you have access to graphing software, drawing the graph of $y = \frac{x^n - 1}{x - 1}$ for different values of n should convince you that this function is 'perfectly well-behaved' near $x = 1$, taking the value n there.

EXERCISE 9E

1. For each of the following GPs find the common ratio and the next two terms.
   a) $3, 6, 12, \ldots$
   b) $2, 8, 32, \ldots$
   c) $32, 16, 8, \ldots$
   d) $2, -6, 18, -54, \ldots$
   e) $1.1, 1.21, 1.331, \ldots$
   f) $x^2, x, 1, \ldots$

2. Find an expression for the nth term of each of the following geometric sequences.
   a) $2, 6, 18, \ldots$
   b) $10, 5, 2.5, \ldots$
   c) $1, -2, 4, \ldots$
   d) $81, 27, 9, \ldots$
   e) $x, x^2, x^3, \ldots$
   f) $pq^2, q^3, p^{-1}q^4, \ldots$

3. Find the number of terms in each of these geometric progressions.
   a) $2, 4, 8, \ldots, 2048$
   b) $1, -3, 9, \ldots, 531441$
   c) $2, 6, 18, \ldots, 1458$
   d) $5, -10, 20, \ldots, -40960$
   e) $16, 12, 9, \ldots, 3.796875$
   f) $x^{-6}, x^{-2}, x^2, \ldots, x^{42}$

4. Find the common ratio and the first term in the GPs where
   a) $u_2 = 4$ and $u_5 = 108$,
   b) $u_3 = 6$ and $u_7 = 96$,
   c) $u_4 = 19683$ and $u_9 = 81$,
   d) $u_3 = 8$ and $u_9 = 64$,
   e) $u_n = 16807$ and $u_{n+4} = 40353607$.
   Note that some of these have more than one answer.

5. Find the sum, for the given number of terms, of each of the following geometric series. Give numerical answers as decimals correct to 4 places.
   a) $2 + 6 + 18 + \cdots$ 10 terms
   b) $2 - 6 + 18 - \cdots$ 10 terms
   c) $1 + \frac{1}{2} + \frac{1}{4} - \cdots$ 8 terms
   d) $1 - \frac{1}{2} + \frac{1}{4} - \cdots$ 8 terms
   e) $3 + 6 + 12 + \cdots$ 12 terms
   f) $12 - 4 + \frac{4}{3} -$ 10 terms
   g) $x + x^2 + x^3 + \cdots$ n terms
   h) $x - x^2 + x^3 - \cdots$ n terms
   i) $x + \frac{1}{x} + \frac{1}{x^3} + \cdots$ n terms
   j) $1 - \frac{1}{x^2} + \frac{1}{x^4} + \cdots$ n terms

6. Find the sums of these GPs. Give numerical answers as rational numbers.

   a) $\displaystyle\sum_{r=0}^{10} 2^r$

   b) $\displaystyle\sum_{r=0}^{10} (-2)^r$

   c) $\displaystyle\sum_{r=0}^{8} 3 \times 4^r$

   d) $\displaystyle\sum_{r=1}^{10} 2^{1-r}$

   e) $\displaystyle\sum_{r=0}^{9} \frac{(-1)^r}{3^r}$

   f) $\displaystyle\sum_{r=0}^{6} \frac{10}{2^r}$

   g) $\displaystyle\sum_{r=1}^{5} 4^{-r}$

   h) $\displaystyle\sum_{r=0}^{n} \frac{1}{2^r}$

   i) $\displaystyle\sum_{r=-2}^{n} 4^{-r}$

   j) $\displaystyle\sum_{r=-4}^{n} (-3)^{-r}$

7. A child negotiates a pocket money deal of 1 pence on 1 February, 2 pence on 2 February, 4 cents on 3 February and so on for 28 days. How much should the child receive in total during February?

8. If x, y and z are the first three terms of a geometric sequence, show that x^2, y^2 and z^2 form another geometric sequence.

9. Different numbers x, y and z are the first three terms of a geometric progression with common ratio r, and also the first, second and fourth terms of an arithmetic progression.

   a) Find the value of r.

   b) Find which term of the arithmetic progression will next be equal to a term of the geometric progression.

10. Different numbers x, y and z are the first three terms of a GP with common ratio r and also the first, second and fifth terms of an AP.

    a) Find the value of r.

    b) Find which term of the arithmetic progression will next be equal to a term of the geometric progression.

11. The first three terms of a GP are x, $x + 4$ and $7x + 4$. Find the possible values of x, and write down the corresponding common ratios.

12. The sum of the first four terms of a geometric progression is equal to 280, and the sum of the first eight terms is equal to 22960. Find two possible values for the common ratio, and write down the corresponding possible values of the first term.

13. The sum of the third, fourth, fifth and sixth terms of a GP is $\frac{15}{4}$ times the sum of the first two terms. The common ratio is positive; what is it?

14. The first, third and seventh terms of a non-constant arithmetic progression form a geometric progression. Find the common ratio of the geometric progression.

15*. The first, second and third terms of a GP are x, $x + 4$ and $x^2 + 14$. Find the value of x.

16*. $3x$, $x - 2$ and $x - 5$ are the first, third and fourth terms of a GP. Find the possible values of x, and the corresponding values of the first three terms of the sequence.

17*. The sequence u_n is a geometric progression of non-zero terms such that

$$4u_{n+6} - 21u_{n+4} + 21u_{n+2} - 4u_n = 0$$

for all n. Find four different possible values for r.

18*. Consider the geometric progression

$$q^{n-1} + q^{n-2}p + q^{n-3}p^2 + \ldots + qp^{n-2} + p^{n-1}.$$

where n is a positive integer.

    a) Find the common ratio and the number of terms.

    b) Show that the sum of the series is equal to $\frac{q^n - p^n}{q - p}$.

   c) Suppose that r_k is a sequence which converges to 1.

      i. What is the limit of the sequence

$$\frac{r_k^n - 1}{r_k - 1}$$

      as k tends to infinity?

      ii. How does this explain the relationship between the formula for the sum of n terms of a GP when $r \neq 1$ and the formula when $r = 1$?

      iii. What is the limit of the sequence

$$\frac{r_k^{-n} - 1}{r_k - 1}$$

      as k tends to infinity?

9.6 The Sum to Infinity of a Geometric Progression

9.6.1. THE PROBLEM WITH RECURRING DECIMALS

When studying decimals, we soon meet the idea of recurring decimals. Statements like

$$0.\dot{3} = \tfrac{1}{3} \qquad\qquad 0.\dot{1}\dot{8} = \tfrac{2}{11}$$

cause no particular difficulty, but the identity

$$0.\dot{9} = 1$$

generally causes students a good deal of concern. Because of the 0 before the decimal point, the number $0.\dot{9}$ 'must' somehow be less than 1. Similarly, students frequently write that the range of real numbers that round to 3 are those numbers between 2.5 and $3.4\dot{9}$, with the idea that $3.4\dot{9}$ is less than 3.5 (and 3.5, of course, rounds to 4).

Food For Thought 9.5

Consider the following points:

- $0.\dot{9}$ is less than or equal to 1.

- $0.\dot{9}$ is greater than $u_n = 0.999\cdots9$, the number with n 9s after the decimal point, for any positive integer n.

These two statements are reasonable enough. Suppose now that a is any number less than 1. Then $1 - a > 0$, and so we can find an integer N such that $10^{-N} < 1 - a$. Since $u_N = 1 - 10^{-N}$, we deduce that $a < u_N$, and hence that $a < 0.\dot{9}$.
We have agreed that $0.\dot{9} \leq 1$. But we have just shown that $0.\dot{9}$ is greater than any number less than 1. Since $0.\dot{9}$ cannot be greater than itself, we deduce that $0.\dot{9} \geq 1$. Putting these two facts together, we deduce that $0.\dot{9} = 1$.

In one sense, the value of $0.\dot{3}$ is just as mysterious as the value of $0.\dot{9}$. What do we mean by a recurring decimal? When we talk about $0.\dot{3}$, we cannot actually write down an infinite number of 3s after the decimal point. What, then, is this number that cannot be written down? The only way to think about $0.\dot{3}$ is as the number that the sequence of terminating decimals

$$0.3\,,\,0.33\,,\,0.333\,,\,0.3333\,,\,0.33333\,,\,\ldots$$

is getting closer and closer to; in other words, $0.\dot{3}$ must be seen as the limit of a sequence. Similarly, $0.\dot{1}\dot{8}$ and $0.\dot{9}$ should be seen as the limits of the sequences

$$0.18\,,\,0.1818\,,\,0.181818\,,\,0.18181818\,,\,\ldots \qquad 0.9\,,\,0.99\,,\,0.999\,,\,0.9999\,,\,0.99999\,,\,\ldots$$

respectively. It is important to note that the sequences defining recurring decimals arise from GPs.

- The sequence $0.3, 0.33, 0.333, \ldots$ is the sequence S_n of sums of the first n terms of a GP with $a = 0.3$ and $r = 0.1$. But then

$$S_n = \frac{0.3(1-0.1^n)}{1-0.1} = \frac{1}{3}\left((1-0.1^n)\right)$$

which converges to $\frac{1}{3}$ as n tends to infinity. Thus $0.\dot{3} = \frac{1}{3}$.

- The sequence $0.18, 0.1818, 0.181818, \ldots$ is the sequence S_n of sums of the first n terms of a GP with $a = 0.18$ and $r = 0.01$ But then

$$S_n = \frac{0.18(1-0.01^n)}{1-0.01} = \frac{2}{11}\left(1-0.01^n\right)$$

which converges to $\frac{2}{11}$ as n tends to infinity. Thus $0.\dot{1}\dot{8} = \frac{2}{11}$.

- The sequence $0.9, 0.99, 0.999, \ldots$ is the sequence S_n of sums of the first n terms of a GP with $a = 0.9$ and $r = 0.1$. But then

$$S_n = \frac{0.9(1-0.1^n)}{1-0.1} = 1 - 0.1^n$$

which converges to 1 as n tends to infinity. Thus $0.\dot{9} = 1$.

Looking at all recurring decimals in this light gives a consistent way to consider the 'impossible' notion of a number with an infinite number of 3s after the decimal point, and which gives us the right values for these decimals.

9.6.2. The Formula for S_∞

The sum of the first n terms of a geometric series is given by the formula

$$S_n = \frac{a(1-r^n)}{1-r}$$

provided that $r \neq 1$. How does this sum behave as n increases?

- If $r > 1$, then r^n increases indefinitely, and hence the sequence S_n also increases indefinitely (assuming that $a > 0$). The sequence S_n diverges.

- If $r = 1$, then the sum S_n is actually equal to an, which also increases indefinitely (again, assuming that $a > 0$). The sequence S_n diverges.

- If $-1 < r < 1$, then r^n converges to 0 as n tends to infinity. The sequence S_n converges.

- If $r = -1$, then the sequence S_n oscillates, alternately taking the values of a and 0. Again, the sequence S_n fails to converge.

- If $r < -1$, then r^n diverges in an oscillating manner, and therefore S_n does so as well.

We can summarise these results as follows:

Key Fact 9.7 The Sum to Infinity of a Geometric Series

Provided that $|r| < 1$, the sequence of sums S_n of a geometric series is convergent. We call the limit the **sum to infinity** of the geometric series, and denote it

$$S_\infty = \sum_{n=1}^{\infty} ar^{n-1} = \frac{a}{1-r}$$

Example 9.6.1. *Express the recurring decimal $0.\dot{2}9\dot{6}$ as a fraction.*

The recurring decimal $0.\dot{2}9\dot{6}$ is the sum of infinity of the GP with first term 0.296 and common ratio 0.001. Thus

$$0.\dot{2}9\dot{6} = \frac{0.296}{1-0.001} = \frac{0.296}{0.999} = \frac{8}{27}$$

Example 9.6.2. *A geometric progression has first term 10 and sum to infinity 15. What is the common ratio?*

With $a = 10$ and $\frac{a}{1-r} = 15$, we deduce that $r = \frac{1}{3}$.

Example 9.6.3 (Zeno's Paradox). *To complete a race, a runner must first cover half the distance along the track. She must then complete half the remaining distance, then half the remaining distance, then half the remaining distance, and so on. Since the runner always has a task to complete (running half the remaining distance) before she can end the race, how can she ever finish?*

The runner has to run first $\frac{1}{2}$, then $\frac{1}{4}$, then $\frac{1}{8}$, then $\frac{1}{16}$, and so on, of the total course length. Since

$$\sum_{n=1}^{\infty} \frac{1}{2^n} = \frac{\frac{1}{2}}{1 - \frac{1}{2}} = 1$$

after doing all this, the runner has covered the entire track.

Actually, this paradox is not really one about geometric progressions. The Greek philosopher Zeno, who lived about 450 BC, was concerned about what he saw as the possibility of a runner having to complete an infinite number of tasks in a finite time. Once we accept the idea of a limit, this is not a problem mathematically. Suppose that the runner is travelling at a constant speed, and that it takes her 5 seconds to run half the track. It then takes her 2.5 seconds to run a quarter of the track, 1.25 seconds to run an eighth, and so forth. The total time it takes her to complete the race is

$$\sum_{n=1}^{\infty} \frac{10}{2^n} = \frac{5}{1 - \frac{1}{2}} = 10$$

seconds. She might have to complete an infinite number of tasks to finish the race, but each task takes less and less time, so that the total time required to complete all the tasks is finite.

For Interest

Philosophers are still not finished with this paradox, and argue about whether it is possible for a human (or any other) consciousness to perceive an infinite number of events in a finite time. We are going to leave that to the philosophers!

EXERCISE 9F

1. Find the sum to infinity of the following geometric series. Give numeric answers as whole numbers or fractions.

   a) $1 + \frac{1}{2} + \frac{1}{4} + \cdots$

   b) $1 + \frac{1}{3} + \frac{1}{9} + \cdots$

   c) $\frac{1}{5} + \frac{1}{25} + \frac{1}{125} + \cdots$

   d) $0.1 + 0.01 + 0.001 + \cdots$

   e) $1 - \frac{1}{3} + \frac{1}{9} - \cdots$

   f) $0.2 - 0.04 + 0.008 - \cdots$

   g) $\frac{3}{2} + \frac{3}{4} + \frac{3}{8} + \cdots$

   h) $\frac{1}{2} - \frac{1}{4} + \frac{1}{8} - \cdots$

   i) $10 - 5 + 2.5 - \cdots$

   j) $50 + 10 + 2 + \cdots$

   k) $x + x^2 + x^3 + \cdots$, where $|x| < 1$

   l) $1 - x^2 + x^4 - \cdots$, where $|x| < 1$

   m) $1 + x^{-1} + x^{-2} + \cdots$, where $|x| > 1$

   n) $x^2 - x + 1 - \cdots$, where $|x| > 1$

2. Express each of the following recurring decimals as exact fractions.

   a) $0.\dot{3}\dot{6}$

   b) $0.\dot{1}2\dot{3}$

   c) $0.\dot{5}$

   d) $0.4\dot{7}\dot{1}$

   e) $0.\dot{1}4285\dot{7}$

   f) $0.\dot{2}8571\dot{4}$

   g) $0.\dot{7}1428\dot{5}$

   h) $0.1\dot{8}5714\dot{2}$

3. Find the common ratio of a GP with:

   a) $a = 5$ and $S_\infty = 6$.

   b) $a = 11$ and $S_\infty = 6$.

4. Find the first term of a GP with

   a) $r = \frac{3}{4}$ and $S_\infty = 12$

   b) $r = -\frac{3}{5}$ and $S_\infty = 12$

5. A beetle starts at a point O on the floor. It walks 1 m east, then $\frac{1}{2}$ m west, then $\frac{1}{4}$ m east, then $\frac{1}{8}$ m west and so on. How far away from O does it end up, and how far has it travelled altogether?

6. A 'supa-ball' is thrown upwards from ground level. It hits the ground after 2 seconds and continues to bounce. The time it is in the air for a particular bounce is always 0.8 of the time for the previous bounce. How long does it take for the ball to stop bouncing?

7. A 'supa-ball' is dropped from a height of 1 metre onto a level table. It always rises to a height equal to 0.9 of the height from which it was dropped. How far does it travel in total until it stops bouncing?

8. A frog sits at one end of a table which is 2 m long. In its first jump the frog goes a distance of 1 m along the table, with its second jump $\frac{1}{2}$ m, with its third jump $\frac{1}{4}$ m and so on. After how many jumps will the frog be within 1 cm of the far end of the table?

9. The first term of a GP is $1 - a$, and the second term is $2 - 3a + a^2$. State the range of values of a for which S_∞ exists, and evaluate S_∞ when a is in that range.

10. The positive numbers a, b, c and d are such that a, b and c are in arithmetic progression, while the numbers a, d and c are in geometric progression. Show that $d \leq b$. When is $b = d$?

11*. The first three terms u_1, u_2 and u_3 of a non-constant GP are such that u_2, u_3 and u_1 (note the change of order) are in arithmetic progression. Show that

$$u_2^2 = u_1 u_3 \qquad\qquad 2u_3 = u_1 + u_2$$

Hence determine the common ratio of the GP, and write down its sum to infinity.

12*. For some positive integer m, the first term, the $(m+1)^{\text{st}}$ and the $(3m+1)^{\text{st}}$ terms of a non-constant GP are in arithmetic progression. The GP has a finite sum to infinity. Determine the common ratio, and express the sum to infinity as a multiple of the first term a of the GP. How large must m be to ensure that the sum of infinity is greater than $10a$?

13*. By considering the expression $(1 - x)S$ evaluate the series

$$S = \sum_{n=0}^{\infty} nx^n, \qquad |x| < 1.$$

> ## Chapter 9: Summary
>
> - A sequence can be defined by a specific formula for the nth term, or else by some rule, such as a recurrence relation.
>
> - A sequence u_r is:
>
>   - ★ **periodic** if there exists a positive integer k such that $u_{k+r} = u_r$ for all r,
>   - ★ **increasing** if $u_r \leq u_{r+1}$ for all r, and **decreasing** if $u_r \geq u_{r+1}$ for all r,
>   - ★ **convergent** to the value λ if (roughly) u_r tends to the value λ as r keeps getting bigger,
>   - ★ **divergent** if it is not convergent,
>   - ★ **alternating** if its values are alternately positive and negative.
>
> - A series is the sum of the terms of a sequence. We can use the sigma notation to write the series $u_a + u_{a+1} + \cdots + u_{b-1} + u_b$ in the compact form
>
> $$\sum_{r=a}^{b} u_r, \qquad a \leq b,$$
>
> - An **arithmetic progression** is a sequence u_n where the successive terms differ by a **common difference** d, so that $u_{n+1} = u_n + d$ for all r. The formula for the nth term of an arithmetic progression with common difference d and first term $u_1 = a$ is
>
> $$u_n = a + (n-1)d \, ;$$
>
> the formula for the sum of the first n terms of the arithmetic progression is
>
> $$S_n = \tfrac{1}{2}n\big[2a + (n-1)d\big].$$
>
> Another formula for this sum is $S_n = \tfrac{1}{2}n(a + \ell)$, where ℓ is the last term in the sequence.
>
> - A **geometric progression** is a sequence u_n where the successive terms differ by a **common ratio** r, so that $u_{n+1} = r u_n$ for all n. The formula for the nth term of a geometric progression with common ratio r and starting term $u_1 = a$ is
>
> $$u_n = ar^{n-1} \, ;$$
>
> the formula for the sum of the first n terms of the geometric progression is
>
> $$S_n = \frac{a(r^n - 1)}{r - 1}$$
>
> provided that $r \neq 1$.
>
> - If $|r| < 1$, the infinite series defined by a geometric progression with common ratio r and starting term a is convergent, with infinite sum
>
> $$S_\infty = \sum_{n=1}^{\infty} ar^{n-1} = \frac{a}{1 - r},$$
>
> this sum is called the **sum to infinity** of the series.

1. The functions f, g and h are defined by

$$f(x) = 2x+1, \quad x \in \mathbb{R} \qquad g(x) = x^5, \quad x \in \mathbb{R} \qquad h(x) = \tfrac{1}{x}, \quad x \in \mathbb{R}, x \neq 0$$

Express each of the following in terms of f, g, h as appropriate.

a) $x \mapsto (2x+1)^5$ b) $x \mapsto 4x+3$ c) $x \mapsto x^{\frac{1}{5}}$ d) $x \mapsto 2x^{-5}+1$

e) $x \mapsto \frac{1}{2x^5+1}$ f) $x \mapsto \tfrac{1}{2}(x-1)$ g) $x \mapsto \sqrt[5]{\frac{2}{x^5}+1}$ h) $x \mapsto \frac{2}{x-1}$

2. The functions f and g are defined by

$$f(x) = x^2 + 6x, \quad x \in \mathbb{R} \qquad g(x) = 2x-1, \quad x \in \mathbb{R}$$

Find the two values of x such that $fg(x) = gf(x)$, giving each answer in the form $p + q\sqrt{3}$.

3. The function f is defined by $f(x) = x^2 - 2x + 7$ with domain $x \leq k$. Given that f is a one-to-one function, find the greatest possible value of k and find the inverse function f^{-1}.

4. Functions f and g are defined by

$$f(x) = x^2 + 2x + 3, \quad x \in \mathbb{R} \qquad g(x) = ax + b, \quad x \in \mathbb{R}$$

Given that $fg(x) = x^2 - 48x + 146$ for all x, find the possible values of a and b.

5. Functions f and g are defined by $f(x) = 4x + 5$, $x \in \mathbb{R}$, and $g(x) = 3 - 2x$, $x \in \mathbb{R}$. Find

a) f^{-1} b) g^{-1} c) $f^{-1}g^{-1}$ d) gf e) $(gf)^{-1}$.

6. Functions f and g are defined by $f(x) = 2x + 7$, $x \in \mathbb{R}$, and $g(x) = x^3 - 1$, $x \in \mathbb{R}$. Find

a) f^{-1} b) g^{-1} c) $g^{-1}f^{-1}$ d) $f^{-1}g^{-1}$
e) fg f) gf g) $(fg)^{-1}$ h) $(gf)^{-1}$

7. Given the function $f(x) = 10 - x$, $x \in \mathbb{R}$, evaluate

a) $f(7)$ b) $f^{(2)}(7)$ c) $f^{(15)}(7)$ d) $f^{(100)}(7)$
As usual, $f^{(2)}$ denotes ff, $f^{(3)}$ denotes fff, and so on.

8. Given the function $f(x) = \frac{x+5}{2x-1}$, $x \in \mathbb{R}, x \neq \tfrac{1}{2}$, find

a) $f^{(2)}(x)$ b) $f^{(3)}(x)$ c) $f^{(4)}(x)$ d) $f^{(10)}(x)$ e) $f^{(351)}(x)$

9. Given the function $f(x) = \frac{2x-4}{x}$, $x \in \mathbb{R}, x \neq 0, 2$, find

a) $f^{(2)}(x)$ b) $f^{-1}(x)$ c) $f^{(3)}(x)$
d) $f^{(4)}(x)$ e) $f^{(12)}(x)$ f) $f^{(82)}(x)$.

10. Show that a function of the form $f(x) = \frac{x+a}{x-1}$, $x \in \mathbb{R}, x \neq 1$, is self-inverse for all values of the constant a.

11. Functions f and g are defined by

$$f(x) = 2x^2 - 5, \quad x \in \mathbb{R} \qquad\qquad g(x) = 7x - 9, \quad x \in \mathbb{R}$$

Solve the equation $f(x) = g^{-1}(12)$.

12. The function f with domain $x \in \mathbb{R}, x \geq 0$ is defined by $f(x) = \frac{16}{(x+3)^2}$.

    a) What is the range of f?

    b) Identify the function f^{-1}.

    c) Find the value of x for which $f(x) = f^{-1}(x)$.

13. Two circles C_1 and C_2 have equations

$$x^2 + y^2 + 2x - 4y + 1 = 0 \qquad\qquad x^2 + y^2 - 4x - 12y = 9$$

respectively.

    a) Find the radii of C_1 and C_2.

    b) Find the distance between the centres of C_1 and C_2.

    c) Explain why C_1 and C_2 touch each other, and find the coordinates of the point of contact X.

14. Determine the coordinates of the centre C and the radius of the circle with equation

$$x^2 + y^2 - 6x + 10y + 18 = 0$$

If Q is the point with coordinates $(-1, 3)$, what is the distance QC? Find the length of the tangents from Q to the circle.

15. The circle C has equation

$$x^2 + y^2 - 20x - 40y + 490 = 0$$

    a) Find the radius of C and the coordinates of its centre.

    b) There are two lines passing through the origin which are tangent to C. Find the equations of these lines, and the coordinates of the points of tangency with C.

    c) Find the distance between the two points of tangency.

16. The points U, V, W have coordinates $(4, 5)$, $(0, -7)$ and $(12, -3)$ respectively.

    a) Find the equation of the perpendicular bisector of UV.

    b) The circle passing through all three points U, V, W has centre C. Find the coordinates of C and the radius of the circle.

    c) Calculate the area of the smaller segment of the circle cut off by the chord UV.

17. A circle S has centre at the point $(3, 1)$ and passes through the point $(0, 5)$.

    a) Find the radius of S and hence write down its Cartesian equation.

    b)   i. Determine the two points on S where the y-coordinate is twice the x-coordinate.

        ii. Calculate the length of the minor arc joining these two points.   (CIE)

18. A sector AOB of a circle has radius r cm and the angle $\angle AOB$ is θ radians. The perimeter of the sector is 40 cm and its area is 100 cm^2.

    a) Write down equations for the perimeter and area of the sector in terms of r and θ.

    b) Use your equations to show that $r^2 - 20r + 100 = 0$, and hence find the value of r and of θ.   (CIE)

19. The diagram shows a sector of a circle with centre O and radius 6 cm.
Angle $\angle POQ = 0.6$. Calculate the length of arc PQ and the area of sector POQ.

    (OCR)

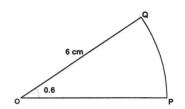

20. A sector OAB of a circle, of radius a and centre O, has $\angle AOB = \theta$. Given that the area of the sector OAB is twice the square of the length of the arc AB, find θ.

    (OCR)

21. The diagram shows a sector of a circle, with centre O and radius r. The length of the arc is equal to half the perimeter of the sector. Find the area of the sector in terms of r.

    (OCR)

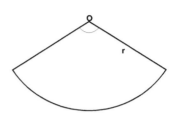

22. The diagram shows two circles, with centres A and B, intersecting at C and D in such a way that the centre of each lies on the circumference of the other. The radius of each circle is 1 unit. Write down theze of angle $\angle CAD$ and calculate the area of the shaded region (bounded by the arc CBD and the straight line CD). Hence show that the area of the region common to the interiors of the two circles is approximately 39% of the area of one circle.

    (OCR)

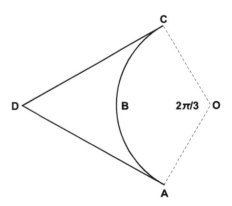

23. In the diagram, ABC is an arc of a circle with centre O and radius 5 cm. The lines AD and CD are tangents to the circle at A and Crespectively. Angle $\angle AOC = \frac{2}{3}\pi$.
Calculate the area of the region enclosed by AD, DC and the arc ABC, giving your answer correct to 3 significant figures.

    (OCR)

24. The diagram shows a semicircle ABC with centre O and radius 6 cm. The point B is such that $\angle BOA = \frac{1}{2}\pi$, and BD is an arc of a circle with centre A. Find

    a) the length of the arc AD,

    b) the area of the shaded region.

    (CIE)

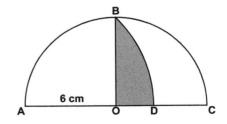

25. A sequence is defined inductively by $u_{r+1} = 3u_r - 1$ and $u_0 = c$.

    a) Find the first five terms of the sequence if (i) $c = 1$, (ii) $c = 2$, (iii) $c = 0$, (iv) $c = \frac{1}{2}$.

    b) Show that, for each of the values of c in part (a), the terms of the sequence are given by the formula $u_r = \frac{1}{2} + b \times 3^r$ for some value of b.

    c) Show that the formula for u_r given in (b) satisfies the recurrence relation defining the sequence.

26. The sequence $u_1, u_2, u_3,...$, where u_1 is a given real number, is defined by $u_{n+1} = \sqrt{(4 - u_n)^2}$.

    a) Given that $u_1 = 1$, evaluate u_2, u_3 and u_4, and describe the behaviour of the sequence.

    b) Given alternatively that $u_1 = 6$, describe the behaviour of the sequence.

    c) For what value of u_1 will all the terms of the sequence be equal to each other?   (OCR, adapt.)

27. The sequence $u_1, u_2, u_3,...$, where u_1 is a given real number, is defined by $u_{n+1} = u_n^2 - 1$.

    a) Describe the behaviour of the sequence for each of the cases $u_1 = 0$, $u_1 = 1$ and $u_1 = 2$.

    b) Given that $u_2 = u_1$, find exactly the two possible values of u_1.

    c) Given that $u_3 = u_1$, show that $u_1^4 - 2u_1^2 - u_1 = 0$. Hence find exactly the four possible values of u_1 in this case.   (OCR, adapt.)

28. The rth term of an arithmetic progression is $1 + 4r$. Find, in terms of n, the sum of the first n terms of the progression.   (OCR)

29. The sum of the first two terms of an arithmetic progression is 18 and the sum of the first four terms is 52. Find the sum of the first eight terms.   (OCR)

30. The sum of the first twenty terms of an arithmetic progression is 50, and the sum of the next twenty terms is -50. Find the sum of the first hundred terms of the progression.   (OCR)

31. An AP has first term a and common difference -1. The sum of the first n terms is equal to the sum of the first $3n$ terms. Express a in terms of n.   (OCR)

32. Find the sum of the arithmetic progression $1, 4, 7, 10, 13, 16, \ldots, 1000$.

    Every third term of the above progression (i.e. $7, 16$, etc.) is removed. Find the sum of the remaining terms.   (OCR)

33. The sum of the first hundred terms of an arithmetic progression with first term a and common difference d is T. The sum of the first 50 odd-numbered terms (the 1st, 3rd, 5th, ..., 99th) is $\frac{1}{2}T - 1000$. Find the value of d.   (OCR)

34. Three sequences are defined inductively by

    a) $u_0 = 0$ and $u_{r+1} = u_r + (2r + 1)$,

    b) $u_0 = 0$, $u_1 = 1$ and $u_{r+1} = 2u_r - u_{r-1}$ for $r \geq 1$,

    c) $u_0 = 1$, $u_1 = 2$ and $u_{r+1} = 3u_r - 2u_{r-1}$ for $r \geq 1$.

    For each sequence calculate the first few terms, and suggest a formula for u_r. Check that the formula you have suggested does in fact satisfy all parts of the definition.

35. In a geometric progression, the fifth term is 100 and the seventh term is 400. Find the first term.

36. The nth term of a sequence is ar^{n-1}, where a and r are constants. The first term is 3 and the second term is $-\frac{3}{4}$. Find the values of a and r.

    Hence find the sum of the first n terms of the sequence.

37. A geometric series has first term 1 and common ratio r. Given that the sum to infinity of the series is 5, find the value of r.

    Find the least value of n for which the sum of the first n terms of the series exceeds 4.9.

38. In a geometric series, the first term is 12 and the fourth term is $-\frac{3}{2}$. Find the sum, S_n, of the first n terms of the series.

    Find the sum to infinity, S_∞, of the series and the least value of n for which the magnitude of the difference between S_n and S_∞ is less than 0.001.

39. A geometric series has non-zero first term a and common ratio r, where $0 < r < 1$. Given that the sum of the first 8 terms of the series is equal to half the sum to infinity, find the value of r, correct to 3 decimal places. Given also that the 17th term of the series is 10, find a.

40. A geometric series G has positive first term a, common ratio r and sum to infinity S. The sum to infinity of the even-numbered terms of G (the $2^{\text{nd}}, 4^{\text{th}}, 6^{\text{th}}, \ldots$ terms) is $-\frac{1}{2}S$. Find the value of r.

    a) Given that the third term of G is 2, show that the sum to infinity of the odd-numbered terms of G (the $1^{\text{st}}, 3^{\text{rd}}, 5^{\text{th}}, \ldots$ terms) is $\frac{81}{4}$.

    b) In another geometric series H, each term is the modulus of the corresponding term of G. Show that the sum to infinity of H is $2S$.

41. An infinite geometric series has first term a and sum to infinity b, where $b \neq 0$. Prove that a lies between 0 and $2b$.

42. The sum of the infinite geometric series $1 + r + r^2 + \cdots$ is k times the sum of the series $1 - r + r^2 - \cdots$, where $k > 0$. Express r in terms of k.

43. Find the sum of the geometric series

    $$(1 - x) + (x^3 - x^4) + (x^6 - x^7) + \cdots + (x^{3n} - x^{3n+1}).$$

    Hence show that the sum of the infinite series $1 - x + x^3 - x^4 + x^6 - x^7 + \cdots$ is equal to $\frac{1}{1+x+x^2}$, and state the values of x for which this is valid.

    Use a similar method to find the sum of the infinite series $1 - x + x^5 - x^6 + x^{10} - x^{11} + \cdots$.

44. Peter borrows £5000 from his bank. He is charged 5% interest on his loan annually and, at the end of each year, he pays an amount £a in an attempt to reduce his debt. If the amount that Peter owes the bank after n years is £u_n, explain why u_n satisfies the recurrence relation

    $$u_{n+1} = 1.05u_n - a, \qquad u_0 = 5000.$$

    a) Find the value of the constant b such that the recurrence relation for u_n can be written in the form

    $$\left(u_{n+1} - b\right) = 1.05(u_n - b).$$

    b) What value of a will mean that Peter never reduces his debt, but always owes the bank £5000 at the end of each year?

    c) Find a formula for u_n in terms of n and b.

    d) Peter decides to repay £500 each year. How many years does it take him to clear his debt?

45. The first three terms of a GP are 1, p and q. Given that p, 6 and q are the first three terms of an AP, show that
    $$p^2 + p - 12 = 0$$
    and hence find the possible values of p and q.

46*. Let $f(x) = x^2 + px + q$ and $g(x) = x^2 + rx + s$. Find an expression for $fg(x)$ and hence find a necessary and sufficient condition on a, b and c for it to be possible to write the quartic expression $x^4 + ax^3 + bx^2 + cx + d$ in the form $fg(x)$, for some choice of p, q, r and s.

    Show further that this condition holds exactly when it is possible to write the quartic expression $x^4 + ax^3 + bx^2 + cx + d$ in the form $(x^2 + ux + v)^2 - k$ for some choice of values for u, v and k.

    Find the real roots of the quartic equation $x^4 - 4x^3 + 10x^2 - 12x + 4 = 0$.   (STEP)

47*.   a) The point A has coordinates $(5, 16)$ and the point B has coordinates $(-4, 4)$. The variable point P has coordinates (x, y) and moves on a path such that $AP = 2BP$. Show that the Cartesian equation of the path of P is

$$(x + 7)^2 + y^2 = 100.$$

b) The point C has coordinates $(a, 0)$ and the point D has coordinates $(b, 0)$. The variable point Q moves on a path such that

$$QC = k \times QD,$$

where $k > 1$. Given that the path of Q is the same as the path of P, show that

$$\frac{a + 7}{b + 7} = \frac{a^2 + 51}{b^2 + 51}.$$

Show further that $(a + 7)(b + 7) = 100$, in the case that $a \neq b$.   (STEP)

48*. The n positive numbers $x_1, x_2, \ldots, x_n$, where $n \geq 3$, satisfy

$$x_1 = 1 + x_2^{-1}, \qquad x_2 = 1 + x_3^{-1}, \qquad \cdots, \qquad x_{n-1} = 1 + x_n^{-1},$$

and also

$$x_n = 1 + x_1^{-1}.$$

Show that:

a) $x_1, x_2, \ldots, x_n > 1$,

b) $x_1 - x_2 = -\frac{x_2 - x_3}{x_2 x_3}$,

c) $x_1 = x_2 = \cdots = x_n$.

Hence find the value of x_1.   (STEP)

The Binomial Theorem

In this chapter we will learn:

- to use the binomial expansion of $(a + b)^n$ where n is a positive integer,

- to use the infinite binomial expansion of $(1 + x)^n$ where n is a rational number and $|x| < 1$, adapting this method to be able to handle expressions of the form $(a + bx)^n$ and know the range of values of x for which this expression is valid.

10.1 Expanding $(x + y)^n$

The Binomial Theorem enables us to calculate $(x + y)^n$ quickly and easily, thereby enabling us to perform more complex calculations than hitherto. It is useful to start by looking at this expression for small values of n.

These are:

$$
\begin{aligned}
(x+y)^2 &= (x+y)(x+y) = x^2 + 2xy + y^2 \\
(x+y)^3 &= (x+y)(x+y)^2 = (x+y)(x^2 + 2xy + y^2) \\
&= \begin{array}{ccccccc} x^3 &+& 2x^2y &+& xy^2 \\ &+& x^2y &+& 2xy^2 &+& y^3 \end{array} \\
&= x^3 \;+\; 3x^2y \;+\; 3xy^2 \;+\; y^3 \\
(x+y)^4 &= (x+y)(x+y)^3 = (x+y)(x^3 + 3x^2y + 3xy^2 + y^3) \\
&= \begin{array}{ccccccccc} x^4 &+& 3x^3y &+& 3x^2y^2 &+& xy^3 \\ &+& x^3y &+& 3x^2y^2 &+& 3xy^3 &+& y^4 \end{array} \\
&= x^4 \;+\; 4x^3y \;+\; 6x^2y^2 \;+\; 4xy^3 \;+\; y^4
\end{aligned}
$$

These results can be summarised as follows. Key parts of the expansions have been written in bold type:

$$
\begin{aligned}
(x+y)^1 &= \mathbf{1}x + \mathbf{1}y \\
(x+y)^2 &= \mathbf{1}x^2 + \mathbf{2}xy + \mathbf{1}y^2 \\
(x+y)^3 &= \mathbf{1}x^3 + \mathbf{3}x^2y + \mathbf{3}xy^2 + \mathbf{1}y^3 \\
(x+y)^4 &= \mathbf{1}x^4 + \mathbf{4}x^3y + \mathbf{6}x^2y^2 + \mathbf{4}xy^3 + \mathbf{1}y^4
\end{aligned}
$$

Study the expansion of $(x + y)^n$ carefully. Notice how the powers start from the left with x^n. The powers of x then successively reduce by 1 with each term, while at the same time the powers of y increase by 1 until reaching the term y^n. Also note that the coefficients that appear in these expansions are part of a very important pattern, called **Pascal's triangle:**

The important thing to note about Pascal's triangle is that (almost) every number in it is obtained very simply by adding together the two numbers immediately above it in the preceding row. Thus the number 10 in Row 5 is obtained by adding together the numbers 6 and 4 above it in Row 4, while the number 4 in Row 4 is obtained by adding together the numbers 1 and 3 above it in Row 3.

The only exceptions to this rule are the numbers at the end of the triangle. These are all equal to 1, and (except for the number 1 in Row 0) each only have one number (equal to 1) above them in the preceding Row.

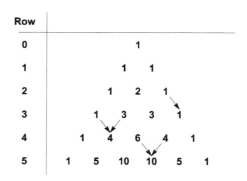

Figure 10.1

It is therefore easy to predict the next row of Pascal's triangle:

$$1 \quad 6 \quad 15 \quad 20 \quad 15 \quad 6 \quad 1$$

and hence the expansions of $(x+y)^5$ and $(x+y)^6$:

$$
\begin{aligned}
(x+y)^5 &= x^5 + 5x^4y + 10x^3y^3 + 10x^2y^3 + 5xy^4 + y^5 \\
(x+y)^6 &= x^6 + 6x^5y + 15x^4y^2 + 20x^3y^3 + 15x^2y^4 + 6xy^5 + y^6
\end{aligned}
$$

Example 10.1.1. *Write down the expansion of $(1+y)^7$.*

Use the next row of Pascal's triangle, continuing the pattern of powers and replacing x by 1:

$$
\begin{aligned}
(1+y)^7 &= (1)^7 + 7(1)^6y + 21(1)^5y^2 + 35(1)^4y^3 + 35(1)^3y^4 + 21(1)^2y^5 + 7(1)y^6 + y^6 \\
&= 1 + 7y + 21y^2 + 35y^3 + 35y^4 + 21y^5 + 7y^6 + y^7
\end{aligned}
$$

Example 10.1.2. *Multiply out the brackets in the expression $(2x+3)^4$.*

Adjusting the expansion of $(x+y)^4$,

$$
\begin{aligned}
(2x+3)^4 &= (2x)^4 + 4 \times (2x)^3 \times 3 + 6 \times (2x)^2 \times 3^2 + 4 \times (2x) \times 3^3 + 3^4 \\
&= 16x^4 + 96x^3 + 216x^2 + 216x + 81
\end{aligned}
$$

Example 10.1.3. *Expand $(x^2+2)^3$.*

This time

$$(x^2+2)^3 = (x^2)^3 + 3 \times (x^2)^2 \times 2 + 3 \times x^2 \times 2^2 + 2^3 = x^6 + 6x^4 + 12x^2 + 8.$$

Example 10.1.4. *Find the coefficient of x^3 in the expansion of $(3x-4)^5$.*

The coefficient of x^3 will be obtained from the term involving $(3x)^3 \times (-4)^2$, which is the third in the list of terms to be found in the expansion of $(3x-4)^5$. Thus the coefficient of this term in the expansion is 10. The term in x^3 is thus

$$10 \times (3x)^3 \times (-4)^2 = 4320x^3$$

and so the coefficient of x^3 is 4320.

Example 10.1.5. *Expand $(1+2x+3x^2)^3$.*

To use our new method, we need to consider $1+2x+3x^2$ as a sum of two terms, rather than of three. This is simply done by adding a bracket, so that

$$(1+2x+3x^2)^3 = \left(1+(2x+3x^2)\right)^3 = 1 + 3(2x+3x^2) + 3(2x+3x^2)^2 + (2x+3x^2)^3$$

We can now expand each of the new bracketed terms:

$$
\begin{aligned}
(1 + 2x + 3x^2) &= 1 + 3(2x + 3x^2) + 3\left[(2x)^2 + 2(2x)(3x^2) + (3x^2)^2\right] \\
&\quad + \left[(2x)^3 + 3(2x)^2(3x^2) + 3(2x)(3x^2)^2 + (3x^2)^3\right] \\
&= 1 + (6x + 9x^2) + (12x^2 + 36x^3 + 27x^4) + (8x^3 + 36x^4 + 54x^5 + 27x^6) \\
&= 1 + 6x + 21x^2 + 44x^3 + 63x^4 + 54x^5 + 27x^6
\end{aligned}
$$

Alternatively, we could have written

$$
(1 + 2x + 3x^2)^3 = \left((1 + 2x) + 3x^2\right)^3 = (1 + 2x)^3 + 3(1 + 2x)^2(3x^2) + 3(1 + 2x)(3x^2)^2 + (3x^2)^3
$$

and expanded these brackets to obtain the same result.

EXERCISE 10A

1. Write down the expansion of each of the following.

   a) $(2x + y)^2$
   b) $(5x + 3y)^2$
   c) $(4 + 7p)^2$
   d) $(1 - 8t)^2$
   e) $(1 - 5x^2)^2$
   f) $(2 + x^3)^2$
   g) $(x^2 + y^3)^3$
   h) $(x^2 + 2y^3)^3$

2. Write down the expansion of each of the following.

   a) $(x + 2)^3$
   b) $(2p + 3q)^3$
   c) $(1 - 4x)^3$
   d) $(1 - x^3)^3$

3. Find the coefficient of x in the expansion of

   a) $(3x + 7)^2$
   b) $(2x + 5)^3$

4. Find the coefficient of x^2 in the expansion of

   a) $(4x + 5)^3$
   b) $(1 - 3x)^4$

5. Expand each of the following expressions.

   a) $(1 + 2x)^5$
   b) $(p + 2q)^6$
   c) $(2m - 3n)^4$
   d) $\left(1 + \frac{1}{2}x\right)^4$

6. Find the coefficient of x^3 in the expansion of

   a) $(1 + 3x)^5$
   b) $(2 - 5x)^4$

7. Expand $(1 + x + 2x^2)^2$. Check your answer by testing your answer for $x = 1$ and $x = 2$.

8. Write down the expansion of $(x + 4)^3$ and hence expand $(x + 1)(x + 4)^3$.

9. Expand $(3x + 2)^2(2x + 3)^3$.

10. In the expansion of $(1 + ax)^4$, the coefficient of x^3 is 1372. Find the constant a.

11. In the expansion of $(a + bx)^3$, the coefficient of x^2 is 60. In the expansion of $(b - ax)^5$, the coefficient of x^3 is -5000. What are the values of a and b?

12. In the expansion of $(a + bx)^4$, the coefficient of x^2 is 24. What is the coefficient of x^4 in $(a + bx)^8$?

13*. Expand $(x + y)^{11}$.

14*. Find the coefficient of $x^6 y^6$ in the expansion of $(2x + y)^{12}$.

10.2 The Factorial Function

Before studying Pascal's triangle in greater detail, we must introduce a very important function, called the **factorial** function. We will frequently meet products like

$$
3 \times 2 \times 1 \qquad \text{or} \qquad 7 \times 6 \times 5 \times 4 \times 3 \times 2 \times 1
$$

and it is useful to have a compact notation for these expressions.

> **Key Fact 10.1** The Factorial Function
>
> For any positive integer n, the integer obtained by multiplying together all the integers from 1 to n inclusive is written $n!$, and called n **factorial**:
>
> $$n! = 1 \times 2 \times 3 \times \cdots \times n, \qquad n \in \mathbb{N}.$$
>
> For reasons of convenience, we shall also define
>
> $$0! = 1.$$

Of course, it is not possible to 'multiply together all the positive integers from 1 to 0 inclusive' (without going backwards instead of forwards), and so this definition of 0! seems strange, to say the least. However there is a much more complicated function, called the **Gamma function $\Gamma(\mathbf{x})$**, which is defined for all positive real numbers x, such that $\Gamma(n+1) = n!$ for all $n \in \mathbb{N}$ and with $\Gamma(1) = 1$. Mathematicians therefore regard the factorial function as a special case of the Gamma function, and so writing $0! = \Gamma(1) = 1$ is perfectly natural, except when we try to understand the factorial function in terms of the definition given above.

The factorials of integers become very big extremely quickly: 1, 2, 6, 24, 120, 720, 5040, 40320, 362880, 3628800 being the first ten. Your calculators probably have a button to calculate factorials, but it can only be used cautiously. Since $14! > 10^{10}$, most calculators can only calculate up to 13! exactly. Beyond that, it does not take long to exceed a standard calculator's capacity. Since

$$69! = 1.7112 \times 10^{98} \qquad 70! = 1.1979 \times 10^{100}$$

most calculators will baulk at evaluating factorials for integers greater than 69.

10.3 The Binomial Coefficients

Pascal's triangle is a useful way of finding the coefficients in the expansion of $(x+y)^n$, but there would be a great deal of effort involved in using it to expand $(x+y)^{100}$, or in determining the coefficient of x^6 in $(2+3x)^{50}$. We need to develop a greater understanding of the patterns in Pascal's triangle to be able to handle such problems easily.

There certainly are patterns to be found in Pascal's triangle. Inspecting Figure 10.1 shows us that:

- the 'first' diagonal (starting at the top and running down the right-hand side of the triangle) yields a constant sequence of 1s,

- the 'second' diagonal (heading down the triangle parallel to the first diagonal, but one layer in) is the sequence $1, 2, 3, 4, \ldots$ of natural numbers,

- the 'third' diagonal (one level further in) yields the triangular numbers.

It is also possible to find powers of 2 and the Fibonacci numbers in the triangle. To be able to find these sequences, and to understand the triangle fully, we need to be able to express all the coefficients in the triangle algebraically. Now that we have the factorial function, this is possible.

There are $n+1$ numbers in the nth row of Pascal's triangle. It is convenient to count these numbers, starting at 0; the $n+1$ numbers will be referred to as the 0th, the 1st, the 2nd, and so on, up to the nth. The above comments about the diagonals of Pascal's triangle can be restated as follows:

- The 0th element of the nth row is 1 for all $n \geq 1$.

- The 1st element of the nth row is n for all $n \geq 1$.

- The 2nd element of the nth row is $\frac{1}{2}n(n-1)$ for all $n \geq 2$.

These formulae are all special cases of this general result:

Key Fact 10.2 The Binomial Coefficients

The mth element of the nth row of Pascal's triangle is denoted either as $\binom{n}{m}$ or as ^nC_m.

It is equal to

$$\binom{n}{m} = {}^nC_m = \frac{n!}{m!(n-m)!}, \qquad 0 \le m \le n.$$

The entries in Pascal's triangle are known collectively as the **Binomial coefficients**.

Example 10.3.1. *Calculate* $^6C_3$ *and* $\binom{7}{0}$

We see that

$$^6C_3 = \frac{6!}{3! \times 3!} = \frac{720}{6 \times 6} = 20 \qquad \binom{7}{0} = \frac{7!}{0! \times 7!} = 1.$$

Notice how the definition of 0! as 1 enables us to use this formula for the Binomial coefficients for $m = 0$ and n (at the edges of the triangle) as well as for $1 \le m \le n$ (inside the triangle).

Example 10.3.2. *Show that* $^nC_1 = n$ *for all* $n \ge 1$ *and that* $^nC_2 = \frac{1}{2}n(n-1)$ *for all* $n \ge 2$.

This time

$$^nC_1 = \frac{n!}{1!(n-1)!} = \frac{n \times (n-1)!}{(n-1)!} = n$$

$$^nC_2 = \frac{n!}{2!(n-2)!} = \frac{n \times (n-1) \times (n-2)!}{2 \times (n-2)!} = \frac{1}{2}n(n-1)$$

as required.

For large numbers, it might be easier to expand the Binomial coefficient than just to calculate the factorials.

Example 10.3.3. *Evaluate* $^{150}C_4$.

We cannot calculate 150! using our calculators, but we can write

$$^{150}C_4 = \frac{150!}{4! \times 146!} = \frac{150 \times 149 \times 148 \times 147}{24} = 20260275.$$

Of course, many calculators have a button which will calculate Binomial coefficients directly! Look for the button, more often labelled nCr.

EXERCISE 10B

---

1. Find the value of each of the following.

   a) $\binom{7}{3}$ b) $\binom{8}{6}$ c) $\binom{9}{5}$ d) $\binom{13}{4}$

   e) $\binom{6}{4}$ f) $\binom{10}{2}$ g) $\binom{11}{10}$ h) $\binom{50}{2}$

2. Find the value of each of the following:

   a) $^{12}C_9$ b) $^5C_3$ c) $^{17}C_3$ d) $^{20}C_{18}$
   e) $^{100}C_{97}$ f) $^{80}C_5$ g) $^{20}C_{15}$ h) $^{30}C_{15}$

3. Show that $^nC_3 = \frac{1}{6}n(n-1)(n-2)$.

4. Explain why $\binom{n}{m} = \binom{n}{n-m}$ for $0 \le m \le n$.

5. Show that $^{n+1}C_2 + {}^nC_2 = n^2$ for all $n \ge 2$, and that $^{n+2}C_3 - {}^nC_3 = n^2$ for all $n \ge 3$.

6. show that $(n+1)\binom{n}{r} = (r+1)\binom{n+1}{r+1}$ for all $0 \le r \le n$.

7*. What is the value of $^nC_0 + {}^nC_1 + \cdots + {}^nC_{n-1} + {}^nC_n$ for any $n \ge 0$?

10.4 Why the Formula Works

Although not necessary at this stage, it is worthwhile taking some time to understand why this formula works! This can be done in two different ways.

Example 10.4.1. *Show that* $\binom{n+1}{m+1} = \binom{n}{m} + \binom{n}{m+1}$ *for all* $0 \le m \le n-1$.

Using the formulae for the Binomial coefficients, and putting the fractions over a common denominator, we see that

$$\binom{n}{m} + \binom{n}{m+1} = \frac{n!}{m!(n-m)!} + \frac{n!}{(m+1)!(n-m-1)!}$$

$$= \frac{n!}{(m+1)!(n-m)!}\Big[(m+1) + (n-m)\Big] = \frac{n!}{(m+1)!(n-m)!} \times (n+1)$$

$$= \frac{(n+1)!}{(m+1)!(n-m)!} = \binom{n+1}{m+1}$$

The vital importance of this identity is to note that the two numbers in Pascal's triangle immediately above the $(m+1)^{\text{th}}$ element in the $(n+1)^{\text{st}}$ row are the mth and the $(m+1)^{\text{st}}$ (the diagram shows the first few rows of Pascal's triangle, with the appropriate numbering of the row elements shown in red). The identity in the above example tells us that the Binomial coefficients obey the defining property of Pascal's triangle. Since the Binomial coefficients $\binom{n}{0} = \binom{n}{n} = 1$, we see that the Binomial coefficients are indeed the correct entries in Pascal's triangle on the edges. Putting these two ideas together, we deduce that the formula for $\binom{n}{m}$ is indeed the correct one for the mth entry in the mth row of the triangle.

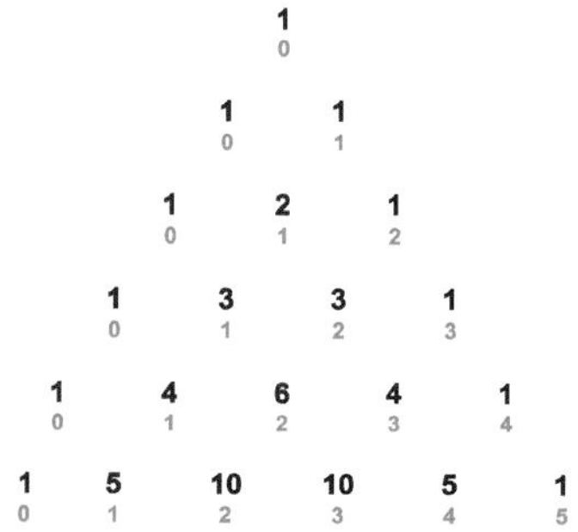

$$
\begin{array}{ccccccccccc}
 & & & & & 1 & & & & & \\
 & & & & & 0 & & & & & \\
 & & & & 1 & & 1 & & & & \\
 & & & & 0 & & 1 & & & & \\
 & & & 1 & & 2 & & 1 & & & \\
 & & & 0 & & 1 & & 2 & & & \\
 & & 1 & & 3 & & 3 & & 1 & & \\
 & & 0 & & 1 & & 2 & & 3 & & \\
 & 1 & & 4 & & 6 & & 4 & & 1 & \\
 & 0 & & 1 & & 2 & & 3 & & 4 & \\
1 & & 5 & & 10 & & 10 & & 5 & & 1 \\
0 & & 1 & & 2 & & 3 & & 4 & & 5 \\
\end{array}
$$

Figure 10.2

While these calculations show that the formula for the Binomial coefficients is correct, it does not explain where that formula came from. Why should anyone expect that the formula for these coefficients should work? To explain this, we need to think about Pascal's triangle in a different manner.

A familiar fairground game, or child's toy, consists of a triangular array of pins nailed into a sloping board. A marble is fed into the slot at the top, hitting the top pin, and makes it ways through the row of pins to one of the lots at the bottom of the game. Each time it hits a pin, it bounces off it, either to left or to right, and lands on the top of one of the two pins immediately below it in the next row. It then bounces off that pin, and so on. The amount that the player wins (or loses) depends on which slot the marble reaches. The winning slots are the ones on the outside, while the middle slots are losing ones. Before we play the game, we might want to know how much more likely it is for the marble to land in a winning slot as opposed to a losing slot.

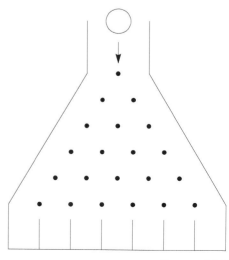

Figure 10.3

The marble must start at the top pin. There is exactly one way for it to reach either of the pins in the row below (it can drop either to the left or the right of the first pin). There is exactly 1 route for the marble to reach the left-hand pin in the next row (dropping to the left of both of the previous pins it reached) and, similarly, 1 route for the marble to reach the right-hand pin in that row. However, there are 2 routes whereby the marble can reach the middle of the three pins in that row (it can drop to the left, then to the right, of the two pins it meets, or else it can first drop to the right, then to the left. Similarly, we see that there are 1, 3, 3 and 1 routes whereby the marble can reach the four pins in the row below (for example, there is 1 route to this pin via the left-hand pin in the row above, and 2 routes to this pin via the middle pin of the row above, making 3 routes in all.

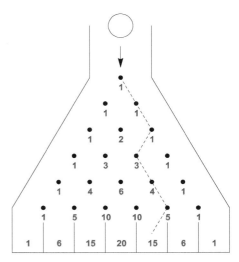

Figure 10.4

It is clear that the number of routes that reach a particular pin is equal to the sum of the numbers of routes that reach the two pins immediately above it (or, in the case of a pin on the edge, the number of routes that reach the single pin above it). This is precisely the rule for determining the values in Pascal's triangle, and so the number of routes that reach any pin, and (ultimately) the final slots is determined by that pin's (or slot's) position in Pascal's triangle. One of the 15 routes whereby the marble can reach the fifth slot at the bottom is shown. If we assume that it is equally likely for the marble to drop to the left or to the right of each pin, then we would deduce that it is 20 times as likely for the marble to end in the middle slot at the bottom as in either of the outside slots.

This mhanicsechanistic view of Pascal's triangle gives us an insight from which we can obtain a formula to calculate all the coefficients in the triangle. We have seen that the number of routes into the different slots at the bottom of our version of the game are given by the numbers $1, 6, 15, 20, 15, 6, 1$ of the 6th row of Pascal's triangle.

If we extended the game so that there were an unlimited number of rows of pins, we could generalise our ideas as follows:

- The number of routes that lead to pin number m in Row n is equal to the Binomial coefficient ^nC_m for any $0 \leq m \leq n$.

- Every time the marble drops to the left of a pin, the number of the pin it next meets is the same as the number of the pin it just left (see Figure 10.2). Every time the marble drops to the right of a pin, the number of the pin it next meets increases by 1.

- Every route that leads to pin number m in Row n involves the marble dropping to the right of a pin m times, and dropping to the left of a pin $n - m$ times.

Thus the Binomial coefficient ^nC_m is equal to the number of ways of choosing m elements from the set $\{0, 1, 2, \ldots, n-1\}$ of n numbers (these m numbers will then be the numbers of the rows in which the marble drops to the right of the pin it meets in that row). Imagine putting the n numbers $0, 1, \ldots, n-1$ into a bag, and drawing m of them out, one at a time. There are n numbers that can be drawn first, then $n-1$ that can be drawn second, then $n-2$ that can be draw third, and so on. By the time we draw the mth number, there are just $n - m + 1$ left to choose from. It would seem that there are

$$n \times (n-1) \times (n-2) \times \cdots \times (n-m+1) = \frac{n!}{(n-m)!}$$

ways in which m numbers can be drawn out of the bag.

But we do not actually care about the order in which the balls are taken out of the bag; if we drew the numbers $0, 2, 3$ (so that the marble drops to the right at the pins in the zeroth, second and third rows), we would obtain the same route if we had chosen these numbers in the order $3, 0, 2$ instead. For our purposes, the order in which the m numbers are chosen is irrelevant. It is easy to see that there are $m!$ orders in which the m numbers can appear, and so we need to divide our previous result for the number of routes by $m!$ to get the correct answer. Thus we have shown that

$$\binom{n}{m} = {^nC_m} = \frac{n!}{m!(n-m)!}, \qquad 0 \leq m \leq n.$$

as required.

We shall return to this sort of argument much later, when we consider the topic of Combinatorics in Chapter 30

It is a remarkable fact that the formula for the Binomial coefficient ^nC_m always produces an integer. It is not obvious, at first sight, that $n!$ should always be divisible by $m!(n-m)!$ for any $0 \le m \le n$. Certainly both $m!$ and $(n-m)!$ divide $n!$, but the fact that they both do is a little unexpected.

Example 10.4.2. *Explain why the product of any 7 consecutive positive integers is divisible by 5040.*

If the 7 consecutive positive integers are $n+1, n+2, \ldots, n+7$, then their product is

$$(n+1) \times (n+2) \times \cdots \times (n+7) = \frac{(n+7)!}{n!} = \binom{n+7}{n} \times 7! = 5040\binom{n+7}{n}$$

which is a multiple of 5040.

10.5 The Binomial Theorem

Putting the various ideas discussed in this Chapter together, we obtain the Binomial Theorem:

Key Fact 10.3 The Binomial Theorem

For any positive integer n, the following expansion holds:

$$(x+y)^n = \sum_{m=0}^{n} \binom{n}{m}x^{n-m}y^m = x^n + \binom{n}{1}x^{n-1}y + \binom{n}{2}x^{n-2}y^2 + \cdots + \binom{n}{n-1}xy^{n-1} + y^n$$

This theorem enables us to consider much larger indices n, and also enables us to focus on small parts of the expansion, without the need to calculate large numbers of intermediate steps.

Example 10.5.1. *Expand* $(2-3x)^7$.

Without needing to refer to Pascal's triangle, we calculate

$$
\begin{aligned}
(2-3x)^7 &= 2^7 + {}^7C_1 \times 2^6 \times (-3x) + {}^7C_2 \times 2^5 \times (-3x)^2 + {}^7C_3 \times 2^4 \times (-3x)^3 \\
&\quad + {}^7C_4 \times 2^3 \times (-3x)^4 + {}^7C_5 \times 2^2 \times (-3x)^5 + {}^7C_6 \times 2 \times (-3x)^6 + (-3x)^7 \\
&= 128 + 7 \times (-192x) + 21 \times 288x^2 + 35 \times (-432x^3) + 35 \times 648x^4 \\
&\quad + 21 \times (-972x^5) + 7 \times 1458x^6 - 2187x^7 \\
&= 128 - 1344x + 6048x^2 - 15120x^3 + 22680x^4 - 20412x^5 + 10206x^6 - 2187x^7
\end{aligned}
$$

Example 10.5.2. *Calculate the coefficient of* $x^{11}y^4$ *in the expansion of* $(x+y)^{15}$.

The coefficient is $^{15}C_4 = \frac{15!}{4!11!} = 1365$.

Example 10.5.3. *What is the constant coefficient in the expansion of* $\left(2x^2 - 5x^{-1}\right)^9$?

The constant term in this expansion is

$$\binom{9}{3} \times (2x^2)^3 \times \left(-5x^{-1}\right)^6 = 10500000$$

and this is therefore also the constant coefficient.

The next idea will become even more fruitful in the next section, but one of the values of the Binomial Theorem is that it enables accurate approximations of complicated calculations to be made.

Example 10.5.4. *Find the first four terms of* $(2 - 3x)^{10}$, *in ascending powers of* x. *By means of a suitable substitution, find an approximation of* 1.97^{10} *correct to the nearest integer.*

The Binomial Theorem tells us that

$$
\begin{aligned}
(2 - 3x)^{10} &= 2^{10} + {}^{10}C_1 \times 2^9 \times (-3x) + {}^{10}C_2 \times 2^8 \times (-3x)^2 + {}^{10}C_3 \times 2^7 \times (-3x)^3 + \cdots \\
&= 1024 - 10 \times 1536x + 45 \times 2304x^2 - 120 \times 3456x^3 + \cdots \\
&= 1024 - 15360x + 103680x^2 - 414720x^3 + \cdots
\end{aligned}
$$

Although the question only asks for the first four terms of the expansion, it is good technique to add $+\cdots$ after these first terms, as a reminder that there are more terms that are being ignored.

The key trick in the next stage is to note that $2 - 3x$ is equal to 1.97 when we put $x = 0.01$. Since x is small, its higher powers are very small indeed, and (even though the Binomial coefficients are quite large) the size of the terms in $x^4, x^5, \ldots, x^{10}$ which have been omitted from the above expansion will be small enough to be ignored. Thus we approximate

$$
1.97^{10} \approx 1024 - 15360 \times 10^{-2} + 103680 \times 10^{-4} - 414720 \times 10^{-6} = 880.35328
$$

and so we obtain $1.97^{20} \approx 880$.

The next term in the Binomial expansion of $(2 - 3x)^{10}$ would have been $1088640x^4$, which takes the value 0.0108864 when $x = 10^{-2}$; this justifies our idea that the remaining terms in the expansion would be small. Indeed, the exact value of 1.97^{10} is 880.3639729, so the first four terms in the Binomial expansion of $(2 - 3x)^{10}$ approximated 1.97^{10} correct to 4 significant figures, and so certainly to the nearest integer.

EXERCISE 10C

1. Find the coefficient of x^3 in the expansion of each of the following.
   a) $(1 + x)^5$
   b) $(1 - x)^8$
   c) $(1 + x)^{11}$
   d) $(1 - x)^{16}$

2. Find the coefficient of x^5 in the expansion of each of the following.
   a) $(2 + x)^7$
   b) $(3 - x)^8$
   c) $(1 + 2x)^9$
   d) $\left(1 + \frac{1}{2}x\right)^{12}$

3. Find the coefficient of $x^6 y^8$ in the expansion of each of the following.
   a) $(x + y)^{14}$
   b) $(2x - y)^{14}$
   c) $(3x + 2y)^{14}$
   d) $\left(4x + \frac{1}{2}y\right)^{14}$

4. Find the first four terms in the expansion in ascending powers of x of the following.
   a) $(1 + x)^{13}$
   b) $(1 - x)^{15}$
   c) $(1 + 3x)^{10}$
   d) $(2 - 5x)^7$

5. Find the first three terms in the expansion in ascending powers of x of the following.
   a) $(1 + x)^{22}$
   b) $(1 - x)^{30}$
   c) $(1 - 4x)^{18}$
   d) $(1 + 6x)^{19}$

6. Find the first three terms in the expansion, in ascending powers of x, of $(1 + 2x)^8$. By substituting $x = 0.01$, find an approximation to 1.02^8.

7. Find the first three terms in the expansion, in ascending powers of x, of $(2 + 5x)^{12}$. By substituting a suitable value for x, find an approximation to 2.005^{12} to 2 decimal places.

8. Expand $(1 + 2x)^{16}$ up to and including the term in x^3. Deduce the coefficient of x^3 in the expansion of $(1 + 3x)(1 + 2x)^{16}$.

9. Expand $(1 - 3x)^{10}$ up to and including the term in x^2. Deduce the coefficient of x^2 in the expansion of $(1 + 3x)^2(1 - 3x)^{10}$.

10. Given that the coefficient of x in the expansion of $(1 + ax)(1 + 5x)^{40}$ is 207, determine the value of a.

11. Simplify $(1 - x)^8 + (1 + x)^8$. Substitute a suitable value of x to find the exact value of $0.99^8 + 1.01^8$.

12. Given that the expansion of $(1 + ax)^n$ begins $1 + 36x + 576x^2 + \cdots$, find the values of a and n.

13. Given that, in the expansion of $(1 + ax)^n$, the coefficient of x is -35 and the coefficient of x^2 is 525, find the values of a and n.

14. a) Show that $(p + q)^5 + (p - q)^5 = 2p^5 + 20p^3q^2 + 10pq^4$.

    b) Hence show that $\left(\sqrt{3} + \sqrt{2}\right)^5 + \left(\sqrt{3} - \sqrt{2}\right)^5 = 178\sqrt{3}$.

    c) Evaluate $\left(\sqrt{3} + \sqrt{2}\right)^5 - \left(\sqrt{3} - \sqrt{2}\right)^5$ exactly.

    d) Using the fact that $0 < \sqrt{3} - \sqrt{2} < 0.4$ and that $178\sqrt{3} = 308.305$, state the integer nearest to $\left(\sqrt{3} + \sqrt{2}\right)^5$ (do not use your calculator).

15*. Given that, in the expansion of $(1 + ax)^n$, where both $a > 0$ and n is a positive integer, the coefficient of x^2 is 525 and the coefficient of x^3 is 4375:

    a) Show that $n(n - 1)a^2 = 1050$ and $(n - 2)a = 25$.

    b) Deduce that $(3n - 4)a^2 = 425$.

    c) Forming and solving a quadratic equation for a, find the values of a and n.

16*. By considering the expansions for $(1 + x)^n$ and for $(1 + x)^{2n}$, evaluate:

    a) $\displaystyle\sum_{m=0}^{n} \binom{n}{m}$

    b) $\displaystyle\sum_{m=0}^{n} (-1)^m \binom{n}{m}$

    c) $\displaystyle\sum_{m=0}^{n} \binom{n}{m}^2$

17*. Recalling the general formula for the Fibonacci sequence found in Question 17 in Exercise 9A, prove that

$$2^{2n} F_{2n+1} = \sum_{m=0}^{n} \binom{2n + 1}{2m + 1} 5^m, \qquad n \geq 0.$$

10.6   The General Binomial Expansion

The Binomial Theorem enables us to expand $(x + y)^n$ for any positive integer n, and this is extremely useful. However, there are many similar expressions that we would like to be able to study, such as $(2 + x)^{-1}$ or $\sqrt{1 + x}$, and the Binomial Theorem, as currently expressed, cannot handle such expressions.

What is remarkable is that the Binomial Theorem can be extended so that we can study expressions of the form $(x + y)^n$ for any real number n whatsoever. Since we have removed any restrictions on the type of number that n can be, there will be some compensatory restrictions put on the numbers x and y, but these restrictions are not onerous.

Let us first note that the Binomial Theorem can be written in a different manner; this new formalism will be capable of extension. We shall restrict our attention to expressions of the form $(1 + x)^n$. The Binomial Theorem states that

$$\begin{aligned}
(1 + x)^n &= \sum_{m=0}^{n} \binom{n}{m} x^m = \binom{n}{0} + \binom{n}{1} x + \binom{n}{2} x^2 + \binom{n}{3} x^3 + \cdots + \binom{n}{n} x^n \\
&= 1 + \frac{n!}{1!(n-1)!} x + \frac{n!}{2!(n-2)!} x^2 + \frac{n!}{3!(n-3)!} x^3 + \cdots + \frac{n!}{n!0!} x^n \\
&= 1 + \frac{n}{1!} x + \frac{n(n-1)}{2!} x^2 + \frac{n(n-1)(n-2)}{3!} x^3 + \cdots + \frac{n(n-1)\cdots 1}{n!} x^n
\end{aligned}$$

so that the coefficient of x^r can be written as

$$\frac{n(n-1)(n-2)\cdots(n-r+1)}{r!}$$

for any $1 \leq r \leq n$, where the numerator is the product of r numbers, starting with n and decreasing by 1 each time.

Note that the expression

$$\frac{n(n-1)(n-2)\cdots(n-r+1)}{r!}$$

makes sense for any positive integer r and any real number n, but also that it equals 0 whenever n is a positive integer and $r > n$. Thus the standard Binomial Theorem expansion for $(1+x)^n$ could be written

$$(1+x)^n = 1 + \sum_{r=1}^{\infty} \frac{n(n-1)(n-2)\cdots(n-r+1)}{r!}x^r = 1 + \frac{n}{1!}x + \frac{n(n-1)}{2!}x^2 + \frac{n(n-1)(n-2)}{3!}x^3 + \cdots \quad (\star)$$

with the infinite sum in fact collapsing to a finite sum for a positive integer n. However, this series may converge for other values of n, in which case we are considering a series with an infinite number of terms. What happens then?

- **Case 1: n $= -1$** Provided that $|x| < 1$, $(1+x)^{-1}$ is the sum to infinity of a GP with initial term $a = 1$ and constant ratio $r = -1$. Thus we see that

$$(1+x)^{-1} = \sum_{r=0}^{\infty}(-x)^r = 1 + \frac{-1}{1!}x + \frac{(-1)(-2)}{2!}x^2 + \frac{(-1)(-2)(-3)}{3!}x^3 + \cdots + \frac{(-1)(-2)\cdots(-n)}{n!}x^n + \cdots$$

  and so the formula $(\star)$ holds when $n = -1$ and $|x| < 1$.

- **Case 2: n $= -2$** Provided that $|x| < 1$, we can regard $(1+x)^{-2}$ as the square of $(1+x)^{-1}$, and hence as the square of the sum of infinity of a GP, so that

$$(1+x)^{-2} = \left(1 - x + x^2 - x^3 + x^4 - \cdots\right)\left(1 - x + x^2 - x^3 + x^4 - \cdots\right)$$

When two infinite series are to be multiplied together like this, every term in the first series gets multiplied by every term in the second series, and the (doubly infinite) collection of products must be added up. Although there are an infinite number of terms to add together, there are only finitely many terms involving any particular power of x, and so we can collect terms together, and write this product of infinite sums as a single infinite sum. Thus

$$
\begin{aligned}
(1+x)^{-2} &= 1 - (1+1)x + (1+1+1)x^2 - (1+1+1+1)x^3 + (1+1+1+1+1)x^4 - \cdots \\
&= 1 - 2x + 3x^2 - 4x^3 + 5x^4 - \cdots + (-1)^n(n+1)x^n + \cdots \\
&= 1 + \frac{(-2)}{1!}x + \frac{(-2)(-3)}{2!}x^2 + \frac{(-2)(-3)(-4)}{3!}x^3 + \cdots + \frac{(-2)(-3)\cdots(-n-1)}{n!}x^n + \cdots
\end{aligned}
$$

for all $|x| < 1$. Thus we see again that the formula $(\star)$ works when $n = -2$ and $|x| < 1$.

- **Case 3: n $= -3$** Similarly,

$$
\begin{aligned}
(1+x)^{-3} &= (1+x)^{-1} \times (1+x)^{-2} \\
&= \left(1 - x + x^2 - x^3 + x^4 - \cdots\right)\left(1 - 2x + 3x^2 - 4x^3 + 5x^4 - \cdots\right) \\
&= 1 - (1+2)x + (1+2+3)x^2 - (1+2+3+4)x^3 + (1+2+3+4+5)x^4 + \cdots \\
&= 1 - 3x + 6x^2 - 10x^3 + 15x^4 - \cdots + \tfrac{1}{2}(n+1)(n+2)(-1)^nx^n + \cdots \\
&= 1 + \frac{(-3)}{1!}x + \frac{(-3)(-4)}{2!}x^2 + \frac{(-3)(-4)(-5)}{3!}x^3 + \cdots + \frac{(-3)(-4)\cdots(-n-2)}{n!}x^n + \cdots
\end{aligned}
$$

for all $|x| < 1$. Again, formula $(\star)$ holds when $n = -3$ and $|x| < 1$.

- **Case 4: n $= \frac{1}{2}$** Suppose that $(1+x)^{\frac{1}{2}}$ can be written as an infinite series

$$(1+x)^{\frac{1}{2}} = A + Bx + Cx^2 + Dx^3 + Ex^4 + \cdots$$

valid for $|x| < 1$. Then

$$
\begin{aligned}
1 + x &= (1+x)^{\frac{1}{2}} \times (1+x)^{\frac{1}{2}} \\
&= \left(A + Bx + Cx^2 + Dx^3 + Ex^4 + \cdots\right) \times \left(A + Bx + Cx^2 + Dx^3 + Ex^4 + \cdots\right) \\
&= A^2 + (AB + AB)x + (AC + B^2 + AC)x^2 + (AD + BC + BC + AD)x^3 \\
&\quad + (AE + BD + C^2 + BD + AE)x^4 + \cdots \\
&= A^2 + 2ABx + (B^2 + 2AC)x^2 + 2(AD + BC)x^3 + (C^2 + 2AE + 2BD)x^4 + \cdots
\end{aligned}
$$

for $|x| < 1$, so we deduce that

$$A^2 = 1 \qquad 2AB = 1 \qquad B^2 + 2AC = 0 \qquad 2(AD + BC) = 0 \qquad C^2 + 2AE + 2BD = 0$$

Since this formula holds for $x = 0$, and we are taking the positive square root, we deduce that $A = 1$. Hence $B = \frac{1}{2}$, $C = -\frac{1}{8}$, $D = \frac{1}{16}$ and $E = -\frac{5}{128}$. Thus it seems that

$$
\begin{aligned}
(1+x)^{\frac{1}{2}} &= 1 + \tfrac{1}{2}x - \tfrac{1}{8}x^2 + \tfrac{1}{16}x^3 - \tfrac{5}{128}x^4 + \cdots \\
&= 1 + \frac{(\frac{1}{2})}{1!}x + \frac{(\frac{1}{2})(-\frac{1}{2})}{2!}x^2 + \frac{(\frac{1}{2})(-\frac{1}{2})(-\frac{3}{2})}{3!}x^3 + \frac{(\frac{1}{2})(-\frac{1}{2})(-\frac{3}{2})(-\frac{5}{2})}{4!}x^4 + \cdots
\end{aligned}
$$

and so it seems, at least considering terms in powers of x up to x^4, that ($\star$) holds for $n = \frac{1}{2}$ as well.

Although the result has not been fully proved, we have shown enough to suggest very strongly that the following result is true:

Key Fact 10.4 The General Binomial Expansion

For any real number n,

$$(1+x)^n = 1 + \frac{n}{1!}x + \frac{n(n-1)}{2!}x^2 + \frac{n(n-1)(n-2)}{3!}x^3 + \cdots + \frac{n(n-1)\cdots(n-r+1)}{r!}x^r + \cdots$$

provided that $|x| < 1$.

Example 10.6.1. *Find the expansion of* $(1 + x)^{-4}$ *in ascending powers of x up to the term in* x^4.

We have

$$
\begin{aligned}
(1+x)^{-4} &= 1 + \frac{(-4)}{1!}x + \frac{(-4)(-5)}{2!}x^2 + \frac{(-4)(-5)(-6)}{3!}x^3 + \frac{(-4)(-5)(-6)(-7)}{4!}x^4 + \cdots \\
&= 1 - 4x + 10x^2 - 20x^3 + 35x^4 + \cdots
\end{aligned}
$$

Example 10.6.2. *Find the expansion of* $(1 + 3x)^{\frac{3}{2}}$ *in ascending powers of x up to and including the term in* x^3. *For what values of x is the expansion valid?*

This time

$$
\begin{aligned}
(1+3x)^{\frac{3}{2}} &= 1 + \frac{(\frac{3}{2})}{1!}(3x) + \frac{(\frac{3}{2})(\frac{1}{2})}{2!}(3x)^2 + \frac{(\frac{3}{2})(\frac{1}{2})(-\frac{1}{2})}{3!}(3x)^3 + \cdots \\
&= 1 + \tfrac{9}{2}x + \tfrac{27}{8}x^2 - \tfrac{27}{16}x^3 + \cdots
\end{aligned}
$$

Since the general expansion for $(1 + y)^n$ is valid for $|y| < 1$, in this case the expansion is valid for $|3x| < 1$, and hence for $|x| < \frac{1}{3}$.

Just as in the simpler case, we can use the general Binomial expansion to obtain approximations of numbers.

Example 10.6.3. *Find the expansion of* $(1 - 2x)^{\frac{1}{2}}$ *in ascending powers of x up to and including the term in* x^3. *By choosing a suitable value of x, obtain an approximation for* $\sqrt{2}$.

We see that

$$
\begin{aligned}
(1-2x)^{\frac{1}{2}} &= 1 + \frac{(\frac{1}{2})}{1!}(-2x) + \frac{(\frac{1}{2})(-\frac{1}{2})}{2!}(-2x)^2 + \frac{(\frac{1}{2})(-\frac{1}{2})(-\frac{3}{2})}{3!}(-2x)^3 + \cdots \\
&= 1 - x - \tfrac{1}{2}x^2 - \tfrac{1}{2}x^3 + \cdots
\end{aligned}
$$

which is valid for $|x| < \frac{1}{2}$.

Choosing the right value of x needs a little skill. It is not good enough to choose $x = -\frac{1}{2}$, so that $(1 - 2x)^{\frac{1}{2}} = \sqrt{2}$. The problem with this approach is that $x = -\frac{1}{2}$ is not small enough for the terms that have been omitted to be small enough to be ignored (putting $x = -\frac{1}{2}$ into the above formula gives an approximate value of 1.4375 for $\sqrt{2}$, a very rough approximation!). The right trick is to find a small value of x such that $1 - 2x$ is 2 times a square. A successful choice is $x = 0.01$, for then $1 - 2x = 0.98 = 2 \times 0.7^2$, and hence $(1 - 2x)^{\frac{1}{2}} = \frac{7}{10}\sqrt{2}$. Thus

$$\tfrac{7}{10}\sqrt{2} \approx 1 - 0.01 - \tfrac{1}{2} \times 0.01^2 - \tfrac{1}{2} \times 0.01^3 = 0.9899495$$

and hence $\sqrt{2} \approx \frac{10}{7} \times 0.9899495 \approx 1.414214$. This is a good approximation of $\sqrt{2}$.

10.7 More Complicated Expansions

The general Binomial expansion can only be used directly to expand terms of the form $(1 + x)^n$ for some x and n. More complicated expressions need to be manipulated into that form before they can be handled.

Example 10.7.1. *Find the Binomial expansion of $\left(4 - 3x^2\right)^{\frac{1}{2}}$, up to and including the term in x^6. Use this expansion to approximate $\sqrt{397}$ to 4 decimal places.*

The expression $4 - 3x^2$ is not in the right form, so it must first be written as $4\left(1 - \frac{3}{4}x^2\right)$. Then

$$
\begin{aligned}
\left(4 - 3x^2\right)^{\frac{1}{2}} &= 4^{\frac{1}{2}}\left(1 - \tfrac{3}{4}x^2\right)^{\frac{1}{2}} \\
&= 2\left[1 + \frac{\left(\frac{1}{2}\right)}{1!}\left(-\tfrac{3}{4}x^2\right) + \frac{\left(\frac{1}{2}\right)\left(-\frac{1}{2}\right)}{2!}\left(-\tfrac{3}{4}x^2\right)^2 + \frac{\left(\frac{1}{2}\right)\left(-\frac{1}{2}\right)\left(-\frac{3}{2}\right)}{3!}\left(-\tfrac{3}{4}x^2\right)^3 + \cdots\right] \\
&= 2\left[1 - \tfrac{3}{8}x^2 - \tfrac{9}{128}x^4 - \tfrac{27}{1024}x^6 + \cdots\right] \\
&= 2 - \tfrac{3}{4}x^2 - \tfrac{9}{64}x^4 - \tfrac{27}{512}x^6 + \cdots
\end{aligned}
$$

Choosing $x = 0.1$ gives $(4 - 3x^2)^{\frac{1}{2}} = \frac{1}{10}\sqrt{397}$. Thus

$$\sqrt{397} \approx 10\left[2 - \tfrac{3}{4} \times 0.1^2 - \tfrac{9}{64} \times 0.1^4 - \tfrac{27}{512} \times 0.1^6\right] \approx 19.9249$$

Example 10.7.2. *Expand $\dfrac{5 + x}{(2 - x + x^2)^2}$ in ascending powers of x up to the term in x^3. For what range of values of x is this expansion valid?*

We must first write

$$\frac{5 + x}{(2 - x + x^2)^2} = \frac{5 + x}{4\left(1 - \frac{1}{2}x + \frac{1}{2}x^2\right)^2} = \tfrac{1}{4}(5 + x)\left(1 - \tfrac{1}{2}x + \tfrac{1}{2}x^2\right)^{-2}$$

Since

$$
\begin{aligned}
(1 - u)^{-2} &= 1 + \frac{(-2)}{1!}(-u) + \frac{(-2)(-3)}{2!}(-u)^2 + \frac{(-2)(-3)(-4)}{3!}(-u)^3 + \cdots \\
&= 1 + 2u + 3u^2 + 4u^3 + \cdots
\end{aligned}
$$

we deduce that

$$
\begin{aligned}
\left(1 - \tfrac{1}{2}x + \tfrac{1}{2}x^2\right)^{-2} &= 1 + 2 \times \tfrac{1}{2}(x - x^2) + 3 \times \tfrac{1}{4}(x - x^2)^2 + 4 \times \tfrac{1}{8}(x - x^2)^3 + \cdots \\
&= 1 + (x - x^2) + \tfrac{3}{4}(x^2 - 2x^3 + \cdots) + \tfrac{1}{2}(x^3 - \cdots) + \cdots \\
&= 1 + x - \tfrac{1}{4}x^2 - x^3 + \cdots
\end{aligned}
$$

183

and hence

$$\frac{5+x}{(2-x+x^2)^2} = \tfrac{1}{4}(5+x)\left(1+x-\tfrac{1}{4}x^2-x^3+\cdots\right)$$

$$= \tfrac{1}{4}\left(5+5x-\tfrac{5}{4}x^2-5x^3+\cdots+x+x^2-\tfrac{1}{4}x^3+\cdots\right)$$

$$= \tfrac{5}{4}+\tfrac{3}{2}x-\tfrac{1}{16}x^2-\tfrac{21}{16}x^3+\cdots$$

For this expansion to be valid, we require $|\tfrac{1}{2}(x-x^2)| < 1$, or $|x-x^2| < 2$. Since $x^2-x = \left(x-\tfrac{1}{2}\right)^2 - \tfrac{1}{4}$, we see that $x^2-x \ge -\tfrac{1}{4} > -2$ for all real x, and that $x^2-x = 2$ when $x = -1, 2$. It follows that the expansion is valid for $-1 < x < 2$.

EXERCISE 10D

1. Expand the following in ascending powers of x up to and including the term in x^2:

   a) $(1+x)^{-3}$
   b) $(1+x)^{-5}$
   c) $(1-x)^{-4}$
   d) $(1-x)^{-6}$

2. Find the expansion of the following in ascending powers of x up to and including the term in x^2:

   a) $(1+4x)^{-1}$
   b) $(1-2x)^{-3}$
   c) $(1-3x)^{-4}$
   d) $\left(1+\tfrac{1}{2}x\right)^{-2}$

3. Find the coefficient of x^3 in the expansions of the following:

   a) $(1-x)^{-7}$
   b) $(1+2x)^{-1}$
   c) $(1+3x)^{-3}$
   d) $(1-4x)^{-2}$
   e) $\left(1-\tfrac{1}{3}x\right)^{-6}$
   f) $(1+ax)^{-4}$
   g) $(1-bx)^{-4}$
   h) $(1-cx)^{-n}$

4. Find the expansion of the following in ascending powers of x up to and including the term in x^2:

   a) $(1+x)^{\frac{1}{3}}$
   b) $(1+x)^{\frac{3}{4}}$
   c) $(1-x)^{\frac{3}{2}}$
   d) $(1-x)^{-\frac{1}{2}}$
   e) $(1+4x)^{\frac{1}{2}}$
   f) $(1+3x)^{-\frac{1}{3}}$
   g) $(1-6x)^{\frac{4}{3}}$
   h) $\left(1-\tfrac{1}{2}x\right)^{-\frac{1}{4}}$

5. Find the coefficient of x^3 in the expansions of the following:

   a) $(1+2x)^{\frac{3}{2}}$
   b) $(1-5x)^{-\frac{1}{2}}$
   c) $(1+\tfrac{3}{2}x)^{\frac{1}{3}}$
   d) $(1-4x)^{\frac{3}{4}}$
   e) $(1-7x)^{-\frac{1}{7}}$
   f) $\left(1+\sqrt{2}x\right)^{\frac{1}{2}}$
   g) $(1+ax)^{\frac{3}{2}}$
   h) $(1-bx)^{-\frac{1}{2}n}$

6. Show that, for small x, $\sqrt{1+\tfrac{1}{4}x} \approx 1+\tfrac{1}{8}x-\tfrac{1}{128}x^2$. Deduce the first three terms in the expansions of the following:

   a) $\sqrt{1-\tfrac{1}{4}x}$
   b) $\sqrt{1+\tfrac{1}{4}x^2}$
   c) $\sqrt{4+x}$
   d) $\sqrt{36+9x}$

7. Show that $\left(1-\tfrac{3}{2}x\right)^{-2} \approx 1+3x+\tfrac{27}{4}x^2+\tfrac{27}{2}x^3$ and state the interval of values of x for which the expansion is valid. Deduce the first four terms in the expansions of the following:

   a) $\dfrac{4}{\left(1-\tfrac{3}{2}x\right)^2}$
   b) $\dfrac{1}{(2-3x)^2}$

8. Find the first four terms in the expansion of each of the following in ascending powers of x. State the interval of values of x for which each expansion is valid:

   a) $\sqrt{1-6x}$
   b) $\dfrac{1}{1+5x}$
   c) $\dfrac{1}{\sqrt[3]{1+9x}}$
   d) $\dfrac{1}{(1-2x)^4}$
   e) $\sqrt{1+2x^2}$
   f) $\sqrt[3]{8-16x}$
   g) $\dfrac{10}{(1+\tfrac{1}{5}x)^2}$
   h) $\dfrac{2}{2-x}$
   i) $\dfrac{1}{(2+x)^3}$
   j) $\dfrac{4x}{\sqrt{4+x^3}}$
   k) $\sqrt[4]{1+8x}$
   l) $\dfrac{12}{(\sqrt{3}-x)^4}$

9. Expand $\sqrt{1+8x}$ in ascending powers of x up to and including the term in x^3. By giving a suitable value to x, find an approximation for $\sqrt{1.08}$. Deduce approximations for

   a) $\sqrt{108}$
   b) $\sqrt{3}$

10. Expand $\sqrt[3]{1+4x}$ in ascending powers of x up to and including the term in x^2.

    a) By putting $x = 0.01$, determine an approximation for $\sqrt[3]{130}$.

    b) By putting $x = -0.00025$, determine an approximation for $\sqrt[3]{999}$.

11. Given that the coefficient of x^3 in the expansion of $\frac{1}{(1+ax)^3}$ is -2160, find a.

12. Find the coefficient of x^2 in the expansion of $\frac{(1-2x)^2}{(1+x)^2}$.

13. Find the first three terms in the expansion in ascending powers of x of $\frac{\sqrt{1+2x}}{\sqrt{1-4x}}$. State the values of x for which the expansion is valid. By substituting $x = 0.01$ in your expansion, find an approximation for $\sqrt{17}$.

14. Given that terms involving x^4 and higher powers may be ignored and that $\frac{1}{(1+ax)^3} - \frac{1}{(1+3x)^4} \approx bx^2 + cx^3$, find the values of a, b and c.

15. Find the expansion of $\frac{2}{1-x-x^2}$ in ascending powers of x up to and including the term in x^4. By substitution of a suitable value of x, find the approximation, correct to 12 decimal places, of $\frac{1}{0.998999}$.

16. Find the first three terms in the expansion in ascending powers of x of:

    a) $\frac{8}{(2+x-x^2)^2}$

    b) $\frac{8}{(1-x+2x^2)^3}$

17. Given that the expansion of $(1 + ax)^n$ is $1 - 2x + \frac{7}{3}x^2 + kx^3 + \cdots$, find the value of k.

18*. Show that

$$\sqrt[4]{\frac{1+x}{1-2x}} = 1 + \frac{3}{4}x + \frac{21}{32}x^2 \cdots$$

By substituting $x = 0.02$, deduce that $\sqrt[4]{17} \approx 2.0305$.

19*. a) Show that

$$\frac{1}{(a+bx)^3} = \frac{1}{a^3} - \frac{3b}{a^4}x + \frac{6b^2}{a^5}x^2 + \cdots$$

    b) Suppose that the coefficient of x is 81 and the coefficient of x^2 is 162. Find the values of a and b.

Chapter 10: Summary

- The Binomial coefficients are defined as follows:

$$\binom{n}{m} = {}^nC_m = \frac{n!}{m!(n-m)!} \qquad 0 \le m \le n.$$

${}^nC_m$ is the number of ways of choosing m objects out from n distinct objects.

- For any $a, b,$ and any positive integer n,

$$(a+b)^n = \sum_{m=0}^{n}\binom{n}{m}a^{n-m}b^m = a^n + \binom{n}{1}a^{n-1}b + \binom{n}{2}a^{n-2}b^2 + \cdots + \binom{n}{n-2}a^2b^{n-2} + \binom{n}{n-1}ab^{n-1} + b^n$$

- For any real number n,

$$(1+x)^n = 1 + \frac{n}{1!}x + \frac{n(n-1)}{2!}x^2 + \frac{n(n-1)(n-2)}{3!}x^3 + \cdots + \frac{n(n-1)\cdots(n-r+1)}{r!}x^r + \cdots$$

provided that $|x| < 1$.

Differentiation

In this chapter we will learn:

- to understand the idea of the gradient of a curve, and use the various notations for derivatives,
- to understand the idea of 'differentiation from first principles', and use it to evaluate the derivative of simple powers of x,
- the algebraic properties of differentiation with respect to sums, differences and scalar multiples of functions,
- apply differentiation to gradients, tangents and normals, increasing and decreasing functions and rates of change,
- locate stationary points, and determine by calculation whether the points are maxima or minima.

11.1 The Gradient of a Curve

We know that the gradient of a straight line curve is given by the expression

$$\frac{\text{RISE}}{\text{RUN}}$$

and that this quantity stays the same, no matter where on the straight line we choose to calculate the rise and run of the curve.

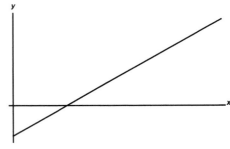

Figure 11.1

Matters are more complicated when the curve is not a straight line. There are no longer any lines on the curve whose gradients can be calculated! Nonetheless, there should still be some notion of gradient. It is well known that (for objects travelling at a constant speed) speed is the ratio of distance covered over time elapsed: speed is the gradient of the straight line that is the distance-time graph of the motion. When an object is accelerating, or decelerating, the speed-time graph is no longer a straight line, but the object still has a speed at any moment in time. It can be seen that the speedometer on a car registers a (changing) speed throughout a car's motion.

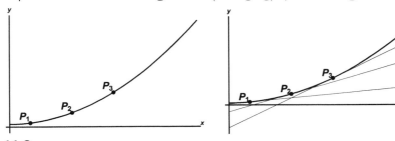

Figure 11.2

The solution to this problem is as follows:

Key Fact 11.1 The Gradient of a Curve

The gradient of a curve at a point is the gradient of the tangent to that curve at that point.

If a curve is a straight line, it will be the same as its tangent at any point on the line, and so the gradient of the tangent to the curve at any point is always equal to the gradient of the original line (so this new way of thinking about gradients does not change what we already know for straight lines).

On the other hand, we can now consider the gradient at points on curves that are not straight lines. The tangents at different points will now be different from each other, and in general not parallel to each other, and so the gradient of the curve will be different at distinct points P_1, P_2, P_3.

This idea is all well and good, but it does not help us to calculate these gradients. The problem is that the current definition is geometric in basis: we can only use it by drawing the graph, drawing the tangent at a point on the curve, and then finally calculating the gradient of that tangent. Drawing a graph is not an easy process, since anything drawn by hand will be inaccurate, and the matter of judging whether or not a particular line is the tangent or not is not an easy decision to make. Which of the two lines shown here is the true tangent?

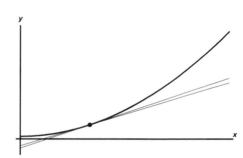

Figure 11.3

What we need is a method for calculating the gradient of a curve at a point, and therefore also of determining the tangent at that point, without the need to draw the curve and the tangent physically. We need an algebraic approach to this problem. To do this requires a fresh insight.

The simplest way to calculate the gradient of a straight line is to know two points on that line. This is why calculating the gradient of tangents is difficult: we only know one point on that line for certain. Suppose that, instead of trying to consider the tangent at the point P, we considered instead the gradients of chords like PQ_1, PQ_2 and PQ_3. It is clear that the chord PQ_1 is more like the tangent at P than is the chord PQ_3, and so the gradient of PQ_1 will be closer to the gradient of the tangent at P than is the gradient of the chord PQ_3.

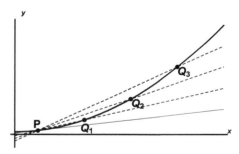

Figure 11.4

What happens to the gradient of the chord PQ if Q is a point on the curve, as the point Q gets closer and closer to 0? Of course, Q cannot be allowed to ever be the same as P (in that case, there would be no chord, and therefore no gradient to calculate). Let us investigate this problem by looking at some examples.

Example 11.1.1. *Let P be the point $(1, 1)$ on the curve $y = x^2$. What is the gradient of the tangent PQ, where Q is the point with x-coordinates:*

   a) 1.5   *b)* 1.1   *c)* 1.01   *d)* 1.001   *e)* $1 + h$?

      The gradients are

      a) $\frac{2.25 - 1}{1.5 - 1} = 2.5$ *b)* $\frac{1.21 - 1}{1.1 - 1} = 2.1$ *c)* $\frac{1.0201 - 1}{1.01 - 1} = 2.01$

      d) $\frac{1.002001 - 1}{1.001 - 1} = 2.001$ *e)* $\frac{1 + 2h + h^2 - 1}{1 + h - 1} = 2 + h$

So long as Q is not equal to P, it will have x-coordinate $1 + h$ for some non-zero number h. Thus the gradient of the chord PQ will be $2 + h$. This gradient is never equal to 2, but gets closer and closer to 2 as h gets closer and closer to 0. In other words, 2 is the limit of the gradient of PQ as h tends to 0.

Key Fact 11.2 Calculating the Gradient of a Tangent

The gradient of the tangent to a curve at a point P on the curve is equal to the limit of the gradient of the chord PQ, where Q is another point on the curve, as Q tends to P.

The real power of this idea lies in the fact that we are not required to draw any pictures to use it. All calculations can be performed in algebra.

11.2 Differentiation By First Principles

Suppose we are interested in finding the gradient of the tangent to the function $y = f(x)$ at the point P. Let us suppose that P has coordinates (x, y). Pick a point Q on the curve other than P. Its x-coordinate will no longer be x; we write it is $x + \delta x$. Note that δ is not a number in its own right, and $x + \delta x$ is not the same as $(1 + \delta)x$: the term δx is used to mean the 'change in x', and is a single quantity, even though it is written with two symbols. Similarly, the y-coordinate of Q will not be the same as the y-coordinate of P, and we shall write it as $y + \delta y$ (again δy means the 'change in y', and is a single quantity). Thus Q has coordinates $(x + \delta x, y + \delta y)$.

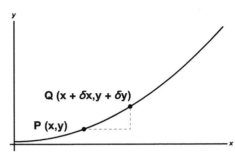

Figure 11.5

Remember throughout all this that P and Q lie on the curve, so that x, y, δx and δy are quantities related by the formulae

$$y = f(x) \qquad y + \delta y = f(x + \delta x)$$

It is clear that, for the chord PQ, we can measure a run of δx and a rise of δy from P to Q, and so the gradient of the chord PQ is

$$\frac{\delta y}{\delta x}$$

To determine the gradient of the tangent at the point P, we need to let the point Q approach P. In other words, we need to let δx tend to 0.

Key Fact 11.3 Differentiation from First Principles

A fixed point P on the curve $y = f(x)$ has coordinates (x, y). If Q is a moveable point on the same curve, with coordinates $(x + \delta x, y + \delta y)$, then the limit of the ratio $\frac{\delta y}{\delta x}$, as δx tends to 0, is called the **derivative** of the function $y = f(x)$ **with respect to x** at the point P. It is written

$$\frac{dy}{dx}$$

The derivative of a function at the point P is equal to the gradient of the tangent to the graph of that function at the point P. The process of obtaining the derivative of a function is called **differentiation**.

Note that, since a function might well have a derivative at all points on the curve, the derivative $\frac{dy}{dx}$ is itself a function of x. This technique of calculating the derivative by considering the gradients of chords is called **differentiation by first principles**.

For Interest

First principles differentiation is vital, in that it can be used to define differentiation accurately, and it can later be used to prove important results about differentiation. Once we have established certain key facts, however, we shall use a more mundane method of differentiation on a day-by-day basis.

It is important to remember that the expression $\frac{dy}{dx}$ is not a fraction, nor is dx equal to d times x.

The expression $\frac{dy}{dx}$ is just a notation representing the derivative of y with respect to x: its structure makes you think of the ratios $\frac{\delta y}{\delta x}$ from which it is obtained. It is sometimes worth thinking of $\frac{dy}{dx}$ as follows:

$$\frac{dy}{dx} = \frac{d}{dx}y$$

where $\frac{d}{dx}$ is an operator which takes any function of x and replaces it with its first derivative with respect to x.

Example 11.2.1. *Using first principles, find the derivatives of the functions*
a) $y = 2x^2 + 3x$ b) $y = 5$

(a) We have

$$y + \delta y = 2(x + \delta x)^2 + 3(x + \delta x) = 2x^2 + 4x\,\delta x + 2(\delta x)^2 + 3x + 3\delta x$$

so that

$$\frac{\delta y}{\delta x} = \frac{4x\,\delta x + 2(\delta x)^2 + 3\delta x}{\delta x} = 4x + 2\delta x + 3$$

which tends to $4x + 3$ as δx tend to 0, so that

$$\frac{dy}{dx} = 4x + 3\,.$$

(b) This time $y + \delta y = 5$, so that $\delta y = 0$, and hence $\frac{\delta y}{\delta x} = 0$, so that $\frac{dy}{dx} = 0$.

The last result is worth noting. The function $y = 5$ has a horizontal graph, and so we should expect its derivative to be 0.

11.3   Differentiation: Functional Notation

The study of differentiation is the starting point of the field of mathematics known as calculus. A moot point in the history of mathematics is to decide who invented it! The two mathematicians Isaac Newton and Gottfried Leibniz both developed the theory of the subject in the second half of the 17th Century, but who developed it first? Without going into the details of this, we shall content ourselves by noting that the two different developments of the calculus are still reflected in mathematics today. There are two different notations to represent differentiation.

The notation we have seen so far, which represents the (first) derivative of the function y with respect to x by the symbol $\frac{dy}{dx}$, is due to Leibniz. Newton's notation was more oriented towards functions.

> **Key Fact 11.4** The Functional Notation for Differentiation
>
> If $y = f(x)$, then a different notation for $\frac{dy}{dx}$ is simply $f'(x)$.

Since the first principles definition for differentiation involved y explicitly, if we are to work with this functional notation, we need to rewrite the definition of differentiation.

The functional notation means that method of differentiation by first principles can be expressed differently. If we have a function $f(x)$, consider the curve $y = f(x)$. Replacing δx by h, we see that

$$\delta y = (y + \delta y) - y = f(x + h) - f(x)$$

and so

$$\frac{\delta y}{\delta x} = \frac{f(x + h) - f(x)}{h}$$

> **Key Fact 11.5** Differentiation of Functions by First Principles
>
> The first derivative of a function $f(x)$ with respect to x is the function $f'(x)$, where $f'(x)$ is the limit of the expression
> $$\frac{f(x+h)-f(x)}{h}$$
> as h tends to 0.

Example 11.3.1. *Find the functions $f'(x)$ for the function $f(x) = 2x^3 - 3x^2 + 7x - 2$.*

Since
$$
\begin{aligned}
\frac{f(x+h)-f(x)}{h} &= \frac{2(x+h)^3 - 3(x+h)^2 + 7(x+h) - 2 - 2x^3 + 3x^2 - 7x + 2}{h} \\
&= \frac{6x^2h + 6xh^2 + 2h^3 - 6xh - 3h^2 + 7h}{h} \\
&= 6x^2 + 6xh + 2h^2 - 6x - 3h + 7
\end{aligned}
$$

letting h tend to 0 tells us that $f'(x) = 6x^2 - 6x + 7$.

> **Food For Thought 11.1**
>
> It is worth noting that not all functions have derivatives! The condition that the limit $\frac{1}{h}\big[f(x+h) - f(x)\big]$ exists as h tends to 0 is not a trivial one, and is not satisfied for all functions, or even for all values of x for a given function. For example, if $f(x) = |x|$ then
> $$\frac{f(h) - f(0)}{h} = \frac{|h|}{h} = \begin{cases} 1 & h > 0 \\ -1 & h < 0 \end{cases}$$
> which does not tend to a single limit (neither 1 nor -1) as h tends to 0. The function $f(x) = |x|$ does not have a derivative at the point $x = 0$ (although it does have one at all other points).
> What is remarkable is that essentially all the other 'standard' functions that we meet do have derivatives.

11.4 Rules for Differentiation

Before we get involved with real functions, we need to be able to differentiate as many functions as possible without having to revert to first principles at all stages. Fortunately, there are some simple rules which, when carefully applied, enable us to differentiate a large class of functions easily.

> **Key Fact 11.6** Rules for Differentiation
>
> * If $y = x^n$ for any real number n, then $\dfrac{dy}{dx} = nx^{n-1}$.
>
> * If $y = f(x) + g(x)$ for two functions $f(x)$ and $g(x)$, then $\dfrac{dy}{dx} = f'(x) + g'(x)$.
>
> * If $y = \alpha f(x)$ for some function $f(x)$ and a constant α, then $\dfrac{dy}{dx} = \alpha f'(x)$.

Because it is so important, we will prove the first of these. The other two results will be left as exercises for the reader.

If $f(x) = x^n$ where n is a positive integer, then the Binomial Theorem tells us that

$$\frac{f(x+h)-f(x)}{h} = \frac{\sum_{r=0}^{n} {}^nC_r x^{n-r}h^r - x^n}{h} = \frac{\sum_{r=1}^{n} {}^nC_r x^{n-r}h^r}{h} = \sum_{r=1}^{n} {}^nC_r x^{n-r}h^{r-1} = nx^{n-1} + \sum_{r=2}^{n} {}^nC_r x^{n-r}h^{r-1}$$

separating the $r = 1$ term out from the rest of the sum. As h tends to 0, all the terms in that final sum tend to 0, leaving just nx^{n-1} on the right-hand side. Thus we deduce that $\frac{dy}{dx} = nx^{n-1}$ as required.

If now $f(x) = x^n$ for a more general real number n, then the general Binomial expansion tells us that

$$\frac{f(x+h)-f(x)}{h} = \frac{(x+h)^n - x^n}{h} = x^n \frac{\left(1+\frac{h}{x}\right)^n - 1}{h} = x^n \frac{1 + \frac{n}{1!}\frac{h}{x} + \frac{(n)(n-1)}{2!}\left(\frac{h}{x}\right)^2 + \frac{(n)(n-1)(n-2)}{3!}\left(\frac{h}{x}\right)^3 + \cdots - 1}{h}$$

$$= x^n \left[\frac{(n)}{1!}\frac{1}{x} + \frac{(n)(n-1)}{2!}\frac{h}{x^2} + \frac{(n)(n-1)(n-2)}{3!}\frac{h^2}{x^3} + \cdots \right]$$

All the terms on the right-hand side tend to 0 as h tends to 0 except the first and so it follows that $\frac{dy}{dx} = nx^{n-1}$, as expected.

For Interest

The fact that the limit as h tends to 0 exists is in fact a very subtle result. Although every term in the Binomial expansion shown here tends to a finite limit as h becomes small, there is a significant technical problem raised by the fact that infinitely many terms are being added together. The details are complex, and not necessary at this stage, so we omit them.

For some values of n, a more elegant demonstration of the rules for differentiation is possible.

Example 11.4.1. *Find the derivatives of $f(x) = x^{-1}$ (for $x \neq 0$) and $g(x) = \sqrt{x}$ (for $x > 0$).*

$$\frac{f(x+h)-f(x)}{h} = \frac{1}{h}\left[\frac{1}{x+h} - \frac{1}{x}\right] = \frac{1}{h}\frac{x-(x+h)}{x(x+h)} = -\frac{1}{x(x+h)}$$

fox $x \neq 0$, and

$$\frac{g(x+h)-g(x)}{h} = \frac{\sqrt{x+h}-\sqrt{x}}{h} = \frac{\sqrt{x+h}-\sqrt{x}}{h} \times \frac{\sqrt{x+h}+\sqrt{x}}{\sqrt{x+h}+\sqrt{x}}$$

$$= \frac{x+h-x}{h(\sqrt{x+h}+\sqrt{x})} = \frac{1}{\sqrt{x+h}+\sqrt{x}}$$

for $x > 0$. These tend to $-x^{-2}$ and $\frac{1}{2\sqrt{x}} = \frac{1}{2}x^{-\frac{1}{2}}$, as expected, as h tends to 0.

We can now watch these rules in action.

Example 11.4.2. *Find $\frac{dy}{dx}$ for each of the following:*

a) $y = x^9$
b) $y = 5x^7$
c) $y = \frac{1}{x^4}$,
d) $y = \frac{1}{\sqrt{x}} + 3x^4$
e) $y = \sqrt[4]{x}$
f) $x(1+x^2)$
g) $(1+\sqrt{x})^2$
h) $\frac{x^2+x+1}{x}$.

(a) $\frac{dy}{dx} = 9 \times x^{9-1} = 9x^8$.

(b) $\frac{dy}{dx} = 5 \times 7x^{7-1} = 35x^6$.

(c) $y = x^{-4}$, so $\dfrac{dy}{dx} = -4x^{-4-1} = -4x^{-5} = -\dfrac{4}{x^5}$.

(d) $y = x^{-\frac{1}{2}} + x^2$, so $\dfrac{dy}{dx} = -\dfrac{1}{2}x^{-\frac{1}{2}-1} + 3 \times 4x^{4-1} = -\dfrac{1}{2}x^{-\frac{3}{2}} + 12x^3 = 12x^3 - \dfrac{1}{2x\sqrt{x}}$.

(e) $y = x^{\frac{1}{4}}$, and so $\dfrac{dy}{dx} = \dfrac{1}{4}x^{\frac{1}{4}-1} = \dfrac{1}{4}x^{-\frac{3}{4}} = \dfrac{1}{4x^{\frac{3}{4}}}$

(f) $y = x + x^3$, and so $\dfrac{dy}{dx} = 1 + 3x^2$

(g) $y = 1 + 2\sqrt{x} + x$, so $\dfrac{dy}{dx} = 2 \times \dfrac{1}{2}x^{-\frac{1}{2}} + 1 = \dfrac{1}{\sqrt{x}} + 1$

(h) $y = x + 1 + x^{-1}$, and so $\dfrac{dy}{dx} = 1 - x^{-2} = 1 + \dfrac{1}{x^2}$.

Note that we can only differentiate (at least for the while) functions which are sums and constant multiples of powers of x; if our function is not in that form, we must first manipulate it into the right form before trying to differentiate it. Note that negative powers of x and square (and other) roots of x have to be written in index form before they can be differentiated. Whether or not to convert the expression for the derivative back into an expression not in index form is a matter of choice and/or style.

EXERCISE 11A

1. In each part of this question, find the gradient of the chord joining the two points with the given x-coordinates on the graphs of $y = 2x^2$, $y = 3x^2$ and $y = -x^2$:

   a) 1 and 1.001
   b) 1 and 0.9999
   c) 2 and 2.002
   d) 2 and 1.999
   e) 3 and 3.000001
   f) 3 and 2.99999

2. Differentiate the following functions:

   a) x^2
   b) $x^2 - x$
   c) $4x^2$
   d) $3x^2 - 2x$
   e) $2 - 3x$
   f) $x - 2 - 2x^2$
   g) $2 + 4x - 3x^2$
   h) $\sqrt{2}x - \sqrt{3}x^2$

3. Find the derivative of each of the following functions $f(x)$ at $x = -3$:

   a) $-x^2$
   b) $3x$
   c) $x^2 + 3x$
   d) $2x - x^2$
   e) $2x^2 + 4x - 1$
   f) $-(3 - x^2)$
   g) $-x(2 + x)$
   h) $(x - 2)(2x - 1)$

4. For each of the following functions $f(x)$, find the value of x for which $f'(x)$ has the given value:

   a) $2x^2$ 3
   b) $x - 2x^2$ -1
   c) $2 + 3x + x^2$ 0
   d) $x^2 + 4x - 1$ 2
   e) $(x - 2)(x - 1)$ 0
   f) $2x(3x + 2)$ 10

5. For each of the following functions $f(x)$, find $f'(x)$.

   a) $3x - 1$
   b) $2 - 3x^2$
   c) 4
   d) $1 + 2x + 3x^2$
   e) $x^2 - 2x^2$
   f) $3(1 + 2x - x^2)$
   g) $2x(1 - x)$
   h) $x(2x + 1) - 1$

6. Differentiate the following functions:

   a) $x^3 + 2x^2$
   b) $1 - 2x^3 + 3x^2$
   c) $x^3 - 6x^2 + 11x - 6$
   d) $2x^3 + 3x^2 + x$
   e) $2x^2(1 - 3x^2)$
   f) $(1 - x)(1 + x + x^2)$

7. Find $f'(-2)$ for each of the following functions $f(x)$:

   a) $2x - x^3$
   b) $2x - x^2$
   c) $1 - 2x - 3x^2 + 4x^3$
   d) $2 - x$
   e) $x^2(1 + x)$
   f) $(1 + x)(1 - x + x^2)$

8. For each of the following functions $f(x)$ find the value(s) of x for which $f'(x)$ is equal to the given number.

   a) x^3 12
   b) $x^3 - x^2$ 8
   c) $3x - 3x^2 + x^3$ 108
   d) $x^3 - 3x^2 + 2x$ -1
   e) $x(1 + x)^2$ 0
   f) $x(1 - x)(1 + x)$ 2

9. Differentiate the following functions:

a) $2\sqrt{x}$

b) $(1 + 2\sqrt{x})^2$

c) $x - \frac{1}{2}\sqrt{x}$

d) $x\left(1 - \frac{1}{\sqrt{x}}\right)^2$

e) $x - \frac{1}{x}$

f) $\frac{x^3 + x^2 + 1}{x}$

g) $\frac{(x+1)(x+2)}{x}$

h) $\left(\frac{\sqrt{x}+x}{\sqrt{x}}\right)^2$

10. Differentiate each of these functions $f(x)$. Give your answer $f'(x)$ in a similar form, without negative or fractional indices:

a) $\frac{1}{4x}$

b) $\frac{3}{x^2}$

c) x^0

d) $\sqrt[4]{x^3}$

e) $6\sqrt[3]{x}$

f) $\frac{4}{\sqrt{x}}$

g) $\frac{3}{x} + \frac{1}{3x^3}$

h) $\sqrt{16x^5}$

i) $x\sqrt{x}$

j) $\frac{1}{\sqrt[3]{8x}}$

k) $\frac{x-2}{x^2}$

l) $\frac{1+x}{\sqrt[4]{x}}$

11. a) Show that $x^n - y^n = (x - y)\left(x^{n-1} + x^{n-2}y + x^{n-3}y^2 + \cdots + xy^{n-2} + y^{n-1}\right)$ for any positive integer n.

b) Use this result to expand $\frac{1}{h}\left[(x+h)^n - x^n\right]$ and hence deduce from first principles that the derivative of x^n is nx^{n-1}, without using the Binomial Theorem.

12*. Using first principles, determine the derivative of the functions

a) x^{-2}

b) $\sqrt{1 + x^2}$

c) $\frac{1}{1+x^4}$.

11.5   Tangents and Normals

Now that we can differentiate functions to determine gradients, we can calculate exact information about tangents to curves. Indeed, we can also determine another important class of lines related to a curve. In addition to tangents, we can determine **normals**. The normal to a curve at a point is the straight line which passes through that point and which is perpendicular to the tangent to the curve at that point. Differentiation will tell us the gradient of the tangent, and standard Coordinate Geometry ideas will give us the gradient of the normal.

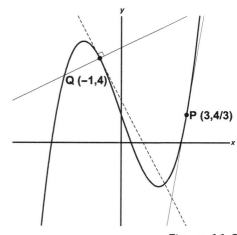

Figure 11.6

Example 11.5.1. *Points P and Q lie on the curve $y = \frac{1}{3}x^3 - 3x + \frac{4}{3}$. The x-coordinates of P and Q are 3 and -1 respectively. Find the equation of the tangent to the curve at P, and the equation of the normal to the curve at Q.*

Since $y = \frac{1}{3}x^3 - 3x + \frac{4}{3}$, we deduce that

$$\frac{dy}{dx} = x^2 - 3$$

At the point P we have $x = 3$, and hence $y = \frac{4}{3}$ and $\frac{dy}{dx} = 6$. Thus the tangent at P has equation

$$
\begin{aligned}
y - \tfrac{4}{3} &= 6(x - 3) \\
y &= 6x - \tfrac{50}{3} \\
18x - 3y &= 50
\end{aligned}
$$

At the point Q we have $x = -1$, and hence $y = 4$ and $\frac{dy}{dx} = -2$. Since the normal at Q is to be perpendicular to the tangent at Q, its gradient must be $\frac{1}{2}$ (so that $-2 \times \frac{1}{2} = -1$), and so the normal has equation

$$
\begin{aligned}
y - 4 &= \tfrac{1}{2}(x + 1) \\
x - 2y + 9 &= 0
\end{aligned}
$$

Example 11.5.2. *The point P on the curve $y = p\sqrt{x} + qx^{-2}$ has x-coordinate 1. The equation of the normal at P is $x + 4y = 13$. Find the values of p and q.*

Since the normal passes through the point P, the coordinates of P are $(1, 3)$, and hence

$$p + q = 3$$

The line $x + 4y = 13$ has gradient $-\frac{1}{4}$, and so the tangent at P has gradient 4. Since $\frac{dy}{dx} = \frac{p}{2\sqrt{x}} - 2qx^{-3}$, we deduce that

$$\tfrac{1}{2}p - 2q = 4$$

Solving these two equations simultaneously, we deduce that $p = 4$ and $q = -1$.

Example 11.5.3. *The tangent to the curve $y = \frac{1}{\sqrt{x}}$ at the point $P(a^2, a^{-1})$ (where $a > 0$) meets the x-axis at A and the y-axis at B. Find the area of the triangle OAB.*

Since $y = x^{-\frac{1}{2}}$, we have $\frac{dy}{dx} = -\frac{1}{2}x^{-\frac{3}{2}}$. At the point P we have $\frac{dy}{dx} = -\frac{1}{2}a^{-3}$, and so the tangent has equation

$$
\begin{aligned}
y - a^{-1} &= -\tfrac{1}{2}a^{-3}(x - a^2) \\
2a^3 y - 2a^2 &= a^2 - x \\
x + 2a^3 y &= 3a^2
\end{aligned}
$$

Looking for the intercepts of this tangent with the axes, we see that A has coordinates $(3a^2, 0)$, while B has coordinates $(0, \frac{3}{2}a^{-1})$. Thus triangle OAB has area

$$\tfrac{1}{2} \times 3a^2 \times \tfrac{3}{2}a^{-1} = \tfrac{9}{4}a$$

Example 11.5.4. *The tangent to the curve $y = x^3 - 11x^2 + 38x - 40$ at the point P, where $x = 3$, meets the curve again at the point Q. What are the coordinates of Q?*

We have $\frac{dy}{dx} = 3x^2 - 22x + 38$, and so $y = 2$ and $\frac{dy}{dx} = -1$ at the point P. Thus the tangent at P has equation $y - 2 = -(x - 3)$, or $x + y = 5$. To find the coordinates of Q we need to solve the equations $y = x^3 - 11x^2 + 38x - 40$ and $x + y = 5$ simultaneously. This leads us to the equation $x^3 - 11x^2 + 38x - 40 = 5 - x$, or

$$x^3 - 11x^2 + 39x - 45 = 0.$$

This is a fairly scary-looking cubic equation, but we already know a lot about its solutions! The tangent at P and the original curve both pass through P, and so $x = 3$ must be a solution of this cubic. Indeed, since the tangent just touches the original curve, we will see that $x = 3$ is a repeated root of this cubic. Factorising,

$$x^3 - 11x^2 + 39x - 45 = (x - 3)(x^2 - 8x + 15) = (x - 3)(x - 3)(x - 5).$$

Since Q is a point distinct from P, its x-coordinate is 5. The coordinates of Q are $(5, 0)$.

EXERCISE 11B

1. The tangent at P to the curve $y = x^2$ has gradient 3. Find the equation of the normal at P.

2. A normal to the curve $y = x^2 + 1$ has gradient -1. Find the equation of the tangent there.

3. Find the point where the normal at $(2, 4)$ to $y = x^2$ cuts the curve again.

4. Find the equation of the tangent to the curve $y = x^2$ which is parallel to the line $y = x$.

5. Find the equation of the tangent to the curve $y = x^2$ which is parallel to the x-axis.

6. Find the equation of the tangent to the curve $y = \frac{1}{2}x - 1$ which is perpendicular to the line $y = x - 1$.

7. Find the equation of the normal to the curve $y = 3x^2 - 2x - 1$ which is parallel to the line $y = x - 3$.

8. Find the equation of the normal to the curve $y = (x - 1)^2$ which is parallel to the y-axis.

9. Find the equation of the normal to the curve $y = 2x^2 + 3x + 4$ which is perpendicular to the line $y = 7x - 5$.

10. Find the equation of the tangent to the curve $y = x^3 + x$ at the point for which $x = -1$.

11. One of the tangents to the curve with equation $y = 4x - x^3$ is the line with equation $y = x - 2$. Find the equation of the other tangent parallel to $y = x - 2$.

12. Find the equation of the tangent at the point $(4, 2)$ to the curve with equation $y = \sqrt{x}$.

13. Find the equation of the tangent at the point $(2, \frac{1}{2})$ to the curve with equation $y = \frac{1}{x}$.

14. Find the equation of the normal at the point $(1, 2)$ to the graph $y = x + x^{-1}$.

15. The graphs of $y = x^2 - 2x$ and $y = x^3 - 3x^2 - 2x$ both pass through the origin. Show that they share the same tangent at the origin.

16. Find the equation of the tangent to the curve with equation $y = x^3 - 3x^2 - 2x - 6$ at the point where it crosses the y-axis.

17. A curve has equation $y = x(x - a)(x + a)$, where a is a constant. Find the equations of the tangents to the graph at the points where it crosses the x-axis.

18. Find the coordinates of the point of intersection of the tangents to the graph of $y = x^2$ at the points at which it meets the line with equation $y = x + 2$.

19. Find the equations of the tangent and the normal to $y = \sqrt[3]{x^2}$ at the point $(8, 4)$.

20. The tangent to the curve with equation $y = \frac{1}{x^2}$ at the point $(\frac{1}{2}, 4)$ meets the axes at P and Q. Find the coordinates of P and Q.

21. The curve $y = 2x^2 - 3x + 1$ crosses the x-axis at the points P and Q. The tangents to the curve at these two points intersect at the point R. Find the coordinates of R. Explain why PQR is a right-angled triangle, and calculate its area.

22. The normal to the curve $y = x^2 + x + 1$ at the point $P(1, 3)$ meets the curve again at Q. What are the coordinates of Q?

23. The tangent to the curve $y = x^3 + 4x^2 - 3x + 2$ at the point P, where $x = 2$, meets the curve again at the point Q. Find the coordinates of Q.

24. The normal to the curve $y = x^3 - 2x^2 + 7$ at the point P, where $x = 1$, meets the curve again at the points Q and R. Find the coordinates of Q and R.

25*. Consider the curve $y = f(x)$, where f is a polynomial. Suppose that P is the point on the curve where $x = a$.

   a) Show that the equation of the tangent at P is $y = f(a) + f'(a)(x - a)$.

   b) Explain why $f(x) - f(a) = (x - a)g(x)$, where g is another polynomial. By letting x tend to a, determine the value of $g(a)$.

   c) Show that $(x - a)^2$ is a factor of the polynomial $f(x) - f(a) - f'(a)(x - a)$.

   d) Complete the sentence: 'if the line $y = mx + c$ is a tangent to the curve $y = f(x)$ at the point $x = a$ then the equation
   $$f(x) = mx + c$$
   has ...'.

26*. The point P lies on the curve $4ay = x^2$ (where $a > 0$) and has coordinates $(2ap, ap^2)$. The point F has coordinates $(0, a)$.

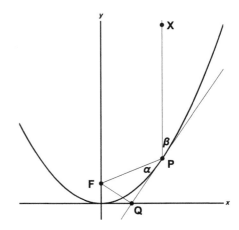

a) Find the equation of the tangent to the curve at the point P.

b) The tangent at P meets the x-axis at the point Q. Show that FQ is perpendicular to the tangent.

c) If α is the angle $\angle APF$, calculate $\tan \alpha$.

d) What relationship exists between α and β, where β is the angle between the tangent at P and the line PX which is parallel to the y-axis?

e) Why do we use parabolic mirrors?

11.6 Higher Order Derivatives

If y is a function, then its derivative $\dfrac{dy}{dx}$ is itself a function, and so could itself be differentiated. The derivative of the derivative of y is called the **second derivative** of y. We need a notation to describe such calculations.

If we are using the function notation, then this is relatively easy. The derivative of the function $f(x)$ was indicated by a single prime, giving $f'(x)$. To differentiate the function a second time, we simply add a second prime symbol, and write it as $f''(x)$.

If we are using Leibniz' notation instead, we need to recall the idea of the differential operator $\dfrac{d}{dx}$, so that $\dfrac{dy}{dx} = \dfrac{d}{dx}y$ can be thought of as applying the differential operator $\dfrac{d}{dx}$ to the function y. To obtain the second derivative, we need to apply the differential operator one more time, obtaining

$$\frac{d}{dx}\left(\frac{dy}{dx}\right)$$

This is an informative, but clumsy, notation. By convention we abbreviate this, and write the second derivative as

$$\frac{d^2 y}{dx^2}$$

> **Key Fact 11.7** Second Derivatives
>
> The second derivative of the function $f(x)$ with respect to x is denoted $f''(x)$. The second derivative of the function $y = f(x)$ can also be written $\dfrac{d^2 y}{dx^2}$.

Example 11.6.1. If $f(x) = x(x+1)^2$, find $f''(x)$. If $y = 2\sqrt{x} + x^2 - 4$, find $\dfrac{d^2 y}{dx^2}$.

We see that $f(x) = x^3 + 2x^2 + x$, so that $f'(x) = 3x^2 + 4x + 1$, and hence $f''(x) = 6x + 4$. In the other case we have $y = 2x^{\frac{1}{2}} + x^2 - 4$, so that

$$\frac{dy}{dx} = x^{-\frac{1}{2}} + 2x \qquad \frac{d^2 y}{dx^2} = -\tfrac{1}{2}x^{-\frac{3}{2}} + 2$$

Of course, we do not need to stop with the second derivative. We can differentiate functions as many times as we like (to be more accurate, as many times as it is possible, since not all functions are differentiable), and we extend the above notation for second derivatives to cope.

> **Key Fact 11.8** Higher Order Derivatives
>
> The successive derivatives of a function y with respect to x are denoted
>
> $$\frac{dy}{dx}; \frac{d^2y}{dx^2}, \frac{d^3y}{dx^3}, \frac{d^4y}{dx^4}, \dots, \frac{d^ny}{dx^n}, \dots$$
>
> while the successive derivatives of a function $f(x)$ with respect to x are denoted
>
> $$f'(x), f''(x), f'''(x), f^{(4)}(x), \dots, f^{(n)}(x), \dots$$

It is not practical, or legible, to keep adding prime symbols, so higher order derivatives are represented by superscript numbers in brackets instead.

EXERCISE 11C

1. Find $\dfrac{dy}{dx}, \dfrac{d^2y}{dx^2}, \dfrac{d^3y}{dx^3}$ and $\dfrac{d^4y}{dx^4}$ for the following functions:

   a) $y = x^2 + 3x - 7$
   b) $y = 2x^3 + x$
   c) $y = x^4 - 2$
   d) $y = \sqrt{x}$
   e) $y = \frac{1}{\sqrt{x}}$
   f) $y = x^{\frac{1}{4}}$

2. Find $f'(x)$, $f''(x)$, $f'''(x)$ and $f^{(4)}(x)$ for the following functions:

   a) $f(x) = x^2 - 5x + 2$
   b) $f(x) = 2x^5 - 3x^2$
   c) $f(x) = \frac{1}{x^4}$
   d) $f(x) = x^2(3 - x^4)$
   e) $f(x) = x^{\frac{3}{4}}$
   f) $f(x) = x^{\frac{3}{8}}$

3. Find an expression for $\dfrac{d^ny}{dx^n}$, where n is a positive integer, when

   a) $y = x^n$

   b) $y = x^{n+2}$

   c) $y = x^m$ where m is a positive integer and $n > m$.

4. Find an expression for $\dfrac{d^ny}{dx^n}$ where

   a) $y = x^{-1}$
   b) $y = x^{2n}$
   c) $y = \sqrt{x}$

11.7 Increasing and Decreasing Functions

As we have seen, the derivative $f'(x)$ of a function $f(x)$ is itself a function, which can (for example) be differentiated. It is important to start to see the relationship between the graph of a function $y = f(x)$ and the graph of its derived function $y = f'(x)$.

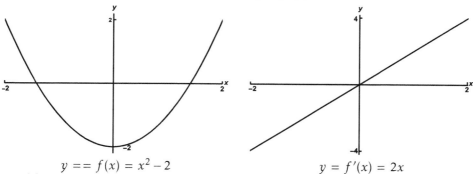

$$y == f(x) = x^2 - 2 \qquad\qquad y = f'(x) = 2x$$

Figure 11.7

Consider the function $f(x) = x^2 - 2$ and compare the graphs of $y = f(x)$ and $y = f'(x)$. If $x < 0$ the graph of $y = f'(x)$ is below the x-axis and so $f'(x)$ is negative. On the other hand, when $x > 0$ the graph of $f'(x)$ is above the x-axis, and so $f'(x)$ is positive. Thus the gradient of $y = f(x)$ is negative for $x < 0$ and positive for $x > 0$, which is reflected in the graph of $y = f(x)$.

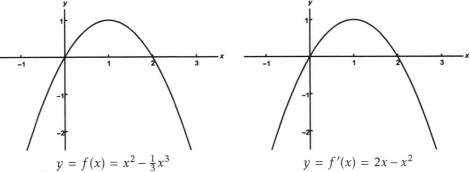

$$y = f(x) = x^2 - \tfrac{1}{3}x^3 \qquad\qquad y = f'(x) = 2x - x^2$$

Figure 11.8

This time, compare the graphs of $y = f(x) = x^2 - \tfrac{1}{3}x^3$ and the graph of its derived function $y = f'(x) = 2x - x^2$. This time $f'(x)$ is negative for $x < 0$ and $x > 2$, and positive for $0 < x < 2$, and so the gradient of $y = f(x)$ is negative for $x < 0$ and $x > 0$, and positive for $0 < x < 2$.

In both cases, we see that properties of the graph $y = f'(x)$ can be used to infer details of properties of the graph $y = f(x)$.

Key Fact 11.9 Derivatives and Monotonic Functions

If $f'(x) > 0$ in an interval $p < x < q$, then $f(x)$ is a strictly increasing function over the interval $p \le x \le q$, in that $f(x) < f(y)$ for any $p \le x < y \le q$.
If $f'(x) \ge 0$ in an interval $p < x < q$, then $f(x)$ is an increasing function over the interval $p \le x \le q$, in that $f(x) \le f(y)$ for any $p \le x < y \le q$.
If $f'(x) < 0$ in an interval $p < x < q$, then $f(x)$ is a strictly decreasing function over the interval $p \le x \le q$, in that $f(x) > f(y)$ for any $p \le x < y \le q$.
If $f'(x) \le 0$ in an interval $p < x < q$, then $f(x)$ is a decreasing function over the interval $p \le x \le q$, in that $f(x) \ge f(y)$ for any $p \le x < y \le q$.
Note that these results can apply to ranges that extend without limit: if $f'(x) > 0$ for all $x > p$, then $f(x)$ is strictly increasing on $x \ge p$, for example.

For Interest

We are assuming here that the function $y = f(x)$ is continuous on the interval $p \le x \le q$. This is a rather technical requirement, but the requirement of continuity ensures that the function does not contain any instantaneous changes of value, or 'jumps' in the graph.
The function such as 'the fractional part of x' is defined for all positive real numbers but is not continuous — although this function has a positive derivative at all non-integer values of x, it is not increasing.

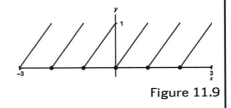

Figure 11.9

Example 11.7.1. *For the function* $f(x) = x^4 - 4x^3$*, find where* $f(x)$ *is increasing and where it is decreasing.*

Start by differentiating and factorising $f'(x)$:

$$f'(x) = 4x^3 - 12x^2 = 4x^2(x - 3)$$

Since x^2 is always positive (except when $x = 0$) it is easy to see that $f'(x) > 0$ for $x > 3$, and that $f'(x) < 0$ for all $x < 3$ except $x = 0$.

Thus $f(x)$ is strictly increasing over the interval $x \geq 3$. Since $f'(x) \leq 0$ for all $x \leq 3$, we might be tempted simply to deduce that $f(x)$ is decreasing over that interval. However, we know that $f(x)$ is strictly decreasing for $x \leq 0$ and for $0 \leq x \leq 3$, and these together imply that $f(x)$ is strictly decreasing for $x \leq 3$.

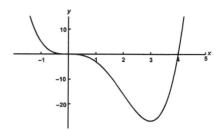

Figure 11.10

For Interest

Although the condition that $f'(x) > 0$ guarantees that $f(x)$ is strictly increasing for $p \leq x \leq q$, it is not necessary. A function can be strictly increasing, and have its derivative being zero at a number of points.

Example 11.7.2. *Find where the function $g(x) = x^{\frac{2}{3}}(1-x)$ is increasing and where it is decreasing.*

If we write $g(x) = x^{\frac{2}{3}} - x^{\frac{5}{3}}$, we deduce that

$$g'(x) = \tfrac{2}{3}x^{-\frac{1}{3}} - \tfrac{5}{3}x^{\frac{2}{3}} = \tfrac{1}{3}x^{-\frac{1}{3}}(2 - 5x)$$

and hence $g'(x) > 0$ for $0 < x < \tfrac{2}{5}$, while $g'(x) < 0$ for $x < 0$ and $x > \tfrac{2}{5}$. Note that, while $g(x)$ does not have a finite derivative at 0, it is continuous at 0. The function $g(x)$ is increasing for $0 \leq x \leq \tfrac{2}{5}$, and decreasing for $x \leq 0$ and $x \geq \tfrac{2}{5}$.

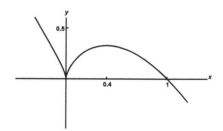

Figure 11.11

11.8 Turning Points

In Example 11.7.1, we saw that the function $f(x) = x^4 - 4x^3$ was strictly decreasing for $x \leq 3$, and strictly increasing for $x \geq 3$. This implies that $f(x) \geq f(3)$ for all possible values of x. Thus $f(3)$ is the minimum value of the function $f(x)$, and that $(3, -27)$ is the minimum point on the graph $y = f(x)$.

A minimum point does not have to be the lowest point on the whole graph: it just has to be the lowest point in its immediate neighbourhood. In Example 11.7.2, $x = 0$ is a minimum for the function $y = g(x) = x^{\frac{2}{3}}(1 - x)$, even though the function takes smaller values that 0 when $x > 1$; the region $x > 1$ is not in the immediate neighbourhood of $x = 0$.

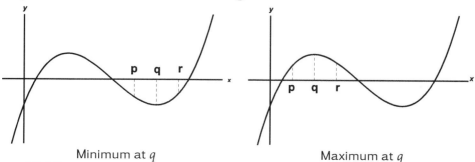

Minimum at q Maximum at q

Figure 11.12

Key Fact 11.10 Maxima and Minima

A function $f(x)$ has a **(local) minimum** at $x = q$ if there exists an interval $p < x < r$ containing q in which $f(x) > f(q)$ for all $p < x < r$ except q.
A function $f(x)$ has a **(local) maximum** at $x = q$ if there exists an interval $p < x < r$ containing q in which $f(x) < f(q)$ for all $p < x < r$ except q.

As observed above, $x = 0$ is a minimum for the function $y = g(x) = x^{\frac{2}{3}}(1 - x)$ discussed in Example 11.7.2. We also note that $x = \frac{2}{5}$ is a maximum for the same function. The function $g(x)$ is differentiable at $x = \frac{2}{5}$, and (since $x = \frac{2}{5}$ is a maximum for the function, the tangent at that point will be horizontal, and so the gradient at that point will be zero. Hence $g'(\frac{2}{5}) = 0$. A similar argument concerning the local minimum at $x = 3$ for the function $y = f(x) = x^4 - 4x^3$ introduced in Example 11.7.1 tells us that $f'(3) = 0$.

Key Fact 11.11 Turning Points

Any point x where the derivative $f'(x)$ both exists and is zero is called **turning point** of the function.

We have seen above how turning points can be maxima or minima, that a maximum or a minimum need not be a turning point (since the function does not have to be differentiable at a maximum or minimum). Most maxima and minima do occur at turning points, however, and so we need to be able to identify the various types of turning point. There are essentially four types (although we shall only be mainly concerned with the first two):

- **Minima** If we consider an interval around the minimum q where the derivative is non-zero (except at q) then, since the function y is decreasing for $x < q$, the derivative $\frac{dy}{dx} < 0$ for $x < q$. Similarly, the function y is increasing for $x > q$, and so $\frac{dy}{dx} > 0$ for $x > q$:

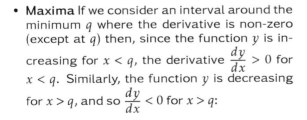

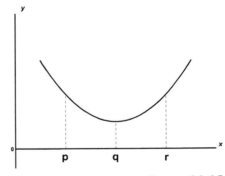

Figure 11.13

- **Maxima** If we consider an interval around the minimum q where the derivative is non-zero (except at q) then, since the function y is increasing for $x < q$, the derivative $\frac{dy}{dx} > 0$ for $x < q$. Similarly, the function y is decreasing for $x > q$, and so $\frac{dy}{dx} < 0$ for $x > q$:

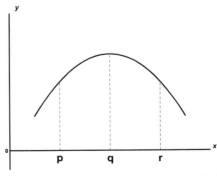

Figure 11.14

- **Inflexions** These are less common turning points, that we include for the sake of completeness. It is possible for a function to have a turning point without the derivative changing sign, and so without the graph 'changing direction'.

In the first case, there is an interval around the turning point q where the derivative is non-zero (except at q) and the function is strictly increasing throughout. Thus $\dfrac{dy}{dx} > 0$ for $x \neq q$. This sort of turning point is called a **positive inflexion**:

x	−	q	+
$\dfrac{dy}{dx}$	+	0	+
	╱	−	╱

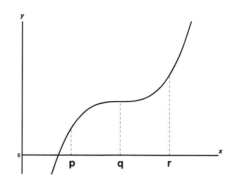

Figure 11.15

In the second case, there is an interval around the turning point q where the derivative is non-zero (except at q) and the function is strictly decreasing throughout. Thus $\dfrac{dy}{dx} < 0$ for $x \neq q$. This sort of turning point is called a **negative inflexion**:

x	−	q	+
$\dfrac{dy}{dx}$	−	0	−
	╲	−	╲

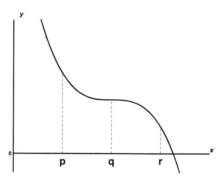

Figure 11.16

Key Fact 11.12 Classifying Turning Points

Turning points can be classified into maxima, minima and positive and negative inflexions by considering the sign of the derivative in an interval around the turning point!

Example 11.8.1. *Find and classify the turning points of the function* $y = x^3 - 6x^2 - 36x + 10$.

Differentiating and factorising the function

$$\frac{dy}{dx} = 3x^2 - 12x - 36 = 3(x^2 - 4x - 12) = 3(x - 6)(x + 2)$$

so the turning points of the function occur at $(-2, 50)$ and $(6, -206)$. We could use our knowledge of the shape of a cubic to deduce that $(-2, 60)$ must be a maximum, and $(6, -206)$ a minimum, but it is good practice (looking ahead to the time where we do not know the shape of the curve in advance of our analysis) to classify these turning points by the above method.

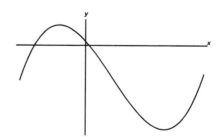

Figure 11.17

Looking at the sign of the derivative at and between the turning points tells us that the turning point at $x = -2$ is a maximum, while that at $x = 6$ is a minimum.

x		−2		6	
$\dfrac{dy}{dx}$	+	0	−	0	+
	╱	−	╲	−	╱

There is a second method that can be used to determine some turning points.

If the function $y = f(x)$ has a turning point at the point q, and if $\frac{d^2y}{dx^2} = f''(x) < 0$ at the point q (and therefore in an interval around it), then $\frac{dy}{dx} = f'(x)$ will be decreasing in an interval around q. Since $\frac{dy}{dx} = 0$ at $x = q$, we deduce that $\frac{dy}{dx} > 0$ for $x < q$, and $\frac{dy}{dx} < 0$ for $x > q$, and hence the turning point $x = q$ is a maximum.

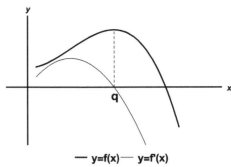

Figure 11.18

If the function $y = f(x)$ has a turning point at the point q, and if $\frac{d^2y}{dx^2} = f''(x) > 0$ at the point q (and therefore in an interval around it), then $\frac{dy}{dx} = f'(x)$ will be increasing in an interval around q. Since $\frac{dy}{dx} = 0$ at $x = q$, we deduce that $\frac{dy}{dx} < 0$ for $x < q$, and $\frac{dy}{dx} > 0$ for $x > q$, and hence the turning point $x = q$ is a minimum.

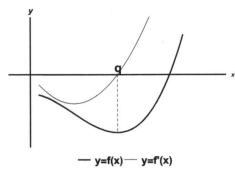

Figure 11.19

Key Fact 11.13 Turning Points and the Second Derivative

A turning point where the second derivative is negative is a maximum, and a turning point where the second derivative is positive is a minimum.

For Interest

When we deduce from the fact that $\frac{d^2y}{dx^2}$ is positive at q that the second derivative is positive in an interval around q, we are in fact assuming that the second derivative is continuous. This type of assumption is acceptable for all the 'nice' functions that we normally meet.

The problem with the second derivative method is that it is not comprehensive in classifying all turning points. We do not know what to do at a turning point where the second derivative is zero. The functions $y = x^4$, $y = 16 - x^4$ and $y = 8 + x^3$ all have turning points at $x = 0$, all have second derivative equal to zero, but the turning points are (respectively) a minimum, a maximum and a positive inflexion.

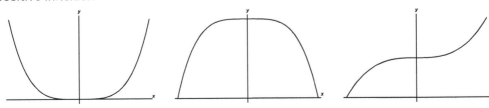

Figure 11.20

> **Food For Thought 11.2**
>
> Just to be confusing, any point on a curve which has zero second derivative is called an **inflexion**. Thus an inflexion can be a maximum, a minimum or a positive or negative inflexion (in the other sense of the word)!

Example 11.8.2. *Find and classify the turning points for the function $f(x) = x^3(x-2)^2$.*

We will discover an easier way to differentiate this function later on. For the present, $f(x) = x^5 - 4x^4 + 4x^3$, and hence

$$f'(x) = 5x^4 - 16x^3 + 12x^2 = x^2(5x^2 - 16x + 12) = x^2(x-2)(5x-6)$$

so the turning points of the function are $(0,0)$, $(2,0)$ and $\left(\frac{6}{5}, \frac{3456}{3125}\right)$. The table

x		0		$\frac{6}{5}$		2	
$\dfrac{dy}{dx}$	$+$	0	$+$	0	$-$	0	$+$
	$\diagup$	$-$	$\diagup$	$-$	$\diagdown$	$-$	$\diagdown$

shows that we have a positive inflexion at $x = 0$, a maximum at $x = \frac{6}{5}$ and a minimum at $x = 2$. The sketch on the right shows the shape of the graph $y = f(x)$. Note that $f''(x) = 20x^3 - 48x^2 + 24x$ is equal to 0, $-\frac{144}{25}$ and 16 at 0, $\frac{6}{5}$ and 2 respectively, so the second derivative method can classify the turning points at $x = \frac{6}{5}$ and $x = 2$, but not the one at $x = 0$.

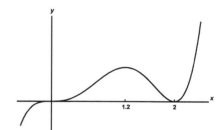

Figure 11.21

Finding turning points can enable us to determine the ranges of functions.

Example 11.8.3. *Find the range of the function $f(x) = x^2 + 2x^{-1}$ for $x > 0$.*

The function clearly tends to infinity as x tends to 0 or as x tends to infinity. We need to determine the minimum value obtained by f. Now

$$f'(x) = 2x - 2x^{-2} \qquad x > 0$$

and hence has a turning point when $2x = 2x^{-2}$, or when $x = 1$. Since $f''(x) = 2 + 4x^{-3}$, we see that $f''(1) = 6 > 0$, and hence $x = 1$ is indeed a minimum for $f(x)$. It is now clear that the range of $f(x)$ is $y \geq 3$.

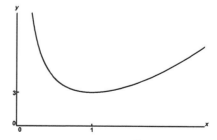

Figure 11.22

EXERCISE 11D

1. For each of the following functions $f(x)$, find $f'(x)$ and the interval in which $f(x)$ is increasing.

   a) $x^2 - 5x + 6$ b) $x^2 + 6x - 4$ c) $7 - 3x - x^2$
   d) $3x^2 - 5x + 7$ e) $5x^2 + 3x - 2$ f) $7 - 4x - 3x^2$

2. For each of the following functions $f(x)$, find $f'(x)$ and the interval in which $f(x)$ is decreasing.

a) $x^2 + 4x - 9$

b) $x^2 - 3x - 5$

c) $5 - 3x + x^2$

d) $2x^2 - 8x + 7$

e) $4 + 7x - 2x^2$

f) $3 - 5x - 7x^2$

3. For each of the following functions $f(x)$, find $f'(x)$ and any intervals in which $f(x)$ is increasing.

a) $x^3 - 12x$

b) $2x^3 - 18x + 5$

c) $2x^3 - 9x^2 - 24x + 7$

d) $x^3 - 3x^2 + 3x + 4$

e) $x^4 - 2x^2$

f) $x^4 + 4x^3$

g) $3x - x^3$

h) $2x^5 - 5x^4 + 10$

i) $3x + x^3$

4. For each of the following functions $f(x)$, find $f'(x)$ and any intervals in which $f(x)$ is decreasing. In part (i), n is an integer.

a) $x^3 - 27x$ for $x \geq 0$

b) $x^4 + 4x^2 - 5$ for $x \geq 0$

c) $x^3 - 3x^2 + 3x - 1$

d) $12x - 2x^3$

e) $2x^3 + 3x^2 - 36x - 7$

f) $3x^4 - 20x^3 + 12$

g) $36x^2 - 2x^4$

h) $x^5 - 5x$

i) $x^n - nx$ $(n \geq 1)$

5. For each of the following functions $f(x)$, find $f'(x)$, the intervals in which $f(x)$ is decreasing, and the intervals in which $f(x)$ is increasing.

a) $x^{\frac{3}{2}}(x-1)$ for $x > 0$

b) $x^{\frac{3}{4}} - 2x^{\frac{7}{4}}$ for $x > 0$

c) $x^{\frac{2}{3}}(x+2)$

d) $x^{\frac{3}{5}}(x^2 - 13)$

e) $x + \frac{3}{x}$ for $n \neq 0$

f) $\sqrt{x} + \frac{1}{\sqrt{x}}$ for $x > 0$

6. For the graphs of each of the following functions:

- find the coordinates of the stationary point,
- determine, with reasoning, whether the turning point is a maximum or a minimum,
- state the range of the function.

a) $x^2 - 8x + 4$

b) $3x^2 + 12x + 5$

c) $5x^2 + 6x + 2$

d) $4 - 6x - x^2$

e) $x^2 + 6x + 9$

f) $1 - 4x - 4x^2$

7. Find the coordinates of the stationary points on the graphs of the following functions, and classify the turning points.

a) $2x^3 + 3x^2 - 72x + 5$

b) $x^3 - 3x^2 - 45x + 7$

c) $3x^4 - 8x^3 + 6x^2$

d) $3x^5 - 20x^3 + 1$

e) $2x + x^2 - 4x^3$

f) $x^3 + 3x^2 + 3x + 1$

g) $x + \frac{1}{x}$

h) $x^2 + \frac{54}{x}$

i) $x - \frac{1}{x}$

j) $x - \sqrt{x}$ for $x > 0$

k) $\frac{1}{x} - \frac{3}{x^2}$

l) $x^2 - \frac{16}{x} + 5$

m) $x^{\frac{1}{3}}(4 - x)$

n) $x^{\frac{1}{5}}(x + 6)$

o) $x^4(1 - x)$

8. Find the ranges of each of these functions $f(x)$, each defined over their largest possible domains.

a) $x^2 + x + 1$

b) $x^4 - 8x^2$

c) $x + \frac{1}{x}$

9. Determine the coordinates of the stationary points of these functions $f(x)$, classifying them as maxima, minima or positive or negative inflexions.

a) $3x - x^3$

b) $x^3 - 3x^2$

c) $3x^4 + 1$

d) $2x^3 - 3x^2 - 12x + 4$

e) $\frac{2}{x^4} - \frac{1}{x}$

f) $x^2 + \frac{1}{x^2}$

g) $\frac{1}{x} - \frac{1}{x^2}$

h) $2x^3 - 12x^2 + 24x + 6$

10. Determine the coordinates of the stationary points of these functions, classifying them as maxima, minima or positive or negative inflexions.

a) $y = 3x^4 - 4x^3 - 12x^2 - 3$

b) $y = x^3 - 3x^2 + 3x + 5$

c) $y = 16x - 3x^3$

d) $y = \frac{4}{x^2} - x$

e) $y = \frac{4 + x^2}{x}$

f) $y = \frac{x-3}{x^2}$

g) $y = 2x^5 - 7$

h) $y = 3x^4 - 8x^3 + 6x^2 + 1$

11*. Differentiating from first principles, explain why $f'(q) \geq 0$, where f is a function which is strictly increasing on the interval $p < x < r$ which contains q (and which is differentiable at q).

12*. Differentiating from first principles, explain why $f'(q) = 0$ for any function which has a maximum at $x = q$ (and which is differentiable at q).

11.9 Applications

11.9.1. Derivatives as Rates of Change

7.4 Derivatives as rates of change

The quantities x and y in a relationship $y = f(x)$ are often called **variables**, because x can stand for any number in the domain and y for any number in the range. When you draw the graph you have a free choice of values of x, and then work out the values of y. So x is called the **independent variable** and y the **dependent variable**.

These variables often stand for physical or economic quantities, and then it is convenient to use other letters which suggest what these quantities are: for example, t for time, V for volume, C for cost, P for population, and so on.

Consider a car accelerating away from rest. For the first 10 seconds of its motion it is accelerating, and after that time it is travelling at a constant speed. The diagram on the right shows an appropriate speed-time diagram for this motion. After 10 seconds, the car is travelling at a constant speed, and so that part of the graph is a straight line. The gradient of that line is 30 (as can be calculated by determining the rise δs and the run δt for the line), and this tells us that the speed of the car during that stage of the motion is 30 ms^{-1}.

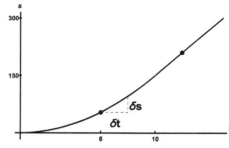

Figure 11.23

However, it is not quite so clear what the speed of the car is at time $t = 6$, for example. An approximation to that speed can be obtained by looking at the average speed over a short period of time δt. If the distance travelled in that time is δs, then the average speed is then $\frac{\delta s}{\delta t}$. But this is the gradient of the chord on the curve between time $t = 6$ and $t = 6 + \delta t$. As δt tends to 0, the average speed tends towards a limit, which is the instantaneous speed v of the car. In other words, we need to replace the simple 'speed equals distance over time' idea with the notion that 'speed is the rate of change of distance with respect to time, namely the derivative of distance with respect to time'. Thus

$$v = \frac{ds}{dt}$$

Key Fact 11.14 Rates of Change

If x and y are the independent and dependent variables respectively in a functional relationship, then the derivative

$$\frac{dy}{dx}$$

measures the **rate of change of y with respect to x**.

Example 11.9.1. *A sprinter in a women's 100 metre race reaches her top speed of 12 ms^{-1} after she has run 36 metres. Up to that distance her speed is proportional to the square root of the distance she has run. Show that until she reaches full speed the rate of change of her speed with respect to distance is inversely proportional to her speed.*

Suppose that after she has run s metres her speed is v ms^{-1}. We know that, for $0 \leq s \leq 36$, $v = k\sqrt{s}$ for some constant k, and that $v = 12$ when $s = 36$. Substituting in, we see that $12 = 6k$, and so $k = 2$. Thus

$$v = 2\sqrt{s}, \qquad 0 \leq s \leq 36.$$

The rate of change of her speed with respect to distance is thus

$$\frac{dv}{ds} = \frac{1}{\sqrt{s}} = \frac{2}{v}$$

The rate of change is indeed inversely proportional to her speed.

11.9.2. SOLVING PROBLEMS

Example 11.9.2. *A line of cars, each 5 metres long, is travelling along an open road at a steady speed of S kmh. There is a recommended separation between each pair of cars given by the formula $0.18S + 0.006S^2$ metres. At what speed should the cars travel to maximise the number of cars that the road can accommodate?*

Although perhaps more challenging conceptually, it is easier notationally to handle this problem in the general case, and write the formula for separation between card as $aS + bS^2$ (with $a = 0.18$ and $b = 0.006$). This will make the algebra clearer. We just have to remember that a and b are constants when it comes to differentiating functions which involve them.

A 'block', being the total length of a car, plus the recommended gap between successive cars, is $5 + aS + bS^2$ m, or $\frac{1}{1000}(5 + aS + bS^2)$ km. In order for the most cars to pass a checkpoint on the road in a given hour. the time T taken for each block to pass that checkpoint must be as small as possible. Since ST is the length of a block, we have

$$T = \tfrac{1}{1000}\left(5S^{-1} + a + bS\right)$$

We want to find the value of S that minimises T. Note that the problem assumes that the cars's speed is positive, so that $S > 0$. Since

$$\frac{dT}{dS} = \tfrac{1}{1000}\left(b - 5S^{-2}\right)$$

we see that the only turning point for T (for $S > 0$) occurs when $S = \sqrt{\frac{5}{b}}$.

If $0 < S < \sqrt{\frac{5}{b}}$ then $bS^2 < 5$, so $b < 5S^{-2}$, and hence $\frac{dT}{dS} < 0$. Similarly, if $S > \sqrt{\frac{5}{b}}$ then $\frac{dT}{dS} > 0$. Hence we deduce that T has a minimum when $S = \sqrt{\frac{5}{b}}$.

Substituting $b = 0.006$, we obtain the optimal speed to be 28.87 kmh. Note that this optimal speed does not depend on the value of a. For $a = 0.18$ we obtain the minimum value of T to be 5.26×10^{-4} hours, or 1.90 seconds. Approximately 1900 cars can pass the checkpoint in an hour at the optimal speed.

Example 11.9.3. *A hollow cone with base radius a cm and height b cm is placed on a table. What is the volume of the largest cylinder that can be hidden underneath it?*

The volume of a cylinder of radius r cm and height h cm is V cm^3, where

$$V = \pi r^2 h.$$

Since the size of the cylinder is limited by its having to lie inside the cone, there are restrictions that must be applied to the values of r and h.

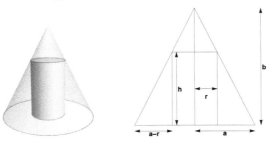

Figure 11.24

Figure 11.24 shows a three-dimensional representation of the problem, and a two-dimensional cross-section illustrating the problem. The height h and radius r of the cylinder are related by the equation

$$\frac{h}{a - r} = \frac{b}{a}$$

so that

$$h = \tfrac{b}{a}(a - r)$$

Thus the volume of a cylinder of radius r fitting snugly inside the cone is

$$V = \frac{b\pi}{a}r^2(a-r) = \frac{\pi b}{a}(ar^2 - r^3)$$

and we need to maximise V over the domain $0 < r < a$. Now

$$\frac{dV}{dr} = \frac{\pi b}{a}(2ar - 3r^2) = \frac{\pi br}{a}(2a - 3r)$$

and so V has turning points at ($r = 0$ and) $r = \frac{2}{3}a$. It is easy to check that $\frac{dV}{dr}$ is positive for $0 < r < \frac{2}{3}a$, and negative for $\frac{2}{3}a < r < a$, and hence the turning point at $\frac{2}{3}a$ is a maximum.

When $r = \frac{2}{3}a$, $h = \frac{1}{3}b$, and hence $V = \frac{4}{27}\pi a^2 b$. Since the volume of the cone is $\frac{1}{3}\pi a^2 b$, this cylinder occupies $\frac{4}{9}$ of the volume of the cone.

EXERCISE 11E

1. a) Find $\frac{dz}{dt}$ where $z = 3t^2 + 7t - 5$.
    b) Find $\frac{d\theta}{dx}$ where $\theta = x - \sqrt{x}$.
    c) Find $\frac{dx}{dy}$ where $x = y + 3y^{-2}$.
    d) Find $\frac{dr}{dt}$ where $r = t^2 + \frac{1}{\sqrt{t}}$.
    e) Find $\frac{dm}{dt}$ where $m = (t+3)^2$.
    f) Find $\frac{df}{ds}$ where $f = 2s^6 - 3s^2$.
    g) Find $\frac{dw}{dt}$ where $w = 5t$.
    h) Find $\frac{dR}{dr}$ where $R = \frac{1-r^3}{r^2}$.

2. A particle moves along the x-axis. Its displacement at time t is $x = 6t - t^2$.

    a) What does $\frac{dx}{dt}$ represent?

    b) Is x increasing or decreasing when   (i) $t = 1$,   (ii) $t = 4$?

    c) Find the greatest (positive) displacement of the particle.

3. Devise suitable notation to express each of the following in mathematical form.

    a) The distance travelled along the motorway is increasing at a constant rate.

    b) The rate at which a savings bank deposit grows is proportional to the amount of money deposited.

    c) The rate at which the diameter of a tree increases is a function of the air temperature.

4. At a speed of S kmh a car will travel y kilometres on each litre of petrol, where

    $$y = 5 + \tfrac{1}{5}S - \frac{1}{800}S^2 .$$

    Calculate the speed at which the car should be driven for maximum economy.

5. A ball is thrown vertically upwards. At time t seconds its height h metres is given by $h = 20t - 5t^2$. Calculate the ball's maximum height above the ground.

6. The sum of two real numbers x and y is 12. Find the maximum value of their product xy.

7. The product of two positive real numbers x and y is 20. Find the minimum possible value of their sum.

8. The volume of a cylinder is given by the formula $V = \pi r^2 h$. Find the greatest and least values of V if $r + h = 6$.

9. A loop of string of length 1 metre is formed into a rectangle with one pair of opposite sides each x cm. Calculate the value of x which will maximise the area enclosed by the string.

10. One side of a rectangular sheep pen is formed by a hedge. The other three sides are made using fencing; 120 metres of fencing are available. The hedge side of the sheep pen is $120 - x$ m long.

   a) Show that the area of the rectangle is $\frac{1}{2}x(120-x)$ m^2.

   b) Calculate the maximum possible area of the sheep pen.

11. A rectangular sheet of metal measures 50 cm by 40 cm. Equal squares of side x cm are cut from each corner and discarded. The sheet is then folded up to make a tray of depth x cm. What is the domain of possible values of x? Find the value of x which maximises the capacity of the tray.

12. An open rectangular box is to be made with a square base, and its capacity is to be 4000 cm^2. Find the length of the side of the base when the amount of material used to make the box is as small as possible. (Ignore 'flaps'.)

13. An open cylindrical wastepaper bin, of radius r cm and capacity V cm^3, is to have a surface area of 5000 cm^2.

   a) Show that $V = \frac{1}{2}r(5000 - \pi r^2)$.

   b) Calculate the maximum possible capacity of the bin.

14. A circular cylinder is to fit inside a sphere of radius 10 cm. Calculate the maximum possible volume of the cylinder. (It is probably best to take as your independent variable the height, or half the height, of the cylinder.)

15. A ship sails on a voyage of 300 km at a constant speed. When the ship's speed is u kmh the cost is $£\left(\frac{1}{25}v^3 + \frac{2025}{v}\right)$ per hour. Find the speed at which the ship should travel in order to minimise costs.

16*. The point P on the hyperbola with equation $y = 1 - x^2$ has x-coordinate $u > 0$. The tangent to the hyperbola at the point P meets the x- and y-axes at points P and Q. What value of $u > 0$ minimises the area of the triangle OPQ?

17*. A line of negative gradient $-m$ passes through the point P (a,b), where $a, b > 0$, and meets the coordinate axes at X and Y.

   a) Find the coordinates of X and Y in terms of a, b and m.

   b) Show that the area of the triangle OXY is $A = \frac{1}{2m}(ma + b)^2$.

   c) Treating the values of a and b as fixed, find the minimum value of A.

Chapter 11: Summary

- The gradient of the tangent to a curve a point is called the (first) derivative of the curve at that point; if the curve is $y = f(x)$, the derivative is written

$$\frac{dy}{dx} = f'(x).$$

- The first derivative of a function $f(x)$ can be derived 'from first principles' using the formula

$$f'(x) = \lim_{h \to 0} \frac{f(x+h) - f(x)}{h}$$

- Differentiation behaves well with respect to sums, differences and scalar multiples of functions, since if functions f, g and h are related by the formula $f(x) = \alpha g(x) + \beta h(x)$ for scalars α and β, then

$$f'(x) = \alpha g'(x) + \beta h'(x).$$

- A function with non-negative (positive) derivative is (strictly) increasing; a function with non-positive (negative) derivative is (strictly) decreasing.

- The derivative $\dfrac{dy}{dx}$ is the rate of change of y with respect to x.

- The second derivative of y with respect to x is the derivative of $\dfrac{dy}{dx}$ with respect to x; given the function $y = f(x)$, its second derivative is written $\dfrac{d^2 y}{dx^2} = f''(x)$.

- A turning point on a function $f(x)$ is a point where $f'(x) = 0$. A turning point is:

  ★ a maximum if $\dfrac{d^2 y}{dx^2} < 0$ at the turning point,

  ★ a minimum if $\dfrac{d^2 y}{dx^2} > 0$ at the turning point.

  Turning points can also be identified without the need to evaluate the second derivative; inspection of the sign of the derivative of y near the turning point q can distinguish between:

  ★ **maxima:**

x	$-$	q	$+$
$\dfrac{dy}{dx}$	$+$	0	$-$
	╱	—	╲

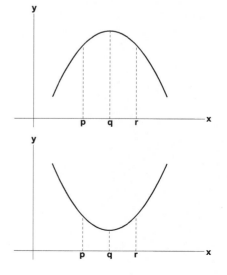

  ★ **minima:**

x	$-$	q	$+$
$\dfrac{dy}{dx}$	$+$	0	$-$
	╲	—	╱

  ★ **and inflexions as well!**

Integration

In this chapter we will learn to:

- understand integration as the reverse process of differentiation, and integrate x^n for all $n \neq -1$, together with constant multiples, sums and differences,

- solve problems involving the evaluation of a constant of integration,

- use definite integration to find the area of a region bounded by a curve and lines parallel to the axes or between two curves,

- calculate a volume of revolution about the x- or y-axis, to include the volume of a solid generated by rotating a region between two curves.

12.1 Finding a function from its derivative

It was shown in the previous chapter that some features of the graph of a function can be interpreted in terms of the graph of its derived function. Suppose now that you know the graph of the derived function. What does this tell you about the graph of the original function?

It is useful to begin by trying to answer this question geometrically. Figure 12.1 shows the graph of the derived function $y = f'(x)$ for some function $f(x)$. Looking at this graph tells us that:

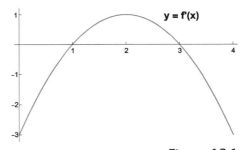

Figure 12.1

- The gradient function $f'(x) < 0$ for $x < 1$, so $f(x)$ is decreasing here.

- At $x = 1$ the gradient changes from negative to positive, so $f(x)$ has a minimum here.

- Since $f'(x) > 0$ here, $f(x)$ is increasing for $1 < x < 3$. Since $f'(x)$ has its maximum at $x = 2$, the graph of $f(x)$ climbs most steeply here.

- Continuing, $f(x)$ has a maximum at $x = 3$, and is decreasing for $x > 3$.

Using this information you can make a sketch like Figure 12.2, which gives an idea of the shape of the graph of $f(x)$. But there is no way of deciding precisely where the graph is located. You could translate it in the y-direction by any amount, and it would still have the same gradient $f'(x)$. So there is no unique answer to the problem; there are many functions $f(x)$ with the given derived function.

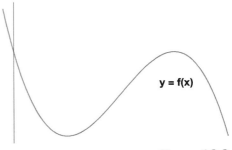

Figure 12.2

This can be shown algebraically. The graph in Figure 12.1 comes from the equation

$$f'(x) = (x-1)(3-x) = 4x - x^2 - 3.$$

What function has this expression as its derivative? We can try to work this out by brute force. Since the derivative of x^2 is $2x$, the function $2x^2$ differentiates to $4x$. Since x^3 differentiates to $3x^2$, the function $\frac{1}{3}x^3$ differentiates to x^3. Since x differentiates to 1, the function $-3x$ differentiates to -3. Thus one possible function $f(x)$ is

$$f(x) = 2x^2 - \tfrac{1}{3}x^3 - 3x.$$

However, since the derivative of 1 is 0, we deduce that we could add any constant c to this function $f(x)$ without affecting its derivative. Thus a complete solution to the problem is to say that $f(x)$ must be equal to

$$f(x) = 2x^2 - \tfrac{1}{3}x^3 - 3x + c$$

for some constant c.

The process of getting from $f'(x)$ to $f(x)$ is called **integration**, and the general expression for $f(x)$ is called the **indefinite integral** of $f'(x)$. Integration is the reverse process of differentiation. The indefinite integral always includes an added constant c, which is called an **arbitrary constant**. The word 'arbitrary' means that, in any application, you can choose its value to fit some extra condition; for example, you can make the graph of $y = f(x)$ go through some given point.

It is easy to find a rule for integrating functions which are powers of x. Since we know the rule for differentiating powers of x, it is easy to work that rule 'backwards', as we did above. We recall that the derivative of the function x^n is the derived function nx^{n-1} for any constant n. What function differentiates to x^n, then? It is clear that x^{n+1} has derivative $(n+1)x^n$, so we deduce that a function that differentiates to x^n is $\frac{1}{n+1}x^{n+1}$. Thus the indefinite integral of x^n is $\frac{1}{n+1}x^{n+1} + c$.

Key Fact 12.1 The Indefinite Integral

The indefinite integral of the function $f(x)$ is the general expression for the function whose derivative is the function $f(x)$. It is denoted with the special symbol

$$\int f(x)\,dx$$

The indefinite integral of a function **always** involves an arbitrary constant. We can integrate most simple functions of x by applying the key rule

$$\int x^n\,dx = \tfrac{1}{n+1}x^{n+1} + c, \qquad n \neq -1.$$

Food For Thought 12.1

Notice an important exception to this rule. The formula makes no sense if $n = -1$, and so we do not (yet) know how to differentiate x^{-1}. Thus while we know how to differentiate all powers of x, we cannot (yet) make the same claim about integration.

Since differentiation 'behaves nicely' with respect to adding and scaling functions (see Key Fact 11.6, so does integration:

Key Fact 12.2 Integration: Linearity

If $f(x)$ and $g(x)$ are functions and p, q are constants, then

$$\int \big(pf(x) + qg(x)\big)\,dx = p\int f(x)\,dx + q\int g(x)\,dx$$

Example 12.1.1. *Calculate* $\int (3x^2 + 7x - 2)\,dx$

We know how to integrate x^2, x and 1, and so

$$\int (3x^2 + 7x - 2)\,dx = 3 \times \tfrac{1}{3}x^3 + 7 \times \tfrac{1}{2}x^2 - 2 \times x + c = x^3 - \tfrac{7}{2}x^2 - 2x + c.$$

Note that we can abuse the linearity of integration when it comes to the arbitrary constant. While it is true that

$$\int x\,dx = \tfrac{1}{2}x^2 + c_1 \qquad \int x^3\,dx = \tfrac{1}{4}x^4 + c_2$$

for arbitrary constants c_1, c_2, we do not need to write

$$\int (5x + 8x^3)\,dx = 5\left(\tfrac{1}{2}x^2 + c_1\right) + 8\left(\tfrac{1}{4}x^4 + c_2\right) = \tfrac{5}{2}x^2 + 2x^4 + 5c_1 + 8c_2 ;$$

we can automatically 'lump together' the term $5c_1 + 8c_2$ into a new arbitrary constant which we shall simply call c. We only need one arbitrary constant for a single integral.

Example 12.1.2. *The graph of $y = f(x)$ passes through $(2,3)$, and $f'(x) = 6x^2 - 5x$. Find its equation.*

The indefinite integral of $f'(x)$ is $6 \times \tfrac{1}{3}x^3 - 5 \times \tfrac{1}{2}x^2 + c$, so the graph has equation

$$y = f(x) = 2x^3 - \tfrac{5}{2}x^2 + c$$

for some constant c. The curve must pass through the point $(2,3)$, so we deduce that $f(2)$ must equal 3, and hence $3 = 2 \times 2^3 - \tfrac{5}{2} \times 2^2 + c = c + 6$, and hence $c = -3$. Thus the equation of the graph is $y = 2x^3 - \tfrac{5}{2}x^2 - 3$.

Example 12.1.3. *A gardener is digging a plot of land. As he gets tired he works more slowly. After t minutes he is digging at a rate of $\frac{2}{\sqrt{t}}$ square metres per minute. How long will it take him to dig an area of 40 square metres?*

Let A m^2 be the area he has dug after t minutes. Then his rate of digging is measured by the derivative $\frac{dA}{dt}$, so we know that $\frac{dA}{dt} = 2t^{-\frac{1}{2}}$; taking the indefinite integral gives

$$A(t) = \int \frac{dA}{dt}\,dt = \int 2t^{-\frac{1}{2}}\,dt = 2 \times \left(\tfrac{1}{1/2}t^{\frac{1}{2}}\right) + c = 4\sqrt{t} + c.$$

Presumably, the gardener has dug nothing at the moment he starts, and so $A = 0$ when $t = 0$. Thus $0 = 4 \times \sqrt{0} + c$, and so $c = 0$. Thus $A(t) = 4\sqrt{t}$. To answer the question, we want to know the value of t which yields $A = 40$. Substituting into the equation, we obtain $40 = 4\sqrt{t}$, and hence $t = 100$. It takes the gardener 100 minutes to dig the area of 40 m^2.

EXERCISE 12A

1. Find a general expression for the function $f(x)$ in each of the following cases.

   a) $f'(x) = 4x^3$,

   b) $f'(x) = 6x^5$,

   c) $f'(x) = 2x$,

   d) $f'(x) = 3x^2 + 5x^4$,

   e) $f'(x) = 10x^9 - 8x^7 - 1$,

   f) $f'(x) = -7x^6 + 3x^2 + 1$.

2. Calculate these indefinite integrals:

   a) $\int (9x^2 - 4x - 5)\,dx$,

   b) $\int (12x^2 + 6x + 4)\,dx$

   c) $\int 7\,dx$,

   d) $\int (16x^3 - 6x^2 + 10x - 3)\,dx$

   e) $\int (2x^3 + 5x)\,dx$,

   f) $\int (x + 2x^2)\,dx$

   g) $\int (2x^2 - 3x - 4)\,dx$,

   h) $\int (1 - 2x - 3x^2)\,dx$

3. Find y in terms of x in each of the following cases:

a) $\dfrac{dy}{dx} = x^4 + x^2 + 1$,

b) $\dfrac{dy}{dx} = 7x - 3$,

c) $\dfrac{dy}{dx} = 2x^2 + x - 8$,

d) $\dfrac{dy}{dx} = 6x^3 - 5x^2 + 3x + 2$,

e) $\dfrac{dy}{dx} = \frac{2}{3}x^3 + \frac{1}{2}x^2 + \frac{1}{3}x + \frac{1}{6}$,

f) $\dfrac{dy}{dx} = \frac{1}{2}x^3 - \frac{1}{3}x^2 + x - \frac{1}{3}$,

g) $\dfrac{dy}{dx} = x - 3x^2 + 1$,

h) $\dfrac{dy}{dx} = x^3 + x^2 + x + 1$.

4. The graph of $y = f(x)$ passes through the origin and $f'(x) = 8x - 5$. Find $f(x)$.

5. A curve passes through the point $(2, -5)$ and satisfies $\dfrac{dy}{dx} = 6x^2 - 1$. Find y in terms of x.

6. A curve passes through $(-4, 9)$ and is such that $\dfrac{dy}{dx} = \frac{1}{2}x^3 + \frac{1}{4}x + 1$. Find y in terms of x.

7. Given that $f'(x) = 15x^2 - 6x + 4$ and $f(1) = 0$, find $f(x)$.

8. Each of the following diagrams shows the graph of a derived function $f'(x)$. In each case, sketch the graph of a possible function $f(x)$:

a)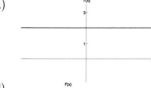

b)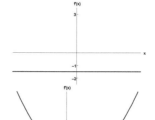

c)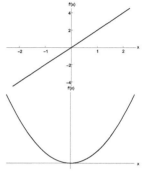

d)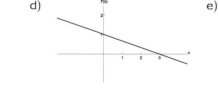

e)

f)

9. The graph of $y = f(x)$ passes through $(4, 25)$ and $f'(x) = 6\sqrt{x}$. Find its equation.

10. Find y in terms of x in each of the following cases:

a) $\dfrac{dy}{dx} == x^{\frac{1}{2}}$,

b) $\dfrac{dy}{dx} = 4x^{-\frac{2}{3}}$,

c) $\dfrac{dy}{dx} = \sqrt[3]{x}$,

d) $\dfrac{dy}{dx} = 2\sqrt{x} - \frac{2}{\sqrt{x}}$,

e) $\dfrac{dy}{dx} = \frac{5}{\sqrt[3]{x}}$,

f) $\dfrac{dy}{dx} = \frac{-2}{\sqrt[3]{x^2}}$.

11. Find a general expression for the function $f(x)$ in each of the following cases.

a) $f'(x) = x^{-2}$,

b) $f'(x) = 3x^{-4}$,

c) $f'(x) = \frac{6}{x^3}$,

d) $f'(x) == 4x - \frac{3}{x^2}$,

e) $f'(x) = \frac{1}{x^3} - \frac{1}{x^4}$,

f) $f'(x) = \frac{2}{x^2} - 2x^2$.

12. The graph of $y = f(x)$ passes through $(\frac{1}{2}, 5)$ and $f'(x) = \frac{4}{x^2}$. Find its equation.

13. A curve passes through the point $(25, 3)$ and is such that $\dfrac{dy}{dx} = \frac{1}{2\sqrt{x}}$. Find the equation of the curve.

14. A curve passes through the point $(1, 5)$ and is such that $\dfrac{dy}{dx} = \sqrt[3]{x} - \frac{6}{x^3}$. Find the equation of the curve.

15. In each of the following cases, find y in terms of x.

a) $\dfrac{dy}{dx} = 3x(x - 2)$,

b) $\dfrac{dy}{dx} = (2x - 2)(6x + 5)$,

c) $\dfrac{dy}{dx} = \frac{4x^3 + 1}{x^2}$,

d) $\dfrac{dy}{dx} = \frac{x + 4}{\sqrt{x}}$,

e) $\dfrac{dy}{dx} = \left(\sqrt{x} + 5\right)^2$,

f) $\dfrac{dy}{dx} = \frac{\sqrt{x} + 5}{\sqrt{x}}$.

16. A tree is growing so that, after t years, its height is increasing at a rate of $\frac{30}{\sqrt[3]{t}}$ cm per year. Assume that, when $t = 0$, the height is 5 cm.

a) Find the height of the tree after 4 years.

b) After how many years will the height be 4.1 metres?

17. A pond, with surface area 48 square metres, is being invaded by a weed. At a time t months after the weed first appeared, the area of the weed on the surface is increasing at a rate of $\frac{1}{3}t$ square metres per month. How long will it be before the weed covers the whole surface of the pond?

18. The function $f(x)$ is such that $f'(x) = 9x^2+4x+c$, where c is a constant. Given that $f(2) = 14$ and $f(3) = 74$, find the value of $f(4)$.

19*. Find a function $f(x)$ such that $f'(-1) = f'(1) = 0$ and such that $f(0) = 3$ and $f(2) = 0$.

20*. If y is such that $\frac{d^2y}{dx^2} = 21x^2 + 15x^4$ and $y(1) = \frac{3}{4}$ and $y(-1) = \frac{1}{4}$, find the function y.

12.2 Calculating Areas

What is remarkable about integration is that it is more than just the reverse of differentiation; it has meaning and value in its own right, since it can be used to calculate areas (and volumes). Many of the formulae you have learnt, such as those for the volume of a sphere or a cone, can be proved by using integration. For the moment, we shall be primarily concerned with areas.

Consider the graph of the function $y = f(x)$, and suppose that the function $A(t)$ is the area between the curve and the x-axis in the range $0 \le x \le t$. For the present, we shall assume that t is always positive, and that the graph of the function always lies above the x-axis, as shown in the diagram. We shall shortly be able to remove these restrictions. What is the derivative $A'(t)$ of the function $A(t)$?

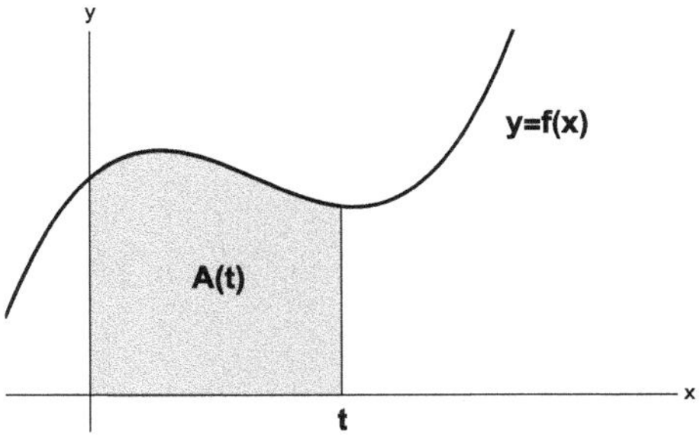

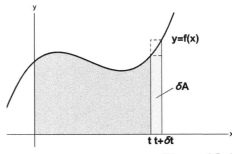

Figure 12.3

Trying to differentiate from first principles, we need to consider the function A at the point t and at a point $t + \delta t$ which is close to t. Since $A(t)$ is the area under the curve for $0 \le x \le t$, and $A + \delta A = A(t+\delta t)$ is the area under the curve for $0 \le x \le t + \delta t$, it is clear that δA is the area under the curve for $t \le x \le t + \delta t$. The quantity δA is the lighter shaded area shown in Figure 12.4.

Figure 12.4

The small area δA is not quite a rectangle, but it lies between two rectangles, both of width δt, one of height y and the other of height $y + \delta y$. Thus

$$y\delta t \le \delta A \le (y + \delta y)\delta t,$$

and hence the ratio

$$y \le \frac{\delta A}{\delta t} \le y + \delta y.$$

In other words, in the limit as δt tends to 0, the ratio $\frac{\delta A}{\delta t}$ tends to $y = f(t)$. In other words $A(t)$ is a function whose derivative is $f(t)$. The key implication of this is that the function $A(t)$ is obtained from $f(t)$ by integrating:

$$A'(t) = f(t), \qquad \int f(t)\,dt = A(t) + c.$$

What is the area under the curve $y = f(x)$ for $a \leq x \leq b$? It is clearly equal to difference between the area $A(b)$ under the curve for $0 \leq x \leq b$ and the area $A(a)$ under the curve for $0 \leq x \leq a$. In other words, the area under the curve for $a \leq x \leq b$ is $A(b) - A(a)$. This is fine when $b > a > 0$. What happens if we want to know the area under the curve for $a \leq x \leq b$ for more general values of a and b?

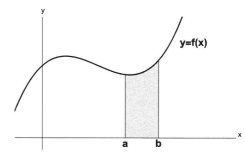

Figure 12.5

When we performed the analysis to determine that $A(t)$ was a function that differentiated to f, there was no particular reason why we chose to consider $A(t)$ as the integral under the curve for $0 \leq x \leq t$. We could have chosen $B(t)$ to be the area under the curve for $-1000 \leq x \leq t$, for example, and this would have enabled us to show that $B'(t) = f(t)$ for $t > -1000$, and that the area under the curve for $a \leq x \leq b$ was equal to $B(b) - B(a)$ for any $-1000 < a < b$.

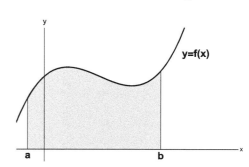

Figure 12.6

Since A and B both differentiate to give f, they can only differ by a constant. Indeed $B(t) = A(t) + k$, where k is the area under the curve for $-1000 \leq x \leq 0$, and consequently $B(b) - B(a) = A(b) - A(a)$. Thus the area under the curve for $a \leq x \leq b$ is equal to $A(b) - A(a)$ for any $-1000 < a < b$. Repeating this for numbers other than -1000 enables us to cope with other negative values of a and b.

We also note that if $F(t)$ and $G(t)$ are functions such that $G(t) = F(t) + k$, then $G(b) - G(a) = F(b) - F(a)$ for all $a < b$. This means that we have even greater flexibility when determining areas:

Key Fact 12.3 Finding Areas By Integrating

To find the area under the curve $y = f(x)$ for the region $a \leq x \leq b$, integrate f to find a function F whose derivative is equal to f. Then the area under the curve for $a \leq x \leq b$ is the so-called **definite integral of f from a to b**:

$$\int_a^b f(x)\,dx = F(b) - F(a).$$

It is useful to have an intermediate notation, allowing us to integrate f to find F before we substitute in $x = b$ and $x = a$. To do this we also write

$$\int_a^b f(x)\,dx = \Big[F(x)\Big]_a^b = F(b) - F(a),$$

where putting the function F inside big squares brackets means that the difference between F evaluated at a and b needs to be calculated.
When considering a definite integral

$$\int_a^b f(x)\,dx,$$

the numbers a and b are called the **limits** and the function $f(x)$ is called the **integrand**.

> **For Interest**
>
> The special symbol $\int$ we use in integration is in fact a tall, stretched S, standing for 'sum'. We have introduced integration as the reverse of differentiation, and that is the simplest method of getting to grips with it. However, as a mathematical concept in its own right, integration is fundamentally about calculating areas, and the connection with differentiation is an added bonus.
>
> Imagine splitting the interval from a to b into a large number of equally spaced strips, each of width δx. The area under the curve is split up into a collection of narrow areas, each of which is almost rectangular. Thus the area under the curve is roughly
>
> $$\sum_x f(x)\,\delta x$$
>
>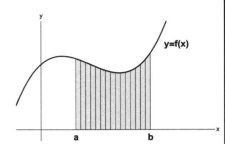
>
> **Figure 12.7**
>
> where the sum is over all the strips, and $f(x)$ represents the height of the approximate rectangle.
>
> In the limit $\delta x \to 0$, as the width of the strips tends to zero, this approximation should tend to the exact area, and this explains the notation:
>
> $$\sum_x f(x)\,\delta x \quad \to \quad \int_a^b f(x)\,dx\,.$$

Example 12.2.1. *Find the area under $y = x^{-2}$ for $2 \le x \le 5$.*

The indefinite integral of x^{-2} is $-x^{-1} + c$. Thus the required area is

$$\int_2^5 x^{-2}\,dx = \left[-x^{-1}\right]_2^5 = \left(-\tfrac{1}{5}\right) - \left(-\tfrac{1}{2}\right) = \tfrac{3}{10}\,.$$

Note that we do not need the '$+c$' term inside the square brackets; if we put it in, it would cancel out in the subsequent calculations.

We need to remember the similarities and the distinctions between indefinite and definite integrals. An indefinite integral

$$\int f(x)\,dx$$

is a function, while a definite integral

$$\int_1^{10} f(x)\,dx$$

is a number.

Example 12.2.2. *Find the area under $y = \sqrt{x}$ from $x = 1$ to $x = 4$.*

The area is

$$\int_1^4 \sqrt{x}\,dx = \left[\tfrac{2}{3}x^{\frac{3}{2}}\right]_1^4 = \tfrac{2}{3} \times 8 - \tfrac{2}{3} \times 1 = \tfrac{14}{3}\,.$$

EXERCISE 12B

1. Find the following indefinite integrals:

a) $\displaystyle\int 4x\,dx,$

b) $\displaystyle\int 15x^2\,dx,$

c) $\displaystyle\int 2x^5\,dx$

d) $\displaystyle\int 9\,dx,$

e) $\displaystyle\int \tfrac{1}{2}x^8\,dx,$

f) $\displaystyle\int \tfrac{2}{3}x^4\,dx.$

2. Evaluate the following definite integrals:

a) $\int_1^2 3x^2\,dx$,

b) $\int_2^5 8x\,dx$,

c) $\int_0^2 x^3\,dx$,

d) $\int_{-1}^1 10x^4\,dx$,

e) $\int_0^{\frac{1}{2}} \frac{1}{2}x\,dx$,

f) $\int_0^1 2\,dx$.

3. Find the following indefinite integrals:

a) $\int (6x+7)\,dx$

b) $\int (6x^2 - 2x - 5)\,dx$

c) $\int (2x^3 + 7x)\,dx$,

d) $\int (3x^4 - 8x^3 + 9x^2 - x + 4)\,dx$

e) $\int (2x+5)(x-4)\,dx$,

f) $\int x(x+2)(x-2)\,dx$.

4. Evaluate the following definite integrals:

a) $\int_0^2 (8x+3)\,dx$,

b) $\int_2^4 (5x-4)\,dx$

c) $\int_{-2}^2 (6x^2 + 1)\,dx$,

d) $\int_0^1 (2x+1)(x+3)\,dx$,

e) $\int_{-3}^4 (6x^2 + 2x + 3)\,dx$,

f) $\int_{-3}^3 (6x^3 + 2x)\,dx$.

5. Find the area under the curve $y = x^2$ from $x = 0$ to $x = 6$.

6. Find the area under the curve $y = 4x^3$ from $x = 1$ to $x = 2$.

7. Find the area under the curve $y = 12x^3$ from $x = 2$ to $x = 3$.

8. Find the area under the curve $y = 3x^2 + 2x$ from $x = -a$ to $x = a$.

9. Find the area under the curve $y = 3x^2 - 2x$ from $x = -4$ to $x = 0$.

10. Find the area under the curve $y = x^4 + 5$ from $x = -a$ to $x = a$.

11. The diagram shows the graph of $y = 4x + 1$ and the region between $x = 1$ and $x = 3$. Find the area of the shaded region by

a) using the formula for the area of a trapezium,

b) using integration.

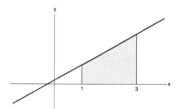

12. The diagram shows the region bounded by $y = \frac{1}{2}x - 3$, by $x = 14$ and the x-axis. Find the area of the shaded region by

a) using the formula for the area of a triangle,

b) using integration.

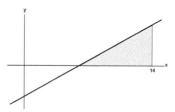

13. Find the area of the region shaded in each of the following diagrams:

a)

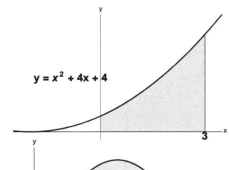

$y = x^2 + 4x + 4$

b)

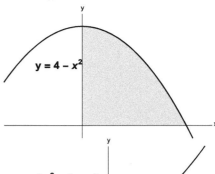

$y = 4 - x^2$

c)

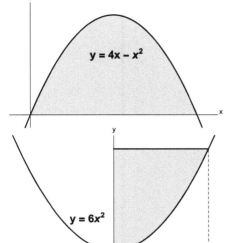

$y = 4x - x^2$

d)

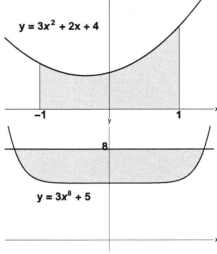

$y = 3x^2 + 2x + 4$

e)

$y = 6x^2$

f)

$y = 3x^8 + 5$

14. Find the following indefinite integrals:

a) $\displaystyle\int \frac{1}{x^3}\,dx,$

b) $\displaystyle\int \left(x^2 - x^{-3}\right)dx,$

c) $\displaystyle\int \sqrt{x}\,dx,$

d) $\displaystyle\int 6x^{\frac{2}{3}}\,dx,$

e) $\displaystyle\int \frac{6x^4+5}{x^2}\,dx$

f) $\displaystyle\int \frac{1}{\sqrt{x}}\,dx.$

15. Evaluate the following definite integrals:

a) $\displaystyle\int_0^8 12\sqrt[3]{x}\,dx,$

b) $\displaystyle\int_1^2 \frac{3}{x^2}\,dx,$

c) $\displaystyle\int_1^4 \frac{10}{\sqrt{x}}\,dx,$

d) $\displaystyle\int_1^2 \left(\frac{8}{x^3} + x^3\right)dx,$

e) $\displaystyle\int_4^9 \frac{2\sqrt{x}+3}{\sqrt{x}}\,dx,$

f) $\displaystyle\int_1^8 \frac{1}{\sqrt[3]{x^2}}\,dx.$

16. Find the area under the curve $y = \frac{6}{x^4}$ between $x = 1$ and $x = 2$.

17. Find the area under the curve $y = \sqrt[3]{x}$ between $x = a^3$ and $x = b^3$.

18. Find the area under the curve $y = \frac{5}{x^2}$ between $x = -3$ and $x = -1$.

19. Given that $\displaystyle\int_0^a 12x^2\,dx = 1372$, find the value of the constant a.

20. Given that $\displaystyle\int_0^9 p\sqrt{x}\,dx = 90$, find the value of the constant p.

21. Find the area of the shaded region in each of the following diagrams.

a)

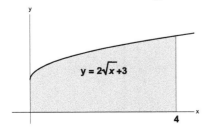

$y = 2\sqrt{x} + 3$

b)

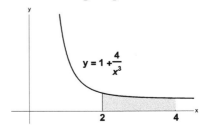

$y = 1 + \frac{4}{x^3}$

22. The diagram shows the graph of $y = 9x^2$. The point P has coordinates $(4, 144)$. Find the area of the shaded region.

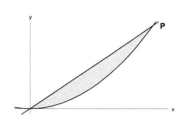

23. The diagram shows the graph of $y = \frac{1}{\sqrt{x}}$. Show that the area of the shaded region is $3 - \frac{5\sqrt{3}}{3}$.

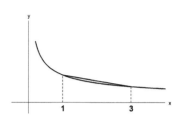

24. Find the area of the region between the curve $y = 9 + 15x - 6x^2$ and the x-axis.

25*. The average height of a function f over an interval $a \leq x \leq b$ is equal to the integral $\displaystyle\int_a^b f(x)\,dx$ divided by the interval width $b - a$:

$$M(a, b) = \tfrac{1}{b-a} \int_a^b f(x)\,dx$$

Calculate $M(a, b)$ for $0 < a < b$ and the functions

a) $f(x) = x^2$, \qquad\qquad b) $f(x) = \frac{1}{\sqrt{x}}$,

writing each in the simplest form possible. In both cases, show that $M(a, b)$ tends to $f(a)$ as b tends to a.

26*. Consider the function $y = x$ for $0 \leq x \leq a$. Divide the interval from 0 to a into n equal strips (in the picture, $n = 10$).

a) What is the width of each strip in terms of a and n?

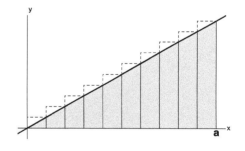

b) The integral $\displaystyle\int_0^a x\,dx$ is to be approximated by n rectangles which 'sit above' the curve (shown by dashed lines in the diagram). Show that doing this gives an approximation of

$$\frac{a}{n} \sum_{j=1}^{n} \frac{aj}{n}$$

c) Evaluate this sum, and show that it tends to $\frac{1}{2}a^2 = \int_0^a x\,dx$ as n tends to infinity.

12.3 Some Properties Of Integrals

The graph in Figure 12.1 is that of $y = (x-1)(3-x)$. The area under the graph between 1 and 3 is

$$\int_1^3 (x-1)(3-x)\,dx = \int_1^3 (4x - x^2 - 3)\,dx = \left[2x^2 - \tfrac{1}{3}x^3 - 3x\right]_1^3 = 0 - (-\tfrac{4}{3}) = \tfrac{4}{3}.$$

What are we to make of the calculation

$$\int_0^3 (x-1)(3-x)\,dx = \left[2x^2 - \tfrac{1}{3}x^3 - 3x\right]_0^3 = 0 - 0 = 0\,?$$

The area between the graph and the axis between $x = 0$ and $x = 3$ is clearly **not** zero. The answer to this problem lies in gaining a deeper understanding of the definite integral.

If the function $f(x)$ is positive on the interval $c < x < d$, then its indefinite integral $F(x)$ has positive derivative $f(x)$ on this interval, and so is increasing. Thus $\int_c^d f(x)\,dx = \left[F(x)\right]_c^d = F(d) - F(c) > 0$. On the other hand, if $f(x)$ is negative for $c < x < d$, then $F(x)$ is decreasing on that interval, and hence $\int_c^d f(x)\,dx < 0$.

Key Fact 12.4 Integration: Signed Area

The definite integral $\displaystyle\int_a^b f(x)\,dx$ is the **signed area** between the function and the x-axis in the interval $a \le x \le b$; it counts area above the x-axis as positive, and area below the x-axis as negative.

Thus, considering the graph of $y = (x-1)(3-x)$ again, the regions A and B both have area $\frac{4}{3}$ but, since the integrand is negative for $0 < x < 1$, the integral $\displaystyle\int_0^1 (x-1)(3-x)\,dx$ is equal to $-\frac{4}{3}$, and the total signed area in the interval $0 \le x \le 3$ is $\frac{4}{3} - \frac{4}{3} = 0$.

Care needs to be taken if we are being asked for the total non-signed area; the total area of regions A and B is $\frac{8}{3}$, and not 0!

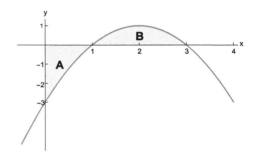

Figure 12.8

This calculation includes another important property of integration; it is easy to combine the definite integrals over different intervals.

Key Fact 12.5 Integration: Combining Intervals

If $a < b < c$, then

$$\int_a^c f(x)\,dx = \int_a^b f(x)\,dx + \int_b^x f(x)\,dx\,.$$

so the integral over the interval is obtained by adding together the integrals over the two subintervals.

This result is easy to understand, since this identity of integrals simply states that

$$F(c) - F(a) = [F(b) - F(a)] + [F(c) - F(b)]$$

where F is an indefinite integral of f. A consequence of the rule for combining intervals is the following:

Key Fact 12.6 Integration: Reversing The Limits

For any function $f(x)$ and any numbers a and b,

$$\int_b^a f(x)\,dx = -\int_a^b f(x)\,dx\,.$$

This might seem an unlikely property for us to want to know about, but it will be useful. There will be times later on when our mathematics naturally leads us to want to know the value of unlikely expression such as $\int_2^{-1} x^3\,dx$ and we will want to be able simply to write this as $-\int_{-1}^{2} x^3\,dx = -\frac{15}{4}$.

Finally, it is worth noting that the indefinite integral's good behaviour with respect to adding and scaling functions also applies to the definite integral.

Key Fact 12.7 Integration: Linearity of the Definite Integral

If $f(x)$ and $g(x)$ are functions, p and q are constants, and if $a < b$, then

$$\int_a^b \big(pf(x) + qg(x)\big)\,dx = p\int_a^b f(x)\,dx + q\int_a^b g(x)\,dx .$$

For Interest

Very occasionally, we are asked to integrate a function $f(x)$ over an infinite interval. Our current technique does not allow us to do this, since the limits a and b of a definite integral are assumed to be finite.

It is possible to make sense of an integral such as $\displaystyle\int_1^{\infty} \frac{1}{x^2}\,dx$, however. To do this we need to evaluate the definite integral $\int_1^s \frac{1}{x^2}\,dx$, and investigate what happens to this integral as s increases without limit. We see that

$$\int_1^s \frac{1}{x^2}\,dx = \left[-x^{-1} \right]_1^s = 1 - s^{-1}$$

tends to 1 as s increases towards infinity, and so we can write

$$\int_1^{\infty} \frac{1}{x^2}\,dx = 1 .$$

This type of integral is called an **infinite integral**. Not all functions have infinite integrals. For example

$$\int_1^s \frac{1}{\sqrt{x}}\,dx = \left[2\sqrt{x} \right]_1^s = 2\sqrt{s} - 2$$

which does not converge as s increases towards infinity. When an infinite integral exists, we have an example of a region which has infinite width but finite area. That not all infinite integrals exist means that some infinitely wide regions have infinite areas, which is not that strange.

12.4 The Area Between Two Graphs

We sometimes want to find the area of a region bounded by the graphs of two functions $f(x)$ and $g(x)$, and by two lines $x = a$ and $x = b$, as in Figure 12.9. Some of the examples in the previous exercise asked us to do just this, but at that stage one of the functions was a straight line, and so some of the areas could be calculated by other geometrical methods.

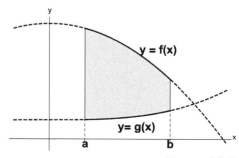

Figure 12.9

This area can be calculated as the difference between the area under the graph $y = f(x)$ for $a \leq x \leq b$ minus the area under the graph $y = g(x)$ for $a \leq x \leq b$:

$$\int_a^b f(x)\,dx - \int_a^b g(x)\,dx$$

but it frequently much simpler to use the linearity of the definite integral and calculate this area as the single integral

$$\int_a^b \Big(f(x) - g(x)\Big)\,dx\,.$$

Example 12.4.1. *Show that the graphs of $f(x) = x^3 - x^2 - 6x + 8$ and $g(x) = x^3 + 2x^2 - 1$ intersect at two points, and find the area enclosed between them.*

The graphs intersect where

$$\begin{aligned} x^3 - x^2 - 6x + 8 &= x^3 + 2x^2 - 1 \\ 3x^2 + 6x - 9 &= 0 \\ (x+3)(x-1) = x^2 + 2x - 3 &= 0 \end{aligned}$$

and so the curves intersect when $x = -3, 1$. The two points of intersection are $(-3, -10)$ and $(1, 2)$.

Either by drawing the graphs, or by observing that $f(0) > g(0)$, we see that $f(x) > g(x)$ for $-3 < x < 1$. Thus the area between the graphs is

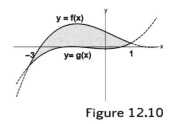

Figure 12.10

$$\begin{aligned} \int_{-3}^1 \Big(f(x) - g(x)\Big)\,dx &= \int_{-3}^1 (9 - 6x - 3x^2)\,dx \\ &= \Big[9x - 3x^2 - x^3\Big]_{-3}^1 \\ &= 5 - (-27) = 32 \end{aligned}$$

12.5 Integrating With Respect To Other Variables

There is nothing sacrosanct about the variable x. It is entirely possible to integrate functions of other variables, and these resulting integrals can have correspondingly different interpretations.

Example 12.5.1. *Calculate the area between the curve $y = x^2$, the y-axis and the lines $y = 1$ and $y = 9$.*

As the left-hand of the two pictures shows, this area is not an 'area under a curve'. It is an 'area to the left of a curve'.

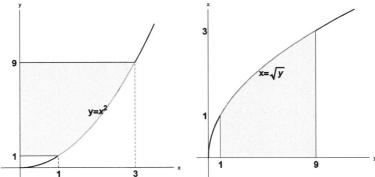

Figure 12.11

If we reflect this picture in the line $y = x$, we obtain the picture on the right. The roles of the x- and y-axes have been reversed, and what we want is the area under the curve $x = \sqrt{y}$. Thus this area is

$$\int_1^9 \sqrt{y}\,dy = \Big[\tfrac{2}{3}y^{\frac{3}{2}}\Big]_1^9 = \tfrac{2}{3} \times 27 - \tfrac{2}{3} \times 1 = \tfrac{52}{3}$$

In general, while the area under a curve is expressed by an integral $\int y\,dx$, the area to the left of a curve is expressed by an integral $\int x\,dy$. To be able to use the second formula, we need to be able to invert the function $y = f(x)$ to be able to write x as a function of y.

EXERCISE 12C

1. Evaluate $\displaystyle\int_0^1 3x(x-1)\,dx$, and comment on your answer.

2. Find the total area of the region shaded in each of the following diagrams:

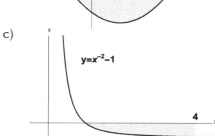

a) $y = (x+1)(x-3)$

b) $y = 3x^2 - 12x + 9$

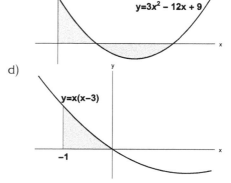

c) $y = x^{-2} - 1$

d) $y = x(x-3)$

3. Find the area enclosed between the curves $y = x^2 + 7$ and $y = 2x^2 + 3$.

4. Find the area enclosed between the straight line $y = 12x + 14$ and the curve $y = 3x^2 + 6x + 5$.

5. Find the area enclosed between the curve $y = \sqrt{x-1}$, the y-axis, the line $y = 1$ and the line $y = 5$.

6. Find the area enclosed between the y-axis, the line $y = 125$ and the curve $y = x^3$.

7. The diagram shows the graphs of $y = 16 + 4x - 2x^2$ and $y = x^2 - 2x - 8$. Find the area of the region, shaded in the diagram, between the curves.

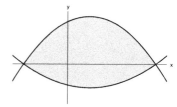

8. Find the area between the curves $y = (x-4)(3x-1)$ and $y = (4-x)(1+x)$.

9. Parts of the graphs of $f(x) = 2x^3 + x^2 - 8x$ and $g(x) = 2x^3 - 3x - 4$ enclose a finite region. Find its area.

10. The diagram shows the graph of $y = \sqrt{x}$. Given that the area of the shaded region is 72, find the value of the constant a.

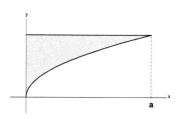

11*. Find the values of the infinite integrals:

a) $\displaystyle\int_2^\infty \frac{6}{x^4}\,dx,$

b) $\displaystyle\int_4^\infty \frac{6}{x\sqrt{x}}\,dx,$

c) $\displaystyle\int_1^\infty x^{-1.01}\,dx.$

12*. Find an expression for $\displaystyle\int_1^s \frac{1}{x^m}\,dx$ in terms of m and s, where m is a positive rational number, $m \neq 1$, and $s > 1$. Show that the infinite integral $\displaystyle\int_1^\infty \frac{1}{x^m}\,dx$ has a meaning if $m > 1$, and state its value in terms of m.

13*. Suppose that $f(x)$ is an increasing invertible function, and let $0 < a < b$. Suppose that $0 < \alpha < \beta$ are such that $f(a) = \alpha$ and $f(b) = \beta$. Use the diagram to explain why

$$\int_a^b f(x)\,dx + \int_\alpha^\beta f^{-1}(y)\,dy \;=\; b\beta - a\alpha\,.$$

Use this result to evaluate the integral

$$\int_9^{64} \sqrt{\sqrt{x}+1}\,dx\,.$$

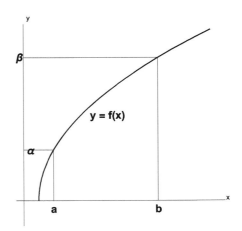

12.6   Volumes Of Revolution

Let O be the origin, and let OA be a line through the origin. Consider the shaded region between the line OA and the x-axis. If we rotate this region about the x-axis through $360°$, it sweeps out a solid cone, shown below.

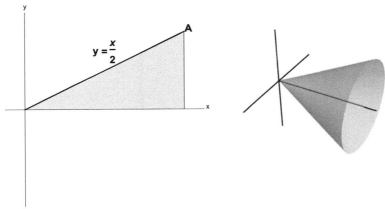

Figure 12.12

A solid shape constructed in this way is called a **solid of revolution**. The volume of a solid of revolution is sometimes called a **volume of revolution**.

Calculating a volume of revolution is similar in many ways to calculating the area of a region under a curve, and can be illustrated by an example.

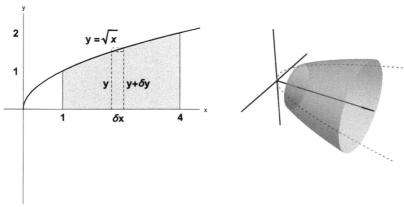

Figure 12.13

Suppose that the region between the graph of $y = \sqrt{x}$ and the x-axis from $x = 1$ to $x = 4$ is rotated about the x-axis to form a solid of revolution. We shall investigate the function $V(x)$, which is the volume of the solid of revolution from $x = 1$ to any value of x (and not just $x = 4$).

Suppose that x is increased by δx. Since y and V are both functions of x, the corresponding increases in y and V can be written as δy and δV. Examine this increase δV in the volume more closely. The area under the graph which is rotated to form the volume δV lies between two rectangles, each of width δx, but with heights y and $y + \delta y$. These rectangles are shown on the left-hand diagram in Figure 12.13. Thus δV will lie between the volumes of revolution of these two rectangles. The solid of revolution formed by each of these rectangles is a coin-shaped cylinder of width δx; one cylinder has radius y and the other has radius $y + \delta y$. Thus δV lies between $\pi y^2 \delta x$ and $\pi (y + \delta y)^2 \delta x$. Dividing by δx, we see that $\frac{\delta V}{\delta x}$ lies between πy^2 and $\pi (y + \delta y)^2$. Letting δx tend to 0, we deduce from first principles that the function V has derivative πy^2:

$$\frac{dV}{dx} = \pi y^2 = \pi x.$$

Thus we deduce that $V = \frac{1}{2}\pi x^2 + c$. Since $V = 0$ when $x = 1$, we deduce that $0 = \frac{1}{2}\pi + c$, so that $c = -\frac{1}{2}\pi$, and so $V = \frac{1}{2}\pi(x^2 - 1)$. The particular volume of revolution of the problem is $V(4) = \frac{15}{2}\pi$. Even more simply, we can write

$$V = \int_1^4 \pi x\, dx = \left[\tfrac{1}{2}\pi x^2\right]_1^4 = 8\pi - \frac{1}{2}\pi = \tfrac{15}{2}\pi.$$

Until we started to integrate $\frac{V}{x}$ to obtain V, the argument we used was completely general, and did not depend in any way on the equation of the original curve.

Key Fact 12.8 Volumes Of Revolution: x-Axis

When the region under the graph of $y = f(x)$ between $x = a$ and $x = b$ (where $a < b$) is rotated about the x-axis, the volume of the solid of revolution formed is

$$\int_a^b \pi y^2\, dx = \int_a^b \pi \big(f(x)\big)^2\, dx.$$

Example 12.6.1. *Find the volume generated when the region under the graph of $y = 1 + x^2$ between $x = -1$ and $x = 1$ is rotated through $360°$ about the x-axis.*

The required volume is V, where

$$V = \int_{-1}^1 \pi y^2\, dx = \pi \int_{-1}^1 (1 + x^2)^2\, dx = \pi \int_{-1}^1 (1 + 2x^2 + x^4)\, dx$$

$$= \pi\left[x + \tfrac{2}{3}x^3 + \tfrac{1}{5}x^5\right]_{-1}^1 = \pi\left[\left(1 + \tfrac{2}{3} + \tfrac{1}{5}\right) - \left(-1 - \tfrac{2}{3} - \tfrac{1}{5}\right)\right]$$

$$= \tfrac{56}{15}\pi.$$

You can also use this method to obtain the formulae for the volumes of a cone and a sphere.

Example 12.6.2. *Show that the volume of a cone with base radius r and height h is $\frac{1}{3}\pi r^2 h$.*

Referring to Figure 12.12, we recall how a cone is obtained as a solid of revolution. In order for the cone to have radius r and height h, the point A needs to have coordinates (h, r), and hence the line OA must have equation $y = \frac{r}{h}x$. Thus the volume of revolution of the cone is

$$\int_0^h \pi y^2 \, dx \;=\; \pi \int_0^h \left(\tfrac{r}{h}x\right)^2 dx = \pi \tfrac{r^2}{h^2} \int_0^h x^2 \, dx$$

$$=\; \pi \tfrac{r^2}{h^2}\left[\tfrac{1}{3}x^3\right]_0^h \;=\; \pi \tfrac{r^2}{h^2} \times \tfrac{1}{3}h^3 \;=\; \tfrac{1}{3}\pi r^2 h$$

Example 12.6.3. *Show that the volume of a sphere of radius r is $\frac{4}{3}\pi r^3$.*

A sphere is the solid of revolution obtained from a diametrical semicirle, which has equation $y = \sqrt{r^2 - x^2}$. Thus it has volume

$$\pi \int_{-r}^r y^2 \, dx \;=\; \pi \int_r^r (r^2 - x^2)\, dx$$

$$=\; \pi\left[r^2 x - \tfrac{1}{3}x^3\right]_{-r}^r \;=\; \pi\left(\tfrac{2}{3}r^3 - \left(-\tfrac{2}{3}r^3\right)\right)$$

$$=\; \tfrac{4}{3}\pi r^3 \,.$$

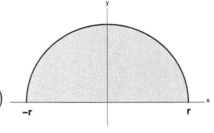

Solids of revolution can be defined by more than one curve.

Example   **12.6.4.**

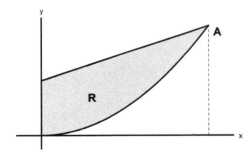

The finite region R is defined by the curves $y = x + 2$, the curve $y = x^2$ and the y-axis. What is the volume of the solid of revolution obtained by rotating R through $360°$ about the x-axis?

The line and curve meet at the point A where $x + 2 = x^2$, and so $0 = x^2 - x - 2 = (x - 2)(x + 1)$. Thus it is clear that A has coordinates $(2, 4)$. The volume of revolution formed by R is equal to the volume of revolution formed by $y = x + 2$ for $0 \le x \le 2$ minus the volume of revolution formed by $y = x^2$ for $0 \le x \le 2$. Thus the desired answer is

$$\pi \int_0^2 (x+2)^2 \, dx - \pi \int_0^2 x^4 \, dx \;=\; \pi \int_0^2 (x^2 + 4x + 4 - x^4)\, dx = \left[\tfrac{1}{3}x^3 + 2x^2 + 4x - \tfrac{1}{5}x^5\right]_0^2$$

$$=\; \tfrac{8}{3} + 8 + 8 - \tfrac{32}{5} \;=\; \tfrac{184}{15} \,.$$

Just as we could calculate areas 'to the left' of a curve by integrating with respect to y, it is possible to create solids of revolution about the y-axis. The formulae for such volumes of revolution are, of course, very similar to those for volumes of revolution about the x-axis.

Key Fact 12.9 Volumes Of Revolution: y-axis

When the region bounded by the graph of $y = f(x)$, the lines $y = c$ and $y = d$ and the y-axis is rotated about the y-axis, the volume of the solid of revolution formed is

$$\pi \int_c^d x^2 \, dy \, .$$

To be able to use this formula, we need to be able to invert the function $y = f(x)$ to write x as a function of y.

Example 12.6.5. *Find the volume generated when the region bounded by $y = x^3$ and the y-axis between $y = 1$ and $y = 8$ is rotated through $360°$ about the y-axis.*

Since $y = x^3$, we have $x = y^{\frac{1}{3}}$, and hence the volume of revolution is

$$\pi \int_1^8 x^2 \, dy \;=\; \pi \int_1^8 y^{\frac{2}{3}} \, dy \;=\; \pi \Big[\tfrac{3}{5} y^{\frac{5}{3}} \Big]_1^8$$
$$=\; \pi \big(\tfrac{3}{5} \times 32 - \tfrac{3}{5} \times 1 \big) \;=\; \tfrac{93}{5} \pi \, .$$

EXERCISE 12D

In all the questions in this Exercise, leave your answers as multiples of π.

1. Find the volume generated when the region under the graph of $y = f(x)$ between $x = a$ and $x = b$ is rotated through $360°$ about the x-axis in the following cases:
   a) $f(x) = x$; $a = 3, b = 5$,
   b) $f(x) = x^2$; $a = 2, b = 5$,
   c) $f(x) = x^3$; $a = 2, b = 6$,
   d) $f(x) = \frac{1}{x}$; $a = 1, b = 4$.

2. Find the volume formed when the region under the graph of $y = f(x)$ between $x = a$ and $x = b$ is rotated through $360°$ about the x-axis.
   a) $f(x) = x + 3$; $a = 3, b = 9$,
   b) $f(x) = x^2 + 1$; $a = 2, b = 5$,
   c) $f(x) = \sqrt{x+1}$; $a = 0, b = 3$,
   d) $f(x) = x(x-2)$; $a = 0, b = 2$.

3. Find the volume generated when the region bounded by the graph of $y = f(x)$, the y-axis and the lines $y = c$ and $y = d$ is rotated about the y-axis to form a solid of revolution.
   a) $f(x) = x^2$; $c = 1, d = 3$,
   b) $f(x) = x + 1$; $c = 1, d = 4$,
   c) $f(x) = \sqrt{x}$; $c = 2, d = 7$,
   d) $f(x) = \frac{1}{x}$; $c = 2, d = 5$,
   e) $f(x) = \sqrt{9-x}$; $c = 0, d = 3$,
   f) $f(x) = x^2 + 1$; $c = 1, d = 4$,
   g) $f(x) = x^{\frac{2}{3}}$; $c = 1, d = 5$,
   h) $f(x) = \sqrt{\frac{75}{x+2}}$; $c = 3, d = 5$.

4. In each case the region enclosed between the following curves and the x-axis is rotated through $360°$ about the x-axis. Find the volume of the solid generated.
   a) $y = (x+1)(x-3)$,
   b) $y = 1 - x^2$,
   c) $y = x^2 - 5x + 6$,
   d) $y = x^2 - 3x$.

5. The region enclosed between the graphs of $y = x$ and $y = x^2$ is denoted by R. Find the volume generated when R is rotated through $360°$ about
   a) the x-axis,
   b) the y-axis.

6. The region enclosed between the graphs of $y = 4x$ and $y = x^2$ is denoted by R. Find the volume generated when R is rotated through $360°$ about
   a) the x-axis,
   b) the y-axis.

7. The region enclosed between the graphs of $y = \sqrt{x}$ and $y = x^2$ is denoted by R. Find the volume generated when R is rotated through $360°$ about
   a) the x-axis,
   b) the y-axis.

8. A glass bowl is formed by rotating about the y-axis the region between the graphs of $y = x^2$ and $y = x^3$. Find the volume of glass in the bowl.

9. The region enclosed by both axes, the line $x = 2$ and the curve $y = \frac{1}{8}x^2 + 2$ is rotated about the y-axis to form a solid. Find the volume of this solid.

10*. The finite region defined by the curve $y = (x-1)(5-x)$ and the line $y = 3$ is called R. Find the volume generated when R is rotated through $360°$ about the line $y = 3$.

11*. The torus (doughnut) is the solid of revolution obtained when the disc defined by the equation $(x-a)^2 + y^2 = b^2$, where $0 < b < a$, is rotated about the y-axis.

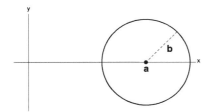 

a) Explain why the volume V of (revolution of) the torus is given by the expression

$$V = \pi \int_{-b}^{b} \left[a + \sqrt{b^2 - y^2}\right]^2 dy - \pi \int_{-b}^{b} \left[a - \sqrt{b^2 - y^2}\right]^2 dy$$

and simplify this to write V as a single integral.

b) Interpreting this integral geometrically, find a formula for the volume V of the torus.

Chapter 12: Summary

- The indefinite integral $F(x) = \int f(x)\,dx$ is the reverse of differentiation, so that $F'(x) = f(x)$. It is defined to within an arbitrary constant.

- The indefinite integral of x^n is $\frac{1}{n+1}x^{n+1} + c$ for any $n \neq -1$.

- The definite integral $\int_a^b y\,dx = \int_a^b f(x)\,dx$ is the signed area under the curve $y = f(x)$ in the region $a \leq x \leq b$.

- The definite integral $\int_c^d x\,dy = \int_c^d f^{-1}(y)\,dy$ is the signed area to the left of the curve $y = f(x)$ in the region $c \leq y \leq d$.

- The indefinite and definite integrals are linear functions, with

$$\int \left[pf(x) + qg(x) \right] dx = p \int f(x)\,dx + q \int g(x)\,dx$$

$$\int_a^b \left[pf(x) + qg(x) \right] dx = p \int_a^b f(x)\,dx + q \int_a^b g(x)\,dx$$

- The area between the curves $y = f(x)$ and $y = g(x)$ in the region $a \leq x \leq b$ is the integral $\int_a^b [f(x) - g(x)]\,dx$.

- The volume of revolution formed by rotating the region under the curve $y = f(x)$ in the interval $a \leq x \leq b$ through $360°$ about the x-axis is

$$\pi \int_a^b y^2\,dx = \pi \int_a^b f(x)^2\,dx.$$

The volume of revolution formed by rotating the region to the left of the curve $y = f(x)$ in the interval $c \leq y \leq d$ through $360°$ about the y-axis is

$$\pi \int_c^d x^2\,dy = \pi \int_c^d \left[f^{-1}(y) \right]^2 dy.$$

Review Exercises 4

1. Find the first three terms in the expansions, in ascending powers of x, of:

   a) $(1 + 4x)^{10}$

   b) $(1 - 2x)^{16}$

2. Find the coefficient of $a^3 b^5$ in the expansions of:

   a) $(3a - 2b)^8$

   b) $\left(5a + \tfrac{1}{2}b\right)^8$.

3. Obtain the first four terms in the expansion of $\left(2 + \tfrac{1}{4}x\right)^8$ in ascending powers of x. By substituting an appropriate value of x into this expansion, find the value of 2.0025^8 correct to three decimal places. (OCR)

4. Find, in ascending powers of x, the first three terms in the expansion of $(2 - 3x)^8$. Use the expansion to find the value of 1.997^8 to the nearest whole number. (OCR)

5. Expand $\left(x^2 + \tfrac{1}{x}\right)^3$, simplifying each of the terms.

6. Expand $\left(2x - \tfrac{3}{x^2}\right)^4$.

7. Expand and simplify $\left(x + \tfrac{1}{2x}\right)^6 + \left(x - \tfrac{1}{2x}\right)^6$.

8. Find the coefficient of x^2 in the expansion of $\left(x^4 + \tfrac{4}{x}\right)^3$.

9. Find the term independent of x in the expansion of $\left(2x + \tfrac{5}{x}\right)^6$.

10. Determine the coefficient of $p^4 q^7$ in the expansion of $(2p - q)(p + q)^{10}$.

11. Write down the first three terms in the binomial expansion of $\left(2 - \tfrac{1}{2x^2}\right)^{10}$ in desending powers of x. Hence find the value of 1.995^{10} correct to three significant figures. (OCR)

12. Two of the following expansions are correct and two are incorrect. Find the two expansions which are incorrect.

   A: $(3 + 4x)^5 = 243 + 1620x + 4320x^2 + 5760x^3 + 3840x^4 + 1024x^5$

   B: $(1 - 2x + 3x^2)^3 = 1 + 6x - 3x^2 + 28x^3 - 9x^4 + 54x^5 - 27x^6$

   C: $(1 - x)(1 + 4x)^4 = 1 + 15x + 80x^2 + 160x^3 - 256x^5$

   D: $(2x + y)^2(3x + y)^3 = 108x^5 + 216x^4 y + 171x^3 y^2 + 67x^2 y^3 + 13xy^4 + y^6$

13. Find and simplify the term independent of x in the expansion of $\left(\tfrac{1}{2x} + x^3\right)^8$. (OCR)

14. Evaluate the term which is independent of x in the expansion of $\left(x^2 - \tfrac{1}{2x^2}\right)^{16}$. (OCR)

231

15. Find the coefficient of x^{-12} in the expansion of $\left(x^3 - \frac{1}{x}\right)^{24}$. (OCR)

16. Expand $(1 + 3x + 4x^2)^4$ in ascending powers of x as far as the term in x^2. By substituting a suitable of x, find an approximation to 1.0304^4.

17. Expand and simplify $(3x + 5)^3 - (3x - 5)^3$. Hence solve the equation

$$(3x + 5)^3 - (3x - 5)^3 = 730$$

18. Find, in ascending powers of t, the first three terms in the expansions of
   a) $(1 + \alpha t)^5$ b) $(1 - \beta t)^8$
   Hence find, in terms of α and β, the coefficient of t^2 in the expansion of $(1 + \alpha t)^5 (1 - \beta t)^8$. (OCR)

19. Prove that
$$\binom{n}{r-1} + 2\binom{n}{r} + \binom{n}{r+1} = \binom{n+2}{r+1}$$

20. a) Expand $(2\sqrt{2} + \sqrt{3})^4$ in the form $a + b\sqrt{6}$, where a and b are integers.
   b) Find the exact value of $(2\sqrt{2} + \sqrt{3})^5$.

21. a) Expand and simplify $(\sqrt{7} + \sqrt{5})^4 + (\sqrt{7} - \sqrt{5})^4$. By using the fact that $0 < \sqrt{7} - \sqrt{5} < 1$, state the consecutive integers between which $(\sqrt{7} + \sqrt{5})^4$ lies.
   b) Without using a calculator, find the consecutive integers between which the value of $(\sqrt{3} + \sqrt{2})^6$ lies.

22. Find the series expansion of $(1 + 2x)^{\frac{5}{2}}$ up to and including the term in x^3, simplifying the coefficients. (OCR)

23. Expand $(1 - 4x)^{\frac{1}{2}}$ as a series of ascending powers of x, where $|x| < \frac{1}{4}$, up to and including the term in x^3, expressing the coefficients in their simplest form. (OCR)

24. Expand $(1 + 2x)^{-3}$ as a series of ascending powers of x, where $|x| < \frac{1}{2}$, up to and including the term in x^3, expressing the coefficients in their simplest form. (OCR)

25. Expand $\frac{1}{(1+2x^2)^2}$ as a series in ascending powers of x, up to and including the term in x^6, giving the coefficients in their simplest form. (OCR)

26. Obtain the first three terms in the expansion, in ascending powers of x, of $(4 + x)^{\frac{1}{2}}$. State the set of values of x for which the expansion is valid. (OCR)

27. If x is small compared with a, expand $\frac{a^3}{(a^2+x^2)^{\frac{3}{2}}}$ in ascending powers of $\frac{x}{a}$ up to and including the term in $\frac{x^4}{a^4}$. (OCR)

28. Given that $|x| < 1$, expand $\sqrt{1 + x}$ as a series of ascending powers of x, up to and including the term in x^2. Show that, if x is small, then $(2 - x)\sqrt{1 + x} \approx a + bx^2$, where the values of a and b are to be stated. (OCR)

29. Expand $(1 - x)^{-2}$ as a series of ascending powers of x, given that $|x| < 1$. Hence express $\frac{1+x}{(1-x)^2}$ in the form $1 + 3x + ax^2 + bx^3 + \cdots$, where the values of a and b are to be stated. (OCR)

30. Obtain the first three terms in the expansion, in ascending powers of x, of $(8 + 3x)^{\frac{2}{3}}$, stating the set of values of x for which the expansion is valid. (OCR)

31. Write down the first four terms of the series expansion in ascending powers of x of $(1 - x)^{\frac{1}{3}}$, simplifying the coefficients. By taking $x = 0.1$, use your answer to show that $\sqrt[3]{900} \approx \frac{15641}{1620}$. (OCR)

32. Give the binomial expansion, for small x, of $(1 + x)^{\frac{1}{4}}$ up to and including the term in x^2, and simplify the coefficients. By putting $x = \frac{1}{16}$ in your expression, show that $\sqrt[4]{17} \approx \frac{8317}{4096}$. (OCR)

33. Expand $\dfrac{2+\left(1+\frac{1}{2}x\right)^6}{2+3x}$ in ascending powers of x up to and including the term in x^2. (OCR)

34. Show that $26\left(1-\frac{1}{26^2}\right)^{\frac{1}{2}} = n\sqrt{3}$, where n is an integer whose value is to be found. Given that $|x| < 1$, expand $(1-x)^{\frac{1}{2}}$ as a series of ascending powers of x, up to and including the term in x^2, simplifying the coefficients. Hence obtain an approximate value for $\sqrt{3}$ in the form $\frac{p}{q}$, where p and q are integers. (OCR)

35. Expand $(1+x)^{-\frac{1}{4}}$ in ascending powers of x as far as the term in x^2, simplifying the coefficients. Prove that $\frac{3}{2}\left(1+\frac{1}{80}\right)^{-\frac{1}{4}} = 5^{\frac{1}{4}}$ and, using your expansion of $(1+x)^{-\frac{1}{4}}$ with $x = \frac{1}{80}$, find an approximate value for $5^{\frac{1}{4}}$, giving five places of decimals in your answer. (OCR)

36*. Show that the coefficient of x^n in the series expansion of $(1+2x)^{-2}$ is $(-1)^n(n+1)2^n$.

37*. Show that the coefficient of x^n in the series expansion of $(1-x)^{-\frac{1}{2}}$ is $\dfrac{(2n)!}{2^{2n}(n!)^2}$.

38. Find the maximum and minimum values of $x^3 - 6x^2 + 9x + 6$, showing carefully how you determine which is which.

39. Aeroplanes in flight experience a resistance known as drag. For a particular aeroplane at low speeds the drag is equal to kS^2, where k is the (constant) drag coefficient and S is the speed of the aeroplane.
    At high speeds, however, k changes with speed, and a typical graph of k against S is shown here. (The transonic region is commonly known as the 'sound barrier'.)

    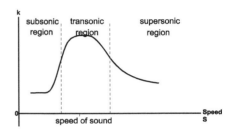

    a) Give the signs of $\dfrac{dk}{dS}$ and $\dfrac{d^2k}{dS^2}$ for each of the three sections of the graph and, in particular, say where each is zero.

    b) Where is k changing most rapidly?

    c) What does the graph imply about k at even higher speeds?

40. A window consists of a lower rectangular part $ABCD$ of width $2x$ m and height y m and an upper part which is a semicircle of radius x m on AB as diameter, as shown in the diagram. The perimeter of the window is 10 m. Find an expression in terms of x and π for the total area of the window, and find the value of x for which the area is a maximum.
    By considering the second derivative of the area, verify that the area is a maximum for this value of x.

    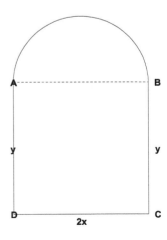

41. Investigate the maxima and minima of the following functions, where $a > 0$.
    a) $x^2(x-a)$ b) $x^3(x-a)$ c) $x^2(x-a)^2$ d) $x^3(x-a)^2$
    Make a conjecture about $x^n(x-a)^m$, where $m, n \in \mathbb{N}$.

42. Find an expression for $f^{(n)}(x)$ where
    a) $f(x) = \frac{1}{x^3}$,   b) $f(x) = \sqrt{x}$.

43. Find the coordinates of any points of inflexion on the curves with equations

    a) $y = x^4 - 8x^3 + 18x^2 + 4$,   b) $y = x^2 - \frac{1}{x} + 2$.

44. Use differentiation to find the coordinates of the stationary points on the curve

$$y = x + \frac{4}{x}$$

and determine whether each stationary point is a maximum point or a minimum point.

Find the set of values of x for which y increases as x increases.   (OCR)

45. The rate at which a radioactive mass decays is known to be proportional to the mass remaining at that time. If, at time t, the mass remaining is m, this means that m and t satisfy the equation

$$\frac{dm}{dt} = -km$$

where k is a positive constant. (The negative sign ensures that $\frac{dm}{dt}$ is negative, which indicates that m is decreasing.)

Write down similar equations which represent the following statements.

    a) The rate of growth of a population of bacteria is proportional to the number, n, of bacteria present.

    b) When a bowl of hot soup is put in the freezer, the rate at which its temperature, $\theta°C$, decreases as it cools is proportional to its current temperature.

    c) The rate at which the temperature, $\theta°C$, of a cup of coffee decreases as it cools is proportional to the excess of its temperature over the room temperature, $\beta°C$.

46. A car accelerates to overtake a truck. Its initial speed is u, and in a time t after it starts to accelerate it covers a distance x, where $x = ut + kt^2$. Use differentiation to show that its speed is then $u + 2kt$, and show that its acceleration is constant.

47. A car is travelling at 20 ms^{-1} when the driver applies the brakes. At a time t seconds later the car has travelled a further distance x metres, where $x = 20t - 2t^2$. Use differentiation to find expressions for the speed and the acceleration of the car at this time. For how long do these formulae apply?

48. A boy stands on the edge of a cliff of height 60 m. He throws a stone vertically upwards so that its distance, h m, above the cliff top is given by $h = 20t - 5t^2$.

    a) Calculate the maximum height of the stone above the cliff top.

    b) Calculate the time which elapses before the stone hits the beach. (It just misses the boy and the cliff on the way down.)

    c) Calculate the speed with which the stone hits the beach.

49. Find the least possible value of $x^2 + y^2$ given that $x + y = 10$.

50. The sum of the two shorter sides of a right-angled triangle is 18 cm. Calculate

    a) the least possible length of the hypotenuse,

    b) the greatest possible area of the triangle.

51.   a) Find the stationary points on the graph of $y = 12x + 3x^2 - 2x^3$ and sketch the graph.

    b) How does your sketch show that the equation $12x + 3x^2 - 2x^3 = 0$ has exactly three real roots?

    c) Use your graph to show that the equation $12x + 3x^2 - 2x^3 = -5$ also has exactly three real roots.

    d) For what range of values of k does the equation $12x + 3x^2 - 2x^3 = k$ have: (i) exactly three distinct real roots,   (ii) only one real root?

52. Find the coordinates of the stationary points on the graph of $y = x^3 - 12x - 12$ and sketch the graph. Find the set of values of k for which the equation $x^3 - 12x - 12 = k$ has more than one real solution.   (OCR)

53. Find the coordinates of the stationary points on the graph of $y = x^3 + x^2$. Sketch the graph and hence write down the set of values of the constant k for which the equation $x^3 + x^2 = k$ has three distinct real roots.

54. Find the coordinates of the stationary points on the graph of $y = 3x^4 - 4x^3 - 12x^2 + 10$, and sketch the graph. For what values of k does the equation $3x^4 - 4x^3 - 12x^2 + 10 = k$ have: (a) exactly four roots, (b) exactly two roots?

55. Find the coordinates of the stationary points on the curve with equation $y = x(x-1)^2$. Sketch the curve.

    Find the set of real values of k such that the equation $x(x-1)^2 = k^2$ has exactly one real root. (OCR, adapt.)

56. The cross-section of an object has the shape of a quarter-circle of radius r adjoining a rectangle of width x and height r, as shown in the diagram.

    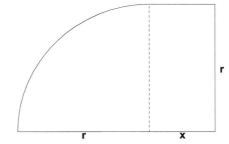

    a) The perimeter and area of the cross-section are P and A respectively. Express each of P and A in terms of r and x, and hence show that $A = \frac{1}{2}Pr - r^2$.

    b) Taking the perimeter P of the cross-section as fixed, find x in terms of r for the case when the area A of the cross-section is a maximum, and show that, for this value of x, A is a maximum and not a minimum. (OCR)

57. A curve has equation $y = \frac{1}{x} - \frac{1}{x^2}$. Use differentiation to find the coordinates of the stationary point and determine whether the stationary point is a maximum point or a minimum point. Deduce, or obtain otherwise, the coordinates of the stationary point of each of the following curves.

    a) $y = \frac{1}{x} - \frac{1}{x^2} + 5$

    b) $y = \frac{2}{x-1} - \frac{2}{(x-1)^2}$

58. The manager of a supermarket usually adds a mark-up of 20% to the wholesale prices of all the goods he sells. He reckons that he has a loyal core of F customers and that, if he lowers his mark-up to $x\%$ he will attract an extra $k(20 - x)$ customers from his rivals. Each week the average shopper buys goods whose wholesale value is £A. Show that with a mark-up of $x\%$ the supermarket will have an anticipated weekly profit of

    $$£\frac{1}{100}Ax\big((F + 20k) - kx\big).$$

    Show that the manager can increase his profit by reducing his mark-up below 20% provided that $20k > F$. (OCR)

59. The costs of a firm which makes climbing boots are of two kinds:

    • Fixed costs (plant, rates, office expenses): £2000 per week;

    • Production costs (materials, labour): £20 for each pair of boots made.

    Market research suggests that, if they price the boots at £30 a pair they will sell 500 pairs a week, but that at £55 a pair they will sell none at all; and between these values the graph of sales against price is a straight line.

    If they price boots at £x a pair ($30 \leq x \leq 55$) find expressions for

    a) the weekly sales,   b) the weekly receipts,   c) the weekly costs (assuming that just enough boots are made).

    Hence show that the weekly profit, £P, is given by

    $$P = -20x^2 + 1500x - 24000.$$

    Find the price at which the boots should be sold to maximise the profit. (OCR)

60. A function with domain $\mathbb{R}$ is said to be **even** if $f(-x) = f(x)$ for all $x \in \mathbb{R}$, and is said to be **odd** if $f(-x) = -f(x)$ for all $x \in \mathbb{R}$. Sketch the graph of an even function $f(x)$ which has a derivative at every point.

Let P be the point on the graph for which $x = p$ (where $p > 0$). Draw the tangent at P on your sketch. Also draw the tangent at the point P' for which $x = -p$.

a) What is the relationship between the gradient at P' and the gradient at P? What can you deduce about the relationship between $f'(p)$ and $f'(-p)$? What does this tell you about the derivative of an even function?

b) Show that the derivative of an odd function is even.

61. Find $\displaystyle\int 6\sqrt{x}\,dx$, and hence evaluate $\displaystyle\int_1^4 6\sqrt{x}\,dx$. (OCR)

62. The diagram shows the graph of $y = 12 - 3x^2$. Determine the x-coordinate of each of the points where the curve crosses the x-axis. Find by integration the area of the region (shaded in the diagram) between the curve and the x-axis. (OCR)

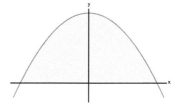

63. a) Find $\displaystyle\int \left(x^{-3} + x^3 \right) dx$.   b) Evaluate $\displaystyle\int_0^8 \frac{1}{\sqrt[3]{x}}\,dx$. (OCR)

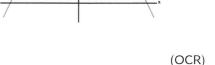

64. The diagram shows the curve $y = x^3$. The point P has coordinates $(3, 27)$ and PQ is the tangent to the curve at P. Find the area of the region enclosed between the curve, PQ and the x-axis.

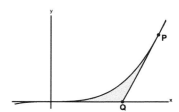

65. The diagram shows the curve $y = (x-2)^2 + 1$ with minimum point P. The point Q on the curve is such that the gradient of PQ is 2. Find the area of the region, shaded in the diagram, between PQ and the curve.

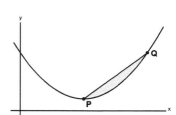

66. a) Find $\displaystyle\int x(x^2 - 2)\,dx$.

b) The diagram shows the graph of $y = x(x^2 - 2)$ for $x \geq 0$. The value of a is such that the two shaded regions have equal areas. Find the value of a. (OCR)

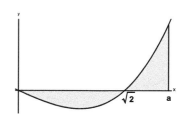

67. Given that $\displaystyle\int_1^p (8x^3 + 6x)\,dx = 39$, find two possible values of p. Use a graph to explain why there are two values.

68. Show that the area enclosed between the curves $y = 9 - x^2$ and $y = x^2 - 7$ is $\frac{128\sqrt{2}}{3}$.

69. The diagram shows a sketch of the graph of $y = x^2$ and the normal to the curve at the point $A\,(1,1)$.

    a) Use differentiation to find the equation of the normal at A. Verify that the point B where the normal cuts the curve again has coordinates $(-\frac{3}{2}, \frac{9}{4})$.

    b) The region which is bounded by the curve and the normal is shaded in the diagram. Calculate its area, giving your answer as an exact fraction.   (OCR)

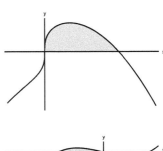

70. The diagram shows the graph of $y = \sqrt[3]{x} - x^2$. Show by integration that the area of the region (shaded in the diagram) between the curve and the x-axis is $\frac{5}{12}$.   (OCR)

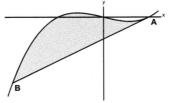

71. The diagram shows a sketch of the graph of the curve $y = x^3 - x$ together with the tangent to the curve at the point $A\,(1,0)$.

    a) Find the equation of the tangent to the curve at A, and verify that the point B where the tangent cuts the curve again has coordinates $(-2, -6)$.

    b) Find the area of the region bounded by the curve and the tangent (shaded in the diagram), giving your answer as a fraction in its lowest terms.   (OCR)

72. The diagram shows part of the curve $y = x^n$, where $n > 1$.
    The point P on the curve has x-coordinate a. Show that the curve divides the rectangle $OAPB$ into two regions whose areas are in the ratio $n : 1$.

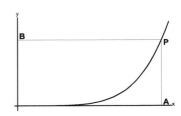

73. Find the stationary points on the graph of $y = x^4 - 8x^2$. Use your answers to make a sketch of the graph. Show that the graphs of $y = x^4 - 8x^2$ and $y = x^2$ enclose two finite regions. Find the area of one of them.

74. The region bounded by the curve $y = x^2 + 1$, the x-axis, the y-axis and the line $x = 2$ is rotated completely about the x-axis. Find, in terms of π, the volume of the solid formed.   (OCR)

75. The ellipse with equation $\frac{x^2}{a^2} + \frac{y^2}{b^2} = 1$, is shown in the diagram. It is said to have **semi-axes** a and b.
    The ellipse is rotated about the x-axis to form an **ellipsoid.** Find the volume of this ellipsoid. Deduce the volume of the ellipsoid formed if, instead, the ellipse had been rotated about the y-axis.

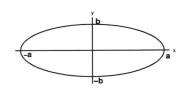

76. The region R is bounded by the part of the curve $y = (x - 2)^{\frac{3}{2}}$ for which $2 \le x \le 4$, the x-axis, and the line $x = 4$. Find, in terms of π, the volume of the solid obtained when R is rotated through $360°$ about the x-axis.   (OCR)

77*. Use the Binomial expansion to show that the coefficient of x^r in the expansion of $(1-x)^{-3}$ is $\frac{1}{2}(r+1)(r+2)$.

    a) Show that the coefficient of x^r in the expansion of $\frac{1-x+2x^2}{(1-x)^3}$ is r^2+1, and hence find the sum of the series

$$1 + \frac{2}{2} + \frac{5}{4} + \frac{10}{8} + \frac{17}{16} + \frac{26}{32} + \frac{37}{64} + \frac{50}{128} + \cdots$$

    b) Find the sum of the series

$$1 + 2 + \frac{9}{4} + 2 + \frac{25}{26} + \frac{9}{8} + \frac{49}{64} + \cdots$$

78*. The line L has equation $y = c - mx$ with $m > 0$ and $c > 0$. It passes through the point $R(a,b)$ and cuts the axes at the point $P(p,0)$ and $Q(0,q)$, where a, b, p and q are all positive. Find p and q in terms of a, b and m.

As L varies with R remaining fixed, show that the minimum value of the sum of the distances of P and Q from the origin is $\left(\sqrt{a}+\sqrt{b}\right)^2$, and find in similar form the minimum distance between P and Q. You may assume that any stationary values of these distances are minima.

Trigonometry

In this chapter we will learn to:

- sketch and use the graphs of the sine, cosine and tangent functions for angles of any size, using degrees or radians,

- solve simple trigonometric equations,

- work with the inverse trigonometric functions $\sin^{-1}$, $\cos^{-1}$ and $\tan^{-1}$,

- understand the relationship of the secant, cosecant and cotangent functions to each other and to the three main trigonometric functions,

- work with trigonometric identities including the Pythagorean identities, compound and double angle formulae and harmonic form identities, using them in the simplification of expressions and solving equations.

13.1   Graphs of $\sin\theta$, $\cos\theta$ and $\tan\theta$

In Chapter 8 we reminded ourselves of the shapes of the sine, cosine and tangent functions for angles between $0°$ and $180°$, or (in radians) between 0 and π. We used these results to solve simple trigonometric problems similar to those we encountered at GCSE (or the equivalent), using the sine and cosine rules to calculate lengths, angles and areas of triangles. In that chapter, we concentrated on working in radians, to develop our understanding of the new method for measuring angle. Of course, we could (and did, at GCSE) do the same calculations working in degrees!

We need to extend our understanding of the trigonometric functions. The sine and cosine functions might have their roots in the geometry of triangles, but they are actually functions with domain equal to the whole real line. It might be impossible to contemplate a triangle containing an angle of $715°$, but we can still assign a meaning to $\sin 715°$ and $\cos 715°$.

Figure 13.1 shows a circle with radius 1 unit centered at the origin O. For any positive angle θ (whether in degrees or radians), rotate the radius line OA anticlockwise through an angle θ; this line meets the circle at P. The point P will have coordinates (x, y), where each of x and y can lie between -1 and 1, depending on the size of θ.

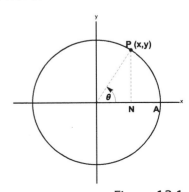

Figure 13.1

> **For Interest**
>
> Frequently Greek letters like θ ('theta') and ϕ ('phi') are used to describe angles.

> **Key Fact 13.1** The Functions $\cos\theta$, $\sin\theta$ And $\tan\theta$: General Definitions
>
> For any angle θ, the point P defines the values of $\cos\theta$, $\sin\theta$ and $\tan\theta$ as follows:
>
> $$\cos\theta = x \qquad \sin\theta = y \qquad \tan\theta = \tfrac{y}{x}.$$

It is clear that this rule works well for acute angles, for then θ is one of the angles in the right-angled triangle ONP which has hypotenuse of length 1. With respect to the angle θ, the adjacent side is $ON = x$, and the opposite side if $PN = y$. The key advantage of these rules is that they work for all values of θ. Note that they also imply that $\tan\theta \equiv \frac{\sin\theta}{\cos\theta}$ for all θ.

Example 13.1.1. *Find the values of:*
a) $\cos 180°$, b) $\sin 270°$, c) $\tan 135°$, d) $\cos -90°$, e) $\sin 810°$.

When $\theta = 180°$, the line ON has been rotated through half a circle, and hence P has coordinates $(-1,0)$. Thus $\cos 180° = -1$. Rotating ON through $270°$ gives P the coordinates $(0,-1)$, and so $\sin 170° = -1$ as well.

If we rotate ON through $135°$, then it ends up pointing in a 'north-westerly direction', at an angle of $45°$ above the horizontal. Recalling the results of Key Fact 8.4 for the sine and cosine of $\frac{1}{4}\pi = 45°$, we see that P has coordinates $(-\frac{1}{\sqrt{2}}, \frac{1}{\sqrt{2}})$, and hence $\tan 135° = -1$.

What happens if θ is negative? The answer is simply to rotate ON clockwise, instead of clockwise. This is consistent with previous work with rotations when studying rotations of shapes; a negative rotation is a clockwise one. Thus, if we rotate ON through $-90°$, it ends up pointing vertically down, so that P has coordinates $(-1,0)$ and hence $\cos -90° = 0$.

Finally, a rotation through $810°$ involves two complete circles and an additional $90°$. Thus P has coordinates $(0,1)$, and hence $\sin 810° = 1$.

Modern calculators will provide the values of the trigonometric functions for all values of θ, whether in degrees or radians. The graphs of $\cos\theta$ and $\sin\theta$ can be readily plotted for all values of θ:

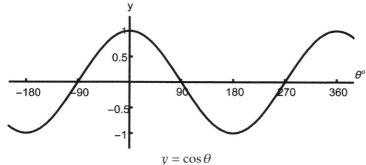

$$y = \cos\theta$$

Figure 13.2

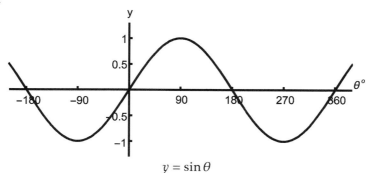

$$y = \sin\theta$$

Figure 13.3

The graphs of $y = \cos\theta$ and $y = \sin\theta$ are almost identical; they have the same shape, but one seems to be a translated version of the other. They share many properties in common. Most important of these is the fact that they keep on repeating themselves. If ON is rotated through

360°, it gets back to where it started, and so the sine and cosine functions will be the same. In other words,

$$\sin(\theta \pm 360°) \equiv \sin\theta \qquad \cos(\theta \pm 360°) \equiv \cos\theta.$$

The functions sin and cos are **periodic** of period 360°. Moreover, if ON is rotated through 180°, then it ends up pointing diametrically away from its starting point, and hence the signs of x and y are changed. Thus the signs of $\sin\theta°$ and $\cos\theta°$ are changed if θ changes by 180:

$$\sin(\theta \pm 180°) \equiv -\sin\theta \qquad \cos(\theta \pm 180°) \equiv -\cos\theta°.$$

We say that sin and cos are **antiperiodic** of period 180°. Notice also that $\cos\theta$ and $\sin\theta$ both take values between -1 and 1.

Example 13.1.2. *The height h in metres of the water in a harbour is given approximately by the formula $h = 6 + 3\cos(30t)°$, where t is the time in hours after noon. Find the height of the water at 9.45 p.m., and find the highest and lowest water levels, and when they first occur after noon.*

At 9.45 p.m. we have $t = 9.75$, and hence $h = 6 + 3\cos 292.5° = 7.148$ m. The maximum water level occurs when the cosine function is equal to 1, and so the high water level is $6 + 3 = 9$ m. This first happens when $30t = 360$, or $t = 12$. High water occurs at midnight. Similarly the low water mark occurs when the cosine function is equal to -1, and so the low water level is $6 - 3 = 3$. This first happens when $30t = 180$, or $t = 6$. Low water occurs at 6 p.m.

The graph of $\tan\theta$ is slightly complicated. Since $\tan\theta = \frac{y}{x}$, it is undefined whenever $\cos\theta = x$ is zero, namely when $\theta = \pm 90°, \pm 270°, \dots$

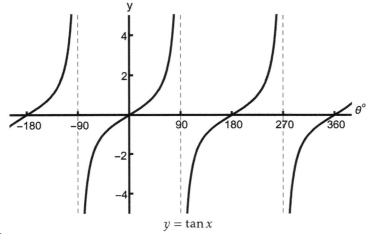

$$y = \tan x$$

Figure 13.4

Like the sine and cosine functions, the graph of $y = \tan\theta$ is also periodic; this time the period is 180°, so that

$$\tan(\theta \pm 180°) \equiv \tan\theta.$$

Example 13.1.3. *Write down the exact values of $\cos 135°$, $\sin 120°$ and $\tan 405°$.*

Recalling properties from Chapter 8, and in particular Key Fact 8.4, $\cos 135° = -\cos 45° = -\frac{1}{\sqrt{2}}$, and $\sin 120° = \sin(180 - 120)° = \sin 60° = \frac{1}{2}\sqrt{3}$. The graphs in Figures 13.2 and 13.3 could have been used to work these out. Finally, the periodicity of the tangent gives $\tan 405° = \tan 45° = 1$.

Example 13.1.4. *Sketch the graph of $y = \sin(2x - 50°)$ for $0° \le x \le 360°$.*

This graph is obtained from the graph of $y = \sin x$ by a combination of a horizontal scale, factor $\frac{1}{2}$, and a horizontal shift. While the following graph is accurate

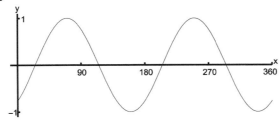

Figure 13.5

it is not particularly informative. It is better to choose to label more interesting points on the x-axis. Marking the values of the intercepts with the x-axis is better (it is easy to work out the coordinates of each turning point, since they occur halfway between successive intercepts)

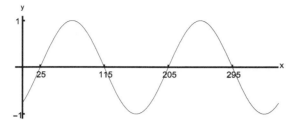

Figure 13.6

Example 13.1.5. *Sketch the graph of* $y = 1 + 2\cos(x + \frac{1}{4}\pi)$ *for* $-\pi \le x \le \pi$.

This graph is obtained from the graph of $y = \cos x$ by a horizontal shift, a vertical shift and a vertical scale, factor 2. The maximum value of this function is 3, which occurs at $x = -\frac{1}{4}\pi$. The minimum value of this function is -1, which occurs at $\frac{3}{4}\pi$.

We can also work out the values of the x-intercepts. These occur when $\cos(x + \frac{1}{4}\pi) = -\frac{1}{2}$, namely when $x + \frac{1}{4}\pi = \pm\frac{2}{3}\pi$, and so when $x = -\frac{11}{12}\pi$ and $\frac{5}{12}\pi$.

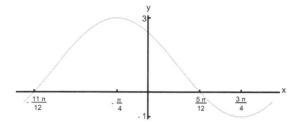

Figure 13.7

As a general rule, try to indicate the key points on the curve: intercepts, turning points and points where the function is undefined (in the case of $\tan x$). We probably do not need to indicate all of them on the graph, just enough to make the overall shape of the curve clear.

> **Food For Thought 13.1**
>
> If an angle is measured in degrees, a degree symbol $^\circ$ will be present. If no degree symbol is present, work in radians.

Exercise 13A

1. In each part of this question sketch the graphs of the given functions on the same set of axes for $-180° \le \theta \le 180°$:

   a) $y = \sin\theta, y = 2\sin\theta,$
   c) $y = \tan\theta, y = -\tan\theta,$

   b) $y = \cos\theta, y = 2 - \cos\theta,$
   d) $y = \sin\theta, y = \sin(90° - \theta).$

2. In each part of this question sketch the graphs of the given functions on the same set of axes for $0 \le \theta \le 2\pi$:

   a) $y = \cos\theta, y = \cos(\theta + \frac{1}{2}\pi),$
   c) $y = \sin\theta, y = \sin 2\theta,$

   b) $y = \tan\theta, y = 2\tan\theta,$
   d) $y = \cos\theta, y = 2 + \cos(2\theta).$

3. Find the maximum value and the minimum value of each of the following functions. In each case, give the least positive values of x (in degrees) at which they occur.

a) $2 + \sin x$,

b) $7 - 4\cos x$,

c) $5 + 8\cos 2x$,

d) $\frac{8}{3 - \sin x}$,

e) $9 + \sin(4x - 20°)$,

f) $\frac{30}{11 - 5\cos(\frac{1}{2}x - 45°)}$.

4. (Do not use a calculator for this question.) In each part of the question a trigonometric function of an angle is given. Find all the other angles x with $0° \leq x \leq 360°$ for which the same trigonometric function of x is equal to the given trigonometric ratio. For example, if you are given $\sin 80°$ then $x = 100°$, since $\sin 100° = \sin 80°$.

a) $\sin 20°$,
b) $\cos 40°$,
c) $\tan 60°$,
d) $\sin 130°$,
e) $\cos 140°$,
f) $\tan 160°$,
g) $\sin 400°$,
h) $\cos(-30)°$,
i) $\tan 430°$,
j) $\sin(-260)°$,
k) $\cos(-200)°$,
l) $\tan 1000°$.

5. (Do not use a calculator for this question.) In each part of the question a trigonometric function of an angle is given. Find all the other angles x, $-180° \leq x \leq 180°$, such that the same function of x is equal to the given trigonometric ratio.

a) $\sin 20°$,
b) $\cos 40°$,
c) $\tan 60°$,
d) $\sin 130°$,
e) $\cos 140°$,
f) $\tan 160°$,
g) $\sin 400°$,
h) $\cos(-30)°$,
i) $\tan 430°$,
j) $\sin(-260)°$,
k) $\cos(-200)°$,
l) $\tan 1000°$.

6. (Do not use a calculator for this question.) In each part of the question a trigonometric function of a number is given. Find all the other numbers x with $0 \leq x \leq 2\pi$ for which the same trigonometric function of x is equal to the given trigonometric ratio. For example, if you are given $\sin \frac{1}{5}\pi$ then $x = \frac{4}{5}\pi$, since $\sin \frac{4}{5}\pi = \sin \frac{1}{5}\pi$.

a) $\sin \frac{1}{10}\pi$,
b) $\cos \frac{1}{7}\pi$,
c) $\tan \frac{1}{7}\pi$,
d) $\sin \frac{5}{9}\pi$,
e) $\cos \frac{6}{7}\pi$,
f) $\tan \frac{10}{11}\pi$,
g) $\sin \frac{13}{12}\pi$,
h) $\cos -\frac{1}{6}\pi$,
i) $\tan \frac{6}{5}\pi$,
j) $\sin -\frac{4}{3}\pi$,
k) $\cos -\frac{8}{5}\pi$,
l) $\tan 15\pi$.

7. Without using a calculator, write down the exact values of the following.

a) $\sin 135°$,
b) $\cos 120°$,
c) $\sin(-30)°$,
d) $\tan 240°$,
e) $\cos 225°$,
f) $\tan(-330)°$,
g) $\cos 900°$,
h) $\tan 510°$,

i) $\sin \frac{5}{4}\pi$,
j) $\cos \frac{7}{2}\pi$,
k) $\tan \frac{9}{4}\pi$,
l) $\sin -\frac{7}{4}\pi$,

m) $\sin \frac{7}{6}\pi$,
n) $\tan \frac{15}{4}\pi$,
o) $\cos -\frac{2}{3}\pi$,
p) $\sin 7\pi$.

8. Without using a calculator, write down the smallest positive angle (in degrees) which satisfies the following equations.

a) $\cos \theta = \frac{1}{2}$,
b) $\sin \phi = -\frac{1}{2}\sqrt{3}$,
c) $\tan \theta = -\sqrt{3}$,
d) $\cos \theta = \frac{1}{2}\sqrt{3}$,
e) $\tan \theta = \frac{1}{3}\sqrt{3}$,
f) $\tan \phi = -1$,
g) $\sin \theta = -\frac{1}{2}$,
h) $\cos \theta = 0$.

9. Without using a calculator, write down the angle (in radians) with the smallest modulus which satisfies the following equations. (If there are two such angles, choose the positive one.)

a) $\cos \theta = -\frac{1}{2}$,
b) $\tan \phi = \sqrt{3}$,
c) $\sin \theta = -1$,
d) $\cos \theta = -1$,
e) $\sin \phi = \frac{1}{2}\sqrt{3}$,
f) $\tan \theta = -\frac{1}{3}\sqrt{3}$,
g) $\sin \phi = -\frac{1}{2}\sqrt{2}$,
h) $\cos \phi = 0$.

10. The water levels in a dock follow (approximately) a twelve-hour cycle, and are modelled by the equation $D = A + B\sin(30t)°$, where D metres is the depth of water in the dock, A and B are positive constants, and t is the time in hours after 8 a.m.

Given that the greatest and least depths of water in the dock are 7.80 m and 2.20 m respectively, find the value of A and the value of B.

Find the depth of water in the dock at noon, giving your answer correct to the nearest cm.

13.2 Symmetries

Let us look again at the diagram we first considered in Figure 13.1. If the point P, corresponding to the angle θ, has coordinates (x, y), then there are three other interesting points on the circle which have very similar coordinates.

The point S has coordinates $(x, -y)$, and corresponds to the angle $-\theta$ or $2\pi - \theta$. Thus

$$\sin(-\theta) \equiv \sin(2\pi - \theta) \equiv -\sin\theta$$
$$\cos(-\theta) \equiv \cos(2\pi - \theta) \equiv \cos\theta$$
$$\tan(-\theta) \equiv \tan(2\pi - \theta) \equiv -\tan\theta.$$

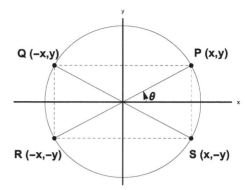

Figure 13.8

Functions $f(x)$ for which $f(-x) = f(x)$ are called **even**. Functions $f(x)$ for which $f(-x) = -f(x)$ are called **odd**. The cosine is an even function, while the sine and tangent are odd functions.

The point Q has coordinates $(-x, y)$, and corresponds to the angle $\pi - \theta$. Thus

$$\sin(\pi - \theta) \equiv \sin\theta \qquad \cos(\pi - \theta) \equiv -\cos\theta \qquad \tan(\pi - \theta) \equiv -\tan\theta.$$

The point R has coordinates $(-x, -y)$, and corresponds to the angle $\pi + \theta$. From this we obtain the already-observed antiperiodicity/periodicity properties:

$$\sin(\pi + \theta) \equiv -\sin\theta \qquad \cos(\pi + \theta) \equiv -\cos\theta \qquad \tan(\pi + \theta) \equiv \tan\theta$$

These results are vital to our understanding of the trigonometric functions.

Key Fact 13.2 Trigonometric Symmetries

Periodic:	$\sin(\theta \pm 2\pi) \equiv \sin\theta$	$\cos(\theta \pm 2\pi) \equiv \cos\theta$	$\tan(\theta \pm 2\pi) \equiv \tan\theta$
Antiperiodic:	$\sin(\theta \pm \pi) \equiv -\sin\theta$	$\cos(\theta \pm \pi) \equiv -\cos\theta$	
Even/Odd?	$\sin(-\theta) \equiv -\sin\theta$	$\cos(-\theta) \equiv \cos\theta$	$\tan(-\theta) \equiv -\tan\theta$
Quadrants:	$\sin(\pi - \theta) \equiv \sin\theta$	$\cos(\pi - \theta) \equiv -\cos\theta$	$\tan(\pi - \theta) \equiv -\tan\theta$
	$\sin(\pi + \theta) \equiv -\sin\theta$	$\cos(\pi + \theta) \equiv -\cos\theta$	$\tan(\pi + \theta) \equiv \tan\theta$
	$\sin(2\pi - \theta) \equiv -\sin\theta$	$\cos(2\pi - \theta) \equiv \cos\theta$	$\tan(2\pi - \theta) \equiv -\tan\theta$

For Interest

So that we always remember that trigonometric calculations can be performed in degrees or radians, we have presented this set of identities in radian form!

The **quadrant identities** are important because they provide a quick method of calculation of the trigonometric functions for general angles. Split the plane up into four quadrants (quarters), and number them 1, 2, 3 and 4, counting anticlockwise from the top-right quadrant. If θ is an acute angle ($0 < \theta < \frac{1}{2}\pi$), then θ lies in the first quadrant, and $\pi - \theta$, $\pi + \theta$ and $2\pi - \theta$ are angles in the second, third and fourth quadrants respectively. The quadrant identities tell us how the values of the trigonometric functions relates to their values for the corresponding first quadrant angle θ.

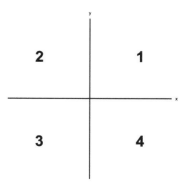

Figure 13.9

We note that any trigonometric function of a second, third or fourth quadrant angle is equal to either $+1$ or -1 times the same trigonometric function of the corresponding first quadrant angle. For example, $\sin(\pi - \theta) \equiv \sin\theta$ is one of the rules for the second quadrant angle $\pi - \theta$, and $\tan(2\pi - \theta) \equiv -\tan\theta$ is one of the rules for the fourth quadrant angle $2\pi - \theta$. The quadrant rules tell us that in each quadrant (except the first) exactly one of the three trigonometric functions is positive; sin is positive in the second quadrant, tan is positive in the third and cos is positive in the fourth.

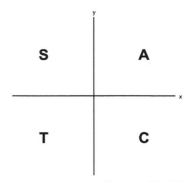

Figure 13.10

All three functions are positive in the first quadrant, only the Sine is positive in the second, only the Tangent is positive in the third, and only Cosine is positive in the fourth quadrant. The mnemonic 'All Silly Tom Cats' is as memorable as any!

Example 13.2.1.   (a) *Express* $\sin 350°$ *and* $\tan 205°$ *in terms of trigonometric functions of acute angles.*

(b) *Find all values* θ, *with* $0 < \theta < 2\pi$, *for which* $\cos\theta = -0.2$.

(a) $\sin 350° = \sin(360 - 10)° = \sin 10°$ and $\tan 205° = \tan(180 + 25)° = -\tan 25°$.

(b) Since $\cos\theta = -0.2 < 0$, θ must lie in either the second or third quadrants. If ϕ is the (first quadrant) acute angle with $\cos\phi = 0.2$, our calculators tell us that $\phi = 1.3694$ to 4 decimal places. The possible values of θ are thus the second and third quadrant angles corresponding to ϕ, namely $\pi - \phi = 1.7722$ and $\pi + \phi = 4.5110$.

Food For Thought 13.2

The symmetries that we have discussed so far are those between a trigonometric function and itself. There are other identities to be discussed, which relate the trigonometric functions to each other. These will be discussed in detail later. However, it is worth noticing the important identity

$$\cos\theta \equiv \sin(\tfrac{1}{2}\pi - \theta)$$

which is easy to understand for acute angles θ by thinking about right-angled triangles. More generally, it reflects the fact that the graph of $y = \cos\theta$ is the mirror image of $y = \sin\theta$ in the line $x = \tfrac{1}{4}\pi$.

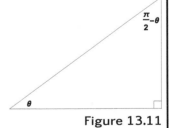

Figure 13.11

13.3   Solving Trigonometric Equations

We have already considered some trigonometric equations, for example by asking when high tide occurred in Example 13.1.2. However, it is not enough just to be able to find one solution; to provide the complete solution to a trigonometric equation, we need to find **all** the solutions. In general, there will be infinitely many of them, so we shall be content with finding all the solutions that lie in a given range.

Example 13.3.1. *Solve the equation* $\cos\theta = \tfrac{1}{3}$, *giving all roots in the interval* $0° \le \theta \le 360°$ *correct to* 1 *decimal place.*

It is clear from the graphs of $y = \cos\theta$ and $y = \frac{1}{3}$ that there will be solutions in this interval; there will be solutions in the first and fourth quadrants (the two quadrants where $\cos\theta$ is positive). Using our calculators, we see that the first quadrant solution is $\cos^{-1}\frac{1}{3} = 70.5°$. Using the symmetry properties of cos, we deduce that the fourth quadrant solution is $(360 - 70.5)° = 289.5°$.

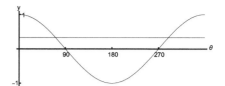

Figure 13.12

Example 13.3.2. *Solve the equation* $\cos 3\theta = -\frac{1}{2}$, *giving all roots in the interval* $-180° \leq \theta \leq 180°$.

If we put $3\theta = \phi$, we are being asked to solve the equation $\cos\phi = -\frac{1}{2}$. However, since θ is allowed to take values between $-180°$ and $180°$, ϕ must be allowed to take values between $-540°$ and $540°$.

Angles with negative cosines lie in the second and third quadrants. We know that $\cos 60° = \frac{1}{2}$, and hence $\cos 120° = -\frac{1}{2}$. This is a second quadrant angle. The corresponding third quadrant angle is 240o. Other values of 3θ can be obtained using the periodicity of the sine function, Thus possible values of ϕ are $-480°, -240°, -120°, 120°, 240°, 480°$, and so possible values of θ are $-160°, -80°, -40°, 40°, 80°, 160°$.

Example 13.3.3. *Solve the equation* $\sin\frac{1}{3}(\theta - \frac{1}{6}\pi) = \frac{1}{2}\sqrt{3}$, *for* θ *in the interval* $0 \leq \theta \leq 2\pi$.

If we put $\phi = \frac{1}{3}(\theta - \frac{1}{6}\pi)$, then we need to solve the equation $\sin\phi = \frac{1}{2}\sqrt{3}$ in the range $-\frac{1}{18}\pi \leq \phi \leq \frac{11}{18}\pi$.

Angles with positive sines lie in the first and second quadrants. We know that $\sin\frac{1}{3}\pi = \frac{1}{2}\sqrt{3}$. The corresponding second quadrant angle is $\frac{2}{3}\pi$, but this is larger than $\frac{11}{18}\pi$. Thus the only possible solution for ϕ is $\frac{1}{3}\pi$, and so the only solution for θ is $\frac{7}{6}\pi$.

Example 13.3.4. *Solve the equation* $\tan\theta = -2$, *for* θ *in the range* $0° \leq \theta \leq 360°$, *correct to 2 decimal places.*

The tangent function is perhaps the easiest one to solve, since it has the simplest periodicity properties — the fact that $\tan\theta$ is periodic of period $180°$ is enough.

Using our calculators gives $\tan^{-1}(-2) = -63.43°$. Although this gives a solution of the equation $\tan\theta = -2$, it is not in the correct range for θ. We obtain other solutions by adding $180°$, so the possible solutions for θ are $116.57°, 296.57°$.

Example 13.3.5. *The height in metres of the water in a harbour is given approximately by the formula* $d = 6 + 3\cos(30t)°$ *where* t *is the time measured in hours from noon. Find the time after noon when the height of the water is 7.5 metres for the second time.*

The height of water is 7.5 m when $6 + 3\cos(30t)° = 7.5$, or $\cos(30t)° = \frac{1}{2}$. The first two positive values for $30t$ are 60 and $360 - 60 = 300$. Thus the water level is 7.5 m for the second time after noon when $t = 10$, namely at 10 p.m.

Exercise 13B

1. Find, in degrees correct to 1 decimal place, the two smallest positive values of θ which satisfy each of the following equations:

a) $\sin\theta = 0.1$,
b) $\sin\theta = -0.84$,
c) $\sin\theta = 0.951$,
d) $\tan\theta = 4$,
e) $\tan\theta = -0.32$,
f) $\tan\theta = 0.11$,
g) $\sin(180° + \theta) = 0.4$,
h) $\cos(90° - \theta) = -0.571$,
i) $\tan(90° - \theta) = -3$,
j) $\sin(2\theta + 60°) = 0.3584$,
k) $\sin(30° - \theta) = 0.5$,
l) $\cos(3\theta - 120°) = 0$.

2. Find all values of θ in the interval $-180° \leq \theta \leq 180°$ which satisfy each of the following equations, giving your answers correct to 1 decimal place where appropriate:

   a) $\sin\theta = -0.67$,
   b) $\cos\theta = -0.12$,
   c) $4\tan\theta + 3 = 0$,
   d) $4\sin\theta = 5\cos\theta$,
   e) $2\sin\theta = \frac{1}{\sin\theta}$,
   f) $2\sin\theta = \tan\theta$.

3. Find all the solutions in the interval $0 \leq \theta \leq 2\pi$ of each of the following equations, giving all answers to 2 decimal places of accuracy:

   a) $\cos 2\theta = \frac{1}{3}$,
   b) $\tan 3\theta = 2$,
   c) $\sin 2\theta = -0.6$,
   d) $\cos 4\theta = -\frac{1}{4}$,
   e) $\tan 2\theta = 0.4$,
   f) $\sin 3\theta = -0.42$.

4. Find the roots in the interval $-\pi \leq x \leq \pi$ of each of the following equations:

   a) $\cos 3x = \frac{2}{3}$,
   b) $\tan 2x = -3$,
   c) $\sin 3x = -0.2$,
   d) $\cos 2x = 0.246$,
   e) $\tan 5x = 0.8$,
   f) $\sin 2x = -0.39$.

5. Find the roots (if there are any) in the interval $-180° \leq \theta \leq 180°$ of the following equations:

   a) $\cos\frac{1}{2}\theta = \frac{2}{3}$,
   b) $\tan\frac{2}{3}\theta = -3$,
   c) $\sin\frac{1}{4}\theta = -\frac{1}{4}$,
   d) $\cos\frac{2}{3}\theta = \frac{1}{3}$,
   e) $\tan\frac{3}{4}\theta = 0.5$,
   f) $\sin\frac{2}{5}\theta = -0.3$.

6. Without using a calculator, find the exact roots of the following equations, if there are any, giving your answers in the interval $0 \leq t \leq 2\pi$:

   a) $\sin(2t - \frac{1}{6}\pi) = \frac{1}{2}$,
   b) $\tan(2t - \frac{1}{4}\pi) = 0$,
   c) $\cos(3t + \frac{3}{4}\pi) = \frac{1}{2}\sqrt{3}$,
   d) $\tan(\frac{3}{2}t - \frac{1}{4}\pi) = -\sqrt{3}$,
   e) $\cos(2t - \frac{5}{18}\pi) = -\frac{1}{2}$,
   f) $\sin(\frac{1}{2}t + \frac{5}{18}\pi) = 1$,
   g) $\cos(\frac{1}{5}t - \frac{5}{18}\pi) = 0$,
   h) $\tan(3t - \pi) = -1$,
   i) $\sin(\frac{1}{4}t - \frac{1}{18}\pi) = 0$.

7. Find, to 1 decimal place, all values of z in the interval $-180° \leq z \leq 180°$ satisfying:

   a) $\sin z = -0.16$,
   b) $\cos z(1 + \sin z) = 0$,
   c) $(1 - \tan z)\sin z = 0$,
   d) $\sin 2z = 0.23$,
   e) $\cos(45° - z) = 0.832$,
   f) $\tan(3z - 17°) = 3$.

8. Find all values of θ in the interval $0° \leq \theta \leq 360°$ for which:

   a) $\sin 2\theta = \cos 36°$
   b) $\cos 5\theta = \sin 70°$,
   c) $\tan 3\theta = \tan 60°$.

9. Find all values of θ in the interval $0 \leq \theta \leq \pi$ for which $2\sin\theta\cos\theta = \frac{1}{2}\tan\theta$.

10. For each of the following values, give an example of a trigonometric function involving (i) sine, (ii) cosine and (iii) tangent, with that value as period.

   a) $90°$
   b) $20°$
   c) $48°$
   d) $120°$
   e) $720°$
   f) $600°$

11. At a certain latitude in the northern hemisphere, the number d of hours of daylight in each day of the year is taken to be $d = A + B\sin(kt)°$, where A, B, k are positive constants and t is the time in days after the spring equinox.

   a) Assuming that the number of hours of daylight follows an annual cycle of 365 days and that successive spring equinoxes are exactly one year apart, find the value of k, giving your answer correct to 3 decimal places.

   b) Given also that the shortest and longest days have 6 and 18 hours of daylight respectively, state the values of A and B. Find, in hours and minutes, the amount of daylight on New Year's Day, which is 80 days before the spring equinox.

   c) A town at this latitude holds a fair twice a year on those days having exactly 10 hours of daylight. Find, in relation to the spring equinox, which two days these are.

13.4   Elementary Trigonometric Identities

There is a large amount of redundancy in trigonometry. From one point of view, we only need one trigonometric function, since (for example) both the cosine and the tangent can be written in terms of the sine. It is, however, convenient to have all three functions (and shortly we will have six!). The consequence of this is that there are many relationships between these functions. The trigonometric functions satisfy a large number of identities, therefore, which both enrich their study (these identities make more complex calculations possible, and make yet it more complicated (since the same function can be expressed in a number of different ways.

The two identities that we shall consider at this stage are both immediate consequences of the definitions of the trigonometric functions. In Figure 13.1 we observed how the point P on the circle of radius 1 have raise to formulae for the $\cos\theta = x$, $\sin\theta = y$ and $\tan\theta = \frac{y}{x}$ in terms of the coordinates (x, y) of P.

Since the circle has radius 1, $x^2 + y^2 = 1$, which implies that $(\cos\theta)^2 + (\sin\theta)^2 = 1$. However, we do not usually write this identity like that. It is nice to adopt a convention which avoids the use of brackets, and which makes it possible to distinguish between square of the cosine, $(\cos\theta)^2$, and the cosine of the square, $\cos\theta^2$, for example. The conventional manner for doing this is to write the positive n^{th} power of $\cos\theta$ as $\cos^n\theta$ instead of $(\cos\theta)^n$, and similarly for $\sin\theta$ and $\tan\theta$.

Key Fact 13.3 Trigonometric Identities

For any angle θ,
$$\tan\theta \equiv \frac{\sin\theta}{\cos\theta} \qquad \cos^2\theta + \sin^2\theta \equiv 1.$$

The identity $\cos^2\theta + \sin^2\theta \equiv 1$ is, not surprisingly, known as a Pythagorean identity.

Food For Thought 13.3

When using the notation $\sin^n\theta$ to represent $(\sin\theta)^n$, it is best to restrict its use to positive integer powers n only. Above all, it should not be used to represent inverse powers. The notation $\sin^{-1}$ is reserved for the inverse function of $\sin$, and does not mean one over the sine function.

These identities have a number of uses. They could, for instance, provide an easier proof of the cosine rule than we presented in Section 8.5.3.

If we have a triangle ABC, choose axes so that A is at the origin and C on the positive x-axis. Then B has coordinates $(c\cos A, c\sin A)$, while C has coordinates $(b, 0)$. Coordinate geometry tells us that

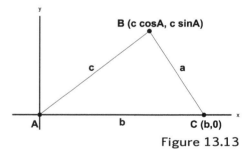

$$\begin{aligned} a^2 &= BC^2 = (b - c\cos A)^2 + (c\sin A)^2 \\ &= b^2 - 2bc\cos A + c^2\cos^2 A + c^2\sin^2 A \\ &= b^2 - 2bc\cos A + c^2[\cos^2 A + \sin^2 A] \\ &= b^2 + c^2 - 2bc\cos A \end{aligned}$$

Figure 13.13

Evaluating functions, solving equations, and establishing other identities are common uses.

Example 13.4.1. *Given that $\sin\theta = \frac{2}{5}$ and that θ is obtuse (second quadrant) find, without using a calculator, exact values for $\cos\theta$ and $\tan\theta$.*

We know that $\cos^2\theta = 1 - \sin^2\theta = 1 - \frac{4}{25} = \frac{21}{25}$. Since θ is obtuse, we know that $\cos\theta$ is negative, and hence $\cos\theta = -\frac{1}{5}\sqrt{21}$. Thus

$$\tan\theta = \frac{\sin\theta}{\cos\theta} = \frac{\frac{2}{5}}{-\frac{1}{5}\sqrt{21}} = -\frac{2}{\sqrt{21}} = -\frac{2}{21}\sqrt{21}.$$

Example 13.4.2. *Given that $\tan\theta = \frac{1}{3}$ and that θ is not acute, calculate the exact values of $\sin\theta$ and $\cos\theta$*

The simplest way to do this is by drawing a right-angled triangle. If the triangle has sides of length 1 and 3 as marked, then $\tan\phi = \frac{1}{3}$. This triangle has hypotenuse of length $\sqrt{1^2 + 3^2} = \sqrt{10}$, and hence $\cos\phi = \frac{3}{\sqrt{10}}$ and $\sin\phi = \frac{1}{\sqrt{10}}$. Since θ is not acute, we deduce that $\theta = \phi + \pi$ is in the third quadrant, and hence $\cos\theta = -\frac{3}{\sqrt{10}}$ and $\sin\theta = -\frac{1}{\sqrt{10}}$.

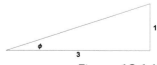

Figure 13.14

A more algebraic method might proceed as follows:

$$\tan\theta = \tfrac{1}{3} \quad\Rightarrow\quad 3\sin\theta = \cos\theta \quad\Rightarrow\quad 9\sin^2\theta = \cos^2\theta = 1-\sin^2\theta \quad\Rightarrow\quad 10\sin^2\theta = 1$$

and hence $\sin^2\theta = \tfrac{1}{10}$. Since θ is known to be third quadrant, we deduce that $\sin\theta = -\tfrac{1}{\sqrt{10}}$, and so $\cos\theta = \tfrac{\sin\theta}{\tan\theta} = -\tfrac{3}{\sqrt{10}}$.

Example 13.4.3. *Solve the equation* $3\cos^2\theta + 4\sin\theta = 4$, *giving all roots in the interval* $-180° \le \theta \le 180°$, *correct to 1 decimal place.*

This equation needs to be manipulated before it can be solved. Substituting $\cos^2\theta = 1 - \sin^2\theta$ turns it into a concealed quadratic in $\sin\theta$:

$$3(1-\sin^2\theta) + 4\sin\theta = 4$$
$$3\sin^2\theta - 4\sin\theta + 1 = 0$$
$$(3\sin\theta - 1)(\sin\theta - 1) = 0$$

Thus either $\sin\theta = \tfrac{1}{3}$, yielding $\theta = 19.5°$, $160.5°$, or else $\sin\theta = 1$, so that $\theta = 90°$.

Example 13.4.4. *Prove that* $\cos\theta - \tfrac{1}{\cos\theta} \equiv -\sin\theta\tan\theta$ *and* $\cos^4\theta - \cos^2\theta \equiv \sin^4\theta - \sin^2\theta$.

A good way of proving identities is to start with the expression on one side, and keep on applying standard identities and elementary algebra until the expression on the other side is obtained. Thus

$$\cos\theta - \frac{1}{\cos\theta} \equiv \frac{\cos^2\theta - 1}{\cos\theta} \equiv \frac{-\sin^2\theta}{\cos\theta} \equiv -\sin\theta \times \frac{\sin\theta}{\cos\theta} \equiv -\sin\theta\tan\theta$$
$$\cos^4\theta - \cos^2\theta \equiv \cos^2\theta(\cos^2\theta - 1) \equiv -\cos^2\theta\sin^2\theta$$
$$\equiv (\sin^2\theta - 1)\sin^2\theta \equiv \sin^4\theta - \sin^2\theta$$

EXERCISE 13C

1. In each part of this question the triangle in the figure has two of the sides a, b and c defined. In each case, work out the length of the missing side, and calculate the exact values of $\sin\theta$, $\cos\theta$ and $\cos\theta$:
   a) $a = 8.8, b = 6.6$,   b) $b = 20, c = 42.5$,
   c) $a = 3, b = 2$,   d) $a = 5\sqrt{3}, c = 14$,
   e) $a = 22, b = 31$,   f) $a = 4\sqrt{2}, b = 16$.

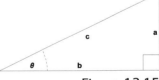

Figure 13.15

2. a) Given that angle A is obtuse and that $\sin A = \tfrac{5}{14}\sqrt{3}$, find the exact value of $\cos A$.

   b) Given that $180° < B < 360°$ and that $\tan B = -\tfrac{21}{20}$, find the exact value of $\cos B$.

   c) Find all possible values of $\sin C$ for which $\cos C = \tfrac{1}{2}$.

   d) Find the values of D for which $-180° < D < 180°$ and $\tan D° = 5\sin D°$.

3. Establish the following identities:

   a) $\tfrac{1}{\sin\theta} - \tfrac{1}{\tan\theta} \equiv \tfrac{1-\cos\theta}{\sin\theta}$,   b) $\tfrac{\sin^2\theta}{1-\cos\theta} \equiv 1 + \cos\theta$,

   c) $\tfrac{1}{\cos\theta} + \tan\theta \equiv \tfrac{\cos\theta}{1-\sin\theta}$,   d) $\tfrac{\tan\theta\sin\theta}{1-\cos\theta} \equiv 1 + \tfrac{1}{\cos\theta}$,

   e) $(1-\sin\theta+\cos\theta)^2 \equiv 2(1-\sin\theta)(1+\cos\theta)$.

4. Solve the following equations for θ, giving all the roots in the interval $0° \le \theta \le 360°$ correct to 1 decimal place:

   a) $4\sin^2\theta - 1 = 0$,   b) $\sin^2\theta + 2\cos^2\theta = 2$,
   c) $10\sin^2\theta - 5\cos^2\theta + 2 = 4\sin\theta$,   d) $4\sin^2\theta\cos\theta = \tan^2\theta$.

5. Find all values of θ, $-180° \le \theta \le 180°$, for which $2\tan\theta - 3 = \tfrac{2}{\tan\theta}$.

6. Solve the following equations for $0 \le \theta \le 2\pi$, giving your answers (where necessary) correct to 2 decimal places.

a) $2\cos^2\theta + \sin\theta - 1 = 0$,

b) $4\sin^2\theta + \cos\theta - 1 = 0$,

c) $4\sin^2\theta + \cos\theta - 3 = 0$,

d) $3\sin^2\theta + \cos\theta = 3 - \cos^2\theta$,

e) $\cos^3\theta = \sin^2\theta\cos\theta$,

f) $3\sin\theta\tan\theta = 2\sin\theta + \cos\theta$,

g) $\cos^4\theta = 4\sin^2\theta$,

h) $\tan^2\theta + 2\tan\theta - 1 = 0$.

7. Solve the following equations for $0° \le \theta \le 360°$, giving your answers correct to 1 decimal place.

a) $4\sin^3\theta - 3\sin\theta + 1 = 0$,

b) $3\cos^3\theta + 3\cos^2\theta - 2\cos\theta - 2 = 0$,

c) $5\sin^3\theta + 4\sin^2\theta - 2\sin\theta = 0$,

d) $\tan^3\theta - 5\tan^2\theta + \tan\theta + 7 = 0$,

e) $\cos^2 2\theta = 2\sin 2\theta + 1$,

f) $\sin 3\theta = 4\cos 3\theta$.

8*. Given that
$$\sin\theta = \frac{3\cos^3\theta - \cos\theta}{11\cos^2\theta - 6}$$
find all possible values of $\tan\theta$.

13.5   Secant, Cosecant and Cotangent

We have already observed that there is a problem with the standard notation for powers of trigonometric functions. While the expression $\sin^3 x$ is fine to represent the cube of the sine function, the expression $\sin^{-1} x$ is used to represent the inverse of that function. We therefore need a method of expressing negative powers of trigonometric functions clearly. The conventional method for doing this is to introduce three new functions which are closely related to the sine, cosine and tangent. Basically, allowing for the niceties of domains, these new functions are simply the reciprocals of the sine, cosine and tangent.

Key Fact 13.4 Secant, Cosecant and Cotangent

The **secant**, **cosecant** and **cotangent** functions are defined by

$$\sec x \equiv \frac{1}{\cos x}, \qquad \cos x \neq 0,$$

$$\operatorname{cosec} x \equiv \frac{1}{\sin x}, \qquad \sin x \neq 0,$$

$$\cot x \equiv \frac{\cos x}{\sin x}, \qquad \sin x \neq 0.$$

Note that $\cot x \equiv \frac{1}{\tan x}$ for all values of x except where $\tan x$ is either undefined or zero.

You won't find sec, cosec or cot keys on your calculator. To find their values you have to use the cos, sin or tan keys and the reciprocal key.

The graphs of $y = \sec\theta$, $y = \operatorname{cosec}\theta$ and $y = \cot\theta$ are shown below. The first two functions have period 2π, while the cotangent has period π.

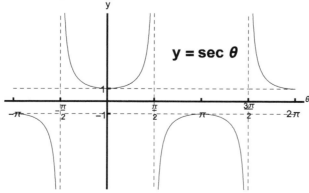

Figure 13.16

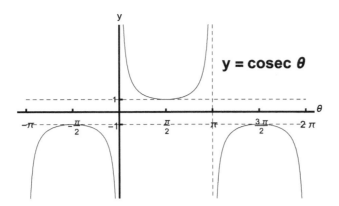

Figure 13.17

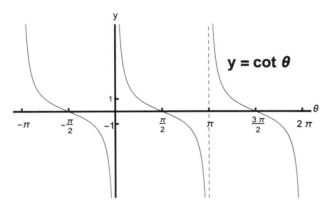

Figure 13.18

As the reciprocals of cos, sin and tan, these functions have extremely similar periodicity properties. It is probably easier to use the symmetry properties of the original trigonometric functions.

Example 13.5.1. *Find the exact values of* $\sec\frac{2}{3}\pi$, $\operatorname{cosec}\frac{5}{6}\pi$ *and* $\cot(-\frac{2}{3}\pi)$.

We have $\cos\frac{2}{3}\pi = -\cos(\pi - \frac{2}{3}\pi) = -\cos\frac{1}{3}\pi = -\frac{1}{2}$, and hence $\sec\frac{2}{3}\pi = -2$. Similarly $\sin\frac{5}{6}\pi = \sin(\pi - \frac{5}{6}\pi) = \sin\frac{1}{6}\pi = \frac{1}{2}$, and hence $\operatorname{cosec}\frac{5}{6}\pi = 2$. Finally $\tan(-\frac{2}{3}\pi) = \tan(\pi - \frac{2}{3}\pi) = \frac{1}{3}\pi = \sqrt{3}$, and hence $\cot(-\frac{2}{3}\pi) = \frac{1}{\sqrt{3}}$.

The Pythagorean identity $\cos^2\theta + \sin^2\theta \equiv 1$ has two new versions, obtained by dividing the original one first by $\cos^2\theta$ and then by $\sin^2\theta$:

Key Fact 13.5 The Pythagorean Identities

$$\cos^2\theta + \sin^2\theta \equiv 1 \qquad 1 + \tan^2\theta \equiv \sec^2\theta \qquad 1 + \cot^2\theta \equiv \operatorname{cosec}^2\theta$$

Food For Thought 13.4

It is worth noting the pairings of cos with sin, tan with sec and cot with cosec. We shall meet these pairings again.

Example 13.5.2. *Prove the identity*

$$\frac{1}{\sec\theta - \tan\theta} \equiv \sec\theta + \tan\theta, \qquad \sec\theta - \tan\theta \neq 0.$$

We have previously discussed how to prove identities by starting with either the left-hand side or the right-hand side and applying known identities and good algebra until the other side is reached. This technique is not easy to use here, since how to

251

start manipulating one side to obtain the other is not particularly obvious. Another (if harder approach) is to start with a true statement, and to deduce from it the desired identity. We shall use this method here. Proofs like these tend to be sequences of identities, where each implies the next.

$$\sec^2\theta - \tan^2\theta \equiv 1$$

$$\Rightarrow \quad (\sec\theta - \tan\theta)(\sec\theta + \tan\theta) \equiv 1$$

$$\Rightarrow \quad \sec\theta + \tan\theta \equiv \frac{1}{\sec\theta - \tan\theta}$$

For Interest

The most common mistake when attempting to prove identities is to do this argument backwards, to start with the answer and from it derive a true statement, like $1 \equiv 1$. For example

$$\frac{1}{\sec\theta - \tan\theta} \equiv \sec\theta + \tan\theta$$

$$1 \equiv (\sec\theta + \tan\theta)(\sec\theta - \tan\theta)$$

$$1 \equiv \sec^2\theta - \tan^2\theta$$

$$1 \equiv 1$$

is a very common offering. This is not a proof. What it is saying is that if the desired identity were true, then $1 = 1$. Unfortunately, the fact that something true can be derived from it does not make a statement true in itself. Indeed, an important principle of mathematical logic states that *absolutely anything* can be deduced from a false statement; the argument shown above has therefore shown nothing.

EXERCISE 13D

1. Find, giving your answers to 3 decimal places,
   a) $\cot 304°$,
   b) $\sec(-48)°$,
   c) $\operatorname{cosec} 62°$.

2. Simplify the following:
   a) $\sec(\frac{1}{2}\pi - x)$,
   b) $\frac{\cos x}{\sin x}$,
   c) $\sec(-x)$,
   d) $1 + \tan^2 x$,
   e) $\cot(\pi + x)$,
   f) $\operatorname{cosec}(\pi + x)$.

3. Find the exact values of
   a) $\sec\frac{1}{4}\pi$,
   b) $\operatorname{cosec}\frac{1}{2}\pi$,
   c) $\cot\frac{5}{6}\pi$,
   d) $\operatorname{cosec}(-\frac{3}{4}\pi)$,
   e) $\cot(-\frac{1}{3}\pi)$,
   f) $\sec\frac{13}{6}\pi$,
   g) $\cot(-\frac{11}{2}\pi)$,
   h) $\sec\frac{7}{6}\pi$.

4. Using a calculator where necessary, find the values of the following, giving any non-exact answers correct to 3 significant figures.
   a) $\operatorname{cosec}\frac{2}{5}\pi$,
   b) $\sec\frac{1}{10}\pi$,
   c) $\cot\frac{1}{12}\pi$,
   d) $\operatorname{cosec}\frac{17}{6}\pi$,
   e) $\sec\frac{7}{8}\pi$,
   f) $\cot\frac{5}{12}\pi$,
   g) $\sec(-\frac{11}{12}\pi)$,
   h) $\cot(-\frac{1}{6}\pi)$.

5. Given that $\sin A = \frac{3}{7}$, where A is acute, and $\cos B = -\frac{1}{4}$, where B is obtuse, find the exact values of
   a) $\sec A$,
   b) $\cot A$,
   c) $\cot B$,
   d) $\operatorname{cosec} B$.

6. Given that $\operatorname{cosec} C = 7$, where C is obtuse, and $\cot D = \frac{1}{10}$, where D is not acute, find the exact values of
   a) $\cos C$,
   b) $\cot C$,
   c) $\sin D$,
   d) $\sec D$.

7. Simplify the following.
   a) $\sqrt{\sec^2\phi - 1}$,
   b) $\frac{\tan\phi}{1+\tan^2\phi}$,
   c) $\frac{\tan\phi}{\sec^2\phi-1}$,
   d) $\frac{1}{\sqrt{1+\cot^2\phi}}$,
   e) $\frac{1}{\sqrt{\operatorname{cosec}^2\phi-1}}$,
   f) $(\operatorname{cosec}\phi - 1)(\operatorname{cosec}\phi + 1)$.

8. a) Express $3\tan^2\theta - \sec\theta$ in terms of $\sec\theta$.

   b) Solve the equation $3\tan^2\phi - \sec\phi = 1$ for $0 \le \phi \le 2\pi$.

9. Solve equation $5\cot x + 2\mathrm{cosec}^2 x = 5$ for $0 \le x \le 2\pi$.

10. Find exact solutions to $2\sin^2 t + \mathrm{cosec}^2 t = 3$ in the range $0 \le t \le 2\pi$.

11. Solve the following equations for $0° \le \theta \le 360°$:

   a) $\sec\theta = 7\mathrm{cosec}\theta$,
   c) $2\sec\theta + 11\mathrm{cosec}\theta = 0$,
   e) $\sec^2\theta = 8 + \tan\theta$,
   g) $\sec^3\theta - 2\sec^2\theta - 11\sec\theta + 12 = 0$,

   b) $\mathrm{cosec}^2\theta = 5\sec^2\theta$,
   d) $\sec\theta\tan\theta = 27\mathrm{cosec}\theta\cot\theta$,
   f) $4 + \tan^2\theta = \sec\theta(13 - 2\sec\theta)$,
   h) $2\cot^3\theta = \mathrm{cosec}^2\theta + 13\cot\theta + 5$.

12. Prove the following identities:

   a) $\mathrm{cosec}\,x + \cot x \equiv \dfrac{1}{\mathrm{cosec}\,x - \cot x}$,
   c) $\dfrac{\sec x}{\tan x + \cot x} \equiv \sin x$,
   e) $\sin x \tan x + \cos x \equiv \sec x$,
   g) $\sec^2 x - \mathrm{cosec}^2 x \equiv \tan^2 x - \cot^2 x$,
   i) $\sqrt{\dfrac{1 - \sin x}{1 + \sin x}} \equiv \sec x - \tan x$,

   b) $\dfrac{\sec x - 1}{\tan x} \equiv \dfrac{\tan x}{\sec x + 1}$,
   d) $\dfrac{1}{1 + \tan^2 x} + \dfrac{1}{1 + \cot^2 x} \equiv 1$,
   f) $\mathrm{cosec}\,x - \sin x \equiv \cot x \cos x$,
   h) $\dfrac{\sin x}{1 + \cos x} + \dfrac{1 + \cos x}{\sin x} \equiv 2\mathrm{cosec}\,x$,
   j) $\dfrac{\tan^3\phi}{1 + \tan^2\phi} + \dfrac{\cot^3\phi}{1 + \cot^2\phi} \equiv \dfrac{1 - 2\sin^2\phi\cos^2\phi}{\sin\phi\cos\phi}$.

13*. Given that

$$\cos\theta(2\cos\theta + 1) = 6 + \sec\theta(7 + 2\sec\theta)$$

find the possible values of $\tan\theta$.

13.6 Inverse Trigonometric Functions

We have already met the notation $\sin^{-1}$, $\cos^{-1}$ and $\tan^{-1}$ a number of times. It is now time to give a more precise definition of the inverse trigonometric functions.

The key problem is that the functions $\cos x$, $\sin x$ and $\tan x$ are not one-to-one. It follows that they do not have inverses. What is meant by the inverses to these functions, then? When we use the $\sin^{-1}$, $\cos^{-1}$ and $\tan^{-1}$ buttons on out calculators, we get a definite answer, so there must be a way around this problem.

The trick is to restrict each of the functions $\sin x$, $\cos x$ and $\tan x$ to smaller domains than their standard ones, in such a way that the restricted functions are one-to-one (and so have inverses), but still have the ranges of their unrestricted 'parents'. We will work in radians.

Figure 13.19 shows how the domain of the cosine function is restricted to the interval $0 \le x \le \pi$ to define the function $\cos^{-1}$:

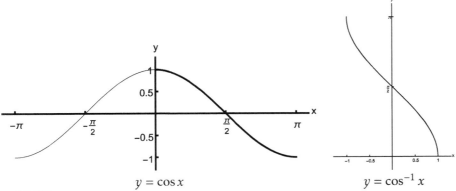

$y = \cos x$ $y = \cos^{-1} x$

Figure 13.19

The graph of $y = \cos^{-1} x$ is the mirror image of the graph of $y = \cos x$ (restricted to $0 \le x \le \pi$) in the line $y = x$.

Similarly, Figure 13.20 shows how the domain of the sine function is restricted to $-\frac{1}{2}\pi \le x \le \frac{1}{2}\pi$ to define $\sin^{-1}$:

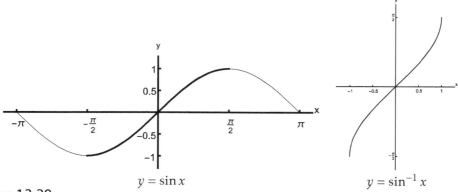

$y = \sin x$ $y = \sin^{-1} x$

Figure 13.20

Once again, the graphs of $y = \sin^{-1} x$ and the restricted portion of $y = \sin x$ are mirror images. Finally, Figure 13.21 shows the graph of the function $\tan^{-1}$, which is obtained by restricting tan to the domain $-\frac{1}{2}\pi < x < \frac{1}{2}\pi$.

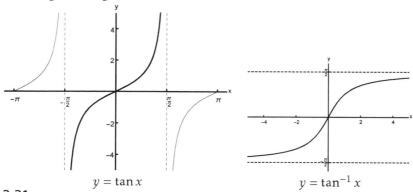

$y = \tan x$ $y = \tan^{-1} x$

Figure 13.21

These are not the only possible choices for the inverse trigonometric functions, but they are the most natural, since they ensure that the images of positive numbers under $\sin^{-1}$, $\cos^{-1}$ and $\tan^{-1}$ are acute angles, which is what we expect to happen.

> **Key Fact 13.6** Inverse Trigonometric Functions
>
> The inverse trigonometric functions have the following domains and ranges:
>
> | | Domain | Range |
> |-----------|------------------|--|
> | $\cos^{-1}$ | $-1 \le x \le 1$ | $0 \le y \le \pi$ |
> | $\sin^{-1}$ | $-1 \le x \le 1$ | $-\frac{1}{2}\pi \le y \le \frac{1}{2}\pi$ |
> | $\tan^{-1}$ | $\mathbb{R}$ | $-\frac{1}{2}\pi < y < \frac{1}{2}\pi$ |
>
> Sometimes the inverse trigonometric functions are written as arccos, arcsin and arctan. This is a different way of removing potential confusions over indices and trigonometric functions.

EXERCISE 13E

Do not use a calculator in Questions 1 to 5.

1. Find:

   a) $\cos^{-1} \frac{1}{2}\sqrt{3}$,   b) $\tan^{-1} 1$,   c) $\cos^{-1} 0$,   d) $\sin^{-1} \frac{1}{2}\sqrt{3}$,

   e) $\tan^{-1}(-\sqrt{3})$,   f) $\sin^{-1}(-1)$,   g) $\tan^{-1}(-1)$,   h) $\cos^{-1}(-1)$.

2. Find:

   a) $\cos^{-1} \frac{1}{\sqrt{2}}$,   b) $\sin^{-1}(-0.5)$,   c) $\cos^{-1}(-0.5)$,   d) $\tan^{-1}\left(\frac{1}{\sqrt{3}}\right)$.

3. Find:

    a) $\sin\left(\sin^{-1} 0.5\right)$,   b) $\cos\left(\cos^{-1}(-1)\right)$,   c) $\tan\left(\tan^{-1}\sqrt{3}\right)$,   d) $\cos\left(\cos^{-1} 0\right)$.

4. Find:

    a) $\cos^{-1}(\cos\frac{3}{2}\pi)$,   b) $\sin^{-1}(\sin\frac{13}{6}\pi)$,   c) $\tan^{-1}(\tan\frac{1}{6}\pi)$,   d) $\cos^{-1}(\cos 2\pi)$.

5. Find:

    a) $\sin\left(\cos^{-1}\frac{1}{2}\sqrt{3}\right)$,   b) $\dfrac{1}{\tan\left(\tan^{-1} 2\right)}$,   c) $\cos\left(\sin^{-1}(-0.5)\right)$,   d) $\tan\left(\cos^{-1}\frac{1}{2}\sqrt{2}\right)$.

6. Use a graphical method to solve, in radians correct to 3 decimal places, the equation $\cos x = \cos^{-1} x$. What simpler equation has this as its only root?

7*. What is the value of $\sin^{-1} x + \cos^{-1} x$ for any $-1 \le x \le 1$? You might find it helpful to start with positive values of x.

13.7 Compound Angle Formulae

Suppose that we know the values of $\sin A$, $\cos A$, $\sin B$ and $\cos B$. Is it possible to calculate the values of $\sin(A + B)$, $\sin(A - B)$, $\cos(A + B)$ and $\cos(A - B)$ without using a calculator to find the angles, which, of course, would only give approximations? There is a general formula which we can use.

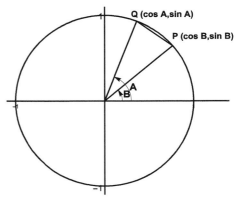

In Figure 13.22, angles A and B are drawn measured anticlockwise from the x-axis. The points P and Q lie on a circle of radius 1, and so have coordinates $(\cos A, \sin A)$ and $(\cos B, \sin B)$ respectively. There are now two different ways to calculate the length of the line PQ. We can use coordinate geometry, since we have the coordinates of the endpoints, or we can apply the cosine rule to the triangle OPQ, noting that the angle $\angle POQ$ is equal to $A - B$. The two different expressions for PQ^2 are $(\cos A - \cos B)^2 + (\sin A - \sin B)^2$ and $1^2 + 1^2 - 2 \times 1 \times 1 \times \cos(A - B)$. Equating these, and simplifying both sides, we obtain

Figure 13.22

$$\cos^2 B - 2\cos A\cos B + \cos^2 B + \sin^2 A - 2\sin A\sin B + \sin^2 B = 2 - 2\cos(A - B)$$
$$(\cos^2 B + \sin^2 B) + (\cos^2 A + \sin^2 A) - 2(\cos A\cos B + \sin A\sin B) = 2 - 2\cos(A - B)$$

and since $\cos^2 A + \sin^2 A = \cos^2 B + \sin^2 B = 1$, we deduce that

$$\cos(A - B) \equiv \cos A\cos B + \sin A\sin B$$

Although Figure 13.22 has been drawn with both A and B acute angles, this proof is general, and works for all angles A and B.

From this formula we can derive a collection of very similar other formulae, using symmetry properties of sine and cosine. Let us start with the formula for $\cos(A + B)$. Now

$$\cos(A + B) \equiv \cos\left(A - (-B)\right) \equiv \cos A\cos(-B) + \sin A\sin(-B) \equiv \cos A\cos B + \sin A(-\sin B)$$
$$\equiv \cos A\cos B - \sin A\sin B$$

using the facts that $\cos(-A) \equiv \cos A$ and $\sin(-A) \equiv -\sin A$.

In Food for Thought 13.2 we noted the identity $\cos\theta \equiv \sin(\frac{1}{2}\pi - \theta)$, noting that it was a consequence of a reflection symmetry between the sine and cosine functions. We are now in a position to prove it fully.

Example 13.7.1. *The* sin *and* cos *functions satisfy the identities:*

$$\cos\theta \equiv \sin(\tfrac{1}{2}\pi - \theta) \qquad \sin\theta \equiv \cos(\tfrac{1}{2}\pi - \theta).$$

We have
$$\cos(\tfrac{1}{2}\pi - \theta) \equiv \cos\tfrac{1}{2}\pi\cos\theta + \sin\tfrac{1}{2}\pi\sin\theta \equiv \sin\theta\,,$$

since we know that $\sin\tfrac{1}{2}\pi = 1$ and $\cos\tfrac{1}{2}\pi = 0$. Thus
$$\sin(\tfrac{1}{2}\pi - \theta) \equiv \cos\left(\tfrac{1}{2}\pi - (\tfrac{1}{2}\pi - \theta)\right) \equiv \cos\theta\,.$$

We can use this result to obtain formulae for $\sin(A+B)$ and $\sin(A-B)$, since

$$\sin(A+B) \equiv \cos(\tfrac{1}{2}\pi - A - B) \equiv \cos(\tfrac{1}{2}\pi - A)\cos B + \sin(\tfrac{1}{2}\pi - A)\sin B \equiv \sin A\cos B + \cos A\sin B$$
$$\sin(A-B) \equiv \sin A\cos(-B) + \cos A\sin(-B) \equiv \sin A\cos B - \cos A\sin B\,.$$

Key Fact 13.7 Compound Angle Formulae For sin and cos

We have the following identities:

$$\cos(A+B) \equiv \cos A\cos B - \sin A\sin B \qquad \cos(A-B) \equiv \cos A\cos B + \sin A\sin B$$
$$\sin(A+B) \equiv \sin A\cos B + \cos A\sin B \qquad \sin(A-B) \equiv \sin A\cos B - \sin A\cos B$$

Example 13.7.2. *Find exact values of* $\cos 75°$ *and* $\cos 15°$.

With $A = 45°$ and $B = 30°$, we have

$$\begin{aligned}
\cos 75° &= \cos(A+B) = \cos A\cos B - \sin A\sin B = \tfrac{1}{\sqrt{2}} \times \tfrac{1}{2}\sqrt{3} - \tfrac{1}{\sqrt{2}} \times \tfrac{1}{2}\\
&= \tfrac{1}{2\sqrt{2}}(\sqrt{3} - 1) = \tfrac{1}{4}(\sqrt{6} - \sqrt{2})\,,\\
\cos 15° &= \cos(A-B) = \cos A\cos B + \sin A\sin B = \tfrac{1}{\sqrt{2}} \times \tfrac{1}{2}\sqrt{3} + \tfrac{1}{\sqrt{2}} \times \tfrac{1}{2}\\
&= \tfrac{1}{2\sqrt{2}}(\sqrt{3} + 1) = \tfrac{1}{4}(\sqrt{6} + \sqrt{2})\,,
\end{aligned}$$

Example 13.7.3. *You are given that* $\sin A = \tfrac{8}{17}$, *that* $\sin B = \tfrac{12}{13}$, *and that* $0 < B < \tfrac{1}{2}\pi < A < \pi$. *Find the exact value of* $\tan(A+B)$.

Now $\cos^2 A = 1 - \left(\tfrac{8}{17}\right)^2 = \tfrac{225}{289}$. Since A is obtuse we deduce that $\cos A = -\tfrac{15}{17}$. Similarly $\cos^2 B = 1 - \left(\tfrac{12}{13}\right)^2 = \tfrac{25}{169}$. Since B is acute it follows that $\cos B = \tfrac{5}{13}$. Thus

$$\begin{aligned}
\sin(A+B) &= \sin A\cos B + \cos A\sin B = \tfrac{8}{17} \times \tfrac{5}{13} + \left(-\tfrac{15}{17}\right) \times \tfrac{12}{13} = \tfrac{40-180}{17\times 13} = -\tfrac{140}{221}\\
\cos(A+B) &= \cos A\cos B - \sin A\sin B = \left(-\tfrac{15}{17}\right) \times \tfrac{5}{13} - \tfrac{8}{17} \times \tfrac{12}{13} = \tfrac{-75-96}{17\times 13} = -\tfrac{171}{221}
\end{aligned}$$

and hence

$$\tan(A+B) = \frac{\sin(A+B)}{\cos(A+B)} = \frac{-140/221}{-171/221} = \frac{140}{171}\,.$$

Example 13.7.4. *Prove that* $\sin(A+B) + \sin(A-B) \equiv 2\sin A\cos B$.

Expanding both terms on the left-hand side,

$$\sin(A+B) + \sin(A-B) \equiv \sin A\cos B + \cos A\sin B + \sin A\cos B - \cos A\sin B \equiv 2\sin A\cos B\,,$$

noting that two of the terms in the expansions cancel each other out.

Example 13.7.5. *Find the exact value of* $\tan x$, *given that* $\sin(x + 30°) = 2\cos(x - 30°)$.

Use the compound angle formulae to write the equation as

$$\sin x \cos 30° + \cos x \sin 30° = 2\left[\cos x \cos 30° + \sin x \sin 30°\right]$$
$$\tfrac{1}{2}\sqrt{3}\sin x + \tfrac{1}{2}\cos x = 2\left[\tfrac{1}{2}\sqrt{3}\cos x + \tfrac{1}{2}\sin x\right]$$
$$\tfrac{1}{2}\sqrt{3}\sin x - \sin x = \sqrt{3}\cos x - \tfrac{1}{2}\cos x$$
$$(\sqrt{3}-2)\sin x = (2\sqrt{3}-1)\cos x$$
$$\tan x = \frac{2\sqrt{3}-1}{\sqrt{3}-2}.$$

The formula for $\tan(A + B)$ is obtained by first expressing $\tan(A + B)$ in terms of $\sin(A + B)$ and $\cos(A + B)$, and using the compound angle formulae for these expressions. Thus

$$\tan(A+B) \equiv \frac{\sin(A+B)}{\cos(A+B)} \equiv \frac{\sin A \cos B + \cos A \sin B}{\cos A \cos B - \sin A \sin B}$$

This expression is not particularly neat, but it can be tidied substantially by taking a factor of $\cos A \cos B$ out of both numerator and denominator. Since

$$\sin A \cos B + \cos A \sin B \equiv \cos A \cos B(\tan A + \tan B) \qquad \cos A \cos B - \sin A \sin B \equiv \cos A \cos B(1 - \tan A \tan B)$$

we see that

$$\tan(A+B) \equiv \frac{\tan A + \tan B}{1 - \tan A \tan B}$$

Key Fact 13.8 Compound Angles: Tangents

We have the identities

$$\tan(A+B) = \frac{\tan A + \tan B}{1 - \tan A \tan B} \qquad \tan(A-B) = \frac{\tan A - \tan B}{1 + \tan A \tan B}$$

Example 13.7.6. *Given that* $\tan(x+y) = 1$ *and that* $\tan x = \tfrac{1}{2}$, *find* $\tan y$.

$$\tan y = \tan\left((x+y)-x\right) = \frac{\tan(x+y)-\tan x}{1+\tan(x+y)\tan x} = \frac{1-\tfrac{1}{2}}{1+\tfrac{1}{2}} = \tfrac{1}{3}.$$

Recall Key Fact 2.8, where we stated a formula for the angle between two lines, given the gradients of those lines. We are now in a position to see why that formula is true.

Example 13.7.7. *If two lines have gradients* m_1 *and* m_2, *where* $m_1 > m_2$, *show that the angle between these lines is*

$$\tan^{-1}\frac{m_1 - m_2}{1 + m_1 m_2}$$

Suppose that the two lines make angles α_1 and α_2 respectively with the x-axis. Then $m_1 = \tan \alpha_1$ and $m_2 = \tan \alpha_2$. The angle between these two lines is $\alpha_1 - \alpha_2$, and

$$\tan(\alpha_1 - \alpha_2) = \frac{\tan \alpha_1 - \tan \alpha_2}{1 + \tan \alpha_1 \tan \alpha_2} = \frac{m_1 - m_2}{1 + m_1 m_2}$$

and the result follows immediately from this.

EXERCISE 13F

---

1. Find the exact values of $\sin 75°$ and $\tan 75°$.

2. Find the exact values of
   a) $\cos 105°$,   b) $\sin 105°$,   c) $\tan 105°$.

3. Express $\cos(x + \frac{1}{3}\pi)$ in terms of $\cos x$ and $\sin x$.

4. Simplify $\sin(\frac{3}{2}\pi + \phi)$ and $\cos(\frac{1}{2}\pi + \phi)$.

5. Express $\tan(\frac{1}{3}\pi + \phi)$ and $\tan(\frac{5}{6}\pi - x)$ in terms of $\tan x$.

6. Given that $\cos A = \frac{3}{5}$ and $\cos B = \frac{24}{25}$, where A and B are acute, find the exact values of:

   a) $\tan A$,   b) $\sin B$,   c) $\cos(A - B)$,   d) $\tan(A + B)$.

7. Given that $\sin A = \frac{3}{5}$ and $\cos B = \frac{12}{13}$, where A is obtuse and B is acute, find the exact values of $\cos(A + B)$ and $\cot(A - B)$.

8. Given that $\tan(A - B) = \frac{1}{3}$ and $\tan A = 4$, find the value of $\tan B$.

9. Given that $\tan(U + V) = 7$ and $\tan V = 5$, find the value of $\tan U$.

10. Given that $\cot(30° - \theta) = 4$, find the value of $\tan \theta$.

11. In each part of this question, find the value of $\cot \theta$.

    a) $\cos(\theta - 60°) = \sin \theta$,   b) $\tan(\theta + 45°) = 5$,
    c) $\sin(\theta + 60°) = 2\sin(\theta - 30°)$,   d) $\sin(45° - \theta) = \cos(30° + \theta)$.

12.   a) By considering $\sin(x + 90°)$ and $\cos(x + 90°)$, show that $\tan(x + 90°) \equiv -\cot x$.

    b) What is the limit of $\tan(x + y)$ as y tends to $90°$ (so that $\tan y$ tends to ∞)?

13. Establish the following identities:

    a) $\cos(180° - \theta) \equiv -\cos \theta$,   b) $\cos(x - 90°) \equiv \sin x$,
    c) $\sin(A + B) + \sin(A - B) \equiv 2\sin A \cos B$,   d) $\cos(A - B) - \cos(A + B) \equiv 2\sin A \sin B$,
    e) $\tan A + \tan B \equiv \frac{\sin(A+B)}{\cos A \cos B}$,   f) $\cos(A + B)\cos(A - B) \equiv 1 - \sin^2 A - \sin^2 B$,
    g) $\frac{\sin(A+B)}{\sin(A-B)} \equiv \frac{\cot B + \cot A}{\cot B - \cot A}$,   h) $\frac{\sin(P-Q)}{\cos P \cos Q} + \frac{\sin(Q-R)}{\cos Q \cos R} + \frac{\sin(R-P)}{\sin R \sin P} \equiv 0$,
    i) $\sin^2 X + \sin^2 Y \equiv 2\sin^2(X + Y) - 2\sin X \sin Y \cos(X + Y)$.

14*.   a) If A, B and C are three angles of a triangle, prove that

$$\tan A + \tan B + \tan C = \tan(A)\tan B \tan C.$$

     b) If A, B, C and D are the four angles of a quadrilateral, prove that

$$\tan A + \tan B + \tan C + \tan D = \tan A \tan B \tan C + \tan A \tan B \tan D$$
$$+ \tan A \tan C \tan D + \tan B \tan C \tan D.$$

For Interest

In the previous Exercise, we established two of the following identities:

$\sin(A + B) + \sin(A - B) \equiv 2\sin A \cos B$, $\sin(A + B) - \sin(A - B) \equiv 2\cos A \sin B$,
$\cos(A + B) + \cos(A - B) \equiv 2\cos A \cos B$, $\cos(A + B) - \cos(A - B) \equiv -2\sin A \sin B$.

By putting $X = A + B$ and $Y = A - B$, we obtain a similar set of identities:

$\sin X + \sin Y \equiv 2\sin \frac{X+Y}{2} \cos \frac{X-Y}{2}$, $\sin X - \sin Y \equiv 2\cos \frac{X+Y}{2} \sin \frac{X-Y}{2}$,
$\cos X + \cos Y \equiv 2\cos \frac{X+Y}{2} \cos \frac{X-Y}{2}$, $\cos X - \cos Y \equiv -2\sin \frac{X+Y}{2} \sin \frac{X-Y}{2}$.

These four identities are known as the **factor formulae**; while they appear in the Pre-U Formula sheet, they are rarely used.

13.8 Multiple Angles

In Question 5 of Exercise 8C we saw that there were different ways of calculating lengths and areas in isosceles triangles, and these observations led to formulae which expressed $\cos 2\theta$ and $\sin 2\theta$ in terms if $\cos\theta$ and $\sin\theta$.

$$\cos 2\theta = 2\cos^2\theta - 1 \qquad \sin 2\theta = 2\sin\theta\cos\theta .$$

Those calculations were geometrically inspired, and our arguments there only work for angles $0° \leq \theta \leq 90°$. Now that we have the compound angles formulae, however, we can establish these identities, and more, in full generality.

If we substitute $B = A$ into the formulae for $\sin(A+B)$, $\cos(A+B)$ and $\tan(A+B)$, we obtain

$$\begin{aligned}
\sin 2A &\equiv \sin(A+A) \equiv \sin A \cos A + \cos A \sin A \equiv 2\sin A \cos A \\
\cos 2A &\equiv \cos(A+A) \equiv \cos A \cos A - \sin A \sin A \equiv \cos^2 A - \sin^2 A \\
\tan 2A &\equiv \tan(A+A) \equiv \frac{\tan A + \tan A}{1 - \tan A \tan A} \equiv \frac{2\tan A}{1 - \tan^2 A}
\end{aligned}$$

The formula $\cos^2 A + \sin^2 A \equiv 1$ (which incidentally, follows from substituting $B = A$ into the formula for $\cos(A - B)$) can be used to express $\cos 2A$ in two other forms, since

$$\begin{aligned}
\cos^2 A - \sin^2 A &\equiv \cos^2 A - (1 - \cos^2 A) \equiv 2\cos^2 A - 1 \\
&\equiv (1 - \sin^2 A) - \sin^2 A \equiv 1 - 2\sin^2 A
\end{aligned}$$

Key Fact 13.9 Double Angle Formulae

The **double angle formulae** are the identities:

$$\begin{aligned}
\sin 2A &\equiv 2\sin A \cos A \\
\cos 2A &\equiv \cos^2 A - \sin^2 A \equiv 2\cos^2 A - 1 \equiv 1 - 2\sin^2 A \\
\tan 2A &\equiv \frac{2\tan A}{1 - \tan^2 A}
\end{aligned}$$

Example 13.8.1. *Given that $\cos A = \frac{1}{3}$, find the exact value of $\cos 2A$ and the possible values of $\cos\frac{1}{2}A$.*

$$\cos 2A = 2\cos^2 A - 1 = 2\times\left(\tfrac{1}{3}\right)^2 - 1 = \tfrac{2}{9} - 1 = -\tfrac{7}{9}$$

The double angle formulae can also be used to express $\cos A$ in terms of $\cos\frac{1}{2}A$. Indeed

$$\tfrac{1}{3} = \cos A = 2\cos^2\frac{1}{2}A - 1$$

so that $\cos^2\frac{1}{2}A = \frac{2}{3}$, and so it follows that $\cos\frac{1}{2}A = \pm\sqrt{\frac{2}{3}}$.

Example 13.8.2. *Solve the equation $2\sin 2\theta = \sin\theta$, for $0° \leq \theta \leq 360°$ correct to 1 decimal place.*

Using the identity $\sin 2\theta \equiv 2\sin\theta\cos\theta$, this equation becomes

$$\begin{aligned}
4\sin\theta\cos\theta &= \sin\theta \\
\sin\theta(4\cos\theta - 1) &= 0
\end{aligned}$$

Thus either $\sin\theta = 0$ or else $\cos\theta = \frac{1}{4}$. Possible solutions are thus $0°$, $75.5°$, $180°$, $284.5°$, $360°$.

Example 13.8.3. *Prove the identity $\cot A - \tan A \equiv 2\cot 2A$.*

One strategy would be to express everything in terms of $\sin A$ and $\cos A$, so that

$$\cot A - \tan A \equiv \frac{\cos A}{\sin A} - \frac{\sin A}{\cos A} \equiv \frac{\cos^2 A - \sin^2 A}{\sin A \cos A} \equiv \frac{\cos 2A}{\frac{1}{2} \sin 2A} \equiv 2 \cot 2A$$

This approach can become quite complicated, and it is worth looking for a higher-level solution. This problem can be handled working entirely with tangents.

$$\cot A - \tan A \equiv \frac{1}{\tan A} - \tan A \equiv \frac{1 - \tan^2 A}{\tan A} \equiv 2 \times \frac{1 - \tan^2 A}{2 \tan A} \equiv 2 \frac{1}{\tan 2A} \equiv 2 \cot 2A$$

Example 13.8.4. *Prove that* $\operatorname{cosec} x + \cot x \equiv \cot \frac{1}{2} x$.

Starting with the left side, and putting everything in terms of sines and cosines,

$$\operatorname{cosec} x + \cot x \equiv \frac{1}{\sin x} + \frac{\cos x}{\sin x} \equiv \frac{1 + \cos x}{\sin x}$$

The right-hand side is expressed in terms of half-angles, so we need to convert everything into half-angles:

$$\operatorname{cosec} x + \cot x \equiv \frac{1 + \cos x}{\sin x} \equiv \frac{1 + 2\cos^2 \frac{1}{2} x - 1}{2 \sin \frac{1}{2} x \cos \frac{1}{2}} \equiv \frac{2 \cos^2 \frac{1}{2} x}{2 \sin \frac{1}{2} x \cos \frac{1}{2} x} \equiv \frac{\cos \frac{1}{2} x}{\sin \frac{1}{2} x} \equiv \cot \frac{1}{2} x$$

Having obtained double angle formula, why stop there? We do not need to know these formulae, but it is worth remembering that they are there.

Example 13.8.5. *Prove the identities*

$$\cos 3A \equiv 4 \cos^3 A - 3 \cos A, \qquad \cos 4A \equiv$$

We start by writing $3A = 2A + A$ and using the compound angle formula:

$$\cos 3A \equiv \cos(2A + A) \equiv \cos 2A \cos A - \sin 2A \sin A$$

Now use the double angle formulae to eliminate the terms in $2A$:

$$\begin{aligned}
\cos 3A &\equiv \cos 2A \cos A - \sin 2A \sin A \equiv (2\cos^2 A - 1)\cos A - (2 \sin A \cos A) \cos A \\
&= 2\cos^3 A - \cos A - 2 \sin^2 A \cos A
\end{aligned}$$

Finally, the identity $\cos^2 A + \sin^2 A \equiv 1$ gets rid of the $\sin^2 A$ term:

$$\cos 3A \equiv 2\cos^3 A - \cos A - 2(1 - \cos^2 A)\cos A \equiv 4\cos^3 A - 3\cos A$$

The derivation of $\cos 4A$ is, surprisingly, easier, since we can work with cosines alone:

$$\begin{aligned}
\cos 4A &\equiv \cos(2A + 2A) \equiv 2\cos^2 2A - 1 \equiv 2(2\cos^2 A - 1)^2 - 1 \\
&\equiv 8\cos^4 A - 8\cos^2 A + 1
\end{aligned}$$

EXERCISE 13G

1. If $\sin A = \frac{2}{3}$ and A is obtuse, find the exact values of $\cos A$, $\sin 2A$ and $\tan 2A$.

2. If $\cos B = \frac{3}{4}$, find the exact values of $\cos 2B$ and $\cos \frac{1}{2} B$.

3. By writing $\cos x$ in terms of $\frac{1}{2} x$, find an alternative expression for $\frac{1 - \cos x}{1 + \cos x}$.

4. Prove that $4 \sin\left(x + \frac{1}{6}\pi\right) \sin\left(x - \frac{1}{6}\pi\right) \equiv 3 - 4\cos^2 x$.

5. If $\cos 2A = \frac{7}{18}$, find the possible values of $\cos A$ and $\sin A$.

6. If $\tan 2A = \frac{12}{5}$, find the possible values of $\tan A$.

7. If $\tan 2A = 1$, find the possible values of $\tan A$. Hence state the exact value of $\tan 22.5°$.

8. Solve these equations for values of A between 0 and 2π inclusive:

    a) $\cos 2A + 3 + 4\cos A = 0$,

    b) $2\cos 2A + 1 + \sin A = 0$,

    c) $\tan 2A + 5\tan A = 0$,

    d) $\sin 2A + 2\sin A - 3\tan A = 0$,

    e) $5\cos 2A - 8\cos A + 3 = 0$,

    f) $5\sin A = \tan \frac{1}{2}A$.

9. Solve these equations for values of A between $-360°$ and $360°$ inclusive:

    a) $5\cos \frac{1}{2}A = 3\sin A$,

    b) $5\tan A = \tan \frac{1}{2}A$.

10. Prove the identities:

    a) $\tan^2 A \equiv \dfrac{\sec 2A - 1}{\sec 2A + 1}$,

    b) $\cos^4 A - \sin^4 A \equiv \cos 2A$,

    c) $\sin A \equiv \dfrac{2\tan \frac{1}{2}A}{1 + \tan^2 \frac{1}{2}A}$,

    d) $\cos A \equiv \dfrac{1 - \tan^2 \frac{1}{2}A}{1 + \tan^2 \frac{1}{2}A}$,

    e) $\dfrac{3\sin A + \sin 2A}{1 + 3\cos A + \cos 2A} \equiv \tan A$,

    f) $\dfrac{\sin 2A}{1 - \cos 2A} \equiv \cot A$,

    g) $\dfrac{\cos 2A}{1 - \sin 2A} \equiv \dfrac{1 + \tan A}{1 - \tan A}$.

11. a) By expressing $\sin 3A$ as $\sin(2A + A)$, find an expression for $\sin 3A$ in terms of $\sin A$.

    b) By substituting $X = \sin A$, solve the cubic equation $8X^3 - 6X + 1 = 0$ exactly.

12*. a) Suppose that A is an acute angle with $\tan A = \frac{1}{5}$. Find expressions for $\tan 2A$, $\tan 4A$ and $\tan(4A - \frac{1}{4}\pi)$.

    b) Deduce that $\frac{1}{4}\pi = 4\tan^{-1} \frac{1}{5} - \tan^{-1} \frac{1}{239}$.

13*. a) Find an expression for $\cos 5\theta$ in terms of $\cos \theta$.

    b) Show that $\cos^5 \theta \equiv \frac{1}{16}[\cos 5\theta + 5\cos 3\theta + 10\cos \theta]$.

For Interest

The formula for $\frac{1}{4}\pi$ found in Question 12 above is called **Machin's Formula**. It is of historical significance, since it was used by John Machin in 1706 to calculate the first 100 digits of π. This was possible because the inverse tangent function has a convergent series expansion

$$\tan^{-1} x \equiv x - \tfrac{1}{3}x + \tfrac{1}{5}x^5 - \tfrac{1}{7}x^7 + \cdots, \qquad |x| < 1.$$

This formula is easy to use for $x = \frac{1}{5}$, since dividing by 5 is easy, so a large number of terms can be calculated quite easily without using a calculator. It is less easy to use for $x = \frac{1}{239}$, but since $\frac{1}{239}$ is small, not so many terms are needed to get a good degree of accuracy.

13.9 Harmonic Form

We know that the graph $y = \sin(x - 10°)$ is the graph of $y = \sin x$ translated $10°$ to the right. Similarly the graph $y = \cos x + 2$ is the graph of $y = \cos x$ translated up by 2. Graphs like $y = \cos 3x$ and $y = 4\sin x$ represent horizontal and vertical scalings of the standard trigonometric graphs.

What is more surprising is that a graph like $y = \sin x + 4\cos x$ is also a transformation of the sine curve; it has been shifted horizontally and then scaled vertically. There is no vertical translation (the graph is symmetric about the x-axis) and there is no horizontal scaling (the function still has period $360°$).

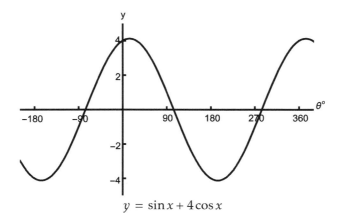

$$y = \sin x + 4\cos x$$

Figure 13.23

For this to be true, it must be possible to write the function $y = \sin x + 4\cos x$ in the form $y = R\sin(x + \alpha)$; the graph of $y = \sin x + 4\cos x$ will then be obtained from that of $y = \sin x$ by first shifting the graph horizontally by $-\alpha$, and then vertically scaling by a factor of R.

How do we find the values of R and α?

We want the expressions $\sin x + 4\cos x$ and $R\sin(x + \alpha)$ to be identically equal, and so we want

$$\sin x + 4\cos x \equiv R\sin(x + \alpha) \equiv R(\sin x\cos\alpha + \cos x\sin\alpha) \equiv R\cos\alpha\sin x + R\sin\alpha\cos x$$

Since these expressions are identically equal, they must be equal when $x = 0$ and $x = 90°$. From this we deduce that

$$\cos\alpha = 1 \qquad R\sin\alpha = 4.$$

and so R needs to be the hypotenuse of a right-angled triangle with sides 1 and 4, with α being one of the angles of the triangle. Hence $R = \sqrt{1^1 + 4^2} = \sqrt{17}$. Now $\cos\alpha$ and $\sin\alpha$ are both positive, and hence α is in the first quadrant, with $\tan\alpha = 4$, and so $\alpha = 75.96° = 76.0°$.

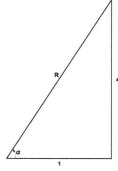

Note that the process of putting $x = 0$ and $x = \frac{1}{2}\pi$ resulted in our 'matching the coefficients' of $\cos x$ and $\sin x$; $R\cos\alpha$, the coefficient of $\sin x$ in $R\sin(x + \alpha)$, had to be equal to 1, the coefficient of $\sin x$ in $\sin x + 4\cos x$, and so on. Matching coefficients is a useful trick.

Figure 13.24

Key Fact 13.10 Harmonic Form : Sine Version

If a and b are constants, then $a\sin x + b\cos x \equiv R\sin(x + \alpha)$ provided that $R\cos\alpha = a$ and $R\sin\alpha = b$. If $R > 0$ this requires

$$R = \sqrt{a^2 + b^2} \quad, \quad \cos\alpha = \frac{a}{\sqrt{a^2+b^2}} \quad, \quad \sin\alpha = \frac{b}{\sqrt{a^2+b^2}}.$$

Note that we do not need a and b to be positive; different signs of a and b will result in α lying in different quadrants.

Example 13.9.1. (a) Find the maximum and minimum values of $3\sin x + 2\cos x$ and find, in radians to 2 decimal places, the smallest positive values of x at which they occur.

(b) Solve the equation $3\sin x + 2\cos x = 1$, for $-\pi \leq x \leq \pi$, to 2 decimal places.

Let us write $3\sin x + 2\cos x$ in the form $R\sin(x + \alpha)$. Matching coefficients, we must have $R\cos\alpha = 3$ and $R\sin\alpha = 2$, so that $R = \sqrt{3^2 + 2^2} = \sqrt{13}$ and $\tan\alpha = \frac{2}{3}$. It is clear in this case that α is in the first quadrant, and so $\alpha = 0.588$. Thus $3\sin x + 2\cos x \equiv \sqrt{13}\sin(x + 0.588)$.

(a) Since $\sin(x+\alpha)$ lies between -1 and 1, it is clear that $\sqrt{13}\sin(x+\alpha)$ has maximum value $\sqrt{13}$ and minimum value $-\sqrt{13}$. The maximum value of $\sqrt{13}$ occurs when $x + 0.588 = \frac{1}{2}\pi$, so when $x = 0.98$, while the minimum value of $-\sqrt{13}$ occurs when $x + 0.588 = \frac{3}{2}\pi$, so when $x = 4.12$.

(b) Since

$$3\sin x + 2\cos x = 1 \quad \Leftrightarrow \quad \sqrt{13}\sin(x + 0.588) = 1 \quad \Leftrightarrow \quad \sin(x + 0.588) = \tfrac{1}{\sqrt{13}},$$

the possible values in the range $-\pi \leq x \leq \pi$ are given by setting $x + 0.588 = 0.281, 2.861$, so that $x = -0.31, 2.27$.

There is nothing special about the form $R\sin(x + \alpha)$. The form $R\cos(x + \alpha)$ is just as useful. Using the compound angle formula for $\cos(x + \alpha)$ and matching coefficients gives us the following:

Key Fact 13.11 Harmonic Form : Cosine Version

If a and b are constants, then $-a\sin x + b\cos x \equiv R\cos(x + \alpha)$ provided that $R\cos\alpha = b$ and $R\sin\alpha = a$. If $R > 0$ this requires

$$R = \sqrt{a^2 + b^2} \quad, \quad \cos\alpha = \tfrac{b}{\sqrt{a^2+b^2}} \quad, \quad \sin\alpha = \tfrac{a}{\sqrt{a^2+b^2}}.$$

Example 13.9.2. *Solve the equation* $3\cos x - 7\sin x = 5$ *for* $0° \leq x \leq 360°$.

To write $3\cos x - 7\sin x \equiv R\cos(x + \alpha)$, we need $R\cos\alpha = 3$ and $R\sin\alpha = 7$. Thus $R = \sqrt{3^2 + 7^2} = \sqrt{58}$ and α is in the first quadrant with $\tan\alpha = \tfrac{7}{3}$, so that $\alpha = 66.80°$. Now

$$3\cos x - 7\sin x = 5 \quad \Leftrightarrow \quad \sqrt{58}\cos(x + 66.80°) = 5 \quad \Leftrightarrow \quad \cos(x + 66.80°) = \tfrac{5}{\sqrt{58}},$$

and hence the desired solutions are given by $x + 66.80° = 48.96°, 311.04°, 408.96°$. Note that the first solution will give too small a value of x, so we have added an extra solution at the other end to replace it. The solutions are $x = 244.2°, 342.2°$.

Food For Thought 13.5

For a given expression, we could seek to express it in one of the following forms:

$$R\sin(x + \alpha) \qquad R\sin(x - \alpha) \qquad R\cos(x + \alpha) \qquad R\cos(x - \alpha)$$

There is no significant difference between them but, for a given problem, the right choice can make calculations easier. Choosing the right form can ensure that α lies in the first quadrant, which simplifies matters. To make the right choice, we have to bear in mind the patterns of signs in the compound angle formulae.

The various formulae for the different forms are very similar to each other, and easily confused. It is much better to remember how they are derived (from the compound angle formulae and matching coefficients) and derive the correct formula each time.

Example 13.9.3. *Find the minimum value of* $3\sin\theta - 10\cos\theta$, *and find the smallest possible value of* θ *(in degrees) for which this value is achieved. Explain why the equation* $3\sin\theta - 10\cos\theta = 11$ *is not soluble.*

In $3\sin\theta - 10\cos\theta$, the coefficient of $\sin\theta$ is positive and the coefficient of $\cos\theta$ is negative. This leads us to choose the form $R\sin(\theta - \alpha)$. We want

$$3\sin\theta - 10\cos\theta \equiv R\sin(\theta - \alpha) \equiv R\cos\alpha\sin\theta - R\sin\alpha\cos\theta$$

and so we need $R\cos\alpha = 3$ and $R\sin\alpha = 10$. Thus $R = \sqrt{109}$ and α is in the first quadrant with $\tan\alpha = \tfrac{10}{3}$, so that $\alpha = 73.3°$.

The minimum value of $3\sin\theta - 10\cos\theta$ is thus $-\sqrt{109}$, and this is first achieved when $\theta - 73.3° = 270°$, so when $\theta = 343.3°$. The maximum value of $3\sin\theta - 10\cos\theta$ is $\sqrt{109}$, which is smaller than 11.

Exercise 13H

1. Find the value of α between 0 and $\frac{1}{2}\pi$ for which $5\sin x + 2\cos x \equiv \sqrt{29}\sin(x + \alpha)$.

2. Find the value of ϕ between 0 and $90°$ for which $3\cos x - 4\sin x = 5\cos(x + \phi)$.

3. Find the value of R such that, if $\tan\beta = \frac{3}{5}$, then $5\sin\theta + 3\cos\theta \equiv R\sin(\theta + \beta)$.

4. Find the value of R and the value of β between 0 and $\frac{1}{2}\pi$, correct to 3 decimal places, such that $6\cos x + \sin x = R\cos(x - \beta)$.

5. Find the value of R and the value of α between 0 and $\frac{1}{2}\pi$ in each of the following cases, when the given expression is written in the given form.

   a) $\sin x + 2\cos x$; $R\sin(x + \alpha)$,
   b) $\sin x + 2\cos x$; $R\cos(x - \alpha)$,
   c) $\sin x - 2\cos x$; $R\sin(x - \alpha)$,
   d) $2\cos x - \sin x$; $R\cos(x + \alpha)$.

6. Express $5\cos\theta + 6\sin\theta$ in the form $R\cos(\theta - \beta)$ where $R > 0$ and $0 < \beta < \frac{1}{2}\pi$. State:

   a) the maximum value of $5\cos\theta + 6\sin\theta$, and the least positive value of θ which gives this maximum,

   b) the minimum value of $5\cos\theta + 6\sin\theta$, and the least positive value of θ which gives this minimum.

7. Express $8\sin x + 6\cos x$ in the form $R\sin(x + \phi)$, where $R > 0$ and $0 < \phi < 90°$. Deduce the number of roots for $0° < x < 180°$ of the following equations:

   a) $8\sin x + 6\cos x = 5$,   b) $4\sin x + 3\cos x = 5$,   c) $12\sin x + 9\cos x = 18$.

8. Solve the following equations for $0 \le \theta \le 2\pi$:

   a) $3\sin x - 2\cos x = 1$,   b) $5\cos\theta + 2\sin\theta = 3$,
   c) $\sin 2\theta + 4\cos 2\theta = 3$,   d) $\tan x + \sec x = 4$.

9. Find the greatest and least values of each of the following expressions and state, correct to one decimal place, the smallest positive value of θ (in degrees) for which each occurs:

   a) $7 + 4\cos\theta - 3\sin\theta$,   b) $2 - 7\cos\theta + 2\sin\theta$,
   c) $\dfrac{6}{12\cos\theta + 5\sin\theta + 15}$,   d) $(2\sin\theta + 7\cos\theta)^2$.

10*. Find the maximum and minimum values of $\sin 4\theta - \sin^2 2\theta$.

11*. Solve the equation $\cos\theta(\cos\theta + 3\sin\theta) = 2$ for $0° \le \theta \le 360°$. Can you do this in two different ways?

Chapter 13: Summary

- **Symmetries:**

Periodicity	$\sin(\theta + 2\pi) \equiv \sin\theta$	$\cos(\theta + 2\pi) \equiv \cos\theta$	$\tan(\theta + \pi) \equiv \tan\theta$
Anti-Periodicity	$\sin(\theta + \pi) \equiv -\sin\theta$	$\cos(\theta + \pi) \equiv -\cos\theta$	
Even/Odd	$\sin(-\theta) \equiv -\sin\theta$	$\cos(-\theta) \equiv \cos\theta$	$\tan(-\theta) \equiv -\tan\theta$
Quadrants	$\sin(\pi - \theta) \equiv \sin\theta$	$\cos(\pi - \theta) \equiv -\cos\theta$	$\tan(\pi - \theta) \equiv -\tan\theta$
	$\sin(\pi + \theta) \equiv -\sin\theta$	$\cos(\pi + \theta) \equiv -\cos\theta$	$\tan(\pi + \theta) \equiv \tan\theta$
	$\sin(2\pi - \theta) \equiv -\sin\theta$	$\cos(2\pi - \theta) \equiv \cos\theta$	$\tan(2\pi - \theta) \equiv -\tan\theta$

- **Interrelations:**

$$\tan\theta \equiv \frac{\sin\theta}{\cos\theta} \quad \sec\theta \equiv \frac{1}{\cos\theta} \quad \mathrm{cosec}\,\theta \equiv \frac{1}{\sin\theta} \quad \cot\theta \equiv \frac{1}{\tan\theta} \equiv \frac{\cos\theta}{\sin\theta}$$

- **Pythagorean Identities:**

$$\cos^2\theta + \sin^2\theta \equiv 1 \qquad 1 + \tan^2\theta \equiv \sec^2\theta \qquad 1 + \cot^2\theta \equiv \mathrm{cosec}^2\theta$$

- **Compound Angles:**

$$\sin(A \pm B) \equiv \sin A \cos B \pm \cos A \sin B$$
$$\cos(A \pm B) \equiv \cos A \cos B \mp \sin A \sin B$$
$$\tan(A \pm B) \equiv \frac{\tan A \pm \tan B}{1 \mp \tan A \tan B}$$

- **Double Angles:**

$$\sin 2A \equiv 2\sin A \cos A$$
$$\cos 2A \equiv \cos^2 A - \sin^2 A \equiv 2\cos^2 A - 1 \equiv 1 - 2\sin^2 A$$
$$\tan 2A \equiv \frac{2\tan A}{1 - \tan^2 A}$$

- **Half Angles:**

$$\sin A \equiv 2\sin\tfrac{1}{2}A \cos\tfrac{1}{2}A \equiv \frac{2\tan\tfrac{1}{2}A}{1 + \tan^2\tfrac{1}{2}A}$$

$$\cos A \equiv \cos^2\tfrac{1}{2}A - \sin^2\tfrac{1}{2}A \equiv 2\cos^2\tfrac{1}{2}A - 1 \equiv 1 - 2\sin^2\tfrac{1}{2}A \equiv \frac{1 - \tan^2\tfrac{1}{2}A}{1 + \tan^2\tfrac{1}{2}A}$$

$$\tan A \equiv \frac{2\tan\tfrac{1}{2}A}{1 - \tan^2\tfrac{1}{2}A}$$

- **Harmonic Form:**

$$a\sin x \pm b\cos x \equiv R\sin(x \pm \alpha) \quad \Leftrightarrow \quad a = R\cos\alpha,\ b = R\sin\alpha.$$
$$\mp a\sin x + b\cos x \equiv R\cos(x \pm \alpha) \quad \Leftrightarrow \quad a = R\sin\alpha,\ b = R\cos\alpha.$$

Exponentials And Logarithms

In this chapter we will learn to:

understand the relationship between logarithms and indices and use the law of logarithms,

use logarithms to solve equations like $a^x = b$ and related equations and inequalities,

use logarithms to transform appropriate relationships to linear form.

14.1   Multiplication And Indices

In the days before calculators were commonplace, performing even elementary calculations such as multiplication and division was a laborious process (try dividing 34.15 by 2.19 using long division). There were a number of calculational aids available, and one of these was the slide rule. This involved two straight pieces of (usually) plastic that were marked with identical, but uneven scales, with numbers running from 1 to 10 along the scale. The two pieces of plastic were held in contact with their scales facing each other, and they could slide along each other. A simplified example is shown below (a real slide rule would have many more marks on each scale, with the gaps between the numbers subdivided):

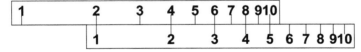

Figure 14.1

Suppose that we wanted to multiply 2 by 4. We would need to slide the bottom piece of plastic so that the 1 on its scale was opposite the 2 on the top scale (as in the Figure above). We then look for the 4 on the bottom scale, and see what number it is opposite on the top scale; the answer is $8 = 2 \times 4$. The same arrangement of the slide rule also tells us that $2 \times 3 = 6$ and $2 \times 5 = 10$.

This is all very well. What happens if we want to multiply 4 by 5? We try putting the 1 on the bottom scale against the 4 on the top scale:

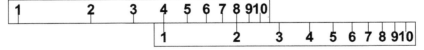

Figure 14.2

and we have a problem. There is no point on the top scale opposite 5 on the bottom scale (our scale does not go up to 20). The solution to this problem is to readjust the bottom scale so that the 10 on that scale is against the 4 on the top scale:

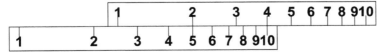

Figure 14.3

We then see that 5 on the bottom scale is against 2 on the top scale. This told us that $4 \times 5 = 2 \times 10^1 = 20$. The slide rule only ever calculated significant figures (that is why its scale did not include a range between 0 and 1); users had to keep track of powers of 10 themselves.

Why did this work? For any x, suppose that $D(x)$ was the distance along one of the scales between 1 and x.

- When multiplying 2 by 4, the scales were set so that the 1 on the bottom scale was a distance $D(2)$ from the 1 on the top scale. Since the 4 on the bottom scale is a distance $D(4)$ from the 1 on the bottom scale, it is a distance $D(2) + D(4)$ from the 1 on the top scale. The scales have been constructed in such a way that $D(2) + D(4) = D(8)$. Similarly $D(2) + D(3) = D(6)$ and $D(2) + D(5) = D(10)$.

- When multiplying 4 by 5, the scales were set (eventually) so that the 10 on the bottom scale was a distance $D(4)$ from the 1 on the top scale. Since the 5 on the bottom scale is a distance $D(10) - D(5)$ to the left of the 10 it is a distance $D(4) - \big(D(10) - D(5)\big) = D(4) + D(5) - D(10)$ away from the 1 on the top scale. The scales have been constructed in such a way that $D(4) + D(5) - D(10) = D(2)$.

The key to the slide rule lies in the choice of scale, and thus the values of the function $D(x)$. We can use the slide rule to multiply because $D(x) + D(y) = D(xy)$ for all $1 \leq x, y \leq 10$; even though we did not have a distance $D(20)$ on the slide rule we could still multiply 4 by 5 because $D(4) + D(5) = D(2) + D(10)$.

A real slide rule had a more complicated scale marked on it, perhaps like this:

Figure 14.4

With this, an experienced user could perform calculations accurate to between 2 and 3 significant figures quickly and easily.

This still does not tell us why it is possible to mark a slide rule with a scale (and therefore define a function D) which enables us to multiply numbers. We have seen situations before where multiplication is achieved through addition. Recall our work in Chapter 1 on indices. We stated there that

$$a^m \times a^n \equiv a^{m+n}, \qquad a > 0,$$

at least for all rational m, n. Thus, provided that we can identify numbers as powers of some fixed number a, then these numbers can be multiplied simply by adding the indices. In particular, the slide rule worked because the function D was chosen (for suitable units of distance) so that $x = 10^{D(x)}$ for all $x \geq 1$, for then

$$10^{D(xy)} = xy = x \times y = 10^{D(x)} \times 10^{D(y)} = 10^{D(x)+D(y)}$$

for all $x, y \geq 1$, so that $D(xy) = D(x) + D(y)$ for all $x, y \geq 1$. The aim of this chapter is to extend these ideas, thereby discovering a rich field of study.

14.2 Exponential Functions

In Chapter 9 we met the idea of exponential growth and decay, defined by an equation of the form $u_i = ar^i$. In this equation a is the initial value, r the rate of growth (if $r > 1$) or decay (if $r < 1$), and i counts units of time after the start. The equation defines a geometric sequence with common ratio r.

Exponential growth does not only occur in situations that increase by discrete steps. Rampant inflation, a nuclear chain reaction, the spread of an epidemic and the growth of cells are phenomena that take place in continuous time, and they need to be described by functions having the real numbers rather than the natural numbers for their domain. The equation $u_i = ar^i$, where $i \in \mathbb{N}$, needs to be replaced by

$$f(x) = ab^x, \qquad x \in \mathbb{R}, \, x \geq 0.$$

Now a stands for the initial value when $x = 0$, and b is a constant which indicates how fast the quantity is growing. (The idea of a 'common ratio' no longer applies in the continuous case, so a different letter is used.) In many applications the variable x represents time. The graph of $f(x)$ is shown below:

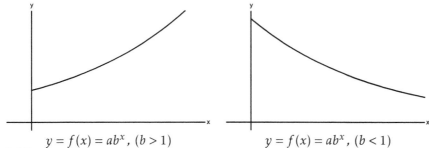

$$y = f(x) = ab^x, \ (b > 1) \qquad\qquad y = f(x) = ab^x, \ (b < 1)$$

Figure 14.5

For exponential growth b has to be greater than 1. For exponential decay, we must have $0 < b < 1$. As x gets larger the graph gets closer to the x-axis but never reaches it. Examples of this behaviour are the level of radioactivity in a lump of uranium ore, and the concentration of an antibiotic in the blood stream.

Example 14.2.1. *The population of the USA grew exponentially from the end of the War of Independence until the Civil War. It increased from 3.9 million at the 1790 census to 31.4 million in 1860. What would the population have been in 1990 if it had continued to grow at this rate?*

If the population x years after 1790 is P million, and if the growth were exactly exponential, then P and x would be related by an equation of the form $P = 3.9b^x$. Since $P = 31.4$ when $x = 70$, the constant b must satisfy the equation $31.4 = 3.9b^{70}$, and hence $b = \left(\frac{31.4}{3.9}\right)^{\frac{1}{70}} = 1.030$. At this rate of increase the population in 1990 would have been $3.9 \times 1.030^{200} \approx 1.510$ million, or 1.51 billion. This calculation could be made easier by noting that the population in 1990 ought to have been $3.9\left(\frac{31.4}{3.9}\right)^{\frac{200}{70}}$; it is not necessary to calculate b.

Example 14.2.2. *Carbon dating in archaeology is based on the decay of the isotope carbon-14, which has a half-life of 5715 years. By what percentage does carbon-14 decay in 100 years?*

The half-life of a radioactive isotope is the time it would take for half of any sample of the isotope to decay. After t years one unit of carbon-14 is reduced to b^t units, where $b^{5715} = 0.5$ (since 0.5 units are left after 5715 years), so $b = 0.5^{\frac{1}{5715}}$. Thus, when $t = 100$ the quantity left is $b^{100} = 0.5^{\frac{100}{5715}} = 0.988$ units, a reduction of 0.012 units, or 1.2%.

In the equation $y = ab^x$ for exponential growth the constant a simply sets a scale on the y-axis, since changing its value simply performs a vertical scaling of the function. The essential features of an exponential relationship can be studied in the function

$$y = f(x) = b^x, \qquad x \in \mathbb{R}.$$

A function of this form is called an **exponential function**, because the variable x appears in the exponent (another word for the index). A number of key point may be made about exponential functions:

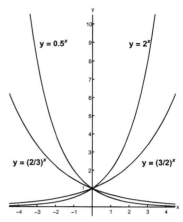

Figure 14.6

- This definition of an exponential function only makes sense if $b > 0$. There is no meaning to $b^{\frac{1}{2}} = \sqrt{b}$ if $b < 0$ (or, at least, not yet).

- The function $y = b^x$ is constant, equal to 1 for all x, if $b = 1$; while an exponential function, this is not very interesting.

- Since $b^0 = 1$ for any $b > 0$, all exponential functions pass through the point $(0, 1)$.

- There is no problem in allowing x to be negative. Since $b^{-x} = \left(\frac{1}{b}\right)^x$ for all x, it is clear that the reflection of the graph $y = b^x$ in the y-axis is the graph $y = \left(\frac{1}{b}\right)^x$.

- Exponential functions are increasing for $b > 1$ and decreasing for $0 < b < 1$.

Figure 14.6 shows the graphs of exponential functions for several values of b.

For Interest

One final point to realise is that, up until now, the expression b^x has only been defined when x is rational, and we have not considered the meaning of irrational powers. How can we assign a meaning to a number like 2^π, for example? We could try to bracket π between two rationals, obtaining approximations to its value. For example, $3.1415926 < \pi < 3.1415927$, and hence

$$8.824977 = 2^{3.1415926} < 2^\pi < 2^{3.1415927} = 8.824978$$

and so $2^\pi = 8.82498$ correct to 5 decimal places. Choosing a pair of rational numbers which are even closer to π will give a better approximation for 2^π.

The problem with this approach is that it assumes that 2^π exists. Alternatively, we could try to define 2^π by considering π as the limit of a sequence of rationals like $3, 3.1, 3.14, 3.141, 3.1415, \ldots$, and finding the limit of the corresponding sequence of powers 2^3, $2^{3.1}, 2^{3.14}, 2^{3.141}, 2^{3.1415}, \ldots$. This works, and produces a theory of powers and indices in which all the laws of indices work fully, but the details are extremely technical.

It is best at this stage to assume that we can calculate real powers of positive numbers, and that the laws of indices work for non-rational indices, so that

$$b^x \times b^y = b^{x+y} \qquad (b^x)^y = b^{xy} \qquad b > 0,\ x, y \in \mathbb{R},$$

and proceed on this assumption.

14.3 Logarithmic Functions

The graphs in Figure 14.6 show that (for $b \neq 1$) the exponential function $x \mapsto b^x$ has as its domain the set of all real numbers, with its range being the positive real numbers. The function is increasing if $b > 1$, and decreasing if $0 < b < 1$. In either case it is one-to-one. It follows that this function has an inverse whose domain is the set of positive real numbers and whose range is all real numbers. This inverse function is called the **logarithm to base b**, and is denoted by $\log_b$.

Key Fact 14.1 The Principle of Logarithms

If $b > 0$ then the functions

$$f(x) = b^x, \qquad x \in \mathbb{R}, \qquad g(x) = \log_b x, \qquad x > 0,$$

are inverses of each other. Thus

$$y = b^x \qquad \Leftrightarrow \qquad x = \log_b y \qquad x \in \mathbb{R},\ y > 0.$$

The graph of $y = \log_b(x)$ is obtained, of course, by reflecting the graph of $y = b^x$ in the line $y = x$. The diagram on the right shows the situation for a value of b that is greater than 1. The graphs for $0 < b < 1$ look rather different, but are less important, since we rarely use logarithms to bases less than 1.

Since the point $(0,1)$ always lies on the curve $y = b^x$, the point $(1,0)$ always lies on the curve $y = \log_b x$. This is an important special case of a more general observation. Since the point (n, b^n) lies on the curve $y = b^x$ for any n, the point (b^n, n) lies on the curve $y = \log_b x$ for any n.

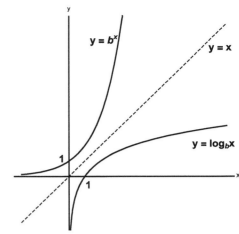

Figure 14.7

Key Fact 14.2 Logarithms of Powers

Let $b > 0$. For any n, $\log_b b^n = n$. In particular, $\log_b 1 = 0$.

This result is not new; it is simply a restatement of the Principle of Logarithms. It is worth noting separately, since it **looks** rather different!

Example 14.3.1. Find $\log_3 81$, $\log_{81} 3$, $\log_3 \frac{1}{81}$ and $\log_{\frac{1}{3}} 81$.

Since $81 = 3^4$, $\log_3 81 = 4$. Now $3 = 81^{\frac{1}{4}}$, so $\log_{81} 3 = \frac{1}{4}$. Next $\frac{1}{81} = 3^{-4}$, so $\log_3 \frac{1}{81} = -4$. Finally, $81 = 3^4 = \left(\frac{1}{3}\right)^{-4}$, and so $\log_{\frac{1}{3}} 81 = -4$.

EXERCISE 14A

1. A rumour spreads exponentially through a college. 100 people have heard it by noon, and 200 by 1 p.m. How many people have heard it

   a) by 3 p.m.,　　　b) by 12.30 p.m.,　　　c) by 1.45 p.m.?　　　　3

2. An orchestra tunes to a frequency of 440 Hz, which sounds the A above middle C. Each octave higher doubles the frequency, and each of the 12 semitones in the octave increases the frequency in the same ratio.

   a) What is this ratio?

   b) Find the frequency of middle C.

   c) Where on the scale is a note with a frequency of 600 Hz?

3. A cup of coffee at $85°$ C is placed in a freezer at $0°$ C. The temperature of the coffee decreases exponentially, so that after 5 minutes it is $30°$ C.

   a) What is its temperature after 3 minutes?

   b) Find, by trial, how long it will take for the temperature to drop to $5°$ C.

4. A radioactive substance decays at a rate of 12% per hour.

   a) Find, by trial, after how many hours half of the radioactive material will be left.

   b) How many hours earlier did it have twice the current amount of radioactive material?

5. With the same axes, sketch the graphs of
   a) $y = 1.25^x$,　　　　b) $y = 0.8^x$,　　　　c) $y = 0.8^{-x}$.

6. Write each of the following statements in the form $y = b^x$:
   a) $\log_2 8 = 3$,　　　　b) $\log_3 81 = 4$,　　　　c) $\log_5 0.04 = -2$,
   d) $\log_7 x = 4$,　　　　e) $\log_x 5 = t$,　　　　f) $\log_p q = r$.

7. Write each of the following in the form $x = \log_b y$:
   a) $2^3 = 8$,　　　　b) $3^6 = 729$,　　　　c) $4^{-3} = \frac{1}{64}$,
   d) $a^8 = 20$,　　　　e) $h^9 = g$,　　　　f) $m^n = p$.

8. Evaluate the following:
   a) $\log_2 16$,　　　　b) $\log_4 16$,　　　　c) $\log_7 \frac{1}{49}$,
   d) $\log_4 1$,　　　　e) $\log_5 5$,　　　　f) $\log_{27} \frac{1}{3}$,
   g) $\log_{16} 8$,　　　　h) $\log_2 2\sqrt{2}$,　　　　i) $\log_{\sqrt{2}} 8\sqrt{2}$.

9. Find the value of y in each of the following.
   a) $\log_y 49 = 2$,　　　　b) $\log_4 y = -3$,　　　　c) $\log_3 81 = y$,
   d) $\log_{10} y = -1$,　　　　e) $\log_2 y = 2.5$,　　　　f) $\log_y 1296 = 4$,
   g) $\log_{\frac{1}{2}} y = 8$,　　　　h) $\log_{\frac{1}{2}} 1024 = y$,　　　　i) $\log_y 27 = -6$.

14.4　Properties Of Logarithms

The point of introducing logarithms was to be able to access the ease that the laws of indices provide when multiplying and dividing. Given the Principle of Logarithms:

$$y = \log_b x \qquad \Leftrightarrow \qquad x = b^y$$

for any base $b > 0$, the laws of indices can be written as follows:

Key Fact 14.3 Laws Of Logarithms

For any base $b > 0$, we have the rules:

Multiplication Rule: 　　　$\log_b(xy) = \log_b x + \log_b y$ for any $x, y > 0$.

Division Rule: 　　　$\log_b\left(\frac{x}{y}\right) = \log_b x - \log_b y$ for any $x, y > 0$.

Power Rule: 　　　$\log_b x^p = p\log_b x$ for any $x > 0$ and $p \in \mathbb{R}$.

pth Root Rule: 　　　$\log_b \sqrt[p]{x} = \frac{1}{p}\log_b x$ for any $x > 0$ and $p \in \mathbb{R}$.

Establishing these rules is a simple application of the Principle of Logarithms and the laws of indices. If $u = \log_b x$ and $v = \log_b y$, then $x = b^u$ and $y = b^v$, so that $xy = b^u \times b^v = b^{u+v}$, which implies that $\log_b(xy) = u + v = \log_b x + \log_b$. This is the multiplication rule, and the division rule is a simple rewriting of the multiplication rule. Similarly, if $u = \log_b x$, so that $x = b^u$, we see that $x^p = (b^u)^p = b^{up}$, and hence $\log_b x^p = pu = p\log_b x$ for any $p \in \mathbb{R}$. This is the power rule; the pth root rule is just the power rule applied to $x^{\frac{1}{p}}$.

Example 14.4.1. *If* $\log_b 2 = r$ *and* $\log_b 3 = s$, *express the following in terms of* r *and* s:
　a) $\log_b 16$,　　　　b) $\log_b 18$,　　　　c) $\log_b 13.5$.

The Laws of Logarithms tell us that

$$\log_b 16 = \log_b 2^4 = 4\log_b 2 = 4r,$$
$$\log_b 18 = \log_b(2 \times 3^2) = \log_b 2 + \log_b 3^2 = \log_b 2 + 2\log_b 3 = r + 2s,$$
$$\log_b 13.5 = \log_b\left(\tfrac{27}{2}\right) = \log_b 27 - \log_b 2 = \log_b 3^3 - \log_b 2 = 3\log_b 3 - \log_b 2 = 3s - r.$$

Example 14.4.2. *Find the connection between* $\log_b c$ *and* $\log_c b$ *for any* $b, c > 0$.

Since

$$\log_b c = x \quad \Leftrightarrow \quad c = b^x \quad \Leftrightarrow \quad c^{\frac{1}{x}} = (b^x)^{\frac{1}{x}} = b^1 = b \quad \Leftrightarrow \quad \log_c b = \tfrac{1}{x}$$

we deduce that $\log_c b = \frac{1}{\log_b c}$.

Logarithms were important historically because they were used to make calculations easier, either (implicitly) through constructing a slide rule (since the distance function $D(x) = \log_{10} x$), or through the use of look-up tables for logarithms. These printed tables of logarithms worked in base 10, and gave values of $\log_{10} x$ for values of x between 1.000 and 9.999, to 4 decimal places. If we wanted to use these tables to calculate the product of 21.5 and 139.2, we would look up $\log_{10} 2.15 = 0.3324$ and $\log_{10} 1.392 = 0.1436$, and calculate

$$
\begin{aligned}
\log_{10} 21.5 &= \log_{10}(2.15 \times 10) = \log_{10} 2.15 + \log_{10} 10 = 0.3324 + 1 = 1.3324 \\
\log_{10} 139.2 &= \log_{10}(1.392 \times 100) = \log_{10} 1.392 + \log_{10} 100 = 0.1436 + 2 = 2.1436 \\
\log_{10}(21.5 \times 139.2) &= 1.3324 + 2.1436 = 3.4760
\end{aligned}
$$

Using the tables again, we would discover that $\log_{10} 2.992 = 0.4760$, and hence that

$$21.5 \times 139.2 = 2.992 \times 10^3 = 2992$$

which is correct to 3 significant figures (the actual answer is 2992.8). There are some definite advantages to the calculator age!

While we no longer need to use logarithms in this messy, hands-on, fashion, we still live with the legacy of logarithm tables. Everyone used logarithms to base 10 for the purpose of calculation, and it became common simply to refer to the logarithm to base 10 by the notation log, rather than $\log_{10}$. The button on most calculators marked LOG calculates logarithms to base 10, for example.

EXERCISE 14B

1. On the same set of axes, plot the graphs of $y = \left(\frac{1}{2}\right)^x$ and $y = \log_{\frac{1}{2}} x$.

2. Write each of the following in terms of $\log p$, $\log q$ and $\log r$. All logarithms have base 10.

   a) $\log pqr$,

   b) $\log pq^2 r^3$,

   c) $\log 100 pr^5$,

   d) $\log \sqrt{\frac{p}{q^2 r}}$,

   e) $\log \frac{pq}{r^2}$,

   f) $\log \frac{1}{pqr}$,

   g) $\log \frac{p}{\sqrt{r}}$,

   h) $\log \frac{qr^7 p}{10}$,

   i) $\log \sqrt{\frac{10 p^{10} r}{q}}$.

3. Express as a single logarithm, simplifying where possible. All the logarithms have base 10.

   a) $2 \log 5 + \log 4$,

   b) $2 \log 2 + \log 150 - \log 6000$,

   c) $3 \log 5 + 5 \log 3$,

   d) $2 \log 4 - 4 \log 2$,

   e) $\log 24 - \frac{1}{2} \log 9 + \log 125$,

   f) $3 \log 2 + 3 \log 5 - \log 10^6$,

   g) $\frac{1}{2} \log 16 + \frac{1}{3} \log 8$,

   h) $\log 64 - 2 \log 4 + 5 \log 2 - \log 2^7$.

4. If $p = \log_b 3$, $q = \log_b 5$ and $r = \log_b 10$, express the following in terms of p, q and r:

   a) $\log_b 2$,

   b) $\log_b 45$,

   c) $\log_b \sqrt{90}$,

   d) $\log_b 0.2$,

   e) $\log_b 750$,

   f) $\log_b 60$,

   g) $\log_b \frac{1}{6}$,

   h) $\log_b 4.05$,

   i) $\log_b 0.15$.

5. Given that x and y are both positive, solve the simultaneous equations $\log_2(xy) = 4 + \log_2(x^3 y) = 2 + \log_2\left(\frac{x}{y}\right)$.

6. If $\log(3p - q + 1) = 0$ and $\log(pq) = \log 300$, find the values of p and q.

14.5 Changing The Base

Although logarithms to any positive base (except 1) can be used, in practical cases there are only two commonly used bases. We have already discussed logarithms to the base 10. The second commonly used base for logarithms is much more elegant mathematically, but its base is unusual. The topic of **natural logarithms**, or logarithms to the base e (where e is only of the special numbers of mathematics, like π; it is approximately equal to 2.7182818) will be deferred until the next chapter, when we will have studied sufficient calculus to realise their importance. The important point to realise is that, to all intents and purposes, the different logarithms are basically the same! There is a close relationship between logarithms to different bases.

Suppose that x, y and z are positive numbers, and let $p = \log_x y$, $q = \log_y z$ and $r = \log_x z$. Then we know that $y = x^p$, $z = y^q$ and $z = x^r$, so that

$$x^r = z = y^q = (x^p)^q = x^{pq}$$

and hence $r = pq$.

Key Fact 14.4 Change of Base

If x, y and z are positive numbers, then

$$\log_x z = \log_x y \times \log_y z \,.$$

Thus the functions $u \mapsto \log_x u$ and $u \mapsto \log_y u$ are related by the formula

$$\log_y u = \frac{1}{\log_x y} \log_x u \,, \qquad u > 0 \,.$$

The result that $\log_y x = \left(\log_x y\right)^{-1}$ we noted earlier on is a consequence of this result, since (putting $z = x$) we have $1 = \log_x x = \log_x y \times \log_y x$.

Thus any logarithm is just a scaled version of the base 10 logarithm $\log = \log_{10}$.

Example 14.5.1. *Working in base 10, calculate* $\log_2 3$ *and* $\log_9 7$.

Using the above results we have

$$\log_2 3 = \frac{\log_{10} 3}{\log_{10} 2} = \frac{0.47712}{0.301033} = 1.5850$$

$$\log_9 7 = \frac{\log_{10} 7}{\log_{10} 9} = \frac{0.84510}{0.95424} = 0.88562$$

correct to 5 significant figures in each case.

14.6 Equations and inequalities

Example 14.6.1. *How many terms of the geometric series* $1 + 1.01 + 1.01^2 + 1.01^3 + \cdots$ *must be taken to give a sum greater than 1 million?*

The sum of n terms of this GP is given by the formula

$$S_n = \frac{1.01^n - 1}{1.01 - 1} = 100\left[1.01^n - 1\right].$$

We need to find the smallest value of n for which

$$100\left[1.01^n - 1\right] > 1000000$$
$$1.01^n > 10001$$

Since the logarithm $\log_{10}$ is an increasing function, we deduce that $n \log_{1.01} > \log_{10} 10001$, and hence $n > \frac{\log_{10} 10001}{\log_{10} 1.01} = 925.64$, so the least possible value of n is 926.

Note that we could have worked in base 1.01, and simply observed that $1.01^n > 10001$ implies $n > \log_{1.01} 10001$.

Example 14.6.2. *Iodine-131 is a radioactive isotope used in treatment of the thyroid gland. It decays so that, after t days, 1 unit of the isotope is reduced to 0.9174^t units. How many days does it take for the amount to fall to less than 0.1 units?*

This requires solution of the inequality

$$0.9174^t < 0.1 \,.$$

Since $\log_{10}$ is an increasing function, taking logarithms gives

$$t \log_{10} 0.9174 \;=\; \log_{10} 0.9174^t \;<\; \log_{10} 0.1 \;=\; -1 \,.$$

Since $0.9174 < 1$, $\log_{10} 0.9174$ is negative, so we need to be careful with the direction of the inequality when dividing out, deducing that $n > \frac{-1}{\log_{10} 0.9174} = 26.7$, so the iodine-131 levels have dropped to 0.1 units after 26.7 days.

The brave could attempt working with logarithms in base 0.9174, but beware! Since $0.9174 < 1$, the logarithm to that base is a **decreasing** function, and so the inequality $0.9174^t < 0.1$ becomes $t > \log_{0.9174} 0.1$.

Example 14.6.3. *Solve the equation $4^x - 5 \times 2^x - 6 = 0$.*

If we put $y = 2^x$, the equation becomes

$$y^2 - 5y - 6 \;=\; (2^x)^2 - 5 \times 2^x - 6 \;=\; 4^x - 5 \times 2^x - 6 \;=\; 0$$

and hence $(y-6)(y+1) = 0$, so that $y = 6$ or -1. Thus $2^x = 6$ or -1. But 2^x cannot be negative, and hence $2^x = 6$, so that $x = \log_2 6 = 2.585$.

Example 14.6.4. *If $b > 1$, solve the simultaneous equations*

$$\log_b(y - x) = 0 \qquad \text{and} \qquad 2\log_b y = \log_b(6x + y) \,.$$

The equation $\log_b(y - x) = 0$ implies that $y - x = 1$, so that $x = y + 1$. The second equation implies

$$\log_b y^2 \;=\; 2\log_b y \;=\; \log_b(6x + y)$$

so that $y^2 = 6x + y = 6(y - 1) + y = 7y - 6$. Thus

$$(y - 1)(y - 6) \;=\; y^2 - 7y + 6 \;=\; 0$$

If $y = 1$ then $x = 0$. If $y = 6$ then $x = 5$. The two possible solutions are $(x, y) = (0, 1)$ and $(5, 6)$.

EXERCISE 14C

1. Solve the following equations, giving answers correct to 3 significant figures:

   a) $3^x = 5$, b) $7^x = 21$, c) $6^{2x} = 60$,

   d) $5^{2x-1} = 10$, e) $4^{\frac{1}{2}x} = 12$, f) $2^{x+1} = 3^x$,

   g) $\left(\frac{1}{2}\right)^{3x+2} = 25$, h) $2^x \times 2^{x+1} = 128$, i) $\left(\frac{1}{4}\right)^{2x-1} = 7$.

2. Solve the following inequalities, giving your answers correct to 3 significant figures:

   a) $3^x > 8$, b) $5^x < 10$, c) $7^{2x+5} \leq 24$,

   d) $0.5^x < 0.001$, e) $0.4^x < 0.0004$, f) $0.2^x > 25$,

   g) $4^x \times 4^{3-2x} \leq 1024$, h) $0.8^{2x+5} \geq 4$, i) $0.8^{1-3x} \geq 10$.

3. How many terms of the geometric series $1 + 2 + 4 + 8 + 16 + \cdots$ must be taken for the sum to exceed 10^{11}?

4. How many terms of the geometric series $2 + 6 + 18 + 54 + \cdots$ must be taken for the sum to exceed 3 million?

5. How many terms of the geometric series $1 + \frac{1}{2} + \frac{1}{4} + \frac{1}{8} + \cdots$ must be taken for its sum to differ from 2 by less than 10^{-8}?

6. How many terms of the geometric series $2 + \frac{1}{3} + \frac{1}{18} + \frac{1}{108} + \cdots$ must be taken for its sum to differ from its sum to infinity by less than 10^{-5}?

7. A kg of radioactive isotope decays so that after t days an amount 0.82^t kg remains. How many days does it take for the amount to fall to less than 0.15 kg?

8. Jacques is saving for a new car which will cost £29000. He saves by putting £400 at the start of each month into a savings account which gives 0.1% interest per month. After how many months will he be able to buy his car? Assume it does not increase in price!

9. To say that a radioactive isotope has a half-life of 6 days means that 1 kg of isotope is reduced to $\frac{1}{2}$ kg in 6 days. Let the daily decay rate be given by r.

   a) For this isotope, find r.

   b) How long will it take for the amount to fall to 0.25 kg?

   c) How long will it take for the amount to fall to 0.1 kg?

10. A biological culture contains 500000 bacteria at 12 noon on Monday. The culture increases by 10% every hour. At what time will the culture exceed 4 million bacteria?

11. A dangerous radioactive substance has a half-life of 90 years. It will be deemed safe when its activity is down to 0.05 of its initial value. How long will it be before it is deemed safe?

12. Solve each of the following equations for x, giving your answers correct to 2 decimal places when needed:

   a) $2^{2x} - 9 \times 2^x + 8 = 0$,
   b) $7^{2x} - 50 \times 7^x + 49 = 0$,
   c) $8^{2x} - 11 \times 8^x + 30 = 0$,
   d) $2^{2x+1} - 7 \times 2^x + 3 = 0$,
   e) $5^{2x} + 7 \times 5^x = 12$,
   f) $9^x + 11 \times 3^x = 30$.

13. Solve each of the following inequalities for x, giving answers correct to 2 decimal places when needed:

   a) $3^{2x} - 2 \times 3^{x+1} + 5 < 0$,
   b) $2^{2x+1} - 2^x - 3 > 0$,
   c) $2^x \times 3^{4-2x} > 1$.

14. By factorising the cubic expression $x^3 - 13x^2 + 44x - 32$, find the exact solutions to the equation $8^x - 13 \times 4^x + 44 \times 2^x - 32 = 0$.

15. By factorising the cubic expression $x^3 - 9x^2 - 2x + 18$, find the solutions to the equation $27^x - 9^{x+1} - 2 \times 3^x + 18 = 0$, giving answers to 3 significant figures where necessary.

16. The variable x satisfies the equation $5^x \times 11^{2x-1} = 7^{x+2}$. Find x correct to 3 decimal places.

17*. Solve the following equations, giving answers correct to 3 decimal places where necessary:

   a) $5^{2x} - 6 \times 5^{x+1} + 124 = 0$,
   b) $3^{4x+1} - 10 \times 3^{3x} = 3 - 10 \times 3^x$,
   c) $17 \times 2^x = 11 \times 3^{x^2}$,
   d) $\log_2 x[9 - \log_2 x] = 20$,
   e) $2\log_{10}(x + 1) = \log_{10}(x + 7)$,
   f) $\log_x 2 + \log_2 x = \frac{5}{2}$,
   g) $\log_x 2 + \log_4 x = \frac{9}{4}$.

14.7 Reducing Exponential Curves To Linear Form

Example 14.7.1. *An investment company claims that the price of its shares has grown exponentially over the past seven years, and provides the following data to support its claim:*

Year	2008	2009	2010	2011	2012	2013	2014
Price (p)	20	36	65	117	210	352	540

Is the company's claim justified?

If we plot the price p against the year x as in Figure 14.8, then the company's claim seems plausible. The problem is that we are not very good at identifying curve shapes by sight. What we need to do is re-draw this graph in a way which makes it easier to decide whether the relationship between p and x is exponential.

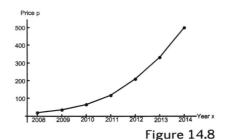

Figure 14.8

Suppose that there was an exponential relationship between p and x. This would mean that there was an equation of the form

$$p = ab^x$$

relating them, for some values of a and b. The trick to analysing this equation is to take logarithms, for then the equation becomes

$$\log_{10} p = \log_{10} a + x \log_{10} b,$$

so that there is a linear relationship between x and $\log_{10} p$.

Plotting $\log_{10} p$ against x tells us a differ-ent story, since it is easy for us to identify when points are lying on a straight line. It is clear from Figure 14.9 that the com-pany's claim was reasonable until 2012, but that share growth has slackened off somewhat in the last two years.

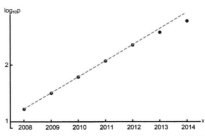

Figure 14.9

Key Fact 14.5 Reduction to Linear Form: Exponential Graphs

An exponential relationship of the form $y = ab^x$ can be more easily identified and stud-ied after taking logarithms, since there is a linear relationship between $\log y$ and x:

$$\log y = \log a + x \log b.$$

Note that logarithms can be taken to any basis. The process is called **reduction to linear form**.

Example 14.7.2. *Use the following census data to justify the statement in Example 14.2.1, that the population in the USA grew exponentially from 1790 to 1860.*

Year:	1790	1800	1810	1820	1830	1840	1850	1860
Population(millions):	3.9	5.3	7.2	9.6	12.9	17.0	23.2	31.4

As in the previous Example, there is no point in simply plotting the population against the year and looking at the shape of the graph. We need to take logarithms first. Before doing this, we shall code the data a little. Let t be the number of decades after 1790, and let P be the population in millions. We are looking for a relationship of the form

$$P = ab^t,$$

which becomes, on taking logarithms, the relationship

$$\log_{10} P = \log_{10} a + t \log_{10} b.$$

With this coding, the census data becomes:

t	0	1	2	3	4	5	6	7
$\log_{10} P$	0.591	0.724	0.857	0.982	1.111	1.230	1.365	1.497

and plotting $\log_{10} P$ against t shows a strong linear relationship between these variables; it is not perfect, but we should not expect that of census data.

The points at $t = 1$ and $t = 7$ pass through the proposed straight line relating $\log_{10} P$ and t, and these can be used to estimate the gradient $\log_{10} b$ of the line. We calculate

$$\log_{10} b = \frac{1.497 - 0.724}{7 - 1} = 0.1288$$

and hence $b = 1.345$. The intercept of the line of best fit with the $\log_{10} P$ axis is 0.60 (we would need a larger-scaled drawing of real graph paper to see this), and hence $\log_{10} a = 0.60$, so that $a = 3.98$. Thus we have discovered the relationship

$$P = 3.98 \times 1.345^t$$

between P and t, which looks convincing.

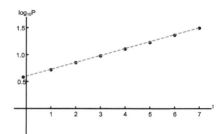

Figure 14.10

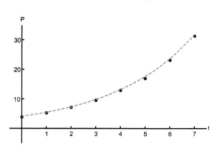

Figure 14.11

An equation like $P = 3.98 \times 1.345^t$ is called a **mathematical model.** It is not an exact equation giving a precise relationship between P and t, but it is instead a relatively simple equation which enables us to approximate P quickly to a good degree of accuracy. For example, if we wanted to know what the population of the USA was in 1836, putting $t = 4.6$ into this equation gives $P = 15.6$; we can be confident (given the goodness of fit of our curve to the given data) that the population of the USA in 1836 was about 15.5 million.

14.8   Power Law Models

Other models can be reduced to linear form by taking logarithms. In particular, we can use the same method to identify power law relationships of the form $y = ax^b$ for constants a and b.

> **Key Fact 14.6** Reduction to Linear Form: Power Law Graphs
>
> A power relationship of the form $y = ax^b$ can be reduced to linear form by taking logarithms, since there is a linear relationship between $\log y$ and $\log x$:
>
> $$\log y = \log a + b \log x.$$
>
> Note that logarithms can be taken to any base.

Example 14.8.1. *These figures have been given for the typical daily metabolic activity of various species of mammal.*

	Weight (kg)	Energy expended (calories per kg)
Rabbit	2	58
Man	70	33
Horse	600	22
Elephant	4000	13

Investigate the relation between the energy expenditure (E calories per kg) and the weight (W kg) of the various animals.

This is the kind of situation where a power law model of the form $E = aW^b$ might be appropriate, so we try plotting $log_{10}E$ against $log_{10}W$. Using logarithms to base 10, the corresponding values for the four animals are:

$log_{10} W$	0.301	1.845	2.778	3.602
$log_{10} E$	1.763	1.519	1.342	1.113

These are plotted on the graph to the right. There are four points, one for each animal. Since all the figures are statistical averages, and energy expenditure can't be very precisely measured, we wouldn't expect the points to lie exactly on a straight line. However, they do suggest a trend that might be generalised to apply to other mammals in a similar environment. This is expressed by the equation of the line, which is approximately

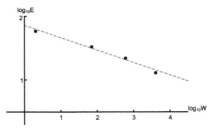

Figure 14.12

$$log_{10} E = 1.845 - -0.19 log_{10} W ,$$

which leads back to the power law relationship

$$E = 10^{1.845} \times W^{-0.19} \approx 70W^{-0.2} .$$

The uncertainty of the data, and the approximations shown up by the graph, mean that this model can do little more than suggest an order of magnitude for the dependent variable E. It would therefore be unwise to give the coefficients in the model to more than 1 significant figure, since that would suggest a degree of accuracy that couldn't be justified.

EXERCISE 14D

1. a) If $log_{10} y = 0.4 + 0.6x$, express y in terms of x.
   b) If $log_{10} y = 12 - 3x$, express y in terms of x.
   c) If $log_{10} y = 0.7 + 1.7x$, express y in terms of x.
   d) If $log_{10} y = 0.7 + 2 log_{10} x$, express y in terms of x.
   e) If $log_{10} y = -0.5 - 5 log_{10} x$, express y in terms of x.

2. Population census data for the USA from 1870 to 1910 were as follows.

Year	1870	1880	1890	1900	1910
Population (millions)	38.6	50.2	63.0	76.0	92.0

Investigate how well these figures can be described by an exponential model.

3. The table shows the mean relative distance X, in astronomical units (1 astronomical unit is the average distance of the Earth from the Sun), of some of the planets from the Earth and the time, T years, taken for one revolution round the sun. By drawing an appropriate graph show that there is an approximate law of the form $T = aX^n$, stating the values of a and n.

	Mercury	Venus	Earth	Mars	Saturn
X	0.39	0.72	1.00	1.52	9.54
T	0.24	0.62	1.00	1.88	29.5

4. Jack takes out a fixed rate savings bond. This means he makes one payment and leaves his money for a fixed number of years. The value of his bond, £B, is given by the formula $B = Ax^n$ where A is the original investment and n is the number of complete years since he opened the account. The table gives some values of B and n. By plotting a suitable graph find the initial value of Jack's investment and the rate of interest he is receiving.

n	2	3	5	8	10
B	982	1056	1220	1516	1752

5. In a spectacular experiment on cell growth the following data were obtained, where N is the number of cells at a time t minutes after the start of the growth.

t	1.5	2.7	3.4	8.1	10
N	9	19	32	820	3100

At $t = 10$ a chemical was introduced which killed off the culture. The relationship between N and t was thought to be modelled by $N = ab^t$, where a and b are constants.

a) Use a graph to determine how these figures confirm the supposition that the relationship is of this form. Find the values of a and b, each to the nearest integer.

b) If the growth had not been stopped at $t = 10$ and had continued according to your model, how many cells would there have been after 20 minutes?

6. In a version of the so-called Ehrenfest game, 100 balls (numbered from 1 to 100) are placed in a container A, and another container B is left empty. Numbers in the range 1 to 100 are drawn at random. When a number is drawn, the corresponding ball is transferred from the container it is currently in to the other container. In one playing of this game, the number T of balls left in container A after x numbers have been drawn was as follows:

x	0	10	20	30	40	50
T	100	92	84	78	72	68

Find a law of the form $T = ab^{-x}$, where a and b are constants, to fit these data as well as possible. Can T be expected to continue to obey this law as x becomes large?

7*. Fit a relationship of the form $y = ak^{x^2}$ to the data:

x	0.5	1	1.5	2	2.5	3
y	3.6	13.8	129.6	2981	1.679×10^5	2.318×10^7

Chapter 14: Summary

Exponential Functions: The exponential function $x \mapsto b^x$, for $x \in \mathbb{R}$, can be defined for any positive real b. For any $b \neq 1$, the function has range $y > 0$. If $b > 1$, the function is increasing. If $0 < b < 1$, the function is decreasing. The laws of indices

$$b^x \times b^y = b^{x+y} \qquad (b^x)^y = b^{xy}$$

hold for all real x, y.

Logarithmic Functions: For $b > 0$ and $b \neq 1$ the inverse of the function $x \mapsto b^x$, for $x \in \mathbb{R}$, is the logarithm $x \mapsto \log_b x$, for $x > 0$. Thus

$$a = \log_b c \qquad \Leftrightarrow \qquad c = b^a .$$

The Laws of Logarithms: For any positive x, y and any real p we have

$$\log_b(xy) = \log_b x + \log_b y \qquad \log_b\left(\tfrac{x}{y}\right) = \log_b x - \log_b y \qquad \log_b x^p = p \log_b x$$

Change of Base: If a, b and c are positive, then

$$\log_a b \times \log_b c = \log_a c$$

and so

$$\log_a x = \frac{\log_b x}{\log_b a}, \qquad x > 0 ,$$

for all positive a and b.

Reduction to Linear Form: An exponential relation $y = ab^x$ implies a linear relationship $\log y = \log a + x \log b$ between $\log y$ and x (to any base). A power law relation $y = ax^b$ implies a linear relationship $\log y = \log a + b \log x$ between $\log y$ and $\log x$ (to any base).

Further Differentiation

In this chapter we will learn to:

- differentiate by the chain rule,

- apply differentiation to related rates of change,

- differentiate products and quotients,

- differentiate trigonometric functions, exponentials and logarithms,

- understand the mathematical importance of the number e, the exponential e^x and the natural logarithm $\ln x$,

15.1 The Chain Rule

With our current state of knowledge, we can only differentiate combinations of powers of x. This is a very limited range of functions, and we shall now extend our range considerably.

There are some functions that we can differentiate at present, but doing so is hard work, and the answers indicate that there might be a more efficient method to be found.

Example 15.1.1. *Differentiate the functions* $(x+2)^3$, $(3x-1)^2$ *and* $(x^3+2)^4$.

All of these functions can be expanded by the Binomial Theorem, differentiated, and the result can be factorised:

$$\frac{d}{dx}(x+2)^3 = \frac{d}{dx}\left(x^3+6x^2+12x+8\right) = 3x^2+12x+12 = 3(x^2+4x+4) = 3(x+2)^2$$

$$\frac{d}{dx}(3x-1)^2 = \frac{d}{dx}\left(9x^2-6x+1\right) = 18x-6 = 6(3x-1) = 3\times 2(3x-1)$$

$$\frac{d}{dx}(x^3+2)^4 = \frac{d}{dx}\left(x^{12}+8x^9+24x^6+32x^3+16\right) = 12x^{11}+72x^8+144x^5+96x^2$$

$$= 12x^2(x^9+6x^6+12x^3+8) = 12x^2(x^3+2)^3 = 3x^2\times 4(x^3+2)^3$$

It would be something of a challenge to use this approach to differentiate $(x^3-2x^2+1)^{101}$, though.

There is an intriguing pattern to be seen in the results of the previous example: $(x+2)^3$ could be differentiated by 'differentiating the cube', obtaining $3(x+2)^2$. $(3x-1)^2$ could be differentiated by 'differentiating the square', obtaining $2(3x-1)$, and then 'differentiating the inside', obtaining 3, and multiplying these two derivatives together. Finally, $(x^3+2)^4$ could be differentiated by 'differentiating the fourth power', obtaining $4(x^3+2)^3$, and then 'differentiating the inside', obtaining $3x^2$, and multiplying these two derivatives together. If we applied this idea to the function $(x^3-2x^3+1)^{101}$, we would obtain

$$\frac{d}{dx}(x^3-2x^2+1)^{101} = 101(x^3-2x^2+1)^{100}\times(3x^2-4x) = 101x(3x-4)(x^3-2x^2+1)^{100},$$

which is a relatively straightforward calculation. The best bit of all is that this method works!

Consider the function $y = (x^3 + 2)^4$ again. If we introduce the function

$$u = x^3 + 2,$$

then y can be written as a function of u:

$$y = u^4.$$

But then we can differentiate y with respect to u, and we can differentiate u with respect to x:

$$\frac{dy}{du} = 4u^3 \qquad\qquad \frac{du}{dx} = 3x^2.$$

The remarkable fact is that $\frac{dy}{dx}$ is obtained from these two derivatives by multiplication:

$$\frac{dy}{dx} = \frac{dy}{du} \times \frac{du}{dx} = 4u^3 \times 3x^2 = 12x^2(x^3 + 2)^3.$$

This is an example of what is called the **chain rule**:

Key Fact 15.1 The Chain Rule

If u is a function of x, and if y can be written as a function both of x and of u, then

$$\frac{dy}{dx} = \frac{dy}{du} \times \frac{du}{dx}.$$

This rule is also sometimes known as the **composite function rule** or the **function of a function rule**; substituting $u = g(x)$ shows how to differentiate $y = fg(x) = f(g(x))$:

$$\frac{d}{dx} f(g(x)) = f'(g(x)) \times g'(x).$$

The notation with u is simpler to understand!

Example 15.1.2. Find $\frac{dy}{dx}$ when a) $y = \sqrt{3x^2 + 2x - 7}$, and b) $y = \frac{1}{1+x+2x^2}$.

(a) If $u = 3x^2 + 2x - 7$ then $y = \sqrt{3x^2 + 2x - 7} = \sqrt{u}$. Thus $\frac{dy}{du} = \frac{1}{2\sqrt{u}}$ and so, since $\frac{du}{dx} = 6x + 2$, we obtain

$$\frac{dy}{dx} = \frac{1}{2\sqrt{u}} \times (6x + 2) = \frac{3x+1}{\sqrt{3x^2+2x-7}}.$$

(b) If $u = 1 + x + 2x^2$ then $y = \frac{1}{1+x+2x^2} = u^{-1}$. Thus $\frac{dy}{du} = -u^{-2}$ and so, since $\frac{du}{dx} = 1 + 4x$, we obtain

$$\frac{dy}{dx} = -u^{-2} \times (1 + 4x) = -\frac{1+4x}{(1+x+2x^2)^2}.$$

Example 15.1.3. *Find any stationary points on the graph* $y = \sqrt{2x+1} + \frac{1}{\sqrt{2x+1}}$, *and classify them.*

The largest possible domain for this function is $x > -\frac{1}{2}$. If we put $u = 2x + 1$, then $y = u^{\frac{1}{2}} + u^{-\frac{1}{2}}$, and so

$$\frac{dy}{dx} = \frac{dy}{du} \times \frac{du}{dx} = \left(\tfrac{1}{2}u^{-\frac{1}{2}} - \tfrac{1}{2}u^{-\frac{3}{2}}\right) \times 2 = (2x+1)^{-\frac{1}{2}} - (2x+1)^{-\frac{3}{2}}$$

$$= (2x+1)^{-\frac{3}{2}}\big((2x+1) - 1\big) = 2x(2x+1)^{-\frac{3}{2}}.$$

The turning point occurs at $x = 0$. It is clear that $\frac{dy}{dx}$ is negative for $-\frac{1}{2} < x < 0$, and positive for $x > 0$, so it follows that the turning point $(0, 2)$ is a minimum.

Why does the chain rule work? A first principles argument gives us the answer. Suppose that u is a function of x, and that y can be written as both a function of x and of u. To find the derivative of y at x, we consider a nearby point with coordinate $x + \delta x$; the corresponding value of y is $y + \delta y$. The values of u at these two points are, similarly u and $u + \delta u$, and so

$$\frac{dy}{dx} = \lim_{\delta x \to 0} \frac{\delta y}{\delta x} \qquad\qquad \frac{du}{dx} = \lim_{\delta x \to 0} \frac{\delta u}{\delta x}$$

However, regarding y as a function of u, the ratio $\frac{\delta y}{\delta u}$ is the ratio of the changes in y and u as u varies slightly; since δu will tend to 0 as δx tends to 0, it follows that

$$\frac{dy}{du} = \lim_{\delta u \to 0} \frac{\delta y}{\delta u} = \lim_{\delta x \to 0} \frac{\delta y}{\delta u}$$

Since elementary algebra tells us that $\frac{\delta y}{\delta x} = \frac{\delta y}{\delta u} \times \frac{\delta u}{\delta x}$, letting δx tend to 0 tells us that

$$\frac{dy}{dx} = \frac{dy}{du} \times \frac{du}{dx}.$$

If y is an invertible function of x, then x can also be regarded as a function of y, and so it is possible to calculate both $\frac{dy}{dx}$ and $\frac{dx}{dy}$. Note that

$$\frac{dy}{dx} \times \frac{dx}{dy} = \frac{dy}{dy} = 1.$$

Key Fact 15.2 Differentiating an Inverse Function

If y is an invertible function of x, then

$$\frac{dx}{dy} = \left(\frac{dy}{dx}\right)^{-1}.$$

Example 15.1.4. *Derive the derivative of $y = x^{\frac{1}{3}}$.*

Note that $x = y^3$, so that $\frac{dx}{dy} = 3y^2$. Thus $\frac{dy}{dx} = \frac{1}{3y^2} = \frac{1}{3}x^{-\frac{2}{3}}$, as expected.

Note that this argument can be used to justify the formula for the derivative of $x^{\frac{1}{3}}$ without the need to prove it from first principles.

Example 15.1.5. *Calculate the equation of the tangent to the curve defined by the formula $y^3 + y + 1 = x$ at the point $(3, 1)$.*

The function $f(t) = t^3 + t + 1$ is invertible (it is increasing everywhere), but we cannot easily find an explicit formula for y as a function of x. Never mind! Since $\frac{dx}{dy} = 3y^2 + 1$,

we have $\frac{dx}{dy} = 4$ at $(3, 1)$, and hence $\frac{dy}{dx} = \frac{1}{4}$ there. Thus the tangent at this point has the equation $y - 1 = \frac{1}{4}(x - 3)$, or $y = \frac{1}{4}(1 + x)$.

EXERCISE 15A

1. Use the substitution $u = 5x + 3$ to differentiate the following with respect to x:

   a) $y = (5x + 3)^6$,   b) $y = (5x + 3)^{\frac{1}{2}}$,   c) $y = \frac{1}{5x+3}$.

2. Use the substitution $u = 1 - 4x$ to differentiate the following with respect to x:

   a) $y = (1 - 4x)^5$,   b) $y = (1 - 4x)^{-3}$,   c) $y = \sqrt{1 - 4x}$.

3. Use the substitution $u = 1 + x^3$ to differentiate the following with respect to x:

   a) $y = (1 + x^3)^5$,   b) $y = (1 + x^3)^{-4}$,   c) $y = \sqrt[3]{1 + x^3}$.

4. Use the substitution $u = 2x^2 + 3$ to differentiate the following with respect to x:

   a) $y = (2x^2 + 3)^6$,   b) $y = \frac{1}{2x^2 + 3}$,   c) $y = \frac{1}{\sqrt{2x^2 + 3}}$.

5. Differentiate $y = (3x^4 + 2)^2$ with respect to x by using the chain rule. Confirm your answer by expanding $(3x^4 + 2)^2$ and then differentiating.

6. Differentiate $y = (2x^3 + 1)^3$ with respect to x:

   a) by using the binomial theorem to expand $y = (2x^3 + 1)^3$ and then differentiating term by term,

   b) by using the chain rule.

   Check that your answers are the same.

7. Use appropriate substitutions to differentiate the following with respect to x:

   a) $y = (x^5 + 1)^4$,   b) $y = (2x^3 - 1)^8$,   c) $y = (\sqrt{x} - 1)^5$.

8. Differentiate the following with respect to x; try to do this without writing down the substitutions.

   a) $y = (x^2 + 6)^4$,   b) $y = (5x^3 + 4)^3$,   c) $y = (x^4 - 8)^7$,   d) $y = (2 - x^9)^5$.

9. Differentiate the following with respect to x:

   a) $y = \sqrt{4x + 3}$,   b) $y = (x^2 + 4)^6$,   c) $y = (6x^3 - 5)^{-2}$,   d) $y = (5 - x^3)^{-1}$.

10. Given that $f(x) = \frac{1}{1 + x^2}$, find a) $f'(2)$,   b) the value of x such that $f'(x) = 0$.

11. Given that $y = \sqrt[4]{x^3 + 8}$, find the value of $\frac{dy}{dx}$ when $x = 2$.

12. Differentiate the following with respect to x:

   a) $y = (x^2 + 3x + 1)^6$,   b) $y = \frac{1}{(x^2 + 5x)^3}$,   c) $y = \sqrt{x^5 - 7x}$,

   d) $y = \left(\frac{1}{x} + 5\right)^3$,   e) $y = (4\sqrt{x} + x^2)^3$,   f) $y = \sqrt[4]{1 - 2\sqrt{x} + x^2}$.

13. Find the equation of the tangent to the curve $y = (x^2 - 5)^3$ at the point $(2, -1)$.

14. Find the equation of the tangent to the curve $y = \frac{1}{\sqrt{x} - 1}$ at the point $(4, 1)$.

15. Find the equation of the normal to the curve $y = \frac{8}{1 - x^3}$ at the point $(-1, 4)$.

16. Use the substitutions $u = x^2 - 1$ and $v = \sqrt{u} + 1$ with the chain rule to differentiate $y = \left(\sqrt{x^2 - 1} + 1\right)^6$.

17. Use two substitutions to find $\frac{d}{dx}\left(\sqrt{1 + \sqrt{4x + 3}}\right)$.

18. A curve has equation $y = (x^2 + 1)^4 + 2(x^2 + 1)^3$. Show that $\frac{dy}{dx} = 4x(x^2 + 1)^2(2x^2 + 5)$ and hence show that the curve has just one stationary point. State the coordinates of the stationary point and determine its nature.

19*. Find an expression for $\frac{dy}{dx}$, given that $y = \dfrac{1}{\sqrt{x + \left(\sqrt{x} + 3\right)^2}}$.

15.2   Related Rates of Change

We often need to consider the rates of change of different, but connected, quantities. Suppose that a spherical balloon is being inflated. We might know the rate at which air is being pumped into the balloon, and therefore the rate at which the balloon's volume is increasing. What does this tell us about the rate of increase of the balloon's radius? The chain rule is exactly what we need to solve these problems.

Example 15.2.1. *Suppose that a spherical balloon is being inflated at a constant rate of 5 ms^{-1}. At a particular moment, the radius of the balloon is 4 metres. Find how fast the radius of the balloon is increasing at that instant.*

First of all, we need to model the problem mathematically. If the volume of the balloon is V m^3, and its radius is r m, then we know that $\frac{dV}{dt} = 5$, and we want to know $\frac{dr}{dt}$ at an instant when $r = 4$.

We also know that the balloon is spherical, and hence there is a relationship between V and r given by the formula $V = \frac{4}{3}\pi r^3$, and hence $\frac{dV}{dr} = 4\pi r^2$. The chain rule tells us that

$$\frac{dV}{dt} = \frac{dV}{dr} \times \frac{dr}{dt},$$

and hence, in this case, $\frac{dr}{dt} = \frac{5}{4\pi r^2}$. At the moment when $r = 4$, the rate of increase of the radius is $\frac{5}{64\pi}$ ms^{-1}.

Example 15.2.2. *The surface area of a cube is increasing at a constant rate of 24 cm^2 s^{-1}. Find the rate at which its volume is increasing at the moment when the volume is 216 cm^3.*

We can be a little more concise than we were above. If the cube has side x cm, surface area S cm^2 and volume V cm^3, then $S = 6x^2$ and $V = x^3$. We are told that $\frac{dS}{dt} = 24$, and we want to know $\frac{dV}{dt}$ when $V = 216$, so when $x = 6$.

Since $\frac{dV}{dt} = \frac{dV}{dx} \times \frac{dx}{dt} = 3x^2\frac{dx}{dt}$, we have $\frac{dV}{dt} = 108\frac{dx}{dt}$ when $x = 6$. Similarly $\frac{dS}{dt} = \frac{dS}{dx} \times \frac{dx}{dt} = 12x\frac{dx}{dt}$, and so $24 = 72\frac{dx}{dt}$, and hence $\frac{dx}{dt} = \frac{1}{3}$, when $x = 6$. Thus $\frac{dV}{dt} = 36$. The cube's volume is increasing at a rate of 36 m^3 s^{-1} at this instant.

EXERCISE 15B

1. The number of bacteria present in a culture at time t hours after the beginning of an experiment is denoted by N. The relation between N and t is modelled by $N = 10\left(1 + \frac{3}{2}t\right)^3$. At what rate per hour will the number of bacteria be increasing when $t = 6$?

2. A metal bar is heated to a certain temperature and then the heat source is removed. At time t minutes after the heat source is removed, the temperature, $\theta°$ C, of the metal bar is given by $\theta = \frac{280}{1+0.02t}$. At what rate is the temperature decreasing 100 minutes after the removal of the heat source?

3. The length of the side of a square is increasing at a constant rate of 1.2 cm s^{-1}. At the moment when the length of the side is 10 cm, find:

    a) the rate of increase of the perimeter,

    b) the rate of increase of the area.

4. The length of the edge of a cube is increasing at a constant rate of 0.5 mm s^{-1}. At the moment when the length of the edge is 40 mm, find:

    a) the rate of increase of the surface area,

    b) the rate of increase of the volume.

5. A circular stain is spreading so that its radius is increasing at a constant rate of 3 mm s^{-1}. Find the rate at which the area is increasing when the radius is 50 mm.

6. A water tank has a rectangular base 1.5 m by 1.2 m. The sides are vertical, and water is being added to the tank at a constant rate of 0.45 m^3 per minute. At what rate is the depth of water in the tank increasing?

7. Air is being lost from a spherical balloon at a constant rate of 0.6 m^3 s^{-1}. Find the rate at which the radius is decreasing at the instant when the radius is 2.5 m.

8. The volume of a spherical balloon is increasing at a constant rate of 0.25 m^3 s^{-1}. Find the rate at which the radius is increasing at the instant when the volume is 10 m^3.

9. A conical funnel has a circular top of diameter 20 cm and a height of 30 cm. When the depth of liquid in the funnel is 12 cm, the liquid is dripping from the funnel at a rate of 0.2 cm^3 s^{-1}. At what rate is the depth of the liquid in the funnel decreasing at this instant?

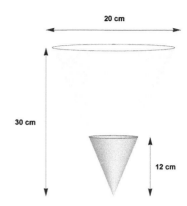

10*. The volume V and surface area S of a sphere of radius r are related by the equation

$$\frac{dV}{dr} = S.$$

Give a geometrical explanation of this fact.

15.3 The Product And Quotient Rules

How do we differentiate a product of two functions? There are many cases where functions can be constructed as the product of two simpler functions. If we know how to differentiate the two component functions, can we work out how to differentiate their product?

The most common mistake made by students is to assume that the derivative $\frac{d}{dx}(uv)$ of a product of u and v is the product $\frac{du}{dx} \times \frac{dv}{dx}$ of the two derivatives. We start by showing this to be false.

Example 15.3.1. *Except by good fortune, $\frac{d}{dx}(uv)$ is not equal to $\frac{du}{dx} \times \frac{dv}{dx}$.*

This is best seen by observing a number of examples. The table below should be enough!

$\mathbf{u}$	$\mathbf{v}$	$\mathbf{uv}$	$\dfrac{\mathbf{du}}{\mathbf{dv}}$	$\dfrac{\mathbf{dv}}{\mathbf{dx}}$	$\dfrac{\mathbf{d}}{\mathbf{dx}}(\mathbf{uv})$	$\dfrac{\mathbf{du}}{\mathbf{dx}} \times \dfrac{\mathbf{dv}}{\mathbf{dx}}$
x^2	x^3	x^5	$2x$	$3x^2$	$5x^4$	$6x^3$
x	$\sqrt{x}$	$x\sqrt{x}$	1	$\frac{1}{2\sqrt{x}}$	$\frac{3}{2}\sqrt{x}$	$\frac{1}{2\sqrt{x}}$
x^3	x^{-3}	1	$3x^2$	$-3x^{-4}$	0	$-9x^{-2}$
$x+1$	$x+2$	x^2+3x+2	1	1	$2x+3$	1

The proper pattern is not easy to identify, but some examples might help.

Example 15.3.2. *Differentiate $(2x+3)(x^2+x+1)$ and $(2-x)\sqrt{x}$.*

We can differentiate these functions by multiplying out the brackets. After we have done this, we will rearrange the answers to put them in a suggestive shape.

$$\frac{d}{dx}\left[(2x+3)(x^2+x+1)\right] = \frac{d}{dx}\left(2x^3+5x^2+5x+\right) = 6x^2+10x+5$$
$$= 2(x^2+x+1)+(4x^2+8x+3) = 2(x^2+x+1)+(2x+3)(2x+1)$$

Note that 2 is the derivative of $2x+3$ and that $2x+1$ is the derivative of x^2+x+1.

$$\frac{d}{dx}\left[(2-x)\sqrt{x}\right] = \frac{d}{dx}\left(2\sqrt{x}-x\sqrt{x}\right) = \frac{1}{\sqrt{x}} - \frac{3}{2}\sqrt{x}$$
$$= -1 \times \sqrt{x} + \left(\frac{1}{\sqrt{x}} - \frac{1}{2}\sqrt{x}\right) = -1 \times \sqrt{x} + (2-x) \times \frac{1}{2\sqrt{x}}$$

Note that -1 is the derivative of $2-x$ and that $\frac{1}{2\sqrt{x}}$ is the derivative of $\sqrt{x}$.

These results suggest the following rule:

> **Key Fact 15.3** The Product Rule
>
> If $y = uv$ is the product of two functions, then
> $$\frac{dy}{dx} = \frac{du}{dx}v + u\frac{dv}{dx} \qquad \text{or} \qquad y' = u'v + uv'.$$

This result can be established by first principles. Suppose that the various functions take the values y, u and v at x. If we move slightly, to the point $x + \delta x$, the three functions take the values $y + \delta y$, $u + \delta u$ and $v + \delta v$, as usual. But

$$y = uv \qquad y + \delta y = (u + \delta u)(v + \delta v) = uv + (\delta u)v + u(\delta v) + (\delta u)(\delta v)$$

and hence $\delta y = (\delta u)v + u(\delta v) + (\delta u)(\delta v)$, and hence

$$\frac{\delta y}{\delta x} = \frac{\delta u}{\delta x}v + u\frac{\delta v}{\delta x} + \frac{\delta u \delta v}{\delta x} = \frac{\delta u}{\delta x}v + u\frac{\delta v}{\delta x} + \frac{\delta u}{\delta x} \times \delta v,$$

so that, letting $\delta x \to 0$,

$$\frac{dy}{dx} = \lim_{\delta x \to 0}\frac{\delta u}{\delta x}v + u\lim_{\delta x \to 0}\frac{\delta v}{\delta x} + \lim_{\delta x \to 0}\frac{\delta u}{\delta x} \times \lim_{\delta x \to 0}\delta v = \frac{du}{dx}v + u\frac{dv}{dx} + \frac{du}{dx} \times 0 = \frac{du}{dx}v + u\frac{dv}{dx}.$$

Example 15.3.3. *Calculate the derivatives of $y = (x-2)^2\sqrt{x}$ and $y = (x-3)^2(x+2)^3$. Find and classify the turning points of $y = (x-2)^2\sqrt{x}$.*

Putting $u = (x-2)^2$ and $v = \sqrt{x}$ gives us

$$\frac{dy}{dx} = 2(x-2) \times \sqrt{x} + (x-2)^2 \times \frac{1}{2\sqrt{x}} = \frac{1}{2\sqrt{x}}(x-2)\big[4x + (x-2)\big] = \frac{1}{2\sqrt{x}}(x-2)(5x-2)$$

and hence $y = (x-2)^2\sqrt{x}$ has turning points at $x = \frac{2}{5}$ and $x = 2$. Since $\frac{dy}{dx}$ is negative for $\frac{2}{5} < x < 2$, and positive for $0 < x < \frac{2}{5}$ and $x > 2$, we deduce that $x = \frac{2}{5}$ is a maximum, while $x = 2$ is a minimum.

Alternatively, putting $u = (x-3)^2$ and $v = (x+2)^3$ gives us

$$\frac{dy}{dx} = 2(x-3) \times (x+2)^3 + (x-3)^2 \times 3(x+2)^2 = (x-3)(x+2)^2\big[2(x+2) + 3(x-3)\big]$$
$$= 5(x-3)(x+2)^2(x-1).$$

Note that we have used the chain rule in determining these derivatives.

> **Food For Thought 15.1**
>
> When using the product rule, it is important to 'tidy up'. After applying the rule, the remaining expression must be factorised and simplified as much as possible, otherwise it will not be possible to identify such things as turning points.

We can also differentiate quotients. There are two ways to approach these. With the use of the chain rule, quotients can be differentiated as slightly more complicated products.

Example 15.3.4. *Differentiate $\frac{x+1}{x^2+3}$ and $\frac{x^2+3x+1}{(x^3+2)^2}$.*

Writing the first function as the product $(x+1)(x^2+3)^{-1}$, the product rule tells us that

$$\frac{d}{dx}\frac{x+1}{x^2+3} = 1 \times (x^2+3)^{-1} + (x+1) \times \big(-2x(x^2+3)^{-3}\big) = (x^2+3)^{-2}\big((x^2+3) - 2x(x+1)\big)$$
$$= \frac{3 - 2x - x^2}{(x^2+3)^2} = \frac{(3+x)(1-x)}{(x^2+3)^2}.$$

287

Similarly, if we write the second function as $(x^2 + 3x + 1)(x^3 + 2)^{-2}$, then

$$\frac{d}{dx}\frac{x^2 + 3x + 1}{(x^3 + 2)^2} = (2x + 3) \times (x^3 + 2)^{-2} + (x^2 + 3x + 1) \times \left(-6x^2(x^3 + 2)^{-3}\right)$$

$$= (x^3 + 2)^{-3}\left((2x + 3)(x^3 + 2) - 6x^2(x^2 + 3x + 1)\right) = \frac{6 + 4x - 6x^2 - 15x^3 - 4x^4}{(x^3 + 2)^3}.$$

Again, note that it is important to 'tidy up' after using the product rule.

It is sometimes convenient to have a rule to use when differentiating quotients.

Key Fact 15.4 The Quotient Rule

If $y = \frac{u}{v}$, then

$$\frac{dy}{dx} = \frac{\dfrac{du}{dx}v - u\dfrac{dv}{dx}}{v^2} \qquad \text{or} \qquad y' = \frac{u'v - uv'}{v^2}.$$

Example 15.3.5. *Find the minimum and maximum values of $f(x) = \frac{x+2}{x^2+x+2}$, and hence sketch the curve $y = \frac{x+2}{x^2+x+2}$.*

The quadratic $x^2 + x + 2$ has discriminant -7, so is never zero, and so the function $f(x)$ has domain $\mathbb{R}$. The quotient rule (with $u = x + 2$ and $v = x^2 + x + 2$) gives

$$f'(x) = \frac{1 \times (x^2 + x + 2) - (x + 2) \times (2x + 1)}{(x^2 + x + 2)^2} = \frac{-4x - x^2}{(x^2 + x + 2)^2}$$

$$= -\frac{x(x + 4)}{(x^2 + x + 3)^2}.$$

The turning points of $f(x)$ occur when $x = 0$ and $x = 4$. Since $f'(x)$ is negative for $x < -4$, positive for $-4 < x < 0$ and negative again for $x > 0$, we deduce that $x = -4$ is a minimum, while $x = 0$ is a maximum. The minimum value of $f(x)$ is $f(-4) = -\frac{1}{7}$, while the maximum value of $f(x)$ is $f(0) = 1$.

We know not only the turning points of $f(x)$, but also the regions where $f(x)$ is increasing and decreasing. The only zero of $f(x)$ occurs at $x = -2$. For large values of $|x|$, $x + 2 \approx x$ and $x^2 + x + 2 \approx x^2$, and hence $f(x) \approx \frac{x}{x^2} = \frac{1}{x}$. This tells us that $f(x)$ tends to 0 as x tends to infinity in either direction. We can now sketch the graph of $y = \frac{x+2}{x^2+x+2}$.

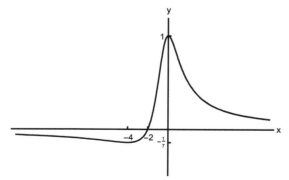

Figure 15.1

EXERCISE 15C

1. Differentiate the following functions with respect to x by using the product rule. Verify your answers by multiplying out the products and then differentiating.

   a) $(x+1)(x-1)$,

   b) $x^2(x+2)$,

   c) $(x^3+4)(x^2+3)$,

   d) $(3x^2+5x+2)(7x+5)$,

   e) $(x^2-2x+4)(x+2)$,

   f) $x^m x^n$.

2. Differentiate the following functions with respect to x using the product rule:

   a) $x^3(x-3)^4$,

   b) $x^7(x+5)^3$,

   c) $(x-1)^3(x+2)^2$,

   d) $x^4(3x-1)^2$,

   e) $2x^3(4x+2)^4$,

   f) $7x^5(2x+11)^3$,

   g) $x^3(3x^2+2x-1)^2$,

   h) $5x^4(2x^3-5)^5$,

   i) $7x^3(x^4+3x^2-x+3)^2$.

3. Differentiate the following functions with respect to x:

   a) $(2x+3)^2(3x-1)^3$

   b) $(2-3x)^3(5+2x)^2$,

   c) $(1+x+x^2)^3(2-3x)^4$,

   d) $(3x^2+2)^4(7x^4-8x+1)^2$,

   e) $(x^4+1)^3(x^3+1)^4$,

   f) $(x^3+2x+3)^2(x^3-5x^2+1)^3$.

4. Differentiate the following functions with respect to x:

   a) $x\sqrt{x+4}$,

   b) $(x+3)\sqrt{5-2x}$,

   c) $2x^3\sqrt[3]{x+1}$,

   d) $(x^2+1)\sqrt{2x+7}$,

   e) $(3x+2)^2\sqrt{x^2-3}$,

   f) $\sqrt{x+2}\sqrt{x-1}$.

5. In each case, differentiate these functions first by using the product rule, and then by using the chain rule:

   a) $(2x+1)^2(x-2)^2$,

   b) $\sqrt{x(x+2)}$,

   c) $x\sqrt{2+x^2}$.

6. a) Assuming that $\dfrac{d}{dx}x^n = nx^{n-1}$, use the product rule to show that $\dfrac{d}{dx}x^{n+1} = (n+1)x^n$.

   b) Still assuming that $\dfrac{d}{dx}x^n = nx^{n-1}$, use the product rule to show that $\dfrac{d}{dx}x^{-n} = -nx^{-n-1}$.

7. Find the coordinates of the stationary point on the curve $y = (x^2-4)\sqrt{4x-1}$ for $x > \frac{1}{4}$.

8. The volume, V, of a solid is given by $V = x^2\sqrt{8-x}$. Use calculus to find the maximum value of V and the value of x at which it occurs.

9. Differentiate with respect to x:

   a) $\dfrac{x}{1+5x}$,

   b) $\dfrac{x^2}{3x-2}$,

   c) $\dfrac{x^2}{1+2x^2}$,

   d) $\dfrac{x}{1+x^3}$,

   e) $\dfrac{x}{x^2+1}$,

   f) $\dfrac{x}{(x+1)^3}$.

10. Differentiate with respect to x:

   a) $\dfrac{x}{\sqrt{x+1}}$,

   b) $\dfrac{\sqrt{x-5}}{x}$,

   c) $\dfrac{\sqrt{3x+2}}{2x}$,

   d) $\dfrac{2-\sqrt{x}}{(5-x)^3}$,

   e) $\dfrac{(x^2+1)^3}{\sqrt{x+1}}$,

   f) $\sqrt{\dfrac{x^2+1}{x^2+2}}$.

11. Find $\dfrac{dy}{dx}$ when $y = \dfrac{\sqrt{1-x}}{\sqrt{1+x}}$ for $-1 < x < 1$, and sketch this curve.

12. Find the equation of the tangent at the point with coordinates $(3, 2)$ to the curve with equation $y = \dfrac{x^2+3}{x+3}$.

13. Find the equation of the normal to the curve $y = \dfrac{2x-1}{x(x-3)}$ at the point on the curve where $x = 2$.

14. Find and classify the turning points of the curve $y = \dfrac{x^2+4}{2x-x^2}$.

15. If $f(x) = \dfrac{x^2-3x}{x+1}$, find $f'(x)$. Find the values of x for which $f(x)$ is decreasing.

16*. Differentiate the following functions with respect to x:

   a) $\dfrac{x(x+3)^2}{x+2}$,

   b) $\dfrac{(x^2+1)\sqrt{x}}{x+1}$,

   c) $\dfrac{x\sqrt{x^6-1}}{\sqrt{x^2+3}}$.

17*. A ladder of length $a\sqrt{2}$ m is leaning against a vertical wall. Its base is resting on a horizontal floor. The distance of the base of the ladder from the base of the wall is x cm, and the height of the top of the ladder above the ground is y m.

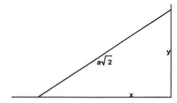

The ladder is sliding down the wall in such a way that the rate of decrease of y is $0.1a$ ms^{-1}. What are the rates of change of the distance x, and of the gradient of the ladder, at the point when the ladder makes an angle of $45°$ with the horizontal?

15.4 Differentiating Trigonometric Functions

If we compare the graphs of $y = \sin\theta$ and $y = \cos\theta$, we can notice a connection between them that we have not previous considered. The graph of $y = \sin\theta$ has turning points precisely where $\cos\theta = 0$, the graph of $y = \sin\theta$ is increasing where $\cos\theta$ is positive, and is decreasing where $\cos\theta$ is negative. It seems that $\cos\theta$ has much in common with the derivative of $\sin\theta$.

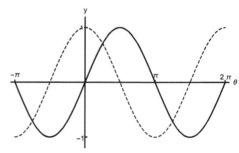

Figure 15.2

There is indeed a very close connection between the derivative of the sine function and the cosine function, and one of the many reasons why mathematicians measure angles in radians is that doing so makes this connection particularly elegant. To show this connection, we need a couple of important inequalities.

Figure 15.3 shows a sector OAB of a circle with radius r and angle $\theta < \frac{1}{2}\pi$ radians. The tangent to the circle at B meets the radius OA extended at D. It is clear that the triangle OAB is contained inside the sector OAB, which is in turn contained in the triangle ABD. Comparing these areas:

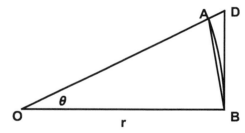

Figure 15.3

$$\tfrac{1}{2}r^2\sin\theta < \tfrac{1}{2}r^2\theta < \tfrac{1}{2} \times r \times r\tan\theta = \tfrac{1}{2}r^2\tan\theta .$$

and hence

$$\sin\theta < \theta < \tan\theta .$$

Provided that $\theta \neq 0$, we can consider the ratio $\frac{\sin\theta}{\theta}$. Remembering that $\tan\theta \equiv \frac{\sin\theta}{\cos\theta}$, these inequalities can be rewritten: since $\sin\theta < \theta$ we deduce that $\frac{\sin\theta}{\theta} < 1$, and since $\theta < \frac{\sin\theta}{\cos\theta}$ we deduce (remember that both $\sin\theta$ and θ are positive) that $\cos\theta < \frac{\sin\theta}{\theta}$:

$$\cos\theta < \frac{\sin\theta}{\theta} < 1 .$$

Since $\cos(-\theta) = \cos\theta$ and $\frac{\sin(-\theta)}{-\theta} = \frac{-\sin\theta}{-\theta} = \frac{\sin\theta}{\theta}$, this last inequality holds for negative θ as well. Figure 15.4 shows the graph of $y = \frac{\sin\theta}{\theta}$ (solid) as well as the graphs of $y = \cos\theta$ and $y = 1$ (dashed). It is clear that $\frac{\sin\theta}{\theta}$ is 'trapped', for $0 < |\theta| < \frac{1}{2}\pi$, between $\cos\theta$ and 1, and both of these functions are nicely behaved at $\theta = 0$, taking the value 1 there. In the limit as θ tends to 0, $\frac{\sin\theta}{\theta}$ must tend to 1.

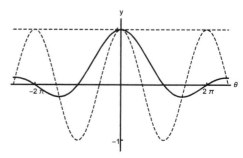

Figure 15.4

> **Key Fact 15.5** The Limit of $\frac{\sin\theta}{\theta}$.
>
> For any $0 < \theta < \frac{1}{2}\pi$, $\sin\theta < \theta < \tan\theta$. For any $0 < |\theta| < \frac{1}{2}\pi$, $\cos\theta < \frac{\sin\theta}{\theta} < 1$, and hence
>
> $$\lim_{\theta \to 0} \frac{\sin\theta}{\theta} = 1 \, .$$
>
> The value of radians as our unit for angle is that this limit is equal to 1.

Now that we have this limit, we can derive the derivatives of all the trigonometric functions without much effort. We only need to differentiate one function from first principles; the other five can be derived using the chain, product and quotient rules.

To differentiate $y = \sin x$, let us consider the value of the function at the points x and $x + \delta x$, as usual. Some compound angle maths is needed here! We can write

$$\sin(x+\delta x) \;=\; \sin\left(x + \tfrac{1}{2}\delta x + \tfrac{1}{2}\delta x\right) \;=\; \sin(x+\tfrac{1}{2}\delta x)\cos\tfrac{1}{2}\delta x + \cos(x+\tfrac{1}{2}\delta x)\sin\tfrac{1}{2}\delta x$$

$$\sin x \;=\; \sin\left(x + \tfrac{1}{2}\delta x - \tfrac{1}{2}\delta x\right) \;=\; \sin(x+\tfrac{1}{2}\delta x)\cos\tfrac{1}{2}\delta x - \cos(x+\tfrac{1}{2}\delta x)\sin\tfrac{1}{2}\delta x$$

and hence

$$\delta y \;=\; \sin(x+\delta x) - \sin x \;=\; 2\cos(x+\tfrac{1}{2}\delta x)\sin\tfrac{1}{2}\delta x$$

$$\frac{\delta y}{\delta x} \;=\; \cos(x+\tfrac{1}{2}\delta x)\frac{2\sin\tfrac{1}{2}\delta x}{\delta x} \;=\; \cos(x+\tfrac{1}{2}\delta x)\frac{\sin\tfrac{1}{2}\delta x}{\tfrac{1}{2}\delta x}$$

so that

$$\frac{dy}{dx} \;=\; \lim_{\delta x\to 0}\frac{\delta y}{\delta x} \;=\; \lim_{\delta x\to 0}\cos(x+\tfrac{1}{2}\delta x) \times \lim_{\delta x\to 0}\frac{\sin\tfrac{1}{2}\delta x}{\tfrac{1}{2}\delta x} \;=\; \cos x \, .$$

Thus $\cos x$ is not just closely related to the derivative of $\sin x$; it is precisely equal to it! Other trigonometric functions can now be differentiated.

Example 15.4.1. *Show that $\frac{d}{dx}\cos x = -\sin x$ and $\frac{d}{dx}\tan x = \sec^2 x$.*

Since $\cos x = \sin(x + \tfrac{1}{2}\pi$, the chain rule tells us that

$$\frac{d}{dx}\cos x \;=\; \frac{d}{dx}\sin(x+\tfrac{1}{2}\pi) \;=\; \cos(x+\tfrac{1}{2}\pi) \;=\; -\sin x \, .$$

We now use that quotient rule to deduce that

$$\frac{d}{dx}\tan x \;=\; \frac{d}{dx}\frac{\sin x}{\cos x} \;=\; \frac{\cos x \times \cos x - \sin x \times (-\sin x)}{\cos^2 x} \;=\; \sec^2 x(\cos^2 x + \sin^2 x) \;=\; \sec^2 x \, .$$

Since $\operatorname{cosec} x$, $\sec x$ and $\cot x$ are the reciprocals of $\sin x$, $\cos x$ and $\tan x$, the chain rule can now be used to obtain the last three derivatives. These proofs will be left as an exercise.

> **Key Fact 15.6** Derivatives Of Trigonometric Functions
>
> The derivatives of the trigonometric functions are as follows:
>
> $$\frac{d}{dx}\sin x = \cos x \qquad\qquad \frac{d}{dx}\cos x = -\sin x$$
>
> $$\frac{d}{dx}\tan x = \sec^2 x \qquad\qquad \frac{d}{dx}\sec x = \sec x\tan x$$
>
> $$\frac{d}{dx}\cot x = -\operatorname{cosec}^2 x \qquad\qquad \frac{d}{dx}\operatorname{cosec} x = -\operatorname{cosec} x\cot x$$

Food For Thought 15.2

It is interesting to note the same pairings between $\sin x$ and $\cos x$, between $\tan x$ and $\sec x$ and between $\cot x$ and $\text{cosec} x$, as we found in the Pythagorean identities.

Example 15.4.2. *Differentiate the following with respect to x:*

a) $\sin^5 x$, b) $\sec \sqrt{x}$, c) $x \tan x$, d) $\frac{\sin x}{1+\cos x}$, e) $\sin^2 x + \cos^2 x$.

(a) Using the chain rule,

$$\frac{d}{dx} \sin^5 x = 5\sin^4 x \times \cos x = 5\sin^4 x \cos x.$$

(b) Using the chain rule,

$$\frac{d}{dx} \sec \sqrt{x} = \sec \sqrt{x} \tan \sqrt{x} \times \frac{1}{2\sqrt{x}} = -\frac{\sec \sqrt{x} \tan \sqrt{x}}{2\sqrt{x}}.$$

(c) Using the product rule,

$$\frac{d}{dx} x \tan x = 1 \times \tan x + x \times \sec^2 x = \tan x + x \sec^2 x.$$

(d) Using the quotient rule,

$$\frac{d}{dx} \frac{\sin x}{1+\cos x} = \frac{\cos x(1+\cos x) - \sin x(-\sin x)}{(1+\cos x)^2} = \frac{1+\cos x}{(1+\cos x)^2} = \frac{1}{1+\cos x}$$

(e) Using the chain rule,

$$\frac{d}{dx}(\sin^2 x + \cos^2 x) = 2\sin x \times \cos x + 2\cos x \times (-\sin x) = 2\sin x \cos x - 2\sin x \cos x = 0$$

The last result is reassuring, since we know that $\sin^2 x + \cos^2 x \equiv 1$. The fact that this function has zero derivative implies that it must be constant, and hence equal everywhere to the value it takes at $x = 0$, namely 1.

Example 15.4.3. *Find the maxima and minima of the function $f(x) = 4\cos x + \cos 2x$, and sketch the curve $y = 4\cos x + \cos 2x$.*

The domain of the function is the whole of $\mathbb{R}$, and the function is periodic of period 2π. Now

$$f'(x) = -4\sin x - 2\sin 2x = -4\sin x - 4\sin x \cos x = -4\sin x(1+\cos x),$$

Thus turning points occur when either $\sin x = 0$ or $\cos x = -1$; turning points occur at integer multiples of π.

Note that $1 + \cos x = 2\cos^2 \frac{1}{2}x \geq 0$ for all x. Thus $f'(x)$ is positive for $-\pi < x < 0$, negative for $0 < x < \pi$, and negative again for $\pi < x < 2\pi$. Thus $x = 0$ is a maximum, while $x = \pi$ is a minimum.

The function $y = 4\cos x + \cos 2x$ has maxima at 0, $\pm 2\pi$, $\pm 4\pi$, ..., at which points $y = 5$. Moreover the function has minima at $\pm \pi$, $\pm 3\pi$, $\pm 5\pi$, ..., at which points $y = -3$. The graph crosses the x-axis when $f(x) = 2\cos^2 x + 4\cos x - 1 = 0$, so when $\cos x = \sqrt{\frac{3}{2}} - 1$; zeroes occur at $x = \pm 1.34$, ± 4.94, ... Although this function is periodic of period 2π, it is not a simple transformation of a sine graph.

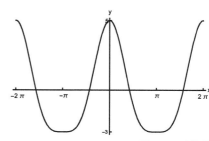

Figure 15.5

Example 15.4.4. *Find all points on the graph $y = x\sin x$ at which the tangent passes through the origin.*

We have $\dfrac{dy}{dx} = \sin x + x\cos x$, so the tangent at the point $P\,(p, p\sin p)$ has gradient $\sin p + p\cos p$. We want to know when $\sin p + p\cos p$ is equal to the gradient of OP, which is $\dfrac{p\sin p}{p} = \sin p$. Thus we need to solve the equation

$$\sin p + p\cos p = \sin p$$

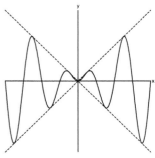

or $p\cos p = 0$. Apart from the point $p = 0$, this equation is satisfied by odd multiples of $\frac{1}{2}\pi$, where $\sin p = \pm 1$.

The required solutions are $(0, 0)$, $(\pm\frac{1}{2}\pi, \frac{1}{2}\pi)$, $(\pm\frac{3}{2}\pi, -\frac{3}{2}\pi)$, $(\pm\frac{5}{2}\pi, \frac{5}{2}\pi)$, ... Apart from the case $p = 0$, then, the tangent at P is either the line $y = x$ or the line $y = -x$. Since $|\sin x| \leq 1$, it is clear that the graph $y = x\sin x$ oscillates between $y = x$ and $y = -x$, and the solutions to this problem are $(0, 0)$ and the points where the curve $y = x\sin x$ touches on these two bounding straight lines.

Figure 15.6

EXERCISE 15D

1. Use the inequalities $\sin\theta < \theta < \tan\theta$ for a suitable value of θ to show that π lies between 3 and $2\sqrt{3}$.

2. What is the value of the limit $\lim_{\theta \to 0} \dfrac{\sin\theta°}{\theta}$?

3. Differentiate the following with respect to x:

   a) $-\sin x$, b) $-\cos x$, c) $\sin 4x$, d) $2\cos 3x$,
   e) $\sin\frac{1}{2}\pi x$, f) $\cos 3\pi x$, g) $\cos(2x - 1)$, h) $5\sin(3x + \frac{1}{4}\pi)$,
   i) $\cos(\frac{1}{2}\pi - 5x)$, j) $-\sin(\frac{1}{4}\pi - 2x)$, k) $-\cos(\frac{1}{2}\pi + 2x)$, l) $\sin\left(\frac{1}{2}\pi(1 + 2x)\right)$.

4. Differentiate the following with respect to x.

   a) $\sin^2 x$, b) $\cos^2 x$, c) $\cos^3 x$, d) $5\sin^2 \frac{1}{2}x$,
   e) $\cos^4 2x$, f) $\sin x^2$, g) $7\cos 2x^3$, h) $\sin^2(\frac{1}{2}x - \frac{1}{3}\pi)$,
   i) $\cos^3 2\pi x$, j) $\sin^3 x^2$, k) $\sin^2 x^2 + \cos^2 x^2$, l) $\cos^2 \frac{1}{2}x$.

5. Show that $\dfrac{d}{dx}\sec x = \sec x\tan x$, $\dfrac{d}{dx}\operatorname{cosec} x = -\operatorname{cosec} x\cot x$ and $\dfrac{d}{dx}\cot x = -\operatorname{cosec}^2 x$.

6. Differentiate the following with respect to x:

   a) $\sec 2x$ b) $\operatorname{cosec} 3x$, c) $\sec(x - \frac{1}{2}\pi)$, d) $\cot(3x - \frac{1}{6}\pi)$,
   e) $\tan(3x + \frac{1}{5}\pi)$, f) $\operatorname{cosec}(\frac{1}{4}\pi - 2x)$, g) $\tan(6x - \frac{1}{6}\pi)$, h) $\cot(\frac{1}{3}\pi - 5x)$.

7. By writing $\cos\theta = \cos 2(\frac{1}{2}\theta)$, show that $\cos\theta \geq 1 - \frac{1}{2}\theta^2$ for θ.

8.   a) Find the equation of the tangent where $x = \frac{1}{3}\pi$ on the curve $y = \sin x$.

   b) Find the equation of the normal where $x = \frac{1}{4}\pi$ on the curve $y = \sec x$.

   c) Find the equation of the tangent where $x = \frac{1}{2}\pi$ on the curve $y = 3\sin^2 2x$.

   d) Find the equation of the tangent where $x = \pi$ on the curve $y = x\sin x$.

9. Find any stationary points in the interval $0 \leq x < 2\pi$ on each of the following curves, and classify them:

   a) $y = \sin x + \cos x$, b) $y = x + \sin x$, c) $y = \sin^2 x + 2\cos x$,
   d) $y = \cos 2x + x$, e) $y = \sec x + \operatorname{cosec} x$, f) $y = \cos 2x - 2\sin x$.

10. Consider the function $f_a(x) = \sin x \cos(a-x) + \cos x \sin(a-x)$. Calculate $f'_x(a)$ using the product rule. What is the value of $f_a(0)$? What can you deduce from this result?

11. Show that $\frac{d}{dx}\left(2\cos^2 x\right)$, $\frac{d}{dx}\left(-2\sin^2 x\right)$ and $\frac{d}{dx}\cos 2x$ are all the same. Why?

12. Find $\frac{d}{dx}\sin^2(x+\frac{\pi}{4})$, and write your answer in its simplest form.

13. Find whether the tangent to $y = \cos x$ at $x = \frac{5}{6}\pi$ cuts the y-axis above or below the origin.

14. Show that, if $y = \sin nx$, where n is constant, then $\frac{d^2y}{dx^2} = -n^2 y$. What can you deduce about the shape of the graph of $y = \sin nx$? Give a more general equation which has the same property.

15. Calculate $\frac{d^2}{dx^2}\sec x$; write your answer as simply as possible.

16. Differentiate the following with respect to x:

   a) $x^3(\sin x + 1)$,　　b) $\sin x \cos x$,　　c) $x \cos x$,　　d) $x^2(\sin x + \cos x)$,

   e) $x\sin^2 x$,　　f) $x^2 \sin^3 2x$,　　g) $\sin^4 2x \cos^3 5x$,　　h) $x^3 \sec^2 x$.

   i) $\dfrac{\sin x}{x}$,　　j) $\dfrac{x}{\sin x}$,　　k) $\left(\dfrac{x}{\sin x}\right)^2$,　　l) $\dfrac{\cos x}{\sqrt{x}}$,

   m) $\dfrac{1}{\tan x + 1}$,　　n) $\dfrac{1}{\sec x + \tan x}$,　　o) $\dfrac{\tan x}{1 + \sec x}$,　　p) $\dfrac{x\sin x}{\tan x + 2}$.

17*. If $y = \sin^{-1} x$ for $-1 \le x \le 1$, calculate $\dfrac{dx}{dy}$ in terms of y, and hence determine $\dfrac{dy}{dx}$.

18*. A right circular cone has semi-vertical angle θ and slant length R.

   a) Show that the volume of the cone is given by the expression
   $$\tfrac{1}{3}\pi R^3 \sin^2\theta \cos\theta .$$

   b) Find the maximum (exact) value of this volume.

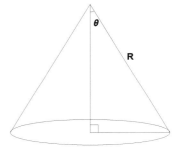

Figure 15.7

19*. An isosceles triangle ABC is inscribed in a circle of radius r. If the angle A is 2θ,

   a) Show that the perimeter of the triangle is $4r\cos\theta + 2r\sin 2\theta$.

   b) Find the greatest (exact) value of the perimeter. What sort of triangle is ABC when the perimeter is largest?

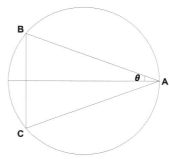

Figure 15.8

15.5　Differentiating Exponentials And Logarithms

15.5.1.　THE RATE OF CHANGE OF AN EXPONENTIAL FUNCTION

In Chapter 14 we considered exponential functions. We now need to understand the behaviour of the derivatives of these functions.

If we consider the graph of $y = a^x$, and draw some tangents, we notice some properties of their gradients:

- Provided that $a > 1$, all gradients are positive.

- The gradients increase as we move from left to right along the graph.

- The gradient tends towards 0 as we head off to infinity to the left, and tend to infinity as we head off to infinity to the right.

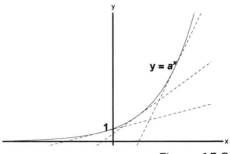

Figure 15.9

In short, the derivative function of a^x has properties which are very similar to those of a^x itself. We need to put detail on this idea. Again, some first principles differentiation is what we need.

Comparing the values of the function $y = a^x$ at points x and $x + \delta x$ as usual, we obtain that

$$\delta y = a^{x+\delta x} - a^x = a^x\left(a^{\delta x} - 1\right)$$

so that

$$\frac{\delta y}{\delta x} = a^x \times \frac{a^{\delta x} - 1}{\delta x}.$$

If we consider the constant

$$K_a = \lim_{\delta x \to 0} \frac{a^{\delta x} - 1}{\delta x},$$

which depends only upon a, and not upon x, we have shown that

$$\frac{d}{dx}a^x = K_a \times a^x, \qquad x \in \mathbb{R}.$$

Key Fact 15.7 The Rate Of Change Of An Exponential Function

The rate of change, or derivative, of an exponential function is a multiple of that function.

What can we say about the constant K_a? We can obtain a good estimate of K_a for different values of a by estimating it by $\frac{a^h-1}{h}$ for small h; $h = 10^{-7}$ works fairly well! If we do this, we obtain the following table of values (to 3 decimal places):

a	0.2	0.5	1	1.5	2	2.5	3	4	6
K_a	−1.609	−0.693	0	0.405	0.693	0.916	1.099	1.386	1.792

Plotting these points shows an intriguing relationship between a and K_a. It appears that K_a behaves like a logarithm of a.

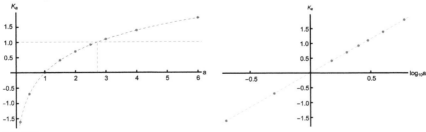

Figure 15.10

Plotting K_a against $\log_{10} a$ confirms this; the transformed points fit on a straight line through the origin, and so K_a is a constant multiple of $\log_{10} a$.

Of course, these calculations have all been performed based on approximate data, but they are suggestive. We need to investigate further.

15.5.2. THE NUMBER e

We have observed that exponential functions have the property that they are proportional to their rates of change. Mathematicians like formulae that are neat and tidy. If there is a way to remove unnecessary constants, they take it. That was one of the reasons for choosing radians as the preferred unit of angle; formulae for differentiation became simple.

We are then naturally drawn to finding the base (let us call it e) for which $K_e = 1$, so that the rate of change of e^x is not just proportional to, but is in fact equal to, itself. The graphs in Figure 15.10 give us confidence that such a base exists, and an approximation to its value. The gradient of the graph of K_a against $\log_{10} a$ is 2.302, and so our estimate for $\log_{10} e$ is $\frac{1}{2.302}$, and hence $e \approx 2.7185$. Given the approximate nature of our data, this is not a bad estimate.

In fact $e = 2.7182818284590....$ It is one of those magical numbers in mathematics, like π. It appears in a wide variety of unexpected places in the subject, which would be much duller without it. Like π, it is irrational. Unlike π, it is easy to calculate to a high degree of accuracy, since

$$e = \sum_{n=0}^{\infty} \frac{1}{n!} = 1 + \frac{1}{1!} + \frac{1}{2!} + \frac{1}{3!} + \cdots .$$

Since $n!$ becomes very large quickly, not many terms of this series are needed to find an accurate formula for e.

> **Key Fact 15.8** The Number e
>
> The irrational number $e = 2.7182818284590...$ is the number such that the exponential function e^x is equal to its own derivative:
>
> $$\frac{d}{dx} e^x = e^x .$$

Example 15.5.1. *Find the derivatives of the following functions:*

a) e^{1+x},   b) e^{-x^2},   c) xe^{-x},   d) $e^{2x} \sec x$,   e) $\frac{e^x}{1+e^x}$.

(a) Using the chain rule, the derivative of e^{1+x} is e^{1+x} (alternatively $e^{1+x} = e \times e^x$, and so its derivative is $e \times e^x = e^{1+x}$).

(b) Using the chain rule, $\frac{d}{dx} e^{-x^2} = -2xe^{-x^2}$.

(c) By the product rule, $\frac{d}{dx} xe^{-x} = 1 \times e^{-x} + x \times (-e^{-x}) = (1-x)e^{-x}$.

(d) By the product rule, $\frac{d}{dx} e^{2x} \sec x = 2e^{2x} \sec x + e^{2x} \sec x \tan x = e^{2x} \sec x (2 + \tan x)$.

(e) Using the quotient rule, $\frac{d}{dx} \frac{e^x}{1+e^x} = \frac{e^x \times (1+e^x) - e^x \times e^x}{(1+e^x)^2} = \frac{e^x}{(1+e^x)^2}$.

Since any positive number b can be written as e^k for some real number k, we see that any function of the form b^x can be written in the form e^{kx} for some real number k. Thus exponential functions can be thought of as functions of the form ae^{kx}. Exponential functions for which $k > 0$ are called **positive**, while exponential functions with $k < 0$ are called **negative**.

Example 15.5.2. *Prove that $e^x \geq 1 + x$ for all $x \geq 0$.*

The function $f(x) = e^x - 1 - x$ has $f'(x) = e^x - 1$. Since $e^x \geq 1$ for all $x \geq 0$, $f'(x) \geq 0$ for all $x \geq 0$, and hence $f(x)$ is an increasing function for $x \geq 0$. Since $f(0) = 0$, it follows that $f(x) \geq 0$ for all $x \geq 0$, which is what we need.

Food For Thought 15.3

We sometimes need to compare the 'size' of exponential and other functions; which of e^x and x^2 increases towards infinity faster as x tends to infinity, for example? The key fact to remember is that positive exponentials always 'beat' polynomials; they increase towards infinity much faster. As an example of this, we note that

$$e^x = e^{\frac{1}{3}x + \frac{1}{3}x + \frac{1}{3}x} \geq (1 + \tfrac{1}{3}x)^3 \geq \tfrac{1}{27}x^3$$

for all $x > 0$, so that $0 \leq x^2 e^{-x} \leq 27x^{-1}$ for all $x > 0$, and hence $x^2 e^{-x}$ tends to 0 as x tends to infinity; e^x has definitely 'beaten' x^2.

Example 15.5.3. *Find the equation of the tangent to the curve $y = e^x$ at the point $(0, 1)$.*

Since $\dfrac{dy}{dx} = e^x$, the gradient at this point is 1, and so the tangent has equation $y - 1 = 1(x - 0)$, or $y = x + 1$.

Note that Example 15.5.2 shows that the exponential curve $y = e^x$ always lies above the tangent at 0 for all positive x. The graph on the right shows that this is true for all real x. In fact, the curve $y = e^x$ lies above **all** of its tangents.

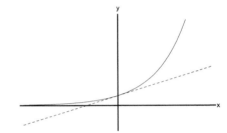

Figure 15.11

Example 15.5.4. *Find and classify the turning points of the function $f(x) = (x^2 - 3x)e^{-\frac{1}{2}x}$, and hence sketch the function $y = (x^2 - 3x)e^{-\frac{1}{2}x}$ for $x \geq 0$.*

Since

$$f'(x) = (2x - 3)e^{-\frac{1}{2}x} + (x^2 - 3x) \times \left(-\tfrac{1}{2}e^{-\frac{1}{2}x}\right) = -\tfrac{1}{2}(x^2 - 7x + 6)e^{-\frac{1}{2}x} = -\tfrac{1}{2}(x - 1)(x - 6)e^{-\frac{1}{2}x}$$

the turning points of $f(x)$ occur at $(1, -2e^{-\frac{1}{2}})$ and $(6, 18e^{-3})$. Since $f'(x)$ is negative for $x < 1$ and $x > 6$, and positive for $1 < x < 6$, the turning point at 1 is a minimum, while the turning point at 6 is a maximum.

The function $f(x)$ has zeros at $x = 0, 3$. Since positive exponentials 'beat' quadratics, $f(x)$ tends to 0 as x tends to infinity. We can produce the sketch:

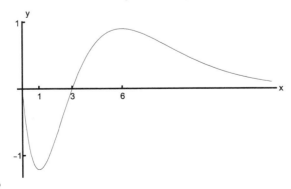

Figure 15.12

EXERCISE 15E

1. Differentiate each of the following functions with respect to x:

   a) e^{3x},

   b) e^{-x},

   c) $3e^{2x}$,

   d) $-4e^{-4x}$,

   e) e^{3x+4},

   f) e^{3-2x},

   g) e^{1-x},

   h) $3e \times e^{2+4x}$,

   i) e^{x^2},

   j) $e^{-\frac{1}{2}x^2}$,

   k) $e^{\frac{1}{x}}$,

   l) $e^{\sqrt{x}}$.

2. Find, in terms of e, the gradients of the tangents to the following curves for the given values of x:

   a) $y = 3e^x$ when $x = 2$,

   b) $y = 2e^{-x}$ when $x = -1$,

   c) $y = x - e^{2x}$ when $x = 0$,

   d) $y = e^{6-2x}$ when $x = 3$.

3. Find the equations of the tangents to the given curves for the given values of x:

   a) $y = e^x$ where $x = -1$,

   b) $y = 2x - e^{-x}$ where $x = 0$,

   c) $y = x^2 + 2e^{2x}$ where $x = 2$,

   d) $y = e^{-2x}$ where $x = 3$.

4. Use the chain rule to differentiate:

   a) $y = 2e^{x^2+x+1}$,

   b) $y = 3\left(e^{-x} + 1\right)^5$,

   c) $y = e^{\sqrt{1-x^2}}$.

5. Given that $y = \frac{5}{1+e^{3x}}$ find the value of $\frac{dy}{dx}$ when $x = 0$.

6. Find any stationary points of the following graphs, and classify them:

   a) $y = 2 - e^x$,

   b) $y = e^2x - e^x$,

   c) $y = x^2 e^{-x^2}$.

7. Sketch the curve of $y = xe^{-\frac{1}{2}x^2}$ for $x \in \mathbb{R}$.

8. Differentiate the following with respect to x:

   a) xe^x,

   b) $e^{x^2}\sec x$,

   c) $x\cos xe^{2x}$,

   d) $e^{-x}\sin x$,

   e) $(x^2 + 3)e^x$,

   f) $x^2(2 + e^x)$,

   g) $x^3 e^{2x}$,

   h) $x\sqrt{e^x + 1}$,

   i) $e^x\sqrt{5x^2 + 2}$,

   j) $e^{ax}\cos(bx + \frac{1}{2}\pi)$,

   k) $\frac{e^x - e^{-x}}{e^x + e^{-x}}$,

   l) e^{e^x},

   m) $\frac{e^x + 5x}{e^x - 2}$,

   n) $\frac{e^x}{2x + 1}$,

   o) $e^{\tan 2x}$,

   p) $e^{\cos^2 3x}$.

9. Find the equations of tangents to the following curves at the given points.

   a) $y = x^3 e^{-2x}$ where $x = 0$,

   b) $y = xe^{\sin x}$ where $x = \pi$,

   c) $y = \frac{e^x}{e^x + 1}$ where $x = 2$.

10. Find the turning points of the function $f(x) = e^x \sin x$ for $x > 0$ and classify them.

11*. Find the x-coordinates of the stationary points on the curve $y = x^n e^{-x}$, where n is a positive integer. Determine the nature of these stationary points, distinguishing between the cases when n is odd and when n is even.

12*. Find the equation of the tangent to the curve $y = e^x$ at the point where $x = a$ for some constant $a \in \mathbb{R}$. Prove that the whole of the graph of $y = e^x$ lies above the tangent.

13*. Suppose that a function $E : \mathbb{R} \to \mathbb{R}$ has the property that $E(0) = 1$ and $E'(x) = E(x)$. For any $a \in \mathbb{R}$ let f_a be the function $F_a(x) = E(x)E(a - x)$.

   a) What is $f_a'(x)$?

   b) What is $f_a(0)$?

   c) Deduce that $E(x + y) = E(x)E(y)$ for all $x, y \in \mathbb{R}$.

15.5.3. Natural Logarithms

Having introduced the exponential function e^x and the base e, we need to consider its inverse function, the logarithm $\log_e$ to the base e. This logarithm is called the **natural logarithm**, and is denoted $\ln x$.

Key Fact 15.9

The natural logarithm $\ln x = \log_e x$ has the following properties:

$$y = e^x \qquad \Leftrightarrow \qquad x = \ln y \qquad (x \in \mathbb{R}, y > 0)$$

In particular, note that $\ln 1 = 0$, $\ln e = 1$, and $\ln e^n = n$ for any n.

For Interest

The name **natural** logarithms says it all; this is the logarithm that mathematicians regard as important. Indeed, university-level mathematics textbooks probably do not mention logarithms to base 10 in any great detail, and the notation log is used simply to denote the natural logarithm, without the need the for ln notation!

We are now able to differentiate logarithms. It is worthwhile deriving this result using the graphical relationship between the functions $y = e^x$ and $y = \ln x$. They are, of course, mirror images of each other in the line $y = x$.

If we want to know the gradient of the line $y = \ln x$ at the point where $x = u$, which has coordinates (u, v), we note that the tangent to $y = \ln x$ is the mirror image in $y = x$ of the tangent to the curve $y = e^x$ at the point (v, u). If we compare these two tangents, then one has rise α and run β, while the other has rise β and run α. Thus while the gradient of one is $\frac{\alpha}{\beta}$, the gradient of the other is $\frac{\beta}{\alpha}$; the gradient of one tangent is the reciprocal of the gradient of the other.

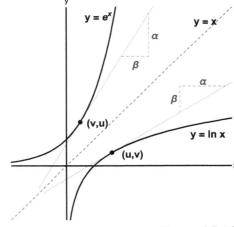

Figure 15.13

The derivative of the function $y = e^x$ at the point (v, u) is e^v, and hence the derivative of the function $y = \ln x$ at the point (u, v) is e^{-v}. But $v = \ln u$, so that $u = e^v$, and hence the derivative of $y = \ln x$ at the point (u, v) is u^{-1}.

Key Fact 15.10 Differentiating The Natural Logarithm

The derivative of the natural logarithm is x^{-1}, so that

$$\frac{d}{dx} \ln x = \frac{1}{x}, \qquad x > 0.$$

This argument could have been shortened to a use of the chain rule. If $y = \ln x$, then $x = e^y$, and hence $\frac{dx}{dy} = e^y$, and hence $\frac{dy}{dx} = e^{-y} = x^{-1}$.

Example 15.5.5. *Find the minimum value of the function* $f(x) = 2x - \ln x$ *for* $x > 0$.

Since $f'(x) = 2 - x^{-1}$, the only turning point occurs when $x = \frac{1}{2}$. Since $f''(x) = x^{-2}$ is always positive, this turning point is a minimum. The minimum value of f is $f(\frac{1}{2}) = 1 - \ln\frac{1}{2}$. But $\frac{1}{2} = 2^{-1}$, so that $\ln\frac{1}{2} = -\ln 2$, and it is a little neater to write the minimum as $1 + \ln 2$.

Example 15.5.6. *Find the derivatives of the following functions with respect to* x:

a) $\ln(3x + 1)$, b) $\ln 3x$, c) $\ln x^3$, d) $\ln\left(x + x^{-1}\right)$.

(a) The chain rule tells us that $\dfrac{d}{dx}\ln(3x + 1) = \dfrac{3}{3x + 1}$.

(b) The chain rule tells us that $\dfrac{d}{dx}\ln 3x = \dfrac{3}{3x} = \dfrac{1}{x}$. Alternatively, we could have observed that $\ln 3x = \ln 3 + \ln x$ before differentiating.

(c) This time, note that $\ln x^3 = 3\ln x$, so its derivative is $\frac{3}{x}$.

(d) We could write $x + x^{-1} = (x^2 + 1)x^{-1}$, so that $\ln\left(x + x^{-1}\right) = \ln(x^2 + 1) - \ln x$, and hence

$$\frac{d}{dx}\ln\left(x + x^{-1}\right) = \frac{2x}{x^2 + 1} - \frac{1}{x} = \frac{x^2 - 1}{x(x^2 + 1)},$$

or we could have used the chain rule.

15.5.4. DIFFERENT BASES

At the start of this section, we collected evidence which showed that $\dfrac{d}{dx}a^x = K_a \times a^x$ for some constant K_a, where $K_a \approx 2.302\log_{10} a$. This needs to be tidied up, and the meaning of 2.302 identified.

Recall that an exponential to any base can be written in terms of a different base, and that, in particular, we can write a^x in the form e^{kx} for some constant k. Indeed, since $a = e^{\ln a}$, it follows that

$$a^x = e^{(\ln a)x}$$

The chain rule then tells us that

$$\frac{d}{dx}a^x = \ln a \times e^{(\ln a)x} = \ln a \times a^x.$$

and hence $K_a = \ln a$. Thus K_a is in fact a natural logarithm, and our previous observation that $K_a \approx 2.302\log_{10} a$ reflects the fact $\ln a = \log_e a = \log_e 10\log_{10} a = \ln 10\log_{10} a$, and hence

$$\frac{\ln a}{\log_{10} a} = \ln 10 = 2.302585\ldots.$$

Just as we can now differentiate all exponentials, we can also differentiate all logarithms. Converting between logarithms to base a and natural logarithms,

$$\log_a x = \frac{\ln x}{\ln a}, \qquad x > 0,$$

and hence

$$\frac{d}{dx}\log_a = \frac{1}{x\ln a}, \qquad x > 0.$$

Key Fact 15.11 Differentiating General Exponentials and Logarithms

For any base $a > 0$,

$$\frac{d}{dx}a^x = \ln a \times a^x \qquad\qquad \frac{d}{dx}\log_a x = \frac{1}{x\ln a}.$$

EXERCISE 15F

1. Differentiate each of the following functions with respect to x:

   a) $\ln 2x$,

   b) $\ln(2x-1)$,

   c) $\ln(1-2x)$,

   d) $\ln x^2$,

   e) $\ln(a+bx)$,

   f) $\ln \frac{1}{x}$,

   g) $\ln \frac{1}{3x+1}$,

   h) $\ln \frac{2x+1}{3x-1}$,

   i) $3\ln x^{-2}$,

   j) $\ln(x(x+1))$,

   k) $\ln(x^2(x-1))$,

   l) $\ln(x^2+x-2)$.

2. Find the equations of the tangents to the following graphs for the given values of x:

   a) $y = \ln x$ where $x = \frac{1}{2}$,

   b) $y = \ln 2x$ where $x = \frac{1}{2}$,

   c) $y = \ln(-x)$ where $x = -\frac{1}{3}$,

   d) $y = \ln 3x$ where $x = e$.

3. Find any stationary values of the following curves and determine whether they are maxima or minima. Sketch the curves.

   a) $y = x - \ln x$,

   b) $y = \frac{1}{2}x^2 - \ln 2x$,

   c) $y = x^2 - \ln x^2$,

   d) $y = x^n - \ln x^n$ for $n \geq 1$.

4. Differentiate the following functions with respect to x:

   a) $y = \ln(1+x^3)$,

   b) $y = \frac{1}{2}\ln(2+x^4)$,

   c) $y = \ln(x^3+4x)$.

5. Prove that the tangent at $x = e$ to the curve with equation $y = \ln x$ passes through the origin.

6. Find the equation of the normal at $x = 2$ to the curve with equation $y = \ln(2x-3)$.

7. For each of the following functions $f(x)$, find the natural domain of f, calculate $f'(x)$, and find the regions where $f'(x)$ is positive and the regions where it is negative:

   a) $f(x) = \ln(x-2) + \ln(x-6)$,

   b) $f(x) = \ln(x-2) + \ln(6-x)$,

   c) $f(x) = \ln(2-x) + \ln(x-6)$.

8. Differentiate the following with respect to x:

   a) $x^2 \ln x$,

   b) $(4+3x^2)\ln x$,

   c) $\ln(\sin x)$,

   d) $e^x \ln x$,

   e) $x\ln(x^2+1)$,

   f) $\ln(\ln x)$,

   g) $\sqrt{x}\ln 2x$,

   h) $(4x+1)^3 \ln 3x$,

   i) $\ln(2\ln \sqrt{x})$,

   j) $\dfrac{\ln x}{x}$,

   k) $\dfrac{\ln(x^2+4)}{x}$,

   l) $\dfrac{\ln(3x+2)}{2x-1}$.

9. P is a point on the graph of $y = 2^{-x}$. The tangent to the curve $y = 2^{-x}$ at the point P meets the x-axis at the point B. Show that the length AB is equal to $\frac{1}{\ln 2} = \log_2 e$, irrespective of the position of P on the curve.

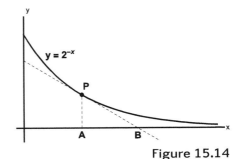

Figure 15.14

301

Chapter 15: Summary

- **The Chain Rule**

$$\frac{dy}{dx} = \frac{dy}{du} \times \frac{du}{dx}.$$

- **The Product Rule** If $y = uv$, then

$$y' = u'v + uv'.$$

- **The Quotient Rule** If $y = \frac{u}{v}$, then

$$y' = \frac{u'v - uv'}{v^2},$$

- **Trigonometric Functions**

$$\frac{d}{dx}\sin x = \cos x \qquad\qquad \frac{d}{dx}\cos x = -\sin x$$

$$\frac{d}{dx}\tan x = \sec^2 x \qquad\qquad \frac{d}{dx}\sec x = \sec x \tan x$$

$$\frac{d}{dx}\cot x = -\operatorname{cosec}^2 x \qquad\qquad \frac{d}{dx}\operatorname{cosec} x = -\operatorname{cosec} x \cot x$$

- **Exponential Functions** With respect to the base $e = 2.718281828459\ldots$, we write $\ln x$ for the natural logarithm $\log_e x$, and

$$\frac{d}{dx}e^x = e^x \qquad\qquad \frac{d}{dx}\ln x = \frac{1}{x}$$

With respect to general bases,

$$\frac{d}{dx}a^x = \ln a \times a^x \qquad\qquad \frac{d}{dx}\ln_a x = \frac{1}{x \ln a}$$

Review Exercises 5

1. By considering the graph of $y = \cos x$, or otherwise, express the following in terms of $\cos x$:

   a) $\cos(360° - x)$,   b) $\cos(x + 180°)$.   (OCR)

2. Solve the following equations for θ, giving your answers in the interval $0° \leq \theta \leq 360°$:

   a) $\tan \theta = 0.4$,   b) $\sin 2\theta = 0.4$.   (OCR)

3. Solve the equation $3 \cos 2x = 2$, giving all the solutions in the interval $0° \leq x \leq 180°$ correct to 1 decimal place.   (OCR)

4. Find all values of θ, $0° \leq \theta \leq 360°$, for which $2 \cos(\theta + 30°) = 1$.   (OCR)

5.   a) Express $\sin 2x + \cos(90° - 2x)$ in terms of a single trigonometric function.

     b) Hence, or otherwise, find all values of x in the interval $0° \leq x \leq 360°$ for which $\sin 2x + \cos(90° - 2x) = -1$.   (OCR)

6. Find the least positive value (in degrees) of the angle A for which:

   a) $\sin A = 0.2$ and $\cos A < 0$,   b) $\tan A = -0.5$ and $\sin A < 0$,

   c) $\cos A = \sin A < 0$,   d) $\sin A = -0.2275$ and $A > 360°$.

7. Prove the following identities:

   a) $\frac{1}{\sin \theta} - \sin \theta \equiv \frac{\cos \theta}{\tan \theta}$,   b) $\frac{1 - \sin \theta}{\cos \theta} \equiv \frac{\cos \theta}{1 + \sin \theta}$,

   c) $\frac{1}{\tan \theta} + \tan \theta \equiv \frac{1}{\sin \theta \cos \theta}$,   d) $\frac{1 - 2 \sin^2 \theta}{\cos \theta + \sin \theta} \equiv \cos \theta - \sin \theta$.

8. For each of the following functions, determine the maximum and minimum values of y and the least positive values of x (in degrees) at which these occur:

   a) $y = 1 + \cos 2x$,   b) $y = 5 - 4 \sin(x + 30°)$,

   c) $y = 29 - 20 \sin(3x - 45°)$,   d) $y = 8 - 3 \cos^2 x$,

   e) $y = \frac{12}{3 + \cos x}$,   f) $y = \frac{60}{1 + \sin^2(2x - 15)°}$.

9. Solve the following equations for θ, giving solutions in the interval $0° \leq \theta \leq 360°$:

   a) $\sin \theta = \tan \theta$,   b) $2 - 2 \cos^2 \theta = \sin \theta$,

   c) $\tan^2 \theta - 2 \tan \theta = 1$,   d) $\sin 2\theta - \sqrt{3} \cos 2\theta = 0$.

10. An oscillating particle has displacement y metres, where y is given by $y = a \sin(kt + \alpha)°$, where a is measured in metres, t is measured in seconds and k and α are constants. The time for a complete oscillation is T seconds. Find:

    a) k in terms of T,

    b) the number, in terms of k, of complete oscillations per second.

303

11. A simple model of the tides in a harbour on the south coast of Cornwall assumes that they are caused by the attractions of the sun and the moon. The magnitude of the attraction of the moon is assumed to be nine times the magnitude of the attraction of the sun. The period of the sun's effect is taken to be 360 days and that of the moon is 30 days. A model for the height, h metres, of the tide (relative to a mark fixed on the harbour wall), at t days, is
$$h = A\cos\alpha t + B\cos\beta t,$$
where the term $A\cos\alpha t$ is the effect due to the sun, and the term $B\cos\beta t$ is the effect due to the moon. Given that $h = 2$ when $t = 0$ (at which time the sun's and the moon's pulls are both at their greatest) determine the values of A, B, α and β. (OCR, adapt.)

12. Establish the identity
$$\tan^{-1} x + \tan^{-1} x^{-1} \equiv \tfrac{1}{2}\pi \text{ or } -\tfrac{1}{2}\pi.$$
When does each option occur?

13. Give the domains and the ranges of the following functions:
    a) $2\sin^{-1} x - 4$,
    b) $2\sin^{-1}(x - 4)$.

14. a) Starting from the identity $\sin^2\phi + \cos^2\phi \equiv 1$, prove that $\sec^2\phi \equiv 1 + \tan^2\phi$.
    b) Given that $180° < \phi < 270°$ and that $\tan\phi = \frac{7}{24}$, find the exact value of $\sec\phi$. (OCR)

15. Solve the equation $\tan x = 3\cot x$, giving all solutions between $0°$ and $360°$. (OCR)

16. a) State the value of $\sec^2 x - \tan^2 x$.
    b) The angle A is such that $\sec A + \tan A = 2$. Show that $\sec A - \tan A = \tfrac{1}{2}$, and hence find the exact value of $\cos A$. (OCR)

17. Given that $\sin\theta = 4\sin(\theta - 60°)$, show that $2\sqrt{3}\cos\theta = \sin\theta$. Hence find the value of θ such that $0° < \theta < 180°$. (OCR)

18. Solve the equation $\sin 2\theta - \cos^2\theta = 0$, giving values of θ in the interval $0° < \theta < 360°$. (OCR, adapt.)

19. a) Prove the identity $\cot\tfrac{1}{2}A - \tan\tfrac{1}{2}A \equiv 2\cot A$.
    b) By choosing a suitable numerical value for A, show that $\tan 15°$ is a root of the quadratic equation $t^2 + 2\sqrt{3}t - 1 = 0$. (OCR)

20. Express $\sin\theta + \sqrt{3}\cos\theta$ in the form $R\sin(\theta + \alpha)$, where $R > 0$ and $0° < \alpha < 90°$. Hence find all values of θ, for $0° < \theta < 360°$, which satisfy the equation $\sin\theta + \sqrt{3}\cos\theta = 1$. (OCR)

21. The function f is defined for all real degrees x by $f(x) = \cos x - \sqrt{3}\sin x$.
    a) Express $f(x)$ in the form $R\cos(x + \phi)$, where $R > 0$ and $0° < \phi < 90°$.
    b) Solve the equation $|f(x)| = 1$, giving your answers in the interval $0° \le x \le 360°$. (OCR)

22. a) Express $12\cos x + 9\sin x$ in the form $R\cos(x - \theta)$, where $R > 0$ and $0 < \theta < \tfrac{1}{2}\pi$.
    b) Find the smallest positive root α of the equation $12\cos x + 9\sin x = 14$, giving your answer correct to three decimal places. (OCR)

23. Express $2\cos x + \sin x$ in the form $R\cos(x - \alpha)$, where $R > 0$ and $0° < \alpha < 90°$. Hence:
    a) solve the equation $2\cos x + \sin x = 1$, giving all solutions between $0°$ and $360°$,
    b) find the exact range of values of the constant k for which the equation $2\cos x + \sin x = k$ has real solutions for x. (OCR)

24. If $\cos^{-1}(3x + 2) = \tfrac{1}{3}\pi$, find the value of x.

25. a) Express $5\sin x + 12\cos x$ in the form $R\sin(x + \theta)$, where $R > 0$ and $0° < \theta < 90°$.
    b) Hence, or otherwise, find the maximum and minimum values of $f(x)$ where $f(x) = \frac{30}{5\sin x + 12\cos x + 17}$. State also the values of x, in the range $0° < x < 360°$, at which they occur. (OCR)

26. Express $3\cos x - 4\sin x$ in the form $R\cos(x+\alpha)$, where $R > 0$ and $0° < \alpha < 90°$. Hence:

    a) solve the equation $3\cos x - 4\sin x = 2$, giving all solutions between $0°$ and $360°$,

    b) find the greatest and least values, as x varies, of the expression $\frac{1}{3\cos x - 4\sin x + 8}$. (OCR)

27. a) Find the equation of the straight line joining the points $A\,(0, 1.5)$ and $B\,(3, 0)$.

    b) Express $\sin\theta + 2\cos\theta$ in the form $r\sin(\theta + \alpha)$, where r is a positive number and α is an acute angle.

    c) The figure shows a map of a moor-land. The units of the coordinates are kilometres, and the y-axis points due north. A walker leaves her car somewhere on the straight road between A and B. She walks in a straight line for a distance of 2 km to a monument at the origin O. While she is looking at it the fog comes down, so that she cannot see the way back to her car. She needs to work out the bearing on which she should walk.
    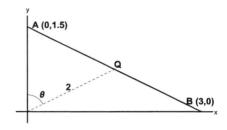
    Write down the coordinates of a point Q which is 2 km from O on a bearing of θ. Show that, for Q to be on the road between A and B, θ must satisfy the equation $2\sin\theta + 4\cos\theta = 3$. Calculate the value of θ between $0°$ and $90°$ which satisfies this equation. (OCR)

28. The figure shows the graphs of

    $$y = 5\cos 2x + 2, \qquad y = \cos x$$

    for $0° \le x \le 180°$.

    a) Find the coordinates of the points A and B where the graph of $y = 5\cos 2x + 2$ meets the x-axis.
    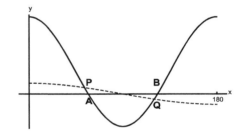

    b) By solving a trigonometric equation, find the coordinates of the points P and Q. (OCR)

29*. Show that $\tan 3\theta \equiv \frac{3\tan\theta - \tan^3\theta}{1 - 3\tan^2\theta}$.

    Given that $\theta = \cos^{-1}\frac{2}{\sqrt{5}}$ and $0 < \theta < \frac{1}{2}\pi$, show that $\tan 3\theta = \frac{11}{2}$.

    Hence, or otherwise, find all solutions of the equations

    a) $\tan\left(3\cos^{-1}x\right) = \frac{11}{2}$,

    b) $\cos\left(\frac{1}{3}\tan^{-1}y\right) = \frac{2}{\sqrt{5}}$. (STEP)

30. Solve each of the following equations to find x in terms of a where $a > 0$ and $a \ne 100$:

    a) $a^x = 10^{2x+1}$,

    b) $2\log(2x) = 1 + \log a$. (OCR, adapt.)

31. Solve the equation $3^{2x} = 4^{2-x}$, giving your answer to three significant figures. (OCR)

32. The function f is given by $f(x) = \log_{10}(1+x)$, where $x \in \mathbb{R}$ and $x > -1$. Express the definition of f^{-1} in a similar form. (OCR, adapt.)

33. Find the root of the equation $10^{2-2x} = 2 \times 10^{-x}$, giving your answer exactly in terms of logarithms. (OCR, adapt.)

34. Given the simultaneous equations

    $$2^x = 3^y, \qquad x + y = 1,$$

    show that $x = \dfrac{\log_{10} 3}{\log_{10} 6}$. (OCR, adapt.)

35. Express $\log_{10}\left(2\sqrt{10}\right) - \frac{1}{3}\log_{10} 0.8 - \log_{10}\left(\frac{10}{3}\right)$ in the form $c + \log d$ where c and d are rational numbers.

(OCR, adapt.)

36. Prove that $\log_b a \times \log_c b \times \log_a c = 1$, where a, b and c are positive numbers.

37. Prove that $\log\left(\frac{p}{q}\right) + \log\left(\frac{q}{r}\right) + \log\left(\frac{r}{q}\right) = 0$ for any positive numbers p, q and r. The logarithms can be taken to any base.

38. If a, b and c are positive numbers in geometric progression, show that (to any base) $\log a$, $\log b$ and $\log c$ are in arithmetic progression.

39. Express $\log_2(x + 2) - \log_2 x$ as a single logarithm. Hence solve the equation $\log_2(x + 2) - \log_2 x = 3$.

40. The strength of a radioactive source is said to 'decay exponentially'. Explain briefly what is meant by exponential decay, and illustrate your answer by means of a sketch-graph.

   After t years the strength S of a particular radioactive source, in appropriate units, is given by $S = 10000 \times 3^{-0.0014t}$. State the value of S when $t = 0$, and find the value of t when the source has decayed to one-half of its initial strength, giving your answer correct to 3 significant figures.

(OCR, adapt.)

41. Students who revise more for a particular examination tend to perform better in that examination. The study habits and test scores of a group of 100 students were compared. It is believed that the relationship between the amount of time, x hours, spent on revision and the score, y %, obtained by the student is of the form $y = kx^n$, where k and n are constants.

   A plot of $\log_{10} y$ against $\log_{10} x$ is drawn for these 100 students. It is found that the straight line of best fit for this data passes through the points $(0, 0.415)$ and $(5, 4.915)$. Find the values of k and n.

   Estimate the percentage score obtained by a student who revises for 40 hours. Give your answer to the nearest percentage point.

42. An experiment was conducted to discover how the mass of a sample of mould varied with time. The following data represents a series of observations, with y g of mould present t days after the start of the experiment.

t	1	2	3	4	5
y	2.40	2.88	3.46	4.15	4.98

   a) A suggested model for these data is given by $y = a + bt^2$, where a and b are constants. Use the results for $y = 1$ and $y = 5$ to find estimates of a and b, correct to one decimal place. Calculate the amount of mould predicted by this model 3 days after the start of the experiment.

   b) A second model is given by $y = kc^t$, where k and c are constants. By plotting $\log_{10} y$ against t, estimate the values of k and c.

   c) Compare the fit of the two models to the data.

43*. Do not use a calculator for this question!

   To nine decimal places, $\log_{10} 2 = 0.301029996$ and $\log_{10} 3 = 0.477121255$.

   a) Calculate $\log_{10} 5$ and $\log_{10} 6$ to three decimal places. By taking logarithms, or otherwise, show that
   $$5 \times 10^{47} < 3^{100} < 6 \times 10^{47}.$$
   Hence write down the first digit of 3^{100}.

   b) Find the first digit of the following numbers: 2^{1000}, 2^{10000} and 2^{100000}.

(STEP)

44. Differentiate $(4x - 1)^{20}$ with respect to x.

(OCR)

45. Find the equation of the tangent to the curve $y = (x^2 - 5)^6$ at the point $(2, 1)$.

46. Find the equation of the normal to the curve $y = \sqrt{2x^2 + 1}$ at the point $(2, 3)$.

47. The radius of a circular disc is increasing at a constant rate of 0.003 cm s^{-1}. Find the rate at which the area is increasing when the radius is 20 cm.

(OCR)

48. Find the equation of the tangent to the curve $y = \frac{50}{(2x-1)^2}$ at the point $(3, 2)$, giving your answer in the form $ax + by + c = 0$, where a, b and c are integers. (OCR)

49. Differentiate $\sqrt{x + \frac{1}{x}}$ with respect to x. (OCR)

50. Using differentiation, find the equation of the tangent at the point $(2, 1)$ on the curve with equation $y = \sqrt{x^2 - 3}$. (OCR)

51. A curve has equation $y = \frac{1}{12}(3x + 1)^4 - 8x$.

    a) Show that there is a stationary point where $x = \frac{1}{3}$ and determine whether this stationary point is a maximum or a minimum.

    b) At a particular point of the curve, the equation of the tangent is $48x + 3y + c = 0$. Find the value of the constant c. (OCR)

52. If a hemispherical bowl of radius 6 cm contains water to a depth of x cm, the volume of the water is $\frac{1}{3}\pi x^2(18 - x)$. Water is poured into the bowl at a rate of 3 cm^3 s^{-1}. Find the rate at which the water level is rising when the depth is 2 cm.

53. A curve has equation $y = (x^2 - 1)^3 - 3(x^2 - 1)^2$. Find the coordinates of the stationary points and determine whether each is a minimum or a maximum. Sketch the curve.

54. The equation of a curve is $y = 2x^2 - \ln x$, where $x > 0$. Find by differentiation the x-coordinate of the stationary point on the curve, and determine whether this point is a maximum point or a minimum point. (OCR)

55. Find the coordinates of the stationary point of the curve $y = \ln(x^2 - 6x + 10)$ and show that this stationary point is a minimum.

56. a) Find the stationary value of $y = \ln x - x$, and deduce that $\ln x \leq x - 1$ for $x > 0$ with equality only when $x = 1$.

    b) Find the stationary value of $\ln x + x^{-1}$, and deduce that $\frac{x-1}{x} \leq \ln x$ for $x > 0$ with equality only when $x = 1$.

    c) By putting $x = \frac{z}{y}$ where $0 < y < z$, deduce Napier's inequality,

$$\frac{1}{z} < \frac{\ln z - \ln y}{z - y} < \frac{1}{y}.$$

57. Find the coordinates of the three stationary points of the curve $y = e^{x^2(x^2 - 18)}$.

58. Draw a sketch of the curve $y = e^{-2x} - 3x$. The curve crosses the x-axis at A $(a, 0)$ and the y-axis at B $(0, 1)$. O is the origin. Write down an equation satisfied by a.

    a) Show the tangent at A meets the y-axis at the point whose y-coordinate is $2ae^{-2a} + 3a$.

    b) Show that $\frac{d^2y}{dx^2} > 0$ and hence that $6a^2 + 3a < 1$.

    c) Show the tangent at B meets the x-axis at $(\frac{1}{5}, 0)$. Deduce that $\frac{1}{5} < a < \frac{1}{12}\sqrt{33} - \frac{1}{4}$. (OCR, adapt.)

59. Show that, if $x > 0$, x^n can be written as $e^{n \ln x}$. Differentiate this last expression by the chain rule, and deduce that $\frac{d}{dx}x^n = nx^{n-1}$ for any real number n.

60. A mobile consists of a bird with flapping wings suspended from the ceiling by two elastic strings. A small weight hangs below it. The weight is pulled down and then released. After t seconds, the distance, y cm, of the weight below its equilibrium position is modelled by the periodic function $y = 5\cos 2t + 10\sin t$.

    a) Verify that the (t, y) graph has a stationary point where $t = \frac{1}{6}\pi$.

    b) Show that all the stationary points of the graph correspond to solutions of the equation $\cos t(2\sin t - 1) = 0$. Find the other two solutions in the interval $0 \leq t \leq \pi$.

    c) State one limitation of the model. Explain why $y = e^{-kt}(5\cos 2t + 10\sin t)$, where k is a small constant, might give a better model. (OCR)

61. In this question $f(x) = \sin\frac{1}{2}x + \cos\frac{1}{3}x$.

    a) Find $f'(x)$.

    b) Find the values of $f(0)$ and $f'(0)$.

    c) State the periods of $\sin\frac{1}{2}x$ and $\cos\frac{1}{3}x$.

    d) Write down another value of x (not 0) for which $f(x) = f(0)$ and $f'(x) = f'(0)$.   (OCR)

62. The diagram shows a sketch, not to scale, of part of the graph of $y = f(x)$, where $f(x) = \sin x + \sin 2x$, and x is measured in radians.

    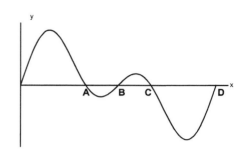

    a) Find, in terms of π, the x-coordinates of the points A, B, C and D, shown in the diagram, where the graph of f meets the positive x-axis.

    b) Show that $f(\pi - \theta)$ may be expressed as $\sin\theta - \sin 2\theta$, and show also that $f(\pi - \theta) + f(\pi + \theta) = 0$ for all values of θ.

    c) Differentiate $f(x)$, and hence show that the greatest value of $f(x)$, for $0 \le x \le 2\pi$, occurs when $\cos x = \frac{1}{8}(\sqrt{33} - 1)$.   (OCR)

63. a) Differentiate $x^3 \sin x$.

    b) Differentiate $\frac{x}{\sqrt{x+3}}$, simplifying your answer as far as possible.   (OCR)

64. Given that $y = xe^{-3x}$, find $\frac{dy}{dx}$. Hence find the coordinates of the stationary point on the curve $y = xe^{-3x}$.   (OCR)

65. Use appropriate rules of differentiation to find $\frac{dy}{dx}$ in each of the following cases: (OCR)

    a) $y = \sin 2x \cos 4x$,   b) $y = \frac{3x^2}{\ln x}$ for $x > 1$,   c) $y = \left(1 - \frac{1}{5}x\right)^{10}$.

66. Use differentiation to find the coordinates of the turning point on the curve whose equation is $y = \frac{4x+2}{\sqrt{x}}$.   (OCR)

67. A curve C has equation $y = \frac{\sin x}{x}$, where $x > 0$. Find $\frac{dy}{dx}$, and hence show that the x-coordinate of any stationary point of C satisfies the equation $x = \tan x$.   (OCR)

68. A curve has equation $y = \frac{x}{\sqrt{2x^2+1}}$. Show that $\frac{dy}{dx} = (2x^2 + 1)^{-\frac{3}{2}}$, and deduce that the curve has no turning points.   (OCR)

69. A length of channel of given depth d is to be made from a rectangular sheet of metal of width $2a$. The metal is to be bent in such a way that the cross-section $ABCD$ is as shown in the diagram, with $AB + BC + CD = 2a$ and with AB and CD each inclined to the line BC at an angle θ.

    Show that $BC = 2(a - d\operatorname{cosec}\theta)$, and that the area of the cross-section $ABCD$ is

    $$A = 2ad + d^2(\cot\theta - 2\operatorname{cosec}\theta).$$

    Show that the maximum value of A, as θ varies, is $d(2a - d\sqrt{3})$. By considering the length of BC, show that the cross-sectional area can only be made equal to this maximum value if $2d \le a\sqrt{3}$.

70*. Suppose that $a > 0$ and that $n \in \mathbb{N}$. Find the value of x for which $x^{n+1}e^{-ax}$ has its maximum value, and hence find a number M such that $0 \le x^n e^{-ax} < Mx^{-1}$ for all $x > 0$. Hence show that $x^n e^{-ax} \to 0$ as $x \to \infty$. Any positive exponential in x 'beats' any power of x.

71*. Prove that the rectangle of greatest perimeter which can be inscribed in a given circle is a square.

The result changes if, instead of maximising the sum of the sides of the rectangle, we seek to maximise the sum of the nth powers of the lengths of those sides, where $n \ge 2$. What happens if $n = 2$? What happens if $n = 3$? Justify your answers.

Differentiating Implicit And Parametric Equations

In this chapter we will learn to:

- understand how curves can be described implicitly or parametrically,
- calculate first and second derivatives of such curves,
- sketch graphs of simple cases of such curves.

16.1 Explicit Equations

All the graphs we have considered to so far have been **explicit**, in that they have had equations of the form
$$y = f(x)$$
for some function $f(x)$, possibly restricted to some domain. However, there are many interesting curves that cannot be expressed in this way, bit still need to be studied. Here are a few examples:

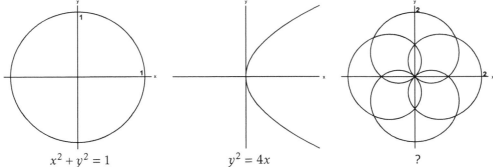

$$x^2 + y^2 = 1 \qquad\qquad y^2 = 4x \qquad\qquad ?$$

Figure 16.1

If we tried to write $x^2 + y^2 = 1$ explicitly, we would end up with something like $y = \pm\sqrt{1 - x^2}$. The $\pm$ term is what stops this being an explicit equation, since a function $f(x)$ can only take a single value, and y needs to be able to assume two values for all values of x between -1 and 1. An explicit equation like $y = \sqrt{1 - x^2}$ would only graph the top half of the curve, and not the whole circle. Similarly, the parabola $y^2 = 4x$ cannot be expressed as an explicit equation, since every positive value of x needs two values of y associated with it. The last curve is even worse; there are some values of x associated with two values of y, but other values of x associated with six or even ten values of y. Yet each of these curves have tangents and normals, and two of them achieve minimum and maximum values, that we need to be able to determine.

We need a new way of dealing with equations that cannot be expressed explicitly. Happily, there are two approaches.

16.2 Parametric Equations

Imagine a person P going round on a turntable of radius 1 unit, at a constant speed. Suppose that P starts at the x-axis and moves anticlockwise in such a way that the angle at the centre t seconds after starting is t radians.

311

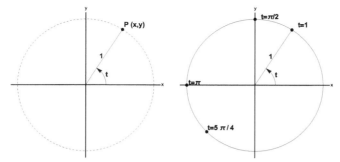

Figure 16.2

Where is P after t seconds? It is clear from Figure 16.2 that the coordinates of P are given by

$$x = \cos t, \ y = \sin t.$$

These equations allow you to find the position of P at any time, and they describe the path of P completely. The second diagram in Figure 16.2 shows the values of t at various points on the first revolution of the turntable. Notice that for each value of $0 \le t < 2\pi$ there is a unique point on the curve. However, the point P returns to its starting point every time t increases by 2π, and begins to repeat its steps. Mathematically, we note that the formulae for both x and y are periodic of period 2π, and so we only need to specify the curve for t in the region $0 \le t \le 2\pi$ to define the whole curve.

Key Fact 16.1 Parametric Equations

If $x = f(t)$ and $y = g(t)$, where f and g are functions of a variable t defined for some common domain of values of t, then the pair of equations $x = f(t)$ and $y = g(t)$ are called **parametric equations**, parametrised by the **parameter** t.

Although, as in the example above, t had the physical significance of time, it does not have to have any particular meaning.

Like any other curve, parametric curves can be drawn using graphical calculators and other graphing software. Let us investigate how much we can do without the benefit of such assistance.

Example 16.2.1. *A curve has parametric equations $x = \sin t, y = \sin 2t$, for values of t between 0 and 2π. Plot the curve, and indicate the points corresponding to values of t that are multiples of $\frac{1}{6}\pi$.*

We draw up a table of values.

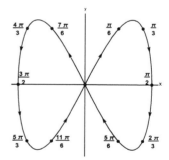

t	0	$\frac{1}{6}\pi$	$\frac{1}{3}\pi$	$\frac{1}{2}\pi$	$\frac{2}{3}\pi$	$\frac{5}{6}\pi$
x	0	0.5	0.866	1	0.866	0.5
y	0	0.866	0.866	0	-0.866	-0.866

t	π	$\frac{7}{6}\pi$	$\frac{4}{3}\pi$	$\frac{3}{2}\pi$	$\frac{5}{3}\pi$	$\frac{11}{6}\pi$	2π
x	0	-0.5	-0.866	-1	-0.866	-0.5	0
y	0	0.866	0.866	0	-0.866	-0.866	0

Figure 16.3

Figure 16.3 illustrates this curve, with the points from the table labelled with their t-values, except for the origin, that corresponds to $t = 0$, π and 2π. The arrows are not an essential part of the sketch, but they indicate the direction of increasing t around the curve, which can be helpful. It is clear that the curve repeats itself once t extends beyond the region $0 \le t \le 2\pi$.

16.2.1. CONVERTING PARAMETRIC TO CARTESIAN EQUATIONS

A curve that is described parametrically can sometimes also be described by a Cartesian equation (a single equation involving x and y alone), by eliminating the parameter from the two parametric equations.

Example 16.2.2. *Write the parametric equation $x = t^2, y = 2t$ in Cartesian form.*

We can write $t = \frac{1}{2}y$ and substitute this into the equation for x, obtaining $x = \frac{1}{4}y^2$, or $y^2 = 4x$. This is the second of the examples shown in Figure 16.1.

Often the goal of expressing a parametric equation in Cartesian form is achieved by solving one or both of the equations to express t as a function of x and y, and then substituting that expression back into one of the equations.

Example 16.2.3. *A curve C is given parametrically by the equations $x = t + \sqrt{t}, y = \sqrt[3]{t} - \sqrt{t}$. Find the Cartesian equation for C.*

Since $y^3 = t - \sqrt{t}$, we deduce that $t = \frac{1}{2}(x + y^3)$ and $\sqrt{t} = \frac{1}{2}(x - y^3)$. Thus we obtain the equation $\frac{1}{2}(x - y^3) = \sqrt{\frac{1}{2}(x + y^3)}$, or $(x - y^3)^2 = 2(x + y^3)$.

Trigonometric identities are often useful.

Example 16.2.4. *Let E be the curve given parametrically by $x = a\cos t, y = b\sin t$, where a and $b are constants and $0 \le t \le 2\pi$. Find the Cartesian equation of E.*

Since $x = a\cos t$ and $y = b\sin t$, $\frac{x}{a} = \cos t$ and $\frac{y}{b} = \sin t$. Since $\cos^2 t + \sin^2 t \equiv 1$, we obtain the equation

$$\frac{x^2}{a^2} + \frac{y^2}{b^2} = \left(\frac{x}{a}\right)^2 + \left(\frac{y}{b}\right)^2 = 1.$$

This is the equation of the ellipse shown on the right. If a and b are equal, this is a circle of radius a.

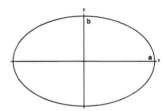

Figure 16.4

Example 16.2.5. *Show that the parametric curve given by $x = \cos 2t, y = \sin t$ for $-\frac{1}{2}\pi \le t \le \frac{1}{2}\pi$ is a portion of a parabola.*

Since $\cos 2t \equiv 1 - 2\sin^2 t$, this curve satisfies the Cartesian equation $x = 1 - 2y^2$, which is a parabola. Since $y = \sin t$, we must have $-1 \le y \le 1$, and so this curve is that portion of the parabola $x = 1 - 2y^2$ for which $-1 \le y \le 1$.
If we were to let t vary over the whole of $\mathbb{R}$, what would we see? The point corresponding to t would oscillate back and forth on this portion of the parabola, moving periodically from one end of the curve to the other and back again.

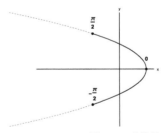

Figure 16.5

EXERCISE 16A

1. Find the coordinates of the point on the curve $x = 5t^2, y = 10t$ when:

   a) $t = 6$, b) $t = -1$.

2. Find the coordinates of the point on the curve $x = 1 - t^{-1}, y = 1 + t^{-1}$ when:

   a) $t = 3$, b) $t = -1$.

3. The parametric equations of a curve are $x = 2\cos t, y = 2\sin t$, for $0 \le t \le 2\pi$. What is the value of t at the point $(0, 2)$?

4. A curve is given by $x = 5\cos t, y = 2\sin t$ for $0 \le t \le 2\pi$. Find the value of t at the point $(-\frac{5}{2}, \sqrt{3})$.

5. Sketch the curve given by $x = t^2$, $y = \frac{1}{t}$ for $t > 0$.

6. Sketch the curve given by $x = 3\cos t, y = 2\sin t$ for $0 \le t \le 2\pi$.

7. Sketch the graph of $x = t^2, y = 6t$ for $-4 \le t \le 4$.

8. Sketch the locus given by $x = \cos^2 t, y = \sin^2 t$ for $0 \le t \le 2\pi$.

9. Find Cartesian equations for curves with these parametric equations:

   a) $x = t^2, y = \frac{1}{t}$,
   b) $x = 3t^2, y = 6t$,
   c) $x = 2\cos t, y = 2\sin t$,
   d) $x = \cos^2 t, y = \sin^2 t$,
   e) $x = \cos^3 t, y = \sin^3 t$,
   f) $x = 1 - \frac{1}{t}, y = 1 + \frac{1}{t}$,
   g) $x = 3t^2, y = 2t^3$,
   h) $x = 2t^2 - 1, y = 4 - 5t^2$,
   i) $x = \frac{t}{1+t}, y = \frac{2t+1}{1-t}$,
   j) $x = \tan t, y = \sec t$,
   k) $x = t^3, y = t^5$,
   l) $x = \tan 2x, y = \tan x$.

16.2.2. Differentiating In Parametric Form

When plotting the curve in Example 16.2.1, it would have been useful to know a few more facts. What are the four coordinates of the four turning points? To determine this, we would need to find the gradient of the function at various points.

Suppose that a curve is defined parametrically. How can we find the gradient at a point on the curve without first finding the Cartesian equation of the curve (which is not always possible)? Happily, there is a simple method for doing this.

Key Fact 16.2 Parametric Differentiation

If a curve $\mathcal{C}$ is given parametrically in terms of the parameter t, then the derivative of the curve at the point with parameter t is given by the formula

$$\frac{dy}{dx} = \frac{dy}{dt} \bigg/ \frac{dx}{dt} \, .$$

This result follows from a simple application of the chain rule:

$$\frac{dy}{dt} = \frac{dy}{dx} \times \frac{dx}{dt} \, .$$

For Interest

Using the chain rule here assumes that y can be written as a function of both t and x, and the whole point of working with a parametric equation is that it may not be possible to write y as a function of x. If we cannot find y as a function of x, how can we hope to calculate $\frac{dy}{dx}$?

The answer is that, while it may not be possible to write y as a function of x in a way which is true throughout the whole curve, it is possible to do this locally. Thus the circle $x = 5\cos t, y = 5\sin t$ can be written as $y = \sqrt{25 - x^2}$ when y is positive, and this would enable us to calculate $\frac{dy}{dx}$ at any point in the top half of the circle. On the other hand, we can describe the bottom half of the circle by the alternate function $y = -\sqrt{25 - x^2}$, and this enables us to calculate the derivative at any point in the lower half of the circle. Reasonably-behaved equations (and we shall only consider equations like this) can be written in explicit form locally, at least in theory. The chain rule works locally (to differentiate a function, we only need to know its behaviour close to the point where we want to calculate a derivative), and so all is well.

Example 16.2.6. *Use parametric differentiation to find the gradient at $t = 3$ on the parabola $x = t^2, y = 2t$.*

We see that $\frac{dx}{dt} = 2t$ and $\frac{dy}{dt} = 2$, and so $\frac{dy}{dx} = \frac{2}{2t} = t^{-1}$. When $t = 3$, the gradient is $\frac{1}{3}$.

Example 16.2.7. *Find the equation of the normal at* $(-8, 4)$ *to the curve which is given parametrically by* $x = t^3, y = t^2$.

We have $\frac{dx}{dt} = 3t^2$ and $\frac{dy}{dt} = 2t$, and hence $\frac{dy}{dx} = \frac{2}{3}t^{-1}$. At the point $(-8, 4)$ we have $t^3 = -8$ and $t^2 = 4$, and hence $t = -2$. The function has derivative $-\frac{1}{3}$ at this point, and hence the normal has gradient 3, and hence has equation $y - 4 = 3(x + 8)$, or $y = 3x + 28$.

Example 16.2.8. *A bicycle wheel of radius a rolls on flat horizontal ground. Sketch the path taken by a fixed point P on the wheel's rim.*

Suppose that the point P starts its motion in contact with the ground at the origin O. When the wheel has rolled so that the radius CP to the point P makes an angle θ with the downward vertical, then the fact that the wheel is rolling, and not slipping, on the ground means that the distance OX from O to the point of contact of the wheel with the ground is equal to the arc-length PX, which is $a\theta$. It is now easy to see that P has coordinates

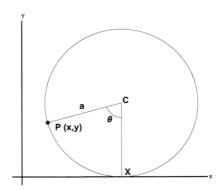

$$x = a(\theta - \sin\theta), \qquad y = a(1 - \cos\theta).$$

Figure 16.6

Thus $\frac{dx}{d\theta} = a(1 - \cos\theta) = 2a\sin^2\frac{1}{2}\theta$, while $\frac{dy}{d\theta} = a\sin\theta = 2a\sin\frac{1}{2}\theta\cos\frac{1}{2}\theta$, and hence

$$\frac{dy}{dx} = \frac{2a\sin\frac{1}{2}\theta\cos\frac{1}{2}\theta}{2a\sin^2\frac{1}{2}\theta} = \cot\frac{1}{2}\theta.$$

Thus there are maxima at $(a\theta, 2a)$ when $\cos\frac{1}{2}\theta = 0$, so when θ is an odd multiple of π, and the gradient is infinite at $(a\theta, 0)$ when $\sin\frac{1}{2}\theta = 0$, so when θ is an even multiple of π. Since

$$x(\theta + 2\pi) = x(\theta) + 2\pi a \qquad y(\theta + 2\pi) = y(\theta),$$

we see that the curve consists of a pattern of width $2\pi a$ which is infinitely repeated. Each pattern corresponds to one rotation of the wheel.

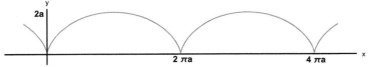

Figure 16.7

This curve is called a **cycloid**, and has many interesting properties. Note that, since $\frac{dy}{dx}$ is infinite then $\theta = 0, 2\pi, \ldots$, the point P is instantaneously stationary when touching the ground (if it were not, the bicycle would be skidding).

EXERCISE 16B

1. Find $\frac{dy}{dx}$ in terms of t for the following curves:

   a) $x = t^3, y = 2t$,

   b) $x = \sin t, y = \cos t$,

   c) $x = 2\cos t, y = 3\sin t$,

   d) $x = t^3 + t, y = t^2 - t$.

2. Find the gradients of the tangents to the following curves at the specified values of t:

   a) $x = 3t^2, y = 6t$ when $t = 0.5$,

   b) $x = t^3, y = t^2$ when $t = 2$,

   c) $x = 1 - \frac{1}{t}, y = 1 + \frac{1}{t}$ when $t = 2$,

   d) $x = t^2, y = \frac{1}{t}$ when $t = 3$.

3. Find the gradients of the normals to the following curves, at the specified values of t:

a) $x = 5t^2, y = 10t$ when $t = 3$,

b) $x = \cos^2 2t, y = \sin^2 2t$ when $t = \frac{1}{3}\pi$,

c) $x = \cos^3 t, y = \sin^3 t$ when $t = \frac{1}{6}\pi$,

d) $x = t^2 + 2, y = t - 2$ when $t = 4$.

4. Show that the equation of the tangent to the curve $x = 3\cos t, y = 2\sin t$ when $t = \frac{1}{4}\pi$ is $3y + 2x = 6\sqrt{2}$.

5. a) Find the gradient of the curve $x = t^3, y = t^2 - t$ at the point $(1, 0)$.

b) Hence find the equation of the tangent to the curve at this point.

6. A curve has parametric equations $x = t - \cos t, y = \sin t$. Find the equation of the tangent to the curve when $t = \pi$.

7. Find the equations of the tangents to these curves at the specified values:

a) $x = t^2, y = 2t$ when $t = 3$,

b) $x = 5\cos t, y = 3\sin t$ when $t = \frac{11}{6}\pi$.

8. Find the equations of the normals to these curves at the specified values.

a) $x = 5t^2, y = 10t$ when $t = 3$,

b) $x = \cos t, y = \sin t$ when $t = \frac{2}{3}\pi$.

9. a) Find the equation of the normal to the hyperbola $x = 4t, y = \frac{4}{t}$ at the point $(8, 2)$.

b) Find the coordinates of the point where this normal crosses the curve again.

10. a) Find the equation of the normal to the parabola $x = 3t^2, y = 6t$ at the point where $t = -2$.

b) Find the coordinates of the point where this normal crosses the curve again.

11*. The third curve pictured in Figure 16.1 has the parametric representation $x = \cos 5t + \cos t$, $y = \sin 5t + \sin t$.

a) Find the equation of the tangent at the point on the curve where $t = \frac{1}{6}\pi$.

b) Show that the curve has a turning point at the point where $t = \frac{1}{2}\pi$.

16.2.3. SECOND DERIVATIVES

We need to be careful when classifying turning points. Consider the parametric equation

$$x = \frac{1 - t^2}{1 + t^2}, \qquad y = \frac{2t}{1 + t^2}.$$

Omitting the details of the calculation, we can show that $\dfrac{dx}{dt} = -\dfrac{4t}{(1 + t^2)^2}$ and that $\dfrac{dy}{dt} = \dfrac{2(1 - t^2)}{(1 + t^2)^2}$, so that

$$\frac{dy}{dx} = -\frac{1 - t^2}{2t}.$$

The point where $t = 1$ has coordinates $(0, 1)$ and is a turning point on this curve. We note that $\dfrac{dy}{dx}$ is negative for $0 < t < 1$ and positive for $t > 1$; does that mean that this turning point is a minimum?

If we considered instead the parametric equation

$$x = \sin u, \qquad y = \cos u,$$

then $\dfrac{dy}{dx} = -\tan u$, and so this curve has a turning point at the point where $u = 0$, which has coordinates $(0, 1)$. Note that $\dfrac{dy}{dx}$ is positive for $-\frac{1}{2}\pi < u < 0$ and negative for $0 < u < \frac{1}{2}\pi$; does this mean that the turning point is a maximum?

Since

$$\left(\tfrac{1-t^2}{1+t^2}\right)^2 + \left(\tfrac{2t}{1+t^2}\right)^2 \equiv \sin^2 u + \cos^2 u \equiv 1$$

these two parametric equations describe the same curve, the unit circle (although the first parametrisation excludes the point $(-1, 0)$), and in both cases we have identified the turning point at $(0, 1)$, which is a maximum for the curve.

The moral of these calculations is that is not easy to identify the nature of a turning point by considering how the sign of the derivative changes as the parameter varies; the pattern of sign changes varies depending on the nature of the parametrisation. Of the two parametrisations of the unit circle that we have been considering, one traverses the circle in an anticlockwise direction as t increases, while the other traverses the circle in a clockwise direction as u increases, and this change of direction affects the pattern of sign-changes that we have used until now to classify turning points.

We must turn back to classifying turning points by calculating the value of the second derivative $\frac{d^2y}{dx^2}$. How can we calculate this parametrically?

Given a parametric equation $x = f(t)$, $y = g(t)$, we can calculate $\frac{dy}{dx}$ as a function of t. Using the chain rule one more time,

$$\frac{dx}{dt} \times \frac{d^2y}{dx^2} = \frac{dx}{dt} \times \frac{d}{dx}\left(\frac{dy}{dx}\right) = \frac{d}{dt}\left(\frac{dy}{dx}\right),$$

which gives us the following result.

> **Key Fact 16.3** Differentiating Parametric Equations Twice
>
> Given a parametric equation, parametrised by t, the formula for the second derivative is
> $$\frac{d^2y}{dx^2} = \frac{d}{dt}\left(\frac{dy}{dx}\right)\bigg/\frac{dx}{dt} .$$

Example 16.2.9. *Find and classify the stationary points on the curve $x = 2 - t^2$, $y = t^3 - 3t$. What can you say about the curve at the point where $t = 0$?*

Since $\frac{dx}{dt} = -2t$ and $\frac{dy}{dt} = 3t^2 - 3 = 3(t^2 - 1)$, we deduce that

$$\frac{dy}{dx} = -\frac{3(t^2 - 1)}{2t} = \tfrac{3}{2}(t^{-1} - t)$$

and hence $\frac{d}{dt}\left(\frac{dy}{dx}\right) = -\tfrac{3}{2}(t^{-2} + 1)$, and so

$$\frac{d^2y}{dx^2} = -\frac{1}{2t} \times -\tfrac{3}{2}(t^{-2} + 1) = \frac{3(t^2 + 1)}{4t^3} .$$

Turning points occur when $t = 1$ (at the point $(1, -2)$) and when $t = -1$ (at the point $(1, 2)$). Since $\frac{d^2y}{dx^2} = \pm\tfrac{3}{2}$ when $t = \pm 1$, the turning point at $t = 1$ is a minimum, and the turning point at $t = -1$ is a maximum.

At $t = 0$ we see that $\frac{dy}{dx}$ is infinite (or, more correctly, undefined). At this point, the tangent is parallel to the y-axis.

16.2.4. Proving Properties About Curves

Parameters are a powerful tool for proving properties about curves. Here is one example of their use.

Example 16.2.10. *A curve is given parametrically by $x = a\cos^3 t$, $y = a\sin^3 t$, where a is a positive constant, for $0 \le t \le 2\pi$. The tangent at any point P on the curve meets the x-axis at A and the y-axis at B. Prove that the length of AB does not depend on the point P.*

This curve is called an **astroid**. Suppose that P is a point on the curve with parameter t. Then P has coordinates $(a\cos^3 t, a\sin^3 t)$. To find the gradient at the point P, we need to calculate

$$\frac{dy}{dx} = \frac{dy}{dt} \bigg/ \frac{dx}{dt} = \frac{3a\sin^2 t \cos t}{-3a\sin t \cos^2 t} = -\tan t.$$

and so the equation of the tangent at P is

$$y - a\sin^3 t = -\tan t(x - a\cos^3 t),$$

which simplifies to

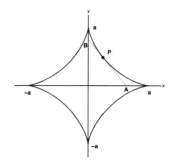

Figure 16.8

$$x\sin t + y\cos t = a(\sin^3 t \cos t + \sin t \cos^3 t) = a\sin t \cos t(\sin^2 t + \cos^2 t) = a\sin t \cos t$$

Thus the coordinates of A and B are $(a\cos t, 0)$ and $(0, a\sin t)$ respectively, and hence the length of AB is

$$\sqrt{(a\cos t - 0)^2 + (0 - a\sin t)^2} = \sqrt{a^2(\cos^2 t + \sin^2 t)} = a.$$

EXERCISE 16C

1. For each of the following curves, calculate $\frac{dy}{dx}$ and $\frac{d^2y}{dx^2}$:

   a) $x = 2t - 3, y = t^2 + 4,$ b) $x = 3t + 1, y = e^{t-2},$ c) $x = t^2 + 1, y = e^t,$
   d) $x = t^2 + 1, y = e^{t^2},$ e) $x = t^3 - t, y = t^3 + 2t^2 - 1,$ f) $x = e^t, y = \sin t.$

2. Given the curve $x = t^3 + 3t + 2, y = t^2 - 6t + 4$, show that $\frac{dy}{dx} = \frac{2(t-3)}{3(t^2+1)}$. Calculate $\frac{d^2y}{dx^2}$ in terms of t. Find and classify the turning point of this curve.

3. Show that the cycloid $x = a(\theta - \sin\theta), y = a(1 - \cos\theta)$ has a maximum at $\theta = \pi$.

4. For the curve $x = e^t, y = e^t \cos t$, show that $\frac{dy}{dx} = \cos t - \sin t$. Calculate $\frac{d^2y}{dx^2}$, and find and classify the turning points in the range $0 \le t \le 4\pi$.

5. The curve in Example 16.2.1 has parametric equation $x = \sin t, y = \sin 2t$. Calculate $\frac{dy}{dx}$ and $\frac{d^2y}{dx^2}$, and hence find and classify its four turning points.

6. Let P be a point on the curve $x = t^2, y = \frac{1}{t}$. If the tangent to the curve at P meets the x- and y-axes at A and B respectively, prove that $PA = 2PB$.

7. A parabola is given parametrically by $x = at^2, y = 2at$. If P is any point on the parabola, let F be the foot of the perpendicular from P onto the axis of symmetry. Let G be the point where the normal from P crosses the axis of symmetry. Prove that $FG = 2a$.

8. Let P be a point on the curve H with equations $x = t, y = t^{-1}$, let S be the point $(\sqrt{2}, \sqrt{2})$. Let N be the point on the tangent to H at P such that SN is perpendicular to PN. Show that the coordinates (x, y) of N satisfy the equations

$$t^2 y + x = 2t \quad , \quad y - t^2 x = \sqrt{2}(1 - t^2).$$

   Deduce that $x^2 + y^2 = 2$, and interpret this result.

9*. Let P be a point on the ellipse with parametric equations $x = 5\cos t, y = 3\sin t$ for $0 \le t \le 2\pi$, and let F and G be the points $(-4, 0)$ and $(4, 0)$ respectively. Prove that:

   a) $FP = 5 + 4\cos t,$ b) $FP + PG = 10.$
   Let the normal at P make angles θ and ϕ with FP and GP respectively. Prove that
   c) $\tan\theta = \frac{4}{3}\sin t,$ d) $\theta = \phi.$

16.3 Implicit Equations

The most general way of describing a curve is neither explicit nor parametric. There is an imbalance in explicit equations, since the variable x has been given a special importance, since y can be calculated uniquely in terms of it. However there is no geometrical reason why one of the two coordinate axes should be more important than the other; equations that give x and y equal weight are worth investigating. We have already seen a number of these: the equation of a circle is $(x-a)^2 + (y-b)^2 = r^2$ for constants a, b and r, and it is possible to write the equation of any straight line in the form $ax + by + c = 0$ for constants a, b and c.

> **Key Fact 16.4** Implicit Equations
>
> An **implicit equation** is one that defines a relationship between the two variables x and y, and has the form
> $$f(x,y) = c$$
> for some function f of two variables and some constant c.

Examples of such equations might be

$$x^2 + y^2 = 1, \qquad x^3 + y^3 + x^2 - y = 0, \qquad 3\cos(x+y) + 2\sin(x-y) = 1 ;$$

their graphs are below:

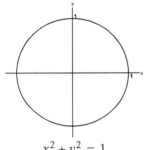 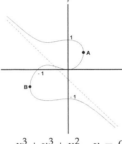 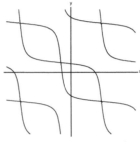

$$x^2 + y^2 = 1 \qquad\qquad x^3 + y^3 + x^2 - y = 0 \qquad 3\cos(x+y) + 2\sin(x-y) = 1$$

Figure 16.9

Comparatively simple-looking implicit equations can yield pretty complicated graphs.

Any explicit equation can be written implicitly, since the equation $y = f(x)$ can be written as $f(x) - y = 0$; the key thing is that most implicit equations cannot be written explicitly. Consider the second of the three equations above,

$$x^3 + y^3 + x^2 - y = 0$$

For any value of x, we have a cubic equation for y. Any value of x will therefore correspond to one, two or three values of y, so the equation cannot be written explicitly. Equally well, any value of y yields a cubic equation for x, and so x cannot be written as a function of y either. However, the following properties of this curve can be established quite easily:

- The equation passes through the origin.

- The curve cuts the x-axis when $x^3 + x^2 = 0$, so at the points $(-1,0)$ and $(0,0)$.

- The curve cuts the y-axis when $y^3 - y = 0$, so at the point $(0,-1)$, $(0,0)$ and $(0,1)$.

There are other interesting features. There are points A and B where the gradient seems to be vertical, there are several turning points, and the curve seems to have an asymptote with gradient -1. These will be discussed later.

16.3.1. DIFFERENTIATING IMPLICIT EQUATIONS

The chain rule enables us differentiate implicit equations. Just as with parametric equations, while we might not be able to express the equation explicitly in the form $y = f(x)$ everywhere, in theory we can do so locally. For the purposes of differentiation, when we consider an implicit equation, y can be regarded as a function of x.

Returning to the second equation shown in Figure 16.9,

$$x^3 + y^3 + x^2 - y = 0,$$

since we can (locally) regard y as a function of x, the equation is in fact an identity, stating that the function $x^3 + y(x)^3 + x^2 - y(x)$ is identically zero. Thus this function will also have zero derivative. Since the derivative of y is $\dfrac{dy}{dx}$ and, by the chain rule, the derivative of y^3 is $3y^2\dfrac{dy}{dx}$, we deduce that

$$3x^2 + 3y^2\frac{dy}{dx} + 2x - \frac{dy}{dx} = 0.$$

Collecting terms, we can solve this equation to express $\dfrac{dy}{dx}$ as a function of x:

$$\frac{dy}{dx} = \frac{x(3x+2)}{1-3y^2}.$$

Being able to express $\dfrac{dy}{dx}$ in terms of both x and y is the best we can hope for. Provided that we know both coordinates of any point on the curve, there is no problem with calculating derivatives. We can now identify the turning points of the curve. These occur when $x(3x+2) = 0$, so when either $x = 0$ or $x = -\frac{2}{3}$. Three of these turning points are thus $(0,-1)$, $(0,0)$ and $(0,1)$. The y-coordinates of the other three (where $x = -\frac{2}{3}$) are the solutions of the cubic equation $y^3 - y + \frac{4}{27} = 0$. They are 0.92, 0.15 and -1.07, correct to 2 decimal places.

We can also identify points where the tangent is vertical by looking for an undefined gradient. This occurs when $1 - 3y^2 = 0$, so when $y = \pm\frac{1}{\sqrt{3}}$. The x-coordinates of these points are also found by solving a cubic equation. These points are shown as A and B on the graph.

Key Fact 16.5 Implicit Differentiation

To differentiate an implicit equation, treat y as a function of x and differentiate the whole equation as a function of x, using the chain rule to differentiate functions of y. This process is called **implicit differentiation**.

Food For Thought 16.1

Since these equations can become quite complicated, particularly when we study second derivatives, there is a substantial increase of clarity if we use the y' notation to denote derivatives. We shall do so for the rest of this chapter.

Example 16.3.1. *Show that $(1,2)$ is on the circle $x^2 + y^2 - 6x + 2y - 3 = 0$, and find the gradient at that point.*

Substituting $x = 1$, $y = 2$ in the left side of the equation gives $1 + 4 - 6 + 4 - 3$, which is equal to 0. Thus $(1,2)$ lies on the circle. Differentiating this equation implicity,

$$2x + 2yy' - 6 + 2y' = 0$$

At the point $(1,2)$ this means that $2 + 4y' - 6 + 2y' = 0$, or $y' = \frac{2}{3}$.

Of course, we could have used coordinate geometry, identifying $(3,-1)$ as the centre of the circle, and hence calculating the gradient of the radius to $(1,2)$ to be $-\frac{3}{2}$, thereby deriving the gradient of the tangent, since it must be perpendicular to the radius.

Example 16.3.2. *Find an expression for y' on the curve $3x^2 - 2y^3 = 1$.*

This equation could be written explicitly, but let us use the new method. Differentiating implicitly,

$$6x - 6y^2y' = 0$$

and hence $y' = \frac{x}{y^2}$.

Example 16.3.3. *Sketch the graph of* $\cos x + \cos y = \frac{1}{2}$ *for* $-\pi \le x, y \le \pi$, *and find the equation of the tangent at the point* $(\frac{1}{2}\pi, \frac{1}{3}\pi)$.

The graph crosses the x-axis when $y = 0$, so when $\cos x = -\frac{1}{2}$, and hence for $x = \pm\frac{2}{3}\pi$. Since $\cos y \le 1$ for all y, it follows that $\cos x \ge -\frac{1}{2}$ for all points on the curve, and hence that $-\frac{2}{3}\pi \le x \le \frac{2}{3}\pi$. Similarly the graph crosses the y-axis when $y = \pm\frac{2}{3}\pi$, and that $-\frac{2}{3}\pi \le y \le \frac{2}{3}\pi$.

Differentiating this equation implicitly,

$$-\sin x - \sin y\, y' = 0, \qquad \text{so} \qquad y' = -\frac{\sin x}{\sin y}.$$

Turning points occur when $\sin x = 0$, so these occur at the intercepts with the y-axis. Additionally, the tangent is vertical when $\sin y = 0$, so this happens at the intercepts with the x-axis.

Finally, since cos is an even function, the graph has reflectional symmetry in both the x- and y-axes. We now have enough to sketch the curve.

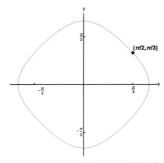

At $(\frac{1}{2}\pi, \frac{1}{3}\pi)$ the gradient is $-\frac{2}{\sqrt{3}}$, and so the equation of the tangent at this point can be shown to be

$$y + \frac{2}{\sqrt{3}}x = \frac{1}{3}\pi(1 + \sqrt{3}).$$

Figure 16.10

We might need to use the product rule to perform implicit differentiation.

Example 16.3.4. *Find the gradient of* $x^2 y^3 = 72$ *at the point* $(3, 2)$.

Differentiating implicitly, and using the product rule,

$$2xy^3 + 3x^2 y^2 y' = 0$$

At the point $(3, 2)$ we have $2 \times 3 \times 8 + 3 \times 9 \times 4y' = 0$, and so $y' = -\frac{4}{9}$.

Another approach to this problem would have been to take logarithms first, and then differentiate. Since $2\ln x + 3\ln y = 0$, we deduce that $\frac{2}{x} + \frac{3}{y}y' = 0$, which gets us to the same answer. This method is known as **logarithmic differentiation**.

Example 16.3.5. *The equation* $x^2 - 6xy + 25y^2 = 16$ *represents an ellipse with its origin at the centre. What ranges of values of* x *and* y *are needed to plot it?*

Differentiating implicitly,

$$2x - 6y - 6xy' + 50yy' = 0$$

and hence

$$y' = \frac{3y - x}{25y - 3x}.$$

Turning points occur when $3y = x$. Substituting this equation into the equation for the ellipse, we see that

$$16y^2 = (3y)^2 - 6 \times 3y \times y + 25y^2 = 16,$$

and hence $y = \pm 1$. Tangents are parallel to the x-axis at the point $(3, 1)$ and $(-3, -1)$.

Vertical tangents occur when $25y = 3x$. Substituting this equation into the equation for the ellipse, we see that

$$\tfrac{16}{25}x^2 = x^2 - 6x\tfrac{3}{25}x + 25\left(\tfrac{3}{25}x\right)^2 = 16,$$

and hence $x = \pm 5$. Tangents are parallel to the y-axis at the points $(5, \frac{3}{5})$ and $(-5, -\frac{3}{5})$.

To be able to plot the whole ellipse, we therefore need the ranges $-5 \le x \le 5$ and $-1 \le y \le 1$. A sketch of the function is shown on the right.

Figure 16.11

Exercise 16D

1. Differentiate the implicit equation $y^2 = 4x$ to find the gradient at $(9, -6)$ on the curve.

2. Differentiate the implicit equation of the ellipse $3x^2 + 4y^2 = 16$ to find the equation of the tangent at the point $(2, -1)$.

3. Differentiate the implicit equation of the hyperbola $4x^2 - 3y^2 = 24$ to find the equation of the normal at the point $(3, -2)$. Find the y-coordinate of the point where the normal meets the curve again.

4. Find the gradient of each of the following curves at the point given:
   a) $x \sin y = \frac{1}{2}$ at $(1, \frac{1}{6}\pi)$,
   b) $ye^x = xy + y^2$ at $(0, 1)$,
   c) $\ln(x + y) = -x$ at $(0, 1)$,
   d) $\cos(xy) = \frac{1}{2}$ at $(1, \frac{1}{3}\pi)$.

5. Find the equation of the tangent to the curve $x^2 - 2xy + 2y^2 = 5$ at the point $(1, 2)$.

6. Find the equation of the normal to the curve $2xy^2 - x^2y^3 = 1$ at the point $(1, 1)$.

7. Find the points on the curve $4x^2 + 2xy - 3y^2 = 39$ at which the tangent is parallel to one of the axes.

8. Consider the curve with equation $x^2 + 4y^2 = 1$.

   a) Find the coordinates of the points where the curve cuts the coordinate axes.

   b) Find the interval of possible values of x and y for points on the curve.

   c) Show that the curve is symmetrical about both the x- and y-axes.

   d) Differentiate the equation with respect to x, and show that $y' = 0$ when $x = 0$. Interpret this geometrically.

   e) Show that the tangent to the curve is vertical when $y = 0$. Interpret this geometrically.

   f) Use your results to sketch the curve.

9. Repeat the steps of the previous question, this time using the curve $x^2 - y^2 = 1$. If there are parts of the question which have no answer, or are impossible, say why that is so.

10. Consider the curve $y^3 = (x - 1)^2$.

    a) Find the coordinates of the points where the curve crosses the axes.

    b) Are there any values which either x or y cannot take?

    c) Differentiate the equation to find an expression for the gradient in terms of x and y. Find the gradient of the curve where it crosses the y-axis.

    d) What happens to the gradient as x gets close to 1?

    e) By making the substitution $x = 1 + X$, and examining the resulting equation between y and X, show that the curve is symmetrical about the line $x = 1$.

    f) Sketch the curve.

11. On the same set of axes sketch the curves $x^4 + y^4 = 1$ and $x^2 + y^2 = 1$.

12. a) Show that the origin lies on the curve $e^x + e^y = 2$.

    b) Differentiate the equation with respect to x, and explain why the gradient is always negative.

    c) Find any restrictions that you can on the values of x and y, and sketch the curve.

13. a) Show that if (a, b) lies on the curve $x^2 + y^3 = 2$, then so does $(-a, b)$. What can you deduce from this about the shape of the curve?

    b) Differentiate $x^2 + y^3 = 2$ with respect to x, and deduce what you can about the gradient for negative and for positive values of x.

    c) Show that there is a stationary point at $(0, \sqrt[3]{2})$ and deduce its nature.

    d) Sketch the curve.

14. Find the coordinates of the points at which the curve $y^5 + y = x^3 + x^2$ meets the coordinate axes, and find the gradients of the curve at each of these points.

15. Find the gradient of the curve $y^3 - 3y^2 + 2y = e^x + x - 1$ at the points where it crosses the y-axis.

16. a) Explain why all points on the curve $(x^2 + y^2)^2 = x^2 - y^2$ lie in the region $|x| \geq |y|$.

   b) Find the coordinates of the points at which the tangent is either parallel to the x-axis or parallel to the y-axis.

   c) By considering where the curve meets the circle $x^2 + y^2 = r^2$, show that $r^2 \leq 1$, so that the curve is bounded.

   d) Sketch the curve, which is called the **lemniscate of Bernoulli**.

16.3.2. SECOND DERIVATIVES

Consider the equation $x^2 + 2x + y^2 = 4$. Differentiating implicitly gives

$$2x + 2 + 2yy' = 0,$$

and hence

$$y' = -\frac{x+1}{y}.$$

We have y' expressed as a function of x and y, and so we can differentiate this expression one more time, obtaining y''. Hence

$$y'' = -\frac{1 \times y - (x+1)y'}{y^2} = -\frac{y - (x+1)y'}{y^2}.$$

Expressing y'' in terms of x, y and y' is a bit much, so we shall substitute our known expression for y':

$$y'' = -\frac{y + (x+1)\frac{x+1}{y}}{y^2} = -\frac{(x+1)^2 + y^2}{y^3}.$$

Finally, completing the square in the original equation shows that $(x+1)^2 + y^2 = 5$, and hence (finally)

$$y'' = -\frac{5}{y^3}.$$

This method works, but it very laborious. It is easier not to solve the original differentiated equation for y' (which forced us to differentiate y' as a quotient), but instead simply to differentiate the original equation twice. Thus

$$\begin{aligned} x^2 + 2x + y^2 &= 4 \\ 2x + 2 + 2yy' &= 0 \\ 2 + 2(y')^2 + 2yy'' &= 0 \end{aligned}$$

For then we know that $y' = -\frac{x+1}{y}$, and therefore that

$$yy'' = -1 - (y')^2 = -1 - \frac{(x+1)^2}{y^2} = -\frac{(x+1)^2 + y^2}{y^2} = -\frac{5}{y^2},$$

and hence that $y'' = -\frac{5}{y^3}$.

This method is particular efficient if we want to classify turning points, since we can then assume that $y' = 0$ before simplifying our algebra.

Example 16.3.6. *Find and classify the turning points of the curve $x^2 + 6xy + 10y^2 = 25$.*

Differentiating this equation twice,

$$\begin{aligned} 2x + 6y + 6xy' + 20yy' &= 0 \\ 2 + 6y' + 6y' + 6xy'' + 20(y')^2 + 20yy'' &= 0 \end{aligned}$$

Turning points occur when $y' = 0$, so that $x = -3y$. Substituting this condition into the original equation

$$y^2 = (-3y)^2 + 6(-3y)y + 10y^2 = 25$$

and so $y = \pm 5$. The turning points occur at $(15, -5)$ and $(-15, 5)$.

At a turning point, the second equation tells us that $1 + (3x + 10y)y'' = 0$ (we can discard all the terms involving y'). Thus $y'' = -\frac{1}{3x+10y} = \frac{1}{5}$ at $(15, -5)$ and $y'' = -\frac{1}{5}$ at $(-15, 5)$; $(15, -5)$ is a minimum, and $(-15, 5)$ is a maximum.

EXERCISE 16E

1. For each of the following equations, find y' and y'':

   a) $x^3 + y^3 = 2$,
   b) $\sin x + \sin y = 1$,
   c) $x^3 - 2xy^2 = 1$,
   d) $x^2 y + xy^2 = 3$,
   e) $e^{x+y} = x - y$,
   f) $xy^2 = x + y$.

2. For each of the following equations, find y'' at the point specified:

   a) $x^4 + y^2 = 2$ at $(1, 1)$,
   b) $x^2 y - xy = 6$ at $(3, 1)$,
   c) $x \sin y = 1$ at $(\sqrt{2}, \frac{1}{4}\pi)$,
   d) $e^{x-y} = x$ at $(1, 1)$.

3. Find and classify the turning points of the following curves:

   a) $x^2 + y^2 + 8x - 2y = 8$,
   b) $xy + y - x^2 = 8$,
   c) $4xy^2 = 1 + 4x^2 y$,
   d) $y^3 + 3xy^2 - x^3 = 3$.

4*. Given that $x^2 - 6xy + y^2 + 14x - 10y + 25 = 0$:

   a) show that $\dfrac{dy}{dx} = \dfrac{x - 3y + 7}{3x - y + 5}$,

   b) find the turning points of the curve, and decide whether they are maxima or minima,

   c) find the points on the curve whose tangents are parallel to the y-axis.

5*. Suppose that $x^{2n} + y^n = 1$. Show that $\dfrac{d^2 y}{dx^2} = -2\dfrac{x^{2n-2}}{y^{2n-1}}[y^n + 2(n-1)]$.

Chapter 16: Summary

- **Parametric Equations** If an equation is given in the parametric form $x = f(t)$, $y = g(t)$, using the parameter t, then

$$\frac{dy}{dx} = \frac{dy}{dt} \bigg/ \frac{dx}{dt} \qquad\qquad \frac{d^2 y}{dx^2} = \frac{d}{dt}\left(\frac{dy}{dx}\right) \bigg/ \frac{dx}{dt}$$

- **Implicit Functions** An implicit equation is one of the form $f(x, y) = c$. Implicit equations are differentiated by determined use of the chain rule. Both $\dfrac{dy}{dx}$ and $\dfrac{d^2 y}{dx^2}$ will be expressed as functions of x and y.

- **Graph Sketching** As well as turning points, points on curves where the tangent is parallel to the y-axis are of interest.

Further Integration

In this chapter we will learn to:

- integrate trigonometric functions, exponential functions and logarithms,

- use trigonometric identities to integrate otherwise intractable functions,

- use substitution to simplify and evaluate definite or indefinite integrals, and recognise and integrate a function of the form $\frac{f'(x)}{f(x)}$.

- integrate algebraic fractions by means of decomposition into partial fractions,

- use integration by parts to integrate suitable products.

17.1   Integrating Standard Functions

Now that we have learned how to differentiate trigonometric, exponential and logarithmic functions, we automatically have a new array of functions that we can integrate. Our current knowledge of how to integrate 'standard functions' is summarised as follows:

$$\int x^n \, dx = \frac{1}{n+1} x^{n+1} + c \quad (n \neq -1) \qquad \int x^{-1} \, dx = \ln x + c \quad (x > 0)$$

$$\int \cos x \, dx = \sin x + c \qquad\qquad \int \sin x \, dx = -\cos x + c$$

$$\int \sec^2 x \, dx = \tan x + c \qquad\qquad \int \sec x \tan x \, dx = \sec x + c$$

$$\int \operatorname{cosec}^2 x \, dx = -\cot x + c \qquad \int \operatorname{cosec} x \cot x \, dx = -\operatorname{cosec} x + c$$

$$\int e^x \, dx = e^x + c \qquad\qquad \int a^x \, dx = \frac{1}{\ln a} a^x + c \quad (a > 0)$$

This is a big step forward. Now that we have the natural logarithm $\ln x$, we can integrate all powers of x. On the other hand, while we know how to differentiate all the six standard trigonometric functions, we still only know how to integrate two of them. We might be able to integrate $\sec^2 x$, but (as yet) we cannot integrate $\sec x$, for example. In this chapter we will investigate various methods for extending the range of functions that we know how to integrate.

17.2   Pattern-Spotting

Integration is hard. Unlike differentiation, where careful application of the various rules and formulae will always yield a result, we do not always know how to integrate functions. Some functions cannot be integrated at all (at least, cannot have their integrals written in terms of the standard functions), and very similar functions need to be integrated in very different ways. Almost because it is hard, though, integration is a challenging and rewarding topic; the satisfaction of working out how to integrate a complicated function is great!

It is important to gain a feeling for the 'easy' functions, and to be able to spot functions which can be integrated without too much fuss. Of course, we will rarely be faced with something as simple as integrating $\sin x$ or e^x; we need to be able to handle easy variants of the standard functions.

Example 17.2.1. *Find the indefinite integral* $\displaystyle\int \sin(3x+1)\,dx$.

What function differentiates to something like $\sin(3x+1)$? Using the chain rule, we know that $\cos(3x+1)$ has derivative $-3\sin(3x+1)$, which is -3 times what we want. All we have to do is rescale the function:

$$\int \sin(3x+1)\,dx \;=\; -\tfrac{1}{3}\cos(3x+1) + c\,.$$

What we have done in this case is use our knowledge of differentiation to 'guess' what the integral will look like. By differentiating back down again, we can adjust our guess accordingly, and obtain the correct answer. Alternatively, we can apply the following template:

Key Fact 17.1 Integration: Pattern-Spotting 1

If $f(x)$ is a function and a and b are constants, then

$$\int f'(ax+b)\,dx \;=\; \tfrac{1}{a}f(ax+b) + c\,.$$

This template works because $\dfrac{d}{dx}f(ax+b) = af'(ax+b)$; we need to rescale by dividing by a.

Example 17.2.2. *Find the integral* $\displaystyle\int x(3x^2+1)^4\,dx$.

This integral could be evaluated by multiplying out the bracket using the Binomial Theorem. Alternatively, and more efficiently, the chain rule tells us that $(3x^2+1)^5$ has derivative $5(3x^2+1)^4 \times 6x = 30x(3x^2+1)^4$, which is 30 times more than the desired answer. Thus

$$\int x(3x^2+1)^4\,dx \;=\; \tfrac{1}{30}(3x^2+1)^5 + c\,.$$

The trick to integrating this function was to note that a multiple of the x term at the front appears when we differentiate $3x^2+1$; this enabled us to 'guess' that the answer was going to be a multiple of $(3x^2+1)^5$; differentiating back down enabled us to determine the multiplying factor $\tfrac{1}{30}$. Alternatively, we can apply the following template:

Key Fact 17.2 Integration: Pattern-Spotting 2

If $f(x)$ is a function and $n \neq -1$ is a number, then

$$\int f'(x) \times \big(f(x)\big)^n\,dx \;=\; \tfrac{1}{n+1}\big(f(x)\big)^{n+1} + c\,.$$

Example 17.2.3. *Evaluate* $\displaystyle\int x^3\sqrt{x^4+2}\,dx$.

With $f(x) = x^4+2$ and $n = \tfrac{1}{2}$, the template tells us that

$$\int 4x^3\sqrt{x^4+2}\,dx \;=\; \tfrac{2}{3}(x^4+2)^{\frac{3}{2}} + c\,.$$

Dividing by 4 gives

$$\int x^3\sqrt{x^4+2}\,dx \;=\; \tfrac{1}{6}(x^4+2)^{\frac{3}{2}} + c\,.$$

Note that we were able to 'divide' the arbitrary constant c by 4 and still write just c. Since the constant c is arbitrary, there is no benefit in writing $\frac{1}{4}c$; we can relabel arbitrary constants if it is convenient to do so.

Food For Thought 17.1

When using these templates, care must be taken only to rescale by constants. While putting $f(x) = x^2 + 5$ and $n = -\frac{1}{2}$ gives us

$$\int \frac{2x}{\sqrt{x^2 + 5}}\,dx = 2\sqrt{x^2 + 5} + c,$$

we cannot 'divide by $2x$' and write the integral $\int \frac{1}{\sqrt{x^2 + 5}}\,dx$ as $x^{-1}\sqrt{x^2 + 5} + dx^{-1}$. We are only allowed to rescale by constants!

EXERCISE 17A

1. Integrate the following with respect to x:

   a) $(2x + 1)^6$,
   b) $(3x - 5)^4$,
   c) $(1 - 7x)^3$,
   d) $(\frac{1}{2}x + 1)^{10}$,

   e) $(5x + 2)^{-3}$,
   f) $2(1 - 3x)^{-2}$,
   g) $\dfrac{1}{(x + 1)^5}$,
   h) $\dfrac{3}{2(4x + 1)^4}$,

   i) $\sqrt{10x + 1}$,
   j) $\dfrac{1}{\sqrt{2x - 1}}$,
   k) $(\frac{1}{2}x + 2)^{\frac{2}{3}}$,
   l) $\dfrac{8}{\sqrt[4]{2 + 6x}}$.

2. Evaluate the following definite integrals:

   a) $\displaystyle\int_1^5 (2x - 1)^3\,dx$,
   b) $\displaystyle\int_1^5 \sqrt{2x - 1}\,dx$,
   c) $\displaystyle\int_1^3 \frac{1}{(x + 2)^2}\,dx$,
   d) $\displaystyle\int_1^3 \frac{2}{(x + 2)^3}$.

3. Given that $\displaystyle\int_{1.25}^p (4x - 5)^4\,dx = 51.2$, find the value of p.

4. The diagram shows the curve $y = (2x - 5)^4$. The point P has coordinates $(4, 81)$ and the tangent to the curve at P meets the x-axis at Q. Find the area of the region (shaded in the diagram) enclosed between the curve, the line PQ and the x-axis.

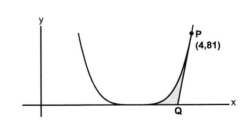

5. Find the area of each of the following shaded regions:

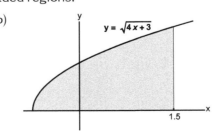

   a) $y = (2x - 1)^4$

   b) $y = \sqrt{4x + 3}$

6. Find the area enclosed between the curves $y = (x - 2)^4$ and $(x - 2)^3$.

7. The diagram shows the curve $y = \sqrt{4-x}$ and the line $y = 2 - \frac{1}{3}x$. The coordinates of A and B, where the curve and the line intersect, are $(0, 2)$ and $(3, 1)$ respectively. Calculate the area of the shaded region between the line and the curve, giving your answer as an exact fraction.

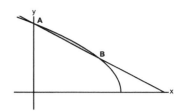

8. Integrate the following functions with respect to x:

   a) $x(x^2 + 1)^{17}$,
   b) $x^2\sqrt{x^3 - 1}$,
   c) $(x + 1)(x^2 + 2x - 3)^5$,

   d) $(4x + 6)\sqrt{x^2 + 3x + 1}$,
   e) $\dfrac{(\sqrt{x} + 1)^7}{\sqrt{x}}$,
   f) $x^{-\frac{2}{3}}\left(x^{\frac{1}{3}} + 1\right)^5$.

9. By differentiating $\ln(x + \sqrt{x^2 + 5})$, find the indefinite integral $\displaystyle\int \dfrac{1}{\sqrt{x^2 + 5}}\,dx$.

10. Find the following indefinite integrals:

   a) $\displaystyle\int e^{3x}\,dx$,
   b) $\displaystyle\int e^{-x}\,dx$,
   c) $\displaystyle\int 3e^{2x}\,dx$,
   d) $\displaystyle\int -4e^{-4x}\,dx$,

   e) $\displaystyle\int e^{3x+4}\,dx$,
   f) $\displaystyle\int e^{3-2x}\,dx$,
   g) $\displaystyle\int e^{1-x}\,dx$,
   h) $\displaystyle\int 3e \times e^{2+4x}\,dx$.

11. Give the exact value of each of these definite integrals:

   a) $\displaystyle\int_1^2 e^{2x}\,dx$,
   b) $\displaystyle\int_{-1}^1 e^{-x}\,dx$,
   c) $\displaystyle\int_{-2}^0 e^{1-2x}\,dx$,
   d) $\displaystyle\int_4^5 2e^{2x}\,dx$,

   e) $\displaystyle\int_{\ln 3}^{\ln 9} e^x\,dx$,
   f) $\displaystyle\int_0^{\ln 2} 2e^{1-2x}\,dx$,
   g) $\displaystyle\int_0^1 2^x\,dx$,
   h) $\displaystyle\int_{-3}^9 3^x\,dx$.

12. Find the area bounded by the graph of $y = e^{2x}$, the x- and y-axes and the line $x = 2$.

13. Calculate $\displaystyle\int_0^N e^{-x}\,dx$. Deduce the value of the infinite integral $\displaystyle\int_0^\infty e^{-x}\,dx$.

14. Find the following indefinite integrals, stating the values of x for which they are valid:

   a) $\displaystyle\int \dfrac{1}{2x}\,dx$,
   b) $\displaystyle\int \dfrac{1}{x-1}\,dx$,
   c) $\displaystyle\int \dfrac{1}{1-x}\,dx$,
   d) $\displaystyle\int \dfrac{1}{4x+3}\,dx$,

   e) $\displaystyle\int \dfrac{4}{1-2x}\,dx$,
   f) $\displaystyle\int \dfrac{4}{1+2x}\,dx$,
   g) $\displaystyle\int \dfrac{4}{-1-2x}\,dx$,
   h) $\displaystyle\int \dfrac{4}{2x-1}\,dx$.

15. Calculate the area under the following graphs:

   a) $y = \dfrac{1}{x+2}$ from $x = -1$ to $x = 0$,
   b) $y = \dfrac{1}{2x-1}$ from $x = 2$ to $x = 5$,

   c) $y = \dfrac{2}{3x-5}$ from $x = 4$ to $x = 6$,
   d) $y = \dfrac{e}{ex-7}$ from $x = 4$ to $x = 5$,

   e) $y = \dfrac{1}{-x-1}$ from $x = -3$ to $x = -2$,
   f) $y = 2 + \dfrac{1}{x-1}$ from $x = 2$ to $x = 6$.

16. The region under the curve with equation $y = x^{-\frac{1}{2}}$ is rotated through $360°$ about the x-axis to form a solid. Find the volume of the solid between $x = 2$ and $x = 3$.

17. Given that $\dfrac{dy}{dx} = \dfrac{3}{2x+1}$ and that the graph of y against x passes through the point $(1, 0)$, find y in terms of x.

18. The graph of $y = x^{-2}$ between $x = 1$ and $x = 2$ is rotated through $360°$ about the y-axis. Find the volume of the solid so formed.

19. Integrate the following with respect to x:

   a) $\cos 2x$,
   b) $\sin 3x$,
   c) $\cos(2x + 1)$,
   d) $\sin(3x - 1)$,

   e) $\sin(1 - x)$,
   f) $\cos(4 - \frac{1}{2}x)$,
   g) $\sin(\frac{1}{2}x + \frac{1}{3}\pi)$,
   h) $-\sin\frac{1}{2}x$,

   i) $\sec 3x \tan 3x$,
   j) $\csc 4x \cot 4x$,
   k) $\sec^2 5x$,
   l) $\dfrac{\sin 2x}{\cos^2 2x}$.

20. Evaluate the following definite integrals:

a) $\displaystyle\int_0^{\frac{1}{2}\pi} \sin x\, dx,$

b) $\displaystyle\int_0^{\frac{1}{4}\pi} \cos x\, dx,$

c) $\displaystyle\int_0^{\frac{1}{4}\pi} \sin 2x\, dx,$

d) $\displaystyle\int_{\frac{1}{4}\pi}^{\frac{1}{3}\pi} \cos 3x\, dx,$

e) $\displaystyle\int_{\frac{1}{6}\pi}^{\frac{1}{3}\pi} \sin(3x + \tfrac{1}{6}\pi)\, dx,$

f) $\displaystyle\int_0^{\frac{1}{2}\pi} \sin(\tfrac{1}{4}\pi - x)\, dx,$

g) $\displaystyle\int_0^1 \cos(1 - x)\, dx,$

h) $\displaystyle\int_0^{\frac{1}{2}} \sin(\tfrac{1}{2}x + 1)\, dx,$

i) $\displaystyle\int_0^{2\pi} \sin \tfrac{1}{2}x\, dx,$

g) $\displaystyle\int_{\frac{1}{6}\pi}^{\frac{1}{4}\pi} \operatorname{cosec} 3x \cot 3x\, dx,$

h) $\displaystyle\int_{\frac{1}{4}}^{\frac{1}{2}} \operatorname{cosec}^2 2x\, dx,$

i) $\displaystyle\int_{0.1}^{0.3} \sec \tfrac{1}{4}x \tan \tfrac{1}{4}x\, dx.$

21*. Calculate the following definite integrals:

a) $\displaystyle\int_0^{\frac{1}{2}\pi} \sin x \cos^3 x\, dx,$

b) $\displaystyle\int_0^{\frac{1}{4}\pi} \sin^3 4x \cos 4x\, dx,$

c) $\displaystyle\int_0^{\frac{1}{3}\pi} \sec^2 x \tan x\, dx,$

d) $\displaystyle\int_0^{\frac{1}{6}\pi} \sec^2 x \tan^2 x\, dx.$

22*. In the interval $0 \le x \le \pi$ the curve $y = \sin x + \cos x$ meets the y-axis at P and the x-axis at Q. Find the coordinates of P and Q, and calculate the area of the region enclosed between the curve and the area bounded by P and Q.

Show also that $(\sin x + \cos x)^2 \equiv 1 + \sin 2x$, and hence calculate the volume of revolution obtained if the above shape is rotated through $360°$ about the x-axis.

17.3 Extending The Reciprocal Integral

The function $\ln x$ has domain $x > 0$, and so the results

$$\frac{d}{dx}\ln x = \frac{1}{x} \qquad \int \frac{1}{x}\, dx = \ln x + c$$

are only valid for $x > 0$. However, while the function $y = x^{-1}$ cannot be defined when $x = 0$, it is perfectly well-defined when $x < 0$, and so we need to be able to integrate x^{-1} for negative values of x.

The function $\ln(-x)$ is defined for $x < 0$, and the chain rule tells that $\dfrac{d}{dx}\ln(-x) = -1 \times \dfrac{1}{-x} = x^{-1}$ for $x < 0$. Thus $\ln(-x)$ is a function which differentiates to x^{-1} for negative values of x. Thus we deduce that

$$\int \frac{1}{x}\, dx = \begin{cases} \ln x + c, & x > 0, \\ \ln(-x) + c, & x < 0. \end{cases}$$

This result can be most conveniently be expressed as follows:

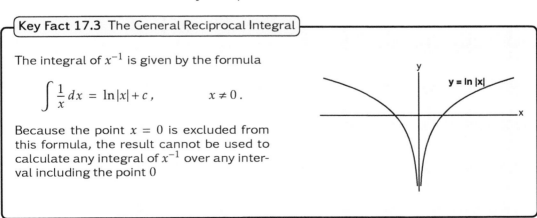

Key Fact 17.3 The General Reciprocal Integral

The integral of x^{-1} is given by the formula

$$\int \frac{1}{x}\, dx = \ln|x| + c, \qquad x \ne 0.$$

Because the point $x = 0$ is excluded from this formula, the result cannot be used to calculate any integral of x^{-1} over any interval including the point 0

Example 17.3.1. *The graphs of* $y = \dfrac{2}{x-2}$ *and* $y = -x - 1$ *intersect when* $x = 0$ *and* $x = 1$. *Find the area of the region between them.*

329

A sketch shows that the curve lies about the straight line, and so the integral we want is

$$\int_0^1 \left(\frac{2}{x-2} - (-x-1)\right)dx \ = \ \int_0^1 \left(\frac{2}{x-2} + x + 1\right)dx \ = \ \left[2\ln|x-2| + \tfrac{1}{2}x^2 + x\right]_0^1$$
$$= \ \left(2\ln 1 + \tfrac{1}{2} + 1\right) - \left(2\ln 2 + 0 + 0\right) \ = \ \tfrac{3}{2} - 2\ln 2 \ .$$

17.4 Using Trigonometric Identities

It is sometimes necessary to rearrange a function before we are able to integrate it. If a function is not in a form we can integrated immediately, some algebraic manipulation might be necessary. We have a large number of trigonometric identities, and these can be used to manipulate many trigonometric expressions into forms that can be integrated.

Example 17.4.1. *Find the indefinite integral of the function* $\cos x \operatorname{cosec}^2 x$.

Using the identity $\tan x \equiv \dfrac{\sin x}{\cos x}$, we see that $\cos x \operatorname{cosec}^2 x \equiv \operatorname{cosec} x \cot x$, and so

$$\int \cos x \operatorname{cosec}^2 x \, dx \ = \ \int \operatorname{cosec} x \cot x \, dx \ = \ -\operatorname{cosec} x + c \ .$$

Pythagorean identities are very commonly used:

Example 17.4.2. *Integrate the functions* $\tan^2 x$ *and* $\cos^3 x$.

We can write

$$\int \tan^2 x \, dx \ = \ \int (\sec^2 x - 1)\, dx \ = \ \tan x - x + c \ .$$

If we write $\cos^3 x \equiv \cos x(1 - \sin^2 x) \equiv \cos x - \sin^2 x \cos x$, then we know how to integrate $\cos x$, and (using Key Fact 17.2) we know how to integrate $\sin^2 x \cos x$. Thus

$$\int \cos^3 x \, dx \ = \ \int (\cos x - \sin^2 x \cos x)\, dx \ = \ \sin x - \tfrac{1}{3}\sin^3 x + c \ .$$

Use of the double and half-angle formulae is common.

Example 17.4.3. *Calculate the integrals* $\displaystyle\int_0^{\frac{1}{2}\pi} \cos^2 x \, dx$ *and* $\displaystyle\int_0^{\frac{1}{4}\pi} \sin^2 x \cos^2 x \, dx$.

Initially, we do not know how to integrate $\cos^2 x$, but we do know how to integrate $\cos 2x$. Thus we write

$$\int_0^{\frac{1}{2}\pi} \cos^2 x \, dx \ = \ \int_0^{\frac{1}{2}\pi} \tfrac{1}{2}(\cos 2x + 1)\, dx \ = \ \left[\tfrac{1}{4}\sin 2x + \tfrac{1}{2}x\right]_0^{\frac{1}{2}\pi} \ = \ \left(0 + \tfrac{1}{4}\pi\right) - \left(0 + 0\right) \ = \ \tfrac{1}{4}\pi \ .$$

For the second integral, we shall use the formulae for $\sin 2x$ and $\cos 2x$.

$$\int_0^{\frac{1}{4}\pi} \sin^2 x \cos^2 x \, dx \ = \ \int_0^{\frac{1}{4}\pi} \left(\tfrac{1}{2}\sin 2x\right)^2 dx \ = \ \tfrac{1}{4}\int_0^{\frac{1}{4}\pi} \sin^2 2x \, dx \ = \ \tfrac{1}{4}\int_0^{\frac{1}{4}\pi} \tfrac{1}{2}(1 - \cos 4x)\, dx$$
$$= \ \tfrac{1}{4}\left[\tfrac{1}{2}x - \tfrac{1}{8}\sin 4x\right]_0^{\frac{1}{4}\pi} \ = \ \tfrac{1}{4}\left[\left(\tfrac{1}{8}\pi - 0\right) - \left(0 - 0\right)\right] \ = \ \tfrac{1}{32}\pi \ .$$

Occasionally, the compound angles formulae can help.

Example 17.4.4. *Calculate* $\displaystyle\int_0^{\frac{1}{3}\pi} \cos 5x \cos 3x \, dx$.

In principle, we could proceed as follows. Both $\cos 3x$ and $\cos 5x$ can be written in terms of $\cos x$. The integrand can therefore be written as a polynomial in $\cos x$. Extensions of the methods that we used to integrate $\cos^2 x$ and $\cos^3 x$ above will enable us to integrate all powers of $\cos x$, so we could calculate the integral this way. However, this would be an enormous amount of work! Happily, there is a shorter method. Since

$$
\begin{aligned}
\cos 8x &= \cos(5x + 3x) = \cos 5x \cos 3x - \sin 5x \sin 3x \\
\cos 2x &= \cos(5x - 3x) = \cos 5x \cos 3x + \sin 5x \sin 3x ,
\end{aligned}
$$

we deduce that $\cos 8x + \cos 2x = 2 \cos 5x \cos 3x$, and hence

$$
\begin{aligned}
\int_0^{\frac{1}{3}\pi} \cos 5x \cos 3x \, dx &= \tfrac{1}{2} \int_0^{\frac{1}{3}\pi} (\cos 8x + \cos 2x) \, dx = \tfrac{1}{2}\left[\tfrac{1}{8} \sin 8x + \tfrac{1}{2} \sin 2x \right]_0^{\frac{1}{3}\pi} \\
&= \tfrac{1}{2}\left(\tfrac{1}{8} \sin \tfrac{8}{3}\pi + \tfrac{1}{2} \sin \tfrac{2}{3}\pi \right) = \tfrac{5}{16} \sin \tfrac{2}{3}\pi = \tfrac{5}{32}\sqrt{3} .
\end{aligned}
$$

EXERCISE 17B

1. Calculate the following integrals:

   a) $\displaystyle\int_{-6}^{-3} \frac{1}{x+2} \, dx,$ b) $\displaystyle\int_{-1}^{0} \frac{1}{2x-1} \, dx,$ c) $\displaystyle\int_{-1}^{0} \frac{2}{3x-5} \, dx,$

   d) $\displaystyle\int_{1}^{2} \frac{e}{ex-7} \, dx,$ e) $\displaystyle\int_{2}^{4} \frac{1}{-x-1} \, dx,$ f) $\displaystyle\int_{-1}^{0} \left(2 + \frac{1}{x-1}\right) dx.$

2. Integrate the following functions with respect to x:

   a) $\sin^2 x,$ b) $\cos^2 \tfrac{1}{2}x,$ c) $\sin^4 x,$ d) $\cos^4 x,$
   e) $\sec^4 x,$ f) $\operatorname{cosec}^4 3x,$ g) $\sin^5 x,$ h) $\sec x \tan^3 x,$
   i) $\cot^2 2x,$ j) $\tan^2 5x,$ k) $\sin^3 2x \cos^2 2x,$ l) $(\sin x + \cos x)^3.$

3. Find a relationship between the indefinite integrals of $\cos^4 x$, $\sin^4 x$ and $\sin^2 2x$. Explain this relationship.

4. The figure shows the graphs of the functions $y = \sin x$ and $y = \sin^2 x$ for $0 \le x \le \pi$. Find the area of the shaded region.

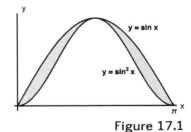

Figure 17.1

5. The graphs of $y = \sin^3 x$ and $y = \cos^3 x$ for $0 \le x \le \tfrac{1}{2}\pi$ are shown in the Figure.

   a) What are the coordinates of the point P?

   b) Find an exact expression for the shaded area.

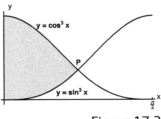

Figure 17.2

6*. Calculate the indefinite integrals of the following functions:

   a) $\sin 3x \sin x,$ b) $\cos 4x \sin 2x,$ c) $\sin 9x \sin 3x,$ d) $\sin 4x \sin 3x.$

7*. Show that

$$
\int_0^{\frac{1}{3}\pi} \tan^n x \, dx = \frac{1}{n-1} 3^{\frac{1}{2}(n-1)} - \int_0^{\frac{1}{3}\pi} \tan^{n-2} x \, dx
$$

for any $n \geq 2$. Hence find an exact expression for $\displaystyle\int_0^{\frac{1}{3}\pi} \tan^6 x\,dx$.

17.5 Integration By Substitution

The chain rule enabled us to differentiate an increased range of functions. Integration by substitution uses the power of the chain rule to perform an increased number of types of integral. Suppose that we wanted to evaluate the integral

$$\int \frac{1}{x + \sqrt{x}}\,dx.$$

Although this integral is currently in a form we cannot handle, careful introduction of a new variable will enable us to cast this integral in a shape that we can deal with.

If we denote this integral by the letter I, then we know that

$$\frac{dI}{dx} = \frac{1}{x + \sqrt{x}}.$$

The tricky term in this integral is the square root, so let us write $x = u^2$. Then, by the chain rule,

$$\frac{dI}{du} = \frac{dI}{dx} \times \frac{dx}{du} = \frac{1}{x + \sqrt{x}} \times 2u = \frac{2u}{u^2 + u} = \frac{2}{u + 1}.$$

Thus we deduce that $I = 2\ln|u + 1| + c$. Replacing u by $\sqrt{x}$ we obtain the value of the integral

$$\int \frac{1}{x + \sqrt{x}}\,dx = I(x) = \ln(\sqrt{x} + 1) + c.$$

Note that, since $\sqrt{x} + 1$ is always positive, we do not need the modulus sign inside the logarithm. The above method is algebraically exact, but not particularly easy to use. There is an easier way of setting down these calculations. To be able to use this simpler approach, we need to 'break the rules' with our notation. Up until now we have know that an expression like $\dfrac{dx}{du}$ was a single quantity, and that it should not be thought of as the 'quotient' of dx by du. The technique of **integration by substitution** is most easily performed by doing just what we have been told not to do. Introducing the variable u, where $x = u^2$, we know that $\dfrac{dx}{du} = 2u$. If we allow ourselves to split up the dx and the du, this last identity can be written as $dx = 2u\,du$. Since the integrand $\dfrac{1}{x + \sqrt{x}}$ can be written as $\dfrac{1}{u^2 + u}$, we can replace all parts of this integral with expressions involving u alone, obtaining

$$\int \frac{1}{x + \sqrt{x}}\,dx = \int \frac{1}{u^2 + u} \times 2u\,du = \int \frac{2}{u + 1}\,du\,;$$

we have replaced an integral of a function of x with respect to x by a simpler integral in terms of u, and we calculate

$$\int \frac{1}{x + \sqrt{x}}\,dx = \int \frac{2}{u + 1}\,du = 2\ln|u + 1| + c = 2\ln(\sqrt{x} + 1) + c$$

expressing the function of u as a function of x to obtain the final answer.

Example 17.5.1. *Find the integral $\displaystyle\int x^{-1} \ln x\,dx$ using the substitution $x = e^u$.*

Since $\dfrac{dx}{du} = e^u$, we write $dx = e^u\,du$. Thus the integral becomes

$$\int x^{-1} \ln x\,dx = \int e^{-u} \times u \times e^u\,du = \int u\,du = \tfrac{1}{2}u^2 + c\,;$$

substituting back for u gives

$$\int x^{-1} \ln x\,dx = \tfrac{1}{2}(\ln x)^2 + c.$$

Example 17.5.2. *Find the integral* $\displaystyle\int \frac{6x}{2x+1}\,dx$ *using the substitution* $2x+1 = u^2$.

Differentiating this formula with respect to u, we deduce that $2\dfrac{dx}{du} = 2u$, and hence we write $dx = u\,du$. Thus

$$
\begin{aligned}
\int \frac{6x}{\sqrt{2x+1}}\,dx &= \int \frac{3(u^2-1)}{u}\,u\,du = 3\int (u^2-1)\,du \\
&= u^3 - 3u + c = (2x+1)^{\frac{3}{2}} - 3(2x+1)^{\frac{1}{2}} + c = \left((2x+1)-3\right)\sqrt{2x+1} + c \\
&= 2(x-1)\sqrt{2x+1} + c
\end{aligned}
$$

Definite integrals can also be evaluated using integration by substitution. Suppose that we wanted to evaluate

$$\int_1^4 \frac{1}{x+\sqrt{x}}\,dx .$$

We saw at the start of this section how to evaluate this indefinite integral, and hence

$$\int_1^4 \frac{1}{x+\sqrt{x}}\,dx = \left[2\ln(\sqrt{x}+1)\right]_1^4 = 2\ln 3 - 2\ln 2 = 2\ln\tfrac{3}{2} .$$

However, there is no need to calculate the full indefinite integral as a function of x; it is sufficient to know it as a function of $u = \sqrt{x}$. When we change the variable from x to u, turning the integral with respect to x into an integral with respect to u, change the limits of the integral at the same time, replacing each limit for x with the corresponding value for u. In this case $u = 1$ when $x = 1$, and $u = 2$ when $x = 4$. Thus, with $x = u^2$, we obtain

$$\int_1^4 \frac{1}{x+\sqrt{x}}\,dx = \int_1^2 \frac{1}{u^2+u} \times 2u\,du = 2\int_1^2 \frac{1}{u+1}\,du = \left[2\ln(u+1)\right]_1^2 = 2\ln 3 - 2\ln 2 = 2\ln\tfrac{3}{2} .$$

In other words integration by substitution replaces a definite integral in x by a definite integral in u. This method works because substituting $x = 1$ and $x = 4$ into the function $2\ln(\sqrt{x}+1)$ is the same as substituting $u = 1$ and $u = 2$ into $2\ln(u+1)$; there is no need to convert the indefinite integral $2\ln(u+1)$, expressed in terms of u, back into expression of the indefinite integral in terms of x.

Example 17.5.3. *Using the substitution* $x = \tan u$, *evaluate the integral* $\displaystyle\int_0^1 \frac{1}{1+x^2}\,dx.$

Since $\dfrac{dx}{du} = \sec^2 u$, we write $dx = \sec^2 u\,du$. When $x = 0$, $u = 0$. When $x = 1$, $u = \tfrac{1}{4}\pi$. Thus

$$\int_0^1 \frac{1}{1+x^2}\,dx = \int_0^{\frac{1}{4}\pi} \frac{1}{1+\tan^2 u} \times \sec^2 u\,du = \int_0^{\frac{1}{4}\pi} du = \left[u\right]_0^{\frac{1}{4}\pi} = \tfrac{1}{4}\pi .$$

Example 17.5.4. *Prove that the area of a circle of radius 1 is equal to* π.

The area of the circle is twice the area under between the x-axis and the curve $y = \sqrt{1-x^2}$. Thus we want to calculate the integral $2\displaystyle\int_{-1}^1 \sqrt{1-x^2}\,dx$. If we use the substitution $x = \sin\theta$, then $\dfrac{dx}{d\theta} = \cos\theta$, and so $dx = \cos\theta\,d\theta$. When $x = -1$, $\theta = -\tfrac{1}{2}\pi$. When $x = 1$, $\theta = \tfrac{1}{2}\pi$. Thus the area is

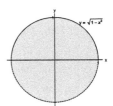

Figure 17.3

$$
\begin{aligned}
2\int_{-1}^1 \sqrt{1-x^2}\,dx &= 2\int_{-\frac{1}{2}\pi}^{\frac{1}{2}\pi} \cos\theta \times \cos\theta\,d\theta = \int_{-\frac{1}{2}\pi}^{\frac{1}{2}\pi} 2\cos^2\theta\,d\theta = \int_{-\frac{1}{2}\pi}^{\frac{1}{2}\pi} (\cos 2\theta + 1)\,d\theta \\
&= \left[\tfrac{1}{2}\sin 2\theta + \theta\right]_{-\frac{1}{2}\pi}^{\frac{1}{2}\pi} = \left(0 + \tfrac{1}{2}\pi\right) - \left(0 - \tfrac{1}{2}\pi\right) = \pi .
\end{aligned}
$$

> **For Interest**
>
> This calculation is not as pointless as it looks. Even if we were to accept π to be defined as the ratio of the circumference of a circle to its diameter, there is no good reason why π should reappear in the formula for the area of the circle.
>
> Mathematicians prefer a non-geometric definition of π. The problem with a geometrical definition is that π can only be calculated by measuring lengths, and such measurements are always inaccurate, no matter how precisely they are performed; we are simply not able to measure a length exactly. Mathematicians prefer a definition of π that is wholly founded in mathematics; they would then like to prove that π has all the properties that we normally associate with it. This integral is one of those proofs.

This type of substitution (expressing x in terms of a trigonometric function) is known as **trigonometric substitution**.

Sometimes, making a substitution of the explicit form $x = f(u)$ is cumbersome, and creates additional calculational effort. Provided that it is possible to write the substitution in this form, it is often easier to define the change of variable implicitly.

Example 17.5.5. *Calculate* $\int \dfrac{x}{\sqrt{x^2 + 1}}\, dx$.

If we put $x = \sqrt{u^2 - 1}$, then $\dfrac{dx}{du} = \dfrac{u}{\sqrt{u^2 - 1}}$, so that $dx = \dfrac{u}{\sqrt{u^2 - 1}}\, du$, and hence

$$\int \frac{x}{\sqrt{x^2 + 1}}\, dx = \int \frac{\sqrt{u^2 - 1}}{u} \times \frac{u}{\sqrt{u^2 - 1}}\, du = \int du = u + c = \sqrt{x^2 + 1} + c.$$

We could instead write $x^2 + 1 = u^2$, in which case $2x\dfrac{dx}{du} = 2u$, and hence $x\, dx = u\, du$, giving the simpler argument

$$\int \frac{x}{\sqrt{x^2 + 1}}\, dx = \int u^{-1} \times u\, du = \int du = u + c = \sqrt{x^2 + 1} + c.$$

Example 17.5.6. *Evaluate the integral* $\int \tan\theta \sec^4\theta\, d\theta$.

If we put $u = \sec\theta$, then $\dfrac{du}{d\theta} = \sec\theta\tan\theta$, and hence we write $du = \sec\theta\tan\theta\, d\theta$. We can write

$$\int \tan\theta\sec^4\theta\, d\theta = \int \sec^3\theta \times \sec\theta\tan\theta\, d\theta = \int u^3\, du = \tfrac{1}{4}u^4 + c = \tfrac{1}{4}\sec^4\theta + c$$

It can be very challenging finding a successful substitution. While **any** substitution, correctly applied, will replace the original integral with an equivalent one, it is not easy to find that substitution which produces an integral that can be evaluated.

Example 17.5.7. *Calculate the integral* $\int \dfrac{1}{e^x + 1}\, dx$.

The term $e^x + 1$ in the denominator suggests that a substitution of the form $u = e^x$ might work. Then $\dfrac{du}{dx} = e^x = u^{-1}$, so that $dx = u^{-1}\, du$, and the integral becomes

$$\int \frac{1}{e^x + 1}\, dx = \int \frac{1}{u + 1} \times u^{-1}\, du = \int \frac{1}{u(u + 1)}\, du.$$

At the present, we do not know how to integrate this function (although we will after the next section). We need a slightly different approach. If we rewrite the integral slightly, noting that

$$\int \frac{1}{e^x + 1}\, dx = \int \frac{e^{-x}}{1 + e^{-x}}\, dx,$$

then the substitution $v = e^{-x}$ gives $\frac{dv}{dx} = -e^{-x}$, so that $dv = -e^{-x} dx$. We note that the term $e^{-x} dx$ is sitting nicely inside our rewritten integral, and we see that

$$\int \frac{1}{e^x + 1} dx = -\int \frac{1}{1 + v} dv = -\ln(1 + v) + c = -\ln(1 + e^{-x}) + c.$$

Example 17.5.8. *Calculate the integral* $\int_0^3 xe^{-x^2} dx$.

Try $u = x^2$. Then $\frac{du}{dx} = 2x$, and we write $du = 2x\,dx$. When $x = 0$, $u = 0$. When $x = 3$, $u = 9$. Thus

$$\int_0^3 xe^{-x^2} dx = \int_0^3 e^{-x^2} \times x\,dx = \int_0^9 e^{-u} \times \tfrac{1}{2} du = \tfrac{1}{2} \int_0^9 e^{-u} du = \tfrac{1}{2}\left[-e^{-u}\right]_0^9 = \tfrac{1}{2}(1 - e^{-9}).$$

Having seen a number of examples of integration by substitution, we are now ready to see the general statement.

> **Key Fact 17.4** Integration By Substitution
>
> If f and g are functions, then
>
> $$\int f'\big(g(x)\big) g'(x)\,dx = f\big(g(x)\big) + c.$$

Viewed in this way, integration is clearly directly related to the chain rule, since that rule tells us that $\frac{d}{dx} f\big(g(x)\big) = f'\big(g(x)\big) g'(x)$; this formula simply reverses the differentiation. We can connect this result to our earlier notation by introducing the variable $u = g(x)$. Then $\frac{du}{dx} = g'(x)$, so we write $du = g'(x)\,dx$, and hence

$$\int f'\big(g(x)\big) g'(x)\,dx = \int f'(u)\,du = f(u) + c = f\big(g(x)\big) + c.$$

We note another important special case; what happens when $f(x) = |\ln x|$.

> **Key Fact 17.5** Integration: Pattern-Spotting 3
>
> For a function g we have
>
> $$\int \frac{kg'(x)}{g(x)} dx = k\ln|g(x)| + c = \ln|g(x)|^k + c.$$

Example 17.5.9. *Calculate the indefinite integrals of* $\frac{x}{x^2+1}$, $\tan x$ *and* $\cot x$.

Putting $g(x) = x^2 + 1$, we deduce that $\int \frac{x}{x^2+1} dx = \tfrac{1}{2}\ln(x^2 + 1) + c$. Note that, since $x^2 + 1 > 0$, we do not need the modulus sign.

The second integral can be calculated in two ways. Putting $g(x) = \cos x$ we have

$$\int \tan x\,dx = -\int \frac{-\sin x}{\cos x} dx = -\ln|\cos x| + c = \ln|\sec x| + c.$$

Alternatively we could write

$$\int \tan x\,dx = \int \frac{\sec x \tan x}{\sec x} dx = \ln|\sec x| + c.$$

Similarly

$$\int \cot x \, dx = \int \frac{\cos x}{\sin x} \, dx = \ln|\sin x| + c.$$

When calculating definite integrals, it is possible that a substitution will result in the limits of the new integral being 'upside-down', with the larger limit at the bottom. Don't forget how to resolve that problem.

Example 17.5.10. *Calculate the definite integral* $\displaystyle\int_1^2 t^{-3} e^{-t^{-2}} \, dt.$

If we substitute $u = t^{-2}$, then $\dfrac{du}{dt} = -2t^{-3}$, and so $du = -2t^{-3} \, dt$. When $t = 1$, $u = 1$, and $t = \frac{1}{4}$ when $t = 2$. Thus

$$\int_1^2 t^{-3} e^{-t^{-2}} \, dt = \int_1^{\frac{1}{4}} e^{-u} \times (-\tfrac{1}{2} \, du) = -\tfrac{1}{2} \int_1^{\frac{1}{4}} e^{-u} \, du$$

Reversing the order of the limit simply changes the sign of the integral, and we obtain the more natural expression

$$\int_1^2 t^{-3} e^{-t^{-2}} \, dt = \tfrac{1}{2} \int_{\frac{1}{4}}^1 e^{-u} \, du = \tfrac{1}{2} \Big[-e^{-u} \Big]_{\frac{1}{4}}^1 = \tfrac{1}{2} \big(e^{-\frac{1}{4}} - e^{-1} \big).$$

17.6 Implicit Curves

Suppose that a curve has parametric equation:

$$x = x(t), \qquad y = y(t).$$

The area under the curve between $x = a$ and $x = \beta$ is, of course $\displaystyle\int_a^b y \, dx$. The problem is that we do not know y as a function of x. Integration by substitution solves this problem for us. Suppose that the points P and Q on the curve are achieved by the values α and β of t.

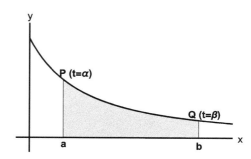

Figure 17.4

The substitution $x = x(t)$ converts the integral for the area into

$$\int_a^b y \, dx = \int_\alpha^\beta y \frac{dx}{dt} \, dt.$$

A similar formula enables us to calculate volumes of revolution as well.

Key Fact 17.6 Parametric Curves: Areas And Volumes Of Revolution

The area under the section of a parametric curve $x = x(t)$, $y = y(t)$ is

$$\int y \frac{dx}{dt} \, dt,$$

while the volume of the solid of revolution obtained by rotating this region through $360°$ about the x-axis is

$$\pi \int y^2 \frac{dx}{dt} \, dt.$$

In both cases the integrals are to be performed over the range of values of t which determine the desired section of curve.

Example 17.6.1. *Find the volume of the solid of revolution formed when the region defined by the parametric curve $x = t^2 + 1$, $y = t - 1$, the line $x = 10$ and the x-axis is rotated through $360°$ about the x-axis.*

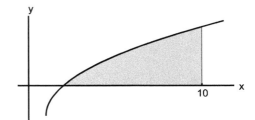

Figure 17.5

Since $y = 0$ when $t = 1$ and $x = 10$ with $y > 0$ when $t = 3$, we see that the desired volume is

$$\pi \int_1^3 y^2 \frac{dx}{dt} \, dt \;=\; \pi \int_1^3 (t-1)^2 \times 2t \, dt \;=\; 2\pi \int_1^3 (t^3 - 2t^2 + t) \, dt$$

$$=\; 2\pi \left[\tfrac{1}{4} t^4 - \tfrac{2}{3} t^3 + \tfrac{1}{2} t^2 \right]_1^3 \;=\; 2\pi \left(\tfrac{27}{4} - \tfrac{1}{12} \right) \;=\; \tfrac{40}{3} \pi .$$

EXERCISE 17C

1. Use the given substitutions to evaluate the following indefinite integrals:

a) $\displaystyle \int \frac{1}{x - 2\sqrt{x}} \, dx$ $x = u^2,$

b) $\displaystyle \int \frac{1}{(3x+4)^2} \, dx$ $3x + 4 = u,$

c) $\displaystyle \int \sin\left(\tfrac{1}{3}x - \tfrac{1}{2}\pi \right)$ $\tfrac{1}{3}\pi - \tfrac{1}{2}x = u,$

d) $\displaystyle \int x(x-1)^5 \, dx$ $x = 1 + u,$

e) $\displaystyle \int \frac{e^x}{e^x + 1} \, dx$ $x = \ln u,$

f) $\displaystyle \frac{1}{3\sqrt{x} + 4x} \, dx$ $x = u^2,$

g) $\displaystyle \int 3x\sqrt{x+2} \, dx$ $x = u^2 - 2,$

h) $\displaystyle \int \frac{x}{\sqrt{x-3}} \, dx$ $x = 3 + u^2,$

i) $\displaystyle \int \frac{1}{x \ln x} \, dx$ $x = e^u,$

j) $\displaystyle \int \frac{1}{\sqrt{4 - x^2}} \, dx$ $x = 2\sin u.$

2. Use a substitution of the form $ax + b = u$ to find the following integrals:

a) $\displaystyle \int x(2x+1)^3 \, dx,$

b) $\displaystyle \int (x+2)(2x-3)^5 \, dx,$

c) $\displaystyle \int x\sqrt{2x-1} \, dx,$

d) $\displaystyle \int \frac{x-2}{\sqrt{x-4}} \, dx,$

e) $\displaystyle \int \frac{x}{(x+1)^2} \, dx,$

f) $\displaystyle \int \frac{x}{2x+3} \, dx.$

3. Use a suitable substitution to find the following integrals:

a) $\displaystyle \int \frac{1}{\sqrt{1 - 9x^2}} \, dx,$

b) $\displaystyle \int \sqrt{16 - 9x^2} \, dx,$

c) $\displaystyle \int \frac{1}{2 + e^{-x}} \, dx,$

d) $\displaystyle \int \frac{x}{\sqrt[3]{1 + x}} \, dx,$

e) $\displaystyle \int \left(1 - x^2 \right)^{-\frac{3}{2}} \, dx,$

f) $\displaystyle \int \frac{1}{2 - \sqrt{x}} \, dx.$

4.   a) Use the substitution $x = \tan u$ to show that $\displaystyle \int \frac{1}{x^2 + 1} \, dx = \tan^{-1} x + c.$

     b) Use the substitution $x = \ln u$ to find $\displaystyle \int \frac{e^x}{1 + e^{2x}} \, dx.$

5. Use the given substitutions to evaluate the following definite integrals:

a) $\displaystyle\int_0^1 \frac{e^x}{e^x+1}\,dx$ $\quad x = \ln u,$ $\qquad$ b) $\displaystyle\int_9^{16} \frac{1}{x-2\sqrt{x}}\,dx$ $\quad x = u^2,$

c) $\displaystyle\int_1^2 x(x-1)^5\,dx$ $\quad x = 1+u,$ $\qquad$ d) $\displaystyle\int_1^2 x\sqrt{x-1}\,dx$ $\quad x = 1+u,$

e) $\displaystyle\int_0^1 \frac{1}{\sqrt{4-x^2}}\,dx$ $\quad x = 2\sin u,$ $\qquad$ f) $\displaystyle\int_6^9 \frac{x^2}{\sqrt{x-5}}\,dx$ $\quad x = 5+u,$

g) $\displaystyle\int_{-4}^4 \sqrt{16-x^2}\,dx$ $\quad x = 4\sin u,$ $\qquad$ h) $\displaystyle\int_1^6 \frac{1}{4+x^2}\,dx$ $\quad x = \tan u,$

i) $\displaystyle\int_e^{e^2} \frac{1}{x(\ln x)^2}\,dx$ $\quad x = e^u,$ $\qquad$ j) $\displaystyle\int_0^{\frac12} \frac{1}{(1-x^2)^{\frac32}}\,dx$ $\quad x = \sin u.$

k) $\displaystyle\int_1^8 \frac{1}{\sqrt[3]{x^2}\left(1+\sqrt[3]{x}\right)}\,dx$ $\quad x = u^3.$

6. Use the substitution $x = \sin^2 u$ to calculate $\displaystyle\int_0^{\frac12} \sqrt{\frac{x}{1-x}}\,dx.$

7. Use the given substitutions to evaluate the following indefinite integrals:

a) $\displaystyle\int 2x(x^2+1)^3\,dx$ $\quad u = x^2+1,$ $\qquad$ b) $\displaystyle\int x\sqrt{4+x^2}\,dx$ $\quad u = 4+x^2,$

c) $\displaystyle\int \sin^5 x\cos x\,dx$ $\quad u = \sin x,$ $\qquad$ d) $\displaystyle\int \tan^3 x\sec^2 x\,dx$ $\quad u = \tan x,$

e) $\displaystyle\int \frac{2x^3}{\sqrt{1-x^4}}\,dx$ $\quad u = 1-x^4,$ $\qquad$ f) $\displaystyle\int \cos^3 2x\sin 2x\,dx$ $\quad u = \cos 2x.$

8. Evaluate each of these integrals, giving an exact answer:

a) $\displaystyle\int_1^2 \frac{e^x}{e^x-1}\,dx,$ $\qquad$ b) $\displaystyle\int_4^5 \frac{x-2}{x^2-4x+5}\,dx,$ $\qquad$ c) $\displaystyle\int_0^{\frac16\pi} \frac{\sin 2x}{1+\cos 2x}\,dx,$

d) $\displaystyle\int_0^{\frac12\pi} \frac{\cos x}{\sqrt{1+3\sin x}}\,dx,$ $\qquad$ e) $\displaystyle\int_0^2 x(x^2+1)^3\,dx,$ $\qquad$ f) $\displaystyle\int_0^{\frac14\pi} \sin x\cos^2 x\,dx,$

g) $\displaystyle\int_1^8 (1+2x)\sqrt{x+x^2}\,dx,$ $\qquad$ h) $\displaystyle\int_0^{\frac13\pi} \frac{\sin x}{(1+\cos x)^2}\,dx,$ $\qquad$ i) $\displaystyle\int_0^3 2x\sqrt{1+x^2}\,dx,$

j) $\displaystyle\int_0^{\frac14\pi} \sec^2 x\tan^2 x\,dx,$ $\qquad$ k) $\displaystyle\int_1^e \frac{(\ln x)^n}{x}\,dx,$ $\qquad$ l) $\displaystyle\int_0^{\frac13\pi} \sec^3 x\tan x\,dx.$

9. a) Use the substitution $u = \sec x + \tan x$ to evaluate $\displaystyle\int \sec x\,dx.$ Determine $\displaystyle\int \operatorname{cosec} x\,dx.$

   b) Use the substitutions $u = \tan\left(\frac12 x + \frac14\pi\right)$ and $v = \tan\frac12 x$ respectively to evaluate the integrals $\displaystyle\int \sec x\,dx$ and $\displaystyle\int \operatorname{cosec} x\,dx.$

10. Explain why the special patterns of integration found in Key Fact 17.1 and Key Fact 17.2 are both instances of integration by substitution.

11. The parametric curve with equation $x = t^3 - 1$, $y = 4 - t^2$ for $t > 0$ meets the x-axis at the point P and the y-axis at the point Q. Find the coordinates of P and Q, and the value of t corresponding to each point. What is the area of the finite region formed by the curve and the x- and y-axes?

12. An ellipse has parametric equation $x = a\cos t$, $y = b\sin t$ for $0 \le t \le 2\pi$. What is the volume of the solid of revolution formed by rotating the ellipse through $360°$ about the x-axis?

13. a) Use a substitution to show that $\displaystyle\int_0^{\frac12\pi} \sin^2 x\,dx$ and $\displaystyle\int_0^{\frac12\pi} \cos^2 x\,dx$ are equal (do not calculate the values of either integral). Hence deduce that both are equal to $\frac14\pi.$

   b) By considering the identity $(\cos^2 x + \sin^2 x)^2 \equiv 1$, use a similar argument to evaluate $\displaystyle\int_0^{\frac12\pi} \cos^4 x\,dx.$

14. Use a substitution to show that $\displaystyle\int_0^\pi x\sin x\,dx = \int_0^\pi (\pi - x)\sin x\,dx$. Hence show that $\displaystyle\int_0^\pi x\sin x\,dx = \tfrac{1}{2}\pi\int_0^\pi \sin x\,dx$, and evaluate this.

15*. Use trigonometric substitution to evaluate the following integrals (note that some of them are infinite):

a) $\displaystyle\int_0^\infty \frac{1}{x^2+4}\,dx,$

b) $\displaystyle\int_0^3 \frac{1}{\sqrt{9-x^2}}\,dx,$

c) $\displaystyle\int_{-\infty}^\infty \frac{1}{9x^2+4}\,dx$

d) $\displaystyle\int_0^1 \frac{1}{\sqrt{x(1-x)}}\,dx,$

e) $\displaystyle\int_0^\infty \frac{1}{(1+x^2)^{\frac{3}{2}}}\,dx,$

f) $\displaystyle\int_1^\infty \frac{1}{x\sqrt{x^2-1}}\,dx$

16*. By completing the square in the denominator, evaluate $\displaystyle\int_0^1 \frac{1}{x^2+x+1}\,dx.$

17*. Prove that $\displaystyle\int \frac{1}{1+\cos^2 x}\,dx = \frac{1}{\sqrt{2}}\tan^{-1}\left(\frac{1}{\sqrt{2}}\tan x\right)+c.$

18*. If $t = \tan\tfrac{1}{2}\theta$, show that

$$\frac{d\theta}{dt} = \frac{2}{1+t^2}, \qquad \sin\theta = \frac{2t}{1+t^2}, \qquad \cos\theta = \frac{1-t^2}{1+t^2}.$$

Hence calculate the integral $\displaystyle\int_0^1 \frac{t(1-t^2)^3}{(1+t^2)^5}\,dt.$

17.7 Algebraic Fractions

We now have enough integration techniques to be able to integrate all algebraic fractions of the types discussed in Chapter 6; techniques of polynomial division and the use of the technique of partial fractions will reduce all algebraic fractions (of the types that we shall meet) to combinations of polynomials, quotients of the form $\frac{1}{(x+a)^n}$ (for positive integers n) and quotients like $\frac{ax+b}{x^2+c}$ for constants a, b and c. Integration by substitution enables us to integrate all expressions of this type.

Example 17.7.1. *Calculate the indefinite integral* $\displaystyle\int \frac{x^3 - 4x^2 + 4x - 2}{x^2 - 5x + 6}\,dx.$

Long division tells us that $x^3 - 4x^2 + 4x - 2 \equiv (x+1)(x^2 - 5x + 6) + 3x - 8$, and hence

$$\frac{x^3 - 4x^2 + 4x - 2}{x^2 - 5x + 6} \equiv x+1+ \frac{3x-8}{x^2-5x+6} \equiv x+1+\frac{3x-8}{(x-2)(x-3)}.$$

Applying the technique of partial fractions to this last fraction, we try to write

$$\frac{3x-8}{(x-2)(x-3)} \equiv \frac{A}{x-2}+\frac{B}{x-3},$$

which is possible provided that $3x - 8 \equiv A(x-3) + B(x-2)$. Putting $x = 2$ gives $A = 2$. Putting $x = 3$ gives $B = 1$. Thus

$$\frac{x^3 - 4x^2 + 4x - 2}{x^2 - 5x + 6} = x+1+\frac{2}{x-2}+\frac{1}{x-3};$$

integrating this gives

$$\int \frac{x^3 - 4x^2 + 4x - 2}{x^2 - 5x + 6}\,dx = \tfrac{1}{2}x^2+x+2\ln|x-2|+\ln|x-3|+c = \tfrac{1}{2}x^2+x+c+\ln\left((x-2)^2|x-3|\right).$$

Example 17.7.2. *Evaluate* $\displaystyle\int_3^5 \frac{2x^2 - 7x + 8}{(x-1)(x-2)^2}\,dx.$

The degree of the numerator is smaller than that of the denominator, so we do not need to do any division first. The method of partial fractions leads us to look for an expansion of the form

$$\frac{2x^2 - 7x + 8}{(x-1)(x-2)^2} \equiv \frac{A}{x-1} + \frac{B}{x-2} + \frac{C}{(x-2)^2} ;$$

that will work provided that $2x^2 - 7x + 8 \equiv A(x-2)^2 + B(x-1)(x-2) + C(x-1)$. Putting $x = 1$ gives $A = 3$; putting $x = 2$ gives $C = 2$. Matching the coefficients of x^2 tells us that $A + B = 2$, and so $B = -1$. In other words

$$\frac{2x^2 - 7x + 8}{(x-1)(x-2)^2} \equiv \frac{3}{x-1} - \frac{1}{x-2} + \frac{2}{(x-2)^2} ;$$

integrating this identity gives

$$\int_3^5 \frac{2x^2 - 7x + 8}{(x-1)(x-2)^2}\, dx = \left[3\ln(x-1) - \ln(x-2) - \frac{2}{x-2} \right]_3^5 = \left[\ln\left(\frac{(x-1)^3}{x-2}\right) - \frac{2}{x-2} \right]_3^5$$

$$= \left(\ln\tfrac{64}{3} - \tfrac{2}{3} \right) - \left(\ln 8 - 2 \right) = \ln\tfrac{8}{3} + \tfrac{4}{3} .$$

Note that, since $x > 2$ and $x > 1$ throughout the range of integration, we did not need the modulus signs inside the logarithms.

The terms in a partial fraction expansion related to an irreducible quadratic denominator are more complicated. They have to be handled in two parts.

Example 17.7.3. *Integrate* $\displaystyle\int \frac{3t + 2}{(t+1)(t^2+2)}\, dt.$

We want to write

$$\frac{3t + 2}{(t+1)(t^2+2)} \equiv \frac{A}{t+1} + \frac{Bt + C}{t^2 + 2} ,$$

which is possible provided that $3t + 2 \equiv A(t^2 + 2) + (Bt + C)(t + 1)$. Putting $t = -1$ gives $A = -\frac{1}{3}$. Comparing coefficients of t^2 gives $A + B = 0$, and so $B = \frac{1}{3}$. Comparing constant coefficients gives $2 = 2A + C$, and so $C = \frac{8}{3}$. Thus

$$\frac{3t + 2}{(t+1)(t^2+2)} \equiv \frac{1}{3}\left(\frac{t + 8}{t^2 + 2} - \frac{1}{t+1} \right).$$

and so

$$\int \frac{3t + 2}{(t+1)(t^2+2)}\, dt = \frac{1}{3}\left(\int \frac{t}{t^2 + 2}\, dt + \int \frac{8}{t^2 + 2}\, dt - \ln|t + 1| \right).$$

The two remaining integrals have to be handled by two separate substitutions. Putting $t^2 + 2 = u$ gives

$$\int \frac{t}{t^2 + 2}\, dt = \frac{1}{2}\int u^{-1}\, du = \frac{1}{2}\ln u + c = \frac{1}{2}\ln(t^2 + 2) + c ,$$

while the substitution $t = \sqrt{2}\tan\theta$ is needed for the second integral:

$$\int \frac{8}{t^2 + 2}\, dt = \int \frac{8}{2\sec^2\theta} \times \sqrt{2}\sec^2\theta\, d\theta = 4\sqrt{2}\,\theta + c = 4\sqrt{2}\tan^{-1}\tfrac{t}{\sqrt{2}} + c ,$$

and hence

$$\int \frac{3t + 2}{(t+1)(t^2+2)}\, dt = \frac{1}{3}\left(\frac{1}{2}\ln(t^2 + 2) + 4\sqrt{2}\tan^{-1}\tfrac{t}{\sqrt{2}} - \ln|t + 1| \right) + c$$

$$= \ln\left(\frac{(t^2 + 2)^{\frac{1}{6}}}{|t + 1|^{\frac{1}{3}}} \right) + \tfrac{4}{3}\sqrt{2}\tan^{-1}\tfrac{t}{\sqrt{2}} + c .$$

340

EXERCISE 17D

1. Find the indefinite integral of each of the following functions:

a) $\dfrac{x^2 + 5}{x - 2}$,

b) $\dfrac{x^2 + 3x + 5}{x + 3}$,

c) $\dfrac{x^2 + 4x - 2}{2x + 9}$,

d) $\dfrac{x^3}{x + 3}$,

e) $\dfrac{x^4 + 1}{x - 1}$,

f) $\dfrac{3x^2 - 5x + 2}{2x - 4}$.

2. Calculate the following integrals:

a) $\displaystyle\int \dfrac{x}{(x + 1)(x + 2)}\, dx$,

b) $\displaystyle\int \dfrac{2x - 3}{x(x + 1)}\, dx$,

c) $\displaystyle\int \dfrac{1}{x^2 - 16}\, dx$,

d) $\displaystyle\int \dfrac{x - 2}{(x + 1)(x + 2)^2}\, dx$,

e) $\displaystyle\int \dfrac{3x + 1}{(x - 3)^2}\, dx$,

f) $\displaystyle\int \dfrac{x^2 + 8}{x^2(x - 4)}\, dx$,

g) $\displaystyle\int \dfrac{3}{x(x^2 + 1)}\, dx$,

h) $\displaystyle\int \dfrac{x^2 + 2x}{(x - 2)(x^2 + 4)}\, dx$,

i) $\displaystyle\int \dfrac{2x + 1}{x(x^2 + 9)}\, dx$.

3. Evaluate:

a) $\displaystyle\int_0^4 \dfrac{3}{(x + 2)(x + 5)}\, dx$,

b) $\displaystyle\int_0^4 \dfrac{2x + 1}{(x + 1)(x - 5)}\, dx$,

c) $\displaystyle\int_1^2 \dfrac{2x + 1}{(x + 2)(2x + 1)}\, dx$,

d) $\displaystyle\int_5^7 \dfrac{1}{(x - 4)^2(x + 1)}\, dx$,

e) $\displaystyle\int_1^2 \dfrac{x^2 + 2x - 1}{x^2(x + 3)}\, dx$,

f) $\displaystyle\int_0^3 \dfrac{x^3 + 2x^2 + x - 1}{(x + 1)(x + 2)}\, dx$,

g) $\displaystyle\int_0^1 \dfrac{x^2 + 4x - 2}{(x + 2)(x^2 + 2)}\, dx$,

h) $\displaystyle\int_0^1 \dfrac{3x^2 + x}{(x - 3)(x^2 + 1)}\, dx$,

i) $\displaystyle\int_1^3 \dfrac{3x - 3}{x(x^2 + 3)}\, dx$.

4. Expand $\dfrac{1}{(x + 2)(x + 3)}$ by partial fractions. Hence evaluate the integrals $\displaystyle\int \dfrac{1}{(x + 2)(x + 3)}\, dx$

and $\displaystyle\int \dfrac{1}{(x + 2)^2(x + 3)^2}\, dx$.

5. Use the substitution $x = u^6$ to evaluate the integral $\displaystyle\int \dfrac{1}{x^{\frac{1}{2}} + x^{\frac{1}{3}}}\, dx$.

6. a) Use the substitution $u = e^x$ to show that

$$\int \dfrac{1}{e^x - 4e^{-x}}\, dx = \int \dfrac{1}{u^2 - 4}\, du.$$

b) Deduce that

$$\int \dfrac{1}{e^x - 4e^{-x}}\, dx = \tfrac{1}{4}\ln\left(\dfrac{e^x - 2}{e^x + 2}\right) + c.$$

7. The region R is defined by the line $y = 1$, the line $x = 2$ and the curve $y = \dfrac{2}{x^2(x + 1)}$. Find the coordinates of the point P, and find the area of the region R.

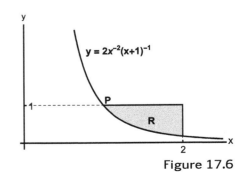

8. Use the substitution $x = u^4$ to evaluate

$$\int_1^{16} \dfrac{1}{\sqrt{x}(\sqrt[4]{x} + 1)(\sqrt[4]{x} + 2)}\, dx.$$

9. Evaluate the integral

$$\int_0^1 \dfrac{1}{(x^2 + 1)(x^2 + 3)}\, dx.$$

341

10*. Find $\displaystyle\int \frac{1}{x^3+1}\,dx$.

11*. Suppose that a is a positive constant.

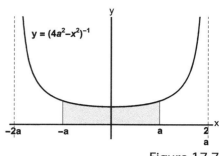

Figure 17.7

a) Find the area of the region defined by the curve $y = \dfrac{1}{4a^2 - x^2}$, the x-axis and the lines $x = -a$ and $x = a$.

b) What is the volume of revolution obtained if this region is rotated through $360°$ about the x-axis?

17.8 Integration By Parts

The last, and extremely important, integration technique to be considered is related to the product rule for differentiation. For example, since

$$\frac{d}{dx}(x\sin x) = \sin x + x\cos x$$

we know that

$$x\sin x = \int \left(\sin x + x\cos x \right) dx = \int \sin x\,dx + \int x\cos x\,dx = -\cos x + c + \int x\cos x\,dx\,;$$

reordering this identity we deduce that

$$\int x\cos x\,dx = x\sin x + \cos x - c\,.$$

The new technique essentially gives a way for discovering that the way to calculate $\displaystyle\int x\cos x\,dx$ is (essentially) to differentiate $x\sin x$; an insight which is not immediately obvious.

Let us investigate the calculations we performed above in a more general way. For functions u and v, the product rule tells us that

$$\frac{d}{dx}(uv) = \frac{du}{dx}v + u\frac{dv}{dx}\,,$$

and this identity can be integrated to give

$$uv = \int \frac{du}{dx}v\,dx + \int u\frac{dv}{dx}\,dx\,.$$

We now simply rearrange this formula.

Key Fact 17.7 Integration By Parts: Indefinite Integrals

For functions u and v,

$$\int u\frac{dv}{dx}\,dx = uv - \int \frac{du}{dx}v\,dx \qquad \text{or} \qquad \int uv'\,dx = uv - \int u'v\,dx\,.$$

We would now calculate $\displaystyle\int x\cos x\,dx$ as follows. If we put $u = x$ and $v' = \cos x$, then $u' = 1$ and $v = \sin x$ (we do not need to worry about an arbitrary constant here). Thus

$$\int x\cos x\,dx = uv - \int u'v\,dx = x\sin x - \int 1 \times \sin x\,dx = x\sin x + \cos x + c\,.$$

It does not matter that, this time, our integral include the term '$+c$', when '$-c$' appeared last time. Since c is an arbitrary constant, its sign does not matter. It is not unusual to find that an integral can be performed in more than one way, with the answers differing by having different-looking arbitrary constants.

It is useful to have a systematic system of notation that will ensure that we perform the calculations properly. We shall integrate $\int xe^{2x}\,dx$. We decide to put $u = x$ and $v' = e^{2x}$. We set this choice out in a small table:

$u = x$	$v' = e^{2x}$
$u' =$	$v =$

We now differentiate the term u on the left-hand side, and integrate the term v' on the right-hand side:

$u = x$	$v' = e^{2x}$
$u' = 1$	$v = \frac{1}{2}e^{2x}$

In this table:

- the function being integrated is uv', the product of the two terms on the top row,

- the so-called **cross term** uv is the product of the entries on the main diagonal (top left and bottom right),

- the product of the terms on the bottom row is $u'v$, the new function to be integrated.

Thus

$$\int xe^{2x}\,dx \;=\; x \times \tfrac{1}{2}e^{2x} - \int 1 \times \tfrac{1}{2}e^{2x}\,dx \;=\; \tfrac{1}{2}xe^{2x} - \tfrac{1}{2}\int e^{2x}\,dx \;=\; \tfrac{1}{2}xe^{2x} - \tfrac{1}{4}e^{2x} + c \;=\; \tfrac{1}{4}(2x-1)e^{2x} + c\,.$$

Note that some authors set this table out differently, with both u and v on the top row.

The skill in using integration by parts lies in choosing the functions u and v'. We need to be able to split the original function into two pieces in such a way that we can integrate v' to obtain v, and moreover so that the new integral $u'v$ is easier to integrate than the original integral.

Most of the time, when the function to be integrated is a polynomial times another function, u should be chosen to be the polynomial. This is because differentiating a polynomial u yields a polynomial u' of smaller degree. This will tend to simplify matters. Care still has to be taken, however, that we can actually integrate v'.

Example 17.8.1. *Calculate the integrals of $x\sec^2 x$ and $x^3 e^{x^2}$.*

In the first case, put $u = x$, $v' = \sec^2 x$. Then

$$\int x\sec^2 x\,dx \;=\; x \times \tan x - \int 1 \times \tan x\,dx$$

$$=\; x\tan x - \int \tan x\,dx \;=\; x\tan x - \ln|\sec x| + c\,.$$

$u = x$	$v' = \sec^2 x$
$u' = 1$	$v = \tan x$

In the second case, however, we cannot simply choose $u = x^3$, since we do not know how to integrate e^{x^2}. We do know how to integrate xe^{x^2}, however, so we put $u = x^2$, and all is well:

$$\int x^3 e^{x^2}\,dx \;=\; x^2 \times \tfrac{1}{2}e^{x^2} - \int 2x \times \tfrac{1}{2}e^{x^2}\,dx$$

$$=\; \tfrac{1}{2}x^2 e^{x^2} - \int xe^{x^2}\,dx \;=\; \tfrac{1}{2}x^2 e^{x^2} - \tfrac{1}{2}e^{x^2} + c$$

$$=\; \tfrac{1}{2}(x^2 - 1)e^{x^2} + c\,.$$

$u = x^2$	$v' = xe^{x^2}$
$u' = 2x$	$v = \tfrac{1}{2}e^{x^2}$

Definite integrals can be calculated using integration by parts; just add the limits.

> **Key Fact 17.8** Integration By Parts: Definite Integrals
>
> If u and v are functions, then
>
> $$\int_a^b u\frac{dv}{dx}\,dx = \left[uv\right]_a^b - \int \frac{du}{dx}v\,dx \qquad \text{or} \qquad \int_a^b uv'\,dx = \left[uv\right]_a^b - \int_a^b u'v\,dx\,.$$

Example 17.8.2. *Evaluate* $\displaystyle\int_2^8 x\ln x\,dx.$

We cannot put $u = x$ here, since we do not know how to integrate $\ln x$. We shall try things the other way round.

$$
\begin{aligned}
\int_2^8 x\ln x\,dx &= \left[\ln x \times \tfrac{1}{2}x^2\right]_2^8 - \int_2^8 x^{-1} \times \tfrac{1}{2}x^2\,dx \\
&= \left[\tfrac{1}{2}x^2\ln x\right]_2^8 - \tfrac{1}{2}\int_2^8 x\,dx \\
&= \left(32\ln 2^3 - 2\ln 2\right) - \tfrac{1}{2}\left[\tfrac{1}{2}x^2\right]_2^8 = 94\ln 2 - \tfrac{1}{2}\left(32 - 2\right) = 94\ln 2 - 15\,.
\end{aligned}
$$

$$\boxed{\begin{aligned} u &= \ln x & v' &= x \\ u' &= x^{-1} & v &= \tfrac{1}{2}x^2 \end{aligned}}$$

Having just said that we do not know how to integrate $\ln x$; we do. We now have the ability to integrate this last function, the one standard function that we have yet to integrate.

Example 17.8.3. *Show that* $\displaystyle\int \ln x\,dx = x\ln x - x + c.$

It might seem that using integration by parts is difficult, since there is no product of functions to split up. We can nevertheless put $v' = 1$ and see what happens.

$$
\begin{aligned}
\int \ln x\,dx &= \ln x \times x - \int x^{-1} \times x\,dx \\
&= x\ln x - \int dx = x\ln x - x + c\,.
\end{aligned}
$$

$$\boxed{\begin{aligned} u &= \ln x & v' &= 1 \\ u' &= x^{-1} & v &= x \end{aligned}}$$

We might need to integrate by parts more than once to reach a result:

Example 17.8.4. *Calculate* $\displaystyle\int x^2 e^{-x}\,dx.$

We start by choosing $u = x^2$ and $v = e^{-x}$, and obtain

$$
\begin{aligned}
\int x^2 e^{-x}\,dx &= x^2 \times (-e^{-x}) - \int 2x \times (-e^{-x})\,dx \\
&= -x^2 e^{-x} + 2\int xe^{-x}\,dx\,.
\end{aligned}
$$

$$\boxed{\begin{aligned} u &= x^2 & v' &= e^{-x} \\ u' &= 2x & v &= -e^{-x} \end{aligned}}$$

This new integral can be integrated by parts, with new definitions for u and v':

$$
\begin{aligned}
\int x^2 e^{-x}\,dx &= -x^2 e^{-x} + 2x \times (-e^{-x}) - 2\int 1 \times (-e^{-x})\,dx \\
&= -(x^2 + 2x)e^{-x} + 2\int e^{-x}\,dx \\
&= -(x^2 + 2x + 2)e^{-x} + c\,.
\end{aligned}
$$

$$\boxed{\begin{aligned} u &= x & v' &= e^{-x} \\ u' &= 1 & v &= -e^{-x} \end{aligned}}$$

Example 17.8.5. *Calculate* $\displaystyle\int_0^\pi e^x \cos x\,dx.$

We need to integrate by parts twice.

$$\int_0^{\pi} e^x \cos x \, dx = \left[e^x \times \sin x \right]_0^{\pi} - \int_0^{\pi} e^x \times \sin x \, dx$$

$u = e^x$	$v' = \cos x$
$u' = e^x$	$v = \sin x$

$$= \left(e^{\pi} \times 0 - 1 \times 0 \right) - \int_0^{\pi} e^x \sin x \, dx = -\int_0^{\pi} e^x \sin x \, dx$$

$$= -\left(\left[e^x \times (-\cos x) \right]_0^{\pi} - \int_0^{\pi} e^x \times (-\cos x) \, dx \right)$$

$u = e^x$	$v' = \sin x$
$u' = e^x$	$v = -\cos x$

$$= -\left(e^{\pi} + 1 \right) - \int_0^{\pi} e^x \cos x \, dx .$$

Algebra now tells us that $\int_0^{\pi} e^x \cos x \, dx = -\frac{1}{2}(e^{\pi} + 1)$.

EXERCISE 17E

1. Use integration by parts to integrate the following functions with respect to x;
    a) $x \sin x$,
    b) $3xe^x$,
    c) $(x+4)e^x$
    d) xe^{2x},
    e) $x \cos 4x$,
    f) $x \ln 2x$,
    g) $x^3 \sin x^2$,
    h) $\frac{x^2}{(x^2+1)^2}$,
    i) $x \sec x \tan x$.

2. Find the following integrals:
    a) $\int x^5 \ln 3x \, dx$,
    b) $\int xe^{2x+1} \, dx$,
    c) $\int \ln 2x \, dx$.

3. Evaluate the following:
    a) $\int_1^e x \ln x \, dx$,
    b) $\int_0^{\frac{1}{2}\pi} x \sin \frac{1}{2}x \, dx$,
    c) $\int_1^e x^n \ln x \, dx \quad (n > 0)$,
    d) $\int_0^1 \frac{x}{\sqrt{1-x}} \, dx$.

4. Find the integrals of the following functions:
    a) $x^2 e^{2x}$,
    b) $x^2 \cos \frac{1}{2}x$,
    c) $x(\ln x)^2$,
    d) $e^x \sin 2x$,
    e) $x^3 e^x$,
    f) $x^2 \sqrt{x+1}$.

5. The function $x\sqrt{2x+1}$ can be integrated by parts, and also through use of the substitution $u = 2x + 1$. Show that the two approaches give the same answer.

6. Use integration by parts to show that $\int_0^{\frac{1}{2}\pi} \sin^2 x \, dx = \int_0^{\frac{1}{2}\pi} \cos^2 x \, dx$.

7. Find the area bounded by the curve $y = xe^{-x}$, the x-axis and the lines $x = 0$ and $x = 2$. Find also the volume of revolution obtained by rotating this region about the x-axis through $360°$.

8. Find the area between the x-axis and the curve $y = x \sin 3x$ for $0 \le x \le \frac{1}{3}\pi$. Give your answer in terms of π. Find also the volume of the solid of revolution obtained when this region is rotated through $360°$ about the x-axis.

9. Evaluate:
    a) $\int_0^{\pi} e^{-x} \cos x \, dx$,
    b) $\int_{-\pi}^{\pi} e^{-4x} \sin 2x \, dx$,
    c) $\int_0^{2\pi} e^{-ax} \cos bx \, dx$.

10*. Evaluate $\int_0^n e^{-x} \sin x \, dx$, and hence determine the infinite integral $\int_0^{\infty} e^{-x} \sin x \, dx$.

11*. Show that $\displaystyle\int \sin^{-1} x \, dx = x \sin^{-1} x + \sqrt{1 - x^2} + c.$

12*. Use the identity $\sin^n x \equiv \sin^{n-2} x(1 - \cos^2 x)$ and integration by parts to show that

$$\int_0^{\frac{1}{2}\pi} \sin^n x \, dx = \frac{n-1}{n} \int_0^{\frac{1}{2}\pi} \sin^{n-2} x \, dx, \qquad n \geq 2.$$

Hence evaluate $\displaystyle\int_0^{\frac{1}{2}\pi} \sin^8 x \, dx.$

Chapter 17: Summary

- **Standard Integrals**

$$\int x^n \, dx = \begin{cases} \frac{1}{n+1} x^{n+1} + c & n \neq -1 \\ \ln x + c & n = -1 \end{cases} \qquad \int \ln x \, dx = x \ln x - x + c$$

$$\int e^x \, dx = e^x + c \qquad\qquad\qquad \int a^x \, dx = \frac{1}{\ln a} a^x + c \quad (a > 0)$$

$$\int \cos x \, dx = \sin x + c \qquad\qquad \int \sin x \, dx = -\cos x + c$$

$$\int \sec^2 x \, dx = \tan x + c \qquad\qquad \int \sec x \tan x \, dx = \sec x + c$$

$$\int \mathrm{cosec}^2 x \, dx = -\cot x + c \qquad\qquad \int \mathrm{cosec}\, x \cot x \, dx = -\mathrm{cosec}\, x + c$$

$$\int \tan x \, dx = \ln|\sec x| + c \qquad\qquad \int \cot x \, dx = \ln|\sin x| + c$$

$$\int \sec x \, dx = \ln|\sec x + \tan x| + c \qquad \int \mathrm{cosec}\, x \, dx = -\ln|\mathrm{cosec}\, x + \cot x| + c$$

$$= \ln\left|\tan\left(\tfrac{1}{2}x + \tfrac{1}{4}\pi\right)\right| + c \qquad\qquad\qquad = \ln\left|\tan \tfrac{1}{2}x\right| + c$$

- **Special Patterns**

$$\int f'(ax + b) \, dx = \tfrac{1}{a} f(ax + b) + c$$

$$\int f'(x)\big(f(x)\big)^n \, dx = \tfrac{1}{n+1}\big(f(x)\big)^{n+1} + c \qquad (n \neq -1)$$

$$\int \frac{k f'(x)}{f(x)} \, dx = \ln|f(x)|^k + c$$

- **Inverse Trigonometric Functions**

$$\int \frac{1}{\sqrt{a^2 - x^2}} \, dx = \sin^{-1} \tfrac{x}{a} + c = -\cos^{-1} \tfrac{x}{a} + c$$

$$\int \frac{1}{x^2 + a^2} \, dx = \tfrac{1}{a} \tan^{-1} \tfrac{x}{a} + c$$

- **Integration By Substitution**

$$\int f'(g(x))g'(x) \, dx = f(g(x)) + c$$

- **Integration By Parts**

$$\int uv' \, dx = uv - \int u'v \, dx$$

- **Partial fractions** and **trigonometric identities** are often useful.

Differential Equations

In this chapter we will learn to:

- formulate simple statements involving a rate of change as a differential equation, using constants of proportionality if necessary,

- find, by integration, the general form of solution for a first-order differential equation for which the variables are separable,

- use initial conditions to find particular solutions,

- interpret the solution of a differential equation in the context of a problem being modelled by the equation.

18.1 Forming and Solving Equations

Many applications of mathematics involve two variables, and we need to determine the relationship between them. Often this relationship is, at least initially, not expressed simply in terms of the two variables, but will involve the rates of change of one variable with respect to the other.

Key Fact 18.1 What Is A Differential Equation?

A **differential equation** is a functional relationship between two variables (let us call them x and y) and the derivatives of one with respect to the other. A differential equation is generally a relation of the form

$$F(x,y,y',y'',\ldots) = 0$$

for some function F. Examples are

$$x\frac{dy}{dx} - y^2 = 0 \qquad \frac{d^2y}{dx^2} + \sin xy = 0 \qquad xy^2 + \cos x + \frac{dy}{dx}\frac{d^3y}{dx^3} = 0$$

First order differential equations are ones which only involve the first derivatives of variable. Here are some more examples of first-order differential equations:

$$\frac{dy}{dx} = 10 - y^2 \qquad x\frac{dy}{dx} = x^3 + y^2 \qquad (\cos x + \cos y)\frac{dy}{dx} = 1$$

A **solution**, or an **integral** of a differential equation is any equation relating x and y which satisfies the equation.

Example 18.1.1. *A curve C has the property that $x > 0$ for all points on the curve and, at each point P on the curve, the tangent at P has y-intercept with a value 1 less than the y-coordinate of P. What is the equation of the curve C?*

Our first task is to determine the differential equation described in words in the question. The tangent to the curve at the point P meets the y-axis at the point T, and we are told that the length TN is always equal to 1. Since $PN = x$, the gradient of the line PT is $\frac{1}{x}$. Since PT is the tangent to the curve at P, we deduce the differential equation

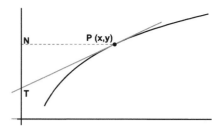

$$\frac{dy}{dx} = \frac{1}{x}.$$

Figure 18.1

This equation is particularly simple, since it tells us what $\frac{dy}{dx}$ is as a function of x. To obtain y, therefore, we simply have to integrate the right-hand side of the equation. We deduce that

$$y = \ln x + c.$$

for some constant c. We do not need the modulus sign inside the logarithm, since we know that $x > 0$ everywhere on the curve.

As things stand, therefore, we do not know the equation of the curve precisely. What we have is a family of solutions, parametrised by a constant of integration. The figure on the right shows just a few of them.
The collection of all the solutions, in this case

$$y = \ln x + c,$$

is called the **general solution** of the differential equation. If we wanted to know exactly which of the curves was the right one, we would need to have some extra information.

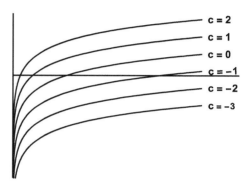

Figure 18.2

Differential equations frequently arise as a consequence of a scientific law or hypothesis. The equation is then a **mathematical model** of the real-world situation.

Example 18.1.2. *A rodent has mass 30 g at birth. It reaches maturity in 3 months. The rate of growth of a rodent is modelled by the differential equation*

$$\frac{dm}{dt} = 120(t-3)^2,$$

where the rodent's mass is m g at time t months after birth. What is the mass of a fully grown rodent?

This differential equation has general solution

$$m = 40(t-3)^3 + c.$$

To find which value of c we want, we need to use the information in the question that $m = 30$ when $t = 0$. This tells us that $30 = 40 \times (-3)^3 + c$, or $c = 1110$. Thus the mass of a rodent t months after birth is given by the formula

$$m = 1110 + 40(t-3)^3.$$

The mass of a full-grown rodent is its mass at 3 months, namely 1110 g.

In this example the variable m and t had to satisfy an **initial condition**, since the value of m was specified at the starting time $t = 0$ of the problem. Satisfying an initial condition is (generally) enough to determine the constant of integration, and hence specify the correct solution to the problem. It is not necessary to specify the behaviour of the problem at the starting point, as above; having information about the system at any point should be enough to specify the solution. A more general term for initial condition, then, is **boundary condition**.

Example 18.1.3. *A botanist working in the UK makes a hypothesis that the rate of growth of a hot-house plant is proportional to the amount of daylight it receives. If t is the time in years after the shortest day of the year, then the number of hours of sunlight in a day is given by the formula* $12 - 4\cos 2\pi t$. *In December one year, on the shortest day, the height of one plant was measured to be 123.0 cm; 55 days later the height was 128.0 cm. What was the height of the plant on the longest day of the year, 6 months later in the following June?*

We know that the rate of growth is proportional to the number of hours of daylight received, but we do not know the constant of proportionality. We will assign a name to it. If the height of the plant at time t is h cm, the differential equation relating h and t must be of the form

$$\frac{dh}{dt} = k(12 - 4\cos 2\pi t).$$

Nothing in the question (as yet) allows us to calculate the value of k. Since k is a constant, however, we can still integrate this equation, obtaining

$$h = k\left(12t - \tfrac{2}{\pi}\sin 2\pi t\right) + c,$$

and equation relating h and t which includes two unknown constants. Happily, we have two boundary conditions that we can apply. The initial condition that $h(0) = 123.0$ implies that

$$123.0 = k(0 - 0) + c,$$

so that $c = 123.0$. After 55 days the value of h is 128.0; this tells us that

$$128.0 = k\left[12 \times \tfrac{55}{365} - \tfrac{2}{\pi}\sin\left(2\pi\tfrac{55}{365}\right)\right] = 123.0 = 1.29158k + 123.0$$

so that $k = 3.8712$. The botanist's model gives the formula

$$h = 123.0 + 3.8712\left(12t - \tfrac{2}{\pi}\sin 2\pi t\right)$$

for the height of the plant; on the longest day in June the following year (when $t = \tfrac{1}{2}$), the plant's height was $h(\tfrac{1}{2}) = 146$ cm, to 3 significant figures.

This approach is typical of many applications of differential equations. The form of the differential equation might be known, but not the values of all the numerical constants. Solving the differential equation in general, and then applying boundary conditions to determine not only the constant of integration but also the constants of the equation, is the way to handle such problems.

18.2 Types Of Differential Equations

The general theory of differential equations is extremely complex, and still growing. There are many types of differential equations so that many different solution techniques are required; indeed some cannot be solved at all (in the sense of having their solutions expressed in terms of 'nice' functions), and only approximate solutions exist.

We shall restrict our attention to a small class of differential equations that can all (in principle) be solved. While being comparatively simple as differential equations go, as a class of equations they are sufficiently varied to be of mathematical interest, and to include within them equations that describe interesting real-world situations.

While we are really only studying one type of differential equation, there are two special cases of this type of equation that we shall mention separately, by way of introduction.

18.2.1. EQUATIONS OF THE FORM $y'(x) = f(x)$

We have already been considering equations of this type. If the differential equation defined the derivative $\frac{dy}{dx}$ explicitly in terms of x, then its general solution is obtained by integration.

Key Fact 18.2 Solving $\frac{dy}{dx} = f(x)$

The general solution of the differential equation

$$\frac{dy}{dx} = f(x)$$

is

$$y = \int f(x)\,dx + c.$$

Since the right-hand side of this equation is an indefinite integral, an arbitrary constant of integration is implied, and so the term '$+c$' could have been omitted from the formula. We have added it for clarity. It is vital that it is included. If the '$+c$' term is omitted, it will probably not be possible to satisfy any initial and boundary conditions that have been imposed.

18.2.2. EQUATIONS OF THE FORM $y'(x) = g(y)$

The previous type of differential equation, the simplest, had the benefit of yielding solutions y which were explicit functions of x. As we know from our study of implicity and parametric equations, an explicit formula for y is not necessary, or even desirable, to describe an equation. It is important that we are prepared, if necessary, to move away from the (very natural) desire to find explicit solutions.

A differential equation of the form

$$\frac{dy}{dx} = g(y)$$

cannot be integrated directly, since we cannot integrate the function $g(y)$ with respect to x (at least, not without knowing y as a function of x, which is what we are trying to discover.). However, if we drop our insistence on looking for y as an explicit function of x, we can handle such equations. Recall that the chain rule tells us (amongst many other things) that

$$\frac{dy}{dx} \times \frac{dx}{dy} = 1.$$

Using this identity, the differential equation $\frac{dy}{dx} = g(y)$ can be written in the form

$$\frac{dx}{dy} = \frac{1}{g(y)}.$$

But this is a differential equation of the previous type, but with the roles of x and y interchanged. We can integrate this equation to obtain x as an explicit function of y.

Key Fact 18.3 Solving $\frac{dy}{dx} = g(y)$

The differential equation

$$\frac{dy}{dx} = g(y)$$

is equivalent to the differential equation

$$\frac{dx}{dy} = \frac{1}{g(y)};$$

its general solution expresses x as an explicit function of y;

$$x = \int \frac{1}{g(y)}\,dy + c.$$

Example 18.2.1. *A hot-air balloon can reach a maximum height of 1.25 km, and the rate at which it gains height decreases as it climbs according to the formula*

$$\frac{dh}{dt} = 20 - 16h \, ,$$

where h is the height of the balloon in km, and t is the time in hours after lift-off. How long does it take the balloon to reach a height of 1 km?

We first rewrite the differential equation as

$$\frac{dt}{dh} = \frac{1}{20 - 16h} \, ,$$

the general solution of this equation is

$$t = c - \tfrac{1}{16} \ln(20 - 16h) \, .$$

Note that, since the maximum height that a balloon can reach is 1.25 km, the quantity $20 - 16h$ is always positive; no modulus sign is required in the integral.

Although it has not been stated explicitly, the question does imply an initial condition. We are assuming that the balloon is at ground level at take-off, and hence that $h = 0$ when $t = 0$. This implies that

$$0 = c - \tfrac{1}{16} \ln 20 \, ,$$

and hence the equation becomes

$$t = \tfrac{1}{16} \ln 20 - \tfrac{1}{16} \ln(20 - 16h) = \tfrac{1}{16} \ln\left(\frac{20}{20 - 16h}\right) = \tfrac{1}{16} \ln\left(\frac{5}{5 - 4h}\right) .$$

When $h = 1$, t is equal to $\tfrac{1}{16} \ln 5 = 0.101$; it takes 6.04 minutes to climb 1 km.

Alternatively, since we only wanted to know the value of t when $h = 1$, we could have performed this calculation as a definite integral. Since $h = 0$ when $t = 0$ and $h = 1$ when $t = T$ (say), we deduce that

$$T = \int_0^1 \frac{1}{20 - 16h} \, dh = \left[-\tfrac{1}{16} \ln(20 - 16h)\right]_0^1 = -\tfrac{1}{16}(\ln 4 - \ln 20) = \tfrac{1}{16} \ln 5 = 0.101 \, .$$

While the definite integral approach obtains the particular answer quickly, we miss the opportunity to discover that the formula for t in term of h can be inverted, so that in fact

$$h = \tfrac{5}{4}\left(1 - e^{-16t}\right) .$$

Example 18.2.2. *Solve the differential equation*

$$y\frac{dy}{dx} = \sqrt{y^2 + 1} \, , \qquad y(0) = \sqrt{8} \, .$$

The differential equation becomes

$$\frac{dx}{dy} = \frac{y}{\sqrt{y^2 + 1}} \, ;$$

using the substitution $u = y^2$ we see that the general solution is

$$x = \int \frac{y}{\sqrt{y^2 + 1}} \, dy = \tfrac{1}{2} \int \frac{1}{\sqrt{u + 1}} \, du = \sqrt{u + 1} + c = \sqrt{y^2 + 1} + c \, .$$

Applying the initial condition that $y = \sqrt{8}$ when $x = 0$, we see that $0 = c + 3$. The solution is $x = \sqrt{y^2 + 1} - 3$, or even

$$(x + 3)^2 - y^2 = 1 \, .$$

Example 18.2.3. *Which functions of x have the property that they are proportional to their rates of change with respect to x?*

When studying the calculus of exponential functions, we found that all exponential functions have this property. The question remains whether there are any other types of function with the same property. Answering this question involves solving the differential equation

$$\frac{dy}{dx} = \alpha y$$

for any constant of proportionality α. It becomes

$$\frac{dx}{dy} = \frac{1}{\alpha y},$$

and hence

$$x = \int \frac{1}{\alpha y} dy + c = \tfrac{1}{\alpha} \ln |y| + c.$$

This equation can be rearranged to read

$$|y| = e^{\alpha(x-c)} = e^{-\alpha c} e^{\alpha x}.$$

At this point we decide that our choice of c as arbitrary constant has turned out to be inconvenient; our general solution looks much more elegant if we introduce a new arbitrary constant $A = e^{-\alpha c}$ and write the general solution as

$$|y| = A e^{\alpha x}.$$

Finally, it is clear from the formula $A = e^{-\alpha c}$ that A, as defined, is positive. If we now forget that A came from a formula involving c, and agree that we will let A be negative if necessary, the general equation becomes

$$y = A e^{\alpha x}.$$

Multiples of exponential functions are the **only** functions whose rates of change are proportional to themselves.

***

Key Fact 18.4 Renaming The Constant Of Integration

It is perfectly acceptable to rename the constant of integration, if it proves convenient!

***

EXERCISE 18A

1. Find general solutions of the following differential equations:

   a) $\dfrac{dy}{dx} = (3x - 1)(x - 3),$

   b) $\dfrac{dx}{dt} = \sin^2 3t,$

   c) $\dfrac{dP}{dt} = 50 e^{\frac{1}{10}t},$

   d) $e^{2t} \dfrac{du}{dt} = 100,$

   e) $\sqrt{x}\dfrac{dy}{dx} = x + 1$ for $x > 0,$

   f) $\sin t \dfrac{dx}{dt} = \cos t + \sin 2t$ for $0 < t < \pi.$

2. Solve the following differential equations with the given initial conditions:

   a) $\dfrac{dx}{dt} = 2 e^{0.4t}, x = 1$ when $t = 0,$

   b) $\dfrac{dv}{dt} = 6(\sin 2t - \cos 3t), v = 0$ when $t = 0,$

   c) $(1 - t^2)\dfrac{dy}{dt} = 2t, y = 0$ when $t = 0,$ for $-1 < t < 1.$

3. Find the solutions of the following differential equations which pass through the given points;

   a) $\frac{dy}{dx} = \frac{x-1}{x^2}$, through $(1,0)$, for $x > 0$,   b) $\frac{dy}{dx} = \frac{1}{\sqrt{x}}$, through $(4,0)$, for $x > 0$,

   c) $(x+1)\frac{dy}{dx} = x - 1$, through $(0,0)$, for $x > -1$.

4. Starting from rest, the driver of an electric car depresses the throttle gradually. If the speed of the car after t seconds is v ms^{-1}, the acceleration $v'(t)$ ms^{-2} is given by $0.2t$. How long does it take for the car to reach a speed of 20 ms^{-1}?

5. The solution curve for a differential equation of the form $y'(x) = x - ax^{-2}$ for $x > 0$, passes through the points $(1,0)$ and $(2,0)$. Find the value of y when $x = 3$.

6. A point moves on the x-axis so that its coordinate at time t satisfies the differential equation $x'(t) = 5 + a\cos 2t$ for some value of a. It is observed that $x = 3$ when $t = 0$, and $x = 0$ when $t = \frac{1}{4}\pi$. Find the value of a, and the value of x when $t = \frac{1}{3}\pi$.

7. The normal to a curve at a point P cuts the y-axis at T, and N is the foot of the perpendicular from P to the y-axis. If, for all P, T is always 1 unit below N, find the equation of the curve.

8. Water is leaking slowly out of a tank. The depth of the water after t hours is h metres, and these variables are related by a differential equation of the form $\frac{dh}{dt} = -ae^{-0.1t}$. Initially the depth of water is 6 metres, and after 2 hours it has fallen to 5 metres. At what depth will the level eventually settle down?

   Find an expression for $\frac{dh}{dt}$ in terms of h.

9*. Four theories are proposed about the growth of an organism:

   a) It grows at a constant rate of k units per year.

   b) It only grows when there is enough daylight, so that its rate of growth at time t years is $k(1 - \frac{1}{2}\cos 2\pi t)$ units per year.

   c) Its growth is controlled by the 10-year sunspot cycle, so that its rate of growth at time t years is $k(1 + \frac{1}{4}\cos\frac{1}{5}\pi t)$ units per year.

   d) Both (b) and (c) are true, so that its rate of growth is $k(1 - \frac{1}{2}\cos 2\pi t)(1 + \frac{1}{4}\cos\frac{1}{5}\pi t)$ units per year.

   The size of the organism at time $t = 0$ is A units. For each model, find an expression for the size of the organism at time t years. Do the models all give the same value for the size of the organism after 10 years?

10. Find general solutions of the following differential equations, writing y as a function of x each time:

   a) $\frac{dy}{dx} = y^2$,   b) $\frac{dy}{dx} = \tan y$ for $|y| < \frac{1}{2}\pi$,

   c) $\frac{dx}{dt} = 4x$,   d) $\frac{dz}{dt} = z^{-1}$ for $z > 0$,

   e) $\frac{dx}{dt} = \csc x$ for $0 < x < \pi$,   f) $u^2\frac{du}{dx} = a$ for $u > 0$.

11. Solve the following differential equations with the given initial conditions:

   a) $\frac{dx}{dt} = -2x$, $x = 3$ when $t = 0$,   b) $\frac{du}{dt} = u^3$, $u = 1$ when $t = 0$.

12. Find the solutions of the following differential equations which pass through the given points. Suggest any restrictions which should be placed on the values of x:

   a) $\frac{dy}{dx} = y + y^2$ through $(0,1)$,   b) $\frac{dy}{dx} = e^y$ through $(2,0)$.

13. A girl lives 500 metres from school. She sets out walking at 2 ms^{-1}, but when she has walked a distance of x metres her speed has dropped to $\left(2 - \frac{1}{400}x\right)$ ms^{-1}. How long does she take to get to school?

14. A boy is eating a 250 g burger. When he has eaten a mass m g, his rate of consumption is $100 - \frac{1}{900}m^2$ g per minute. How long does he take to finish his meal?

15. A sculler is rowing a 2 kilometre course. She starts rowing at 5 ms^{-1}, but gradually tires, so that when she has rowed x m her speed has dropped to $5e^{-0.0001x}$ ms^{-1}. How long will she take to complete the course?

16. A tree is planted as a seedling of negligible height. The rate of increase in its height, in metres per year, is given by the formula $0.2\sqrt{25 - h}$, where h is the height of the tree, in metres, t years after it is planted.

    a) Explain why the height of the tree can never exceed 25 metres.

    b) Write down a differential equation connecting h and t, and solve it to find an expression for t as a function of h.

    c) How long does it take for the tree to put on: (i) its first metre of growth, (ii) its last metre of growth?

    d) Find an expression for the height of the tree after t years. Over what interval of values of t is this model valid?

17*. Astronomers observe a luminous cloud of stellar gas which appears to be expanding. When it is observed a month later, its radius r is estimated to be 5 times the original radius. After a further 3 months, the radius appears to be 5 times as large again.

It is thought that the expansion is described by a differential equation of the form $\dfrac{dr}{dt} = cr^m$ where c and m are constants. There is, however, a difference of opinion about the appropriate value to take for m. Two hypotheses are proposed: either $m = \frac{1}{3}$ or $m = \frac{1}{2}$.

Investigate which of these models fits the observed data better.

18*. A reaction occurs between two chemicals, called A and B, in a beaker. The quantities of A and B in the beaker vary over time, with chemical A changing into chemical B and vice versa.

A model of this chemical reaction states that the rate of change $\dfrac{da}{dt}$ of the **proportion** of chemical A in the beaker is proportional to both the proportion a of A and the proportion $1 - a$ of B. When the reaction starts, there are equal quantities of A and B in the beaker.

    a) Write down a differential equation relating the proportion a of chemical A and time t. Your answer should include a constant of proportionality.

    b) Using partial fractions, solve this equation, and deduce that a satisfies an equation of the form

$$a = \frac{1}{1 + e^{-kt}}.$$

    for a positive constant k.

    c) What will the long-term result of this reaction be?

18.2.3. Equations Of The Form $y'(x) = f(x)g(y)$: Separation Of Variables

The first two types of differential equations have been special cases of the most general type of differential equation that we shall consider.
Consider a differential equation of the form

$$\frac{dy}{dx} = f(x)g(y).$$

If we divide this equation by $g(y)$, it becomes

$$\frac{1}{g(y)}\frac{dy}{dx} = f(x).$$

Suppose that we can integrate $\frac{1}{g(y)}$ with respect to y and integrate $f(x)$ with respect to x. In other words, we can find functions $F(x)$ and $G(y)$ such that $\dfrac{dF}{dx} = f(x)$ and $\dfrac{dG}{dy} = \dfrac{1}{g(y)}$. The differential equation can now be written as

$$\frac{dG}{dy} \times \frac{dy}{dx} = \frac{dF}{dx},$$

and the chain rule tells us that the left-hand side of this equation is equal to $\frac{dG}{dx}$. The solution of the differential equation is therefore

$$G(y) = F(x) + c.$$

The above argument is correct, but not a very good guide for solving these equations in practice. We need to stop half-way through our analysis of the differential equation to determine the functions F and G before we can resume the argument, and evaluating either of these functions might be a complicated process. It would be better to have a formalism whereby the calculation of these functions can be seen as an integral part of solving the differential equation. We can achieve this by a little abuse of notation.

A differential equation of the form

$$\frac{dy}{dx} = f(x)g(y)$$

is solved by the process known as **separation of variables**; by multiplication and division (alone), all instances of the variable x are moved to one side of the equation, and all instances of the variable y are moved to the other side. **This includes the 'terms' dx and dy inside the derivative: we pretend that we can separate them algebraically.** After dividing by $g(y)$ and 'multiplying' by dx, the differential equation turns into the 'equation'

$$\frac{1}{g(y)}\,dy = f(x)\,dx.$$

You will recall similar 'equations' were used when performing integrations by substitution in Chapter 17. While this equation has no real meaning, it regains meaning immediately once we integrate both sides:

$$\int \frac{1}{g(y)}\,dy = \int f(x)\,dx + c.$$

This is, of course, the same equation $G(y) = F(x) + c$ that we derived previously, but the algebra involved in reaching it was a little clearer. This technique is more easily written down.

Example 18.2.4. *The gradient of the tangent to a curve C at each point P on the curve is equal to the square of the gradient of the gradient of the line OP. Find the equation of the curve, if the curve passes through the point $(2,1)$.*

If the point P has coordinates (x, y), then the line OP has gradient $\frac{y}{x}$, and so we are interested in the differential equation

$$\frac{dy}{dx} = \frac{y^2}{x^2}.$$

Separating variables gives us

$$y^{-2}\,dy = x^{-2}\,dx$$

on integrating, we obtain

$$-y^{-1} = \int y^{-2}\,dy = \int x^{-2}\,dx = -x^{-1} + c.$$

Since $y = 1$ when $x = 2$, we see that $-1 = -\frac{1}{2} + c$, so that $c = -\frac{1}{2}$, so the equation becomes $y^{-1} = x^{-1} + \frac{1}{2}$, or $y = \frac{2x}{x+2}$.

We can also use definite integrals to satisfy initial or boundary conditions.

Example 18.2.5. *Find the equation of the curve satisfying the differential equation*

$$y\frac{dy}{dx} = (y^2 + 3)\cos^2 x$$

such that $y = 1$ when $x = 0$.

Separating variables yields

$$\frac{y}{y^2 + 3} \, dy = \cos^2 x \, dx.$$

Since $y = 1$ when $x = 0$, we obtain an equation involving definite integrals:

$$\int_1^y \frac{y}{y^2 + 3} \, dy = \int_0^x \cos^2 x \, dx.$$

The bottom y limit is the y value corresponding to the bottom x limit: similarly for the top limits. Both of these integrals need to be evaluated carefully. If we put $u = \sqrt{y^2 + 3}$ to evaluate the left-hand side, and use trigonometric identities on the right-hand side, we obtain

$$\int_2^{\sqrt{y^2+3}} \frac{u}{u} \, du = \tfrac{1}{2} \int_0^x (1 + \cos 2x) \, dx$$

$$\left[u\right]_2^{\sqrt{y^2+3}} = \tfrac{1}{2} \left[x + \tfrac{1}{2} \sin 2x\right]_0^x$$

$$\sqrt{y^2 + 1} - 2 = \tfrac{1}{2}(x + \tfrac{1}{2} \sin 2x)$$

$$\sqrt{y^2 + 1} = 2 + \tfrac{1}{2}x + \tfrac{1}{4} \sin 2x$$

Example 18.2.6. *Find the solutions to the differential equation*

$$x\frac{dy}{dx} + 3y = 2 - y^2, \qquad x \geq 0,$$

such that:

a) $y = 1.5$ when $x = 1$,   b) $y = 4$ when $x = 1$.

We need to handle the $3y$ term on the left-hand side before separating variables. Thus

$$x\frac{dy}{dx} = 2 - 3y + y^2 = (y-1)(y-2)$$

$$\frac{1}{(y-1)(y-2)} \, dy = \frac{1}{x} \, dx$$

$$\int \left(\frac{1}{y-2} - \frac{1}{y-1}\right) dy = \int \frac{1}{(y-1)(y-2)} \, dy = \int \frac{1}{x} \, dx$$

$$\ln\left|\frac{y-2}{y-1}\right| = \ln|y-2| - \ln|y-1| = \ln x + c$$

$$\left|\frac{y-2}{y-1}\right| = e^c x = Ax$$

(changing the arbitrary constant from c to A). At this point we need to be a little careful. Inspection of the graphs of $\left|\frac{y-2}{y-1}\right| = Ae^x$ for any value of A shows that the graph splits into three curves, separated by the lines $y = 1$ and $y = 2$. We will want to find the correct curve for each of our boundary conditions. This is achieved through careful removal of the modulus sign.

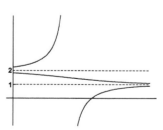

Figure 18.3

(a) The first boundary condition tells us that $A = 1$. Since $1 < \frac{3}{2} < 2$, we want the curve that lies between $y = 1$ and $y = 2$. Since $\left|\frac{y-2}{y-1}\right| = \frac{2-y}{y-1}$ for this range of y, the equation is

$$\frac{2-y}{y-1} = x, \qquad \text{or} \qquad y = \frac{2+x}{1+x}.$$

(b) The second boundary condition tells us that $A = \frac{2}{3}$. This time we want the curve that lies above the line $y = 2$. Since $\left|\frac{y-2}{y-1}\right| = \frac{y-2}{y-1}$ for this range of y, the equation is

$$\frac{y-2}{y-1} = \frac{2}{3}x, \qquad \text{or} \qquad y = \frac{2(3-x)}{3-2x}.$$

We note that this solution is only valid for $0 \le x < \frac{3}{2}$.

Example 18.2.7. *In a particular model of infection, the proportion P, $0 < P < 1$, of a population that has a particular disease is presumed to satisfy the following property: the rate $\dfrac{dP}{dt}$ of infection*

- *is proportional to the proportion P of infected people,*

- *is proportional to the proportion $1 - P$ of uninfected people,*

- *decays exponentially with time, as the population's resistance to this disease increases.*

One example of this model provides the differential equation

$$\frac{dP}{dt} = e^{-t}P(1-P).$$

If, initially, 25% of the population has the disease, what proportion of the population will eventually have it?

Separating variables and integrating, remembering that $0 < P < 1$ at all times,

$$\int \frac{1}{P(1-P)}\,dP = \int e^{-t}\,dt$$

$$\int \left(\frac{1}{P} + \frac{1}{1-P}\right)dP = \int e^{-t}\,dt$$

$$\ln\left(\frac{P}{1-P}\right) = \ln P - \ln(1-P) = c - e^{-t}$$

$$\frac{P}{1-P} = e^{c-e^{-t}} = Ae^{-e^{-t}}$$

Since $P = \frac{1}{4}$ when $t = 0$, we deduce that $Ae^{-1} = \frac{1}{3}$, and so $A = \frac{1}{3}e$. Letting t tend to infinity, the final proportion P_∞ of infected people must satisfy the equation

$$\frac{P_\infty}{1 - P_\infty} = Ae^{-0} = A = \frac{1}{3}e,$$

and hence $P_\infty = \frac{e}{e+3} = 47.5\%$.

EXERCISE 18B

1. Find the general solution of each of the following differential equations:

   a) $\dfrac{dy}{dx} = \dfrac{x^2}{y^2}$,   b) $\dfrac{dy}{dx} = \dfrac{x}{y}$,   c) $\dfrac{dy}{dx} = xy$,   d) $\dfrac{dy}{dx} = \dfrac{1}{xy}$.

2. Find the equation of the curve which satisfies the differential equation $\dfrac{dy}{dx} = \dfrac{y}{x(x+1)}$ and passes through the point $(1, 2)$.

3. Find the general solution of the differential equation $\dfrac{dy}{dx} = -\dfrac{x}{y}$. Describe the solutions geometrically, and find the equation of the curve which passes through $(-4, 3)$.

4. Solve the differential equation $\dfrac{dy}{dx} = \dfrac{x+1}{2-y}$, and describe the solution curves.

5. Find the equations of the curves which satisfy the given differential equations and pass through the given points:

a) $\dfrac{dy}{dx} = \dfrac{3y}{2x}$, through $(2, 4)$,

b) $\dfrac{dy}{dx} = -\dfrac{3y}{2x}$, through $(2, 4)$,

c) $\dfrac{dy}{dx} = \dfrac{\sin x}{\cos y}$, through $(\tfrac{1}{3}\pi, 0)$,

d) $\dfrac{dy}{dx} = \dfrac{\tan x}{\tan y}$, through $(\tfrac{1}{3}\pi, 0)$.

6. Solve the equation $v\dfrac{dv}{dx} = -\omega^2 x$, where ω is a constant. Find the particular solution for which $v = 0$ when $x = a$.

7. Find the general solution of the equations:

a) $\dfrac{dy}{dx} = \dfrac{2x(y^2 + 1)}{y(x^2 + 1)}$,

b) $\dfrac{dy}{dx} = \tan x \cot y$.

8. Find the equations of the curves which satisfy the following differential equations and pass through the given points:

a) $\dfrac{dy}{dx} = \dfrac{y(y - 1)}{x}$, through $(1, 2)$,

b) $\dfrac{dy}{dx} = \cot x \cot y$, through $(\tfrac{1}{6}\pi, 0)$,

c) $\dfrac{dy}{dx} = \dfrac{1 + y^2}{y(1 - x^2)}$, through $(\tfrac{3}{2}, 2)$,

d) $\dfrac{dy}{dx} = y \tan x$, through $(0, 2)$.

9. Find the general solution of the differential equations:

a) $4 + x\dfrac{dy}{dx} = y^2$,

b) $e^y\dfrac{dy}{dx} - 1 = \ln x$,

c) $y \cos x \dfrac{dy}{dx} = 2 - y\dfrac{dy}{dx}$.

10. The gradient at each point of a curve is n times the gradient of the line joining the origin to that point $(1, 2)$. Find the general equation of such a curve.

11. The size n of an insect population, which fluctuates during the year, is modelled by the equation $\dfrac{dn}{dt} = 0.01n(0.05 - \cos 0.02t)$, where t is the number of days from the start of observations. The initial number of insects is 5000.

   a) Solve the differential equation to find n in terms of t.

   b) Show that the model predicts that the number of insects will fall to a minimum after about 76 days, and find this minimum value.

12. The outward velocity v ms^{-1} of a spacecraft moving vertically x metres above the centre of the earth can be modelled by the equation

$$v\dfrac{dv}{dx} = -\dfrac{10R^2}{x^2},$$

where the radius of the earth is R metres. The initial velocity at blast-off, when $x = R$, is V ms^{-1}.

Find an expression for v^2 in terms of V, x and R and show that, according to this model, V^2 must be no less than $20R$ if the spacecraft is to escape from the earth's gravitational field.

13. Find all solutions of the differential equation

$$x^2\left(\dfrac{dy}{dx}\right)^2 + 2xy\dfrac{dy}{dx} + y^2 - 1 = 0.$$

What are the two solutions that pass through the origin?

14*. Show that $\dfrac{dy}{dx} - x$ is a factor of

$$\left(\dfrac{dy}{dx}\right)^3 + (xy - x - y)\left(\dfrac{dy}{dx}\right)^2 + (xy - x^2 y - xy^2)\dfrac{dy}{dx} + x^2 y^2$$

Hence find all solutions of the differential equation

$$\left(\dfrac{dy}{dx}\right)^3 + (xy - x - y)\left(\dfrac{dy}{dx}\right)^2 + (xy - x^2 y - xy^2)\dfrac{dy}{dx} + x^2 y^2 = 0.$$

15*. a) By substituting $p = \dfrac{dy}{dx} + x$ show that $\dfrac{d^2y}{dx^2} - 2\dfrac{dy}{dx} = 2x$ may be written as $\dfrac{dp}{dx} = 2p + 1$.

b) Hence find the general solution of the differential equation $\dfrac{d^2y}{dx^2} - 2\dfrac{dy}{dx} = 2x$. Your answer should include two constants of integration.

16*. a) By substituting $y = xu$ show that $x^2\dfrac{dy}{dx} = x^2 + 3xy + y^2$ may be written as $x\dfrac{du}{dx} = (1+u)^2$.

b) Hence solve the differential equation $x^2\dfrac{dy}{dx} = x^2 + 3xy + y^2$, given that $y = 1$ when $x = 1$.

Chapter 18: Summary

- Differential equations of the form $\dfrac{dy}{dx} = f(x)$ are solved by simple integration,

$$y = \int f(x)\,dx + c.$$

- Differential equations of the form $\dfrac{dy}{dx} = g(y)$ can be converted into equations of the previous type,

$$\dfrac{dy}{dx} = g(y) \quad \Leftrightarrow \quad \dfrac{dx}{dy} = \dfrac{1}{g(y)} \quad \Leftrightarrow \quad x = \int \dfrac{1}{g(y)}\,dy + c.$$

- Differential equations of the form $\dfrac{dy}{dx} = f(x)g(y)$ can be solved by separation of variables,

$$\int \dfrac{1}{g(y)}\,dy = \int f(x)\,dx + c.$$

- The **general solution** of a differential equation always involves a constant of integration.

- Constants of integration can be determined by satisfying initial or **boundary conditions**.

Review Exercises 6

1. The parametric equations of a curve are $x = \cos t$, $y = 2\sin t$ where the parameter t takes all values such that $0 \le t \le \pi$.

   a) Find the value of t at the point A where the line $y = 2x$ intersects the curve.

   b) Show that the tangent to the curve at A has gradient -2 and find the equation of this tangent in the form $ax = by = c$, where a and b are integers. (OCR)

2. The parametric equations of a curve are $x = 2\cos t$, $y = 5 + 3\cos 2t$, where $0 < t < \pi$.

   Express $\dfrac{dy}{dt}$ in terms of t, and hence show that the gradient at any point of the curve is less than 6. (OCR)

3. A curve is defined by the parametric equations: $x = t - \frac{1}{t}$, $y = t + \frac{1}{t}$ for $t \ne 0$.

   a) Use parametric differentiation to determine $\dfrac{dy}{dx}$ as a function of the parameter t.

   b) Show that the equation of the normal to the curve at the point where $t = 2$ may be written as $3y + 5x = 15$.

   c) Determine the Cartesian equation of the curve. (OCR)

4. A curve is defined parametrically by $x = t^3 + t$, $y = t^2 + 1$.

   a) Find $\dfrac{dy}{dx}$ in terms of t.

   b) Find the equation of the normal to this curve at the point where $t = 1$. (OCR)

5. The parametric equations of a curve are $x = t - e^{-t}$, $y = t + e^{-t}$, where t takes all real values.

   Express $\dfrac{dy}{dx}$ in terms of t, and hence find and classify the turning point on the curve.

6. A curve is defined parametrically for $0 \le t \le \pi$ by $x = 2(1 + \cos t)$, $y = 4\sin^2 t$.

   a) Determine the equation of the tangent to the curve at the point where $t = \frac{1}{3}\pi$.

   b) Obtain the Cartesian equation of the curve in simplified form. (OCR)

7. The curves in this question are all examples of **Lissajous figures**. By first finding the co-ordinates of the points where either x or y takes the values -1, 0 or 1, sketch the curves completely. Indicate on your sketches, with arrows, the direction on each curve in which t is increasing.

   a) $x = \cos t$, $y = \cos 2t$, b) $x = \sin t$, $y = \cos 2t$,
   c) $x = \sin t$, $y = \sin 3t$, d) $x = \sin t$, $y = \cos 3t$,
   e) $x = \cos 2t$, $y = \sin 3t$, f) $x = \cos 2t$, $y = \cos 3t$,
   g) $x = \sin 2t$, $y = \sin 3t$, h) $x = \sin 2t$, $y = \cos 3t$.

8. Find the equation of the normal at the point $(2,1)$ on the curve $x^3 + xy + y^3 = 11$, giving your answer in the form $ax + by + c = 0$. (OCR)

361

9. A curve has implicit equation $x^2 - 2xy + 4y^2 = 12$.

    a) Find an expression for $\dfrac{dy}{dx}$ in terms of y and x. Hence determine the coordinates of the points where the tangents to the curve are parallel to the x-axis.

    b) Find the equation of the normal to the curve at the point $(2\sqrt{3}, \sqrt{3})$.   (OCR)

10. A curve has equation $y^3 + 3xy + 2x^3 = 9$. Obtain the equation of the normal at the point $(2, -1)$.   (OCR)

11. A curve is defined implicitly by the equation $4y - x^2 + 2x^2 y = 4x$.

    a) Use implicit differentiation to find $\dfrac{dy}{dx}$.

    b) Find the coordinates of the turning points on the curve, and classify the turning points.

      (OCR, adapt.)

12. Show that the tangent to the ellipse $\dfrac{x^2}{a^2} + \dfrac{y^2}{b^2} = 1$ at the point $P\,(a\cos\theta, b\sin\theta)$ has equation $bx\cos\theta + ay\sin\theta = ab$.

    a) The tangent to the ellipse at P meets the x-axis at Q and the y-axis at R. The midpoint of QR is M. Find a Cartesian equation for the locus of M as θ varies.

    b) The tangent to the ellipse at P meets the line $x = a$ at T. The origin is at O and A is the point $(-a, 0)$. Prove that OT is parallel to AP.   (OCR)

13. The equation of a curve is $x^2 + 4xy + 5y^2 = 9$. Show by differentiation that the maximum and minimum values of y occur at the intersections of $x + 2y = 0$ with the curve. Find the maximum and minimum values of y.   (OCR)

14. The curve C, whose equation is $x^2 + y^2 = e^{x+y} - 1$, passes through the origin O. Show that $\dfrac{dy}{dx} = -1$ at O. Find the value of $\dfrac{d^2y}{dx^2}$ at O.   (OCR)

15*. A curve C has equation $y = x + 2y^4$.

    a) Find $\dfrac{dy}{dx}$ in terms of y.

    b) Show that $\dfrac{d^2y}{dx^2} = \dfrac{24y^2}{(1 - 8y^3)^3}$.

    c) Write down the value of $\dfrac{dy}{dx}$ at the origin. Hence, by considering the sign of $\dfrac{d^2y}{dx^2}$, draw a diagram to show the shape of C in the neighbourhood of the origin.   (OCR)

16*. A curve is given by $x^2 + y^2 + 2axy = 1$ where a is a constant satisfying $0 < a < 1$. Show that the gradient of the curve at the point P with coordinates (x, y) is

$$-\frac{x + ay}{ax + y},$$

provided that $ax + y \neq 0$. Show that θ, the acute angle between OP and the normal to the curve at P, satisfies

$$\tan\theta = a|y^2 - x^2|.$$

Show further that, if $\dfrac{d\theta}{dx} = 0$ at P, then

    a) $a(x^2 + y^2) + 2xy = 0$,   b) $(1 + a)(x^2 + y^2 + 2xy) = 1$,   c) $\tan\theta = \dfrac{a}{\sqrt{1-a^2}}$.   (STEP)

17. By using the substitution $u = 2x - 1$, or otherwise, find $\displaystyle\int \frac{2x}{(2x-1)^2}\,dx$.   (OCR)

18. Use integration by parts to find the value of $\displaystyle\int_1^2 x\ln x\,dx$.   (OCR)

19. Find $\displaystyle\int \frac{1}{4x^2 + 9}\,dx$.   (OCR)

20. By using a suitable substitution, or otherwise, evaluate $\int_0^1 x(1-x)^9\,dx$. (OCR)

21. Use integration by parts to determine $\int_0^{\frac{1}{3}} xe^{2x}\,dx$. (OCR)

22. Use the given substitution, and then use integration by parts to complete the integration:

    a) $\int \cos^{-1} x\,dx,\ (x=\cos u)$,   b) $\int \tan^{-1} x\,dx,\ (x=\tan u)$,   c) $\int (\ln x)^2\,dx,\ (x=e^u)$.

23. Use the substitution $x=\sin u$ to find $\int_0^1 \sin^{-1} x\,dx$.

24. Find $\int \dfrac{1}{e^x + 4e^{-x}}\,dx$, by means of the substitution $u=e^x$, followed by another substitution, or otherwise. (OCR, adapt.)

25. Find $\int \dfrac{6x}{1+3x^2}\,dx$. (OCR)

26. Calculate the exact value of $\int_0^3 \dfrac{x}{1+x^2}\,dx$. (OCR)

27. By using the substitution $u=\sin x$, or otherwise, find $\int \sin^3 x \sin 2x\,dx$, giving your answer in terms of x. (OCR)

28. By means of the substitution $u=1+\sqrt{x}$, or otherwise, find $\int \dfrac{1}{1+\sqrt{x}}\,dx$, giving your answer in terms of x. (OCR)

29. Integrate with respect to x, firstly by using a substitution of the form $ax+b=u$, and secondly by parts, and show that your answers are equivalent.

    a) $x\sqrt{4x-1}$,   b) $x\sqrt{2-x}$,   c) $x\sqrt{2x+3}$.

30. Use the substitution $u=\ln x$ to show that $\int_e^{e^2} \dfrac{1}{x\sqrt{\ln x}}\,dx = 2\sqrt{2}-2$. (OCR)

31. Use the substitution $u=4+x^2$ to show that $\int_0^1 \dfrac{x^3}{\sqrt{4+x^2}}\,dx = \frac{1}{3}(16-7\sqrt{5})$. (OCR)

32. Use the substitution $u=3x-1$ to find $\int x(3x-1)^4\,dx$. (OCR)

33. Show, by means of the substitution $x=\tan\theta$, that $\int_0^1 \dfrac{1}{(x^2+1)^2}\,dx = \int_0^{\frac{1}{4}\pi} \cos^2\theta\,d\theta$. Hence find the exact value of $\int_0^1 \dfrac{1}{(x^2+1)^2}\,dx$.

34. Find:

    a) $\int x(1+x)^6\,dx$,   b) $\int x(ax+b)^{12}\,dx$.

35. Evaluate $\int_0^1 xe^{-x}\,dx$ showing all your working. (OCR)

36. Showing your working clearly, use integration by parts to evaluate $\int_0^\pi 4x\sin\frac{1}{2}x\,dx$. (OCR)

37. By using the substitution $u = 3x + 1$, or otherwise, show that

$$\int_0^1 \frac{x}{(3x+1)^2}\,dx = \tfrac{2}{9}\ln 2 - \tfrac{1}{12}\,.$$

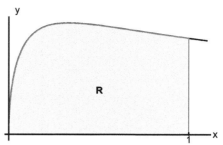

The diagram shows the finite region R in the first quadrant which is bounded by the curve $y = \dfrac{6\sqrt{x}}{3x+1}$, the x-axis and the line $x = 1$.

Find the volume of the solid formed when R is rotated completely about the x-axis, giving your answer in terms of π and $\ln 2$. (OCR)

38. Use integration by parts to determine the exact value of $\displaystyle\int_0^{\frac{1}{2}\pi} 3x\sin 2x\,dx$. (OCR)

39. Show that

$$\int_2^3 \frac{2}{(x-1)^2(x^2+1)}\,dx = a + b\ln 2,$$

where a and b are constants whose values you should find. (OCR, adapt.)

40*. The figure shows part of a *cycloid*, given by the parametric equations

$$x = a(t - \sin t), \qquad y = a(1 - \cos t),$$

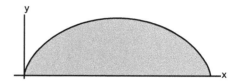

for $0 \le t \le 2\pi$. Calculate the area of the region enclosed between this arch of the cycloid and the x-axis.

Find also the volume of the solid of revolution formed when this region is rotated through $360°$ about the x-axis.

41*. Show that the area enclosed by the astroid in Example 16.2.10 is given by the integral $\displaystyle\int_0^{\frac{1}{2}\pi} 12a^2\sin^4 t\cos^2 t\,dt$. Use the substitution $t = \tfrac{1}{2}\pi - u$ to show that the area could also be written as $\displaystyle\int_0^{\frac{1}{2}\pi} 12a^2\cos^4 t\sin^2 t\,dt$.

Prove that $\sin^4 t\cos^2 t + \cos^4 t\sin^2 t \equiv \tfrac{1}{8}(1 - \cos 4t)$, and deduce that the area enclosed by the astroid is equal to $\tfrac{3}{4}a^2\displaystyle\int_0^{\frac{1}{2}\pi}(1 - \cos 4t)\,dt$. Evaluate this area.

42*. Calculate $\displaystyle\int_1^2 \frac{2x^3 + 3x^2 + 28}{(x+2)(x^2+4)}\,dx$, giving an exact answer.

43*. Use the substitution $x = (t^2 - 1)^{-1}$, where $t > 1$, to show that, for $x > 0$,

$$\int \frac{1}{\sqrt{x(x+1)}}\,dx = 2\ln\left(\sqrt{x} + \sqrt{x+1}\right) + c\,.$$

You may use without proof the result that $\displaystyle\int \frac{1}{t^2 - a^2}\,dt = \tfrac{1}{2a}\ln\left|\frac{t-a}{t+a}\right| + c$.

The section of the curve

$$y = \frac{1}{\sqrt{x}} - \frac{1}{\sqrt{x+1}}$$

between $x = \tfrac{1}{8}$ and $x = \tfrac{9}{16}$ is rotated through $360°$ about the x-axis. Show that the volume enclosed is $2\pi\ln\tfrac{5}{4}$. (STEP)

44. Find the solution of the differential equation $x\dfrac{dy}{dx} = 2x^2 + 7x + 3$ for which $y = 10$ when $x = 1$

(OCR)

45. In a chemical reaction, the amount z grams of a substance after t hours is modelled by the differential equation $\frac{dz}{dt} = 0.005(20 - z)^2$. Initially $z = 0$. Find an expression for t in terms of z, and show that $t = 15$ when $z = 12$. (OCR)

46. The gradient of a curve is given by $\frac{dy}{dx} = 3x^2 - 22x + 15$, and the curve passes through the point $(0, 100)$. Find the equation of the curve. Find the coordinates of the two stationary points, stating (with a reason) the nature of each stationary point.

47. The area of a circle of radius r metres is A m^2.

    a) Find $\frac{dA}{dr}$ and write down an expression, in terms of r, for $\frac{dr}{dA}$.

    b) The area increases with time t seconds in such a way that $\frac{dA}{dt} = \frac{2}{(t+1)^3}$. Find an expression, in terms of r and t, for $\frac{dr}{dt}$.

    c) Solve the differential equation $\frac{dA}{dt} = \frac{2}{(t+1)^3}$ to obtain A in terms of t, given that $A = 0$ when $t = 0$.

    d) Show that, when $t = 1$, $\frac{dr}{dt} = 0.081$ correct to 2 significant figures. (OCR)

48. The rate of destruction of a drug by the kidneys is proportional to the amount of drug present in the body. The constant of proportionality is denoted by k. At time t the quantity of drug in the body is x. Write down a differential equation relating x and t, and show that the general solution is $x = Ae^{-kt}$, where A is an arbitrary constant.

Before $t = 0$ there is no drug in the body, but at $t = 0$ a quantity Q of the drug is administered. When $t = 1$ the amount of drug in the body is $Q\alpha$, where a is a constant such that $0 < \alpha < 1$. Show that $x = Q\alpha^t$.

When $t = 1$ and again when $t = 2$ another dose Q is administered. Show that the amount of drug in the body immediately after $t = 2$ is $Q(1 + \alpha + \alpha^2)$.

If the drug is administered at regular intervals for an indefinite period, and if the greatest amount of the drug that the body can tolerate is T, show that Q should not exceed $T(1 - \alpha)$. (OCR, adapt.)

49.   a) The number of people, x, in a queue at a travel centre t minutes after it opens is modelled by the differential equation $\frac{dx}{dt} = 1.4t - 4$ for values of t up to 10. Interpret the term '-4' on the right side of the equation. Solve the differential equation, given that $x = 8$ when $t = 0$.

    b) An alternative model gives the differential equation $\frac{dx}{dt} = 1.4t - 0.5x$ for the same values of t. Verify that $x = 13.6e^{-0.5t} + 2.8t - 5.6$ satisfies this differential equation. Verify also that when $t = 0$ this function takes the value 8. (OCR)

50.   a) Two quantities x and y are related by the differential equation $y\frac{dy}{dx} = -16x$. Solve this equation to get an implicit equation of the solution curve for which $y = 0$ when $x = 0.1$.

    b) Sketch your solution curve from part (a), showing the values of x and y at which the curve cuts the coordinate axes. (OCR)

51. At time $t = 0$ there are 8000 fish in a lake. At time t days the birth-rate of fish is equal to one-fiftieth of the number N of fish present. Fish are taken from the lake at the rate of 100 per day. Modelling N as a continuous variable, show that $50\frac{dN}{dt} = N - 5000$.

Solve the differential equation to find N in terms of t. Find the time taken for the population of fish in the lake to increase to 11000.

When the population of fish has reached 11000, it is decided to increase the number of fish taken from the lake from 100 per day to F per day. Write down, in terms of F, the new differential equation satisfied by N. Show that if $F > 220$, then $\frac{dN}{dt} < 0$ when $N = 11000$. If $F > 220$, give a reason why the population of fish in the lake continues to decrease. (OCR)

52. A metal rod is 60 cm long and is heated at one end. The temperature at a point on the rod at distance x cm from the heated end is denoted by $T°$ C. At a point halfway along the rod, $T = 290$ and $\frac{dT}{dx} = -6$.

   a) In a simple model for the temperature of the rod, it is assumed that $\frac{dT}{dx}$ has the same value at all points on the rod. For this model, express T in terms of x and hence determine the temperature difference between the ends of the rod.

   b) In a more refined model, the rate of change of T with respect to x is taken to be proportional to x. Set up a differential equation for T, involving a constant of proportionality k. Solve the differential equation and hence show that, in this refined model, the temperature along the rod is predicted to vary from $380°$ C to $20°$ C. (OCR)

53. During a manufacturing procedure, hot pieces of metal are plunged into baths of water to cool them down. The rate of cooling is modelled by the equation $\frac{dT}{dt} = -k(T - T_0)$, where T is the temperature of the metal after t minutes in the bath, and T_0 is a constant, being the temperature of the water bath, and k is a constant of proportionality.

   a) It is given that $T = \lambda T_0$ when $t = 0$, where $\lambda \geq 5$ is a constant. Solve the differential equation to find T in terms of t. Sketch the graph of the solution.

   b) It is noted that the rate of cooling halves every 30 seconds. Show that $k = 2\ln 2$.

   c) When the temperature of the metal has reached $1.05T_0$, the metal is cool enough to be passed on to the next stage of production. Find an expression for the number of minutes the metal needs to be in the cooling bath for until it is cool enough to be passed on down the production line.

54. Find the general solution of the differential equation $\frac{dy}{dx} = \frac{x(y^2 + 1)}{(x-1)y}$, expressing y in terms of x. (OCR, adapt.)

55. Solve the differential equation $\frac{dy}{dx} = xye^{2x}$, given that $y = 1$ when $x = 0$.

56. The rate at which the water level in a cylindrical barrel goes down is modelled by the equation $\frac{dh}{dt} = -\sqrt{h}$, where h is the height in metres of the level above the tap and t is the time in minutes. When $t = 0$, $h = 1$. Show by integration that $h = (1 - \frac{1}{2}t)^2$. How long does it take for the water flow to stop?.

   An alternative model might be to write $h = 1 - \sin kt$. Find the value of k which gives the same time before the water flow stops as the previous model. Show that this model satisfies the differential equation $\frac{dh}{dt} = -k\sqrt{2h - h^2}$. (OCR, adapt.)

57. A tropical island is being set up as a nature reserve. Initially there are 100 nesting pairs of fancy terns on the island. In the first year this increases by 8. In one theory being tested, the number N of nesting pairs after t years is assumed to satisfy the differential equation $\frac{dN}{dt} = \frac{1}{5000}N(500 - N)$.

   a) Show that, according to this model, the rate of increase of N is 8 per year when $N = 100$. Find the rate of increase when $N = 300$ and when $N = 450$. Describe what happens as N approaches 500, and interpret your answer.

   b) Use your answers to part (a) to sketch the solution curve of the differential equation for which $N = 100$ when $t = 0$.

   c) Obtain the general solution of the differential equation, and the solution for which $N = 100$ when $t = 0$. Use your answer to predict after how many years the number of pairs of nesting fancy terns on the island will first exceed 300. (OCR)

58. Obtain the general solution of the differential equation $y\frac{dy}{dx}\tan 2x = 1 - y^2$. (OCR, adapt.)

59. Find the general solution of the differential equation $\frac{dy}{dx} = \frac{y^2}{x^2 - x - 2}$ in the region $x > 2$. Find also the particular solution which satisfies $y = 1$ when $x = 5$. (OCR)

60. Find the solution of the differential equation $\dfrac{dy}{dx} = \dfrac{\sin^2 x}{y^2}$ which also satisfies $y = 1$ when $x = 0$.

(OCR)

61. Solve the differential equation $\dfrac{dy}{dx} = \dfrac{x}{y}e^{x+y}$, in the form $f(y) = g(x)$, given that $y = 0$ when $x = 0$.

62. The organiser of a sale, which lasted for 3 hours and raised a total of £1000, attempted to create a model to represent the relationship between s and t, where £s is the amount which had been raised at time t hours after the start of the sale. In the model s and t were taken to be continuous variables. The organiser assumed that the rate of raising money varied directly as the time remaining and inversely as the amount already raised. Show that, for this model, $\dfrac{ds}{dt} = k\dfrac{3-t}{s}$, where k is a constant. Solve the differential equation, and show that the solution can be written in the form $\dfrac{s^2}{1000^2} + \dfrac{(3-t)^2}{3^2} = 1$. Hence:

a) find the amount raised during the first hour of the sale,

b) find the rate of raising money one hour after the start of the sale.

(OCR)

63. A biologist studying fluctuations in the size of a particular population decides to investigate a model for which $\dfrac{dP}{dt} = kP\cos kt$, where P is the size of the population at time t days and k is a positive constant.

a) Given that $P = P_0$ when $t = 0$, express P in terms of k, t and P_0.

b) Find the ratio of the maximum size of the population to the minimum size.

(OCR)

64. For $x \geq 0$ and $0 \leq y < \frac{1}{2}\pi$, the variables y and x are connected by the differential equation

$$\frac{dy}{dx} = \frac{\ln x}{x\cos y}$$

and $y = 0$ when $x = 1$. Solve this differential equation. What is the range of values of x for which is solution is valid?

65. Show that, if $y^2 = x^k f(x)$, then $2xy\dfrac{dy}{dx} = ky^2 + x^{k+1}\dfrac{df}{dx}$.

a) By setting $k = 1$ in this result, find the solution of the differential equation

$$2xy\frac{dy}{dx} = y^2 + x^2 - 1$$

for which $y = 2$ when $x = 1$. Describe this solution geometrically.

b) Find the solution of the differential equation

$$2x^2 y\frac{dy}{dx} = 2\ln x - xy^2$$

for which $y = 1$ when $x = 1$

(STEP)

Vector Geometry

In this chapter we will learn:

- the standard notations for vectors, and understand the terms 'position vector' and 'displacement vector',

- how to carry out addition, subtraction and scaling of vectors, understanding these operations geometrically,

- about the modulus of a vector,

- how to calculate the scalar product of two vectors, using it to calculate the angle between vectors, and to solve problems concerning perpendicular vectors,

- to understand both the vector and Cartesian form of the equation of a straight line,

- to determine whether two lines are parallel, intersect or are skew,

- to determine the angle between two lines, and the point of intersection of two lines when it exists.

19.1   Planar Translations

In Chapter 7 we studied graph transformations. In particular we saw how the graph of the function $y = f(x) + a$ was obtained from that of $y = f(x)$ by translating the graph vertically through a distance of a units, while the graph of $y = f(x - a)$ was obtained by translating the graph horizontally through a distance of a units. A practical way of performing either of these transformations would be to draw the graph on a transparent sheet placed over the coordinate grid, and then move the transparent sheet.

The essential feature of a translation is that the sheet moves over the grid without turning. A general translation would move the sheet u units across and v units up the grid. This is shown on the right where several points all move in the same direction through the same distance. Such a translation is called a **vector** and is written $\begin{pmatrix} u \\ v \end{pmatrix}$.

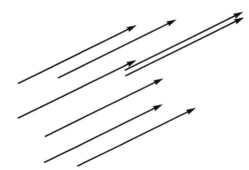

Figure 19.1

As observed in Chapter 7, a horizontal translation through a distance a is represented by the vector $\begin{pmatrix} a \\ 0 \end{pmatrix}$, while a vertical translation through b is represented by the vector $\begin{pmatrix} 0 \\ b \end{pmatrix}$.

In practice, drawing several arrows, as above, is not a convenient way of representing a vector. It is usual to draw just a single arrow, as here. Note that the position of the arrow in the (x, y)-plane is of no significance. This arrow is just one of infinitely many that could be drawn to represent the vector.

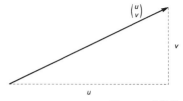

Figure 19.2

While there are many different types of vectors to be found in physics: velocity vectors, acceleration vectors, force vectors, for example, from a mathematical perspective, all vectors are the same; only the ways in which they are interpreted differ.

19.2 Vector Algebra

It is often convenient to use a single letter to stand for a vector. In print, bold type is used to distinguish vectors from numbers. For example, in $\mathbf{p} = \begin{pmatrix} u \\ v \end{pmatrix}$, $\mathbf{p}$ is a vector but u and v are numbers, called the **components** of the vector $\mathbf{p}$ in the x- and y-directions. In handwriting, vectors are indicated by a wavy line underneath the letter: $\underset{\sim}{p} = \begin{pmatrix} u \\ v \end{pmatrix}$. It is important to get into the habit of writing vectors in this way, so that it is quite clear in your work which letters stand for vectors and which stand for numbers.

If s is any number and $\mathbf{p}$ is any vector, then $s\mathbf{p}$ is another vector. If $s > 0$, the vector $s\mathbf{p}$ is a translation in the same direction as $\mathbf{p}$ but s times as large; if $s < 0$ it is in the opposite direction and $|s|$ times as large. A number such as s is often called a **scalar**, because it usually changes the scale of the vector. It is clear from the diagram that $s\mathbf{p} = \begin{pmatrix} su \\ sv \end{pmatrix}$.

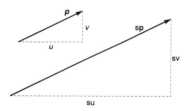

Note that the scaled vector $(-1)\mathbf{p} = \begin{pmatrix} -u \\ -v \end{pmatrix}$ is a vector of the same magnitude as $\mathbf{p}$ but pointing in the opposite direction. It is denoted by $-\mathbf{p}$.

Figure 19.3

Vectors are added by performing one translation after another. To find the sum $\mathbf{p} + \mathbf{q}$ of two vectors $\mathbf{p}$ and $\mathbf{q}$, we represent them by a pair of arrows placed 'tip-to-tail', so that the translations represented by the vectors $\mathbf{p}$ and $\mathbf{q}$ can be performed one after the other and be seen as a single translation. If the vector $\mathbf{p}$ is represented as a vector from the point U to the point V, and the vector $\mathbf{q}$ is represented as a vector from the point V to the point W, then the vector $\mathbf{p} + \mathbf{q}$ is represented as a vector from U to W. This is known as the **triangle law** of vector addition.

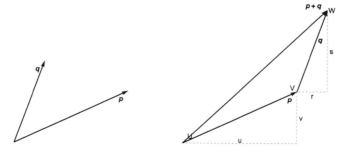

Figure 19.4

It is therefore clear that, if $\mathbf{p} = \begin{pmatrix} u \\ v \end{pmatrix}$ and $\mathbf{q} = \begin{pmatrix} r \\ s \end{pmatrix}$, then $\mathbf{p} + \mathbf{q} = \begin{pmatrix} u+r \\ v+s \end{pmatrix}$.

If this notion of vector addition is to make sense, it should be the case that

$$\mathbf{p} + \mathbf{q} = \begin{pmatrix} u + r \\ v + s \end{pmatrix} = \begin{pmatrix} r + u \\ s + v \end{pmatrix} = \mathbf{q} + \mathbf{p},$$

so that the order in which vectors are added does matter. The truth of this fact can be seen by considering the parallelogram $UVWZ$, from which it is clear the vector $\mathbf{p} + \mathbf{q}$ translates from U to W via the point V, the vector $\mathbf{q} + \mathbf{p}$ translates U to the same point W, but this time via the point Z. This property is called the **commutative rule for addition of vectors.**

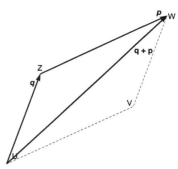

Figure 19.5

Example 19.2.1. *If* $\mathbf{p} = \begin{pmatrix} 2 \\ -3 \end{pmatrix}$, $\mathbf{q} = \begin{pmatrix} 1 \\ 2 \end{pmatrix}$ *and* $\mathbf{r} = \begin{pmatrix} 5 \\ 3 \end{pmatrix}$, *find a number s such that* $\mathbf{p} + s\mathbf{q} = \mathbf{r}$.

We can write $\mathbf{p} + s\mathbf{q}$ as

$$\begin{pmatrix} 2 \\ -3 \end{pmatrix} + s\begin{pmatrix} 1 \\ 2 \end{pmatrix} = \begin{pmatrix} s + 2 \\ 2s - 3 \end{pmatrix}.$$

For this vector to be equal to $\mathbf{r}$, we need both the x- and y-components of the two vectors to be equal. This means that the equations

$$s + 2 = 5 \qquad 2s - 3 = 3$$

must both be satisfied, which happens when $s = 3$. Thus we deduce that $\mathbf{r} = \mathbf{p} + 3\mathbf{q}$.

The idea of addition of vectors can be extended to adding three or more vectors. We therefore need to clarify what is meant by $\mathbf{p} + \mathbf{q} + \mathbf{r}$; is this to be equal to $(\mathbf{p} + \mathbf{q}) + \mathbf{r}$ or to $\mathbf{p} + (\mathbf{q} + \mathbf{r})$? Happily, we do not have to make a choice, since both of these expressions are equal. This is easiest to see using components. If $\mathbf{p} = \begin{pmatrix} a \\ b \end{pmatrix}$, $\mathbf{q} = \begin{pmatrix} c \\ d \end{pmatrix}$ and $\mathbf{r} = \begin{pmatrix} e \\ f \end{pmatrix}$, then

$$\mathbf{p} + (\mathbf{q} + \mathbf{r}) = \begin{pmatrix} a \\ b \end{pmatrix} + \begin{pmatrix} c + e \\ d + f \end{pmatrix} = \begin{pmatrix} a + c + e \\ b + d + f \end{pmatrix} = \begin{pmatrix} a + c \\ b + d \end{pmatrix} + \begin{pmatrix} e \\ f \end{pmatrix} = (\mathbf{p} + \mathbf{q}) + \mathbf{r}.$$

This property is called the **associative property of addition of vectors.**

To complete the algebra of vector addition, the symbol $\mathbf{0} = \begin{pmatrix} 0 \\ 0 \end{pmatrix}$ is needed for the **zero vector**, which has the properties that, for any vector $\mathbf{p}$,

$$0\mathbf{p} = \mathbf{0} \qquad \mathbf{p} + \mathbf{0} = \mathbf{p} \qquad \mathbf{p} + (-\mathbf{p}) = \mathbf{0}.$$

We also need to know that vector addition is compatible with scalar multiplication. The following diagrams, and properties of similar triangles, make it clear that

$$s(\mathbf{p} + \mathbf{q}) = s\mathbf{p} + s\mathbf{q} \qquad (s + t)\mathbf{p} = s\mathbf{p} + t\mathbf{p}$$

for all vectors $\mathbf{p}$ and $\mathbf{q}$ and all scalars s and t. This is called the **distributive property of scalar multiplication over vector addition.**

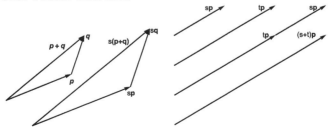

Figure 19.6

We note that subtraction of vectors is implicit in the combination of vector addition and scalar multiplication.

The difference $\mathbf{q} - \mathbf{p}$ between two vectors can be seen as either the vector $\mathbf{x}$ that satisfies the equation

$$\mathbf{x} = \mathbf{q} - \mathbf{p} \qquad \Leftrightarrow \qquad \mathbf{p} + \mathbf{x} = \mathbf{q}$$

or else is the vector obtained by adding $-\mathbf{p} = (-1)\mathbf{p}$ to the vector $\mathbf{q}$.

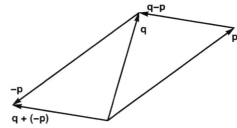

Figure 19.7

19.3 Fundamental Unit Vectors

Using the rules of vector algebra to the components of a vector, we see that a vector $\mathbf{p} = \begin{pmatrix} u \\ v \end{pmatrix}$ can be written as

$$\mathbf{p} = \begin{pmatrix} u \\ v \end{pmatrix} = \begin{pmatrix} u \\ 0 \end{pmatrix} + \begin{pmatrix} 0 \\ v \end{pmatrix} = u\begin{pmatrix} 1 \\ 0 \end{pmatrix} + v\begin{pmatrix} 0 \\ 1 \end{pmatrix}$$

The vectors $\begin{pmatrix} 1 \\ 0 \end{pmatrix}$ and $\begin{pmatrix} 0 \\ 1 \end{pmatrix}$ are called the **fundamental unit vectors** in the x- and y-directions, and they are denoted by the vectors $\mathbf{i}$ and $\mathbf{j}$, so that we write

$$\mathbf{p} = \begin{pmatrix} u \\ v \end{pmatrix} = u\mathbf{i} + v\mathbf{j}.$$

Figure 19.8

The vectors $u\mathbf{i}$ and $v\mathbf{j}$ are called the **component vectors** of $\mathbf{p}$ in the x- and y-directions. We now have two alternative notations for performing algebra with vectors. For example, to calculate $3\mathbf{p} - 2\mathbf{q}$, where $\mathbf{p} = \begin{pmatrix} 2 \\ 5 \end{pmatrix}$ and $\mathbf{q} = \begin{pmatrix} 1 \\ -3 \end{pmatrix}$, we can write either of

$$3\begin{pmatrix} 2 \\ 5 \end{pmatrix} - 2\begin{pmatrix} 1 \\ -3 \end{pmatrix} = \begin{pmatrix} 6 \\ 15 \end{pmatrix} - \begin{pmatrix} 2 \\ -6 \end{pmatrix} = \begin{pmatrix} 4 \\ 21 \end{pmatrix} \qquad 3(2\mathbf{i} + 5\mathbf{j}) - 2(\mathbf{i} - 3\mathbf{j}) = 6\mathbf{i} + 15\mathbf{j} - 2\mathbf{i} + 6\mathbf{j} = 4\mathbf{i} + 21\mathbf{j}.$$

There is no difference between the two methods of expression; sometimes one is more convenient than the other.

EXERCISE 19A

When you are asked to illustrate a vector equation geometrically, you should show vectors as arrows on a grid of squares, either on paper or on screen.

1. Illustrate the following equations geometrically:

   a) $\begin{pmatrix} 4 \\ 1 \end{pmatrix} + \begin{pmatrix} -3 \\ 2 \end{pmatrix} = \begin{pmatrix} 1 \\ 3 \end{pmatrix}$,

   b) $3\begin{pmatrix} 1 \\ -2 \end{pmatrix} = \begin{pmatrix} 3 \\ -6 \end{pmatrix}$,

   c) $\begin{pmatrix} 0 \\ 4 \end{pmatrix} + 2\begin{pmatrix} 1 \\ -2 \end{pmatrix} = \begin{pmatrix} 2 \\ 0 \end{pmatrix}$,

   d) $\begin{pmatrix} 3 \\ 1 \end{pmatrix} - \begin{pmatrix} 5 \\ 1 \end{pmatrix} = \begin{pmatrix} -2 \\ 0 \end{pmatrix}$,

   e) $3\begin{pmatrix} -1 \\ 2 \end{pmatrix} - \begin{pmatrix} -4 \\ 3 \end{pmatrix} = \begin{pmatrix} 1 \\ 3 \end{pmatrix}$,

   f) $4\begin{pmatrix} 2 \\ 3 \end{pmatrix} - 3\begin{pmatrix} 3 \\ 2 \end{pmatrix} = \begin{pmatrix} -1 \\ 6 \end{pmatrix}$,

   g) $\begin{pmatrix} 2 \\ -3 \end{pmatrix} + \begin{pmatrix} 4 \\ 5 \end{pmatrix} + \begin{pmatrix} -6 \\ -2 \end{pmatrix} = \begin{pmatrix} 0 \\ 0 \end{pmatrix}$,

   h) $2\begin{pmatrix} 3 \\ -1 \end{pmatrix} + 3\begin{pmatrix} -2 \\ 3 \end{pmatrix} + \begin{pmatrix} 0 \\ -7 \end{pmatrix} = \begin{pmatrix} 0 \\ 0 \end{pmatrix}$.

2. Rewrite each of the equations in Question 1 using fundamental vector notation.

3. Express each of the following vectors as column vectors, and illustrate your answers geometrically.

   a) $\mathbf{i} + 2\mathbf{j}$,

   b) $3\mathbf{i}$,

   c) $\mathbf{j} - \mathbf{i}$,

   d) $4\mathbf{i} - 3\mathbf{j}$.

4. Show that there is a number s such that $s\begin{pmatrix} 1 \\ 2 \end{pmatrix} + \begin{pmatrix} -3 \\ 1 \end{pmatrix} = \begin{pmatrix} -1 \\ 5 \end{pmatrix}$. Illustrate your answer geometrically.

5. If $\mathbf{p} = 5\mathbf{i} - 3\mathbf{j}$, $\mathbf{q} = 2\mathbf{j} - \mathbf{i}$ and $\mathbf{r} = \mathbf{i} + 5\mathbf{j}$, show that there is a number s such that $\mathbf{p} + s\mathbf{q} = \mathbf{r}$. Illustrate your answer geometrically.

   Rearrange this equation so as to express $\mathbf{q}$ in terms of $\mathbf{p}$ and $\mathbf{r}$. Illustrate the rearranged equation geometrically.

6. Find numbers s and t such that $s\left(\begin{smallmatrix}5\\4\end{smallmatrix}\right)+t\left(\begin{smallmatrix}-3\\-2\end{smallmatrix}\right)=\left(\begin{smallmatrix}1\\2\end{smallmatrix}\right)$. Illustrate your answer geometrically.

7. If $\mathbf{p}=4\mathbf{i}+\mathbf{j}$, $\mathbf{q}=6\mathbf{i}-5\mathbf{j}$ and $\mathbf{r}=3\mathbf{i}+4\mathbf{j}$, find numbers s and t such that $s\mathbf{p}+t\mathbf{q}=\mathbf{r}$. Illustrate your answer geometrically.

8. Show that it is not possible to find numbers s and t such that

$$\begin{pmatrix}4\\-2\end{pmatrix}+s\begin{pmatrix}3\\1\end{pmatrix}=\begin{pmatrix}-6\\3\end{pmatrix}\quad\text{and}\quad\begin{pmatrix}3\\4\end{pmatrix}+t\begin{pmatrix}-1\\2\end{pmatrix}=\begin{pmatrix}1\\1\end{pmatrix}.$$

Give geometrical reasons.

9. If $\mathbf{p}=2\mathbf{i}+3\mathbf{j}$, $\mathbf{q}=4\mathbf{i}-5\mathbf{j}$ and $\mathbf{r}=\mathbf{i}-4\mathbf{j}$, find a set of numbers f, g and h such that $f\mathbf{p}+g\mathbf{q}+h\mathbf{r}=\mathbf{0}$. Illustrate your answer geometrically. Give a reason why there is more than one possible answer to this question.

10. If $\mathbf{p}=3\mathbf{i}-\mathbf{j}$, $\mathbf{q}=4\mathbf{i}+5\mathbf{j}$ and $\mathbf{r}=2\mathbf{j}-6\mathbf{i}$,

   a) is it possible to find numbers s and t such that $\mathbf{q}=s\mathbf{p}+t\mathbf{r}$,

   b) is it possible to find numbers u and v such that $\mathbf{r}=u\mathbf{p}+v\mathbf{q}$?

   Give a geometrical reason for your answers.

19.4 Position vectors

If E and F are two points on a grid, there is a unique translation which takes us from E to F. This translation can be represented by the arrow which starts at E and ends at F, and it is denoted by the symbol $\overrightarrow{EF}$, or possibly just **EF**. Although this translation is unique, its name is not. If G and H are two other points on the grid such that the lines EF and GH are parallel and equal in length (so that $EFHG$ is a parallelogram), then the translation $\overrightarrow{EF}$ also takes you from G to H, so that it could also be denoted by $\overrightarrow{GH}$. In a vector equation $\overrightarrow{EF}$ could be replaced by $\overrightarrow{GH}$ without affecting the truth of the statement.

Vectors written like this are sometimes called **displacement vectors**. They are not a different kind of vector, just translation vectors written in a different way. There is, however, one especially important displacement vector. This is the vector $\overrightarrow{OA}$ that starts at the origin O and ends at a point A, so that $\overrightarrow{OA}=\overrightarrow{EF}=\overrightarrow{GH}$. The translation from O to A is called the **position vector** of A.

There is a close link between the coordinates of A and the components of its position vector. If A has coordinates (u,v), then to get from O to A you must move u units in the x-direction and v units in the y-direction, so that the vector $\overrightarrow{OA}$ has components u and v.

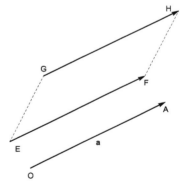

Figure 19.9

Key Fact 19.1 Position Vectors

The position vector of the point A with coordinates (u,v) is

$$\overrightarrow{OA}=\begin{pmatrix}u\\v\end{pmatrix}=u\mathbf{i}+v\mathbf{j}\,.$$

It is a useful convention to use the same letter for a point and its position vector. For example, the position vector of the point A can be denoted by $\overrightarrow{OA}$, or by **a**. This 'alphabet convention' will be used wherever possible in this book. It has the advantages that it economises on letters of the alphabet and avoids the need for repetitive definitions.

19.5 Algebra With Position Vectors

Multiplication by a scalar has a simple interpretation in terms of position vectors. If the vector $s\mathbf{a}$ is the position vector $\overrightarrow{OD}$ of a point D, then:

- If $s > 0$, D lies on the directed line OA (produced if necessary) such that $OD = sOA$.

- If $s < 0$, D lies on the directed line AO produced such that $OD = |s|OA$.

This is shown on the right for $s = 1.5$ and $s = -0.3$.

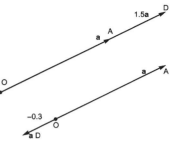

Figure 19.10

To identify the point with position vector $\mathbf{a} + \mathbf{b}$ is not quite so easy, because adding vectors requires that they be placed 'tip-to-tail', and the position vectors **OA** and **OB** both start at O, and so are not 'tip-to-tail'. We must construct the parallelogram $OACB$, in which case

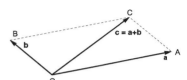

$$\overrightarrow{OC} = \overrightarrow{OA} + \overrightarrow{AC} = \overrightarrow{OA} + \overrightarrow{OB} = \mathbf{a} + \mathbf{b}.$$

Figure 19.11

This is called the **parallelogram rule of addition** for position vectors.

Subtraction can be shown in either of two ways. The vector $\mathbf{b} - \mathbf{a}$ can be seen as the vector $\overrightarrow{AB}$. Completing the parallelogram $OABE$, the vector $\mathbf{e} = \mathbf{b} - \mathbf{a}$ is the position vector of the point E. Alternatively completing the parallelogram $OBEF$, where $\overrightarrow{OF} = -\mathbf{a}$, shows how $\overrightarrow{OE}$ is the sum of the vectors $\mathbf{b}$ and $-\mathbf{a}$.

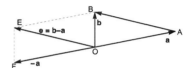

Figure 19.12

Example 19.5.1. *Points A and B have position vectors $\mathbf{a}$ and $\mathbf{b}$. Find the position vectors of the midpoint M of AB and the point T on AB such that $AT = \frac{2}{3}AB$. Such a point T is called a point of trisection of AB.*

Since the displacement vector $\overrightarrow{AB} = \mathbf{b} - \mathbf{a}$, we must have $\overrightarrow{AM} = \frac{1}{2}(\mathbf{b} - \mathbf{a})$, and hence

$$\overrightarrow{OM} = \overrightarrow{OA} + \overrightarrow{AM} = \mathbf{a} + \tfrac{1}{2}(\mathbf{b} - \mathbf{a}) = \tfrac{1}{2}(\mathbf{a} + \mathbf{b}).$$

Similarly, the displacement vector $\overrightarrow{AT} = \frac{2}{3}\overrightarrow{AB} = \frac{2}{3}(\mathbf{b} - \mathbf{a})$, and hence

$$\overrightarrow{OT} = \mathbf{a} + \tfrac{2}{3}(\mathbf{b} - \mathbf{a}) = \tfrac{1}{3}\mathbf{a} + \tfrac{2}{3}\mathbf{b}.$$

An alternative method for determining $\overrightarrow{OM}$ lies in recalling an important geometric property of parallelograms. If the parallelogram $OACB$ is completed (see Figure 19.11) we note that M, the midpoint of AB, is also the midpoint of OC (since the diagonals of a parallelogram bisect each other). Thus

$$\overrightarrow{OM} = \tfrac{1}{2}\overrightarrow{OC} = \tfrac{1}{2}(\mathbf{a} + \mathbf{b}).$$

The results of this example can be used to prove an important theorem about triangles.

Example 19.5.2. *In triangle ABC the midpoints of BC, AC and AB are D, E and F respectively. Prove that the lines AD, BE and CF (called the **medians** of the triangle) meet at a point G, and that G is a point of trisection of each of the medians*

We know that $\mathbf{d} = \frac{1}{2}(\mathbf{b}+\mathbf{c})$. If G is the point of trisection of AD such that $AG = \frac{2}{3}AD$, then

$$\begin{aligned}
\mathbf{g} &= \tfrac{1}{3}\mathbf{a} + \tfrac{2}{3}\mathbf{d} \\
&= \tfrac{1}{3}\mathbf{a} + \tfrac{2}{3} \times \tfrac{1}{2}(\mathbf{b}+\mathbf{c}) \\
&= \tfrac{1}{3}(\mathbf{a}+\mathbf{b}+\mathbf{c})
\end{aligned}$$

Since this position vector is symmetric in $\mathbf{a}$, $\mathbf{b}$ and $\mathbf{c}$, it is clear that G is also the point of trisection of BE closer to E, and the point of trisection of CF closer to F. In particular, this means that the point G lies on all three medians.

The three medians meet at the point G, where $\mathbf{g} = \frac{1}{3}(\mathbf{a}+\mathbf{b}+\mathbf{c})$. This point is called the **centroid** of the triangle.

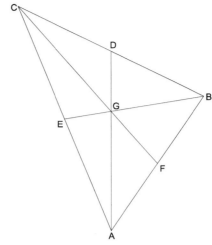

Figure 19.13

For Interest

If we cut the triangle out of card, then the centroid is the point on the triangle where we could balance the triangle on a fingertip.

EXERCISE 19B

1. The points A and B have coordinates $(3,1)$ and $(1,2)$. Plot on squared paper the points C, D, E, F, G, H defined by the following vector equations, and state their coordinates.

   a) $\mathbf{c} = 3\mathbf{a}$,
   b) $\mathbf{d} = -\mathbf{b}$,
   c) $\mathbf{e} = \mathbf{a} - \mathbf{b}$,
   d) $\mathbf{f} = \mathbf{b} - 3\mathbf{a}$,
   e) $\mathbf{g} = \mathbf{b} + 3\mathbf{a}$,
   f) $\mathbf{h} = \frac{1}{2}(\mathbf{b} + 3\mathbf{a})$.

2. Points A and B have coordinates $(2,7)$ and $(-3,-3)$ respectively. Use a vector method to find the coordinates of C and D, where

   a) C is the point such that $\overrightarrow{AC} = 3\overrightarrow{AB}$,
   b) D is the point such that $\overrightarrow{AD} = \frac{3}{5}\overrightarrow{AB}$.

3. C is the point on AB produced such that $\overrightarrow{AB} = \overrightarrow{BC}$. Express $\overrightarrow{OC}$ in terms of $\mathbf{a}$ and $\mathbf{b}$. Use a vector method to confirm that B is the midpoint of AC.

4. C is the point on AB such that $AC : CB = 4 : 3$. Express $\mathbf{c}$ in terms of $\mathbf{a}$ and $\mathbf{b}$.

5. If C is the point on AB such that $\overrightarrow{AC} = t\overrightarrow{AB}$, prove that $\mathbf{c} = t\mathbf{b} + (1-t)\mathbf{a}$.

6. Write a vector equation connecting $\mathbf{a}$, $\mathbf{b}$, $\mathbf{c}$ and $\mathbf{d}$ to express the fact that $\overrightarrow{AB} = \overrightarrow{DC}$. Deduce from your equation that

   a) $\overrightarrow{DA} = \overrightarrow{CB}$,

   b) if E is the point such that $OAEC$ is a parallelogram, then $OBED$ is a parallelogram.

7. ABC is a triangle. D is the midpoint of BC, E is the midpoint of AC, F is the midpoint of AB and G is the midpoint of EF. Express the displacement vectors $\overrightarrow{AD}$ and $\overrightarrow{AG}$ in terms of $\mathbf{a}$, $\mathbf{b}$ and $\mathbf{c}$. What can you deduce about the points A, D and G?

8. $OABC$ is a parallelogram, M is the midpoint of BC, and P is the point of trisection of AC closer to C. Express $\mathbf{b}$, $\mathbf{m}$ and $\mathbf{p}$ in terms of $\mathbf{a}$ and $\mathbf{c}$. Deduce that $\mathbf{p} = \frac{2}{3}\mathbf{m}$, and interpret this equation geometrically.

9. ABC is a triangle, D is the midpoint of BC, E is the midpoint of AD and F is the point of trisection of AC closer to A. G is the point on FB such that $\overrightarrow{FG} = \frac{1}{4}\overrightarrow{FB}$. Express $\mathbf{d}, \mathbf{e}, \mathbf{f}$ and $\mathbf{g}$ in terms of $\mathbf{a}, \mathbf{b}$ and $\mathbf{c}$, and deduce that G is the same point as E. Draw a figure to illustrate this result.

10. OAB is a triangle, Q is the point of trisection of AB closer to B and P is the point on OQ such that $\overrightarrow{OP} = \frac{2}{5}\overrightarrow{OQ}$. AP produced meets OB at R. Express $\overrightarrow{AP}$ in terms of $\mathbf{a}$ and $\mathbf{b}$, and hence find the number k such that $\overrightarrow{OA} + k\overrightarrow{AP}$ does not depend on $\mathbf{a}$. Use your answer to express $\mathbf{r}$ in terms of $\mathbf{b}$. Use a similar method to identify the point where S where BP produced meets OA.

11*. OAB is a triangle and P is a point lying inside the triangle. The line OP produced meets AB at X, the line AP produced meets OB at Y, and the line BP produced meets OA at Z.

   a) Find an expression for $\mathbf{x}$ in terms of $\mathbf{a}$ and $\mathbf{b}$, and deduce that $\mathbf{p}$ can be expressed as $\alpha\mathbf{a} + \beta\mathbf{b}$ where $\alpha, \beta > 0$ and $\alpha + \beta < 1$.

   b) Assuming that $\mathbf{p} = \alpha\mathbf{a} + \beta\mathbf{b}$ (where $\alpha, \beta > 0$ and $\alpha + \beta < 1$), find expressions for $\mathbf{x}, \mathbf{y}$ and $\mathbf{z}$ in terms of $\mathbf{a}, \mathbf{b}, \alpha$ and β.

   c) Hence prove that $\dfrac{OZ}{ZA} \times \dfrac{AX}{XB} \times \dfrac{BY}{YO} = 1$. This is a special case of a theorem known as **Ceva's Theorem**. The full theorem allows for the possibility that the point P lies outside the triangle.

19.6 Vectors In Three Dimensions

The power of vector methods is best appreciated when they are used to do geometry in three dimensions. This requires setting up axes in three directions, as in Figure 19.14. The figure includes a drawing of a unit cube to assist in visualising the diagram. The usual convention is to take x- and y-axes in a horizontal plane (shown shaded), and to add a z-axis pointing vertically upwards. These axes are said to be 'right-handed': if the outstretched index finger of your right hand points in the x-direction, and you bend your middle finger to point in the y-direction, then your thumb naturally points up in the z-direction.

A vector $\mathbf{p}$ in three dimensions is a translation of the whole of space relative to a fixed coordinate framework. It is written as

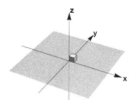

Figure 19.14

$$\mathbf{p} = \begin{pmatrix} u \\ v \\ w \end{pmatrix}$$

which is a translation of u, v and w units in the x-, y- and z-directions respectively. It can also be written in terms of three fundamental unit vectors

$$\mathbf{i} = \begin{pmatrix} 1 \\ 0 \\ 0 \end{pmatrix} \qquad \mathbf{j} = \begin{pmatrix} 0 \\ 1 \\ 0 \end{pmatrix} \qquad \mathbf{k} = \begin{pmatrix} 0 \\ 0 \\ 1 \end{pmatrix},$$

with each vector pointing along one the three axes; we can write

$$\mathbf{p} = \begin{pmatrix} u \\ v \\ w \end{pmatrix} = u\mathbf{i} + v\mathbf{j} + w\mathbf{k}.$$

All the basic ideas of vector algebra: vector addition, scalar multiplication, and properties of commutativity, associativity and distributivity, transfer from two dimensions to three dimensions without any particular difficulty.

Example 19.6.1. *Points A and B have coordinates $(-5, 3, 4)$ and $(-2, 9, 1)$. Investigate whether or not the point C with coordinates $(-4, 5, 2)$ lies on the line passing through A and B.*

The displacement vector $\overrightarrow{AB}$ is

$$\overrightarrow{AB} = \mathbf{b} - \mathbf{a} = \begin{pmatrix} -2 \\ 9 \\ 1 \end{pmatrix} - \begin{pmatrix} -5 \\ 3 \\ 4 \end{pmatrix} = \begin{pmatrix} 3 \\ 6 \end{pmatrix} - 3 = 3\begin{pmatrix} 1 \\ 2 \\ -1 \end{pmatrix},$$

while the displacement vector $\overrightarrow{AC}$ is

$$\overrightarrow{AC} = \mathbf{c} - \mathbf{a} = \begin{pmatrix} -4 \\ 5 \\ 2 \end{pmatrix} - \begin{pmatrix} -5 \\ 3 \\ 4 \end{pmatrix} = \begin{pmatrix} 1 \\ 2 \\ -2 \end{pmatrix},$$

which is not a multiple of $\overrightarrow{AB}$. Thus C cannot lie on the line through A and B.

Note, however, that the point D with coordinates $(-4, 5, 3)$ does lie on AB, since $\overrightarrow{AD} = \frac{1}{3}\overrightarrow{AB}$.

Example 19.6.2. *Points P, Q and R have coordinates $(1, 3, 2)$, $(3, 1, 4)$ and $(4, 1, -5)$ respectively.*

(a) *Find the displacement vectors $\overrightarrow{PQ}$ and $\overrightarrow{QR}$ in terms of the basic vectors $\mathbf{i}, \mathbf{j}$ and $\mathbf{k}$.*

(b) *Find $2\overrightarrow{PQ} - \frac{1}{2}\overrightarrow{PR} + \frac{1}{2}\overrightarrow{QR}$ in terms of the basic vectors $\mathbf{i}, \mathbf{j}$ and $\mathbf{k}$, and the coordinates of the point reached if we start at R and carry out the translation $2\overrightarrow{PQ} - \frac{1}{2}\overrightarrow{PR} + \frac{1}{2}\overrightarrow{QR}$.*

(a)
$$\overrightarrow{PQ} = \mathbf{q} - \mathbf{p} = (3\mathbf{i} + \mathbf{j} + 4\mathbf{k}) - (\mathbf{i} + 3\mathbf{j} + 2\mathbf{k}) = 2\mathbf{i} - 2\mathbf{j} + 2\mathbf{k}$$
$$\overrightarrow{QR} = \mathbf{r} - \mathbf{q} = (4\mathbf{i} + \mathbf{j} - 5\mathbf{k}) - (3\mathbf{i} + \mathbf{j} + 4\mathbf{k}) = \mathbf{i} - 9\mathbf{k}$$

(b) First note that $\overrightarrow{PR} = \mathbf{r} - \mathbf{p} = 3\mathbf{i} - 2\mathbf{j} - 7\mathbf{k}$. Thus

$$2\overrightarrow{PQ} - \frac{1}{2}\overrightarrow{PR} + \frac{1}{2}\overrightarrow{QR} = 2(2\mathbf{i} - 2\mathbf{j} + 2\mathbf{k}) - \frac{1}{2}(3\mathbf{i} - 2\mathbf{j} - 7\mathbf{k}) + \frac{1}{2}(\mathbf{i} - 9\mathbf{k}) = 3\mathbf{i} - 3\mathbf{j} + 3\mathbf{k}$$

Applying this translation to the position vector $\mathbf{r}$, the point reached has position vector

$$\mathbf{r} + (3\mathbf{i} - 3\mathbf{j} + 3\mathbf{k}) = (4\mathbf{i} + \mathbf{j} - 5\mathbf{k}) + (3\mathbf{i} - 3\mathbf{j} + 3\mathbf{k}) = 7\mathbf{i} - 2\mathbf{j} - 2\mathbf{k},$$

and so the point reached has coordinates $(7, -2, -2)$.

EXERCISE 19C

1. If $\mathbf{p} = 2\mathbf{i} - \mathbf{j} + 3\mathbf{k}$, $\mathbf{q} = 5\mathbf{i} + 2\mathbf{j}$ and $\mathbf{r} = 4\mathbf{i} + \mathbf{j} + \mathbf{k}$, calculate the vector $2\mathbf{p} + 3\mathbf{q} - 4\mathbf{r}$, giving your answer as a column vector.

2. A and B are points with coordinates $(2, 1, 4)$ and $(5, -5, -2)$. Find the vector $\overrightarrow{AB}$, writing it both as a column vector and in terms of $\mathbf{i}, \mathbf{j}$ and $\mathbf{k}$.

3. For each of the following sets of points A, B and C, determine whether the point C lies on the line AB.
   a) $A\,(3, 2, 4)$, $B\,(-3, -7, -8)$, $C\,(0, 1, 3)$,   b) $A\,(3, 1, 0)$, $B\,(-3, 1, 3)$, $C\,(5, 1, -1)$.
   If the answer is yes, draw a diagram showing the relative positions of A, B and C on the line.

4. a) Using the points $A\,(2, -1, 3)$, $B\,(3, 1, -4)$ and $C\,(-1, 1, -1)$, write $\overrightarrow{AB}$, $2\overrightarrow{AC}$ and $\frac{1}{2}\overrightarrow{BC}$ as column vectors.

    b) If we start from B and the translation $\overrightarrow{AB} + 2\overrightarrow{AC} + \frac{1}{2}\overrightarrow{BC}$ takes us to D, find the coordinates of D.

5. Four points A, B, C and D have position vectors $3\mathbf{i} - \mathbf{j} + 7\mathbf{k}$, $4\mathbf{i} + \mathbf{k}$, $\mathbf{i} - \mathbf{j} + \mathbf{k}$ and $-2\mathbf{j} + 7\mathbf{k}$ respectively. Find the displacement vectors $\overrightarrow{AB}$ and $\overrightarrow{DC}$. What can we deduce about the quadrilateral $ABCD$?

377

6. Two points A and B have position vectors $\begin{pmatrix} 4 \\ -1 \\ 2 \end{pmatrix}$ and $\begin{pmatrix} 1 \\ 5 \\ 3 \end{pmatrix}$. C is the point on the line segment AB such that $\dfrac{AC}{CB} = 2$. Find

    a) the displacement vector $\overrightarrow{AB}$,   b) the displacement vector $\overrightarrow{AC}$,

    c) the position vector of C.

7. Four points A, B, C and D have coordinates $(0, 1, -2)$, $(1, 3, 2)$, $(4, 3, 4)$ and $(5, -1, -2)$ respectively. Find the position vectors of

    a) the midpoint E of AC,   b) the point F on BC with $\dfrac{BF}{FD} = \dfrac{1}{3}$.

Use your answers to draw a sketch showing the relative positions of A, B, C and D.

19.7 The Modulus Of A Vector

Any translation can be described by giving its magnitude and direction. The notation used for the magnitude of a vector $\mathbf{p}$, ignoring its direction, is $|\mathbf{p}|$. Another word for the magnitude of a vector is its **modulus**.

Two vectors $\mathbf{p}$ and $\mathbf{q}$ can have equal modulus, so that $|\mathbf{p}| = |\mathbf{q}|$, while not being equal: they can have different directions. An example of a pair of such vectors is $\mathbf{i}$ and $\mathbf{j}$, both of which have modulus 1.

If s is a scalar, then it follows from the definition of $s\mathbf{p}$ that $|s\mathbf{p}| = |s|\,|\mathbf{p}|$. This is true whether s is positive or negative (or zero).

The symbol for the modulus of a vector is the same as the one for the modulus of a real number, because the concepts are similar. In fact, a real number x behaves just like the vector $x\mathbf{i}$ in one dimension, where $\mathbf{i}$ is one of the fundamental unit vectors. The vector $x\mathbf{i}$ represents a displacement on the number line, and the modulus $|x| = |x\mathbf{i}|$ then measures the magnitude of the displacement, whether it is in the positive or the negative direction.

A vector of modulus 1 is called a **unit vector**. The fundamental unit vectors $\mathbf{i}, \mathbf{j}, \mathbf{k}$ are examples of unit vectors, but there are others; indeed, there is a unit vector in every direction.

19.8 Scalar Products

To date we have been able to add and subtract vectors, and multiply them by scalars. We have not discussed whether or not it is possible to multiply two vectors together. There are many applications in Physics, in particular, where vector quantities need to be combined, and they are done so in a variety of different ways.

We shall start the process of multiplying vectors by considering a very important quantity, called the **scalar product** or **dot product** of two vectors. This is not a proper case of vector multiplication, since the result of combining two vectors will be a scalar, and not another vector (hence its name), but the scalar product is nonetheless a very useful concept in the theory of vectors.

One of the reasons the scalar product is so important is that it can be defined in an algebraic sense, yet also has deep geometric meaning. The algebraic definition enables the basic properties of scalar product to be established, while the geometric interpretation gives the scalar product its reason for being. The strange part of the matter is that the connection between the algebraic and geometric interpretations of the scalar product is very unexpected, and one of the more remarkable features of vector algebra.

Key Fact 19.2 The Scalar Product — Algebraic Definition

The **scalar product**, or **dot product**, of two vectors $\mathbf{p}$ and $\mathbf{q}$ is written $\mathbf{p} \cdot \mathbf{q}$, and is equal to the sum of the products of the corresponding coefficients of both vectors. In two dimensions, this means that

$$\begin{pmatrix} a \\ b \end{pmatrix} \cdot \begin{pmatrix} c \\ d \end{pmatrix} = ac + bd\,,$$

while in three dimensions this means that

$$\begin{pmatrix} a \\ b \\ c \end{pmatrix} \cdot \begin{pmatrix} d \\ e \\ f \end{pmatrix} = ad + be + cf\,.$$

Note that it is implicit in this definition that the scalar product can only be found between two vectors of the same dimension. The two vectors must both have two or three (or four, or five, or ...) components each. There is no meaning that can be assigned to the expression

$$\begin{pmatrix} 1 \\ 3 \end{pmatrix} \cdot \begin{pmatrix} -2 \\ 3 \\ 7 \end{pmatrix}$$

for example. Whenever we talk about the scalar product of two vectors, we shall always assume that the vectors in question have the same dimension.

Example 19.8.1. *Calculate* $\mathbf{p} \cdot \mathbf{q}$, $\mathbf{p} \cdot \mathbf{r}$, $\mathbf{p} \cdot (\mathbf{q} + \mathbf{r})$ *and* $(2\mathbf{p}) \cdot \mathbf{q}$ *for the vectors* $\mathbf{p} = \begin{pmatrix} 1 \\ 2 \end{pmatrix}$, $\mathbf{q} = \begin{pmatrix} 3 \\ -2 \end{pmatrix}$, $\mathbf{r} = \begin{pmatrix} 4 \\ 0 \end{pmatrix}$.

Since $\mathbf{q} + \mathbf{r} = \begin{pmatrix} 7 \\ -2 \end{pmatrix}$ and $2\mathbf{p} = \begin{pmatrix} 2 \\ 4 \end{pmatrix}$, we deduce that

$$\mathbf{p} \cdot \mathbf{q} = 1 \times 3 + 2 \times (-2) = -1 \qquad \mathbf{p} \cdot \mathbf{r} = 1 \times 4 + 2 \times 0 = 4$$
$$\mathbf{p} \cdot (\mathbf{q} + \mathbf{r}) = 1 \times 7 + 2 \times -2 = 3 \qquad (2\mathbf{p}) \cdot \mathbf{q} = 2 \times 3 + 4 \times -2 = -2$$

Notice that $\mathbf{p} \cdot (\mathbf{q} + \mathbf{r}) = \mathbf{p} \cdot \mathbf{q} + \mathbf{p} \cdot \mathbf{r}$ and $(2\mathbf{p}) \cdot \mathbf{q} = 2(\mathbf{p} \cdot \mathbf{q})$ in the above example. These are special cases of some of the standard algebraic properties of the scalar product. These properties can be summarised as follows.

Key Fact 19.3 The Scalar Product — Algebraic Properties

The following identities hold

$$\mathbf{p} \cdot \mathbf{q} = \mathbf{q} \cdot \mathbf{p} \qquad\qquad (s\mathbf{p}) \cdot \mathbf{q} = \mathbf{p} \cdot (s\mathbf{q}) = s(\mathbf{p} \cdot \mathbf{q})$$
$$\mathbf{p} \cdot (\mathbf{q} + \mathbf{r}) = \mathbf{p} \cdot \mathbf{q} + \mathbf{p} \cdot \mathbf{r} \qquad (\mathbf{p} + \mathbf{q}) \cdot \mathbf{r} = \mathbf{p} \cdot \mathbf{r} + \mathbf{q} \cdot \mathbf{r}$$

for any vectors $\mathbf{p}$, $\mathbf{q}$ and $\mathbf{r}$ (of the same dimension) and any scalar s.

In other words, the scalar product is commutative, compatible with scalar multiplication of vectors, and distributive over addition. These identities can all be shown to hold simply by applying the algebraic definitions, expressing the vectors in terms of components. Thus, for example, if $\mathbf{p} = \begin{pmatrix} a \\ b \end{pmatrix}$, $\mathbf{q} = \begin{pmatrix} c \\ d \end{pmatrix}$, $\mathbf{r} = \begin{pmatrix} e \\ f \end{pmatrix}$, and s is a scalar, then

$$\mathbf{p} \cdot \mathbf{q} = \begin{pmatrix} a \\ b \end{pmatrix} \cdot \begin{pmatrix} c \\ d \end{pmatrix} = ac + bd = ca + db = \begin{pmatrix} c \\ d \end{pmatrix} \cdot \begin{pmatrix} a \\ b \end{pmatrix} = \mathbf{q} \cdot \mathbf{p}$$

$$(s\mathbf{p}) \cdot \mathbf{q} = \begin{pmatrix} sa \\ sb \end{pmatrix} \cdot \begin{pmatrix} c \\ d \end{pmatrix} = (sa)c + (sb)d = sac + sbd = s(ac + bd) = s(\mathbf{p} \cdot \mathbf{q})$$

$$\mathbf{p} \cdot (\mathbf{q} + \mathbf{r}) = \begin{pmatrix} a \\ b \end{pmatrix} \cdot \begin{pmatrix} c + e \\ d + f \end{pmatrix} = a(c + e) + b(d + f) = (ac + bd) + (ae + bf) = \mathbf{p} \cdot \mathbf{q} + \mathbf{p} \cdot \mathbf{r}$$

As we know, vectors can be expressed in terms of the fundamental unit vectors $\mathbf{i}$, $\mathbf{j}$ (and $\mathbf{k}$ in three dimensions). Applying the definition of the scalar product to these vectors gives the following:

Key Fact 19.4 The Scalar Product — Fundamental Unit Vectors

The two fundamental unit vectors in two dimensions satisfy the identities:

$$\mathbf{i} \cdot \mathbf{i} = \mathbf{j} \cdot \mathbf{j} = 1 \qquad\qquad \mathbf{i} \cdot \mathbf{j} = 0$$

The three fundamental unit vectors in three dimensions satisfy the identities:

$$\mathbf{i} \cdot \mathbf{i} = \mathbf{j} \cdot \mathbf{j} = \mathbf{k} \cdot \mathbf{k} = 1 \qquad\qquad \mathbf{i} \cdot \mathbf{j} = \mathbf{i} \cdot \mathbf{k} = \mathbf{j} \cdot \mathbf{k} = 0$$

Food For Thought 19.1

It is worth noting that the algebraic properties of commutativity, compatibility with scalar multiplication and distributivity over addition, together with the given scalar products of the fundamental unit vectors, is enough information to derive the scalar product of all vectors. For example, if $\mathbf{p} = a\mathbf{i} + b\mathbf{j} + c\mathbf{k}$ and $\mathbf{q} = d\mathbf{i} + e\mathbf{j} + f\mathbf{k}$, then

$$
\begin{aligned}
\mathbf{p} \cdot \mathbf{q} &= (a\mathbf{i} + b\mathbf{j} + c\mathbf{k}) \cdot (d\mathbf{i} + e\mathbf{j} + f\mathbf{k}) \\
&= ad\mathbf{i} \cdot \mathbf{i} + ae\mathbf{i} \cdot \mathbf{j} + af\mathbf{i} \cdot \mathbf{k} + bd\mathbf{j} \cdot \mathbf{i} + de\mathbf{j} \cdot \mathbf{j} + be\mathbf{j} \cdot \mathbf{k} + cd\mathbf{k} \cdot \mathbf{i} + ce\mathbf{k} \cdot \mathbf{j} + cf\mathbf{k} \cdot \mathbf{k}
\end{aligned}
$$

using the distributivity property, and the compatibility of the scalar product with scalar multiplication. But then

$$
\begin{aligned}
\mathbf{p} \cdot \mathbf{q} &= ad \times 1 + ae \times 0 + af \times 0 + bd \times 0 + be \times 1 + bf \times 0 + cd \times 0 + ce \times 0 + cf \times 1 \\
&= ad + be + cf
\end{aligned}
$$

as required.

19.9   The Geometric Interpretation Of Scalar Products

On its own, the scalar product is an algebraic curiosity. Its real usefulness comes from the fact that the scalar product of two vectors has a very simple geometric interpretation.

Key Fact 19.5 Scalar Products — Geometric Interpretation

If $\mathbf{p}$ and $\mathbf{q}$ are two vectors, then the scalar product $\mathbf{p} \cdot \mathbf{q}$ is equal to the product of the moduli of $\mathbf{p}$ and $\mathbf{q}$, and the cosine of the angle between the two vectors.

$$\mathbf{p} \cdot \mathbf{q} = |\mathbf{p}||\mathbf{q}| \cos\theta .$$

Note that any two non-parallel vectors lie in a common plane (the diagram presumes that this plane is the plane of the page). Choosing θ, $2\pi - \theta$ or $-\theta$, for example, the angle between two vectors is (almost) a uniquely defined concept. Since $\cos\theta = \cos(-\theta) = \cos(2\pi - \theta)$, the cosine of the angle between two vectors is uniquely defined.

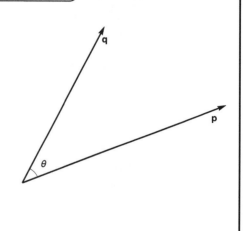

It is an entirely legitimate question to wonder why the algebraic and geometric representations of the scalar product should be the same. Let us show that this is indeed true for two-dimensional vectors.

Suppose that the vectors $\mathbf{p}$ and $\mathbf{q}$ have moduli r and s respectively, and that they make angles α and α and β with the positive x-axis, so that the angle between them is $\theta = \beta - \alpha$. Applying a little trigonometry, we can write

$$\mathbf{p} = \begin{pmatrix} r\cos\alpha \\ r\sin\alpha \end{pmatrix} \qquad \mathbf{q} = \begin{pmatrix} s\cos\beta \\ s\sin\beta \end{pmatrix}$$

and hence

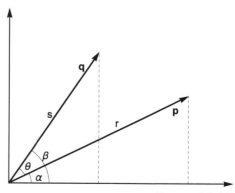

Figure 19.15

$$
\begin{aligned}
\mathbf{p} \cdot \mathbf{q} &= (r\cos\alpha)(s\cos\beta) + (r\sin\alpha)(s\sin\beta) = rs(\cos\alpha\cos\beta + \sin\alpha\sin\beta) = rs\cos(\alpha - \beta) \\
&= |\mathbf{p}||\mathbf{q}| \cos\theta .
\end{aligned}
$$

Special cases of this formula need to be noted. If we consider the scalar product of $\mathbf{p}$ with itself, then the angle θ must be 0, and hence it follows that $\mathbf{p} \cdot \mathbf{p} = |\mathbf{p}|^2$. This result is also clear by Pythagoras, since $\mathbf{p} \cdot \mathbf{p} = a^2 + b^2$ for the vector $\mathbf{p} = \left(\begin{smallmatrix} a \\ b \end{smallmatrix} \right)$. Even more interesting is the observation that, since $\cos \frac{1}{2}\pi = 0$, the scalar product of two perpendicular vectors is zero.

Key Fact 19.6 Scalar Products — Magnitudes and Perpendicularity

For any vector $\mathbf{p}$ we have $\mathbf{p} \cdot \mathbf{p} = |\mathbf{p}|^2$. If $\mathbf{p}$ and $\mathbf{q}$ are non-zero vectors, then $\mathbf{p} \cdot \mathbf{q} = 0$ precisely when $\mathbf{p}$ and $\mathbf{q}$ are perpendicular.

Example 19.9.1. *Show that the vectors $\left(\begin{smallmatrix} 3 \\ 2 \end{smallmatrix} \right)$ and $\left(\begin{smallmatrix} -2 \\ 3 \end{smallmatrix} \right)$ are perpendicular.*

Their scalar product is $3 \times (-2) + 2 \times 3 = 0$.

Example 19.9.2. *Find the angle between the vectors $\mathbf{p} = 2\mathbf{i} - 2\mathbf{j} + \mathbf{k}$ and $\mathbf{q} = 12\mathbf{i} + 4\mathbf{j} - 3\mathbf{k}$, giving the answer correct to the nearest tenth of a degree.*

We have

$$
\begin{aligned}
|\mathbf{p}|^2 &= \mathbf{p} \cdot \mathbf{p} = 2^2 + (-2)^2 + 1 = 9 \\
|\mathbf{q}|^2 &= \mathbf{q} \cdot \mathbf{q} = 12^2 + 4^2 + (-3)^2 = 169 \\
\mathbf{p} \cdot \mathbf{q} &= 2 \times 12 + (-2) \times 4 + 1 \times (-3) = 13
\end{aligned}
$$

Since $\mathbf{p} \cdot \mathbf{q} = |\mathbf{p}||\mathbf{q}| \cos \theta$, we deduce that $\cos \theta = \dfrac{13}{3 \times 13} = \frac{1}{3}$, and hence $\theta = 70.5°$.

Example 19.9.3. *A barn has a rectangular floor $ABCD$ of dimensions 6 m by 12 m. The edges AP, BA, CR and DS are each vertical and of height 5 m. The roof ridge UV is symmetrically placed above $PQRS$, and is a height 7 m above the ground $ABCD$. Calculate the angle (to the nearest tenth of a degree) between the lines AS and UR.*

If we take the fundamental unit vectors $\mathbf{i}, \mathbf{j}$ and $\mathbf{k}$ to point in the directions of BC, BA and BQ respectively, then $\overrightarrow{AS} = 12\mathbf{i} + 5\mathbf{k}$ and $\overrightarrow{UR} = 12\mathbf{i} - 3\mathbf{j} - 2\mathbf{k}$. Thus

$$
\begin{aligned}
\left| \overrightarrow{AS} \right| &= \sqrt{12^2 + 5^2} = 13 \\
\left| \overrightarrow{UR} \right| &= \sqrt{12^2 + 3^2 + 2^2} = \sqrt{157} \\
\overrightarrow{AS} \cdot \overrightarrow{US} &= 12 \times 12 = 5 \times (-2) = 134
\end{aligned}
$$

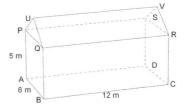

Figure 19.16

If θ is the angle between AS and UR, then

$$
\cos \theta = \frac{134}{13 \times \sqrt{157}}
$$

and hence $\theta = 34.6°$.

To show that the geometric interpretation of the scalar product is compatible with the algebraic one in three dimensions is harder to prove, but is possible using the Cosine Rule. Given any two vectors $\mathbf{p}$ and $\mathbf{q}$, where

$$
\mathbf{p} = a\mathbf{i} + b\mathbf{j} + c\mathbf{k} \quad , \qquad \mathbf{q} = d\mathbf{i} + e\mathbf{j} + f\mathbf{k} \quad ,
$$

so that $\mathbf{p} - \mathbf{q} = (a-d)\mathbf{i} + (b-e)\mathbf{j} + (c-f)\mathbf{k}$, then Pythagoras' Theorem in three dimensions shows that

$$\begin{aligned} |\mathbf{p} - \mathbf{q}|^2 &= (a-d)^2 + (b-e)^2 + (c-f)^2 = (a^2 + b^2 + c^2) + (d^2 + e^2 + f^2) - 2(ad + be + cf) \\ &= |\mathbf{p}|^2 + |\mathbf{q}|^2 - 2\mathbf{p} \cdot \mathbf{q} \end{aligned}$$

Supposing that $\mathbf{p}$ and $\mathbf{q}$ are the position vectors of points P and Q, we deduce, using the cosine rule, that

$$\begin{aligned} OP^2 + OQ^2 - 2\mathbf{p} \cdot \mathbf{q} &= |\mathbf{p} - \mathbf{q}|^2 = PQ^2 \\ &= OP^2 + OQ^2 - 2\,OP\,OQ \cos \angle POQ \end{aligned}$$

so that

$$\mathbf{p} \cdot \mathbf{q} = OP\,OQ \cos \angle POQ = |\mathbf{p}||\mathbf{q}| \cos \theta$$

where $\theta = \angle POQ$ is the angle between the vectors $\mathbf{p}$ and $\mathbf{q}$.

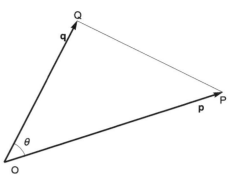

Figure 19.17

For Interest

It is interesting to note that the geometric interpretation of the scalar product does not depend on the choice of coordinate system, while the algebraic interpretation of the scalar product is specific a particular choice of xy-coordinate system. A consequence of this is the remarkable fact that the value of the scalar product does not depend on the choice of coordinate axes!

EXERCISE 19D

1. Let $\mathbf{a} = \left(\begin{smallmatrix} 3 \\ 2 \end{smallmatrix}\right)$, $\mathbf{b} = \left(\begin{smallmatrix} -4 \\ 2 \end{smallmatrix}\right)$ and $\mathbf{c} = \left(\begin{smallmatrix} 1 \\ 4 \end{smallmatrix}\right)$. Calculate $\mathbf{a} \cdot \mathbf{b}$, $\mathbf{a} \cdot \mathbf{c}$ and $\mathbf{a} \cdot (\mathbf{b} + \mathbf{c})$, and verify that $\mathbf{a} \cdot (\mathbf{b} + \mathbf{c}) = \mathbf{a} \cdot \mathbf{b} + \mathbf{a} \cdot \mathbf{c}$.

2. Let $\mathbf{a} = 2\mathbf{i} - \mathbf{j}$, $\mathbf{b} = 4\mathbf{i} - 3\mathbf{j}$ and $\mathbf{c} = -2\mathbf{i} - \mathbf{j}$. Calculate $\mathbf{a} \cdot \mathbf{b}$, $\mathbf{a} \cdot \mathbf{c}$ and $\mathbf{a} \cdot (\mathbf{b} + \mathbf{c})$, and verify that $\mathbf{a} \cdot (\mathbf{b} + \mathbf{c}) = \mathbf{a} \cdot \mathbf{b} + \mathbf{a} \cdot \mathbf{c}$.

3. Let $\mathbf{p} = \left(\begin{smallmatrix} 3 \\ -1 \\ 4 \end{smallmatrix}\right)$, $\mathbf{q} = \left(\begin{smallmatrix} -1 \\ -9 \\ 3 \end{smallmatrix}\right)$ and $\mathbf{r} = \left(\begin{smallmatrix} 33 \\ -13 \\ -28 \end{smallmatrix}\right)$. Calculate $\mathbf{p} \cdot \mathbf{q}$, $\mathbf{p} \cdot \mathbf{r}$ and $\mathbf{q} \cdot \mathbf{r}$. What can you deduce about the vectors $\mathbf{p}$, $\mathbf{q}$ and $\mathbf{r}$?

4. Which of the following vectors are perpendicular to each other?
    a) $2\mathbf{i} - 3\mathbf{j} + 6\mathbf{k}$,   b) $2\mathbf{i} - 3\mathbf{j} - 6\mathbf{k}$,   c) $-3\mathbf{i} - 6\mathbf{j} + 2\mathbf{k}$,   d) $6\mathbf{i} - 2\mathbf{j} - 3\mathbf{k}$.

5. Let $\mathbf{p} = \mathbf{i} - 2\mathbf{k}$, $\mathbf{q} = 3\mathbf{j} + 2\mathbf{k}$ and $\mathbf{r} = 2\mathbf{i} - \mathbf{j} + 5\mathbf{k}$. Calculate $\mathbf{p} \cdot \mathbf{q}$, $\mathbf{p} \cdot \mathbf{r}$ and $\mathbf{p} \cdot (\mathbf{q} + \mathbf{r})$, and verify that $\mathbf{p} \cdot (\mathbf{q} + \mathbf{r}) = \mathbf{p} \cdot \mathbf{q} + \mathbf{p} \cdot \mathbf{r}$.

6. Find the modulus of each of the following vectors.
    a) $\left(\begin{smallmatrix} -3 \\ 4 \end{smallmatrix}\right)$,   b) $\left(\begin{smallmatrix} -2 \\ 1 \end{smallmatrix}\right)$,   c) $\left(\begin{smallmatrix} -1 \\ -2 \end{smallmatrix}\right)$,   d) $\left(\begin{smallmatrix} 0 \\ -1 \end{smallmatrix}\right)$,
    e) $\left(\begin{smallmatrix} 1 \\ -2 \\ 2 \end{smallmatrix}\right)$,   f) $\left(\begin{smallmatrix} 4 \\ -3 \\ 12 \end{smallmatrix}\right)$,   g) $\left(\begin{smallmatrix} 0 \\ -3 \\ 4 \end{smallmatrix}\right)$,   h) $\left(\begin{smallmatrix} 2 \\ -1 \\ 1 \end{smallmatrix}\right)$,
    i) $\mathbf{i} - 2\mathbf{k}$,   j) $3\mathbf{j} + 2\mathbf{k}$,   k) $2\mathbf{i} - \mathbf{j} + 5\mathbf{k}$,   l) $2\mathbf{k}$.

7. Let $\mathbf{a} = \left(\begin{smallmatrix} 4 \\ -3 \end{smallmatrix}\right)$. Find the modulus of $\mathbf{a}$, and find a unit vector in the same direction as $\mathbf{a}$.

8. Find unit vectors in the same directions as $\left(\begin{smallmatrix} 1 \\ -2 \\ 2 \end{smallmatrix}\right)$, and $2\mathbf{i} - \mathbf{j} + 2\mathbf{k}$.

9. Use a vector method to calculate the angles between the following pairs of vectors, giving your answers in degrees to one place of decimals, where appropriate.

a) $\begin{pmatrix} 2 \\ 1 \end{pmatrix}$ and $\begin{pmatrix} 1 \\ 3 \end{pmatrix}$,

b) $\begin{pmatrix} 4 \\ -5 \end{pmatrix}$ and $\begin{pmatrix} -5 \\ 4 \end{pmatrix}$,

c) $\begin{pmatrix} 4 \\ -6 \end{pmatrix}$ and $\begin{pmatrix} -6 \\ 9 \end{pmatrix}$

d) $\begin{pmatrix} -1 \\ 4 \\ 5 \end{pmatrix}$ and $\begin{pmatrix} 2 \\ 0 \\ -3 \end{pmatrix}$,

e) $\begin{pmatrix} 1 \\ 2 \\ -3 \end{pmatrix}$ and $\begin{pmatrix} 2 \\ 3 \\ -4 \end{pmatrix}$,

f) $\begin{pmatrix} 2 \\ -1 \\ 3 \end{pmatrix}$ and $\begin{pmatrix} 5 \\ -2 \\ -4 \end{pmatrix}$.

10. Let $\mathbf{r}_1 = \begin{pmatrix} x_1 \\ y_1 \end{pmatrix}$ and $\mathbf{r}_2 = \begin{pmatrix} x_2 \\ y_2 \end{pmatrix}$. Calculate $|\mathbf{r}_1 - \mathbf{r}_2|$, and interpret your result geometrically.

11. Find the angle between the line joining the points $(1, 2)$ and $(3, -5)$ and the line joining the points $(2, -3)$ and $(1, 4)$.

12. Find the angle between the line joining the points $(1, 3, -2)$ and $(2, 5, -1)$ and the line joining the points $(-1, 4, 3)$ and $(3, 2, 1)$.

13. Find the angle between the diagonals of a cube.

14. $ABCD$ is the base of a square pyramid of side 2 units, and V is the vertex. The pyramid is symmetrical, and of height 4 units. Calculate the acute angle between AV and BC, giving your answer in degrees correct to 1 decimal place.

15. Two aeroplanes are flying in directions given by the vectors $300\mathbf{i} + 400\mathbf{j} + 2\mathbf{k}$ and $-100\mathbf{i} + 500\mathbf{j} - \mathbf{k}$. A person from the flight control centre is plotting their paths on a map. Find the acute angle between their paths on the map.

16. The roof of a house has a rectangular base of side 4 metres by 8 metres. The ridge line of the roof is 6 metres long, and centred 1 metre above the base of the roof. Calculate the acute angle between two opposite slanting edges of the roof.

17. Let AB be the diameter of a circle with centre O, and let C be a point on the circumference of that circle. Using the vectors $\mathbf{x} = \overrightarrow{AC}$ and $\mathbf{y} = \overrightarrow{BC}$, show that $\angle ACB = 90°$.

18. Suppose that OAB is a triangle and that C is the midpoint of AB. Show that

a) $4\mathbf{c} \cdot \mathbf{c} = |\mathbf{a}|^2 + |\mathbf{b}|^2 + 2\mathbf{a} \cdot \mathbf{b}$,

b) $4|\mathbf{c} - \mathbf{a}|^2 = |\mathbf{a}|^2 + |\mathbf{b}|^2 - 2\mathbf{a} \cdot \mathbf{b}$

Hence deduce a relationship between OA^2, OB^2, OC^2 and AC^2. This geometrical result is known as **Apollonius' Theorem**.

19*. Suppose that ABC is a triangle inscribed in a circle with centre O. Let $\mathbf{a}$, $\mathbf{b}$ and $\mathbf{c}$ be the position vectors of A, B and C, as usual.

a) What can be said about $|\mathbf{a}|$, $|\mathbf{b}|$ and $|\mathbf{c}|$?

b) Show that $\mathbf{b} + \mathbf{c}$ is vector perpendicular to $\overrightarrow{BC}$.

c) The **altitude** from the point A is the line through A perpendicular to BC. Show that the point with position vector $\mathbf{a} + \mathbf{b} + \mathbf{c}$ lies on the altitude from A.

d) Show that the three altitudes of a triangle are concurrent. The point H where the three lines meet is called the **orthocentre** of the triangle.

e) The point O is the centre of a circle passing through the vertices of A, and is called the **outcentre** of the triangle. What can we say about the outcentre O, the orthocentre H and the centroid G (see Example 19.5.2) of a triangle?

20*. Suppose that two different coordinate systems have been created. In addition to the standard xy-coordinate system, there is also the XY-coordinate system. which is rotated at an angle θ to the xy-coordinate system, as shown in Figure 19.18. New fundamental unit vectors $\mathbf{I}$ and $\mathbf{J}$ are defined for the new coordinate system, in addition to the normal fundamental unit vectors $\mathbf{i}$ and $\mathbf{j}$ for the old coordinate system.

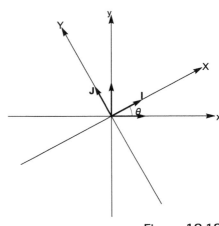

Figure 19.18

383

a) Express the fundamental unit vectors $\mathbf{I}$ and $\mathbf{J}$ in terms of $\mathbf{i}, \mathbf{j}$ and θ.

b) Suppose that a vector $\mathbf{p}$ can be written as $a\mathbf{i} + b\mathbf{j}$ and also as $A\mathbf{I} + B\mathbf{J}$. Find an expression for a and b in terms of A, B and θ.

c) Suppose that vectors $\mathbf{p}$ and q can be written

$$\mathbf{p} = a\mathbf{i} + b\mathbf{j} = A\mathbf{I} + B\mathbf{J} \quad , \quad \mathbf{q} = c\mathbf{i} + d\mathbf{j} = C\mathbf{I} + D\mathbf{J} .$$

Show that $ac + bd = AC + BD$, and hence that the algebraic definition of the scalar product is independent of the choice of coordinate system.

19.10 The Vector Equation Of A Line In Two Dimensions

Figure 19.19 shows a line through a point A in the direction of a non-zero vector $\mathbf{p}$. If R is any point on the line, the displacement vector $\overrightarrow{AR}$ is a multiple of $\mathbf{p}$, so

$$\mathbf{r} = \overrightarrow{OR} = \overrightarrow{OA} + \overrightarrow{AR} = \mathbf{a} + t\mathbf{p}$$

where t is a scalar. The value of t measures the ratio of the displacement $\overrightarrow{AR}$ to $\mathbf{p}$, and takes a different value for each point R on the line.

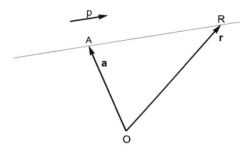

Figure 19.19

Key Fact 19.7 The Vector Equation Of A Line

Points on a line through A in the direction of $\mathbf{p}$ have position vectors

$$\mathbf{r} = \mathbf{a} + t\mathbf{p} ,$$

where t is a variable scalar. This is called the **vector equation** of the line. The vector $\mathbf{p}$ is called a **direction vector** for the line.

Example 19.10.1. *Find a vector equation for the line through* $(2, -1)$ *with gradient* $\frac{3}{4}$, *and deduce its Cartesian equation.*

The position vector of the point $(2, -1)$ is $\left(\begin{smallmatrix} 2 \\ -1 \end{smallmatrix}\right)$. There are many vectors pointing along a line with gradient $\frac{3}{4}$, but the simplest one goes 4 units across the grid and 3 units up; this is the vector $\left(\begin{smallmatrix} 4 \\ 3 \end{smallmatrix}\right)$. Thus an equation of the line is

$$\mathbf{r} = \begin{pmatrix} 2 \\ -1 \end{pmatrix} + t\begin{pmatrix} 4 \\ 3 \end{pmatrix} \quad , \quad t \in \mathbb{R} .$$

If R has coordinates (x, y), then $\mathbf{r} = \left(\begin{smallmatrix} x \\ y \end{smallmatrix}\right)$. Thus we must have

$$\begin{pmatrix} x \\ y \end{pmatrix} = \begin{pmatrix} 2 + 4t \\ -1 + 3t \end{pmatrix}$$

which means that we have the simultaneous equations

$$x = 2 + 4t, \qquad y = -1 + 3t .$$

These can be recognised as the parametric equation of a straight line. Eliminating the scalar t from these equations gives us the Cartesian equation for the line:

$$3x - 4y = 3(2 + 4t) - 4(-1 + 3t) = 10 .$$

Example 19.10.2. *Find a vector equation for the line through* $(3, 1)$, *parallel to the* y-axis, *and deduce its Cartesian equation.*

A vector in the direction of the line is $\mathbf{j}$, and the line passes through the point with position vector $\mathbf{a} = 3\mathbf{i} + \mathbf{j}$. Thus the vector equation of the line is

$$\mathbf{r} = 3\mathbf{i} + \mathbf{j} + t\mathbf{j} = 3\mathbf{i} + (t+1)\mathbf{j},$$

and from this we deduce that $x = 3$ and $y = 1 + t$. It is clear that the Cartesian equation of this line is $x = 3$.

Example 19.10.3. *Find the points common to the pairs of lines:*

a) $\mathbf{r} = \begin{pmatrix} 1 \\ 2 \end{pmatrix} + s\begin{pmatrix} 1 \\ 1 \end{pmatrix}$ and $\mathbf{r} = \begin{pmatrix} 3 \\ -2 \end{pmatrix} + t\begin{pmatrix} 1 \\ 4 \end{pmatrix}$,
    b) $\mathbf{r} = \begin{pmatrix} 3 \\ 1 \end{pmatrix} + s\begin{pmatrix} 4 \\ -2 \end{pmatrix}$ and $\mathbf{r} = \begin{pmatrix} 1 \\ 2 \end{pmatrix} + t\begin{pmatrix} -6 \\ 3 \end{pmatrix}$.

(a) Position vectors of points on these two lines can be written

$$\mathbf{r} = \begin{pmatrix} 1+s \\ 2+s \end{pmatrix} \qquad \mathbf{r} = \begin{pmatrix} 3+t \\ -2+4t \end{pmatrix}$$

If these are to be position vectors of the same point, the position vectors must be the same, and hence

$$1 + s = 3 + t \qquad 2 + s = -2 + 4t.$$

These are simultaneous equations for s and t, with solution $s = 4$, $t = 2$. Thus the position vector that is common to both lines is $\begin{pmatrix} 5 \\ 6 \end{pmatrix}$, and so the point of intersection of the two lines is $(5, 6)$.

(b) The same procedure as for the previous pair of lines leads to the pair of equations
$$3 + 4s = 1 - 6t \qquad 1 - 2s = 2 + 3t,$$

a pair of simultaneous equations. However, both of these equations can be simplified to read $2s + 3t = -1$ thus the two equations are identical. This means that there is really only one equation to solve, and any value of s can be matched by a value of t. There are infinitely many points where these two lines meet. The only way that two lines can meet at an infinite number of points is if the two lines are the same, and this is what is happening here.

Looking at this second case in further detail, we see that the two vector equations can be written

$$\mathbf{r} = \begin{pmatrix} 3 \\ 2 \end{pmatrix} + 2s\begin{pmatrix} 2 \\ -1 \end{pmatrix} = \begin{pmatrix} 1 \\ 2 \end{pmatrix} + (2s+1)\begin{pmatrix} 2 \\ -1 \end{pmatrix} \qquad \mathbf{r} = \begin{pmatrix} 1 \\ 2 \end{pmatrix} - 3t\begin{pmatrix} 2 \\ -1 \end{pmatrix}$$

and so it is clear that the second equation is just a reparametrised version of the first equation, with $2s + 1 = -3t$.

Food For Thought 19.2

While the vector equation of a line is convenient and useful, it is not **unique**. There are infinitely many choices for the point A on the line through which the line passes, and there are infinitely many choices for a vector pointing along the line (they all have the same direction, but can have different magnitudes). Thus there are infinitely many different vector equations for the line.

Key Fact 19.8 Identifying Identical Lines

The lines with vector equations $\mathbf{r} = \mathbf{a} + s\mathbf{p}$ and $\mathbf{r} = \mathbf{b} + t\mathbf{q}$ are parallel, and therefore point in the same direction, if $\mathbf{p}$ and $\mathbf{q}$ are multiples of each other. If, in addition, $\mathbf{b} - \mathbf{a}$ is a multiple of $\mathbf{q}$, then the lines are in fact identical. This is because if $\mathbf{b} - \mathbf{a} = u\mathbf{q}$ and $\mathbf{p} = v\mathbf{q}$ then

$$\mathbf{r} = \mathbf{a} + s\mathbf{p} = \mathbf{b} - u\mathbf{q} + vs\mathbf{q} = \mathbf{b} + (vs - u)\mathbf{q}$$

and so the first line is a reparametrisation of the second line.

Example 19.10.4. *Show that the lines with vector equations* $\mathbf{r} = 2\mathbf{i} - 3\mathbf{j} + s(-\mathbf{i} + 3\mathbf{j})$ *and* $\mathbf{r} = 4\mathbf{i} + t(2\mathbf{i} - 6\mathbf{j})$ *are parallel, and find the equation of the parallel line through* $(1,1)$.

Both lines are in the direction of the vector $-\mathbf{i} + 3\mathbf{j}$, and so are certainly parallel. The desired equation of the new line is

$$\mathbf{r} = \mathbf{i} + \mathbf{j} + s(-\mathbf{i} + 3\mathbf{j}).$$

Example 19.10.5. *Find a vector equation for the line with Cartesian equation* $2x + 5y = 1$, *and use it to find where the line meets the circle* $x^2 + y^2 = 10$.

The gradient of the line is $-\frac{2}{5}$, so we can use the direction vector $\begin{pmatrix} 5 \\ -2 \end{pmatrix}$. A point on the line is $(3, -1)$, and so a vector equation of the line is

$$\mathbf{r} = \begin{pmatrix} 3 \\ -1 \end{pmatrix} + s \begin{pmatrix} 5 \\ -2 \end{pmatrix}.$$

The line meets the circle at points $\mathbf{r}$ with $|\mathbf{r}|^2 = 10$, so we need to solve the equation

$$
\begin{aligned}
(3 + 5s)^2 + (-1 - 2s)^2 &= 10 \\
9 + 30s + 25s^2 + 1 + 4s + 4s^2 &= 10 \\
29s^2 + 34s &= 0
\end{aligned}
$$

and hence either $s = 0$ or $s = -\frac{34}{39}$. The position vectors of the points where the line meets the circle are thus $\begin{pmatrix} 3 \\ -1 \end{pmatrix}$ and $\begin{pmatrix} -2\frac{25}{29} \\ 1\frac{10}{29} \end{pmatrix}$.

EXERCISE 19E

1. Write down vector equations for the line through the given point in the specified direction. Then eliminate t to obtain the Cartesian equation.

   a) $(2, -3)$, $\begin{pmatrix} 1 \\ 2 \end{pmatrix}$,

   b) $(4, 1)$, $\begin{pmatrix} -3 \\ 2 \end{pmatrix}$,

   c) $(5, 7)$, parallel to the x-axis,

   d) $(0, 0)$, $\begin{pmatrix} 2 \\ -1 \end{pmatrix}$,

   e) (a, b), $\begin{pmatrix} 0 \\ 1 \end{pmatrix}$,

   f) $(\cos\alpha, \sin\alpha)$, $\begin{pmatrix} -\sin\alpha \\ \cos\alpha \end{pmatrix}$

2. Find vector equations for lines with the following Cartesian equations.

   a) $x = 2$,

   b) $x + 3y = 7$,

   c) $2x - 5y = 3$.

3. Find the coordinates of the points common to the following pairs of lines, if any.

   a) $\mathbf{r} = \begin{pmatrix} 2 \\ 0 \end{pmatrix} + s \begin{pmatrix} 5 \\ 3 \end{pmatrix}$ and $\mathbf{r} = \begin{pmatrix} 3 \\ -1 \end{pmatrix} + t \begin{pmatrix} 1 \\ 1 \end{pmatrix}$,

   b) $\mathbf{r} = \begin{pmatrix} 5 \\ 1 \end{pmatrix} + s \begin{pmatrix} -1 \\ 2 \end{pmatrix}$ and $\mathbf{r} = \begin{pmatrix} 3 \\ -5 \end{pmatrix} + t \begin{pmatrix} 1 \\ 0 \end{pmatrix}$,

   c) $\mathbf{r} = \begin{pmatrix} 2 \\ -1 \end{pmatrix} + s \begin{pmatrix} 1 \\ -3 \end{pmatrix}$ and $\mathbf{r} = \begin{pmatrix} 4 \\ 0 \end{pmatrix} + t \begin{pmatrix} -2 \\ 6 \end{pmatrix}$,

   d) $\mathbf{r} = \begin{pmatrix} -1 \\ -4 \end{pmatrix} + s \begin{pmatrix} 3 \\ 4 \end{pmatrix}$ and $\mathbf{r} = \begin{pmatrix} 11 \\ -1 \end{pmatrix} + t \begin{pmatrix} -4 \\ 3 \end{pmatrix}$,

   e) $\mathbf{r} = \begin{pmatrix} 7 \\ 1 \end{pmatrix} + s \begin{pmatrix} 6 \\ -4 \end{pmatrix}$ and $\mathbf{r} = \begin{pmatrix} 10 \\ -1 \end{pmatrix} + t \begin{pmatrix} -9 \\ 6 \end{pmatrix}$,

   f) $\mathbf{r} = \begin{pmatrix} 2 \\ 1 \end{pmatrix} + s \begin{pmatrix} 3 \\ 0 \end{pmatrix}$ and $\mathbf{r} = \begin{pmatrix} -1 \\ 3 \end{pmatrix} + t \begin{pmatrix} 0 \\ -2 \end{pmatrix}$.

4. Write down in parametric form the coordinates of any point on the line through $(2, -1)$ in the direction $\mathbf{i} + 3\mathbf{j}$. Use these to find the point where this line intersects the line $5y - 6x = 1$.

5. Find the coordinates of the point where the line with vector equation $\mathbf{r} = \begin{pmatrix} -3 \\ 4 \end{pmatrix} + t \begin{pmatrix} 2 \\ -1 \end{pmatrix}$ intersects the line with Cartesian equation $2x + y = 7$.

6. Which of the following points lie on the line joining $(2, 0)$ to $(4, 3)$?

   a) $(8, 9)$,

   b) $(12, 13)$,

   c) $(-4, -1)$,

   d) $(-6, -12)$,

   e) $(3\frac{1}{3}, 2)$.

7. Find vector equations for the lines joining the following pairs of points.

   a) $(3, 7)$, $(5, 4)$,

   b) $(2, 3)$, $(2, 8)$,

   c) $(-1, 2)$, $(5, -1)$,

   d) $(-3, -4)$, $(5, 8)$,

   e) $(-2, 7)$, $(4, 7)$,

   f) $(1, 3)$, $(-4, -2)$.

8. A quadrilateral $ABCD$ has vertices $A\,(4,-1)$, $B\,(-3,2)$, $C\,(-8,-5)$ and $D\,(4,-5)$.

   a) Find vector equations for the diagonals, AC and BD, and find their point of intersection.

   b) Find the points of intersection of BA produced and CD produced, and of CB produced and DA produced.

9. Show that the vectors $a\mathbf{i}+b\mathbf{j}$ and $-b\mathbf{i}+a\mathbf{j}$ are perpendicular to each other. Is this still true:

   a) if a is zero but b is not,   b) if b is zero but a is not,   c) if both a and b are zero?
   Find a vector equation for the line through $(1,2)$ perpendicular to the line with vector equation $\mathbf{r}=7\mathbf{i}+2\mathbf{j}+t(3\mathbf{i}+4\mathbf{j})$.

10. Find a vector in the direction of the line ℓ with Cartesian equation $3x-y=8$. Write down a vector equation for the line through $P\,(1,5)$ which is perpendicular to ℓ. Hence find the coordinates of the foot of the perpendicular from P to ℓ.

11. Use the method of the previous Question to find the coordinates of the foot of the perpendicular from $(-3,-2)$ to $5x+2y=10$.

12. Find a vector equation for the line joining the points $(-1,1)$ and $(4,11)$. Use this to write parametric coordinates for any point on the line. Hence find the coordinates of the points where the line meets the parabola $y=x^2$.

13. Find the coordinates of the points where the line through $(-5,-1)$ in the direction $\binom{2}{3}$ meets the circle $x^2+y^2=65$.

14*. Let ABC be a triangle with outcentre O, and use O as the origin of a system of vectors. Let D, E and F be the midpoints of BC, AC and AB respectively. You may find it helpful to refer back to Question 19 of Exercise 19D in what follows:

   a) Show that EF is parallel to BC.

   b) Find the vector equation of the perpendicular bisector of EF.

   c) The perpendicular bisectors of DE, DF and EF all meet at a point N, which will be the outcentre of the triangle DEF. Find the position vector of the point N, called the **nine-point centre** of the triangle ABC.

   d) Show that the outcentre O, the centroid G, the orthocentre H and the nine-point centre N are collinear (the line on which they lie is called the **Euler line of the triangle** ABC).

   e) The circle with centre N passing through the midpoints D, E and F is called the **nine-point circle** of the triangle ABC. The points D, E and F are three of the nine points referred to. Show that the midpoints of the lines AH, BH and CH also lie on the nine-point circle. (The nine-point circle also passes through the feet of the perpendiculars from A, B and C; that makes a total of nine special points through which the circle passes — hence its name!)

   f) What is the relationship between the radius of the nine-point circle and the radius of the outcircle of the triangle ABC?

19.11 The Vector Equation Of A Line In Three Dimensions

Everything that we have learnt about the vector equation of a line in two dimensions carries over into three dimensions in an obvious way. However there are two important differences between two dimensions and three dimensions.

- There is no natural three-dimensional equivalent of the gradient of a line.

- In two dimensions, lines either meet at a single point, or else they are parallel and distinct, or else they are identical. In three dimensions, there is a further option, in that non-parallel lines may fail to meet altogether. Consider, for example, the two lines defined by joining up some of the vertices of the cube shown in the figure. These lines will never meet (if we extended the 'top' line, it would appear to intersect the bottom one, but that is just a trick of the fact that we are trying to represent a three-dimensional object two-dimensionally).

Figure 19.20

> **Key Fact 19.9** Skew Lines
>
> Non-parallel lines that never meet are called **skew** lines.

The following examples show some of the situations which can occur when working with lines in three dimensions.

Example 19.11.1. *Points A and B have coordinates $(-5, 3, 4)$ and $(-2, 9, 1)$. The line AB meets the xy-plane at C. Find the coordinates of C.*

The displacement vector $\overrightarrow{AB}$ is

$$\overrightarrow{AB} = \mathbf{b} - \mathbf{a} = \begin{pmatrix} -2 \\ 9 \\ 1 \end{pmatrix} - \begin{pmatrix} -5 \\ 3 \\ 4 \end{pmatrix} = \begin{pmatrix} 3 \\ 6 \\ -3 \end{pmatrix},$$

so $\begin{pmatrix} 1 \\ 2 \\ -1 \end{pmatrix}$ can be used as a direction vector for the line, which thus has vector equation

$$\mathbf{r} = \begin{pmatrix} -5 \\ 3 \\ 4 \end{pmatrix} + t\begin{pmatrix} 1 \\ 2 \\ -1 \end{pmatrix} = \begin{pmatrix} t - 5 \\ 2t + 3 \\ 4 - t \end{pmatrix}.$$

A point on this line lies in the xy-plane if its z-coordinate is zero. This will happen when $4 - t = 0$, so when $t = 4$. The point of intersection of this line with the xy-plane has position vector $\begin{pmatrix} -1 \\ 11 \\ 0 \end{pmatrix}$, and so has coordinates $(-1, 11, 0)$.

Example 19.11.2. *Find the value of u for which the lines $\mathbf{r} = (\mathbf{j} - \mathbf{k}) + s(\mathbf{i} + 2\mathbf{j} + \mathbf{k})$ and $\mathbf{r} = (\mathbf{i} + 7\mathbf{j} - 4\mathbf{k}) + t(\mathbf{i} + u\mathbf{k})$ intersect.*

Points on the lines can be written as $s\mathbf{i} + (1 + 2s)\mathbf{j} + (s - 1)\mathbf{k}$ and $(1 + t)\mathbf{i} + 7\mathbf{j} + (tu - 4)\mathbf{k}$ respectively, and so a point will lie on both lines if values of s and t can be found such that

$$s\mathbf{i} + (1 + 2s)\mathbf{j} + (s - 1)\mathbf{k} = (1 + t)\mathbf{i} + 7\mathbf{j} + (tu - 4)\mathbf{k};$$

for this to happen we require that

$$s = 1 + t \qquad 1 + 2s = 7 \qquad s - 1 = tu - 4$$

simultaneously. The first two equations can be solved to find $s = 3$ and $t = 2$. For the last equation to be true as well we need $2 = 2u - 4$, and hence we need $u = 3$. It is easy to check that the point of intersection of these lines has coordinates $(3, 7, 2)$.

> **Food For Thought 19.3**
>
> This example gives an algebraic clue as to why lines can be skew in three dimensions. For two lines to intersect, the two parameters which define the two lines must satisfy **three** simultaneous equations. In general, this is one equation too many, and so it will often be impossible to satisfy all three equations at the same time.
> Sets of three or more equations in two variables might not always have solutions. If they do, they are called **consistent**. Skew lines are associated with inconsistent sets of equations.

Example 19.11.3. *Show that the lines $\mathbf{r} = \mathbf{i} + s(2\mathbf{i} + \mathbf{j} - 3\mathbf{k})$ and $\mathbf{r} = (3\mathbf{i} - 4\mathbf{k}) + t(4\mathbf{i} + 3\mathbf{j} - \mathbf{k})$ are skew.*

If the lines are to intersect, we need to solve the simultaneous equations

$$1 + 2s = 3 + 4t \qquad s = 3t \qquad -3s = -4 - 4t.$$

The first two equations are simultaneously satisfied when $s = 3$, $t = 1$. However, since $-9 \neq -8$, these values do not satisfy the third equation, and so the two lines do not meet. Since the direction vectors of the two lines are not parallel, it follows that the lines are skew.

Example 19.11.4. *Find the values of a and b such that the line with vector equation $\mathbf{r} = (2\mathbf{i} + 4\mathbf{j} - \mathbf{k}) + s(a\mathbf{i} + b\mathbf{j} + 12\mathbf{k})$ is perpendicular to the vector $4\mathbf{i} + 6\mathbf{j} + \mathbf{k}$, and also intersects the line passing through the points with coordinates $(1, 2, 7)$ and $(-5, 5, 1)$. Find the angle between the two lines.*

Since the first line is perpendicular to the vector $4\mathbf{i} + 6\mathbf{j} + \mathbf{k}$, it follows that

$$0 = (4\mathbf{i} + 6\mathbf{j} + \mathbf{k}) \cdot (a\mathbf{i} + b\mathbf{j} + 12\mathbf{k}) = 4a + 6b + 12,$$

The second line has vector equation

$$\mathbf{r} = (\mathbf{i} + 2\mathbf{j} + 7\mathbf{k}) + t(2\mathbf{i} - \mathbf{j} + 2\mathbf{k}).$$

For the two lines to intersect, we need to solve the simultaneous equations

$$2 + as = 1 + 2t \qquad 4 + bs = 2 - t \qquad 12s - 1 = 7 + 2t.$$

The last equation tells us that $t = 6s - 4$, and so the first two equations become

$$(12 - a)s = 9 \qquad (6 + b)s = 2.$$

Thus

$$0 = (6 + b)(12 - a)s - (12 - a)(6 + b)s = 9(6 + b) - 2(12 - a) = 30 + 2a + 9b.$$

Solving the simultaneous equations

$$2a + 3b + 6 = 0 \qquad 2a + 9b + 30 = 0$$

simultaneously, we deduce that $a = 3$, $b = -4$.

The angle between the lines is the angle between the vectors $\mathbf{x} = 3\mathbf{i} - 4\mathbf{j} + 12\mathbf{j}$ and $\mathbf{y} = 2\mathbf{i} - \mathbf{j} + 2\mathbf{k}$. Since

$$|\mathbf{x}|^2 = 3^2 + 4^2 + 12^2 = 169 \qquad |\mathbf{y}|^2 = 2^2 + 1^2 + 2^2 = 9 \qquad \mathbf{x} \cdot \mathbf{y} = 6 + 4 + 24 = 34,$$

and hence the angle is

$$\cos^{-1} \frac{34}{13 \times 3} = 29.3°.$$

EXERCISE 19F

1. Write down vector equations for the following straight lines which pass through the given points and lie in the given directions.

   a) $(1, 2, 3)$, $\begin{pmatrix} 0 \\ 1 \\ 2 \end{pmatrix}$,　　　 b) $(0, 0, 0)$, $\begin{pmatrix} 0 \\ 0 \\ 1 \end{pmatrix}$,　　　 c) $(2, -1, 1)$, $\begin{pmatrix} 3 \\ -1 \\ 1 \end{pmatrix}$,　　　 d) $(3, 0, 2)$, $\begin{pmatrix} 4 \\ -2 \\ 3 \end{pmatrix}$.

2. Find vector equations for the lines joining the following pairs of points.

   a) $(2, -1, 2)$, $(3, -1, 4)$,　　　 b) $(1, 2, 2)$, $(2, -2, 2)$,　　　 c) $(3, 1, 4)$, $(-1, 2, 3)$.

3. Which of these equations of straight lines represent the same straight line as each other?

   a) $\mathbf{r} = \begin{pmatrix} 1 \\ 4 \\ 2 \end{pmatrix} + t\begin{pmatrix} 2 \\ -1 \\ 2 \end{pmatrix}$,　　　 b) $\mathbf{r} = \begin{pmatrix} 3 \\ 3 \\ 4 \end{pmatrix} + t\begin{pmatrix} 2 \\ -1 \\ 2 \end{pmatrix}$,

   c) $\mathbf{r} = (5\mathbf{i} + 2\mathbf{j} + 6\mathbf{k}) + t(-2\mathbf{i} + \mathbf{j} - 2\mathbf{k})$,　　　 d) $\mathbf{r} = (\mathbf{i} + 4\mathbf{j} + 2\mathbf{k}) + t(-2\mathbf{i} + \mathbf{j} - 2\mathbf{k})$,

   e) $\mathbf{r} = (-\mathbf{i} + 5\mathbf{j}) + t(2\mathbf{i} - \mathbf{j} + 2\mathbf{k})$,　　　 f) $\mathbf{r} = (-\mathbf{i} + 5\mathbf{j}) + t(-2\mathbf{i} + \mathbf{j} - 2\mathbf{k})$.

4. Find whether or not the point $(-3, 1, 5)$ lies on each of the following lines.

   a) $\mathbf{r} = \begin{pmatrix} 1 \\ 3 \\ 1 \end{pmatrix} + t\begin{pmatrix} -2 \\ -1 \\ 2 \end{pmatrix}$,　　　 b) $\mathbf{r} = \begin{pmatrix} 0 \\ 1 \\ 2 \end{pmatrix} + t\begin{pmatrix} 1 \\ 0 \\ 3 \end{pmatrix}$,　　　 c) $\mathbf{r} = \begin{pmatrix} 1 \\ -2 \\ 4 \end{pmatrix} + t\begin{pmatrix} -4 \\ -3 \\ -1 \end{pmatrix}$.

5. Determine whether each of the following sets of points lies on a straight line.

   a) $(1, 2, -1)$, $(2, 4, -3)$, $(4, 8, -7)$,　　　 b) $(5, 2, -3)$, $(-1, 6, -11)$, $(3, -2, 4)$.

6. Investigate whether or not it is possible to find numbers s and t which satisfy the following vector equations.

a) $s\begin{pmatrix} 3 \\ 4 \\ 1 \end{pmatrix} + t\begin{pmatrix} 2 \\ -1 \\ 0 \end{pmatrix} = \begin{pmatrix} 0 \\ 11 \\ 2 \end{pmatrix}$,   b) $s\begin{pmatrix} 1 \\ 2 \\ -3 \end{pmatrix} + t\begin{pmatrix} 5 \\ 1 \\ 1 \end{pmatrix} = \begin{pmatrix} 1 \\ -7 \\ 11 \end{pmatrix}$,   c) $\begin{pmatrix} -1 \\ -2 \\ 3 \end{pmatrix} + s\begin{pmatrix} 1 \\ 2 \\ -1 \end{pmatrix} + t\begin{pmatrix} 3 \\ -1 \\ 4 \end{pmatrix} = \begin{pmatrix} 5 \\ 3 \\ 4 \end{pmatrix}$.

7. Find the points of intersection, if any, of each of the following pairs of lines.

a) $\mathbf{r} = \begin{pmatrix} 1 \\ 3 \\ 1 \end{pmatrix} + s\begin{pmatrix} -2 \\ -1 \\ 2 \end{pmatrix}$, $\mathbf{r} = \begin{pmatrix} 0 \\ -2 \\ 8 \end{pmatrix} + t\begin{pmatrix} 1 \\ -1 \\ 1 \end{pmatrix}$,   b) $\mathbf{r} = \begin{pmatrix} 1 \\ -1 \\ 2 \end{pmatrix} + s\begin{pmatrix} -1 \\ 2 \\ -1 \end{pmatrix}$, $\mathbf{r} = \begin{pmatrix} 1 \\ 3 \\ -1 \end{pmatrix} + t\begin{pmatrix} 2 \\ -8 \\ 5 \end{pmatrix}$.

8. If $\mathbf{p} = 2\mathbf{i} - \mathbf{j} + 3\mathbf{k}$, $\mathbf{q} = 5\mathbf{i} + 2\mathbf{j}$ and $\mathbf{r} = 4\mathbf{i} + \mathbf{j} + \mathbf{k}$, find a set of numbers f, g, h such that $f\mathbf{p} + g\mathbf{q} + h\mathbf{r} = \mathbf{0}$. What does this tell you about the translations represented by the three vectors $\mathbf{p}, \mathbf{q}$ and $\mathbf{r}$?

9. A and B are points with coordinates $(2, 1, 4)$ and $(5, -5, -2)$. Find the coordinates of the point C such that $\overrightarrow{AC} = \frac{2}{3}\overrightarrow{AB}$.

10. Four points A, B, C and D, with position vectors $\mathbf{a}$, $\mathbf{b}$, $\mathbf{c}$ and $\mathbf{d}$ are vertices of a tetrahedron. The midpoints of BC, CA, AB, AD, BD, CD are denoted by P, Q, R, U, V, W. Find the position vectors of the midpoints of PU, QV and RW. What do you notice about the answer? State your conclusion as a geometrical theorem.

11. If E and F are two points with position vectors $\mathbf{e}$ and $\mathbf{f}$, find the position vector of the point H such that $\overrightarrow{EH} = \frac{3}{4}\overrightarrow{EF}$. With the notation of the previous Question, express in terms of $\mathbf{a}$, $\mathbf{b}$, $\mathbf{c}$ and $\mathbf{d}$ the position vectors of G, the centroid of triangle ABC, and of H, the point on DG such that $DH : HG = 3 : 1$. Can you deduce a geometric theorem about tetrahedra from this?

12. For each of the following sets of points A, B, C and D, determine whether the lines AB and CD are parallel, intersect each other, or are skew.

a) $A\,(3, 2, 4)$, $B\,(-3, -7, -8)$, $C\,(0, 1, 3)$, $D\,(-2, 5, 9)$,

b) $A\,(3, 1, 0)$, $B\,(-3, 1, 3)$, $C\,(5, 0, -1)$, $D\,(1, 0, 1)$,

c) $A\,(-5, -4, -3)$, $B\,(5, 1, 2)$, $C\,(-1, -3, 0)$, $D\,(8, 0, 6)$.

13. A student displays her birthday cards on strings which she has pinned to opposite walls of her room, whose floor measures 3 metres by 4 metres. Relative to one corner of the room, the coordinates of the ends of the first string are $(0, 3.3, 2.4)$ and $(3, 1.3, 1.9)$ in metre units. The coordinates of the ends of the second string are $(0.7, 0, 2.3)$ and $(1.5, 4, 1.5)$. Assuming that the strings are straight lines, find the difference in the heights of the two strings where one passes over the other.

19.12   The Distance From A Point To A Line

If a point does not lie on a line, it is natural to ask how far from the line it is. Considering Figure 19.21, it is clear that the shortest distance from the point P to a line is the distance PN, where N is the point on the line for which NP is perpendicular to the line. This is because the distance PX from P to any other point on the line is the hypotenuse of a right-angled triangle for which PN is one of the other two sides, and so $PX \geq PN$.

Thus one way of finding the shortest distance from the point P to the line is to identify the point N on the line for which $\overrightarrow{PN}$ is perpendicular to the direction vector of the line.

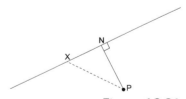

Figure 19.21

> **Key Fact 19.10 The Distance From A Point To A Line**
>
> The shortest distance from the point P to a line is called the **perpendicular distance**, the distance PN from P to the point N on the line where PN is perpendicular to that line.

Example 19.12.1. *Find the shortest distance from the point* Q $(3,1)$ *to the line* ℓ *with vector equation* $\mathbf{r} = \left(\begin{smallmatrix} 3 \\ 2 \end{smallmatrix}\right) + t\left(\begin{smallmatrix} -1 \\ 3 \end{smallmatrix}\right)$.

A general point X on the line ℓ has position vector $\mathbf{x} = \left(\begin{smallmatrix} 3-t \\ 2+3t \end{smallmatrix}\right)$, and so the position vector

$$\overrightarrow{PX} = \mathbf{x} - \mathbf{p} = \left(\begin{matrix} -t \\ 1+3t \end{matrix}\right).$$

If X is to be the point on ℓ which is closest to Q, we need to satisfy the equation

$$0 = \overrightarrow{XP} \cdot \left(\begin{matrix} -1 \\ 3 \end{matrix}\right) = \left(\begin{matrix} -t \\ 1+3t \end{matrix}\right) \cdot \left(\begin{matrix} -1 \\ 3 \end{matrix}\right) = t + 3(1+3t) = 3 + 10t$$

so we need $t = -0.3$. Thus it follows that $\overrightarrow{XP} = \left(\begin{smallmatrix} 0.3 \\ 0.1 \end{smallmatrix}\right)$, and hence the shortest distance from Q to the line ℓ is

$$\left\| \left(\begin{matrix} 0.3 \\ 0.1 \end{matrix}\right) \right\| = \tfrac{1}{10}\sqrt{3^2 + 1^2} = \tfrac{1}{10}\sqrt{10}.$$

A more geometric approach to this problem is as follows. Suppose that the equation of the line is $\mathbf{r} = \mathbf{a} + t\mathbf{p}$, where $\mathbf{a}$ is the position vector of a point A on the line, and where $\mathbf{p}$ is unit vector along the line. Then the shortest distance XN from the point X, with position vector $\mathbf{x}$, and the line is the length XN, which is equal to $XA\sin\theta$ by simple trigonometry. Now

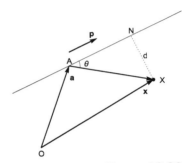

Figure 19.22

$$(\mathbf{x} - \mathbf{a}) \cdot \mathbf{p} = |\mathbf{x} - \mathbf{a}| |\mathbf{p}| \cos\theta = XA\cos\theta$$

and so the perpendicular distance XN from X to the line is given by the formula

$$XN^2 = |\mathbf{x} - \mathbf{a}|^2 - \big((\mathbf{x} - \mathbf{a}) \cdot \mathbf{p}\big)^2.$$

Key Fact 19.11 The Distance From A Point To A Line — A Formula

The perpendicular distance d from a point X, with position vector $\mathbf{x}$, to the line with equation $\mathbf{r} = \mathbf{a} + t\mathbf{p}$, where $\mathbf{p}$ is a unit vector, is

$$d = \sqrt{|\mathbf{x} - \mathbf{a}|^2 - \big((\mathbf{x} - \mathbf{a}) \cdot \mathbf{p}\big)^2}.$$

Example 19.12.2. *Find the distance of the point* Q, *with coordinates* $(1, 2, 3)$, *from the straight line with equation* $\mathbf{r} = (3\mathbf{i} + 4\mathbf{j} - 2\mathbf{k}) + t(\mathbf{i} - 2\mathbf{j} + 2\mathbf{k})$.

Since $1^1 + (-2)^2 + 2^2 = 9$, a unit vector in the direction of the line is $\mathbf{p} = \tfrac{1}{3}\mathbf{i} - \tfrac{2}{3}\mathbf{j} + \tfrac{2}{3}\mathbf{k}$. With $\mathbf{x} = \mathbf{i} + 2\mathbf{j} + 3\mathbf{k}$ and $\mathbf{a} = 3\mathbf{i} + 4\mathbf{j} - 2\mathbf{k}$, we calculate that

$$
\begin{aligned}
\mathbf{x} - \mathbf{a} &= -2\mathbf{i} - 2\mathbf{j} + 5\mathbf{k} \\
|\mathbf{x} - \mathbf{a}|^2 &= 2^2 + 2^2 + 5^2 = 33 \\
(\mathbf{x} - \mathbf{a}) \cdot \mathbf{p} &= (-2) \times \tfrac{1}{3} + (-2) \times (-\tfrac{2}{3}) + 5 \times \tfrac{2}{3} = 4
\end{aligned}
$$

and hence the perpendicular distance d is

$$d = \sqrt{33 - 4^2} = \sqrt{17}.$$

EXERCISE 19G

1. Find the distance of $(3,4)$ from the straight line $3x + 4y = 0$.

2. Find the distance of $(1,0,0)$ from the line $\mathbf{r} = t(12\mathbf{i} - 3\mathbf{j} - 4\mathbf{k})$.

3. Find the distance of the point $(1,1,4)$ from the line $\mathbf{r} = \mathbf{i} - 2\mathbf{j} + \mathbf{k} + t(-2\mathbf{i} + \mathbf{j} + 2\mathbf{k})$.

4. Find the distance of the point $(1,6,-1)$ from the line with vector equation

$$\mathbf{r} = \begin{pmatrix} 1 \\ 7 \\ -1 \end{pmatrix} + t \begin{pmatrix} 3 \\ 4 \\ 5 \end{pmatrix}.$$

5. Find a vector equation of the line ℓ containing the points $(1,3,1)$ and $(1,-3,-1)$. Find the perpendicular distance of the point with coordinates $(2,-1,1)$ from ℓ.

6. If $a, b > 0$, use a vector method to find the shortest distance from the origin $(0,0)$ to the line $\frac{x}{a} + \frac{y}{b} = 1$. Confirm your answer using trigonometry.

7. (See Chapter 2) Use a vector method to show that the closest distance from the point (u,v) to the line $ax + by + c = 0$ is

$$\left| \frac{au + bv + c}{\sqrt{a^2 + b^2}} \right|.$$

8*. Consider the skew lines ℓ_1 and ℓ_2 with respective equations

$$\mathbf{r} = \begin{pmatrix} 0 \\ -1 \\ 10 \end{pmatrix} + s \begin{pmatrix} 1 \\ 1 \\ 3 \end{pmatrix} \qquad \mathbf{r} = \begin{pmatrix} -8 \\ 11 \\ 2 \end{pmatrix} + t \begin{pmatrix} 2 \\ 0 \\ -1 \end{pmatrix}.$$

Let P be a point on ℓ_1, and let Q be a point on ℓ_2, such that PQ is perpendicular to both lines.

a) Write down parametrised expressions for the position vectors $\mathbf{p}$ and $\mathbf{q}$ of P and Q.

b) Write down two equations for the parameters determining $\mathbf{p}$ and $\mathbf{q}$, and solve them to determine the position vectors $\mathbf{p}$ and $\mathbf{q}$.

c) Find the distance PQ, the shortest distance between the skew lines ℓ_1 and ℓ_2.

Chapter 19: Summary

- A vector is a quantity that has both magnitude and direction. It can be expressed in terms of components, either as a column vector, or using the fundamental unit vectors $\mathbf{i}, \mathbf{j}$ (and $\mathbf{k}$ if needed). Two vectors are equal precisely when they have the same magnitude and direction or, equivalently, precisely when they have the same components.

- Vectors can be added and multiplied by scalars. Algebraically this is performed by adding or scaling the components of the vectors. Geometrically vectors are added using the triangle law. Vector addition is commutative, associative and distributive over scalar multiplication, in that

$$\mathbf{p} + \mathbf{q} = \mathbf{q} + \mathbf{p} \qquad\qquad \mathbf{p} + (\mathbf{q} + \mathbf{r}) = (\mathbf{p} + \mathbf{q}) + \mathbf{r}$$
$$s(\mathbf{p} + \mathbf{q}) = s\mathbf{p} + s\mathbf{q} \qquad\qquad (s + t)(\mathbf{p} = s\mathbf{p} + t\mathbf{q}$$

- The modulus $|\mathbf{a}|$ of a vector is its magnitude. The modulus of the two-dimensional vector $\begin{pmatrix} u \\ v \end{pmatrix} = u\mathbf{i} + v\mathbf{j}$ is $\sqrt{u^2 + v^2}$, while the modulus of the three-dimensional vector $\begin{pmatrix} u \\ v \\ w \end{pmatrix} = u\mathbf{i} + v\mathbf{j} + w\mathbf{k}$ is $\sqrt{u^2 + v^2 + w^2}$. A vector of modulus 1 is called a unit vector.

- The position vector (relative to O) of a point A is the displacement vector $\overrightarrow{OA}$, often written as $\mathbf{a}$. The modulus of $\overrightarrow{AB}$ is the length AB.

- The scalar product of two vectors $\mathbf{a}$ and $\mathbf{b}$ (of the same dimension) is equal to

$$\mathbf{a} \cdot \mathbf{b} = |\mathbf{a}||\mathbf{b}|\cos\theta,$$

where θ is the angle between $\mathbf{a}$ and $\mathbf{b}$. In particular, $\mathbf{a} \cdot \mathbf{a} = |\mathbf{a}|^2$. If $\mathbf{a} = \begin{pmatrix} p \\ q \end{pmatrix}$ and $\mathbf{b} = \begin{pmatrix} r \\ s \end{pmatrix}$, then $\mathbf{a} \cdot \mathbf{b} = pr + qs$. If $\mathbf{a} = \begin{pmatrix} p \\ q \\ r \end{pmatrix}$ and $\mathbf{b} = \begin{pmatrix} s \\ t \\ u \end{pmatrix}$, then $\mathbf{a} \cdot \mathbf{b} = ps + qt + ru$.

- Non-zero vectors are perpendicular precisely when their scalar product is zero.

- The scalar product satisfies the identities

$$\mathbf{p} \cdot \mathbf{q} = \mathbf{q} \cdot \mathbf{p} \qquad\qquad (s\mathbf{p}) \cdot \mathbf{q} = \mathbf{p} \cdot (s\mathbf{q}) = s(\mathbf{p} \cdot \mathbf{q})$$
$$\mathbf{p} \cdot (\mathbf{q} + \mathbf{r}) = \mathbf{p} \cdot \mathbf{q} + \mathbf{p} \cdot \mathbf{r} \qquad\qquad (\mathbf{p} + \mathbf{q}) \cdot \mathbf{r} = \mathbf{p} \cdot \mathbf{r} + \mathbf{q} \cdot \mathbf{r}$$

- The straight line passing through the point A with position vector $\mathbf{a}$ in the direction of the vector $\mathbf{p}$ has vector equation $\mathbf{r} = \mathbf{a} + t\mathbf{p}$. The vector $\mathbf{p}$ is called the direction vector for the line.

- The angle between two lines is the angle between their direction vectors.

- In two dimensions, two lines are either parallel or identical, or they meet at a unique point. In three dimensions, two lines can also be skew; they can fail to be parallel, and yet do not intersect.

Complex Numbers

In this chapter we will learn to:

- understand the definition of a complex number, and the meaning of its real part, imaginary part, modulus, argument and conjugate,

- perform algebraic operations on complex numbers written in Cartesian form,

- learn how to solve any quadratic equation, and simple cubic equations,

- recognise that complex roots occur in conjugate pairs in polynomials with real coefficients,

- represent complex numbers geometrically on the Argand diagram, and indicate simple loci graphically.

20.1 Extending The Number System

Mathematicians have always wanted to discover new numbers. If we think back to the beginning of this book, in Chapter 1 we considered a hierarchy of numbers:

- The natural numbers $\mathbb{N}$ are the most fundamental; we can count things with them, and we can add numbers, and (sometimes) subtract. However, it is not possible to subtract any pair of numbers, and this was a serious problem.

- To be able to subtract at all times, mathematicians then invented/discovered (depending on your philosophical perspective) the number 0 and the negative integers, obtaining the number system of all integers $\mathbb{Z}$. It was now possible to add, subtract and multiply.

- To be able to divide by non-zero numbers, the rationals $\mathbb{Q}$ were invented/discovered. All four basic mathematical operations are now possible.

- To be able to take square roots of positive numbers, and solve many equations, mathematicians needed the real numbers $\mathbb{R}$.

At this point we have a rich field of numbers with which to work, and we have seen that the real numbers permit us to study trigonometry, exponentials and logarithms, and to perform calculus.

That might seem to be enough, but mathematicians are not satisfied (they seldom are). Mathematicians want to be able to solve as many equations as possible, and scientists appreciate the convenience that this mathematical power can bring. The fact that equations like $x^2 = -2$ and $\cos x = 3$ cannot be solved in real numbers needs to be addressed. Previously, when a number system was not large enough to handle all the demands that mathematicians placed on it, that number system was extended in a manner which enabled these new demands to be met (so, for example, the integers $\mathbb{Z}$ were extended to the rationals $\mathbb{Q}$ to enable division). To be able to solve more general equations than can be handled by real numbers, the mathematical response is to invent a new kind of number, called a **complex number**. It turns out that this can be done very simply, by introducing just one new number, usually denoted by i, whose square is -1. Requiring that this number combines with the real numbers using the usual rules of algebra, this creates a whole new system of numbers.

Notice first that you don't need a separate symbol for the square root of -2, since the rules of algebra require that $\sqrt{-2} = \sqrt{2} \times \sqrt{-1}$, so that $\sqrt{-2}$ is just $\sqrt{2}i$.

Since you must be able to combine i with all the real numbers, the complex numbers must include all numbers of the form $a + bi$, where a and b are real. It turns out that this is all that is needed.

Key Fact 20.1 The Complex Numbers

The **complex numbers** consist of numbers of the form $a + bi$, where a and b are real numbers and i is a special (new) number such that $i^2 = -1$. The set of all complex numbers is denoted $\mathbb{C}$:

$$\mathbb{C} = \left\{ a + bi \, \middle| \, a, b \in \mathbb{R} \right\}.$$

Food For Thought 20.1

The existence of the number i disturbs some people. Throughout our mathematical careers, up until this point, we learn that the square of a number is always positive, and that -1 cannot have a square root. The idea of a square root of -1 is therefore baffling.

Although we rarely discuss the point, the true nature of real numbers is equally mysterious. It is relatively simple to get our heads around the idea of a fraction (we can slice a cake into 17 equal pieces, and therefore create $\frac{12}{17}$ of a cake, should we wish), but what do we really mean by a number like π, which is expressed by an infinite non-recurring decimal expansion? The fact that our calculators give us a comfortable, 8 or 9 significant figure view of the world tends to disguise the problem, since we can work with these numbers without really addressing the question of what they are.

It is important to take the same approach to i. Rest assured that it is possible to create a number system which behaves like the complex numbers, and learn what their properties are. You will then see why mathematicians wanted to create them!

The various parts of a complex number have names. A complex number is precisely determined by its two constituent real numbers,

$$a + bi = c + di \qquad \Leftrightarrow \qquad a = c \quad \text{and} \quad b = d.$$

in just the same way that a point (a, b) in the plane is precisely determine by its x- and y-coordinates a and b (we shall return to this idea later on).

Example 20.1.1. *If $2 + yi$ and $x - 5i$ are complex numbers, where x and y are real, and $2 + yi = x - 5i$, find x and y.*

Since $2 + yi = x - 5i$, we deduce that $2 = x$ and $y = -5$. The equation $2 = x$ arose from the operation called **equating real parts**, while the equation $y = -5$ came from **equating imaginary parts**.

Key Fact 20.2 Complex Numbers: Real and Imaginary Numbers

If $a + bi$ is a complex number, then a is called its **real part**, written $\mathrm{Re}(a + bi)$, and b is called its **imaginary part**, written $\mathrm{Im}(a + bi)$.

Complex numbers of the form $a = a + 0i$ are called **real numbers**, while complex numbers of the form $bi = 0 + bi$ are called **imaginary numbers**.

We sometimes want to describe complex numbers by specifying their real and imaginary parts, and sometimes we would like a more compact notation. Single letters like z and w (anything except x and y, that are generally reserved for real numbers) are frequently used to represent a complex number. We might talk about the number $z = 2 + 3i$ for example, in which case $\mathrm{Re}z = 2$ and $\mathrm{Im}z = 3$.

Two questions need to be asked before going further: is algebra with complex numbers consistent, and are complex numbers useful? The answers are *'yes, but ...'* and *'yes, very'*. Complex numbers have an important place in modern science.

20.2 Operations With Complex Numbers

It is remarkable, and not at all obvious, that when you add, subtract, multiply or divide two complex numbers $a + bi$ and $c + di$, the result is another complex number.

- **Addition and subtraction** According to the usual rules of algebra,

$$(a + bi) \pm (c + di) = a + bi \pm c \pm di = a \pm c + bi \pm di = (a \pm c) + (b \pm d)i\,,$$

  so that addition and subtraction is performed by adding or subtracting corresponding real and imaginary parts:

$$\operatorname{Re}(z_1 \pm z_2) = \operatorname{Re}z_1 \pm \operatorname{Re}z_2 \qquad \operatorname{Im}(z_1 \pm z_2) = \operatorname{Im}z_1 \pm \operatorname{Im}z_2\,.$$

- **Multiplication** Again using the usual rules of algebra,

$$(a + bi)(c + di) = ac + a \times di + bi \times c + bi \times di = ac + adi + bci + bdi^2 = (ac - bd) + (ad + bc)i\,.$$

  and so the product of two complex numbers is another complex number, but the rules describing the real and complex parts of a product are quite complex:

$$\operatorname{Re}(z_1 z_2) = \operatorname{Re}z_1 \times \operatorname{Re}z_2 - \operatorname{Im}z_1 \times \operatorname{Im}z_2 \qquad \operatorname{Im}(z_1 z_2) = \operatorname{Re}z_1 \times \operatorname{Im}z_2 + \operatorname{Im}z_1 \times \operatorname{Re}z_2\,.$$

  An important special case of this multiplication is the following

$$(a + bi)(a - bi) = \left(aa - b(-b)\right) + i\left(a(-b) + ba\right) = a^2 + b^2 + 0i = a^2 + b^2\,,$$

  so that the product of $a + bi$ and $a - bi$ is a real number, and the sum of two squares can be factorised in complex numbers.

- **Uniqueness** If $a + bi = 0$, then $0 = (a + bi)(a - bi) = a^2 + b^2$. Thus the sum of the squares of two real numbers is equal to 0. Since $a^2 \geq 0$ (with equality only when $a = 0$), and $b^2 \geq 0$ (with equality only when $b = 0$), the fact that $a^2 + b^2 = 0$ tells us that $a^2 = b^2 = 0$, and hence that $a = b = 0$. In other words,

$$z = 0 \qquad \Leftrightarrow \qquad \operatorname{Re}z = \operatorname{Im}z = 0\,.$$

  Hence the notion that complex numbers are determined by their real and imaginary parts is a consequence of the algebraic properties of complex numbers:

$$z_1 = z_1 \quad \Leftrightarrow \quad z_1 - z_2 = 0 \quad \Leftrightarrow \quad \operatorname{Re}(z_1 - z_2) = \operatorname{Im}(z_1 - z_2) = 0$$
$$\Leftrightarrow \quad \operatorname{Re}z_1 = \operatorname{Re}z_2\,, \operatorname{Im}z_1 = \operatorname{Im}z_2\,,$$

  as we observed in the previous section.

- **Division** If $z = c + di$ is not equal to zero, than we cannot have both c and d equal to 0, and hence $c^2 + d^2 > 0$. Since $z(c - di) = (c + di)(c - di) = c^2 + d^2$, we deduce that

$$\frac{1}{z} = \frac{1}{c^2 + d^2}(c - di) = \frac{c}{c^2 + d^2} - \frac{d}{c^2 + d^2}i\,.$$

  Thus division by non-zero numbers can be performed:

$$\frac{a + bi}{c + di} = \frac{(a + bi)(c - di)}{(c + di)(c - di)} = \frac{(ac + bd) + (bc - ad)i}{c^2 + d^2} = \frac{ac + bd}{c^2 + d^2} + \frac{bc - ad}{c^2 + d^2}i\,,$$

  provided that $c + di \neq 0$. There is no need to learn this formula for division until we have a better notation for expressing the inverse z^{-1} of a non-zero complex number z but you should be able to reproduce this technique. Note its similarity to the technique of 'rationalising the denominator' used with surds.

Thus we can perform the standard mathematical operations of addition, subtraction, multiplication and division on complex numbers, which is good news. On the other hand, there is no notion of 'positive' or 'negative' complex numbers. If there were, then i would have to be either positive or negative. If $i > 0$ then i^2 would be the square of a positive number, and so would be positive. This would imply that -1 is positive, which is not true. Thus i would have to be negative. But that implies that $-i$ would be positive, which makes $-1 = (-i)^2$ positive again!

Food For Thought 20.2

Since there is no concept of positive or negative complex numbers, there can be no meaningful inequalities concerning complex numbers.

EXERCISE 20A

---

1. If $p = 2 + 3i$ and $q = 2 - 3i$, express the following in the form $a + bi$, for real numbers a and b:

   a) $p + q$,   b) $p - q$,   c) pq,   d) $(p + q)(p - q)$,

   e) $p^2 - q^2$,   f) $p^2 + q^2$,   g) $(p + q)^2$,   h) $(p - q)^2$.

2. If $r = 3 + i$ and $s = 1 - 2i$, express the following in the form $a + bi$, for real numbers a and b:

   a) $r + s$,   b) $r - s$,   c) $2r + s$,   d) $r + si$,

   e) rs,   f) r^2,   g) $\frac{r}{s}$,   h) $\frac{s}{r}$,

   i) $\frac{r}{i}$,   j) $(1 + i)r$,   k) $\frac{s}{1+i}$,   l) $\frac{1-i}{s}$.

3. If $(2 + i)(x + yi) = 1 + 3i$, where x and y are real numbers, write two equations connecting x and y, and solve them. Compare your answer with that given by dividing $1 + 3i$ by $2 + i$.

4. Evaluate the following:

   a) $\text{Re}(3 + 4i)$,   b) $\text{Im}(4 - 3i)$,   c) $\text{Re}(2 + i)^2$,

   d) $\text{Im}(3 - i)^2$,   e) $\text{Re}\frac{1}{1+i}$,   f) $\text{Im}\frac{1}{i}$.

5. If s and t are complex numbers, which of the following are always true?

   a) $\text{Re}s + \text{Re}t = \text{Re}(s + t)$,   b) $\text{Re}(3s) = 3\text{Re}s$,   c) $\text{Re}(is) = \text{Im}s$,

   d) $\text{Im}(is) = \text{Re}s$,   e) $\text{Re}s \times \text{Re}t = \text{Re}(st)$,   f) $\frac{\text{Im}s}{\text{Im}t} = \text{Im}\left(\frac{s}{t}\right)$.

6. If ω is the complex number $\omega = -\frac{1}{2} + i\frac{1}{2}\sqrt{3}$, calculate ω^3.

7*. By considering $(a + bi)(c + di)(a - bi)(c - di)$, express $(a^2 + b^2)(c^2 + d^2)$ as the sum of two squares. Hence write $1586 = 13 \times 122$ as the sum of the squares of two positive integers (there is more than one way).

8*. For any θ and ϕ, find a simplified form for

$$(\cos\theta + i\sin\theta)(\cos\phi + i\sin\phi).$$

20.3 Conjugates

Given a complex number $z = a + bi$, its (complex) **conjugate** is the complex number (read as 'z-star')

$$z^\star = a - bi,$$

The complex conjugate is an important operation, and it is important to understand its properties. If $z = a + bi$ and $w = c + di$ are complex numbers, then $a - (-b)i = a + bi$ and

$$z + z^\star = 2a \qquad\qquad z - z^\star = 2bi$$
$$z \pm w = (a \pm c) + i(b \pm d) \qquad\qquad z^\star \pm w^\star = (a \pm c) - (b \pm d)i$$
$$zw = (ac - bd) + i(ad + bc) \qquad\qquad z^\star w^\star = (ac - bd) - i(ad + bc)$$
$$\frac{1}{z} = \frac{1}{a^2+b^2}(a - bi) \qquad\qquad \frac{1}{z^\star} = \frac{1}{a^2+b^2}(a + bi)$$

These calculations, and their key implications, can be summarised as follows:

> **Key Fact 20.3** The Complex Conjugate
>
> The complex conjugate operator on complex numbers:
>
> $$z = x + yi \qquad \mapsto \qquad z^\star = x - yi$$
>
> has the following properties. For any complex numbers z and w:
>
> $(z^\star)^\star = z,$ $\qquad\qquad$ $zz^\star = (\mathrm{Re}z)^2 + (\mathrm{Im}z)^2 \geq 0,$
>
> $z + z^\star = 2\mathrm{Re}z,$ $\qquad\qquad$ $z - z^\star = 2i\mathrm{Im}z,$
>
> $(z \pm w)^\star = z^\star \pm w^\star,$ $\qquad\qquad$ $\left(\frac{z}{w}\right)^\star = \frac{z^\star}{w^\star}.$

In summary, the complex conjugate behaves nicely with respect to addition, subtraction, multiplication and division, and can be used to identify the real and imaginary parts of a complex number.

Example 20.3.1. *Show that a complex number is real precisely when $z = z^\star$.*

If z is real, then $z = x + 0i = x$, so that $z^\star = x - 0i = x = z$. On the other hand, if $z^\star = z$, then $2i\mathrm{Im}z = z - z^\star = 0$. Since z has no imaginary part, it must be real.

20.4 Solving Equations

When solving quadratic equations with real coefficients,

$$ax^2 + bx + c = 0,$$

we needed to study the discriminant $\Delta = b^2 - 4ac$. If $\Delta \geq 0$, it was possible to solve the equation, since we can calculate the square root $\sqrt{b^2 - 4ac}$. If $\Delta < 0$, up until now we have had to say that the equation had no solutions.

Since we are now able to take the square roots of negative numbers, such equations are no longer insoluble.

Example 20.4.1. *Solve the quadratic equation $z^2 + 4z + 13 = 0$.*

In the usual terminology, $a = 1$, $b = 4$ and $c = 13$. Thus $b^2 - 4ac = -36$. Using the quadratic formula, we can write the solutions as

$$z = \frac{-b \pm \sqrt{b^2 - 4ac}}{2a} = \frac{-4 \pm \sqrt{-36}}{2} = \frac{-4 \pm 6i}{2} = -2 \pm 3i.$$

Alternatively we could complete the square, observing that

$$z^2 + 4z + 13 = (z+2)^2 + 9 = (z+2)^2 + 3^2 = (z+2+3i)(z+2-3i),$$

Thus the equation becomes $(z+2+3i)(z+2-3i) = 0$, and hence $z = -2 \pm 3i$.

This method works for any quadratic equation with real coefficients. The solutions to the quadratic equation

$$ax^2 + bx + c = 0 \qquad (a, b, c \in \mathbb{R})$$

are:

- the distinct real numbers $\frac{-b \pm \sqrt{b^2 - 4ac}}{2a}$ if $b^2 - 4ac > 0$,

- the single real number $-\frac{b}{2a}$ if $b^2 - 4ac = 0$,

- the distinct complex numbers $\frac{-b \pm i\sqrt{4ac - b^2}}{2a}$ if $b^2 - 4ac < 0$.

The discriminant no longer tells us when the equation is soluble; instead it tells us when the roots are real or complex. Note that, when the roots are complex numbers, then they have the form $\alpha \pm i\beta$ for real α and β; they are a pair of complex numbers of the form w, $w^\star$. Pairs of numbers like this are called **complex conjugate pairs**. Thus the roots of a quadratic equation with real coefficients are either real or they form a complex conjugate pair.

Example 20.4.2. (a) *Solve the cubic equation $z^3 - z^2 - z - 2 = 0$.*

(b) *By considering $(\pm 1 + i)^4$, solve the quartic equation $z^4 + 4 = 0$.*

To solve a cubic, we need to hunt for a root using the Remainder Theorem. After some search, we find that $2^3 - 2^2 - 2 - 2 = 0$, and hence $z - 2$ is a factor of the cubic, so the first equation becomes

$$0 = z^3 - z^2 - z - 2 = (z - 2)(z^2 + z + 1)$$

so that either $z = 2$ or $z^2 + z + 1 = 0$. We can solve this quadratic, so the roots to the cubic are $2, -\frac{1}{2} + i\frac{1}{2}\sqrt{3}, -\frac{1}{2} - 2\frac{1}{2}\sqrt{3}$.

To solve the quartic, we see that

$$(\pm 1 + i)^2 = 1 \pm 2i + i^2 = 1 \pm 2i - 1 = \pm 2i \qquad (\pm 1 + i)^4 = (\pm 2i)^2 = -4$$

and hence both $1 + i$ and $-1 + i$ are solutions of $z^4 + 4 = 0$. Since this quartic expression only involves even powers of z, it follows that $-(1 + i) = -1 - i$ and $-(-1 + i) = 1 - i$ are also solutions. In other words, the linear polynomials

$$z - 1 - i \quad , \quad z - 1 + i \quad , \quad z + 1 - i \quad , \quad z + 1 + i$$

are all factors of $z^4 + 4$. A product of four linear polynomials is quartic, and matching the coefficient of z^4 tells us that

$$z^4 + 4 = (z - 1 - i)(z - 1 + i)(z + 1 - i)(z + 1 + i),$$

and hence that $1 \pm i, -1 \pm i$ are the four solutions.

This last example contained two polynomials with real coefficients. The cubic equation had one real root and a complex conjugate pair of roots, which the quartic had two complex conjugate pairs of roots. It looks like we have a pattern here!

Suppose that a is real and that n a non-negative integer. Since the complex conjugate behaves well with respect to multiplication, we see that

$$(z^2)^\star = z^\star z^\star = (z^\star)^2$$
$$(z^3)^\star = (z^2)^\star z^\star = (z^\star)^3$$

and so on, leading to $(z^n)^\star = (z^\star)^n$. Thus

$$\left(a z^n\right)^\star = a^\star (z^n)^\star = a(z^\star)^n.$$

If $p(z)$ is a polynomial with real coefficients, then

$$p(z) = \sum_{j=0}^{n} a_j z^j = a_n z^n + a_{n-1} z^{n-1} + \cdots + a_1 z + a_0,$$

where n a non-negative integer and $a_0, a_1, \ldots, a_{n-1}, a_n$ are all real. Since the complex conjugate also behaves well with respect to addition, we deduce that

$$p(z*) = \sum_{j=0}^{n} a_j (z^\star)^j = \sum_{j=0}^{n} \left(a_j z^j\right)^\star = \left(\sum_{j=0}^{n} a_j z^j\right)^\star = p(z)^\star$$

Thus, if u is a root of the equation $p(z) = 0$, then $p(u^\star) = p(u)^\star = 0^\star = 0$, and so $u^\star$ is also a solution. These calculations can be summarised as follows:

Key Fact 20.4 Complex Roots Of Real Polynomials

If $p(z)$ is a polynomial with real coefficients, then $p(z^\star) = p(z)^\star$ for any $z \in \mathbb{C}$. Thus if u is a complex root of $p(z) = 0$, then so is $u^\star$. The roots of $p(z)$ are either real (if $u = u^\star$), or they come in complex conjugate pairs.

Example 20.4.3. *Given that* $-1 + 3i$ *is a root of the quartic equation* $z^4 - 2z^3 + 11z^2 - 22z + 90 = 0$.

This quartic has real coefficients. Since $-1 + 3i$ is a root, so is $(-1 + 3i)^\star = -1 - 3i$. Thus $z + 1 - 3i$ and $z + 1 + 3i$ are both factors of the quartic, and hence the quadratic

$$(z + 1 - 3i)(z + 1 + 3i) = (z + 1)^2 + 3^2 = z^2 + 2z + 10$$

must be a factor. Dividing $z^2 + 2z + 10$ into the quartic:

$$z^4 - 2z^3 + 11z^2 - 22z + 90 = (z^2 + 2z + 10)(z^2 - 4z + 9)$$

Since $z^2 - 4z + 9 = (z - 2)^2 + 5 = (z - 2 - i\sqrt{5})(z - 2 + i\sqrt{5})$, the equation has become

$$(z + 1 - 3i)(z + 1 + 3i)(z - 2 - i\sqrt{5})(z - 2 + i\sqrt{5}) = 0 ,$$

and so the solutions are $-1 \pm 3i$ and $2 \pm i\sqrt{5}$ (two complex conjugate pairs).

Example 20.4.4. *Solve the equation* $z^5 - 6z^3 - 2z^2 + 17z - 10 = 0$.

Denote the left side by $p(z)$ and begin by trying to find some real factors, using the Remainder Theorem.

Since $p(1) = 0$, $z - 1$ is a factor; we calculate $p(z) = (z - 1)q(z)$, where $q(z) = z^4 + z^3 - 5z^2 - 7z + 10$.

Since $q(1) = 0$, $z - 1$ is a factor; we calculate $q(z) = (z - 1)r(z)$, where $r(z) = (z^3 + 2z^2 - 3z - 10)$.

This time $r(2) = 0$, and so $z - 2$ is a factor, and $r(z) = (z - 2)(z^2 + 4z + 5)$. Completing the square, $z^2 + 4z + 5 = (z + 2)^2 + 1 = (z + 2 + i)(z + 2 - i)$.

Thus $p(z) = (z-1)^2(z-2)(z+2+i)(z+2-i)$, and so the solutions of the equation $p(z) = 0$ are 1 (twice), 2, $-2 + i$ and $-2 - i$

EXERCISE 20B

1. If $p = 3 + 4i$, $q = 1 - i$ and $r = -2 + 3i$, solve the following equations for z:
   a) $p + z = q$,
   b) $2r + 3z = p$,
   c) $qz = r$,
   d) $pz + q = r$.

2. Solve these pairs of simultaneous equations for the complex numbers z and w:
   a) $\quad (1 + i)z + (2 - i)w = 3 + 4i$
   $\quad\quad iz + (3 + i)w = -1 + 5i$
   b) $\quad\quad 5z - (3 + i)w = 7 - i$
   $\quad\quad (2 - i)z + 2iw = -1 + i$

3. Solve the following quadratic equations, giving answers in the form $a + bi$, where a and b are real numbers:
   a) $z^2 + 9 = 0$,
   b) $z^2 + 4z + 5 = 0$,
   c) $z^2 - 6z + 25 = 0$,
   d) $2z^2 + 2z + 13 = 0$.

4. Write down the conjugates of:
   a) $1 + 7i$,
   b) $2 + i$,
   c) 5,
   d) $3i$.
   For each of these complex numbers z find the values of $z + z^\star$, $z - z^\star$, $zz^\star$ and $\frac{z}{z^\star}$.

5. Write the following polynomials as products of linear factors:
   a) $z^2 + 25$,
   b) $9z^2 - 6z + 5$,
   c) $4z^2 + 12z + 13$,
   d) $z^4 - 16$,
   e) $z^4 - 8z^2 - 9$,
   f) $z^3 + z - 10$,
   g) $z^3 - 3z^2 + z + 5$,
   h) $z^4 - z^2 - 2z + 2$.

6. Prove that $1 + i$ is a root of the equation $z^4 + 3z^2 - 6z + 10 = 0$. Find all the other roots.

7. Prove that $-2 + i$ is a root of the equation $z^4 + 24z + 55 = 0$. Find all the other roots.

8. Let $z = a + bi$, where a and b are real numbers. If $\frac{z}{z^\star} = c + di$, where c and d are real, prove that $c^2 + d^2 = 1$.

9. Complete the sentence 'z is purely imaginary precisely when …'. Your answer should be an equation involving z and $z^{\star}$.

10. If $z = a + bi$, where a and b are real, use the binomial theorem to find the real and imaginary parts of z^5 and $(z^{\star})^5$.

11*. In a recent lesson, Peter was asked to find the solutions of an equation $f(z) = 0$, where $f(z)$ is a quartic polynomial with real coefficients. Peter remembered that $-3 + i$ was one of the solutions, but he failed to write down the polynomial $f(z)$ completely. Given that $f(z) = z^4 + z^3 - 13z^2 + az + b$ for some (real) numbers a, b, help Peter by finding the values of a and b and solving the equation for him.

20.5 Argand Diagrams

Earlier in this chapter we mentioned that a complex number $z = a + bi$ was specified by its real and imaginary parts a, b in the same way that a point (a, b) on the plane was specified by its x- and y-coordinates. Both the complex number $z = a + bi$ and the point (a, b) need two real numbers to describe it.

This idea leads to a method for representing complex numbers pictorially. Let a complex number $z = a + bi$ be represented as a point on the plane with coordinates (a, b). In this context, we no longer talk about the x- and y-axes; they are now called the **real** and **imaginary** axes respectively. Real numbers correspond to points lying on the real axis, and purely imaginary numbers correspond to points lying on the imaginary axis.

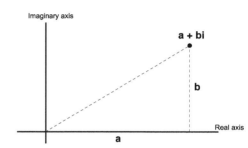

Figure 20.1

Representing complex numbers in this way is called drawing an **Argand diagram**, named after an 18th century French mathematician. We do not normally label either of the axes.

Example 20.5.1. *Show in an Argand diagram the roots of*

a) $z^4 + 4 = 0$, b) $z^5 - 6z^3 - 2z^2 + 17z - 10 = 0$.

we found the roots of these polynomials in Example 20.4.2 and Example 20.4.4. Argand diagrams of their roots are as follows:

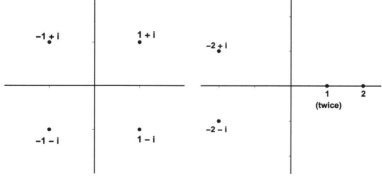

Figure 20.2

Note that complex conjugate pairs are plotted symmetrically with respect to the real axis.

If we compare the rules for addition/subtraction of both complex numbers and vectors,

$$\begin{pmatrix} a \\ b \end{pmatrix} \pm \begin{pmatrix} c \\ d \end{pmatrix} = \begin{pmatrix} a \pm c \\ b \pm d \end{pmatrix} \qquad (a + bi) \pm (c + di) = (a \pm c) + (b \pm d)i$$

we see that complex numbers can be added in the Argand diagram using the same parallelogram rule as is used to add vectors (if we associate to a complex number z the vector from the origin 0 to z in the Argand diagram):

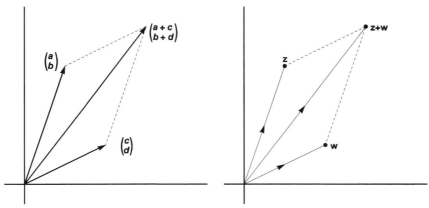

Figure 20.3

while complex numbers are subtracted in the Argand diagram using very much the same triangle rule as is used for vectors:

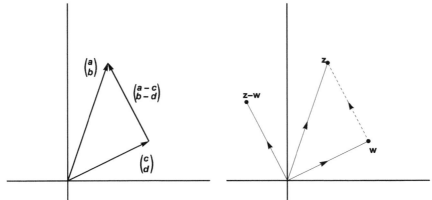

Figure 20.4

20.6 Modulus And Argument

Any vector has a modulus, or length. We have just seen that complex numbers, represented in the Argand diagram, exhibit some similarities to vectors. There will therefore be benefit in defining the **modulus** of a complex number.

Key Fact 20.5 The Modulus

Given a complex number $z = x + yi$, its modulus is the non-negative real number

$$|z| = \sqrt{x^2 + y^2}\,.$$

A complex number z is zero precisely when its modulus $|z|$ is zero, and the identity

$$|z|^2 = (\text{Re}z)^2 + (\text{Im}z)^2 = zz^\star$$

holds for any complex number z. Thus

$$z^{-1} = \frac{z^\star}{|z|^2}\,, \qquad z \neq 0\,.$$

We have met this notation before for the modulus of a real number, but there is no danger of confusion. If $z = x$ is a real number, then $z = z^\star$, and hence $zz^\star = x^2$, so that $|z| = |x|$, and the two notations coincide. We have also met this notation describing the modulus of a vector; making the connection in an Argand diagram between a complex number and its 'position vector' relative to 0 ensures that the two notations coincide as well, since $|x + yi| = \left|\binom{x}{y}\right|$.

But beware! If z is complex, then it is not true that $|z| = \sqrt{z^2}$, as is true for real numbers.

Key Fact 20.6 The Modulus In The Argand Diagram

The modulus $|z|$ is the distance of the complex number z from 0 in an Argand diagram. For any two complex numbers z and w, the modulus $|z - w|$ is the distance between z and w in the Argand diagram; if $z = a + bi$, $w = c + di$, then

$$|z - w| = \sqrt{(a-c)^2 + (b-d)^2}\,.$$

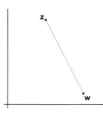

Figure 20.5

Inspection of the parallelogram in Figure 20.3 leads us to the following result, since $|z|$, $|w|$ and $|z + w|$ are seen to form three sides of a triangle.

Key Fact 20.7 The Triangle Inequality For Complex Numbers

If z and w are complex numbers, then $|z + w| \le |z| + |w|$.

Another important quantity associated with a complex number is its **argument**. Just as a vector can be described in terms of its modulus and the angle it makes with a fixed direction, so can a complex number.

Key Fact 20.8 The Argument

The **argument** $\arg z$ of a non-zero complex number z is the angle that the line from 0 to z makes with the positive real axis in the Argand diagram. The usual choice for the argument, called the **principal branch of the argument**, requires that $-\pi \le \arg z \le \pi$.

Provided that $x = \operatorname{Re} z \ne 0$,

$$\tan(\arg z) = \frac{y}{x} = \frac{\operatorname{Im} z}{\operatorname{Re} z}\,.$$

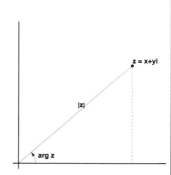

Figure 20.6

Example 20.6.1. *Calculate the modulus and argument for the following complex numbers:*

  a) $1 + i$,   *b)* $-1 + i\sqrt{3}$,   *c)* -5,   *d)* $-i$,   *e)* $3 - 3i$.

(a) If $z = 1 + i$ then $|z| = \sqrt{1^2 + 1^2} = \sqrt{2}$, while $\tan(\arg z) = 1$. It is clear that z is in the first quadrant of the Argand diagram, and so $\arg z = \tfrac{1}{4}\pi$.

(b) If $z = -1 + i\sqrt{3}$ then $|z| = \sqrt{1^2 + \sqrt{3}^2} = 2$, while $\tan(\arg z) = -\sqrt{3}$. It is clear that z is in the second quadrant, and so $\arg z = \tfrac{2}{3}\pi$.

(c) -5 lies on the negative real axis, and so has modulus 5 and argument π.

(d) $-i$ lies on the negative imaginary axis, and so has modulus 1 and argument $-\tfrac{1}{2}\pi$. The formula for the tangent of the argument does not work this time.

(e) If $z = 3 - 3i$ then $|z| = \sqrt{3^2 + 3^2} = 3\sqrt{2}$, while $\tan(\arg z) = -1$. Since z lies in the fourth quadrant, we see that $\arg z = -\tfrac{1}{4}\pi$.

20.7 Loci

Complex numbers can be linked with coordinate geometry, and can be used to describe geometrical shapes in the Argand diagram. There are a standard set of loci that we need to be able to recognise:

- $|z - a| = r$ This locus consists of all points z whose distance from a in the Argand diagram is equal to r. In other words, the locus is the circle with centre a and radius r.

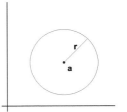

- $\arg(z - a) = \theta$ The angle that $z - a$ makes with the positive real axis must be θ. This locus is a **half-line**, or **ray**. starting at a and making an angle θ with the real axis.

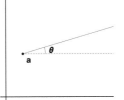

- $\mathrm{Re}\,z = \alpha$ The locus of all complex numbers with real part equal to α is a straight line parallel to the imaginary axis. An equation of the form $\mathrm{Re}(wz) = \alpha$ for some fixed complex number w will have locus equal to a line which is, in general, not parallel to either axis.

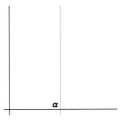

- $|z - a| = |z - b|$ This is the locus of all points equidistant from a and b in the Argand diagram. This is the straight line which is the perpendicular bisector of the line segment from a to b.

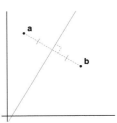

Example 20.7.1. *Sketch the following loci:*
 a) $|z - 1 - i| = 1$,   b) $|z| < |z - 2|$,   c) $\mathrm{Im}\,z = 1.1$

    (a) This locus is the circle with centre $1 + i$ and radius 1.

    (b) This locus is the set of points that are closer to 0 than they are to 2. The locus of this inequality is the half-plane to the left of the perpendicular bisector of the line segment from 0 to 1, namely the region with $\mathrm{Re}\,z < 1$.

    (c) The set of numbers with imaginary part equal to -1 form a line parallel to the real axis.

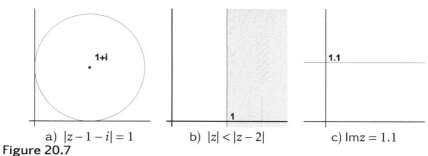

a) $|z-1-i|=1$ b) $|z|<|z-2|$ c) $\text{Im} z = 1.1$

Figure 20.7

Other loci might have to be determined by algebra.

Example 20.7.2. *Find the loci of the following:*
  a) $\text{Im}((1+i)z) = 1$,   b) $|z-3| = 2|z|$,   c) $|z| = \text{Re} z + 2$.

(a) If we write $z = x + yi$, then $(1+i)z = (1+i)(x+yi) = (x-y)+i(x+y)$. The equation $\text{Im} z = 1$ therefore reads $x + y = 1$, so the locus is a straight line of gradient -1.

(b) If we write $z = x + yi$, the equation becomes

$$
\begin{aligned}
(x-3)^2 + y^2 &= |z-3|^2 &= 4|z|^2 = 4(x^2+y^2) \\
4(x^2+y^2) - (x-3)^2 - y^2 &= 0 \\
4x^2 + 4y^2 - x^2 + 6x - 9 - y^2 &= 0 \\
3x^2 + 3y^2 + 6x - 9 &= 0 \\
x^2 + y^2 + 2x - 3 &= 0 \\
(x+1)^2 + y^2 &= 4,
\end{aligned}
$$

and so the locus is a circle with centre -1 and radius 2.

(c) If we write $z = x + yi$, the equation reads

$$
\begin{aligned}
\sqrt{x^2 + y^2} &= x + 2 \\
x^2 + y^2 &= (x+2)^2 \\
x^2 + y^2 - (x+2)^2 &= 0 \\
x^2 + y^2 - x^2 - 4x - 4 &= 0 \\
x &= \tfrac{1}{4}y^2 - 1,
\end{aligned}
$$

and so the locus is a parabola.

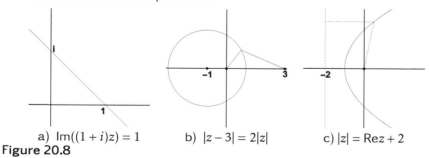

a) $\text{Im}((1+i)z) = 1$ b) $|z-3| = 2|z|$ c) $|z| = \text{Re} z + 2$

Figure 20.8

In problems such as this, it is possible to perform all these calculations without reverting to the Cartesian coordinates of the complex number z. However, we are more familiar with the form of equations of lines and other geometric shapes when expressed in Cartesian form; while the algebra is slightly more involved, the end product is easier to recognise.

EXERCISE 20C

1. Draw Argand diagrams to represent the following relationships:

   a) $(3+i)+(-1+2i) = (2+3i)$,

   b) $(1+4i)-(3i) = (1+i)$.

2. Draw Argand diagrams to illustrate the following properties of complex numbers:

   a) $z+z^\star = 2\text{Re}z$,

   b) $z-z^\star = 2i\text{Im}z$,

   c) $(s+t)^\star = s^\star + t^\star$,

   d) $\text{Re}z \le |z|$,

   e) $\arg z + \arg z^\star = 0$.

3. Draw Argand diagrams showing the roots of the following equations:

   a) $z^4 - 1 = 0$,

   b) $z^3 + 1 = 0$,

   c) $z^3 + 6z + 20 = 0$,

   d) $z^4 + 4z^3 + 4z^2 - 9 = 0$,

   e) $z^4 + z^3 + 5z^2 + 4z + 4 = 0$.

4. Represent the roots of the equation $z^4 - z^3 + z - 1 = 0$ in an Argand diagram, and show that they all have the same modulus.

5. Identify the following loci in an Argand diagram:

   a) $|z| = 5$,

   b) $\text{Re}z = 3$,

   c) $z + z* = 6$,

   d) $z - z* = 2i$,

   e) $|z-2| = 2$,

   f) $|z-4| = |z|$,

   g) $|z+2i| = |z+4|$,

   h) $|z+4| = 3|z|$,

   i) $1 + \text{Re}z = |z-1|$,

   j) $(\arg z)^2 = 1$,

   k) $\arg(z^2) = 2$,

   l) $-\frac{1}{2}\pi < z < \frac{1}{2}\pi$.

6. Find the point of intersection of the loci $\arg(z-2i) = \frac{1}{4}\pi$ and $|z-2| = 4$.

7. Identify in an Argand diagram the points corresponding to the following inequalities.

   a) $|z| > 2$,

   b) $|z-3i| \le 1$,

   c) $|z+1| \le |z-i|$,

   d) $|z| > 2|z-3|$.

8. a) Show that $|zw| = |z| \times |w|$ for any complex numbers z and w.

   b) Show that, if z is a complex number and n is a positive integer, $|z^n| = |z|^n$. Hence show that all the roots of the equation $z^n + a^n = 0$, where a is a positive real number, have modulus a.

9. Recalling the triangle inequality $|s+t| \le |s| + |t|$ for any two complex numbers s and t, prove that $|z-w| \ge |z| - |w|$ for any two complex numbers z and w.

10. Let P be a point in an Argand diagram corresponding to the complex number z, and suppose that $|z+5| + |z-5| = 26$. Prove that $12 \le OP \le 13$.

11. If s and t are two complex numbers, prove the following:

   a) $|s+t|^2 = |s|^2 + |t|^2 + (st^\star + s^\star t)$,

   b) $|s-t|^2 = |s|^2 + |t|^2 - (st^\star + s^\star t)$,

   c) $|s+t|^2 + |s-t|^2 = 2(|s|^2 + |t|^2)$.

   Interpret this last result geometrically.

12*. Identify the locus $\arg(z-1) = \arg(z+1) + \frac{1}{2}\pi$. Remember circle theorems!

13*. If s and t are two complex numbers, prove the following:

   a) $(s^\star t)^\star = st^\star$,

   b) $st^\star + s^\star t$ is a real number, and $st^\star - s^\star t$ a purely imaginary number,

   c) $(st^\star + s^\star t)^2 - (st^\star - s^\star t)^2 = 4|st|^2$,

   d) $(|s| + |t|)^2 - |s+t|^2 = 2|st| - (st^\star + s^\star t)$.

   Use these results to prove that $|s+t| \le |s| + |t|$.

14*. If a and k are positive real numbers, consider the locus $|z+a| = k|z-a|$. Describe the locus when:

   a) $k = 1$,

   b) $k \ne 1$.

   If you have access to some graphing software, draw a number of these loci on the same Argand diagram for different values of k. Does the resulting pattern look familiar? Ask your Physics teacher about this!

20.8   Solving More Complicated Equations

One of the strengths of complex numbers is that we are able to use them to take the square roots of negative real numbers. Can we take the square roots of other complex numbers?
Since $(2+2i)^2 = 2^2 + 8i - 2^2 = 8i$ and $(2+3i)^2 = 2^2 + 12i - 3^2 = -5 + 12i$, we see that $2+2i$ is a square root of $8i$, and that $2+3i$ is square root of $-5+12i$. This is not just luck.

Example 20.8.1. *Show that any non-zero complex number $z = a + bi$ has exactly two square roots, one of which is the negative of the other.*

If $b = 0$ then the roots are either $\pm\sqrt{a}$ (if $a > 0$) or $\pm i\sqrt{-a}$ (if $a < 0$); let us now assume that $b \neq 0$. This means that $a^2 + b^2 > a^2$, and hence $\sqrt{a^2 + b^2} > |a|$. We are looking for a number $w = c + di$ such that $w^2 = z$. Thus we need

$$(c^2 - d^2) + 2icd = w^2 = z = a + bi,$$

so that the real numbers c and d must satisfy the simultaneous equations

$$c^2 - d^2 = a \qquad 2cd = b.$$

Multiplying the first equation by $4c^2$ yields

$$\begin{aligned} 4c^4 - b^2 = 4c^4 - 4c^2d^2 &= 4ac^2 \\ 4c^4 - 4ac^2 - b^2 &= 0 \\ (2c^2 - a)^2 &= a^2 + b^2 \end{aligned}$$

Since c is real, c^2 must be non-negative, and so $c^2 = \frac{1}{2}\left[\sqrt{a^2 + b^2} + a\right]$. Thus there are two possible square roots of z, of the form $c + di$ where

$$c = \pm\sqrt{\frac{\sqrt{a^2 + b^2} + a}{2}}, \qquad d = \frac{b}{2c}.$$

It is clear that one of these roots is the negative of the other.

We do not need to learn the formulae for the square roots; it is enough to be able to reproduce this argument in individual cases.

Since we can take the square root of any complex number, we can solve any quadratic equation with complex coefficients.

Example 20.8.2. *Solve the quadratic equation $(2-i)z^2 + (4+3i)z + (-1+3i) = 0$.*

Using the quadratic formula we see that the roots are

$$\begin{aligned} z &= \frac{-(4+3i) \pm \sqrt{(4+3i)^2 - 4(2-i)(-1+3i)}}{2(2-i)} = \frac{-(4+3i) \pm \sqrt{7 + 24i - 4(1 + 7i)}}{2(2-i)} \\ &= \frac{-(4+3i) \pm \sqrt{3 - 4i}}{2(1-i)} \end{aligned}$$

If $\sqrt{3 - 4i} = c + di$ then $c^2 - d^2 = 3$ and $2cd = -4$, so that $c^4 - 4 = c^4 - c^2d^2 = 3c^2$, and hence $c^4 - 3c^2 - 4 = 0$. We deduce that $c^2 = 4$ ($c^2 = -1$ is not acceptable) and so $c = \pm 2$. Thus $d = \mp 1$, and so the square roots of $3 - 4i$ are $\pm(2 - i)$. Thus the roots of the quadratic are

$$\begin{aligned} z &= \frac{-(4+3i) \pm (2-i)}{2(2-i)} = \frac{-2 - 4i}{2(2-i)}, \frac{-6 - 2i}{2(2-i)} = \frac{(-2 - 4i)(2+i)}{2(2-i)(2+i)}, \frac{(-6 - 2i)(2+i)}{2(2-i)(2+i)} \\ &= \frac{-10i}{10}, \frac{-10 - 10i}{10} = -i, -1 - i. \end{aligned}$$

Much effort could have been saved by tidying up the coefficient of z^2 first. Multiplying the equation by $2 + i$ gives

$$\begin{aligned} (2+i)(2-i)z^2 + (2+i)(4+3i)z + (2+i)(-1+3i) &= 0 \\ 5z^2 + (5+10i)z + (-5+5i) &= 0 \\ z^2 + (1+2i)z + (-1+i) &= 0 \end{aligned}$$

and hence the roots are

$$z = \frac{-(1+2i) \pm \sqrt{(1+2i)^2 - 4 \times 1 \times (-1+i)}}{2} = \frac{-(1+2i) \pm \sqrt{(-3+4i) - 4(-1+i)}}{2}$$

$$= \frac{-(1+2i) \pm \sqrt{1}}{2} = \frac{-(1+2i) \pm 1}{2} = \frac{-2i}{2}, \frac{-2-2i}{2} = -i, -1-i$$

Note that, since the coefficients of this quadratic equation are complex, the two roots no longer form a conjugate pair.

For Interest

One of the most beautiful results concerning complex numbers, and one of the most compelling reasons to work with them, is the fact that they can handle so much more than quadratic equations. The so-called **Fundamental Theorem of the Algebra** states that any polynomial of degree n with complex coefficients has n complex zeros. With complex numbers available to us, we can solve all polynomial equations!

For this to be true, we have to count roots in a special way. If a root is repeated twice, it contributes 2 to the sum of roots. If it is repeated three times, it contributes 3 to the sum, and so forth. The polynomial $(z-1)^{100}$ has, in one sense, only one zero (=1). However that root is repeated 100 times, which allows us to say that the polynomial has 100 zeros.

The Fundamental Theorem of the Algebra does not tell us anything about how to find those roots; it merely tells us that they exist.

EXERCISE 20D

1. Find the square roots of:

   a) $-2i$, b) $-3+4i$, c) $5+12i$, d) $8-6i$.

2. Solve the following quadratic equations:

   a) $z^2 + z + (1-i) = 0$, b) $z^2 + (1-i)z + (-6+2i) = 0$,
   c) $z^2 + 4z + (4+2i) = 0$, d) $(1+i)z^2 + 2iz + 4i = 0$,
   e) $(2-i)z^2 + (3+i)z - 5 = 0$.

3. Find the fourth roots of:

   a) -64, b) $7+24i$.

   Show your answers on an Argand diagram.

4. If $(x+yi)^3 = 8i$, where x and y are real numbers, prove that either $x = 0$ or $x = \pm\sqrt{3}y$. Hence find all the cube roots of $8i$. Show your answers on an Argand diagram.

5. If $(x+yi)^3 = 2-2i$, where x and y are real numbers, prove that

$$x(x^2 - 3y^2) = y(y^3 - 3x^2) = 2.$$

   Show that these equations have one solution for which $x = y$, and hence find one cube root of $2 - 2i$.

   Find the quadratic equation satisfied by the other cube roots of $2 - 2i$, and solve it. Show all the roots on an Argand diagram.

Chapter 20: Summary

- **Complex numbers** $\mathbb{C}$ are numbers of the form $z = a + bi$ where a and b are real and i is a number where $i^2 = -1$. The real number a is the **real part** of z, while b is the **imaginary part** of z. The normal operations of addition, subtraction, multiplication and division can all be performed within the complex numbers.

- The (**complex**) **conjugate** of $z = a + bi$ is the complex number $z^\star = a - bi$.

- The **modulus** $|z|$ and **argument** $\arg z$ of a complex number z are the length that the line from 0 to z makes in the Argand diagram, and the angle that that line makes with the positive real axis, respectively. To be exact, $-\pi < \arg z \leq \pi$.

  For any complex number z, $zz^\star = |z|^2$.

  For any complex numbers z and w, the triangle inequality $|z + w| \leq |z| + |w|$ holds.

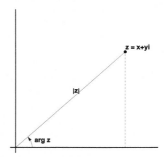

- Any complex number z has a square root, and so all quadratic equations with complex coefficients can be solved, giving complex solutions. Indeed, any polynomial with complex coefficients can be solved completely, and all its roots are complex.

- The zeros of a polynomial with real coefficients are either real or else occur in complex conjugate pairs.

- Complex numbers exist, and are of vital importance to mathematics and science.

Numerical Methods

In this Chapter we will learn to:

- investigate the location of roots $f(x) = 0$ by a change of sign in $y = f(x)$ over an interval,

- implement the direct iteration method for the numerical evaluation of an approximation to a root of $x = F(x)$, understand and recognise informally the relationship between the magnitude of the derivative of F at the root and the convergence or divergence of the iterative scheme,

- implement the Newton-Raphson iteration method for the numerical evaluation of an approximation to a root of $f(x) = 0$, and understand the geometric derivation of this method,

- understand the concept of rate of convergence of an iterative scheme, and in particular how this concept is realised for the above two schemes.

21.1   Introduction

There are many equations that 'we cannot solve". For example, we equations

$$x = \cos x \qquad x^5 - 20x + 5 = 0 \qquad 4xe^{-x} = 1$$

are "insoluble". This does not mean that solutions do not exist; a quick sketch of their graphs show that there must be one or more solutions in each of these cases:

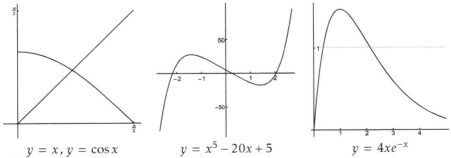

$$y = x, y = \cos x \qquad y = x^5 - 20x + 5 \qquad y = 4xe^{-x}$$

Figure 21.1

In this context, to say that an equation is soluble means that we cannot find 'nice' formulae for its roots which use standard mathematical operations and functions. The quadratic formula, for example, tells us how to solve quadratic equations, and there are similar (but more complicated) formulae for solving cubics and quartics. Famously, the mathematician Évariste Galois, a 19th century French mathematician but unsuccessful duellist (he died aged 20), showed that it was not possible to solve quintic equations 'nicely'; an example of an 'insoluble' quintic is given above.

Since we cannot find exact answers to these problems, the next best thing is to try to find approximate solutions. Investigating a number of strategies for doing this is the aim of this Chapter.

21.2   The Sign-Change Principle

We briefly remind ourselves of the key terminology. Any equation can be rearranged so that it is in the form $f(x) = 0$ for some function f. A **root** of the equation $f(x) = 0$ is a value of x for which $f(x)$ is equal to 0. A **zero** of $f(x)$ is a root of the equation $f(x) = 0$. The **solution** to an equation $f(x) = 0$ is the set of all roots.

Example 21.2.1. *Sketch the curve* $y = x^5 - 20x + 5$.

A table of values

x	−3	−2	−1	0	1	2	3
y	−178	13	24	5	−14	−3	188

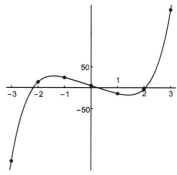

leads to a sketch like the one on the right. We could have identified the turning points at $x = \pm\sqrt{2}$, but this is less important at the moment.
We have drawn the graph crossing the axis between $x = -3$ and $x = -2$, and between $x = 0$ and $x = 1$, and between $x = 2$ and $x = 3$. We felt confident in doing this because the function $x^5 - 5x + 20$ changed sign between these three pairs of values.

Figure 21.2

If the function $f(x)$ changes sign between $x = p$ and $x = q$, its graph must cross the x-axis somewhere in between, giving us a zero of the function f:

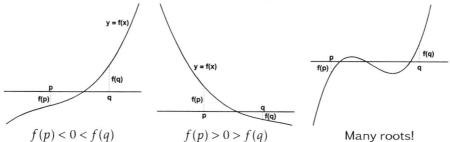

$$f(p) < 0 < f(q) \qquad f(p) > 0 > f(q) \qquad \text{Many roots!}$$

Figure 21.3

There may be more than one root between $x = p$ and $x = q$, but that does not matter!

However, we have avoided mentioning one vitally important condition without which this idea will not work. It is perfectly possible for a function $f(x)$ to be defined at $x = p$ and $x = q$, have opposite signs at those two points, and yet not have a zero in between them. This point is often overlooked, since it relates to the fact that not all functions are 'well-behaved'. Not all points in between $x = p$ and $x = q$ have to belong to the domain of f and, even if they do, the function f might still not have a zero between them. The functions

$$y = x^{-1} \quad (x \neq 0) \qquad \text{and} \qquad y = f(x) = \begin{cases} e^x & x \leq 1 \\ -e^{-x} & x > 1 \end{cases}$$

demonstrate these problems.

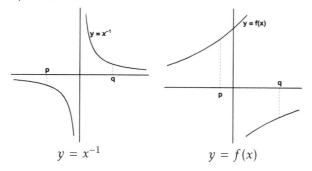

$$y = x^{-1} \qquad\qquad y = f(x)$$

Figure 21.4

We need to ensure that our function f is defined everywhere between $x = p$ and $x = q$, and that it does not have any jumps and breaks in its graph in that interval of values. The first of these conditions is covered by requiring that the interval $p \leq x \leq q$ belongs to the domain of f, and the second is covered by the technical requirement that $f(x)$ be **continuous** on that interval. Continuity is, as we have mentioned previously, a complex and technical condition.

Fundamentally, we can (and do) think of continuous functions as one 'whose graph we can draw without taking or pencil off the paper'. Happily most of the functions that we meet on a day-to-day basis are continuous, or at least continuous on the intervals in which we shall be interested.

Key Fact 21.1 The Sign-Change Principle

If the function $f(x)$ is such that the interval $p \leq x \leq q$ belongs to its domain, and if $f(x)$ is continuous on that interval, and if $f(p)$ and $f(q)$ have opposite signs, then there exists a zero of $f(x)$ between p and q.

Example 21.2.2. *Show that the equation $x = \cos x$ has a root between 0.73 and 0.74.*

We first need to cast this equation into the right form; it becomes $f(x) = x - \cos x = 0$. The function $f(x)$ has $\mathbb{R}$ as its domain and is continuous everywhere; the nit-picking technical details are satisfied! Using our calculators, we observe that $f(0.73) = -0.01517\ldots$ and $f(0.74) = 0.001531\ldots$. Since there is a sign change, and since f is continuous on the necessary interval, we deduce the presence of a root of the equation.

It is important that we set out solutions to this type of problem well; we must make clear to our readers that we know why we are reaching our decision! This solution should be finished off with a sentence like the one above: we should not just calculate $f(0.73)$ and $f(0.74)$ and say nothing else!

Example 21.2.3. *Show that, to 6 decimal places, 0.357403 is a root of $4xe^{-x} = 1$.*

First, cast this equation in the correct shape; it becomes $f(x) = 4xe^{-x} - 1 = 0$.

Checking that this value for the root is accurate to 6 decimal places is actually checking that the root α lies in the interval $0.3574025 < \alpha < 0.3574035$. Using our calculators, $f(0.3574025) = -8.202 \times 10^{-7}$, while $f(0.3574035) = 9.778 \times 10^{-7}$. This sign change, and the continuity of f, ensure that there is a root α of the equation between 0.3574025 and 0.3574035, and hence that $\alpha = 0.357403$ to 6 decimal places.

There is always more than one way of attempting this problem. We could have written the original equation in the form $g(x) = e^x - 4x = 0$, and looked for a change of sign in $g(x)$ instead. We could even have tried $h(x) = x^{-1}e^x - 4 = 0$; the function $h(x)$ has the point 0 missing from its domain, but is continuous for positive x, and so is continuous on the interval of interest in this question.

Having found that a root lies in a particular interval, we could perform further sign-change checks to reduce the size of the interval in which the root lies, thereby obtaining a more accurate estimate of the root.

For example, consider the continuous function $f(x) = x^5 - 20x + 5$, whose graph was shown in Figure 21.1:

- Since $f(0) = 5$ and $f(1) = -14$, there is a root between 0 and 1.

- Since $f(0.3) = -0.998$, the root lies between 0 and 0.3.

- Since $f(0.2) = 1.00$, the root lies between 0.2 and 0.3.

- Since $f(0.25) = 0.000977$, the root lies between 0.25 and 0.3.

This process of testing and refinement has shown us that the root is certainly equal to 0.3 to 1 decimal place; given the value of $f(0.25)$, it is likely to be pretty close to 0.25 (its actual value is 0.250196 to 6 decimal places). Finding roots by this process of continued testing and refinement is very laborious and slow; we want to find more efficient techniques.

21.3   Direct Iteration

Example 21.3.1. *Find the first 25 terms in the sequence of numbers x_n defined by the formula*

$$x_0 = 0, \qquad x_{n+1} = e^{-x_n}, \qquad n \geq 0.$$

Modern calculators equipped with an ANS button are great for performing these calculations, since we are performing the same operation again and again, each time applying the same function to the previous answer. We obtain the following table of values:

n	x_n	n	x_n	n	x_n	n	x_n
0	0	7	0.57961	14	0.56691	21	0.56715
1	1	8	0.56012	15	0.56728	22	0.56714
2	0.36788	9	0.57114	16	0.56707	23	0.56714
3	0.69220	10	0.56488	17	0.56719	24	0.56714
4	0.50047	11	0.56843	18	0.56712		
5	0.60624	12	0.56641	19	0.56716		
6	0.54540	13	0.56756	20	0.56714		

Looking at this data, for $n \geq 22$ it seems that all subsequent values will be equal to 0.56714 (to 5 decimal places, anyway). This is particularly easy to see because the sequence is **oscillatory**; alternate values go up and down, oscillating above and below some middle value. Moreover the sequence is clearly **convergent**; the values are tending towards this middle value. When a sequence is both convergent and oscillatory, once two successive values are the same (to a desired degree of accuracy), all subsequent values will be the same (to that degree of accuracy), and the middle value to which the sequence converges will be specified to that same degree of accuracy.

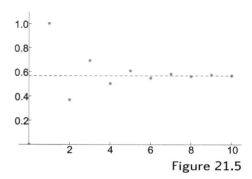

Figure 21.5

What is the relevance of this limiting number 0.56714? If we consider the continuous function $f(x) = x - e^{-x}$, we calculate that $f(0.567135) = -1.299 \times 10^{-5}$ and $f(0.567145) = 2.679 \times 10^{-6}$; this change of sign (and the continuity of f) tells us that 0.56724 is the solution, to 5 decimal places, of the equation $x = e^{-x}$. We were able to obtain 5 decimal place accuracy in finding the root of this equation relatively quickly, with about 24 identical calculations (which is particularly easy to do if our calculator has an ANS button); it took us much less time to obtain this level of accuracy that it would have taken us using search techniques like those of the previous section.

These calculations give an example of the following idea:

Key Fact 21.2 Direct Iteration

If $F(x)$ is a continuous function, consider the sequence of numbers x_n defined by the recurrence relation

$$x_{n+1} = F(x_n), \qquad n \geq 0,$$

where x_0 can be chosen freely. In this context, a recurrence relation of this type is called an **iterative scheme.**

If the sequence x_n converges to the number α, then α is a root of the equation $x = F(x)$. This particular iterative scheme is called **direct iteration.**

Continuity is vital for this idea to work; one of the consequences of a function being continuous is that if x_n converges to α, then the sequence $F(x_n)$ converges to $F(\alpha)$. In our case this tells us that the sequence x_{n+1} converges to $F(\alpha)$. But x_{n+1} is just the sequence x_n with the first term x_0 removed, and so it also converges to α; thus $\alpha = F(\alpha)$.

Example   21.3.2.

(a) *Find the solution of the equation $x = \cos x$ correct to 4 decimal places.*

(b) *Show that there is a solution of the cubic equation $x^3 - 3x - 5 = 0$ lying between 2 and 3, and determine it, correct to 5 decimal places.*

(a) This equation is already in the form $x = F(x)$, where $F(x) = \cos x$. Example 21.2.2 tells us that a root lies between 0.73 and 0.74; we shall try the iterative scheme

$$x_0 = 0.74, \qquad x_{n+1} = \cos x_n, \qquad n \geq 0.$$

The first few values in the sequence are $x_0 = 0.74$, $x_1 = 0.738469$, $x_2 = 0.739500$, $x_3 = 0.738805$, $x_4 = 0.739274$, $x_5 = 0.738958$, $x_6 = 0.739171$, $x_7 = 0.739028$, $x_8 = 0.739124$, $x_9 = 0.739059$.

We can stop now. The sequence is clearly oscillatory and convergent. Since x_8 and x_9 are both equal to 0.7391 to 4 decimal places, and since the root α of the equation must lie between them, it follows that $\alpha = 0.7391$ to 4 decimal places.

(b) Now $2^3 - 3 \times 2 - 5 = -3 < 0 < 13 = 3^3 - 3 \times 3 - 5$, and this sign change (and the continuity of the cubic) tells us that there is a root between 2 and 3. The cubic equation must be manipulated into the shape $x = F(x)$ before we can apply direct iteration. There are many ways of doing this, but the one we shall consider is to write $x^3 = 3x + 5$, and hence $x = \sqrt[3]{3x + 5}$, and therefore consider the iterative scheme

$$x_0 = 2, \qquad x_{n+1} = \sqrt[3]{3x_n + 5}, \qquad n \geq 0.$$

The first few terms in this sequence are $x_0 = 2$, $x_1 = 2.22398$, $x_2 = 2.26837$, $x_3 = 2.27697$, $x_4 = 2.27862$, $x_5 = 2.27894$, $x_6 = 2.27900$, $x_7 = 2.27902$, $x_8 = 2.27902$, $x_9 = 2.27902$.

This sequence is behaving rather differently. It is not oscillatory; instead is an increasing sequence. It is harder to be sure that a monotonic sequence has finally converged, since it is possible for a sequence to keep on increasing, even if by minute amounts at a time. The best way to be sure is to look for a sign-change once we feel confident that we have found the answer. If we write $f(x) = x^3 - 3x - 5$, then $f(2.279015) = -4.76 \times 10^{-5}$ and $f(0.279025) = 7.82 \times 10^{-5}$, this sign change confirms that 2.27902 is a root of the cubic equation, correct to 5 decimal places.

Not all iterative schemes work.

- The cubic equation $x^3 - 3x - 5 = 0$ could have been rewritten as $x = \frac{1}{3}(x^3 - 5)$, leading to the iterative scheme

$$x_0 = 2, \qquad x_{n+1} = \tfrac{1}{3}(x^3 - 5), \qquad n \geq 0.$$

The first few terms in this sequence are $2, 1, -1.3333, -2.4568, -6.6096, -97.9165, \dots$. This sequence is monotonic (decreasing) but **divergent**.

- The cubic equation $x^3 + x - 7 = 0$ has a root near $x = 1.7$. If we try the possible iterative scheme

$$x_0 = 1.7, \qquad x_{n+1} = 7 - x_n^3, \qquad n \geq 0.$$

then the first few terms in the sequence are $1.7, 2.087, -2.090, 16.130, -4189.871, 7.355 \times 10^{10}, \dots$. This term is oscillatory, but divergent.

- Finally, suppose that we tried to solve the equation $xe^x = 1$ using the iterative scheme

$$x_0 = 0.5, \qquad x_{n+1} = -\ln x_n, \qquad n \geq 0.$$

We calculate $x_1 = 0.693$, $x_2 = 0.367$, $x_3 = 1.004$, $x_4 = -0.00371$, at which point the iteration breaks down, since we cannot take the logarithm of a negative number. This can happen if the function F in the iteration scheme has domain not equal to the whole of $\mathbb{R}$, since it is possible that a term in the sequence might end up outside the domain. Such iterative schemes are **pathological**, and best avoided!

EXERCISE 21A

1. Show that the equation $2x^3 - 3x^2 - 2x + 5 = 0$ has a root between -1.5 and -1.

2. The equation $e^{-x} - x + 2 = 0$ has one root, α. Find an integer N such that $N < \alpha < N + 1$.

3. Given $f(x) = 3x + 13 - e^x$, evaluate $f(3)$ and $f(4)$, correct to 3 significant figures. Explain the significance of the answers in relation to the equation $3x + 7 = e^x$.

4. Show that the equation $x^3 - 3x^2 + 2x + 7 = 0$ has one root equal to -1.08675, correct to 6 significant figures. Determine the quadratic satisfied by the other two roots (with coefficients correct to 4 significant figures), and hence find the other two roots of the cubic, correct to 3 significant figures.

5. For part of this question, find three possible rearrangements of the equation $f(x) = 0$ into the form $x = F(x)$.

   a) $f(x) = x^5 - 5x + 6$,   b) $f(x) = e^x - \frac{5}{x}$,   c) $f(x) = x^5 + x^3 - 1999$.

6. For each direct iterative scheme below, of the form $x_{n+1} = F(x_n)$:

   - Rearrange the equation $x = F(x)$ into the form $f(x) = 0$, where f is a polynomial function.
   - Find the terms $x_0, x_1, x_2, x_3, x_4, x_5$.
   - Describe the behaviour of the sequence.
   - If the sequence converges, investigate whether x_5 is an approximate root of $f(x) = 0$.

   a) $x_0 = 0$, $x_{n+1} = \sqrt[11]{x_n^7 - 6}$,   b) $x_0 = 3$, $x_{n+1} = \left(\frac{17 - x_n^2}{x_n}\right)^2$,

   c) $x_0 = 7$, $x_{n+1} = \sqrt[3]{500 + \frac{10}{x_n}}$,   d) $x_0 = 4$, $x_{n+1} = \sqrt[3]{40 - x_n}$.

7. Show that the equation $x^5 + x - 19 = 0$ can be arranged into the form $x = \sqrt[3]{\frac{19-x}{x^2}}$, and that the equation has a root α between $x = 1$ and $x = 2$.

   Use an iteration based on this arrangement, with initial approximation $x_0 = 2$, to find the values of $x_1, x_2, \ldots, x_6$. Investigate whether this sequence is converging to α.

8. a) Show that the equation $x^2 + 2x - e^x = 0$ has a root in the interval $2 < x < 3$.

   b) Use an iterative method based on the rearrangement $x = \sqrt{e^x - 2x}$, with initial value $x_0 = 2$, to find the value of x_{10} to 4 decimal places. Describe what is happening to the terms of this sequence of approximations.

9. Show that the equation $e^x = x^3 - 2$ can be arranged into the form $x = \ln(x^3 - 2)$. Show also that it has a root between 2 and 3.

   Use the iteration $x_{n+1} = \ln(x_n^3 - 2)$, commencing with $x_0 = 2$ as an initial approximation to the root, to show that this arrangement is not a suitable one for finding this root.

   Find an alternative arrangement of $e^x = x^3 - 2$ which can be used to find this root, and use it to calculate the root correct to 2 decimal places.

10. a) Determine the value of the positive integer N such that the equation $12 - x - \ln x = 0$ has a root α such that $N < \alpha < N + 1$.

    b) Define the iterative scheme of approximations to α by $x_0 = N + \frac{1}{2}$, $x_{n+1} = 12 - \ln x_n$. Find the number of steps required before two consecutive terms of this sequence are the same when rounded to 4 significant figures. Show that this common value is equal to α to this degree of accuracy.

11. Sketch the graphs of $y = x^2$ and $y = \cos x$, and state the number of roots of the equation $x^2 = \cos x$. Use a suitable iteration and starting point to find the positive root of the equation $x^2 = \cos x$, giving your answer correct to 3 decimal places.

    Show that the iterative scheme $x_{n+1} = \cos^{-1} \sqrt{x_n}$, starting from $x = 0$, does not converge.

12*. Consider the two functions

$$F_+(x) = x + \tfrac{1}{2}x^2 \quad , \qquad F_-(x) = x - \tfrac{1}{2}x^2 .$$

What are the values of $F_+'(0)$ and $F_-'(0)$? Do either of the direct iteration schemes

   $x_0 = 0.1$, $x_{n+1} = F_+(x_n)$, $n \geq 0$,   or $x_0 = 0.1$, $x_{n+1} = F_-(x_n)$, $n \geq 0$,

converge?

21.3.1. SPIDER DIAGRAMS

Can we tell in advance whether or not a particular iteration scheme is going to be oscillatory or monotonic, or whether it is going to be convergent? There is a nice graphical way to understand the direct iteration process, which will enable us to answer these questions.

We are trying to solve the equation $x = F(x)$. Suppose that the graphs of $y = F(x)$ and $y = x$ have been drawn on the same set of axes, as in Figure 21.6, and suppose that α is the root of the equation $x = F(x)$ that we are trying to approximate. A single step in the iteration scheme $x_{n+1} = F(x_n)$ can be seen graphically as follows:

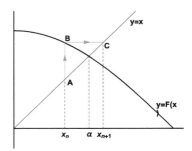

Figure 21.6

- Start at the point A on the line $y = x$, which has x-ordinate x_n.

- Move parallel to the y-axis until we meet the graph of $y = F(x)$ at the point B. The point B has coordinates $(x_n, F(x_n)) = (x_n, x_{n+1})$.

- Move parallel to the x-axis until we meet the line $y = x$ again at the point C. The point C has x-coordinate x_{n+1}.

If we consider the whole sequence of approximations, this pattern of moving from the line $y = x$ to the line $y = f(x)$ and back again builds up a characteristic spiral pattern. We see that the sequence x_n is oscillatory, with the terms in the sequence alternately above and below α. In this case the sequence is also convergent. Pictorially, the sequence can be thought of as 'spiralling in' to the root α. For what should now be an obvious reason, graphs like these are called **spider diagrams**.

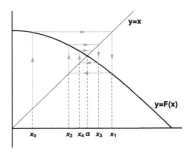

Figure 21.7

Leaving aside pathological functions, there are essentially four types of spider diagram, depending on whether the associated sequence is monotonic or oscillatory, and whether the sequence is convergent or divergent:

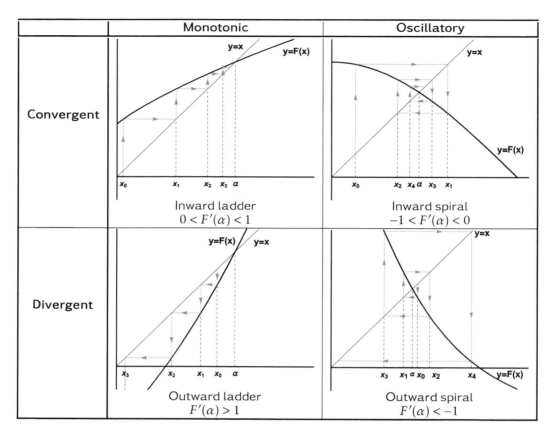

The spider diagram is a spiral for oscillatory sequences and a ladder for monotonic sequences. The ladder can head either towards or away from the root α depending on whether the sequence converges or diverges.

Inspection of the above four diagrams shows us that the different types of sequence can be distinguished by the steepness of the curve $y = F(x)$. Of course, this means that we are restricting our attention to functions F that can be differentiated, making F even 'nicer'! What is important is the size of the derivative of F at the point α.

Key Fact 21.3 Identifying Iteration Types

Near the root α of the equation $x = F(x)$, the direct iteration scheme $x_{n+1} = F(x_n)$ is:

- **monotonic** if $F'(\alpha) > 0$ and **oscillatory** if $F'(\alpha) < 0$,

- **convergent** of $|F'(\alpha)| < 1$ and **divergent** if $|F'(\alpha)| > 1$.

For the moment, let us satisfy ourselves why the sign of $F'(\alpha)$ distinguishes monotonic sequences from oscillatory ones. Since

$$F'(\alpha) = \lim_{h \to 0} \frac{F(\alpha + h) - F(\alpha)}{h} = \lim_{h \to 0} \frac{F(\alpha + h) - \alpha}{h}$$

(remember that $F(\alpha) = \alpha$) we deduce that, once h is small enough, $\frac{F(\alpha+h)-\alpha}{h}$ will be close to $F'(\alpha)$ and hence (provided that $F'(\alpha) \neq 0$) will have the same sign as $F'(\alpha)$.

- If $F'(\alpha) < 0$, this means that $\frac{F(\alpha+h)-\alpha}{h}$ is negative for small enough h, and hence (putting $h = x - \alpha$) that $\frac{F(x)-\alpha}{x-\alpha}$ is negative provided that x is close enough to α. In other words $F(x) - \alpha$ and $x - \alpha$ will have opposite signs. For our direct iteration scheme, this implies that $x_{n+1} - \alpha$ and $x_n - \alpha$ have opposite signs provided that x_n is close enough to α. Thus, so long as the sequence remains close to α, it is oscillatory, since successive terms are on opposite sides of α.

- If $F'(\alpha) > 0$, then similar calculations will tell us that $x_{n+1} - \alpha$ and $x_n - \alpha$ will have the same sign, provided that x_n is close enough to α. Thus, provided that it remains close enough to α for this analysis to be valid, the sequence remains on the same side of α; this will be enough to show that it must be monotonic.

Food For Thought 21.1

It is important to realise that all this theory assumes that terms in the approximating sequence are 'sufficiently close' to whichever root α we are currently considering. If the approximating sequence x_n stops being that close to α, all bets are off, and different behaviour may occur.

For example, in the case of the function $F(x)$ shown on the right, any iterative scheme will be monotonic and divergent with respect to β (since $F'(\beta) > 1$), but monotonic and convergent with respect to α (since $0 < F'(\alpha) < 1$). If the first value x_0 lies between α and β, then the sequence x_n will converge to α, no matter how close x_0 is to β.

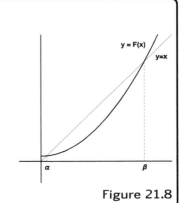

Figure 21.8

Example 21.3.3. *The cubic equation $2x^3 - 3x^2 - 2x + 2 = 0$ has a root α between 0 and 1. Will the direction iteration scheme*

$$x_0 = \tfrac{1}{2}, \qquad x_{n+1} = x_n^3 - \tfrac{3}{2}x_n^2 + 1, \qquad n \geq 0,$$

converge to this root?

We are interested in the function $F(x) = x^3 - \tfrac{3}{2}x^2 + 1$, for which

$$F'(x) = 3x^2 - 3x = 3x(x-1) = 3(x - \tfrac{1}{2})^2 - \tfrac{3}{4},$$

and so $-\tfrac{3}{4} \leq F'(x) < 0$ for all $0 < x < 1$. In particular, then, $-1 < F'(\alpha) < 0$. This iterative scheme should be both monotonic and convergent.

21.3.2. RATES OF CONVERGENCE

Suppose, for example, that α is a root of the equation $x = F(x)$, and that $F'(\alpha) = \tfrac{1}{2}$. Since this means that

$$\lim_{x \to \alpha} \frac{F(x) - \alpha}{x - \alpha} = \lim_{x \to \alpha} \frac{F(x) - F(\alpha)}{x - \alpha} = F'(\alpha) = \tfrac{1}{2}$$

we deduce that, once x is close enough to α, the quotient $\frac{F(x) - \alpha}{x - \alpha}$ will roughly equal to $\tfrac{1}{2}$. For example, this means that we can find some number $\delta > 0$ such that $\frac{F(x) - \alpha}{x - \alpha}$ is roughly $\tfrac{1}{2}$ provided that x is within δ of α; in other words,

$$\alpha - \delta < x < \alpha + \delta, x \neq \alpha \quad \Rightarrow \quad \frac{F(x) - \alpha}{x - \alpha} \approx \tfrac{1}{2} \quad \Rightarrow \quad F(x) - \alpha \approx \tfrac{1}{2}(x - \alpha).$$

This fact has important implications for the direct iteration scheme $x_{n+1} = F(x_n)$, since it implies that

$$|x_n - \alpha| < \delta \quad \Rightarrow \quad x_{n+1} - \alpha \approx \tfrac{1}{2}(x_n - \alpha), \qquad n \geq 0.$$

- If x_n is within δ of α, then $x_{n+1} - \alpha \approx \tfrac{1}{2}|x_n - \alpha|$ will be less than $\tfrac{1}{2}\delta$, and hence x_{n+1} is also within δ of α. Thus, provided that x_0 is within δ of α, so is x_1, and therefore so is x_2, and therefore so is x_3, and so on. We see that the whole sequence of approximations x_n lies within δ of α.

- If $|x_0 - \alpha| < \delta$, then $x_1 - \alpha \approx \tfrac{1}{2}(x_0 - \alpha)$. But then $x_2 - \alpha \approx \tfrac{1}{2}(x_1 - \alpha) \approx \left(\tfrac{1}{2}\right)^2 (x_0 - \alpha)$, and hence $x_3 - \alpha \approx \tfrac{1}{2}(x_2 - \alpha) \approx \left(\tfrac{1}{2}\right)^3 (x_0 - \delta)$, and so on. Thus, we have an approximation

$$|x_n - \alpha| \approx \left(\tfrac{1}{2}\right)^n \delta, \qquad n \geq 0.$$

This gives us important information about the direct iterative scheme. Not only is it convergent, the error between x_n and the root α is about the size of a geometric progression with common ratio $\frac{1}{2}$. This gives us vital information about the rate at which the sequence of approximations converges to α. Since $\left(\frac{1}{2}\right)^{43} < 5 \times 10^{-13}$, we can be pretty sure (it is likely that δ will be less than 1) that we have 12 decimal place accuracy if we calculate x_{43}.

There was nothing special about $\frac{1}{2}$; we could have repeated this argument for any value of $F'(\alpha)$ between -1 and 1.

Key Fact 21.4 Exponential Rate of Convergence Of Direct Iteration

If α is a root of the equation $x = F(x)$, and if $|F'(\alpha)| < 1$ then the approximate inequality

$$|x_n - \alpha| \approx |F'(\alpha)|^n (x_0 - \alpha), \qquad n \geq 0,$$

holds, provided that x_0 is sufficiently close to α in the first place, and so the error between x_n and α tends to 0 at a geometric rate. Thus the errors in direct iteration tend to 0 exponentially; for this reason the rate of convergence is called **exponential**.

One of the immediate consequences of this calculation is that direct iteration is convergent when $|F'(\alpha)| < 1$, as observed in the previous Subsection. A practical use of this result is that a direct iteration technique is better at converging to α the smaller the value of $F'(\alpha)$.

Example 21.3.4. *Find a direct iteration scheme which solves the equation $xe^x = 1$ quickly.*

In Example 21.3.1 it took us 25 terms of the iteration scheme

$$x_0 = 0, \qquad x_{n+1} = e^{-x_n}, \qquad n \geq 0,$$

to find the root $\alpha = 0.56714$ to 5 DP. Adding kx to both sides, the equation $x = e^{-x}$ can be rewritten as $(k+1)x = kx + e^{-x}$, which becomes $x = G(x) = \frac{1}{k+1}(kx + e^{-x})$. Thus $G'(x) = \frac{1}{k+1}(k - e^{-x})$, and so $G'(\alpha) = \frac{k-\alpha}{1+k}$. Since α is roughly 0.5, putting $k = 0.5$ should give good convergence. This leads us to the iteration scheme

$$x_0 = 0, \qquad x_{n+1} = \tfrac{1}{3}(x_n + 2e^{-x_n}), \qquad n \geq 0.$$

This scheme is oscillatory, with $x_4 = x_5 = 0.56714$ to 5 decimal places; this is a huge efficiency gain!

One interesting consequence of this analysis of rates of convergence is that, in many cases, we can always find a convergent direct iteration scheme for a root.

Example 21.3.5. *If the function $F(x)$ is invertible and if α is a root of the equation $x = F(x)$, show that, in most cases, one of the iteration schemes*

$$x_{n+1} = F(x_n), \qquad n \geq 0, \qquad \text{or} \qquad x_{n+1} = F^{-1}(x_n), \qquad n \geq 0,$$

will converge to α, provided that x_0 is chosen suitably.

If $y = F(x)$, then $x = F^{-1}(y)$. The chain rule tells us that $\dfrac{dy}{dx}\dfrac{dx}{dy} = 1$, from which we deduce that $F'(\alpha)(F^{-1})'(\alpha) = 1$. Unless $|F'(\alpha)| = 1$, one of the numbers $F'(\alpha)$ and $(F^{-1})'(\alpha)$ will have modulus less than 1, and the matching direct iteration scheme will be convergent at α.

EXERCISE 21B

1. Consider the iterative scheme

   $$x_0 = 0.2, \qquad x_{n+1} = x_n^3 + 2x_n^2 + \tfrac{1}{2}x_n, \qquad n \geq 0.$$

   Calculate x_n and $2^n x_n$ for $0 \leq n \leq 10$, and postulate an inequality of the form $0 \leq x_n \leq A2^{-n}$, where A is an integer.

2. In each part of this question, sketch the graph of $y = F(x)$, and hence decide whether the iteration $x_{n+1} = F(x_n)$, with initial approximation x_0, is suitable for finding the root of the equation $x = F(x)$ near to $x = x_0$. When this iteration scheme is suitable, find the root. When the iteration scheme is unsuitable, find $F^{-1}(x)$ and use it to find the root. Give your answers to 3 decimal places in parts (a) and (b), and to 4 decimal places in the remaining parts.

   a) $F(x) = \frac{3}{x} - 1, \quad x_0 = 1,$

   b) $F(x) = 5 - e^{3x}, \quad x_0 = 0,$

   c) $F(x) = \frac{1}{2}\tan x, \quad x_0 = 1,$

   d) $F(x) = 30 - \frac{1}{10}x^6, \quad x_0 = -2,$

   e) $F(x) = 2\sin x, \quad x_0 = \frac{1}{2}\pi.$

3. In each part of this question, find a constant k for which the iterative scheme $x_{n+1} + kx_{n+1} = kx_n + F(x_n)$, or

   $$x_{n+1} = \tfrac{1}{k+1}(kx_n + F(x_n)), \qquad n \geq 0,$$

   is a better iterative scheme to determine the root of $x = F(x)$ near the given value of x_0. In each case, find the root to 4 significant figures.

   a) $F(x) = 2 - 5\ln x, \quad x_0 = 1,$

   b) $F(x) = x^2 + 6\ln x - 50, \quad x_0 = 6,$

   c) $F(x) = \frac{1}{48}(x^4 - x^7 - 192), \quad x_0 = -2,$

   d) $F(x) = x\ln x - e^{-x} - 20, \quad x_0 = 12.$

21.4 The Newton-Raphson Formula

21.4.1. QUADRATIC CONVERGENCE

In the 1970s, when pocket calculators were first becoming cheap enough to be bought by students, they were fairly elementary. Operations like addition, subtraction, multiplication and division were possible, and there was a single memory, which could store one number only. How did people use these calculators to calculate square roots? Students were taught an iterative scheme which was extraordinarily efficient.

To calculate the square root of k, for example, a student took a first guess u, and then calculated the average of that guess and k divided by that guess; the result $\frac{1}{2}(u + \frac{k}{u})$ became the new guess. In our current notation, students used the iterative scheme

$$x_{n+1} = \tfrac{1}{2}\left(x_n + \tfrac{k}{x_n}\right), \qquad n \geq 0.$$

When calculating $\sqrt{2}$, with $x_0 = 1$, the first few terms in this sequence are 1, 1.5, 1.416666667, 1.414215686, 1.414213562; we have achieved 10 significant figure accuracy at the term x_4.

This iteration scheme is a case of direct iteration with the function $F(x) = \frac{1}{2}(x + \frac{k}{x})$; since $F'(x) = \frac{1}{2}(1 - \frac{k}{x^2})$, we see that $F'(\sqrt{k}) = 0$. The fact that the derivative of F at the root is 0 indicates that something quite special is happening; the error analysis for direct iteration does not really work (putting $F'(\alpha) = 0$ into the approximation $F(x) - \alpha \approx F'(\alpha)(x - \alpha)$ just gives us that $F(x) - \alpha \approx 0$, which is true, but not helpful).

The fact that $F'(\sqrt{k}) = 0$ indicates that the rate of convergence of this iteration scheme is faster than **any** exponential decay. Let us find out how good the convergence actually is.

For simplicity, we shall focus on the method for calculating the square root of 2, so that $k = 2$. A little algebra shows us that

$$x_{n+1} - \sqrt{2} = \tfrac{1}{2}(x_n + \tfrac{2}{x_n}) - \sqrt{2} = \tfrac{1}{2x_n}(x_n^2 - 2\sqrt{2}x_n + 2) = \tfrac{1}{2x_n}(x - \sqrt{2})^2$$

Provided that x_n is positive, this tells us that $x_{n+1} \geq \sqrt{2}$. If we start with $x_0 = 1$, it follows that $x_n \geq 1$ for all $n \geq 0$, and hence that

$$0 \leq x_{n+1} - \sqrt{2} \leq \tfrac{1}{2}(x - \sqrt{2})^2 \leq (x_n - \sqrt{2})^2.$$

Thus $|x_1 - \sqrt{2}| < |x_0 - \sqrt{2}|^2$, $|x_2 - \sqrt{2}| \leq |x_1 - \sqrt{2}|^2 \leq |x_0 - \sqrt{2}|^4$, $|x_3 - \sqrt{2}| \leq |x_2 - \sqrt{2}|^2 = |x_0 - \sqrt{2}|^8$ and so on. After a little thought we realise that

$$|x_n - \sqrt{2}| \leq |x_0 - \sqrt{2}|^{2^n} = (\sqrt{2} - 1)^{2^n}, \qquad n \geq 0.$$

so the errors head towards 0 extremely fast, much faster than any exponential decay - the nth error is an exponential power of an exponentially large quantity (2^n), and in some sense is 'doubly' exponentially small.

Key Fact 21.5 Quadratic Convergence

Any iteration scheme, with limit α, which exhibits behaviour of the form

$$|x_{n+1} - \alpha| \leq A|x_n - \alpha|^2, \qquad n \geq 0,$$

for some constant A, is said to display **quadratic convergence**. Provided that x_0 is close enough to α, a quadratically convergent iteration scheme converges faster than any rate of exponential convergence.

In this final Section of this Chapter we shall investigate a particularly simple iteration technique which, in favourable circumstances, is quadratically convergent.

21.4.2. THE DETAILS OF THE FORMULA

Suppose that are attempting to solve the equation $f(x) = 0$, where $f(x)$ is a differentiable function. Let α be a zero of this function, and that u is an approximation to α.

Consider drawing the tangent at P, the point $(u, f(u))$ on the curve with x-coordinate u, and finding the x-coordinate v of the point where this tangent meets the x-axis. It seems reasonable that v will be another approximation to α.

If the graph of $y = f(x)$ were a straight line, v would be equal to α, whatever the value of u. The straighter that the graph of $y = f(x)$ is, the closer v is to α.

What we need is the mathematical formula for determining v in terms of u. The tangent to the curve $y = f(x)$ at the point P has gradient $f'(u)$ and passes through the point $(u, f(u)$; thus it has equation

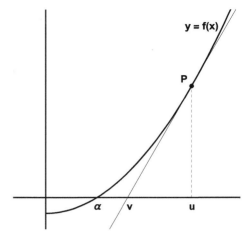

Figure 21.9

$$y - f(u) = f'(u)(x - u).$$

This tangent passes through the point $(v, 0)$, and so $-f(u) = f'(u)(v - u)$, from which we deduce that

$$v = u - \frac{f(u)}{f'(u)}.$$

If we iterate this process, we obtain an iterative scheme

> **Key Fact 21.6** The Newton-Raphson Formula
>
> The **Newton-Raphson Formula** is the iterative scheme
>
> $$x_{n+1} = x_n - \frac{f(x_n)}{f'(x_n)}, \qquad n \geq 0,$$
>
> for solving the equation $f(x) = 0$.

Example 21.4.1. *Find the positive root of the equation $x^3 + 2x^2 - 2 = 0$, giving the answer to 4 decimal places.*

The function $f(x) = x^3 + 2x^2 - 2$ has $f(0) = -2$ and $f(1) = 1$; once $x > 1$ we have $f(x) = x^3 + 2(x^2 - 1) > 0$, so there is only one positive root to this cubic equation (the other two roots are, in fact, complex), and it lies between 0 and 1. The Newton-Raphson formula in this case defines the iterative scheme

$$x_{n+1} = x_n - \frac{f(x_n)}{f'(x_n)} = x_n - \frac{x_n^3 + 2x_n^2 - 2}{3x_n^2 + 4x_n} = \frac{2(x_n^3 + x_n^2 + 1)}{3x_n(x_n + 4)}, \qquad n \geq 0.$$

It is not necessary to perform the algebraic simplification, given the power of modern calculators, but it is sometimes convenient.

The presence of the term x_n in the denominator tells us that we cannot use 0 as the initial value for x_0. If we put $x_0 = 1$ we obtain $x_1 = 0.857143$, $x_2 = 0.839545$, $x_3 = 0.839287$ and $x_4 = 0.839287$. To 4 decimal places, the root is 0.8393 (as can be checked by looking for a sign change).

Example 21.4.2. *Find the solution of the equation $x \sin x = 1$ in the range $0 < x < \frac{1}{2}\pi$.*

Since the function $f(x) = x \sin x - 1$ is such that $f(0) < 0 < f(\frac{1}{2}\pi)$, there is a solution to the desired equation in the range. Since $f'(x) = \sin x + x \cos x$ is positive for $0 < x < \frac{1}{2}\pi$, there is only one root in this range. The Newton-Raphson formula

$$x_{n+1} = x_n - \frac{x_n \sin x_n - 1}{\sin x_n + x_n \cos x_n} = \frac{x_n^2 \cos x_n + 1}{\sin x_n + x_n \cos x_n}, \qquad n \geq 0,$$

with the starting value $x_0 = 1$, yields $x_1 = 1.114729$, $x_2 = 1.114157$, $x_3 = 1.114157$. The root is 1.11416, correct to 5 decimal places.

Food For Thought 21.2

Like any iterative scheme, it is important to choose x_0 carefully. If x_0 is not chosen near the root α that we are looking for, then unexpected behaviour might occur (but this is the same for any other iterative scheme). Crucially for the Newton-Raphson formula, its main danger lies in the fact that the formula requires us to divide by $f'(x_n)$; thus the change between x_n and x_{n+1} can be large if the derivative $f'(x_n)$ is close to zero, and results can be unexpected.

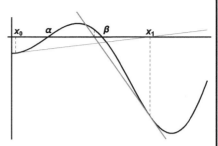

Figure 21.10

In the previous Example, for example, choosing $x_0 = 0.2$ yields a sequence which converges rapidly to 2.7886, choosing $x_0 = 0.1$ yields a sequence converging to 12.6455, and choosing $x_0 = 0.01$ yields a sequence converging to 50.2854. The equation $x \sin x = 1$ has many solutions, and applying the Newton-Raphson formula at a point where the gradient is close to zero results in the iterative scheme zeroing in on a root we had not expected!

Example 21.4.3. *The iterative scheme to calculate* $\sqrt{k}$,

$$x_{n+1} = \tfrac{1}{2}\left(x_n + \tfrac{k}{x_n}\right), \qquad n \geq 0,$$

is an instance of the Newton-Raphson formula.

With $f(x) = x^2 - k$, the Newton-Raphson formula reads

$$x_{n+1} = x_n - \frac{x_n^2 - k}{2x_n} = \frac{x_n^2 + k}{2x_n} = \tfrac{1}{2}\left(x_n + \tfrac{k}{x_n}\right),$$

and so we are done.

21.4.3. RATES OF CONVERGENCE

The iterative scheme for $\sqrt{k}$ converged quadratically, and was an example of the Newton-Raphson formula. Our examples for this formula have all shown fast rates of convergence. These three statements are connected, and one of the particular strengths of the Newton-Raphson formula is that is exhibits quadratic convergence.

As usual, then, let α be a root of the equation $f(x) = 0$. Provided that x is close to α, we have

$$\frac{f(x)}{x - \alpha} = \frac{f(x) - f(\alpha)}{x - \alpha} \approx f'(\alpha), \qquad \frac{f'(x) - f'(\alpha)}{x - \alpha} \approx f''(\alpha)$$

and hence we deduce that

$$f(x) \approx f'(\alpha)(x - \alpha) \quad , \quad f'(x) - f'(\alpha) \approx f''(\alpha)(x - \alpha),$$

More simply, we can assume that

$$f'(x) \approx f'(\alpha).$$

Thus we deduce that

$$(x - \alpha)f'(x) - f(x) \approx (x - \alpha)[f'(x) - f'(\alpha)] \approx f''(\alpha)(x - \alpha)^2$$

and hence, looking at the Newton-Raphson formula

$$x_{n+1} - \alpha = x_n - \alpha - \frac{f(x_n)}{f'(x_n)} = \frac{(x_n - \alpha)f'(x_n) - f(x_n)}{f'(x_n)} \approx \frac{f''(\alpha)(x_n - \alpha)^2}{f'(x_n)} \approx \frac{f''(\alpha)}{f'(\alpha)}(x_n - \alpha)^2,$$

which confirms that fact that the Newton-Raphson formula exhibits quadratic rates of convergence.

EXERCISE 21C

1. Show that the equation $x^3 - 7x + 2 = 0$ has a root between 0 and 1. Using the Newton-Raphson formula with $x_0 = 0$, evaluate x_1, x_2, x_3 and x_4 to 6 decimal places, identify the root to the same degree of accuracy.

2. Show that the equation $2x^4 - 3x - 1 = 0$ has a solution between $x = 1$ and $x = 2$. Using the Newton-Raphson formula, find this root, accurate to 4 decimal places.

3. Use the Newton-Raphson formula to find the root of the equation $9 - x - x^3 = \ln x$, giving your answer correct to 3 decimal places.

4. A cube of clay of side $2x$ cm is remodelled into a cube of side 2 cm and a cylinder of height 5 cm and radius x cm. Use the Newton-Raphson formula to determine the value of x, giving your answer to 3 decimal places.

5. Find all three real solutions of the cubic equation $x^3 - 25x^2 + 4x + 10 = 0$, using the Newton-Raphson formula to obtain answers accurate to 4 decimal places.

6. Using the Newton-Raphson formula, find the solution to the equation $\tan x = e^{-x}$ in the range $0 < x < \frac{1}{2}\pi$. What is the solution to this equation in the range $\pi < x < \frac{3}{2}\pi$? Give both answers accurate to 4 decimal places.

7. Use the Newton-Raphson formula to solve the equation $2^x + 3^x = 6^x$ for $x > 0$.

8. Use the Newton-Raphson formula to find the smallest positive solution of the equation $\cos 5x = 0.2$, correct to 4 decimal places. Compare your answer with a solution obtained by trigonometry.

9*. Use the Newton-Raphson formula to find two positive numbers x such that $x^{1/x} = 1.3$, giving both answers correct to 4 decimal places.

10*. If u_n is a sequences such that $u_{n+1} = Au_n^2$ for $n \geq 0$ and some constant A, show that

$$u_n = A^{2^n - 1} \times u_0^{2^n} \quad n \geq 0.$$

How small must u_0 be for u_n to converge quadratically to zero?

Chapter 21: Summary

- **The Sign-Change Principle** If f is a function defined and continuous for $p \leq x \leq q$, and if $f(p)$ and $f(q)$ have opposite signs, then f has a zero between p and q.

- **Direct Iteration** The iterative scheme

$$x_{n+1} = F(x_n), \qquad n \geq 0,$$

will, if x_0 is sufficiently close to the root α of the equation $x = F(x)$:

  ★ be monotonic (either towards or away from α) if $F'(\alpha) > 0$,
  ★ be oscillatory about α if $F'(\alpha) < 0$,
  ★ converge exponentially to α if $|F'(\alpha)| < 1$, with $|x_n - \alpha| \approx |F'(\alpha)|^n |x_0 - \alpha|$,
  ★ diverge away from α if $|F'(\alpha)| > 1$.

- The **Newton-Raphson formula**

$$x_{n+1} = x_n - \frac{f(x_n)}{f'(x_n)}, \qquad n \geq 0,$$

converges quadratically to a solution α of the equation $f(\alpha) = 0$, provided that x_0 is close enough to α.

1. The vectors $\overrightarrow{AB}$ and $\overrightarrow{AC}$ are $\begin{pmatrix} -1 \\ 0 \\ 3 \end{pmatrix}$ and $\begin{pmatrix} 2 \\ 4 \\ 3 \end{pmatrix}$ respectively. The vectors $\overrightarrow{AD}$ is the sum of the $\overrightarrow{AB}$ and $\overrightarrow{AC}$. Determine the acute angle, in degrees correct to one decimal place, between the diagonals of the parallelogram $ABDC$. (OCR)

2. The vectors $\overrightarrow{AB}$ and $\overrightarrow{AC}$ are $\begin{pmatrix} -2 \\ 6 \\ -3 \end{pmatrix}$ and $\begin{pmatrix} -2 \\ -3 \\ 6 \end{pmatrix}$ respectively.

   a) Determine the lengths of the vectors.

   b) Find the scalar product $\overrightarrow{AB} \cdot \overrightarrow{AC}$.

   c) Use your result to calculate the acute angle between the vectors. Give the angle in degrees correct to one decimal place. (OCR)

3. The position vectors of three points A, B and C with respect to a fixed origin O are $2\mathbf{i} - 2\mathbf{j} + \mathbf{k}$, $4\mathbf{i} + 2\mathbf{j} + \mathbf{k}$ and $\mathbf{i} + \mathbf{j} + 3\mathbf{k}$ respectively. Find unit vectors in the directions of $\overrightarrow{CA}$ and $\overrightarrow{CB}$. Calculate angle $\angle ACB$ in degrees, correct to 1 decimal place. (OCR)

4. a) Find the angle between the vectors $2\mathbf{i} + 3\mathbf{j} + 6\mathbf{k}$ and $3\mathbf{i} + 4\mathbf{j} + 12\mathbf{k}$.

   b) The vectors $\mathbf{a}$ and $\mathbf{b}$ are non-zero.

      i. Given that $\mathbf{a} + \mathbf{b}$ is perpendicular to $\mathbf{a} - \mathbf{b}$, prove that $|\mathbf{a}| = |\mathbf{b}|$.
      ii. Given instead that $|\mathbf{a} + \mathbf{b}| = |\mathbf{a} - \mathbf{b}|$, prove that $\mathbf{a}$ and $\mathbf{b}$ are perpendicular. (OCR)

5. The three-dimensional vector $\mathbf{r}$, which has positive components, has magnitude 1 and makes angles of $60°$ with each of the unit vectors $\mathbf{i}$ and $\mathbf{j}$.

   a) Write $\mathbf{r}$ as a column vector.

   b) State the angle between $\mathbf{r}$ and the unit vector $\mathbf{k}$.

6. The points A, B and C have position vectors given respectively by $\mathbf{a} = 7\mathbf{i} + 4\mathbf{j} - 2\mathbf{k}$, $\mathbf{b} = 5\mathbf{i} + 3\mathbf{j} - 3\mathbf{k}$, $\mathbf{c} = 6\mathbf{i} + 5\mathbf{j} - 4\mathbf{k}$.

   a) Find the angle $\angle BAC$ b) Find the area of the triangle ABC.
   (OCR)

7. The points A, B, C have coordinates $(3,1,-3)$, $(5,1,-3)$ and $(7,20,2)$ respectively. Find the vectors $\overrightarrow{AB}$ and $\overrightarrow{AC}$. Find numbers λ, μ such that $\overrightarrow{OA} = \lambda \overrightarrow{AB} + \mu \overrightarrow{AC}$. What does this tell you about the points A, B C and the origin O?

8. Prove that, if $(\mathbf{c} - \mathbf{b}) \cdot \mathbf{a} = 0$ and $(\mathbf{c} - \mathbf{a}) \cdot \mathbf{b} = 0$, then $(\mathbf{b} - \mathbf{a}) \cdot \mathbf{c} = 0$. Show that this can be used to prove the following geometrical results.

   a) The lines through the vertices of a triangle ABC perpendicular to the opposite sides meet in a point.

b) If the tetrahedron $OABC$ has two pairs of perpendicular opposite edges, the third pair of edges is perpendicular.

Prove also that, in both cases, $OA^2 + BC^2 = OB^2 + CA^2 = OC^2 + AB^2$.

9. Two lines have equations $\mathbf{r} = \begin{pmatrix} 1 \\ 3 \\ 2 \end{pmatrix} + \lambda \begin{pmatrix} 4 \\ -2 \\ 1 \end{pmatrix}$ and $\mathbf{r} = \begin{pmatrix} 3 \\ 8 \\ 7 \end{pmatrix} + \mu \begin{pmatrix} 2 \\ -3 \\ -1 \end{pmatrix}$. Show that these lines intersect, and find the position vector of the point of intersection. (OCR)

10. An aeroplane climbs so that its position relative to the airport control tower t minutes after take-off is given by the vector $\mathbf{r} = \begin{pmatrix} -1 \\ -2 \\ 0 \end{pmatrix} + t \begin{pmatrix} 4 \\ 5 \\ 0.6 \end{pmatrix}$, the units being kilometres. The x- and y-axes point towards the east and north respectively. Calculate the closest distance of the aeroplane from the control tower during this flight, giving your answer correct to 2 decimal places. To the nearest second, how many seconds after leaving the ground is the aeroplane at its closest to the airport control tower?

11. Lines ℓ_1 and ℓ_2 have vector equations

$$\mathbf{r} = \begin{pmatrix} 2 \\ -3 \\ 1 \end{pmatrix} + \lambda \begin{pmatrix} 5 \\ 1 \\ 2 \end{pmatrix} \qquad \mathbf{r} = \begin{pmatrix} m \\ 2 \\ 5 \end{pmatrix} + \mu \begin{pmatrix} 2 \\ 1 \\ -1 \end{pmatrix}$$

respectively, where λ and μ are scalar parameters, and m is a constant.

a) The points P and Q have coordinates $(7, -2, 1)$ and $(5, 4, 3)$ respectively.

   i. Determine the vector $\overrightarrow{PQ}$, and show that the length $PQ = 2\sqrt{11}$.

   ii. Verify that $\overrightarrow{PQ}$ is perpendicular to both ℓ_1 and ℓ_2.

   iii. Show that P lies on ℓ_1, and the value of m for which Q lies on ℓ_2. Write down the shortest distance from ℓ_1 to ℓ_2 in this case.

b) Find the size of the acute angle between the lines ℓ_1 and ℓ_2, giving your answer correct to the nearest $0.1°$.

c) Determine the value of m, different to the value you found in part (a), for which ℓ_1 and ℓ_2 intersect. (OCR)

12. The line ℓ has vector equation $\mathbf{r} = 2\mathbf{i} + s(\mathbf{i} + 3\mathbf{j} + 4\mathbf{k})$.

a)   i. Show that the line ℓ intersects the line with equation $\mathbf{r} = \mathbf{k} + t(\mathbf{i} + \mathbf{j} + \mathbf{k})$, and determine the position vector of the point of intersection.

   ii. Calculate the acute angle, to the nearest degree, of these two lines.

b) Find the position vector of the points on ℓ which are exactly $5\sqrt{10}$ units from the origin.

c) Determine the position vector of the point on ℓ which is closest to the point with position vector $6\mathbf{i} - \mathbf{j} + 3\mathbf{k}$. (OCR)

13. The centre line of an underground railway tunnel follows a line given by $\mathbf{r} = t \begin{pmatrix} 10 \\ 8 \\ -1 \end{pmatrix}$ for $0 \leq t \leq 40$, the units being metres. The centre line of another tunnel at present stops at the point with position vector $\begin{pmatrix} 200 \\ 100 \\ -25 \end{pmatrix}$, and it is proposed to extend this line in a direction $\begin{pmatrix} 5 \\ 7 \\ u \end{pmatrix}$. The constant u has to be chosen so that, at the point where one tunnel passes over the other, there is at least 15 meters difference in depth between the centre lines of the two tunnels. What restriction does this impose on the value of u?

Another requirement is that the tunnel must not be inclined at more than $5°$ to the horizontal. What values of u satisfy both requirements?

14. The non-collinear points A, B and C have position vectors $\mathbf{a}$, $\mathbf{b}$ and $\mathbf{c}$ respectively. The points P and Q have position vectors $\mathbf{p}$ and $\mathbf{q}$ respectively, given by

$$\mathbf{p} = \lambda \mathbf{a} + (1 - \lambda)\mathbf{b} \qquad \mathbf{q} = \mu \mathbf{a} + (1 - \mu)\mathbf{c},$$

where $0 < \lambda < 1$ and $\mu > 1$. Draw a diagram showing A, B, C, P and Q.

Given that $CQ \times BP = AB \times AC$, find μ in terms of λ and show that, for all values of λ, the line PQ passes through the fixed point D, with position vector $\mathbf{d} = -\mathbf{a} + \mathbf{b} + \mathbf{c}$. What can be said about the quadrilateral $ABDC$? (STEP)

15. Given that z is a complex number such that $z + 3z^{\star} = 12 + 8i$, find z. (OCR)

16. Given that $3i$ is a root of the equation $3z^3 - 5z^2 + 27z - 45 = 0$, find the other two roots. (OCR)

17. Two of the roots of a cubic equation, in which all the coefficients are real, are 2 and $1 + 3i$. State the third root and find the cubic equation. (OCR)

18. It is given that $3 - i$ is a root of the quadratic equation $z^2 - (a + bi)z + 4(1 + 3i) = 0$, where a and b are real.

    a) find the values of a and b,

    b) find the other root of the quadratic equation, given that it is of the form ki, where k is real. (OCR)

19. Find the roots of the equation $z^2 = 21 - 20i$. (OCR)

20. Verify that $(3 - 2i)^2 = 5 - 12i$. Find the two roots of the equation $(z - i)^2 = 5 - 12i$. (OCR)

21. Consider the complex number $w = -\frac{1}{2} + \frac{1}{2}i\sqrt{3}$. Calculate w^2 and w^3. Deduce that $w^4 - w^3 + w^2 + 2 = 0$.

    Write down two roots of the equation $z^4 - z^3 + z^2 + 2 = 0$, and hence solve this equation completely.

22. Two complex numbers, z and w, satisfy the inequalities $|z - 3 - 2i| \leq 2$ and $|w - 7 - 5i| \leq 1$. By drawing an Argand diagram, find the least possible value of $|z - w|$. (OCR)

23. Consider the complex number $z = \frac{1}{2}(1 + i)$. Show that

$$1 + z + z^2 + \cdots + z^{4n-1} = (1 + i)\left[1 - z^{4n}\right]$$

    for any positive integer n. Hence evaluate the infinite sum

$$\sum_{m=0}^{\infty} z^m$$

24.   a) The complex number z satisfies the equation $\left(z + \frac{2i}{k}\right)\left(\frac{1}{z} - \frac{2i}{k}\right) = 1$, where k is a positive real number. Obtain a quadratic equation for z, and show that its solution can be expressed in the form $ikz = a \pm \sqrt{bk^2 + ck + d}$ for suitable real numbers a, b, c and d. Show that z is purely imaginary when $k \leq 1$.

    b) A second complex number α is defined in terms of z by $\alpha = 1 + \frac{2i}{kz}$. What can be said about α when $k \leq 1$? Show that $|\alpha| = 1$ when $k \geq 1$.

    c) A third complex number β is defined by $\frac{1}{\beta} = 1 - \frac{i}{k}$. By finding the real and imaginary parts of $\beta - \frac{1}{2}ki$, show that β lies on a circle with centre $\frac{1}{2}ki$ and radius $\frac{1}{2}k$. (OCR)

25. Given that $5x - 6 \equiv A(x^2 + 4) + (Bx + C)(x + 2)$, find the values of A, B and C by substituting $x = -2$, $2i$ and $-2i$ into this equation. Hence split

$$\frac{5x - 6}{(x + 2)(x^2 + 4)}$$

    into partial fractions.

26*. Define the modulus of a complex number z and give the geometric interpretation of $|z_1 - z_2|$ for two complex numbers z_1 and z_2. On the basis of this interpretation establish the inequality

$$|z_1 + z_2| \leq |z_1| + |z_2|.$$

    Use this result to derive a corresponding inequality for $|z_1 + z_2 + \cdots + z_n|$ for n complex numbers $z_1, z_2, \ldots, z_n$.

    The complex numbers $a_1, a_2, \ldots, a_n$ satisfy $|a_j| \leq 3$ for $i = 1, 2, \ldots, n$. Prove that the equation

$$a_1 z + a_2 z^2 + \cdots + a_n z^n = 1$$

    has no solution z with $|z| \leq \frac{1}{4}$. (STEP)

27. Find the positive integer N such that $40e^{-x} = x^2$ has a root between N and $N+1$.

28. a) On the same diagram, sketch the graphs of $y = 2^{-x}$ and $y = x^2$.

 b) One of the points of intersection of these graphs has a positive x-coordinate. Find this x-coordinate correct to 2 decimal places and give a brief indication of your method. (OCR)

29. Find, correct to 2 decimal places, the x-coordinate of the turning point on the curve with equation $y = 5\cos x + x^2$, $x > 0$.

30. The region, R, of the plane enclosed by the axes, the curve $y = e^x + 4$ and the line $x = 2$ has area A. Find, correct to 4 significant figures, the value of m, $0 < m < 2$, such that the portion of R between the y-axis and the line $x = m$ has area $\frac{1}{2}A$.

31. Show that the equation $3.5x = 1.6^x$ has a real solution between 6 and 7. By rearranging the equation into the form $x = a + b\ln x$, determine this root correct to 2 decimal places.

32. a) Given that $f(x) = e^{2x} - 6x$, evaluate $f(0)$ and $f(1)$, giving each answer correct to 3 decimal places. Explain how the equation $f(x) = 0$ could still have a root in the interval $0 < x < 1$ even though $f(0)f(1) > 0$.

 b) Rewrite the equation $f(x) = 0$ in the form $x = F(x)$, for some suitable function F. Taking $x_0 = 0.5$ as an initial approximation, use an iterative method to determine one of the roots of this equation correct to 3 decimal places. How could you demonstrate that this root has the required degree of accuracy?

 c) Deduce the value, to 2 decimal places, of one of the roots of the equation $e^x - 3x = 0$.

33. a) Show that the equation $x^3 - 3x^2 - 1 = 0$ has a root α between $x = 3$ and $x = 4$.

 b) The iterative formula $x_{n+1} = 3 + \frac{1}{x_n^2}$ is used to calculate a sequence of approximations to this root. Taking $x_0 = 3$ as an initial approximation to α, determine the values of x_1, x_2, x_3 and x_4 correct to 5 decimal places. State the value of α to 3 decimal places and justify this degree of accuracy.

34. a) Show that the equation $x + \ln x - 4 = 0$ has a root α in the interval $2 < x < 3$.

 b) Find which of the two iterative forms $x_{n+1} = e^{4-x_n}$ and $x_{n+1} = 4 - \ln x_n$ is more likely to give a convergent sequence of approximations to α, giving a reason for your answer. Use your chosen form to determine α correct to 2 decimal places.

35. a) Find the positive integer N such that the equation $(t-1)\ln 4 = \ln(9t)$ has a solution $t = r$ in the interval $N < t < N+1$.

 b) Write down two possible rearrangements of this equation in the form $t = F(t)$ and $t = F^{-1}(t)$. Show which of these two arrangements is more suitable for using iteratively to determine an approximation to r to 3 decimal places, and find such an approximation.

36. a) Find the coordinates of the points of intersection of the graphs with equations $y = x$ and $y = g(x)$, where $g(x) = \frac{5}{x}$.

 b) Show that the iterative process defined by $x_0 = 2$, $x_{n+1} = g(x_n)$ cannot be used to find good approximations to the positive root of the equation $x = \frac{5}{x}$.

 c) Describe why the use of the inverse function $g^{-1}(x)$ is also inappropriate in this case.

 d) Find an effective iterative scheme for this problem, and find the positive root of the equation, correct to 6 decimal places.

37. Given the one-to-one function $F(x)$, explain why roots of the equation $F(x) = F^{-1}(x)$ are also roots of the equation $x = F(x)$.

 Use this to solve the following equations, giving your answers correct to 5 decimal places.

 a) $x^3 - 1 = \sqrt[3]{1+x}$, b) $\frac{1}{10}e^x = \ln(10x)$.

38. Use the Newton-Raphson formula to find the root, to 4 decimal places, of the equation $\sin(\sin x) = 5 - e^x$ in the region $1 < x < 2$.

39*. For practice, Philip was using the Newton-Raphson method to find roots of the equation $\cos x = 0$. He was using the iterative scheme

$$x_{n+1} = x_n - \frac{\cos x_n}{-\sin x_n} = x_n + \cot x_n, \qquad n \geq 0.$$

a) The first value that Philip chose for x_0 made his calculator declare a Maths Error on the first iteration. What happened? What was the smallest nonnegative value of x_0 that Philip could have chosen.

b) Philip made a small correction to avoid this problem. This time his iterations gave him $x_1 = \pi$, and therefore his calculator declared a Maths Error at the second iteration. What value had Philip chosen this time? Given your answer correct to 4 decimal places.

Part 2

Mechanics

General Kinematics

In this chapter we will learn:

- to recognise distance and speed as scalar quantities, and displacement, velocity and acceleration as vector quantities,

- to sketch and interpret displacement-time and velocity-time graphs, and understand how velocity is represented on a displacement-time graph, and how displacement and acceleration are represented on a velocity-time graph,

- to use the formulae for motion with constant acceleration,

- to use differentiation and integration with respect to time to solve simple problems concerning displacement, velocity and acceleration,

- to be able to perform calculations in one, two and three dimensions.

22.1 Displacement And Velocity

A Roman legion marched out of the city of Alexandria along a straight road, with a velocity of 100 paces per minute due east. Where was the legion 90 minutes later?

Notice the word **velocity**, rather than speed. This is because we are told not only how fast the legion marched, but also in which direction. Velocity is speed in a particular direction. Two cars travelling in opposite directions on a north-south motorway might have the same speed of 90 kilometres per hour, but they have different velocities. One has a velocity of 90 km h^{-1} north and the other, a velocity of 90 km h^{-1} south.

The answer to the question in the first paragraph is, of course, that the legion was 9000 paces (9 Roman miles) east of Alexandria. The legion made a **displacement** of 9000 paces east. Displacement is distance in a particular direction.

It is also possible to travel a distance, and yet experience no displacement. Take one lap around a running track, for instance.

Quantities with magnitude and direction are, as we know, **vectors**, and quantities that have magnitude, but no direction, are called **scalars**. We observe that displacement and velocity are vectors, and that distance and speed are scalars.

Key Fact 22.1 Displacement And Velocity

- **Displacement** is a vector quantity and **distance** is a scalar quantity. The magnitude of a displacement is a distance.

- **Velocity** is a vector quantity and **speed** is a scalar quantity. The magnitude of a velocity is a speed.

The calculation $9000 = 100 \times 90$, that was used to determine the position of the Roman legion above, is a special case of a general rule.

> **Key Fact 22.2** Constant Velocity And Displacement
>
> An object moving with constant velocity $\mathbf{u}$ for time t makes a displacement $\mathbf{s}$, where
>
> $$\mathbf{s} = t\mathbf{u}.$$

This is an extension of the concept that distance is equal to speed multiplied by time (that concept is now reflected in the formula $|\mathbf{s}| = t|\mathbf{u}|$). Note that we are using the notation for vectors discussed in Chapter 19. Using vectors includes the fact that velocity and displacement are in the same direction as well.

Of course, for these relationships between displacement, time and velocity to be true, these three quantities have to be measured in consistent units. The so-called SI (standing for *Système Internationale*) system of units for these quantities are the metre (m), the second (s) and the metre per second (m s^{-1}), and are accepted internationally as the scientific standard set of units. That does not mean that we cannot perform calculations in other units.

Example 22.1.1. *An airliner flies from Cairo to Harare, a displacement of 5340 kilometres south, at a speed of 800 km h^{-1}. How long does the flight last?*

The velocity and the displacement are both due south, and so in this problem we can dispense with vector considerations, and just work with distance and speed. The distance to be travelled is $s = 5340$ at speed $u = 800$; the time taken is $\frac{s}{t} = 6.675$ hours, or 6 hours and 40.5 minutes.

This process of conversion from decimal time to hours and minutes (which we could have continued into hours, minutes and seconds) is a frequent source of student error. There are 60 minutes in an hour, and so there are $60 \times 0.675 = 40.5$ minutes, or 40 minutes and 30 seconds, in 0.675 hours.

It is clear that this model is not likely to be particularly accurate. Airplanes slow down at the beginning and end of each flight, so will not travel at a constant maximum speed.

Example 22.1.2. *A cyclist is travelling at 18 km h^{-1} along a road which heads due north. At a particular point in time, the cyclist is 150 m due east of a windmill in a nearby field. How far away from the windmill is the cyclist one minute later?*

A speed of 18 km h^{-1} is a speed of $18 \times \frac{1000}{3600} = 5$ ms^{-1} (there are 1000 metres in a kilometre, and 3600 seconds in an hour). In a minute, therefore, the cyclist has undergone a displacement of $5 \times 60 = 300$ m in a northerly direction. If we introduce unit vectors $\mathbf{i}$ and $\mathbf{j}$ pointing due east and due north, then since the initial displacement of the cyclist from the windmill is $150\mathbf{i}$ m, the displacement of the cyclist from the windmill after 1 minute is $150\mathbf{i} + 300\mathbf{j}$ m. The distance of the cyclist from the windmill is the magnitude $|150\mathbf{i} + 300\mathbf{j}|$ m of the displacement vector of the cyclist from the windmill. Thus the distance of the cyclist from the windmill at that time is

$$\sqrt{150^2 + 300^2} = 150\sqrt{5} = 335.4 \text{ m}.$$

22.2 Acceleration

A car starting from rest cannot immediately reach its top speed. There has to be period of time during which its velocity is changing. The rate at which velocity increases is called **acceleration**.

In the simplest case, velocity increases at a constant rate. Suppose that a train was accelerating from rest to 144 km h^{-1} in 100 seconds at a constant rate. Now 144 km h^{-1} is equal to 40 ms^{-1}, and hence the speed has to increase by 0.4 ms^{-1} every second. The SI unit of acceleration is ' ms^{-1} per second', or ' ms^{-1} s^{-1}, most commonly written as ms^{-2}. Thus the acceleration of the train is 0.4 ms^{-2}.

If the train's initial speed was 10 ms^{-1}, and it accelerated at 0.5 ms^{-2} for 60 seconds, then its speed would have increased by $0.5 \times 60 = 30$ ms^{-1}, and hence its final speed would be 40 ms^{-1}. This calculation is an example of a general result:

Key Fact 22.3 Acceleration

Acceleration is another vector quantity. Unfortunately, the modulus $|a|$ of acceleration **a** does not have its own title; it is also frequently referred to as acceleration.
An object subject to a constant acceleration **a** for a fixed time t experiences a change of velocity equal to $t\mathbf{a}$, so that
$$\mathbf{v} = \mathbf{u} + t\mathbf{a}$$
where **u** is the object's velocity before the acceleration, and **v** is its velocity after the acceleration.

In English there are separate words to describe negative accelerations, when an object is slowing down. An object subject to an acceleration of -5 ms^{-2} can also be said to have a **deceleration** of 5 ms^{-2}, or even a **retardation** of 5 ms^{-2}. The terms deceleration and retardation are used to describe the modulus of a negative acceleration.

22.3   One-Dimensional Motion

Frequently, a mathematical problem will be concerned with the behaviour of an object which is moving along a straight line. If we consider an object moving along the x-axis, then the object at the point $(x, 0)$ has position (its displacement from the origin O) equal to the vector $x\mathbf{i}$. (We remind the reader that, as in Chapter 19, we are using the symbols **i**, **j** and **k** to represent unit vectors pointing along the positive x-, y- and z-axes respectively.) Since the object cannot move off the x-axis, there is no reason to write the vector **i** down, and we will denote the object's displacement by the number x.

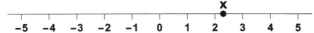

Figure 22.1

This can be confusing, since a single number is begin used to describe a vector. However, the only sort of vectors that we can have either point to the right or to the left. If $x > 0$, the displacement is to the right of 0, if $x < 0$, the displacement is to the left. A displacement x can be positive or negative; this is what enables x to represent a vector. Similarly, a negative velocity is to the left, while a positive velocity is to the right. Speed, being the magnitude of velocity, is always positive, however; an object moving one-dimensionally can have velocity -2 ms^{-1}, but must have speed 2 ms^{-1}, for example.

Key Fact 22.4 One-Dimensional Motion

A particle moving on a straight line will have its position represented by a number x. Displacements, distances, velocities, and speeds will all be represented by numbers. The vector nature of displacements, velocities and accelerations is reflected in the fact that these numbers can be both positive and negative.

22.4   Displacement-Time And Velocity-Time Graphs

We do not always have to use equations to describe mathematical models. Another method is to use graphs. There are two kinds of graph that are often useful in kinematics.

A **displacement-time graph**, like the one shown in Figure 22.2, plots the displacement s of a moving object against time t. Objects travelling with constant velocity will be represented by straight-line graphs. Stationary objects will be represented by horizontal lines. Accelerating objects will be represented by curves.

Since displacement is a vector quantity, it can be negative, and so it is permissible for a displacement-time graph to dip below the t-axis!

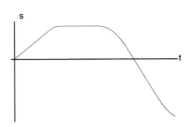

Figure 22.2

The second kind of graph is a **velocity-time graph**, as in Figure 22.3. This graph plots the velocity v of the moving object against time t. Objects travelling with constant velocity will be represented by horizontal lines. An object is stationary when its velocity-time graph meets the t-axis. Accelerating objects will be represented by slanting lines, and objects with constant acceleration will be represented by straight-line graphs.

Velocity is a vector quantity and can be negative, and so velocity-time graphs can dip below the t-axis.

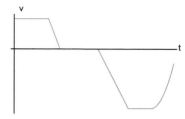

Figure 22.3

The above displacement-time and velocity-time graphs describe the same motion.

Key Fact 22.5 Using Displacement-Time And Velocity-Time Graphs

- In a displacement-time graph, the gradient of a straight-line segment is the current velocity of the object.

- In a velocity-time graph, the gradient of a straight-line segment is the current acceleration of the object.

- In a velocity-time graph, the displacement from the start up to time t is equal to the area under the velocity-time graph between the times of 0 and t.

The first two of these facts are immediate consequences of the one-dimensional versions of the relationships outlined in Key Facts 22.2 and 22.3 . The third is more tricky. An object travelling with constant velocity u will undergo a displacement of ut in time t, which is equal to the area of a rectangle of height u and width t, which is the area under the appropriate velocity-time graph for the correct time range. The fact that the area under the graph represents distance travelled for all velocity-time diagrams is more complex, and will be justified fully later.

Figure 22.4

Example 22.4.1. *A sprinter in a 100 metre race pushes off the starting block with speed 6 ms^{-1}, and then accelerates at a constant rate. He attains his maximum speed of 10 ms^{-1} after running 40 m, and continues at this top speed until the end of the race. How long does it take him to run the whole race?*

We do not know (yet) the amount of time the sprinter spends accelerating; call it T. We do know that the sprinter covers the last 60 m of the race at speed 10 ms^{-1}, and so that part of the race lasts $\frac{60}{10} = 6$ seconds. Since the sprinter covers 40 m during the first stage of the race, we deduce that

$$\tfrac{1}{2} \times (6 + 10) \times T = 40,$$

and hence $T = 5$. The runner completes the race is 11 seconds.

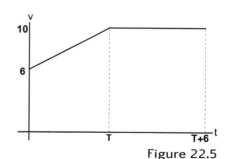

Figure 22.5

Example 22.4.2. *A train travelling between stations (which are 10 km apart) starts at one station. It accelerates from rest, at a constant acceleration of 0.2 ms^{-2}, until it reaches its maximum speed of 20 ms^{-1}. It travels at this constant speed for a period of time, and then decelerates to rest at a constant rate over a period of 50 seconds. It has then reached the other station. Draw a velocity-time diagram for the train during its journey. What is the acceleration of the train while it is coming to rest? How long did the whole journey take?*

The train accelerates from rest to 20 ms^{-1} at an acceleration of 0.2 ms^{-2}, and hence must do so in a period of 100 seconds. We do not yet know the length of time that the train travels at a constant speed; we call it T, and can draw the velocity-time diagram.

The train decelerates from 20 ms^{-1} to rest in 50 seconds, and hence experiences an acceleration of $\frac{-20}{50} = -0.4$ ms^{-2} (this is sometimes referred to as a **retardation** of 0.4 ms^{-2}).

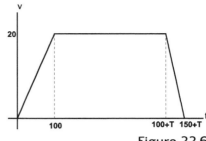

Figure 22.6

We could calculate the area under the graph by splitting it into two triangular regions and one rectangle; alternatively we could simply calculate its area using the formula for a trapezium:

$$\tfrac{1}{2} \times (T + 150 + T) \times 20 = 10000$$

which tells us that $2T + 150 = 1000$, so that $T = 425$. The journey lasts 425 seconds.

EXERCISE 22A

1. A train maintains a constant velocity of 60 ms^{-1} due south for 20 minutes. What is its displacement in that time? Give the distance in kilometres.

2. How long will it take for a cruise liner to sail a distance of 530 nautical miles at a speed of 25 knots? (A knot is a speed of 1 nautical mile per hour.)

3. Some Antarctic explorers walking towards the South Pole expect to average 1.8 kilometres per hour. What is their expected displacement in a day in which they walk for 14 hours?

4. Light travels at a speed of 3.00×10^8 ms^{-1}. Light from the star Sirius takes 8.65 years to reach the earth. What is the distance of Sirius from the earth in kilometres?

5. The speed limit on a motorway is 120 km h^{-1}. What is this in SI units?

6. A sheep is running in a large field. The shepherd is standing still in the middle of the field. Initially, the sheep has a displacement $10\mathbf{i} + 7\mathbf{j}$ metres from the shepherd, where $\mathbf{i}$ and $\mathbf{j}$ are unit vectors pointing due east and north respectively. The sheep has velocity $-2\mathbf{i} + 1\mathbf{j}$ ms^{-1}.

    a) What is the distance of the sheep from the shepherd after 2 seconds?

    b) Describe the displacement of the sheep from the shepherd after 5 seconds.

7. A plane takes from a runway at an airport. The runway is facing east. At the point of take-off, the plane has a displacement of $100\mathbf{j}$ m from the control tower, where $\mathbf{i}$, $\mathbf{j}$ and $\mathbf{k}$ are unit vectors pointing due east, north and vertically up, respectively. The plane's velocity on take-off is $75\mathbf{i} + 20\mathbf{k}$ ms^{-1}, which can be assumed to be constant for the first minute of flight.

    a) What is the plane's altitude after 1 minute of flight?

    b) What is the plane's displacement from the control tower at that time, and what is its distance from the control tower?

8. The straightest railway line in the world runs across the Nullarbor Plain in southern Australia, a distance of 500 kilometres. A train takes $12\frac{1}{2}$ hours to cover the distance. Model the journey by drawing:

    a) a velocity-time graph,   b) a displacement-time graph.

    Label your graphs to show the numbers 500 and $12\frac{1}{2}$ and to indicate the units used. Suggest some ways in which your models may not match the actual journey.

9. A police car accelerates from 15 ms^{-1} to 35 ms^{-1} in 5 seconds. The acceleration is constant. Illustrate this with a velocity-time graph. Calculate the acceleration of the car. Find the distance travelled by the car in this time.

10. A marathon competitor running at 5 ms^{-1} puts on a sprint when she is 100 metres from the finish, and covers this distance in 16 seconds. Assuming that her acceleration is constant, find how fast she is running as she crosses the finishing line.

11. A train travelling at 20 ms^{-1} starts to accelerate with constant acceleration. It covers the next kilometre in 25 seconds. Calculate the acceleration. Find also how fast the train is moving at the end of this time. Illustrate the motion of the train with a velocity-time graph.

    How long does the train take to cover the first half kilometre?

12. A long-jumper takes a run of 30 metres to accelerate to a speed of 10 ms^{-1} from a standing start. Find the time he takes to reach this speed, and hence calculate his acceleration. Illustrate his run-up with a velocity–time graph.

13. Starting from rest, an aircraft accelerates to its take-off speed of 60 ms^{-1} in a distance of 900 metres. Assuming constant acceleration, find how long the take-off run lasts. Calculate the acceleration.

14. A train is travelling at 80 ms^{-1} when the driver applies the brakes, producing a deceleration of 2 ms^{-2} for 30 seconds. How fast is the train then travelling, and how far does it travel while the brakes are on?

15. A balloon at a height of 300 m is descending at 10 ms^{-1} and decelerating at a rate of 0.4 ms^{-2}. How long will it take for the balloon to stop descending, and what will its height be then?

16. Two villages are 900 metres apart. A car leaves the first village travelling at 15 ms^{-1} and accelerates at $\frac{1}{2} \text{ ms}^{-2}$ for 30 seconds. How fast is it then travelling, and what distance has it covered in this time?

    The driver now sees the next village ahead, and decelerates so as to enter it at 15 ms^{-1}. What constant deceleration is needed to achieve this? How much time does the driver save by accelerating and decelerating, rather than by covering the whole distance at 15 ms^{-1}?

17. A car rounds a bend at 10 ms^{-1}, and then accelerates at $\frac{1}{2} \text{ ms}^{-2}$ along a straight stretch of road. There is a junction 400 m from the bend. When the car is 100 m from the junction, the driver brakes and brings the car to rest at the junction with constant deceleration. Draw a velocity-time graph to illustrate the motion of the car. Find how fast the car is moving when the brakes are applied, and the deceleration needed for the car to stop at the junction.

18. A motorbike and a car are waiting side by side at traffic lights. When the lights turn to green, the motorbike accelerates at 2.5 ms^{-2} up to a top speed of 20 ms^{-1}, and the car accelerates at 1.5 ms^{-2} up to a top speed of 30 ms^{-1}. Both then continue to move at constant speed. Draw velocity-time graphs for each vehicle, using the same axes, and sketch the displacement-time graphs as well.

    a) After what time will the motorbike and the car again be side by side?

    b) What is the greatest distance that the motorbike is in front of the car?

19*. A cyclist is free-wheeling down a long straight hill. The times between passing successive kilometre posts are 100 seconds and 80 seconds. Assuming his acceleration is constant, find this acceleration.

20*. A particle is moving along a straight line with constant acceleration. In an interval of T seconds it moves D metres; in the next interval of $3T$ seconds it moves $9D$ metres.

    How far does it move in a further interval of T seconds?

22.5 Constant Acceleration And SUVAT Equations

Although graphs are a useful way to represent one-dimensional problems, they can be a little cumbersome. By the end of this chapter we will discover techniques that will enable us to dispense with all diagrams, and solve kinematics problems entirely in algebra, but it is useful to discuss some of the ideas from these graphs before we do so.

One particularly useful area concerns problems of constant acceleration. There are many problems that we can consider in which an object experiences acceleration at a constant rate, and the equations that define its motion are sufficiently simple to make it worth learning them.

Suppose, therefore, that an object is travelling along a straight line with constant acceleration a for a period of time t. Before this period of acceleration occurs, the object has velocity u. After the period of acceleration, the object has velocity v.

If we consider a velocity-time diagram that represents this information, the fact that the graph has gradient a implies that

$$\frac{v-u}{t} = a \qquad \text{or} \qquad v = u + at \, .$$

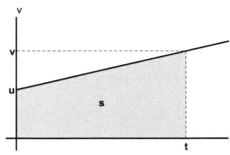

We see this result in Key Fact 22.3 . Since s is the area under the graph, the formula for the area of a trapezium tells us that

$$s = \tfrac{1}{2}(u+v)t \, .$$

Figure 22.7

Food For Thought 22.1

The object has experienced a displacement s in time t, and therefore has been moving with **average velocity** $\frac{s}{t}$. It is interesting to note that the above equation tells us that the average velocity $\frac{s}{t}$ of the object is equal to the average (mean) $\frac{1}{2}(u+v)$ of the initial and final velocities of the object. This neat match of uses of the word 'average' does not always happen; it only happens when acceleration is constant.

These two formulae are the key ideas behind velocity-time diagrams. The benefit we gain from writing them down algebraically is that we can manipulate them to obtain new equations, that do not have a ready geometric interpretation for velocity-time or displacement-time graphs. We see that

$$s = \tfrac{1}{2}(u+v)t = \tfrac{1}{2}(u+(u+at))t = ut + \tfrac{1}{2}at^2 \, ,$$
$$s = \tfrac{1}{2}(u+v)t = \tfrac{1}{2}((v-at)+v)t = vt - \tfrac{1}{2}at^2 \, ,$$

for example. We also note that

$$v^2 - u^2 = (v-u)(v+u) = at \times \frac{2s}{t} = 2as$$

Key Fact 22.6 SUVAT Equations

The quantities s, u, v, a and t satisfy the so-called SUVAT equations:

$$v = u + at \qquad s = ut + \tfrac{1}{2}at^2 \qquad v^2 = u^2 + 2as$$
$$s = \tfrac{1}{2}(u+v)t \qquad s = vt - \tfrac{1}{2}at^2$$

It is important to note that each of the five SUVAT equations connects four out of the five variables s, u, v, a and t. In order to calculate any of the five quantities, it is enough to know any three of the others (and then choose the appropriate equation to use).

Example 22.5.1. *The barrel of a shotgun is 0.9 m long, and the shot emerges from the barrel with a speed of 240 ms^{-1}. Assuming that it is constant, find:*

(a) the acceleration of the shot in the barrel, and

(b) the length of time that the shot is in the barrel after firing.

Since the shot is initially at rest, $u = 0$. We are told that $s = 0.9$ and $v = 240$. We want to find a, so we shall use the equation $v^2 = u^2 + 2as$. Thus

$$240^2 = 0^2 + 2 \times a \times 0.9 \, ,$$

and hence $a = 32000$. We now want to calculate t. Since we know all the other four variables, we can choose whichever formula is most convenient. The simplest is probably $v = u + at$. Using it gives $240 = 0 + 32000t$, so that $t = 0.0075$. Thus the acceleration of the bullet is 32000 ms^{-2}, and the bullet spends 0.0075 seconds in the barrel.

Example 22.5.2. *The driver of a car travelling at* 96 *km h^{-1} suddenly sees a stationary bus* 100 *metres ahead. With the brakes full on, the car can decelerate at* 4 *ms^{-2} in the prevailing road conditions. Can the driver stop in time?*

Firstly, the initial speed of the car is $96 \times \frac{1000}{3600} = \frac{80}{3}$ ms^{-1}, so we have $u = \frac{80}{3}$ and $a = -4$. If we try to find the value of v when $s = 100$, the equation $v^2 = u^2 + 2as$ yields

$$v^2 = \tfrac{6400}{9} - 2 \times 4 \times 100 = -\tfrac{800}{9},$$

which is clearly nonsense. The reason for this absurdity is that the car will have stopped long before the bus. After it has stopped it will remain stationary (until the bus has moved away). The model we are using is no longer valid.

A better approach would be to determine the stopping distance of the car. With $u = \frac{80}{3}$ and $a = -4$, we would like to know the value of s when $v = 0$. The same SUVAT equation now gives

$$0^2 = \tfrac{6400}{9} - 2 \times 4 \times s$$

so that $s = \frac{800}{9} = 88.9$. The car stops after travelling 88.9 m, roughly 11 m short of the bus.

22.6   Free Fall Under Gravity

The earth exerts a gravitational attraction on all objects near it. For objects near the surface of the earth, this attraction is such that all objects fall towards the earth with a constant acceleration (we are assuming that we can ignore other factors, such as air resistance). This gravitational acceleration is denoted g. Its value is $g \approx 9.8$ ms^{-2} (there is in fact a good degree of variability in its value, between 9.76 and 9.83 depending where on the earth it is being measured. In this Pre-U course we shall make the (very rough) approximation that $g = 10$ ms^{-1}. While this approximation does mean that our answers are less accurate than with a more precise figure, it has the advantage of producing calculations which are not unnecessarily complex to calculate. Indeed, there are times when we won't even want to give g a value; we will work with the symbol g algebraically.

Example 22.6.1. *A stone is dropped from the top of a* 50 *m cliff. How long does the stone take to hit the ground?*

The stone is travelling in a straight line, and is always moving downwards. The simplest way to model this problem is to measure distances and velocities downwards from the top of the cliff so that, for example, s is the distance fallen by the stone, and the acceleration a of the stone is $g = 10$ ms^{-2}. We have $u = 0$ (we presume that 'dropped' means 'dropped from rest'), $a = 10$, $s = 50$, and we want to know t. The equation $s = ut + \frac{1}{2}at^2$ gives us

$$50 = 0 + \tfrac{1}{2} \times 10 \times t^2,$$

Figure 22.8

and hence $t = \sqrt{10}$. The stone hits the ground after approximately 3.16 seconds.

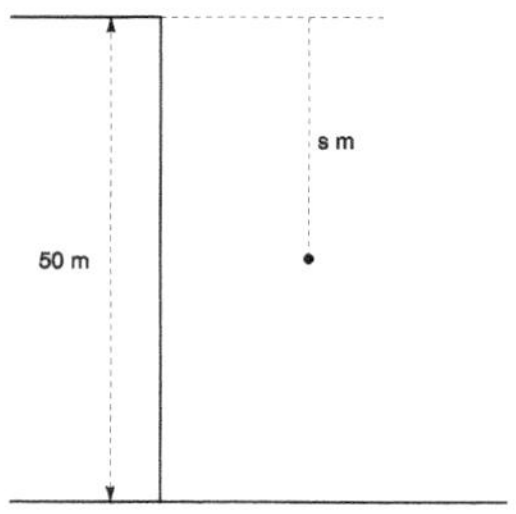

It is important to realise that u, v and a are vector quantities so they can be negative.

Example 22.6.2. *A ball is thrown vertically upwards with a speed of* 5 *ms^{-1} from the top of a building. If the top of the building is* 30 *m above the ground, and the ball manages to miss the building on its way down, find the length of time ball the ball spends in the air. At what speed does it hit the ground?*

442

This time we shall measure distances, velocities and accelerations vertically upwards, so that s is the height of the ball above the level of the roof of the building. We are told that $u = 5$ and (since acceleration is downwards) $a = -g = -10$. To find out when the ball hits the ground, we need to know when $s = -30$. The equation $s = ut + \frac{1}{2}at^2$ tells us that

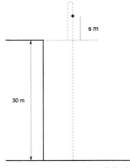

$$-30 = 5t - \frac{1}{2} \times 5t^2$$
$$5(t-3)(t+2) = 5t^2 - 5t - 60 = 0$$

Figure 22.9

and so the ball hits the ground when $t = 3$, after spending 3 seconds in the air. Using the equation $v^2 = u^2 + 2as$ gives us

$$v^2 = 5^2 - 2 \times 10 \times (-30) = 625,$$

so the ball hits the ground with a speed of 25 ms^{-1}.

Why do the SUVAT equations also give us the solution of $t = -2$? We are not supposing that we could go back in time. The point is that the SUVAT equations know nothing about buildings and balls; they simply investigate when an object will be in a particular place travelling with particular speed and acceleration. The second SUVAT equation we used above told us that $v^2 = 625$, when $s = -30$. Technically, we should have deduced that $v = -25$ at that point (since positive velocities are upward in this question) before deciding on an impact speed of 25 ms^{-1}. What is the meaning of the positive solution $v = 25$?

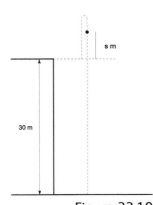

Figure 22.10

If someone shot the ball upwards from ground level with velocity 25 ms^{-1}, then it would reach the top of the building with upward speed of 5 ms^{-1} after 2 seconds of flight. The solution $t = -2$ indicates how the ball could have been travelling at this same constant acceleration of $a = -10$ to reach the top of the building with the desired speed.

Example 22.6.3. *A particle is fired vertically upwards from ground level with speed V. What is the maximum height that it attains?*

Measuring positive distances vertically upwards, we have $u = V$, $a = -g$. We want to know the value of s when $v = 0$ (the particle will be stationary when it reaches its maximum height). The equation $v^2 = u^2 + 2as$ gives $0^2 = V^2 - 2gs$, and hence the maximum possible height is $\frac{V^2}{2g}$.

EXERCISE 22B

1. Interpret each of the following in terms of the motion of a particle along a line, and select the appropriate constant acceleration formula to find the answer. The quantities u, v, s and t are all positive or zero, but a may be positive or negative:

   a) $u = 9, a = 4, s = 5$; find v,
   b) $u = 10, v = 14, a = 3$; find s,
   c) $u = 17, v = 11, s = 56$; find a,
   d) $u = 14, a = -2, t = 5$; find s,
   e) $v = 20, a = 1, t = 6$; find s,
   f) $u = 10, s = 65, t = 5$; find a,
   g) $u = 18, v = 12, s = 210$; find t,
   h) $u = 9, a = 4, s = 35$; find t,
   i) $u = 20, s = 110, t = 5$; find v,
   j) $s = 93, v = 42, t = \frac{3}{2}$; find a,
   k) $u = 24, v = 10, a = -0.7$; find t,
   l) $s = 35, v = 12, a = 2$; find u,
   m) $v = 27, s = 40, a = -4.5$; find t,
   n) $a = 7, s = 100, v - u = 20$; find u.

2. A train goes into a tunnel at 20 ms^{-1} and emerges from it at 55 ms^{-1}. The tunnel is 1500 m long. Assuming constant acceleration, find how long the train is in the tunnel for, and the acceleration of the train.

3. A motor-scooter moves from rest with acceleration 0.1 ms^{-2}. Find an expression for its speed, v ms^{-1}, after it has gone s metres. Illustrate your answer by sketching a graph of v against s.

4. A cyclist riding at 5 ms^{-1} starts to accelerate, and 200 metres later she is riding at 7 ms^{-1}. Find her acceleration (assumed to be constant).

5. A train travelling at 55 ms^{-1} has to reduce speed to 35 ms^{-1} to pass through a junction. If the deceleration is not to exceed 0.6 ms^{-2}, how far ahead of the junction should the train begin to slow down?

6. An ocean liner leaves the harbour entrance travelling at 3 ms^{-1}, and accelerates at 0.04 ms^{-2} until it reaches its cruising speed of 15 ms^{-1}.

   a) How far does it travel in accelerating to its cruising speed?

   b) How long does it take to travel 2 km from the harbour entrance?

7. A downhill skier crosses the finishing line at a speed of 30 ms^{-1} and immediately starts to decelerate at 10 ms^{-2}. There is a barrier 50 metres beyond the finishing line.

   a) Find an expression for the skier's speed when she is s metres beyond the finishing line.

   b) How fast is she travelling when she is 40 metres beyond the finishing line?

   c) How far short of the barrier does she come to a stop?

   d) Draw a graph of v against s to illustrate the motion.

8. A boy kicks a football up a slope with a speed of 6 ms^{-1}. The ball decelerates at 0.3 ms^{-2}. How far up the slope does it roll?

9. A cyclist comes to the top of a hill 165 metres long travelling at 5 ms^{-1} and free-wheels down it with an acceleration of 0.8 ms^{-2}. Write expressions for his speed and the distance he has travelled after t seconds. Hence find how long he takes to reach the bottom of the hill, and how fast he is then travelling.

10. A car travelling at 10 ms^{-1} is 25 metres from a pedestrian crossing when the traffic light changes from green to amber. The light remains at amber for 2 seconds before it changes to red. The driver has two choices: to accelerate so as to reach the crossing before the light changes to red, or to try to stop at the light. What is the least acceleration which would be necessary in the first case, and the least deceleration which would be necessary in the second?

11. A freight train $\frac{1}{4}$ km long takes 20 seconds to pass a signal. The train is decelerating at a constant rate, and by the time the rear truck has passed the signal it is moving 10 kilometres per hour slower than it was when the front of the train passed the signal. Find the deceleration in km h^{-2}, and the speed at which the train is moving when the rear truck has just passed the signal.

12. A cheetah is pursuing an impala. The impala is running in a straight line at a constant speed of 16 ms^{-1}. The cheetah is 10 m behind the impala, running at 20 ms^{-1} but tiring, so that it is decelerating at 1 ms^{-2}. Find an expression for the gap between the cheetah and the impala t seconds later. Will the impala get away?

13. A brick falls from rest from the top of a 25 m high building. How long does it take to hit the ground, and what is its impact speed?

14. A ball is thrown vertically upwards from the ground at a speed of 11 ms^{-1}. For what amount of time is the ball more than 2 above the ground?

15. Two balls are released from the top of a 30 high cliff. One of these balls is released with an upwards speed of 5 ms^{-1}; the second is released with a downwards speed of 10 ms^{-1}. What is the time difference between the times when the two balls hit the ground?

16. A ball is released from rest at the top of a skyscraper. In the last two seconds before it hits the ground, it falls two thirds of the total height of the building. Find the exact time before the ball hits the ground, and calculate the height of the building in terms of g.

17*. A ball is thrown vertically downwards from the top of a 60 m building with a speed of 10 ms^{-1}. At the same time, a second ball is thrown vertically upwards from the bottom of the same building with a speed of 20 ms^{-1}, starting directly underneath the first ball. How much time elapses until the two balls meet in mid-air?

Gravitational force is greater or larger on different planets, due to their sizes. This can be most simply modelled by noting that the value of g is different of different planets.

    a) If the same experiment took place on the surface of Mars (where the value of g is 3.75 ms^{-2}), what would be answer be?

    b) What would happen if the experiment took place on the surface of Jupiter (where the value of g is 26.0 ms^{-2})?

18*. A train is slowing down with constant acceleration. It passes a signal at A, and after successive intervals of t seconds it passes points B and C, where $AB = s_1$ m and $BC = s_2$ m (where $s_1 > s_2$).

    a) How fast is the train moving when is passes A?

    b) Explain why $s_2 > \frac{1}{3}s_1$.

    c) How far from A does the train come to a stop?

Your answers should be expressed in terms of s_1, s_2 and t.

22.7 Constant Velocity In Two And Three Dimensions

We have already expressed the basic equation relating to constant velocity in vector form (see Key Fact 22.2). This equation can be used to study a number of questions relating to the motion of one or more objects in two or three dimensions (or in any higher number of dimensions, if we really want to).

Suppose that an object P is travelling with constant velocity $\mathbf{u}$. Its position vector at time t with respect to some fixed point O (the vector describing its displacement from O) is given by the vector $\mathbf{r}_t$. We add the subscript t to remind ourselves that $\mathbf{r}_t$ is a function of t. The function $\mathbf{r}_t$, as t varies (over the range of values over an appropriate range) describes the **trajectory** of P: where it is at all times.

After time t, the object P has been travelling with constant velocity $\mathbf{u}$, and hence has experienced a displacement of $t\mathbf{u}$. Thus we obtain a relationship between the position vectors of P at time 0 and at time t.

Key Fact 22.7 Constant Velocity Trajectories

If an object is travelling with constant velocity $\mathbf{u}$, then its trajectory is given by the equation

$$\mathbf{r}_t = \mathbf{r}_0 + t\mathbf{u}, \qquad t \in \mathbb{R}.$$

Remember that $\mathbf{r}_0$ is the displacement of the object at time $t = 0$, while $\mathbf{r}_t$ is the displacement of the object at time t.

Example 22.7.1. *An object is moving with constant velocity $\mathbf{i} + 3\mathbf{j}$ ms^{-1}. Initially its displacement from a fixed point O is $-3\mathbf{i} + 2\mathbf{j}$ m. What is its displacement from O after 3 seconds? At what time $t > 0$ is the object 5 m away from O?*

The trajectory of the object is given by the formula

$$\mathbf{r}_t = (-3\mathbf{i} + 2\mathbf{j}) + t(\mathbf{i} + 3\mathbf{j}) = (t - 3)\mathbf{i} + (3t + 2)\mathbf{j}.$$

The object's displacement after 3 seconds is thus $3\mathbf{i} + 10\mathbf{j}$ metres. The distance of the object from O is equal to

$$|\mathbf{r}_t| = \sqrt{(t-3)^2 + (3t+2)^2} = \sqrt{10t^2 + 6t + 13};$$

We need to find the value of t for which $|\mathbf{r}_t| = 5$; this occurs when $10t^2 + 6t + 13 = 25$, or $5t^2 + 3t - 6 = 0$. The solutions of this quadratic are $t = -1.436$ and $t = 0.836$. We are just asked for the positive solution.

Example 22.7.2. *A boat is sailing with constant velocity 15 knots in a north-easterly direction. At noon it is 30 nautical miles due south of a lighthouse.*

(a) *What is the distance of the boat from the lighthouse at 1 p.m?*

(b) *At what time will the lighthouse be due west of the boat?*

(c) *How close does the boat come to the lighthouse?*

This time, we have been given the velocity in terms of its speed and its bearing. If we use the usual unit vectors $\mathbf{i}$ and $\mathbf{j}$ which point east and north respectively, then a north-easterly pointing vector is parallel to $\mathbf{i} + \mathbf{j}$. We want a velocity vector $\mathbf{u} = \alpha(\mathbf{i} + \mathbf{j})$ which points northeast and which has modulus 15. But since $15^2 = |\mathbf{u}|^2 = \alpha^2 + \alpha^2 = 2\alpha^2$, we deduce that $\alpha = \frac{15}{\sqrt{2}} = \frac{15}{2}\sqrt{2}$, and hence that the boat has velocity $\mathbf{u} = \frac{15}{2}\sqrt{2}(\mathbf{i} + \mathbf{j})$.

If we assume that the lighthouse is at the origin of our coordinate system, then the initial displacement of the boat is $-30\mathbf{j}$ nautical miles, and hence the displacement of the boat at time t hours after noon is given by the formula

$$\mathbf{r}_t = -30\mathbf{j} + \frac{15}{2}t\sqrt{2}(\mathbf{i} + \mathbf{j}) = \frac{15}{2}t\sqrt{2}\mathbf{i} + \left(\frac{15}{2}t\sqrt{2} - 30\right)\mathbf{j} = \frac{15}{2}\sqrt{2}\big(t\mathbf{i} + (t - 2\sqrt{2})\mathbf{j}\big).$$

(a) At 1 p.m. the boat's displacement is $\frac{15}{2}\sqrt{2}\big(\mathbf{i} + (1 - 2\sqrt{2})\mathbf{j}\big)$ nautical miles. Taking the modulus of this vector, the distance of the boat from the lighthouse is

$$\frac{15}{2}\sqrt{2}\sqrt{1^2 + (1 - 2\sqrt{2})^2} = 22.1 \text{ nautical miles.}$$

(b) The lighthouse will be due west of the boat when the boat is due east of the lighthouse, which will occur when $\mathbf{r}_t$ is a positive multiple of $\mathbf{i}$ which happens when the $\mathbf{j}$ component of $\mathbf{r}_t$ is zero; this happens when $t = 2\sqrt{2}$. The lighthouse is due west of the boat at time $2:50$ (to the nearest minute).

(c) We want to know when the distance $d_t = |\mathbf{r}_t|$ of the boat from the lighthouse is least. We see that

$$d_t = \frac{15}{2}\sqrt{2}\sqrt{t^2 + (t - 2\sqrt{2})^2} = \frac{15}{2}\sqrt{2}\sqrt{2t^2 - 4t\sqrt{2} + 8} = 15\sqrt{t^2 - 2\sqrt{2} + 4}.$$

We could try to minimise d_t by looking for its turning points. Calculating $\frac{d}{dt}d_t$ is possible, but involves using the chain rule. There is an easier way.
Suppose that the distance is minimised at time t_0, so that $d_t \geq d_{t_0}$ for all t. Then $d_t^2 \geq d_{t_0}^2$ for all t, so we see that d_t^2 is also minimised at time t_0. In order to minimise d_t, all we have to do is minimise d_t^2, and $d_t^2 = 225(t^2 - 2t\sqrt{2} + 4)$ is a quadratic. This could be minimised by differentiation; alternatively completing the square shows us that

$$d_t^2 = 225\Big[(t - \sqrt{2})^2 + 2\Big].$$

We deduce that the closest approach of the boat to the lighthouse occurs when $t = \sqrt{2}$; the distance of closest approach is $15\sqrt{2} = 21.2$ nautical miles.

Example 22.7.3. *Two planes are flying near a radio beacon. At one instant, plane A has displacement $-1000\mathbf{i} - 300\mathbf{j} + 1015\mathbf{k}$ metres from the beacon, while plane B has displacement $1800\mathbf{i} + 100\mathbf{j} + 1075\mathbf{k}$ metres from the beacon. Both planes are flying with constant velocities: plane A has velocity $80\mathbf{i} + 60\mathbf{j} + \mathbf{k}$ ms^{-1} and plane B has velocity $-60\mathbf{i} + 40\mathbf{j} - 2\mathbf{k}$ ms^{-1}, where the unit vectors $\mathbf{i}, \mathbf{j}$ and $\mathbf{k}$ point east, north and vertically up respectively. Show that the planes will collide.*

Ten seconds before the collision, the pilot of plane A notices the impending collision and takes evasive action by levelling out, changing his plane's velocity to $80\mathbf{i} + 60\mathbf{j}$ ms^{-1}. By how much do the two planes miss each other?

The trajectories of the two planes are given by the formulae

$$\begin{aligned}
\mathbf{a}_t &= -1000\mathbf{i} - 300\mathbf{j} + 1015\mathbf{k} + t(80\mathbf{i} + 60\mathbf{j} + \mathbf{k}) = (80t - 1000)\mathbf{i} + (60t - 300)\mathbf{j} + (t + 1015)\mathbf{k} \\
\mathbf{b}_t &= 1800\mathbf{i} + 100\mathbf{j} + 1075\mathbf{k} + t(-60\mathbf{i} + 40\mathbf{j} - 2\mathbf{k}) = (1800 - 60t)\mathbf{i} + (100 + 40t)\mathbf{j} + (1075 - 2t)\mathbf{k}
\end{aligned}$$

The two planes will collide only if they are in the same place at the same time. This means there must be a (positive) time t for which $\mathbf{a}_t = \mathbf{b}_t$. We need to solve the simultaneous equations

$$80t - 1000 = 1800 - 60t \qquad 60t - 300 = 100 + 40t \qquad t + 1015 = 1075 - 2t\,.$$

These equations are all satisfied by $t = 20$; the planes will collide in 20 seconds time.

At the time 10 seconds before the collision, plane A has displacement (putting $t = 10$ into the above formulae)

$$\mathbf{a}_{10} = -200\mathbf{i} + 300\mathbf{j} + 1025\mathbf{k}\,,$$

With the changed velocity for A, t seconds after the initial time, plane A has new displacement

$$\hat{\mathbf{a}}_t = -200\mathbf{i} + 300\mathbf{j} + 1025\mathbf{k} + (t-10)(80\mathbf{i} + 60\mathbf{j}) = (80t - 1000)\mathbf{i} + (60t - 300)\mathbf{j} + 1025\mathbf{k}$$

for $t \geq 10$, and hence the distance between the two planes is now $D_t = |\hat{\mathbf{a}}_t - \mathbf{b}_t|$, and

$$D_t^2 = (2800 - 140t)^2 + (400 - 20t)^2 + (50 - 2t)^2 = 20004t^2 - 800200t + 8002500$$

Differentiation shows that this expression is minimised when $t = \frac{800200}{2 \times 20004} = 20.00$, at which point $D_t = 10.0$. The two planes miss each other by 10 m.

22.8 Constant Acceleration In More Than One Dimension

Although all the SUVAT equations have a natural vector form, we do not need all of them, and can work with a more restricted set of equations. Note that, in a problem with constant acceleration, both displacement $\mathbf{r}$ and velocity $\mathbf{v}$ are functions of time.

Key Fact 22.8 Constant Acceleration Trajectories

Suppose that an object is moving with a constant acceleration $\mathbf{a}$. If the object has displacement $\mathbf{r}_t$ with respect to some fixed origin at time t, and has velocity $\mathbf{v}_t$ at time t, then

$$\mathbf{r}_t = \mathbf{r}_0 + \mathbf{v}_0 t + \tfrac{1}{2}\mathbf{a}t^2 \qquad \mathbf{v}_t = \mathbf{v}_0 + \mathbf{a}t\,.$$

The formulae for velocity is a simple restatement of Key Fact 22.3 . The first, like the one-dimensional SUVAT equations $s = ut + \frac{1}{2}at^2$ and $s = \frac{1}{2}(u + v)t$, is a consequence of the fact that the area under a velocity-time graph is equal to the displacement. This fact will be established by the end of this chapter.

Example 22.8.1. *A rocket is flying horizontally over a plain. Its initial velocity is $600\mathbf{i} - 10\mathbf{j}$ ms^{-1}, where $\mathbf{i}$ and $\mathbf{j}$ are unit vectors pointing east and north respectively. At this stage of its motion, the rocket is accelerating with constant acceleration $10\mathbf{i} + 30\mathbf{j}$ ms^{-2}. When the rocket is flying on a bearing of $070°$, it will stop accelerating. For how long must the rocket accelerate? What is the rocket's speed at the moment it stops accelerating, and what is its displacement relative to its initial position?*

The velocity of the rocket, t second after the onset of acceleration, is

$$\mathbf{v}_t = (600\mathbf{i} - 10\mathbf{j}) + t(10\mathbf{i} + 30\mathbf{j}) = (600 + 10t)\mathbf{i} + (30t - 10)\mathbf{j}\,.$$

The rocket is on a bearing of $070°$ when its velocity is parallel to $\sin 70°\mathbf{i} + \cos 70°\mathbf{j}$; we want to know when

$$\frac{600 + 10t}{30t - 10} = \tan 70°$$
$$600 + 10t = (30t - 10)\tan 70°$$
$$(30\tan 70° - 10)t = 600 + 10\tan 70°$$

and hence this happens when $t = 8.66$. The rocket must accelerate for 8.66 seconds. At this time the rocket has velocity $686.6\mathbf{i} + 249.9\mathbf{j}$ ms^{-1}, and hence speed 731 ms^{-1}; its displacement is

$$(600t + 5t^2)\mathbf{i} + (15t^2 - 10t)\mathbf{j} = 5570\mathbf{i} + 1040\mathbf{j} \text{ metres}$$

to 3 significant figures.

EXERCISE 22C

1. A particle P moving with constant velocity $\mathbf{v}$ has displacements as indicated. Calculate $\mathbf{v}$ in each case:

   a) $\mathbf{r}_0 = 2\mathbf{i}, \mathbf{r}_3 = 5\mathbf{i} + 9\mathbf{j},$ b) $\mathbf{r}_0 = \mathbf{i} + 3\mathbf{j}, \mathbf{r}_5 = -4\mathbf{i} + 13\mathbf{j},$
   c) $\mathbf{r}_0 = \mathbf{i} + \mathbf{j}, \mathbf{r}_3 = 2\mathbf{i} - 4\mathbf{j},$ d) $\mathbf{r}_0 = -3\mathbf{i} - 2\mathbf{j}, \mathbf{r}_6 = \mathbf{j}.$

2. A particle P is moving with constant acceleration $\mathbf{a}$. Its initial velocity is $\mathbf{u}$. Find its velocity and speed after t seconds, when:

   a) $\mathbf{u} = 2\mathbf{i}, \mathbf{a} = \mathbf{j}, t = 4,$ b) $\mathbf{u} = -2\mathbf{i} + \mathbf{j}, \mathbf{a} = 3\mathbf{i} - 2\mathbf{j}, t = 3,$
   c) $\mathbf{u} = -3\mathbf{i} + 4\mathbf{j}, \mathbf{a} = 3\mathbf{i} + 10\mathbf{j}, t = 1,$ d) $\mathbf{u} = 2\mathbf{i} - 4\mathbf{j}, \mathbf{a} = 3\mathbf{j}, t = 5$

3. A particle has velocity $2\mathbf{i} + 17\mathbf{j}$ at one instant and velocity $7\mathbf{i} - 2\mathbf{j}$ at a time 4 seconds later. Assuming the particle's acceleration to be constant, find that acceleration. Also find the displacement of the particle from its initial position after those 4 seconds.

4. A particle has initial velocity $4\mathbf{i} - 7\mathbf{j}$, and is accelerating in the direction $\mathbf{i} + 2\mathbf{j}$. After 5 seconds, the particle's speed is parallel to $\mathbf{i} + \mathbf{j}$. Find the magnitude of the particle's acceleration, and the particle's displacement over this 5 second time period.

5. Starting from the point O at the same time, Fred and George set out across a field at night-time. Fred moves with velocity $\mathbf{i} + \mathbf{j}$ ms^{-1}, while George moves with velocity $-2\mathbf{i} + 3\mathbf{j}$ ms^{-1}. They each hold the end of a piece of thread which is 100 m long.

   a) Write down the displacement vectors of Fred and George t seconds after they start.

   b) What is the angle between Fred and George's two paths?

   c) How long do the pair have until the thread becomes taut and breaks?

6. A toy plane is flying horizontally east with speed 6 ms^{-1} at a height of 1 m above the ground. It is subject to a constant acceleration of $-0.1\mathbf{i} + 0.03\mathbf{j} - 0.02\mathbf{k}$ ms^{-2}, where the unit vectors $\mathbf{i}, \mathbf{j}$ and $\mathbf{k}$ point east, north and vertically up.

   a) With the origin O at ground level immediately below the plane's starting point, write down the displacement vector of the plane as a function of time t seconds.

   b) When does the plane crash?

   c) What is the plane's speed when it crashes?

   d) What was the plane's bearing (ignoring the plane's vertical motion) at the point of impact?

7. A motorboat is sailing with a constant velocity of $8\mathbf{i} + 11\mathbf{j}$ knots ($\mathbf{i}$ and $\mathbf{j}$ are unit vectors pointing east and north, respectively) when it spots a freighter sailing due east with a speed of 5 knots. The displacement of the freighter from the motorboat is $\mathbf{i} + 4\mathbf{j}$ nautical miles. Will the motorboat intercept the freighter?

   The motorboat can release a torpedo successfully if it can be fired within $\frac{1}{5}$ nautical miles of the target. Can the motorboat hit the freighter?

22.9   General Motion: Differentiation

So far we have been concerned with the motion of objects with constant acceleration, but the real world does not always allow us that luxury; there are many circumstances where acceleration varies with time, but we still want to be able to understand such motion. There have been a couple of stages in this chapter where we have avoided proving key facts. To be specific, we have promised that the result that displacement is the area under the curve of a velocity-time graph, will be proved 'later on'. Now is the time. To do this, we need to have a complete understanding of the relationship between displacement, velocity and acceleration. For the present, we shall restrict ourselves to one-dimensional motion.

We know that the average velocity of an object over a period of time is equal to the displacement of that object over that period of time divided by the time interval. That, however, does not give us a clear picture of what the instantaneous speed of the object at any time is. Any moving object has an instantaneous speed at any time, for example, a car's speedometer will always register, even if it is always changing. We need to appreciate what that instantaneous speed is.

Consider the displacement-time graph of a particle's motion. What is the speed of the particle at time t (at the point P)? The average speed between times t and $t + h$ is equal to the displacement over that time period, $s(t + h) - s(t)$, divided by the time period h; thus the average speed over the time period from t to $t + h$ is the fraction

$$\frac{s(t+h) - s(t)}{h},$$

which is the gradient of the chord on the displacement-time graph between times t and $t + h$.

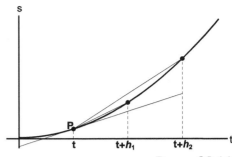

Figure 22.11

The larger h is, the more likely this expression will be inaccurate as an estimate of the speed of the object at time t. The smaller h is, the more likely it is that the average speed is primarily concerned with the motion of the object at the time t. Considering the diagram, the fraction $\frac{1}{h_1}(s(t+h_1) - s(t))$ is likely to be a better estimate of the object's speed at time t than is the fraction $\frac{1}{h_2}(s(t+h_2) - s(t))$. We would expect the average velocity $\frac{1}{h}[s(t+h) - s(t)]$ between times t and $t + h$ to get closer and closer to the instantaneous velocity of the object at time t as h approaches 0. Comparing these diagrams and observations to similar ones made when we were considering differentiation leads us to the following observation:

Key Fact 22.9 Velocity As A Derivative

If s is the position of an object moving along the x-axis, then the velocity v of the object is the derivative of s with respect to time t:

$$v = \frac{ds}{dt}.$$

Velocity is the rate of change of displacement with respect to time, and hence is the gradient of a displacement-time graph.

Similar arguments can be made about the relationship of velocity and acceleration:

Key Fact 22.10 Acceleration As A Derivative

If s is the displacement of an object moving along the x-axis, and if v is its velocity, then the acceleration a of the object is the derivative of v with respect to time t:

$$a = \frac{dv}{dt} = \frac{d^2s}{dt^2}.$$

Acceleration is the rate of change of velocity with respect to time, and hence is the gradient of a velocity-time graph.

Example 22.9.1. *A space probe is launched by rockets. For the first stage of its ascent, which is in a vertical line and lasts for 40 seconds, the height x metres of the rocket after t seconds is modelled by the equation $x = 50t^2 + \frac{1}{4}t^3$. How high is the probe at the end of the first stage, and how fast is it then moving? What is its acceleration at that time?*

The height of the rocket at the end of the first stage is given by substituting $t = 40$ into the formula for x, which gives $x = 50 \times 40^2 + \frac{1}{4} \times 40^3 = 96000$. The rocket is 96 km high after the first stage is complete. To find its velocity at this time we must differentiate, obtaining

$$v = \frac{dx}{dt} = 100t + \tfrac{3}{4}t^2.$$

Its value when $t = 40$ is $100 \times 40 + \frac{3}{4} \times 40^2 = 5200$; the rocket's velocity is 5.2 km s^{-1} vertically up. Finally, the acceleration of the rocket is

$$a = \frac{dv}{dt} = 100 + \tfrac{3}{2}t,$$

449

which equals $100 + \frac{3}{2} \times 40 = 160$; the rocket's upwards acceleration is 160 ms^{-2}.

Note that displacement was represented by the letter x, rather than the letter s. It is important not to become too attached to any one symbol; a more appropriate symbol than s might be useful in a particular problem. We may choose to measure the distance d below the top of a cliff, or the height h reached by a cricket ball. For that matter, we might meet a problem in which one of the standard letters has already been assigned a meaning; in such circumstances we need to be flexible enough to change the labels for the standard quantities!

22.10   The 'Dot' Notation

One way of avoiding symbolic confusion, and also of saving space, is to adopt a notation frequently used by mathematicians and physicists when writing down equations in mechanics. The operation of differentiation with respect to time t (specifically) is denoted by a superscript dot over the quantity being differentiated; instead of $\frac{ds}{dt}$, we can write $\dot{s}$. If we need to differentiate twice with respect to t, two dots are used instead, so that instead of $\frac{d^2s}{dt^2}$ we can write $\ddot{s}$. The relationships between displacement, velocity and acceleration can now be written as follows:

$$v = \dot{s}, \qquad a = \ddot{s} = \dot{v}.$$

The benefit of this notation is twofold. Firstly, it is more compact, since it takes less space to write $\dot{s}$ than it does to write $\frac{ds}{dt}$. In this regard the 'dot' notation is useful in the same way that the 'dash' notation, writing y' for $\frac{dy}{dx}$, was convenient for general differentiation. Recall, for example, how much simpler it was to write the quotient rule using the 'dash' notation. Secondly, if s is displacement, the symbols $\dot{s}$ and $\ddot{s}$ are sufficiently clear that we do not need additional symbols such as v and a to represent them; we know that $\dot{s}$ is velocity, and $\ddot{s}$ is acceleration.

EXERCISE 22D

In Questions 1 to 9, s metres is the displacement at time t seconds of a particle moving in a straight line; v is the velocity in ms^{-1} and a is the acceleration in ms^{-2}. Only zero and positive values of t should be considered.

1. Given that $s = t^3 + 4t + 6$, find expressions for v and a in terms of t. Find the displacement, velocity and acceleration when $t = 2$.

2. Given that $s = 3 + 20t - t^4$, find expressions for v and a in terms of t. Find the displacement, velocity and acceleration when $t = 1$, and also when $t = 3$.

3. Given that $s = t(t-2)(t-5)$, find the displacement, velocity and acceleration when $t = 0$.

4. Given that $v = 3\sqrt{t}$, find the velocity and acceleration when $t = 4$.

5. Given that $s = 16 - 2t^3$, find the time when the displacement is zero. Find the velocity and acceleration at this instant.

6. Given that $s = 120 - 15t - 6t^2 + t^3$, find the time when the velocity is zero. Find the displacement at this instant.

7. Given that $v = t^2 - 12t + 40$, find the velocity when the acceleration is zero.

8. Given that $v = 32 - 18t^{-2}$, find the acceleration when the velocity is 30 ms^{-1}.

9. Given that $s = 2t^4 + 8t$, find the displacement and the acceleration when the velocity is 35 ms^{-1}.

10. A car is accelerating from rest. At time t seconds after starting, the velocity of the car is v ms^{-1}, where $v = 6t - \frac{1}{2}t^2$, for $0 \le t \le 6$.

    a) Find the velocity of the car 6 seconds after starting.

b) Find the acceleration of the car when its velocity is 10 ms^{-1}.

11. A train leaves a station and travels in a straight line. After t seconds the train has travelled a distance x metres, where $s = (320t^3 - 2t^4) \times 10^{-5}$. This formula is valid until the train comes to rest at the next station.

   a) Find when the train comes to rest, and hence find the distance between the two stations.

   b) Find the acceleration of the train 40 seconds after the journey begins.

   c) Find the deceleration of the train just before it stops.

   d) Find when the acceleration is zero, and hence find the maximum velocity of the train.

12. A flare is launched from a hot-air balloon and moves in a vertical line. At time t seconds after launch, the height of the flare is s metres, where $s = 1464 - 40t - 2560(t+5)^{-1}$ for $t \geq 0$.

   a) Find the height and velocity of the flare immediately after it is launched.

   b) Find the acceleration of the flare immediately after it is launched, when its velocity is zero, and when $t = 20$.

   c) Find the terminal speed of the flare.

   d) Find when the flare reaches the ground.

13. The displacement s of an object is given by the formula $s = a + bt + ct^2$, where a, b and c are constants. Calculate $\dot{s}$ and $\ddot{s}$, and show that the particle is subject to constant acceleration. What the physical meanings of the constants a, b and c?

14*. The displacement s of an object has the form $s = a \sin \omega t$, where a and ω are constants.

   a) Describe the motion of the object.

   b) Show that $\ddot{x} = -\omega^2 x$.

   c) Describe the position of the object when it is stationary.

   d) What is the top speed of the object?

   e) Explain why the object's acceleration has greatest magnitude when the object is stationary.

15*. Let s be the displacement of an object at time t from its starting position at time 0, and suppose that object's initial velocity is u. Consider the quantity $y = s - \frac{1}{2}t(\dot{s} + u)$.

   a) Calculate $\dot{y}$, and show that $\ddot{y} = -\frac{1}{2}t\dddot{s}$ (three 'dots' means the third derivative with respect to time).

   b) If the object moves in such a way that its average velocity between times 0 and t is always equal to the average of its velocities at times 0 and t, show that the object must be experiencing constant acceleration.

22.11   General Motion: Integration

Of course, we can go the other way: since we differentiate displacement with respect to time to obtain velocity, we can retrieve displacement from velocity by integrating with respect to time. Similarly, velocity can be retrieved from acceleration by integration with respect to time. Obtaining displacement from velocity, then, is a matter of solving the differential equation

$$\frac{dx}{dt} = v(t) \, ,$$

for a known function $v(t)$. The general solution of this differential equation involves an arbitrary constant, that will need to be determined by the application of an appropriate initial or boundary condition.

Example 22.11.1. *A train is travelling on a straight track at 48 ms^{-1} when the driver sees an amber light ahead. He applies the brakes for a period of 30 seconds in such a way that the deceleration of the train during that period is given by the formula $\frac{1}{125}t(30 - t)$ ms^{-2}, where t is the number of seconds after the brakes were first applied. Find how fast the train is travelling after 30 seconds, and how far it has travelled in that time?*

If x m is the displacement of the train from the point where the brakes were first applied after t seconds, we have acceleration

$$a = \ddot{x} = -\tfrac{1}{125}t(30-t) = \tfrac{1}{125}t^2 - \tfrac{6}{25}t.$$

Integrating to find the velocity of the train gives

$$v = \dot{x} = \tfrac{1}{375}t^3 - \tfrac{3}{25}t^2 + c.$$

We are told that $v = 48$ when $t = 0$, and hence $c = 48$. Thus $v = 48 + \tfrac{1}{375}t^3 - \tfrac{3}{25}t^2$. Integrating one more time gives

$$x = 48t + \tfrac{1}{1500}t^4 - \tfrac{1}{25}t^3 + d.$$

Since x is the displacement from the point where the brakes were first applied, $x = 0$ when $t = 0$, and so $d = 0$. Thus $x = 48t + \tfrac{1}{1500}t^4 - \tfrac{1}{25}t^3$.

We can find the velocity and displacement of the train at the end of this period of acceleration by substituting $t = 30$ into the formula for v and x. Doing so gives us values of $v = 12$ and $x = 900$. The train has slowed to 12 ms^{-1}, and has travelled 900 m during the deceleration.

We did not need to calculate the full formula for the displacement x. To determine the displacement during the 30 second period, we could have calculated the definite integral

$$\int_0^{30} \left(\tfrac{1}{375}t^3 - \tfrac{3}{25}t^2 + 48\right)dt = \left[\tfrac{1}{1500}t^4 - \tfrac{1}{25}t^3 + 48t\right]_0^{30} = (540 - 1080 + 1440) - 0 = 900.$$

We recall that the definite integral is used to calculate area. This yields the following long-awaited result.

> **Key Fact 22.11** The Area Under A Velocity-Time Graph
>
> For an object moving in a straight line, with velocity v given as a function of time t, the displacement of the object between times t_1 and t_2 is given by the integral
>
> $$\int_{t_1}^{t_2} v(t)\,dt.$$
>
> This displacement is thus represented by the area under the velocity-time graph for the interval $t_1 \le t \le t_2$.

Example 22.11.2. *An object is moving with constant acceleration a. Let s be its displacement from its starting position at time t, and let v be its velocity at time t. Suppose that its initial velocity (its velocity at time 0) is u. Find formulae for v and s as functions of time t.*

Since the object experiences constant acceleration a, it follows that $\ddot{s} = a$. Integrating gives us that $v = \dot{s} = c + at$ for some constant c. Since $v = u$ when $t = 0$, it follows that $c = u$, and hence $v = u + at$. Integrating one more time gives us that $s = ut + \tfrac{1}{2}at^2 + d$; since $s = 0$ when $t = 0$ we deduce that $d = 0$, and hence $s = ut + \tfrac{1}{2}at^2$.

Thus the key SUVAT equations (and the other three can be derived from these two) can be developed entirely through the calculus.

22.12   General Motion: Higher Dimensions

All of these calculations can be performed for two- and three-dimensional problems. Velocity is still the rate of change of displacement, and acceleration is still the rate of change of velocity; we just have to be able to differentiate vectors. This is easy. We just differentiate each component separately.

> **Key Fact 22.12** Vector Differentiation
>
> If a vector **a** is a function of time, with components $\mathbf{a} = x\mathbf{i} + y\mathbf{j}$, then the rate of change of **a** with respect to time t is
> $$\dot{\mathbf{a}} = \dot{x}\mathbf{i} + \dot{y}\mathbf{j}.$$

Example 22.12.1. *An object is moving on a plane with velocity* $\mathbf{v} = (2t+3)\mathbf{i} + (1+\cos t)\mathbf{j}$ *ms*$^{-1}$*. Its initial displacement with respect to the origin O is* $3\mathbf{i}$ *m. Find expressions for the displacement* **s** *and the acceleration* **a** *of the object at time t.*

The acceleration is easy to determine by differentiation of each component,

$$\mathbf{a} = 2\mathbf{i} - \sin t\mathbf{j} \text{ ms}^{-2}.$$

To obtain the displacement **s**, we need to integrate **v**. We will obtain a constant of integration for each of the two components that we need to integrate.

$$\mathbf{s} = (t^2 + 3t + a)\mathbf{i} + (t + \sin t + b)\mathbf{j}.$$

Since $\mathbf{s} = 3\mathbf{j}$ when $t = 0$, we deduce that $a = 0$ and $b = 3$; thus

$$\mathbf{s} = (t^2 + 3t)\mathbf{i} + (3 + t + \sin t)\mathbf{j}.$$

> **Food For Thought 22.2**
>
> Why do we need two constants of integration? Firstly, when we differentiate vectors, we differentiate each component separately, and so a constant term can be lost from each component. We need two constants of integration to be able to undo this loss. From a physical perspective, the need for two constants is also clear. If we know the velocity of an object at all times, integrating that velocity will give us the displacement of the object at all times **relative to its initial position**. We need to specify the initial position of the particle (providing two arbitrary constants) if we want to know the actual displacement of the particle at all times.
>
> It is therefore clear that, if we integrate three-dimensional vectors, we will need three constants of integration, and not just two.

EXERCISE 22E

In Questions 1 to 12, x m is the displacement at time t s of a particle moving in a straight line; v is the velocity in ms^{-1} and a is the acceleration in ms^{-2}. Only zero and positive values of t should be considered.

1. Given that $v = 3t^2 + 8$ and that the displacement is 4 m when $t = 0$, find an expression for x in terms of t. Find the displacement and the velocity when $t = 2$.

2. Given that $a = 10 - 6t^2$ and that the velocity is 4 ms^{-1} and the displacement is 12 m when $t = 1$, find expressions for v and x in terms of t. Find the displacement, velocity and acceleration when $t = 0$.

3. Given that $v = 9 - t^2$ and that the displacement is 2 m when $t = 0$, find the displacement when the velocity is zero.

4. Given that $a = 3t - 12$, and that the velocity is 30 ms^{-1} and the displacement is 4 m when $t = 0$, find the displacement when the acceleration is zero.

5. Given that $v = 3t^2 + 4t + 3$, find the distance travelled between $t = 0$ and $t = 2$.

6. Given that $v = 12 - 8t^3$, find the distance travelled between $t = 0$ and $t = 1$.

7. Given that $a = 4t - 1$ and that the velocity is 5 ms^{-1} when $t = 0$, find the distance travelled between $t = 0$ and $t = 3$.

8. Given that $a = 12 - 3\sqrt{t}$ and that the velocity is 15 ms^{-1} when $t = 1$, find the distance travelled between $t = 1$ and $t = 25$.

9. Given that $v = 3(t-3)(t-5)$, find the distance travelled

   a) between $t = 0$ and $t = 3$,

   b) between $t = 3$ and $t = 5$,

   c) between $t = 5$ and $t = 6$.

   Hence find the total distance travelled between $t = 0$ and $t = 6$. How far is the particle from its starting point when $t = 6$?

10. Given that $a = t^{-2}$ and that the velocity is 4 ms^{-1} when $t = 1$, find the velocity when $t = 100$. State the terminal speed of the particle.

11. Given that $a = -4t^{-3}$ and that the velocity is 2 ms^{-1} and the displacement 0 when $t = 1$, find the displacement when $t = 4$. Show that the velocity is always positive but the displacement never exceeds 2 m.

12. Given that $v = 13 + 5t$ find the distance travelled as the velocity increases from 13 ms^{-1} to 33 ms^{-1}. Show that the acceleration is constant. Verify that using the formula $v^2 = u^2 + 2as$ gives the same answer for the distance travelled.

13. A car starts from rest and for the first 4 seconds of its motion the acceleration a ms^{-2} at time t seconds after starting is given by $a = 6 - 2t$.

   a) Find the maximum velocity of the car.

   b) Find the velocity of the car after 4 seconds, and the distance travelled up to this time.

14. A train is travelling at 32 ms^{-1}. The driver brakes, producing a deceleration of $k\sqrt{16-t}$ ms^{-2} after t seconds. The train comes to rest in 16 seconds. Find k, and how far the train travels before coming to rest.

15. A truck starts from rest. Its acceleration up to its maximum speed is given by $a = (p - qt)^n$, where p, q and n are constant. Express the maximum speed in terms of p, q and n.

16. An object is moving in a straight line with acceleration $a = 6t - 2$ ms^{-2} at time t seconds. Its displacement relative to a fixed point O is 3 m when $t = 1$, and is equal to 11 m when $t = 2$. Find the formula for the displacement x m at time t seconds.

17. An object moving in a straight line has velocity $v = e^{-t}\sin t$, and $x = 0$ when $t = 0$. Find the object's displacement and acceleration as functions of t, and show that $\ddot{x} + 2\dot{x} + 2x = 1$.

18. At time t seconds, an object has acceleration $\mathbf{a} = 2t\mathbf{i} + 4\mathbf{j} - 6t\mathbf{k}$ ms^{-2}. Its velocity is $3\mathbf{i} - \mathbf{j}$ ms^{-1} when $t = 0$, and its displacement is $\mathbf{k}$ m at the same time. What is an expression for its displacement at time t?

19. Two particles are moving with velocities given by
$$\mathbf{v} = (3t-1)\mathbf{i} + 7\mathbf{j}, \qquad \mathbf{V} = -2\mathbf{i} + (t-1)\mathbf{j}.$$
When $t = 0$, both objects are at the point with position vector $\mathbf{i} + 2\mathbf{j}$

   a) At what time are the two objects moving in perpendicular directions?

   b) What is the distance between the two particles when $t = 1$?

20*. An object is moving in two dimensions. Its position vector, relative to a fixed origin, has the form
$$\mathbf{x} = a\cos\omega t\,\mathbf{i} + a\sin\omega t\,\mathbf{j}, \qquad t \geq 0,$$
where $\mathbf{i}$ and $\mathbf{j}$ are the usual unit vectors, and a, ω are positive constants.

   a) Describe the motion of the object. Does the object move around the origin in a clockwise or anticlockwise direction?

   b) Calculate the velocity and acceleration vectors $\dot{\mathbf{x}}$ and $\ddot{\mathbf{x}}$.

   c) What is the speed of the object? Calculate the scaler product $\mathbf{x} \cdot \dot{\mathbf{x}}$. What does this tell you about the velocity of the object?

   d) In what direction is the acceleration $\ddot{\mathbf{x}}$ pointing?

Chapter 22: Summary

- An object moving with constant velocity $\mathbf{u}$ has displacement $\mathbf{s}_t = \mathbf{s}_0 + t\mathbf{u}$.

- An object moving with constant acceleration $\mathbf{a}$ has velocity $\mathbf{v}_t = \mathbf{v}_0 + t\mathbf{a}$ and displacement $\mathbf{s}_t = \mathbf{s}_0 + t\mathbf{v}_0 + \frac{1}{2}\mathbf{a}t^2$.

- **SUVAT equations** for constant acceleration in one dimension:

$$v = u + at \qquad s = ut + \tfrac{1}{2}at^2 \qquad v^2 = u^2 + 2as$$
$$s = \tfrac{1}{2}(u + v)t \qquad s = vt - \tfrac{1}{2}at^2$$

- Velocity is the rate of change of displacement, and acceleration is the rate of change of velocity:

$$\mathbf{v} = \dot{\mathbf{s}}, \qquad \mathbf{a} = \dot{\mathbf{v}} = \ddot{\mathbf{s}}.$$

Force And Equilibrium

In this chapter we will learn to:

- understand the vector nature of force, and use directed segments to represent forces,

- calculate the resultant of two or more forces acting at a point, and use vector addition to solve problems involving resultants and components of forces,

- find and use perpendicular components of a force, for example in calculating the resultant of a system of forces, or to calculate the magnitude and direction of a force,

- identify the forces acting in a given situation, including weight, tension, normal reaction and friction,

- use the principle that a particle is in equilibrium precisely when the vector sum of the forces acting is zero,

- use the model of a 'smooth contact' and understand its limitations,

- represent the contact force between two rough surfaces by two components: the normal reaction and the frictional force,

- understand the notion of the coefficient of friction, the relationship it imposes between the normal reaction and the frictional force, and the concept of limiting friction,

- use the law of friction to solve problems involving the equilibrium of a particle.

23.1 Introduction

The previous chapter was concerned with kinematics, which is the aspect of mechanics which studies **how** objects move. This chapter is concerned with statics, which is the study of **why** objects stay where they are.

Objects move or stay still in accordance with the **forces** that act on them. We all have a fairly clear idea about the existence and effects of some forces. When we pick up a heavy weight, we feel the force of gravity. When we sit in an accelerating car, we feel the effect of the car's driving force. When flying a kite, we feel the tension in the control line. If we walk into a door, we feel the reaction force from the door! Without the force of friction preventing the wheels from slipping, we could never ride our bicycles around corners. Our first task is to understand the nature of forces.

23.2 Force Is A Vector

Imagine pushing an empty tea chest which is resting on the floor. If we vary the effort with which we push, we will expect differing outcomes. If we change the direction in which we push, we will expect different outcomes.

Figure 23.1

In the first case above, a large (indicated by a longer arrow) push to the right will probably result in the chest moving to the right quite quickly. A smaller push to the left will result in a smaller response, in the opposite direction. In the third diagram, although the force is a large one, much of the force is 'trying to' push the chest into the floor, and so a different response is likely. In the final diagram, it is possible that the empty chest will topple over when pushed at the top as shown.

A force, therefore, must have a size (magnitude) and a direction. In other words, a force is a **vector**. We also see that the point where the force acts on an object makes a difference: objects can be made to rotate and tilt. It is easier to shut a door by pushing on the door handle than it is by pushing near the hinges.

At this level, however, we do not want or need to introduce the added complication of rotating objects. We want to study motion in a way which makes this aspect of mechanics unnecessary. We achieve this by adopting a particular model for objects.

Key Fact 23.1 Point Objects

We shall model objects as a point. A point has no dimensions, just position.

Whether our problem is concerned with the motion of a car, a cricket ball, a brick or an elephant, this model assumes that the actual dimensions of the object have no importance. Whether this is a valid assumption to make raises the question of the usefulness of the model. If we are throwing a cricket ball, then the dimensions of the ball itself are small compared to the distance over which it is likely to be thrown, and so it is perhaps reasonable to pretend that the ball itself has no size. If our problem concerned the fate of a hapless elephant falling down a mineshaft, then the size of the elephant would probably have a significant effect on the problem, and the point object model might be inappropriate.

Working with the point object model of mechanics has one immediate advantage; since an object has no size, there is no choice about where a force can act on it, so we do not need to worry about where a force acts: all that matters is its magnitude and its direction.

The SI unit for force is the **Newton**, abbreviated as N. For the present, we shall not concern ourselves with how large a force of 1 N is; that will become clear when we consider dynamics in the next chapter.

23.3   Adding Forces

Since force is a vector, we can add forces by adding vectors.

Key Fact 23.2

If a number of forces act on an object, the **resultant** force is the vector sum of the forces acting on it.

As we know, the sum of vectors can be determined by geometrical methods.

Example 23.3.1. *Two perpendicular forces, of magnitude 5 N and 2.6 N, act on a particle. Determine the resultant force on the particle.*

The resultant of the two forces can be determined by placing the two vectors 'tip-to-tail'. Suppose that the resultant force has magnitude X N, and acts at an angle of θ to the direction of action of the 5 N force.

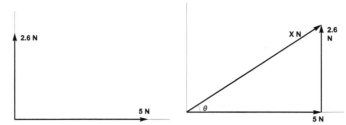

Figure 23.2

Pythagoras' Theorem tells us that

$$X^2 = 5^2 + 2.6^2$$

and hence the resultant force has magnitude $X = 5.64$ N. Simple trigonometry tells us that

$$\tan\theta = \frac{2.6}{5}$$

and hence that $\theta = 27.5°$.

Example 23.3.2. *Figure 23.3 shows three forces acting on a particle. Determine the resultant force.*

Add the forces one by one, starting with the 3 N and the 4 N forces. Putting these forces 'tip to tail', we see that the sum of these vectors has magnitude $X = \sqrt{3^2 + 4^2} = 5$ N, at an angle θ to the 'horizontal', where $\tan\theta = \frac{3}{4}$, and so $\theta = 36.87°$.

Adding the third vector to the sum of the first two, we note that $\alpha = \theta - 20° = 16.87°$. The resultant force has magnitude R N, where (by the cosine rule)

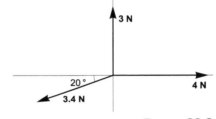

Figure 23.3

$$R^2 = 5^2 + 3.4^2 - 2 \times 5 \times 3.4 \times \cos\alpha$$

so that $R = 2.01$ N. The sine rule tells us that

$$\frac{\sin\beta}{3.4} = \frac{\sin\alpha}{R},$$

we obtain $\sin\beta = 0.4919$, so $\beta = 29.47°$. The resultant force has magnitude 2.01 N at an angle of $\beta + \theta = 66.3°$ to the 'horizontal' (or on a bearing of 023.7°).

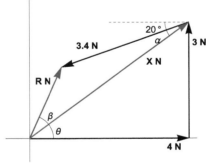

Figure 23.4

Example 23.3.3. *The three forces shown in Figure 23.5 act on an object, and the resultant force is zero. Describe the magnitude and direction of the force **F**.*

Since the three forces acting on the object have zero resolvent, when placed 'tip-to-tail' they must end up at their starting point; in other words the three vectors form a **vector triangle**. The cosine rule tells us that

$$F^2 = 5^2 + 2^2 - 2 \times 5 \times 2 \times \cos 30°$$

and hence $F = 3.42$ N.

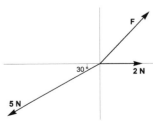

Figure 23.5

The sine rule now tells us that

$$\frac{\sin(180° - \alpha)}{5} = \frac{\sin 30°}{F}$$

and hence $\beta = 47.0°$. The third force has magnitude 3.42 N, and acts in a direction at an angle of 47.0° 'to the horizontal' (on a bearing of 043.0°).

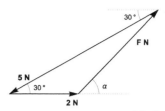

Figure 23.6

Trigonometry can be used as above to solve all questions about adding forces, but the technique is extremely laborious. If more than three forces are to be added, the calculations become even worse. We need a more efficient method of adding forces and determining the resolvent force; the technique of taking components is just as useful when adding forces as it was when adding abstract vectors.

Example 23.3.4. *By taking components, find the resolvent of the three forces being added in Figure 23.3.*

Introduce the standard unit vectors **i** and **j** where **i** points 'horizontally to the right' and **j** points 'vertically up'. The three forces in this question can now be written 4**i** N, 3**j** N and $-3.4\cos 20°\mathbf{i} - 3.4\sin 20°\mathbf{j}$ N. Thus the resultant force is

$$4\mathbf{i}+3\mathbf{j}-3.4\cos 20°\mathbf{i}-3.4\sin 20°\mathbf{j} = (4-3.4\cos 20°)\mathbf{i}+(3-3.4\sin 20°)\mathbf{j} = 0.80505\mathbf{i}+1.83713\mathbf{j} \text{ N},$$

This resultant force has magnitude $\sqrt{0.80505^2 + 1.83713^2} = 2.01$ N, and acts at an angle $\tan^{-1}\frac{1.83713}{0.80505} = 66.3°$ 'to the horizontal'.

Example 23.3.5. *By taking components, determine the third force **F** in Example 23.3.3.*

With the unit vectors **i** and **j** pointing in the usual directions, the three vectors acting on the object are 2**i** N, $-5\cos 30°\mathbf{i} - 5\sin 30°\mathbf{j}$ N and $F\mathbf{N}$. Since the resolvent force on the object is zero, we deduce that

$$2\mathbf{i} - 2.5\sqrt{3}\mathbf{i} - 2.5\mathbf{j} + \mathbf{F} = \mathbf{0},$$

so that $\mathbf{F} = (2.5\sqrt{3} - 2)\mathbf{i} + 2.5\mathbf{j} = 2.33013\mathbf{i} + 2.5\mathbf{j}$ N. The third force has magnitude $\sqrt{2.33013^2 + 2.5^2} = 3.42$ N, acting at an angle $\tan^{-1}\frac{2.5}{2.33013} = 47.0°$ 'to the horizontal'.

For Interest

As we can see from these examples, the component-based calculations are much simpler.

EXERCISE 23A

1. For each of the following systems of forces, determine the resultant force using vector addition.

a)   b)   c)

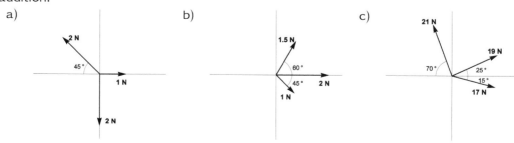

2. For each of the following systems of forces, the resultant force is zero. Draw a triangle of forces, and identify the unknown force **F**:

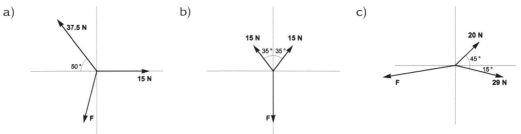

a)

b)

c)

3. Repeat the calculations for Questions 1 and 2 using components.

4. For each of the following systems of forces, the resultant force is zero. Determine the unknown quantities:

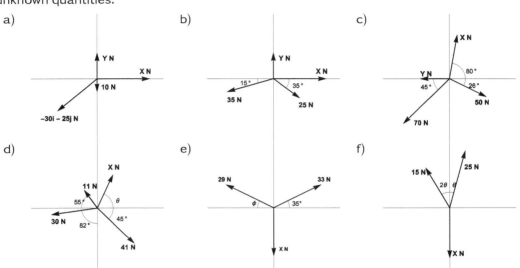

a)

b)

c)

d)

e)

f)

5. Find the resultant of the two vectors **P** and **Q** in the following cases:

   a) **P** has magnitude 15 N and bearing 025°, **Q** has magnitude 10 N and bearing 075°,

   b) **P** has magnitude 20 N and bearing 030°, **Q** has magnitude 15 N and bearing 115°,

   c) **P** has magnitude 25 N and bearing 045°, **Q** has magnitude 20 N and bearing 200°,

   d) **P** has magnitude 10 N and bearing 065°, **Q** has magnitude 5 N and bearing 310°.

6. A car is being pushed by two people. The magnitude and direction of each force is shown in the Figure. Find the resultant of the two forces.

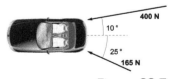

Figure 23.7

7. A particle of weight 4 N is attached to one end of a piece of string. The other end of the string is attached to a fixed point O. With the string taut, P travels in a circular path in a vertical plane. The string exerts a force **T** on the particle in the direction PO as shown in the Figure. The resultant of **T** and the weight of P is denoted **R**.

   a) The magnitude of **T** is 28 N when P is at A, the lowest point of the circular path. State the direction of **R** when P is in this position, and find its magnitude.

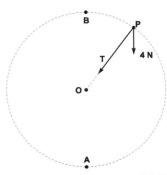

Figure 23.8

b) The magnitude of **T** is 4 N when P is at B, the highest point of the circular path. State the direction of **R** when P is in this position, and find its magnitude.

c) The magnitude of **T** is 16 N when OP is horizontal. Find the magnitude and direction of **R** when P is in this position.

8. In each of the following cases, find the magnitudes of the forces **P** and **Q**, whose resultant is **R**:

- **R** has magnitude 20 N due north, **P** and **Q** have bearings 040° and 320°,

- **R** has magnitude 25 N due east, **P** and **Q** have bearings 110° and 310°,

- **R** has magnitude 30 N due south, **P** and **Q** have bearings 075° and 225°,

- **R** has magnitude 35 N due west, **P** and **Q** have bearings 220° and 300°,

23.4   Types Of Force

Certain types of force are very common, and we need to be familiar with them.

- **Gravity** The gravitational attraction of the earth on another object acts vertically downwards towards the centre of the earth. The size of the force is proportional to the mass of the object in question. The formula relating the mass m kilogrammes of the object and the gravitational force W N acting on it is given by the formula

$$W = mg,$$

where g is the acceleration at the earth's surface due to gravity. Recall that, if we need to assign g a numerical value, we write $g = 10 \text{ ms}^{-2}$. The gravitational force on an object is often called its **weight** (this is a not quite correct, but useful, term).

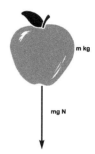

Figure 23.9

- **Tension** When a string or rod is pulled in way that might stretch it, it exerts a force called **tension** in response. A boy playing with a yo-yo will exert an upwards force on the string. The string will exert a tension T in response, and this tension will be felt by the boy, and will also act on the yo-yo, opposing the force of gravity W acting on it. We say that a string is **light** if we intend to assume that the string has no mass (or, more realistically, negligible mass compared with the other objects in the system); if a string is light, the tension in the string is the same throughout its length.

Figure 23.10

- **Thrust** When the ends of a rigid object such as a pole or a bar are pushed, in an attempt to compress it, the pole exerts a **thrust** in response. Like tension, thrust will be assumed to be constant throughout the rod. The gravitational weight of the top of the lamp stand acts on the lamp pole, which exerts a thrust T in response. This thrust T is also exerted on the ground.

Figure 23.11

- **Contact Forces: Normal Reaction** (Figure 23.12) When two objects touch, they exert a force on each other. The first of these forces is called the **normal reaction**, which is exerted in a direction perpendicular (normal) to the plane of contact of the two objects. The table top exerts a normal reaction R on the kettle (which prevents the kettle from 'falling through' the table). The normal reaction acts to oppose the gravitational attraction W that also acts on the kettle.

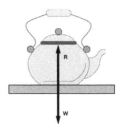

Figure 23.12

- **Contact Forces: Friction** Surfaces can be **rough** or **smooth**. If surfaces are smooth, they can exert normal reaction contact forces only. If a surface is rough, it can also exert a **friction force**. A friction force will always be exerted parallel to the surface, and in such a direction as to oppose any possible motion.

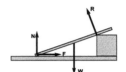

Figure 23.13

A pencil is propped against a box on a table. The box is smooth, but the table is rough. There are four forces acting on the pencil: its weight W, the normal reaction R at the point of contact of the box with the pencil, the normal reaction force N of the table, and a friction force F from the table. Since, if it moves at all, the pencil will slide down and slip off the book, the friction force is pointed in a way that will oppose the tendency of the pencil to slide. Note that the normal reaction R is acting normally to the pencil.

There are more complicated reaction forces. A door hinge can exert a reaction force in any direction, for example.

23.5 Elements of Mechanical Models

The real world is very complicated, and an accurate description of how objects behave in it involves taking into account a wide variety of factors. However, some factors only have a very small effect, and can be ignored, provided that it sensible to do so. For example, if we are throwing a ball, the fact that the earth is spherical is unlikely to affect whether or not we will hit the stumps; nor will the fact that the earth is rotating matter. However, if we were launching an intercontinental ballistic missile, both of these factors would become very relevant. Similarly, if we dropped a small ball bearing from a height of several metres onto the floor, the size of the ball bearing, and the effects of air resistance, would be negligible; dropping a sheet of paper would be a very different matter.

Mathematical modelling is a matter of striking a balance; we want a description of the real world which is sufficiently simple for us to be able to solve the relevant equations, and yet one which is accurate enough to yield results that are useful.

In this course we shall be considering very simple models of mechanics. While the models we will be working with are inaccurate, they are nonetheless useful, since they enable us to understand some of the basic principles behind mechanics without becoming overburdened with details.

Our models will comprise the following elements.

- **Point Particles** As we have already said, we won't be concerned with the shape of objects. We will only try to describe an object like a ball, book or car in terms of its position, and take no account of which way it is facing, its shape, whether it is rotating, and so on. This is clearly an extremely large simplification, and is probably the most physically unrealistic of the simplifications that we make. We have removed the ability of footballers to curve the ball. On the bright side, though, a tall pile of books will never topple over. Under moderate circumstances, however, we nonetheless can obtain useful information from modelling objects as particles.

- A **bead** is a particle that has a hole drilled through it, so that it can slide along a **wire**, which is a thin rigid shape. A bead on a wire is a particle that is constrained so that it can only move along the path of the wire.

- **Rods** Tow-bars on caravans, struts supporting objects and broom handles are all examples of objects that will be modelled as rods. A rod is something that is regarded as only having length, and no width and breadth. Rods do not change their length; they can be both under tension and in compression, in which case they exert forces along their length.

- **Light** objects are assumed to have no mass. In reality a light object will have a mass that is extremely small compared to other masses in the system.

- **Strings** are flexible objects that have length, but no width or breadth. Strings are generally light. We shall only be considering **inextensible** strings. These strings never stretch, but always remain the same length. Strings can be under tension, exerting tension along their length, but they cannot be under compression; if they are not under tension, strings go slack.

- **Surfaces** are flat regions on which objects can move. Surfaces always exert normal reaction forces on objects that touch them. **Rough** surfaces also exert friction forces, while **smooth** surfaces do not. An ice rink is a good example of a smooth surface, a plank of wood an example of a rough one. The **surface of the earth** will be modelled as a horizontal surface.

- A **peg** is a small fixed object against which other objects can rest. They can be either rough or smooth.

- A **pulley** is an object over which a string can be run to allow the string to change direction while still under tension. A peg can be used for the same purpose. Pulleys can be rough or smooth.

- The force of **gravity** will be assumed to be constant on a particle, acting vertically downwards.

- In most cases, objects will fall **without being affected by air resistance.**

Example 23.5.1. *Model the motion of a ball after it has been hit by a bat.*

We start by modelling the ball as a point particle. No air resistance acts on the particle, and so the only force acting is the force of gravity, which is constant and acts vertically downwards. Whatever the initial velocity of the ball might be, subsequent motion will not move the ball out of the vertical plane defined by that initial velocity and the downward vertical. Thus it is possible to regard this as a two-dimensional problem. If we set up a coordinates system, the surface of the earth is represented by the x-axis, with the y-axis pointing vertically upwards. The position of the ball can be given by its coordinates (x, y).

As we shall see in Chapter 27, this model predicts a parabolic path for the ball; real life experience shows that the true path is more like the asymmetric path with the shorter range.

Figure 23.14

The true path has been calculated taking air resistance into account.

Example 23.5.2. *A book of weight 5 N rests on a rough lectern which is angled at a $15°$ to the horizontal. The book is prevented from sliding down the slope by a horizontal force of 1 N.*

Breaking the problem down to its essentials, the book is modelled as a point particle, and the lectern is modelled as a plane surface. No motion is taking place, and so the problem can be modelled two-dimensionally, with the lectern represented as a straight line at $15°$ to the horizontal, and the book as a point particle at rest on this line.

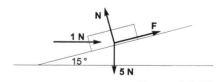

Figure 23.15

The book is acted on by a normal reaction N perpendicular to the lectern, a friction force F parallel to the lectern, its weight 5 N and the additional horizontal force of 1 N. Although we still drew the book as a rectangle, to represent its being a book, we could have simply marked it as a point.

1. A boy is sliding down a slide, which is inclined at $30°$ to the horizontal. Draw a diagram to represent this problem, marking clearly all forces acting on the boy.

2. A car is towing a caravan. In addition to the driving force of the car's engine, there are resistance forces acting on both the car and the caravan. Draw a diagram to show the fores acting on the car, and a separate diagram to show the forces acting on the caravan. How would your diagrams differ if the car was decelerating rather than accelerating?

3. Two particles, each of weight 10 N, are attached to opposite ends of a light inextensible string. The string is looped over a smooth pulley, and both particles are hanging at rest. Draw a diagram to indicate the forces acting on the two particles, and another diagram to indicate the forces acting on the pulley.

4. A camera is resting on horizontal ground on a light tripod. Draw a diagram to represent the forces acting on the camera.

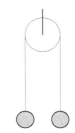

Figure 23.16

5. A ladder rests on a rough horizontal floor, and is leaning against a smooth vertical wall. Draw a diagram, indicating all the forces acting on the ladder.

6. A boy is sitting on a swing. Draw a diagram to show the forces acting on the boy, another diagram to show the forces acting on the seat of the swing.

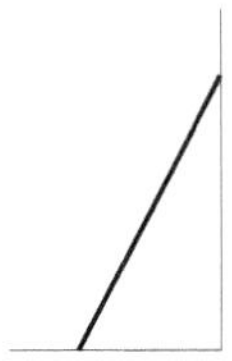

Figure 23.17

7. A 10 kg mass and a 2 kg mass are attached at opposite ends of a light inextensible string, which is passed over a smooth pulley. The 10 kg mass is lying on a rough sloping surface, while the 2 kg mass hangs vertically below the pulley. Draw a diagram indicating all the forces acting on both particles.

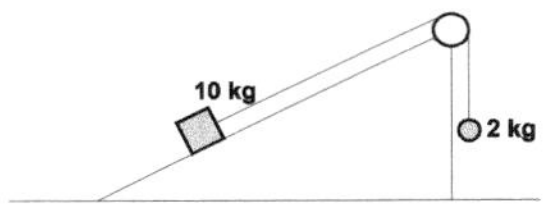

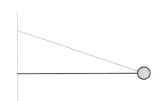

Figure 23.18

8. A 10 kg brass sphere is hangs from a wall. It is attached to the end of a horizontal rod which is fastened to the wall at its other end, and is held in place by a thin wire, as shown in the diagram. Draw a diagram to indicate the forces acting on the sphere.

Figure 23.19

> **Food For Thought 23.1**
>
> The ability to draw and label clear force diagrams is essential to success in mechanics.

23.6 Equilibrium

Since the time of Aristotle, it had been thought that objects only moved because they were being pushed or pulled and that, if no force was being applied, motion stopped. In the 17th century, Isaac Newton proposed a series of ideas which totally contradicted this; force did not produce velocity, but rather **change** velocity. Thus, if there is no overall force acting, there is no change of velocity. Although this idea was a special case of a more general idea he proposed at the same time, Newton felt that this change of approach to force was sufficiently dramatic that it needed stating separately from the more general result.

Key Fact 23.3 Newton's First Law

Every object remains at rest, or moves with constant velocity, unless an external force acts to change that state.

Note that, although Newton's Laws are called Laws, they are in truth only models of the real world, albeit pretty good ones. When the resultant forces acting on a particle are zero, Newton's first law states that a particle's velocity does not change. We say that the particle is in **equilibrium**. If the particle is stationary, we call the equilibrium **static**. If the particle is in motion, we all the equilibrium **dynamic**.

Key Fact 23.4 Equilibrium

An object is in equilibrium (either static or dynamic) if the resultant force acting on it is zero.

To determine whether or not a particle is in equilibrium, we need to determine the resultant force acting on it. As previously in this chapter, this can be done by vector methods, or much more simply by taking components. Rather than calculating all components of the resultant forces at the same time, we find it convenient to calculate resultant forces one component at a time. This technique is called **resolving**.

Key Fact 23.5 Resolving

If a force of F N acts in a direction that makes an angle θ with a given direction d, then the effect of the force in that direction is $F\cos\theta$. This is called the **resolved part** of the force in that direction.
If we consider mutually perpendicular unit vector $\mathbf{i}$ and $\mathbf{j}$ pointing parallel to and perpendicular to the direction d, then the force can be written in components as $F\cos\theta\mathbf{i} + F\sin\theta\mathbf{j}$. Thus the resolved part of the force in the direction d is just the $\mathbf{i}$ component of the force.

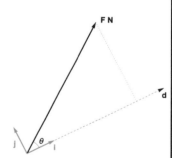

Figure 23.20

Example 23.6.1. *A kettle of weight W N rests on a horizontal table. Find the magnitude of the normal reaction between the table and the kettle.*

The resultant force on the kettle must be zero. We can avoid writing all the forces as vectors simply by resolving vertically, from which we deduce that $R - W = 0$, so that $R = W$ N.

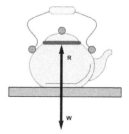

Figure 23.21

Example 23.6.2. *A box of mass 15 kg is at rest on a smooth horizontal floor. A rope is attached to the box, and is pulling on the box at an angle of 30° above the horizontal. It is held in place by a horizontal force of magnitude 20 N. What is the magnitude of the tension in the rope, and what is the magnitude of the normal reaction of the floor on the box?*

The four forces acting on the box are marked. The tension in the rope is T N, while the normal reaction force is R N. Since the floor is smooth, we may assume that no other force acts between the floor and the box. Since the box is at rest, it is in equilibrium, and hence the resultant force acting on the box is zero. Indeed, if we resolve forces **in any direction**, then the resultant resolved force in that direction must be zero. We need to decide on some convenient directions in which to resolve.

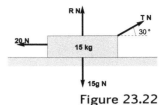

Figure 23.22

Start by resolving horizontally. We deduce that

$$T \cos 30° - 20 = 0$$

and hence $T = 23.1$ N. Resolving forces vertically gives

$$R + T \sin 30° - 15g = 0$$

so that $R = 150 - \frac{1}{2}T = 138$ N (to 3 SF).

Example 23.6.3. *A sphere of mass 20 kg is at rest between two smooth wedges. One wedge is angled at 55° to the horizontal; the other is angled at 35° to the horizontal. Find the normal reactions between the two wedges and the sphere.*

We could solve this problem by resolving forces horizontally and vertically. Resolving horizontally tells us that

$$R_1 \sin 35° - R_2 \sin 55° = 0,$$

while resolving forces horizontally tells us that

$$R_1 \cos 35° + R_2 \cos 55° = 20g.$$

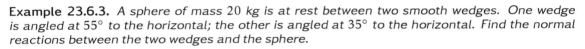

Figure 23.23

Thus $R_2 = \dfrac{\sin 35°}{\sin 55°} R_1$, and hence

$$R_1 \cos 35° + \frac{\sin 35°}{\sin 55°} R_1 \cos 55° = 20g$$
$$R_1 (\sin 55° \cos 35° + \sin 35° \cos 55°) = 20g \sin 55°$$
$$R_1 = R_1 \sin(55° + 35°) = 20g \sin 55°$$

so that $R_1 = 164$ N (3 SF). Thus $R_2 = \dfrac{\sin 35°}{\sin 55°} R_1 = 115$ N (3 SF).

An alternative approach would be to notice that faces of the two wedges are perpendicular to each other, and hence that the normal reactions R_1 and R_2 act in perpendicular directions; if we choose the directions in which we resolve carefully, we should be able to calculate R_1 and R_2 one at a time.

A little angle-calculation tells us that the angle between the line of action of R_1 and the downward vertical is 35°; this is the angle that will enable us to resolve the weight in various directions. Resolving parallel to the 55° wedge, gives us

$$R_1 - 20g \cos 35° = 0,$$

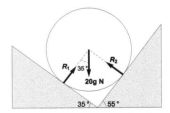

Figure 23.24

while resolving forces parallel to the 35° wedge gives us

$$R_2 - 20g \sin 35° = 0.$$

We have obtained the same answers as before, with less effort.

Example 23.6.4. *A particle of mass 10 kg is at rest on a smooth slope that is inclined at 15° to the horizontal. It is held in place by the application of a force of P N. What is the magnitude of P if this force is applied:*

(a) *horizontally,*

(b) *at an angle of* $20°$ *above the horizontal,*

(c) *parallel to the slope?*

In which direction should the force P be applied if the magnitude of P is to be as small as possible?

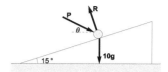

All three parts of this problem are basically the same, except in the angle of application of the force P. We will try to solve the problem generally, rather than repeating almost identical calculations. Let us suppose that P acts on the particle at an angle of θ above the horizontal.

Figure 23.25

The key point that simplifies our calculations is that we are not interested in the value of the normal reaction force R, so we might as well resolve in a direction that removes R from the calculation. This is done by resolving **parallel to the slope.**

Note that P, which is acting at an angle of θ above the horizontal, is therefore acting at an angle of $\theta + 15°$ to the slope. Resolving forces parallel to the slope then gives

$$P\cos(\theta + 15°) = 10g\sin 15°.$$

and so $P = \dfrac{100\sin 15°}{\cos(\theta + 15°)}$ N. We can now solve the individual parts of the question:

(a) If P acts horizontally, then $\theta = 0$, and so $P = 100\tan 15° = 26.8$ N.

(b) If P acts at an angle of $20°$ above the horizontal, then $\theta = 20°$, and so $P = \dfrac{100\sin 15°}{\cos 35°} = 31.6$ N.

(c) If P acts parallel to the slope, then $\theta = -15°$, and so $P = 100\sin 15° = 25.9$ N.

It is clear that P is at least, equal to $100\sin 15°$, when $\cos(\theta + 15°) = 1$ and that is when $\theta = -15°$. The force P is minimised when it acts parallel to the slope.

If we wished, we could resolve forces perpendicular the slope now, and retrieve the value of the normal reaction R.

Sometimes there is no nice direction in which to resolve, and we must resort to algebraic hard work.

Example 23.6.5. *A load of weight W N is hung from two light wires. These wires are fixed at angles of θ_1 and θ_2 above the horizontal. Find expressions for the tensions in the two wires in terms of W, θ_1 and θ_2.*

Resolving forces horizontally tells us that

$$T_1\cos\theta_1 - T_2\cos\theta_2 = 0$$

and resolving forces vertically tells us that

$$T_1\sin\theta_1 + T_2\sin\theta_2 = W.$$

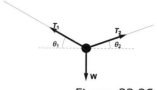

Figure 23.26

Eliminating T_2 from these equations (by multiplying the first by $\sin\theta_2$, the second by $\cos\theta_2$, and adding) gives

$$\begin{aligned} T_1(\cos\theta_1\sin\theta_2 + \sin\theta_1\cos\theta_2) &= W\cos\theta_2 \\ T_1\sin(\theta_1 + \theta_2) &= W\cos\theta_2 \end{aligned}$$

and hence $T_1 = \dfrac{W\cos\theta_2}{\sin(\theta_1 + \theta_2)}$. Hence $T_2 = \dfrac{W\cos\theta_1}{\sin(\theta_1 + \theta_2)}$.

Had we done this question with specific numerical values of θ_1 and θ_2, it is likely that we would have missed the appearance of $\sin(\theta_1 + \theta_2)$ in the final formulae. This is one of the benefits of an algebraic approach.

EXERCISE 23C

1. A laundry basket of mass 5 kg is being pulled, with constant speed, along a corridor by a rope inclined at $20°$ to the horizontal. Given that the frictional force has magnitude 33 N, find the tension in the rope.

2. A car of mass 850 kg is being pushed along a level road with a force of magnitude T N, directed upwards at $25°$ to the horizontal, and also pulled by a horizontal force of 283 N. There is a constant force of 600 N opposing the motion. The car is moving at constant speed. Find the value of T, and the total normal contact force from the road.

3. A lamp is supported in equilibrium by two chains fixed to two points A and B at the same level. The lengths of the chains are 0.3 m and 0.4 m and the distance between A and B is 0.5 m. Given that the tension in the longer chain is 36 N, show by resolving horizontally that the tension in the shorter chain is 48 N. By resolving vertically, find the mass of the lamp.

4. A child's toy of mass 5 kg is pulled along level ground by a string inclined at $30°$ to the horizontal. Denoting the tension in the string by T N, find, in terms of T, an expression for the normal contact force between the toy and the floor, and deduce that T cannot exceed 100.

5. A block of wood of mass 4.5 kg rests on a table. A force of magnitude 35 N, acting upwards at an angle of θ to the horizontal, is applied to the block but does not move it. Given that the normal contact force between the block and the table has magnitude 30 N, calculate:

   a) the value of θ,
   b) the frictional force acting on the block.

6. A concrete slab of mass m kg is being raised vertically, at a constant speed, by two cables. One of the cables is inclined at $10°$ to the vertical and has a tension of 2800 N; the other cable has a tension of 2400 N. Calculate the angle at which this cable is inclined to the vertical, and also find the value of m, assuming there is no air resistance.

7. A man is pulling a chest of mass 40 kg along a horizontal floor with a force of 140 N inclined at $30°$ to the horizontal. His daughter is pushing with a force of 50 N directed downwards at $10°$ above the horizontal. The chest is moving with constant speed. Calculate the magnitude, F N, of the frictional force, and the magnitude, R N, of the normal contact force from the ground on the chest. Show that the fraction $\frac{F}{R}$ lies between 0.50 and 0.51.

8. A particle is in equilibrium under the action of the three forces shown in the diagram. By resolving in the direction of the force of magnitude Y N, show that $Y = 5$. Calculate the value of X.

9. Calculate the magnitude of the horizontal force needed to maintain a crate of mass 6 kg in equilibrium, when it is resting on a frictionless plane inclined at $20°$ to the horizontal. Calculate also the magnitude of the normal contact force acting on the crate.

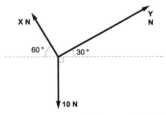

Figure 23.27

10. A skier of mass 78 kg is pulled at constant speed up a slope, of inclination $12°$, by a force of magnitude 210 N acting upwards at an angle of $20°$ to the slope. Find the magnitudes of the frictional force and the normal contact force acting on the skier.

11. A particle of mass m kg is placed on a smooth plane inclined at angle θ to the horizontal. Find the magnitude of the force required to keep the particle in equilibrium if it acts at an angle of α to the slope. What is the least possible force needed to keep the particle in equilibrium?

12. The lid of a desk is hinged along one edge so that it can be tilted at various angles to the horizontal. A book of mass 1.8 kg is placed on the lid. The lid is tilted to an angle of $15°$, as shown in the Figure. Find the frictional force, given that the book does not move.
As the desk lid is tilted further, the book begins to move when the lid is inclined at θ to the horizontal. Given that the maximum magnitude that the frictional force can attain is 8.45 N, find the maximum value of θ for which equilibrium remains unbroken.

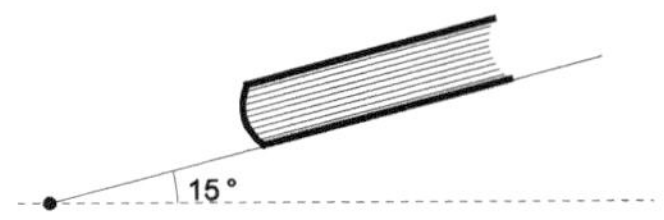

Figure 23.28

13. A metal sphere of weight 500 N is suspended from a fixed point O by a chain. The sphere is pulled to one side by a horizontal force of magnitude 250 N and the sphere is held in equilibrium with the chain inclined at an angle θ to the vertical. Find the tension in the string and the value of θ.

14. A picture of mass 12 kg is supported in equilibrium by two strings, inclined at $20°$ and $70°$ to the horizontal. Calculate the tension in each string.

15. A box of mass 12 kg is dragged, at a constant speed, up a path inclined at $30°$ to the horizontal. The force pulling the box has magnitude $2X$ N and acts at $10°$ to the path, as shown in the Figure. The frictional force has magnitude X N. Calculate the value of X and the magnitude of the normal contact force of the path on the box.

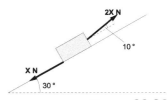

Figure 23.29

16. A boat on a trailer is held in equilibrium on a slipway inclined at $20°$ to the horizontal, by a cable inclined at θ to a line of greatest slope of the slipway, as shown on the Figure. The combined mass of the boat and trailer is 1250 kg. The cable may break if the tension exceeds 7000 N. Find the maximum value of θ.

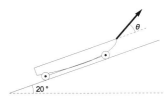

Figure 23.30

17. The two ends of a light inextensible string of length 26 m are attached to two points A and B. The points A and B are the same vertical height above the ground, and are a distance of 24 m apart. A light ring is threaded onto the string, and a mass of m kg is attached to the ring. The ring can slide smoothly on the string. When the system is in equilibrium, the two sections of the string make angles of θ_A and θ_B with the horizontal at A and B respectively.

   a) Explain why $\theta_A = \theta_B$.

   b) Find an expression for the tension T in the string in terms of θ_A, m and g.

18*. A weight of mass M kg hangs from the end of a light string. The other end of the string is attached to the end C of a rod AC, while the other end A of the rod is fixed to a vertical wall. The rod AC makes an angle θ with the wall. The system is held in equilibrium by a light string, which is attached to the rod at C, and also attached to the wall again at B, where the lengths AB and AC are equal. Find an expression for the tension T N in the string in terms of M, θ and g.

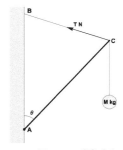

Figure 23.31

23.7 Friction

Imagine that you are trying to push a heavy box along a horizontal platform as in Figure 23.32. One of two things might happen. If you push hard enough, the box will start to move in the direction you are pushing in. If you don't push as hard, the box will stay where it is. In either case your push will be opposed by a frictional force.

This frictional force acts horizontally, in the plane where the base of the box is in contact with the platform. Its direction is opposite to the direction in which the box is moving, or in which it would move if it could. Whether or not the box moves, there are four forces acting on the box: the pushing force, friction, the gravitational attraction on the box (its 'weight') and the normal reaction force from the platform.

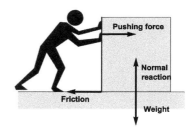

Figure 23.32

We have used these ideas in problems already but, up until now, we have simply assumed that we knew exactly what the friction force was in each situation. In this section, we will investigate the relationship between the force of friction and the other forces acting on the box.

- When you don't push the box, there is no external sideways force on the box, and so there will be no friction force being exerted. Friction only acts to oppose other forces.

- When you start pushing, the box stays stationary. Since the box is in equilibrium, the resultant force on the box is zero. Thus the normal reaction force must exactly equal the weight, and the friction force must exactly match the pushing force. As the pushing force increases, so does the friction force.

- There is a limit to the amount of friction force that can be produced. This depends on the physical properties of the box and the platform it is in contact with. Once the pushing force exceeds this maximum value, there will be a resultant horizontal force on the box, and it will start to move.

Key Fact 23.6 Friction

When an object is in contact with a fixed surface, and forces are acting upon it that might result in the object moving across the surface, these forces will be opposed by a friction force. Its direction of action is always opposite to the direction of possible motion.

The frictional force cannot exceed a certain magnitude, called the **limiting friction**. If an object is at rest, and equilibrium is possible with a frictional force not greater than the limiting friction, the object will remain at rest in equilibrium.

If the object is at rest, and the forces are in equilibrium with the limiting friction, then the object is said to be in **limiting equilibrium**, and is said to be **on the point of slipping**.

Example 23.7.1. *A dustbin of mass 20 kg is placed on a path which is at an angle of 13° to the horizontal. The limiting friction between the bin and the path is 50 N.*

(a) *Will the bin slide down the path?*

(b) *A force parallel to the slope is applied to the bin so that it is on the point of moving up the path. How large is this force?*

(a) There are three forces on the bin: its weight, the normal reaction force and friction. There is no possibility of motion perpendicular to the surface, and only the weight of the bin and the friction force have components parallel to the path. Resolving parallel to the path, the bin will be in equilibrium provided that $F = 20g\cos 77° = 45.0$ N. Since this value is less than the limiting friction, equilibrium is possible. The bin will not slide down the path.

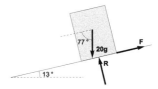

Figure 23.33

(b) Since the bin is on the point of sliding up the slope, friction has the limiting value of 50 N, and acts down the slope. If the applied force is P N, then resolving forces parallel to the slope tells us that
$$P - 50 - 20g\cos 77° = 0$$
and so $P = 95.0$ N.

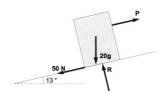

Figure 23.34

The next question to ask is, how large is the limiting friction? It might depend on a number of factors, such as

- the materials that the surfaces in contact consist of,

- the shape and area of the region of contact between the surfaces,

- the other forces acting on the object.

The first of these is obviously important. Other things being equal, wood sliding across gravel produces much more friction than polished steel sliding across ice. Any model of friction has to take account of the difference in roughness of various materials. Experiments suggest that shape and area do not have much effect on the size of the limiting friction. However, there are exceptions to this. For example, a new car tyre with a well-designed tread can produce more friction than a worn tyre, even though both are made of the same material.

The effect of the other forces certainly needs to be taken into account. We can show this by carrying out a simple experiment. Two people are standing next to each other. One is holding a slim book, while the is holding a heavy dictionary. Both books are in covers of the same material. The two people are holding these books by the strange method of clenching them tightly between their fists, as shown in the figure.

If a book has weight W, and if the friction force between the cover of the book and each fist is F, then $F = \frac{1}{2}W$. The friction force has therefore to be greater for the heavier book.

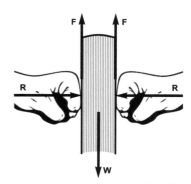

Figure 23.35

Both people try to relax their grips on the books, reducing the forces R from their knuckles. When, for each person, their book is on the point of slipping between their fists, friction is limiting.

These two people will find that the person holding the dictionary will have to maintain a much higher value of R to ensure that their book does not slip, while the person holding the lighter book will be able to relax their grip more.

The consequence of this is that a greater friction force F is possible in the presence of a greater normal reaction force R.

Notice that the same effect is the case for the box being pushed across the platform in Figure 23.32. If the box is made heavier, then we need to push harder before it starts to move. The limiting friction depends on the normal reaction force, and in this case the normal contact force has the same magnitude as the weight of the box.

If we carry out more precise experiments, we find that there is a direct proportional relationship connecting the limiting friction and the normal reaction force. If we double the normal force, the limiting friction is doubled. The rule for calculating limiting friction can then be summarised as follows.

Key Fact 23.7 The Coefficient of Friction

The limiting frictional force between two surfaces is proportional to the normal reaction force. If the normal reaction force is R, then the value of limiting friction is μR, where μ is a constant. Thus the friction force F is always such that

$$F \le \mu R ,$$

with equality when friction is limiting. The constant μ is called the **coefficient of friction**. Its value depends mainly on the materials of which the surfaces consist.

The symbol μ is the Greek letter m, pronounced mu. It is always used to denote the coefficient of friction. For most surfaces, the value of μ lies between 0.3 and 0.9, but smaller or larger values (even greater than 1) can occur.

If μ is very small, we can get useful approximate results by taking μ to be 0, so that friction is ignored. In that case, the surfaces are said to be **smooth**. If μ is greater than 0, the surfaces are said to be **rough**, and we will need to consider friction.

Example 23.7.2. *A person tries to pull a small cupboard across the floor. The mass of the cupboard is 76 kg and the coefficient of friction is 0.5. What is the maximum force that can be applied to the cupboard before it starts to move?*

Suppose that the cupboard is in equilibrium, and that the applied force is P N. Resolving forces vertically, we deduce that $R = 76g = 760$ N. Resolving forces horizontally, we deduce that $F = P$. Thus equilibrium is possible provided that $P = F \le \mu R = 380$ N. Thus the maximum applied force possible is 380 N.

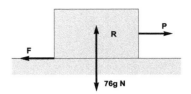

Figure 23.36

Example 23.7.3. *A particle of mass m kg lies at rest on a rough slope which is inclined at an angle of θ to the horizontal. What is the smallest possible value of the coefficient of friction μ for this to be possible?*

Clearly, friction must act up the slope to prevent the particle sliding down. If the normal reaction and the friction force on the particle are R and F respectively then, resolving forces perpendicular to the slope gives

$$R = mg\cos\theta\,,$$

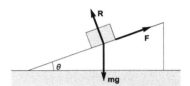

Figure 23.37

and resolving forces parallel to the slope gives

$$F = mg\sin\theta\,.$$

For this to be possible, we must have $F \le \mu R$, and hence $mg\sin\theta \le \mu mg\cos\theta$, and hence

$$\mu \ge \tan\theta\,.$$

Example 23.7.4. *A particle of mass 10 kg rests on a rough horizontal surface. It is acted upon by two forces: a horizontal force of magnitude 200 N, and a force of magnitude X N acting at an angle of $10°$ below the horizontal. The coefficient of friction between the particle and the surface is 0.2. What is the range of values of X that will enable the particle to remain at rest?*

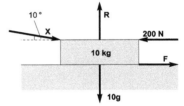

Figure 23.38

With the force X being applied, the particle will be unable to stay in equilibrium, and will slide to the left. When X is just big enough to prevent motion, friction will be limiting and pointing to the right. Resolving forces vertically yields

$$R = 10g + X\sin 10°\,,$$

while resolving forces horizontally yields

$$X\cos 10° + F = 200\,.$$

When friction is limiting, we have $F = 0.2R$, and hence

$$\begin{aligned} X\cos 10° + 0.2(10g + X\sin 10°) &= 200 \\ X(\cos 10° + 0.2\sin 10°) &= 180 \end{aligned}$$

and hence $X = 177$ N (to 3 SF).

For larger values of X, the tendency of the combined forces will be to push the particle to the right, and so friction will act in a leftwards direction. This time we deduce that

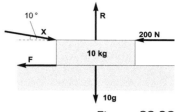

$$R = 10g + X\sin 10° \qquad X\cos 10° = F + 200 ;$$

with limiting friction, $F = \mu R$, we deduce that

$$X\cos 10° = 0.2(10g + X\sin 10°) + 200$$
$$X(\cos 10° - 0.2\sin 10°) = 220$$

Figure 23.39

and hence $X = 231$ (to 3 SF). Thus equilibrium is possible provided that $177 \le X \le 231$.

EXERCISE 23D

1. An airline passenger pushes a 15 kg suitcase along the floor with his foot. A force of 60 N is needed to move the suitcase. Find the coefficient of friction.

2. A horizontal cable from a winch is attached to a small boat of mass 800 kg which rests on horizontal ground. The coefficient of friction is $\frac{3}{4}$. The tension in the cable is increased in steps of 100 N. What is the frictional force when the tension is:

   a) 5900 N, b) 6000 N.

   Describe what happens in each of these cases.

3. The diagram shows a block of weight 50 N at rest on a plane inclined at an angle α to the horizontal, under the action of a force of magnitude P N acting up the plane. Find, in terms of P, the magnitude and direction of the frictional force acting on the block when:
   a) $P > 50\sin\alpha$, b) $P < 50\sin\alpha$
   In each case, determine the least value of the coefficient of friction which will enable the block to remain at rest.

Figure 23.40

4. The diagram shows a block of mass 4 kg at rest on a plane inclined at $35°$ to the horizontal, under the action of a force of magnitude P N acting up the plane. The coefficient of friction between the block and the plane is 0.45. Find the range of possible values of P.

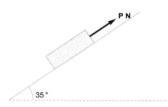

Figure 23.41

5. A bowl of mass 500 grams is placed on a table, which is tilted at various angles to the horizontal. The coefficient of friction is 0.74. What is the greatest angle at which the table can be tilted to the horizontal before the bowl slips?

6. A solid cylinder of mass 6 kg is lightly held, with its axis vertical, in the jaws of a vice, and is on the point of slipping downwards. The magnitude of the horizontal force exerted by each of the jaws is 70 N. Calculate the coefficient of friction between the vice and the cylinder.

7. A builder holds up a vertical piece of plate glass of weight 40 N by pressing the two sides with forces of P N from the palms of his hands. If the coefficient of friction is $\frac{1}{4}$, what is the least value of P needed if the glass is not to slip?

8. A shopper picks up a 2 kg packet of rice with the thumb and index finger of one hand. The coefficient of friction between her fingers and the wrapping is 0.3. What horizontal force must she exert to prevent the packet from slipping?

9. A block at rest on a horizontal floor, and is subject to various forces. The total contact force X of the floor on the block is the resultant of the normal reaction R and the frictional force F. The angle between the resultant force X and the normal to the plane (the direction of the normal reaction force N) is θ. Find an inequality relating θ and the coefficient of friction μ. Note that some authors refer to $\tan^{-1}\mu$ as the **angle of friction**.

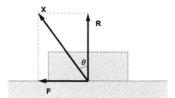

Figure 23.42

10. An object of mass 50 kg rests on a rough plane, which is at an angle of θ to the horizontal. It is held in this position by a light string parallel to the plane, whose other end is attached to a point at the top of the plane. The string will break if it has to exert a tension of more than 150 N. If the coefficient of friction between the object and the slope is 0.1 and the string does not break, what is the largest possible value of θ?

11. A block of mass m kg is at rest on a slope which is at an angle of θ to the horizontal. The coefficient of friction between the block and the slope is μ, where $\mu > \tan\theta$. A force of P N is applied to the block, acting vertically downwards. Will the block ever slip?

12*. A block of mass m kg can just rest on a rough slope when the slope is inclined at an angle of α to the horizontal. The slope is tilted further, so that it is inclined at an angle of β to the horizontal. The block is held in place by a horizontal force P. Show that the smallest possible value of P is $mg\tan(\beta - \alpha)$.

If $\alpha < 45°$ and $\beta < 90° - \alpha$, find the largest possible value of P.

13*. A light string of length $2a$ has one end attached to a rough horizontal rod. A mass of $2m$ kg is fixed to the midpoint of the string, and the other end of the string is attached to a ring of mass m kg, which is threaded on the horizontal rod. Show that the maximum distance between the two ends of the string, for equilibrium to be maintained, is

$$\frac{4a\mu}{\sqrt{1 + 4\mu^2}} \, .$$

Chapter 23: Summary

- A force is a vector; the **resultant** force acting on an object is the vector sum of the forces acting on that object.

- **Newton's First Law** states that, if no resultant force acts, an object either remains at rest or else continues to move with constant velocity. An object on which no resultant force is acting is said to be in **equilibrium**. Equilibrium can be either static or dynamic, according to whether the object is at rest or not.

- Like any other vector, a force can be analysed by considering its components. The process of identifying the component of a vector in a particular direction is called **resolving**.

- An object in contact with a surface experiences two contact forces: the **normal reaction** force, that acts perpendicularly to the surface, and the **friction force**, that acts parallel to the slope, in such a direction as to oppose any motion that might happen. There is an upper limit on the size of the friction force, called the **limiting friction**. If an object is in equilibrium, and the friction force required to maintain equilibrium is the limiting friction, the object is said to be in **limiting equilibrium**, or to be **on the point of slipping**.

- The magnitude F of the friction force and the magnitude R of the normal reaction force are related by the inequality

$$F \leq \mu R \,,$$

where μ is a constant, called the **coefficient of friction**. The value of μ depends on the materials involved in both the object and the contact surface. The value of limiting friction is μR.

Newton's Laws Of Motion

In this chapter we will learn to:

- apply Newton's Laws of motion to the linear motion of bodies of constant mass moving under the action of constant forces,

- model the motion of a body moving vertically or in an inclined plane as motion with constant acceleration, and understand any limitations of this model.

24.1   Newton's Second Law

In previous chapters, we have studied two of the three branches of Mechanics. In Chapter 22 we studied **kinematics**. This is the study of how things move, and the relationship between quantities like displacement, velocity and acceleration. Kinematics is not concerned about why objects move; it simply describes how they do move. Then, in Chapter 23 we studied **statics**. This is the study of what makes objects stay still. Newton's first and third laws were key in this study. The first law specified that the condition for (static) equilibrium was that the resultant force on a particle be zero, while the Third Law was useful in determining exactly what forces acted on a particular particle.

We now move on to the third aspect of mechanics: **dynamics**. This is the study of why things move. It tells us how the forces on a particle determine the acceleration that the particle experiences. Ideas from kinematics can then be used to determine the subsequent motion of that particle. Dynamics is the field of mechanics that makes the connection between forces and motion.

As in previous chapters, we shall continue only to consider the motion of objects that can be modelled as particles. As a consequence, there is just one principle that is needed to study dynamic systems: Newton's Second Law.

If a force is applied to an object, the object experiences an acceleration. It is reasonable to suppose that the size of that acceleration is proportional to the size of the force, and is also inversely proportional to the mass of the object; a greater force will produce a larger acceleration, but a heavier object will have to be pushed harder. Thus the force F applied is proportional to both the mass m of the object and the acceleration a experienced by that object:

$$F \propto m\mathbf{a}.$$

It is at this point that we discover the reason for the choice of Newton as the unit of force. Wherever possible, SI units are chosen to be as compatible as possible, in order to ensure that constants of proportionality are equal to 1. Thus we define 1 Newton of force to be that amount of force that will give a particle of mass 1 kg an acceleration of 1 ms^{-2}. With these units, Newton's second law of motion can be expressed as follows:

Key Fact 24.1 Newton's Second Law

If a resultant force of **F** Newtons acts on an object of mass m kg, then the object experiences an acceleration of **a** ms^{-2}, where

$$\mathbf{F} = m\mathbf{a}.$$

This relationship has been written as a vector identity (since both force and acceleration are vector quantities); the direction of the resultant force determines the direction of the acceleration of the particle.

For Interest

Newton's first law is, from one point of view, a special case of Newton's second law. It simply states that zero resultant force results in zero acceleration; in other words **a** = **0** whenever **F** = **0**. Why did Newton feel it necessary to include his first law as a separate law in addition to the second?

While, mathematically, the first law says nothing that is not stated in the second, the first law was important historically, since it marked an important difference in Newton's description of the world from the then currently accepted interpretation. Before Newton, the generally accepted description of mechanics has been provided by the Greek philosopher Aristotle. Aristotle's description of the world was that

CONSTANT FORCE PRODUCES CONSTANT VELOCITY.

For example, if a horse stops pulling a cart, the cart stops moving. From our current perspective, we can say that Aristotle forgot to include the resistance forces to motion experienced by the cart. Newton felt it important to make it absolutely clear that his interpretation of mechanics was fundamentally different from that of Aristotle; thus he had a first as well as a second law.

Aristotle: Constant speed   Newton: Constant speed

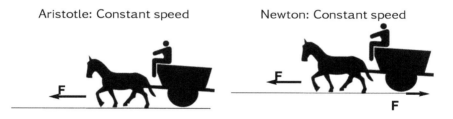

Applications of Newton's second law are often made in conjunction with kinematic calculations, frequently using SUVAT equations.

Example 24.1.1. *A car of mass 1200 kg is pushed with a force of 150 N. Calculate the acceleration of the car, and find how long it will take to reach a speed of 1.5 ms^{-1} from rest.*

Substituting $F = 150$ and $m = 1200$ into Newton's second law gives $150 = 1200a$, or $a = \frac{1}{8}$ ms^{-2}. To reach a speed of 1.5 ms^{-1} from rest, we substitute $v = 1.5$, $u = 0$ and $a = \frac{1}{8}$ into the equation $v = u + at$ to obtain $t = 12$. It takes the car 12 seconds to reach this speed.

Figure 24.1

> **Food For Thought 24.1**
>
> It is a useful convention, when labelling diagrams which contain force arrows as well as arrows indicating accelerations, that accelerations are distinguished from forces by being drawn with double-headed arrows. This simple device prevents confusion. Try to avoid marking forces, accelerations and velocities all on the same diagram.

Example 24.1.2. *In the sport of curling, a stone of mass 18 kg is placed on ice and given a push. It this produces a speed of 2 ms^{-1}, and the stone travels a distance of 30 metres before coming to rest, calculate the deceleration, and find the resistance force between the stone and the ice.*

Using the equation $v^2 = u^2 + 2as$ with $u = 2$, $v = 0$, $s = 30$, we deduce that $0 = 4 + 60a$, so that $a = -\frac{1}{15}$ ms^{-2}. Since $a < 0$, the stone is decelerating, and the resistance force must be acting in the direction that opposes the motion (the 'negative' direction). Using Newton's second law, the resistance force is $R = 18 \times \frac{1}{15} = 1.2$ N.

Figure 24.2

Example 24.1.3. *A wagon of mass 250 kg is pulled by a horizontal cable along a straight level track against a resisting force of 150 N. The wagon starts from rest. After 10 seconds it has covered a distance of 60 m. Find the tension in the cable.*

If the tension in the cable is T N and the acceleration of the wagon is a ms^{-2}, then Newton's Second Law tells us that

$$T - 150 = 250a.$$

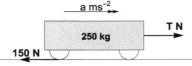

To find T, we must determine a. With $u = 0$, $t = 10$, $s = 60$, the equation $s = ut + \frac{1}{2}at^2$ reads

$$60 = 0 \times 10 + \tfrac{1}{2}a \times 10^2 = 50a$$

and hence $a = 1.2$ ms^{-2}. Thus it follows that $T = 150 + 250 \times 1.2 = 450$ N.

EXERCISE 24A

1. The engine of a car of mass 800 kg which is travelling along a straight horizontal road, is producing a driving force of 1200 N. Assuming that there are no forces resisting the motion, calculate the acceleration of the car.

2. For the first stage of its motion on the runway, before take-off, an aircraft of mass 2200 kg has a constant acceleration of 4.2 ms^{-2} Calculate the magnitude of the force necessary to provide this acceleration.

3. A wooden block of mass m kg is at rest on a table, 1.6 metres from an edge. The block is pulled directly towards the edge by a horizontal string. The tension in the string has magnitude $0.2m$ N. Calculate the time taken for the block to reach the edge of the table.

4. A particle P of mass m kg is moving in a straight line with constant deceleration. It passes point A with speed 6 ms^{-1}, and point B with speed 3.6 ms^{-1}. Given that the distance between A and B is 12 m, calculate, in terms of m, the magnitude of the force resisting the motion of P.

5. A runaway sledge of mass 10 kg travelling at 15 ms^{-1} reaches a horizontal snow field. It travels in a straight line before it comes to rest. Given that the force of friction slowing the sledge down has magnitude 60 N, calculate how far the sledge travels in the snow field.

6. A boy slides a box of mass 2 kg across a wooden floor. The initial speed of the box is 8 ms^{-1} and it comes to rest in 5 m. Calculate the deceleration of the box and find the frictional force between the box and the floor.

7. A car of mass of 1000 kg runs out of petrol and comes to rest just 30 m from a garage. The car is pushed, with a force of 120 N, along the horizontal road towards the garage. Calculate the acceleration of the car and find the time it takes to reach the garage.

8. A jet plane of mass 30 tonnes touches down with a speed of 55 ms^{-1} and comes to rest after moving for 560 m in a straight line on the runway. Assuming that the only forces stopping the plane are provided by the reverse thrust of its two engines, and that these forces are equal and directed opposite to the direction of motion, calculate the magnitude of the thrust in each engine.

9. Three men are trying to move a 100 kg skip. Two of the men are pushing horizontally with forces of magnitude 120 N and 150 N and one man is pulling with a horizontal force of magnitude X N. The frictional force resisting the motion is 385 N. Given that the skip moves with acceleration 0.1 ms^{-2}, find the value of X.

10. A motorcyclist moves with an acceleration of 5 ms^{-2} along a horizontal road against a total resistance of 120 N. The total mass of the rider and the motorcycle is 400 kg. Find the driving force provided by the engine.

11. A student is dragging a luggage trunk of mass 85 kg along a corridor with an acceleration of 0.18 ms^{-2}. The horizontal force the student exerts is 180 N. Find the frictional force between the floor and the trunk.

12. A particle of mass 5 kg is pulled, with constant speed, along a rough surface by a horizontal force of magnitude 45 N. Calculate the magnitude of the frictional force. Assuming that this force remains constant, calculate the acceleration of the particle when the magnitude of the horizontal force is increased to 55 N.

13. A railway engine of mass 5000 kg is moving at 0.25 ms^{-1} when it strikes the buffers in a siding. Given that the engine is brought to rest in 0.4 s, find the force, assumed constant, exerted on the engine by the buffers.

14. A particle of mass 2.5 kg is pulled along a horizontal surface by a string parallel to the surface with an acceleration of 2.7 ms^{-2}. Given that the frictional force resisting motion has magnitude 4 N, calculate the tension in the string. At the instant that the particle is moving with speed 3 ms^{-1}, the string breaks. Calculate how much further the particle moves before coming to rest.

15. A porter is pushing a heavy crate of mass M kg along a horizontal floor with a horizontal force of 180 N. The resistance to motion has magnitude $3M$ N. Given that the acceleration of the crate is 0.45 ms^{-2}, find the value of M.

16. One horse pulls, with a force of X N, a cart of mass 800 kg along a horizontal road at constant speed. Three horses, each pulling with a force of X N, give the cart an acceleration of 0.8 ms^{-2}. Find the time it would take two horses to increase the speed of the cart from 2 ms^{-1} to 5 ms^{-1}, given that each horse pulls with a force of X N, and that the resistance to motion has the same constant value at all times.

17. Four forces act on the corners of a square object of mass 2.5 kg. All four forces act in the plane of the square, and act towards the centre of the square. The forces have magnitudes 1 N, 1 N, 1 N and 2 N. What is the magnitude of the acceleration experienced by the object, and in which direction is it?

18. Three mutually perpendicular forces of magnitude 3 N, 6 N and 10 N act on an object of mass 2 kg. What is the magnitude of the acceleration produced?

19*. A man is pushing a crate along a rough horizontal surface. If he pushes with a horizontal force X N, the crate starts moving with acceleration a ms^{-2}. If the man doubles his effort, and pushes with a horizontal force $2X$ N, the crate starts to move with three times the acceleration. It may be assumed that friction provides a resistance to the motion that is the same in both situations. Find an expression for the magnitude of the resistance force. What acceleration would the man achieve if lubrication was applied to the ground, halving the resistance force due to friction, and he pushed with his original force of X N?

20*. A particle of mass 1 kg is moving in a straight line. At time t seconds, the velocity of the particle is v ms^{-1}. At any moment in time, the particle is subject to a force of $1 - v$ Newtons. Explain why the velocity of the particle satisfies the differential equation

$$\frac{dv}{dt} = 1 - v.$$

Initially, the particle is at rest. At exactly what time will the particle have a speed of $\frac{3}{4}$ ms1? Describe how the velocity of the particle varies with time.

24.2 Vertical Motion

We observed in Chapter 22 that the acceleration due to gravity was constant. More precisely, two objects near the surface of the earth, at the same latitude and longitude on the earth, will fall with the same acceleration (provided that they are not subject to any other forces, such as air resistance). The actual value of that acceleration varies according to where on the surface of the earth these two objects are: the altitude at that point on the earth's surface makes a difference. However, as a simple approximation, we decided to model the real world by stating that all objects near the earth's surface fall with an acceleration of g ms^{-2} where $g \approx 9.8$ (unless subject to additional forces), irrespective of where on the earth the experiment is conducted. We decided to simplify matters further by making the further approximation that $g \approx 10$, and electing to use this approximate value of g whenever numerical calculations were needed.

Now that we have Newton's second law to consider, we need to ask ourselves what produces this acceleration. Newton's answer was that the force of gravity was the cause of the acceleration. The gravitational attraction of the earth on an object of mass m kg was a force of $W = mg$ N; this force must produce an acceleration in that object of magnitude a ms^{-2}, where $W = ma$. But this implies that $a = g$, and so the acceleration experienced by the object is g ms^{-2}.

Key Fact 24.2 Gravity

The fact that the gravitational force $W = mg$ N acting on an object of mass m kg involves the acceleration g ms^{-2} is an immediate consequence of Newton's second law.

For Interest

Actually, things are a little more complicated than this. It is possible to distinguish between the **inertial mass** and the **gravitational mass** of an object. The inertial mass of an object is that mass m which occurs in the $F = ma$ equation of Newton's second law. The gravitational mass of an object is that quantity which is proportional to the force that gravity applies to it: in other words, the m in the mg formula. There is no rigorous proof that the inertial and gravitational masses of an object must be the same. However, the experimental evidence for this fact is overwhelming, and it is one of the fundamental assumptions of the theory of general relativity that these two quantities are identical.

Example 24.2.1. *A load of mass 55 kg is being winched up to a rescue helicopter. Find the tension in the cable when the helicopter is rising:*

(a) at a steady speed of 4 ms^{-1},

(b) with an acceleration of 0.8 ms^{-2}?

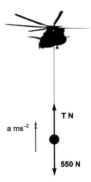

The two forces acting on the load are the tension T N in the cable and the gravitational attraction $55g = 550$ N. Newton's second law states that

$$T - 550 = 55a$$

when the load has acceleration a ms^{-2}. When the helicopter is rising at a steady rate, $a = 0$, and hence $T = 550$ N. When $a = 0.8$, the tension is $T = 550 + 55 \times 0.8 = 594$ N.

Figure 24.3

Example 24.2.2. *A pulley system is used to lift a heavy crate. There are six vertical sections of rope, each having tension T, and the crate has an upward acceleration a. Find the mass of the crate, expressing your answer in terms of T, a and g.*

481

Denote the mass of the crate by m. The forces and the acceleration are shown in the figure. The resultant upwards force on the crate is $6T - mg$ and so, by Newton's second law,

$$6T - mg = ma .$$

Making m the subject of this equation, we deduce that

$$m = \frac{6T}{g+a} .$$

Figure 24.4

Example 24.2.3. *Machinery of total mass 280kg is being lowered to the bottom of a mine by means of two ropes attached to a cage of mass 20 kg. For the first 3 seconds of the descent, the tension in each rope is 900 N. Then, for a further 16 seconds, the tension in each rope is 1500 N. For the final 8 seconds, the tension in each rope is 1725 N. Find the depth of the mine shaft.*

The mass of the machinery and cage combined is 300 kg, so the gravitational attraction on the cage and machinery is 3000 N. If, at any stage, the tension in the cables is T N, and the corresponding downwards acceleration is a ms^{-2}, then Newton's second law tells us that

$$3000 - 2T = 300a .$$

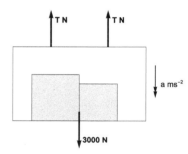

Figure 24.5

For the initial 3 seconds, we are told that $T = 900$, and hence $a = 4$. The cage accelerates from rest to a speed of $3 \times 4 = 12$ ms^{-1}.

For the middle 16 seconds, we are told that $T = 1500$, and hence $a = 0$. The cage continues to descend with constant speed 12 ms^{-1}. For the final 8 seconds, we are told that $T = 1725$, and hence $a = -1.5$. The cage decelerates from its speed of 12 ms^{-1} to its final speed of $12 - 8 \times 1.5 = 0$, and comes to rest at the bottom of the mine shaft.

Using SUVAT equations, the depth of the mine shaft is

$$\left(\tfrac{1}{2} \times 4 \times 3^2\right) + \left(12 \times 16\right) + \left(12 \times 8 - \tfrac{1}{2} \times 1.5 \times 8^2\right) = 18 + 192 + 48 = 258$$

metres.

Note that we have considered the lift cage and its contents as a single object. In Chapter 25 we will analyse systems like this in greater detail, in which case the reaction forces between the lift cage and its contents will become important.

EXERCISE 24B

1. A crane is lifting a load of mass 350 kg. The tension in the cable as the load is lifted is 4200 N. Calculate the acceleration of the load.

2. A lift bringing miners to the surface of a mine shaft is moving with an acceleration of 1.2 ms^{-2}. The total mass of the cage and the miners is 1600 kg . Find the tension in the lift cable.

3. The total mass of a hot-air balloon, occupants and ballast is 1300 kg. What is the upthrust on the balloon when it is travelling vertically upwards with constant velocity? The occupants now release 50 kg of ballast. Assuming no air resistance, find the immediate acceleration of the balloon. (The upthrust is the upward buoyancy force, which does not change when the ballast is thrown out.)

4. A steel ball of mass 1.8 kg is dropping vertically through water with an acceleration of 5.6 ms^{-2}. Find the magnitude of the force resisting the motion of the ball.

5. In a simulation of a spacecraft's lift-off an astronaut of mass 85 kg experiences a constant force of 7000 N from the seat. Calculate the acceleration of the astronaut in the simulation.

6. A boy of mass 45 kg is stranded on a beach as the tide comes in. A rescuer of mass 75 kg is lowered down, by rope, from the top of the cliff. They are raised together, initially with a constant acceleration of 0.6 ms^{-2}. Find the tension in the rope for this stage of the ascent.

   As they near the top of the cliff, the tension in the rope is 1020 N and they are moving with a constant deceleration. Calculate the magnitude of this deceleration.

7. The resisting force, R N, experienced by a parachutist travelling with speed v ms^{-1} may be modelled as $R = 135v$. It may be assumed that the parachutist moves vertically downwards at all times. At the instant that she is moving with a speed of 8 ms^{-1} she has a deceleration of 2 ms^{-2}. Find her mass.

   At what speed must the parachutist be travelling if she is experiencing no acceleration at all?

8. A stone of mass 0.1 kg drops vertically into a lake, with an entry speed of 15 ms^{-1}, and sinks a distance of 18 metres in 2 seconds. Find the resisting force, assumed constant, acting on the stone.

9. A load of mass M is raised with constant acceleration, from rest, by a rope. The load reaches a speed of v in a distance of s. The tension in the rope is T. Find an expression for s in terms of M, T, v and g.

10. A container of total mass 200 kg is being loaded on to a cargo ship by using a pulley system, similar to that used in Example 24.2.2, but with only two vertical sections of rope. In this operation the container is lifted vertically off the ground to a height of h metres. For the first 3 seconds of the ascent the tension in each cable is 1200 N. For the next second it travels at constant speed. For the final 6 seconds, before it comes to rest, the tension in each rope is T N. Find the values of h and T.

11. A load of weight 7 kN is being raised from rest with constant acceleration by a cable. After the load has been raised 20 metres, the cable suddenly becomes slack. The load continues upwards for a distance of 4 metres before coming to instantaneous rest. Assuming no air resistance, find the tension in the cable before it became slack.

24.3   More Complex Situations

We can now consider problems where a greater variety of forces act on a particle. Contact forces, such as the normal reaction and friction forces, frequently appear in problems. Just as statics problems with these forces were handled by resolving forces in various directions, dynamics problems can be solved by similar methods, plus the application of Newton's second law.

Example 24.3.1. *A block of mass 40 kg rests on a smooth horizontal surface. Two forces are applied to the block. One is horizontal, and of magnitude 15 N. The second is of magnitude 20 N, and applied at an angle of 20° below the horizontal. Determine the magnitude of the normal reaction of the surface on the block, and the acceleration of the block.*

As usual, a carefully labelled diagram is vital. Clearly, the block can only move horizontally. When we now resolve forces horizontally and vertically, we need to interpret our results differently.

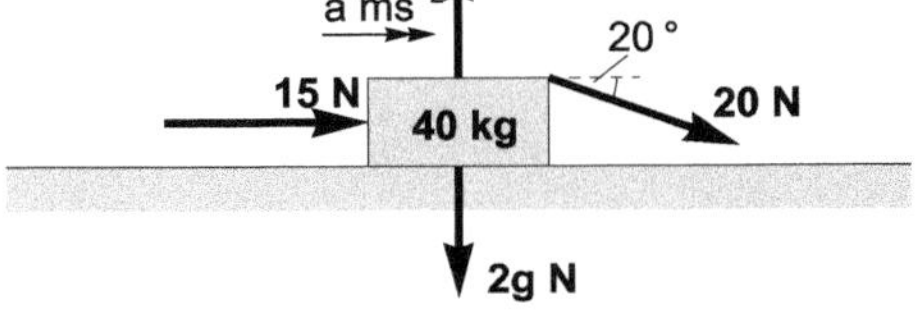

There is no vertical motion, and so the resultant vertical force must be zero. Thus, resolving forces vertically tells us that

Figure 24.6

$$R = 2g + 20\sin 20° = 26.8 \text{ N}.$$

The resultant horizontal force must be responsible for the acceleration a ms^{-2} experienced by the block. Using Newton's second law gives

$$15 + 20\cos 20° = 40a$$

and hence $a = 0.845$ ms^{-2}.

Example 24.3.2. *A particle of mass 3 kg is on a smooth slope, which is at an angle of 25° to the horizontal. Initially the particle is 10 m away from the bottom of the slope, moving uphill with a speed of 5 ms⁻¹. What is the maximum height above the bottom of the hill that is reached by the particle, and how much time elapses before the particle reaches the bottom of the slope?*

Since the slope is smooth, and all motion takes place up and down the slope, the value of the normal reaction R is unimportant. We only need to resolve parallel to the slope, and apply Newton's second law in that direction. We obtain

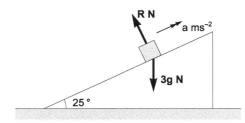

Figure 24.7

$$3a = -3g\sin 25°,$$

and hence $a = -g\sin 25°$.

The rest of the question is a matter of applying the correct SUVAT equations. With $u = 5$, $v = 0$, $a = -g\sin 25°$, the equation $v^2 = u^2 + 2as$ gives us $s = \dfrac{5^2}{2g\sin 25°} = 2.958$, so that the particle travels a distance of 2.958 m up the slope before coming to rest. Thus the maximum height reached by the particle is $(10 + 2.958)\sin 25° = 5.48$ m.

With $u = 5$, $s = -10$ and $a = -g\sin 25°$, the equation $s = ut + \frac{1}{2}at^2$ gives us

$$-10 = 5t - 5t^2\sin 25°.$$

The positive solution of this quadratic equation is $t = 3.66$, and so the particle reaches the bottom of the hill after 3.66 seconds.

Consider an object in contact with a rough surface. In statics problems, the relationship between the normal reaction R and friction contact forces F was that

$$F \le \mu R,$$

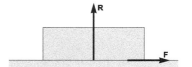

Figure 24.8

where μ is the coefficient of friction. When $F = \mu R$, we said that friction was limiting, and observed that the object was on the point of slipping.

If the maximum possible friction force μR is not sufficient to keep the object in equilibrium, slipping will occur, and the object will start to move. At this stage, the problem becomes one of dynamics. Our model of friction is that, while slipping occurs, the frictional force F is equal to μR; friction remains limiting whether the object is on the point of slipping or is actually slipping.

Key Fact 24.3 Friction Dynamics

While an object is slipping on a rough surface, friction is limiting, in that the relationship between the normal reaction R and the friction force F is

$$F = \mu R.$$

For Interest

This is a not particularly accurate model of reality. For most materials, reality is more complicated. The true picture is that a an object and a surface will have **two** coefficients of friction. While slipping does not occur, $F \le \mu_s R$, where μ_s is the **coefficient of static friction**. Once slipping occurs, $F = \mu_k R$, where μ_k is the **coefficient of kinetic friction**. For many materials, μ_k is smaller than μ_s. This is because the physical causes of friction are complex, and what is going on when slipping occurs is very different to what is going on while slipping does not occur.

However, and this is a great relief, for dry metal objects, there is very little difference between the two coefficients, and so our simple model does have a range of validity.

Example 24.3.3. *A boy kicks a stone of mass* 100 *grams across the playground. The coefficient of friction between the stone and the playground is* 0.25. *If the stone comes to rest* 31 *m away, find the speed with which the boy kicked it.*

We assume that the playground surface is horizontal. The gravitational attraction on the stone is $0.1g = 1$ N. Resolving forces vertically, we see that

$$R = 1\,\text{N}.$$

While slipping occurs, friction is limiting, and hence the friction force $F = \mu R = 0.25$ N.

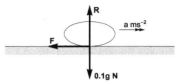

Figure 24.9

Resolving forces horizontally, and using Newton's Second Law, we obtain

$$0.1a = -F = -0.25$$

and hence $a = -2.5$ ms^{-2}. With $v = 0, s = 31, a = -2.5$, the SUVAT equation $v^2 = u^2 + 2as$ tells us that $u^2 = 155$, so that $u = 12.4...$. The initial speed of the stone is 12.4 ms^{-1}.

Example 24.3.4. *A particle of mass* 20 *kg is sliding with speed* 10 *ms*$^{-1}$ *across a rough horizontal floor. After travelling* 50 *m, it comes to rest. What is the coefficient of friction between the particle and the floor?*

Resolving forces vertically tells us that $R = 20g$. While slipping occurs, $F = \mu R = 20\mu g$. Resolving forces horizontally, and using Newton's second law, gives

$$20a = -F = -20\mu g$$

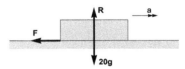

Figure 24.10

and hence the particle experiences an acceleration of $-\mu g$. Using the SUVAT equation $v^2 = u^2 + 2as$, we see that $0^2 = 10^2 - 2\mu g \times 50$, so that $\mu g = 1$, and hence $\mu = 0.1$.

Example 24.3.5. *A rough slope is at an angle of* 30° *to the horizontal. A particle of mass* 3 *kg is placed at rest on that slope, and a horizontal force of magnitude* 40 *N is applied to the particle. The coefficient of friction between the particle and the slope is* 0.2. *How long does it take for the particle to reach a speed of* 5 *ms*$^{-1}$*?*

When the particle reaches the speed of 5 *ms*$^{-1}$*, the horizontal force of* 40 *N is removed. Describe the subsequent motion of the particle.*

Motion only takes place parallel to the slope, and so the resultant force perpendicular to the slope must be zero. Thus

$$R = 3g\cos 30° + 40\sin 30° = 15\sqrt{3} + 20\,.$$

Since slipping occurs, friction is limiting, and so $F = \mu R = 3\sqrt{3} + 5$. Resolving forces parallel to the slope gives

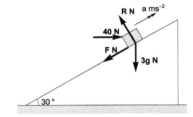

Figure 24.11

$$3a = 40\cos 30° - F - 3g\sin 30° = 20\sqrt{3} - F - 15\,,$$

so that $a = \frac{1}{3}(17\sqrt{3} - 20) = 3.148...$ The particle moves up the slope with acceleration 3.15 ms^{-2}, and so reaches a speed of 5 ms^{-1} from rest after time $\frac{5}{a} = 1.59$ s.

When the 40 N force is removed, the value of the normal reaction on the particle changes, and hence so does the friction force. It is vital, therefore, to draw a new diagram, and sensible to give the new normal reaction and friction forces different names, so that they do not get confused with the previous ones. Similarly, we have a new acceleration! Resolving perpendicular to the slope gives

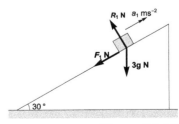

Figure 24.12

$$R_1 = 3g\cos 30° = 15\sqrt{3}\,,$$

485

and hence $F_1 = 3\sqrt{3}$. Thus, resolving parallel to the slope yields

$$3a_1 = -3g\sin 30° - F = -15 - 3\sqrt{3},$$

so that the particle experiences an acceleration of $a_1 = -5 - \sqrt{3} = -6.73$ ms^{-2}, and so comes to instantaneous rest after $\frac{5}{-a_1} = 0.743$ seconds.

Referring back to Chapter 23, we see that, since $\mu < \tan 30°$, the particle will not remain at rest on the slope, but will slide back down the slope. A new diagram is needed again. We can use the symbols R_1 and F_1 for the normal reaction and friction forces, since their magnitudes do not change (why?); it is important to note the changed direction of the friction force, however. Resolving forces parallel to the slope, we obtain

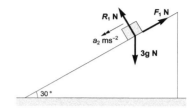

Figure 24.13

$$3a_2 = 3g\sin 30° - F_1 = 15 - 3\sqrt{3},$$

so that the particle slides back down the slope with acceleration $a_2 = 5 - \sqrt{3} = 3.27$ ms^{-2}.

Key Fact 24.4 Friction Opposes Motion

We observed in Chapter 23 that friction acts to prevent motion in cases where static equilibrium is possible. This principle can be extended to situations where slipping occurs. When slipping occurs, friction always acts in a direction so as to oppose the motion.

Example 24.3.6. *A particle of mass m slides on a rough slope, angled at θ to the horizontal. The particle starts at the point A on the slope, moving uphill. A little while later, the particle returns to the point A. The speed of the particle when it passes the point A on the way uphill is twice the speed of the particle when it passes the point A on the way downhill. Find an expression for the coefficient of friction μ between the particle and the slope in terms of the angle θ.*

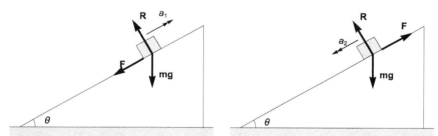

Figure 24.14

The normal reaction $R = mg\cos\theta$ between the particle and the slope is the same when the particle is going uphill as when it is going downhill, as is the magnitude of the friction force $F = \mu R$. However, the friction force is pointing in opposite directions during the two stages of the motion. Note that, since we are told that the particle returns to the point A, we already know that $\mu < \tan\theta$, since the particle does not remain in static equilibrium when coming to rest at the top of its motion.

Resolving forces parallel to the slope, and applying Newton's second law, gives the equations

$$ma_1 = -mg\sin\theta - F \qquad ma_2 = mg\sin\theta - F,$$

so that the particle has accelerations $a_1 = -g(\sin\theta + \mu\cos\theta)$ and $a_2 = g(\sin\theta - \mu\cos\theta)$ during the two stages of the motion.

On the way up, the particle passes A with speed v_1, and decelerates to rest after travelling a distance of s up the slope. Thus $0^2 = v_1^2 + 2a_1 s$. On the way down, the particle starts from rest, and travels the same distance s, reaching the point A travelling with speed v_2. Thus $v_2^2 = 0^2 + 2a_2 s$. Since $v_1 = 2v_2$, we deduce that

$$-2a_1 s = v_1^2 = 4v_2^2 = 8a_2 s$$

and hence $-a_1 = 4a_2$. Thus

$$\begin{aligned} g(\sin\theta + \mu\cos\theta) &= 4g(\sin\theta - \mu\cos\theta) \\ 5\mu\cos\theta &= 3\sin\theta \end{aligned}$$

and hence $\mu = \frac{3}{5}\tan\theta$.

EXERCISE 24C

1. A crate stands on the floor of a moving train. The crate has a tendency to slide backwards relative to the train. State the direction of the frictional force, and whether the train is accelerating or decelerating.

   The acceleration or deceleration has magnitude 4 ms^{-2} and the crate is on the point of sliding. Find the coefficient of friction between the crate and the floor.

2. A cyclist and his bicycle have a total mass of 90 kg. He is travelling along a straight horizontal road, at 7 ms^{-1} when he applies the brakes, locking both wheels. He comes to rest in a distance of 5 m. Find the coefficient of friction between the tyres and the road surface.

3. The coefficient of friction between a waste skip of mass 500 kg and the horizontal ground on which it stands is 0.6. What is the maximum mass of waste material that the skip can contain if it is to be moved by a horizontal force of magnitude 7350 N? If the skip is fully laden, and the horizontal force is increased to 7500 N, what is the resulting acceleration of the skip?

4. A car is travelling on a horizontal straight road at 12 ms^{-1} when its brakes are applied, locking all four wheels. The coefficient of friction between the road and the wheels is 0.8. Find the distance travelled by the car from the instant that the brakes are applied until it comes to rest.

5. An ice-hockey puck is struck from one end of a rink of length 27 m towards the other end. The initial speed is 6 ms^{-1}, and the puck rebounds from the boundary fence at the other end with a speed which is $\frac{3}{4}$ times the speed with which it struck the fence, before just returning to its starting point. Calculate the coefficient of friction between the puck and the ice.

6. A railway engine is travelling at 50 ms^{-1}, without carriages or trucks, when the power is shut off and the brakes applied, locking the wheels of the engine. The engine comes to rest in 25 seconds. Calculate the coefficient of friction between the wheels and the track.

7. A block of mass 5 kg accelerates at 0.8 ms^{-2}, down a plane inclined at 15° to the horizontal, under the action of a force of magnitude 30 N acting down the plane. Calculate the coefficient of friction between the block and the plane.

8. A crate of mass 350 kg is released from rest at the top of a polished chute of length 80 m, which is inclined at an angle of 20° to the horizontal. The coefficient of friction between the crate and the chute is 0.36. Calculate the frictional force on the crate, and the speed of the crate at the bottom of the chute, given that the crate:

   a) is empty,   b) contains objects of total mass 150 kg.

9. A child starts from rest at the top of a playground slide and reaches a speed of 5.5 ms^{-1} at the bottom of the sloping part, which makes an angle of 35° with the horizontal. The coefficient of friction between the child and the slide is 0.25. Find the length of the sloping part of the slide, and the length of time for which the child is on the sloping part.

10. A car travels down a hill which is inclined at 6° to the horizontal, with its engine switched off. When the car's speed reaches 10 ms^{-1} the brakes are applied, locking all four wheels. The car comes to rest in a distance of 8 m. Find the coefficient of friction between the tyres and the road.

11. A small magnet of mass 0.05 kg is held against the metal door of a refrigerator and then released from rest. The magnetic effect is only partially effective and so the magnet moves vertically downwards, remaining in contact with the door. The magnet travels 1.4 m in 2 seconds. Assuming the acceleration of the magnet is constant, find the frictional force on the magnet.

    Given that the coefficient of friction between the door and the magnet is 0.3, calculate the normal contact force exerted by the door on the magnet.

12. A cyclist free-wheels down a slope inclined at $7°$ to the horizontal. When her speed gets to 4 ms^{-1} she applies the brakes, locking both wheels. The cyclist comes to rest 1 s after applying the brakes. Find the coefficient of friction between the tyres and the slope.

13. The Figure shows a force of magnitude 20 N acting downwards at $25°$ to the horizontal on a block of mass 4 kg, which is at rest in limiting equilibrium on a horizontal surface. Calculate the coefficient of friction between the block and the surface.
    The direction of the force of magnitude 20 N is now reversed. Calculate the acceleration with which the block starts to move.

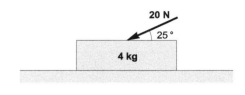

14. The diagram shows a horizontal force of magnitude 10 N acting on a block of mass 6 kg, which is at rest in limiting equilibrium on a plane inclined at $20°$ to the horizontal. Calculate the coefficient of friction between the block and the plane.
    The direction of the horizontal force is now reversed. Find the acceleration with which the block starts to move.

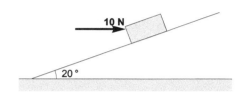

15*. A block of mass 20 kg is placed on a slope at an acute angle of α to the horizontal, where $\sin \alpha = \frac{3}{5}$. The coefficient of friction between the block and the slope is μ, where $\mu < \frac{3}{4}$. It is kept from moving by a horizontal force of P N. Find the range of values of P for which the block remains in equilibrium on the slope.

    For a certain value of P, the block accelerates up the slope with the same magnitude of acceleration as if the horizontal force P was removed (and the block slid down the slope). Find a formula relating P and μ.

Chapter 24: Summary

- **Newton's Second Law** states that a resultant force F N on an object of mass m kg produces an acceleration a ms^{-2} in the object, where $F = ma$.

- Our model of dynamic friction assumes that the friction force F, the normal reaction R and the coefficient of friction μ are related by the formula $F = \mu R$ whenever slipping occurs, as well as in cases of static limiting equilibrium.

- Friction always acts in that direction which opposes any motion that is occurring.

1. A car starts from rest at the point A and moves in a straight line with constant acceleration for 20 seconds until it reaches the point B. The speed of the car at B is 30 ms^{-1}. Find:

   a) the acceleration of the car,

   b) the speed of the car as it passes the point C, where C is between A and B and $AC = 40$ m. (OCR)

2. A motorist travelling at u ms^{-1} joins a straight motorway. On the motorway she travels with a constant acceleration of 0.07 ms^{-2} until her speed has increased by 2.8 ms^{-1}.

   a) Calculate the time taken for this increase in speed.

   b) Given that the distance travelled while this increase takes place is 1050 m, find u. (OCR)

3. A cyclist, travelling with constant acceleration along a straight road, passes three points A, B and C, where $AB = BC = 20$ m. The speed of the cyclist at A is 8 ms^{-1} and at B is 12 ms^{-1}. Find the speed of the cyclist at C. (OCR)

4. As a car passes the point A on a straight road, its speed is 10 ms^{-1}. The car moves with constant acceleration a ms^{-2} along the road for T seconds until it reaches the point B, where its speed is V ms^{-1}. The car travels at this speed for a further 10 seconds, when it reaches the point C. From C it travels for a further T seconds with constant acceleration $3a$ ms^{-2} until it reaches a speed of 20 ms^{-1} at the point D. Sketch the velocity-time graph for the motion, and show that $V = 12.5$.

   Given that the distance between A and D is 675 m, find the values of a and T. (OCR)

5. The figure shows the velocity-time graph for the motion of a cyclist; the graph consists of three straight line segments. Use the information given on the graph to find the acceleration of the cyclist when $t = 2$ and the total distance travelled by the cyclist for $0 \le t \le 30$. Time is measured in seconds, and velocity in metres per second.
   Without making any detailed calculations, sketch the displacement-time graph for this motion. (OCR)

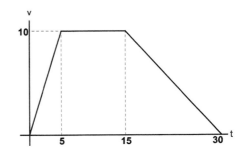

6. A car is waiting at traffic lights with a van behind it. There is a 1 metre gap between them. When the lights turn green, the car accelerates at 1.5 ms^{-2} until it reaches a speed of 15 ms^{-1}; it then proceeds at this speed. The van does the same, starting when the gap between the vehicles is 4 metres.

   Find a formula for the distance travelled by the car in the first t seconds $(0 \le t \le 10)$, and hence the time interval between the car starting and the van starting. Find also the distance between the vehicles when they are both going at 15 ms^{-1}. (OCR)

7. Two runners, Ayesha and Fatima, are leading the field in a long-distance race. They are both running at 5 ms^{-1}, with Ayesha 10 m behind Fatima. When Fatima is 50 m from the tape, Ayesha accelerates but Fatima doesn't. What is the least acceleration Ayesha must produce to overtake Fatima?

   If instead Fatima accelerates at 0.1 ms^{-2} up to the tape, what is the least acceleration Ayesha must produce in order to win?

8. A woman stands on the bank of a frozen lake with a dog by her side. She skims a bone across the ice at a speed of 3 ms^{-1}. The bone slows down with deceleration 0.4 ms^{-2}, and the dog chases it with acceleration 0.6 ms^{-2}. How far out from the bank does the dog catch up with the bone?

9. A man is running for a bus at 3 ms^{-1}. When he is 100 m from the bus stop, the bus passes him going at 8 ms^{-1}. If the deceleration of the bus is constant, at what constant rate should the man accelerate so as to arrive at the bus stop at the same instant as the bus?

10. a) A train travels from a station P to the next station Q, arriving at Q exactly 5 minutes after leaving P. The velocity-time graph for the train's journey is approximated by three straight line segments, as shown in the figure.

   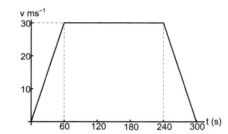

   i. Write down the acceleration of the train during the first minute of the journey.

   ii. Find the distance from P to Q.

   b) On one occasion, when the track is being repaired, the train is restricted to a maximum speed of 10 ms^{-1} for the 2000 m length of track lying midway between P and Q. The train always accelerates and decelerates at the rate shown in the figure. When not accelerating or decelerating or moving at the restricted speed of 10 ms^{-1}, the train travels at 30 ms^{-1}. Sketch the velocity-time graph for the train's journey from P to Q when the speed restriction is in force, and hence find how long the train takes to travel from P to Q on this occasion.

   c) The second figure shows the velocity-time graph for the train accelerating from rest up to a maximum speed of V ms^{-1}, and then immediately decelerating to a speed of 10 ms^{-1}. The acceleration and deceleration have the same value as shown in the first figure. Show that the distance travelled is $2V^2 - 100$ metres.

   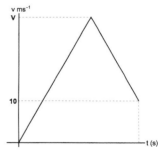

   Determine whether the train in (b) could, by exceeding the normal speed of 30 ms^{-1} when possible, make up the time lost due to the speed restriction when travelling from P to Q. Assume that the acceleration and deceleration must remain as before. (OCR)

11. If a ball is placed on a straight sloping track and then released from rest, the distances that it moves in successive equal intervals of time are found to be in the ratio 1 : 3 : 5 : 7 : .... Show that this is consistent with the theory that the ball rolls down the track with constant acceleration.

12. A boy drops a stone down a well. Assume that the stone is released from rest, and that the depth of the well, from ground level to the surface of the water, is d m.

   a) Find an expression for the time the stone takes to fall in to the water.

   b) Assuming that sound travels at 300 m s^{-1}, find an expression for the time that elapses from the moment when the boy drops the stone until he hears the splash.

   c) If the boy measures a time of 2.5 seconds until he hears the splash, how deep is the well?

13. The acceleration $\mathbf{a}$ ms^{-2} of a particle P at time t seconds is given by

$$\mathbf{a} = 6t\mathbf{i} + (3t - 1)\mathbf{j}$$

When $t = 0$ the particle P has velocity $4\mathbf{i}$ ms^{-1}. Let $\mathbf{V}$ be the velocity of P at time $t = 3$. Find the magnitude of $\mathbf{V}$, and find the angle that $\mathbf{V}$ makes with the vector $\mathbf{i}$, giving your answer in degrees accurate to 1 decimal place.

14. A particle starts from O and moves along a straight line. At time t seconds its displacement from O is x cm and its velocity is $(10t - t^2)$ cm s^{-1}.

    a) Find x in terms of t.

    b) Find an expression for the acceleration of the particle in terms of t.

    c) Find the distance covered and the velocity at the moment when the acceleration is zero.

    d) Find the average velocity of the particle during the first 3 seconds. Show that this is less than the actual velocity after 1.5 seconds. (OCR)

15. A particle is travelling on the x-axis. Its velocity is $6(1 - t)(t - 3)$ ms^{-1} at time t seconds.

    a) Find the time at which the speed of the particle in the positive direction is greatest. What is the speed at that time?

    b) At time $t = 0$, the particle is 5 m from O in the positive direction. Calculate the position of the particle when it is first instantaneously at rest.

    c) How many times does the particle pass through the origin O?

16. A particle starts from rest. Its acceleration after t seconds is $(1 + 2t)^{-3}$ ms^{-2}. Find its speed and how far it has moved after 2 seconds.

17. A particle moving in a straight line has displacement x metres after t seconds for $0 \le t \le 5$, where $x = t^3 - 12t^2 + 21t + 18$.

    a) Find the displacement, velocity and acceleration when the time is zero.

    b) Find the time, velocity and acceleration when the displacement is zero.

    c) Find the time, displacement and acceleration when the velocity is zero.

    d) Find the time, displacement and velocity when the acceleration is zero.

18. A particle moving on the x-axis has displacement x metres from the origin O after t seconds for $0 \le t \le 5$, where $x = t^2(t - 2)(t - 5)$.

    a) For what values of t is the particle on the positive side of O?

    b) For what values of t is the particle moving towards O?

    c) For what values of t is the acceleration of the particle directed towards O?

19. The displacement, x metres, of a particle moving on the x-axis at a time t seconds after it starts to move is given by $x = t^5$ for $0 \le t \le 1$, and by $x = 4t^{-1} - 3t^{-k}$ for $t \ge 1$.

    a) Verify that both formulae give the same value for x when $t = 1$.

    b) Find the value of k for which there is no sudden change of velocity when $t = 1$.

    For the rest of the question, take k to have the value you found in part (b).

    c) Show that the particle stays on the same side of O throughout the motion.

    d) What is the greatest distance of the particle from O?

20*. A particle is travelling in a straight line. It accelerates from its initial velocity u to velocity v, where $v > |u| > 0$, travelling a distance d_1 with uniform acceleration of magnitude $3a$. It then comes to rest after travelling a further distance d_2 with uniform acceleration of magnitude a. Show that

    a) if $u > 0$ then $3d_1 < d_2$,

    b) if $u < 0$ then $d_2 < 3d_1 < 2d_2$.

Show also that the average speed of the particle (that is, the total distance travelled divided by the total time) is greater in the case $u > 0$ than in the case $u < 0$.

N.B. In this question d_1 and d_2 are the distances travelled by the particle, which are not the same, in the second case, as the displacements from the starting point. (STEP)

21. A particle is in equilibrium under the action of the three coplanar forces shown in the diagram. Find the magnitudes of P and Q. (OCR)

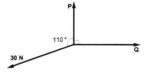

22. Susie uses a strap to pull her suitcase, at a constant speed in a straight line, along the horizontal floor of an airport departure lounge. The strap is inclined at $50°$ to the horizontal and the frictional force exerted on the case by the floor has magnitude 20 N. Find the tension in the strap. (OCR)

23. The diagram shows a particle of mass 2.6 kg maintained in equilibrium in a vertical plane by forces of $5P$ N and $12P$ N which are perpendicular. Find:

    a) α, the angle at which the force of $5P$ N is inclined to the vertical,

    b) the value of P. (OCR)

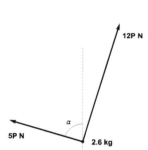

24. A particle is in equilibrium under the action of the three coplanar forces whose magnitudes and directions are shown in the diagram. Find the values of P and Q. The force of magnitude 4 N is now removed from the system. State the direction in which the particle begins to move. (OCR)

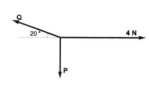

25. The diagram shows a small metal ball, of mass 2 kg, resting in the horizontal groove between two smooth planes inclined at $20°$ and $40°$ to the horizontal. Find the magnitudes of the contact forces P and Q. (OCR)

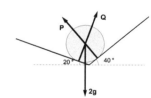

26. A particle P rests in equilibrium on a smooth horizontal surface under the action of the four horizontal forces shown in the diagram. The angles between the forces of magnitudes 1.2 N and 2 N, and between the forces of magnitudes X N and Y N, are each $90°$. The angle between the forces of magnitudes 2 N and Y N is $130°$. Find the values of X and Y.

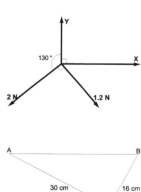

The force of magnitude 1.2 N is now removed. What is the direction of the motion of the particle? (OCR, adapt.)

27. The diagram shows a particle P attached to points A and B by two light inextensible strings, AP of length 30 cm and BP of length 16 cm. The points A and B are at the same horizontal level and P hangs freely with angle $\angle APB$ equal to $90°$. Given that the tension in the string BP is 15 N, find:

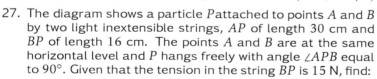

    a) the tension in the string AP,

    b) the mass of P.

    Particle P is now replaced by a heavier particle Q. Given that the tension in either string must not exceed not exceed 120 N, find the greatest possible mass of Q. (OCR)

28. A book, which may be modelled as a particle of weight 8 N, rests in equilibrium on a desk top inclined at $28°$ to the horizontal. Find the frictional force acting on the book. The coefficient of friction between the book and the desk top is 0.6. Determine whether the equilibrium is limiting. (OCR)

29. A heavy ring of mass 5 kg is threaded on a fixed rough horizontal rod. The coefficient of friction between the rod and the ring is $\frac{1}{2}$. A light string is attached to the ring and pulled downwards with a force acting at a constant angle of 30° to the horizontal. The magnitude of the force is T N, and is gradually increased from zero. Find the value of T that is just sufficient to make the equilibrium limiting. (OCR)

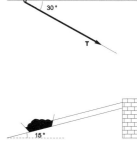

30. A straight path is inclined at an angle of 15° to the horizontal. A loaded skip of total mass 1500 kg is at rest on the path and is attached to a wall at the top of the path by a rope. The rope is taut and parallel to a line of greatest slope of the path, as shown in the diagram. Calculate the normal reaction and the friction force exerted on the skip by the path when the tension in the rope is 2000 N.

After the rope is cut the skip is on the point of slipping down the path. Calculate the coefficient of friction between the skip and the path. (OCR)

31. A straight footpath makes an angle of α with the horizontal. An object P of weight 1250 N rests on the footpath. The coefficient of friction between the object and the footpath is 0.1. The least magnitude of a force, acting up the footpath, which will hold the object at rest on the footpath is 50 N. By treating the object as a particle, show that the value of α satisfies $10\sin\alpha - \cos\alpha = 0.4$. (OCR)

32. A log, of mass 80 kg, rests on horizontal ground. When a force of magnitude 240 N is applied to the log in an upward direction that makes an angle of 20° with the horizontal, the log is on the point of moving. Modelling the log as a particle, calculate the coefficient of friction between the log and the ground. (OCR)

33*. A loaded crate of mass m kg is to be moved along rough horizontal ground. A student was asked to compare the least 'pushing' force needed with the least 'pulling' force needed. The student modelled the crate as a particle, and decided to compare 'pushing' and 'pulling' forces inclined at the same angle θ to the horizontal. The coefficient between the crate and the ground is μ. If the least 'pushing' force has magnitude X N, and $\mu\tan\theta < 1$, find X. What happens when $\mu\tan\theta \geq 1$?

The least 'pulling' force has magnitude Y Newtons. Find Y. If $\mu\tan\theta < 1$, which is greater, X or Y?

34*. A particle of weight W is placed on a rough plane inclined at an angle θ to the horizontal. The coefficient of friction between the particle and the plane is μ. A horizontal force X acting on the particle is just sufficient to prevent the particle from sliding down the plane; when a horizontal force kX acts on the particle, the particle ia about the slide up the plane. Both horizontal forces act in the vertical plane containing the line of greatest slope.

Prove that

$$(k-1)(1+\mu^2)\sin\theta\cos\theta = \mu(k+1),$$

and hence that $k \geq \dfrac{(1+\mu)^2}{(1-\mu)^2}$. (STEP)

35. A marker buoy of mass 5 kg is dropped into the sea from a helicopter at a height of 40 m. After the buoy enters the water it experiences a buoyancy force of 300 N. If there is no loss of speed as the buoy enters the water, find how far it sinks below the surface. Find also how long after it is dropped the buoy returns to the surface.

Discuss how these answers would be affected if the resistance of the air and the water were included in the calculation.

36. A naval gun has a barrel 4 m long. When fired horizontally, a shell of mass 2 kg emerges from the muzzle with a speed of 500 ms⁻¹. The force from the expanding gases inside the barrel may be taken to have a constant value of 80 kN. Calculate the resistance to motion of the shell from the sides of the barrel.

Would the answer be substantially different if the barrel were angled at $40°$ to the horizontal?

37. A hot-air balloon of mass 500 kg is descending at a speed of 5 ms^{-1} with an acceleration of 0.2 ms^{-2}. What mass of ballast must be thrown out to reduce the acceleration to zero? If twice this amount of ballast is thrown out, how much further will the balloon descend before it starts to climb?

38. A bed has to be pushed across a room. If one person pushes, the bed will move with an acceleration a_1. If two or three people push, it will move with acceleration a_2 or a_3 respectively. Assuming that each person pushes with the same magnitude of force, and all push in the same direction, and that the resistance to the motion of the bed is the same in all cases, show that $a_1 + a_3 = 2a_2$.

39. A man on a bicycle, of total mass 100 kg, is free-wheeling at a constant speed of 15 ms^{-1} down a hill with a gradient of 10%. He wants to slow down to a safer speed, so he applies the brake lightly to produce a constant braking force of 84 N. The air resistance is proportional to the square of the speed.

    a) Calculate the deceleration when he first applies the brake.

    b) Calculate the deceleration when his speed has dropped to 12 ms^{-1}.

    c) At what speed will his deceleration be reduced to zero?

40. Explain why a runner's acceleration cannot exceed 10μ ms^{-1}, where μ is the coefficient of friction between her shoes and the track.

    The highest speed that a runner can maintain in an 800 m race is 8 ms^{-1}. Show that the fastest time she can hope to achieve from a standing start is $\left(100 + \dfrac{2}{5\mu}\right)$ seconds. By how much could she better her time by changing running shoes, increasing μ from 0.5 to 1.0?

41. A valley is formed between two hills, which are at angles α and β to the horizontal. A skier starts from rest on the slope of the first hill, at a height h above the valley floor. Find his acceleration down the first hill, and his deceleration up the opposite hill, supposing that there is no friction, and no loss of speed at the skier moves from the first hill to the second. Show that, if he exerts no force with his ski sticks, he ends up at the same height h as he started.

    Suppose now that $\alpha = 15^{c}irc$, that $\beta = 10°$, and that the coefficient of friction between the skier and the snow is 0.1. Show that he ends up at a height of about $0.4h$ above the valley floor.

42. A laundry basket of mass 3 kg is being pulled along a rough horizontal floor by a light rope inclined upward at an angle of $30°$ to the floor. The tension in the rope is 8 N.

    Considering the laundry basket as a particle, calculate the magnitude of the normal contact force exerted on the laundry basket by the floor.

    Given that the acceleration of the laundry basket is 0.2 ms^{-2}, find the coefficient of friction between the laundry basket and the floor. (OCR)

43. A parcel of mass 3 kg is released from rest at the top of a straight chute which is fixed at $40°$ to the horizontal. Given that the coefficient of friction between the parcel and the chute is 0.2, and neglecting any other resistances, calculate the acceleration of the parcel as it slides down the chute. (OCR)

44. A coin of mass 8 grams is placed flat on a rough board, which is inclined at an angle of $25°$ to the horizontal. The coin moves downwards with acceleration 1.5 ms^{-2}. Find the coefficient of friction between the coin and the board. (OCR)

45. Initially a small block of wood is at a point O on a rough plane inclined at $15°$ to the horizontal. The block is projected directly up the plane with initial speed 4 ms^{-1}. The coefficient of friction between the block and the plane is $\frac{1}{10}$. The block comes instantaneously to rest at A. Find the distance OA. Find the speed of the block as it passes through O when moving back down the plane. (OCR)

46. A wooden box is pulled along a rough horizontal floor by means of a constant force of magnitude 150 N acting at an angle of $40°$ above the horizontal. The box may be modelled as a particle of mass 45 kg, and air resistance may be neglected. Draw a diagram showing all the forces acting on the box, and show that the normal contact force of the floor on the

box is approximately 354 N. The coefficient of friction between the box and the floor is 0.3. Calculate the time taken for the box to move 40 m from rest. (OCR, adapt.)

47. A girl sitting on a wooden board slides down a line of greatest slope, which is inclined at $10°$ to the horizontal, on a snow-covered mountain. The combined mass of the girl and the board is 65 kg, and the magnitude of the frictional force between the board and the slope is 125 N. Air resistance may be ignored. Show that the coefficient of friction between the board and the slope is 0.20 correct to 2 significant figures, and verify that the girl and the board are slowing down.

    The girl passes a point A travelling at 5 ms^{-1}. Calculate her speed at the point B, where B is 40 m down the slope from A.

    Later in the day the girl, still sitting on the board, is pulled up the same slope, with constant speed, by a rope inclined at $30°$ above the horizontal. The surface of the slope may now be assumed to be smooth. Calculate the magnitude of the force exerted on the board by the slope. (OCR)

48. A schoolboy slides a box, of mass 6 kg, down a straight path inclined at $20°$ to the horizontal. The initial speed of the box is 5 ms^{-1}, and the coefficient of friction between the box and the path is 0.8. Assuming constant acceleration, find the distance travelled before the box comes to rest. (OCR)

49*. A particle of unit mass is projected vertically upwards in a medium whose resistance is k times the square of the velocity of the particle. If the initial velocity is u, prove that the velocity v after rising through a distance s satisfies the formula

$$v^2 = u^2 e^{-2ks} + \tfrac{g}{k}(e^{-2ks} - 1).$$

You may use the fact that the upwards acceleration of the particle can be written as $v\dfrac{dv}{ds}$.

Find an expression for the maximum height of the particle above the point of projection.

Does the above equation relating v and s still hold on the downward path? Justify your answer. (STEP)

Linked Systems

In this chapter we will learn to:

- understand the application of Newton's third law to systems of connected particles,

- solve simple problems which may be modelled as the motion of two or three connected particles.

25.1   Forces In Pairs

Imagine two cars travelling along a motorway, one in front of the other. The front car slows down just as the car behind it accelerates. The two cars collide, and both are damaged.

Figure 25.1

The front car is damaged because it experiences a large force from behind. The rear car experiences a large force from the opposite direction, from the front. These forces are shown in the above figure. The third of Newton's laws of motion states that the two forces are equal in magnitude.

Key Fact 25.1 Newton's Third Law

If an object A exerts a force on an object B, the B exerts a force on A which is equal in magnitude, but opposite in direction. This happens whether or not A and B are moving.

Newton's original statement was (when translated from the Latin) that 'action and reaction are always equal and opposite'. However, it is not always clear which force should be the action, and which the reaction. It is simpler to have a statement that does not give precedence to either of the forces.

The important point about Newton's third law is that it applies to all types of force. Consider a cyclist of weight W_c N sitting on a bicycle of weight W_b N.

 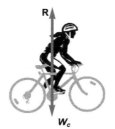 

Figure 25.2

The middle diagram has 'grayed out' the bicycle, so that we can consider the forces acting on the cyclist alone. The cyclist experiences a gravitational attraction of W_c N (her weight), and also a normal reaction force of R N from the bicycle. The normal reaction force is what keeps the cyclist in the saddle (provided that she maintains her balance).

From the point of view of the bicycle, there are different forces to consider. The bicycle experiences a gravitational attraction of W_b N, as well as two normal reactions of R_1 N and R_2 N from the road. In addition to these, however, the bicycle also experiences a normal reaction force from the presence of the cyclist in the saddle. Newton's third law tells us that this normal reaction is equal and opposite to the normal reaction R N acted on the cyclist by the bicycle. It is important to realise that this normal reaction force is **not** the weight of the cyclist. The gravitational attraction on the cyclist acts on the cyclist, and not on the bicycle.

Although we have not drawn the diagram, the road itself is also subject to two normal reaction forces R_1 and R_2 from the wheels of the bicycle. Both of these act vertically downwards.

In this diagram, we have not considered what happens when the cyclist is accelerating. The mutual reaction forces between the cyclist and the bicycle and between the bicycle and the road would have to include horizontal components.

If the cyclist is moving steadily forward, and has no vertical component of motion, then the resultant vertical force on the cyclist will cancel out. This will mean that the normal reaction force R will equal the weight W_c of the cyclist. Similarly, the resultant vertical force on the bicycle will be zero, so that $R + W_b = R_1 + R_2$. If the cyclist has an overall vertical acceleration, however, the normal reaction R will not be the same as the cyclist's weight W_b; nor will the forces on the bicycle cancel out.

Food For Thought 25.1

It is important to be prepared to draw more than one diagram. If we had drawn a single diagram, with both reaction forces R marked, it would have been difficult to be sure which reaction force was acting on the cyclist and which on the bicycle.

For Interest

The force that makes the moon orbit about the earth is the force of the earth's gravity. Without gravity, Newton's first law would have the moon travel in a straight line, rather than in (roughly) a circle.

The force on the moon has a magnitude of approximately 2×10^{20} N. By Newton's third law, the moon exerts an equal gravitational force on the earth. The most obvious evidence of this force is in the oceans. Tides are largely caused by the gravitational effect of the moon.

Why doesn't the moon's gravitational force make the earth rotate about the moon? To some extent, it does. The best description of the true story is that both earth and moon rotate about a common point (the **centre of mass** of the two objects). However, the earth is so much heavier than the moon that the centre of mass of the earth and the moon lies below the earth's surface, and so (to all practical purposes) the moon does rotate about the earth.

Similarly, if we drop a brick, then the brick exerts a gravitational attraction on the earth, and the earth falls towards the brick at the same time as the brick is falling towards the earth. However, the relative masses of the earth and a brick are such that the earth's motion may safely be ignored (the earth is probably 10^{25} times more massive than a brick).

25.2 Directly Linked Systems

Example 25.2.1. *A pick-up truck of mass* 1200 *kg tows a trailer of mass* 400 *kg. There is air resistance of* 140 *N on the truck, but the resistance to the motion of the trailer is negligible. A coupling connects the trailer to the truck. Find the force in the coupling, and the driving force on the truck, when the truck and trailer accelerate at* 0.5 *ms*⁻².

It is important to realise that there are three ways of looking at this problem. We can consider the pickup and trailer as a single unit, we can consider the pickup on its own, and we can consider the trailer on its own.

There is a tension T N in the coupling. Newton's third law tells us that the tension pulls equally on the pickup as on the trailer.

- **Pickup and trailer together** In this case, the tension forces in the coupling cancel each other out, and hence the only forces acting on the truck and the trailer as a unit are the driving force D N and the resistance force 140 N

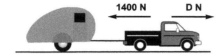

Figure 25.3

The resultant force acting on the pickup and trailer together is $D - 140$ N, and the truck and trailer have a combined mass of $1200 + 400 = 1600$ kg. Newton's third law tells us that

$$D - 140 = 1600 \times 0.5 = 800,$$

and hence the driving force is $D = 940$ N.

- **Pickup and trailer separately** In this case, the tension in the coupling needs to be considered.

Figure 25.4

The only force acting on the trailer is the tension T N, and hence Newton's second law for the trailer reads

$$T = 400 \times 0.5 = 200.$$

The forces acting on the pickup are the driving force D N, the resistance 140 N and the tension in the coupling T N. Thus Newton's Third Law gives

$$D - 140 - T = 1200 \times 0.5 = 600.$$

From the first equation, the tension in the coupling is $T = 200$ N. From the second equation, the driving force is $D = 140 + T + 600 = 940$ N.

Considering the pickup and the trailer separately enabled us to find both T and D. Considering the pickup and trailer as a single object gave us the driving force, but could not identify the coupling force. Sometimes, considering the combined system is convenient, and a combination of both methods is effective.

It is worth noting that the equation of motion for the combined system is simply the sum of the two equations of motion for the separate components of the system: if we add the equations $T = 200$ and $D - 140 - T = 600$, we obtain $D - 140 = 800$. There are three equations of motion (one for the combined system, and one for each of the two components), and any two of these equations implies the third. Thus we can solve the full problem by considering any two of the three possible equations.

> **Key Fact 25.2** Internal And External Forces
>
> When a system is made up of two parts, each of which was the same velocity and acceleration, we can apply Newton's second law either to the object as a whole or to the parts separately.
>
> For the object as a whole, forces of interaction between the two parts are **internal forces**, and are not included in the equation.
>
> For the separate parts, the forces of interaction of each on the other are **external forces**, and are included in the equation.

Example 25.2.2. *A bar magnet of mass 0.2 kg hangs from a string. A metal sphere, of mass 0.5 kg, is held underneath the magnet by a magnetic force of 20 N. The string is then pulled upwards with a force of T N. Find the largest possible value of T if the sphere is not to separate from the magnet.*

So long as the magnet and the sphere are in contact, there are two forces acting between them; the magnetic force of 20 N and the normal reaction force of R N between them. Suppose that the sphere and magnet accelerate upwards with acceleration a ms^{-2}. For the sphere and the magnet to remain in contact, the normal reaction force R must be positive. Our aim is therefore to determine the value of R. There is no point, this time, in considering the sphere and magnet as a combined system, since doing so would give us no information about R. We therefore choose to consider the forces on the magnet and on the sphere separately.

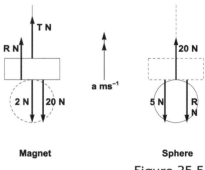

Magnet   Sphere

Figure 25.5

The figure shows force diagrams for the magnet and the sphere separately. Note that the magnetic and normal reaction forces act in opposite directions in the two diagrams. Newton's second law for the magnet states that

$$T + R - 20 - 2 = 0.2a,$$

while Newton's second law for the sphere states that

$$20 - R - 5 = 0.5a.$$

We are not interested in the value of a, so we shall eliminate it from these equations. Thus

$$5(T + R - 20 - 2) = a = 2(20 - R - 5)$$
$$5T + 5R - 110 = 30 - 2R$$

and hence $5T + 7R = 140$.

Since contact between the magnet and the sphere is maintained, we must have $R \geq 0$. Thus $5T \leq 140$, and hence $T \leq 28$. The largest force that can be exerted by the string is 28 N.

More than two objects can be in contact with each other. In such problems, we need to be prepared to take into account the reaction forces between any two touching objects in the system. The motion of the constituent objects can be considered separately, or it may be useful to consider the motion of a collection of more than one object (in which case the interaction forces between the objects in the collection can be ignored).

Example 25.2.3. *A reckless truck driver loads two identical untethered crates stacked one upon the other as shown in the figure. No sliding takes place. Each crate has mass 250kg. Calculate the magnitude of the frictional force exerted on the upper crate by the lower, and on the lower crate by the deck of the truck, when the acceleration of the truck is 1.5 ms^{-2}. If the coefficient* *of friction μ between the two crates is the same as the coefficient of friction between the lower crate and the deck of the truck, what is the smallest possible value of μ?*

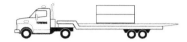

Figure 25.6

Consider the following large-scale diagrams, considering the top crate individually, and the two crates as a single unit.

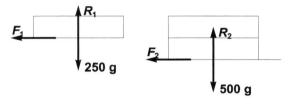

Figure 25.7

Newton's second law applied to the top crate alone states that

$$F_1 = 250 \times 1.5 = 375.$$

The friction force between the two crates is 375 N. Newton's second law applied to the two crates as a single unit states that

$$F_2 = 500 \times 1.5 = 750.$$

and so the friction force between the lower crate and the deck of the truck is 750 N. Since there is no vertical motion, resolving forces vertically for both subdiagrams gives

$$R_1 = 250g \qquad R_2 = 500g.$$

Since $F_1 \leq \mu R_1$ and $F_2 \leq \mu R_2$ we deduce that $\mu g \geq 1.5$ (in both cases) and hence $\mu \geq 0.15$.

Example 25.2.4. *A 20 kg mass is resting on top of a 40 kg mass, and the 40 kg mass is resting on the floor of a 100 kg lift, which is moving vertically with acceleration a ms⁻². Let the tension in the lift cable be T N, let the magnitude of the normal reaction between the two masses be R_1 N, and let the normal reaction between the floor and the 40 kg mass be R_2. What are the values of T, R_1 and R_2 when*

a) $a = 1$,   b) $a = -1.5$,   c) $a = 0$?

The figure shows a force diagram for the complete system of the lift and the two masses on the left, and force diagrams for the individual masses on the right.

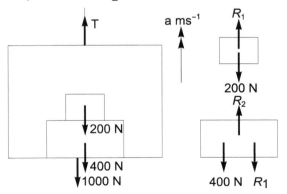

Figure 25.8

Considering the complete system, Newton's second law tells us that

$$T - 200 - 400 - 1000 = (20 + 40 + 100)a = 160a$$

so that $T = 160(a+10)$. Considering the 20 kg mass on its own, we obtain the equation

$$R_1 - 200 = 20a$$

so that $R_1 = 20(a + 10)$. Finally, considering the 40 kg mass on its own, we obtain the equation

$$R_2 - 400 - R_1 = 40a$$

so that $R_2 = 30(a + 10)$. Thus the values of T, R_1 and R_2 are:

(a) 1760 N, 220 N and 330 N when $a = 1$,

(b) 1360 N, 170 N and 255 N when $a = -1.5$,

(c) 1600 N, 200 N and 300 N when $a = 0$.

For Interest

This example explains a commonly observed phenomenon: we feel heavier when in a lift that is accelerating upwards, and feel lighter, with that 'pit of the stomach' feeling, when descending in an accelerating lift. This is because what we experience as weight is actually the magnitude of the reaction force that is preventing us falling through the floor. When we stand on a pair of bathroom scales, what the machine measures is the force it is exerting in holding us up (the normal reaction). When a jockey sits in a weighing chair, what is registered as her weight is the tension in the string that is supporting her. This example shows that the normal reactions are greater in a lift accelerating upwards than in a lift accelerating downwards, which shows how our weight varies in an accelerating lift.

Weight is relative: it is not the magnitude of the gravitational attraction on the object (which is what as described as weight), but it is the force that is being exerted on us to keep us in place. Astronauts in outer space are not **weightless** because there is no gravity is acting upon them (there is); they are weightless because they are falling freely, and nothing is impeding their fall.

EXERCISE 25A

1. Consider the cyclist discussed in Figure 25.2. Draw force diagrams for the cyclist and for the bicycle which will describe the situation when the bicycle is accelerating horizontally.

2. A car of mass 1200 kg, towing a caravan of mass 800 kg, is travelling along a motorway at a constant speed of 20 ms^{-1}. There are air resistance forces on the car and the caravan, of magnitude 100 N and 400 N respectively. Calculate the magnitude of the force on the caravan from the towbar, and the driving force on the car.

   The car brakes suddenly, and begins to decelerate at a rate of 1.5 ms^{-2}. Calculate the force on the car from the towbar. What effect will the driver notice?

3. A dynamo of mass 1500 kg is placed in a cage of mass 500 kg, which is raised vertically by a cable from a crane. The tension in the cable is 20400 N. Find the acceleration of the cage, and the contact force between the cage and the dynamo.

4. Three barges travel down a river in line. Only the rear barge has an engine, which produces a forward force of 400 kN. The masses of the front, middle and rear barges are 1600 tonnes, 1400 tonnes and 2000 tonnes respectively, and the water exerts on them resistance forces of 100 kN, 20 kN and 30 kN respectively. Find the forces in the couplings joining the barges.

5. A car of mass 1000 kg is towing a trailer of mass 250 kg along a straight road. There are constant resistances to the motion of the car and the trailer of magnitude 150 N and 50 N respectively. The driving force on the car has magnitude 800 N. Calculate the acceleration of the car and the trailer, and the tension in the towbar, when

   a) the road is horizontal,

   b) the road is inclined at $\sin^{-1} 0.04$ to the horizontal and the car is travelling uphill.

6. When a car of mass 1350 kg tows a trailer of mass 250 kg along a horizontal straight road, the resistive forces on the car and trailer have magnitude 200 N and 50 N respectively. Find the magnitude of the driving force on the car when the car and trailer are travelling at constant speed, and state the tension in the towbar in this case.

   Find the acceleration or deceleration of the car and the trailer, and the tension in the towbar, when the driving force exerted by the car has magnitude

   a) 330 N,   b) 170 N,   c) zero.

   Find also the deceleration of the car and the trailer, and the magnitude of the force in the towbar, stating whether this force is a tension or thrust, when the driver applies the brakes and the braking force exceeds the driving force by

   d) 30 N,   e) 70 N,   f) 150 N.

7. A car of mass M pulls a trailer of mass m down a straight hill which is inclined at angle α to the horizontal. Resistive forces of magnitudes P and Q act on the car and the trailer respectively, and the driving force on the car is F. Find an expression for the acceleration of the car and trailer, in terms of F, P, Q, M, m and α.

   Show that the tension in the towbar is independent of α.

   In the case when $F = P + Q$, show that the acceleration is $g\sin\alpha$, and that the tension in the towbar is Q.

8. Five spheres, each of mass m, are joined together by four inextensible strings. The spheres hang in a vertical line as shown in the Figure, and are held at rest by a force applied to the uppermost sphere, of magnitude $5mg$, acting vertically upwards. Find the tension in each of the strings.
   The force on the uppermost sphere is now removed. If the total air resistance acting vertically upwards on the spheres is $\frac{1}{2}mg$, find the acceleration of the system in the subsequent motion.
   Find also the tension in each of the four strings if

   a) the air resistance on each individual sphere is $\frac{1}{10}mg$,

   b) the air resistance on the uppermost sphere is $\frac{3}{10}mg$ and the air resistance on each of the other four spheres is $\frac{1}{20}mg$.

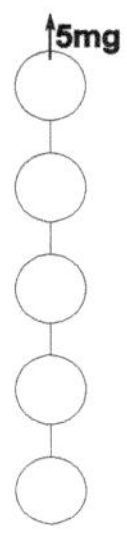

Figure 25.9

9*. A smooth fixed plane is inclined at θ to the horizontal. A smooth wedge of mass M and angle θ is held on the surface so that its upper face is horizontal, and a particle of mass m rests on this face. The system is released from rest. Show that the resultant acceleration of the particle is

$$\frac{g(M+m)\sin^2\theta}{M+m\sin^2\theta}.$$

25.3 Strings, Ropes, Chains And Cables

Consider a 1.5 kg mass hanging on the end of a piece of rope, that is fastened by a hook to the ceiling.
If we had to take the mass of the rope into account, even a simple situation like this one would become complicated. The hook in the ceiling has to support the 1.5 kg mass and the rope. If the rope had mass m kg, then the ceiling hook would have to exert a force of $1.5g + mg$ on the rope for the system to be in equilibrium. There would be an equal and opposite reaction, from the rope on the hook; in other words, the tension in the rope at the top would be $1.5g + mg$ N.

Figure 25.10

503

On the other hand, at the bottom the rope only has to exert a force of $1.5g$ on the mass to maintain equilibrium, and so the tension in the rope is $1.5g$ N at the bottom. If the mass of the rope has to be taken into account, the tension in the string varies along its length (things would be different if the string were being held horizontal in some way).

To make our models simple, we choose to ignore the mass of any rope, string or similar object. We indicate that we are doing so by calling the rope **light**. In our previous discussion, we may assume that the tension T in the rope is the same (equal to $1.5g$ N) at both ends. The tension in a string does not change along its length.

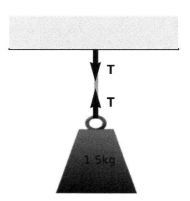

Figure 25.11

Key Fact 25.3 Light Strings

A light string may be assumed to have no mass. A light string exerts forces of equal magnitude on the objects attached to its two ends. These forces act along the line of the string, and are directed inwards at each end. The magnitude of the force at either end is called the **tension** in the string.

The difference between a rod and a string, rope or cable is that a rod can exert a thrust, whereas a string can only exert tension. In the circumstances where a rod would exert thrust, a string simply stops being taut, and therefore exerts no force at all.

Another important assumption that we will be making about strings is that they do not stretch, and always remain the same length. We represent this property by saying that the string is **inextensible**.

Key Fact 25.4 Inextensible Strings

An inextensible string is one that always remains the same length. A consequence of this is the fact that, provided that the string remains taut, particles at each end of the string have the same speed, and the same acceleration.

Example 25.3.1. *Two trucks of masses 250 tonnes are being drawn forward along a railway track. The rear truck is subject to a force of 50 kN resisting its motion, while the lead truck experiences a resistance force of 60 kN. The driver of the train pulling the trucks wants to decelerate, but has to do so in a way that ensures that the coupling chain between the two trucks remains taut at all times. What is the greatest deceleration possible, and what is the driving force on the lead truck at this acceleration?*

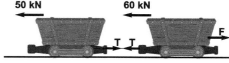

Figure 25.12

Most of the calculations for this problem are much the same as for the problems we were considering in the previous section. Suppose that the acceleration of the trucks is a ms^{-2}, that the driving force on the lead truck is F N, and that the tension in the coupling between the trucks is T N. Newton's second law, applied to the two trucks separately, gives

$$T - 50000 = 250000a \qquad F - T - 60000 = 250000a.$$

so that

$$T = 50000(1 + 5a) \qquad F = 100000(1 + 5a) + 10000.$$

These calculations would have been the same if the coupling had been a rigid bar instead of a chain. However, since the coupling is a chain, we must have non-negative tension in the coupling. Since $T \geq 0$, we deduce that $a \geq -0.2$. The greatest deceleration possible is 0.2 ms^{-2}. At this deceleration, the driving force is 10 kN.

25.4   Pegs And Pulleys

Another property of a string is that it is flexible, so that it can be passed round a fixed peg. The string then has two straight sections and a curved section where it is in contact with the peg, as in the figure. Just as for a straight string, there will be tension in this string all along its length, including the curved section as it bends around the peg.

If the contact between the string and the peg is rough, there could be some friction acting on the string round the circumference of the peg, and in that case there would be a difference in tensions in the two straight sections of the string. But if the contact is smooth, the tensions in the two straight sections are the same.

Figure 25.13

Another possibility is for the string to pass round a pulley, that can rotate on a fixed axis. If the surface is rough, the pulley will rotate with the string. The same applies when a chain passes round a cog wheel. To make the pulley go round, the tensions in the two straight sections would have to be different. However, if the mass of the pulley is small, and if it runs on smooth bearings, the difference in the tensions is very small, so it can be neglected in a first approximation.

Key Fact 25.5 Smooth Pegs And Pulleys

When a string passes around a smooth peg, or over a light smooth pulley, the tension in the string is the same on both sides of the peg or pulley.

Smooth pegs and light pulleys are further examples of mathematical models often used in mechanics. We will never find them in practice, but we can use the models in calculations with only a small loss of accuracy.

Example 25.4.1. *Repairs are being carried out in a tall building. A wheel is attached at the top of the scaffolding with its axis horizontal. A rope runs over the rim of the wheel and has buckets of mass 2 kg tied to it at both ends. One bucket is filled with 8.5 kg of rubble and then released, so that it descends to ground level. With what acceleration does it move?*

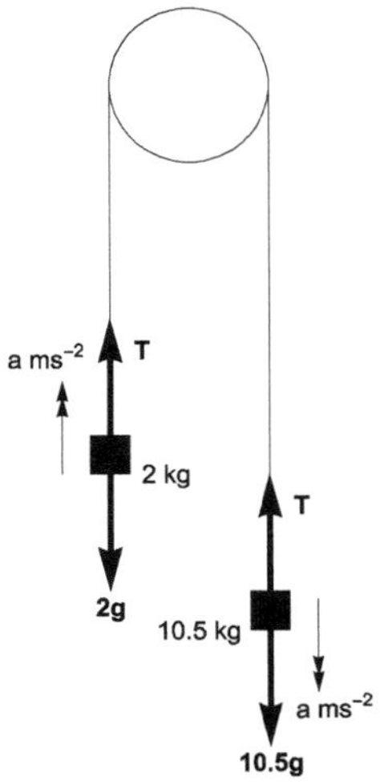

As always, modelling approximations have to be made. We shall assume that the rope is light and inextensible, and that the pulley is smooth. Then the tension T in the string will be the same at both ends, and the upward acceleration a ms^{-2} of the empty bucket will have the same magnitude as the downward acceleration of the filled bucket.

For the empty bucket, Newton's second law states that

$$T - 2g = 2a,$$

while Newton's second law for the filled bucket states that

$$10.5g - T = 10.5a.$$

Figure 25.14

Solving these equations gives $a = \frac{17}{25}g = 6.8$ ms^{-2} and $T = \frac{84}{25}g = 33.6$ N.

Example 25.4.2. *A box of mass 2 kg is placed on a table. A string attached to the box passes over a smooth peg at the edge of the table, and a ball of mass 1 kg is tied to the other end. The two straight sections of the string are horizontal and vertical. If the coefficient of friction between the box and the table is 0.2, find the acceleration of the box and the ball.*

Since the peg is smooth, the tension T in the string is the same on either side of the peg. Since the string is inextensible, both the box and the ball have the same acceleration a.

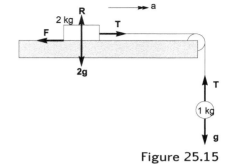

Newton's second law for the ball reads (resolving forces vertically)

$$g - T = a \,,$$

Newton's second law for the box reads (resolving forces horizontally)

Figure 25.15

$$T - F = 2a \,,$$

where F is the friction force acting on the box. Resolving forces horizontally on the box, we see that the normal reaction $R = 2g$. Since the box is slipping, friction is limiting, and hence $F = 0.2R = 0.4g$. Adding these two equations reads

$$0.6g = g - F = 3a$$

and hence $a = 0.2g$. The downward acceleration of the 1 kg particle is 2 ms^{-2}.

Food For Thought 25.2

When two objects in a linked system were in direct contact, and both objects were moving the same direction, it was possible to consider the system as a whole and write down Newton's second law for the combined system. This is no longer possible when considering problems with pegs and pulleys; while it is possible, for example, to add the two equations of motion in the previous example to obtain the equation

$$0.6g = g - F = 3a$$

this equation does not have any physical meaning; it is not a case of Newton's second law You should not attempt to 'resolve forces along the string' to obtain this equation.

Example 25.4.3. *On a construction site a truck of mass 400 kg is pulled up a $10°$ slope by a chain. The chain runs parallel to the slope up to the top, where it passes over a cog wheel of negligible mass. It then runs horizontally and is attached to the rear of a locomotive of mass 2000 kg. Neglecting any resistances, calculate the driving force needed to accelerate the truck up the slope at 0.1 ms^{-2}.*

What is the magnitude of the resultant force from the chain acting on the cogwheel during this motion?

The Figure below shows the forces acting on the truck and on the locomotive. The tension in the chain is T N, the driving force on the locomotive is D N and the normal reaction forces on the locomotive and the truck are R_1 N and R_2 N respectively.

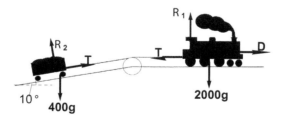

Figure 25.16

Both the truck and the locomotive are travelling with an acceleration of 0.1 ms^{-2}. The forces acting on the truck perpendicular to the slope are irrelevant (resolving forces perpendicular to the slope will determine R_2, but we do not need to know R_2 to solve the problem). Resolving forces on the truck parallel to the slope and applying Newton's second law gives

$$T - 400g \sin 10° = 400 \times 0.1 = 40 \,.$$

Again, we are not interested in the size of R_1, and so will only consider the horizontal components of the forces acting on the locomotive. Applying Newton's second law gives

$$D - T = 2000 \times 0.1 = 200,$$

and hence, adding these equations, $D - 400g \sin 10° = 240$, and hence $D = 935$ N.

When considering the forces on the cogwheel, the tensions in the cable act in the opposite directions to those shown in the previous figure. Two tensions of magnitude T N are acting on the cogwheel, one horizontal and the other at an angle of $10°$ to the horizontal. Letting $\mathbf{i}$ be the unit vector pointing horizontally to the right, and letting $\mathbf{j}$ be the unit vector pointing vertically upwards, we see that the resultant force acting on the cogwheel is

Figure 25.17

$$T\mathbf{i} + (-T\cos 10°\mathbf{i} - T\sin 10°\mathbf{j}) = T(1 - \cos 10°)\mathbf{i} - T\sin 10°\mathbf{j} \text{ N},$$

so this force has magnitude

$$T\sqrt{(1 - \cos 10°)^2 + \sin^2 10°} = T\sqrt{2(1 - \cos 10°)} = 2T\sin 5° = 163 \text{ N}.$$

Example 25.4.4. *A particle of mass m rests in equilibrium on a rough slope which is at an angle of θ to the horizontal. The coefficient of friction μ between the particle and the slope can written $\mu = \tan\alpha$, where $0° < \alpha < 45°$.*

The particle is now attached to a light inextensible string, which is passed over a smooth pulley at the top of the slope and attached to a second particle of mass m which hangs vertically beneath the pulley. When the system is released from rest, the second particle accelerates downwards. Find inequalities relating the values of θ and α, and show that this situation is only possible if $\theta \le 30°$.

While motion is taking place, let the normal reaction and friction forces on the mass on the slope be R and F respectively, and let the tension in the string be T. Suppose that the acceleration of the two particles is a.
Resolving forces on the first particle perpendicular to the slope yields

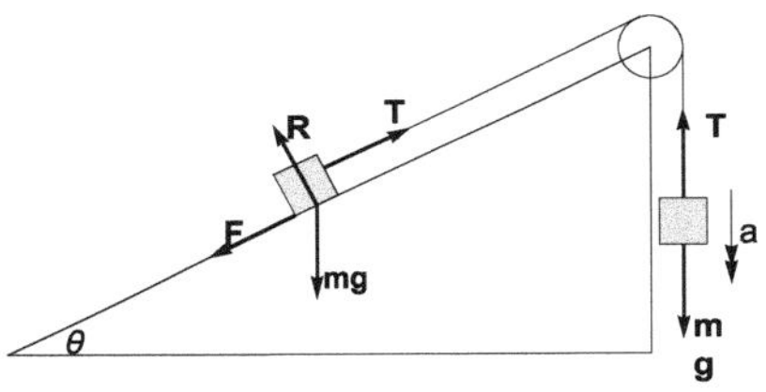

Figure 25.18

$$R = mg\cos\theta.$$

Since slipping is taking place, friction is limiting, and so $F = \mu R = \mu mg \cos\theta$. Resolving forces on the first particle parallel to the slope, and using Newton's second law, yields

$$T - \mu mg\cos\theta - mg\sin\theta = T - F - mg\sin\theta = ma.$$

Applying Newton's second law to the vertical forces acting on the second particle yields

$$mg - T = ma.$$

Eliminating T from these equations yields

$$2ma = mg(1 - \mu\cos\theta - \sin\theta)$$
$$2a\cos\alpha = g(\cos\alpha - \sin\alpha\cos\theta - \cos\alpha\sin\theta) = g\left(\cos\alpha - \sin(\theta + \alpha)\right).$$

We are told that $a \ge 0$, and hence $\sin(\theta + \alpha) \le \cos\alpha = \sin(90° - \alpha)$, from which we deduce that $\theta + \alpha \le 90° - \alpha$, or $\alpha \le 45° - \frac{1}{2}\theta$. Note that, since $0 \le \pi + \alpha \le 180°$, the inequality $\sin(\theta + \alpha) \le \sin(90° - \alpha)$ could be satisfied by $\theta + \alpha \ge 180° - (90° - \alpha) = 90° + \alpha$, but this implies that $\theta \ge 90°$, which is not possible.

In addition to these considerations, we must use the fact that the first particle was at rest on the rough surface before the string was attached to it. Standard statics considerations tell us that this will happen provided that $\mu mg\cos\theta \ge mg\sin\theta$, or provided that $\theta \le \alpha$. Thus we must have

$$\theta \le \alpha \le 45° - \tfrac{1}{2}\theta.$$

Thus $\frac{3}{2}\theta \le 45°$, and so $\theta \le 30°$, when this motion is possible.

EXERCISE 25B

1. In the system illustrated the string passes over a smooth fixed peg. The particles are held in the positions shown, with the string taut; they are then released from rest. Find the tension in the string and the acceleration of the particles.

   Initially, both masses are 1 m above the ground. Once the 3 kg mass hits the ground, the string becomes loose and the other particle moves freely under gravity. Assuming that the string is long enough that the 2 kg particle never hits the pulley, how high above the ground does the 2 kg particle rise?

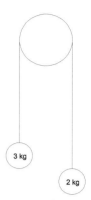

Figure 25.19

2. In the cases illustrated in the following diagrams the strings pass over small light pulleys. The contacts between the blocks and the surfaces are rough, except where they are indicated as smooth. The blocks are rest and the strings taut. In each case find the tension in the string and the frictional force exerted by each surface on the block with which it is in contact.

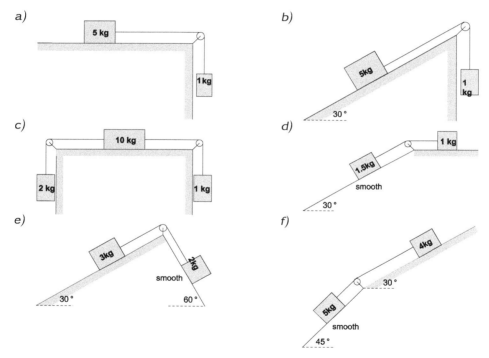

3. Suppose that in each of the cases illustrated in Question 2 the pulleys can rotate freely, and that all the contacts between the blocks and the surfaces are smooth (not just those surfaces marked as smooth). The blocks are held in the positions shown, with the strings taut, then are then released from rest. Find the acceleration of the blocks in each case.

4. Suppose instead that in each of the cases illustrated in Question 2 the pulleys can rotate freely, and that the coefficient of friction between the blocks and the rough surfaces is $\frac{1}{20}$. The blocks are held in the positions shown, with the strings taut, then are then released from rest. Find the acceleration of the blocks in each case.

5. A light inextensible tape is wound round two smooth cylinders as shown. The higher cylinder is fixed, but the lower cylinder sits in a loop formed by the tape. If the 5 kg mass descends at a constant speed, calculate the mass of the lower cylinder.

6. Now assume that the mass of the lower cylinder is 12 kg. The system is held at rest in the position shown, with the tape taut, and then released. Find the accelerations of the lower cylinder and of the 5 kg mass.

7. Two particles are connected by a light inextensible string which passes of a smooth fixed peg. The heavier particle is held so that the string is taut, and the parts of the string not in contact with the pulley are vertical. When the system is released from rest the particles have an acceleration of $\frac{1}{2}g$. Find the ratio of the masses of the particles.

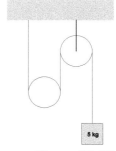

Figure 25.20

8. A particle of mass 3 kg is attached to one end of each of two strings, s_1 and s_2. A particle of mass 2.5 kg is attached to the other end of s_1, and a particle of mass 1 kg is attached to the other end of s_2. The particles are held in the positions shown, with the strings taut and s_1 passing over a smooth fixed peg. The system is released from rest. Find the acceleration of the particles, and the tensions in s_1 and s_2.

9. A particle of mass m is placed on a rough track which goes up at an acute angle α to the horizontal, where $\sin \alpha = \frac{3}{5}$. The coefficient of friction between the particle and the track is $\frac{1}{2}$. A string is attached to the particle, and a particle of mass M is attached to the other end of the string. The string runs up the track, passes over a smooth bar at the top of the track, and then hangs vertically. Find the interval of values of M for which the system can rest in equilibrium.
Find expressions for the acceleration with which the system will move if the value of M lies outside this interval.

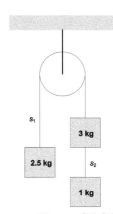

Figure 25.21

10. Particles of masses m_1 and m_2 are connected by a light inextensible string. The string is passed over three light smooth pegs, the middle one of which is free to move. A particle of mass M is suspended from the movable peg. All portions of the string that are not wrapped around one or other of the pegs are vertical. The system is released from rest. If the movable pulley remains stationary, show that

$$M = \frac{4 m_1 m_2}{m_1 + m_2} \, .$$

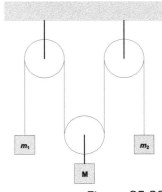

Figure 25.22

Chapter 25: Summary

- **Newton's Third Law** states that if one object exerts a force on another object, then that second object exerts an equal and opposite force on the first object. This applies to moving systems just as much as to stationary ones.

- A linked system can often be considered as a single unit. When doing so, **internal** forces such as tension, normal reaction and friction between the components of the system can be ignored; only **external** forces need to be considered. When a linked system is studied by considering its components separately, internal and external forces must be considered.

- If a string is **light**, the tension in the string does not vary along its length. If a taut string is **inextensible**, the objects at each end of the string have the same speeds and the same accelerations.

- A **smooth** pulley or peg is one over which a string can pass without the tension in the string changing.

Linear Momentum And Impulse

In this chapter we will learn:

- about the vector nature of linear momentum of particle or a system of particles moving in a straight line,

- how the application of an impulse, whether instantaneous or brought about by a force acting over a period of time, brings about a change in momentum,

- to use the principle of conservation of momentum to understand problems concerning the direct impact of two particles travelling in a straight line,

- understand how Newton's law of restitution can be used to model more complex collision problems.

26.1 Momentum And Impulse

There are many examples in the real world where two freely moving objects collide. A ball bounces on the ground, two snooker balls collide with each other, or two dodgem cars collide. Equally, there are examples where two moving objects coalesce into one. A bullet hits a moving target, or two pieces of putty strike each other and stick together. Alternatively, there are cases where an object splits into two or more parts. A space rocket might eject its fuel tanks or, more subtly, a chemical rocket might be powered by an explosive reaction which ejects matter behind the rocket at high speed, propelling the rocket forward.

These examples are all difficult to model exactly for a number of reasons. To begin with, it is very difficult fully to understand the collision between two particles while still modelling them as point particles. When a tennis ball is dropped onto the ground, it bounces back up again because the ball is deformed by the impact with the ground. The physical property that enables objects such as tennis balls to regain their shape, and therefore rebound from each other, is called **elasticity**. Internal forces act within the material of the ball to restore the ball to its original shape, and this results in any changing reaction force between the ball and the ground, which results in the ball being bounced back up in the air, having regained its original shape:

Figure 26.1

Over the very short period of time during which the ball is in contact with the ground, the ball is subject to a variable normal reaction force $F(t)$, which might have a graph looking like this:

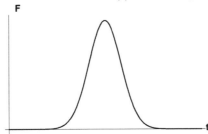

Figure 26.2

511

There is no normal reaction until the ball touches the ground, then the force $F(t)$ increases as the ball becomes more deformed, and then decreases again as the ball regains its natural shape, becoming zero when the ball leaves the ground again. If the height of the ball above the ground is x metres, then Newton's second law tells us that

$$m\ddot{x} = F(t) - mg ,$$

where the mass of the ball is m kg. Without knowing the exact nature of the function $F(t)$ we cannot solve this equation.

However, we do not really need to solve this equation exactly. We really want to know what the speed of the ball up from the ground will be after the collision, and will not (at this stage) be concerned with the specifics of the deformation of the ball, and therefore the behaviour of x in the short time period during which the collision is occurring. Indeed, it might be possible to ignore the details of the collision altogether, and regard the collision as happening instantaneously. Since the ball has its original shape after the collision, it is now possible to continue to model the ball as a single point particle.

Suppose that a particle of mass m is moving under the influence of a variable force $\mathbf{F}(t)$. If the position vector of the particle is $\mathbf{r}$, then its equation of motion is

$$m\ddot{\mathbf{r}} = \mathbf{F}(t) .$$

We are supposing that the force $\mathbf{F}$ is acting over time interval $a \le t \le b$; we shall suppose that the particle has velocity $\mathbf{u}$ before the time $t = a$, and that it has velocity $\mathbf{v}$ after the time $t = b$. If we integrate the particle's equation of motion over the time $a \le t \le b$, we see that

$$I = \int_a^b \mathbf{F}(t)\,dt = \left[m\dot{\mathbf{r}} \right]_a^b = m(\mathbf{v} - \mathbf{u}) ;$$

the integral of $\mathbf{F}$ with respect to time represents the change in a new quantity, the mass times the velocity of the particle.

Key Fact 26.1 Momentum and Impulse: Definition

The **momentum** of a particle is the product of its mass and its velocity. Its units are kg ms^{-1}. A constant force $\mathbf{F}$ acting on a particle over a period of time t exerts an **impulse** of $I = \mathbf{F}t$. The units of impulse are N s.

For Interest

It is very unlikely that an object will ever be acted upon by a constant force for a fixed period of time. As discussed above in the case of the bouncing ball, it is more likely to happen that the force changes with respect to time. The true impulse produced by a force that varies with time is its integral $\int \mathbf{F}(t)\,dt$ with respect to time. However, since we are only interested in the overall effect of the impulse, the manner in which the impulse is applied over the period of time during which it is acting is not relevant, and it is sufficient to approximate a time-dependent force by a force which is constant over time. Thus, instead of considering a time-dependent force over a period of time, we can consider the (constant) average force applied over the same time interval. This yields the same impulse, and is much easier to handle, mathematically.

Newton's Second Law can be summarised as follows:

> **Key Fact 26.2** Newton's Second Law for Impulses
>
> An impulse $\mathbf{I}$ acting on a particle produces a change in the particle's momentum. If the particle has velocities $\mathbf{u}$ and $\mathbf{v}$ before and after the impulse is applied, and if the particle has mass m, then
> $$\mathbf{I} = m\mathbf{v} - m\mathbf{u}.$$

Example 26.1.1. *An object of mass 3 kg is travelling with velocity $4\mathbf{i} - 2\mathbf{j}$ ms^{-1} when it is acted on by a force of $-3\mathbf{i} + 2\mathbf{j}$ N for a total of 5 seconds. What its the object's subsequent velocity?*

This problem could be handled using previous techniques, applying Newton's second law and SUVAT equations to find the new components of the object's velocity. It is easier to use impulses and moments. The object receives an impulse of $5(-3\mathbf{i} + 2\mathbf{j}) = -15\mathbf{i} + 10\mathbf{j}$ Ns, and its original momentum is $3(4\mathbf{i} - 2\mathbf{j}) = 12\mathbf{i} - 6\mathbf{j}$ kg m s^{-1}. Thus the object's new momentum is

$$(12\mathbf{i} - 6\mathbf{j}) + (-15\mathbf{i} + 10\mathbf{j}) = -3\mathbf{i} + 4\mathbf{j} \text{ kg m s}^{-1},$$

and hence its new velocity is $-\mathbf{i} + \frac{4}{3}\mathbf{j}$ ms^{-1}.

A collision can be modelled by disregarding the exact details of the forces acting, and only considering the overall impulse generated by those forces. Instead of a force acting over a short period of time, we can model the collision by assuming that a particle receives an instantaneous impulse, which therefore produces an instantaneous change in momentum, and hence of velocity, in the particle.

Example 26.1.2. *During a collision, a particle which has mass 2 kg and velocity $-3\mathbf{i} - 2\mathbf{j}$ ms^{-1} receives an impulse parallel to the vector $\mathbf{i} + \mathbf{j}$. If the particle's new velocity is $12\mathbf{i} + v\mathbf{j}$ ms^{-1}, find the value of v and the magnitude of the impulse.*

If the impulse is $\alpha(\mathbf{i} + \mathbf{j})$ N s, then we know that

$$\alpha(\mathbf{i} + \mathbf{j}) = 2(12\mathbf{i} + v\mathbf{j}) - 2(-3\mathbf{i} - 2\mathbf{j}) = 30\mathbf{i} + (2v + 4)\mathbf{j},$$

so that $\alpha = 30$ and $2v + 4 = 30$, so that $v = 13$. The magnitude of the impulse is $\alpha\sqrt{2} = 13\sqrt{2} = 18.4$ N s.

In cases where constant forces are acting, ideas of impulse and momentum can be used to solve problems more normally handled by Newton's Second Law.

Example 26.1.3. *A particle is sliding down a rough slope, which is angled at $20°$ to the horizontal. The coefficient of friction between the particle and the slope is $\frac{1}{2}$. If the particle's initial speed down the slope is 5 ms^{-1}, how long does it take to come to rest, and how far has it travelled down the slope in that time?*

Resolving forces perpendicular to the slope yields $N = mg\cos 20°$, where m is the mass of the object. While sliding occurs, friction is limiting, and hence $F = \frac{1}{2}N = \frac{1}{2}mg\cos 20°$. Resolving forces parallel to the slope, the resultant force on the particle up the slope is

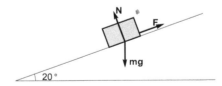

Figure 26.3

$$F - mg\sin 20° = mg\left(\tfrac{1}{2}\cos 20° - \sin 20°\right).$$

If the particle takes t seconds to come to rest, it does so after is has received an impulse of

$$mgt\left(\tfrac{1}{2}\cos 20° - \sin 20°\right) \text{ N s}.$$

This impulse is exactly enough to reduce the particle's momentum down the slope from $5m$ kg m s^{1} to zero, and hence

$$mgt\left(\tfrac{1}{2}\cos 20° - \sin 20°\right) = 5m,$$

and hence $t = 3.91$ seconds. Using the SUVAT equations, in this time the particle travels $\frac{1}{2}(5 + 0)t = 9.78$ m down the slope.

Example 26.1.4. *A garden hose, that has a circular cross-section of radius 0.5 cm, emits water horizontally at a speed of 5 ms^{-1}. The jet of water from the hose strikes a vertical wall, and loses all its speed. What is the force exerted on the wall?*

In 1 second, the hose emits a cylinder of water of volume $\pi \times 0.005^2 \times 5$ m^3 which is travelling with speed 5 ms^{-1}. Thus the horizontal momentum of the water that strikes the wall in 1 second is

$$\pi \times 0.005^2 \times 5 \times 1 \times 5 \; = \; ; 1.96 \times 10^{-3} \text{ kg m s}^1 \, .$$

Since the wall reduces the velocity of the water to zero, it exerts an impulse of 1.96×10^{-3} N s on the water during that second, and so the water exerts an impulse of the same magnitude on the wall. Thus the force exerted on the wall by the water jet is 1.96×10^{-3} N.

For Interest

It is interesting to note that Newton's second law can be expressed as

$$F \; = \; ma \; = \; m\frac{dv}{dt} \; = \; \frac{d}{dt}(mv) \; = \; \frac{dp}{dt}$$

where p represents momentum and force equals rate of change of momentum. In many ways this is a more accurate expression of Newton's second law than is the more familiar $F = ma$, since it can be used to cope with problems where the mass of the moving object is not constant, such as the problem of a raindrop falling through a cloud, collecting water vapour as it falls, and therefore increasing in size.

EXERCISE 26A

1. A 6 N force acts on a 2 kg mass for 5 seconds. Find

   a) the impulse which acted on the mass,

   b) the change in momentum produced,

   c) the final velocity of the mass, given that it was initially at rest.

2. A 2 kg ball moving with an initial speed of 3 ms^{-1} is acted upon by a constant force F for a period of 3 seconds. After the interaction, the ball is moving with a speed of 6 ms^{-1} in the opposite direction. Find the value of F.

3. A 0.25 kg ball is travelling with speed 3 ms^{-1} when it is struck by a bat. After the impact, the ball is travelling with a speed of 9 ms^{-1} in a direction perpendicular to its original motion. Determine the magnitude and direction of the impulse that the bat applies to the ball.

4. A 0.5 kg ball is dropped from rest from a height of 1 m onto a horizontal floor. When it bounces up again, it reaches a maximum height of 0.8 m. How big an impulse did the ground exert on the ball?

5. A particle of mass 5 kg is moving horizontally at a speed of 10 ms^{-1} when it hits a vertical wall. The particle is brought to rest by the impact. Find the impulse exerted on the particle by the wall.

6. An impulse $4\mathbf{i} - 8\mathbf{j}$ N s is applied to an object moving with velocity $\mathbf{i} + 7\mathbf{j}$ ms^{-1}. After the impulse, the object's velocity is $3\mathbf{i} + 3\mathbf{j}$ N s. What is the mass of the particle?

7. A particle of mass 4 kg is travelling in a straight line with speed 2.5 ms^{-1} when it receives an impulse I N s. After the impulse the particle's speed is 2 ms^{-1}. What is the magnitude of I if the particle:

   a) is moving in the same direction as it was before the impulse was applied,

   b) is moving in exactly the opposite direction,

   c) has been deflected through an angle of 30° by the impulse?

8. A toy rocket of mass 0.2 kg can exert an upwards force of 10 N, and burns for 5 seconds. Assuming that the rocket's mass does not change during this time,

   a) what is the overall impulse acting on the rocket during the burn period,

   b) assuming that it starts from rest, what it the rocket's final speed?

   Do you think that the assumption that the rocket's mass stays constant is reasonable?

9. A particle of mass m kg is resting on a rough horizontal surface. The coefficient of friction between the particle and the surface is μ. If the particle receives a horizontal impulse I, find an expression for the time taken for the particle to come to rest.

10. A machine-gun fires 420 bullets per minute, each of mass 30 gm with a speed of 500 ms^{-1}. What is the average force that must be applied to the gun to keep it still?

11. A mechanical digger moving at 5 km/h picks up 360 kg of earth every second. What force must the digger exert to be able to do this?

12. A football has been kicked directly at the goalkeeper. The ball is travelling at 30 ms^{-1}, and has mass 0.4 kg. The goalkeeper is standing in the middle of the goalmouth, which is 7 m wide, and is 1 m in front of the goal line.

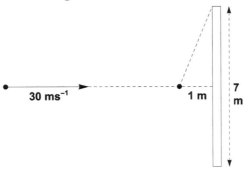

Figure 26.4

What is the magnitude of the smallest impulse that the goalkeeper must apply to the ball if the ball is to be deflected to miss the goal?

13*.   a) A force $F_1(t) = 10\sin 2\pi t$ N acts over the time interval $0 \leq t \leq \frac{1}{2}$. What is the total impulse exerted? For what value of X would the force $F_2(t) = X\sin 50\pi t$ N, acting over the time interval $0 \leq t \leq \frac{1}{50}$, exert the same impulse?

   b) The forces F_1 and F_2 (with the value of X just determined) both act (for their respective time periods) on a 1 kg mass which is originally at rest. What would the end velocities of the two masses be?

   c) How would the motion of the two masses differ from each other?

26.2   Conservation Of Momentum

When two particles interact, Newton's third law states that any action of one upon the other is matched by an equal and opposite reaction.

Suppose that the particles have masses m_1 and m_2, and displacement vectors $\mathbf{r}_1$ and $\mathbf{r}_2$ respectively. Suppose that no external forces act. If the force on the first particle due to its interaction with the first is $\mathbf{F}$, then the force on the second particle due to its interaction with the first is $-\mathbf{F}$. Newton's second law, applied to each particle, tells us that

$$m_1\ddot{\mathbf{r}}_1 = \mathbf{F} \qquad m_2\ddot{\mathbf{r}}_2 = -\mathbf{F}\,;$$

adding these two equations tells us that

$$\frac{d}{dt}\left[m_1\dot{\mathbf{r}}_1 + m_2\dot{\mathbf{r}}_2\right] = m_1\ddot{\mathbf{r}}_1 + m_2\ddot{\mathbf{r}}_2 = \mathbf{F} - \mathbf{F} = \mathbf{0}\,,$$

from which we deduce that $m_1\dot{\mathbf{r}}_1 + m_2\dot{\mathbf{r}}_2$ remains constant throughout the motion; but this is just the sum of the momenta of the two individual particles. In other words, the total momentum of the system of two particles remains unchanged.

Key Fact 26.3 Conservation of Momentum

For any system of two (or more) particles, in the absence of any external forces, the total momentum of the system remains unchanged.

The principle of conservation of momentum is simply Newton's first law, restated in terms of momentum.

26.3 Collisions

As we have already discussed, what happens when objects collide is a complex matter, and one best described in terms of momentum and impulse. We shall restrict our attention to problems when particles collide under **smooth direct impact**; the impact is **direct** in that both particles are travelling in the same straight line, and it is **smooth** in that there are no friction forces acting during the collision. The only reaction forces will be directed along the common line of travel of both particles.

When two objects collide, they deform. During the process of collision, each particle will be exerting a force on the other; these forces will be of equal magnitude but in opposite directions. If F is the magnitude of this force, then F will not be constant, but will vary over the short period of time it takes for the collision to occur.

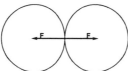

Figure 26.5

The impulse **I** that the left-hand object exerts on the right-hand object is thus $I = \int F\,dt\,\mathbf{i}$, where the integral is over the time interval of the collision. Here **i** is a unit vector pointing 'to the right'. Similarly, the impulse that the right-hand object exerts on the left-hand object has magnitude $-\int F\,dt\,\mathbf{i}$; it has the same magnitude, **but is pointed in the opposite direction.**

If we adopted a simpler model where forces of constant magnitude F acted for time T, the two impulses would be $FT\mathbf{i}$ and $-FT\mathbf{i}$; these are still of equal magnitude but in opposite directions.

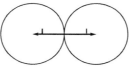

Figure 26.6

Thus Newton's third law can be restated as saying that each impulsive action is matched by an equal and opposite impulsive reaction.

If there are no external impulses acting on a system of particles, the fact that all action and reaction impulses are equal and opposite means that there is no overall impulse acting on that system, which leads (again) to the observation that momentum is conserved for such a system.

Example 26.3.1. *A particle of mass 3 kg is moving at 5 ms^{-1} when it collides with a second particle, that has mass 1 kg and is moving with speed 2 ms^{-1} in the same direction as the first particle. After the first collision the first particle's speed is reduced to 4 ms^{-1}. Find the velocity of the second particle after the collision.*

All collision problems of this type are best solved using a simple 'Before/After' diagram as in the figure. Indicate the masses of the two particles, and their velocities before and after the collision.

Conservation of momentum then tells us that

$$3 \times 5 + 1 \times 2 = 3 \times 4 + 1 \times v$$

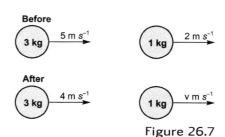

Figure 26.7

and hence $v = 5$. The second particle's velocity after the collision is 5 ms^{-1}, moving in the same direction as the first particle.

Example 26.3.2. *Two particles, both of mass m kg, are travelling in opposite directions when they collide. The first particle has speed v ms^{-1}, while the second has speed $2v$ ms^{-1}. As a result of the collision, the first particle rebounds with speed v ms^{-1}. Show that the second particle is brought to rest by the collision. What is the impulse on the first particle from the second?*

The same type of diagram is used. **It is advisable to have all velocity arrows still pointing in the same direction, with velocities heading 'the other way' shown as negative. This will ensure that momentum calculations (which are vector calculations) are performed correctly.** If the velocity of the second particle after the collision is V ms^{-1}, then

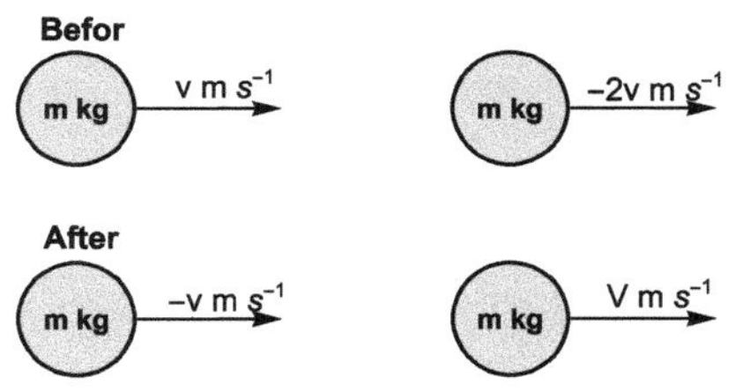

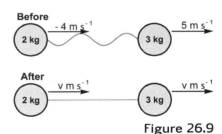

Figure 26.8

$$mv + 2m(-v) = m(-v) + mV$$

from which it is clear that $V = 0$; the second particle is stationary after the collision.

The momentum of the first particle changes from mv kg m s^{-1} before the collision to $-mv$ kg m s^{-1} after the collision. The first particle loses $2mv$ kg m s^{-1} of momentum during the collision, and hence has experienced an impulse of magnitude $2mv$ N s to the left. Note that the first particle's momentum has increased by $2mv$ kg m s^{-1}, which reflects the fact that the second particle has received an impulse of $2mv$ N s to the right (equal and opposite to the impulse on the first particle).

Strings becoming suddenly taut provide impulsive tension. Such problems can then be solved using ideas of impulse and momentum.

Example 26.3.3. *Particles of masses 2 kg and 3 kg are at rest on a horizontal table. The particles are joined by a light inextensible string. The particles are projected away from each other, with respective speeds of 4 ms^{-1} and 5 ms^{-1}. What is the common velocity of the two particles immediately after the string becomes taut, and what was the impulsive tension in the string?*

If the common velocity of the particles after the collision is v ms^{-1}, then

$$2 \times -4 + 3 \times 5 = 2v + 3v = 5v$$

and hence $v = \frac{7}{5}$. Both particles have a velocity of 1.4 ms^{-1} in the original direction of travel of the 3 kg particle.

Figure 26.9

The 3 kg particle suffered a loss of momentum of $3 \times 5 - 3 \times 1.4 = 10.8$ kg m s^{-1}, and so the impulsive tension in the string was 10.8 N s.

This last problem is, to all intents and purposes, as one in which two objects collide and then coalesce into a single particle.

Example 26.3.4. *Two pieces of putty are moving towards each other. The two pieces of putty have masses 0.2 kg and 0.1 kg, and their respective speeds are 3 ms^{-1} and 2 ms^{-1} respectively. When the two pieces of putty collide, they join to form a single particle. What is their common velocity?*

If the two particles join to form a single particle, that particle has mass 0.3 kg. If the common velocity is v ms^{-1}, then conservation of momentum gives

$$0.4 = 0.2 \times 3 + 0.1 \times (-2) = 0.3v$$

and hence $v = \frac{4}{3}$ ms^{-1}.

Equally well, a particle can split into two pieces, perhaps explosively.

Example 26.3.5. *A rocket is travelling at speed* $100\ ms^{-1}$ *when it undergoes a stage separation. Half of its mass is ejected behind it at a speed of* $1\ ms^{-1}$ *away from the rocket. What is the speed of the remainder of the rocket after the stage separation?*

Before the separation, the rocket and the stage (which both have mass m kg) have speed 100 ms^{-1}. After the separation, the rocket has speed v ms^{-1}, while the stage has speed 90 ms^{-1}. Conservation of momentum tells us that

$$2m \times 100 = m \times 90 + m \times v$$

and hence $v = 110$. The new speed of the rocket is 110 ms^{-1}.

Food For Thought 26.1

When applying the principle of conservation of momentum to collisions, we assumed that there were no external impulses acting. This does not mean that there are not external forces acting. Objects are still affected by gravity, or by normal reaction or frictional forces. Why do these forces not affect the momentum of the system during the collision?

The explanation is that we are assuming that the collision takes place instantaneously. Rather than trying to model the exact situation (in which large, but variable, reaction forces act on the colliding particles over a very short period of time), we have chosen to model collisions via impulses, that are assumed to act instantaneously. Consider an simple, if imperfect, example of a reaction force during a collision: a force of T N acting for a period of T^{-1} seconds. This produces an impulse of 1 N s, whatever the value of T. An impulse acting during an instantaneous collision could be modelled by this force as T tends to 0; the overall impulse stays the same, but the magnitude of the force tends in infinity, while the period of application of the force tends to 0.

If we are considering collisions that take value instantaneously, then ordinary finite forces like gravity and contact forces exert no impulse during the collision (since the time-interval in question is of zero length); only impulses, which are the idealisation of an 'infinitely force acting over zero time', can affect the outcome of a collision.

26.4 Kinetic Energy

A moving particle possesses energy due to the fact that it is moving. This energy is called **kinetic energy**. The kinetic energy of a particle of mass m kg, travelling with speed v ms^{-1}, is equal to $\frac{1}{2}mv^2$ Joules (the SI unit of energy). The kinetic energy of a system of particles is simply the sum of the kinetic energies of the particles in the system.

Example 26.4.1. *A particle of mass 3 kg is moving with speed* $4\ ms^{-1}$ *when it strikes, in direct central impact, a second particle of mass 1 kg. Before the impact, the second particle was stationary. After the impact, the smaller particle is moving with twice the speed of the larger particle. Find this speed, and find the kinetic energy of the system of two particles before and after the collision.*

If the speed of the 3 kg particle is v ms^{-1} after the collision, then the 1 kg particle has speed $2v$ ms^{-1} after the collision. Conservation of momentum tells us that

$$12 = 3 \times 4 + 1 \times 0 = 3 \times v + 1 \times 2v = 5v,$$

so that two particles have speeds 2.4 ms^{-1} and 4.8 ms^{-1} after the collision.

The kinetic energy of the system before the collision is $\frac{1}{2} \times 3 + 4^2 = 24$ J, while the kinetic energy of the system after the collision is $\frac{1}{2} \times 3 \times 2.4^2 + \frac{1}{2} \times 1 \times 4.8^2 = 20.16$ J.

Note that the kinetic energy the system has gone down as a result of the collision. As in the rest of physics (ignoring relativistic effects) energy as a whole is conserved. This does not mean that kinetic energy must be conserved, though. However, since there is no external agency that might be adding energy to system during the collision, we deduce that the kinetic energy of a system cannot increase during the collision, although it might decrease, with some energy being lost as heat and sound.

Key Fact 26.4 Kinetic Energy

If E_{before} is the kinetic energy of a system of particle before a collision, and E_{after} is the kinetic energy of the system of particles after the collision, then

$$E_{after} \leq E_{before}.$$

EXERCISE 26B

1. Two particles collide in direct smooth impact. The particles have masses m_1 and m_2, and have velocities u_1 and u_2 before the collision, and v_1 and v_2 after the collision. In each of the following parts, some of the values of m_1, m_2, u_1, u_2, v_1 and v_2 have been supplied. Find the missing variable in each case.

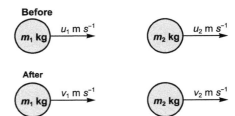

   a) $m_1 = 1$, $m_2 = 2$, $u_1 = 5$, $u_2 = 0$, $v_1 = 0$,
   b) $m_1 = 5$, $u_1 = u$, $u_2 = 0$, $v_2 = u$, $v_1 = -u$,
   c) $m_1 = m_2$, $u_1 = u$, $u_2 = 0$, $v_2 = v_1 + 1$,
   d) $m_1 = 2$, $m_2 = 4$, $u_1 = 3$, $u_2 = -1$, $v_1 = -v_2$,
   e) $m_1 = 100m_2$, $u_1 = V$, $u_2 = -V$, $v_1 = v_2$.

2. A railway truck of mass 2000 kg travelling at 3 ms^{-1} hits another truck of mass 1000 kg which is stationary. The two trucks couple automatically and move on as one. What is their common speed after they have coupled?

3. A trolley of mass 250 kg is moving at 6 ms^{-1}. A man of mass 80 kg steps onto the trolley. What is the speed of the trolley now?

4. A bullet is fired with a speed of 600 ms^{-1} into a block of concrete of mass 1.5 kg, and becomes embedded in it. If this impact gives the block a speed of 12 ms^{-1}, find the mass of the bullet.

5. Two spheres of masses 2 kg and 3 kg are resting on a smooth horizontal surface. They are joined by a light inextensible string which is initially slack. An impulse of 2.5 N s is applied to the smaller sphere, in a direction directly away from the other sphere. What is the speed with which the smaller sphere begins to move, and what is the joint speed of both spheres when then string becomes taut?

6. Consider the two spheres in the previous question. This time, the impulse of 2.5 N s is applied to the smaller sphere, in a direction directly towards the larger sphere, so that the spheres collide. After the collision, the larger sphere's velocity is 1 ms^{-1} more than the velocity of the smaller sphere. What are the velocities of the two particles after the collision? Describe the subsequent motion of the system.

7. Ten particles, all of mass 1 kg, are lying at rest on a horizontal surface. All ten particles are lying in a straight line. One of the two outermost particles receives an impulse of 10 N s, directed towards the other nine particles. Whenever two of these particles collide, they coalesce into a single particle. After nine collisions, all ten particles will be moving as a single particle. What is the speed of that single particle?

8. A particle of mass m_1 is travelling at velocity u when it collides directly with a stationary particle of mass m_2. After the collision, the two particles have velocities v_1 and v_2 respectively, where $v_1 < v_2$. Use the principle of conservation of momentum to show that

$$m_1 m_2 \left[u^2 - (v_2 - v_1)^2 \right] = (m_1 + m_2) \left[m_1 v^2 - m_1 v_1^2 - m_2 v_2^2 \right].$$

   Use the fact that the combined kinetic energy of the two particles does not increase as a result of the collision, derive a relationship between $v_2 - v_1$ and u.

9*. Extend the ideas of the previous question. Suppose that two particles of masses m_1 and m_2 are travelling with velocities u_1 and u_2 respectively, where $u_1 > u_2$ when they collide in a direct smooth impact, and suppose that the velocities of the particles after the collision are v_1 and v_2 respectively, where $v_2 > v_1$. Find an expression for

$$m_1 m_2 \left[(u_1 - u_2)^2 - (v_2 - v_1)^2 \right]$$

in terms of the masses of the particles and the combined kinetic energies of the two particles before and after the collision. Using the fact that the kinetic energy of the system does not increase as a result of the collision, find a relationship between $u_1 - u_2$ and $v_2 - v_1$.

10*. A rocket travelling in a straight line emits fuel behind it at a speed of u ms^{-1} relative to itself. In the process, the rocket's mass decreases. At time t, the rocket has mass m and speed v. At time $t + \delta t$ the rocket has mass $m + \delta m$ and speed $v + \delta v$, and it has emitted fuel of mass $-\delta m$ at a speed of $v - u$. Using the principle of Conservation of Momentum between times t and $t + \delta t$, use a first principles differentiation argument to show that v and m satisfy the differential equation

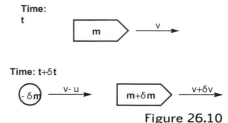

Figure 26.10

$$m \frac{dv}{dm} + u = 0 .$$

If the starting mass of the rocket is M, and the rocket is initially at rest, find an expression for the speed of the rocket as a function of m.

If half the starting mass of the rocket is fuel, show that the speed of the rocket, once all its fuel has been burnt, is $u \ln 2$.

26.5   Newton's Law Of Restitution — General Collisions

In Question 9 of the last Exercise, an interesting fact was shown. If two objects collide in direct impact, and if their velocities before the impact were u_1 and u_2, and if their velocities after the impact were v_1 and v_2, then

$$v_2 - v_1 \le u_1 - u_2 .$$

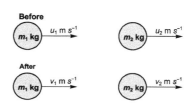

Figure 26.11

This inequality is worth investigating further. The quantity $u_1 - u_2$ must be positive, since otherwise the two particles would be moving away from, and not towards, each other before the collision. The quantity $u_1 - u_2$ is the relative speed of the two particles before the collision, and is the speed at which the two particles are moving towards each other. The speed $u_1 - u_2$ is called the **speed of approach** of the two particles.

Similarly, the quantity $v_2 - v_1$ (note the different order of the subscripts) is positive, since otherwise the two particles would not be moving apart from each other after the collision. The quantity $v_2 - v_1$ is the relative speed of the two particles after the collision, and is the speed at which the particles are moving away from each other. The speed $v_2 - v_1$ is called the **speed of separation** of the two particles.

The fact that energy is not created during this collision has shown us that the speed of separation of the two particles never exceeds the speed of approach of the particles.

This phenomenon can be observed in the behaviour of a ball bouncing on the ground. If we drop a ball from a fixed height h m onto an unmoving floor then, after the ball has bounced, the maximum height h_1 m reached by the ball will never exceed the original height h m from which it was dropped. If the ball has speed u ms^{-1} just before it hits the floor and speed v ms^{-1} just after it has bounced then, using SUVAT equations, $u = \sqrt{2gh}$ and $v = \sqrt{2gh_1}$. Thus it follows that $v \le u$.

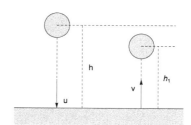

Figure 26.12

The speed v at which the ball rises from the ground is less than or equal to the speed u at which the ball approaches the ground; again, the speed of separation of the ball and the ground is less than or equal to the speed of approach of the ball and the ground.

Sir Isaac Newton conducted a number of experimental observations and found that there was a simple relationship between the speeds of approach and separation of two particles: when any two particles collide, their speeds of approach and of separation are proportional. In other words, there is a constant of proportionality, written e, such that the speed of separation is equal to e times the speed of approach of the two particles. This constant is (to a large degree) independent of the initial speeds of the two particles, and only depends on (physical properties of) the particles themselves.

This relationship is based on experiment, and is not always valid. If the speeds of the particles were such that one of the particles was shattered as a result of the impact, or even permanently distorted as a result of the impact, the relationship no longer holds. Newton assumed (as shall we) that the collisions were of a nature that neither particle was permanently changed as a result of the collision, and that each would spring back to its initial shape and structure after being squashed as part of the collision. Such collisions are called **elastic**.

Key Fact 26.5 Newton's (Experimental) Law Of Restitution

For any two particles colliding in elastic direct impact, there is a quantity e, where $0 \leq e \leq 1$, such that the speed of separation of the particles is equal to e times the speed of approach of the particles:

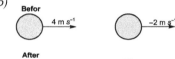

$$v_2 - v_1 = e(u_1 - u_2).$$

The quantity e is called the **coefficient of restitution** between the two particles.

Example 26.5.1. *What is the coefficient of restitution between the two particles in the following examples of elastic collision?*

a)

b)

(a) The speed of approach is $6 - 0 = 6$ ms^{-1} and the speed of separation is $5 - 2 = 3$ ms^{-1}, and so $e = \frac{1}{2}$.

(b) The speed of approach is $4 - (-2) = 6$ ms^{-1} and the speed of separation is $3 - 1 = 2$ ms^{-1}, and so $e = \frac{1}{3}$.

Food For Thought 26.2

These collisions are called elastic, but that does not mean that they have to be particularly 'springy'! Two particles for which $e = 1$ are called **perfectly elastic**: perfectly elastic collisions occur in the idealised situation where no kinetic energy is lost during the collision. Two ball bearings collide in a manner that is almost perfectly elastic, and a pair of snooker balls would also have a coefficient of restitution close to 1.

On the other hand, collisions between particles with $e = 0$ are called **perfectly inelastic**. In such collisions, the speed of separation is always zero, and hence the two particles end up moving at the same velocity. In other words, the particles coalesce into a single particle. The collision between two pieces of putty would be perfectly inelastic. Since the notion of an elastic collisions covers all situations from a pair of ball bearings to couple of pieces of putty, it is clear that Newton's law of restitution has a wide field of application.

Newton's law of restitution enables us to solve general collision problems. If two particles, with known masses and initial velocities, meet in direct elastic collision, there are two quantities to be determined: their velocities after the collision. We can now use both conservation of momentum and Newton's law of restitution to obtain a pair of simultaneous equations for these final velocities, and these equations can be solved.

Example 26.5.2. *Two identical spheres of the same mass m kg meet in direct perfectly elastic impact. Before the impact, the first particle is moving with velocity u ms^{-1}, while the second is stationary. What the velocities of the two particles after the collision?*

Using the standard notation for the velocities and masses, we are told that the masses are identical, which certainly means that they have the same masses, and so $m_1 = m_2 = m$. Moreover, we know that $u_1 = u$ and $u_2 = 0$ (we are told that the second particle is stationary). Since the collision is perfectly elastic, we know that $e = 1$. Thus we have the two equations

$$mv_1 + mv_2 = mu + m0 = mu \qquad v_2 - v_1 = 1(u - 0) = u \, ,$$

the first arising from conservation of momentum, and the second being Newton's law of restitution. If we solve these equations, we obtain $v_1 = 0$ and $v_2 = u$. Thus the first particle is stationary after the collision, while the second particle is now moving at the same speed as the first particle was initially.

This behaviour is (very nearly) what happens when playing snooker or pool. If a target ball is hit cleanly straight-on by the cue ball, then after the collision the cue ball will be stationary and the target ball will be moving with the speed previously observed by the cue ball. Effects like back-spin and top-spin, that cause the cue ball to either move backwards or continue forwards after the collision, are more complicated. They are due to the fact that the cue ball is spinning, and that there is friction between the spinning cue ball and the cloth of the table. Such effects are well beyond the range of factors we are currently considering.

Another common example of perfectly elastic collisions can be seen in Newton's Cradle, a common executive toy. A collection of identical metal balls are hung from strings so that they are all at the same height and simultaneously touching each other. One of the outermost balls is then pulled to one side (keeping the strings supporting it taut) and then released. When the free ball strikes the stationary balls, a sequence of perfectly elastic collisions occurs, resulting in the ball at the far end of the collection moving away from the pack, with the rest of the balls stationary. This process repeats continuously, with the ball at the far end swinging up and then back, striking the line of balls, which causes the first ball to move away from the pack again, and so on. Bored office-workers can be identified by the sound of clicking from their desktop Newton's Cradle models!

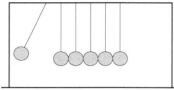

Figure 26.13

Example 26.5.3. *Two particles, of masses 0.2 kg and 0.4 kg, are moving towards each other along a straight line on a smooth horizontal surface. Just before they collide, the first particle has speed 2 ms^{-1}, while the second has speed 3 ms^{-1}. The coefficient of restitution between the two particles is $\frac{1}{5}$. Find*

    (a) the velocities of the particles immediately after the collision,

    (b) the magnitude of the impulse exerted by each particle on the other during the collision.

(a) If the velocities of the particles after the collision are v_1 and v_2, then conservation of momentum tells us that

$$0.2v_1 + 0.4v_2 = 0.2 \times 2 + 0.3 \times (-3) = -0.5$$

or

$$v_1 + 2v_2 = -2.5 \, ,$$

while Newton's law of restitution tells us that

$$-v_1 + v_2 = \tfrac{1}{5}(2 - (-3)) = 1 \, .$$

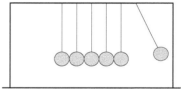

Figure 26.14

Solving these two equations simultaneously tells us that $v_1 = -1.5$ and $v_2 = -0.5$. The first particle changes direction, but the second does not.

(b) Before the collision, the first particle's momentum was $0.2 \times 2 = 0.4$ kg m s^{-1}. After the collision, the first particle's momentum is $0.2 \times (-1.5) = -0.3$ kg m s^{-1}. Thus the first particle experiences a change in momentum of 0.7 kg m s^{-1} as a result of the collision, and hence must have received an impulse of 0.7 N s during the collision. The second particle must have received the same impulse, but in the opposite direction.

Food For Thought 26.3

It is worth noting that in this example, as elsewhere in this chapter, all collision diagrams have been drawn with all velocity arrows pointing in the same direction. Particles moving in the opposite direction are represented by negative velocities. It is best practice to draw all diagrams this way, since then the formulae for momentum and for the speeds of approach and separation are always the same.

If arrows are drawn in different directions in the same diagram, we would need to think much more carefully when applying conservation of momentum and Newton's law of restitution. In the case shown in the figure the speed of approach would be $u_1 + u_2$ instead of $u_1 - u_2$, for example.

Figure 26.15

We started this section by observing that the speed of approach of two particles always exceeded their speed of separation, due to the fact that kinetic energy was at best conserved during a collision.

Example 26.5.4. *A particle of mass 3 kg is moving with speed 4 ms^{-1} when it meets in direct elastic impact a second particle of mass 2 kg, that is stationary before the impact. The coefficient of restitution between the two particles is equal to e. Calculate the change in kinetic energy of the two particles, and show that kinetic energy is only conserved when $e = 1$.*

We have the equations

$$3v_1 + 2v_2 = 12$$
$$-v_1 + v_2 = 4e$$

which give $v_1 = \frac{4}{5}(3 - 2e)$, $v_2 = \frac{12}{5}(1 + e)$.

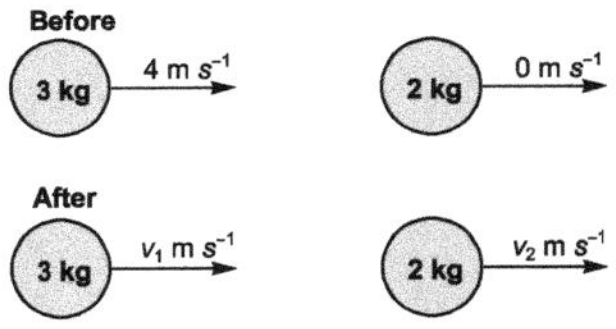

Before

3 kg — 4 m s^{-1} 2 kg — 0 m s^{-1}

After

3 kg — v_1 m s^{-1} 2 kg — v_2 m s^{-1}

Figure 26.16

The kinetic energy of the particles before the collision was $E_{\text{before}} = \frac{1}{2} \times 3 \times 4^2 = 24$ J, while the kinetic energy of the particles after the collision is

$$
\begin{aligned}
E_{\text{after}} &= \tfrac{1}{2} \times 3 \times v_1^2 + \tfrac{1}{2} \times 2 \times v_2^2 = \tfrac{24}{25}(3 - 2e)^2 + \tfrac{144}{25}(1 + e)^2 \\
&= \tfrac{24}{25}\left[(3 - 2e)^2 + 6(1 + e)^2\right] = \tfrac{24}{25}(15 + 10e^2) = \tfrac{24}{5}(3 + 2e^2)
\end{aligned}
$$

Joules, which implies that the loss of kinetic energy is

$$E_{\text{after}} - E_{\text{before}} = \tfrac{48}{5}(1 - e^2) \text{ Joules,}$$

Since $0 \le e \le 1$, this quantity is always non-negative, and is zero precisely when $e = 1$.

Newton's law of restitution can even be used in situations where using conservation of momentum is inappropriate. For a single particle bouncing against an unmoving surface (a floor or a wall), Newton's law of restitution becomes particularly simple.

Example 26.5.5. *A tennis ball is struck, and it is travelling horizontally with speed 5 ms^{-1} when it hits a vertical wall. The coefficient of restitution between the ball and the wall is 0.8. What is the speed at which the ball is moving when it bounces back from the wall?*

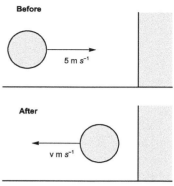

Suppose that the ball rebounds with speed v. We are assuming that the wall does not move. That being the case, momentum is not conserved. Newton's law of restitution tells us that $v = 5e = 4$, so the tennis ball is moving with speed 4 ms^{-1} when it bounces back from the wall.

Figure 26.17

Food For Thought 26.4

Conservation of momentum, being a consequence of Newton's second law, should always be true. How then can we have a situation like the above in which momentum is not conserved? The fault lies in our model, since we have been assuming that the wall remains stationary throughout the collision. In actual fact, the wall is attached to the rest of the earth, and the momentum of the earth will change as a result of the collision with the tennis ball. However, the mass of the earth is so large, compared to the mass of the tennis ball, that it is a reasonable approximation to ignore the change in the earth's, and therefore the wall's, motion. Ignoring the motion of the earth makes using conservation of momentum impossible. Newton's law of restitution can still be used, however. Since ignoring the motion of the earth means that there is only one unknown quantity (the speed of the ball after it bounces) to determine, the single equation produced by Newton's law of restitution is enough to solve the problem.

Example 26.5.6. *A ball is dropped from rest at a height h m above a hard horizontal floor. The coefficient of restitution between the ball and the floor is e. Find an expression for the height to which the ball rises after its first, second and third bounces.*

Find an expression for the amount of time taken by the ball until it hits the ground for the third time.

The ball falls through a height of h m before hitting the floor. Using SUVAT equations, the ball will have speed $\sqrt{2gh}$ ms^{-1} just before impact. After hitting the floor, the ball will bounce back with speed $e\sqrt{2gh} = \sqrt{2g(e^2h)}$ ms^{-1}. Applying SUVAT equations again, this means that the ball will rise to a height of e^2h m after its first bounce. It is clear now that the ball will rise to a height of $e^2 \times e^2h = e^4h$ m after the second bounce, and to a height of e^6 m after the third bounce.

When falling from a height of h m, the ball takes $\sqrt{\dfrac{2h}{g}}$ seconds to hit the ground. It follows that:

- the ball takes $\sqrt{\dfrac{2h}{g}}$ seconds until the first bounce,

- the ball takes $\sqrt{\dfrac{2e^2h}{g}} = e\sqrt{\dfrac{2h}{g}}$ seconds after the first bounce until it reaches its maximum height above the ground, and the same time again until it hits the ground for a second time, so it follows that the ball takes $2e\sqrt{\dfrac{2h}{g}}$ s between the first and second bounces,

- arguing similarly, the ball takes $2e^2\sqrt{\dfrac{2h}{g}}$ seconds between the second and third bounces, and so on.

Thus the time taken until the ball hits the ground for the third time is

$$\sqrt{\frac{2h}{g}} + 2e\sqrt{\frac{2h}{g}} + 2e^2\sqrt{\frac{2h}{g}} = (1 + 2e + 2e^2)\sqrt{\frac{2h}{g}} \text{ seconds.}$$

For Interest

The interested student should consider the behaviour of the ball as it keeps on bouncing. How many times does it bounce, and for how long is it bouncing? See Question 8 of the next set of exercises.

EXERCISE 26C

1. Two particles meet in direct elastic impact as shown in the Figure. Their velocities before the collision are u_1 ms^{-1} and u_2 ms^{-2}, and their velocities after the collision are v_1 ms^{-2} and v_2 ms^{-1}. In each of the cases below, find the coefficient of restitution between the particles:

   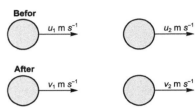

   Figure 26.18

   a) $u_1 = 5, u_2 = 0, v_1 = 0, v_2 = 2$,

   b) $u_1 = 10, u_2 = -2, v_1 = 6, v_2 = 9$,

   c) $u_1 = 2u, u_2 = -2u, v_1 = -u, v_2 = u$,

   d) $u_1 = 7, u_2 = 4, v_1 = 6, v_2 = 9$.

2. In each of the following cases, find the unknown variables. All velocities are measured in ms^{-1}, and all masses in kg:

   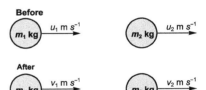

   Figure 26.19

   a) $u_1 = 8, u_2 = 0, m_1 = 1, m_2 = 2, e = \frac{1}{2}$,

   b) $u_1 = 6, u_2 = -2, m_1 = 3, m_2 = 5, e = \frac{1}{3}$,

   c) $u_1 = u, u_2 = -u, m_1 = 3m, m_2 = 4m, e = \frac{1}{4}$,

   d) $u_1 = u, u_2 = -u, m_1 = 3m, m_2 = 5m, v_1 = -u$,

   e) $u_1 = u, u_2 = -u, m_1 = m, v_1 = -\frac{1}{2}u, v_2 = u$.

3. Particles X and Y lie at rest on a smooth horizontal plane near a vertical wall, with the line formed by X and Y being at right angles to the wall, and Y being near to the wall than X. The particles both have mass 2 kg. The coefficient of restitution between the two particles is 0.5 and the coefficient of restitution between particle Y and the wall is 0.7. Find the final velocities of the particles when Y is acted upon by an impulse of 10 N s directly towards the wall. Find the loss of kinetic energy due to the collision.

4. A particle is travelling horizontally with speed u ms^{-1} when it strikes a stationary particle of the same mass as itself in direct elastic collision. The coefficient of restitution between the particles is e. Show that the original particle does not change direction as a result of this collision. If, after the collision, the speed of the second particle is twice that of the first particle, determine the value of the coefficient of restitution e.

5. Particle B is three times the mass of particle A. The coefficient of restitution between them is e. They lie at rest on the same horizontal plane. Suppose that, when A is projected towards B, A is brought to rest as a result of the collision. Determine the coefficient of restitution between the particles, and show that the kinetic energy of the two particles after the collision is a third of its value before the collision.

6. A particle is moving at 8 ms^{-1} when it collides in direct elastic impact with a second particle which is moving in the opposite direction with speed 4 ms^{-1}. The coefficient of restitution between the particles is $\frac{2}{3}$. If the kinetic energy of the second particle is quadrupled as a result of the collision, find an exact expression for the ratio of the masses of the particles.

7. Particles A, B and C, all of the same mass, are at rest lying in a straight line in alphabetical order. Particle A is then projected directly at particle B with speed u ms^{-1}. The coefficient of restitution between any two of the particles is $\frac{1}{4}$. How many collisions between pairs of particles will there be, and find the final velocities of the three particles after all the collisions have taken place.

8. A particle is dropped from a height of h m onto a horizontal floor. The coefficient of restitution between the particle and the floor is e. Find an expression for the total time elapsed before the particle comes to rest. What is the total distance travelled by the particle during that time?

9. Three particles, of masses $5m$, m and $2m$, respectively, lie at rest on a horizontal table in the order stated. The $5m$ kg particle is projected directly towards the m kg particle. The coefficients of restitution between any two balls are the same.

    a) After two collisions, the lightest particle is stationary. What is the value of the coefficient of restitution e?

    b) Show that there are four collisions in total, and find the final velocities of the three particles.

10*. A sphere of mass m_1 kg, moving with speed u_1 ms^{-1}, collides in direct elastic impact with a sphere of mass m_2 that is moving with speed u_2 in the same direction. The coefficient of restitution between the two spheres is e. Show that the loss of kinetic energy E due to the collision satisfies the equation

$$2(m_1 + m_2)E = m_1 m_2 (u_1 - u_2)^2 (1 - e^2).$$

Chapter 26: Summary

- The **momentum** of a particle is equal to its mass times its velocity.

- A constant force $\mathbf{F}$ N acting for a time t seconds exerts an **impulse** Ft N s. An object acted upon by an impulse experiences a change in momentum, in kg m s^{-1}, equal to the impulse acting on it.

- The principle of conservation of momentum states that, in the absence of external forces, momentum is conserved. This is a simple restatement of Newton's second law.

- Momentum is conserved, but kinetic energy rarely is, in collisions between particles.

- In smooth elastic direct impact collisions, Newton's law of restitution states that the speed of separation of the two particles is equal to e times the speed of approach of those particles,

$$v_2 - v_1 = e(u_1 - u_2),$$

where the constant e (which depends on the nature of the two particles) is called the **coefficient of restitution**.

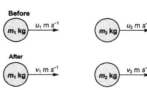

Figure 26.20

The Motion Of Projectiles

In this chapter we will learn:

- to model the motion of a projectile as a particle moving with constant acceleration, and understand any limitations of this model,

- to use horizontal and vertical equations of motion to solve problems on the motion of projectiles, including finding the magnitude and direction of the velocity at a given time or position, the range on a horizontal plane and the greatest height reached,

- to derive and use the Cartesian equation of the trajectory of a projectile, including problems in which the initial speed and/or angle of projection may be unknown.

27.1 Vector Kinematics and Projectile Motion

As discussed in Chapter 22, displacement, velocity and acceleration are all vector quantities, and we have already studied how to solve kinematic problems in two or three dimensions using calculus. In particular, we studied the kinematic equations describing the motion of a particle undergoing constant acceleration. This chapter is concerned with the particular implications of these equations when the constant acceleration is that of gravity.

Consider an object falling freely under gravity. We shall make the following assumptions:

- the object can be modelled as a point particle,

- the force of gravity is constant at all times, acting vertically downwards,

- the surface of the earth is flat,

- no air resistance is experienced.

Since the only force acting on the object is that of gravity, the resultant force acting on the object is the constant force $m\mathbf{g}$, where m is the mass of the object, and $\mathbf{g}$ is a fixed vector pointing vertically downwards. Newton's second law gives us the equation of motion (recall the 'dot' notation introduced in Chapter 22):

$$m\ddot{\mathbf{r}} = m\mathbf{g}$$

for the object, where $\mathbf{r}$ is the displacement vector of the particle relative its starting position at time $t = 0$. Thus

$$\ddot{\mathbf{r}} = \mathbf{g}.$$

Since $\mathbf{g}$ is a constant vector, it is easy to integrate this equation, obtaining

$$\dot{\mathbf{r}} = \mathbf{u} + \mathbf{g}t$$

for some constant vector $\mathbf{u}$; since $\dot{\mathbf{r}} = \mathbf{u}$ when $t = 0$, it is clear that $\mathbf{u}$ is the initial velocity of the object. Integrating one more time gives

$$\mathbf{r} = \mathbf{c} + \mathbf{u}t + \tfrac{1}{2}\mathbf{g}t^2$$

for some constant vector **c**. Since the object starts its motion at the origin, we deduce that $\mathbf{r} = \mathbf{0}$ when $t = 0$, and hence that $\mathbf{c} = \mathbf{0}$. Thus the displacement of the particle at time t is given by the equation

$$\mathbf{r} = \mathbf{u}t + \tfrac{1}{2}\mathbf{g}t^2,$$

at least until the particle hits the ground (or the model ceases to be valid for some other reason).

Looking at this last equation enables us to make a substantial simplification in our notation. The motion of the object is taking place in a three-dimensional world, but we see that the motion of the particle can be described completely by the two vectors **u** and **g**. These two vectors define a vertical plane in which all motion takes place; this means that the vector motion of the object can be described using two-dimensional vectors.

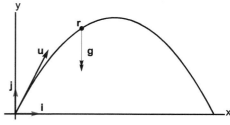

Figure 27.1

Objects falling freely under gravity in this manner are frequently called **projectiles**. The path that a projectile follows in space is called its **trajectory**. Its shape is a parabola.

Food For Thought 27.1

The assumptions made in this model are substantial. We have previously discussed some of the limitations of assuming that an object is a point particle and aerodynamic effects that might provide the object with uplift, or that might make the ball swerve, are being ignored.

Assuming that gravity is constant is reasonable, provided that the object does not reach an altitude comparable with the earth's radius. Provided that our problems deal with throwing cricket balls and dropping bricks off buildings, and do not attempt to model intercontinental ballistic missiles, all should be well. Additionally, provided that the altitude of the object remains relatively low, the distance covered by the particle before it hits the ground will be comparatively short, and assuming that the earth is flat, instead of round, will be acceptable.

The issue of air resistance is perhaps the most contentious. For an object to be treated as a point particle, it needs to be relatively small. This means that, in all likelihood, its mass will be quite small, and the result of this is that even small air resistance forces will have an appreciable effect. Figure 23.14 in Example 23.5.1 showed the difference that air resistance makes to the motion of a ball.

Unfortunately, however, the kinematics of an object falling that is being affected by air resistance is complicated; the shape of the object matters, since it affects the magnitude of the resistance force. The full problem of air resistance is too big to include in a school-level study, so we take the only possible option; we assume that particles are moving in the absence of air resistance, and accept the inevitable limitations of the model. Alternatively, we can conduct our experiments on the surface of the moon, where the model is valid!

It is easiest to handle the equations of projectile motion using components. Introduce fixed unit vectors **i** and **j** pointing horizontally in the direction of motion and vertically upwards respectively. This defines a corresponding coordinate system for the vertical plane. A general point in the plane can be described by a displacement vector $\mathbf{r} = x\mathbf{i} + y\mathbf{j}$ for some real numbers x and y. Since the force of gravity acts vertically downwards, we deduce that $\mathbf{g} = -g\mathbf{j}$. As elsewhere in mechanics, it is useful to retain the symbol g in projectile calculations, only substituting $g = 10\ \text{ms}^{-2}$ if necessary. Since vectors are differentiated by differentiating each of the components, we deduce that $\dot{\mathbf{r}} = \dot{x}\mathbf{i} + \dot{y}\mathbf{j}$.

> **Key Fact 27.1** Displacement and Velocity in Coordinates
>
> If a particle has displacement $\mathbf{r} = x\mathbf{i} + y\mathbf{j}$, with components x and y, then the velocity of the particle is $\dot{\mathbf{r}} = \dot{x}\mathbf{i} + \dot{y}\mathbf{j}$, with components $\dot{x}$ and $\dot{y}$. These vectors could also be written as
>
> $$\mathbf{r} = \begin{pmatrix} x \\ y \end{pmatrix} \qquad \dot{\mathbf{r}} = \begin{pmatrix} \dot{x} \\ \dot{y} \end{pmatrix}.$$
>
> The components of an object's velocity are obtained by differentiating the components of its displacement with respect to time.

Example 27.1.1. *A stone is thrown horizontally from the edge of a cliff with speed $18~ms^{-1}$. Find an expression for the displacement and velocity of the particle at time t. What is its speed 3 seconds into its motion?*

Since the stone is thrown horizontally with speed $18~ms^{-1}$, its initial velocity is $\mathbf{u} = 18\mathbf{i}$. Thus the displacement vector $\mathbf{r}$ of the stone is

$$\mathbf{r} = 18t\mathbf{i} - \tfrac{1}{2}gt^2\mathbf{j};$$

in components we can write

$$x = 18t, \qquad y = -\tfrac{1}{2}gt^2.$$

The velocity of the particle is given by

$$\dot{\mathbf{r}} = 18\mathbf{i} - gt\mathbf{j};$$

in components we can write

$$\dot{x} = 18, \qquad \dot{y} = -gt.$$

After 3 seconds the stone has velocity $18\mathbf{i} - 30\mathbf{j}~ms^{-1}$; its speed is thus $\sqrt{18^2 + 30^2} = \sqrt{1224} = 35.0~ms^{-1}$.

Example 27.1.2. *A ball is thrown with initial velocity $10\mathbf{i} + 15\mathbf{j}~ms^{-1}$, starting at ground level. For how long is the ball in the air?*

Since $\mathbf{u} = 10\mathbf{i} + 15\mathbf{j}$, we deduce that the displacement of the particle is

$$\mathbf{r} = (10\mathbf{i} + 15\mathbf{j})t - \tfrac{1}{2}gt^2\mathbf{j} = 10t\mathbf{i} + (15t - 5t^2)\mathbf{j}.$$

The origin of our coordinate system is at the point of the ball's projection, which is at ground level. Since the y-axis points vertically upwards, we deduce that ground level is represented by the x-axis. Thus the ball hits the ground when it reaches the height $y = 0$. This occurs when

$$15t - 5t^2 = 0$$

Since $15t - 5t^2 = 5t(3 - t)$, this happens when $t = 0$ or 3. We know that the particle is at ground level when $t = 0$ (it is initially projected from ground level). It therefore hits the ground again when $t = 3$, and hence is in the air for 3 seconds.

Instead of being given the velocity's components directly, we are frequently given information about the speed and the direction of a particle's initial motion. It is a standard calculation with vectors to retrieve the components of the particle's initial velocity from that information.

If a particle has initial speed $V~ms^{-1}$, and is travelling at an angle of θ above the horizontal, then its initial velocity is

$$\mathbf{u} = V\cos\theta\mathbf{i} + V\sin\theta\mathbf{j} \quad ms^{-1}.$$

Consequently the subsequent motion of the particle can be expressed in components as follows:

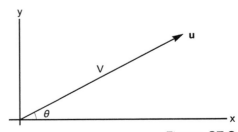

Figure 27.2

Key Fact 27.2 The Trajectory of a Projectile in Components

The motion of a projectile which is initially travelling with speed V at an angle of θ above the horizontal is described by the equations

$$x = Vt\cos\theta \qquad\qquad y = Vt\sin\theta - \tfrac{1}{2}gt^2$$
$$\dot{x} = V\cos\theta \qquad\qquad \dot{y} = V\sin\theta - gt$$

Note that the equations describing x do not involve y, and those describing y do not involve x. Horizontal and vertical motion take place independently of each other. The horizontal motion of the particle is that of an object moving with constant speed, while the vertical motion is that of an object subject to a constant acceleration of $-g$.

Example 27.1.3. *A catapult flings a stone from ground level with a speed of 50 ms^{-1} at an angle of 10° above the horizontal. For how long is the stone in the air, and how far does it travel?*

The trajectory of the stone is given by the equations

$$x = 50t\cos 10° \qquad\qquad y = 50t\sin 10° - \tfrac{1}{2}gt^2 .$$

The stone hits the ground again when $y = 0$. Solving the equation $50t\sin 10° - \tfrac{1}{2}gt^2 = 0$ shows us that the particle hits the ground after time $\frac{100}{g}\sin 10° = 10\sin 10° = 1.74$ seconds. In this time it travels a distance $50\cos 10° \times 10\sin 10° = 85.5$ metres.

Food For Thought 27.2

It is, of course, totally possible to solve these problems by considering the horizontal and vertical motion entirely separately, and simply solving relevant SUVAT equations to determine the behaviour. For example, the previous example could have been solved by substituting $u = 50\sin 10°$, $a = -g$ and $s = 0$ into the SUVAT equation $s = ut + \tfrac{1}{2}at^2$ to determine the time of flight. There is benefit, however, to emphasising the two-dimensional nature of the problem, and working with the equation of the trajectory of the particle. All the kinematics of the SUVAT equations are encapsulated in the equation of the trajectory, and problem-solving is then generally a simple matter of substitution.

Example 27.1.4. *In a game of tennis a player serves the ball horizontally from a height of 2 metres above the ground. The trajectory of the ball has to satisfy two conditions:*

- *it has to pass over the net, which is 0.9 metres high at a distance of 12 metres from the server,*

- *it has to hit the ground less than 18 metres from the server.*

At what speeds can it be hit?

Up to now we have insisted that the point of projection should be the coordinate origin. This time it is more natural to have the origin at the server's feet. This means that the initial displacement of the ball is $2\mathbf{j}$ metres, and so the trajectory of the ball is described by the equations

$$x = ut \qquad\qquad y = 2 - \tfrac{1}{2}gt^2 = 2 - 5t^2 ,$$

where the initial speed of the ball is u ms^{-1}.

- The ball reaches the net when $x = 12$, at time $t = \frac{12}{u}$ seconds. At this time $y = 2 - \frac{720}{u^2}$, and this must be greater than 0.9. Thus we deduce that $2 - \frac{720}{u^2} > 0.9$, which implies that $\frac{720}{u^2} < 1.1$, and hence $u > \sqrt{\frac{720}{1.1}} = 25.6$.

- The ball hits the ground when $y = 2 - 5t^2 = 0$, at time $t = \sqrt{\frac{2}{5}}$. At this time $x = u\sqrt{\frac{2}{5}}$, so we deduce that $u\sqrt{\frac{2}{5}} < 18$, and so $u < 18\sqrt{\frac{5}{2}} = 28.5$.

The initial speed of the tennis ball must lie between 25.6 ms^{-1} and 28.5 ms^{-1}.

Example 27.1.5. *A cricketer scores a six by hitting the ball at an angle of $30°$ to the horizontal. The ball passes over the boundary 90 metres away at a height of 5 metres above the ground. Neglecting air resistance, find the speed at which the ball was hit.*

If the initial speed was u ms^{-1}, the equations of horizontal and vertical motion are

$$x = ut\cos 30° = \tfrac{1}{2}ut\sqrt{3} \qquad y = ut\sin 30° - \tfrac{1}{2}gt^2 = \tfrac{1}{2}ut - 5t^2.$$

Since, at the boundary, $x = 90$ and $y = 5$, we know that

$$90 = \tfrac{1}{2}ut\sqrt{3} \qquad 5 = \tfrac{1}{2}ut - 5t^2$$

for some particular value of t. The first equation tells us that $ut = \frac{180}{\sqrt{3}} = 60\sqrt{3}$, and hence $5 = 30\sqrt{3} - 5t^2$, so that $t = \sqrt{6\sqrt{3} - 1}$. Thus the required value of u is $\frac{60\sqrt{3}}{\sqrt{6\sqrt{3}-1}} = 33.9$. The ball was hit with speed 33.9 ms^{-1}.

Example 27.1.6. *A boy uses a catapult to send a small ball through his friend's open window. The window is 8 metres up a wall 12 metres away from the boy.*

(a) *If the ball enters the window descending at an angle of $45°$ to the horizontal, find the initial velocity of the ball.*

(b) *If the catapult fires balls with a speed of 20 ms^{-1}, find the possible directions in which the boy may fire to reach the window.*

Suppose that the horizontal and vertical components of the initial velocity of the ball are p ms^{-1} and q ms^{-1} respectively. Then $x = pt$ and $y = qt - \tfrac{1}{2}gt^2 = qt - 5t^2$, and hence $\dot{x} = p$ and $\dot{y} = q - 10t$.

(a) If the ball passes through the window at time $t = T$, then $pT = 12$ and $qT - 5T^2 = 8$. Since the ball is descending at an angle of $45°$ to the horizontal at that time, $\dot{y} = -\dot{x}$ at that time, and hence $q - 10T = -p$. From these three equations for p, q and T, we deduce that $p = \frac{12}{T}$ and $q = \frac{5T^2+8}{T}$, and hence

$$\frac{12}{T} + \frac{5T^2+8}{T} = p + q = 10T$$

so that $12 + (5T^2 + 8) = 10T^2$, and hence $5T^2 = 20$, so that $T = 2$. Thus we deduce that $p = 6$ and $q = 14$.

The initial velocity of the ball is $6\mathbf{i} + 14\mathbf{j}$ ms^{-1}, and hence the ball starts by moving with speed $\sqrt{6^2 + 14^2} = 15.2$ ms^{-1} at an angle of $\tan^{-1}\frac{14}{6} = 66.8°$ to the horizontal.

(b) If the ball passes through the window at time T, then (as before) $p = \frac{12}{T}$ and $q = \frac{5T^2+8}{T}$. Since the ball's initial speed is 20 ms^{-1}, it follows that

$$
\begin{aligned}
400 &= p^2 + q^2 = \tfrac{144}{T^2} + \tfrac{(5T^2+8)^2}{T^2} \\
400T^2 &= 144 + (5T^2 + 8)^2 = 25T^4 + 80T^2 + 208 \\
25T^4 - 320T^2 + 208 &= 0 \\
(5T^2 - 32)^2 &= 816
\end{aligned}
$$

and hence $T^2 = \tfrac{1}{5}\left[32 \pm \sqrt{816}\right]$. Since the initial velocity of the ball is $p\mathbf{i} + q\mathbf{j}$ ms^{-1}, the ball is projected at an angle of θ to the horizontal, where θ is acute and $\tan\theta = \frac{q}{p} = \frac{5T^2+8}{12} = \tfrac{1}{12}\left[40 \pm \sqrt{816}\right]$. The possible values for θ are $43.6°$ and $80.1°$.

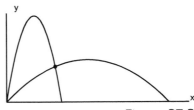

Figure 27.3

EXERCISE 27A

1. A particle is projected horizontally with speed 13 ms^{-1}, from a point high above a horizontal plane. Find the horizontal and vertical components of the velocity of the particle after 2 seconds.

2. The time of flight of an arrow fired with initial speed 30 ms^{-1} horizontally from the top of a tower was 2.4 seconds. Calculate the horizontal distance from the tower to the arrow's landing point. Calculate also the height of the tower.

3. Show that the arrow in Question 2 enters the ground with a speed of about 38 ms^{-1} at an angle of about 39° to the horizontal.

4. A stone is thrown from the point O on top of a cliff with velocity $\binom{15}{0}$ ms^{-1} Find the position vector of the stone after 2 seconds.

5. A particle is projected with speed 35 ms^{-1} at an angle of 40° above the horizontal. Calculate the horizontal and vertical components of the displacement of the particle after 3 seconds. Calculate also the horizontal and vertical components of the velocity of the particle at this instant.

6. A famine relief aircraft, flying over horizontal ground at a height of 245 metres, drops a sack of food.

   a) Calculate the time that the sack takes to fall.

   b) Calculate the vertical component of the velocity with which the sack hits the ground.

   c) If the speed of the aircraft is 70 ms^{-1}, at what distance before the target zone should the sack be released?

7. A girl stands at the water's edge and throws a flat stone horizontally from a height of 80 cm.

   a) Calculate the time the stone is in the air before it hits the water.

   b) Find the vertical component of the velocity with which the stone hits the water.

   The girl hopes to get the stone to bounce off the water surface. To do this the stone must hit the water at an angle to the horizontal of 15° or less.

   c) What is the least speed with which she can throw the stone to achieve this?

   d) If she throws the stone at this speed, how far away will the stone hit the water?

8. A batsman tries to hit a six, but the ball is caught by a fielder on the boundary. The ball is in the air for 3 seconds, and the fielder is 60 metres from the bat. Calculate the horizontal and vertical components of the velocity of the ball immediately after it is hit, and hence find the magnitude and direction of this velocity.

9. A stone thrown with speed 17 ms^{-1} reaches a greatest height of 5 metres. Calculate the angle of projection.

10. A particle projected at 30° to the horizontal rises to a height of 10 metres. Calculate the initial speed of the particle, and its least speed during the flight.

11. In the first 2 seconds of motion a projectile rises 5 metres and travels a horizontal distance of 30 metres. Calculate its initial speed.

12. The nozzle of a fountain projects a jet of water with speed 12 ms^{-1} at 70° to the horizontal. On the way down, the water is caught in a cup 5 metres above the level of the nozzle. Calculate the time taken by the water to reach the cup.

13. A stone was thrown with speed 15 ms^{-1}, at an angle of 40° above the horizontal. It broke a small window 1.2 seconds after being thrown. Calculate the distance of the window from the point at which the stone was thrown.

14. A football, kicked from ground level, enters the goal after 2 seconds with velocity $12\mathbf{i} - 9\mathbf{j}$ ms^{-1}. Neglecting air resistance, calculate

  a) the speed and angle at which the ball was kicked,

  b) the height of the ball as it enters the goal,

  c) the greatest height of the ball above the ground.

15. A golfer strikes a ball in such a way that it leaves the point O at an angle of elevation of θ and with speed of 40 ms^{-1}. After 5 seconds the ball is at a point P which is 120 metres horizontally from O and h metres above O. Assuming that the flight of the ball can be modelled by the motion of a particle with constant acceleration, find the value of θ and the value of h. Give one force on the golf ball that this model does not allow for.

16. A tennis player hits the ball towards the net with velocity $\binom{15}{5}$ ms^{-1} from a point 8 metres from the net and 0.4 metres above the ground. The ball is in the air for 0.8 seconds before hitting the opponent's racquet. Find, at the instant of impact with the opponent's racquet,

  a) the velocity of the ball,

  b) the horizontal distance of the ball from the net and its height above the ground.

17. A projectile reaches its greatest height after 2 seconds, when it is 35 metres from its point of projection. Determine the initial velocity.

18. A tennis ball A is dropped from the top of a vertical tower which is 15 metres high. At time t seconds later the tennis ball is at a height h metres above the ground. Assuming that the motion may be modelled by that of a particle, express h in terms of t.

  The point O is 20 metres from the tower and is at the same horizontal level as the foot of the tower. At the instant that A is dropped, a second ball B is projected from O, towards the tower, with speed V ms^{-1} at an angle of elevation θ. The motion of B, before any impact, may be modelled by that of a particle, and takes place in a vertical plane containing the tower. Given that the two balls collide when $t = 1.5$ and before B hits the ground, show that $V \sin \theta = 10$ and find the value of $V \cos \theta$.

  Deduce the values of V and θ.

19. The behaviour of a water droplet in an ornamental fountain is modelled by the motion of a particle moving freely under gravity with constant acceleration. The particle is projected from the point O with speed 9.1 ms^{-1}, in a direction which makes an angle of 76° with the horizontal. The horizontal and vertical displacements of the particle from O after t seconds are x metres and y metres respectively.

  a) Write down expressions for x and y in terms of t and hence show that $y = 4x - x^2$ is an approximation for the equation of the path of the particle.

  b) Find the range of the particle on the horizontal plane through O.

  c) Make a sketch showing the path of a particle.

20. A ski-jumper takes off from the ramp travelling at an angle of 10° below the horizontal with speed 72 kmh. Before landing she travels a horizontal distance of 70 metres. Find the time she is in the air, and the vertical distance she falls.

21. A particle is projected from the ground with initial speed V. At some future time t it passes through a point with coordinates (x, y) (where the origin O is the point of projection). If the particle is projected at an angle of θ to the horizontal, write down equations relating x, y, V, θ, g and t. Eliminate t from these equations to show that

$$y = x \tan \theta - \tfrac{g}{2V^2} x^2 \sec^2 \theta .$$

By considering this as a quadratic equation in $\tan \theta$, show that $y \le \dfrac{V^4 - g^2 x^2}{2gV^2}$.

22*. A new type of archery contest requires the competitor stand on the ground and fire a single arrow through two hoops. The two hoops and the player are in a straight line. The first hoop is a horizontal distance d from the archer and a height h above the ground. The second hoop is a horizontal distance $D > d$ from the archer and a height H above the ground.

  a) Suppose that the archer looses her arrow at a velocity with horizontal component u and vertical component v. If the arrow is to pass through the first hoop at time t seconds after it is loosed, and through the second hoop at time T seconds after it is loosed,

     i. Write down equations involving d, h, t, g, u and v, and equations involving D, H, T, g, u and v,

     ii. By eliminating t and T, find an equation relating d, h, g, u and v, and another relating D, H, g, u and v.

b) Assuming that the archer can loose an arrow with any speed she wishes, show that this contest can be won provided that $H < \frac{D}{d}h$.

c) In the case that $H = h$ and $D = 3d$, find an expression for the speed of the arrow that must be shot to win the contest.

23*. A hurdler needs to jump over a hurdle of height h. At the point at which the hurdler starts her leap, she is a horizontal distance h away from the hurdle. She leaps with a speed of V, at an angle of θ above the horizontal.

a) Show that $V^2 = \frac{gd^2 \sec^2 \theta}{2(d \tan \theta - h)}$. What does this tell you about the range of possible values of θ?

b) By considering the function $f(u) = \frac{gd^2(u^2+1)}{2(du-h)}$, show that the least possible value of V is $g\left(h + \sqrt{h^2 + d^2}\right)$.

24*. Obtain the result of the previous question by using the ideas of Question 21.

27.2 Some General Formulae

When you have more complicated problems to solve, it is useful to know formulae for some of the standard properties of trajectories. We shall adopt the notational conventions of Key Fact 27.2 ; a particle starting at the origin, travelling with speed V at an angle of θ above the horizontal has displacement vector $\mathbf{r} = x\mathbf{i} + y\mathbf{j}$ at time t seconds after launch, where

$$x = Vt\cos\theta \qquad\qquad y = Vt\sin\theta - \tfrac{1}{2}gt^2$$
$$\dot{x} = V\cos\theta \qquad\qquad \dot{y} = V\sin\theta - gt$$

The following formulae are based on the assumption that O is at ground level. If this is not the case, adjustments would need to be made.

- **Time of Flight:** The particle reaches the ground again when $0 = y = Vt\sin\theta - \tfrac{1}{2}gt^2$, and so the total length of the flight is

$$t_{max} = \frac{2V\sin\theta}{g}.$$

- **Greatest Height:** The particle will reach its maximum height when $0 = \dot{y} = V\sin\theta - gt$, namely when $t = \tfrac{1}{2}t_{max} = \frac{V\sin\theta}{g}$. The maximum height reached by the particle is the height at has attained at that time, namely

$$h = V\tfrac{V\sin\theta}{g}\sin\theta - \tfrac{1}{2}g\left(\tfrac{V\sin\theta}{g}\right)^2 = \frac{V^2\sin^2\theta}{2g}.$$

Note that the time taken to reach the maximum height is equal to the time taken to reach the ground again afterwards; the trajectory is symmetric about the point where the particle reaches its maximum height.

- **Range on Horizontal Ground:** During the time of flight t_{max} the particle covers a distance

$$r = Vt_{max}\cos\theta = V\tfrac{2V\sin\theta}{g}\cos\theta = \frac{2V^2\sin\theta\cos\theta}{g} = \frac{V^2\sin 2\theta}{g}.$$

This distance R is known as the **range** of the particle.

- **Maximum Range on Horizontal Ground:** Suppose that the initial speed V is fixed, but that θ can vary. It is clear that

$$0 \le r = \frac{V^2\sin 2\theta}{g} \le \frac{V^2}{2g},$$

and that $r = \frac{V^2}{2g}$ when $\sin 2\theta = 1$, so when $\theta = 45°$.

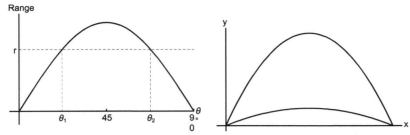

Figure 27.4

Thus the maximum range that can be achieved is $r_{max} = \frac{V^2}{2r}$, and this maximum range is achieved when $\theta = 45°$. Note also that, for any $0 < r < r_{max}$ there are two values of θ which yield that range; one value is $0 < \theta_1 < \frac{1}{4}pi$, and the other is $\frac{1}{4}\pi < \theta_2 = \frac{1}{2}\pi - \theta_1 < \frac{1}{2}\pi$.

• **Equation of the Trajectory:**   We can think of the equations for x and y

$$x = Vt\cos\theta \qquad\qquad y = Vt\sin\theta - \tfrac{1}{2}gt^2$$

as parametric equations for the trajectory, using time as the parameter. The Cartesian equation can be found by eliminating t; substituting $t = \frac{x}{V\cos\theta}$ into the equation for y yields

$$y = V\tfrac{x}{V\cos\theta}\sin\theta - \tfrac{1}{2}g\left(\tfrac{x}{V\cos\theta}\right)^2 = x\tan\theta - \tfrac{g}{2V^2}x^2\sec^2\theta .$$

We note that this is the equation for a parabola; completing the square yields

$$y = \tfrac{V^2}{2g}\sin^2\theta - \tfrac{g}{2V^2}\left(x\sec\theta - \tfrac{V^2}{g}\sin\theta\right)^2 = h - \tfrac{g}{2V^2}(x - \tfrac{1}{2}r)^2\sec^2\theta$$

where h and r are, as above, the maximum height and the range of the particle's trajectory (we note that $y = 0$ when $x = r$, confirming r as the range of the trajectory). This analysis of the trajectory is another way in which we can derive these formulae for the maximum height h and range r.

Key Fact 27.3 Projectile Trajectories: Standard Formulae

For a projectile having initial velocity of magnitude V at an angle θ to the horizontal, under gravity but neglecting air resistance:

• the greatest height reached is $h = \dfrac{V^2\sin^2\theta}{2g}$,

• the time to return to its original height is $\dfrac{2V\sin\theta}{g}$,

• the range on horizontal ground is $r = \dfrac{V^2\sin 2\theta}{g}$,

• the maximum range on horizontal ground is $\dfrac{V^2}{g}$,

• the equation of the trajectory is

$$y = x\tan\theta - \tfrac{g}{2V^2}x^2\sec^2\theta .$$

Example 27.2.1. *A basketball player throws the ball into the net, which is 3 metres horizontally from and 1 metre above the player's hands. The ball is thrown at 50° to the horizontal. How fast is it thrown?*

Taking the player's hands as the origin, you are given that $y = 1$ when $x = 3$ and that $\theta = 50°$. Substituting these numbers into the equation of the trajectory yields

$$1 = 3\tan 50° - \frac{10 \times 3^2}{2u^2 \cos^2 50°}$$

$$\frac{45}{u^2 \cos^2 50°} = 3\tan 50° - 1$$

$$u^2 = \frac{45}{(3\tan 50° - 1)\cos^2 50°} = 42.2918...$$

and hence $u = 6.50$. The ball needs to be thrown at a speed of 6.50 ms^{-1}.

Example 27.2.2. *A boy is standing on the beach and his sister is at the top of a cliff 6 metres away at a height of 3 metres. He throws her an apple with a speed of 10 ms^{-1}. In what direction should he throw it?*

You are given that $y = 3$ when $x = 6$ and that $u = 10$. Substituting the given numbers into the equation of the trajectory:

$$3 = 6\tan\theta - \frac{10 \times 6^2}{2 \times 10^2}\sec^2\theta = 6\tan\theta - \tfrac{9}{5}\sec^2\theta$$

$$5 = 10\tan\theta - 3\sec^2\theta = 10\tan\theta - 3(\tan^2\theta + 1)$$

and hence

$$(3\tan\theta - 4)(\tan\theta - 2) = 3\tan^2\theta - 10\tan\theta + 8 = 0$$

Thus the angle should be thrown either at an angle of $\tan^{-1}\tfrac{4}{3} = 53.1°$ or at an angle of $\tan^{-1} 2 = 63.4°$.

EXERCISE 27B

Assume that all motion takes place above horizontal ground unless otherwise stated.

1. A golfer strikes the ball with speed 60 ms^{-1}. The ball lands in a bunker at the same level 210 metres away. Calculate the possible angles of projection.

2. A projectile is launched at $45°$ to the horizontal. It lands 1.28 km from the point of projection. Calculate the initial speed.

3. A footballer taking a free kick projects the ball with a speed of 20 ms^{-1} at $40°$ to the horizontal. Calculate the time of flight of the ball. How far from the point of the free kick would the ball hit the ground?

4. A stone being skimmed across the surface of a lake makes an angle of $15°$ with the horizontal as it leaves the surface of the water, and remains in the air for 0.6 seconds before its next bounce. Calculate the speed of the stone when it leaves the surface of the lake.

5. A projectile launched with speed 75 ms^{-1} is in the air for 14 seconds. Calculate the angle of projection.

6. An astronaut who can drive a golf ball a maximum distance of 350 metres on Earth can drive it 430 metres on planet Zog. Calculate the acceleration due to gravity on Zog.

7. An archer releases an arrow with speed 70 ms^{-1} at an angle of $25°$ to the horizontal. Calculate the range of the arrow. Determine the height of the arrow above its initial level when it has travelled a horizontal distance of 50 metres, and find the other horizontal distance for which it has the same height.

8. A particle projected at an angle of $40°$ passes through the point with coordinates $(70, 28)$ metres. Find the initial speed of the particle.

9. A hockey player taking a free hit projects the ball with speed 12.5 ms^{-1}. A player 10 metres away intercepts the ball at a height of 1.8 metres. Calculate the angle of projection.

10. The equation of the path of a projectile is $y = 0.5x - 0.02x^2$. Determine the initial speed of the projectile.

11. A tennis player strikes the ball at a height of 0.5 metres. It passes above her opponent 10 metres away at a height of 4 metres, and lands 20 metres from the first player, who has not moved since striking the ball. Calculate the angle of projection of the ball.

12. In a game of cricket, a batsman strikes the ball at a height of 1 metre. It passes over a fielder 7 metres from the bat at a height of 3 metres, and hits the ground 60 metres from the bat. How fast was the ball hit?

13. The greatest height reached by a projectile is one-tenth of its range on horizontal ground. Calculate the angle of projection.

14. A soldier at position P fires a mortar shell with speed $\sqrt{ag}$ at an angle θ above the horizontal, where a is a constant. P is at a vertical height b above a horizontal plane. The shell strikes the plane at the point Q, and O is the point at the level of the plane vertically below P, as shown in the diagram. Letting $OQ = x$, obtain the equation

$$x^2 \tan^2 \theta - 2ax \tan \theta + (x^2 - 2ab) = 0.$$

Show that the maximum value of x, as θ varies, is $\sqrt{a(a + 2b)}$, and that this is achieved when $\tan \theta = \sqrt{\frac{a}{a+2ab}}$.
The sound of the shell being fired travels along the straight line PQ at a constant speed $\sqrt{cg}$. Given that the shell is fired to achieve its maximum range, show that if a man standing at Q hears the sound of firing before the shell arrives at Q, so giving him time to take cover, then $c > \frac{1}{2}(a + b)$.

Figure 27.5

15*. A gun fires a shell from ground level at an angle of $\theta > 45°$ above the horizontal. The shell just strikes the top of a cliff. At the moment of impact, the shell is travelling in a direction of $45°$ below the horizontal. If α is the angle of elevation of the top of the cliff from the gun, find an expression for $\tan \alpha$ in terms of $\tan \theta$. Would the answer be different if the gun was fired on the surface of the moon?

16*. A cricketer throws a ball with speed V. The ball is released at a height a above the ground, in a direction making an angle θ with the horizontal. Show that the horizontal range of the ball is

$$r = \frac{V^2 \sin \theta \cos \theta + V \cos \theta \sqrt{V^2 \sin^2 \theta + 2ga}}{g}.$$

By considering $\dfrac{dr}{d\theta}$ when $\theta = 45°$, explain why the maximum range for the ball is obtained by choosing some value of θ less than $45°$.

17*. Consider an object moving under gravity which is affected by air resistance. One model of air resistance states that the resistance force is proportional to the speed of the object, and pointed in a direction to resist motion. Thus the equation of motion of a particle of mass m might be $m\ddot{\mathbf{r}} = -mg\mathbf{j} - mk\dot{\mathbf{r}}$, or

$$\ddot{\mathbf{r}} + k\dot{\mathbf{r}} = -g\mathbf{j}$$

for some positive constant k. Suppose that the particle's initial velocity is $u\mathbf{i}$, and that it starts from the coordinate origin.

a) If we define $\mathbf{s} = e^{kt}\dot{\mathbf{r}}$, use the product rule to show that $\dot{\mathbf{s}} = -ge^{kt}\mathbf{j}$. Hence find an expression for the velocity $\dot{\mathbf{r}}$ of the object.

b) Integrate this expression to find an expression for the displacement $\mathbf{r}$ of the object.

c) Describe the particle's eventual motion.

Chapter 27: Summary

- A particle moving under gravity, with initial speed V angled at θ to the horizontal, has trajectory given by the equations

$$x = Vt\cos\theta \qquad y = Vt\sin\theta - \tfrac{1}{2}gt^2.$$

- The components of its velocity are

$$\dot{x} = V\cos\theta \qquad \dot{y} = V\sin\theta - gt.$$

- Time of flight (on level ground): $\dfrac{2V\sin\theta}{g}$.

- Maximum height: $\dfrac{V^2\sin^2\theta}{2g}$.

- Range (on level ground): $\dfrac{V^2\sin 2\theta}{g}$.

- Maximum range (on level ground): $\dfrac{V^2}{g}$.

- Equation of trajectory: $y = x\tan\theta - \dfrac{g}{2V^2}x^2\sec^2\theta$.

1. A girl of mass 55 kg is standing in a lift which is moving with an upwards acceleration of 0.15 ms^{-2}. The force exerted on the floor of the lift by the girl has magnitude R N. Draw a diagram showing the forces acting on the girl, who may be modelled as a particle, and find the value of R. (OCR)

2. A child of mass 30 kg is standing in a lift which is descending. The force exerted on the floor of the lift by the child has magnitude 270 N. Find the magnitude of the acceleration of the lift and state whether the lift is speeding up or slowing down. (OCR)

3. Two bodies, of masses 3 kg and 5 kg, are attached to the ends of a light inextensible string. The string passes over a smooth fixed pulley and the particles are moving vertically with both vertical parts of the string taut. Find the tension in the string. (OCR)

4. Two children P and Q, of masses 40 kg and 50 kg respectively, are holding on to the ends of a rope which passes over a thick horizontal branch of a tree. The parts of the rope on either side of the branch are vertical and child Q is moving downwards. A model is to be used in which the children may be considered as particles, and in which the rope is light and inextensible and is moving freely in a smooth groove on the branch. Show that the acceleration of each child has magnitude 1.11 ms^{-2}, and find the tension in the rope.

   When child Q is moving at 2 ms^{-1} she lets go of the rope. Child P continues to rise for a further distance h metres before falling back to the ground. Calculate the value of h.

   Choose one of the assumptions stated in the model and comment briefly on how realistic you think it is. (OCR, adapt.)

5. Two small bodies P and Q, of masses 6 kg and 2 kg respectively, are attached to the ends of a light inextensible string. The string passes over a pulley fixed at a height of 4 m above the ground. Initially Q is held on the ground and P hangs in equilibrium at a height of 2 m above the ground. Both hanging parts of the string are vertical. Q is released. The modelling assumptions are that there is no air resistance and that the pulley is smooth. Find the speed of Q when P hits the ground, and find also the greatest height, above the ground, reached by Q in the subsequent motion.

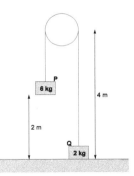

   When Q reaches its highest point the string is cut. Find the speed of Q just before it hits the ground.

   Without further calculation, sketch the velocity-time graph of the motion of Q from the start until it hits the ground. Show clearly, by shading, a region on your sketch whose area is equal to the greatest height, above the ground, reached by Q. (OCR)

6. Two particles P and Q, of masses 2 kg and m kg respectively, are connected by a light inextensible string. Particle P is held on a smooth horizontal table. The string passes over a smooth pulley R fixed at the edge of the table, and Q is at rest vertically below R. When P is released the acceleration of each particle has magnitude 0.81 ms^{-2}. Assuming that air resistance may be ignored, find the tension in the string and the value of m. (OCR)

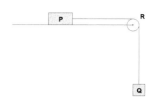

7. The figure shows a light inextensible string passing over a fixed smooth pulley. Particles A and B, of masses 0.03 kg and 0.05 kg respectively, are attached to the ends of the string. The system is held at rest with A and B at the same horizontal level and the string taut. The two parts of the string not in contact with the pulley are vertical. The system is released at time $t = 0$, where t is measured in seconds. The particle B moves downwards for 2 s before being brought to rest as it hits the floor. The string then becomes slack and B remains at rest. Neglecting air resistance, show that the string becomes taut again when $t = 3$.

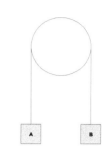

Draw, on separate diagrams, the velocity-time graphs for A and B, for $0 \le t \le 3$, clearly indicating the velocity of A when $t = 2$ and when $t = 3$. (OCR)

8. Particles A and B, of masses 0.5 kg and 0.8kg respectively, are joined by a light inextensible string. A is held at rest on a smooth horizontal platform. The string passes over a smooth pulley at the edge of the platform, and B hangs vertically below the pulley. A is 1.3 m from the pulley. A is released, with the string taut, and the particles start to move. Find the tension in the string, and the speed of A immediately before it reaches the pulley, stating any assumptions you are making.

Immediately before A reaches the pulley it becomes detached from the string. Given that B reaches the floor 1.21 s after the release of A, calculate the initial height of B above the floor. (OCR)

9. Two particles P and Q, of masses 4 kg and 6 kg respectively, are connected by a light inextensible string which passes over a light smooth pulley A. Particle P is held at rest on a rough horizontal table and particle Q rests on a smooth plane inclined at $30°$ to the horizontal, as shown in the figure.

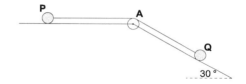

The string is taut and lies in a vertical plane perpendicular to the line of intersection of the table and the inclined plane. The particles are released from rest and in the subsequent motion each particle has an acceleration of magnitude 1.9 ms^{-2}, provided P has not reached A. Find the tension in the string and the coefficient of friction between P and the table.

One second after the system is released from rest the string breaks, and P subsequently comes to rest before reaching A. At the instant when the string breaks P is 0.8 m away from A. Find the distance from A at which P comes to rest. (OCR)

10. Two trucks A and B, of masses 6000 kg and 4000 kg respectively, are connected by a horizontal coupling. An engine pulls the trucks along a straight horizontal track, exerting a constant horizontal force of magnitude X N on truck A, as shown in the Figure.

The resistance to motion for truck A may be modelled by a constant horizontal force of magnitude 360 N; for truck B the resistance may be modelled by a constant horizontal force of magnitude 240 N. Given that the tension in the coupling is T N and that the acceleration of the trucks is a ms^{-2}, show that $T = \frac{2}{5}X$, and express a in terms of X.

Given that the trucks are slowing down, obtain an inequality satisfied by X.

The model is changed so that the resistance for truck B is modelled by a constant force of magnitude 200 N. The resistance for truck A remains unchanged. For this changed model find the range of possible values of X for which the force in the coupling is compressive (i.e. the force in the coupling acting on B is directed from A to B). (OCR)

11. A load P, of mass 200 kg, is suspended by the vertical cable of a crane. Another load Q, of mass 120 kg, is suspended from P by another vertical cable. Both cables may be considered as light and inextensible, and any resistances to motion may be neglected. Find the tension in the vertical cable supporting the load P

    a) when the loads are hanging in equilibrium,

    b) when the loads accelerate vertically upwards at 0.4 ms^{-2}.   (OCR, adapt.)

12. A van of mass 1200 kg is towing a car of mass 800 kg up a slope inclined at $8°$ to the horizontal. The resistance to the motion of the van may be modelled by a single force of magnitude 500 N acting parallel to the slope. For the car the resistance may be modelled by a single force of magnitude 200 N acting parallel to the slope. The van is travelling at constant speed. Stating one assumption that you have made, find, in either order,

    a) the tension in the towrope between the van and the car,

    b) the driving force acting on the van.

The driving force acting on the van is now increased to 4000 N. Find the time taken for the van to increase its speed from 10 ms^{-1} to 14 ms^{-1}.   (OCR)

13*. A smooth ring R, of mass M kg, is threaded on a light inextensible string. Beads A and B, each of mass m kg, are attached to the ends of the string, and are themselves threaded on a smooth horizontal rod. Initially the particles are held at rest, with the string taut, with ABR forming an equilateral triangle, as shown in the figure. Let O be the point on the rod halfway between the initial positions of A and B. The particles are released, and the ring R starts to fall vertically downwards, while particles beads A and B move symmetrically in towards O. Let the magnitudes of the initial accelerations of A and B be $a_1 \text{ ms}^{-2}$, and let the magnitude of the initial acceleration of R be $a_2 \text{ ms}^{-2}$.

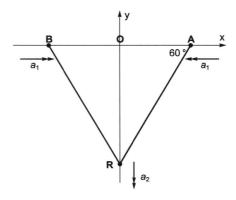

    a) By considering the equations of motion of A and R, show that $2\sqrt{3}ma_1 + Ma_2 = Mg$.

    b) Introduce a coordinate system with O as origin and AB lying along the x-axis. Throughout the motion, the coordinates of A, B and R will be $(u, 0)$, $(-u, 0)$ and $(0, -v)$ respectively, where u and v are functions of time. Explain why $u^2 + v^2$ must remain constant throughout the motion. By differentiating $u^2 + v^2$ twice, and using the fact that the particles are initially stationary, find a relationship between a_1 and a_2.

    c) Deduce that the initial acceleration of R is

$$a_2 = \frac{M}{M + 6m}g.$$

14*. A triangular wedge is fixed to a horizontal surface. The base angles of the wedge are α and $\frac{1}{2}\pi - \alpha$. Two particles, of masses M and m, lie on different faces of the wedge, and are connected by a light inextensible string which passes over a smooth pulley at the apex of the wedge, as shown in the Figure. The contacts between the particles and the wedge are smooth.

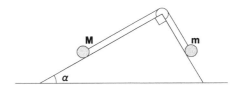

    a) Show that if $\tan\alpha > \frac{m}{M}$ the particle of mass M will slide down the face of the wedge.

    b) Given that $\tan\alpha = \frac{2m}{M}$, show that the magnitude of the acceleration of the particles is

$$\frac{g \sin\alpha}{\tan\alpha + 2},$$

and that this is maximised at $4m^3 = M^3$.   (STEP)

15. A train of mass m is moving with speed V on a horizontal track, when it collides with a truck of mass km, for some constant $k > 0$, which is at rest. Find an expression for the common speed of the train and the truck after the collision, and for the kinetic energy lost in the collision.

16. For how many seconds would a force of 8 N have to act on a 2 kg mass in order to change its velocity from 2 ms^{-1} to 7 ms^{-1}?

17. A particle of mass 3 kg is at rest on a rough plane, which is tilted at an angle of $10°$ to the horizontal. The coefficient of friction of the plane is $\frac{1}{2}$. The particle receives an impulse of 15 N s pointing down the line of greatest slope of the plane. For how long, and how far, does the particle travel before coming to rest again?

18. A ball of mass 0.5 kg is travelling with a speed of 5 ms^{-1} when it receives an impulse of magnitude I. After receiving the impulse, the ball is travelling with a speed of 12 ms^{-1} in a direction perpendicular to its original direction of motion. What is the value of I?

19. A particle of mass m kg is moving with speed v ms^{-1} directly towards a vertical wall. At the point P, when the particle is a distance x m from the wall, it receives an impulse. The effect of this impulse is that the particle strikes the wall at the point Q, a distance of 1 m away from its original expected point of impact, still travelling with speed v ms^{-1}. Find the magnitude and direction of the impulse in terms of m, v and x. For what value of x is the magnitude of the impulse equal to mv N s?

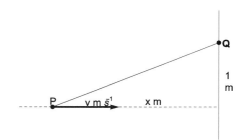

20. A particle of mass $2m$ is moving with speed $2v$ in a straight line on a smooth horizontal surface, when it collides with a second particle. The second particle has mass m, and is moving with speed v in the same direction as the first particle. If exactly $\frac{1}{18}$ of the kinetic energy of the two particles is lost in the collision, what is the coefficient of restitution between the two particles?

21. A smooth ball of mass 0.45 kg is moving on a smooth horizontal table with a speed of 12 ms^{-1} when it hits a fixed smooth vertical wall, which runs perpendicularly to the direction of motion of the ball. The ball rebounds from the wall with a speed of 9 ms^{-1}. Find the coefficient of restitution between the ball and the wall, and find the loss of kinetic energy due to this impact.

22. Two particles, one of mass $3m$ and the other of mass m, are travelling directly towards each other with the same speed V. After the collision the lighter particle has reversed its direction of travel, and its speed is twice that of the heavier particle. What is the coefficient of restitution between the two particles, and what is the magnitude of the impulse that each particle exerts on the other?

23. Two small balls A and B have masses m_1 and m_2 respectively. They lie on a smooth horizontal surface, and the two particles are travelling directly towards each other, both moving with speed u. Let e be the coefficient of restitution between the two balls.

   a) Write down expressions for the velocities of A and B immediately after the collision.

   b) After the collision, ball A is stationary. What is the value of the coefficient of restitution? Explain why $m_2 \le m_1 \le 3m_2$.

24. Three perfectly elastic small balls, P, Q and R lie at rest in a straight line on a smooth horizontal table, with Q between P and R. The balls P and R have mass λm, while Q has mass m, where $\lambda > 1$. Ball Q is projected towards ball P with speed V.

   a) Find the velocities of P and Q after this collision. Explain why there will now be a collision between Q and R.

   b) What condition on λ ensures that, after this collision between Q and R, there is yet another collision betweem P and Q?

25. Two particles P and Q move on a smooth horizontal table. The mass of P is m and the mass of Q is $9m$. Initially particle Q is moving with speed V when it collides with P, which is stationary. The coefficient of restitution between the two spheres is $\frac{1}{2}$. After this collision, particle Q strikes a smooth vertical wall and rebounds. The wall is perpendicular to the direction of motion of Q, and the coefficient of restitution between Q and the wall is also $\frac{1}{2}$.

    a) Find expressions for the velocities of P and Q after the first collision, and for the velocity of Q after its collision with the wall.

    b) If the two particles are a distance d away from the wall when they first collide, how far away are they from the wall when they collide for a second time?

26*. Two colliding bodies moving in a straight line have equal mass. If they are perfectly elastic (so that $e = 1$), prove that the effect of this impact is for the two particles to exchange their velocities. Is the converse result true?

    A row of n perfectly elastic spheres lie in a straight line on a smooth table. They all have the same mass, but are not necessarily regularly spaced along that line, although no two are initially in contact with each other. The m spheres nearest to one end (where $m < n$) are now given a speed of u towards the other $n - m$ spheres. Prove that, eventually, the m spheres nearest the other end will have the same speed. What will the speed of the other $n - m$ spheres be?

27*. Three particles P_1, P_2 and P_3 of masses m_1, m_2 and m_3 respectively lie at rest in a straight line on a smooth horizontal table. Particle P_1 is projected towards P_2 with speed v, and brought to rest by the collision. After P_2 collides with P_3, the latter moves forward with speed v. The coefficients of restitution in the two collisions are e and e' respectively. Show that

$$e' = \frac{m_2 + m_3 - m_1}{m_1}.$$

    Show also that $2m_1 \geq m_2 + m_3 \geq m_1$ for such collisions to be possible. If m_1, m_3 and v are fixed, but m_2 can vary, find (in terms of m_1, m_3 and v) the largest and smallest possible values of the final kinetic energy of the system. (STEP)

28. A girl throws a stone which breaks a window 2 seconds later. The speed of projection is 20 ms^{-1} and the angle of projection is $60°$. Assuming that the motion can be modelled by a particle moving with constant acceleration, find the horizontal and vertical components of the velocity of the stone just before impact. (OCR)

29. A ball is projected from a point on horizontal ground. The speed of projection is 30 ms^{-1} and the greatest height reached is 20 metres. Assuming no air resistance, find the angle of projection above the horizontal and the speed of the ball as it passes through the highest point. (OCR)

30. A ball is thrown with speed 28 ms^{-1} at an angle of $40°$ above the horizontal. After 3 seconds the ball is at P. Ignoring air resistance, find the magnitude and direction of the velocity of the ball as it passes through P. (OCR)

31. A particle is projected at a speed of 45 ms^{-1} at an angle of $30°$ above the horizontal. Find:

    a) the speed and direction of motion of the particle after 4 seconds,

    b) the maximum height, above the point of projection, reached by the particle.

    State one assumption made in modelling the motion of a particle. (OCR)

32. A ball is projected from the point O, with velocity $\binom{u}{v}$ ms^{-1}. The highest point reached in the subsequent motion is 30 metres above the level of O, and at the highest point the speed of the ball is 20 ms^{-1}. Assuming the ball moves with constant acceleration, find the values of u and v. The ball passes through the point S which is above the level of O and 80 metres horizontally from O. Find the direction of motion of the ball at S. (OCR)

33. An athlete throws a heavy ball. The ball is released with an initial speed of 10.3 ms^{-1} at an angle of $35°$ above the horizontal. The point of release is 1.68 metres above the ground.

    a) Neglecting air resistance show that the equation of the path of the ball is approximately $y = 0.7x - 0.07x^2$, where y metres is the height of the ball above the release point when it has travelled a horizontal distance of x metres.

    b) Find how far the ball has been thrown horizontally before it strikes the horizontal, flat ground.

    c) State one further aspect of the motion of the ball which is not incorporated in the model. (OCR)

34. A fielder can throw a cricket ball faster at low angles than at high angles. This is modelled by assuming that, at an angle θ, he can throw a ball with a speed $k\sqrt{\cos\theta}$, where k is a constant.

    a) Show that the horizontal distance he can throw is given by $\frac{2k^2}{g}(\sin\theta - \sin^3\theta)$.

    b) Find the maximum distance he can throw the ball on level ground.

35. A boy is trying to throw a pellet of bread to a young bird sitting on a ledge in a wall, at a height of 11 metres above the ground. The boy is standing 5 metres away from the wall and throws the pellet from a height of 1.5 metres above the ground. When the pellet reaches the ledge it is moving horizontally. Treating the pellet as a particle moving with constant acceleration, find:

    a) the vertical component of the initial velocity,

    b) the time taken for the pellet to reach the ledge,

    c) the speed of the pellet when it reaches the ledge.

State a force that has been neglected in the above model. (OCR)

36. a) At a point O on its path, a projectile has speed V and is travelling at an angle α above the horizontal. Derive the equation of the trajectory of the projectile in the form

$$y = x\tan\alpha - \frac{gx^2}{2V^2}(1 + \tan^2\alpha),$$

where the x- and y-axes pass through O and are directed horizontally and vertically upwards respectively, and state briefly one simplifying assumption that is necessary in obtaining this result.

    b) An aircraft is flown on a path given by $y = 0.28x - (2.4 \times 10^{-4})x^2$, in such a way that the acceleration of the aircraft has the constant value 10 ms^{-2} vertically downwards. The units of x and y are metres. By comparing the equation of the aircraft's path with the standard trajectory equation in (a), find the speed and direction of motion of the aircraft at the point $(0,0)$. Calculate the time of flight between the two points on the aircraft's path at which $y = 0$. (OCR, adapt.)

(By flying an aircraft on a parabolic path with appropriate speed, it is possible to simulate within the fuselage a weightless environment. This has been used for astronaut training.)

37. A player in a rugby match kicks the ball from the ground over a crossbar which is at a height of 3 metres above the ground and at a horizontal distance of 30 metres from the ball as shown in the diagram. The player kicks the ball so that it leaves the ground at an angle of $25°$ above the horizontal. Find the minimum speed at which the ball must be kicked. In fact the player kicked the ball with an initial speed of 25 ms^{-1}.

    a) Find the time that elapsed between the ball leaving the ground and it passing vertically above the crossbar.

    b) Find the angle to the horizontal made by the direction of motion of the ball as it passed over the crossbar. You should make it clear whether the ball is ascending or descending at this time.

    c) State two assumptions that you have made in modelling the motion of the ball which may not be reasonable in practice. (OCR)

38. A particle P is projected with speed 10.1 ms^{-1} from a point O on horizontal ground. The angle of projection is α above the horizontal. At time t seconds after the instant of projection, the horizontal distance travelled by P is x metres and the height of P above the ground is y metres. Neglecting air resistance, write down expressions for x and y in terms of α and t. Hence:

   a) show that P reaches the ground when $t = 2.02 \sin \alpha$, approximately,

   b) find, in terms of α, the value of x when P reaches the ground,

   c) state the value of t, in terms of α, for which P is at its maximum height and show that the maximum height of P above the ground is $5.10 \sin^2 \alpha$ metres, approximately,

   d) find an expression for y in terms of x and α.

Given that $\alpha = 45°$, use your answer to part (d) to find the horizontal distance travelled by P when this horizontal distance is 8 times the height of P above the ground.   (OCR, adapt.)

39. A stone is projected from the point O with speed 20 ms^{-1} at an angle θ above the horizontal, where $\sin \theta = \frac{3}{5}$. The point A is on horizontal ground and is 30 metres directly below O. The stone hits the ground at the point B. Modelling the motion of the stone as that of a particle moving with constant acceleration, find:

   a) the distance AB,

   b) the distance of the stone below the level of O at the instant that its direction of motion makes an angle of $50°$ with the horizontal.

T seconds after projection, the stone is at the point R, where $\angle RAB = 20°$. Find the value of T.   (OCR)

40*. A gun is sited on a horizontal plain, and can fire shells in any direction and at any elevation as speed v. The gun is a distance d from a straight railway line which crosses the plain, where $v^2 > gd$. The gunner aims to hit the line, choosing the direction and elevation so as to maximise the time of flight of the shell. Show that

$$g^2 T^2 = 2v^2 + 2\sqrt{v^4 - g^2 d^2},$$

where T is the time of flight of the shell.   (STEP)

Part 3

Probability & Statistics

Analysis of Data

In this chapter we will learn:

- to use and interpret different measures of location and spread in comparing and contrasting sets of data, calculating them from both raw and summary statistics

- to understand and use the effect of linear transformations on mean and standard deviation,

- to identify outliers, and determine the skewness of a dataset.

28.1 Data Types

The collection, organisation and analysis of numerical information are all part of the subject called **statistics.** Pieces of numerical and other information are called **data.** Alternatively, 'data' is 'a collection of facts from which it is hoped that conclusions may be drawn'.

> **For Interest**
>
> Purists argue that *data* is the plural of the Latin word *datum*, and should be regarded as a plural noun. However, current English usage accepts *data* as a singular noun like 'information'. We intend to use data in both senses as convenient.

In order to collect data, we need to measure or observe some property. This property is called a **variable.** Suppose, for instance, we were interested in collecting data about cars. There are many variables that could be recorded:

- Variables such as colour or type (saloon or hatchback) are known as **qualitative variables.** The values that they can take are not numeric, but are descriptive.

- A special type of qualitative variable is a **Boolean variable.** This is one that takes only the values 'True' or 'False'. The response to the question 'does this car have a sunroof?' is a Boolean variable. These variables are named after George Boole (1815 - 1864), a mathematician and logician.

- All other types of variables can be described in numbers, and are called **quantitative variables.** Examples are the number of doors to the car, or the engine capacity.

Although it is technically possible to provide numeric representations of qualitative data, a Boolean variable could be recorded numerically by coding 'True' as the number 0, and 'False' as the number 1, for example. We shall not consider Boolean and qualitative variables in this book. Studying quantitative variables allows us to perform more calculations, and calculate more interesting quantities than studying qualitative data permits.

Restricting our attention to quantitative variables alone, we still need to distinguish between data types. The variables 'number of doors' and 'engine capacity' are examples of different types of quantitative variables:

- A quantitative variable that can only take a collection of clearly distinguished values is called **discrete**. The number of doors to a car can only take positive integer values, and so each possible value (1, 2, 3, ...) is clearly distinguished from the other. In real life, more often than not, discrete variables will be found to take integer values only, but this is not necessary. A variable that can only take the values 1.2, π, 3.5 and 1000 would be discrete, even though it does not take just integer values.

- All other quantitative variables are called **continuous**. Such variables can take values in a range of values, generally an interval of real numbers. The engine capacity of a car, or its weight, are example of such. Continuous random variables are generally the results of inexact measurements; we can never measure the volume, or the weight, of an object exactly, no matter how exact we try to be.

For Interest

These statements represent something of a simplification. Is a variable that can take only rational values discrete or continuous? An example of this might be the ratio of carbon and iron atoms in the car: not a variable the average car buyer will be interested in, perhaps. This variable can take positive rational values, but is the variable discrete or continuous? It is hard to assert that different rationals can be **clearly** distinguished, since there exist rationals as close together to each other as we like. The numbers 1 and $1 + \frac{1}{N}$ are both rational for and positive integer N, for example, but it is also clear that the rationals do not exhaust a full **range**, or **interval**, of values.

If we made the effort to define discrete and continuous variables precisely, then a rational-valued variable would be a discrete one. However, the technical details required to make the correct distinction are too great for the present, and so we shall continue to work with situations where the distinction between discrete and continuous variables is obvious.

A good deal of time is spent in GCSE and similar studies concerning the representation and graphing of data; a reminder of the various techniques is in order.

Discrete data can be given as a list of values. The numbers on the right represent the outcomes of 50 throws of a six-sided die. It is not easy to comprehend data in large lists of this type, and so it is useful to summarise it.

1	2	2	1	4	3	1	5	2	3
2	5	6	3	1	5	4	3	5	2
1	5	5	6	3	2	1	6	2	1
6	4	2	3	5	2	5	1	1	1
6	5	3	3	5	6	2	6	5	6

This data can be conveniently represented either in a **frequency table** or graphically with a **bar-chart**.

Score	Frequency
1	10
2	10
3	8
4	3
5	11
6	8

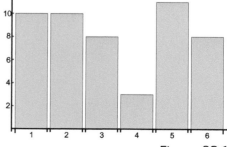

Figure 28.1

If there is a large amount of data, and in particular if the data takes a large number of different values, it can be more efficient to group the data into classes. By doing so, we lose information (since we no longer know exactly how the frequency within each class is distributed), but the loss of exactness is repaid by increased clarity. Information can now be represented either in a frequency table or in a **histogram**.

Class	Frequency	Frequency Density
10-19	13	1.3
20-19	17	1.7
30-39	25	2.5
40-49	39	3.9
50-59	28	2.8
60-69	17	1.7
70-99	11	0.367

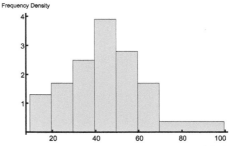

Figure 28.2

Recall that, in a histogram, the vertical axis is **frequency density**, which is the frequency divided by the class-width; frequency is represented by the area, and not the height, of the graph. Note also that a histogram, essentially, assumes that the data is continuous. There are no 'gaps' between the classes, and so the $40-49$ class is regarded as running between 39.5 and 49.499, and the box representing that class is plotted accordingly.

On the other hand, **continuous data** can only be represented in grouped frequency tables and by histograms.

Class	Frequency	Frequency Density
$20 \leq x < 25$	6	1.2
$25 \leq x < 30$	14	2.8
$30 \leq x < 35$	10	2
$35 \leq x < 40$	16	3.2
$40 \leq x < 45$	19	3.8
$45 \leq x < 50$	17	3.6
$50 \leq x < 55$	16	3.2
$55 \leq x < 60$	13	2.6
$60 \leq x < 65$	9	1.8
$65 \leq x < 70$	7	1.4

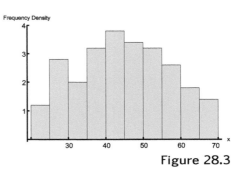

Figure 28.3

Note the different manner in which the classes are defined, which has had an effect on the lower and upper bounds of each class, and consequently where they have been plotted in the histogram.

For Interest

In practice, data-related questions in Pre-U examinations tend to relate to discrete datasets.

28.2 Measures of Location

Suppose that we wanted to know the typical playing time for a CD. We could start by taking a few CDs and finding out the playing time for each one, obtaining a list of values such as

$$49, 56, 55, 68, 61, 57, 61, 52, 63$$

where the values have been given in minutes, to the nearest whole minute. We can see that CD playing times are in the region of 1 hour, and not 2 hours or 10 minutes. It would be useful to be able to give a numeric value that expresses the time that is most representative of CD playing times. If we had such a value, we could compare it with a similar value for the playing times of (for example) vinyl LPs. Such a value is called a **measure of location** or, in everyday language, an **average**. There is more than one way of calculating this average.

28.2.1. THE MEDIAN

Perhaps the simplest measure of location is the 'middle' value; half the data is greater than this value and half the data is less than it. This value is called the **median**. For discrete datasets, like the one above, the first task is to order the data:

$$49, 52, 55, 56, 57, 61, 61, 63, 68$$

There are 9 data points, and so it is clear that the median is the 5th number, namely 57. If there are an even number of data points, then there is no single 'middle' value. In the case of the six values

$$47, 49, 59, 62, 65, 68$$

that are the playing times of another set of six CDs, the median is taken to be half-way between the 3rd and 4th values, which is $\frac{1}{2}(59 + 62) = 60.5$. There is a simple algorithm that enables us to determine the median for general datasets.

Key Fact 28.1 The Median : Discrete Data

To obtain the median of a dataset of n values, first order them, and then calculate $\frac{1}{2}n$. If $r = \frac{1}{2}n$ is an integer, the median of the dataset is half-way between the rth and $(r+1)^{\text{st}}$ data points. If $\frac{1}{2}n$ is not an integer, round it up to the nearest integer r. Then the median is the rth data point.

Example 28.2.1. *Find the medians of the 50 dice rolls discussed at the start of the previous section, as described in Figure 28.1.*

When data has been presented in a frequency table, it has, in effect, already been sorted. We know that the first ten numbers are 1, the next ten numbers are 2, and so on. The size of the dataset is $n = 50$, and so we calculate $\frac{1}{2}n = 25$. The median is halfway between the 25th and 26th numbers in the dataset.

Adding a **cumulative frequency (CF)** column to the frequency table is often helpful. Cumulative frequency is the 'running total' of frequency so far.

From the CF column, it is easy to see that the 20th datapoint is the 'last' 2, while the 28th datapoint is the 'last' 3. Thus the 25th and 26th numbers are both 3, and so the median is $\frac{1}{2}(3 + 3) = 3$.

Score	Frequency	CF
1	10	10
2	10	20
3	8	28
4	3	31
5	11	42
6	8	50

When data has been grouped, we will no longer be able to calculate the median of a dataset exactly (after all, we no longer know the data exactly). We can again use cumulative frequency to **estimate** the median, however.

The table on the right shows the playing time x (in minutes) of a larger collection of 95 CDs. Because the data has been grouped, we can only estimate the median. There are $n = 95$ datapoints, and so we calculate $\frac{1}{2}n = 47.5$. We want to know where there '47.5^{th} datapoint' is to be found. In other words, we want to know when the CF 'reaches the value of 47.5'. Looking at the cumulative frequency column in the table, it is clear that this must occur somewhere in the $60 - 64$ class.

Playing time x	Frequency	CF
$40 - 44$	1	1
$44 - 49$	7	8
$50 - 54$	12	20
$55 - 59$	24	44
$60 - 64$	29	73
$65 - 69$	14	87
$70 - 74$	5	92
$75 - 79$	3	95

We see that we have reached a cumulative frequency of 44 by the end of the $55 - 59$ class, or equivalently the start of the $60 - 64$ class; this occurs when $x = 59.5$. Similarly, we have reached a cumulative frequency of 73 by the end of the $60 - 64$ class; this occurs when $x = 64.5$.

Starting from the left-hand point 59.5 of the $60 - 64$ class, we need a further $47.5 - 44 = 3.5$ in frequency to reach the median out of a total available frequency of 29 in that class. If we assume that the datapoints are even distributed around the class (and we cannot really assume anything else), then we will have reached the median after we have covered $\frac{3.5}{29}$ of the width of the class. Since the class has width 5, our estimate for the median is

$$59.5 + \frac{3.5}{29} \times 5 = 60.1 \text{ mins.}$$

This process of estimating the proportion of the class that is required to reach the desired cumulative frequency is known as **interpolation**.

> **Key Fact 28.2** The Median : Grouped Data
>
> To estimate the median for data (either discrete or continuous) that has been grouped, find the class in which a cumulative frequency of $\frac{1}{2}n$ is achieved, and interpolate within that class.

Example 28.2.2. *Estimate the median of the dataset described in Figure 28.2*

With $n = 150$ data points, we have $\frac{1}{2}n = 75$, and a cumulative frequency of 75 occurs within the $40 - 49$ class. Since we have a cumulative frequency of 55 at the start of this class, we need 20 out of the total frequency of 39 to reach a cumulative frequency of 75, and so we estimate the median to occur $\frac{20}{29}$ of the way across this class. This class starts at the value 39.5, and has width 10. Thus we estimate the median to be

Class	Frequency	CF
10-19	13	13
20-19	17	30
30-39	25	55
40-49	39	94
50-59	28	122
60-69	17	139
70-99	11	150

$$39.5 + \tfrac{20}{39} \times 10 = 44.6$$

28.2.2. THE MODE OR MODAL CLASS

The next measure of location is called the **mode**; it is simply the most frequently occurring value. This is easy to find if data has been presented in a frequency table, since we simply need to find the value which has the largest frequency.

With grouped data, we do not have a mode. Instead we can find the **modal class**, which is the class with the greatest frequency.

While fairly easy to calculate, the mode is not a particularly reliable measure. It might not exist, or it might have more than one value. If we consider the collection of CD playing times that we started this section with,

$$49, 52, 55, 56, 57, 61, 61, 63, 68$$

then it is clear that the mode is 61, since that value has a frequency of 2, and every other value occurs just once, On the other hand, the second collection of six playing times,

$$47, 49, 59, 62, 65, 68$$

has no mode, since all six values occur once each. Yet again, if we combined the two datasets into a single dataset,

$$47, 49, 49, 52, 55, 56, 57, 59, 61, 61, 62, 63, 65, 68, 68$$

there are now three values that are contenders for the mode: 49, 61 and 68 all have frequency 2. This type of problem occurs most frequently with small datasets; the mode is therefore more useful with large ones.

EXERCISE 28A

---

1. Find the median mass of 6.6 kg, 3.2 kg, 4.8 kg, 7.6 kg, 5.4 kg, 7.1 kg, 2.0 kg, 6.3 kg and 4.3 kg. A mass of 6.0 kg is added to the set. What is the median of the 10 masses?

2. Find the median of the following set of numbers:

68	34	59	94	34	30	33	37	49	53	18	51	20	40	23	41
46	36	22	40	65	47	36	44	32	31	58	41	41	28	35	24
52	53	46	22	31	29	37	36	39	45	27	55	37	34	30	40
30	41	60	30	38	42	61	63	50	51	39	40	55	42	41	68
74	73	31	53	59	39	29	47	39	28	50	52	36			

3. Calculate the median values of the following two datasets:

   a) The speeds, in kmh, of twenty cars measured on a city street are: 41, 15, 4, 27, 21, 32, 43, 37, 18, 25, 29, 34, 28, 30, 25, 52, 12, 36, 6, 25.

   b) The times taken, in hours, to carry out repairs to 17 pieces of machinery are: 0.9, 1.0, 2.1, 4.2, 0.7, 1.1, 0.9, 1.2, 2.3, 1.6, 2.1, 0.3, 0.8, 2.7, 0.4.

4. Two biased four-sided dice, with faces numbered 1, 2, 3 and 4, are rolled 100 times. Each time their two scores are added and the sum is recorded. The frequency table below summarises the results:

Score	2	3	4	5	6	7	8
Frequency	5	8	7	23	14	18	25

What is the median score?

5. A group of students took a quiz. Their marks (out of 8) are summarised as follows:

Mark	0	1	2	3	4	5	6	7	8
Frequency	15	12	27	28	43	43	38	25	19

What is the median mark?

6. A team of researchers used a sample of 38 students at a university. Amongst other things, the students' genders (F or M) and masses (in kg) were recorded. This data is given below (the record $(F, 54)$ means that a woman had a mass of 54 kg):

$(F,54)$	$(M,65)$	$(M,78)$	$(F,67)$	$(F,66)$	$(F,63)$	$(F,79)$	$(M,61)$
$(M,78)$	$(F,54)$	$(M,69)$	$(M,70)$	$(F,70)$	$(F,66)$	$(F,61)$	$(F,58)$
$(M,81)$	$(F,62)$	$(M,82)$	$(M,84)$	$(F,55)$	$(M,60)$	$(F,52)$	$(M,78)$
$(F,64)$	$(M,85)$	$(F,48)$	$(F,72)$	$(F,58)$	$(M,87)$	$(M,87)$	$(M,82)$
$(F,65)$	$(F,69)$	$(M,65)$	$(F,63)$	$(M,67)$	$(M,81)$		

Find the median mass of the men and of the women, and compare your results.

7. The following grouped frequency table shows the scores received by 275 students who sat a statistics examination.

Score	$0-9$	$10-19$	$20-29$	$30-34$	$35-39$	$40-49$	$50-59$
Frequency	6	21	51	36	48	82	31

Estimate the median score.

8. The records of the sales in a small grocery store for the 360 days that it opened during the year 2002 are summarised in the following table:

Sales, x in \$100s	$x < 2$	$2 \leq x < 3$	$3 \leq x < 4$	$4 \leq x < 5$
Number of days	15	27	64	72

Sales, x in \$100s	$5 \leq x < 6$	$6 \leq x < 7$	$7 \leq x < 8$	$x \geq 8$
Number of days	86	70	16	10

Estimate the median value for the store's sales that year.

9. The following are ignition times in seconds, correct to the nearest 0.1s, of samples of 80 flammable materials. They are arranged in numerical order as follows:

1.2	1.4	1.4	1.5	1.5	1.6	1.7	1.8	1.8	1.9
2.1	2.2	2.3	2.5	2.5	2.5	2.5	2.6	2.7	2.8
3.1	3.2	3.5	3.6	3.7	3.8	3.8	3.9	3.9	4.0
4.1	4.2	4.3	4.5	4.5	4.6	4.7	4.7	4.8	4.9
5.1	5.1	5.1	5.2	5.2	5.3	5.4	5.5	5.6	5.8
5.9	5.9	6.0	6.3	6.4	6.4	6.4	6.4	6.7	6.8
6.8	6.9	7.3	7.4	7.4	7.6	7.9	8.0	8.6	8.8
8.8	9.2	9.4	9.6	9.7	9.8	10.6	11.2	11.8	12.8

a) Group the data into eight classes of equal width, the first two being $1.0 - 2.4$ and $2.5 - 3.9$, and form a grouped frequency table. Use this grouped frequency table to estimate the median ignition time.

b) Calculate the median directly from the initial data, and comment on any difference between the two results.

10. The number of rejected CDs produced each day by a machine was monitored for 100 days. The results are summarised in the following table.

Number of rejects	$0-9$	$10-19$	$20-29$	$30-39$	$40-49$	$50-59$
Number of days	5	8	19	37	22	9

Estimate the median number of rejects.

11. For the following distributions state, where possible, the mode or the modal class.

a)

x	0	1	2	3	4
Freq.	7	4	2	5	1

b)

x	70	75	80	85	90
Freq.	5	5	5	5	5

c)

x	$2-3$	$4-5$	$6-7$	$8-9$	$10-11$
Freq.	7	4	4	4	1

d)

x	1	2	3
Freq.	23	39	3

28.2.3. THE MEAN

The third measure of location is called the **mean**, and is what most people mean when they talk about the 'average' of a set of numbers. It is obtained by adding the numbers in the dataset together, and dividing the sum by the number of elements in the dataset. For example, the mean playing time of the nine CDs discussed at the beginning of Section 28.2 is

$$\tfrac{1}{9}(49 + 56 + 55 + 68 + 61 + 57 + 61 + 52 + 63) = \tfrac{522}{9} = 58 \text{ minutes.}$$

Before proceeding, it is worth reminding ourselves of some useful notation. In Chapter 9, we introduced the Σ-**notation** as a convenient method for describing sums. The expression

$$x_1 + x_2 + x_3 + x_4 + x_5 + x_6 + x_7 + x_8 + x_9$$

can more compactly and conveniently be written as $\displaystyle\sum_{i=1}^{9} x_i$.

If we have a dataset with n numbers in it, then we could describe the datapoints in the dataset by the symbols $x_1, x_2, \ldots, x_n$. Then the sum of the elements in the dataset can simply be written as

$$\sum_{i=1}^{n} x_i .$$

In the case of the nine CD playing times, we have a dataset with $n = 9$ values, which are $x_1 = 49$, $x_2 = 56$, $x_3 = 55$ and so on. The mean of that dataset can thus be written as $\frac{1}{n}\displaystyle\sum_{i=1}^{n} x_i$.

Often it is convenient to abuse this notation somewhat; we can assume that all sums are over the entire dataset unless we state otherwise. Thus we can abbreviate the Σ-notation somewhat, writing simply $\displaystyle\sum_{i} x_i, \sum x_i$ or even just $\displaystyle\sum x$ instead of the more precise $\displaystyle\sum_{i=1}^{n} x_i$.

Key Fact 28.3 The Mean : Discrete Data

The **mean** of a dataset with the n values $x_1, x_2, \ldots, x_n$ is denoted $\overline{x}$, and is equal to

$$\overline{x} = \frac{1}{n}\sum_{i} x_i .$$

The Σ-notation can, of course, be used to perform many more calculations for a dataset than simply to evaluate the mean.

Example 28.2.3. *For the dataset with the four elements* $x_1 = 1, x_2 = 3, x_3 = 4$ *and* $x_4 = 5$, *evaluate:*

a) $\displaystyle\sum_i x_i,$ b) $\displaystyle\sum_i x_i^2,$ c) $\bar{x},$ d) $\displaystyle\sum_i (x_i - \bar{x}),$ e) $\displaystyle\sum_i (x_i - \bar{x})^2.$

(a) $\displaystyle\sum_i x_i = 1 + 3 + 4 + 5 = 13.$

(b) $\displaystyle\sum_i x_i^2 = 1^2 + 3^2 + 4^2 + 5^2 = 51.$

(c) $\bar{x} = \frac{1}{4} \times 13 = 3.25.$

(d) $\displaystyle\sum_i (x_i - \bar{x}) = -2.25 - 0.25 + 0.75 + 1.75 = 0.$

(e) $\displaystyle\sum_i (x_i - \bar{x})^2 = (-2.25)^2 + (-0.25)^2 + 0.75^2 + 1.75^2 = 8.75.$

When data is presented in a frequency table, our formula for the mean needs adjusting slightly. The table on the right gives the frequency distribution of the number of siblings (brothers and sisters) of the children at a school. Of the 204 values, 36 are 0s, 94 are 1s, 48 are 2s, and so on. Their sum will be

$$(0 \times 36) + (1 \times 94) + (2 \times 48) + \cdots = 284.$$

Siblings x	Frequency f	xf
0	36	0
1	94	94
2	48	96
3	15	45
4	7	28
5	3	15
6	1	6
	204	284

You can include this calculation in the table by adding a third column in which each value of the variable, x, is multiplied by its frequency, f.

The sum of the Frequency f column gives the total number $n = \displaystyle\sum_i f_i$ of data points in the dataset.

In this case, $n = 204$. The sum of the xf column gives the total sum $\displaystyle\sum_i x_i f_i$ of the data points in

the dataset. In this case we are using the symbol x to represent the **different** values that the data points in a dataset can attain. In this case, the sum is 284. Thus the mean number of siblings that a child at this school has is $\frac{284}{204} = 1.39$ (even though you cannot have a fractional number of children, the mean should not be rounded to an integer).

Key Fact 28.4 The Mean : Frequency Tables

If a dataset is described by a frequency table, where the possible values of the data points are $x_1, x_2, \ldots$, and if each of these values is achieved with frequencies $f_1, f_2, \ldots$, then the mean of the dataset is

$$\bar{x} = \frac{1}{n} \sum_i x_i f_i, \qquad \text{where} \qquad n = \sum_i f_i.$$

If the data have been grouped, then we can estimate the mean using the same formula, where $x_1, x_2, \ldots$ are the midpoints of the various classes.

Example 28.2.4. *Estimate the mean playing time for the dataset of 95 CDs discussed on page 552.*

As well as the Class and Frequency columns, we need a Midpoint column for the midpoint of each class, as well as the calculation column xf. The $40-44$ minute class includes play times between 39.5 and 44.5; it has width 5 and midpoint 42. The other midpoints are calculated similarly.

We estimate the mean playing time of this dataset to be $\frac{5690}{95} = 59.9$ minutes.

Playing Time	Freq. f	Midpoint x	xf
$40-44$	1	42	42
$45-49$	7	47	329
$50-54$	12	52	624
$55-59$	24	57	1368
$60-64$	29	62	1798
$65-69$	14	67	938
$70-74$	5	72	360
$75-79$	3	77	231
	95		5690

28.2.4. CODING

Although calculators are sufficiently powerful to calculate means and many other statistical quantities for us without the need for working, there are still occasions when calculations need to be done by hand. More importantly, being able to perform these calculations manually introduces us to concepts that lead us to a deeper understanding of the theory. The technique of **coding** is just one of those.

The previous example showed us that even a fairly simple dataset involved working with moderately large numbers. A more complicated dataset will involve even larger numbers. These are inconvenient to handle, even with a calculator. It would be highly desirable if there were a way of calculating medians and means more simply.

Consider the dataset described by the first table on the right. Calculating the mean of x could be done directly, and

$$\bar{x} = \frac{921 \times 13 + 931 \times 17 + 941 \times 22 + 951 \times 18}{13 + 17 + 22 + 18}$$

$$= 937.4.$$

x	f
921	13
931	17
941	22
951	18

y	f	yf
0	13	0
1	17	17
2	22	44
3	18	54
	70	115

This is a complex calculation, and not one to do in our heads.

If we note that the possible values of x are regularly spaced, then assistance is at hand. Define the variable $y = \frac{1}{10}(x - 921)$, and we obtain the second frequency table for the distribution of y (that takes the values 0, 1, 2 and 3 only). Replacing the variable x by the (simpler) variable y is called **coding**. Calculations for y can (nearly all) be done in our heads: the mean of y is $\bar{y} = \frac{115}{70} = 1.64$. Now, since $x = 921 + 10y$, we can deduce that

$$\bar{x} = 921 + 10\bar{y} = 937.4,$$

Key Fact 28.5 Measures of Location : Coding

If a dataset has data points x_1, x_2, ..., and if we code this dataset via the formula $x = ay + b$ (for some constants a and b), obtaining a new dataset with datapoint y_1, y_2, ..., then the means $\bar{x}$ and $\bar{y}$ of the two datasets are related by the formula

$$\bar{x} = a\bar{y} + b.$$

Why does coding work? Note that

$$\sum_i x_i = \sum_i (ay_i + b) = a\sum_i y_i + nb$$

and dividing through by n gives us the formula for $\bar{x}$.

EXERCISE 28B

1. The test marks of 8 students were 18, 2, 5, 0, 17, 15, 16 and 11. Find the mean test mark.

2. The same group of researchers mentioned in Question 6 of Exercise 28A also measured the height of the 38 students (to the nearest cm). Their data concerning heights was:

$(F,164)$	$(M,186)$	$(M,175)$	$(F,165)$	$(F,175)$	$(F,164)$	$(F,168)$	$(M,168)$
$(M,175)$	$(F,164)$	$(M,178)$	$(M,175)$	$(F,179)$	$(F,168)$	$(F,173)$	$(F,174)$
$(M,187)$	$(F,168)$	$(M,178)$	$(M,194)$	$(F,157)$	$(M,173)$	$(F,160)$	$(M,183)$
$(F,173)$	$(M,196)$	$(F,160)$	$(F,169)$	$(F,159)$	$(M,170)$	$(M,192)$	$(M,175)$
$(F,169)$	$(F,169)$	$(M,179)$	$(F,164)$	$(M,188)$	$(M,192)$		

Find the mean male height and the mean female height. The mean height of adult males is about 175 cm. Comment on your answer in the light of this information.

3. a) Find $\bar{x}$ given that $\displaystyle\sum_{i=1}^{20} x_i = 226$.

   b) Find $\bar{y}$ given that $\displaystyle\sum_{i=1}^{12} (y_i - 100) = 66$.

4. The number of misprints on each page of the draft of a book containing 182 pages is summarised in the following table:

Number of misprints	0	1	2	3	4
Number of pages	144	24	10	2	2

Find the mean number of misprints on a page.

5. The following table gives the frequency distribution for the lengths of rallies (measured by the number of shots) in a tennis match.

Length of rally	1	2	3	4	5	6	7	8
Frequency	2	20	15	12	10	5	3	1

Find the mean length of a rally.

6. The table below gives the number of shoots produced by 50 plants in a botanical research laboratory.

No. of shoots	$0-4$	$5-9$	$10-14$	$15-19$	$20-24$	$25-29$	$30-34$	$35-39$	$40-44$
Frequency	1	1	1	6	17	16	4	2	2

Estimate the mean number of shoots per plant.

7. The speeds, in km/h, of 200 vehicles travelling on a motorway were measured using a radar device. The results are summarised in the following grouped frequency table.

Speed (km/h)	$45-60$	$60-75$	$75-90$	$90-105$	$105-120$	$120-150$
Frequency	12	32	56	72	20	8

Estimate the mean speed.

8. Calls made by a telephone saleswoman were monitored. The lengths (in minutes, to the nearest minute) of 30 calls are summarised in the following table:

Length of call	$0-2$	$3-5$	$6-8$	$9-11$	$12-15$
Number of calls	17	6	4	2	1

   a) Write down the class boundaries.

   b) Estimate the mean length of the calls.

9. The price of a CD is denoted by £x. For 60 CDs bought in different stores it is found that $\sum(x - 12) = 53.40$. Calculate the mean price of these CDs. The mean price of a further 40 CDs is found to be £11.64. Find the mean price of the 100 CDs.

10. The volumes of the contents of 48 half-litre bottles of orangeade were measured, correct to the nearest millilitre. The results are summarised in the following table:

Volume (ml)	480 – 489	490 – 499	500 – 509	510 – 519	520 – 529	530 – 539
Frequency	8	11	15	8	4	2

Estimate the mean volume of the contents of the 48 bottles.

11. A die is rolled 30 times, with the following results:

Score	1	2	3	4	5	6
Frequency	5	a	6	2	7	b

Given that the mean score is 3.8, what are the values of a and b?

12. A (probably unfair) die is rolled a number of times, with the following results:

Score	1	2	3	4	5	6
Frequency	a	a	a	b	b	a

Given that the mean score is exactly 4, what is the smallest possible size of the dataset? What is the median die roll?

13. One number is added to a dataset, and the mean of the dataset is unchanged. What must that extra value have been?

14. Explain why $\sum_i (x_i - \bar{x})$ is equal to 0 for any dataset.

15*. If the number 9 is added to a dataset, the mean is increased by 10%. If, instead, the number 1 is added to the original dataset, the mean is reduced by 10%. How many numbers were in the original dataset, and what was their mean?

28.2.5. A Comparison of The Median, Mode and Mean

The three measures of location each have their advantages and disadvantages:

Advantages

- The median is not affected by the occasional 'rogue' value. If a data entry error recorded the value of a datapoint as 1000, instead of its correct value of 10, this would not substantially affect the median. Similarly, we can calculate the median (to a reasonable degree of accuracy) even if a few datapoints are missing.

- If the mode exists, then it is an actual value in the dataset.

- The mean is easy to calculate; the data does not have to be sorted in order to calculate it. Its theory is more developed mathematically; most of the deep theories of statistics concerning measures of location are framed in terms of the mean.

Disadvantages

- The median is fairly complicated to calculate. Data must be sorted (or categorised into a frequency table) before it can be calculated. Sorting data is a time-consuming business. The mathematical theory of the median is less well-developed than is that of the mean.

- The mode might not exist, or it might have multiple values.

- The mean puts equal weight on all values, and hence is sensitive to data entry issues.

Example 28.2.5. *A class of eighteen pupils have ages 16:2, 17:0, 17:1, 16:10, 17:0, 17:2, 16:9, 16:8, 16:1, 17:3, 16:2, 17:1, 16:6, 16:10, 16:11, 16:11, 16:9, 16:5. Their teacher is 62:10 (an age of a:b should be read as one of a years and b months). The class and their teacher are having a lesson. What is the best measure of the average age of people in the room?*

To work with this data, we would do best to convert the various ages into months; when sorted, the class (and its teacher) have ages of 193, 194, 194, 197, 198, 200, 201, 201, 202, 202, 203, 203, 204, 204, 205, 205, 206, 207 and 754 months.

There is no mode, since the ages of 16:2, 16:9, 16:10, 16:11, 17:0 and 17:1 all have a frequency of 2!

If we consider the class without its teacher, then the median age is 16:10 and the mean age is 16:9 to the nearest month. If we include the teacher in the calculation, the median age is still 16:10, but the mean age has risen to 19:2.

Clearly, then, the median gives the best idea of the average age in the room. The teacher's age is of a very different nature to the age of her pupils, and the median does not give her age too much weight. On the other hand, the mean is substantially affected by the inclusion of the teacher in the calculations.

This example notwithstanding, the mean is probably the most commonly used measure of location.

28.3   Measures of Spread

We have seen how a set of data can be summarised by choosing an appropriate average value, or 'measure of location': the median, the mode or the mean.

Now consider the two sets of data **A** and **B** shown on the right. Both data sets have mean, mode and median all equal to 60. If you were given nothing but a measure of location for each set you might be tempted to think that the two sets of data were similar.

A: 48   52   60   60   60   68   72
B: 0   10   60   60   60   110 120

Yet if you look in detail at the two sets of data you can see that they are quite different. The most striking difference between the two data sets is that set B is much more spread out than set A. Measures of location do not give any indication of these differences, so it is necessary to devise some new measures to summarise the spread of data.

28.3.1. THE RANGE

The most obvious method of measuring spread is to calculate the difference between the lowest value and the highest value. This difference is called the **range.**

The range of data set A is $72 - 48 = 24$, whereas the range of data set B is $120 - 0 = 120$. Calculating the ranges shows clearly that data set B is more spread out than data set A.

For Interest

The range is a number, not an interval! The range of the dataset A is 24, and not $48-72$.

The range is something of a blunt instrument when measuring spread. It has succeeded in distinguishing between datasets A and B, but it cannot do the same for the datasets C and D given here. Both of these have mean and median equal to 8 and range 12.

C: 2   4   6   8   10   12   14
D: 2   8   8   8   8   8   14

Although both data sets C and D have the same range, the patterns of their distributions are quite distinct. Data set C is evenly spread within the interval 2 to 14 whereas data set D has most of its values 'bunched' centrally. Because the range is calculated from extreme values only, it ignores the pattern of spread for the rest of the values. This is a major criticism of the range as a measure of spread. While easy to calculate, the range ignores the *pattern* of spread, since it considers only the extreme values. It would also be very sensitive to 'rogue' data points.

28.3.2. QUARTILES AND THE INTERQUARTILE RANGE

The median splits a dataset into two equal pieces. The **quartiles** of a dataset are intended to indicate a further subdivision of the dataset. The **first, or lower, quartile** Q_1 is the point where one quarter of the data is smaller than it, and three quarters of the data is greater, and the **third, or upper, quartile** Q_3 is the point where three quarters of the data is smaller than it, and one quarter of the data is greater than it. In between these two quartiles is the median M (sometimes also known as the second quartile Q_2).

> **Key Fact 28.6** The Interquartile Range
>
> The interquartile range of a dataset is the difference between the first and third quartiles:
> $$\text{IQR} = Q_3 - Q_1 .$$
> It is the width of the range within which the 'middle half' of the data lies.

For some sizes of dataset, the location of the quartiles is fairly obvious. What we want is a quick and easy formula for calculating the first and third quartiles.

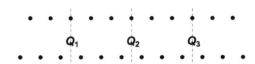

Figure 28.4

> **Key Fact 28.7** Quartiles : Discrete Data
>
> To obtain the first quartile Q_1 of a dataset of n values, first order them, and then calculate $\frac{1}{4}n$. If $r = \frac{1}{4}n$ is an integer, then Q_1 is halfway between the rth and $(r+1)^{\text{st}}$ datapoints. If $\frac{1}{4}n$ is not an integer, round it up to the nearest integer r. Then Q_3 is the rth datapoint.
> To obtain the third quartile Q_3 of a dataset of n values, perform the same calculations, but use $\frac{3}{4}n$ instead of $\frac{1}{4}n$.

This method is not perfect, and not all authors use it. Its main advantage is that the calculations to determine the quartiles Q_1 and Q_3 and the median $Q_2 = M$ are essentially the same. For the first quartile, we perform those calculations on the fraction $\frac{1}{4}n$. For the median $Q_2 = M$, we perform the same calculations on the fraction $\frac{1}{2}n$. For the third quartile Q_3 we perform the same calculations on the fraction $\frac{3}{4}n$.

This method can be extended to split the data into **deciles** (tenths) or even **percentiles** (hundredths), instead of simply quarters. The jth percentile would be found by performing the same calculations on the fraction $\frac{j}{100}n$.

> **For Interest**
>
> It is worth noting that, with the exception of the median, there is no universally accepted rule for calculating the quartiles of a discrete dataset. For small values of n, these quantities are not particularly useful, anyway. For large values of n, the differences between the various calculation methods used by different authors become less and less. Do not worry, then, when other books recommend different calculation techniques.

Example 28.3.1. *Find the quartiles and the interquartile range for each of the two datasets below:*

  a) 7, 9, 12, 13, 8, 11   b) 7, 8, 22, 20, 15, 18, 19, 13, 11 .

(a) With $n = 6$, we have $\frac{1}{4}n = 1.5$ and $\frac{3}{4}n = 4.5$, and so the first and third quartiles are the 2nd and 5th numbers in the dataset. Ordering the dataset, we see that $Q_1 = 8$ and $Q_3 = 12$, so that the IQR is 6.

(b) With $n = 9$, we have $\frac{1}{4}n = 2.25$ and $\frac{3}{4}n = 6.75$, and so the first and third quartiles are the 3rd and 7th numbers in the dataset. Ordering the dataset, we see that $Q_1 = 11$ and $Q_3 = 19$, and hence the IQR is 8.

Example 28.3.2. *Find the interquartile range for the 50 dice rolls described in Figure 28.1.*

With $n = 50$ we see that $\frac{1}{4}n = 12.5$ and $\frac{3}{4}n = 37.5$, Thus Q_1 is the 13th datapoint, while Q_3 is the 38th datapoint. Introducing the cumulative frequency column, we deduce that $Q_1 = 2$ and $Q_3 = 5$. Thus the interquartile range is 3.

Score	Frequency	CF
1	10	10
2	10	20
3	8	28
4	3	31
5	11	42
6	8	50

Example 28.3.3. *In Example 28.2.3 (above) there is information about the number of siblings that children at a particular school had. What is the interquartile range of the number of siblings?*

This time $n = 204$, and so $\frac{1}{4}n = 51$ and $\frac{3}{4}n = 153$. Thus Q_1 is the average of the 51st and 52nd datapoints, while Q_3 is the average of the 153rd and 154th datapoints. Completing the cumulative frequency column for this data, we see that $Q_1 = 1$ and $Q_3 = 2$. The interquartile range is 1.

Siblings x	Frequency f	CF
0	36	36
1	94	130
2	48	178
3	15	193
4	7	200
5	3	203
6	1	204

The first and third quartiles are calculated for continuous (or simply grouped) datasets by a simple extension of the methods used to calculate the medians of such datasets.

Key Fact 28.8 Quartiles : Grouped Data

To estimate the first quartile for data (either discrete or continuous) that has been grouped, find the class in which a cumulative frequency of $\frac{1}{4}n$ is achieved, and interpolate within that class. To estimate the third quartile, perform the same calculations, but with $\frac{3}{4}n$.

Example 28.3.4. *Estimate the interquartile range for the dataset described in Figure 28.2.*

With $n = 150$ we have $\frac{1}{4}n = 37.5$ and $\frac{3}{4}n = 112.5$. A cumulative frequency of 37.5 falls within the $30 - 39$ class. Within that class, we need to 'pick up' a cumulative frequency of 7.5 out of a total frequency of 25 available in that class. Thus

Class	Frequency	CF
10-19	13	13
20-19	17	30
30-39	25	55
40-49	39	94
50-59	28	122
60-69	17	139
70-99	11	150

$$Q_1 = 29.5 + \tfrac{7.5}{25} \times 10 = 32.5 \,.$$

Similarly

$$Q_3 = 49.5 + \tfrac{18.5}{28} \times 10 = 56.1 \,.$$

and hence the interquartile range is 23.6.

The aim of the interquartile range is to tell whether a dataset is widely or tightly spread. Considering the last example, is an interquartile range of 23.6 large or small? The answer is that we cannot tell without more information. Normally we will be comparing the spreads of two or more data sets. You can then make a more sensible comment on whether a particular interquartile range is large or small by comparing its size with the other interquartile ranges.

Example 28.3.5. *Two people undertook separate traffic surveys at different locations. Each person noted down the speed of 50 cars that passed their observation point. The results are given below.*

Speed v (km/h)	A Freq.	A CF	B Freq.	B CF
$0 \le v < 20$	7	7	1	1
$20 \le v < 40$	11	18	3	4
$40 \le v < 60$	13	31	5	9
$60 \le v < 80$	12	43	20	29
$80 \le v < 100$	5	48	18	47
$100 \le v < 120$	2	50	3	50

(a) *Estimate the median speed and the interquartile range of speeds at each observation point.*

(b) *Comment on the differences in speeds at the two locations.*

(a) Dataset A gives $n = 50$, so that $\frac{1}{4}n = 12.5$, $\frac{1}{2}n = 25$ and $\frac{3}{4}n = 37.5$. Thus

$$Q_1 = 20 + \frac{12.5-7}{11} \times 20 = 30$$
$$M = 40 + \frac{25-18}{13} \times 20 = 50.8$$
$$Q_3 = 60 + \frac{37.5-31}{12} \times 20 = 70.8$$

and hence A has an interquartile range of 40.8.
Dataset B gives $n = 50$ as well, and hence

$$Q_1 = 60 + \frac{12.5-9}{20} \times 20 = 63.5$$
$$M = 60 + \frac{25-9}{20} \times 20 = 76$$
$$Q_3 = 80 + \frac{37.5-29}{18} \times 20 = 89.4$$

and hence B has interquartile range 25.9.

(b) The median speed for A is lower, and the interquartile range for A is greater than the corresponding quantities for B. At location A, the cars travel more slowly, but there is greater variation in their speeds. At location B, cars travel at a faster, more consistent, speed.

EXERCISE 28C

1. Find the range and interquartile range of each of the following data sets:

   a) 7, 4, 14, 9, 12, 2, 19, 6, 15,

   b) 7.6, 4.8, 1.2, 6.9, 4.8, 7.2, 8.1, 10.3, 4.8, 6.7.

2. The lengths, in cm, of 15 leaves that were taken from a particular tree are given below.

   42   54   63   76   93   50   61   71   92   57   62   76   53   64   59

   Find the interquartile range of the leaf lengths.

3. The number of times each week that a factory machine broke down was noted over a period of 50 consecutive weeks. The results are given in the following table.

Number of breakdowns	0	1	2	3	4	5	6
Number of weeks		2	12	14	8	8	4	2

   Find the interquartile range of the number of breakdowns in a week.

4. A company employs 2410 people whose annual salaries are summarised as follows:

Salary (in \$1000s)	-10	$10-20$	$20-30$	$30-40$	$40-50$
Number of Staff	16	31	502	642	875

Salary (in \$1000s)	$50-60$	$60-80$	$80-100$	>100
Number of Staff	283	45	12	4

Find the upper and lower quartiles for the salary.

5. The traffic noise levels in two city streets were measured one weekday, between 5.30 a.m. and 8.30 p.m. There were 92 measurements on each street, made at equal time intervals, and the results are summarised in the following grouped frequency table.

Noise level (dB)	<65	$65-67$	$67-69$	$69-71$	$71-73$	$73-75$	$75-77$	$77-79$	>79
Street 1 Freq.	4	11	18	23	16	9	5	4	2
Street 2 Freq.	2	3	7	12	27	16	10	8	7

Find the median and interquartile range for the noise levels for both streets. Use these statistics to compare the noise levels in the two streets.

6. The audience size in a theatre performing a long-running detective play was monitored over a period of one year. The sizes for Monday and Wednesday nights are summarised in the following table.

Audience size	$50-99$	$100-199$	$200-299$	$300-399$	$400-499$	$500-599$
No. of Mondays	12	20	12	5	3	0
No. of Wednesdays	2	3	20	18	5	4

Compare the audience sizes on Mondays and Wednesdays.

7. A pair of fair 6-sided dice is rolled 70 times. Each time, the total score is recorded. The resultant data is summarised below:

Score	2	3	4	5	6	7	8	9	10	11	12
Freq.	1	8	9	9	8	12	6	7	5	3	2

Find the upper and lower quartiles.

8. A pair of fair 6-sided dice is rolled 80 times. Each time, the difference between the two scores is recorded. The resultant data is summarised below:

Difference	0	1	2	3	4	5
Freq.	11	16	27	13	6	7

Calculate the median, and the upper and lower quartiles.

9. A set of three fair 4-sided dice is rolled 100 times. Each time, the total score is recorded. The resultant data is recorded below:

Score	3	4	5	6	7	8	9	10	11	12
Freq.	1	6	14	13	17	20	17	8	2	2

Find the interquartile range of the score on the dice.

10*. The following frequency table describes a dataset with 100 entries:

x	1	2	3	4	5	6
Freq.	15	a	13	b	13	12

where a and b are positive integers.

a) What is the upper quartile Q_3?

b) Given that $Q_1 = 2$ and the median is 4, what are the possible values of a?

c) If, instead, we are told that the median is 3.5, what is the interquartile range?

28.3.3. VARIANCE AND STANDARD DEVIATION

3.7 Variance and standard deviation One of the reasons for using the interquartile range in preference to the range as a measure of spread is that it takes some account of how the interior values are spread rather than concentrating solely on the spread of the extreme values. Just as there were circumstances where the mean was a preferred measure of location to the median, the interquartile range, that can be thought of as a measure of spread related to the median, does not always fit the bill. We would like to have a measure of spread that was related to the mean, so that we could use that measure in cases where the mean was the preferred measure of location.

This alternative measure of spread starts by considering by how much each data point differs from the mean. To do this we calculate the quantity $x_i - \bar{x}$ for each x_i.

The first dataset considered in Section 28.2 concerned the playing times of 9 CDs.

$$49, 56, 55, 68, 61, 57, 61, 52, 63$$

The mean of this dataset was found to be 58 minutes. If the mean is subtracted from each of the original data values we get the following values.

$$-9, -2, -3, 10, 3, -1, 3, -6, 5.$$

To obtain a measure of how big these deviations from the mean are, it is no good just adding them up, since $-9 - 2 - 3 + 10 + 3 - 1 + 3 - 6 + 5 = 0$. Indeed, as we know

$$\sum_i (x_i - \bar{x}) = 0$$

for any dataset. The problem here is that the positive deviations cancel out the negative ones. However, we are not really worried whether or not the deviations are positive or negative (since they must add to 0, there must be some of each); what we want is some measure of how big they are. We could consider the mean of their absolute values:

$$\frac{1}{n} \sum_i |x_i - \bar{x}|,$$

which calculates the average (mean) difference between a data point and the mean. For our dataset of 9 CD playing times, this would evaluate to $\frac{1}{9}(9+2+3+10+3+1+3+6+5) = 4.67$ minutes. This would indeed be a possible measure of spread. However it is not one that responds well to mathematical analysis, and so it is not the preferred measure. A better measure is to calculate the mean of the squares of the differences, obtaining

$$\frac{1}{n} \sum_i (x_i - \bar{x})^2$$

as a measure of spread. In the case of the 9 CDs, this evaluates to $\frac{1}{9}(9^2 + 2^2 + 3^2 + 10^2 + 3^2 + 1^2 + 3^2 + 6^2 + 5^2) = 30.4$. A slight problems arises with units. A dataset is generally measured in some unit, and the mean $\bar{x}$ of a dataset, and hence deviations from the mean, will have the same unit. The mean of the square of these deviations will not have the same unit (if, for example, members of a dataset are measured in minutes, it will be measured in minutes^2). We can get round this problem by observing that $\frac{1}{n}\sum_i (x_i - \bar{x})^2$ is a mean of positive numbers, and hence is itself positive. If we take its square root, we obtain a measure of spread that has the same units as the original dataset.

Key Fact 28.9 Variance & Standard Deviation

The **variance** of a discrete dataset is generally denoted s^2, and is calculated by the formula

$$s^2 = \frac{1}{n} \sum_i (x_i - \bar{x})^2,$$

where $\bar{x}$ is the mean of the dataset. Its square root s is called the **standard deviation** of the dataset.

The standard deviation of the playing times of the nine CDs is $\sqrt{30.4\ldots} = 5.52$, correct to 3 significant figures.

> **For Interest**
>
> Really old books on statistics call the standard deviation the **root mean square deviation**, or the **RMS deviation**. That is exactly what it is: the square **root** of the **mean** of the **squares** of the **deviations** from the mean!

The above formula for the variance is important, particularly because it guarantees that the variance is always non-negative, and hence that its square root can be taken to determine the standard deviation. However, it is a very cumbersome formula to use in practice. To start with, we need to determine the mean $\overline{x}$. Then we need to determine the deviations $x_i - \overline{x}$ from the mean, which can be messy, particularly if $\overline{x}$ has a complicated decimal expansion. We then need to calculate the squares of these deviations and evaluate their mean. All this provides a rich field for data error to creep in. Happily, there is another formula for the variance that is much simpler to use.

> **Key Fact 28.10** The Variance : A Simpler Formula
>
> An alternative formula for the variance of a discrete dataset with mean $\overline{x}$ is
> $$s^2 = \frac{1}{n} \sum_i x_i^2 - \overline{x}^2 .$$

Using this alternative formula with the data on the playing times of CDs gives

$$
\begin{aligned}
s^2 &= \frac{1}{n} \sum_i x_i^2 - \overline{x}^2 \\
&= \frac{1}{9}\left[49^2 + 56^2 + 55^2 + 68^2 + 61^2 + 57^2 + 61^2 + 52^2 + 63^2\right] - 58^2 \\
&= \frac{1}{9} \times 30550 - 3364 = 30.4\ldots
\end{aligned}
$$

correct to 3 significant figures, the same answer that we found by using the original formula.

> **Food For Thought 28.1**
>
> This does not, of course, prove that the two formulae for variance are always equivalent to each other. Since
> $$\sum_i (x_i - \overline{x})^2 = \sum_i \left(x_i^2 - 2x_i\overline{x} + \overline{x}^2\right) = \sum_i x_i^2 - 2\sum_i x_i\overline{x} + \sum_i \overline{x}^2$$
> $$= \sum_i x_i^2 - 2\overline{x}\sum_i x_i + n\overline{x}^2$$
>
> and since $\overline{x} = \frac{1}{n}\sum_i x_i$, we see that
> $$\sum_i (x_i - \overline{x})^2 = \sum_i x_i^2 - 2n\overline{x}^2 + n\overline{x}^2 = \sum_i x_i^2 - n\overline{x}^2 .$$
>
> Dividing this formula by n shows that the two formulae for s^2 are equal.

Example 28.3.6. *For a particular dataset of 12 numbers,*

$$\sum x = 36, \qquad \sum x^2 = 130 .$$

Find the mean and variance of the dataset.

The mean is $\overline{x} = \frac{1}{12} \times 36 = 3$, while the variance is

$$s^2 = \frac{1}{12} \times 130 - 3^2 = \frac{11}{6}.$$

Example 28.3.7. *The 12 boys and 13 girls in a class of 25 students were given a test. The mean mark for the 12 boys was 31 and the standard deviation of the boys' marks was 6.2. The mean mark for the girls was 36 and the standard deviation of the girls' marks was 4.3. Find the mean mark and standard deviation of the marks of the whole class of 25 students.*

Let $x_1, x_2, \ldots, x_{12}$ be the marks of the 12 boys in the test and let $y_1, y2, \ldots, y_{13}$ be the marks of the 13 girls in the test.

Since the mean of the boys' marks is 31, $\frac{1}{12} \sum x = 31$, and so $\sum x = 12 \times 31 = 372$. As the standard deviation of the boys' marks is 6.2, the variance is $6.2^2 = 38.44$. Thus

$$38.44 = \frac{1}{12} \sum x^2 - 31^2$$

and hence $\sum x^2 = 12(31^2 + 38.44) = 11993.28$. Similarly

$$\sum y = 13 \times 36 = 468 \qquad \sum y^2 = 13(36^2 + 4.3^2) = 17088.37$$

Thus the overall mean is

$$\frac{1}{25}\left(\sum x + \sum y\right) = \frac{1}{25}(372 + 468) = 33.6$$

and the overall variance is

$$\frac{1}{25}\left(\sum x^2 + \sum y^2\right) - 33.6^2 = \frac{1}{25}(11993.28 + 17088.37) - 33.6^2 = 34.306$$

so that the overall standard deviation is $\sqrt{34.306} = 5.86$, correct to 3 significant figures.

Since the variance and standard deviation are close relatives of the mean, they suffer from the same faults that the mean does, as well as the same benefits. In particular, the variance is sensitive to 'rogue' values and data input error, and so care must be exercised in its calculation.

When data is presented in a frequency table, we need to change the formulae for the variance, just as we changed the formula for the mean. If we reconsider the data first discussed in Example 28.2.3 (above) concerning the number of siblings that children at a school a school had, then we realised that the correct expression for the sum of all the datapoints was $\sum_i x_i f_i$, since each distinct value x_i occurs f_i times in this dataset.

Siblings x	Freq. f	xf	x^2f
0	36	0	0
1	94	94	94
2	48	96	192
3	15	45	135
4	7	28	112
5	3	15	75
6	1	6	36
	204	284	644

Similarly, in order to sum the squares of all the datapoints, we need to evaluate $\sum_i x_i^2 f_i$. This requires an additional column in the frequency table. The mean and variance are

$$\overline{x} = \frac{284}{204} = 1.39\ldots \qquad , \qquad s^2 = \frac{644}{204} - \overline{x}^2 = 1.218\ldots = 1.22$$

with the standard deviation being $\sqrt{1.218\ldots} = 1.10$.

Key Fact 28.11 Variance And Standard Deviation : Frequency Tables

If a dataset is presented in a frequency table, with distinct possible values $x_1, x_2,$ ... occurring with frequencies $f_1, f_2, \ldots$, then the variance of the dataset is

$$s^2 = \frac{1}{n}\sum_i (x_i - \overline{x})^2 f_i = \frac{1}{n}\sum_i x_i^2 f_i - \overline{x}^2 \qquad n = \sum_i f_i, \quad \overline{x} = \frac{1}{n}\sum_i x_i f_i.$$

The standard deviation is still the square root of the variance.
If the data is continuous and/or grouped, then the above formulae give us an estimate for the variance, provided that x_i is the midpoint of each class.

Example 28.3.8. *Recall the 95 CDs, discussed earlier in this chapter. Estimate the standard deviation of the playing time for the dataset.*

We need one further calculation column in the frequency table.

Play Time	Freq. f	Midpoint x	xf	x^2f
40 – 44	1	42	42	42
45 – 49	7	47	329	15463
50 – 54	12	52	624	32448
55 – 59	24	57	1368	77976
60 – 64	29	62	1798	111476
65 – 69	14	67	938	62846
70 – 74	5	72	360	25920
75 – 79	3	77	231	17787
	95		5690	345680

Then $\bar{x} = \frac{5690}{95} = 59.9$ mins, and $s^2 = \frac{345680}{95} - \bar{x}^2 = 51.4$ mins^2, so $s = 7.17$ mins.

28.3.4. CODING

Just as coding was helpful when calculating the mean, it can simplify the calculation of the variance.

Key Fact 28.12 Measures of Spread : Coding

If a dataset has data points x_1, x_2, ..., and if we code this dataset via the formula $x = ay + b$ (for some constants a and b), obtaining a new dataset with data point y_1, y_2, ..., then the variances s_x^2 and s_y^2 of the two datasets are related by the formula

$$s_x^2 = a^2 s_y^2.$$

Since b alters the location of the data, without altering its spread, it is perhaps not surprising that the coded formula for the variance depends on a only.

Example 28.3.9. *The heights, x cm, of a sample of 80 female students are summarised by the equations*

$$\sum \frac{x-160}{10} = 24, \qquad \sum \left(\frac{x-160}{10}\right)^2 = 87.20.$$

Find the standard deviation of the heights of the 80 students.

If we code x by writing $y = \frac{x-160}{10}$, then $\sum y = 24$ and $\sum y^2 = 87.20$, from which we deduce that $\bar{y} = 0.3$ and $s_y^2 = \frac{87.20}{80} - 0.3^2 = 1$. Since $x = 10y + 160$, we deduce that $\bar{x} = 163$ and $s_x^2 = 100$. Thus the required standard deviation is $s_x = 10$.

EXERCISE 28D

1. The number of absences each day among employees in an office was recorded over a period of 96 days, with the following results. Calculate the mean and variance of the number of daily absence.

No. of Absences	0	1	2	3	4	5
No. of Days	54	24	11	4	2	1

2. Plates of a certain design are painted by a particular factory employee. At the end of each day the plates are inspected and some are rejected. The table shows the number of plates rejected over a period of 30 days. Show that the standard deviation of the daily number of rejects is approximately equal to one-quarter of the range.

Number of rejects	0	1	2	3	4	5	6
Number of days	18	5	3	1	1	1	1

3. The times taken in a 20 km race were noted for 80 people. The results are summarised in the following table.

Time (mins)	$60-80$	$80-100$	$100-120$	$120-140$	$140-160$	$160-180$	$180-200$
No. of people	1	4	26	24	10	7	8

Estimate the variance of the times of the 80 people in the race.

4. The mass of coffee in each of 80 packets of a certain brand was measured correct to the nearest gram. The results are shown in the following table.

Mass (grams)	$244-246$	$247-249$	$250-252$	$253-255$	$256-258$
Number of packets	10	20	24	18	8

Estimate the mean and standard deviation of the masses. State two ways in which the accuracy of these estimates could be improved.

5. Here are 10 values of a variable x. Find the variance using the coding formula $u = x - 20$.

$$18.9 \quad 20.7 \quad 19.3 \quad 20.1 \quad 21.3 \quad 19.6 \quad 20.5 \quad 20.9 \quad 18.8 \quad 20.8$$

6. The coding formula $u = x + 20$ is used to find the standard deviation of the values of x given in a frequency table. It is found that $\sum f_i = 40$, $\sum u_i f_i = 112$ and $\sum u_i^2 f_i = 10208$. Find the mean and variance of the values of x.

7. At the start of a new school year, the heights of the 100 new pupils entering the school are measured. The results are summarised in the following table.

Height (h cm)	$100-110$	$110-120$	$120-130$	$130-140$	$140-150$	$150-160$	$160-170$
Number of pupils	2	10	22	29	22	12	3

By using the formula $u = h - 135$, obtain estimates of the mean and variance of the heights of the 100 pupils.

8. The ages, in completed years, of the 104 workers in a company are summarised as follows:

Age (years)	$16-20$	$21-25$	$26-30$	$31-35$	$36-40$	$41-50$	$51-60$	$61-70$
Frequency	5	12	18	14	25	16	8	6

Estimate the mean and standard deviation of the workers' ages.

In another company, with a similar number of workers, the mean age is 28.4 years and the standard deviation is 9.9 years. Briefly compare the age distribution in the two companies.

9. Twenty observations of t are summarised by $\sum t = 19.52$, $\sum t^2 = 51.5245$. Find the mean and the value of s^2.

10. A random sample has $n = 15$, $s = 1.9$ and $\sum x^2 = 248.55$. Find the value of $\bar{x}$.

11*. Prove the coding formula for variance: if a dataset for x is coded by the formula $x = ay + b$ (for constants a and b), then $s_x^2 = a^2 s_y^2$.

12*. What can you say about a dataset if it has standard deviation equal to zero?

28.4 Outliers and Skewness

We have noted at various times that the mean and standard deviation are sensitive to what we have been calling 'rogue' values, possibly caused by data error. Statisticians call these values **outliers**. It is important to be able to identify outliers; if it is clear that a particular datapoint is in error, then we would want to exclude it from our analysis. The datapoint may not be an error; if we consider the class and its teacher in Example 28.2.5, then the teacher **is** definitely that old, and we would not want to ignore the fact that an older person was present. It is important to be aware, however, if a dataset has unusual features.

There is no hard-and-fast rule for identifying outliers. That said, there are a couple of 'rules of thumb' that have been established. One rule involves the quartiles of a dataset, while the other involves the mean and standard deviation.

Key Fact 28.13 Outliers

Rule 1 A data point that is more than 1.5 times the interquartile range beyond the quartiles is an outlier:

$$x \text{ is an outlier} \quad \text{if} \quad x < Q_1 - 1.5(Q_3 - Q_1) \quad \text{or} \quad x > Q_3 + 1.5(Q_3 - Q_1).$$

Rule 2 A datapoint which is more than 2 standard deviations from the mean is an outlier:

$$x \text{ is an outlier} \quad \text{if} \quad |x - \bar{x}| > 2s.$$

Considering the ages of the pupils and their teacher in Example 28.2.5 we calculate that Q_1 is 16 : 6, while Q_3 is 17 : 1; thus the interquartile range is 7 months, and anyone more than $1.5 \times 7 = 10.5$ months older than the upper quartile 17 : 1 would be an outlier. Thus anyone aged 18 : 0 or more would be an outlier for this dataset; the teacher is certainly one!

Example 28.4.1. *A coin is tossed repeatedly until it finally shows heads, and the number x of tosses required is recorded. This experiment is repeated 100 times, and the results are shown in the table.*

x	1	2	3	4	5	6	7
Freq.	49	24	14	8	4	0	1

Since $Q_1 = 1$ and $Q_3 = 3$, outliers are less than $1 - 1.5(3-1) = -2$ or greater than $3 + 1.5(3-1) = 6$. Thus the single value of 7 is an outlier by the first criterion.

On the other hand, we can calculate $\bar{x} = 1.98$ and $s = 1.25$. By the second criterion, outliers would be values less than $\bar{x} - 2s = -0.518$ or greater than $\bar{x} + 2s = 4.48$. The second criterion would class the outcomes of 5 as outliers as well.

Identifying outliers is important, but it does not tell the whole story. The following graph shows the mortality rates at different ages in France in 1910 (source: Wolfram Alpha™).

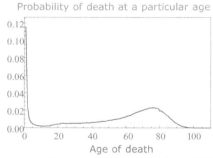

Mortality Rates in France by Age: 1910

Figure 28.5

The modal class would, on this data, be $0 - 1$ years. Infant mortality was a significant factor in the 19th Century (and not just in France). However, we see that, once a person had survived childhood, he or she had a fair life expectancy. With a little more data, we discover that $Q_1 = 29.7$ years and $Q_3 = 74.6$ years. To be an outlier for this dataset, someone would have had to live for 142 years! This data set has no outliers, but its shape is clearly unusual.

The following Figures show three different shapes which occur frequently when drawing bar charts or histograms.

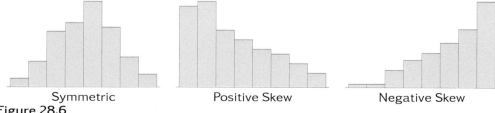

Symmetric   Positive Skew   Negative Skew

Figure 28.6

- The first distribution is **symmetrical**.

- The second distribution is not symmetrical; it has a 'tail' which stretches towards the higher values. Such a distribution is said to be **positively skewed**.

- The first distribution is not symmetrical, either; it has a 'tail' which stretches towards the lower values. Such a distribution is said to be **negatively skewed**.

Drawing a bar chart or a histogram to represent a dataset quickly establishes whether a dataset is skewed or not; we get an overall idea from the shape of the graph. It would be useful to have a quantitative method for determining the skewness of a dataset without drawing any graphs.

- If a dataset is symmetrical, we would expect the mean and the median to be about the same, in the centre of the distribution. Provided that the dataset has a unique mode, the mode is likely to have about the same value as the median and mode. Additionally, the lower quartile Q_1, the median Q_2 and the upper quartile Q_3 are likely to be even spaced.

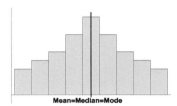

- If a dataset if positively skewed, then the data to the right of the median is spread out over a greater range than is the data to the left of the median. This means that frequencies are likely to be smaller to the right of the median than they are to the left, which will probably mean that the mode (if it exists) is less than the median.

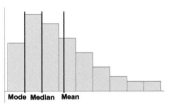

Data points will tend to be spread further away from the median on its right than on its left, and the effect of this is that the mean is likely to be greater than the median. Additionally, the greater spread of data to the right of the mean will mean that the upper quartile Q_3 is further away from the median Q_2 than is the lower quartile Q_1.

- If a dataset is negatively skewed, then the arguments applied to a positively skewed dataset operate in the opposite direction; it is likely that the mode will be greater than the median, and that the mean will be less than the median. Additionally, the lower quartile Q_1 is likely to be further away from the median Q_2 than is the upper quartile Q_3.

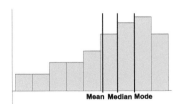

Key Fact 28.14 Skewness

The following are rules of thumb which can be used to identify skewness:

- If a dataset is positively skewed, then (usually)

$$\text{MODE} < \text{MEDIAN} < \text{MEAN} \quad \text{and} \quad Q_2 - Q_1 < Q_3 - Q_2.$$

- If a dataset is negatively skewed, then (usually)

$$\text{MODE} > \text{MEDIAN} > \text{MEAN} \quad \text{and} \quad Q_2 - Q_1 > Q_3 - Q_2.$$

Example 28.4.2. *Referring again to data about the siblings of children at a school, first discussed on page 556, determine the skewness of the dataset.*

Since the mode is 1, the median is 1 and the mean is 1.39, the fact that the median is less than the mode shows that the dataset is positively skewed. Moreover, $Q_1 = Q_2 = 1$ and $Q_3 = 2$. Thus $Q_2 - Q_1 < Q_3 - Q_2$, which is more evidence of skewness.

There are a number of expressions that can be calculated to put a numerical value on skewness. The following formulae

$$\frac{(Q_3 - Q_2) - (Q_2 - Q_1)}{Q_3 - Q_1} \quad \text{or} \quad \frac{3(\bar{x} - Q_2)}{s}$$

can both be used. The more positive the quantity, the greater the (positive) skewness. The more negative the quantity, the greater the (negative) skewness. The nearer the quantity is to 0, the more symmetric is the dataset. It is worth noting that professional statisticians do not make much use of these quantitative measures of skewness.

EXERCISE 28E

1. A **five-number summary** for a dataset consists of the least value, the lower quartile, the median, the upper quartile and the greatest value of that dataset. Describe the skewness, and determine whether outliers are present, for the datasets described by the following five-number summaries:

   a) 6.0 kg, 10.2 kg, 12.7 kg, 13.2kg, 15.7 kg,

   b) $-25°$ C, $-8°$ C, $-6°$ C, $3°$ C, $11°$ C,

   c) 37 m, 48 m, 60 m, 72 m, 110 m.

2. The following figures are the amounts (in \$) spent on food by a family for 13 weeks.

98.25	93.70	102.83	99.24	108.28	105.47	97.29
101.82	108.42	88.73	92.76	102.42	90.85	

   Calculate the quartiles of this dataset, and describe any skewness of the data.

3. The lower and upper quartiles of a dataset are 56 and 84. Which of the following datapoints are outliers?

   a) 140   b) 10   c) 100

4. When searching for a particular species of insect, quadrats (1 m by 1 m squares) are marked out, and the numbers of insects of that species found in each quadrat is recorded. The results from 50 quadrats are summarised below:

0	1	5	2	19	47	21	8	7	4	0	1	1
0	0	0	0	0	0	1	3	15	11	4	3	7
2	2	0	0	0	0	0	1	0	0	1	0	0
1	4	6	6	0	1	2	2	0	0	0		

   a) Determine the mean, median, standard deviation, lower quartile and upper quartile.

   b) Calculate $\frac{(Q_3-Q_2)-(Q_2-Q_1)}{Q_3-Q_1}$ and $\frac{3(\bar{x}-Q_2)}{s}$.

   c) Comment on the skewness of the data.

Chapter 28: Summary

- Data can be either **discrete** or **continuous**.

- **Measures of Location**

  - ★ The **mode** or **modal class** is the value or class that occurs most often.
  - ★ The **median** is the middle value when the data has been sorted. For a dataset of discrete data with n points, calculate $\frac{1}{2}n$. If this is an integer, find the midpoint of the corresponding term and the next term in the dataset. If $\frac{1}{2}n$ is not an integer, round up to the next integer and take the term corresponding to that value. If the data is grouped, calculate $\frac{1}{2}n$ and use interpolation.
  - ★ The **mean** of a dataset is the value

  $$\overline{x} = \frac{1}{n}\sum_i x_i = \frac{1}{n}\sum_i f_i x_i \quad \text{where} \quad n = \sum_i f_i \,.$$

- **Measures of Spread**

  - ★ The **range** is the difference between the largest and the smallest value of a dataset.
  - ★ The **quartiles** Q_1, Q_2 (the median) and Q_3 split the data into four parts, when the data has been sorted. To calculate Q_j, calculate $\frac{j}{4}n$. If this is an integer, find the midpoint of the corresponding term and the next term in the dataset. If $\frac{j}{4}n$ is not an integer, round up to the next integer and take the term corresponding to that value. If the data is grouped, calculate $\frac{j}{4}n$ and use interpolation.
  - ★ The **interquartile range** is $Q_3 - Q_1$.
  - ★ The **variance** of a dataset is

  $$s^2 = \frac{1}{n}\sum_i (x - \overline{x})^2 = \frac{1}{n}\sum_i x_i^2 - \overline{x}^2 = \frac{1}{n}\sum_i f_i(x_i - \overline{x})^2 = \frac{1}{n}\sum_i f_i x_i^2 - \overline{x}^2\,,$$

  while the **standard deviation** is the square root of the variance.

- **Coding** If two datasets are related by the coding formula $x = ay + b$, then

  $$\overline{x} = a\overline{y} + b \qquad s_x^2 = a^2 s_y^2\,.$$

- An **outlier** is a datapoint which is

  - ★ either greater than $Q_3 + 1.5(Q_3 - Q_1)$ or less than $Q_1 - 1.5(Q_3 - Q_1)$,
  - ★ or more than twice the standard deviation away from the mean.

- **Skewness**, either positive or negative, can be determined using either the quartiles or the mean, median and mode.

Correlation and Regression

In this chapter we will learn:

- about the concepts of dependent and independent variables, (linear) correlation, residuals, and regression lines for bivariate data,

- to construct and use scatter graphs,

- to use the product-moment correlation coefficient as a measure of correlation, and to use covariance and variance in the construction of regression lines.

29.1 Scatter Diagrams

There are occasions where we need to **compare** sets of paired data. Such data is called **bivariate**. For example, we might want to investigate the possibility of a relationship between

- the weight x kg hung from the end of a spring and the length y cm of the stretched spring,

- the age x years of an olive tree, and the yield y kg of olives at harvest,

- the number x of minutes spent on a piece of homework, and the number y of errors in that homework.

Let us consider a particular example. A teacher is studying the marks obtained by his 12 students in recent tests in French and German; he wonders whether there is a relationship between the French mark x and the German mark y. The marks obtained by his students are as follows:

Pupil	A	B	C	D	E	F	G	H	I	J	K	L	Mean
French mark x	41	36	39	38	50	46	43	36	38	47	30	30	39.5
German mark y	35	21	32	23	38	26	41	25	28	29	20	18	28

The simplest way for us to start to understand this data, is to graph it. Treat each pair of marks from a student as a pair of coordinates (x, y) and plot those points on a pair of axes. The resulting graph is called a **scatter diagram**.

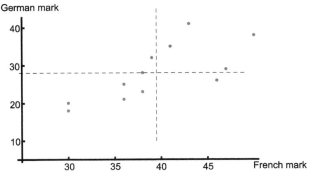

Figure 29.1

To assist us in our study of this diagram, dashed lines have been drawn to indicate the mean values of x and y. We cannot expect to identify a very precise relationship between the French and German marks, but we do notice that, in the main, a pupil who scores well in French also scores well in German, and a student who scores badly in French also scores badly in German.

The same teacher then decided to compare his students' marks in French with the number of goals they scored in the previous Saturday's football matches, and also with the number of hours they had spend on their English coursework in the previous week. Without listing all the figures involved, the associated scatter diagrams were:

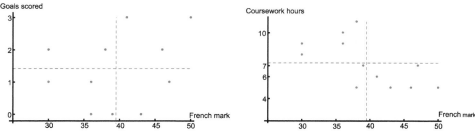

Figure 29.2

It would seem from this data that there is no particular relationship between performance in French and goal-scoring ability, but there is a relationship between performance in French and time spent on other work; in this second case the people who spent more time on their coursework tended to perform worse in French.

The relationships that we have found are called **correlations**. We are interested in what might be called a **paired dataset**, every element of which consists of two values; a value x and a value y, understood to measure different variables. The question is whether there is some relationship between the values of x and their associated values of y.

Key Fact 29.1 Linear Correlation

The variables being measured in a paired dataset are called **positively (linearly) correlated** if the increase in value of one tends to result in an increase in value of the second. The variables in a paired dataset are called **negatively (linearly) correlated** if the increase in value of one tends to result in the decrease in value of the second. The variables in paired datasets that exhibit neither of these behaviours are called **(linearly) uncorrelated**.

(Linearly) correlated variables tend to have scatter diagrams that cluster around straight line graphs, or more generally monotonic curves. If the scatter diagram clusters around an increasing function, the variables are positively correlated, and if the scatter diagram clusters around a decreasing function, then the variables are negatively correlated.

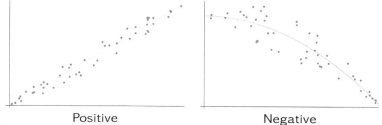

Positive   **Negative**

Figure 29.3

(Linearly) uncorrelated variables can be more complicated. Variables x and y can have a clear relationship between them, but still not be (linearly) correlated, in that it is not always the case that y increases when x does, or that y decreases when x increases.

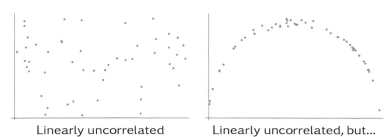

Linearly uncorrelated   Linearly uncorrelated, but...

Figure 29.4

In standard usage, the term **correlation** is taken to mean **linear correlation**. The absence of correlation does not preclude the possibility of two datasets being highly dependent on each other.

29.2   The Product-Moment Correlation Coefficient

What we need is a measure of the degree of correlation of the two variables in a paired dataset (and whether that correlation is positive or negative).

Consider a 'cross-hairs' centered at the point $(\overline{x},\overline{y})$ corresponding to the means of the two variables. If the two variables are positively correlated, we would expect most of the scatter plots to lie in the top-right and bottom-left quadrants (marked with a +) defined by these cross-hairs. If the two variables are negatively correlated, we would expect most of the scatter plots to lie in the top-left and bottom-right quadrants (marked with a -). We need to develop a measure that records positive values for scatter plots (x,y) in the top-right and bottom-left quadrants, and negative values for scatter plots in the top-left and bottom right quadrants. Just such a quantity is

$$\left(x-\overline{x}\right)\left(y-\overline{y}\right).$$

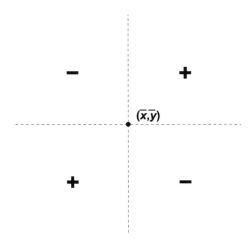

Figure 29.5

For a paired dataset of points $(x_1,y_1),(x_2,y_2),\ldots,(x_n,y_n)$, we define

$$S_{xy} \;=\; \sum_i x_i y_i - n\overline{xy} \qquad\qquad S_{xx} \;=\; \sum_i x_i^2 - n\overline{x}^2 \qquad\qquad S_{yy} \;=\; \sum_i y_i^2 - n\overline{y}^2$$

We note that $S_{xx} = ns_x^2$ and $S_{yy} = ns_y^2$ are multiples of the variances of x and y, while

$$\sum_i \left(x_i - \overline{x}\right)\left(y_i - \overline{y}\right) \;=\; \sum_i \left(x_i y_i - \overline{y}x_i - \overline{x}y_i + \overline{xy}\right) \;=\; \sum_i x_i y_i - \overline{y}\sum_i x_i - \overline{x}\sum_i y_i + n\overline{xy}$$

$$=\; \sum_i x_i y_i - \overline{y}\times n\overline{x} - \overline{x}\times n\overline{y} + n\overline{xy} \;=\; \sum_i x_i y_i - n\overline{xy} \;=\; S_{xy}$$

and so S_{xy} is the sum of all the terms $(x-\overline{x})(y-\overline{y})$ from the paired dataset. $\frac{1}{n}S_{xy}$ is called the **covariance** of x and y. We should therefore expect S_{xy} to be positive when x and y are positively correlated, and to be negative when x and y are negatively correlated. To ensure that our measure of correlation is unaffected by simple data transformations such as scaling and translation, we need to scale S_{xy}.

Key Fact 29.2 The Product-Moment Correlation Coefficient

The **product-moment correlation coefficient** between the two variables x and y in a paired dataset is the quantity

$$r = r_{xy} \;=\; \frac{S_{xy}}{\sqrt{S_{xx} \times S_{yy}}}.$$

Example 29.2.1. *Find the product-moment correlation coefficient of the marks in French and German from the beginning of this chapter.*

After quite a lot of calculator work, we find that $\sum x = 474$, $\sum y = 336$, $\sum x^2 = 19156$, $\sum y^2 = 9994$ and $\sum xy = 13639$. Thus $\bar{x} = 39.5$ and $\bar{y} = 28$ (as we know) and

$$S_{xx} = 433 \qquad S_{yy} = 586 \qquad S_{xy} = 367,$$

so the product-moment correlation coefficient between x and y is $\frac{367}{\sqrt{433 \times 586}} = 0.729$.

Since $r = 0.729$ is positive, we deduce that French and German marks are positively correlated (or exhibit positive correlation). The question we must ask is: how good is that correlation?

Suppose that x and y are perfectly correlated so that there is a linear relationship between x and y of the form $y = ax + b$ for some constants a and b. Results about coding tell us that $S_{yy} = ns_y^2 = na^2s_x^2 = a^2 S_{xx}$. More generally,

$$S_{xy} = \sum_i x_i y_i - n\bar{x}\bar{y} = \sum_i x_i(ax_i + b) - n\bar{x}(a\bar{x} + b)$$

$$= a\sum_i x_i^2 + b\sum_i x_i - na\bar{x}^2 - nb\bar{x} = a\left(\sum_i x_i^2 - \bar{x}^2\right) = aS_{xx}$$

and hence

$$S_{xy} = \frac{aS_{xx}}{\sqrt{S_{xx} \times a^2 S_{xx}}} = \frac{a}{|a|} = \begin{cases} 1 & a > 0, \\ -1 & a < 0. \end{cases}$$

Key Fact 29.3 The Product-Moment Correlation Coefficient : Interpretation

If x and y are perfectly correlated, obeying an exact linear relationship, then r_{xy} is equal to 1 if the correlation is positive, and equal to -1 if the correlation is negative. In general, $-1 \le r_{xy} \le 1$.

The closer that r_{xy} is to 1 (or -1), the better the correlation. The closer that r_{xy} is to 0, the more the two variables are uncorrelated.

For Interest

How large does r_{xy} have to be for the correlation to be strong? The scatter diagram on the right is of two totally uncorrelated datasets of 50 points each, but their product-moment correlation coefficient is 0.23. Clearly, a positive value of r_{xy} is not enough to guarantee positive correlation.

Figure 29.6

To study correlation in full detail, we need to ask the question: 'What is the probability that two uncorrelated datasets could nonetheless produce a product-moment correlation coefficient this big entirely by chance?'. If the probability of a particular value occurring by chance is very small, we can feel justified in claiming a correlation between the datasets. It turns out that the size of product-moment correlation coefficient required for significance depends on the size of the data as well as the level of assurance that we require (if there are only 5 data points, we need $r_{xy} > 0.93$ to be 99% certain that the variables are correlated, but if we have 1000 data points a value of $r_{xy} > 0.07$ is sufficient. In practice (we will be working with small datasets), if we operate on the rule of thumb that a value of r_{xy} of absolute value greater than 0.7 indicates strong correlation, that an absolute value of r_{xy} between 0.5 and 0.7 indicates moderate correlation, and that anything else is at best weak evidence for correlation, we will not go far wrong.

29.2.1. CODING

Coding was a useful tool when calculating means and variances. It is particularly useful when calculating correlation coefficients. Since the product-moment correlation coefficient measures the closeness of fit of a paired dataset to a straight line, it seems likely that this goodness of fit should not be affected by the linear changes of variable afforded by coding.

> **Key Fact 29.4** Product-Moment Correlation Coefficient : Coding
>
> If the variables x and y in a paired dataset are coded as $x = au + b$ and $y = cv + d$ for constants a, b, c and d (where a and c are positive), obtaining a coded paired dataset with variables u and v, then
> $$r_{uv} = r_{xy}.$$
> In short, correlation coefficients are unaffected by coding.

The proof of this result is straightforward. Since $\overline{x} = a\overline{u} + b$, we see that $x_i - \overline{x} = a\left(u_i - \overline{u}\right)$ for all datapoints. Similarly $y_i - \overline{y} = c\left(v_i - \overline{v}\right)$ for all i. Thus

$$S_{xy} = \sum_i \left(x_i - \overline{x}\right)\left(y_i - \overline{y}\right) = ac\sum_i \left(u_i - \overline{u}\right)\left(v_i - \overline{v}\right) = acS_{uv}$$

and we already know from our study of the coding of variance that $S_{xx} = a^2 S_{uu}$ and $S_{yy} = c^2 S_{vv}$. Thus

$$r_{xy} = \frac{S_{xy}}{\sqrt{S_{xx} \times S_{yy}}} = \frac{acS_{uv}}{\sqrt{a^2 S_{uu} \times c^2 S_{vv}}} = \frac{S_{uv}}{\sqrt{S_{uu} \times S_{vv}}} = r_{uv}$$

as required.

Example 29.2.2. *A paired dataset, with variables x and y, has been coded by the formulae*

$$x = w + 10 \qquad y = 3z + 1.$$

The summary statistics for the coded dataset are

$$n = 50 \qquad \sum w = 75 \qquad \sum z = 110 \qquad \sum w^2 = 123 \qquad \sum z^2 = 252 \qquad \sum wz = 157.$$

Evaluate the means $\overline{x}$, $\overline{y}$ and the correlation coefficient r_{xy}.

We have $\overline{w} = \frac{75}{50} = 1.5$ and $\overline{z} = \frac{110}{50} = 2.2$. Thus

$$S_{ww} = 123 - 50\overline{w}^2 = 10.5 \qquad S_{zz} = 252 - 50 \times \overline{z}^2 = 10 \qquad S_{wz} = 157 - 50 \times \overline{wz} = -8$$

and hence $r_{wz} = \frac{-8}{\sqrt{10.5 \times 10}} = -0.781$. Thus we deduce that $\overline{x} = 11.5$, $\overline{y} = 7.6$ and $r_{xy} = -0.781$.

EXERCISE 29A

1. A company is being traded on the Stock Exchange. During one day of trading its share price fluctuated rapidly. There were a number of different purchases of shares in this company during the day. At each deal x thousand shares were purchased, at a cost of y pence a share.

Number of shares x	75	62	71	61	70	59	65	69
Price per share y	37	55	25	20	47	62	24	52

Calculate the product-moment correlation coefficient. Draw a scatter diagram of the data, and contrast the information this provides with the value of the product-moment correlation coefficient.

2. Ten people were asked for their opinions about two television programmes. They were asked to mark each programme on a scale of 1 to 5, indicating their enjoyment of the programme (with 5 being the best possible score). The scores recorded by these people are shown in the following table. Draw a scatter diagram to represent this data, and calculate the product-moment correlation coefficient between the scores for the two programmes.

Person	A	B	C	D	E	F	G	H	I	J
Programme X	5	0	3	1	2	2	5	3	4	2
Programme Y	3	2	1	3	3	4	5	2	2	3

3. This question is a classic problem in statistics. There any many datasets concerning the relationship between storks and babies! This one relates the number of pairs of storks with the birth rate in 17 different countries in Europe in 1990 (adapted from Robert Matthews, *Teaching Statistics*, 2000):

Country	A	B	C	D	E	F	G	H	I
Storks (prs.)	100	300	1	5000	9	140	3300	2500	4
Births (10^3/yr.)	83	87	118	117	59	774	901	106	188

Country	J	K	L	M	N	O	P	Q
Storks (prs.)	5000	5	30000	1500	5000	8000	150	25000
Births (10^3/yr.)	124	551	610	120	367	439	82	1576

Find the product-moment correlation coefficient between the number of storks and the birth rate in European countries; what do you think about your result?

4. The ages x years (given to one decimal place) and the heights y cm (to the nearest cm) of 10 boys were as follows:

x	6.6	6.8	6.9	7.5	7.8	8.2	10.1	11.4	12.8	13.5
y	119	112	116	123	122	123	135	151	141	141

Given that $\sum x^2 = 889.80$, $\sum y^2 = 166091$ and $\sum xy = 12023.3$, calculate the product-moment correlation coefficient between x and y, and comment upon this result.

5. An horse trainer records his horses' weights when they enter a race and their finishing position in the race.

Weight x kg	457	480	510	438	512	570	492	501	502	550	510	449
Position y	2	4	3	2	5	4	1	3	4	2	3	3

Find the product-moment correlation coefficient between the horses' weights and their finishing position.

6. For a given dataset $\sum x = 975$, $\sum y = 401$, $\sum x^2 = 61500$, $\sum y^2 = 9571$, $\sum xy = 11305$ and $n = 23$. Find the product-moment correlation coefficient for the data.

7. Calculate the product-moment correlation coefficient for a dataset if $n = 26$, $\sum x = 185$, $\sum y = 79$, $\sum x^2 = 1402$, $\sum y^2 = 283$ and $\sum xy = 601$.

8. A student records that, for his paired dataset, $n = 15$, $\sum u = 400$, $\sum v = 615$, $\sum u^2 = 11253$, $\sum v^2 = 133490$ and $\sum uv = 7152$. Why must there be an error in this data?

9. The variables x and y are inversely proportional, in that $y = 10x^{-1}$. This relationship might lead to the paired dataset given in the table below:

x	1	2	3	4	5	6	7	8
y	10	5	3.33	2.5	2	1.67	1.43	1.25

Calculate the product-moment correlation coefficient between x and y, and comment on your result.

10. A total of 150 cars were sold in a month by a car dealership. The cars sold had x doors, where x could be 3, 4 or 5. Anybody who bought one of these cards had y children, where y was a number between 0 and 2. The table shows that frequencies of the various possible combinations (so that 15 4-door cars were sold to people with just 1 child, for example).

		No of doors x		
		3	4	5
No.	0	33	21	10
of children	1	10	15	25
y	2	2	15	19

Find the product-moment correlation coefficient r_{xy}.

11*. Consider the paired frequency table on the right, where x and y can both take the values of 1 and 2 alone, and a, b, c and d are nonnegative integers. Prove that

		x	
		1	2
y	1	a	b
	2	c	d

$$r_{xy} = \frac{ad - bc}{\sqrt{(a+b)(c+d)(a+c)(b+d)}}.$$

12*. Consider a paired dataset where, for simplicity, $\bar{x} = \bar{y} = 0$. Consider the quadratic function

$$F(t) = \sum_i (tx_i - y_i)^2.$$

a) Express $F(t)$ in terms of S_{xx}, S_{yy} and S_{xy}.

b) Use the fact that $F(t) \geq 0$ for all $t \in \mathbb{R}$ to deduce that $S_{xy}^2 \leq S_{xx}S_{yy}$, and hence prove that $-1 \leq r_{xy} \leq 1$.

c) How might you adjust this argument to show that $-1 \leq r_{xy} \leq 1$ for all paired datasets?

29.3 Correlation and Causation

Just because two variables are correlated does not mean that one directly affects the other. Storks do not bring babies, no matter how strong the correlation is between their numbers and birthrates (see Question 3 in Exercise 29A above). If we can establish a correlation between two variables, we might want to try to find out whether there is a **causal connection** between them (is there a direct reason why the increase of one should imply the increase or decrease of the other?). A correlation had been established between smoking and lung cancer long before the causal connection between them (the medical reasons why smoking caused cancer) were established.

Correlations might exist because of some third, previously unconsidered, variable that is causally related to both of the original variables. One possible explanation of the stork/babies phenomenon is to consider the (human) population of each country. A greater population will, of course, result in more babies. At the same time, a greater population will provide more houses, and so more chimneys in towns; a perfect breeding habitat for storks!

On the other hand, correlations might be entirely spurious! The internet is a great resource for spurious correlations, for example, there is correlation of 0.87 between the per capita consumption of beef and the number of deaths caused by lightning in United States. The important lesson to learn is that establishing a correlation is the beginning, not the end, of understanding the relationship between variables.

29.4 Linear Regression

29.4.1. DEPENDENT AND INDEPENDENT VARIABLES

There are many experiments that can be conducted with the view to determining the effect of the change of one variable upon another, for example:

- How does the length y cm of a spring change if we adjust the weight x kg attached to its end?

- How does the price £y of a three bedroomed house change as the distance x km from Central London changes?

- Does the height x cm of the father affect the height y cm of his son on his eighteenth birthday?

- Does a student's performance $y\%$ in an examination depend on her performance $x\%$ in an earlier mock examination?

In each of these cases, if we collect some data, we will probably find a correlation between x and y. However the variables x and y have rather different roles in these experiments. If we were to investigate the relationship between the length y cm of a spring the weight x kg attached to its end, then we could do this by choosing different weights to apply. In other words, we could choose the value of x, and discover what the resulting value of y is. Similarly, we could find the price £y of a three bedroom house a distance x km from Central London by looking in estate agents' windows at different values for the distance x km from London; for $x = 47$ we might try estate agents in Luton, for example.

Thus variables found in experiments can be of two types:

- **Independent variables** are ones that do not depend on other variables. In an experiment, we are free to choose any (reasonable) value for an independent variable. We can choose to attach a 1 kg test weight to a spring, or to look at the prices of housing a distance of 100 km from London, or consider the offspring of fathers who are 180 cm tall, or check the examination performance of people who obtained 70% in their mock examination.

- **Dependent variables** are just that; their values depend on the values of other variables. We would expect the length of a spring to respond to the test weight hanging from it, and for the price of a house to depend on its proximity to London. Also, it would be difficult to set the value of a dependent variable except by suitably varying the independent variables upon which it depends. It would be a much greater task to find the distance from London of three bedroom houses costing £250000, for example (except by collecting data from all the nation's estate agents).

We are interested in investigating the relationships between two variables, one independent variable x and one dependent variable y (all of the above examples are of this type). We hope to be able to understand enough of this relationship to be able to predict; if we are 75 km away from Central London, what might we expect the price of a three bedroom house to be?

29.4.2. THE LEAST SQUARES PRINCIPLE

Consider an experiment with one independent variable x and one dependent variable y. We hope that there will be fair degree of correlation between x and y, in which case there should be some type of linear relationship between x and y. In other words, we would like to be able to determine a formula of the form

$$y = ax + b$$

that will express the optimal relationship between x and y. In particular, we hope to be able to use this formula to predict the value of y for a given value of x.

If the correlation coefficient between x and y was ± 1, there would be no problem in determining the equation relating the two variables. In this case the relationship would be linear and exact, and determining the equation of that line defining that relationship would be elementary. The problem is more complicated if the correlation coefficient is not perfect. Which of these three lines, for example, is the best one to use to describe the relationship between x and y?

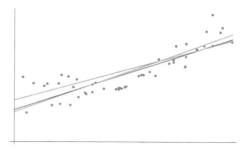

Figure 29.7

Let us answer this question by answering a simpler one: which one number best describes a dataset with values $x_1, x_2, \ldots, x_n$? The mean $\overline{x}$ is a plausible answer, as one of the measures of location considered in the previous chapter. It could be argued that the median might be another answer. However the mean is a good answer for a particular reason that we shall now explore.

Any real number u could have assigned to it a measure of 'how close it is to all the numbers in the dataset' by summing the squares of the difference of u from all numbers in the dataset. In other words, the function

$$E(u) = \sum_i (x_i - u)^2$$

quantifies the 'closeness' of u to all the points in the dataset. Since

$$E(u) \ = \ \sum_i (u^2 - 2ux_i + x_i^2) \ = \ nu^2 - 2u \sum_i x_i + x_i^2 \ = \ nu^2 - 2n\bar{x}u + \sum_i x_i^2$$

$$= \ nu^2 - 2n\bar{x}u + n(\bar{x}^2 + s^2) \ = \ n(u - \bar{x})^2 + ns^2$$

where s^2 is the variance of the dataset, we see that the smallest possible value of $E(u)$ is ns^2, and this occurs when $u = \bar{x}$. Thus the mean $\bar{x}$ is the point that minimises the sum of the squares of the differences from the points in the dataset.

This principle of estimating quantities by minimising a sum of squares or deviations (errors) was first proposed by Gauss, and it is called the *principle of least squares*. We shall attempt to use this principle to find the best line to draw through a correlated dataset.

Suppose that we have a paired dataset, and that we are trying to find the best possible line to fit this dataset. We therefore have two parameters to determine. We want to find the most suitable values of a and b so that the line

$$y \ = \ a + bx$$

is the best possible. If we consider a general line with equation $y = a + bx$, we can expect the points from the dataset to lie above and below the line.

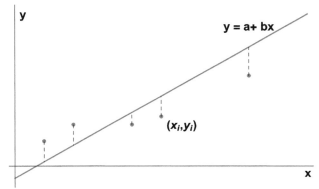

Figure 29.8

We want a measure of how close the points in the dataset are to this line. We shall do this by summing the squares of deviations from the line. Since x is an independent variable (and its values could have been chosen by us as part of the experiment), it is reasonable to suppose that deviations of each datapoint should be measured in terms of the dependent variable y. We shall assume, therefore, that the deviation created by each data point is the **vertical** distance between it and the line. For a data point (x_i, y_i), the point on the line with the same x-coordinate is $(x_i, a + bx_i)$ and so the vertical distance between the data point and the line is the quantity

$$y_i - a - bx_i$$

This quantity is called a **residual**; it is the difference between the observed and the predicted values of the dependent variable y.

Using the principle of least squares, we shall adopt as our measure of goodness of fit for the line $y = a + bx$, the sum of the squares of the residuals:

$$E(a, b) \ = \ \sum_i (y_i - a - bx_i)^2$$

and our aim is to find the values of a and b that minimise $E(a, b)$.

29.4.3. THE LEAST SQUARES LINE OF BEST FIT

> **Key Fact 29.5** Linear Regression : The Least Squares Line Of Best Fit
>
> The **least squares line of best fit** of y on x through a paired dataset has the equation $y = a + bx$ where
>
> $$b \ = \ \frac{S_{xy}}{S_{xx}} \qquad \text{and} \qquad a \ = \ \bar{y} - b\bar{x}.$$
>
> This process of finding the equation of a straight line is called **linear regression**.

Proving this is a challenging problem, since we have never previously had to minimise a function of two variables. However, careful square completion enables us to work out the solution. With a lot of algebra we see that

$$
\begin{aligned}
E(a,b) &= \sum_i (y_i^2 + a^2 + b^2 x_i^2 - 2ay_i - 2bx_iy_i + 2abx_i) \\
&= \sum_i y_i^2 + na^2 + b^2 \sum_i x_i^2 - 2a \sum_i y_i - 2b \sum_i x_iy_i + 2ab \sum_i x_i \\
&= \sum_i y_i^2 + na^2 + b^2 \sum_i x_i^2 - 2na\overline{y} - 2b \sum_i x_iy_i + 2nab\overline{x} \\
&= [S_{yy} + n\overline{y}^2] + na^2 + b^2[S_{xx} + n\overline{x}^2] - 2na\overline{y} - 2b[S_{xy} + n\overline{x}\,\overline{y}] + 2nab\overline{x} \\
&= b^2 S_{xx} - 2bS_{xy} + S_{yy} + n[a^2 + b^2\overline{x}^2 + \overline{y}^2 - 2a\overline{y} - 2b\overline{x}\,\overline{y} + 2ab\overline{x}] \\
&= b^2 S_{xx} - 2bS_{xy} + S_{yy} + n[a + b\overline{x} - \overline{y}]^2 \\
&= S_{xx}\left[b - \tfrac{S_{xy}}{S_{xx}}\right]^2 + S_{yy} - \tfrac{S_{xy}^2}{S_{xx}} + n[a + b\overline{x} - \overline{y}]^2 \\
&= S_{xx}\left[b - \tfrac{S_{xy}}{S_{xx}}\right]^2 + n[a + b\overline{x} - \overline{y}]^2 + \tfrac{S_{xx}S_{yy} - S_{xy}^2}{S_{xx}} .
\end{aligned}
$$

Thus $E(a,b)$ is the sum of three terms, the first two of which are positive multiples of squares, and the last of which does not depend on either a or b. We will therefore minimise $E(a,b)$ if we can choose values of a and b to make the first two terms equal to zero. It is clear that this can be done by choosing a and b such that

$$
b = \frac{S_{xy}}{S_{xx}}, \qquad a = \overline{y} - b\overline{x}.
$$

and so there is a unique line that, by the principle of least squares, is the best possible line.

Example 29.4.1. *The following data show the yield y g of the product of a chemical reaction when the reaction is run at different temperatures x° C.*

Temperature x	110	120	130	140	150	160	170
Yield y	2.1	2.4	3.1	3.4	4.4	5.5	4.9

Find the product-moment correlation coefficient between x and y, and the least squares line of best fit for yield y on temperature x, and show this line on a scatter diagram of the data.

Our initial calculations are often best done in tabular form.

x	y	x²	y²	xy
110	2.1	13100	4.41	231
120	2.4	14400	5.76	268
130	3.1	16900	9.61	403
140	3.4	19600	11.56	476
150	4.4	22500	19.36	660
160	5.5	25600	30.25	880
170	4.9	18900	24.01	833
980	25.8	140000	104.96	3771

We calculate $n = 7$, $\sum x = 980$, $\sum y = 25.8$, $\sum x^2 = 140000$, $\sum y^2 = 104.96$ and $\sum xy = 3771$, so that $\overline{x} = \frac{980}{7} = 140$ and $\overline{y} = \frac{25.8}{7} = 3.686$, while

$$
\begin{aligned}
S_{xx} &= 140000 - 7\overline{x}^2 = 2800 \\
S_{yy} &= 104.96 - 7\overline{y}^2 = 9.869 \\
S_{xy} &= 3771 - 7\overline{x}\,\overline{y} = 159
\end{aligned}
$$

The correlation coefficient is $r_{xy} = \frac{S_{xy}}{\sqrt{S_{xx}S_{yy}}} = 0.957$ (so a linear relationship between y and x is strongly indicated). We now calculate $b = \frac{159}{2800} = 0.05679$ and $a = 3.686 - 140b = -4.264$. Thus the least squares line of best fit for y on x has equation $y = 0.0568x - 4.264$.

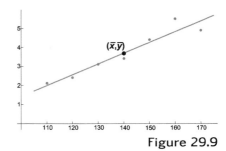

Figure 29.9

It is interesting to note that the point $(\overline{x}, \overline{y})$ (also plotted on the scatter diagram) lies on the regression line. This is no accident.

> **Key Fact 29.6** Linear Regression : The Two Means
>
> If we construct the least squares line of best fit of y on x for a paired dataset, then the point $(\overline{x}, \overline{y})$ lies on that line.

Since $a = \overline{y} - b\overline{x}$, the equation of the least squares line can be rewritten as

$$\begin{aligned} y &= \overline{y} - b\overline{x} + bx \\ y - \overline{y} &= b(x - \overline{x}) \end{aligned}$$

from which it is clear that it passes through the point $(\overline{x}, \overline{y})$.

29.4.4. INTERPOLATION AND EXTRAPOLATION

Example 29.4.2. *The amount of electrical energy y (in some convenient unit) to heat a building for a day varies according to the average daytime temperature $x°$ C for that day. Data for a total of 10 days was recorded:*

Day	1	2	3	4	5	6	7	8	9	10
Temperature x° C	12	14	15	15	17	20	18	22	18	19
Energy y	35	37	32	29	28	28	27	24	24	26

Obtain the least squares line of best fix for y on x, and use it to estimate the amount of electrical energy required to heat this building when the average temperature is $16°$ C, and also when the average temperature is $1°$ C. Can we trust these estimates?

This dataset gives the summary statistics $n = 10$, $\sum x = 170$, $\sum y = 290$, $\sum x^2 = 2972$, $\sum y^2 = 8584$, $\sum xy = 4829$. Thus we calculate that $\overline{x} = 17$, $\overline{y} = 29$, while

$$S_{xx} = 2972 - 10\overline{x}^2 = 82 \qquad S_{xy} = 4829 - 10\overline{x}\,\overline{y} = -101$$

and hence $b = \frac{-101}{82} = -1.232$, while $a = 29 - 17b = 49.94$. Thus the least squares regression line of y on x is $y = 49.94 - 1.232x$.

When $x = 16$, this formula gives us an estimate of $y = 30.2$. When $x = 1$, this formula gives us an estimate of $y = 48.7$.

While the correlation between x and y is good, with $r_{xy} = -0.846$, we would be unwise to believe the prediction that this equation gives us when the temperature is $1°$ C. We have no reason to believe, from this data alone, that the linear relationship between x and y will continue at temperatures as small as $1°$ C. The scatter diagram shows three possible scenarios for how electricity usage might vary with temperature at low temperatures. We cannot assume that the linear model must work.

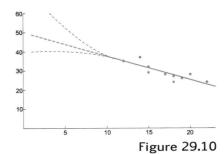

Figure 29.10

The key issue to consider is whether or not the value of x that we wish to substitute into the formula for the line of best fit is within the range of x values that were used to calculate that line of best fit. In the above example, we were given data with values of x between 12 and 22. Using the line of best fit to predict a value of y for a value of x within this range (namely, for $12 \leq x \leq 22$) is called **interpolation**. Using a value of x that lies outside that range of values of x ($x < 12$ or $x > 22$) is called **extrapolation**.

Key Fact 29.7 Linear Regression : Interpolation and Extrapolation

The line of best fit is reliable only when interpolating (using values of the independent variable within the range of x defined by the dataset); values of y obtained by extrapolation are less likely to be reliable.

For Interest

It is worth knowing that the calculations which determine both the product-moment correlation coefficient and the least squares regression line are very sensitive; a slight change in values of the data can have a remarkably large effect. It is important, therefore, to ensure that all calculations are performed to a high degree of accuracy (and only rounded to the desired degree of accuracy at the end).

EXERCISE 29B

1. Calculate the least square regression line of y on x for each of the following datasets. Plot the scatter diagrams of each, and include the regression line on each scatter diagram:

a)

x	1	2	3	3	4	5	5	7	8	9
y	1	3	2	4	4	5	3	2	5	7

b)

x	20	20.2	21.5	21.7	22.5	23.4	24.8
y	5	7	4	10	8	13	13

c)

x	2	5.5	6.5	12	13	15
y	4	8	5	9	11	14

d)

x	11	11	12	13	14	16	18	18
y	65	64	64	65	62	59	58	57

2. Calculate the least squares regression line of y on x for each of the following datasets, whose summary statistics are as follows:

a) $n = 10$, $\sum x = 61$, $\sum y = 610$, $\sum x^2 = 463$, $\sum y^2 = 39960$, $\sum xy = 3256$,

b) $n = 11$, $\sum x = 34$, $\sum y = 13.6$, $\sum x^2 = 126$, $\sum y^2 = 19.34$, $\sum xy = 35.8$,

c) $n = 100$, $\sum x = 319$, $\sum y = 726$, $\sum x^2 = 1253$, $\sum y^2 = 6094$, $\sum xy = 2720$,

d) $n = 88$, $\sum x = 194$, $\sum y = 133.5$, $\sum x^2 = 520$, $\sum y^2 = 215.31$, $\sum xy = 262.3$,

3. Experiments were conducted to compare the chemical content (x g l^{-1}) of a particular chemical salt in solution and the crystallisation temperature ($y°$ K). The results of these experiments were as follows:

x	0.4	0.4	1.3	2.3	3.1	5.2	4.3	4.7
y	3.2	2.5	4.3	5.4	6.7	8.5	7.7	8.1

Calculate the least squares line of best fit of y on x

4. Show that the least squares line of best fit of y on x for a paired dataset with two elements is simply the straight line through those points.

5. It is thought that two variables x and y are related by an equation of the form

$$y = a + bx^{-1}.$$

Ten readings of these variables were taken, and the following results were obtained:

x	95.86	82.97	100.86	94.96	114.40	76.55	94.11	95.29	117.84	82.72
y	31.16	32.12	31.25	31.98	31.33	32.51	31.39	31.97	31.39	31.86

Introducing the variable $t = 200x^{-1}$, the following summary data can be obtained:

$$\sum t = 21.29 \qquad \sum y = 317.0 \qquad \sum t^2 = 46.06 \qquad \sum y^2 = 10050 \qquad \sum ty = 675.6$$

Use this summary data to derive the least squares line of best fit of y on t, and hence write down the proposed equation relating x and y. What value of y would you expect to obtain if the matching value of x was 90? Could you use this equation to estimate the value of y when $x = 130$?

6. A paired dataset with five values is shown on the right, where u is some number.

x	1	2	3	4	5
y	9	7	u	3	1

a) For what value of u is the correlation coefficient r_{xy} equal to 1?

b) The least squares line of best fit of y on x is $y = 11.4 - 2x$. What is the value of u?

7. What is the relationship between the gradient b of the least squares line of best fit of a paired dataset, the standard deviations s_x and s_y of the two variables, and the product-moment correlation coefficient r_{xy} of that dataset. What is the gradient of the least squares line of best fit of an uncorrelated dataset?

8. On the planet Zod, the wholesale cost x Zoddybits per gram and the retail cost y Zoddybits per gram of gratolox (a highly desired gemstone) were recorded for a number of years:

Wholesale x	100	98	96	97	95	92	89	87	88	90	86	88
Retail y	120	117	115	118	114	115	110	109	111	113	109	107

Find the equation of the least squares regression line of y on x. When the wholesale price of gratolox is 93 Zoddybits a gram, what would we expect the retail price to be?

9. A paired dataset can be summarised as follows:

$$n = 10 \qquad \sum h = 72 \qquad \sum t = 89 \qquad \sum h^2 = 734 \qquad \sum t^2 = 1197 \qquad \sum ht = 923$$

Find the least squares line of best fit of h on t, and use it to predict the value of h when $t = 7.5$. You may assume that to do so does not require extrapolation.

10. Consider the paired dataset on the right. Find the least squares line of best fit of y on x.

x	−3	−2	−1	0	2	3
y	5	2	0	−1	−2	−5

It is desired, instead, to find the least squares line of best fit of y on x **that passes through the origin**. In other words, we need to find the line $y = cx$ such that the new least squares error function

$$\mathcal{E}(c) = \sum_i (y_i - cx_i)^2$$

is as small as possible. What is the equation of this line?

11*. Recall the least squares function $E(a, b)$ discussed in Section 29.4.3. What is the smallest possible value of $E(a, b)$, and what does this fact imply about the correlation coefficient r_{xy} of the paired dataset?

29.4.5. Coding

Just as coding has been useful in calculating the various statistical quantities we have been studying to date, it is also helpful when calculating regression lines. If we have a paired dataset for the variables x and y, coding for x and y and obtained a dataset for variables u and v, then there is a simple relationship between the least squares line of best fit of y on x and the least squares line of best fit for v on u.

Key Fact 29.8 Linear Regression : Coding

If a paired dataset involving the variables x and y has been coded by the formulae

$$u = px + q \qquad\qquad v = ry + s$$

and if the least squares line of best fit for v on u has equation

$$v = \alpha + \beta u$$

then the least squares line of best fit for y on x has the equation

$$ry + s = \alpha + \beta(px + q).$$

In other words, the new regression line is obtained simply by substituting the coding formulae into the old regression line.

Showing this result is algebraically complex. If the least squares lines of best fit of y on x has equation $y = a + bx$, we need to show that

$$a = \tfrac{1}{r}(\alpha + \beta q - s) \qquad\qquad b = \tfrac{p}{r}\beta$$

for the result to be true. Since coding ensures that $S_{uv} = prS_{xy}$ and $S_{uu} = p^2 S_{xx}$, we see that

$$\tfrac{p}{r}\beta = \tfrac{p}{r}\frac{S_{uv}}{S_{uu}} = \tfrac{p}{r}\frac{prS_{xy}}{p^2 S_{xx}} = \frac{S_{xy}}{S_{xx}} = b$$

as required. The other identity will be left as an exercise.

Example 29.4.3. *Calculate the least squares line of best fit of y on x for the data concerning the chemical reaction described in Example 29.4.1 by first coding the data using the formulae $x = 140 + 10u, y = 3.5 + v$.*

After coding we have the data

u	−3	−2	−1	0	1	2	3
Yield y	−1.4	−1.1	−0.4	−0.1	0.9	2.0	1.4

and this leads to the summary data $n = 7$, $\sum u = 0$, $\sum v = 1.3$, $\sum u^2 = 28$, $\sum v^2 = 10.11$, $\sum uv = 15.9$ (these can almost be done in our heads). Thus we obtain $\bar{u} = 0, \bar{v} = 0.1857$ and

$$S_{uu} = 28 \qquad\qquad S_{uv} = 15.9$$

and hence the least squares line of best fit of v on u has equation $v = \alpha + \beta u$, where

$$\beta = \tfrac{15.9}{28} = 0.5679 \qquad\qquad \alpha = 0.1857 - 0\beta = 0.1857$$

so the equation is $v = 0.1857 + 0.5679u$. Thus the least squares line of best fit of y on x is

$$
\begin{aligned}
y - 3.5 &= 0.1857 + 0.5679 \times \tfrac{1}{10}(x - 140) \\
y &= 0.0568x - 4.264
\end{aligned}
$$

as before.

29.4.6. TWO LINES OF REGRESSION

There are examples where it is not obvious which of the two variables being investigated is the independent one. If we consider the case introduced previously, of the teacher comparing French and German test marks, either the French mark or the German mark could be the independent variable. Suppose, for example, that the same class took end-of-term examinations in both French and German, but that one student was absent from the French examination, while the other was absent from the German examination. The teacher might want, in the interests of fairness, to have some estimate of how those students might have performed in their missing examinations. In one case, the teacher wants to predict a German mark y on the basis of a French mark x, and so the regression line of y on x would be appropriate.

In the second case the teacher wants to predict a French mark x on the basis of a German mark y, and so the regression line of x on y would be appropriate. This is the line of the form $x = \alpha + \beta y$, where α and β have been chosen to minimise $\sum_i (x_i - \alpha - \beta y_i)^2$, the sum of the squares of the residuals. In this case, of course, the residuals $x_i - \alpha - \beta y_i$ are the horizontal distances between the datapoints and the line. The formula for the regression line of x on y is clearly similar to that for the regression line of y on x, but with the roles of x and y swapped.

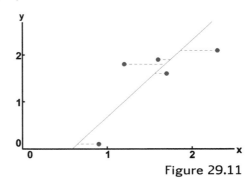

Figure 29.11

Example 29.4.4. *Find the least squares line of best fit of German marks on French marks from the dataset at the beginning of this chapter. Use it to estimate the German mark of a student who obtains a mark of 47 in the French test. Also find the least squares line of best fit of French marks on German marks from the same dataset, and use it to estimate the French mark of a student who obtains a mark of 24 in the German test.*

In Example 29.2.1 it was shown that

$$\overline{x} = 39.5 \qquad \overline{y} = 28 \qquad S_{xx} = 433 \qquad S_{yy} = 586 \qquad S_{xy} = 367$$

and so we calculate that the least squares line of best fit of y on x has equation $y = a + bx$, where

$$b = \tfrac{367}{433} = 0.8476 \qquad\qquad a = 28 - 39.5b = -5.4792$$

to four decimal places each. Thus the least squares line of best fit of y on x is

$$y = -5.4792 + 0.8476x$$

When $x = 47$, this formula predicts that $y = 34.3$, so we would predict that a student who obtains 47 in French will score 34.3 in German.

On the other hand, the least squares line of best fit of x on y will have equation $x = \alpha + \beta x$, where

$$\beta = \frac{S_{yx}}{S_{yy}} = \tfrac{367}{586} = 0.6263 \qquad\qquad \alpha = \overline{x} - \beta\overline{y} = 39.5 - 28\beta = 21.9641$$

to four decimal places each. Thus the least square line of best fit of x on y is

$$x = 21.9641 + 0.6263y$$

When $y = 24$, this formula gives $x = 37.0$, so we would predict that a student who obtains 24 in German will score 37.0 in French.

It is important, in these cases, to remember that these two regression lines are not the same. They both pass through the common point $(\overline{x}, \overline{y})$, but they have different gradients. Take care in such cases as this to use the right regression line.

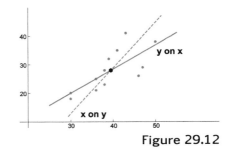

Figure 29.12

Cambridge Pre-U Mathematics

EXERCISE 29C

1. In the financial year $2004-05$, the mean income workers in the UK of different ages was as follows:

Age x (nearest 5 yrs.)	25	30	35	40	45	50	55
Salary ($£y \times 1000$s)	11.8	17.0	19.5	20.1	20.2	20.3	19.3

(Source: HMRC). Find the least squares line of best fit of salary on age, writing it in the form $y = a + bx$.

a) To estimate the salary patterns for the financial year $2010-11$, the salary figures should be increased by 22% to account for inflation. What are the values of a and b for the $2010-11$ least squares line of best fit?

b) If everyone in the country had a £1000 salary increase for the financial year $2005-06$ (they did not!), what would the values of a and b have been for the $2005-06$ line of best fit?

2. A paired dataset can be summarised as follows:

$$n = 20 \qquad \sum x = 395 \qquad \sum y = 220 \qquad \sum x^2 = 8500 \qquad \sum y^2 = 2800 \qquad \sum xy = 3900$$

Find the least squares lines of best fit of y on x and of x on y. Which would be the more useful if:

a) x is age in years, and y is the reaction time in milliseconds of a person,

b) x is the cost (in £1000) and y is the floor-space (in m^2) of a building.

3. In the year 2014 the following information describes the percentage of people in the UK who use the Internet every day.

Age x (nearest 10 years)	20	30	40	50	60	70
Percentage y%	88	85	77	67	68	60

(Source: ONS) Explain why a linear relationship between x and y might be reasonable.

Coding $x = 40 + 10u$ and $y = 70 + v$, find the least squares line of best fit of x on y, and use it to estimate the age-group 70% of which use the Internet every day.

4. Fourteen girls took two exam papers in the same subject, and their marks (as percentages) were as follows. Each girl's marks are in the same column.

Paper 1, x	65	73	42	52	84	60	70	79	60	83	57	77	54	66
Paper 2, y	78	88	60	73	92	77	84	89	70	99	73	88	70	85

Calculate the equation of the least squares line of regression of y on x.

Two girls were absent for one paper. Amanda scored 67 on Paper 1, missing Paper 2. Briony scored 81 on Paper 2, missing Paper 1. In whose case can you use your regression line to estimate the mark she should have obtained in her missing paper, and what was that mark?

5. Following a leak of radioactivity from a nuclear power station an index of exposure to radioactivity was calculated for each of eight geographical areas close to the power station. In the subsequent 10 years the incidence of death due to cancer (measured in deaths per 100000 person-years) was recorded. The data were as follows:

Area	1	2	3	4	5	6	7	8
Index x	7.6	23.5	3.9	14.8	5.9	6.8	5.3	4.8
Deaths y	62	75	54	73	37	41	55	42

a) Find the linear regression line of best fit of y on x.

b) In another region close to the power station the index of exposure was 6.0. Estimate the number of deaths per 100000 person-years in that region.

590

c) Estimate the index of exposure that might result in 40 deaths per 100000 person-years.

6. The table records the year x and the annual total emissions y of all greenhouse gases in the UK; the unit for y is the equivalent of a million ton of CO_2.

Year x	2006	2007	2008	2009	2010	2011	2012	2013
Total emissions y	762	751	732	670	687	645	657	643

(Source: ONS) Coding x and y suitably, find the least squares line of best fit for x on y, and use it to estimate the year in which the annual emissions of greenhouse gases in the UK drops to 500 millions tons of CO_2. Is this a sensible use of the regression line?

7. Complete the details of Key Fact 29.8 .

8. Given a paired dataset, consider the least squares line of best fit of y on x, and also the least squares line of best fit of x on y.

   a) Give the coordinates of a point which is sure to lie on both lines.

   b) Since they have a point in common, the two lines are equal precisely when they have the same gradient. What must be true about the dataset for these two lines of regression to be equal?

9*. Show that the equation of the least squares line of best fit for the dataset represented in the first of the frequency tables below is $y = 0.825 - 0.5x$.

		x	
		0	1
y	0	7	27
	1	33	13

		x	
		45	55
y	10	7	27
	12	33	13

With the least possible further calculation, find the equation of the least squares line of best fit for the dataset represented by the second of these frequency tables.

For Interest

There are further methods that can be used than liner regression but they are beyond the scope of this book. It is possible to fit curves of more complicated shapes to data using the least squares method. For example, the least squares quadratic of best fit to a dataset is the curve with equation $y = ax^2 + bx + c$, where a, b and c are to be chosen to minimise

$$E(a,b,c) = \sum_i [y_i - ax_i^2 - bx_i - c]^2$$

The mathematics to determine the values of a, b and c is more complicated than was required for linear regression, but it does enable us to fit a more complicated curve.

Chapter 29: Summary

- A paired dataset $(x_1, y_1), (x_2, y_2), \ldots, (x_n, y_n)$ has the quantities

$$S_{xx} = \sum_i x_i^2 - n\bar{x}^2 \qquad S_{yy} = \sum_i y_i^2 - n\bar{y}^2 \qquad S_{xy} = \sum_i x_i y_i - n\overline{xy}$$

  associated with it; these are equal to ns_x^2, ns_y^2 and n times the covariance of x and y respectively.

- (Linear) correlation, both positive and negative, is readily identified by drawing scatter diagrams:

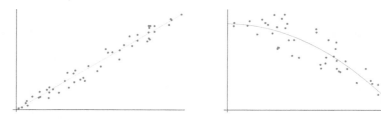

- The product-moment correlation coefficient r_{xy} for a paired dataset is

$$r_{xy} = \frac{S_{xy}}{\sqrt{S_{xx} \times S_{yy}}} \,,$$

  it always lies between -1 and 1. The product-moment correlation coefficient is unaffected by coding of x and y.

- The least squares regression line of y on x has equation

$$y = a + bx \qquad \text{where} \qquad b = \frac{S_{xy}}{S_{xx}}, \quad a = \bar{y} - b\bar{x} \,;$$

  it is the line which minimises the sums of the squares of the residuals $y_i - a - bx_i$:

$$E(a, b) = \sum_i (y_i - a - bx_i)^2 \,.$$

Permutations and Combinations

In this chapter we will learn to:

- solve problems about selections,

- solve problems about arrangements, including problems involving repetitions and restrictions.

30.1 Counting

Mathematicians are continually wanting to count things:

- If ten people compete in race, how many different ways are there in which gold, silver and bronze medals can be awarded?

- How many different ways are there in which a pack of 16 cards can be shuffled?

- How many integers are there between 1 and 1000 (inclusive) that are divisible by neither 2 nor 3?

- In how many different ways can the letters ABRACADABRA be rearranged?

- If ten points are chosen on the circumference of a circle, and every point is joined to every other point by a straight line, how many triangles are created in the process?

- How many different ways are there of sitting six people at a circular table at a dinner party, if there are three married couples attending, and nobody should sit next to his or her partner?

- How many different completed Sudoku grids are there?

The process of finding the answers to questions such as these (720, 20922789888000, 333, 83160, 120, 192, 6670903752021072936960) is part of the branch of mathematics known as **combinatorics**.

Problems of this nature can be solved by a number of techniques, the most elementary of which is called **exhaustion**, namely that of listing the solutions.

Example 30.1.1. *Now many different ways are there of rearranging the letters ABC?*

This problem is small enough for us to be able to list all six solutions ABC, ACB, BAC, BCA, CAB, CBA.

On the other hand, we do not want to have to list all the different ways of shuffling a pack of 52 cards. It would take a very long time to list all 8×10^{67} solutions, and it would be challenging to ensure that we had not missed one out.

When counting solutions, it is sometimes challenging to be sure that we have found all of them. Equally difficult is ensuring that we do not **double-count**; we must not count a particular solution more than once.

Example 30.1.2. *Show that there are* 333 *numbers between* 1 *and* 1000 *(inclusive) that are divisible by neither* 2 *nor* 3.

There are 500 even numbers between 1 and 1000, and 333 multiples of 3. This does not mean, however, that there are $1000 - (500 + 333) = 167$ numbers that are divisible by neither 2 nor 3, since there are numbers that are divisible by both 2 and 3 (the multiples of 6). In the calculation $100 - (500 + 333)$, we have effectively subtracted 2 for each multiple of 6 (1 as a multiple of 2, and 1 as a multiple of 3). Since there are 166 multiples of 6, there are in fact $500 + 333 - 166 = 667$ numbers that are divisible by either 2 or 3, and hence there are 333 numbers that are multiples of neither.

Example 30.1.3. *How many numbers are there between* 1 *and* 1000 *(inclusive) that are divisible by none of* 2, 3 *or* 5?

There are 500 multiples of 2, 333 multiples of 3 and 200 multiples of 5. There are also 166 multiples of 6, 100 multiples of 10 and 66 multiples of 15. Finally, there are 33 multiples of 30.

Putting this information into a Venn diagram enables us to avoid double-counting, and we deduce that there are 266 numbers between 1 and 1000 that are not multiples of 2, 3 or 5.

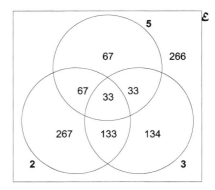

Figure 30.1

When faced with questions of this sort, we want to try to avoid simple exhaustion (problems rapidly become too complex to be handled that way) while avoiding double-counting.

Example 30.1.4. *How many ways are there are ordering the letters ABCD so that no letter is in its true alphabetical position (so that A is not in the first position, B is not in the second position, and so on)?*

It is possible to list all acceptable orderings

BADC   BCDA   BDAC   CDAB   CDBA   CADB   DCBA   DCAB   DABC

finding a total of 9 possible ways, but it is not particularly easy to be certain that we have found all the possible orderings. A more elegant method is desirable.

30.2 Permutations

Up to now, we have dealt with problems simple enough for exhaustion to provide an answer. This approach is not practical, however, when the number of possibilities to be counted becomes large. We would not want to work out how many different hands, containing five cards, can be dealt from an ordinary deck of 52 cards, for example. We need a more theoretical approach to handle such questions

It is useful to start with an easier situation. Suppose that you have the three letters A, B and C, one on each of three separate cards, and that you are going to arrange them in a line to form 'words'. How many three-letter words are there?

In this case the number of words is small enough for you to write them out in full.

ABC   ACB   BCA   BAC   CAB   CBA

You could also show the possible choices by using a tree diagram. You have 3 choices for the first letter: one of A, B or C. Having chosen the first letter, you then have just 2 choices for the second letter (whichever of the three letters has not already been chosen). Once the third letter has been chosen, there is only one letter available to be the third letter in the word.

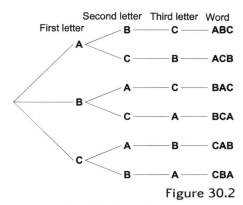

Figure 30.2

So altogether there are $3 \times 2 \times 1 = 6$ possible words that you can make with three letters.

Using a similar argument you can find the number of words that you can make from four letters A, B, C and D.

- You have 4 possibilities for the first letter.

- Having chosen the first letter, you then have 3 possibilities for the second letter.

- Having chosen the first two letters, you then have 2 possibilities for the third letter.

- You then have only 1 possibility for the last letter.

Therefore there are $4 \times 3 \times 2 \times 1 = 24$ possible words. They are

ABCD	ABDC	ACBD	ACDB	ADBC	ADCB
BACD	BADC	BCAD	BCDA	BDAC	BDCA
CABD	CADB	CBAD	CBDA	CDAB	CDBA
DABC	DACB	DBAC	DBCA	DCAB	DCBA

You can now generalise this result to the case where there are n distinct letters. At the same time, we should realise that we do not need just to consider rearranging letters into 'words'. We are considering the number of rearrangements of any collection of n distinct objects, be they letters, numbers or hedgehogs. Each rearrangement of a collection of objects is called a **permutation** of those objects.

Key Fact 30.1 Permutations

The number of permutations of n distinct objects is

$$n! = n \times (n-1) \times (n-2) \times \cdots \times 3 \times 2 \times 1$$

Recall our introduction of the factorial function in Chapter 10.

As mentioned in Chapter 10, the value of $n!$ increases very rapidly. While $16! = 20922789888000$ is large enough (this was the answer to the question of the number of ways of shuffling a deck of 16 cards), the number of ways of shuffling an ordinary deck of 52 cards is

$$52! = 80658175170943878571660636856403766975289505440883277824000000000000 \approx 8.07 \times 10^{67}$$

That 52! is so large is one of the reasons why card games are so popular!

Suppose now that we have more letters than we need to make a word. For example, suppose that we have the seven letters A, B, C, D, E, F and G but that we want to make a four-letter word.

- We have 7 choices for the first letter.

- Having chosen the first letter, we have 6 choices for the second letter.

- Having chosen the first two letters, you have 5 choices for the third letter.

- Having chosen the first three letters, you have 4 choices for the fourth (and last) letter.

The number of permutations of 4 letters chosen from 7 letters (that is, the number of four-letter words) is therefore $7 \times 6 \times 5 \times 4$. This result can be written concisely in terms of factorials.

$$7 \times 6 \times 5 \times 4 = \frac{7 \times 6 \times 5 \times 4 \times 3 \times 2 \times 1}{3 \times 2 \times 1} = \frac{7!}{3!} = \frac{7!}{(7-4)!}.$$

This is an illustration of a general rule.

Key Fact 30.2 The Permutation Symbol

The number of different permutations of r objects which can be made from n distinct objects is denoted ${}^nP_r$, and is equal to

$$ {}^nP_r = \frac{n!}{(n-r)!}, \qquad 0 \le r \le n.$$

Example 30.2.1. *Eight runners are hoping to take part in a race, but the track has only six lanes. In how many ways can six of the eight runners be assigned to lanes?*

The number of permutations is

$$ {}^8P_6 = \frac{8!}{(8-6)!} = \frac{8!}{2!} = 20160$$

Example 30.2.2. *Eight people, A, B, ..., H, are arranged randomly in a line. In how many ways can they be arranged so that A and B are not next to each other?*

There are 8 places where A can go. If A is placed at either end of the line, then there is only one place in the line adjacent to A, and so there are 6 places where B can go. If A is not placed in the middle of the line, there are two places adjacent to A, and so there are 5 places where B can go. Thus there are $2 \times 6 + 6 \times 5 = 42$ ways to position A and B so that they are not next to each other. There are then $6! = 120$ ways of arranging the remaining six people in the remaining six places, and so there are $42 \times 6! = 30240$ ways of arranging the eight people.

Another, more elegant, approach uses a trick. We shall first find out the number of arrangements that have A and B next to each other. There are $7!$ ways of arranging the 7 people $B, C, ..., H$. For each of these arrangements, A can be inserted either immediately to the left or to the right of B, yielding a permutation of the eight people with A and B next to each other. Thus we deduce that there are $2 \times 7!$ permutations of these eight people. Since there are $8!$ permutations of the eight people altogether, there must be $8! - 2 \times 7! = 30240$ permutations for which A and B are not together. In this second method, we effectively regarded A and B as a single 'block' (that could appear either as AB or as BA) and considered the number of permutations of the blocks $AB/BA, C, D, ... H$. It is frequently easier to count permutations when a particular property is true rather than when it is false!

Now that we have information about permutations, we can return to Example 30.1.4, and establish the result more elegantly.

Example 30.2.3. *Show that there are exactly 9 permutations of the four letters A, B, C and D so that no letter is in its correct alphabetical position.*

There are 4! = 24 permutations altogether. There are 3! = 6 permutations of the four letters which have A in its correct place, and similarly for B, C or D. There are 2! = 2 permutations of the four letters which have both A and B in their correct place (and similarly for any other pair of two letters). There is only one permutation that has any three of the four letters in their correct place, since it is the permutation ABCD where all letters are correctly placed (once three letters are correct, the fourth must be so as well).

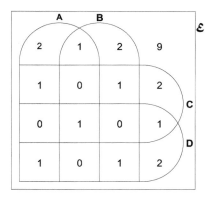

Figure 30.3

If we let **A** be the set of permutations for which A is in the correct place, with similar meanings for **B**, **C** and **D**, we can derive the Venn diagram shown. The numbers in each region of the Venn diagram represent the number of permutations that belong to each region. It is therefore clear that there are 9 permutations that belong to none of the four sets, as required.

It is quite interesting to see an example of a fully general Venn diagram involving four sets.

In this section emphasis is placed on the fact that the objects being arranged have to be distinct. That is, you have to be able to identify each object uniquely. The next section shows how to tackle the permutation problem when the objects are not distinct.

30.3   Permutations of Non-Distinct Objects

Recall that there were 4! = 24 permutations of the letters A, B, C and D. Suppose now that the letters B, C and D are all replaced by the letter Z. How many permutations will there be now?

Suppose temporarily that B was replaced by Z_1, C by Z_2 and D by Z_3, so that we can still distinguish the different Zs. The 24 permutations of A, B, C and D now become

$$
\begin{array}{cccccc}
AZ_1Z_2Z_3 & AZ_1Z_3Z_2 & AZ_2Z_1Z_3 & AZ_2Z_3Z_1 & AZ_3Z_1Z_2 & AZ_3Z_2Z_1 \\
Z_1AZ_2Z_3 & Z_1AZ_3Z_2 & Z_2AZ_1Z_3 & Z_2AZ_3Z_1 & Z_3AZ_1Z_2 & Z_3AZ_2Z_1 \\
Z_1Z_2AZ_3 & Z_1Z_3AZ_2 & Z_2Z_1AZ_3 & Z_2Z_3AZ_1 & Z_3Z_1AZ_2 & Z_3Z_2AZ_1 \\
Z_1Z_2Z_3A & Z_1Z_3Z_2A & Z_2Z_1Z_3A & Z_2Z_3Z_1A & Z_3Z_1Z_2A & Z_3Z_2Z_1A
\end{array}
$$

There are 4 positions where A can appear. Then the letters Z_1, Z_2, Z_3 can occur in any order in the remaining three positions. Each of the four rows in the above array shows the possible permutations of A, Z_1, Z_2 and Z_3, with A occurring in the same place for each permutation in any row.

If we remove the subscripts, and so can no longer distinguish between the Zs, then all six permutations in the first row become just one permutation AZZZ, the permutations in the second row all become ZAZZ, those in the third row become ZZAZ, while the permutations in the final row become ZZZA. Each of the different permutations of A, Z, Z and Z is effectively repeated 3! = 6 times when we distinguish between the Zs, since there are 3! = 6 permutations of three distinct objects. Thus there are exactly $\frac{4!}{3!} = 4$ permutations of A, Z, Z and Z, these being

$$AZZZ \quad ZAZZ \quad ZZAZ \quad ZZZA$$

This argument can be generalised. If there are n objects, r of which are identical, then each of the permutations of these objects would be repeated $r!$ times if the r identical objects were made indistinguishable. Since there are $n!$ permutations of n distinct objects, we deduce that there are $\frac{n!}{r!}$ permutations in this case.

Key Fact 30.3 Permutations With Identical Objects

There are $\frac{n!}{r!}$ permutations of n objects of which r are identical.

This idea can be extended still further! If we consider the letters A, A, B, B, B and C, how many permutations are there of these letters? Suppose that we make the As distinguishable and also make the Bs distinguishable, and consider the resulting 6! permutations:

- Every permutation of the form $\ldots A_1 \ldots A_2 \ldots$ will be matched by a permutation of the form $\ldots A_2 \ldots A_1 \ldots$, where all the other letters in the permutation are unchanged; the two As have just swapped positions.

- Every permutation of the form $\ldots B_1 \ldots B_2 \ldots B_3 \ldots$ will be matched by five other permutations: $\ldots B_1 \ldots B_3 \ldots B_2 \ldots, \ldots B_2 \ldots B_1 \ldots B_3 \ldots, \ldots B_2 \ldots B_3 \ldots B_1 \ldots, \ldots B_3 \ldots B_1 \ldots B_2 \ldots$ and $\ldots B_3 \ldots B_2 \ldots B_1 \ldots$, where all the other letters in the permutation are unchanged; the three Bs are occupying all possible permutations of each other.

Thus there are $\frac{6!}{2! \times 3!} = 60$ permutations.

Key Fact 30.4 Permutations with Identical Objects — General Case

The number of distinct permutations of n objects, of which p are identical to each other, and then q of the remainder are identical, and r of the remainder are identical, and so on, is

$$\frac{n!}{p! \times q! \times r! \times \cdots}, \qquad \text{where } p + q + r + \cdots = n.$$

Example 30.3.1. *Find the number of distinct permutations of the letters of the word MISSISSIPPI.*

The number of letters is 11, of which there are 4 Ss, 4 Is, 2 Ps and 1 M. The number of distinct permutations of the letters is therefore

$$\frac{11!}{4! \times 4! \times 2! \times 1!} = 34650.$$

EXERCISE 30A

1. Seven different cars are to be loaded on to a transporter truck. In how many different ways can the cars be arranged?

2. How many numbers are there between 1245 and 5421 inclusive which contain each of the digits 1, 2, 4 and 5 once and once only?

3. An artist is going to arrange five paintings in a row on a wall. In how many ways can this be done?

4. Ten athletes are running in a 100-metre race. In how many different ways can the first three places be filled?

5. By writing out all the possible arrangements of D_1, E_1, E_2, D_2, show that there are $\frac{4!}{2! \times 2!} = 6$ different arrangements of the word DEED.

6. A typist has five letters and five addressed envelopes. In how many different ways can the letters be placed in each envelope without getting every letter in the right envelope?

7. How many different arrangements can be made of the letters in the word STATISTICS?

8. a) Calculate the number of arrangements of the letters in the word NUMBER.

    b) How many of these arrangements begin and end with a vowel?

9. How many different numbers can be formed by taking one, two, three and four digits from the digits 1, 2, 7 and 8, if repetitions are not allowed? Of these numbers, how many are greater than 200?

10. Eight people attend a dinner party, and are seated around a circular dining table. Three of the eight people want to sit together. In how many ways can the eight guests sit down for dinner?

11. A bus contains 12 seats that face forwards, 12 seats that face backwards, and 18 seats that face sideways. A group of 10 passengers gets on to an empty bus. In how many ways can they be seated, if 4 passengers have booked forward-facing seats, 2 have booked backward-facing seats and the remainder have booked side-facing seats?

12. Four boys and three girls stand in a line. How many ways are there for them to stand, if the pattern of boys and girls is symmetrical (BBGGGBB is acceptable, but BBBGGGB is not)?

13. I eat a yoghurt for breakfast every day. This week I have three raspberry, two strawberry and two peach yoghurts. In how many different orders can I eat them?

   I do not want to eat my two peach yoghurts on consecutive days. In how many ways can I do this?

14*. Five men and eight women stand in a line. In how many ways can they do this? In how many ways can they do this if no two men stand together?

30.4 Combinations

In the last section we considered permutations (arrangements), for which the order of the objects is significant when you count the number of different possibilities. In some circumstances, however, the order of selection does not matter. For example, if you were dealt a hand of 13 cards from a standard pack of 52 playing cards, you would not be interested in the order in which you received the cards. When a selection is made from a set of objects and the order of selection is unimportant it is called a **combination**.

Example 30.4.1. *How many different collections of three letters can be chosen from A, B, C and D?*

We start by considering the $^4P_3 = 24$ permutations of 3 letters that can be chosen from A, B, C and D:

ABC	ACB	BAC	BCA	CAB	CBA
ABD	ADB	BAD	BDA	DAB	DBA
ACD	ADC	CAD	CDA	DAC	DCA
BCD	BDC	CBD	CDB	DBC	DCB

In the above array, the permutations in each row involve the same collection of three letters out of the four available; since the order of elements matters when considering permutations, each collection of three letters has been presented $3! = 6$ times, once for each permutation of those three letters. Thus there are exactly $\frac{24}{3!} = 4$ sets of three letters that can be chosen from four.

We showed that there were

$$\frac{^4P_3}{3!} = \frac{4!}{(4-3)! \times 3!}$$

sets of three letters than can be chosen from the four available. We could have obtained this result using a different argument, using ideas of permutations. There are $\frac{4!}{1! \times 3!}$ permutations of the letters N, Y, Y and Y (since three of the four letters are identical. These permutations can be used to determine the choices of sets of three letters: for any permutation of N, Y, Y and Y, pick the letter A if the first letter in the permutation is Y, pick the letter B if the second letter in the permutation is Y, pick the letter C if the third letter in the permutation is Y, and pick the letter D if the fourth letter in the permutation is Y. Since there are three copies of Y, we shall end up by picking exactly three letters out of the four available. Thus, for example, the permutation YNYY corresponds to selecting the letters A, C and D. Thus $\frac{4!}{1! \times 3!}$, the number of permutations of YYYN, is also the number of choices of three letters out of four.

These results can be generalised.

Key Fact 30.5 Combinations and Binomial Coefficients

A **combination** is a selection in which the order of the objects selected is unimportant. The number of different combinations of r objects selected from n distinct objects is the Binomial coefficient

$$^nC_r = \binom{n}{r} = \frac{n!}{r! \times (n-r)!}. \qquad 0 \le r \le n.$$

This interpretation of the Binomial coefficients was referred to previously in Chapter 10

Example 30.4.2. *The manager of a football team has a squad of 16 players. He needs to choose 11 to play in a match. How many possible teams can be chosen?*

The number of teams is $^{16}C_{11} = \frac{16!}{11! \times 5!} = 4368$.

This example is not entirely realistic because players will not be equally capable of playing in every position, but it does show how many possible teams there are. It is important to decide whether this question is about permutations or combinations. Clearly the important issue here is the people in the team and not their order of selection. Therefore this question is about combinations rather than permutations.

Alternatively, the manager could have selected the team by choosing which five players to drop. This approach would tell us that the number of teams was $^{16}C_5 = 4368$.

Example 30.4.3. *A team of 5 people, which must contain 3 men and 2 women, is chosen from 8 men and 7 women. How many different teams can be selected?*

There are $^8C_3 = \frac{8!}{5!3!} = 56$ ways of choosing 3 men for the team, and $^7C_2 = \frac{7!}{5!2!} = 21$ ways of choosing 2 women for the team. Thus there are $56 \times 21 = 1176$ possible teams.

You can now apply some of these counting methods to probability examples.

Example 30.4.4. *Five cards are dealt without replacement from a standard pack of 52 cards. Find the probability that exactly three of the five cards are hearts.*

There are $^{52}C_5 = \frac{52!}{47!5!}$ possible hands of five cards that can be dealt, all equally likely. This is an extremely large sample space, and so we certainly do not want to try to list all the possible hands containing three hearts!

We want to know how many five-card hands there are that contain exactly three hearts. Such a hand must be put together by choosing three out of the 13 heart cards, and then choosing two out of the 39 cards that are not hearts. Thus the number of five-card hands containing exactly three hearts is

$$^{13}C_3 \times {}^{39}C_2$$

and hence the probability of being dealt a card containing three hearts is

$$\frac{^{13}C_3 \times {}^{39}C_2}{^{52}C_5} = 0.0815$$

EXERCISE 30B

1. How many different three-card hands can be dealt from a pack of 52 cards?

2. Four letters are chosen from the word RANDOMLY. What is the probability that they are all consonants?

3. From a group of 30 boys and 32 girls, two girls and two boys are to be chosen to represent their school. How many possible selections are there?

4. Codes of three letters are made up using the letters A, C, T and G. Find how many different codes are possible:

   a) if all three letters must be different,

   b) if letters may be repeated.

5. A history exam paper contains eight questions, four in Part A and four in Part B. Candidates are required to attempt five questions. In how many ways can this be done if

   a) there are no restrictions,

   b) at least two questions from Part A and at least two questions from Part B must be attempted?

6. A committee of three people is to be selected from four women and five men. The rules state that there must be at least one man and one woman on the committee. In how many different ways can the committee be chosen?

   Subsequently one of the men and one of the women marry each other. The rules also state that a married couple may not both serve on the committee. In how many ways can the committee be chosen now?

7. A box of one dozen eggs contains one that is bad. If three eggs are chosen at random, what is the probability that one of them will be bad?

8. In a game of bridge the pack of 52 cards is shared equally between all four players. What is the probability that one particular player has no hearts?

9. A bag contains 20 chocolates, 15 toffees and 12 peppermints. If three sweets are chosen at random, what is the probability that they are

   a) all different,
   b) all chocolates,
   c) all the same,
   d) all not chocolates?

10. A team of four is to be chosen from 5 girls and 6 boys. In how many ways can the team be chosen if:

    a) there are no restrictions,

    b) 3 girls and 1 boy are required,

    c) more girls than boys are required?

11. a) 20 points are marked on the circumference of a circle. How many chords can be obtained by joining them in pairs? How many triangles are created by joining them in triples?

    b) How many different diagonals does a 20-sided polygon have, if a diagonal is any line joining two non-consecutive vertices?

12*. n points are marked on the circumference of a circle. Every one of these n points is joined to every other point by a chord. The n points are positioned so that no three chords are concurrent.

    a) How many chords have been drawn?

    b) Every point inside the circle where two chords intersect is called a vertex. How many vertices are there?

    c) Into how many regions has the circle been divided?

13*. Let f_n be the number of ways of ascending a flight of n steps, if you are allowed to go up one or two steps at a time.

    a) Show that $f_1 = 1, f_2 = 2$, and explain why

    $$f_{n+2} = f_{n+1} + f_n, \qquad n \geq 1,$$

    so that $f_n = F_{n+1}$ is the $(n+1)^{\text{st}}$ Fibonacci number.

    b) For any $0 \leq k \leq \frac{1}{2}n$, how many different ways are there of ascending a flight of stairs if you go up two steps a total of k times, and one step the remaining $n - 2k$ times?

    c) Explain why

    $$F_{n+1} = \sum_{k=0}^{\frac{1}{2}n} \binom{n-k}{k}$$

    for any $n \geq 0$ (if $\frac{1}{2}n$ is a fraction, the largest value of k to be summed over is the integer part of $\frac{1}{2}n$).

30.5 Applications

In this section we shall consider problems involve counting permutations and combinations where some additional condition is applied. We have already seen some examples of this type of problem. Solving these questions often involves applying some trick or other. We shall consider some examples.

Example 30.5.1. *Find the number of ways of arranging 6 women and 3 men to stand in a row so that all 3 men are standing together.*

Regard the three men as a single unit. At first, then, we have 7 objects to arrange: the 6 women and the block of men. There are 7! ways in which this can be done.

There are, of course, 3! ways of arranging the 3 men within their block. Thus there are $7! \times 3! = 30240$ ways of arranging the men and women as required.

Example 30.5.2. *Find the number of ways of arranging 6 women and 3 men in a row so that no two men are standing next to one another.*

The easiest way to ensure that no two men stand next to each other is to arrange the women first. There are 6! ways in which they can be arranged. For any one of these arrangements, there are 7 'gaps': five between successive women and one at each end. Here is one such arrangement, with the 'gaps' marked as boxes.

$$\square \quad W_3 \quad \square \quad W_4 \quad \square \quad W_1 \quad \square \quad W_6 \quad \square \quad W_5 \quad \square \quad W_2 \quad \square$$

The 3 men must now go into some of these 7 gaps! Since no two men are to stand next to each other, at most one man goes into each gap. We must therefore choose 3 gaps for the men to go into. There are $^7C_3$ ways of doing this. There are then 3! ways of deciding how the three men go into these three gaps. Thus the total number of arrangements is

$$6! \times {}^7C_3 \times 3! = 151200.$$

Note that we could also have obtained the $^7C_3 \times 3! = 7 \times 6 \times 5$ ways of arranging the men into gaps by saying that the first man has 7 choices, the second man 6 choices and the third man 5 choices of gaps to go into.

It is also worth noting that the answers to the last two examples, when added together, do not give 9!, which is the total number of arrangements of 9 people without any restriction at all. This is because there is a third possibility. If two men were standing together and the third man was separated from these two by some women, then it would not be the case that all the men were together but neither would it be the case that the three men were all apart from one another.

Example 30.5.3. *A group of 12 people consisting of 6 married couples is arranged at random in a line for a photograph. Find the probability that each wife is standing next to her husband.*

The number of unrestricted arrangements is 12!. Each of them is equally likely.

If each husband and wife 'couple' is to stand together, then you can consider each couple as a unit. There are therefore 6 such units. The number of permutations of these units is 6!.

But the first couple H_1, W_1 can be arranged in 2! ways, either H_1W_1 or W_1H_1. This applies equally to the other five couples. Therefore the number of arrangements in which each couple stands together is $6! \times (2!)^6$. The desired probability is thus

$$\frac{6! \times 2^6}{12!} = \frac{1}{10395} = 9.62 \times 10^{-5}$$

Example 30.5.4. *Four letters are to be selected from the letters in the word RIGIDITY. How many different combinations are there?*

The letters are not all distinct, since there are three Is, so the answer is not simply $^8C_4$. The easiest way through this problem is to consider various cases:

- If no Is are chosen, we are simply choosing 4 symbols out of R, G, D, T, Y. There are $^5C_4 = 5$ ways of doing this, the combinations being

$$\text{RGDT} \quad \text{RGDY} \quad \text{RGTY} \quad \text{RDTY} \quad \text{GDTY}$$

- If one I is chosen, we are now choosing 3 symbols out of R, G, D, T, Y. There are $^5C_3 = 10$ ways of doing this, the combinations being

$$\begin{array}{ccccc} \text{IRGD} & \text{IRGT} & \text{IRGY} & \text{IRDT} & \text{IRDY} \\ \text{IRTY} & \text{IGDT} & \text{IGDY} & \text{IGTY} & \text{IDTY} \end{array}$$

- If two Is are chosen, we are now choosing 2 symbols out of R, G, D, T, Y. There are $^5C_2 = 10$ ways of doing this, the combinations being

$$\begin{array}{ccccc} \text{IIRG} & \text{IIRD} & \text{IIRT} & \text{IIRY} & \text{IIGD} \\ \text{IIGT} & \text{IIGY} & \text{IIDT} & \text{IIDY} & \text{IITY} \end{array}$$

- If all three Is are chosen, we must choose 1 symbol out of R, G, D, T, Y. There are $^5C_1 = 5$ ways of doing this, the combinations being

$$\text{IIIR} \quad \text{IIIG} \quad \text{IIID} \quad \text{IIIT} \quad \text{IIIY}$$

Thus the total number of ways of choosing 4 letters is $5 + 10 + 10 + 5 = 30$.

It is worth noting the some counting questions do not involve either permutations or combinations.

Example 30.5.5. *How many factors does the number* $11243232 = 2^5 \times 3^3 \times 7 \times 11 \times 13^2$ *have?*

If n is a factor of 11243232, then $2, 3, 7, 11$ and 13 are the only prime numbers that can divide it, and not all of them need to be factors. Indeed, the prime factorisation of n must be of the form

$$n = 2^a \times 3^b \times 7^c \times 11^d \times 13^e$$

where a, b, c, d, e are non-negative integers. Since n has to be a factor of 11243232, we must have

$$0 \le a \le 5 \qquad 0 \le b \le 3 \qquad 0 \le c \le 1 \qquad 0 \le d \le 1 \qquad 0 \le e \le 2$$

Moreover, it is clear that we have a different factor of 11243232 for each choice of integers a, b, c, d, e which satisfy these inequalities. Thus 11243232 has a total of $6 \times 4 \times 2 \times 2 \times 3 = 288$ factors (there are 6 choices for the integer a, 4 choices for the integer b, and so on).

EXERCISE 30C

1. The letters of the word CONSTANTINOPLE are written on 14 cards, one on each card. The cards are shuffled and then arranged in a straight line.

   a) How many different possible arrangements are there?

   b) How many arrangements begin with P?

   c) How many arrangements start and end with O?

   d) How many arrangements are there where no two vowels are next to each other?

2. A coin is tossed 10 times.

   a) How many different sequences of heads and tails are possible?

   b) How many different sequences containing six heads and four tails are possible?

   c) What is the probability of getting six heads and four tails?

3. Eight cards are selected with replacement from a standard pack of 52 playing cards, which contains 12 picture cards, 20 odd-numbered cards and 20 even-numbered cards.

   a) How many different sequences of eight cards are possible?

b) How many of the sequences in part (a) will contain three picture cards, three odd-numbered cards and two even-numbered cards?

c) Use parts (a) and (b) to determine the probability of getting three picture cards, three odd-numbered cards and two even-numbered cards if eight cards are selected with replacement from a standard pack of 52 playing cards.

4. Eight women and five men are standing in a line.

a) How many arrangements are possible if any individual can stand in any position?

b) In how many arrangements will all five men be standing next to one another?

c) In how many arrangements will no two men be standing next to one another?

5. Each of the digits 1, 1, 2, 3, 3, 4, 6 is written on a separate card. The seven cards are then laid out in a row to form a 7-digit number.

a) How many distinct 7-digit numbers are there?

b) How many of these 7-digit numbers are even?

c) How many of these 7-digit numbers are divisible by 4?

d) How many of these 7-digit numbers start and end with the same digit?

6. Three families, the Mehtas, the Campbells and the Lams, go to the cinema together to watch a film. Mr. & Mrs. Mehta take their daughter Indira, Mr. & Mrs. Campbell take their sons Paul and John, and Mrs. Lam comes without her husband, bringing her children Susi, Kim and Lee. The families occupy a single row with eleven seats.

a) In how many ways could the eleven people be seated if there were no restriction?

b) In how many ways could the eleven people sit down so that the members of each family are all sitting together?

c) In how many of the arrangements will no two adults be sitting next to one another?

7. The letters of the word POSSESSES are written on nine cards, one on each card. The cards are shuffled and four of them are selected and arranged in a straight line.

a) How many possible selections are there of four letters?

b) How many arrangements are there of four letters?

8. I have 5 books, each by a different author. The authors are Austen, Brontë, Clarke, Dickens and Eliot.

a) If I arrange the books in a random order on my bookshelf, find the probability that the authors are in alphabetical order with Austen on the left.

b) If I choose two of the books at random, find the probability that I choose the books written by Austen and Brontë.

c) How many ways are there of arranging the books on my bookshelf so that no book is adjacent to its alphabetical neighbour or neighbours (so that the Brontë novel is not adjacent to either the Austen or the Clarke book, and so on)?

9. What positive integers have an odd number of factors?

10*. Suppose that n, k are integers, with $1 \leq k \leq n$.

a) How many subsets of $\{1, 2, 3, \ldots, n+1\}$ are there which have $k+1$ elements?

b) How many subsets of $\{1, 2, 3, \ldots, n+1\}$ are there which have $k+1$ elements and whose greatest element is $m+1$?

c) Prove that

$$\binom{n+1}{k+1} = \sum_{m=k}^{n} \binom{m}{k}$$

11*. How many ways are there of climbing a flight of 15 steps if I take either one or two steps at a time, but I never take two steps at a time twice in a row?

Chapter 30: Summary

- The number of permutations of n distinct objects is $n! = n \times (n-1) \times \cdots \times 2 \times 1$.

- The number of permutations of r objects which can be made from n distinct objects is

$$^{n}P_{r} = \frac{n!}{(n-r)!}, \qquad 0 \le r \le n.$$

- The number of permutations of n objects, amongst which one collection of p objects are indistinguishable, another collection of q objects are indistinguishable, another collection of r objects are indistinguishable, and so on, is

$$\frac{n!}{a!b!c!\cdots}, \text{where} \quad p+q+r+\cdots = n.$$

- The number of ways of choosing r objects from a set of n objects is

$$^{n}C_{r} = \binom{n}{r} = \frac{n!}{r!(n-r)!}, \qquad 0 \le r \le n.$$

1. The costs, x, of all telephone calls costing over $0.40 made by a household over a period of three months are as follows.

0.92	0.66	0.46	0.42	0.54	0.41	0.49	0.59	0.75	0.52	0.42
0.40	0.49	0.52	0.64	0.48	0.57	0.46	0.49	0.42	0.65	0.73
0.40	1.12	0.94	0.76	0.48	0.85	1.66	0.40	0.50		

You may assume that $\sum x = 19.14$.

a) For this data obtain the median, the mean and the mode.

b) Which of the median, mean and mode would be the best to use to give the average cost of a phone call costing over $0.40? Give a reason for your answer.

c) In the same period, the number of calls which cost $0.40 or under was 125, with mean cost $0.142. Find the mean cost of all the calls for the period.

2. The number of times each week that a factory machine broke down was noted over a period of 50 consecutive weeks. The results are given in the following table.

No. of breakdowns	0	1	2	3	4	5	6
No. of weeks	2	12	14	8	8	4	2

a) Find the mean number of breakdowns in this period. Is this value exact or an estimate?

b) Give the mode and median of the number of breakdowns.

3. The following table shows data about the time taken (in seconds, to the nearest second) for each one of a series of 75 similar chemical experiments.

Time (s)	50-60	61-65	66-70	71-75	76-86
No. of experiments	4	13	26	22	10

a) A calculation using the data in the table gave an estimate of 69.64 seconds for the mean time of the experiments. Explain why this value is an estimate.

b) Estimate the median of the times taken for completing the experiment.

c) It was discovered later that the four experiments in the class 50-60 had actually taken 57, 59, 59 and 60 seconds. State, without more calculation, what effect (if any) there would be on the estimates of the median and mean if this information were taken into account. (OCR, adapt.)

4. An ordinary dice was thrown 50 times and the resulting scores were summarised in a frequency table. The mean score was calculated to be 3.42. It was later found that the frequencies 12 and 9, of two consecutive scores, had been swapped. What is the correct value of the mean?

5. Three hundred pupils were asked to keep a record of the total time they spent watching television during the final week of their summer holiday. The times are summarised in the following table.

No. t of hours	$0 \leq t < 5$	$5 \leq t < 10$	$10 \leq t < 15$	$15 \leq t < 20$
Frequency	4	21	43	62
No. t of hours	$20 \leq t < 25$	$25 \leq t < 30$	$30 \leq t < 35$	$35 \leq t < 40$
Frequency	90	56	18	6

a) Estimate the mean viewing time.

b) State two sources of inaccuracy in your estimate of the mean.

c) Find an estimate of the median viewing time.

d) What do the values of the mean and median indicate about the skewness of the data?

6. It is sometimes said that for any set of quantitative data, the median Q_2, mode m and mean $\bar{x}$ are such that either $\bar{x} \leq Q_2 \leq m$ or $m \leq Q_2 \leq \bar{x}$. Is this true of the data in Question 2? Show that the statement is untrue for the data in the table on the right.

x	1	2	3	4	5
f	2	1	11	9	7

7. The table gives the prices (in dollars) of shares in 10 firms on Monday and Tuesday of a particular week. The Monday price is m, the Tuesday price is t, and $d = t - m$.

Firm	A	B	C	D	E	F	G	H	I	J
m	151	162	200	233	287	302	303	571	936	1394
t	144	179	182	252	273	322	260	544	990	1483
d	−7	17	−18	19	−14	20	−43	−27	54	89

a) Calculate $\bar{m}, \bar{t}$ and $\bar{d}$. Does $\bar{d} = \bar{t} - \bar{m}$?

b) Calculate the medians of m, t and d. Is the median of d equal to the difference of the medians of t and m?

8. Seven mature robins (*Erithacus rubecula*) were caught and their wingspans were measured. The results, in centimetres, were as follows.

$$23.1 \quad 22.7 \quad 22.1 \quad 24.2 \quad 23.9 \quad 20.9 \quad 25.2$$

Here are the corresponding figures for seven mature house sparrows (*Passer domesticus*).

$$22.6 \quad 24.1 \quad 23.5 \quad 21.8 \quad 21.0 \quad 24.4 \quad 22.8$$

Find the mean and standard deviation of each species' wingspan, and use these statistics to compare the two sets of figures.

9. The depth of water in a lake was measured at 50 different points on the surface of the lake. The depths, x metres, are summarised by $\sum x = 934.5$ and $\sum x^2 = 19275.81$.

a) Find the mean and variance of the depths.

b) Some weeks later the water level in the lake rose by 0.23 m. What would be the mean and variance of the depths taken at the same points on the lake as before?

10. The lengths of 120 nails of nominal length 3 cm were measured, each correct to the nearest 0.05 cm. The results are summarised in the following table.

Length (cm)	2.85	2.90	2.95	3.00	3.05	3.10	3.15
Frequency	1	11	27	41	26	12	2

a) Estimate the standard deviation.

b) It is claimed that for a roughly symmetrical distribution the statistic obtained by dividing the interquartile range by the standard deviation is approximately 1.3. Calculate the value of this statistic for these data, and comment.

11. Three statistics students, Ali, Les and Sam, spent the day fishing. They caught three different types of fish and recorded the type and mass (correct to the nearest 0.01 kg) of each fish caught. At 4 p.m. they summarised the results as follows.

| | Number of fish by type | | | All fish caught | |
	Perch	Tench	Roach	Mean mass (kg)	Standard deviation (kg)
Ali	2	3	7	1.07	0.42
Les	6	2	8	0.76	0.27
Sam	1	0	1	1.00	0

a) State how you can deduce that the mass of each fish caught by Sam was 1.00 kg.

b) The winner was the person who had caught the greatest total mass of fish by 4 p.m. Determine who was the winner, showing your working.

c) Before leaving the waterside, Sam catches one more fish and weighs it. He then announces that if this extra fish is included with the other two fish he caught, the standard deviation is 1.00 kg. Find the mass of this extra fish. (OCR)

12. The heights of 94 policemen based at a city police station were measured, and the results (in metres) are summarised in the following table.

Height (m)	1.65 – 1.69	1.70 – 1.74	1.75 – 1.79	1.80 – 1.84	1.85 – 1.89
Frequency	2	4	11	23	38

Height (m)	1.90 – 1.94	1.95 – 1.99	2.00 – 2.04	2.05 – 2.09
Frequency	9	4	2	1

a) Estimate the median and quartiles.

b) What do these values indicate about the shape of the distribution?

c) Estimate the mean $\bar{x}$ and standard deviation s.

d) A possible measure of skewness is $\frac{3(\bar{x}-Q_2)}{s}$. Calculate this number and state how it confirms your answer to part (b).

13. The following table gives the ages in completed years of the 141 persons in a town involved in road accidents during a particular year.

Age (years)	12 – 15	16 – 20	21 – 25	26 – 30	31 – 40	41 – 50	51 – 70
Frequency	15	48	28	17	14	7	12

Working in years, and giving your answers to 1 decimal place, calculate estimates of

a) the mean and standard deviation,   b) the median

of the ages. Which do you consider to be the better representative average of the distribution, the mean or the median? Give a reason for your answer.

14. A particular chemical process can be used to manufacture product X, but can be performed at a variety of temperatures, with different results. The experiment was peformed, with the same quantity of reagents in each case, a total of 5 times. If the experiment was performed at $x°$ C, then y g of product X was produced. The results of these experiments can be summarised in the data $\sum x = 190$, $\sum y = 192$, $\sum x^2 = 9900$, $\sum xy = 8450$. Find the regression line of y on x in the form $y = a + bx$.

Estimate the quantity of product X that will be produced if the experiment is conducted at $100°$ C. Is this estimate sensible?

15. The frequency table below records the data in a paired dataset with 100 entries involving the variables x and y:

x	y	Freq.
1	3	29
3	−1	43
4	−2	15
6	−7	13

a) Evaluate the product-moment correlation coefficient r_{xy}.

b) Find the least squares regression line of y on x.

c) What is the expected value of y when $x = 2$?

16. In a paired dataset with n pairs of values involving variables x and y, the values of the x variable are the numbers $1, 2, \ldots, n$ in some order, and the values of the variables y are also the numbers $1, 2, \ldots, n$ in some order.

a) Show that $S_{xx} = S_{yy} = \frac{1}{12}n(n^2 - 1)$. You may assume that the sum $1^2 + 2^2 + \cdots + n^2$ is $\frac{1}{6}n(n+1)(2n+1)$.

b) Show that the product-moment correlation coefficient of x and y is

$$r_{xy} = 1 - \frac{6}{n(n^2 - 1)} \sum_i (x_i - y_i)^2 .$$

c) What is the maximum possible value of $\sum_i (x_i - y_i)^2$?

17. In a laboratory-based investigation of the photosynthesis rate y of the plant *Lorrea tridenta* and its reaction to the level of irradiance x, results were obtained which can be summarised as follows:

$$n = 11 \qquad \sum x = 56.2 \qquad \sum x^2 = 335.18 \qquad \sum y = 614 \qquad \sum y^2 = 41244 \qquad \sum xy = 3688.3$$

a) Calculate the equation of the regression line of y on x.

b) Comment on the adequacy of the linear model.

c) Estimate the photosynthesis rate when the level of irradiance is 5.2. (UCLES)

18. The resting metabolic rate (RMR) x (in kcal/24h) and body weight y (in kg) of 12 randomly selected women are recorded. Suppose that $\sum(x - 50) = 48.2$, $\sum(y - 1200) = 90$, and that

$$\sum(x - 50)^2 = 639.98 \quad \sum(y - 1200)^2 = 276650 \quad \sum(x - 50)(y - 1200) = 9031.6$$

Calculate the product-moment correlation coefficient for the sample. (UCLES)

19. A group of people were asked to test a new company's range of pizzas. They were asked to grade each pizza in two different ways: how much they liked it (on a scale of $0 - 4$, with 0 being the worst score), and how spicy is was (on a scale of $0 - 3$, with 3 being the spiciest rating). The outcome of the feedback from the group of pizza-testers was as follows:

		Liking				
		0	1	2	3	4
Spiciness	0	7	2	1	0	0
	1	5	17	15	8	0
	2	5	26	43	27	33
	3	2	5	35	61	68

Calculate the product-moment correlation coefficient for these data, and comment on the result.

20. The scores obtained by 10 sumo wrestlers in two sumo wrestling competitions are given in the table below.

Wrestler	1	2	3	4	5	6	7	8	9	10
First match x	10	10	13	6	9	7	6	9	5	6
Second match y	12	9	11	8	8	9	8	11	8	5

These results are summarised as $\sum x = 81$, $\sum x^2 = 713$, $\sum y = 89$, $\sum y^2 = 829$, $\sum xy = 753$.

a) Show these data clearly on a scatter diagram.

b) Obtain the value of the product-moment correlation coefficient between x and y.

    c) Obtain the least squares estimates of the values of the parameters a and b in the regression line $y = a + bx$.   (UCLES)

21. Plants of a certain species are dissected. The number of carpels x, and the number of stamens y are counted for each flower. For a random sample of 15 flowers the numbers found are shown in the table:

No. of carpels x	19	21	24	25	26	29	30	31
No. of stamens y	41	70	32	34	35	72	57	64
No. of carpels x	31	33	34	36	36	37	38	
No. of stamens y	67	74	69	76	74	75	70	

These data are summarised by

$$\sum x = 450 \qquad \sum x^2 = 13992 \qquad \sum y = 910 \qquad \sum y^2 = 59018 \qquad \sum xy = 28259$$

    a) Calculate the equations of the estimated regression lines of y on x and of x on y.

    b) Calculate an estimate of the number of carpels in a flower with 50 stamens.   (UCLES)

22. A paired dataset involving the variables x and y has the date given in the table on the right, where a is some number. The least squares regression line of y on x passes through the point $(3, 4)$. What is the value of a?

x	0	3	3	4	5
y	1	2	a	a	7

23. A paired dataset involving the variables x and y has the date given in the table on the right, where a is some number.

x	1	2	3
y	2	a	5

    a) Find expressions for S_{xx}, S_{yy} and S_{xy} in terms of a.

    b) If this dataset is such that $r_{xy} = \frac{1}{2}\sqrt{3}$, find the possible values of a.

24. The judges in a 'Beautiful Baby' competition have to arrange 10 babies in order of merit. In how many different ways could this be done? Two babies are to be selected to be photographed. In how many ways can this selection be made?

25. In how many ways can a committee of four men and four women be seated in a row if

    a) they can sit in any position,   b) no one is seated next to a person of the same sex?

26. How many distinct arrangements are there of the letters in the word RATATATAT?

27. Six people are going to travel in a six-seater minibus but only three of them can drive. In how many different ways can they seat themselves?

28. There are eight different books on a bookshelf: three of them are hardbacks and the rest are paperbacks.

    a) In how many different ways can the books be arranged if all the paperbacks are together and all the hardbacks are together?

    b) In how many different ways can the books be arranged if all the paperbacks are together?

29. Four boys and two girls sit in a line on stools in front of a coffee bar.

    a) In how many ways can they arrange themselves so that the two girls are together?

    b) In how many ways can they sit if the two girls are not together?   (OCR)

30. Ten people travel in two cars, a saloon and a Mini. If the saloon has seats for six and the Mini has seats for four, find the number of different ways in which the party can travel, assuming that the order of seating in each car does not matter and all the people can drive.   (OCR)

31. Giving a brief explanation of your method, calculate the number of different ways in which the letters of the word TRIANGLES can be arranged if no two vowels may come together.   (OCR)

32. A class contains 30 children, 18 girls and 12 boys. Four complimentary theatre tickets are distributed at random to the children in the class. What is the probability that

     a) all four tickets go to girls,

     b) two boys and two girls receive tickets?   (OCR)

33. a) How many different 7-digit numbers can be formed from the digits 0, 1, 2, 2, 3, 3, 3 assuming that a number cannot start with 0 ?

     b) How many of these numbers will end in 0?   (OCR)

34. There is a row of chairs, numbered from 1 to 7. Calculate the number of ways in which four girls and three boys can be seated on these chairs if there are more girls than boys in chairs numbered 1 to m for each $1 \leq m \leq 7$.

35. Find the number of ways in which

     a) 3 people can be arranged in 4 seats,   b) 5 people can be arranged in 5 seats.

     In a block of 8 seats, 4 are in row A and 4 are in row B. Find the number of ways of arranging 8 people in the 8 seats given that 3 specified people must be in row A.   (OCR)

36. Eight different cards, of which four are red and four are black, are dealt to two players so that each receives a hand of four cards. Calculate

     a) the total number of different hands which a given player could receive,

     b) the probability that each player receives a hand consisting of four cards all of the same colour.   (OCR)

37. A piece of wood of length 10 cm is to be divided into three pieces so that the length of each piece is a whole number of cm, for example 2 cm, 3 cm and 5 cm.

     a) List all the different sets of lengths which could be obtained.

     b) If one of these sets is selected at random, what is the probability that the lengths of the pieces could be lengths of the sides of a triangle?   (OCR)

38. Nine persons are to be seated at three tables holding 2, 3 and 4 persons respectively. In how many ways can the groups sitting at the tables be selected, assuming that the order of sitting at the tables does not matter?   (OCR)

39. a) Calculate the number of different arrangements which can be made using all the letters of the word BANANA.

     b) The number of combinations of 2 objects from n is equal to the number of combinations of 3 objects from n. Determine n.   (OCR)

40. A 'hand' of 5 cards is dealt from an ordinary pack of 52 playing cards. Show that there are nearly 2.6 million distinct hands and that, of these, 575757 contain no card from the heart suit.

     On three successive occasions a card player is dealt a hand containing no heart. What is the probability of this happening? What conclusion might the player justifiably reach?   (OCR)

41*. Notice that $7! \times 6! = 10!$. Find three integers, m, n and r, where $r > 10$, for which $m! \times n! = r!$.

42*. How many integers greater than or equal to zero and less than a million are not divisible by 2 or 5? What is the average value of these numbers?

     How many integers greater than or equal to zero and less than 4179 are not divisible by 3 or 7? What is the average value of these integers?   (STEP)

43*. 47321 is a five-digit number whose digits sum to $4 + 7 + 2 + 3 + 1 = 17$.

     a) Show that there are 15 five-digit numbers whose digits sum to 43. You should explain your reasoning carefully.

     b) How many five-digit numbers are there whose digits sum to 39?   (STEP)

Probability

In this chapter we will learn to:

- evaluate probabilities in simple cases by calculation using permutations and combinations,

- understand and use Venn diagrams for up to three events,

- understand the meaning of mutually exclusive and independent events, and calculate and use conditional probabilities in simple cases,

- use the correct notation to refer to the probabilities of events, and to describe the probabilities of intersections and unions of events, and to express conditional probabilities correctly.

31.1 Assigning Probability

In many situations we might be unsure of the outcome of some activity or experiment, although we know what the possible outcomes are. For example, we do not know what number we will get when we roll a dice, but we do know that we will get 1, 2, 3, 4, 5 or 6. We know that if we toss a coin twice, then the possible outcomes are (H,H), (H,T), (T,H) and (T,T). If we are testing a transistor to see if it is defective, then we know that the possible outcomes are 'defective' and 'not defective'.

The list of all the possible outcomes is called the **sample space** of the experiment. The list is usually written in curly brackets, { }.

Thus the sample space for rolling the dice is $\{1,2,3,4,5,6\}$, the sample space for tossing a coin twice is $\{(H,H), (H,T), (T,H), (T,T)\}$, and that for testing a transistor is {defective, not defective}. It is a useful convention, when describing pairs of outcomes like H, H, to put them in brackets, as if they were coordinates.

Each of the outcomes of an experiment has a probability assigned to it. Sometimes we can assign the probability using symmetry. For example, the sample space for throwing a dice is $\{1,2,3,4,5,6\}$, and we might assign each outcome the probability $\frac{1}{6}$, in the belief that the dice is fair, and that each outcome is equally likely.

Food For Thought 31.1

The method of calculating probabilities by assuming that all outcomes in the sample space are equally likely is the most common method of calculations about games of chance, and one with that should be familiar already. On occasion, earlier in this book, probabilities have been discussed. In those cases it has always been possible to calculate them using the assumption that all outcomes in the sample space are equally likely.

Now suppose that the dice is not fair, so that we cannot use the symmetrical method of assumed fairness for assigning probabilities. In this case we will have to carry out an experiment and throw the dice a large number of times. Suppose that we threw the dice 1000 times and recorded the frequencies of the six possible outcomes:

Outcome	1	2	3	4	5	6
Frequency	100	216	182	135	170	197

We would then assign the probabilities $\frac{100}{1000}$, $\frac{216}{1000}$, $\frac{182}{1000}$, $\frac{135}{1000}$, $\frac{170}{1000}$ and $\frac{197}{1000}$ to the outcomes 1, 2, 3, 4, 5 and 6 respectively. These are called the **relative frequencies** of the outcomes, and we can use them as estimates of the probabilities. Of course, if we were to roll the dice another 1000 times, the results would probably not be exactly the same, but we might hope that they would not be too different. Rolling the dice even more times might improve the relative frequency as an approximation to the true probability of something happening.

For Interest

A deep mathematical result, called the **Weak Law of Large Numbers**, tells us that this is exactly what happens. If an experiment is performed repeatedly, then (under moderate assumptions about the type of experiment being conducted) the relative frequency of a particular result converges, as the number of tests tends to infinity, to the true probability of that result.

The Weak Law of Large Numbers is the main result that makes the whole theory of probability practical. The true, or theoretical probability of any particular outcome is the long-term proportion of its actual occurrence in real life.

Sometimes we cannot assign a probability by using symmetry or by carrying out an experiment. For example, there is a probability that my house will be struck by lightning next year, and I insure against this happening. The insurance company will have to have a probability in mind when it calculates the premium I have to pay, but it cannot calculate it by symmetry (not all houses are equally likely to be struck by lightning), or carry out an experiment for a few years (I want insurance cover now, and not a few years later). It will assign its probability using its experience of such matters and its records.

Whether this is to be done by applying some principle of symmetry, the use of experiment or past experience, the starting point of any study of the probabilistic nature of an experiment is to assign probabilities to the various outcomes in the sample space.

Key Fact 31.1 Assigning Probabilities

To assign probabilities to a sample space $\mathcal{E}$ is to associate a number $p(\omega)$ with each element $\omega \in \mathcal{E}$. The number $p(\omega)$ is the probability that the outcome is ω. Two principles must be observed:

- each probability $p(\omega)$ must be a number between 0 and 1,

- the sum of all the probabilities $p(\omega)$ must equal 1.

Example 31.1.1. *How would you assign probabilities to the following experiments or activities?*

(a) *Choosing a card from a standard pack of playing cards.*

(b) *The combined experiment of tossing a coin and rolling a die.*

(c) *Four international football teams, Argentina, Cameroon, Nigeria, Turkey (A, C, N and T), play a knockout tournament. Who will be the winner?*

(d) *Toss a coin twice. How many heads do we get?*

(a) The sample space would consist of the list of the 52 playing cards {AC,2C,3C, ...,KS} in some order (Here A means ace, C means clubs, and so on). Assuming that these cards are equally likely to be picked, the probability assigned to each of them is $\frac{1}{52}$.

(b) The sample space is

$$\left\{ \begin{array}{l} (H,1),(H,2),(H,3),(H,4),(H,5),(H,6), \\ (T,1),(T,2),(T,3),(T,4),(T,5),(T,6) \end{array} \right\},$$

and each of the outcomes would be assigned a probability of $\frac{1}{12}$, assuming that both the coin and the die are fair.

(c) The sample space is { A wins, C wins, N wins, T wins}. You have to assign probabilities subjectively, according to your knowledge of the teams and the game. The probabilities $p(A)$, $p(C)$, $p(N)$ and $p(T)$ must all be non-negative and satisfy $p(A) + p(C) + p(N) + p(T) = 1$.

(d) This one takes a little care, since while the sample space is $\{0, 1, 2\}$, these three outcomes are not equally likely, and so we cannot assign them all a probability of $\frac{1}{3}$. If we consider instead a more detailed sample space { (H,H), (H,T), (T,H), (T,T)}, then each of these four events may be assumed to be equally likely. Since two of these outcomes give us one head, while the other two each give zero or two heads, we deduce that the correct probabilities are $p(0) = \frac{1}{4}$, $p(1) = \frac{1}{2}$, $p(2) = \frac{1}{4}$.

31.2 Probabilities of events

Sometimes we might be interested, not in one particular outcome, but in two or three or more of them. For example, suppose we roll a die twice. We might be interested in whether the result is the same both times (in other words, whether we roll 'doubles'). The list of outcomes in which you are interested is called an **event**, and is written in curly brackets. The sample space here is

$$\{ (1,1), (1,2), (1,3), (1,4), (1,5), (1,6), \ldots, (6,1), (6,2), (6,3), (6,4), (6,5), (6,6) \}$$

and the event of 'throwing doubles' is $\{(1,1), (2,2), (3,3), (4,4), (5,5), (6,6)\}$. Since this event is comprised of 6 members of the sample space, all equally likely, we would suspect that the probability of 'throwing doubles' is $\frac{6}{36}$, or $\frac{1}{6}$.

This is an example of a general rule. The use of curly brackets (set notation) is not accidental!

Key Fact 31.2 Events

An event A is a subset of the sample space $\mathcal{E}$. The probability of an event A, written $\mathbb{P}[A]$ or (more simply) $P(A)$, is the sum of the probabilities of the outcomes that comprise A:

$$\mathbb{P}[A] = \sum_{\omega \in A} p(\omega)$$

Often a list of outcomes can be constructed in such a way that all of them are equally likely. If all the outcomes are equally likely, then the probability of any event A can be found by finding the number of outcomes which make up event A and dividing by the total number of outcomes:

$$\mathbb{P}[A] = \frac{n(A)}{n(\mathcal{E})}.$$

Example 31.2.1. *A fair 20-sided die has eight faces coloured red, ten coloured blue and two coloured green. The die is rolled.*

(a) *Find the probability that the bottom face is red.*

(b) *Let A be the event that the bottom face is not red. Find the probability of A.*

(a) Each face has an equal probability of being the bottom face: as there are 20 faces, each of them has a probability of $\frac{1}{20}$. There are eight red faces, each with probability $\frac{1}{20}$, so $\mathbb{P}[\text{red}] = \frac{8}{20} = \frac{2}{5}$.

(b) The event of not rolling red is that of rolling either blue or green. There are a total of 12 non-red faces, and so

$$\mathbb{P}[A] = \mathbb{P}[\text{not red}] = \mathbb{P}[\text{blue or green}] = \frac{12}{20} = \frac{3}{5}$$

Note that $\mathbb{P}[A] = \frac{1}{2} + \frac{1}{10} = \mathbb{P}[\text{blue}] + \mathbb{P}[\text{green}]$.

Example 31.2.2. *The numbers $1, 2, \ldots, 9$ are written on separate cards. The cards are shuffled and the top one is turned over. Calculate the probability that the number on this card is prime.*

The sample space for this activity is $\{1,2,3,4,5,6,7,8,9\}$. As each outcome is equally likely each has probability $\frac{1}{9}$.

Let B be the event that the card turned over is prime. Then $B = \{2,3,4,7\}$, and so $\mathbb{P}[B] = \frac{4}{9}$.

Example 31.2.3. *Mary has three playing cards, two queens and a king. Siobhan selects one of the cards at random, and returns it to Mary, who shuffles the cards. Siobhan then selects a second card. Siobhan wins if both cards selected are kings. Find the probability that Siobhan wins.*

Imagine that the queens are different, and call them Q_1 and Q_2, and call the king K. Then the sample space is:

$$\{ (Q_1,Q_1), (Q_1,Q_2), (Q_1,K), (Q_2,Q_1), (Q_2,Q_2), (Q_2,K), (K,Q_1), (K,Q_2), (K,K)\}$$

Each of the outcomes in the sample space has probability $\frac{1}{9}$.

Let S be the event that Siobhan wins. Then $S = \{(K,K)\}$ and so $\mathbb{P}[S] = \frac{1}{9}$.

Example 31.2.4. *A die with six faces has been made from brass and aluminium, and is not fair. The probability of a 6 is $\frac{1}{4}$, the probabilities of 2, 3, 4, and 5 are each $\frac{1}{6}$, and the probability of 1 is $\frac{1}{12}$. The die is rolled. Find the probability of rolling:*

a) 1 or 6,   b) *an even number.*

(a) $\mathbb{P}[1 \text{ or } 6] = \mathbb{P}[\{1,6\}] = p(1) + p(6) = \frac{1}{12} + \frac{1}{4} = \frac{1}{3}$.

(b) $\mathbb{P}[\text{an even number}] = \mathbb{P}[\{2,4,6\}] = p(2) + p(4) + p(6) = \frac{1}{6} + \frac{1}{6} + \frac{1}{4} = \frac{7}{12}$.

Sometimes a little cunning is required!

Example 31.2.5. *Draw two cards from an ordinary pack. Find the probability that they are not both kings.*

The problem is that the sample space is very large. There are 52 ways of picking the first card, and then 51 ways of picking the second, so there $52 \times 51 = 2652$ possibilities, and so the sample space therefore consists of 2652 outcomes These outcomes are equally likely, and so each is assigned a probability of $\frac{1}{2652}$.

To avoid counting all the outcomes which are not both kings, it is easier to look at the number of outcomes which *are* both kings. These possible outcomes are

$$\left\{ \begin{array}{l} (KC,KD),(KC,KH),(KC),KS),(KD,KC),(KD,KH,(KD),KS), \\ (KH,KC),(KH,KD),(KH),KS),(KS,KC),(KS,KD,(KS),KH) \end{array} \right\}$$

There are thus 12 outcomes that are both kings. So the number that are not both kings is $2652 - 12 = 2640$. All 2640 of these outcomes have probability $\frac{1}{2652}$, so

$$\mathbb{P}[\text{not both kings}] = \frac{2640}{2652} = \frac{220}{221}.$$

It is always worth watching for this short cut, and it is also useful to have some language to describe it.

Key Fact 31.3 Complements

If A is an event, the event 'not A' is the event consisting of those outcomes in the sample space which are not in A. In other words, the event 'not A' is the set-theoretic complement of the event A in the universal set (sample space) $\mathcal{E}$. The event 'not A' is therefore called the **complement** of A, and is denoted A'.
Since the sum of the probabilities assigned to outcomes in the sample space is 1,

$$\mathbb{P}[A] + \mathbb{P}[A'] = 1.$$

Example 31.2.6. *An unfair die has been made so that the probability of rolling j is proportional to j, for $1 \leq j \leq 6$. What is the probability of not throwing 6?*

With sample space $\{1,2,3,4,5,6\}$ we have probabilities $p(j) = kj$ for $1 \leq j \leq 6$ for some constant k. Since

$$1 = p(1) + p(2) + p(3) + p(4) + p(5) + p(6) = k(1 + 2 + 3 + 4 + 5 + 6) = 21k$$

we deduce that $k = \frac{1}{21}$. Then $\mathbb{P}[\{6\}'] = 1 - \mathbb{P}[\{6\}] = 1 - \frac{6}{21} = \frac{5}{7}$.

Example 31.2.7. *A crow sits on a fence-post of a very long fence. At then end of every minute it flies to one of the neighbouring two fence-posts. It is just as likely to fly to the post to the left as it is to fly to the post to the right. What is the probability that it is **not** at the fence-post it started at after 20 minutes?*

Every minute, the crow flies either left or right, ending up at the next fence-post. We won't write it down because it is very large but the sample space can be regarded as the collection of sequences of 20 letters, where each letter is either L or R. One such sequence is LLLRRRRLRLRLRLRRRRRL. This sequence would represent the flight-path of a crow who flies left three times, then right four times, then left, then right, then left, then right, then left, then right, then left, then right five times, then finally left. Since each letter can be either L or R, there are 2^{20} such sequences, and they are all equally likely.

Let A be the event of the crow ending up at its original fence-post. For the crow to end up where it started, it must have flown left ten times, and right ten times, in some order. The number of ways in which the crow can do this is therefore the number of sequences in the sample space which contain ten Ls and ten Rs. Using the ideas of the previous chapter, there are $^{20}C_{10}$ such sequences, and hence

$$\mathbb{P}[A] = \frac{^{20}C_{10}}{2^{20}}$$

and hence

$$\mathbb{P}[A'] = 1 - \frac{^{20}C_{10}}{2^{20}} = 0.824$$

31.3 Addition of Probabilities

Roll a single fair 6-sided die. Let A be the event that a prime number is rolled, and let B be the event that a square number is rolled. What is the probability that either A or B occurs?

With a sample space of $\{1,2,3,4,5,6\}$, we have $A = \{2,3,5\}$, while $B = \{1,4\}$. Using the notation of set theory, the event that either A or B occurs is the union $A \cup B = \{1,2,3,4,5\}$, and so

$$\mathbb{P}[A \text{ or } B] = \mathbb{P}[A \cup B] = \frac{5}{6} = \frac{1}{2} + \frac{1}{3} = \mathbb{P}[A] + \mathbb{P}[B]$$

Roll a single fair 20-sided die. Let A be the event that a multiple of 4 is rolled. Let B be the event that a perfect square is rolled. What is the probability that either A or B occurs?

This time the sample space is $\{1,2,3,\ldots,20\}$ and $A = \{4,8,12,16,20\}$ and $B = \{1,4,9,16\}$. The event that either A or B occurs is the set-theoretic union $A \cup B = \{1,4,8,9,12,16,20\}$, which contains 7 elements, and so

$$\mathbb{P}[A \text{ or } B] = \mathbb{P}[A \cup B] = \frac{7}{20} \neq \frac{1}{4} + \frac{1}{5} = \mathbb{P}[A] + \mathbb{P}[B].$$

Sometimes is it true that $\mathbb{P}[A \cup B] = \mathbb{P}[A] + \mathbb{P}[B]$, sometimes it is not. Why is this?

Consider the sum $\mathbb{P}[A] + \mathbb{P}[B]$. Since $\mathbb{P}[A]$ is the sum of the probabilities p_x for all $x \in A$, and $\mathbb{P}[B]$ is the sum of the probabilities p_x for all $x \in B$, the expression $\mathbb{P}[A] + \mathbb{P}[B]$ certainly adds up all the probabilities p_x for all $x \in A \cup B$, but it double-counts the probabilities p_x for those x belonging to the intersection $A \cap B$ of A and B.

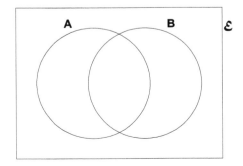

$$\mathbb{P}[A] + \mathbb{P}[B] = \sum_{\omega \in A} p(\omega) + \sum_{\omega \in B} p(\omega)$$

$$= \sum_{\omega \in A \cup B} p(\omega) + \sum_{\omega \in A \cap B} p(\omega)$$

Figure 31.1

and so

> **Key Fact 31.4** Addition of Probabilities
>
> For any two events A and B, we have
> $$\mathbb{P}[A \cup B] + \mathbb{P}[A \cap B] = \mathbb{P}[A] + \mathbb{P}[B]$$
> where $A \cup B$ is the event that either A or B (or both) occur, while $A \cap B$ is the event that both A and B occur.

Apart from its intrinsic interest, this result means that we do not need to know all the probabilities $p(\omega)$ to calculate the probabilities of events; it is sufficient to know the probabilities of other, key, events.

Example 31.3.1. *The probability that it will rain tomorrow is $\frac{1}{4}$. The probability that I will take an umbrella to work tomorrow is $\frac{1}{3}$. The probability that I will take an umbrella to work tomorrow and it will rain is $\frac{1}{10}$. What is the probability that it is dry tomorrow, and I do not take an umbrella to work?*

If A is the event that it will rain tomorrow, and B is the event that I take an umbrella to work tomorrow, then $\mathbb{P}[A] = \frac{1}{4}$ and $\mathbb{P}[B] = \frac{1}{3}$. We are also told that $\mathbb{P}[A \cap B] = \frac{1}{10}$. Thus

$$\mathbb{P}[A \cup B] = \mathbb{P}[A] + \mathbb{P}[B] - \mathbb{P}[A \cap B] = \frac{1}{4} + \frac{1}{3} - \frac{1}{10} = \frac{29}{60},$$

and hence $\mathbb{P}[(A \cup B)'] = \frac{31}{60}$. The event that it does not rain tomorrow is A', and the event that I do not take an umbrella to work is B'. Since $A' \cap B' = (A \cup B)'$, we have found the probability that we want.

In our previous studies of probability, we have almost certainly met examples (probably in other words) of events A and B where we calculated $\mathbb{P}[A \cup B]$ by adding together the probabilities $\mathbb{P}[A]$ and $\mathbb{P}[B]$. It is certainly convenient simply to be able to add probabilities, without the need for the correction factor of $\mathbb{P}[A \cap B]$ For which events is it true that $\mathbb{P}[A \cup B]$ is simply the sum of $\mathbb{P}[A]$ and $\mathbb{P}[B]$?

> **Key Fact 31.5** Mutually Exclusive Events
>
> Events A and B are mutually exclusive when
> $$\mathbb{P}[A \cap B] = 0.$$
> When A and B are mutually exclusive, then
> $$\mathbb{P}[A \cup B] = \mathbb{P}[A] + \mathbb{P}[B]$$

Example 31.3.2. *At a fête, a game involves rolling two dice. If the total of the two dice is 3, or if the individual score of both dice is over 4, the player receives a toffee. If both dice are the same, or the total of the two dice is 4, then the player receives a mint. What is the probability that the player receives:*

   a) a toffee,   *b) a mint,*   *c) a sweet?*

With the usual sample space $\{(1,1),(1,2),(1,3),\ldots,(6,4),(6,5),(6,6)\}$ let

$A = \{\text{total of }10\} = \{(1,2),(2,1)\}$
$B = \{\text{both over }4\} = \{(5,5),(5,6),(6,5),(6,6)\}$
$C = \{\text{both same}\} = \{(1,1),(2,2),(3,3),(4,4),(5,5),(6,6)\}$
$D = \{\text{total of }4\} = \{(1,3),(2,2),(3,1)\}$

Thus $\mathbb{P}[A] = \frac{1}{18}$, $\mathbb{P}[B] = \frac{1}{9}$, $\mathbb{P}[C] = \frac{1}{6}$ and $\mathbb{P}[D] = \frac{1}{12}$. Since $A \cap B = \varnothing$, A and B are mutually exclusive, and so

$$\mathbb{P}[\text{win a toffee}] = \mathbb{P}[A \cup B] = \frac{1}{18} + \frac{1}{9} = \frac{1}{6}$$

On the other hand, $C \cap D = \{(2,2)\}$, so that $\mathbb{P}[C \cap D] = \frac{1}{36}$, and hence

$$\mathbb{P}[\text{win a mint}] = \mathbb{P}[C \cup D] = \frac{1}{6} + \frac{1}{12} - \frac{1}{36} = \frac{2}{9}.$$

Looking carefully, we see that $(A \cup B) \cap (C \cup D) = \{(5,5),(6,6)\}$, and so

$$\mathbb{P}[\text{win a sweet}] = \mathbb{P}[(A \cup B) \cup (C \cup D)] = \frac{1}{6} + \frac{2}{9} - \frac{1}{18} = \frac{1}{3}.$$

For Interest

Mathematicians use the word 'or' **inclusively**: 'A or B' means 'either A or B or both'. It can be confusing, when learning the meaning of the set-theoretic union, that common usage of English often gives the notion of exclusivity to the word 'or': 'either you or I will win this game (but not both of us)'. There are times when mathematicians (and computer scientists) want to work with the **exclusive 'or'** ('either one or the other, but not both'); when they do so, it will be made explicitly clear that the exclusive 'or' is needed. When in doubt, you should assume that the word 'or' is being used inclusively.

31.4 Venn Diagrams

Events are subsets of the sample space $\mathcal{E}$, and the operations of complementation and taking unions and intersections are set-theoretic operations. Thus Venn diagrams can be used to represent events, provided that only a small number of events are to be discussed at one time.

Example 31.4.1. *If $\mathbb{P}[A] = \frac{2}{3}$ and $\mathbb{P}[B] = \frac{1}{2}$, what is the smallest possible value of $\mathbb{P}[A \cap B]$?*

Using a Venn diagram to represent events A and B, and using the sample space $\mathcal{E}$ as the universal set, we shall assume that $\mathbb{P}[A \cap B] = x$, where x is to be determined. We use the Venn diagram by adding probabilities to the differing regions, to represent the probability of corresponding events. Since $\mathbb{P}[A] = \frac{2}{3}$, we have $\mathbb{P}[A \cap B'] = \frac{2}{3} - x$. Since $\mathbb{P}[B] = \frac{1}{2}$, we have $\mathbb{P}[B \cap A'] = \frac{1}{2} - x$. Thus $\mathbb{P}[A \cup B] = \left(\frac{2}{3} - x\right) + x + \left(\frac{1}{2} - x\right) = \frac{7}{6} + x$, from which we deduce that $\mathbb{P}[(A \cup B)'] = x - \frac{1}{6}$.

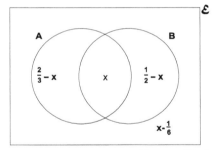

Figure 31.2

Since all probabilities must be positive, we deduce that $x \geq \frac{1}{6}$. The smallest possible value of $\mathbb{P}[A \cap B]$ is $\frac{1}{6}$.

Example 31.4.2. *In a class of 30 pupils, 19 are studying Mathematics, 17 are not studying English. There are twice as many students studying just Mathematics as there are studying just English. What is the probability that a randomly chosen student is studying both Mathematics and English?*

Suppose there are x students studying Mathematics, but not English. Then there are $19 - x$ students studying both Mathematics and English, and $17 - x$ students studying neither Mathematics nor English. Since there are 30 students in the class, there must be $x - 6$ students studying English, but not Mathematics.

The final condition tells us that $x = 2(x-6)$, and hence $x = 12$. Thus there are 7 students studying both subjects, and hence the probability that a randomly chosen student is studying both subjects is $\frac{7}{30}$.

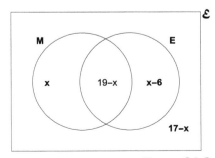

Figure 31.3

Of course, this problem could have been solved without the use of Venn diagrams. Starting with the assumption that $\mathbb{P}[M \cap E'] = x$, we could deduce that $\mathbb{P}[M \cap E] = \frac{19}{30} - x$ and $\mathbb{P}[(M \cup E)'] = \frac{17}{30} - x$, and deduce from these that $\mathbb{P}[M' \cap E] = x - \frac{1}{5}$. The condition $x = \mathbb{P}[M \cap E'] = 2\mathbb{P}[M' \cap E]$ gives us $x = \frac{2}{5}$, and hence $\mathbb{P}[M \cap E] = \frac{19}{30} - \frac{2}{5} = \frac{7}{30}$.

Problems with three different events are more complicated than those with two events, and are often most simply dealt with using Venn diagrams.

Example 31.4.3. *In a group of 32 people, 10 like pepperoni pizza, 15 like margherita pizza, and 19 like Hawaiian pizza. A total of 5 people like both pepperoni and margherita pizzas, 8 people like both margherita and Hawaiian pizzas, while a total of 7 people like both pepperoni and Hawaiian pizzas. In addition, a total of 5 people like none of these pizzas. What is the probability that a person, chosen randomly from this group of 32 people, likes all three types of pizza?*

Starting by assuming that x people like all three pizzas, and letting P, M and H be the sets of those people liking pepperoni, margherita and Hawaiian pizzas respectively, we can deduce that the numbers of people in each of the different set intersections is as shown in the Figure. Adding up all these numbers, we deduce that $29 + x = 32$, and hence $x = 3$. Thus there are 3 people who like all three pizzas, and hence the probability that a randomly chosen person likes all three types of pizza is $\frac{3}{32}$.

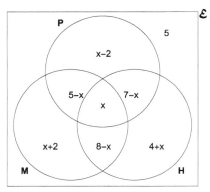

Figure 31.4

EXERCISE 31A

1. A fair dice is thrown once. Find the probabilities that the score is

    a) bigger than 3,
    b) bigger than or equal to 3,
    c) an odd number,
    d) a prime number,
    e) bigger than 3 and a prime number,
    f) bigger than 3 or a prime number,
    g) bigger than 3 or a prime number, but not both.

2. A card is chosen at random from an ordinary pack. Find the probability that it is

    a) red,
    b) a picture card (K,Q,J),
    c) an honour (A,K,Q,J,10),
    d) a red honour,
    e) red or an honour.

3. Two fair dice are thrown simultaneously. Find the probability that

    a) the total is 7,
    b) the total is at least 8,
    c) the total is prime,
    d) neither score is a 6,
    e) at least one score is 6,
    f) exactly one score is 6,
    g) we get 'doubles',
    h) the difference between the scores is odd.

4. A fair dice is thrown twice. If the second score is the same as the first, the second throw does not count, and the dice is thrown again until a different score is obtained. The two different scores are added to give a total.

    List the possible outcomes, and find the probability that

    a) the total is 7,
    b) the total is at least 8,
    c) at least one of the two scores is a 6,
    d) the first score is higher than the last.

5. A bag contains ten counters, of which six are red and four are green. A counter is chosen at random; its colour is noted and it is replaced in the bag. A second counter is then chosen at random. Find the probabilities that

    a) both are red,
    b) both are green,
    c) just one is red,
    d) at least one is red,
    e) the second is red.

6. Suppose that A and B are events, and that $\mathbb{P}[A] = \frac{1}{3}$, $\mathbb{P}[A \cap B] = \frac{1}{6}$ and $\mathbb{P}[A \cup B] = \frac{3}{4}$. What is $\mathbb{P}[B]$?

7. Suppose that $\mathbb{P}[A] = 2\mathbb{P}[A \cap B]$, that $\mathbb{P}[A \cup B] = 2\mathbb{P}[A]$, and that $\mathbb{P}[(A \cup B)'] = \frac{1}{9}$. What is $\mathbb{P}[A \cap B]$?

8. If A and B are events and $\mathbb{P}[A] = \frac{2}{3}$, while $\mathbb{P}[B] = \frac{3}{4}$, what are the smallest and greatest possible values of $\mathbb{P}[A \cap B]$?

9. Three men and five women stand in a line. All arrangements of the eight people are equally likely. What is the probability that either all three men or all five women are standing together?

10. Incey-Wincey Spider is climbing up the spout. Every day, either Incey-Wincey manages to climb one metre up the spout, or else the rain comes down and washes Incey-Wincey one metre down the spout. These two occurrences are equally likely. What is the sample space for the number of metres that Incey-Wincey will have climbed up the spout after eight days, and what are the probabilities of the various outcomes?

    After a while, Incey-Wincey moves to a new spout. If Incey-Wincey manages to reach a height of 6 meters above his starting point, he can leave the spout. What is the probability that Incey-Wincey has left the spout after eight days?

11. If three fair 6-sided dice are rolled, what is the probability that the total score is:

    a) equal to 3,   b) equal to 5,   c) equal to 8,   d) even?

12. Using Venn diagram, find the probability that an integer chosen randomly between 1 and 200 is divisible by neither 2, 3 nor 5?

13*. John tosses three fair coins, and Mary tosses two fair coins. Let A be the event that John tosses more heads than Mary does, and let B be the event that John tosses more tails than Mary does. What is the relationship between the events A' and B? What is $\mathbb{P}[A]$?

14*. Let $\mathcal{E}$ be a sample space. For any event $A \subseteq \mathcal{E}$, consider the so-called **indicator function** $I_A : \mathcal{E} \to \{0, 1\}$ defined by the formula

$$I_A(\omega) = \begin{cases} 1 & \omega \in A, \\ 0 & \omega \notin A. \end{cases}$$

   a) Show that $I'_A \equiv 1 - I_A$ for any event A (we have used the symbol $\equiv$ to represent an identity),

   b) Show that $I_{A \cap B} \equiv I_A \times I_B$ for any two events A and B,

   c) Write down and simplify an expression for $I_{(A' \cap B')'}$. How does this expression prove that $(A' \cap B')' = A \cup B$?

   d) What is a simpler expression for

$$\sum_{\omega \in \mathcal{E}} I_A(\omega) p(\omega) \, ?$$

   e) Use indicator functions to prove that $\mathbb{P}[A \cup B] = \mathbb{P}[A] + \mathbb{P}[B] - \mathbb{P}[A \cap B]$ for any two events A, B.

15*. Write down an expression for $\mathbb{P}[A \cup B \cup C]$ in terms of probabilities of intersections of collections of A, B and C.

31.5 Conditional Probability

Consider a class of 30 pupils, of whom 17 are girls and 13 are boys. Suppose further that five of the girls and six of the boys are left-handed, and all of the remaining pupils are right-handed. If a pupil is selected at random from the whole class, then the chance that he or she is left-handed is $\frac{6+5}{30} = \frac{11}{30}$.

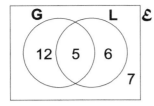 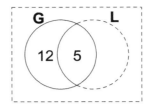

Figure 31.5

However, suppose now that a pupil is selected at random from the girls in the class. There are 17 girls to choose from, of whom 5 are left-handed. The chance that this girl will be left-handed is thus $\frac{5}{17}$. So, being told that the selected pupil is a girl alters the chance that the pupil will be left-handed. This is an example of **conditional probability**. The probability has been calculated on the basis of an extra 'condition' that we have been given.

There is special notation that is used to describe conditional probability. Let L be the event that a left-handed person is chosen, and let G be the event that a girl is chosen. The symbol $\mathbb{P}[L|G]$, or $P(L|G)$, stands for the probability that the pupil chosen is left-handed, **given that** the pupil chosen is a girl. In this case $\mathbb{P}[L|G] = \frac{5}{17}$, although $\mathbb{P}[L] = \frac{11}{30}$.

Fortunately, it is possible to calculate conditional probabilities (where some extra information is known) using (unconditional) probabilities where you have no extra information. Notice that, in the above example, the probability $\mathbb{P}[L|G]$ can be written as

$$\mathbb{P}[L|G] = \frac{5}{17} = \frac{5/30}{17/30}$$

The fraction $\frac{5}{30}$ in the numerator is the probability of choosing a left-handed girl if we are selecting from the whole class, and the fraction $\frac{17}{30}$ in the denominator is the probability of choosing a girl if you are selecting from the whole class. In symbols this could be written as

$$\mathbb{P}[L|G] = \frac{\mathbb{P}[L \cap G]}{\mathbb{P}[G]}.$$

This equation applies to any two events A and B for which $\mathbb{P}[B] > 0$.

Key Fact 31.6 Conditional Probability

If A and B are two events and $\mathbb{P}[B] > 0$, then the **conditional probability of A given B** is

$$\mathbb{P}[A|B] = \frac{\mathbb{P}[A \cap B]}{\mathbb{P}[B]}.$$

This equation can also be written

$$\mathbb{P}[A \cap B] = \mathbb{P}[A|B] \times \mathbb{P}[B].$$

This is known as the **multiplication law of probability**.

Example 31.5.1. *Suppose that a jar contains seven red disks and four white disks. Two disks are selected without replacement (the first disk is not put back before the second disk is selected). What is the probability that both disks are red? What is the probability that the second disk chosen is red?*

This type of problem is often solved using **tree diagrams**, that are a way of using conditional probability diagrammatically.

Each time a disk is chosen, the result is either red (R) or white (W). Initially there are 7 red disks and 4 white disks, so the probability that the first disk is red is $\frac{7}{11}$, while the probability that the first disk is white is $\frac{4}{11}$.

If the first disk chosen is red, then the situation has changed. There are now 10 disks to choose from, of which 6 are red. Thus, given that the first disk chosen is red, the probabilities that the second disk is red or white are $\frac{6}{10}$ and $\frac{4}{10}$ respectively.

Similarly, if the first disk chosen is white, there are now 10 disks left to choose from, of which 7 are red. Thus, given that the first disk chosen is white, the probabilities that the second disk is red or white are $\frac{7}{10}$ are $\frac{3}{10}$ respectively.

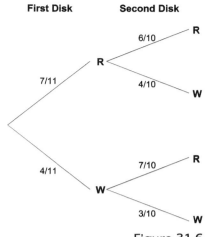

Figure 31.6

All this information is given graphically in the tree diagram above. The first layer of branches give the possible outcomes (red or white) for the choice of the first disk, while the second layer of branches give the possible outcomes (red or white) for the choice of the second disk. In each case, each choice at any stage is labelled with its matching probability.

The ends of the branches represent the (in this case) four possible outcomes: (R,R), (R,W), (W,R) and (W,W) (reading vertically downwards). To calculate probabilities, we use the two 'rules':

- the probability of any one outcome is the product of the probabilities that label the branches that must be followed to reach that outcome,

- the probability of any collection of outcomes is the sum of the probabilities of each of those outcomes.

and so

$$\mathbb{P}[(R,R)] = \tfrac{7}{11} \times \tfrac{6}{10} = \tfrac{42}{110} = \tfrac{21}{55}$$
$$\mathbb{P}[\text{the second disk is red}] = \mathbb{P}[(R,R) \text{ or } (W,R)] = \mathbb{P}[(R,R)] + \mathbb{P}[(W,R)]$$
$$= \tfrac{7}{11} \times \tfrac{6}{10} + \tfrac{4}{11} \times \tfrac{7}{10} = \tfrac{70}{110} = \tfrac{7}{11}$$

We are probably already familiar with this method, but why does it work? We might suspect (correctly) that the second rule of adding the probabilities of different outcomes works because different outcomes are mutually exclusive, but the reason for the first rule is less clear. To see why this method works, we need to be a little more detailed.

Let R_1 and W_1 be the events that the first disk is red and white respectively, and let R_2 and W_2 be the events that the second disk is red and white respectively. Then the outcomes (R,R), (R,W), (W,R) and (W,W) are the events $R_1 \cap R_2$, $R_1 \cap W_2$, $W_1 \cap R_2$ and $W_1 \cap W_2$ respectively (note also that $W_1 = R_1'$ and $W_2 = R_2'$).

The probabilities labelling the first layer of branches are $\mathbb{P}[R_1]$ and $\mathbb{P}[W_1]$, while the probabilities labelling the branches in the second layer are $\mathbb{P}[R_2|R_1]$ and $\mathbb{P}[W_2|R_1]$ for the first pair, and $\mathbb{P}[R_2|W_1]$ and $\mathbb{P}[W_2|W_1]$ for the second pair.

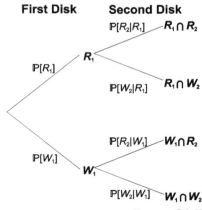

Figure 31.7

Then the calculation of the probability of both disks being red is simply an application of the multiplication law of probability:

$$\mathbb{P}[R_1 \cap R_2] = \mathbb{P}[R_1] \times \mathbb{P}[R_2|R_1] = \tfrac{7}{11} \times \tfrac{6}{10} = \tfrac{21}{55}$$

Moreover, it is clear that any two of the events $R_1 \cap R_2, R_1 \cap W_2, W_1 \cap R_2$ and $W_1 \cap W_2$ are mutually exclusive, and so the second 'rule' is clear:

$$
\begin{aligned}
\mathbb{P}[R_2] &= \mathbb{P}[(R_1 \cap R_2) \cup (W_1 \cap R_2)] = \mathbb{P}[R_1 \cap R_2] + \mathbb{P}[W_1 \cap R_2] \\
&= \mathbb{P}[R_1] \times \mathbb{P}[R_2|R_1] + \mathbb{P}[W_1] \times \mathbb{P}[R_2|W_1]\mathbb{P}[W_1] = \tfrac{7}{11} \times \tfrac{6}{10} + \tfrac{4}{11} \times \tfrac{7}{10} = \tfrac{7}{11}
\end{aligned}
$$

For Interest

In the above argument, we used the identity that

$$\mathbb{P}[R_2] = \mathbb{P}[(R_1 \cap R_2) \cup (W_1 \cap R_2)] = \mathbb{P}[R_1 \cap R_2] + \mathbb{P}[W_1 \cap R_2]$$

We could do this because the events R_1 and R_2 together form what is called a **disjoint partition** of the sample space, since

$$R_1 \cup W_1 = \mathcal{E}, \qquad R_1 \cap W_1 = \emptyset$$

In these conditions state that exactly one of R_1 and W_1 must always happen. For then

$$R_2 = \mathcal{E} \cap R_2 = (R_1 \cup W_1) \cap R_2 = (R_1 \cap R_2) \cup (W_1 \cap R_2)$$

and the disjointness of R_1 and R_2 ensure that $R_1 \cap R_2$ and $W_1 \cap R_2$ are mutually exclusive. Disjoint partitions of the sample space are a useful way to introduce conditional probabilities into a calculation!

If B is any event, then B and B' together form a disjoint partition of the sample space. We can use this fact to derive the following result.

Key Fact 31.7 The Conditional Probability Formula

If A and B are two events, then

$$\mathbb{P}[A] = \mathbb{P}[A \cap B] + \mathbb{P}[A \cap B'] = \mathbb{P}[A|B]\mathbb{P}[B] + \mathbb{P}[A|B']\mathbb{P}[B']$$

This result is particularly useful for dealing with problems described by tree diagrams, as the following examples will show.

One of the main examples of working with conditional probabilities instead of tree diagrams is that tree diagrams can become extremely complicated. The algebraic approach of conditional probabilities enable us to handle these more complicated situations comparatively easily.

Example 31.5.2. *Every day, I drive to work with probability $\tfrac{1}{10}$, or I cycle to work with probability $\tfrac{3}{10}$; otherwise I walk to work. If I drive, the probability that I am early for work is $\tfrac{1}{4}$, and the probability that I am late for work is $\tfrac{1}{6}$. If I cycle, the probability that I am early for work is $\tfrac{1}{2}$, and the probability that I am late for work is $\tfrac{1}{4}$. If I walk, the probability that I am early for work is $\tfrac{1}{5}$, while the probability that I am late for work is $\tfrac{3}{5}$. What is the probability that:*

(a) *I walk to work tomorrow, and am on time,*

(b) *I am late for work tomorrow,*

(c) *I cycle to work tomorrow, and an not late?*

Let D, C and W be the events that I drive, cycle and walk to work respectively, and let E, O and L be the events that I am early, on time or late for work. We have been told that

$$
\begin{array}{lll}
\mathbb{P}[D] = \tfrac{1}{10} & \mathbb{P}[C] = \tfrac{3}{10} & \mathbb{P}[W] = \tfrac{6}{10} \\[4pt]
\mathbb{P}[E|D] = \tfrac{1}{4} & \mathbb{P}[O|D] = \tfrac{7}{12} & \mathbb{P}[L|D] = \tfrac{1}{6} \\[4pt]
\mathbb{P}[E|C] = \tfrac{1}{2} & \mathbb{P}[O|C] = \tfrac{1}{4} & \mathbb{P}[L|C] = \tfrac{1}{4} \\[4pt]
\mathbb{P}[E|W] = \tfrac{1}{5} & \mathbb{P}[O|W] = \tfrac{1}{5} & \mathbb{P}[L|W] = \tfrac{3}{5}
\end{array}
$$

Thus

$$\begin{aligned}
\mathbb{P}[W \cap O] &= \mathbb{P}[W] \times \mathbb{P}[O|W] = \tfrac{6}{10} \times \tfrac{1}{5} = \tfrac{3}{25} \\
\mathbb{P}[L] &= \mathbb{P}[D \cap L] + \mathbb{P}[C \cap L] + \mathbb{P}[W \cap L] = \mathbb{P}[D]\mathbb{P}[L|D] + \mathbb{P}[C]\mathbb{P}[L|C] + \mathbb{P}[W]\mathbb{P}[L|W] \\
&= \tfrac{1}{10} \times \tfrac{1}{6} + \tfrac{3}{10} \times \tfrac{1}{4} + \tfrac{6}{10} \times \tfrac{3}{5} = \tfrac{271}{600} \\
\mathbb{P}[C \cap L'] &= \mathbb{P}[C \cap (E \cup O)] = \mathbb{P}[C \cap E] + \mathbb{P}[C \cap O] \\
&= \mathbb{P}[C]\mathbb{P}[E|C] + \mathbb{P}[C]\mathbb{P}[O|C] = \tfrac{3}{10} \times \tfrac{1}{2} + \tfrac{3}{10} \times 14 = \tfrac{9}{40}
\end{aligned}$$

The alternative to this approach would be to construct a tree diagram with multiple branches like the one below (which is still missing the probabilities):

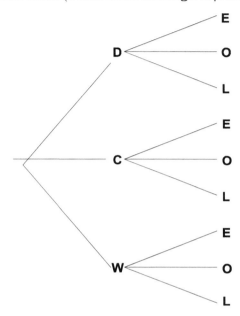

Figure 31.8

Example 31.5.3. *There are n sweets in a bag, of which 3 are mints. Peter takes one sweet at random, eats it, then eats another. The probability that he has eaten no mints is twice the probability that he has eaten two mints. How many sweets were in the bag initially?*

Let M_1 and M_2 be the events Peter first and second sweets, respectively, are mints. Since 3 out of n sweets are mints, it is clear that $\mathbb{P}[M_1] = \tfrac{3}{n}$. If Peter's first sweet is a mint, there are now 2 mints in the bag, and $n - 3$ other sweets in the bag, and so $\mathbb{P}[M_2|M_1] = \tfrac{2}{n-1}$. If Peter's first sweet is not a mint, then there are still 3 mints and $n - 4$ other sweets in the bag, and so $\mathbb{P}[M_2'|M_1'] = \tfrac{n-4}{n-1}$. Thus

$$\begin{aligned}
\mathbb{P}[M_1 \cap M_2] &= \mathbb{P}[M_1]\mathbb{P}[M_2|M_1] = \tfrac{3}{n} \times \tfrac{2}{n-1} = \tfrac{6}{n(n-1)} \\
\mathbb{P}[M_1' \cap M_2'] &= \mathbb{P}[M_1']\mathbb{P}[M_2'|M_1'] = \tfrac{n-3}{n} \times \tfrac{n-4}{n-1} = \tfrac{(n-3)(n-4)}{n(n-1)}
\end{aligned}$$

and so we deduce that

$$\begin{aligned}
\mathbb{P}[M_1' \cap M_2'] &= 2\mathbb{P}[M_1 \cap M_2] \\
(n-3)(n-4) &= 2 \times 6 \\
n^2 - 7n &= 0
\end{aligned}$$

and hence $n = 7$ (for the problem to make sense, n must be at least 3).

One of the exciting applications of conditional probability is the way it enables us to **reverse causation**, in some sense. We could envisage a situation where an island is inhabited by two species of poisonous snake. The first type is more common, but non-aggressive. The second type is rarer, but very aggressive. A man walking on the island is bitten by a snake. Which species is the more likely culprit?

The information we are given comes in a particular order; we know (if we have details about what 'more common' and 'rarer' mean) which snake is more likely to be encountered on a walk. We also know (if we have details about what 'non-aggressive' and 'very aggressive' mean) what the chances are of being bitten, when encountering a snake of either type. Now we turn the problem on its head: someone has been bitten by a snake; which species is more likely to have bitten the man? This sort of probabilistic detective work is handled well by conditional probabilities.

Example 31.5.4. *One quarter of students in a school do not revise thoroughly for their examinations. The school knows that 80% of students who revise thoroughly will gain distinctions, but that only 15% of students who do not revise will gain distinctions.*

One student gained a distinction in her examination. What is the probability that she revised thoroughly? Another student failed to gain a distinction in his examination. What is the probability that he revised thoroughly?

Let R be the event that a student revised thoroughly, and let D be the event that a student gets a distinction. We are told that $\mathbb{P}[R] = \frac{3}{4}$, and that $\mathbb{P}[D|R] = 0.8$, while $\mathbb{P}[D|R'] = 0.15$. We want to know the probabilities $\mathbb{P}[R|D]$ and $\mathbb{P}[R|D']$. Now

$$\mathbb{P}[D] = \mathbb{P}[R]\mathbb{P}[D|R] + \mathbb{P}[R]\mathbb{P}[D'|R'] = \tfrac{3}{4} \times 0.8 + \tfrac{1}{4} \times 0.15 = \tfrac{51}{80}$$

and so

$$\mathbb{P}[R|D] = \frac{\mathbb{P}[D \cap R]}{\mathbb{P}[D]} = \frac{\mathbb{P}[R]\mathbb{P}[D|R]}{\mathbb{P}[D]} = \frac{3/4 \times 0.8}{51/80} = \tfrac{16}{17}$$

$$\mathbb{P}[R|D'] = \frac{\mathbb{P}[D' \cap R]}{\mathbb{P}[D']} = \frac{\mathbb{P}[R]\mathbb{P}[D'|R]}{\mathbb{P}[D']} = \frac{3/4 \times 0.2}{29/80} = \tfrac{12}{29}$$

Example 31.5.5. *The Doctor's Dilemma. One in a thousand people who have a particular set of symptoms suffer from a particular disease. A patient who goes to his doctor exhibiting these symptoms can be given a test. The test comes back as positive for 99% of patients who have the disease, but also comes back as positive in 0.5% of patients without the disease.*

A patient goes to his doctor with the symptoms of this illness and is given the test. The test comes back positive. What is the probability that the patient has the disease?

Let D be the event that the patient has the disease, and let P be the event that the test is positive. We are told that

$$\mathbb{P}[D] = 0.001, \qquad \mathbb{P}[P|D] = 0.99, \qquad \mathbb{P}[P|D'] = 0.005.$$

Thus

$$\mathbb{P}[P] = \mathbb{P}[D]\mathbb{P}[P|D] + \mathbb{P}[D']\mathbb{P}[P|D']$$
$$= 0.001 \times 0.99 + 0.999 \times 0.005 = 0.005985$$
$$\mathbb{P}[D|P] = \frac{\mathbb{P}[P \cap D]}{\mathbb{P}[P]} = \frac{\mathbb{P}[D]\mathbb{P}[P|D]}{\mathbb{P}[P]} = \frac{0.001 \times 0.99}{0.005985} = 0.1654$$

Even though the test is very good at identifying people with the disease, the fact there is a slight chance of misdiagnosis for the large number of patients without the disease means that this test is only 16.5% effective in accurately identifying people with the disease.

On the bright side, we also see that

$$\mathbb{P}[D \cap P'] = \mathbb{P}[D] - \mathbb{P}[P \cap D] = 0.00001$$
$$\mathbb{P}[D|P'] = \frac{\mathbb{P}[D \cap P']}{\mathbb{P}[P']} = \frac{0.00001}{1 - 0.005985} = 1.01 \times 10^{-5}$$

so this test is very unlikely to fail to diagnose someone with the disease, since the chance that someone with a negative test result actually has the disease is about 1 in 100000.

This test has managed to improve matters somewhat. Compared to the initial position, where the probability that a symptomatic patient has the disease is 1 in 1000, the probability that a symptomatic patient who tests positive has the disease is about 16.5%. However, a doctor will need to be able to differentiate between the symptomatic, positive-testing, patients with and without the disease: those with the disease needing treatment, and the others needing reassurance.

31.6 Independent Events

Consider again a jar containing seven red discs and four white discs. Two discs are selected, but this time with replacement. This means that the first disc is returned to the jar before the second disc is selected.

Let R_1 be the event that the first disc is red, R_2 be the event that the second disc is red, W_1 be the event that the first disc is white and W_2 be the event that the second disc is white. The tree diagram for this problem is similar to the one found in Figure 31.6, but the probabilities in the second 'layer' are different.

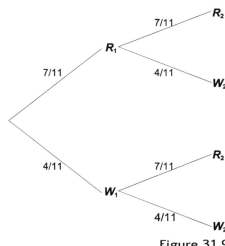

Figure 31.9

Looking at Figure 31.7 we see immediately that

$$\mathbb{P}[R_2|R_1] \ = \ \mathbb{P}[R_2|W_1] \ = \ \tfrac{7}{11} \ = \ \mathbb{P}[R_1]$$
$$\mathbb{P}[W_2|R_1] \ = \ \mathbb{P}[W_2|W_1] \ = \ \tfrac{4}{11} \ = \ \mathbb{P}[W_1]$$

but these identities are not the important ones. Since

$$\mathbb{P}[R_2] \ = \ \mathbb{P}[R_2|R_1]\mathbb{P}[R_1] + \mathbb{P}[R_2|W_1]\mathbb{P}[W_1] \ = \ \tfrac{7}{11}$$

and so $\mathbb{P}[W_2] = \tfrac{4}{11}$, we deduce that

$$\mathbb{P}[R_2|R_1] \ = \ \mathbb{P}[R_2|W_1] \ = \ \mathbb{P}[R_2], \qquad \mathbb{P}[W_2|R_1] \ = \ \mathbb{P}[W_2|W_1] \ = \ \mathbb{P}[W_2].$$

Thus the probability of R_2 does not depend on whether R_1 occurs or not, and similarly the probability of W_2 does not depend on whether R_1 occurs or not.

Events where the outcome of one has no effect on the chances of the other's occurring are called **independent**.

Key Fact 31.8 Independent Events

Two events A and B are called **independent** if the probability of one event occurring is unaffected by the occurrence of the other event, written $\mathbb{P}[A|B] = \mathbb{P}[A]$.

Since

$$\mathbb{P}[A|B] \ = \ \frac{\mathbb{P}[A \cap B]}{\mathbb{P}[B]}, \qquad \mathbb{P}[B|A] \ = \ \frac{\mathbb{P}[A \cap B]}{\mathbb{P}[B]}$$

we deduce a more general result:

Key Fact 31.9 Multiplication Law for Independent Events

Events A and B are equivalent if any one of the three equivalent identities hold:

$$\mathbb{P}[A|B] \ = \ \mathbb{P}[A] \qquad \mathbb{P}[B|A] \ = \ \mathbb{P}[B] \qquad \mathbb{P}[A \cap B] \ = \ \mathbb{P}[A]\mathbb{P}[B].$$

Example 31.6.1. *In a carnival game, a contestant first has to spin a fair coin and then roll a fair cubical dice whose faces are numbered 1 to 6. The contestant wins a prize if the coin shows heads and the dice score is below 3. Find the probability that a contestant wins a prize.*

This question could be answered simply by counting options within the sample space

$$\{(H,1),(H,2),(H,3),(H,4),(H,5),(H,6),(T,1),(T,2),(T,3),(T,4),(T,5),(T,6)\}$$

but it is more efficient to use the fact that the outcome of the dice throw is unaffected by the outcome of the coin toss. Thus, if H is the event that the coin shows heads, and L is the event that the dice score is less than 3, then H and L are independent events. Since $\mathbb{P}[H] = \tfrac{1}{2}$ and $\mathbb{P}[L] = \tfrac{1}{3}$, it follows that $\mathbb{P}[H \cap L] = \tfrac{1}{6}$.

Many questions that we previously solved by considering the sample space in detail can be solved much more efficiently using properties of independent events.

Example 31.6.2. *A fair cubical die with faces numbered 1 to 6 is rolled twice. What is the probability of rolling:*

a) *double 6,*   b) *at least one 6,*   c) *'doubles'?*

(a) *The probability of rolling 6 twice is $\frac{1}{6} \times \frac{1}{6} = \frac{1}{36}$.*

(b) *The probability of rolling no 6s is $\frac{5}{6} \times \frac{5}{6}$, and so the probability of rolling at least one 6 is $1 - \frac{25}{36} = \frac{11}{36}$*

(c) *Whatever the first die roll is, we roll doubles if the second die roll matches the first. Thus the probability of rolling doubles is $\frac{1}{6}$.*

The law of multiplication for independent events can be extended to more than two events, provided they are all independent of one another.

Example 31.6.3. *A fair cubical dice with faces numbered 1 to 6 is thrown four times. Find the probability that exactly three of the four throws result in a 6.*

We are assuming that the outcomes of different die rolls are independent of each other. The event B that exactly three of the four dice rolls is 6 is the union of events $A_1 \cup A_2 \cup A_3 \cup A_4$, where A_1 is the event that the first die roll is not 6, but the other three rolls are 6, while A_2 is the event that the second die roll is not 6, while the other three are, with similarly definitions for A_3 and A_4. It is clear that A_1, A_2, A_3 and A_4 are mutually exclusive events, so that $\mathbb{P}[B] = \mathbb{P}[A_1] + \mathbb{P}[A_2] + \mathbb{P}[A_3] + \mathbb{P}[A_4]$. If S_j is the event that the jth die roll is a 6, then it is clear that $A_1 = S_1' \cap S_2 \cap S_3 \cap S_4$. Since the outcomes of the different dice rolls are independent of each other, we may deduce that

$$\mathbb{P}[A_1] = \mathbb{P}[S_1'] \times \mathbb{P}[S_2] \times \mathbb{P}[S_3] \times \mathbb{P}[S_4] = \frac{5}{6} \times \frac{1}{6} \times \frac{1}{6} \times \frac{1}{6}.$$

Indeed, we can show that

$$\mathbb{P}[A_1] = \frac{5}{6} \times \frac{1}{6} \times \frac{1}{6} \times \frac{1}{6} \qquad \mathbb{P}[A_2] = \frac{1}{6} \times \frac{5}{6} \times \frac{1}{6} \times \frac{1}{6}$$
$$\mathbb{P}[A_3] = \frac{1}{6} \times \frac{1}{6} \times \frac{5}{6} \times \frac{1}{6} \qquad \mathbb{P}[A_4] = \frac{1}{6} \times \frac{1}{6} \times \frac{1}{6} \times \frac{5}{6}$$

and hence

$$\mathbb{P}[B] = 4 \times \left(\frac{1}{6}\right)^3 \times \frac{5}{6} = \frac{5}{324}$$

For Interest

Although is it true that

$$\mathbb{P}[A_1 \cap A_2 \cap \cdots \cap A_n] = \mathbb{P}[A_1] \times \mathbb{P}[A_2] \times \cdots \times \mathbb{P}[A_n]$$

when the events $A_1, A_2, \ldots, A_n$ are independent, the converse is not always true, except in the case when $n = 2$.

For example, consider a pack of cards consisting of the Ace, 2, 3, 4, 5, 6, 7 and 8 each of Hearts, Diamonds and Spades, plus one Joker and the Ace and King of Clubs. Pick one card at random from this pack. Let H be the event of picking either a Heart or the Joker, let D be the event of drawing either a Diamond or the Joker, and let S be the event of picking either a Spade or the Joker. Thus

$$\mathbb{P}[H] = \mathbb{P}[D] = \mathbb{P}[S] = \frac{9}{27} = \frac{1}{3}$$

and so

$$\mathbb{P}[H \cap D \cap S] = \mathbb{P}[\text{pick the Joker}] = \frac{1}{27} = \mathbb{P}[H] \times \mathbb{P}[D] \times \mathbb{P}[S]$$

Mathematicians would not regard these three events as independent, because the events H and D are not independent of each other.

31.7 Buffon's Needle

The Comte de Buffon discovered this experiment in the 18th century. Suppose that a large sheet of paper is ruled with parallel lines a distance 6 cm apart. Drop a needle, which is 6 cm long, onto the sheet of paper. What is the probability that the needle will intersect one of the parallel lines on the sheet?

In the simulation on the right, a needle has been dropped onto the sheet 30 times, and the needle has crossed a line a total of 19 times. The proportion of intersections here is $\frac{19}{30}$.

It is interesting to discover that the probability of an intersection is $\frac{2}{\pi}$, and the Comte de Buffon used this as a method for obtaining an approximate value of π. Our relative frequency of $\frac{19}{30}$ would approximate π as $2 \div \frac{19}{30} = 3.158$, which is not bad for just 30 needle throws!

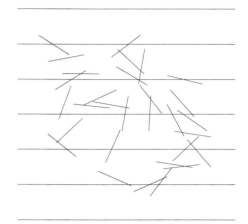

Figure 31.10

Why does this work? The answer lies in slightly more probability theory than we currently have, but it is worthwhile to follow the argument, nonetheless.

When a needle lands on the sheet of paper, let y be the shortest distance from the midpoint of the needle to one of the lines, and let θ be the angle that the needle makes with the lines. It is clear that the needle intersects a line provided that $y < 3\sin\theta$. Now y can take any value between 0 and 3 cm, and θ can take any value between 0 and $\frac{1}{2}\pi$, and all distances y and all angles θ are equally likely. Moreover, the angle θ is independent of the distance y.

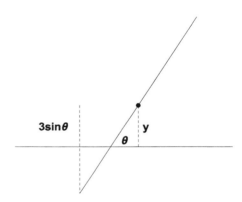

Figure 31.11

What is new here is that both y and θ can take a continuous range of values. We shall handle this by saying that the sample space is the rectangle $0 \le x \le \frac{1}{2}\pi$, $0 \le y \le 3$. The event of the needle intersecting with a line is the event represented by the shaded region below the line $y = 3\sin x$. Standard integration gives the area of this region as

$$\int_0^{\frac{1}{2}\pi} 3\sin x\, dx = \left[-3\cos x\right]_0^{\frac{1}{2}\pi} = 3$$

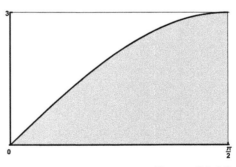

Figure 31.12

while the area of the whole rectangle is $\frac{3}{2}\pi$. If all values of θ and values of y are equally likely, it is reasonable to assume that the probability of an event is proportional to the area it represents in the sample space. Thus the probability of a needle intersecting a line is

$$3 \div \tfrac{3}{2}\pi = \tfrac{2}{\pi}$$

> **For Interest**
>
> We can only hope that the Comte was satisfied with a reasonably low level of accuracy. While this method can obtain π to a small degree of accuracy after comparatively few throws, getting a good degree of accuracy of π takes a very large number of throws. To be 99% sure of obtaining π to 5 decimal places, approximately 5.53×10^{12} throws are required. At one throw a second, that would take 175000 years!

We have put this calculation in here largely for interest, but also because we shall shortly meet the normal distribution, and the idea that areas can be used to describe probabilities is key there.

EXERCISE 31B

1. A bag contains six red and four green counters. Two counters are drawn, without replacement. Find the probabilities that:
    a) both are red,
    b) both are green,
    c) just one is red,
    d) at least one is red,
    e) the second is red.
    Does it make any difference to any of your answers if the two counters are drawn simultaneously rather than one after the other?

2. Two cards are drawn, without replacement, from an ordinary pack. Find the probabilities that
    a) both are picture cards (K, Q, J),
    b) neither is a picture card,
    c) at least one is a picture card,
    d) at least one is red.

3. Events A, B and C satisfy these conditions:

    $$\mathbb{P}[A] = 0.6, \quad \mathbb{P}[B] = 0.8, \quad \mathbb{P}[B|A] = 0.45, \quad \mathbb{P}[B \cap C] = 0.28$$

    Calculate
    a) $\mathbb{P}[A \cap B]$,
    b) $\mathbb{P}[C|B]$,
    c) $\mathbb{P}[A|B]$.

4. A class consists of seven boys and nine girls. Two different members of the class are chosen at random. A is the event that the first person is a girl, and B is the event that the second person is a girl. Find the probabilities:
    a) $\mathbb{P}[B \mid A]$,
    b) $\mathbb{P}[B'|A]$,
    c) $\mathbb{P}[B \mid A']$,
    d) $\mathbb{P}[B' \mid A']$,
    e) $\mathbb{P}[B]$.
    Is it true that
    f) $\mathbb{P}[B|A] + \mathbb{P}[B'|A] = 1$,
    g) $\mathbb{P}[B|A] + \mathbb{P}[B|A'] = 1$?

5. A weather forecaster classifies all days as wet or dry. She estimates that the probability that 1 June next year is wet is 0.4. If any particular day in June is wet, the probability that the next day is wet is 0.6; otherwise the probability that the next day is wet is 0.3. Find the probability that, next year,
    a) the first two days of June are both wet,
    b) June 2nd is wet,
    c) at least one of the first three days of June is wet.

6. Two chess players, K1 and K2, are playing each other in a series of games. The probability that K1 wins the first game is 0.3. If K1 wins any game, the probability that he wins the next is 0.4; otherwise the probability is 0.2. Find the probability that K1 wins
    a) the first two games,
    b) at least one of the first two games,
    c) the first three games,
    d) exactly one of the first three games.

    The result of any game can be a win for K1, a win for K2, or a draw. The probability that any one game is drawn is 0.5, independent of the results of all previous games. Find the probability that, after two games,
    e) K1 won the first and K2 the second,
    f) each won one game,
    g) each has won the same number of games.

7. A fair cubical dice is thrown four times. Find the probability that

   a) all four scores are 4 or more,

   b) at least one score is less than 4,

   c) at least one of the scores is a 6.

8. **The Chevalier du Meré's Problem.** A seventeenth-century French gambler, the Chevalier du Meré, had run out of takers for his bet that, when a fair cubical dice was thrown four times, at least one 6 would be scored (see the previous question). He therefore changed the game to throwing a pair of fair dice 24 times. What is the probability that, out of these 24 throws, at least one is a double 6?

9. **The Birthday Problem.** What is the probability that, out of 23 randomly chosen people, at least two share a birthday? Assume that all 365 days of the year are equally likely and ignore leap years. (Hint: find the probabilities that two people have different birthdays, that three people have different birthdays, and so on.)

10. Given that $\mathbb{P}[A] = 0.75$, $\mathbb{P}[B|A] = 0.8$ and $\mathbb{P}[B|A'] = 0.6$, calculate $\mathbb{P}[B]$ and $\mathbb{P}[A|B]$.

11. There are two races on the planet Zod, the Aardry and the Bevo. The Aardry make up a proportion p of the Zod Planetary Parliament, with the remainder of seats taken by Bevo. When voting in Parliament, the Aardry never change their minds on a subject, whereas that Bevo change their mind between successive votes with probability r.

    A member of the Zod Planetary Parliament has just been seen to vote in the same way twice in a row. What is the probability that it will vote the same way another time?

12. **Resolving the Doctor's Dilemma.** Recall the diagnostic test discussed in Example 31.5.5. The doctor decides to apply a repeat test to all patients with symptoms who tested positive for the first test. What is the probability that a patient who tested positive first time and tested positive again has the disease?

13*. For any events A and B, express $\mathbb{P}[A \cap B]$ and $\mathbb{P}[B]$ in terms of $\mathbb{P}[A]$, $\mathbb{P}[A']$, $\mathbb{P}[B|A]$ and $\mathbb{P}[B|A']$. Deduce **Bayes' Theorem:**

$$\mathbb{P}[A|B] = \frac{\mathbb{P}[A]\mathbb{P}[B|A]}{\mathbb{P}[A]\mathbb{P}[B|A] + \mathbb{P}[A']\mathbb{P}[B|A']}$$

14*. **The Prosecutor's Fallacy.** An accused prisoner is on trial. The defence lawyer asserts that, in the absence of further evidence, the probability that the prisoner is guilty is 1 in a million. The prosecuting lawyer produces a further piece of evidence and asserts that, if the prisoner were guilty, the probability that this evidence would have been obtained is 999 in 1000, and if he were not guilty the probability would only be 1 in 1000. Assuming that the court admits the legality of the evidence, and that the lawyer's figures are correct, what is the probability that the prisoner is guilty? Comment on your answer.

15*. **Pòlya's Urn.** Initially there is one white marble and one black marble in an urn. Every minute a marble is taken at random from the urn, and replaced **together with another marble of the same colour.** After n minutes there will be $n + 2$ marbles in the urn, and there will be at least one marble of each colour; there could be anything from 1 to $n + 1$ black marbles in the urn. For any $1 \le r \le n + 1$, let $A(n, r)$ be the event that there are r black marbles in the urn after n minutes.

    a) Show that $\mathbb{P}[A(1,1)] = \mathbb{P}[A(1,2)] = \frac{1}{2}$.

    b) Show that $\mathbb{P}[A(2,1)] = \mathbb{P}[A(2,2)] = \mathbb{P}[A(2,3)] = \frac{1}{3}$.

    c) What are the values of $\mathbb{P}[A(3,r)]$, for $1 \le r \le 4$?

    d) Suggest a value for $\mathbb{P}[A(n,r)]$ for any $1 \le r \le n + 1$. What does this suggest to you about the proportion of black balls in the urn after n minutes?

    e) Suppose that, after 999998 minutes there are 500000 black marbles and 500000 white marbles in the urn. Will the proportion of black marbles in the urn change greatly after the next minute? What does this suggest to you about the proportion of black balls in the urn after n minutes when n is large?

    f) If you have answered the parts of this question correctly you are probably rather confused about what is going on! Try some internet research to see all this ties together. There are some nice computer simulations to be found.

Chapter 31: Summary

- A sample space $\mathcal{E}$ is the collection of all possible outcomes of an experiment. Each element $\omega \in \mathcal{E}$ has assigned to it a probability $p(\omega)$, which is the event that outcome ω occurs. We have $p(\omega) \geq 0$ for all ω, and

$$\sum_{\omega \in \mathcal{E}} p(\omega) = 1 .$$

- An **event** is any subset of $\mathcal{E}$, its probability, written $\mathbb{P}[A]$ or $P(A)$, is

$$\mathbb{P}[A] = P(A) = \sum_{\omega \in A} p(\omega) .$$

  If all events in the sample space $\mathcal{E}$ are equally likely to occur, then $\mathbb{P}[A] = \dfrac{n(A)}{n(\mathcal{E})}$ for any event A, where $n(B)$ is the number of elements in the set B.

- The **complement** of the event A is the event that A does not occur; it is the set-theoretical complement A' of A. Given two events A and B, the event that both occur is their intersection $A \cap B$, and the event that either A or B (or both) occurs is their union $A \cup B$. The following identities hold:

$$\mathbb{P}[A] + \mathbb{P}[A'] = 1 \qquad \mathbb{P}[A \cup B] + \mathbb{P}[A \cap B] = \mathbb{P}[A] + \mathbb{P}[B] .$$

- Events A and B are **mutually exclusive** when $\mathbb{P}[A \cap B] = 0$, in which case $\mathbb{P}[A \cup B] = \mathbb{P}[A] + \mathbb{P}[B]$.

- Events A and B are **independent** when $\mathbb{P}[A \cap B] = \mathbb{P}[A]\mathbb{P}[B]$.

- The probability of the event A, conditional upon the event B, is written $\mathbb{P}[A|B]$, and is equal to

$$\mathbb{P}[A|B] = \frac{\mathbb{P}[A \cap B]}{\mathbb{P}[B]} .$$

  The events A and B are independent when $\mathbb{P}[A|B] = \mathbb{P}[A]$.

- If A and B are two events, the conditional probability formula states that

$$\mathbb{P}[A] = \mathbb{P}[A|B]\mathbb{P}[B] + \mathbb{P}[A|B']\mathbb{P}[B'] .$$

Random Variables

In this chapter we will learn to:

- use formulae for the probabilities of the binomial and geometric distributions, recognising the notations $B(n,p)$ and $\text{Geo}(p)$, model given situations by one of these as appropriate,

- use tables of cumulative binomial probabilities,

- construct a probability distribution table relating to a given situation involving a discrete random variable X, and calculate the expectation, variance and standard deviation of X,

- use formulae for the expectation and variance of the binomial and geometric distributions.

32.1 Discrete Random Variables

Most people have played board games at some time. Dice are often used to determine each player's move. Here are some examples:

Game A: A turn consists of throwing a die and then moving a number of squares equal to the score on the die.

Game B: A person is allowed a second throw of the die if the first throw is a 6, and may move a number of squares equal to the score on the first die, plus the score on the second die if a second throw was allowed.

Game C: Two dice are thrown, and the player moves a number of squares equal to the sum of the scores on the two dice.

In each of these games, the number of squares moved in a turn is a **variable**, because it can take different values. However, the value it takes is determined by chance, and so we call it a **random variable**.

> **Key Fact 32.1** Random Variables — The Big Picture
>
> A **random variable** is a numeric quantity whose value depends on chance.

The number of squares that a player can move in one of the above three games fits this definition.

Game A: We know that a fair 6-sided die rolls the values 1, 2, 3, 4, 5 and 6 with equal probability $\frac{1}{6}$. It is convenient to say that the random variable X, the number of squares that a player can move, can take any of the values 1, 2, 3, 4, 5 and 6, each with probability $\frac{1}{6}$. The outcome of rolling a 3, the event $\{3\}$ from the sample space $\{1,2,3,4,5,6\}$, can now be written simply as $X = 3$ (at this stage, it is conventional to drop the curly brackets), and we write $\mathbb{P}[X = 3] = \frac{1}{6}$ to denote the fact that the probability of throwing a 3 is $\frac{1}{6}$. Full information about this random variable can be found in the following table, that records possible values of X, and the corresponding probabilities that X takes those values:

x	1	2	3	4	5	6
$\mathbb{P}[X = x]$	$\frac{1}{6}$	$\frac{1}{6}$	$\frac{1}{6}$	$\frac{1}{6}$	$\frac{1}{6}$	$\frac{1}{6}$

Game B: This time we have a more complicated sample space, that we can write as $\{1, 2, 3, 4, 5, (6, 1), (6, 2), (6, 3), (6, 4), (6, 5), (6, 6)\}$. The first five of these outcomes all occur with probability $\frac{1}{6}$, while the last six occur with probability $\left(\frac{1}{6}\right)^2 = \frac{1}{36}$ since the dice rolls are independent of each other. An outcome of $(6, 2)$, for example, means that the number of moves available to the player is $6 + 2 = 8$.

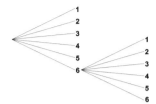

Figure 32.1

If Y is the number of squares that the player can move, then Y can take any of the values $1, 2, 3, 4, 5, 7, 8, 9, 10, 11$ and 12, and the following table gives the key information about Y:

y	1	2	3	4	5	7	8	9	10	11	12
$\mathbb{P}[Y = y]$	$\frac{1}{6}$	$\frac{1}{6}$	$\frac{1}{6}$	$\frac{1}{6}$	$\frac{1}{6}$	$\frac{1}{36}$	$\frac{1}{36}$	$\frac{1}{36}$	$\frac{1}{36}$	$\frac{1}{36}$	$\frac{1}{36}$

Game C: Let Z be the number of squares that the player can move. The diagram on the right represents the sample space for this problem, and the values that Z takes for the various outcomes of the sample space. We see that, this time, Z can take all integer values between 2 and 12, and the table below shows that key information about Z:

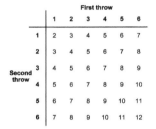

Figure 32.2

z	2	3	4	5	6	7	8	9	10	11	12
$\mathbb{P}[Z = z]$	$\frac{1}{36}$	$\frac{2}{36}$	$\frac{3}{36}$	$\frac{4}{36}$	$\frac{5}{36}$	$\frac{6}{36}$	$\frac{5}{36}$	$\frac{4}{36}$	$\frac{3}{36}$	$\frac{2}{36}$	$\frac{1}{36}$

We have seen that a random variable X consists of a set of values (the values that the random variable can take), plus a collection of associated probabilities. For the present, we are assuming that the set of values that the random variable X can take is **discrete**; just as in Chapter 28, this means that the values of X are clearly distinguishable from each other. There might be a finite number of values only, or there might a list of possible values, like the positive integers. The fact that X must take a value for all outcomes in the underlying sample space has an implication for the collection of associated probabilities.

Key Fact 32.2 Discrete Random Variables — The Details

A **discrete random variable** X consists of a discrete set S consisting of the possible values that the variable X can take, and the corresponding probabilities of X taking each value. The function

$$f(x) = \mathbb{P}[X = x], \qquad x \in S,$$

is called the **probability distribution function** or simply the **mass function** of X.
An alternative notation is to write the set $S = \{x_1, x_2, \ldots\}$. We write x_i to represent a general element of S (the values of i will either lie between 1 and N for some positive integer N, or else i can be any positive integer). We then write

$$p_i = f(x_i) = \mathbb{P}[X = x_i].$$

It should be noted that there are quantities that depend on probability that do not take numeric values. For example, the eye colour of the first person I meet on the street tomorrow morning can be regarded as depending on chance, but takes non-numeric values like blue, hazel, and so on. Although objects like this are of importance to statisticians, we are not going to consider them. The fact that they do not take numeric values means that we cannot analyse them in the same manner.

Example 32.1.1. *A bag contains two red and three blue marbles. Two marbles are selected at random without replacement and the number, X, of blue marbles is counted. Find the probability distribution of X. What is the probability that X is even?*

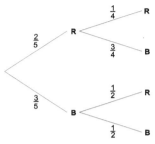

The number of blue marbles can be 0, 1 or 2. Considering the tree diagram, it is clear that

$$\mathbb{P}[X = 0] = \mathbb{P}[\{(R, R)\}] = \tfrac{2}{5} \times \tfrac{1}{4} = \tfrac{1}{10}$$
$$\mathbb{P}[X = 1] = \mathbb{P}[\{(R, B), (B, R)\}] = \tfrac{2}{5} \times \tfrac{3}{4} + \tfrac{3}{5} \times \tfrac{1}{2} = \tfrac{3}{5}$$
$$\mathbb{P}[X = 2] = \mathbb{P}[\{(B, B)\}] = \tfrac{3}{5} \times \tfrac{1}{2} = \tfrac{3}{10}.$$

Figure 32.3

Thus the probability generating function for X is:

x	0	1	2
$\mathbb{P}[\mathbf{X} = \mathbf{x}]$	$\tfrac{1}{10}$	$\tfrac{3}{5}$	$\tfrac{3}{10}$

Example 32.1.2. *A random variable, X, can take the values 1, 2, 3 or 4, and has the probability distribution function*

x	1	2	3	4
$\mathbb{P}[\mathbf{X} = \mathbf{x}]$	0.1	0.2	0.3	0.4

Two independent observations are made of X and the random variable Y is equal to the difference of these two values. Find the probability distribution of Y. Which value of Y is most likely?

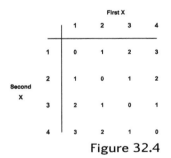

The table illustrates the possible values of Y, according to the possible two values of X. It is clear that Y can take the values 0, 1, 2 or 3. We see that

$$\begin{aligned}
\mathbb{P}[Y = 0] &= \mathbb{P}[\{(0, 0), (1, 1), (2, 2), (3, 3)\}] \\
&= \mathbb{P}[(0, 0)] + \mathbb{P}[(1, 1)] + \mathbb{P}[(2, 2)] + \mathbb{P}[(3, 3)] \\
&= 0.1 \times 0.1 + 0.2 \times 0.2 + 0.3 \times 0.3 + 0.4 \times 0.4 \\
&= 0.30
\end{aligned}$$

Figure 32.4

while

$$\begin{aligned}
\mathbb{P}[Y = 1] &= \mathbb{P}[\{(1, 2), (2, 1), (2, 3), (3, 2), (3, 4), (4, 3)\}] \\
&= 0.1 \times 0.2 + 0.2 \times 0.1 + 0.2 \times 0.3 + 0.3 \times 0.2 + 0.3 \times 0.4 + 0.4 \times 0.3 = 0.40 \\
\mathbb{P}[Y = 2] &= \mathbb{P}[\{(1, 3), (3, 1), (2, 4), (4, 2)\}] = 0.1 \times 0.3 + 0.3 \times 0.1 + 0.2 \times 0.4 + 0.4 \times 0.2 = 0.22 \\
\mathbb{P}[Y = 3] &= \mathbb{P}[\{(1, 4), (4, 1)\}] = 0.1 \times 0.4 + 0.4 \times 0.1 = 0.08
\end{aligned}$$

and so Y has the probability distribution function

y	0	1	2	3
$\mathbb{P}[\mathbf{Y} = \mathbf{y}]$	0.30	0.40	0.22	0.08

from which it is clear that the most likely value of Y is 1.

EXERCISE 32A

1. A fair coin is thrown four times. The random variable X is the number of heads obtained. Find the probability distribution of X.

2. Two fair dice are thrown simultaneously. The random variable D is the difference between the two scores. Find the probability distribution of D.

3. A fair dice is thrown once. The random variable X is related to the number N thrown on the dice as follows. If N is even, then X is $\frac{1}{2}N$; otherwise X is $2N$. Find the probability distribution of X.

4. Two fair dice are thrown simultaneously. The random variable H is the highest common factor of the two scores. Find the probability distribution of H.

5. When a four-sided dice is thrown, the score is the number on the bottom face. Two fair four-sided dice, each with faces numbered 1 to 4, are thrown simultaneously. The random variable M is the product of the two scores multiplied together. Find the probability distribution of M.

6. A bag contains six red and three green counters. Two counters are drawn from the bag, without replacement. Find the probability distribution of the number of green counters obtained.

7. Stephen picks a card at random from an ordinary pack. If the card is an Ace, he stops; if not, he continues to pick cards at random, without replacement, until either an ace is picked, or four cards have been drawn altogether. The random variable C is the total number of cards drawn. Calculate the probability distribution of C.

8. Use a spreadsheet to draw diagrams to illustrate the probability distributions of the total number of heads obtained when $3, 4, 5, \ldots$ fair coins are thrown.

9*. Obtain the probability distribution of the total score when three fair cubical dice are thrown simultaneously.

32.2 Key Properties of a Probability Distribution

All probability distributions of discrete random variables have the following important properties.

> **Key Fact 32.3** Properties of a Probability Distribution
>
> If X is a random variable, then the probability distribution function $f(x) = \mathbb{P}[X = x]$ must have the following properties:
>
> - $p_i = f(x_i) = \mathbb{P}[X = x_i] \geq 0$ for all i,
>
> - The sum of $f(x)$ over all possible values of x is 1: $\displaystyle\sum_i p_i = 1$.
>
> As before, we are using $S = \{x_1, x_2, \ldots\}$ to represent the set of possible values of X.

These properties are not that surprising. The first merely reflects the fact that all the values $f(x)$ are probabilities, while the second reflects the fact that X has to take some value, and hence

$$\sum_i p_i = \sum_{x \in S} f(x) = \sum_{x \in S} \mathbb{P}[X = x] = \mathbb{P}[X \text{ takes some value}] = 1$$

Example 32.2.1. *The table below gives the probability distribution of the random variable T.*

t	1	2	3	4	5
$\mathbb{P}[T = t]$	c	$2c$	$2c$	$2c$	c

Find: a) the value of c, b) $\mathbb{P}[T \leq 3]$, c) $\mathbb{P}[T > 1]$.

(a) Since the probabilities must add to 1, $c + 2c + 2c + 2c + c = 1$, and so $c = \frac{1}{8}$.

(b) $\mathbb{P}[T \le 3] = \mathbb{P}[T = 1] + \mathbb{P}[T = 2] + \mathbb{P}[T = 3] = c + 2c + 2c = 5c = \frac{5}{8}$.

(c) $\mathbb{P}[T > 1] = 1 - \mathbb{P}[T = 1] = 1 - c = \frac{7}{8}$.

Example 32.2.2. *A computer is programmed to give single-digit numbers X between 0 and 9 inclusive in such a way that the probability of getting an odd digit is half the probability of getting an even digit. Find the probability distribution of X.*

Let the probability of getting an odd digit be c. Then the probability of getting an even digit is $2c$.

Since the probabilities must sum to 1,

$$1 = \sum_{x=0}^{9} \mathbb{P}[X = x] = 2c + c + 2c + c + 2c + c + 2c + c + 2c + c = 15c$$

so that $c = \frac{1}{15}$. Hence $\mathbb{P}[X = x] = \frac{1}{15}$ for $x = 1, 3, 5, 7, 9$, while $\mathbb{P}[X = x] = \frac{2}{15}$ for $x = 0, 2, 4, 6, 8$.

Food For Thought 32.1

To be really precise, a random variable is a real-valued function X on the underlying sample space $\mathcal{E}$. The set S of possible values of X is the range of the function $X : \mathcal{E} \to \mathbb{R}$. The random variable X is discrete when the set S consists of clearly distinguishable values: either a finite set or the positive integers, for example.

The probability distribution function can be obtained from the probabilities for the various outcomes of the sample space by noting that

$$\mathbb{P}[X = x] = \sum_{\omega : X(\omega) = x} p(\omega) = \mathbb{P}[X^{-1}\{x\}]$$

where $X^{-1}\{x\}$ is the event $\{\omega \in \mathcal{E} \,|\, X(\omega) = x\}$, and the above sum is meant to be performed over all values of ω such that $X(\omega) = x$.

If $x, y \in S$ and $x \ne y$ then $X^{-1}(x) \cap X^{-1}(y) = \emptyset$ (it is not possible for $\omega \in \mathcal{E}$ to be such that $X(\omega)$ equals both x and y), and hence $X^{-1}(x)$, for $x \in S$, is a disjoint partition of $\mathcal{E}$. This implies that

$$\sum_i p_i = \sum_{x \in S} \mathbb{P}[X = x] = 1$$

32.3 The Cumulative Distribution Function

In previous mathematical studies, we will have met the notion of **cumulative frequency**, namely a 'running total' of the frequency of whatever we are measuring. There is a similar notion of **cumulative probability**, that is particularly neatly expressed for random variables.

Key Fact 32.4 The Cumulative Distribution Function

If X is a random variable, then the **cumulative distribution function** $F(x)$ (the symbol F is always used) for X is the function

$$F(x) = \mathbb{P}[X \le x].$$

In principle, x could be any real number, but for discrete random variables x can (in the interests of simplicity) be restricted to the set S of possible outcomes of X.

The important thing to realise is that the cumulative distribution function F contains exactly the same information about the random variable as does the probability generating function f. To see this, note that

$$F(x) = \mathbb{P}[X \leq x] = \sum_{y \leq x} \mathbb{P}[X = y] = \sum_{y \leq x} f(y)$$

so we see that the cumulative distribution function F can be derived from the probability generating function f. To go in the other direction, note that

$$f(x) = \mathbb{P}[X = x] = \mathbb{P}[X \leq x] - \mathbb{P}[X < x] = F(x) - \mathbb{P}[X < x]$$

which almost describes f in terms of F. Because of the strict inequality, the term $\mathbb{P}[X < x]$ is not the same as $F(x) = \mathbb{P}[X \leq x]$. However, it **is** equal to $F(\hat{x}) = \mathbb{P}[X \leq \hat{x}]$, where $\hat{x}$ is the largest value of S (the set of possible values of X) which is less than x, and hence

$$f(x) = F(x) - F(\hat{x}).$$

Example 32.3.1. *If X is the outcome of the roll of a fair cubical die, write down the cumulative density function F.*

Since $S = \{1, 2, 3, 4, 5, 6\}$, we know that $f(x) = \frac{1}{6}$ for $1 \leq x \leq 6$, and hence

$$F(x) = \sum_{n=1}^{x} f(n) = \frac{1}{6}x, \qquad x = 1, 2, 3, 4, 5, 6.$$

Example 32.3.2. *A discrete random variable X, taking values 1, 2, 3 and 4, has cumulative distribution function F, where*

$$F(1) = \frac{1}{2}, \qquad F(2) = \frac{3}{4}, \qquad F(3) = \frac{7}{8}, \qquad F(4) = 1.$$

Find the probability distribution function for X, and calculate the probability that $2 \leq X \leq 3$.

Since X only takes the values 1, 2, 3 and 4, we deduce that

$$\begin{aligned}
f(1) &= F(1) = \frac{1}{2} \\
f(2) &= F(2) - F(1) = \frac{1}{4} \\
f(3) &= F(3) - F(2) = \frac{1}{8} \\
f(4) &= F(4) - F(3) = \frac{1}{8}
\end{aligned}$$

Thus

$$\mathbb{P}[2 \leq X \leq 3] = \mathbb{P}[X = 2, 3] = f(2) + f(3) = \frac{3}{8}.$$

Alternatively, we could have noted that $\mathbb{P}[2 \leq X \leq 3] = F(3) - F(1) = \frac{3}{8}$.

The same calculations can be used for discrete random variables that can take an infinite number of values.

Example 32.3.3. *Suppose that the random variable X takes values in the positive integers $\mathbb{N}$, and that the cumulative distribution function F is*

$$F(n) = \frac{n}{n+1}, \qquad n \in \mathbb{N}.$$

Find the probability distribution function of X.

We see that $f(1) = F(1) = \frac{1}{2}$, while

$$f(x) = F(x) - F(x-1) = \frac{x}{x+1} - \frac{x-1}{x} = \frac{1}{x(x+1)}, \qquad x \geq 2,$$

so we deduce that the probability distribution function is

$$f(x) = \mathbb{P}[X = x] = \frac{1}{x(x+1)}, \qquad x \in \mathbb{N}.$$

EXERCISE 32B

1. In the following probability distribution, c is a constant. Find the value of c.

x	0	1	2	3
$\mathbb{P}[X = x]$	$\frac{1}{4}$	$\frac{1}{5}$	$\frac{1}{2}$	c

2. In the following probability distribution, d is a constant. Find the value of d.

x	0	1	2	3
$\mathbb{P}[X = x]$	d	0.1	0.2	0.4

3. In the following probability distribution, d is a constant. Find the value of d.

x	0	1	2	3	4
$\mathbb{P}[X = x]$	d	0.2	0.15	0.2	$2d$

4. The score S on a spinner is a random variable with distribution given by $\mathbb{P}[S = s] = k$ $(s = 1, 2, 3, 4, 5, 6, 7, 8)$, where k is a constant. Find the value of k.

5. A cubical dice is biased so that the probability of an odd number is three times the probability of an even number. Find the probability distribution of the score.

6. A cubical dice is biased so that the probability of any particular score between 1 and 6 (inclusive) being obtained is proportional to that score. Find the probability of scoring a 1.

7. For a biased cubical dice the probability of any particular score between 1 and 6 (inclusive) being obtained is inversely proportional to that score. Find the probability of scoring a 1.

8. In the following probability distribution, c is a constant. Find the value of c.

x	0	1	2	3
$\mathbb{P}[X = x]$	0.6	0.16	c	c^2

9. If the random variable X takes integer values only and $F(4) = F(5)$, where F is the cumulative distribution function of X, what can we say about $\mathbb{P}[X = 5]$?

10. If the random variable X has cumulative distribution function F and x, y are such that $F(x) < F(y)$, what can we say about x and y?

11. The random variable X takes the values 0, 1, 2 and 3 only, and has the cumulative distribution function shown below. Find the value of c. Is there any restriction on the value of d?

x	0	1	2	3
$\mathbb{P}[X = x]$	$1 - c$	d	$2d$	$c + \frac{1}{3}$

12*. The random variable T can take any positive integer value, and $\mathbb{P}[T = t] = k3^{-t}$ for any $t \in \mathbb{N}$. What is the value of k, and what is $\mathbb{P}[T \geq 3]$?

13*. The random variable U can take any integer value, and its cumulative distribution function is

$$F(u) = \mathbb{P}[U \leq u] = \begin{cases} \frac{1}{2} \times 3^u, & u \in \mathbb{Z}, u < 0, \\ \frac{1}{2}(2 - 3^{-u}), & u \in \mathbb{Z}, u \geq 0. \end{cases}$$

What is $\mathbb{P}[|U| \leq 4]$? Write down the probability distribution function of U.

32.4 Using a Probability Distribution as a Model

So far, the discussion of probability distributions in this chapter has been very mathematical. At this point it might be helpful to point out the practical application of probability distributions. Probability distributions are useful because they provide models for experiments. Let the random variable X be the number of squares that a player playing Game A (see the beginning of this Chapter) can move each turn. Since the possible outcomes of $1, 2, 3, 4, 5$ and 6 have equal probability $\frac{1}{6}$, we might expect them to occur with approximately equal frequency. Thus, if we consider 360 rounds of Game A, we might expect $1, 2, 3, 4, 5$ and 6 to occur each about $360 \times \frac{1}{6} = 60$ times.

If, instead, we looked at the random variable Y, the number of squares that a player playing Game B can move each turn, then the different outcomes $1, 2, 3, 4, 5, 7, 8, 9, 10, 11$ and 12 are not equally likely, and so we would not expect them to occur with equal frequencies. In Chapter 31 we met the concept that

$$\text{probability} \approx \text{relative frequency} = \frac{\text{frequency}}{\text{total frequency}}$$

This relationship can be rearranged to read

$$\text{frequency} \approx \text{total frequency} \times \text{probability}$$

Thus, after 360 rounds of Game B, we should expect each of $1, 2, 3, 4$ and 5 to occur about $360 \times \frac{1}{6} = 60$ times, and each of $7, 8, 9, 10, 11$ and 12 to occur about $360 \times \frac{1}{36} = 10$ times.

Of course, since these games are games of chance, it is highly unlikely that the frequencies obtained from 360 rounds of Game A, or of 360 rounds of Game B, we would be exactly as predicted above.

If we were playing Game A and obtained frequencies of $62, 57, 63, 59, 58$ and 61 for the values $1, 2, 3, 4, 5$ and 6, then we would probably not worry very much: these observed frequencies are close enough to the expected values. On the other hand, if 360 rounds of Game A gave frequencies of $50, 50, 52, 49, 48$ and 111, we would suspect that the die was biassed in favour of throwing 6. In this second case, the lack of balance between the frequencies was pretty clear; how would we react, for example, if we obtained frequencies of $55, 55, 64, 62, 57$ and 67, would we feel confident that the die was unbiased, or is it possible that frequencies like this could have occurred with a fair die by chance?

The subject of Statistics is primarily concerned with determining when experimental data has meaning (and what the meaning is). The idea of using probability to determine what the ideal outcome ought to be is clearly the starting point. If we are going to say that some result is not as expected, we had better know what the expected result is!

EXERCISE 32C

1. A card is chosen at random from a pack and replaced. This experiment is carried out 520 times. State the expected number of times on which the card is:

   a) a club,
   b) an ace,
   c) a picture card (K, Q, J),
   d) either an ace or a club,
   e) neither an ace nor a club.

2. The biased die of Question 5 from Exercise 32B is rolled 420 times. How many times you would expect to obtain:

   a) a one,
   b) an even number,
   c) a prime number.

3. The table below gives the cumulative distribution function for a random variable R.

r	0	1	2	3	4	5
$F(r) = \mathbb{P}[R \leq r]$	0.116	0.428	0.765	0.946	0.995	1.000

   One hundred observations of R are made. Calculate the expected frequencies of each outcome, giving each answer to the nearest whole number.

4*. A random variable G has a probability distribution given by the following formulae:

$$\mathbb{P}[G = g] = \begin{cases} 0.3 \times (0.7)^g & g = 1, 2, 3, 4, \\ k & g = 5, \\ 0 & \text{for all other values of } g. \end{cases}$$

Find the value of k, and find the expected frequency of the result $G = 3$ when 1000 independent observations of G are made.

5*. When a fair coin is flipped eight times, what is the probability that either seven or eight heads are obtained? In an actual experiment, a coin is tossed eight times and seven heads are obtained. Do you think it likely that the coin is fair?

32.5 Expectation

A key quantity that can be calculated for a random variable is its **expectation**. We start by defining it, and shall investigate what it is.

> **Key Fact 32.5** Expectation
>
> If X is a discrete random variable, then its **expectation** (or **expected value**), is written $\mathbb{E}[X]$ (or simply $E(X)$). The expectation of X is given by the formula
>
> $$\mathbb{E}[X] = \sum_{x \in S} x \times \mathbb{P}[X = x] = \sum_{i} x_i p_i$$
>
> where the sum is over all possible values x of the random variable X, in other words for all x in the set $S = \{x_1, x_2, \ldots\}$ of all possible outcomes of X.

In Chapter 28 we calculated the mean values of sets of data.

Example 32.5.1. *Consider the random variable X which is the outcome of a roll of a fair six-sided die. The probability distribution function of X is*

x	1	2	3	4	5	6
$\mathbb{P}[\mathbf{X} = \mathbf{x}]$	$\frac{1}{6}$	$\frac{1}{6}$	$\frac{1}{6}$	$\frac{1}{6}$	$\frac{1}{6}$	$\frac{1}{6}$

and so the expectation of X is

$$\mathbb{E}[X] = 1 \times \tfrac{1}{6} + 2 \times \tfrac{1}{6} + 3 \times \tfrac{1}{6} + 4 \times \tfrac{1}{6} + 5 \times \tfrac{1}{6} + 6 \times \tfrac{1}{6} = \tfrac{1}{6}(1 + 2 + 3 + 4 + 5 + 6) = 3.5$$

Thus the expectation $\mathbb{E}[X]$ of X is the mean of the set of values $1, 2, 3, 4, 5$ and 6 which are on the faces of the die.

If we rolled the die 600 times, we would expect to roll $1, 2, 3, 4, 5$ and 6 the same number of times, namely 100, and so we would expect the total score from these 600 rolls to be

$$1 \times 100 + 2 \times 100 + 3 \times 100 + 4 \times 100 + 5 \times 100 + 6 \times 100 = 2100$$

Thus the average value scored on each roll would be

$$\tfrac{2100}{600} = 3.5$$

The expectation of X, which is the mean of the numbers on the faces of the die, is the expected average score per roll of the die.

Example 32.5.2. *Now consider the random variable Y which is the outcome of a roll of a fair die, where the six sides of the die are labelled with the numbers $1, 2, 2, 3, 3$ and 3. This random variable has probability generating function*

y	1	2	3
$\mathbb{P}[\mathbf{Y} = \mathbf{y}]$	$\frac{1}{6}$	$\frac{1}{3}$	$\frac{1}{2}$

and its expectation is

$$\mathbb{E}[Y] = 1 \times \tfrac{1}{6} + 2 \times \tfrac{1}{3} + 3 \times \tfrac{1}{2} = \tfrac{7}{3},$$

which is the mean

$$\tfrac{1}{6}(1 + 2 + 2 + 3 + 3 + 3)$$

of the numbers on the faces of the die. If we rolled this die 600 times, we might expect to roll 1 a total of 100 times, to roll 2 200 times, and to roll 3 300 times. Thus we would expect the total score from these 600 rolls to be

$$1 \times 100 + 2 \times 200 + 3 \times 300 = 1400$$

and so the expected average score per roll of the die is

$$\tfrac{1400}{600} = \tfrac{7}{3}.$$

Key Fact 32.6 Expectation: Interpretation

The expectation of a random variable is its 'expected value', the average outcome obtained from a large number of repeated observations of the random variable.

Food For Thought 32.2

The mean of a finite dataset is the expectation of a random variable where (at its simplest) each value in the dataset has an equal chance of occurring. If the dataset contains repeated values, then the probability of any value's occurrence is proportional to that frequency of that value in the dataset.

The expectation of a random variable is a much more theoretical concept than is the mean of a dataset, even although they might well give the same answers, so it is useful to have notational shorthand to distinguish between expectations and means. If we are calculating the expectation of a random variable X, we will often simply denote it by the Greek letter μ, or possibly by μ_X if we wish to be clear as to which random variable's expectation is being discussed. As in Chapter 28, we will continue to denote means of datasets with symbols like $\bar{x}$.

Example 32.5.3. *Consider the three games discussed at the beginning of the chapter. What are the expected number of squares that can be moved by a player in each game? If all three games are played on the same sized board, which game is likely to take the least time?*

We have already discussed Game A; the number of squares available to a player is the random variable X in Example 32.5.1; we have $\mu_X = 3.5$.

The number of moves available to a player in Game B is given by the random variable Y with probability distribution function

y	1	2	3	4	5	7	8	9	10	11	12
$\mathbb{P}[Y = y]$	$\tfrac{1}{6}$	$\tfrac{1}{6}$	$\tfrac{1}{6}$	$\tfrac{1}{6}$	$\tfrac{1}{6}$	$\tfrac{1}{36}$	$\tfrac{1}{36}$	$\tfrac{1}{36}$	$\tfrac{1}{36}$	$\tfrac{1}{36}$	$\tfrac{1}{36}$

and this random variable has expectation

$$
\begin{aligned}
\mu_Y = \mathbb{E}[Y] &= 1 \times \tfrac{1}{6} + 2 \times \tfrac{1}{6} + 3 \times \tfrac{1}{6} + 4 \times \tfrac{1}{6} + 5 \times \tfrac{1}{6} + 7 \times \tfrac{1}{36} \\
&\quad + 8 \times \tfrac{1}{36} + 9 \times \tfrac{1}{36} + 10 \times \tfrac{1}{36} + 11 \times \tfrac{1}{36} + 12 \times \tfrac{1}{36} \\
&= (1 + 2 + 3 + 4 + 5)\tfrac{1}{6} + (7 + 8 + 9 + 10 + 11 + 12)\tfrac{1}{36} = 4\tfrac{1}{12}.
\end{aligned}
$$

The number of moves available to a player in Game C is given by the random variable Z with probability distribution function

z	2	3	4	5	6	7	8	9	10	11	12
$\mathbb{P}[Z = z]$	$\tfrac{1}{36}$	$\tfrac{2}{36}$	$\tfrac{3}{36}$	$\tfrac{4}{36}$	$\tfrac{5}{36}$	$\tfrac{6}{36}$	$\tfrac{5}{36}$	$\tfrac{4}{36}$	$\tfrac{3}{36}$	$\tfrac{2}{36}$	$\tfrac{1}{36}$

and so its expectation is

$$\begin{aligned}
\mu_Z = \mathbb{E}[Z] &= 2 \times \tfrac{1}{36} + 3 \times \tfrac{2}{36} + 4 \times \tfrac{3}{36} + 5 \times \tfrac{4}{36} + 6 \times \tfrac{5}{36} + 7 \times \tfrac{6}{36} \\
&\quad + 8 \times \tfrac{5}{36} + 9 \times \tfrac{4}{36} + 10 \times \tfrac{3}{36} + 11 \times \tfrac{2}{36} + 12 \times \tfrac{1}{36} \\
&= 7 \, .
\end{aligned}$$

We could have observed that, since the probability distribution of Z is symmetric about the value 7, the expectation of Z must also be 7. Why is this?

Since Z has the largest expectation, we would expect Game C to end most quickly.

Example 32.5.4. *A random variable R has the probability distribution shown below.*

r	1	2	3	4
$\mathbb{P}[R = r]$	0.1	a	0.3	b

Given that $\mathbb{E}[R] = 3$, find a and b.

There are two variables to determine, and we have two conditions that we can apply to determine them. Since the probabilities must add to 1, we deduce that

$$0.1 + a + 0.3 + b = 1 \qquad\qquad \Rightarrow \qquad a + b = 0.6 \, .$$

Since the expectation of R is 3, we have

$$\sum_r r \times \mathbb{P}[R = r] = 1 \times 0.1 + 2a + 3 \times 0.3 + 4b = 3 \qquad\qquad \Rightarrow \qquad a + 2b = 1 \, .$$

Solving these two equations simultaneously gives $a = 0.2$ and $b = 0.4$.

32.6 Functions of Random Variables

Consider the random variables A, B and C with probability distribution functions

a	−1	0	1	2
$\mathbb{P}[A = a]$	$\frac{1}{8}$	$\frac{1}{2}$	$\frac{1}{4}$	$\frac{1}{8}$

b	−1	1	3	5
$\mathbb{P}[B = b]$	$\frac{1}{8}$	$\frac{1}{2}$	$\frac{1}{4}$	$\frac{1}{8}$

c	0	1	2
$\mathbb{P}[C = c]$	$\frac{1}{2}$	$\frac{3}{8}$	$\frac{1}{8}$

We could study these random variables, and (for example) calculate their expectations directly, obtaining

$$\begin{aligned}
\mathbb{E}[A] &= \tfrac{1}{8} \times -1 + \tfrac{1}{2} \times 0 + \tfrac{1}{4} \times 1 + \tfrac{1}{8} \times 2 = \tfrac{3}{8} \\
\mathbb{E}[B] &= \tfrac{1}{8} \times -1 + \tfrac{1}{2} \times 1 + \tfrac{1}{4} \times 3 + \tfrac{1}{8} \times 5 = \tfrac{7}{4} \\
\mathbb{E}[C] &= \tfrac{1}{2} \times 0 + \tfrac{3}{8} \times 1 + \tfrac{1}{8} \times 2 = \tfrac{5}{8}
\end{aligned}$$

but to do so would lose some valuable insights into the relationships between these random variables and, in some cases, miss out on some useful calculational shortcuts.

Notice that the four probabilities for A and B are the same; the sets of values with which these probabilities occur are different. Now the function $a \mapsto 2a + 1$ maps the outcome set $S_A = \{-1, 0, 1, 2\}$ of A to the outcome set $S_B = \{-1, 1, 3, 5\}$ of B. Moreover, since

$$\mathbb{P}[A = -1] = \mathbb{P}[B = -1] \qquad \mathbb{P}[A = 0] = \mathbb{P}[B = 1] \qquad \mathbb{P}[A = 1] = \mathbb{P}[B = 3] \qquad \mathbb{P}[A = 2] = \mathbb{P}[B = 5]$$

so that $\mathbb{P}[B = 2a + 1] = \mathbb{P}[A = a]$ for all integers a, we can write B as a function of the random variable A as follows: $B = 2A + 1$. We see that

$$\mathbb{E}[B] = \tfrac{1}{8} \times -1 + \tfrac{1}{2} \times 1 + \tfrac{1}{4} \times 3 + \tfrac{1}{8} \times 5 = \sum_{a=-1}^{2} (2a + 1)\mathbb{P}[A = a]$$

can be calculated without determining the probabilities of B.

The function $a \mapsto |a|$ maps the outcome set $S_A = \{-1, 0, 1, 2\}$ of A to the outcome set $S_C = \{0, 1, 2\}$ of C. Moreover, since

$$\mathbb{P}[A = 0] = \mathbb{P}[C = 0] \qquad \mathbb{P}[A = -1] + \mathbb{P}[A = 1] = \mathbb{P}[C = 1] \qquad \mathbb{P}[A = 2] = \mathbb{P}[C = 2]$$

so that $\mathbb{P}[C = |a|] = \mathbb{P}[A = a] + \mathbb{P}[A = -a]$ for all integers a, we can write C as a function of the random variable A as follows: $C = |A|$. The relationship between the probabilities of A and C is a little more complicated this time, since the modulus function is not one-to-one, and so more than one probability of A needs to be combined to obtain a probability of B. We see that

$$\mathbb{E}[C] = \tfrac{1}{2} \times 0 + \left(\tfrac{1}{8} + \tfrac{1}{4}\right) \times 1 + \tfrac{1}{8} \times 2 = \sum_{a=-1}^{2} |a| \mathbb{P}[A = a]$$

can be calculated without determining the probabilities of A.

Key Fact 32.7 Functions of a Random Variable

If X is a (discrete) random variable, and if g is a real-valued function such that the outcome space S_X of X lies in the domain of g, then we can construct the (discrete) random variable $g(X)$, whose outcome space $S_{g(X)}$ is the set $\{g(a) : a \in S_A\}$, and which has the probability distribution function

$$\mathbb{P}[g(X) = b] = \sum_{a : g(a) = b} \mathbb{P}[X = a], \qquad b \in S_{g(X)}.$$

where the sum is intended to be taken over all values of a such that $g(a) = b$.

Food For Thought 32.3

Since a random variable X is, we recall, a real-valued function $X : \mathcal{E} \to \mathbb{R}$ on the sample space, there is no problem constructing the random variable $gX : \mathcal{E} \to \mathbb{R}$. Since

$$(gX)^{-1}\{u\} = \{\omega \in \mathcal{E} : (gX)(\omega) = u\} = \bigcup_{g(v) = u} \{\omega \in \mathcal{E} : X(\omega) = v\}$$

$$= \bigcup_{v : g(v) = u} X^{-1}\{v\}$$

is a disjoint union of sets $X^{-1}\{v\}$ for any u, we see that

$$\mathbb{P}[gX = u] = \sum_{v : g(v) = u} \mathbb{P}[X = v],$$

and hence we see that the composite function gX is the random variable we have written $g(X)$.

Example 32.6.1. *If X is the random variable with probability distribution function*

x	-2	-1	0	1	2
$\mathbb{P}[X = x]$	0.1	0.2	0.1	0.3	0.3

(a) *calculate $\mathbb{E}[3X - 2]$, $\mathbb{E}[X^3]$ and $\mathbb{E}[4 - X^2]$,*

(b) *find the probability distribution function of X^4,*

(c) *find the cumulative distribution function $F_{|X|}$ of $|X|$.*

(a) We see that

$$\begin{aligned}
\mathbb{E}[3X - 2] &= (-8) \times 0.1 + (-5) \times 0.2 + (-2) \times 0.1 + 1 \times 0.3 + 4 \times 0.3 = -0.5 \\
\mathbb{E}[X^3] &= (-8) \times 0.1 + (-1) \times 0.2 + 0 \times 0.1 + 1 \times 0.3 + 8 \times 0.3 = 1.7 \\
\mathbb{E}[4 - X^2] &= 0 \times 0.1 + 3 \times 0.2 + 4 \times 0.1 + 3 \times 0.3 + 0 \times 0.3 = 1.9
\end{aligned}$$

(b) The outcome space of X^4 is $\{0, 1, 16\}$, and the probability distribution function of X^4 is shown on the right. Note how

x	0	1	16
$\mathbb{P}[X^4 = x]$	0.1	0.5	0.4

$$\mathbb{P}[X^4 = 1] = \mathbb{P}[X = -1] + \mathbb{P}[X = -1] \qquad \mathbb{P}[X^4 = 16] = \mathbb{P}[X = -2] + \mathbb{P}[X = 2].$$

(c) The random variable $|X|$ has outcome space $\{0, 1, 2\}$, and

$$\begin{aligned}
F_{|X|}(0) &= \mathbb{P}[|X| \le 0] = \mathbb{P}[X = 0] = 0.1 \\
F_{|X|}(1) &= \mathbb{P}[|X| \le 1] = \mathbb{P}[-1 \le X \le 1] = 0.2 + 0.1 + 0.3 = 0.6 \\
F_{|X|}(2) &= \mathbb{P}[|X| \le 2] = \mathbb{P}[-2 \le X \le 2] = 1
\end{aligned}$$

EXERCISE 32D

1. A pack of cards has had all its honour cards (A, K, Q, J and 10) removed, leaving 32 cards. A single card is drawn, and X is the number on that card. What is $\mathbb{E}[X]$?

2. Consider the same restricted deck of cards as in the previous question, and draw a single card from the deck. Let Y be the value on the card, if that value is odd. If the value on the card is even, let Y be equal to 9 minus that value. What is the expectation of Y?

3. The random variable X takes the value 1 with probability p, and takes the value -1 with probability $1 - p$. Find the values of

   a) $\mathbb{E}[X]$,   b) $\mathbb{E}[2X + 3]$,   c) $\mathbb{E}[|X|]$,   d) $\mathbb{E}[X^2]$,   e) $\mathbb{E}[X^2] - \mathbb{E}[X]^2$.

4. The random variable X has probability distribution function

x	-2	-1	0	1	2
$\mathbb{P}[X = x]$	0.2	0.1	0.3	0.2	0.2

   What are the values of $\mathbb{E}[X]$ and $\mathbb{E}[X^2 - 2X]$?

5. A random variable X takes the value 1 with probability p, and the value 0 with probability $1 - p$ (this is called a **Bernoulli trial**). Which is bigger: $\mathbb{E}[X^2]$ or $\mathbb{E}[X]^2$?

6. Three coins are tossed. What is the expectation of the number of heads that are obtained?

7. An integer n between 1 and 10 is chosen, with each possibility being equally likely. Let X be the highest common factor of n and 10. Calculate $\mathbb{E}[X]$ and $\mathbb{E}[X^2]$.

8. A bag contains three red marbles and five blue marbles. Two marbles are chosen from the bag, without replacement. What is the expected number of red marbles that have been drawn?

9. The random variable Y has the probability distribution function

y	1	2	3	4	5
$\mathbb{P}[Y = y]$	a	a	a	a	b

   What are the values of a and b if:

   a) $\mathbb{E}[Y] = 3$,   b) $\mathbb{E}[Y^2] = 18$,   c) $\mathbb{E}[Y^2] = 4\mathbb{E}[Y]$?

10. Consider the random variable Y from the previous question. Allowing a and b to vary through all permissible values, what is the largest possible value of $\mathbb{E}[Y]$, and what is the smallest possible value of $\mathbb{E}[Y]$?

11. The letters of the word BANANA are rearranged randomly. Let X be the number of copies of the letter A that appear before the first consonant. What are the values of $\mathbb{E}[X]$ and $\mathbb{E}[|X-1|]$?

12. The random variable X takes the values 1, 2, 3 and 4, and its probability distribution function is such that $\mathbb{P}[X=x]$ is proportional to x^2. Calculate $\mathbb{E}[X]$ and $\mathbb{E}[2X+1]$.

13. Throw two fair 6-sided dice. Let X be the difference between their scores. What is $\mathbb{E}[X]$?

14. Toss two coins, and roll one fair 6-sided die. Let X be the number of heads obtained, minus the score on the die. What is $\mathbb{E}[X]$?

15. Let N be a positive integer. The random variable X takes the values $1, 2, \dots, N$, each with probability $\frac{1}{N}$. What is the expectation of X?

16. In a gambling game, a player pays £1, and is then dealt two cards from an ordinary deck of cards. If she is dealt two Aces, she is paid £25. If she is dealt two red cards, she is paid £3. If the player is dealt two red Aces, she receives both prizes. If she is dealt any other cards, she loses her stake. The player makes a profit of £X. What is the probability distribution of the random variable X, and what is $\mathbb{E}[X]$?

17. In a lottery competition, six different numbers are drawn at random from the numbers 1 to 50. To win the jackpot of £M, a player must have predicted all six of the numbers. Each play of the lottery competition costs £1. A player makes a profit of £P from one draw of the game (we shall assume that a player can only participate once in each lottery draw). How big must M be in order for the player to have a positive expected profit?

18*. The **indicator function** I_A of an event A is the random variable which takes the value 1 when A occurs, and takes the value 0 when A does not occur. Find a simple expression for $\mathbb{E}[I_A]$.

19*. The random variable X takes integer values between 1 and 1000. Explain why

$$\mathbb{E}[X] \;=\; \sum_{x=1}^{1000} \mathbb{P}[X \geq x] \,.$$

32.7 Variance

The following graphs illustrate the probability distribution functions for the numbers of moves X, Y and Z available to a player playing each of Games A, B and C (as described at the start of this chapter).

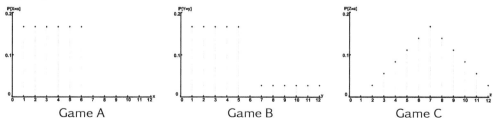

| Game A | Game B | Game C |

Figure 32.5

As well as having different expectations, we see that X, Y and Z have different degrees of spread. Just as the spread in a dataset can be measured by the standard deviation or variance, so it is possible to define a corresponding measure of spread for a random variable. The symbol used for the standard deviation of a random variable is σ. The square σ^2 of the standard deviation is called the **variance** of a random variable, and is denoted by $\mathrm{Var}[X]$.

> **Key Fact 32.8** The Variance of a Random Variable
>
> The variance $\mathrm{Var}[X]$ of a random variable X is given by the formula
>
> $$\mathrm{Var}[X] = \mathbb{E}\left[\left(X - \mathbb{E}[X]\right)^2\right].$$
>
> Since $(X - \mathbb{E}[X])^2 \geq 0$, the variance of a random variable cannot be negative, and so we can calculate its square root. The square root of the variance of X is called the **standard deviation** of X, and is denoted by σ_X (or simply σ if there is no possibility of confusion):
>
> $$\sigma_X = \sqrt{\mathrm{Var}[X]}.$$

Example 32.7.1. *Calculate the variance of the random variable X associated with Game A.*

We have already calculated that $\mathbb{E}[X] = 3.5$, and hence the variance of X is

$$(1-3.5)^2 \times \tfrac{1}{6} + (2-3.5)^2 \times \tfrac{1}{6} + (3-3.5)^2 \times \tfrac{1}{6} + (4-3.5)^2 \times \tfrac{1}{6} + (5-3.5)^2 \times \tfrac{1}{6} + (6-3.5)^2 \times \tfrac{1}{6} = \tfrac{35}{12}.$$

As we observed in Chapter 28, the similar formula for calculating the variance s^2 of a dataset was more complicated than was necessary; for practical purposes we used an easier formula to calculate the variance of a dataset. A similar position can be found here. For simplicity, let us write $\mu = \mathbb{E}[X]$. Then

$$
\begin{aligned}
\mathbb{E}\left[\left(X - \mathbb{E}[X]\right)^2\right] &= \mathbb{E}\left[(X - \mu)^2\right] = \sum_i p_i(x_i - \mu)^2 \\
&= \sum_i p_i(x_i^2 - 2\mu x_i + \mu^2) = \sum_i \left(p_i x_i^2 - 2\mu p_i x_i + \mu^2 p_i\right) \\
&= \sum_i p_i x_i^2 - 2\mu \sum_i p_i x_i + \mu^2 \sum_i p_i
\end{aligned}
$$

But

$$\sum_i p_i = 1 \qquad \sum_i p_i x_i = \mathbb{E}[X] = \mu \qquad \sum_i p_i x_i^2 = \mathbb{E}[X^2]$$

and hence

$$\mathrm{Var}[X] = \mathbb{E}\left[\left(X - \mathbb{E}[X]\right)^2\right] = \mathbb{E}[X^2] - 2\mu \times \mu + \mu^2 \times 1 = \mathbb{E}[X^2] - \mu^2 = \mathbb{E}[X^2] - \mathbb{E}[X]^2$$

> **Key Fact 32.9** The Variance of a Random Variable — An Easier Formula
>
> For any random variable X, we have
>
> $$\mathrm{Var}[X] = \mathbb{E}[X^2] - \mathbb{E}[X]^2.$$
>
> which implies that $\mathbb{E}[X^2] \geq \mathbb{E}[X]^2$ for any random variable X.

Example 32.7.2. *Calculate the variances for the random variables Y and Z relating to Games B and C above.*

We have already calculated that $\mathbb{E}[Y] = \tfrac{49}{12}$ and $\mathbb{E}[Z] = 7$. Now

$$
\begin{aligned}
\mathbb{E}[Y^2] &= \tfrac{1}{6}(1^2 + 2^2 + 3^2 + 4^2 + 5^2) + \tfrac{1}{36}(7^2 + 8^2 + 9^2 + 10^2 + 11^2 + 12^2) = \tfrac{889}{36} \\
\mathbb{E}[Z^2] &= \tfrac{1}{36} \times 2^2 + \tfrac{2}{36} \times 3^2 + \tfrac{3}{36} \times 4^2 + \tfrac{4}{36} \times 5^2 + \tfrac{5}{36} \times 6^2 + \tfrac{6}{36} \times 7^2 = \tfrac{329}{6} \\
&\quad + \tfrac{5}{36} \times 8^2 + \tfrac{4}{36} \times 9^2 + \tfrac{3}{36} \times 10^2 + \tfrac{2}{36} \times 11^2 + \tfrac{1}{36} \times 12^2
\end{aligned}
$$

and so

$$\mathrm{Var}[Y] = \tfrac{889}{36} - \left(\tfrac{49}{12}\right)^2 = \tfrac{385}{48} \qquad \mathrm{Var}[Z] = \tfrac{329}{6} - 7^2 = \tfrac{35}{6}$$

It is interesting (and no accident) that $\mathrm{Var}[Z]$ is equal to $2\mathrm{Var}[X]$; the reason why this is true lies beyond the single mathematics syllabus.

There is a simple relationship between the variance of a random variable and the variance of a dataset, just as there was for the expectation of a random variable and the mean of a dataset. To see this, consider the same random variables X and Y as before

x	1	2	3	4	5	6
$\mathbb{P}[X=x]$	$\frac{1}{6}$	$\frac{1}{6}$	$\frac{1}{6}$	$\frac{1}{6}$	$\frac{1}{6}$	$\frac{1}{6}$

y	1	2	3
$\mathbb{P}[Y=y]$	$\frac{1}{6}$	$\frac{1}{3}$	$\frac{1}{2}$

Then

$$\mathbb{E}[X] = \tfrac{1}{6}(1+2+3+4+5+6) = \tfrac{1}{n}\sum_i x_i = \overline{x} \qquad \mathbb{E}[X^2] = \tfrac{1}{6}(1^2+2^2+3^2+4^2+5^2+6^2) = \tfrac{1}{n}\sum_i x_i^2$$

and so

$$\mathrm{Var}[X] = \tfrac{1}{n}\sum_i x_i^2 - \overline{x}^2 = s_x^2$$

is the variance of the dataset 1, 2, 3, 4, 5, 6.

On the other hand

$$\mathbb{E}[Y] = \tfrac{1}{6}\times 1 + \tfrac{1}{3}\times 2 + \tfrac{1}{2}\times 3 = \tfrac{1}{6}(1+2+2+3+3+3) = \overline{y}$$
$$\mathbb{E}[Y^2] = \tfrac{1}{6}\times 1^2 + \tfrac{1}{3}\times 2^2 + \tfrac{1}{2}\times 3^2 = \tfrac{1}{6}(1^2+2^2+2^2+3^2+3^2+3^2) = \tfrac{1}{n}\sum_i y_i^2$$

and so

$$\mathrm{Var}[Y] = \tfrac{1}{n}\sum_i y_i^2 - \overline{y}^2 = s_y^2$$

is the variance of the dataset 1, 2, 2, 3, 3, 3.

> **Food For Thought 32.4**
>
> The variance of a finite dataset is the variance of a random variable where (at its simplest) each value in the dataset has an equal chance of occurring. If the dataset contains repeated values, then the probability of any value's occurrence is proportional to that frequency of that value in the dataset.
> To distinguish between the variances of random variables and those of datasets, we shall denote the variances of random variables by σ^2, using the Greek letter, but shall continue to refer to the variance of a dataset as s^2, as we did in Chapter 28

Example 32.7.3. *In a certain field, each mushroom that's growing gives rise to a number X of mushrooms in the following year, independently of any other mushrooms in the field. None of the mushrooms present in one year survive until the next year. The random variable X has the following probability distribution:*

x	0	1	2
$\mathbb{P}[X=x]$	0.2	0.6	0.2

If there were two mushrooms present in one year, find the probability distribution of Y, the number of mushrooms present in the following year. Hence find the mean and variance of Y.

The possible values of Y are shown on the right, where the first value of X is the value of X for one mushroom, and the second value of X is the value of X for the second mushroom. Thus it follows that the probability distribution function of Y is as follows:

$$\mathbb{P}[Y=0] = 0.2\times 0.2 = 0.04$$
$$\mathbb{P}[Y=1] = 2\times 0.2\times 0.6 = 0.24$$
$$\mathbb{P}[Y=2] = 2\times 0.2\times 0.2 + 0.6\times 0.6 = 0.44$$
$$\mathbb{P}[Y=3] = 2\times 0.6\times 0.2 = 0.24$$
$$\mathbb{P}[Y=4] = 0.2\times 0.2 = 0.04$$

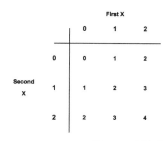

Figure 32.6

and so

$$\begin{aligned}
\mathbb{E}[Y] &= 0.04 \times 0 + 0.24 \times 1 + 0.44 \times 2 + 0.24 \times 3 + 0.04 \times 4 = 2 \\
\mathbb{E}[Y^2] &= 0.04 \times 0^2 + 0.24 \times 1^2 + 0.44 \times 2^2 + 0.24 \times 3^2 + 0.04 \times 4^2 = 4.8
\end{aligned}$$

and hence $\text{Var}[Y] = 2.8 - 2^2 = 0.8$.

Example 32.7.4. *The random variable T has probability distribution function*

t	0	1	2
$\mathbb{P}[T=t]$	a	b	$\frac{1}{2}$

Given that $\text{Var}[T] = \frac{55}{64}$, *find the values of a and b.*

Since

$$\mathbb{E}[T] = a \times 0 + b \times 1 + \tfrac{1}{2} \times 2 = b + 1 \qquad \mathbb{E}[T^2] = a \times 0^2 + b \times 1^2 + \tfrac{1}{2} \times 2^2 = b + 2$$

we deduce that

$$\text{Var}[T] = b + 2 - (b+1)^2 = 1 - b - b^2 .$$

Thus we deduce that

$$\begin{aligned}
1 - b - b^2 &= \tfrac{55}{64} \\
b^2 + b - \tfrac{9}{64} &= 0 \\
\left(b - \tfrac{1}{8}\right)\left(b + \tfrac{9}{8}\right) &= 0
\end{aligned}$$

Since $0 \le b \le 1$, we deduce that $b = \frac{1}{8}$. Since the probabilities for T must add to 1, we deduce that $a + b + \frac{1}{2} = 1$, and hence $a = \frac{3}{8}$.

EXERCISE 32E

In this exercise all random variables are discrete. Give numerical answers to 4 significant figures when appropriate.

1. Find the mean of the random variables X and Y which have the following probability distributions.

   a)

x	0	1	2	3	4
$\mathbb{P}[X=x]$	$\frac{1}{8}$	$\frac{3}{8}$	$\frac{1}{8}$	$\frac{1}{4}$	$\frac{1}{8}$

   b)

y	-2	-1	0	1	2	3
$\mathbb{P}[Y=y]$	0.15	0.25	0.3	0.05	0.2	0.05

2. The random variable T has the probability distribution given in the following table:

t	1	2	3	4	5	6	7
$\mathbb{P}[T=t]$	0.1	0.2	0.1	0.2	0.1	0.2	0.1

   Find $\mathbb{E}[T]$ and $\text{Var}[T]$.

3. Find the exact expectation and variance of the random variable Y, which has the following probability distribution:

y	3	4	5	6	7
$\mathbb{P}[Y=y]$	$\frac{1}{18}$	$\frac{5}{18}$	$\frac{7}{18}$	$\frac{1}{18}$	$\frac{4}{18}$

4. The six faces of a fair cubical dice are numbered $1, 1, 1, 2, 3$ and 3. When the dice is thrown once, the score is the number appearing on the top face. This is denoted by X.

a) Find the mean and standard deviation of X.

b) The dice is thrown twice and Y denotes the sum of the scores obtained. Find the probability distribution of Y. Hence find $\mathbb{E}[Y]$ and $\text{Var}[Y]$.

5. A construction company can bid for one of two possible projects and the finance director has been asked to advise on which to choose. She estimates that project A will yield a profit of £150000 with probability 0.5, a profit of £250000 with probability 0.2 and a loss of £100000 with probability 0.3. Project B will yield a profit of £100000 with probability 0.6, a profit of £200000 with probability 0.3 and a loss of £50000 with probability 0.1. Determine which project the finance director should support.

6. Some of the eggs at a market are sold in boxes of six. The number, X, of broken eggs in a box has the probability distribution given in the following table:

x	0	1	2	3	4	5	6
$\mathbb{P}[X = x]$	0.80	0.14	0.03	0.02	0.01	0	0

a) Find the expectation and variance of X.

b) Find the expectation and variance of the number of unbroken eggs in a box.

c) Comment on the relationship between your answers to the previous two parts.

7. Find $\mathbb{E}[H]$ and $\text{Var}[H]$ for the random variable H defined in Question 4 of Exercise 32A.

8. The random variable X has the probability distribution given in the following table:

x	1	2	3	4	5
$\mathbb{P}[X = x]$	a	0.3	0.2	0.1	0.2

Find the values of a, μ and σ for the distribution.

9. The random variable Y has the probability distribution given in the following table.

y	2	3	4	5	6	7
$\mathbb{P}[Y = y]$	0.05	0.25	a	b	0.1	0.3

Given that $\mathbb{E}[Y] = 4.9$, show that $a = b$, and find the standard deviation of Y.

10. A game is played by throwing a fair dice until either a 6 is obtained or four throws have been made. Let X denote the number of throws made. Find

 a) the probability distribution of X, *b)* the standard deviation of X.

 The number of 6s obtained in the game is denoted by Y. Find $\mathbb{E}[Y]$.

 If the player throws a 6 in the course of the game, then the player wins 100 points. If a 6 is not thrown, then 150 points are lost. Find the expectation of the number of points received by a player after one game.

11. The die of Question 4 is thrown and then an unbiased coin is thrown the number of times indicated by the score on the dice. Let H denote the number of heads obtained.

 a) Show that $\mathbb{P}[H = 2] = \frac{1}{6}$.

 b) Find the probability distribution of H.

 c) Show that $\mathbb{E}[H] = \frac{1}{2}\mathbb{E}[X]$, where X denotes the score on the die.

 d) Calculate $\text{Var}[H]$.

12*. A random variable R has the following probability distribution function:

r	−1	0	1
$\mathbb{P}[R = r]$	a	b	c

and is such that $\text{Var}[R] = 0$.

 a) Calculate $\mathbb{E}[R]$ and $\text{Var}[R]$ in terms of a, and c. Hence deduce that we can write

$$a = 2x^2 + x \qquad b = 1 - 4x^2 \qquad c = 2x^2 - x$$

 for some real number x.

 b) Use the fact that a, b and c are all nonnegative to find the possible values of x.

 c) What does this tell you about a random variable with zero variance?

32.8 Coding: Linear Functions of a Random Variable

The expectation does not 'behave nicely' with functions of random variables. We have seen, for example, that

$$\mathbb{E}[X^2] \neq \mathbb{E}[X]^2$$

except for very special random variables. In general, it is not true that $\mathbb{E}[f(X)] = f(\mathbb{E}[X])$ for a random variable X and a function f.

One exception to this observation occurs for **linear** functions, namely functions of the form $f(x) = ax + b$ for constants a and b. Consider the random variables A and B discussed at the beginning of Section 32.6. We recall that $B = 2A + 1$, and that $\mathbb{E}[A] = \frac{3}{8}$, $\mathbb{E}[B] = \frac{7}{4}$. In this case, then, $\mathbb{E}[2A + 1] = 2\mathbb{E}[A] + 1$.

This result holds in general. Recall that applying a linear function to a dataset was referred to as 'coding' in Chapter 28.

Key Fact 32.10 Coding of Random Variables

If X is a random variable, and a and b are constants, then

$$\mathbb{E}[aX + b] = a\mathbb{E}[X] + b \qquad \text{Var}[aX + b] = a^2 \text{Var}[X] \qquad \sigma_{aX+b} = |a|\sigma_X$$

These results are easy to establish: since

$$\mathbb{E}[aX + b] = \sum_i (ax_i + b)p_i = \sum_i (ax_i p_i + bp_i) = a\sum_i x_i p_i + b\sum_i p_i = a\mathbb{E}[X] + b$$

$$\mathbb{E}\left[(aX + b)^2\right] = \sum_i (ax_i + b)^2 p_i = \sum_i (a^2 x_i^2 + 2abx_i + b^2)p_i = \sum_i (a^2 x_i^2 p_i + 2abx_i p_i + b^2 p_i)$$

$$= a^2 \sum_i x_i^2 p_i + 2ab \sum_i x_i p_i + b^2 \sum_i p_i = a^2\mathbb{E}[X^2] + 2ab\mathbb{E}[X] + b^2$$

we obtain the result for $\mathbb{E}[aX + b]$ and also see that

$$\begin{aligned}
\text{Var}[aX + b] &= \mathbb{E}\left[(aX + b)^2\right] - \mathbb{E}[aX + b]^2 = a^2\mathbb{E}[X^2] + 2ab\mathbb{E}[X] + b^2 - \left(a\mathbb{E}[X] + b\right)^2 \\
&= a^2\mathbb{E}[X^2] + 2ab\mathbb{E}[X] + b^2 - \left(a^2\mathbb{E}[X]^2 + 2ab\mathbb{E}[X] + b^2\right) = a^2\left(\mathbb{E}[X^2] - \mathbb{E}[X]^2\right) \\
&= a^2\text{Var}[X]
\end{aligned}$$

The results concerning the variance and the standard deviation should not be particularly surprising. These quantities measure the spread of a probability distribution, and so are unaffected by a change of position. Consequently it is not surprising that the variance and standard deviation of $aX + b$ is independent of b. Since a scales the random variable X, it must affect the variance and standard deviation.

Example 32.8.1. *A fair six-sided die has sides labelled* $1, 4, 7, 10, 13$ *and* 16*. What is the mean and variance of the value obtained after a single roll.*

If X is the score on a standard six-sided die, and if Y is the score on this die, then it is clear that $Y = 3X - 2$. We have already calculated that $\mathbb{E}[X] = \frac{7}{2}$ and $\text{Var}[X] = \frac{35}{12}$, and hence

$$\mathbb{E}[Y] = 3 \times \frac{7}{2} - 2 = \frac{17}{2} \qquad \text{Var}[Y] = 9 \times \frac{35}{12} = \frac{105}{4}.$$

32.9 The Discrete Uniform Distribution

We have considered discrete random variables in general. There are some types of random variable that occur sufficiently frequently that they have their own names, and need to be studied individually. For our purposes, there are three that need to be considered.

We should already be familiar with the first of these distributions, since we encounter it every time we roll a die! If X is the random variable representing the outcome of one roll of a fair six-sided die, then X can take any of the values 1, 2, 3, 4, 5 and 6 with equal probability $\frac{1}{6}$.

x	1	2	3	4	5	6
$\mathbb{P}[X = x]$	$\frac{1}{6}$	$\frac{1}{6}$	$\frac{1}{6}$	$\frac{1}{6}$	$\frac{1}{6}$	$\frac{1}{6}$

Key Fact 32.11 The Discrete Uniform Distribution $U(N)$

The random variable X, which takes any of the values $1, 2, \ldots, N$ with equal probability $\frac{1}{N}$, so that

$$\mathbb{P}[X = x] = \tfrac{1}{N}, \qquad 1 \leq x \leq N,$$

is said to have the **discrete uniform distribution from 1 to n**. We write $X \sim U(N)$ to represent this fact in symbols (the symbol $\sim$ can be read as 'is distributed as').

This is a particularly simple distribution, and so performing calculations with it is fairly easy. The cumulative distribution function of X is

$$F(x) = \tfrac{x}{N}, \qquad\qquad x \in \mathbb{N}, 1 \leq x \leq N,$$

and other, similarly, probabilities can be calculated easily.

Example 32.9.1. If $X \sim U(10)$, what is $\mathbb{P}[2 \leq X < 6]$?

$$\mathbb{P}[2 \leq X < 7] = \mathbb{P}[2 \leq X \leq 6] = \mathbb{P}[X \leq 6] - \mathbb{P}[X \leq 1] = F(6) - F(1) = \tfrac{6-1}{10} = \tfrac{1}{2}.$$

Finding the mean of this distribution is easy; the alert will notice that we have already calculated it in Question 15 of Exercise 32D. If $X \sim U(N)$, then

$$\mathbb{E}[X] = \sum_{x=1}^{N} x \times \tfrac{1}{N} = \tfrac{1}{N} \sum_{x=1}^{N} x = \tfrac{1}{N} \times \tfrac{1}{2}N(N+1) = \tfrac{1}{2}(N+1)$$

The Pre-U formula book tells us that $\sum_{x=1}^{N} x^2 = \tfrac{1}{6}N(N+1)(2N+1)$ for any $N \in \mathbb{N}$. The proof of this result is part of the further mathematics syllabus. Assuming this result,

$$\begin{aligned}
\mathbb{E}[X^2] &= \sum_{x=1}^{N} x^2 \times \tfrac{1}{N} = \tfrac{1}{N} \times \tfrac{1}{6}N(N+1)(2N+1) = \tfrac{1}{6}(N+1)(2N+1) \\
\mathrm{Var}[X] &= \tfrac{1}{6}(N+1)(2N+1) - \tfrac{1}{4}(N+1)^2 = \tfrac{1}{12}(N+1)\big\{2(2N+1) - 3(N+1)\big\} \\
&= \tfrac{1}{12}(N+1)(N-1) = \tfrac{1}{12}(N^2 - 1)
\end{aligned}$$

Key Fact 32.12 The Discrete Uniform Distribution : Mean and Variance

If $X \sim U(N)$, then $\qquad \mathbb{E}[X] = \tfrac{1}{2}(N+1) \qquad\qquad \mathrm{Var}[X] = \tfrac{1}{12}(N^2 - 1).$

32.10 The Geometric Distribution

Imagine repeating the same experiment again and again. Each of these experiments are called **trials**. Each trial will either succeed or fail, and the probability of a trial succeeding is a fixed probability p. This probability does not vary between the different trials, and the outcomes of different trials are independent of each other. For example, we may roll the same fair six-sided die over and over.

> **Key Fact 32.13** The Geometric Distribution Geo(p)
>
> Given such a sequence of trials, the random variable X, which is the number of trials until we achieve the first success, is said to have the **geometric distribution** with parameter p. We write $X \sim$ Geo(p).

The number of tosses of a fair coin needed to obtain a head would have distribution Geo($\frac{1}{2}$), regarding tossing a head as a success in the trial of tossing a coin. The number of rolls of a die needed to roll a 6 would have the distribution Geo($\frac{1}{6}$); this time rolling a 6 is seen as a success. If the probability of a building being hit by lightning in any thunderstorm is 0.001, and is X is the number of thunderstorms that have to happen before the building is struck by lightning, then $X \sim$ Geo(0.001); this time we have decided that being struck by lightning is a success.

What is the probability distribution function of $X \sim$ Geo(p)? It is first clear that X can only take positive integer values, but that there is no limit to the possible size of X. The geometric distribution gives an example of a discrete random variable with an infinite set of output values. If $x \in \mathbb{N}$, we will have a first success at the xth trial precisely when the first $x-1$ trials are failures, and the xth is a success. In other words

$$\mathbb{P}[X = x] = (1-p)^{x-1}p = pq^{x-1}, \qquad x \in \mathbb{N}.$$

It is usual when talking about repeated trials such that these to introduce the symbol q to represent the probability of a trial being a failure; this makes many of the formulae simpler, but we do need to remember from time to time that $p + q = 1$. Note that the probabilities for X form a geometric sequence (hence the name of the distribution). To be able to calculate probabilities for a geometric distribution, we need to be able to add up geometric series.

Example 32.10.1. *The random variable $X \sim$ Geo(p). What is the cumulative distribution function F for X?*

Summing a geometric series, we see that

$$F(x) = \sum_{y=1}^{x} \mathbb{P}[X = y] = \sum_{y=1}^{x} pq^{y-1} = \frac{p(1 - q^x)}{1 - q} = 1 - q^x$$

for any $x \in \mathbb{N}$. Seeing this answer indicates another approach to this problem. Since $1 - F(x) = \mathbb{P}[X > x]$ is the probability that no success has occurred in the first x trials, hence it is the probability that the first x trials are all failures. Thus $1 - F(x) = q^x$, which gives us the correct result.

Calculating the mean and variance of a geometric distribution is more challenging. We recall from Chapter 10 that

$$(1-x)^{-2} = \sum_{n=0}^{\infty}(n+1)x^n \qquad (1-x)^{-3} = \sum_{n=0}^{\infty} \tfrac{1}{2}(n+1)(n+2)x^n$$

provided that $|x| < 1$. If the random variable X has the geometric distribution Geo(p), then

$$\mathbb{E}[X] = \sum_{n=1}^{\infty} n\mathbb{P}[X = n] = \sum_{n=1}^{\infty} npq^{n-1} = p\sum_{n=0}^{\infty}(n+1)q^n = p(1-q)^{-2} = \tfrac{1}{p}$$

$$\mathbb{E}[X(X+1)] = \sum_{n=1}^{\infty} n(n+1)\mathbb{P}[X = n] = \sum_{n=1}^{\infty} n(n+1)pq^{n-1} = p\sum_{n=0}^{\infty}(n+1)(n+2)q^n = 2p(1-q)^{-3} = \tfrac{2}{p^2}$$

so that

$$\mathbb{E}[X^2] = \mathbb{E}[X(X+1)] - \mathbb{E}[X] = \tfrac{2-p}{p^2} \qquad \text{Var}[X] = \tfrac{2-p}{p^2} - \tfrac{1}{p^2} = \tfrac{q}{p^2}$$

> **Key Fact 32.14** The Geometric Distribution : Mean and Variance
>
> If $X \sim$ Geo(p), then $\qquad \mathbb{E}[X] = \tfrac{1}{p} \qquad \text{Var}[X] = \tfrac{q}{p^2}$

Example 32.10.2. *I am collecting a set of cards. There are 40 in a set, and I currently have all but one of the cards. Let X be the number of cards that I now have to collect before I complete my set, Assuming that the different cards occur with equal probability, calculate:*

a) $\mathbb{E}[X]$ *and* $\text{Var}[X]$,   b) $\mathbb{P}[X \leq 50]$,   c) $\mathbb{P}[|X - \mu| < \sigma]$.

The number X of cards needed to complete my set is $X \sim \text{Geo}(\frac{1}{40})$, and hence

(a) $\mathbb{E}[X] = \frac{1}{p} = 40$ and $\text{Var}[X] = \frac{q}{p^2} = 1560$,

(b) $\mathbb{P}[X \leq 50] = 1 - q^{50} = 1 - \left(\frac{39}{40}\right)^{50} = 0.718$,

(c) We have $\mu = 40$ and $\sigma^2 = 1560$, so that

$$
\begin{aligned}
\mathbb{P}[|X - \mu| < \sigma] &= \mathbb{P}[|X - 40| < \sqrt{1560}] = \mathbb{P}[0.503 < X < 79.49] = \mathbb{P}[1 \leq X \leq 79] \\
&= F(79) = 1 - q^{79} = 0.865.
\end{aligned}
$$

EXERCISE 32F

1. A fair eight-sided die has the numbers from 1 to 8 on its faces. Let X be the outcome of a single roll of this die. What is the expectation and variance of X. What is the probability that X falls within one standard deviations of its mean?

2. A fair eight-sided die has the numbers 3, 7, 11, 15, 19, 23, 27, 31 on its faces. Let Y be the outcome of a single roll of this die. What is the expectation and variance of Y? Write down the probability that Y lies within one standard deviation of its mean?

3. Five roads lead from a junction. Only one of them will get me home. If I attempt any of the others, I will eventually have to retrace my steps to the junction I started at. What is the probability that I will choose the correct junction on my third attempt?

4. I pick a card from a standard deck of 52 cards (with replacement). What is the probability that I have obtain an Ace somewhere between my eighth and fifteenth (inclusive) picks? What is the probability that I do not pick an Ace until I have chosen at least eighteen cards?

5. A hockey player scores with 75% of her shots. If she takes a sequence of shots at goal, what is the probability that she does not fail to score until her sixth shot?

6. A student wants to 'borrow' a bicycle, which is locked with a combination lock. There are m possible codes for this lock, only one of which works. The student tries randomly chosen combinations on the lock; let M be the number of codes that the student has to try before the lock opens. Find the probability distribution function of M if:

   a) the student does not eliminate unsuccessful codes from future selections,

   b) the student does eliminate unsuccessful codes.

   If $m = 1000$, what is the expected number of codes that have to be tried in cases (a) and (b)?

7. A pair of fair six-sided dice are rolled. Let X be the number of dice that have been rolled until 'double 6' is obtained. What is the probability that X is greater than 17? What are the mean and variance of X?

8. Eggs are shipped in boxes of 6. There is a 1% chance that any egg is cracked, independently of all other eggs.

   a) What is the probability that a randomly selected box contains no cracked eggs?

   b) What is the distribution of the number N of boxes of eggs that have to be selected before a box containing a cracked egg is found? What is the expectation of N? What is the probability that $N > 12$?

   c) What is the expectation of the number M of boxes of eggs that have to be selected before a box containing six cracked eggs is found?

9. Let $X \sim \text{Geo}(p)$ for some $0 < p < 1$.

   a) Evaluate $\mathbb{P}[X = 10 + j | X > 10]$ for all $j \in \mathbb{N}$.

   b) Given that it takes more than 10 trials until the first success, let Y be the number of trials **more than** 10 that are needed to obtain the first success. What is the distribution of Y?

   c) 'I have played this game 10 times in a row and lost each time; it must be my turn to win now!' Comment. This question illustrates what is known as the **memory-free** nature of the Geometric distribution.

10. Maisie guesses all the answers to a multiple-choice test.

    a) If each question contains four different choices, find the probability that Maisie gets her first correct answer on her third question.

    b) If each question has four different choices, find the probability that Maisie's first correct answer occurs within the first six questions.

    c) If each question has six different choices, find the probability that Maisie's first correct answers occurs at the tenth question.

11. I roll a fair six-sided die repeatedly until I roll a 6. If I roll a 6 for the first time on my n^{th} roll, I then toss n fair coins. What is the probability that I gain no heads?

12*. A gambling game has the following rules. A player pays £3, and then rolls a fair sided die repeatedly. If she throws n successive 6s before the first non-6, she receives a prize of £3^n, so she always gets at least £1 back. What is her expected profit from a round of this game?

Suppose now that the player pays £λ to play, and receives £λ^n if she manages to roll n successive 6s. Here λ can be any number between 1 and 6.

    a) What values of λ ensure that the player expects to break even on each game?

    b) If you were the manager of the casino running this game, what value of λ maximises your expected profit from each game?

32.11 The Binomial Distribution

32.11.1. DEFINITIONS

The spinner on the right is an equilateral triangle. When it is spun it comes to rest on one of its three edges. One of the three edges is black. The spinner is resting on the black edge in the figure. This will be described as 'showing black'. The spinner is fair, so the probability that the spinner shows black is $\frac{1}{3}$ and the probability that it does not is $\frac{2}{3}$.

Figure 32.7

Suppose that the spinner is spun on 5 separate occasions. Let the random variable X be the number of times out of 5 that the spinner shows black. Clearly X can take any value from 0 to 5. Some of the terms we introduced when discussing the Geometric distribution will be useful here. The act of spinning the spinner once will be called a **trial**. We call the trial a **success** when the spinner shows black, and a **failure** otherwise. Thus X could now be defined as the number of successes in the 5 trials. These trials are identical (they all have the same probability of success) and are independent of each other.

For any $1 \le j \le 5$, let S_j be the event that the jth trial is a success. Thus the event that $X = 5$ is the event that all 5 trials are successes, namely the event $S_1 \cap S_2 \cap S_3 \cap S_4 \cap S_5$. Since the five trials are independent of each other, we deduce that

$$\mathbb{P}[X = 5] = \mathbb{P}[S_1 \cap S_2 \cap S_3 \cap S_4 \cap S_5] = \mathbb{P}[S_1]\mathbb{P}[S_2]\mathbb{P}[S_3]\mathbb{P}[S_4]\mathbb{P}[S_5] = \frac{2}{3} \times \frac{2}{3} \times \frac{2}{3} \times \frac{2}{3} \times \frac{2}{3} = \frac{32}{243} \, .$$

The probability $\mathbb{P}[X = 4]$ is more complicated to calculate. In order for X to be equal to 4, there must be 4 successes, and therefore one failure, out of the 5 trials. Thus the event $X = 4$ is the union of the $5 = {}^5C_4$ events $S_1 \cap S_2 \cap S_3 \cap S_4 \cap S_5'$, $S_1 \cap S_2 \cap S_3 \cap S_4' \cap S_5$, $S_1 \cap S_2 \cap S_3' \cap S_4 \cap S_5$, $S_1 \cap S_2' \cap S_3 \cap S_4 \cap S_5$ and $S_1' \cap S_2 \cap S_3 \cap S_4 \cap S_5$. Each of these events have probability $\left(\frac{1}{3}\right)^4 \times \frac{2}{3}$ (since for each of them, in some order, there must be four successes and one failure), and the events are mutually exclusive, so that

$$\mathbb{P}[X = 4] = 5 \times \left(\frac{1}{3}\right)^4 \times \frac{2}{3} = \frac{10}{243} \, .$$

Similarly, we see that, in order for X to be equal to 3, there must be three successes and two failures in the five trials. Any particular sequence of three successes and two failures (such as $S_1' \cap S_2 \cap S_3' \cap S_4 \cap S_5$) has probability $\left(\frac{1}{3}\right)^3 \times \left(\frac{2}{3}\right)^2$ of occurring. Since there are ${}^5C_3 = 10$ different orders in which three successes and two failures can be ordered, we deduce that

$$\mathbb{E}[X = 3] = 10 \times \left(\frac{1}{3}\right)^3 \times \left(\frac{2}{3}\right)^2 = \frac{40}{243}$$

Continuing these ideas, we can complete the probability distribution function for X:

x	0	1	2	3	4	5
$\mathbb{P}[X = x]$	${}^5C_0\left(\frac{1}{3}\right)^0\left(\frac{2}{3}\right)^5$	${}^5C_1\left(\frac{1}{3}\right)^1\left(\frac{2}{3}\right)^4$	${}^5C_2\left(\frac{1}{3}\right)^2\left(\frac{2}{3}\right)^3$	${}^5C_3\left(\frac{1}{3}\right)^3\left(\frac{2}{3}\right)^2$	${}^5C_4\left(\frac{1}{3}\right)^4\left(\frac{2}{3}\right)^1$	${}^5C_5\left(\frac{1}{3}\right)^5\left(\frac{2}{3}\right)^0$
	$= \frac{32}{243}$	$= \frac{80}{243}$	$= \frac{80}{243}$	$= \frac{40}{243}$	$= \frac{10}{243}$	$= \frac{1}{243}$

The result is this table can be summarised in a single formula:

$$\mathbb{P}[X = x] = {}^5C_x\left(\tfrac{1}{3}\right)^x \times \left(\tfrac{2}{3}\right)^{5-x}, \qquad 0 \le x \le 5.$$

Although the case of the spinner is not important in itself, it is an example of an important and extremely common situation.

Key Fact 32.15 The Binomial Distribution

When considering a sequence of n identical independent trials, each with probability p of success, then the number X of successes in this sequence of n trials is said to have the **Binomial distribution** with **parameters** n and p, and the probability distribution function of X is given by the formula

$$\mathbb{P}[X = x] = {}^nC_x p^x q^{n-x}, \qquad 0 \le x \le n.$$

Food For Thought 32.5

This distribution is called the Binomial distribution both because it contains the Binomial coefficients ${}^nC_x$, but also because the Binomial theorem shows us that

$$\sum_{x=0}^{n} \mathbb{P}[X = x] = \sum_{x=0}^{n} {}^nC_x p^x q^{n-x} = (p+q)^n = 1^n = 1.$$

For comparison, the number of times the spinner showed black in five spins had the distribution $B(5, \tfrac{1}{3})$.

Example 32.11.1. *Given that* $X \sim B(8, \tfrac{1}{4})$, *find* *a)* $\mathbb{P}[X = 6]$, *b)* $\mathbb{P}[X \le 2]$, *c)* $\mathbb{P}[X > 0]$.

(a) $\mathbb{P}[X = 6] = {}^8C_6\left(\tfrac{1}{4}\right)^6 \times \left(\tfrac{3}{4}\right)^2 = 0.00385$.

(b) $\mathbb{P}[X \le 2] = \mathbb{P}[X = 0] + \mathbb{P}[X = 1] + \mathbb{P}[X = 2] = {}^8C_0\left(\tfrac{1}{4}\right)^0\left(\tfrac{3}{4}\right)^8 + {}^8C_1\left(\tfrac{1}{4}\right)^1\left(\tfrac{3}{4}\right)^7 + {}^8C_2\left(\tfrac{1}{4}\right)^2\left(\tfrac{3}{4}\right)^6$

$\qquad = 0.1001... + 0.2669... + 0.3114... = 0.679$

(c) Rather than adding $\mathbb{P}[X = 1], \mathbb{P}[X = 2], \ldots, \mathbb{P}[X = 8]$ together, we calculate

$$\mathbb{P}[X > 0] = 1 - \mathbb{P}[X = 0] = 1 - \left(\tfrac{3}{4}\right)^8 = 1 - 0.1001 = 0.900$$

EXERCISE 32G

In this exercise give probabilities correct to 4 decimal places.

1. The random variable X has a binomial distribution with $n = 6$ and $p = 0.2$. Calculate
   a) $\mathbb{P}[X = 3]$,
   b) $\mathbb{P}[X = 4]$,
   c) $\mathbb{P}[X = 6]$.

2. Given that $Y \sim B(7, \tfrac{2}{3})$, calculate
   a) $\mathbb{P}[Y = 4]$,
   b) $\mathbb{P}[Y = 6]$,
   c) $\mathbb{P}[Y = 0]$.

3. Given that $Z \sim B(9, 0.45)$, calculate
   a) $\mathbb{P}[Z = 3]$,
   b) $\mathbb{P}[Z = 4 \text{ or } 5]$,
   c) $\mathbb{P}[Z \ge 7]$.

4. Given that $D \sim B(12, 0.7)$, calculate
   a) $\mathbb{P}[D < 4]$,
   b) the smallest value of d such that $\mathbb{P}[D > d] < 0.9$.

5. Given that $H \sim B(9, \frac{1}{2})$, calculate the probability that H is

   a) exactly 5,　　　　b) 5 or 6,　　　　c) at least 8,　　　　d) more than 2.

6. Given that $S \sim B(7, \frac{1}{6})$, find the probability that S is

   a) exactly 3,　　　　b) at least 4.

7*. If $X \sim B(n, p)$, show that

$$\mathbb{P}[X = x+1] = \mathbb{P}[X = x] \times \frac{p(n-x)}{q(x+1)}, \qquad x = 0, 1, \ldots, n-1 .$$

Why is this formula useful?

8*. Use the formula of Question 7 to prove that the **mode** m of a binomial distribution (that is, the value of x such that $\mathbb{P}[X = x]$ has the highest probability) satisfies the inequality $(n+1)p - 1 < m \le (n+1)p$. When is there equality?

32.11.2. CUMULATIVE PROBABILITY TABLES

Some of the last questions in the last exercise were beginning to become a little laborious to calculate. For example, if $X \sim B(10, 0.15)$, then to find $\mathbb{P}[X \le 5]$ we need to add $\mathbb{P}[X = 0]$, $\mathbb{P}[X = 1]$, ..., $\mathbb{P}[X = 5]$ together. This involves a lot of number-crunching, with a large possibility of calculation error. The real problem is that, unlike the other discrete random variables that we have considered, there is no simple formula for the cumulative distribution function $F(x) = \mathbb{P}[X \le x]$. (If there were, then answering the above question would have been simple, since it wants to know $F(5)$.)

Where mathematical formulae fail, brute force can work. The tables found on pages 768 to 773 provide data for the cumulative distribution function $F(x)$ for distributions $N(n, p)$ for a range of values of n between 5 and 30, and for the commonest values of p, to 4 decimal place accuracy. Of course, these tables are not complete. Not all values of n and p have been included, since there are infinitely many of both. However, these tables enable us to calculate answers to more complex questions relatively easily, and we are not likely to meet questions which take us outside the safety zone of the tables.

Example 32.11.2. *I throw* 20 *identical fair* 6*-sided dice. What is the probability that I roll between* 2 *and* 9 *sixes?*

The number X of 6s that I roll has distribution $B(20, \frac{1}{6})$. Using the tables, we see that

$$\mathbb{P}[2 \le X \le 9] = F(9) - F(1) = 0.9994 - 0.1304 = 0.8690 = 0.869$$

Example 32.11.3. *A crow sits on a fence post. Every minute it flies to one of the two fence posts on either side of it. It flies to the fence post to its right with probability* 0.4, *and to the fence post to its left with probability* 0.6. *What is the probability that it is within* 10 *fence posts of its starting point after* 25 *minutes?*

This needs a little thought. Let X be the number of times that the crow flies to the fence post on its right. Then $X \sim B(25, 0.4)$. Suppose that the crow's final position after 25 minutes is Y posts to the right of its starting point. Every time the crow flies to the right, Y increases by 1; every time the crow flies to the left, Y decreases by 1. After a little thought, this means that $Y = 2X - 25$. Thus

$$\begin{aligned} \mathbb{P}[-10 \le Y \le 10] &= \mathbb{P}[-10 \le 2X - 25 \le 10] = \mathbb{P}[7.5 \le X \le 17.5] \\ &= \mathbb{P}[8 \le X \le 17] = F(17) - F(7) = 0.9988 - 0.1536 \\ &= 0.8542 = 0.845 \end{aligned}$$

Example 32.11.4. *A card is selected at random from a standard pack of* 52 *playing cards. The suit of the card is noted and the card is replaced. This process is repeated to give a total of* 16 *selections. Find the probability that:*

(a) *exactly* 5 *hearts occur in the* 16 *selections,*

(b) *at least three hearts occur in the* 16 *selections,*

(c) *more than four, but not more than ten, hearts occur in the* 16 *selections.*

Since the selected card is always replaced before the next card is selected, the probability that a heart is chosen is always $\frac{1}{4}$, and so the number X of hearts chosen has distribution $B(16, \frac{1}{4})$. Thus

(a) $\mathbb{P}[X = 5] = {}^{16}C_5 0.25^5 \times 0.75^{11} = 0.180$. Note that the cumulative distribution tables also tell us that $F(5) - F(4) = 0.8103 - 0.6302 = 0.1801 = 0.180$. It is a close call which method is harder work.

(b) $\mathbb{P}[X \geq 3] = 1 - \mathbb{P}[X \leq 2] = 1 - F(2) = 1 - 0.1971 = 0.8029 = 0.803$.

(c) $\mathbb{P}[4 < X \leq 10] = F(10) - F(4) = 0.9997 - 0.6302 = 0.3695 = 0.370$.

EXERCISE 32H

1. In a certain school, 30% of the students are in the age group 16-19.

   a) Ten students are chosen at random. What is the probability that fewer than four of them are in the 16-19 age group?

   b) If the ten students were chosen by picking ten who were sitting together at lunch, explain why a binomial distribution might no longer have been suitable.

2. A factory makes large quantities of coloured sweets, and it is known that on average 20% of the sweets are coloured green. A packet contains 20 sweets. Assuming that the packet forms a random sample of the sweets made by the factory, calculate the probability that fewer than seven of the sweets are green.

   If you knew that, in fact, the sweets could have been green, red, orange or brown, would it have invalidated your calculation?

3. A coin is biassed, and the probability of tossing heads is $\frac{1}{3}$. This coin is tossed 30 times, and the random variable P is the proportion of heads that have been tossed.

   a) What is the distribution of $30P$?

   b) Calculate $\mathbb{P}[0.3 \leq P \leq 0.4]$ and $\mathbb{P}[0.32 \leq P \leq 0.34]$.

4. A six-sided die is such that the probability that it rolls a 6 is p. I roll the die 30 times, and I win £10 if I roll more than eight 6s; otherwise I lose £1. If my profit from this game is £X, write down the probability distribution of X, and calculate $\mathbb{E}[X]$ in each of the following cases:

   a) $p = \frac{1}{6}$,   b) $p = \frac{1}{5}$,   c) $\frac{1}{10}$.

5. Two fair six-sided die has the numbers $1, 1, 1, 2, 2$ and 3 on their faces.

   a) What is the probability that, when the two dice are rolled, they show the same number?

   b) I play a game in which I throw two of these dice continually until they both show the same number. I win the game if it takes more than 4 throws for this to happen. What is the probability that I win the game?

   c) If I play five games, what is the probability that I win two of them?

6. Eggs produced at a farm are packaged in boxes of six. Assume that, for any egg, the probability that it is broken when it reaches the retail outlet is 0.1, independent of all other eggs. A box is said to be bad if it contains at least two broken eggs. Calculate the probability that a randomly selected box is bad.

   Ten boxes are chosen at random. Find the probability that just two of these boxes are bad.

   It is known that, in fact, breakages are more likely to occur after the eggs have been packed into boxes, and while they are being transported to the retail outlet. Explain why this fact is likely to invalidate the calculation.

7. On a particular tropical island, the probability that there is a hurricane in any given month can be taken to be 0.08. Use a binomial distribution to calculate the probability that there is a hurricane in more than two months of the year. State two assumptions needed for a binomial distribution to be a good model. Why may one of the assumptions not be valid?

8. It is given that, at a stated time of day, 35% of the adults in the country are wearing jeans. At that time, a sample of twelve adults is selected. Use a binomial distribution to calculate the probability that exactly five out of these twelve are wearing jeans. Explain carefully two assumptions that must be made for your calculation to be valid. (If you say 'sample is random' you must explain what this means in the context of the question.)

9. Explain why a binomial distribution would not be a good model in the following problem. (Do not attempt any calculation.)

    Thirteen cards are chosen at random from an ordinary pack. Find the probability that there are four clubs, four diamonds, three hearts and two spades.

10. Explain why the binomial distribution $B(6, 0.5)$ would not be a good model in each of the following situations. (Do not attempt any calculations.)

    a) It is known that 50% of the boys in a certain school are over 170 cm in height. They are arranged, for a school photograph, in order of ascending height. A group of six boys standing next to each other is selected at random. Find the probability that exactly three members of the sample are over 170 cm in height.

    b) It is known that, on average, the temperature in London reaches at least 20°C on exactly half the days in the year. A day is picked at random from each of the months January, March, May, July, September and November. Find the probability that the temperature in London reaches 20°C on exactly three of these six days.

11. A bag contains six red and four green counters. Four counters are selected at random, without replacement. The events A, B, C and D represent obtaining a red counter on the first, second, third and fourth selection, respectively.

    Show that $\mathbb{P}[A] = \mathbb{P}[B] = \mathbb{P}[C] = \mathbb{P}[D] = 0.6$.

    Explain why the total number of red counters could not be well modelled by the distribution $B(4, 0.6)$.

For Interest

It is important to note that, just because events have the same probability, this does not automatically mean that they are independent.

32.11.3. MEAN AND VARIANCE

If a random variable X has the Binomial distribution $B(n, p)$, what is its expectation and variance? A little thought tells us the answer to the question about the expectation. Each of the n trials has a probability p of success. Over a sequence of n trials we should expect that the proportion p of those n will be successes. This means that we expect the number of successes to be np. If our understanding of expectation is reasonable, then we should have

$$\mathbb{E}[X] = np.$$

Mathematicians are not content with accepting an idea because it is reasonable; they want to know why it is true as well as reasonable. To prove the result about expectation takes a little algebra. Some manipulation of the Binomial coefficients gives

$$\mathbb{E}[X] = \sum_{x=0}^{n} x \times {}^{n}C_{x}p^{x}q^{n-x} = \sum_{x=1}^{n} x \times \frac{n!}{x!(n-x)!}p^{x}q^{n-x} = \sum_{x=1}^{n} \frac{n!}{(x-1)!(n-x)!}p^{x}q^{n-x}$$

$$= \sum_{x=1}^{n} n \times \frac{(n-1)!}{(x-1)!(n-x)!}p^{x}q^{n-x} = \sum_{x=1}^{n} n \times {}^{n-1}C_{x-1}p^{x}q^{n-x} = np\sum_{x=1}^{n} {}^{n-1}C_{x-1}p^{x-1}q^{n-x}$$

$$= np\sum_{y=0}^{n-1} {}^{n-1}C_{y}p^{y}q^{n-1-y} = np(p+q)^{n-1} = np$$

as required. A similar, but more involved, calculation can calculate the variance of X.

> **Key Fact 32.16** The Binomial Distribution : Mean and Variance
>
> If $X \sim B(n, p)$, then: $\quad \mathbb{E}[X] = np, \quad \text{Var}[X] = npq$.

Example 32.11.5. *Nails are sold in packets of* 100. *Occasionally a nail is faulty. The number of faulty nails in a randomly chosen packet is denoted by* X. *Assuming that a faulty nail occurs independently and at random, calculate the mean and standard deviation of* X, *given that the probability that any one nail is faulty is* 0.02.

We can model the number of faulty nails in a randomly chosen packet by saying that $X \sim B(100, 0.02)$. Thus

$$\mathbb{E}[X] = 100 \times 0.02 = 2, \qquad \text{Var}[X] = 100 \times 0.02 \times 0.98 = 1.96,$$

and hence $\sigma_X = 1.4$.

Example 32.11.6. *If* $X \sim B(10, 0.3)$, *has mean* μ *and standard deviation* σ, *find* $\mathbb{P}[X < \mu + \sigma]$.

We have $\mu = 10 \times 0.3 = 3$ and $\sigma^2 = 10 \times 0.3 \times 0.7 = 2.1$, so $\sigma = 1.449$. Thus

$$\mathbb{P}[X < \mu + \sigma] = \mathbb{P}[X < 3 + 1.449] = \mathbb{P}[X \leq 4] = F(4) = 0.8497 .$$

Example 32.11.7. *If the random variable* $Y \sim B(n, p)$ *is such that* $\mathbb{E}[Y] = 24$ *and* $\text{Var}[Y] = 8$, *find the values of* n *and* p.

We need to solve the simultaneous equations

$$np = 24 \qquad npq = 8$$

From these it is clear that $q = \frac{1}{3}$, and so $n = 36$, $p = \frac{1}{3}$.

EXERCISE 32I

1. Given that $X \sim B(20, 0.14)$, calculate

   a) $\mathbb{E}[X]$ and $\text{Var}[X]$,   b) $\mathbb{P}\big[X \leq \mathbb{E}[X]\big]$.

2. A batch of capsules of a certain drug contains 2% of damaged capsules. A bottle contains 42 of these capsules. Calculate the mean and standard deviation of the number of damaged capsules in such a bottle, assuming that each capsule was randomly selected for inclusion in the bottle.

3. In a certain examination 35% of all candidates pass. Calculate the expectation and variance of the number of passes in a group of 30 randomly chosen candidates who take the examination.

4. The random variable X has a binomial distribution with mean 3 and variance 2.25. Find $\mathbb{P}[X = 3]$.

5. The random variables X and Y are such that $X \sim B(n, p)$ and $Y \sim B(m, p)$. Given that $\mathbb{E}[X] = 3$, $\text{Var}[X] = 2.4$ and $\mathbb{E}[Y] = 2$, find $\text{Var}[Y]$.

6. For the random variable Y, for which $Y \sim B(16, 0.8)$, calculate $\mathbb{P}[Y > mu + \sigma]$.

7*. If $X \sim B(n, p)$, use algebra to show that $\mathbb{E}[X^2 - X] = n(n - 1)p^2$, and deduce that $\text{Var}[X] = npq$.

Chapter 32: Summary

- A discrete random variable X consists of a discrete set S consisting of the possible values that the variable X can take, and the corresponding probabilities of X taking each value. The function

$$f(x) = \mathbb{P}[X = x] \qquad x \in S,$$

is called the probability distribution function or mass function of X. The probability distribution function f satisfies

$$f(x) \geq 0 \qquad x \in S, \qquad \sum_{x \in S} f(x) = 1.$$

If $S = \{x_1, x_2, \ldots\}$, we sometimes write $p_i = f(x_i) = \mathbb{P}[X = x_i]$.

- The cumulative distribution function of a random variable X is the function

$$F(x) = \mathbb{P}[X \leq x], \qquad x \in \mathbb{R}.$$

- For any discrete random variable, its expectation is the quantity

$$\mathbb{E}[X] = \sum_{x \in S} x f(x) = \sum_i x_i p_i.$$

For any appropriate function g, we can calculate the expectation of the random variable $g(X)$:

$$\mathbb{E}[g(X)] = \sum_{x \in S} g(x) f(x) = \sum_i g(x_i) p_i.$$

The variance of the random variable X is the quantity

$$\mathrm{Var}[X] = \mathbb{E}\left[\left(X - \mathbb{E}[X]\right)^2\right] = \mathbb{E}[X^2] - \mathbb{E}[X]^2.$$

The standard deviation of a random variable is the square root of its variance: $\sigma_X = \sqrt{\mathrm{Var}[X]}$.

- $\mathbb{E}[aX + b] = a\mathbb{E}[X] + b$, $\mathrm{Var}[aX + b] = a^2 \mathrm{Var}[X]$ and $\sigma_{aX+b} = |a|\sigma_X$ for any random variable X and constants a, b.

- The discrete uniform distribution $U(N)$ has sample space $\{1, 2, \ldots, N\}$, probability distribution function

$$f(j) = \tfrac{1}{N}, \qquad 1 \leq j \leq N,$$

mean $\frac{1}{2}(N + 1)$ and variance $\frac{1}{12}(N^2 - 1)$.

- A random variable X has the geometric distribution $\mathrm{Geo}(p)$ when it has sample space $\mathbb{N}$ and probability distribution function

$$f(n) = (1 - p)^{n-1} p = q^{n-1} p, \qquad n \geq 0,$$

where $q = 1 - p$. If a sequence of independent identical trials, all with probability p of success, are held, then X is the number of trials until the first success. The mean and variance of X are $\mathbb{E}[X] = p^{-1}$ and $\mathrm{Var}[X] = qp^{-2}$.

- A random variable X has the Binomial distribution $B(n, p)$ when it has sample space $\{0, 1, \ldots, n\}$ and probability distribution function

$$f(j) = {}^nC_j p^j (1 - p)^{n-j} = {}^nC_j p^j q^{n-j}, \qquad 0 \leq j \leq n,$$

where $q = 1 - p$. If a sequence of n independent identical trials, all with probability p of success, are held, then X is the number of successes achieved. The mean and variance of X are $\mathbb{E}[X] = np$ and $\mathrm{Var}[X] = npq$.

The Normal Distribution

In this chapter we will learn to:

- understand the use of a normal distribution to model a continuous random variable, and use normal distribution tables,

- solve problems concerning a normally distributed random variable $X \sim N(\mu, \sigma^2)$, both calculating probabilities and identifying parameters such as the mean and variance.

33.1 Continuous Random Variables

In Chapter 32, we met the idea of a discrete random variable and its probability distribution. What we needed was a discrete set of values, and a collection of probabilities, determining the probability of the random variable achieving any of those values. For example, the outcome X of the roll of a standard die can take any of the values 1, 2, 3, 4, 5 or 6, all with probability $\frac{1}{6}$.

However, not all types of data are discrete, and the same is true of random variables. Let W be the weight, in grams, of an egg picked at random from the packing line of a chicken farm. There might well be a least value a and a greatest value b that W can take, but it is clear that an egg could weigh anything in the interval from a to b. There are an infinite number of numbers in the interval between a and b, and it is not possible to assign a probability to each of this infinite number of possible weights.

Food For Thought 33.1

It is not possible to know a weight precisely. We can never know, for example, if some object weighs 235 g exactly. No matter how sensitive or precise our weighing machine is, we can only measure weight to some degree of accuracy (to the nearest kilogram, the nearest gram, the nearest microgram, or whatever).

It is this fundamental lack of exactness that distinguishes continuous data from discrete data. If data is discrete, then provided our system of measurement is sufficiently precise to distinguish between the (known) possible values that the data can take, we can measure the data values precisely (if we know that the data can only take integer values and our system of measurement is known to be sufficiently precise that any measured value must be within 0.5 of the true value, then we would interpret a measured value of 2.31 as representing the exact data value of 2). In the continuous case, we do not have this luxury; we cannot assign a specific set of probabilities to a fixed set of possible values.

We need some model that can describe random variables that can take values in a continuous range. These are called **continuous random variables**. The full theory of continuous random variables is beyond the syllabus of the Pre-U course, but we do need to be aware of the key ideas of how to model such a random variable, since we need to study the most important continuous random variable of them all.

Like weight, length is another continuous data type. Suppose that we are interested in the lengths (in millimetres) of leaves that fall from a particular tree. As a start. we could collect a random sample of 50 leaves, and record their lengths, obtaining the following data:

60	31	72	57	99	46	68	47	54	57
42	48	39	40	67	89	70	68	42	54
52	50	85	56	50	53	57	83	79	63
63	72	57	53	90	52	58	47	34	102
70	60	94	43	85	67	78	66	57	44

Although at first sight it appears that the length of a leaf takes discrete integer values, this is clearly not true. Leaves could have any length, and not just lengths in whole numbers of millimetres. When recording the data above, the length has been measured to the nearest millimetre. For example, when the length is given as 63 mm, it means that the length, L, of the leaf lies in the interval $62.5 \leq L < 63.5$. It seems, sensible, then, to talk about the probability of a leaf having length L lying in a particular region, rather than having a particular value. Thus we shall start our analysis of this problem by grouping the data into classes of width 10 mm.

The **relative frequency** of each class is then the **experimental probability** of a randomly chosen tree leaf having a length L lying in that class. Note that (for example) for L to lie in the class $60 - 69$ mm, so we must have $59.5 \leq L < 69.5$. Each class is 10 mm wide, and the midpoints of the classes are $34.5, 44.5, \ldots, 104.5$.

The graph on the right, while correctly plotting the relative frequency of each class, is not particularly informative. It does not make it clear the nature of the various classes.

Length	Frequency	Relative Frequency
30 – 39	3	0.06
40 – 49	9	0.18
50 – 59	15	0.3
60 – 69	9	0.18
70 – 79	6	0.12
80 – 89	4	0.08
90 – 99	3	0.06
100 – 109	1	0.02

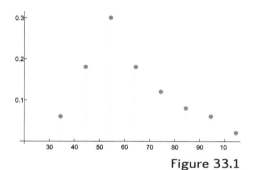

Figure 33.1

A much more useful way in which the probability distribution of the length of the leaves can be illustrated is to use a histogram. Since the classes all have width 10 mm, the relative frequency density for each class is simply one tenth of the relative frequency of that class. Note that we are plotting relative frequency density, and not frequency density, since relative frequency is what corresponds to probability.

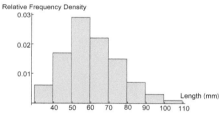

Figure 33.2

The key fact about a histogram plotting relative frequency density is that the experimental probability for L to be in a particular region is the **area under the graph** in that region. For example, the experimental probability that $54.5 \leq L < 71.5$ is the area of the darker shaded region, that is equal to

$$5 \times 0.03 + 10 \times 0.018 + 2 \times 0.012 = 0.354$$

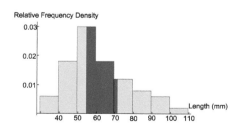

Figure 33.3

> **Key Fact 33.1** Continuous Random Variables: Histograms
>
> If we have plotted the (relative frequency) histogram of a particular continuous random variable, then the experimental probability that the variable takes a value in a particular region is the area under the graph in that region.

One consequence of the idea that area represents probability is the fact that, for example, the probability that $L = 51.2$ is zero. It is clear that $\mathbb{P}[L = 51.2] \leq \mathbb{P}[51.2 - \varepsilon < L < 51.2 + \varepsilon]$ for any $\varepsilon > 0$. Since the relative frequency density never exceeds 0.03, then this second probability cannot be greater than 0.03 times the width of the interval from $51.2 - \varepsilon$ to $51.2 + \varepsilon$, so that $\mathbb{P}[L = 51.2] \leq 0.03 \times 2\varepsilon = 0.06\varepsilon$. Since this is true for all $\varepsilon > 0$, we must have $\mathbb{P}[L = 51.2] = 0$. The fact that this model implies that the probability of obtaining specific values is zero fits well with the previously observed fact that we can never know for certain whether a particular value has been obtained, but only whether L lies in a particular range.

Key Fact 33.2 Continuous Random Variables: Specific Values

If X is a continuous random variable, then $\mathbb{P}[X = a] = 0$ for any value of a, and so

$$\mathbb{P}[a \leq X \leq b] = \mathbb{P}[a \leq X < b] = \mathbb{P}[a < X \leq b] = \mathbb{P}[a < X < b].$$

for any $a < b$.

The model we have used to date to model the lengths of tree leaves is rather crude. We have not considered a very large dataset of information, and we have grouped the data into quite broad classes. We could improve our understanding of the relative frequency distribution of the lengths of tree leaves by increasing the size of the dataset, and reducing the width of the classes. Figure 33.4 shows the result of increasing the size of the dataset to 100, and of halving the interval widths.

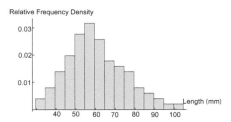

Figure 33.4

If this process were to be continued indefinitely, then the outline of the histogram would become a smooth curve instead of a series of steps. The sort of curve we might see is shown in Figure 33.5. The distribution of the leaf length is roughly symmetrical, and so we might expect symmetry in the eventual curve. The curve gives a model for the length of a tree leaf.

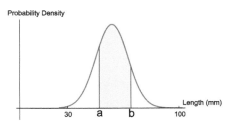

Figure 33.5

Key Fact 33.3 Continuous Random Variables: The Model

A model for a continuous random variable X can be provided by a positive function $f(x)$. The probability that the random variable X lies in the interval from a to b is given by the area under the curve:

$$\mathbb{P}[a \leq X \leq b] = \int_a^b f(x)\,dx.$$

Note that the total area under the curve $f(x)$ must be 1.

33.2 The Normal Distribution

The shape of the final curve in Figure 33.5 was no accident; this shape is fundamental to the study of continuous random variables, and is of vital importance in statistical calculations.

Suppose that we conduct a sequence of n independent identical trials, all with probability p of success, and let $P_{n,p}$ be the proportion of successes that occur in these trials. It is clear that $nP_{n,p} \sim B(n, p)$, and so we know the probability distribution of $P_{n,p}$ precisely. $P_{n,p}$ is a discrete random variable which takes values between 0 and 1 (the actual values are rational numbers with denominator n). If we consider the probability distribution histogram for $P_{n,p}$, we start to notice an interesting fact. In Figure 33.6 below, the horizontal scale is in units of the standard deviation of $P_{n,p}$, and the zero of the horizontal axis is the mean of $P_{n,p}$.

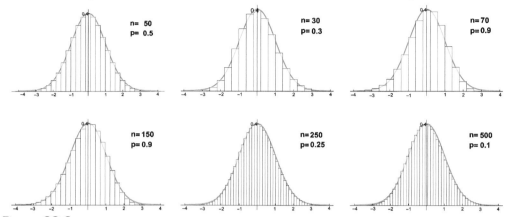

Figure 33.6

These probability histograms are all closely approximated by the same curve (marked in red on each graph), and the approximation becomes better as n increases.

Let us consider the probability distribution of the continuous random variable that is described by this special, 'bell-shaped', curve. This distribution is called the **normal distribution**. This distribution was introduced by Carl Friedrich Gauss (1777-1855), and it is sometimes called the **Gaussian distribution** in his honour. There are many other continuous random variables with different distributions, and there is nothing abnormal about them.

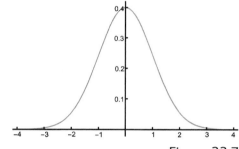

Figure 33.7

This distribution has the following key properties:

- the mode (where the probability density is greatest), the mean and the median (where the cumulative probability equals $\frac{1}{2}$) are all equal to 0,

- the distribution is symmetrical about 0,

- the probability density tails off rapidly as we move away from the mean.

We saw in Figure 33.6 how the same normal distribution curve approximated the distribution of $P_{n,p}$, where the random variable had been coded so that its mean was 0 and its standard deviation was 1. To take a random variable X and code it so that the resulting variable has mean 0 and standard deviation 1 is called **standardisation**; it is achieved by the following formula

$$Z = \frac{X-\mu}{\sigma},$$

where μ and σ are the mean and standard deviation of X. We have seen how the standardised versions of various $P_{n,p}$ could be approximated by the same normal distribution (with mean 0 and variance 1). Pushing the coding backwards we could approximate the different $P_{n,p}$ with different normal distributions, each with their own mean and variance, but with the same fundamental curve shape. Thus there is a normal distribution for each value of mean μ and variance σ^2. If a random variable X has this distribution, we write $X \sim N(\mu, \sigma^2)$. The random variable $Z \sim N(0,1)$ is called the **standard normal distribution**. Since these distributions are all related to each other by coding, their probability density functions will be obtained one from the other by simple graph transformations:

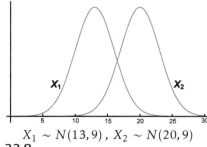 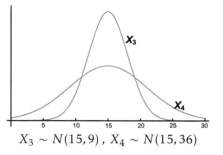

$X_1 \sim N(13,9)$, $X_2 \sim N(20,9)$ $\qquad$ $X_3 \sim N(15,9)$, $X_4 \sim N(15,36)$

Figure 33.8

A change of mean is implemented by a horizontal shift, while a change of variance is a combination of a horizontal and a vertical scale (the horizontal scale changes the spread, while the scale ensures that the area under the curve is still 1).

The key fact to note is that all normal distributions are essentially the same, if we measure the values of the random variable in units of standard deviations from the mean.

Thus, for example, the probability of lying within 1 standard deviation σ of the mean μ is about $\frac{2}{3}$, the probability of lying within 2σ of the mean μ is about 95% and the probability of lying within 3σ of μ is nearly 1, no matter what the values of μ and σ are.

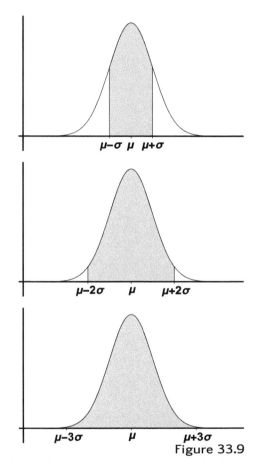

> **Key Fact 33.4** The Normal Distribution
>
> The distribution $X \sim N(\mu,\sigma^2)$ is described by the function
>
> $$f(x) = \frac{1}{\sigma\sqrt{2\pi}}e^{-\frac{1}{2\sigma^2}(x-\mu)^2}, \qquad x \in \mathbb{R}.$$

Note that the probability density function for $N(\mu,\sigma^2)$ is positive for all values of X. Does it makes sense, therefore, to use the normal distribution to model the length of a tree leaf, that can never be negative, since any normal distribution allows for a non-zero probability of being negative?

Figure 33.9

We can do so, since the fact that the curve falls off sharply implies that a reasonable model for the length of tree leaf might be the distribution $X \sim N(61.4,16.8^2)$ (see Figure 33.5 above and Example 33.5.1 below). For X to be negative would require X be more than 3.65 standard deviations away from the mean, and the probability of that happening is so small (about 3×10^{-4}) that it can be treated as zero.

> **For Interest**
>
> We have seen how the normal distribution arises from the Binomial distribution. The Binomial distribution is not special in this respect. If we consider the average of a large number n of identical independent trials, where each trial can have almost any probability distribution, we end up with the normal distribution. This result is known as the Central Limit Theorem.

33.3 The Standard Normal Distribution

Recall that the standard normal distribution $N(0,1)$ has mean 0 and variance 1, and that any other normal distribution can be expressed in terms of the standard normal distribution by the process of standardisation.

> **Key Fact 33.5** The Normal Distribution : Standardisation
>
> If $X \sim N(\mu, \sigma^2)$, then $Z = \frac{X-\mu}{\sigma}$ has the standard normal distribution: $Z \sim N(0,1)$. It is conventional to reserve the letter Z to refer to the standard normal distribution.

To be able to calculate probabilities associated with the standard normal distribution, we need to know its cumulative distribution function. This function is always written $\Phi(z)$ (since Φ is the Greek capital 'F', this is just a special way of writing $F(z)$, the more normal notation for the cumulative distribution function). The formula for $\Phi(z)$ is

$$\Phi(z) = \frac{1}{\sqrt{2\pi}} \int_{-\infty}^{z} e^{-\frac{1}{2}x^2}\, dx, \qquad z \in \mathbb{R}.$$

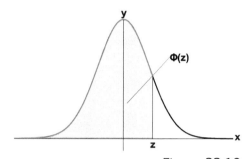

Figure 33.10

and we immediately run into a problem; we cannot perform that integral. The solution to this difficulty is the same as came to our aid with the Binomial distribution; we use precalculated tables. The table in Appendix 3 enables us to calculate $\Phi(z)$. The table tells us that $\Phi(2) = 0.9772$; this means that, for a random variable Z with the standard normal distribution, $Z \sim N(0,1)$, we have $\mathbb{P}[Z \le 2] = 0.9772$.

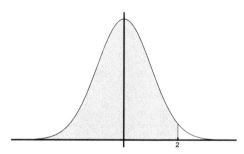

Figure 33.11

The table enables us to calculate $\Phi(z)$ for values of z, given correct to 3 decimal places, between 0 and 3. Here is an extract from that table.

z	0	1	2	3	4	5	6	7	8	9	1	2	3	4	5	6	7	8	9
														ADD					
0.6	0.7257	0.7291	**0.7324**	0.7357	0.7389	0.7422	0.7454	0.7486	0.7517	0.7549	3	7	10	**13**	16	19	23	26	29

Figure 33.12

Suppose we want to determine $\Phi(0.624) = \mathbb{P}[Z \le 0.624]$. The first two digits 0.6 of 0.624 indicate that we need to find the entry 0.6 in the z column, and take values from that row (the one in the above figure). The figure in the second decimal place of 0.624 is 2, which means that we need to take the value from the first column marked 2, namely 0.7324. The third decimal place of 0.624 is 4, so we need to find the corresponding entry in the right-hand column marked 4 (in the section of the table marked ADD), which is 13. This means that we have to add 14 ten-thousandths to 0.7324, obtaining $0.7324 + 0.0013 = 0.7337$. Thus $\Phi(0.624) = 0.7337$.

To find the probability that Z lies in an interval, we use the formula

$$\mathbb{P}[a \le Z \le b] = \mathbb{P}[Z \le b] - \mathbb{P}[Z \le a] = \Phi(b) - \Phi(a), \qquad a < b.$$

Note that this formula works because $\mathbb{P}[Z = a] = 0$, and hence $\mathbb{P}[a \le Z \le b] = \mathbb{P}[a < Z \le b]$, and so is equal to $\Phi(b) - \Phi(a)$. For example

$$\mathbb{P}[1.20 \le Z \le 2.34] = \Phi(2.34) - \Phi(1.20) = 0.9904 - 0.8849 = 0.1055 = 0.106$$

When using the table, it is important to show the four decimal places as evidence of working, but final answers should be rounded to three decimal places.

How do we calculate $\Phi(z)$ when $z < 0$? Negative values of z are not included in the table, but it is not necessary that they are, since we can use the symmetry properties of $\Phi(z)$ to evaluate Φ for them.

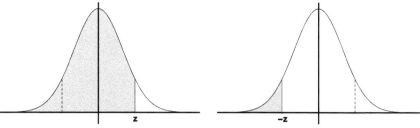

Figure 33.13

The symmetric nature of the function $f(x)$ means that the area under the curve to the left of $-z$ is the same as the area under the graph to the right of z. Thus

> **Key Fact 33.6** The Normal Distribution : Negative Arguments
>
> If $z > 0$ then
> $$\Phi(-z) = \mathbb{P}[Z \leq -z] = \mathbb{P}[Z \geq z] = 1 - \Phi(z).$$

When working with the normal distribution, it might be helpful (at least initially) to draw a small sketch of the bell-curve, to ensure that you are making the right calculations.

Example 33.3.1. *The random variable Z has the standard normal distribution $N(0,1)$. Find the following probabilities:*

a) $\mathbb{P}[0.7 \leq Z < 1.45]$,   b) $\mathbb{P}[Z \leq -2.3]$,   c) $\mathbb{P}[Z > 0.732]$,   d) $\mathbb{P}[-1.4 \leq Z \leq 1]$.

(a) We see that

$$
\begin{aligned}
\mathbb{P}[0.7 \leq Z < 1.4] &= \Phi(1.4) - \Phi(0.7) \\
&= 0.9192 - 0.7580 = 0.1612 \\
&= 0.161
\end{aligned}
$$

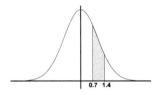

(b) Using the identity $\Phi(-z) = 1 - \Phi(z)$,

$$
\begin{aligned}
\mathbb{P}[Z \leq -2.3] &= 1 - \mathbb{P}[Z \leq 2.3] \\
&= 1 - \Phi(2.3) = 1 - 0.9893 \\
&= 0.0107 = 0.011
\end{aligned}
$$

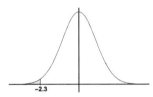

(c) This time

$$
\begin{aligned}
\mathbb{P}[Z > 0.732] &= 1 - \mathbb{P}[Z \leq 0.732] \\
&= 1 - \Phi(0.732) = 1 - (0.7673 + 0.0006) \\
&= 0.2321 = 0.232
\end{aligned}
$$

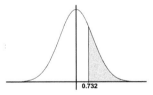

(d) Finally,

$$
\begin{aligned}
\mathbb{P}[-1.4 \leq Z \leq 1] &= \mathbb{P}[Z \leq 1] - \mathbb{P}[Z \leq -1.4] \\
&= \mathbb{P}[Z \leq 1] - \left(1 - \mathbb{P}[Z \leq 1.4]\right) \\
&= \Phi(1) - 1 + \Phi(1.4) \\
&= 0.8413 - 1 + 0.9192 = 0.7605 \\
&= 0.761
\end{aligned}
$$

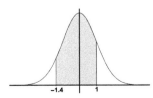

We can also be able to use the table 'backwards'. This is possible because the function Φ is one-to-one.

For Interest

The cumulative distribution function Φ is strictly increasing, and hence one-to-one, because

$$\Phi(z) = \int_{-\infty}^{z} f(x)\,dx$$

and hence

$$\Phi'(x) = f(x) > 0 \qquad x \in \mathbb{R}.$$

Example 33.3.2. *The random variable Z has the standard normal distribution, so that $Z \sim N(0,1)$. Find the values of s, t and u such that*

a) $\mathbb{P}[Z \le s] = s$,   b) $\mathbb{P}[Z > t] = 0.8$,   c) $\mathbb{P}[-u \le Z \le u] = 0.3$

(a) The table tells us that

$$\Phi(0.524) = 0.6999 \qquad \Phi(0.525) = 0.7002\,.$$

Thus, to 3 decimal places, $s = 0.524$.

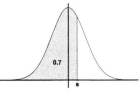

(b) Since $\mathbb{P}[Z > t] = 0.8 > 0.5$, it is clear that $t < 0$. Using the symmetry properties of Φ we know that $-t > 0$ and that $\Phi(-t) = 0.8$.
The table tells us that $\Phi(0.842) = 0.8$, so we deduce that $-t = 0.842$, and so $t = -0.842$

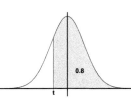

(c) We have to use the symmetry properties of Φ again to see that

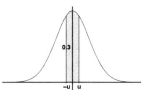

$$
\begin{aligned}
\mathbb{P}[-u \le Z \le u] &= \mathbb{P}[Z \le u] - \mathbb{P}[Z \le -u] \\
&= \mathbb{P}[Z \le u] - (1 - \mathbb{P}[Z \le u]) \\
&= 2\Phi(u) - 1\,.
\end{aligned}
$$

Thus we need to find u such that $\Phi(u) = \frac{1}{2}(1 + 0.3) = 0.65$. Since

$$\Phi(0.385) = 0.6499 \qquad \Phi(0.386) = 0.6502\,,$$

we deduce that $u = 0.385$.

EXERCISE 33A

---

1. The random variable Z has the standard normal distribution: $Z \sim N(0,1)$. Find the following probabilities:

   a) $\mathbb{P}[Z < 1.23]$,   b) $\mathbb{P}[Z \le 2.468]$,   c) $\mathbb{P}[Z < 0.157]$,
   d) $\mathbb{P}[Z \ge 1.236]$,   e) $\mathbb{P}[Z > 2.378]$,   f) $\mathbb{P}[Z \ge 0.588]$,
   g) $\mathbb{P}[Z > -1.83]$,   h) $\mathbb{P}[Z \ge -2.057]$,   i) $\mathbb{P}[Z > -0.067]$,
   j) $\mathbb{P}[Z \le -1.83]$,   k) $\mathbb{P}[Z < -2.755]$,   l) $\mathbb{P}[Z \le -0.206]$,
   m) $\mathbb{P}[Z < 1.645]$,   n) $\mathbb{P}[Z \ge 1.645]$,   o) $\mathbb{P}[Z > -1.645]$,
   p) $\mathbb{P}[Z \le -1.645]$.

2. The random variable Z is distributed such that $Z \sim N(0,1)$. Find these probabilities:

   a) $\mathbb{P}[1.15 < Z < 1.35]$,   b) $\mathbb{P}[1.111 \le Z \le 2.222]$,
   c) $\mathbb{P}[0.387 < Z < 2.418]$,   d) $\mathbb{P}[0 \le Z < 1.55]$,
   e) $\mathbb{P}[-1.815 < Z < 2.333]$,   f) $\mathbb{P}[-0.847 < Z < 2.034]$.

3. The random variable Z is distributed such that $Z \sim N(0,1)$. Find these probabilities:

 a) $\mathbb{P}[-2.505 < Z < 1.089]$,   b) $\mathbb{P}[-0.55 \le Z \le 0]$,
 c) $\mathbb{P}[-2.82 < Z < -1.82]$,   d) $\mathbb{P}[-1.749 \le Z \le -0.999]$,
 e) $\mathbb{P}[-2.568 < Z < -0.123]$,   f) $\mathbb{P}[-1.96 \le Z < 1.96]$,
 g) $\mathbb{P}[-2.326 < Z < 2.326]$,   h) $\mathbb{P}[|Z| \le 1.3]$,
 i) $\mathbb{P}[|Z| > 2.4]$.

4. The random variable $Z \sim N(0,1)$. In each part, find the value of s, t, u or v.

 a) $\mathbb{P}[Z < s] = 0.6700$,   b) $\mathbb{P}[Z < t] = 0.8780$,
 c) $\mathbb{P}[Z < u] = 0.9842$,   d) $\mathbb{P}[Z < v] = 0.8455$,
 e) $\mathbb{P}[Z > s] = 0.4052$,   f) $\mathbb{P}[Z > t] = 0.1194$,
 g) $\mathbb{P}[Z > u] = 0.0071$,   h) $\mathbb{P}[Z > v] = 0.2241$,
 i) $\mathbb{P}[Z \ge s] = 0.9977$,   j) $\mathbb{P}[Z \ge t] = 0.9747$,
 k) $\mathbb{P}[Z > u] = 0.8496$,   l) $\mathbb{P}[Z > v] = 0.5$,
 m) $\mathbb{P}[Z < s] = 0.0031$,   n) $\mathbb{P}[Z < t] = 0.0142$,
 o) $\mathbb{P}[Z < u] = 0.0468$,   p) $\mathbb{P}[Z < v] = 0.4778$,
 q) $\mathbb{P}[-s < Z < s] = 0.90$,   r) $\mathbb{P}[-t < Z < t] = 0.80$,
 s) $\mathbb{P}[-u < Z < u] = 0.99$,   t) $\mathbb{P}[|Z| > v] = 0.5$.

33.4   Standardising A Normal Distribution

Recall that a coded normal distribution is still normal, so that if $X \sim N(\mu, \sigma^2)$, then the standardised random variable

$$Z = \tfrac{X - \mu}{\sigma}$$

that has mean 0 and variance 1, has the standard normal distribution: $Z \sim N(0,1)$. Thus we can use information about the standard normal distribution to answer questions about any normal distribution.

Example 33.4.1. *Given that $X \sim N(4, 25)$, find the following probabilities:*
 a) $\mathbb{P}[X < 4.5]$,   b) $\mathbb{P}[5 \le X \le 6]$,   c) $\mathbb{P}[2 \le X \le 7]$,   d) $\mathbb{P}[X > 1]$.

Let $Z = \tfrac{1}{5}(X - 4)$ be the standardised normally distributed random variable.

 (a) $\mathbb{P}[X < 4.5] = \mathbb{P}[Z < \tfrac{1}{5}(4.5 - 4)] = \mathbb{P}[Z < 0.1] = \Phi(0.1)$
         $= 0.5398 = 0.540$.

 (b) $\mathbb{P}[5 \le X \le 6] = \mathbb{P}[\tfrac{1}{5}(5 - 4) \le Z \le \tfrac{1}{5}(6 - 4)] = \mathbb{P}[0.2 \le Z \le 0.4]$
         $= \Phi(0.4) - \Phi(0.2) = 0.6554 - 0.5793 = 0.0761 = 0.076$.

 (c) $\mathbb{P}[2 \le X \le 7] = \mathbb{P}[\tfrac{1}{5}(2 - 4) \le Z \le \tfrac{1}{5}(7 - 4)] = \mathbb{P}[-0.4 \le Z \le 0.6]$
         $= \mathbb{P}[Z \le 0.6] - \mathbb{P}[Z \le -0.4] = \Phi(0.6) - (1 - \Phi(0.4))$
         $= 0.7257 - 1 + 0.6554 = 0.0811 = 0.081$.

 (d) $\mathbb{P}[X > 1] = \mathbb{P}[Z > \tfrac{1}{5}(1 - 4)] = \mathbb{P}[Z > -0.6] = \mathbb{P}[Z < 0.6]$
        $= \Phi(0.6) = 0.7257 = 0.726$.

Example 33.4.2. *Given that $N \sim N(6, 4)$ find, to 3 significant figures, the values of s and t such that*
 a) $\mathbb{P}[X \le s] = 0.6500$,   b) $\mathbb{P}[X > t] = 0.8200$,

Let $Z = \tfrac{1}{2}(X - 6)$ be the standardised normally distributed random variable.

 (a) The requirement that $\mathbb{P}[X \le s] = 0.6500$ is equivalent to $\mathbb{P}[Z \le \tfrac{1}{2}(s - 6)] = 0.6500$. Since $\Phi(0.385) = 0.6499$ and $\Phi(0.386) = 0.6502$, we deduce that $\tfrac{1}{2}(s - 6) = 0.385$, we deduce that $s = 6 + 2 \times 0.385 = 6.77$.

 (b) The requirement that $\mathbb{P}[X > t] = 0.8200$ is equivalent to $\mathbb{P}[Z > \tfrac{1}{2}(t - 6)] = 0.8200$. From this it is clear that $\tfrac{1}{2}(t - 6)$ must be negative, and that $\mathbb{P}[Z < \tfrac{1}{2}(6 - t)] = 0.8200$. Since $\Phi(0.915) = 0.8199$ and $\Phi(0.916) = 0.8201$, we choose $\tfrac{1}{2}(6 - t) = 0.915$, so that $t = 4.17$. Note that we could have chosen 0.916 instead of 0.915, since their Φ values were equidistant from 0.8200, but this would have given us the same answer for t.

For Interest

Sometimes, intermediate values of z are determined by **interpolation**, and we might argue that since 0.8200 is halfway between $\Phi(0.915)$ and $\Phi(0.916)$, the correct value of z is halfway between 0.915 and 0.916, namely 0.9155.

This approach is not necessary when using these tables. When evaluating $\Phi(z)$, we simply calculate z correct to 3 decimal places, and look up the value, without trying for a more accurate calculation. A similar approach is perfectly acceptable for using the tables backwards. If the exact value of Φ that we are looking for is not to be found in the table, use the value of z that gives a value of Φ closest to out desired value; if there are two equally good choices for z, pick either.

It should be pointed out that the table is not exact; the corrections in $\Phi(z)$ for the third decimal place in z (the ADD columns) are the best possible, but not perfect. If a calculator, or a spreadsheet, with the capability to calculate Φ and Φ^{-1} is available, the answers obtained to questions might differ from time in the time, but generally only in the last decimal place. Calculations in the text, and the answers to exercises, have been calculated to be consistent with the data obtained from the table.

Example 33.4.3. *If X is normally distributed with mean 4.1, and $\mathbb{P}[X \leq 6.770] = 98\%$, find the value of the standard deviation σ.*

The standardised normally distributed random variable is $Z = \frac{1}{\sigma}(X - 4.1)$. We are told that

$$\Phi\left(\tfrac{2.67}{\sigma}\right) = \mathbb{P}[Z \leq \tfrac{1}{\sigma}(6.770 - 4.1)] = \mathbb{P}[X \leq 6.770] = 0.98\,,$$

and hence $\frac{2.67}{\sigma} = 2.054$. Thus $\sigma = 2.67 \div 2.054 = 1.30$ to 3 significant figures.

It is worth noting the small table in Appendix 3 that gives us quick access to values of z for particularly 'nice' (and certainly common) values of $\Phi(z)$; for example, we can read that $\Phi(2.326) = 0.99$ without going through the detail of working with the larger table.

Example 33.4.4. *A normally distributed random variable X is such that $\mathbb{P}[X > 4.2] = 0.5$ and $\mathbb{P}[|X - 4.2| < 0.627] = 0.95$. Calculate the mean and standard deviation of X.*

Since $\mathbb{P}[X > 4.2] = 0.5$, 4.2 is the median of X, and is therefore also the mean. Thus $\mu = 4.2$. The standardised normally distributed random variable is $Z = \frac{1}{\sigma}(X - \mu) = \frac{1}{\sigma}(X - 4.2)$. We are told that

$$2\Phi\left(\tfrac{0.627}{\sigma}\right) - 1 = \mathbb{P}\left[|Z| < \tfrac{0.627}{\sigma}\right] = \mathbb{P}[|X - 4.2| < 0.627] = 0.95$$

so that $\Phi(\frac{0.627}{\sigma}) = 0.975$. Using the smaller table, we see that $\frac{0.627}{\sigma} = 1.960$, and hence $\sigma = 0.320$ to 3 significant figures.

EXERCISE 33B

---

1. Given that $X \sim N(20, 16)$, find the following probabilities:

   a) $\mathbb{P}[X \leq 26]$,   b) $\mathbb{P}[X > 30]$,   c) $\mathbb{P}[X \geq 17]$,   d) $\mathbb{P}[X < 13]$.

2. Given that $X \sim N(24, 9)$, find the following probabilities:

   a) $\mathbb{P}[X \leq 29]$,   b) $\mathbb{P}[X > 31]$,   c) $\mathbb{P}[X \geq 22]$,   d) $\mathbb{P}[X < 16]$.

3. Given that $X \sim N(50, 16)$, find the following probabilities:

   a) $\mathbb{P}[54 \leq X \leq 58]$,   b) $\mathbb{P}[40 < X \leq 44]$,   c) $\mathbb{P}[47 < X < 57]$,
   d) $\mathbb{P}[39 \leq X < 53]$,   e) $\mathbb{P}[44 \leq X \leq 56]$.

4. The random variable X can take negative and positive values. X is distributed normally with mean 3 and variance 4. Find the probability that X has a negative value.

5. The random variable X has a normal distribution. The mean is μ (where $\mu > 0$) and the variance is $\frac{1}{4}\mu^2$.

   a) Find $\mathbb{P}[X > 1.5\mu]$, b) Find the probability that X is negative.

6. Given that $X \sim N(44, 25)$, find s, t, u and v correct to 2 decimal places when

   a) $\mathbb{P}[X \le s] = 0.9808$, b) $\mathbb{P}[X \ge t] = 0.7704$,
   c) $\mathbb{P}[X \ge u] = 0.0495$, d) $\mathbb{P}[X \le v] = 0.3336$.

7. Given that $X \sim N(15, 4)$, find s, t, u, v and w correct to 2 decimal places when

   a) $\mathbb{P}[X \le s] = 0.9141$, b) $\mathbb{P}[X \ge t] = 0.5746$, c) $\mathbb{P}[X \ge u] = 0.1041$,
   d) $\mathbb{P}[X \le v] = 0.3924$, e) $\mathbb{P}[|X - 15| < w] = 0.9$.

8. Given that $X \sim N(35.4, 12.5)$, find the values of s, t, u and v correct to 1 decimal place when

   a) $\mathbb{P}[X < s] = 0.96$, b) $\mathbb{P}[X > t] = 0.9391$,
   c) $\mathbb{P}[X > u] = 0.2924$, d) $\mathbb{P}[X < v] = 0.1479$.

9. X has a normal distribution with mean 32 and variance σ^2. Given that the probability that X is less than 33.14 is 0.6406, find σ^2. Give your answer correct to 2 decimal places.

10. X has a normal distribution, and $\mathbb{P}[X > 73.05] = 0.0289$. Given that the variance of the distribution is 18, find the mean.

11. X is distributed normally, $\mathbb{P}[X \ge 59.1] = 0.0218$ and $\mathbb{P}[X \ge 29.2] = 0.9345$. Find the mean and standard deviation of the distribution, correct to 3 significant figures.

12. $X \sim N(\mu, \sigma^2)$, $\mathbb{P}[X \ge 9.81] = 0.1587$ and $\mathbb{P}[X \le 8.82] = 0.0116$. Find μ and σ, correct to 3 significant figures.

33.5 Using The Normal Distribution

The normal distribution is often used as a model for practical situations. In the following examples, you need to translate the given information into the language of the normal distribution before you can solve the problems.

Example 33.5.1. *Look back to the data on leaf lengths given in Section 33.1. We were given 50 leaf lengths, and created a histogram in Figure 33.2 to represent that data. By the end of that section, we produced a model for leaf length that was normal. Was that a reasonable model to use? For example, assuming that the distribution is normal, how many of the 50 leaves would you expect to (have a length between 59.5 and 69.5 mm, and so) be in the $60 - 69$ mm class?*

We can calculate the mean and the standard deviation of the original data as 61.4 and 16.8, both correct to 1 decimal place. If we model the leaf length L with the normally distributed random variable $X \sim N(61.4, 16.8^2)$, we can calculate the expected frequency for each class that this model predicts. With $Z = \frac{X-61.4}{16.8}$ as the associated standard normal random variable, as usual, we have

$$
\begin{aligned}
\mathbb{P}[59.5 \le X \le 69.5] &= \mathbb{P}\left[\frac{59.5 - 61.4}{16.8} \le Z \le \frac{69.5 - 61.4}{16.8}\right] = \mathbb{P}[-0.113 \le Z \le 0.482] \\
&= \Phi(0.482) - \Phi(-0.113) = \Phi(0.482) - (1 - \Phi(0.113)) \\
&= 0.6851 + 0.5450 - 1 = 0.2301
\end{aligned}
$$

Thus, in a group of 50 leaves, the expected number lying in the $60 - 69$ class would be 11. As we recall, the actual frequency of that class was 9.

Is this an acceptable level of error? To get an idea of this, we need to calculate the expected frequencies of all the classes, and not just one. If we do this, we obtain the following frequencies:

Length (mm)	$29-39$	$39-49$	$49-59$	$59-69$	$69-79$	$79-89$	$89-99$	$99-109$
Observed	3	9	15	9	6	4	3	1
Expected	4.81	7.16	10.78	11.51	8.71	4.67	1.78	0.58

Since a normal distribution would allow for values of X less than 29.5 or greater than 109.5 (albeit with very small probabilities), we have included the expected frequency of leaves less than 29.5 in the $30 - 39$ class, and have included the expected frequency of leaves longer than 109.5 in the $99 - 109$ class. This ensures that the expected frequencies add up to 50. Given the small amount of data to start with, the model is fairly accurate.

Example 33.5.2. *A biologist has been collecting data on the heights of a particular species of cactus (Notocactus rutilans). He has observed that 34.2% of the cacti are below 12 cm in height and 18.4% of the cacti are above 16 cm in height. He assumes that the heights are normally distributed. Find the mean and standard deviation of the distribution.*

Let the mean and standard deviation of the distribution be μ and σ, as usual. Then, if H is the height in cm of a randomly chosen cactus of this species, so that $H \sim N(\mu, \sigma^2)$, the biologist's observations can now be written as

$$\mathbb{P}[H < 12] = 0.342 \qquad \mathbb{P}[H > 16] = 0.184 .$$

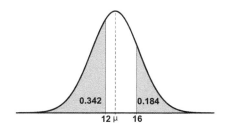

Figure 33.14

Note that it is clear from these probabilities that $12 < \mu < 16$. After standardising, these equations become

$$\mathbb{P}\left[Z < \frac{12-\mu}{\sigma}\right] = 0.342 \qquad \mathbb{P}\left[\frac{16-\mu}{\sigma}\right] = 0.184 ,$$

or

$$\Phi\left(\frac{\mu-12}{\sigma}\right) = 1 - 0.342 = 0.658 \qquad \Phi\left(\frac{16-\mu}{\sigma}\right) = 1 - 0.184 = 0.816$$

Thus we deduce that $\frac{\mu-12}{\sigma} = 0.407$ and $\frac{16-\mu}{\sigma} = 0.900$. Solving these equations gives $\mu = 13.2$ and $\sigma = 3.06$, correct to 3 significant figures.

Example 33.5.3. *Two friends, Sarah and Hannah, often go to the Post Office together. They travel on Sarah's scooter. Sarah always drives Hannah to the Post Office and drops her off there. Sarah then drives around until she is ready to pick Hannah up some time later. Their experience has been that the time Hannah takes in the Post Office can be approximated by a normal distribution with mean 6 minutes and standard deviation 1.3 minutes. How many minutes after having dropped Hannah off should Sarah return if she wants to be at least 95% certain that Hannah will not keep her waiting?*

Suppose that Sarah in fact always returns after 7 minutes. What is the probability that, in 5 randomly chosen trips to the Post Office, Hannah keeps her waiting more often than not?

Let T be the time Hannah takes in the Post Office on a randomly chosen trip. Then $T \sim N(6, 1.3^2)$.

To answer the first question, we want Sarah to wait t minutes, where t has been chosen so that the probability that Hannah takes less than t minutes in the Post Office is at least 95%. In other words, we want $\mathbb{P}[T \le t] \ge 0.95$. After standardising, this expression becomes

$$\Phi\left(\frac{t-6}{1.3}\right) = \mathbb{P}[Z \le \tfrac{t-6}{1.3}] \ge 0.95 .$$

Therefore $\frac{t-6}{1.3} \ge 1.645$, that, on rearranging, gives $t \ge 8.14$. Sarah should not return for at least 8.14 minutes if she wants to be at least 95% sure that Hannah will not keep her waiting.

In the second part of this example, the probability that Hannah keeps Sarah waiting on a visit to the Post Office is now

$$\mathbb{P}[T > 7] = \mathbb{P}[Z > \tfrac{7-6}{1.3}] = 1 - \Phi(0.769) = 1 - 0.7791 = 0.2209$$

The number N of times, out of 5 trips to the Post Office, that Hannah keeps Sarah waiting now has the Binomial distribution $B(5, 0.2209)$; we want to know

$$\mathbb{P}[N \ge 3] = {}^5C_3 \times 0.2209^3 \times 0.7791^2 + {}^5C_4 \times 0.2209^4 \times 0.7791 + 0.2209^5$$
$$= 0.078$$

to 3 decimal places.

674

Example 33.5.4. *A machine manufactures bolts, whose lengths observe a normal distribution with mean 15 mm and variance 1.4 mm². These bolts are sold in boxes of 50. A bolt is too short for its intended purpose if it is less than 12 mm long.*

(a) *What is the probability that a randomly selected bolt is too short?*

(b) *What is the probability that a randomly selected box of 50 bolts contains no short bolts?*

(c) *What is the probability that, out of 10 randomly selected boxes of bolts, at most one box contains a short bolt?*

Let $L \sim N(15, 1.4)$ be the length of a bolt. The probability of a bolt being short is thus

$$\mathbb{P}[L < 12] = \mathbb{P}\left[Z < \tfrac{12-15}{\sqrt{1.4}}\right] = \Phi(-2.535) = 1 - 0.9944 = 0.0056 = 0.006 \,.$$

while the probability that a box contains no short bolts is $0.9944^{50} = 0.7552 = 0.755$. Thus the number N of boxes out of 10 that contain a short bolt has distribution $B(10, 0.2448)$, and so

$$\mathbb{P}[N \leq 1] = 0.7552^{10} + 10 \times 0.7552^{9} \times 0.2448 = 0.256 \,.$$

EXERCISE 33C

1. The time spent waiting for a prescription to be prepared at a chemist's shop is normally distributed with mean 15 minutes and standard deviation 2.8 minutes. Find the probability that the waiting time is

   a) more than 20 minutes,   b) less than 8 minutes,

   c) between 10 minutes and 18 minutes.

2. The heights of a group of sixteen-year-old girls are normally distributed with mean 161.2 cm and standard deviation 4.7 cm. Find the probability that one of these girls will have height

   a) more than 165 cm,   b) less than 150 cm,

   c) between 165 cm and 170 cm,   d) between 150 cm and 163 cm.

   In a sample of 500 girls of this age estimate how many will have heights in each of the above four ranges.

3. The lengths of replacement car wiper blades are normally distributed with mean of 25 cm and standard deviation 0.2 cm. For a batch of 200 wiper blades estimate how many would be expected to have length:

   a) greater than 25.3 cm,   b) between 24.89 cm and 25.11 cm,

   c) between 24.89 cm and 25.25 cm.

4. The time taken by a garage to replace worn-out brake pads follows a normal distribution with mean 90 minutes and standard deviation 5.8 minutes.

   a) Find the probability that the garage takes longer than 105 minutes.

   b) Find the probability that the garage takes less than 85 minutes.

   c) The garage claims to complete the replacements in 'a to b minutes'. If this claim is to be correct for 90% of the repairs, find a and b correct to 2 significant figures, assuming that the interval from a to b is symmetrical about the mean.

5. The fluorescent light tubes made by the company Well-lit have lifetimes which are normally distributed with mean 2010 hours and standard deviation 20 hours. The company decides to promote its sales of the tubes by guaranteeing a minimum life of the tubes, replacing free of charge any tubes that fail to meet this minimum life. If the company wishes to have to replace free only 3% of the tubes sold, find the guaranteed minimum it must set.

6. The lengths of sweetpea flower stems are normally distributed with mean 18.2 cm and standard deviation 2.3 cm.

675

a) Find the probability that the length of a flower stem is between 16 cm and 20 cm.

b) 12% of the flower stems are longer than h cm, and 20% of the flower stems are shorter than k cm. Find h and k.

c) Stem lengths less than 14 cm are unacceptable at a florist's shop. In a batch of 500 sweetpeas estimate how many would be unacceptable.

7. The T-Q company makes a soft drink sold in '330 ml' cans. The actual volume of drink in the cans is distributed normally with standard deviation 2.5 ml. To ensure that at least 99% of the cans contain more than 330 ml, find the volume that the company should supply in the cans on average.

8. The packets in which sugar is sold are labelled '1 kg packets'. In fact the mass of sugar in a packet is distributed normally with mean mass 1.08 kg. Sampling of the packets of sugar shows that just 2.5% are 'underweight' (that is, contain less than the stated mass of 1 kg). Find the standard deviation of the distribution.

9. The life of the Powerhouse battery has a normal distribution with mean 210 hours. It is found that 4% of these batteries operate for more than 222 hours. Find the variance of the distribution, correct to 2 significant figures.

10. In a statistics examination, 15% of the candidates scored more than 63 marks and 10% of the candidates scored fewer than 32 marks. Assuming that the marks were distributed normally find the mean mark and the standard deviation.

11*. A machine bags rice into bags. When working properly, the weight W of the bags it produces is normally distributed with mean 454 g and variance 25 g^2.

a) Provided that the machine is working properly, what is the probability that it produces a bag of rice weighing less than 440 g?

b) In a sample of 10 bags from the machine, one is found to weight less than 440 g. What is the probability that this could happen, if the machine were working as designed? Do you think that the machine needs an overhaul?

12*. An unknown, but fixed, proportion p of the population will vote for Laberalitive Party at the next election. An opinion poll of n people is conducted (so n people are chosen independently of each other, and asked whether or not they will vote for the Laberalitive Party). Let X be the number of people who say 'yes'.

a) Write down, in terms of n and p, a suitable distribution for the random variable X.

b) The proportion P of those polled who say 'yes' is the random variable $\frac{1}{n}X$. What are the mean and variance of P?

c) You may assume that it is reasonable to approximate the random variable P by the random variable Q, which is normally distributed with the same mean and variance as P. Write down an expression for $\mathbb{P}[|Q - p| < 0.03]$ in terms of n, p and Φ.

d) If $p = \frac{1}{4}$, how big must n be (to the nearest integer) for $\mathbb{P}[|Q - p| < 0.03]$ to be bigger than 95%?

e) What value of n (to 3 significant figures) will ensure that $\mathbb{P}[|Q - p| < 0.03] > 95\%$, no matter what the value of p is?

If you have reached the end of this question, you now know why opinion polls commonly question about 1000 people, and claim a $\pm 3\%$ accuracy for their results.

Chapter 33: Summary

- A continuous random variable is a random variable X that can take values over a continuous range. It is described by a probability density function f, a positive function such that the probability $\mathbb{P}[a < X < b]$ is the area under the curve $y = f(x)$ between $x = a$ and $x = b$.

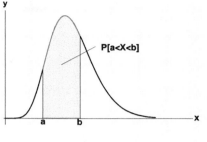

- The standardised normal distribution $N(0,1)$ is described by a probability density function whose graph is bell-shaped. The area under the graph to the left of x is written as $\Phi(x)$:

$$\Phi(z) = \mathbb{P}[X \leq z], \qquad x \in \mathbb{R}.$$

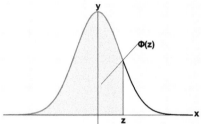

- The function Φ satisfies the equation $\Phi(z) + \Phi(-z) = 1$, and hence

$$\mathbb{P}[Z \leq z] = \Phi(z)$$
$$\mathbb{P}[Z \leq -z] = \Phi(-z) = 1 - \Phi(z)$$
$$\mathbb{P}[|Z| \leq z] = 2\Phi(z) - 1$$

$$\mathbb{P}[Z \geq z] = 1 - \Phi(z)$$
$$\mathbb{P}[Z \geq -z] = 1 - \Phi(-z) = \Phi(z) =$$
$$\mathbb{P}[|Z| \geq z] = 2\big(1 - \Phi(z)\big)$$

for any $z \geq 0$.

- If X is normally distributed with mean μ and variance σ, then $Z = \frac{1}{\sigma}(X - \mu)$ is normally distributed with mean 0 and variance 1. Thus

$$\mathbb{P}[X \leq z] = \mathbb{P}\left[Z \leq \frac{z - \mu}{\sigma}\right] = \Phi\left(\frac{z - \mu}{\sigma}\right).$$

Review Exercises 11

1. Bag A contains 1 red ball and 1 black ball, and bag B contains 2 red balls; all four balls are indistinguishable apart from their colour. One ball is chosen at random from A and is transferred to B. One ball is then chosen at random from B and is transferred to A. Find the probability that, after both transfers, the black ball is in bag A. (OCR, adapt.)

2. The probability that an event A occurs is $\mathbb{P}[A] = 0.3$. The event B is independent of A and $\mathbb{P}[B] = 0.4$. Calculate $\mathbb{P}[A \cup B]$.

   Event C is defined to be the event that neither A nor B occurs. Calculate $\mathbb{P}[C|A']$. (OCR, adapt.)

3. Two cubical fair dice are thrown, one red and one blue. The scores on their faces are added together. Determine which, if either, is greater:

   a) the probability that the total score will be 10 or more given that the red dice shows a 6,

   b) the probability that the total score will be 10 or more given that at least one of the dice shows a 6. (OCR)

4. Half of the A-Level students in a community college study science and 30% study mathematics. Of those who study science, 40% study mathematics.

   a) What proportion of the A-level students study both mathematics and science?

   b) Calculate the proportion of those students who study mathematics but do not study science. (OCR)

5. Three friends, Ahmed, Benjamin and Chi, live in a town where there are only three cafés. They arrange to meet at a café one evening but do not specify the name of the café. The probabilities that they will each choose a particular café are independent. Ahmed lives close to Café Expresso and so the probability that he will choose to go there is $\frac{5}{9}$ whereas Café Kola and Café Pepsi have equal chances of being visited by him.

   Benjamin lives a long distance from Café Kola and the probability that he will choose this one is $\frac{1}{7}$, but he will choose either of the other two cafés with equal probability.

   Each café has an equal chance of being visited by Chi.

   a) Show that the probability that the three friends meet at Café Expresso is $\frac{5}{63}$.

   b) Calculate the probability that

      i. the three friends will meet at the same café,
      ii. at most two friends will meet at the same café. (OCR)

6. Two events A and B are such that $\mathbb{P}[A] = \frac{3}{4}$, $\mathbb{P}[B|A] = \frac{1}{5}$ and $\mathbb{P}[B'|A'] = \frac{4}{7}$. Find $\mathbb{P}[A \cap B]$, $\mathbb{P}[B]$, and $\mathbb{P}[A|B]$. (OCR, adapt.)

7. Students have to pass a test before they are allowed to work in a laboratory. Students do not retake the test once they have passed it. For a randomly chosen student, the probability of passing the test at the first attempt is $\frac{1}{3}$. On any subsequent attempt, the probability of failing is half the probability of failing on the previous attempt.

   a) Show that the probability of a student passing the test in 3 or fewer attempts is $\frac{26}{27}$.

   b) Find the conditional probability that a student passed at the first attempt, given that the student passed in 3 attempts or fewer. (OCR)

8. Events A and B are such that $\mathbb{P}[A] = \frac{13}{25}$, $\mathbb{P}[B] = \frac{9}{25}$, and $\mathbb{P}[A|B] = \frac{5}{9}$.

   a) Determine the following: (i) $\mathbb{P}[A \cap B]$, (ii) $\mathbb{P}[B|A]$, (iii) $\mathbb{P}[A \cup B]$, (iv) $\mathbb{P}[A'|B']$.

   b) Determine $\mathbb{P}[A \cup B']$. (OCR, adapt.)

9. a) The probability that an event A occurs is $\mathbb{P}[A] = 0.4$. B is an event independent of A and $\mathbb{P}[A \cup B] = 0.7$. Find $\mathbb{P}[B]$.

   b) C and D are two events such that $\mathbb{P}[D|C] = \frac{1}{5}$ and $\mathbb{P}[C|D] = \frac{1}{4}$. Given that $\mathbb{P}[C \cap D] = p$, express $\mathbb{P}[C]$ and $\mathbb{P}[D]$ in terms of p.

   c) Given also that $\mathbb{P}[C \cup D] = \frac{1}{5}$, find the value of p. (OCR, adapt.)

10. A batch of forty tickets for an event at a stadium consists of ten tickets for the North stand, fourteen tickets for the East stand and sixteen tickets for the West stand. A ticket is taken from the batch at random and issued to a person, X. Write down the probability that X has a ticket for the North stand. A second ticket is taken from the batch at random and issued to Y. Subsequently a third ticket is taken from the batch at random and issued to Z. Calculate the probability that:

    a) both X and Y have tickets for the North stand,

    b) X, Y and Z all have tickets for the same stand,

    c) two of X, Y and Z have tickets for one stand, with the third in a different stand. (OCR)

11. In a lottery there are 24 prizes allocated at random to 24 prize-winners. Ann, Ben and Cal are three of the prize-winners. Of the prizes, 4 are cars, 8 are bicycles and 12 are watches. Show that the probability that Ann gets a car and Ben gets a bicycle or a watch is $\frac{10}{69}$.

    Giving each answer either as a fraction or as a decimal correct to 3 significant figures, find:

    a) the probability that both Ann and Ben get cars, given that Cal gets a car,

    b) the probability that either Ann or Cal (or both) gets a car,

    c) the probability that Ann gets a car and Ben gets a car or a bicycle,

    d) the probability that Ann gets a car given that Ben gets either a car or a bicycle. (OCR)

12. In a certain part of the world there are more wet days than dry days. If a given day is wet, the probability that the following day will also be wet is 0.8. If a given day is dry, the probability that the following day will also be dry is 0.6.

    Given that Wednesday of a particular week is dry, calculate the probability that:

    a) Thursday and Friday of the same week are both wet days,

    b) Friday of the same week is a wet day.

    In one season there were 44 cricket matches, each played over three consecutive days, in which the first and third days were dry. For how many of these matches would you expect that the second day was wet? (OCR)

13. A study of the numbers of male and female children in families in a certain population is being carried out.

    a) A simple model is that each child in any family is equally likely to be male or female, and that the sex of each child is independent of the sex of any previous children in the family. Using this model calculate the probability that, in a randomly chosen family of 4 children,

        i. there will be 2 males and 2 females,

        ii. there will be exactly 1 female, given that there is at least 1 female.

b) An alternative model is that the first child in any family is equally likely to be male or female, but that, for any subsequent children, the probability that they will be of the same sex as the previous child is $\frac{3}{5}$. Using this model, calculate the probability that, in a randomly chosen family of 4 children,

   i. all four will be of the same sex,

   ii. no two consecutive children will be of the same sex,

   iii. there will be 2 males and 2 females.   (OCR, adapt.)

14. A dice is known to be biased in such a way that, when it is thrown, the probability of a 6 showing is $\frac{1}{4}$. This biased dice and an ordinary fair dice are thrown. Find the probability that:

  a) the fair dice shows a 6 and the biased dice does not show a 6,

  b) at least one of the two dice shows a 6,

  c) exactly one of the two dice shows a 6, given that at least one of them shows a 6.   (OCR)

15. Spares of a particular component are produced by two firms, Bestbits and Lesserprod. Tests show that, on average, 1 in 200 components produced by Bestbits fail within one year of fitting, and 1 in 50 components produced by Lesserprod fail within one year of fitting.

Given that 20% of the components sold and fitted are made by Bestbits and 80% by Lesserprod, what is the probability that a component chosen at random from those sold and fitted will fail within a year of fitting?

Find the proportion of components sold and fitted that would need to be made by Bestbits for this probability to be 0.01.   (OCR)

16. A game is played using a regular 12-faced fair die, with faces labelled 1 to 12, a coin and a simple board with nine squares as shown in the diagram.

Initially, the coin is placed on the shaded rectangle. The game consists of rolling the die and then moving the coin one rectangle towards L or R according to the outcome on the die. If the outcome is a prime number, the move is towards R, otherwise it is towards L. The game stops when the coin reaches either L or R. Find, giving your answers correct to 3 decimal places, the probability that the game:

  a) ends on the fourth move at R,

  b) ends on the fourth move,

  c) ends on the fifth move,

  d) takes more than six moves.   (OCR)

17. You have $2n$ balls, n black and n white, which are indistinguishable apart from their colour. Box X contains 3 of the black balls, and $n-3$ white balls. Box Y contains $n-3$ black balls, and 3 white balls.

A ball is taken at random from box X and put into box Y. A ball is then taken at random from box Y.

  a) Calculate in terms of n the probability that the ball taken from box Y is white.

  b) Calculate in terms of n the probability that the first ball is black, given that the second ball is white.   (OCR)

18*. Each day, I have to take k different types of medicine, one tablet of each. The tablets are identical in appearance. When I go on holiday for n days, I put n tablets of each type in a container and, on each day of the holiday, I select k tablets at random from the container.

  a) In the case $k = 3$, show that the probability that I will select one tablet of each type on the first day of a three-day holiday is $\frac{9}{28}$. Write down the probability that I will be left with one tablet of each type on the last day of the holiday (irrespective of the tablets I took on the first day).

  b) In the case $k = 3$, find the probability that I will select one tablet of each type on the first day of an n-day holiday.

c) In the case $k = 2$, find the probability that I will select one tablet of each type on each day of an n-day holiday, and use Stirling's approximation

$$n! \approx \sqrt{2n\pi}\left(\frac{n}{e}\right)^n$$

to show that this probability is approximately $2^{-n}\sqrt{n\pi}$. (STEP)

19. Three cards are selected at random, without replacement, from a shuffled pack of 52 playing cards. Find the probability distribution of the number of honours $(A, K, Q, J, 10)$ obtained.

20. An electronic device produces an output of 0, 1 or 3 volts, each time it is operated, with probabilities $\frac{1}{2}$, $\frac{1}{3}$ and $\frac{1}{6}$ respectively. The random variable X denotes the result of adding the outputs for two such devices (which act independently of each other).

    a) Find the probability distribution function of X.

    b) In 360 independent operations of the device, state on how many occasions you would expect the outcome to be 1 volt. (OCR, adapt.)

21. The probabilities of the scores on a biased dice are shown in the table below.

Score	1	2	3	4	5	6
Probability	k	$\frac{1}{9}$	$\frac{1}{9}$	$\frac{1}{9}$	$\frac{1}{9}$	$\frac{1}{2}$

    a) Find the value of k.

    Two players, Hazel and Ross, play a game with this biased dice and a fair dice. Hazel chooses one of the two dice at random and rolls it. If the score is 5 or 6 she wins a point.

    b) Calculate the probability that Hazel wins a point.

    c) Hazel chooses a dice, rolls it and wins a point. Find the probability that she chose the biased dice. (OCR)

22. In an experiment, a fair cubical dice was rolled repeatedly until a six resulted, and the number of rolls was recorded. The experiment was conducted 60 times.

    a) Show that you would expect to get a six on the first roll ten times out of the 60 repetitions of the experiment.

    b) Find the expected frequency for two rolls correct to one decimal place. (OCR, adapt.)

23. The probability distribution of the random variable Y is given in the table on the right, where c is a constant. Prove that there is only one possible value of c, and state this value.

y	1	2	3	4	5
$\mathbb{P}[Y = y]$	c	$3c$	c^2	c^2	$\frac{15}{32}$

24. A brand of sweets comes with a free card in each packet. There are 20 different types of card, and the different types of card are randomly distributed amongst the packets of sweets. I am just starting my collection, and so start with no cards at all. How many packets of sweets should I expect to buy before I have:

    a) one,   b) two,   c) three,   d) ten

    different types of card?

    I have managed to collect 19 out of 20 cards. How many more packets should I expect to have to buy to obtain the final missing card?

25. The probability of a novice archer hitting a target with any shot is 0.3. Given that the archer shoots six arrows, find the probability that the target is hit at least twice. (OCR)

26. A computer is programmed to produce at random a single digit from the list 0, 1, 2, 3, 4, 5, 6, 7, 8, 9. The program is run twenty times. Let Y be the number of zeros that occur.

    a) State the distribution of Y and give its parameters.

    b) Calculate $\mathbb{P}[Y < 3]$.

27. A dice is biased so that the probability of throwing a 6 is 0.2. The dice is thrown eight times. Let X be the number of 6s thrown.

a) State the distribution of X and give its parameters.

b) Calculate $\mathbb{P}[X > 3]$.

28. Joseph and four friends each have an independent probability 0.45 of winning a prize. Find the probability that:

    a) exactly two of the five friends win a prize,

    b) Joseph and only one friend win a prize. (OCR)

29. A bag contains two biased coins: coin A shows Heads with probability 0.6, and coin B shows Heads with probability 0.25. A coin is chosen at random from the bag, and tossed three times.

    a) Find the probability that the three tosses of the coin show two Heads and one Tail in any order.

    b) Find the probability that the coin chosen was coin A, given that the three tosses result in two Heads and one Tail. (OCR)

30. a) A fair coin is tossed 4 times. Calculate the probabilities that the tosses result in 0, 1, 2, 3 and 4 heads.

    b) A fair coin is tossed 8 times. Calculate the probability that the first 4 tosses and the last 4 tosses result in the same number of heads.

    c) Two teams each consist of 3 players. Each player in a team tosses a fair coin once and the team's score is the total number of heads thrown. Find the probability that the teams have the same score. (OCR)

31. State the conditions under which the binomial distribution may be used for the calculation of probabilities.

    The probability that a girl chosen at random has a weekend birthday in 1993 is $\frac{2}{7}$. Calculate the probability that, among a group of ten girls chosen at random,

    a) none has a weekend birthday in 1993,

    b) exactly one has a weekend birthday in 1993.

    Among 100 groups of ten girls, how many groups would you expect to contain more than one girl with a weekend birthday in 1993? (OCR)

32. Show that, when two fair dice are thrown, the probability of obtaining a 'double' is $\frac{1}{6}$, where a 'double' is defined as the same score on both dice. Four players play a board game which requires them to take it in turns to throw two fair dice. Each player throws the two dice once in each round. When a double is thrown the player moves forward six squares. Otherwise the player moves forward one square. Find

    a) the probability that the first double occurs on the third throw of the game,

    b) the probability that exactly one of the four players obtains a double in the first round,

    c) the probability that a double occurs exactly once in 4 of the first 5 rounds. (OCR)

33. Six hens are observed over a period of 20 days and the number of eggs laid each day is summarised in the table on the right. Show that the mean number of eggs per day is 5.

Number of eggs	3	4	5	6
Number of days	2	2	10	6

    It may be assumed that a hen never lays more than one egg in any day. State one other assumption that needs to be made in order to consider a Binomial model, with $n = 6$, for the total number of eggs laid in a day. State the probability that a randomly chosen hen lays an egg on a given day. Calculate the expected frequencies of 3, 4, 5 and 6 eggs over this 20 day period. (OCR)

34. A Personal Identification Number (PIN) consists of 4 digits in order, each of which is one of the digits 0, 1, 2, ..., 9. Susie has difficulty remembering her PIN. She tries to remember it and writes down what she thinks it is. The probability that the first digit is correct is 0.8 and the probability that the second digit is correct is 0.86. The probability that the first two digits are correct is 0.72. Find:

    a) the probability that the second digit is correct given that the first digit is correct,

    b) the probability that the first digit is correct and the second digit is incorrect,

c) the probability that the first digit is incorrect and the second digit is correct,

d) the probability that the second digit is incorrect given that the first digit is incorrect.

The probability that all four digits are correct is 0.7. On 12 separate occasions Susie writes down independently what she thinks is her PIN. Find the probability that the number of occasions on which all four digits are correct is less than 10. (OCR)

35. The number of times a certain factory machine breaks down each working week has been recorded over a long period. From these data, the following probability distribution for the number, X, of weekly breakdowns was produced.

x	0	1	2	3	4	5	6
$\mathbb{P}[X = x]$	0.04	0.24	0.28	0.16	0.16	0.08	0.04

a) Find the mean and standard deviation of X.

b) What would be the expected total number of breakdowns that will occur over the next 48 working weeks?

36. Some of the eggs sold in a store are packed in boxes of 10. For any egg, the probability that it is cracked is 0.05, independently of all other eggs. A shelf contains 80 of these boxes. Calculate the expected value of the number of boxes on the shelf which do not contain a cracked egg.

37. The random variable X is such that $X \sim B(5, p)$. Given that $\mathbb{P}[X = 0] = 0.01024$, find the values of $\mathbb{E}[X]$, $\text{Var}[X]$ and $\mathbb{P}\big[X = \mathbb{E}[X]\big]$.

38. The independent random variables X and Y have the following probability distributions.

x	0	1	2	3
$\mathbb{P}[X = x]$	0.3	0.2	0.4	0.1

y	3	4	5
$\mathbb{P}[Y = y]$	0.5	0.2	0.3

Find $\mathbb{E}[X]$, $\text{Var}[X]$, $\mathbb{E}[Y]$ and $\text{Var}[Y]$.

The sum of one random observation of X and one independent random observation of Y is denoted by Z.

a) Obtain the probability distribution of Z.

b) Show that $\mathbb{E}[Z] = \mathbb{E}[X] + \mathbb{E}[Y]$ and $\text{Var}[Z] = \text{Var}[X] + \text{Var}[Y]$.

39. Recall that possible criterion for a data point to be an outlier of a dataset is that it lies outside the interval from $\mu - 2\sigma$ to $\mu + 2\sigma$. For a set of observations of a random variable X, where $X \sim B(20, 0.4)$, determine whether the following values constitute outliers according to this criterion.

a) 2,   b) 5,   c) 10,   d) 15.

Find $\mathbb{P}[X < \mu - 2\sigma])$ and $\mathbb{P}[X > \mu + 2\sigma]$.

40. An absent-minded mathematician is attempting to log on to a computer, which is done by typing the correct password. Unfortunately he can't remember his password. If he types the wrong password he tries again. The computer allows a maximum of four attempts altogether. For each attempt the probability of success is 0.4, independently of all other attempts.

a) Calculate the probability that he logs on successfully.

b) The total number of attempts he makes, successful or not, is denoted by X (so that the possible values of X are 1, 2, 3 or 4). Find the probability distribution of X.

c) Calculate the expectation and variance of X. (OCR)

41. A committee of six men and four women appoints two of its members to represent it. Assuming that each member is equally likely to be appointed, obtain the probability distribution of the number of women appointed. Find the expected number of women appointed.

42. The discrete random variable X takes the values 1, 2, 3, 4 and 5 only, with the probabilities shown in the table on the right.

x	1	2	3	4	5
$\mathbb{P}[X = x]$	a	0.3	0.1	0.2	b

a) Given that $\mathbb{E}[X] = 2.34$, show that $a = 0.34$, and find the value of b.

b) Find $\text{Var}[X]$. (OCR)

43*. The number of eggs, X, laid by the female tawny owl (*Strix aluco*) has the probability distribution given in the table on the right:

x	2	3	4
$\mathbb{P}[X = x]$	0.1	0.2	0.7

For any egg, the probability that it hatches is 0.8, independently of all other eggs. Let Y denote the number of hatched eggs in a randomly chosen nest.

a) Obtain the probability distribution of Y.

b) Find $\mathbb{E}[Y]$ and $\text{Var}[Y]$.

44*. I choose at random an integer in the range 10000 to 99999, all choices equally likely. Given that my choice does not contain the digits $0, 6, 7, 8$ or 9, show that the expected number of different digits in my choice is 3.3616. (STEP)

45*. I seat n boys and 3 girls in a line at random, so that each order of the $n + 3$ children is as likely to occur as any other. Let K be the maximum number of consecutive girls in the line so, for example, $K = 1$ if there is at least one boy between each pair of girls.

a) Find $\mathbb{P}[K = 3]$.

b) Show that

$$\mathbb{P}[K = 1] = \frac{n(n - 1)}{(n + 2)(n + 3)}.$$

c) Find $\mathbb{E}[K]$. (STEP)

46. Given that $X \sim N(10, 2.25)$, find $\mathbb{P}[X > 12]$. (OCR)

47. The random variable X has the distribution $X \sim , N(10, 8)$. Find $\mathbb{P}[X > 6]$. (OCR)

48. W is a normally distributed random variable with mean 0.58 and standard deviation 0.12. Find $\mathbb{P}[W < 0.79]$. (OCR)

49. X is a random variable with the distribution $X \sim N(140, 56.25)$. Find the probability that X is greater than 128.75. (OCR)

50. The manufacturers of a new model of car state that, when travelling at 56 miles per hour, the petrol consumption has a mean value of 32.4 miles per gallon with standard deviation 1.4 miles per gallon. Assuming a normal distribution, calculate the probability that a randomly chosen car of that model will have a petrol consumption greater than 30 miles per gallon when travelling at 56 miles per hour. (OCR)

51. A normally distributed random variable, X, has mean 20.0 and variance 4.15. Find the probability that $18.0 < X < 21.0$. (OCR)

52. The lifetime of a Fotobrite light bulb is normally distributed with mean 1020 hours and standard deviation 85 hours. Find the probability that a Fotobrite bulb chosen at random has a lifetime between 1003 and 1088 hours. (OCR)

53. The area that can be painted using one litre of Luxibrite paint is normally distributed with mean 13.2 m^2 and standard deviation 0.197 m^2. The corresponding figures for one litre of Maxigloss paint are 13.4 m^2 and 0.343 m^2. It is required to paint an area of 12.9 m^2. Find which paint gives the greater probability that one litre will be sufficient, and obtain this probability. (OCR)

54. The random variable X is normally distributed with mean and standard deviation both equal to a. Given that $\mathbb{P}[X < 3] = 0.2$, find the value of a. (OCR)

55. The time required to complete a certain car journey has been found from experience to have mean 2 hours 20 minutes and standard deviation 15 minutes.

a) Use a normal model to calculate the probability that, on one day chosen at random, the journey requires between 1 hour 50 minutes and 2 hours 40 minutes.

b) It is known that delays occur rarely on this journey, but that when they do occur they are lengthy. Give a reason why this information suggests that a normal distribution might not be a good model. (OCR)

56. The weights of eggs, measured in grams, can be modelled by a $X \sim N(85.0, 36)$ distribution. Eggs are classified as large, medium or small, where a large egg weighs 90.0 grams or more, and 25% of eggs are classified as small. Calculate

   a) the percentage of eggs which are classified as large,

   b) the maximum weight of a small egg. (OCR)

57. The random variable X is normally distributed with standard deviation 3.2. The probability that X is less than 74 is 0.8944.

   a) Find the mean of X.

   b) Fifty independent observations of X are made. Find the expected number of observations that are less than 74. (OCR)

58. A random variable X has a $N(m, 4)$ distribution. Its associated normal curve is shown in the diagram. Find the value of m such that the shaded area is 0.800, giving your answer correct to 3 significant figures.

   (OCR)

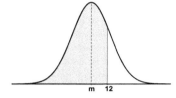

59. A machine cuts a very long plastic tube into short tubes. The length of the short tubes is modelled by a normal distribution with mean m cm and standard deviation 0.25 cm. The value of m can be set by adjusting the machine. Find the value of m for which the probability is 0.1 that the length of a short tube, picked at random, is less than 6.50 cm.

   The machine is adjusted so that $m = 6.40$, the standard deviation remaining unchanged. Find the probability that a tube picked at random is between 6.30 and 6.60 cm long. (OCR)

60. A university classifies its degrees as Class 1, Class 2.1, Class 2.2, Class 3, Pass and Fail. Degrees are awarded on the basis of marks which may be taken as continuous and modelled by a normal distribution with mean 57.0 and standard deviation 10.0. In a particular year, the lowest mark for a Class 1 degree was 70.0, the lowest mark for a Class 2.1 degree was 60.0, and 4.5% of students failed. Calculate

   a) the percentage of students who obtained a Class 1 degree,

   b) the percentage of students who obtained a Class 2.1 degree,

   c) the lowest possible mark for a student who obtained a Pass degree. (OCR)

61. The number of hours of sunshine at a resort has been recorded for each month for many years. One year is selected at random and H is the number of hours of sunshine in August of that year. H can be modelled by a normal variable with mean 130.

   a) Given that $\mathbb{P}[H < 179] = 0.975$, calculate the standard deviation of H.

   b) Calculate $\mathbb{P}[100 < H < 150]$. (OCR)

62. The mass of grapes sold per day in a supermarket can be modelled by a normal distribution. It is found that, over a long period, the mean mass sold per day is 35.0 kg, and that, on average, less than 15.0 kg are sold on one day in twenty.

   a) Show that the standard deviation of the mass of grapes sold per day is 12.2 kg, correct to 3 significant figures.

   b) Calculate the probability that, on a day chosen at random, more than 53.0 kg are sold.

   (OCR)

63. The random variable X is normally distributed with mean μ and variance σ^2. It is given that $\mathbb{P}[X > 81.89] = 0.010$ and $\mathbb{P}[X < 27.77] = 0.100$. Calculate the values of μ and σ. (OCR)

64. Two firms, Goodline and Megadelay, produce delay lines for use in communications. The delay time for a delay line is measured in nanoseconds (ns).

   a) The delay times for the output of Goodline may be modelled by a normal distribution with mean 283 ns and standard deviation 8 ns. What is the probability that the delay time of one line selected at random from Goodline's output is between 275 and 286 ns?

b) It is found that, in the output of Megadelay, 10% of the delay times are less than 274.6 ns and 7.5% are more than 288.2 ns. Again assuming a normal distribution, calculate the mean and standard deviation of the delay times for Megadelay. Give your answers correct to 3 significant figures. (OCR)

65. The random variable Y has the distribution $N(\mu, 16)$. Given that $\mathbb{P}[Y > 57.50] = 0.1401$, find the value of μ giving your answer correct to 2 decimal places. (OCR)

66. The playing time, T minutes, of classical compact discs is modelled by a normal variable with mean 61.3 minutes. Calculate the standard deviation of T if 5% of discs have playing times greater than 78 minutes. (OCR)

67. The random variable Y is such that $Y \sim N(8, 25)$. Show that, correct to 3 decimal places, $\mathbb{P}[|Y - 8| < 6.2] = 0.785$.

Three random observations of Y are made. Find the probability that exactly two observations will lie in the interval defined by $|Y - 8| < 6.2$. (OCR)

68. Squash balls, dropped onto a concrete floor from a given point, rebound to heights which can be modelled by a normal distribution with mean 0.8 m and standard deviation 0.2 m. The balls are classified by height of rebound, in order of decreasing height, into these categories: Fast, Medium, Slow, Super-Slow and Rejected.

   a) Balls which rebound to heights between 0.65 m and 0.9 m are classified as Slow. Calculate the percentage of balls classified as Slow.

   b) Given that 9% of balls are classified as Rejected, calculate the maximum height of rebound of these balls.

   c) The percentages of balls classified as Fast and as Medium are equal. Calculate the minimum height of rebound of a ball classified as Fast, giving your answer correct to 2 decimal places. (OCR)

69*. The random variable X has mean μ and standard deviation σ. The distribution of X is symmetrical about μ and the fixed numbers a and b satisfy

$$\mathbb{P}[X \le \mu + \sigma] = a \qquad \mathbb{P}[X \le \mu + \tfrac{1}{2}\sigma] = b.$$

The numbers a and b do not depend on the particular values of μ and σ, but do not assume that X is normally distributed.

   a) Find expressions (in terms of a and b) for

$$\mathbb{P}[\mu - \tfrac{1}{2}\sigma \le X \le \mu + \sigma] \qquad \text{and} \qquad \mathbb{P}[X \le \mu + \tfrac{1}{2}\sigma \mid X \ge \mu - \tfrac{1}{2}\sigma].$$

   b) My local supermarket sells cartons of skimmed milk and cartons of full-fat milk: 60% of the cartons it sells contain skimmed milk, and the rest contain full-fat milk.
   The volume of skimmed milk in a carton is modelled by X ml, where $\mu = 500$ and $\sigma = 10$.
   The volume of full-fat milk in a carton is modelled by X ml, where $\mu = 495$ and $\sigma = 10$.

   i. Today I bought one carton of milk, chosen at random, from this supermarket. When I get home, I find that it contains less than 505 ml. Determine an expression (in terms of a and b) for the probability that this carton of milk contains more than 500 ml.

   ii. Over the years, I have bought a very large number of cartons of milk, all chosen at random from this supermarket. 70% of the cartons I have bought have contained at most 505 ml of milk. Of all the cartons that have contained at least 495 ml of milk, one third of them have contained full-fat milk. Use this information to estimate the values of a and b. (STEP)

Part 4

Solving Problems

Problem-solving Techniques

34.1 Developing A Library Of Dirty Tricks

An important point to realise is that, for all but the most simple problems, there is probably more than one solution method available. Some solutions are quick and easy, and some are lengthy and detailed. Part of the art of Mathematics is to be able to consider a variety of different solution techniques, and be prepared to adopt an alternative approach. Increased experience of problems develops a mathematician's collection of problem-solving strategies, a library of 'dirty tricks' that can be applied to problems. Being aware of different solution strategies makes it easier to solve unfamiliar problems; if one technique does not seem to be working, we have other methods to try!

We shall discuss a number of different problems in various areas of the subject, investigating the effectiveness of alternative approaches. While some of these problems are harder than questions that we would normally see at our current level, they demonstrate the value of lateral thinking when solving problems!

34.2 Polynomials And Algebraic Functions

Example 34.2.1. *Factorise the polynomials $x^3 + 8$ and $x^4 + 1$.*

- Factorising a difference of two squares is a standard task; here we are asked to factorise a sum of two cubes. It is important to remember the factor theorem at this stage, and note that since $(-2)^3 + 8 = 0$, $x + 2$ is a factor, and hence $x^3 + 8 = (x + 2)(x^2 - 2x + 4)$. We cannot factorise the quadratic $x^2 - 2x + 4$ any further.

- A difference of two fourth powers can be readily factorised as

$$x^4 - y^4 = (x^2 - y^2)(x^2 + y^2) = (x - y)(x + y)(x^2 + y^2);$$

  how are we to handle a sum of two fourth powers? A useful trick, attributed to the French mathematician Marie-Sophie Germain (1776 - 1831) enables us to write this sum of two fourth powers as a difference of two squares:

$$x^4 + 1 = (x^2 + 1)^2 - 2x^2 = \left(x^2 + \sqrt{2}x + 1\right)\left(x^2 - \sqrt{2}x + 1\right);$$

  the coefficients of our polynomials do not have to be rational!

We do not have to restrict our attention to rational coefficients when factorising polynomials, we have seen that real numbers can be useful. Why stop there?

Example 34.2.2. *Evaluate the integral $\displaystyle\int_1^2 \frac{x^2 - 3}{x(x^2 + 1)}\, dx.$*

Attempting to expand the integrand by partial fractions, we try

$$\frac{x^2 + 3}{x(x^2 + 1)} \equiv \frac{A}{x} + \frac{Bx + C}{x^2 + 1},$$

which will work provided that $x^2 + 3 \equiv A(x^2 + 1) + (Bx + C)x$.

Substituting $x = 0$ tells us that $A = 3$. It is tempting to think that there are no further 'neat' values of x to substitute in (and therefore start equating coefficients), but there are, if we use complex numbers.

Substituting $x = i$ yields $2 = -B + Ci$. Substituting $x = -i$ yields $2 = -B - Ci$, so that $B = -2$ and $C = 0$. Thus

$$\int_1^2 \frac{x^2 + 3}{x(x^2 + 1)}\, dx = \int_1^2 \left(\frac{3}{x} - \frac{2x}{x^2 + 1} \right) dx = \left[3\ln x - \ln(x^2 + 1) \right]_1^2$$

$$= \left[\ln\left(\frac{x^3}{x^2 + 1} \right) \right]_1^2 = \ln \tfrac{8}{5} - \ln \tfrac{1}{2} = \ln \tfrac{16}{5}$$

For that matter, we could have attempted a more general partial fraction expansion that the one we did, writing

$$\frac{x^2 + 3}{x(x^2 + 1)} \equiv \frac{P}{x} + \frac{Q}{x - i} + \frac{R}{x + i},$$

which requires $x^2 + 3 \equiv P(x^2 + 1) + Qx(x + i) + Rx(x - i)$ to work. Substituting $x = 0, i, -i$ in turn yields $P = 3$, $Q = -1$ and $R = -1$. Thus

$$\frac{x^2 + 3}{x(x^2 + 1)} \equiv \frac{3}{x} - \frac{1}{x - i} - \frac{1}{x + i} \equiv \frac{3}{x} - \frac{(x + i) + (x - i)}{x^2 + 1} \equiv \frac{3}{x} - \frac{2x}{x^2 + 1}.$$

Sometimes, calculations can be improved by realising that 'factorisation' does not just mean 'factorisation with rational coefficient'. It is true that rational factorisation is enough most of the time; but not always.

34.3   Symmetry

Example 34.3.1. *Calculate the integrals* $\int_0^{\frac{1}{2}\pi} \cos^2\theta\, d\theta$, $\int_0^{\frac{1}{2}\pi} \cos^4\theta\, d\theta$ *and* $\int_0^{\frac{1}{2}\pi} \cos^6\theta\, d\theta$.

- **Integration By Parts:** The standard method for integrating $\cos^2 x$ involves using the double angle formula:

$$\int_0^{\frac{1}{2}\pi} \cos^2\theta\, d\theta = \tfrac{1}{2}\int_0^{\frac{1}{2}\pi} (1 + \cos 2\theta)\, d\theta = \tfrac{1}{2}\left[\theta + \tfrac{1}{2}\sin 2\theta \right]_0^{\frac{1}{2}\pi} = \tfrac{1}{4}\pi.$$

Higher powers of $\cos\theta$ are calculated by integration by parts. We write

$$\int_0^{\frac{1}{2}\pi} \cos^4\theta\, d\theta = \int_0^{\frac{1}{2}\pi} \cos^2\theta\, d\theta - \int_0^{\frac{1}{2}\pi} \cos^2\theta \sin^2\theta\, d\theta$$

$$\begin{array}{|ll|} \hline u = \sin\theta & v' = \cos^2\theta\sin\theta \\ u' = \cos\theta & v = -\tfrac{1}{3}\cos^3\theta \\ \hline \end{array}$$

$$= \int_0^{\frac{1}{2}\pi} \cos^2\theta\, d\theta - \left[-\tfrac{1}{3}\sin\theta\cos^3\theta \right]_0^{\frac{1}{2}\pi} - \tfrac{1}{3}\int_0^{\frac{1}{2}\pi} \cos^4\theta\, d\theta$$

so that

$$\int_0^{\frac{1}{2}\pi} \cos^4\theta\, d\theta = \tfrac{3}{4}\int_0^{\frac{1}{2}\pi} \cos^2\theta\, d\theta = \tfrac{3}{16}\pi.$$

If we wanted to integrate $\int_0^{\frac{1}{2}\pi} \cos^6\theta\, d\theta$, another application of integration by parts would yield

$$\int_0^{\frac{1}{2}\pi} \cos^6\theta\, d\theta = \int_0^{\frac{1}{2}\pi} \cos^4\theta\, d\theta - \int_0^{\frac{1}{2}\pi} \cos^4\theta \sin^2\theta\, d\theta$$

$$\begin{array}{|ll|} \hline u = \sin\theta & v' = \cos^4\theta\sin\theta \\ u' = \cos\theta & v = -\tfrac{1}{5}\cos^5\theta \\ \hline \end{array}$$

$$= \int_0^{\frac{1}{2}\pi} \cos^4\theta\, d\theta - \left[-\tfrac{1}{5}\sin\theta\cos^5\theta \right]_0^{\frac{1}{2}\pi} - \tfrac{1}{5}\int_0^{\frac{1}{2}\pi} \cos^6\theta\, d\theta,$$

so that

$$\int_0^{\frac{1}{2}\pi} \cos^6\theta\, d\theta = \tfrac{5}{6}\int_0^{\frac{1}{4}\pi} \cos^4\theta\, d\theta = \tfrac{5}{32}\pi.$$

- **Symmetry:** A different approach would be to use symmetry. As we know, there are many symmetry properties enjoyed by the trigonometric functions, in particular $\sin(\frac{1}{2}\pi - \theta) \equiv \cos\theta$. Using the substitution $\phi = \frac{1}{2}\pi - \theta$ tells us that

$$\int_0^{\frac{1}{2}\pi} \sin^n\theta \, d\theta = \int_{\frac{1}{2}\pi}^0 \cos^n\phi \, (-d\phi) = \int_0^{\frac{1}{2}\pi} \cos^n\theta \, d\theta$$

for any integer n. Since $\cos^2\theta + \sin^2\theta \equiv 1$, we deduce that

$$\tfrac{1}{2}\pi = \int_0^{\frac{1}{2}\pi} \cos^2\theta \, d\theta + \int_0^{\frac{1}{2}\pi} \sin^2\theta \, d\theta = 2\int_0^{\frac{1}{2}\pi} \cos^2\theta \, d\theta \,,$$

and hence $\int_0^{\frac{1}{2}\pi} \cos^2\theta \, d\theta = \int_0^{\frac{1}{2}\pi} \sin^2\theta \, d\theta = \frac{1}{4}\pi$. We also note that

$$\begin{aligned}
2\int_0^{\frac{1}{2}\pi} \cos^4\theta \, d\theta &= \int_0^{\frac{1}{2}\pi} \cos^4\theta \, d\theta + \int_0^{\frac{1}{2}\pi} \sin^4\theta \, d\theta = \int_0^{\frac{1}{2}\pi} \left(\cos^4\theta + \sin^4\theta\right) d\theta \\
&= \int_0^{\frac{1}{2}\pi} \left[(\cos^2\theta + \sin^2\theta)^2 - 2\cos^2\theta\sin^2\theta\right] d\theta = \int_0^{\frac{1}{2}\pi} \left[1 - \tfrac{1}{2}\sin^2 2\theta\right] d\theta \,.
\end{aligned}$$

While we could choose to evaluate this last integral by using the double angle formula, we could use a $\phi = 2\theta$ substitution and the identity $\sin(\pi - \phi) \equiv \sin\phi$ to show that

$$\int_0^{\frac{1}{2}\pi} \sin^2 2\theta \, d\theta = \tfrac{1}{2}\int_0^{\pi} \sin^2\phi \, d\phi = \tfrac{1}{2}\int_0^{\frac{1}{2}\pi} \sin^2\phi \, d\phi + \tfrac{1}{2}\int_{\frac{1}{2}\pi}^{\pi} \sin^2(\pi-\phi) \, d\phi = \int_0^{\frac{1}{2}\pi} \sin^2\phi \, d\phi = \tfrac{1}{4}\pi$$

from which we deduce that

$$\int_0^{\frac{1}{2}\pi} \cos^4\theta \, d\theta = \tfrac{3}{16}\pi \,.$$

A similar argument shows that

$$\begin{aligned}
2\int_0^{\frac{1}{2}\pi} \cos^6\theta \, d\theta &= \int_0^{\frac{1}{2}\pi} \cos^6\theta \, d\theta + \int_0^{\frac{1}{2}\pi} \sin^6\theta \, d\theta = \int_0^{\frac{1}{2}\pi} \left[\cos^6\theta + \sin^6\theta\right] d\theta \\
&= \int_0^{\frac{1}{2}\pi} \left[(\cos^2\theta + \sin^2\theta)^3 - 3\cos^4\theta\sin^2\theta - 3\cos^2\theta\sin^4\theta\right] d\theta \\
&= \int_0^{\frac{1}{2}\pi} \left[1 - 3\cos^2\theta\sin^2\theta(\cos^2\theta + \sin^2\theta)\right] d\theta = \int_0^{\frac{1}{2}\pi} \left[1 - \tfrac{3}{4}\sin^2 2\theta\right] d\theta
\end{aligned}$$

so that

$$\int_0^{\frac{1}{2}\pi} \cos^6\theta \, d\theta = \tfrac{5}{32}\pi \,.$$

It is clear that the success of this use of symmetry is due to the fact that we are calculating definite integrals over intervals over which the functions $\sin\theta$ and $\cos\theta$ have good symmetry properties, but we have been able to calculate these integrals without integrating by parts, which is complicated.

- **Taking Things Further:** While symmetry is a useful argument for calculating the integrals of small powers of $\sin\theta$ and $\cos\theta$, it could be said that integration by parts has the last laugh, because it can be used successively to integrate large powers of the trigonometric functions, which could not be handled quite so simply by symmetry. Indeed

$$\begin{aligned}
\int_0^{\frac{1}{2}\pi} \cos^n\theta \, d\theta &= \int_0^{\frac{1}{2}\pi} \cos^{n-2}\theta \, d\theta - \int_0^{\frac{1}{2}\pi} \cos^{n-2}\theta\sin^2\theta \, d\theta \\
&= \int_0^{\frac{1}{2}\pi} \cos^{n-2}\theta \, d\theta - \left[-\tfrac{1}{n-1}\sin\theta\cos^{n-1}\theta\right]_0^{\frac{1}{2}\pi} - \tfrac{1}{n-1}\int_0^{\frac{1}{2}\pi} \cos^n\theta \, d\theta
\end{aligned}$$

so that

$$\int_0^{\frac{1}{2}\pi} \cos^n\theta\, d\theta = \frac{n-1}{n} \int_0^{\frac{1}{2}\pi} \cos^{n-2}\theta\, d\theta\,, \qquad n \geq 2\,.$$

and so, for example,

$$\int_0^{\frac{1}{2}\pi} \cos^{10}\theta\, d\theta = \tfrac{9}{10} \int_0^{\frac{1}{2}\pi} \cos^8\theta\, d\theta = \tfrac{9}{10} \times \tfrac{7}{8} \int_0^{\frac{1}{2}\pi} \cos^6\theta\, d\theta = \tfrac{9}{10} \times \tfrac{7}{8} \times \tfrac{5}{32}\pi = \tfrac{63}{512}\pi\,.$$

For Interest

Going beyond the Single Pre-U syllabus, the prize goes to using complex numbers to solve this problem. It can be shown, for example, that

$$256\cos^8\theta \equiv 2\cos 8\theta + 16\cos 6\theta + 56\cos 4\theta + 112\cos 2\theta + 70$$

(the coefficients on the right come from the entries 1, 8, 28, 56, 70 in the 8th row of Pascal's triangle) and hence

$$\int_0^{\frac{1}{2}\pi} \cos^8\theta\, d\theta = \tfrac{70}{256} \times \tfrac{1}{2}\pi = \tfrac{35}{256}\pi\,.$$

The interested reader should look up *De Moivre's Theorem* to find the details.

Example 34.3.2. *Calculate the integrals* $\displaystyle\int_{-1}^{1} \frac{x^3 + 2x - 7}{x^2 + 1}\, dx$ *and* $\displaystyle\int_0^{\pi} x(\pi - x)\cos x\, dx$. *The substitution* $x = \tan u$ *might be of help with the first integral, and the substitution* $x = \tfrac{1}{2}\pi + y$ *may help with the second.*

- **Polynomial division:** If we divide $x^3 + 2x - 7$ by $x^2 + 1$, we obtain

$$\frac{x^3 + 2x - 7}{x^2 + 1} \equiv x + \frac{x-7}{x^2+1}$$

Since the substitution $x = \tan u$ gives us

$$\int \frac{1}{x^2+1}\, dx = \int \frac{1}{\sec^2 u} \sec^2 u\, du = \int du = u + c = \tan^{-1} x + c\,,$$

we see that

$$\begin{aligned}\int_{-1}^{1} \frac{x^3 + 2x - 7}{x^2 + 1}\, dx &= \int_{-1}^{1} \left(x + \frac{x}{x^2+1} - \frac{7}{x^2+1} \right) dx = \left[\tfrac{1}{2}x^2 + \tfrac{1}{2}\ln(x^2+1) - 7\tan^{-1} x \right]_{-1}^{1} \\ &= -\tfrac{7}{2}\pi\,.\end{aligned}$$

- **Integration by parts:** Persistent integration by parts will evaluate the second integral.

$$\begin{aligned}\int_0^{\pi} x(\pi - x)\cos x\, dx &= \left[x(\pi - x)\sin x \right]_0^{\pi} + \int_0^{\pi} (\pi - 2x)\sin x\, dx = \int_0^{\pi} (\pi - 2x)\sin x\, dx \\ &= \left[-(\pi - 2x)\cos x \right]_0^{\pi} - 2\int_0^{\pi} \cos x\, dx = -2\left[\sin x \right]_0^{\pi} = 0\,.\end{aligned}$$

- **Evenness and Oddness:** Recall that a function f is **even** if $f(-x) = f(x)$ for all x, and is **odd** if $f(-x) = -f(x)$ for all x. It is particularly easy to integrate odd functions over suitable regions: if $f(x)$ is odd and $a > 0$, then

$$\int_{-a}^{a} f(x)\, dx = 0\,.$$

It is easy to see why; a simple change of variable $t = -x$ shows that

$$\int_{-a}^{0} f(x)\,dx = \int_{a}^{0} f(-t)\,(-dt) = \int_{0}^{a} f(-t)\,dt = -\int_{0}^{a} f(t)\,dt,$$

and hence

$$\int_{-a}^{a} f(x)\,dx = \int_{0}^{a} f(x)\,dx + \int_{-a}^{0} f(x)\,dx = 0.$$

Since $\dfrac{x^3 + 2x}{x^2 + 1}$ is an odd function, it follows that $\displaystyle\int_{-1}^{1} \dfrac{x^3 + 2x}{x^2 + 1}\,dx = 0$, and hence

$$\begin{aligned}
\int_{-1}^{1} \frac{x^3 + 2x - 7}{x^2 + 1}\,dx &= \int_{-1}^{1} \frac{x^3 + 2x}{x^2 + 1}\,dx - 7\int_{-1}^{1} \frac{1}{x^2 + 1}\,dx = -7\int_{-1}^{1} \frac{1}{x^2 + 1}\,dx \\
&= \left[-7\tan^{-1} x \right]_{-1}^{1} = -\tfrac{7}{2}\pi.
\end{aligned}$$

The function $x(\pi - x)\cos x$ is not odd, but it is the translate of an odd function. The substitution $x = \tfrac{1}{2}\pi + y$ gives us

$$\int_{0}^{\pi} x(\pi - x)\cos x\,dx = -\int_{-\frac{1}{2}\pi}^{\frac{1}{2}\pi} \left(\tfrac{1}{4}\pi^2 - y^2 \right)\sin y\,dy = 0,$$

since $\left(\tfrac{1}{4}\pi^2 - y^2 \right)\sin y$ is an odd function.

Example 34.3.3. *Suppose that two numbers are chosen from the set $1, 2, 3, \ldots 10$. What is the probability that the two numbers add up to 10?*

Probability is a rich field for problems where symmetry makes calculations simpler.

- **Enumerating the sample space:** One approach to this problem would be simply to observe that there are $^{10}C_2 = 45$ different pairs of numbers that might be chosen. If these 45 pairs, only 5 add up to 11 ($\{1,10\}$, $\{2,9\}$, $\{3,8\}$, $\{4,7\}$ and $\{5,6\}$). Thus the probability of this happening is $\frac{9}{45} = \frac{1}{9}$. This method obtains the correct answer, without giving us any particular insight into what is going on. Is the fact that the denominator 9 is 1 less than 10 relevant, for example?

- **Conditional probability:** Suppose that the two numbers are chosen sequentially, and let X be the first number chosen, and Y the second. There is no restriction on the value of X, so that X can take any value between 1 and 10, with $\mathbb{P}[X = i] = \frac{1}{10}$ for each $1 \le i \le 10$. If the first number chosen is i, then the two numbers will only add up to 11 if the second number chosen is $11 - i$. Thus, if A is the event that the two numbers add up to 11, then $\mathbb{P}[A|X = i] = \mathbb{P}[Y = 11 - i|X = i]$. Given that i is the first number chosen, Y can take any of the other 9 values with equal probability, and hence $\mathbb{P}[A|X = i] = \mathbb{P}[Y = 11 - i|X = 1] = \frac{1}{9}$. Hence

$$\mathbb{P}[A] = \sum_{i=1}^{10} \mathbb{P}[A|X = i]\mathbb{P}[X = i] = \sum_{i=1}^{10} \tfrac{1}{9} \times \tfrac{1}{10} = \tfrac{1}{9}.$$

- **Using symmetry:** It really does not matter what the first number chosen is; once it has been chosen, there are 9 possible second numbers that can be chosen, with all 9 being equally likely. Only one of these numbers will add together with the first number to total 11. Thus the probability of the two numbers adding to 11 is $\frac{1}{9}$.

For Interest

We have to make sure that symmetry really exists before we can apply it. Suppose now that we repeated the exercise, but this time chose two distinct numbers from 1 to 99. What is the probability that the two numbers add to 100?

This time, not all the first choice numbers 'are the same'; if we choose any number n other than 50, then the number $100 - n$ which, together with n, adds to 100 is distinct from n. If the first number we chose was 50, there would be no second number possible. There is still some symmetry, in that the situation is similar for all first choice numbers except 50. Thus a combination of conditional probability and symmetry gives us

$$\mathbb{P}[A] = \mathbb{P}[A|X \neq 50]\mathbb{P}[X \neq 50] + \mathbb{P}[A|X = 50]\mathbb{P}[X = 50] = \tfrac{1}{98} \times \tfrac{98}{99} + 0 \times \tfrac{1}{99} = \tfrac{1}{99},$$

where A is the event that the two numbers add to 100 and the random variable X is the value of the number chosen first.

Indeed, if we choose two different numbers from the list $1, 2, \ldots n$, then the probability that these two numbers add to $n + 1$ is either $\frac{1}{n-1}$ or $\frac{1}{n}$, depending on whether n is even or odd.

Example 34.3.4. *Peter tosses 5 fair coins, while Mary tosses 4 fair coins. What is the probability that Peter obtains more heads than Mary does?*

- **Enumerating the sample space:** We could list all the possible outcomes (a, b), where (a, b) represents the outcome that Peter throws a heads, while Mary throws b heads. The possible outcomes where Peter throws more heads than Mary are thus

$$(1,0), (2,0), (2,1), (3,0), (3,1), (3,2), (4,0), (4,1), (4,2), (4,3), (5,0), (5,1), (5,2), (5,3), (5,4).$$

However, these different outcomes (as listed) are not equally likely. If we listed the outcomes of Peter's five coin tosses and Mary's 4 coin tosses in the order that they occurred (for example, $\{HHTHT, TTTH\}$), then these $2^5 \times 2^4 = 512$ different listings would be equally like; the example given here would be one of those outcomes contributing to a final 'score' of $(3, 1)$. There are ${}^5C_a \times {}^4C_b$ ways in which Peter can throw a heads, and Mary b heads. Thus the total number of ways in which Peter can throw more heads than Mary is

$$\sum_{a=1}^{5} \left(\sum_{b=0}^{a-1} {}^5C_a \times {}^4C_b \right) = \sum_{a=1}^{5} {}^5C_a \left(\sum_{b=0}^{a-1} {}^4C_b \right)$$
$$= 5 \times 1 + 10 \times 5 + 10 \times 11 + 5 \times 15 + 1 \times 16 = 256$$

out of the $2^5 \times 2^4 = 512$ possible sequences of coin tosses, and hence the probability that Peter throws more heads than Mary is $\frac{256}{512} = \frac{1}{2}$.

- **Symmetry:** Suppose that Peter throws a heads, while Mary throws b heads. Then Peter and Mary throw $5 - a$ and $4 - b$ tails respectively. Since

$$a > b \quad \Leftrightarrow \quad 4 - b > 4 - a \quad \Leftrightarrow \quad 4 - b \geq 5 - a$$

(using the fact that a and b are both integers), we deduce that $\mathbb{P}[a > b] = \mathbb{P}[4 - b \geq 5 - a] = 1 - \mathbb{P}[5 - a > 4 - b]$. In other words, the probability that Peter throws more heads than Mary is one minus the probability that Peter throws more tails than Mary. Now we can use symmetry to note that, since the coins are all fair, the probabilities that Peter throws more heads than Mary and that Peter throws more tails than Mary are the same; hence they are both equal to $\frac{1}{2}$.

Example 34.3.5. *A shell is fired from a gun based at ground level. It has reached an altitude of 10 m after travelling a horizontal distance of 100 m, and is travelling horizontally after it is 1 km away from the gun. What is the horizontal distance that the shell travels for the time that it is more than 10 m above the ground?*

- **Algebra:** The trajectory of the shell is given by the equations

$$y = ux - \tfrac{1}{2}vx^2$$

for some positive constants u and v. The particle is travelling horizontally when $\frac{dy}{dx} = 0$.

Since $\frac{dy}{dx} = u - vx$, we deduce that $u = 1000v$. We also know that

$$10 = 100u - 5000v = 100000v - 5000v = 95000v$$

so that $u = \frac{2}{19}$ and $v = \frac{1}{9500}$. If we solve the equation $y = 10$, we have

$$
\begin{aligned}
\tfrac{2}{19}x - \tfrac{1}{19000}x^2 &= 10 \\
2000x - x^2 &= 190000 \\
x^2 - 2000x + 190000 &= 0 \\
(x - 100)(x - 1900) &= 0
\end{aligned}
$$

so we see that $y \geq 10$ for $100 \leq x \leq 1900$, and so the shell travels a distance of 1800 m above the altitude of 10 m,

- **Symmetry:** The trajectory of the shell is a parabola. Since the particle is travelling horizontally after travelling a distance of 1000 m, its total range is 2000 m. Since it is 10 m above the ground after travelling 100 m, it will be 10 m above the ground 100 m before impact. Thus the total distance travelled about the altitude of 10 m is $2000 - 100 - 100 = 1800$ m.

34.4 Algebra or Geometry?

We have many ways of handing problems using algebra. However, there are times where it is sensible to stand back and think whether applying some geometrical insight will solve a problem more efficiently.

Example 34.4.1. *Find the values of k for which the circles $x^2 + y^2 = 1$ and $x^2 + y^2 + 2x + 4x + k = 0$ are tangential to each other.*

- **Algebra:** For the two circles to be tangential to each other, they must meet at a single point, and so we could try to solve their equations simultaneously. If

$$x^2 + y^2 = 1 \qquad x^2 + y^2 + 2x + 4y + k = 0$$

then subtracting these equations yields $2x + 4y + k + 1 = 0$. Hence

$$
\begin{aligned}
\left(\tfrac{1}{2}(-4y - k - 1)\right)^2 + y^2 &= 1 \\
(4y + k + 1)^2 + 4y^2 &= 4 \\
20y^2 + 8(k + 1)y + k^2 + 2k - 3 &= 0
\end{aligned}
$$

Since we are looking for a single solution to these simultaneous equations, the discriminant of this quadratic should be zero. Thus

$$
\begin{aligned}
\left(8(k + 1)\right)^2 - 4 \times 20(k^2 + 2k - 3) &= 0 \\
64k^2 + 128k + 64 - 80k^2 - 160k + 240 &= 0 \\
16k^2 + 32k - 304 &= 0 \\
k^2 + 2k - 19 &= 0 \\
(k + 1)^2 &= 20
\end{aligned}
$$

and hence $k = -1 \pm 2\sqrt{5}$.

- **Geometry** The two circles have radii 1 and $\sqrt{5 - k}$ and centres $(0, 0)$ and $(-1, -2)$ respectively. Thus the distance between the centres is $\sqrt{5}$, and the centre of the second circle lies outside the first circle.

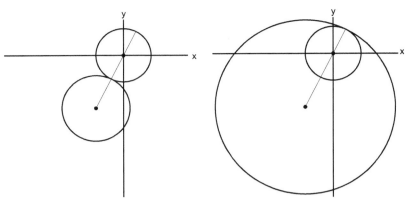

Figure 34.1

Considering the Figure, it is clear that these two circles will be tangential when either $1 + \sqrt{5-k} = \sqrt{5}$ or when $\sqrt{5-k} = 1 + \sqrt{5}$. Thus

$$\sqrt{5-k} = \sqrt{5} \pm 1$$
$$5-k = \left(\sqrt{5} \pm 1\right)^2 = 6 \pm 2\sqrt{5}$$
$$k = -1 \pm 2\sqrt{5}$$

Example 34.4.2. *Find the point of inflexion of the cubic equation* $y = x^3 + 3x^2 + 2x - 7$.

- **Algebra:** Calculating the second derivative gives $\dfrac{d^2 y}{dx^2} = 6x + 6$, and so the second derivative vanishes when $x = -1$, at the point $(-1, -7)$.

- **Geometry:** Writing $y + 7 = (x+1)^3 - (x+1)$, we see that the curve $y = x^3 + 3x^2 + 2x - 7$ is obtained by translating the curve $y = x^3 - x$ through $\binom{-1}{-7}$.

  If $f(x)$ is an odd function, then $f(-x) = -f(x)$. But then $-f'(-x) = -f'(x)$, so that $f'(-x) = f'(x)$, and hence $-f''(-x) = f''(x)$. Thus $-f''(0) = f''(0)$, and hence $f''(0) = 0$. The second derivative of an odd function is zero when $x = 0$.

  Thus the inflexion of the curve $y = x^3 - x$ occurs at the origin, and hence the inflexion of the curve $y = x^3 + 3x^2 + 2x - 7$ occurs at $(-1, -7)$. The point of inflexion of a cubic is its centre of rotational symmetry.

Example 34.4.3. *Recall that the circumcircle of a triangle is the unique circle that passes through all three vertices of that triangle. Find the radius of the circumcircle of the triangle ABC, where A $(-2, 10)$, B $(9, -1)$ and C $(10, 2)$.*

- **Algebra:** We saw in Example 8.1.4 the algebraic approach to this problem; find the three unknown coefficients in the equation of the circumcircle

$$x^2 + y^2 + ax + by + c = 0$$

  by fitting this circle to pass through the three points A, B and C. Doing so yields $a = -4$, $b = -6$, so that $c = -52$. Thus the circle has equation

$$x^2 + y^2 - 4x - 6y - 52 = 0$$
$$(x-2)^2 + (y-3)^2 = 65,$$

  and so the circumcircle has radius $\sqrt{65}$.

- **Geometry 1:** Example 8.1.4 showed us another method for solving this problem. The centre x of the circumcircle must be the same distance R from each of A, B and C. Thus X lies on the perpendicular bisectors of each of AB, AC and BC.

  The line AB has midpoint $(3.5, 4.5)$ and gradient -1; its perpendicular bisector has equation $y = x + 1$.

  The line AC has midpoint $(4, 6)$ and gradient $-\frac{2}{3}$; its perpendicular bisector has equation $y = \frac{3}{2}x$.

  These two lines intersect at the point X $(2, 3)$, and so the radius of the circumcircle is $AX = \sqrt{4^2 + 7^2} = \sqrt{65}$.

- **Geometry 2:** When we proved the sine rule on page 128, we actually proved that

$$\frac{a}{\sin A} = \frac{b}{\sin B} = \frac{c}{\sin C} = 2R$$

for any triangle ABC, where R is the radius of the outcircle. We calculate

$$a = \sqrt{1^2 + 3^2} = \sqrt{10} \qquad b = \sqrt{12^2 + 8^2} = \sqrt{208} \qquad c = \sqrt{11^2 + 11^2} = \sqrt{242},$$

and hence the cosine rule tells us that

$$\cos A = \frac{b^2 + c^2 - a^2}{2bc} = \frac{208 + 242 - 10}{2\sqrt{208 \times 242}} = \frac{440}{88\sqrt{26}} = \frac{5}{\sqrt{26}}$$

and hence $\sin^2 A = 1 - \frac{25}{26}$, and so $\sin A = \frac{1}{\sqrt{26}}$. Thus

$$R = \frac{a}{2\sin A} = \sqrt{10} \times \tfrac{1}{2}\sqrt{26} = \sqrt{65}$$

Example 34.4.4. *The line $y = mx + c$ is tangential to the circle $(x - \alpha)^2 + (y - \beta)^2 = \rho^2$. Show that*

$$(m\alpha - \beta + c)^2 = (1 + m^2)\rho^2.$$

- **Algebra:** Attempting to solve these equations simultaneously leads to the quadratic equation

$$(x - \alpha)^2 + (mx + c - \beta)^2 = \rho^2$$
$$(1 + m^2)x^2 - 2(\alpha + m\beta - mc)x + \alpha^2 + (\beta - c)^2 - \rho^2 = 0.$$

Since the line is tangential to the circle, this equation can only have a single real root. This equation is a quadratic equation in x, $Ax^2 + Bx + C = 0$, where $A = 1 + m^2$, $B = -2(\alpha + m\beta - mc)$ and $C = \alpha^2 + (\beta - c)^2 - \rho^2$, and hence this quadratic must have zero discriminant. Hence

$$B^2 - 4AC = 4(\alpha + m\beta - mc)^2 - 4(1 + m^2)\big(\alpha^2 + (\beta - c)^2 - \rho^2\big) = 0$$
$$(\alpha + m\beta - mc)^2 - (1 + m^2)\big(\alpha^2 + (\beta - c)^2\big) + (1 + m^2)\rho^2 = 0$$

and hence

$$\begin{aligned}
(1 + m^2)\rho^2 &= (1 + m^2)\big(\alpha^2 + (\beta - c)^2\big) - (\alpha + m\beta - mc)^2 \\
&= (1 + m^2)(\alpha^2 + b^2 + c^2 - 2bc) - \alpha^2 - m^2\beta^2 - m^2c^2 - 2m\alpha\beta + 2m\alpha c + 2m^2\beta c \\
&= m^2\alpha^2 + \beta^2 + c^2 - 2m\alpha\beta + 2m\alpha c - 2bc = (m\alpha - \beta + c)^2.
\end{aligned}$$

- **Geometry:** If T is the point on the line with x-coordinate α, then T has coordinates $m\alpha + c$, and hence the length $TC = |m\alpha - \beta + c|$. Angle-chasing shows us that the angles $\angle PCT$ and $\angle TPX$ are the same; we shall call this common angle θ. Considering the right-angled triangle TPX, it is clear that $\tan\theta = m$. Considering the right-angled triangle PCT, we see that $PT = PC\tan\theta = m\rho$. Pythagoras' Theorem, applied to the right-angled triangle PCT, tells us that

$$(m\alpha - \beta + c)^2 = CT^2 = PC^2 + PT^2 = (1 + m^2)\rho^2.$$

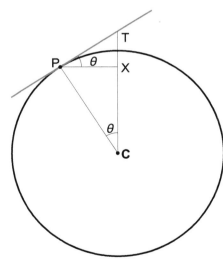

Figure 34.2

Example 34.4.5. *A particle of weight W Newtons is attached at R to two light inextensible strings PR and QR. The other ends of the strings are attached to fixed points P and Q on a horizontal bar. The particle hangs in equilibrium with PR and QR making angles of α and β with the horizontal respectively, where $0 < \alpha + \beta < 180°$. If the tensions in PR and QR are T_P and T_Q respectively, find expressions for T_P and T_Q in terms of W, α and β.*

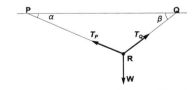

Figure 34.3

- **Algebra** The standard approach to this problem would probably be to resolve forces horizontally and vertically, obtaining the simultaneous equations

$$T_P \cos\alpha - T_Q \cos\beta = 0 \qquad\qquad T_P \sin\alpha + T_Q \sin\beta = W .$$

Eliminating T_Q from this equations yields

$$\begin{aligned} W\cos\beta &= \sin\beta(T_P \cos\alpha - T_Q \cos\beta) + \cos\beta(T_P \sin\alpha + T_Q \sin\beta) \\ &= (\sin\beta\cos\alpha + \cos\beta\sin\alpha)T_P = T_P \sin(\alpha+\beta) \end{aligned}$$

and hence $T_P = \dfrac{W\cos\beta}{\sin(\alpha+\beta)}$. It now follows that $T_Q = \dfrac{W\cos\alpha}{\sin(\alpha+\beta)}$.

- **Geometry** An alternative approach would be to rearrange the three forces T_P, T_Q and W to form a triangle (which must happen, since the particle is in equilibrium).

The sine rule now tells us that

$$\frac{T_P}{\sin(90°-\beta)} = \frac{T_Q}{\sin(90°-\alpha)} = \frac{W}{\sin(\alpha+\beta)},$$

and hence $T_P = \dfrac{W\cos\beta}{\sin(\alpha+\beta)}$ and $T_Q = \dfrac{W\cos\alpha}{\sin(\alpha+\beta)}$.

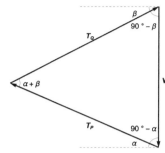

Figure 34.4

Example 34.4.6. *A sphere of weight 15 N rests between two smooth ramps, one inclined at 25° to the horizontal, and the other inclined at 65° to the horizontal. Find the magnitudes of the normal reactions between the ramps and the sphere.*

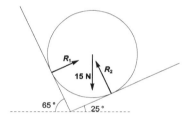

Figure 34.5

- **Algebra:** An awkward approach to this problem creates greater algebraic effort. Resolving forces on the sphere horizontally gives

$$R_1 \cos 25° = R_2 \cos 65°$$

and resolving forces vertically gives

$$R_1 \sin 25° + R_2 \sin 65° = 15 .$$

Solving these simultaneous equations yields

$$R_1 = \cos 25°(R_1 \cos 25° - R_2 \cos 65°) + \sin 25°(R_1 \sin 25° + R_2 \sin 65°) = 15\sin 25° = 6.34\,\text{N}$$

(note that $\cos 25° \cos 65° - \sin 25° \sin 65° = \cos 90° = 0$), and thus $R_2 = 15\cos 25° = 13.6$ N.

- **Geometry:** The two ramps are perpendicular to each other. If we resolve parallel to the two ramps, we will be able to identify the two normal reactions much more simply. Resolving parallel to the right-hand ramp tells us that

$$R_1 = 15\sin 25° = 6.34\,\text{N}$$

while resolving parallel to the left-hand ramp tells us that

$$R_2 = 15\cos 25° = 13.6\,\text{N}.$$

No algebra was needed at all!

Example 34.4.7. *A gun fires a shell from ground level with muzzle velocity u ms^{-1}. What is the maximum range of the shell?*

- **Algebra:** Considering the trajectory of the shell using coordinates is the standard approach to this question. If the angle of elevation of the gun is θ, then the particle's trajectory is given by the equations

$$x = ut\cos\theta \qquad y = ut\sin\theta - \tfrac{1}{2}gt^2.$$

The shell strikes the ground when $y = 0$, at time $t = \dfrac{2u\sin\theta}{g}$, at which time $x = \dfrac{u^2\sin 2\theta}{g}$.

Thus the maximum range of $\frac{u^2}{g}$ occurs when $\theta = 45°$.

- **Geometry:** If the shell's flight lasts t seconds, and the initial velocity of the shell is $\mathbf{u}$ ms^{-1}, then the final displacement of the shell at the time of impact is $R\mathbf{i} = \mathbf{u}t + \tfrac{1}{2}\mathbf{g}t^2$. Pythagoras' Theorem tells us that

$$R^2 = u^2 t^2 - \tfrac{1}{4}g^2 t^4 = \tfrac{u^4}{g^2} - \tfrac{1}{2}\left(gt^2 - \tfrac{u^2}{g}\right)^2$$

and hence the maximum possible value of R^2 is $\frac{u^4}{g^2}$, and hence the greatest possible range is $\frac{u^2}{g}$.

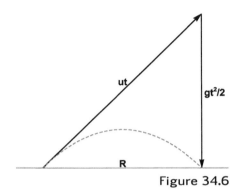

Figure 34.6

The following example comes straight from the Further Mathematics Pre-U.

Example 34.4.8. *A gun fires a shell with muzzle speed u ms^{-1} at an angle of θ to the horizontal. The gun is sited on a hillside, which can be modelled as a plane surface inclined at an angle of α to the horizontal (where $\alpha < \theta$). The gun is fired pointing directly uphill. What is the range of the gun?*

- **Algebra:** The straightforward approach is to use equation of the trajectory of the shell:

$$x = ut\cos\theta \qquad y = ut\sin\theta - \tfrac{1}{2}gt^2.$$

We need to know when the shell hits the hill again, which will occur when $y = x\tan\alpha$, and hence when $t \neq 0$ and

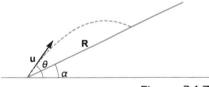

Figure 34.7

$$ut\sin\theta - \tfrac{1}{2}gt^2 = ut\cos\theta\tan\alpha,$$

namely when $t = \frac{2u}{g}(\sin\theta - \cos\theta\tan\alpha) = \dfrac{2u\sin(\theta - \alpha)}{g\cos\alpha}$. At this time

$x = \dfrac{2u^2\sin(\theta - \alpha)\cos\theta}{g\cos\alpha}$, and so the uphill range R is

$$R = x\sec\alpha = \dfrac{2u^2\sin(\theta - \alpha)\cos\theta}{g\cos^2\alpha}.$$

- **Geometry:** If the flight of the shell lasts t seconds, the final displacement $\mathbf{u}t + \tfrac{1}{2}\mathbf{g}t^2$ of the shell is directly up the slope of the hill. The three angles in the triangle XYZ are marked, and so the sine rule gives

$$\frac{R}{\sin(90° - \theta)} = \frac{ut}{\sin(90° + \alpha)} = \frac{\tfrac{1}{2}gt^2}{\sin(\theta - \alpha)}.$$

or

$$\frac{R}{\cos\theta} = \frac{ut}{\cos\alpha} = \frac{gt^2}{2\sin(\theta - \alpha)}.$$

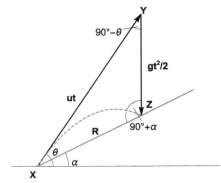

Figure 34.8

The first equality gives $t = \dfrac{R\cos\alpha}{u\cos\theta}$, while the second gives $t = \dfrac{2u\sin(\theta-\alpha)}{g\cos\alpha}$. Hence

$$\frac{R\cos\alpha}{u\cos\theta} = \frac{2u\sin(\theta-\alpha)}{g\cos\alpha}$$

and hence

$$R = \frac{2u^2\sin(\theta-\alpha)\cos\theta}{g\cos^2\alpha}.$$

34.5 Making It Count

Combinatorics problems, and their application to probability, can be particularly challenging. The theory of combinatorics, such as it is, is pretty straightforward (the formulae for permutations and combinations are not particularly demanding) but the problems of counting can be substantial. When counting the numbers of ways in which something can occur, we need to tread a path between the two key requirements of the problem:

- to count all possibilities,

- not to double-count any possibilities.

Sometimes it proves profitable to count exactly the opposite of what we are looking for.

Example 34.5.1. *Four letters are chosen at random from the letters of the word BREAKDOWN. What is the probability that there is at least one vowel amongst the letters?*

- **Counting In:** There are $^9C_4 = 126$ different ways in which four letters can be chosen from the nine distinct letters in the word BREAKDOWN. There are $^6C_1 = 6$ ways of choosing four letters including all three vowels. There are $3 \times {}^6C_2 = 3 \times 15 = 45$ ways of choosing four letters to include exactly two vowels (there are 3 ways of choosing the two vowels, and $^6C_2$ ways of choosing the two consonants). There are $3 \times {}^6C_3 = 3 \times 20 = 60$ ways of choosing four letters to include exactly one vowel. Thus there are $6 + 45 + 60 = 111$ ways of choosing four letters containing at least one vowel. Thus the probability of choosing at least one vowel is $\frac{111}{126}$.

- **Counting Out:** There are $^6C_4 = 15$ ways of choosing four consonants, and hence the probability of not choosing a vowel is $\frac{15}{126}$. Hence the probability of choosing at least one vowel is $1 - \frac{15}{126} = \frac{111}{126}$.

Example 34.5.2. *How many rearrangements are there of the letters STRETCHED for which no two consecutive letters are the same?*

- **Counting In:** There are $5! = 120$ ways of ordering the letters S, R, C, H and D; for each of these 120 arrangements, we need to determine in how many ways the two Es and two Ts can be arranged.

  For example, suppose that the letters S, R, C, H, D have been arranged in that order. Between these five letters there are 6 'spaces' into which the Es and Ts could go. In the diagram below, each space is marked with a star:

  $$\star \quad S \quad \star \quad H \quad \star \quad R \quad \star \quad C \quad \star \quad D \quad \star$$

  (a) If both Es go into the same space (there are 6 ways in which this could happen), then exactly one of the Ts must go between the two Es to separate them. The remaining T can go into one of 7 spaces (one of the remaining original five spaces, or on one side or the other of the sequence of letters ETE in the space already chosen). In this case there are $6 \times 7 = 42$ ways of placing the letters E, E, T, T so that no two consecutive letters are the same.

  (b) If the two Es are in different spaces (there are $^6C_2 = 15$ ways in which this can happen), then there are now 8 spaces (around the letters S, R, C, H, D, E, E) into which the two Ts can go; there are $^8C_2 = 28$ ways in which this can be done without obtaining consecutive Ts. In this case there are $15 \times 28 = 420$ ways of placing the letters E, E, T, T so that no two consecutive letters are the same.

Thus there are $120(42+420) = 55440$ ways of arranging the letters in STRETCHED so that no two consecutive letters are the same.

- **Counting Out:** Let A be the set of arrangements of the letters for which the two Es are consecutive, and let B be the set of arrangements of the letters for which the two Ts are consecutive.

  (a) There are $\frac{8!}{2!} = 20160$ permutations of the letters and letter pair S, R, C, H, D, T, T, EE, and hence $|A| = 21060$.

  (b) There are $\frac{8!}{2!} = 20160$ permutations of the letters and letter pair S, R, C, H, D, E, E, TT, and hence $|B| = 21060$.

  (c) There are $7! = 5040$ permutations of the letters and letter pairs S, R, C, H, D, EE, TT, and hence $|A \cup B| = 5040$.

Thus we deduce that $|A \cup B| = |A| + |B| - |A \cap B| = 8! - 7! = 35280$. This is the number of rearrangements of the letters in STRETCHED for which some two consecutive letters are the same. Since there are $\frac{9!}{2!2!} = 90720$, we deduce that there are $90720 - 35280 = 55440$ rearrangements of the letters in STRETCHED for which no two consecutive letters are the same.

Alternatively, there are occasions where a problem needs to looked at from a different perspective.

Example 34.5.3. *Twenty marbles are arranged at random in a flat box with four compartments, arranged in two rows of two columns each. Given that there must be 12 marbles in the top row, and 9 marbles in the first column, what is the probability that the marbles are arranged as follows:*

5	7
4	4

?

Explain why

$$\sum_{k=1}^{9} {}^{12}C_k \times {}^{8}C_{k-1} = {}^{20}C_9 .$$

Since we are only interested in arrangements of marbles that have 12 marbles in the top row (and therefore 8 marbles in the bottom row), we could pretend that 12 of the marbles are coloured red, with the other 8 being coloured blue. A red marble will always be put in the top row, and a blue marble will always be put in the bottom row.

Now suppose that we are using this box to store marbles for an important marbles competition. The 9 marbles in the first column will be the ones that we shall use in the competition, with the other 11 not being needed.

The problem can now be restated: if we have a collection of 12 red marbles and 8 blue marbles, and want to select a set of 9 marbles from this collection, what is the probability that our set of 9 marbles will contain exactly 5 red marbles?

The solution is now easy. There are ${}^{12}C_5$ ways of choosing 5 out of 12 red marbles, and ${}^{8}C_4$ ways of choosing 4 out of 8 blue marbles, while there are ${}^{20}C_9$ ways of choosing 9 marbles from the total set of 20. The desired probability is therefore

$$\frac{{}^{12}C_5 \times {}^{8}C_4}{{}^{20}C_9} = \frac{792 \times 70}{167960} = 0.330 .$$

Since there have to be 12 marbles in the top row, and there have to be 9 marbles in the first column, the possible arrangements for marbles in the box is comparatively limited. The only possible arrangements of marbles are:

k	$12-k$
$9-k$	$k-1$

$1 \leq k \leq 9$.

In terms of red and blue marbles, the number X of red marbles that can be chosen in a set of 8 can take any of the values between 1 and 9 inclusive. Just like above, we can show that

$$\mathbb{P}[X = k] = \frac{{}^{12}C_k \times {}^{8}C_{k-1}}{{}^{20}C_9}, \qquad 1 \leq k \leq 9.$$

Since $\displaystyle\sum_{k=1}^{9} \mathbb{P}[X = k] = 1$, we deduce that

$$\sum_{k=1}^{9} {}^{12}C_k \times {}^{8}C_{k-1} = {}^{20}C_9 .$$

Thinking about the symmetry of a problem, or identifying unimportant aspects of it, can simplify calculations.

Example 34.5.4. *An ordinary pack of 52 playing cards is dealt between four players. What is the probability that one player is dealt both the Ace and King of Spades?*

(MAT, adapt.)

- **Brute force:** Suppose that the four players are called North, East, South and West. If North is dealt both the Ace and King of Spades, then there are ${}^{50}C_{11}$ different hands that North can receive. There are then ${}^{39}C_{13}$ hands that East can receive, and then ${}^{26}C_{13}$ hands that South can receive. West must receive the remaining 13 cards. Thus there are

$$ {}^{50}C_{11} \times {}^{39}C_{13} \times {}^{26}C_{13} $$

  different ways in which North can be dealt both Ace and King of Spades, while there are

$$ {}^{52}C_{13} \times {}^{39}C_{13} \times {}^{26}C_{13} $$

  different ways in which the cards can be dealt amongst the four players. Thus the probability that North is dealt both Ace and King of Spades is

$$ \frac{{}^{50}C_{11} \times {}^{39}C_{13} \times {}^{26}C_{13}}{{}^{52}C_{13} \times {}^{39}C_{13} \times {}^{26}C_{13}} = \frac{{}^{50}C_{11}}{{}^{52}C_{13}} = \frac{13 \times 12}{52 \times 51} = \frac{1}{17} $$

  Since each of North, East, South and West can be dealt both the Ace and King of Spades, the probability that one of the four players is dealt both Ace and King of spades is $4 \times \frac{1}{17} = \frac{4}{17}$.

- **A lighter touch:** If we want to know the probability that North is dealt both Ace and King of Spades, we do not care about the hands that the other three players are dealt. We can simply ask: what is the probability that someone dealt 13 cards from a pack of 52 will receive both Ace and King of Spades? This probability is clearly

$$ \frac{{}^{50}C_{11}}{{}^{52}C_{13}} = \frac{13 \times 12}{52 \times 51} = \frac{1}{17} . $$

  As above, the probability that any one of the four players is dealt the Ace and King of Spades is clearly four times the probability that North receives these cards, namely $\frac{4}{17}$.

- **Lighter still:** One of the players must be dealt the Ace of Spades. Since it does not matter which player is dealt these cards, we could ask instead: if one player is dealt 12 cards from a pack from which the Ace of Spades has been removed, what is the probability that player receives the King of Spades? This probability can be calculated in at least two different ways. The simplest method gives the probability as

$$ \frac{{}^{50}C_{11}}{{}^{51}C_{12}} = \frac{12}{51} = \frac{4}{17} . $$

  Alternatively, we could consider dealing the twelve cards to this player one at a time. The probability that the King of Spades is the first card dealt is

$$ \tfrac{1}{51} \times \tfrac{50}{50} \times \tfrac{49}{49} \times \tfrac{48}{48} \times \cdots \times \tfrac{40}{40} = \tfrac{1}{51} , $$

  while the probability that the King of Spades is the second card dealt is

$$ \tfrac{50}{51} \times \tfrac{1}{50} \times \tfrac{49}{49} \times \tfrac{48}{48} \times \cdots \times \tfrac{40}{40} = \tfrac{1}{51} , $$

  while the probability that the King of Spades is the third card dealt is

$$ \tfrac{50}{51} \times \tfrac{49}{50} \times \tfrac{1}{49} \times \tfrac{48}{48} \times \cdots \times \tfrac{40}{40} = \tfrac{1}{51} , $$

  and so on. The numerator of each probability is $1 \times 50 \times 49 \times \cdots \times 40$ (although the terms appear in different orders), making each probability equal to $\frac{1}{51}$. Since the King of Spades could be dealt as anything from the first to the twelfth card, it follows that the desired probability is $12 \times \frac{1}{51} = \frac{4}{17}$.

Another important strategy is to break a problem down into cases that can be handled more easily.

Example 34.5.5. *A bag contains two red, two green, two white, two blue, two yellow and two black marbles. Four marbles are taken out of the bad and arranged in a row, with the first-chosen marble on the left and the last-chosen marble on the right. Marbles of the same colour are indistinguishable. How many different arrangements of marbles are possible?*

A pattern of marbles could involve just two colours (two marbles of each colour). There are $^6C_2 = 15$ pairs of colours that could be chosen, and $^4C_2 = 6$ ways of arranging each set of four marbles of two colours. There are $15 \times 6 = 90$ possible arrangements like this.

A pattern could involve two marbles of a single colour, and two separately coloured marbles. There are 6 possible choices for the colour of the identical pair of marbles, and $^5C_2 = 10$ choices for the other two colours. Then are then $^4C_2 \times 2 = 12$ arrangements of these coloured marbles. This makes a total of $6 \times 10 \times 12 = 720$ possible arrangements of this type.

A pattern could involve four differently coloured marbles. There are $^6C_4 = 15$ possible choices of colours, and then $4! = 24$ arrangements of these marbles, making a total of $15 \times 24 = 360$ arrangements of this type.

The total number of arrangements is $90 + 720 + 360 = 1170$.

34.6 To Conclude

In summary, this Chapter shows that there are many different ways of solving problems We hope that we have shown some of the variety of solution techniques possible. It is often worth trying to solve a problem in more than one way (although, perhaps not during an examination!). Ultimately, Mathematics is the business of problem-solving; developing a flexible approach to problems, and being prepared to try an alternative technique if one's first attempt fails, is what the subject is all about.

Part 5

Appendices

Answers to Exercises

Exercise 1A — (page 5)

2). Since $0.\dot{9} = 1$, numbers with a terminating decimal expansion can be written with a recurring expansion instead, for example $0.564 = 0.563\dot{9}$. All other numbers have a unique decimal expansion.

3). $0.\dot{1}2\dot{3} = \frac{41}{333}$, $0.2\dot{2}\dot{7} = \frac{5}{22}$.

4). This is the standard GCSE argument for obtaining the fractional form of a recurring decimal.

5). A remainder can be any number between 0 and 16, so there are 17 possible remainders, and so a fraction with denominator 17 must recur, with a recurring pattern which is no more than 17 digits long. When dividing by a general denominator n, there are at most n possible remainders, so the decimal expansion must either terminate or recur.

Exercise 1B — (page 8)

1). a) 3,   b) 4,   c) 6,   d) 30,   e) 28,   f) $x\sqrt[3]{y}$,   g) 5,   h) $16x$.

2). a) $3\sqrt{2}$,   b) $3\sqrt{5}$,   c) $15\sqrt{3}$,   d) $xy^2\sqrt{xy}$,   e) $20\sqrt{5}$,   f) $5\sqrt[3]{2}$,   g) $2xy\sqrt[4]{2}$,   h) $(x+y)\sqrt{x}$.

3). a) $5\sqrt{2}$,   b) $\sqrt{5}$,   c) $13\sqrt{5}$,   d) $(x+y)\sqrt{x}$,   e) $4\sqrt{11}$,   f) $\sqrt{13}$,   g) x.

4). a) 2,   b) $\sqrt{2}$,   c) $\frac{1}{4}$,   d) $\frac{1}{2}$,   e) $\frac{\sqrt{5}}{5}$,   f) $\sqrt{15}$,   g) $\frac{2\sqrt{6}}{3}$,   h) $\frac{\sqrt{6}}{9}$,   i) $2+\sqrt{3}$,   j) $\frac{3\sqrt{5}+5}{20}$,   k) $4\sqrt{2}-2\sqrt{6}$ l) $2\sqrt{3}+3\sqrt{2}-\sqrt{30}$.

5). 25.4950975680.

6). $x = 3\sqrt{5}, y = 4$. 8). 0.

9). $10 - 3\sqrt{11} < 9 - 4\sqrt{5} < 8 - 3\sqrt{7} < 7 - 4\sqrt{3}$.

Exercise 1C — (page 10)

1). a) 2^{26},   b) 2^{12},   c) 2^6,   d) 2^6,   e) 2^2,   f) $2^1 = 2$,   g) $2^0 = 1$,   h) 1.

2). a) a^{12},   b) c^4,   c) e^{20},   d) $15g^8$,   e) $72a^8$,   f) $128x^7y^{11}$,   g) $4c$,   h) $7r^3s$,   i) $\frac{1}{9}h^{-4}$,   j) $8j^6$,   k) $9n^{-9}$,   l) $\frac{1}{64}q^6$.

3). a) $x = -2$,   b) $y = 0$,   c) $z = 4$,   d) $x = -2$,   e) $y = 120$,   f) $t = 0$.

4). 2^{11}.

5). $3^{-\frac{9}{2}} = \frac{1}{243}\sqrt{3}$.

6). $x = -3$.

7). Because $(a^m)^n = a^{mn}$.

8). 3^{4^3}.

Exercise 1D — (page 11)

1). a) 5,   b) 6,   c) 3,   d) $\frac{1}{2}$,   e) $\frac{1}{10}$,   f) 3,   g) 16,   h) $\frac{1}{625}$,   i) 8,   j) 81,   k) 8,   l) 32,   m) $\frac{1}{1000}$,   n) 625,   o) $\frac{9}{4}$,   p) $\frac{2}{3}$.

2). a) a^2,   b) $12b^{-1}$,   c) $12c^{\frac{3}{4}}$,   d) 1,   e) $4x^6$,   f) 2,   g) $5pq^2$,   h) $2m^{\frac{13}{12}}n^{\frac{5}{4}}$,   i) $2^{\frac{5}{4}}x^{-1}y^{\frac{5}{4}}$.

3). a) $x = 64$,   b) $x = 27$,   c) $x = 8$,   d) $x = 9$,   e) $x = \frac{1}{4}$,   f) $x = \frac{1}{27}$,   g) $x = 0, 2$,   h) $x = 0, 2$,   i) $x = \frac{5}{2}$,   j) $y = -\frac{3}{2}$,   k) $z = \frac{1}{4}$,   l) $x = \frac{3}{2}$,   m) $z = -\frac{7}{3}$,   n) $t = \frac{6}{5}$,   o) $y = -\frac{7}{4}$.

4). $3^{\frac{1}{3}}$.

Exercise 2A — (page 18)

1). a) 13,   b) 5,   c) $5\sqrt{2}$,   d) $2\sqrt{13}$,   e) $17a$,   f) $2\sqrt{5}$,   g) 23,   h) $9a$,   i) $(p-q)\sqrt{2}$,   j) $5q\sqrt{2}$.

5). a) $(4, 13)$,   b) $(1, 8)$,   c) $(-\frac{1}{2}, -\frac{9}{2})$,   d) $(-\frac{11}{2}, \frac{9}{2})$,   e) $(2p + 3, 2p - 3)$,   f) $(p + 4, -2)$,   g) $(3p, 3q)$,   h) $(a + 3, b + 1)$.

6). $(2, 3)$.

7). $(7, 10)$.

8). The common midpoint is $(5, \frac{1}{2})$.

9). A; $BA = AC = \sqrt{26}$.

10). a) 2,   b) -3,   c) $\frac{1}{2}$,   d) $-\frac{3}{4}$,   e) -2,   f) -1,   g) $\frac{3-p}{1-q}$,   h) 0.

11). AB, BC both have gradient $\frac{1}{2}$; A, B and C are collinear.

12). AP and PB have gradients $\frac{y}{x-3}$ and $\frac{y-6}{x-5}$; $\frac{y}{x-3} = \frac{y-6}{x-5} \Rightarrow y = 3x - 9$.

13). 5.

14). a) $M\left(\frac{1}{2}(a+p), \frac{1}{2}(b+q)\right)$, $N\left(\frac{1}{2}(a+u), \frac{1}{2}(b+v)\right)$,   b) MN and BC both have gradient $\frac{v-q}{u-p}$.

15). a) $MN = 5, BC = 10$.

16). a) PQ, QR, RS and SP have gradients $-1, \frac{3}{5}, -1$ and $\frac{3}{5}$,   b) $PQRS$ is a parallelogram.

17). a) Common gradient 4,   b) Common gradient $\frac{1}{4}$,   c) $OP = OR = \sqrt{17}$,   d) Rhombus.

18). a) $ON = LM = 2\sqrt{13}$,   b) Common gradient $\frac{2}{3}$,   c) $OM = LN = \sqrt{65}$,   d) Rectangle.

19). a) PQ, QR, RS and SP have gradients $-\frac{1}{3}, 4, -\frac{1}{3}$ and $\frac{3}{4}$,   b) Trapezium.

20). $TM = TN = 2\sqrt{5}$.

21). a) $DE = \sqrt{10}, EF = 2\sqrt{10}, FG = 2\sqrt{10}, GD = \sqrt{10}$,   b) Kite.

22). $5, -3$.

23). a) $L\left(\frac{1}{2}(p+u), \frac{1}{2}(q+v)\right), M\left(\frac{1}{2}(a+u), \frac{1}{2}(b+v)\right), N\left(\frac{1}{2}(a+p), \frac{1}{2}(b+q)\right)$,   b) AG and AL both have gradient $\frac{2b-q-v}{2a-p-u}$,   c) G is on all 3 medians.

24). a) $AB = (a^2 + b^2)^{(1/2)}, CD = (c^2 + d^2)^{(1/2)}$.

Exercise 2B — (page 23)

1). a) Yes,   b) No,   c) Yes,   d) No,   e) Yes,   f) No,   g) Yes,   h) Yes.

2). a) $y = 5x - 7$,   b) $y = 1 - 3x$,   c) $2y = x + 8$,   d) $3x + 8y = 2$,   e) $y = -3x$,   f) $y = 8$,   g) $3x + 4y + 19 = 0$,   h) $2y = x + 3$,   i) $3x - 8y + 1 = 0$,   j) $x + 2y = 11$,   k) $y = 3 - 2x$,   l) $y = 3x + 1$,   m) $y = 7x - 4$,   n) $y = 2 - x$,   o) $5x + 8y + 1 = 0$,   p) $3x + 5y = 9$,   q) $y = 7x - 7d$,   r) $y = mx + 4$,   s) $y = 3x + c$,   t) $y = mx - mc$.

3). a) $y = 3x + 1$,   b) $y = 2x - 3$,   c) $2x + 3y - 12 = 0$,   d) $x - 3 = 0$,   e) $3x - 5y - 45 = 0$,   f) $y = 8 - 3x$,   g) $y = -3$,   h) $x + 3y - 2 = 0$,   i) $5x + 3y + 14 = 0$,   j) $2x + 7y + 11 = 0$,   k) $x + 3 = 0$,   l) $x + y + 1 = 0$,   m) $y = 3x + 1$,   n) $5x + 3y + 13 = 0$,   o) $3x + 5y = 0$,   p) $qx - py = 0$,   q) $x + 3y - p - 3q = 0$,   r) $x - p = 0$,   s) $y = x + q - p$,   t) $qx + py - pq = 0$.   4). a) -2,   b) $\frac{3}{4}$,   c) $-\frac{5}{2}$,   d) 0,   e) $\frac{3}{2}$,   f) ∞,   g) -1,   h) 3,   i) $-\frac{1}{2}$,   j) $\frac{7}{3}$,   k) m,   l) $-\frac{p}{q}$.   5). $y = \frac{1}{2}x + 2$.

6). $y + 2x = 5$.   7). $3x + 8y = 19$.   8). $x + y = 12$.   9). $y = 7$.   10). $y = mx - md$.   11). a) $(x, y) = (7, 3)$,   b) $(x, y) = (2, 7)$,   c) $(x, y) = \left(-\frac{1}{4}, -\frac{7}{8}\right)$,   d) $(x, y) = (-3, -1)$,   e) $(x, y) = (2, 4)$,   f) $(x, y) = (6, 5)$,   g) No solutions (parallel lines),   h) $(x, y) = (2, -1)$,   i) $(x, y) = (u, 2u + 3)$ for any real u, (identical lines),   j) $(x, y) = \left(\frac{c}{a(1+2b)}, \frac{2c}{1+2b}\right)$,   k) $(x, y) = \left(\frac{d-c}{2m}, \frac{1}{2}(c+d)\right)$,   l) $(x, y) = \left(\frac{1}{a-b}, \frac{1}{a-b}\right)$.   12). $M(2, 1)$ and $M(4, 2)$. $AM = MN = NC = \sqrt{5}$.   14). $a = b = c = 0$.   15). $\frac{1}{2m}(mp + q)^2$; ℓ passes through the origin O.   16). $u = \frac{1-m^2}{1+m^2}a, v = \frac{2m}{1+m^2}a$.   17). a) $(2a_1 - b_1 - c_1)(2y - b_2 - c_2) = (2a_2 - b_2 - c_2)(2x - b_1 - c_1)$, or $(2a_1 - b_1 - c_1)(y - a_2) = (2a_2 - b_2 - c_2)(x - a_1)$,   c) G lies on all three lines.

Exercise 2C — (page 28)

1). a) $-\frac{1}{2}$,   b) $\frac{1}{3}$,   c) $-\frac{1}{4}$,   d) $\frac{6}{5}$,   e) 1,   f) $-\frac{4}{7}$,   g) m,   h) $-\frac{1}{m}$,   i) $-\frac{q}{p}$,   j) ∞,   k) $\frac{1}{m}$,   l) $\frac{c-b}{a}$.

2). a) $x+4y = 14$, b) $y = 2x+7$, c) $x-5y = 27$, d) $x = 7$, e) $3x-2y = -11$, f) $5x+3y = 29$, g) $y = -3$, h) $x + 2y = 6$, i) $x + my = 0$, j) $x + my = a + mb$, k) $nx + y = nc + d$, l) $bx - ay = 2a - b$.

3). $x + 3y = 13, (1, 4)$.

4). $3x + 2y = 5, (3, -2)$.

5). $36.87°$.

6). $x + 2y = 8$.

7). a) $x = 8, x - 2y - 2 = 0$, b) $(8, 3)$, c) The altitude through P has equation $x + 3y = 17$, which passes through $(8, 3)$.

8). a) $7y = x + 9, y = \frac{1}{2}x + 2 (-2, 1)$, b) $XP = XQ = XR = 5$, c) Yes.

9). a) $(c_2 - b_2)y + (c_1 - b_1)x = 0$, Yes, b) All three perpendicular bisectors pass through O.

10). a) $(c_1 - b_1)(x - a_1) + (c_2 - b_2)(y - a_2) = 0$, c) All three altitudes pass through H, d) O, G and H all lie on $(a_1 + b_1 + c_1)y = (a_2 + b_2 + c_2)x$.

Exercise 3A — (page 33)

1). a) $(2, 3), x = 2$, b) $(5, -4), x = 5$, c) $(-3, -7), x = -3$, d) $\left(\frac{3}{2}, 1\right), x = \frac{3}{2}$, e) $\left(-\frac{3}{5}, 2\right), x = -\frac{3}{5}$, f) $\left(-\frac{7}{3}, -4\right), x = -\frac{7}{3}$, g) $(3, c), x = 3$, h) $(p, q), x = p$, i) $\left(-\frac{b}{a}, c\right), x = -\frac{b}{a}$.

2). a) $-1, x = -2$, b) $2, x = 1$, c) $5, x = -3$, d) $-7, x = -\frac{1}{2}$, e) $3, x = 4$, f) $q, x = -p$, g) $-q, x = p$, h) $r, x = t$, i) $c, x = -\frac{b}{a}$.

3). a) $x = 3 \pm \sqrt{3}$, b) $x = -4, 0$, c) $x = -3 \pm \sqrt{\frac{5}{2}}$, d) $x = \frac{1}{3}(7 \pm 2\sqrt{2})$, e) $x = -p \pm \sqrt{q}$, f) $x = -b \pm \sqrt{\frac{c}{a}}$.

4). a) $(x+1)^2 + 1$, b) $(x-4)^2 - 19$, c) $\left(x + \frac{3}{2}\right)^2 - \frac{37}{4}$, d) $(x-3)^2 - 4$, e) $(x+7)^2$, f) $2(x+3)^2 - 23$, g) $3(x-2)^2 - 9$, h) $11 - 4(x+1)^2$, i) $2\left(x + \frac{5}{4}\right)^2 - \frac{49}{8}$.

5). a) $(x-7)(x+5)$, b) $(x-22)(x+8)$, c) $(x+24)(x-18)$, d) $(2x-3)(3x+2)$, e) $(7-2x)(2+7x)$, f) $(4x+3)(3x-2)$.

6). a) $3, x = 2$, b) $\frac{11}{4}, x = \frac{3}{2}$, c) $13, x = 3$, d) $-\frac{9}{8}, x = \frac{5}{4}$, e) $-\frac{13}{3}, x = -\frac{1}{3}$, f) $\frac{85}{12}, x = -\frac{7}{6}$.

Exercise 3B — (page 36)

1). a) $x = \frac{1}{2}[-3 \pm \sqrt{29}]$, b) $x = 2 \pm \sqrt{11}$, c) $x = -3$, d) $x = -3, -\frac{1}{2}$, e) $\frac{1}{2}[-3 \pm \sqrt{41}]$, f) No solutions.

2). a) $\Delta = 29$, 2 solutions, b) $\Delta = 0$, 1 solution, c) $\Delta = -7$, no solutions, d) $\Delta = -24$, no solutions, e) $\Delta = p^2 + 4q$, 2 solutions, f) $\Delta = -3p^2$, no solutions.

3). a) $k < \frac{9}{4}$, b) $k = \frac{49}{4}$, c) $k > \frac{9}{20}$, d) $k > -\frac{25}{12}$, e) $k = \frac{4}{3}$, f) $k > \frac{25}{28}$, g) $k > 4$ or $k < -4$, h) $-6 < k < 6$, i) $k = \pm\frac{7}{2}$.

4). The quadratic is a 'smile' with two real roots, so crosses the x-axis twice.

5). The quadratic is a 'frown' with two real roots, so crosses the x-axis twice.

6). $\alpha + \beta = -b, \alpha\beta = c$.

7). $\alpha + \beta = -\frac{b}{a}, \alpha\beta = \frac{c}{a}$.

9). Always 2 roots.

10). $p = q = 0$.

11). $u = -3 (x = 1, 2)$ or $u = 7 (x = -4, -3)$.

Exercise 3C — (page 38)

1). a) $(x, y) = (3, 4), (-4, -3)$,
b) $(x, y) = (3, 4), (4, 3)$,
c) $(x, y) = (4, -3), (0, 5)$,
d) $(x, y) = (1, 0), (\frac{1}{2}, \frac{1}{2})$,
e) $(x, y) = (1, 3), (2, 5)$,
f) $(x, y) = (1, 5), (-\frac{11}{5}, -\frac{23}{5})$,
g) $(x, y) = (5, -2), (27, 42)$,
h) $(x, y) = (\frac{1}{2}, -1), (-\frac{13}{8}, -\frac{37}{20})$.

2). a) 2, b) 0, c) 2, d) 1, e) 0, f) 1.

3). $(x, y) = (1, 3), (\frac{6}{5}, \frac{12}{5})$.

4). a) $x = \pm 1, \pm 2$,   b) $x = \pm 1, \pm 3$,   c) $x = 2, -1$,   d) $x = \sqrt[3]{3}, -\sqrt[3]{4}$,   e) $x = 5, -2$,   f) $t = \frac{1}{2}, -3$,
g) $x = 3, -4$,   h) $t = 9$,   i) $x = 1, -\frac{8}{3}$,   j) $x = 5, -\frac{11}{3}$,   k) $x = \frac{1}{2}, -\frac{4}{11}$,   l) $y = \pm 1$,   m) $x = 16$,
n) $x = 9, 25$,   o) $t = 49$,   p) $x = 27, -8$,   q) $t = 64, -1$.
5). $x = \pm 1, \pm 3$.
6). $x = 1, -3, 2, -4$.
7). $x = 2, -\frac{1}{2}, 3, -\frac{1}{3}$.
8). $x = \pm \frac{1}{2}$.

Exercise 3D — (page 40)

1).   (a) 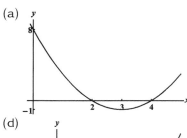   (b) 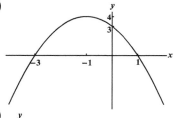   (c)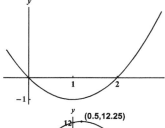

   (d) 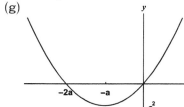   (e) 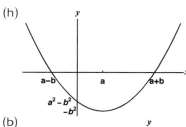   (f)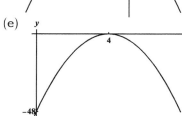

   (g) 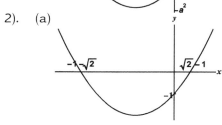   (h)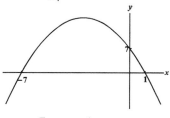

2).   (a)   (b)   (c)

$-1 - \sqrt{2} < x < \sqrt{2} - 1$ $x < -7$ or $x > 1$ Nowhere

3). a) $y = 3x^2 - 18x + 15$,   b) $y = 4x^2 - 20x - 56$,   c) $y = -\frac{1}{2}x^2 - 4x - 6$,   d) $y = 4x^2 - 8x + 7$,
e) $y = -x^2 + 6x - 2$.
4). $y = x^2 + 2x - 3$.
5).

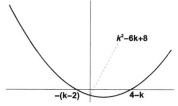

Exercise 3E — (page 42)

a) $x > 14$,   b) $x < 4$,   c) $x \le \frac{5}{2}$,   d) $x \ge 7$,   e) $x > -4$,   f) $x \le -\frac{16}{5}$,   g) $x < -\frac{7}{2}$,
h) $x \le -4$.
1). a) $x > 7$,   b) $x \le 22$,   c) $x \le -\frac{23}{2}$,   d) $x \le 6$,   e) $x \ge -\frac{11}{4}$,   f) $x > -2$,   g) $x < \frac{10}{3}$,
h) $x \ge -4$.
2). a) $x \ge -9$,   b) $x \ge 4$,   c) $x > 6$,   d) $x > \frac{9}{4}$,   e) $x \le \frac{6}{7}$,   f) $x \ge -1$,   g) $x < -\frac{3}{4}$,   h) $x > -3$,
i) $x \le -\frac{1}{4}$.
3). a) $x > \frac{11}{2}$,   b) $x < -3$,   c) $x \le 5$,   d) $x \le \frac{16}{9}$.

Exercise 3F — (page 45)

1). a) $2 < x < 3$,   b) $x < 4$ or $x > 7$,   c) $1 < x < 3$,   d) $x \le -10$ or $x \ge 4$,   e) $x < -3$ or $x > \frac{1}{2}$,
f) $-\frac{5}{3} \le x \le \frac{2}{3}$,   g) $x \le -2$ or $x \ge -\frac{5}{4}$,   h) $x < -3$ or $x > 1$,   i) $x < \frac{3}{2}$ or $x > 5$,   j) $-5 < x < 5$,   k) $-\frac{4}{3} < x < \frac{3}{4}$,   l) $x \le -\frac{2}{3}$ or $x \ge \frac{2}{3}$.

2). a) $x < -\frac{1}{2}(3+\sqrt{29})$ or $x > \frac{1}{2}(\sqrt{29}-3)$,   b) No solutions,   c) $\frac{1}{2}(5-\sqrt{17}) < x < \frac{1}{2}(5+\sqrt{17})$,   d) $\mathbb{R}$,
e) $x < -3$ or $x > 3$,   f) $x = -1$,   g) $\frac{1}{4}(3-\sqrt{17}) < x < \frac{1}{4}(3+\sqrt{17})$,   h) $-\frac{1}{2}(3+\sqrt{41}) < x < \frac{1}{2}(\sqrt{41}-3)$,
i) $x \le -\frac{1}{4}(7+\sqrt{41})$ or $x \ge \frac{1}{4}(\sqrt{41}-7)$,   j) $x < a$ or $x > b$,   k) $-a \le x \le b$,   l) $-\sqrt{ab} < x < \sqrt{ab}$.

3). a) $x < -3$ or $x > -2$,   b) $3 < x < 4$,   c) $-3 \le x \le 5$,   d) $x \le -3$ or $x \ge 3$,   e) $x \le 1$ or $x \ge \frac{3}{2}$,
f) $-\frac{2}{3} < x < \frac{3}{2}$,   g) $x < -\frac{1}{2}(5+\sqrt{17})$ or $x > \frac{1}{2}(\sqrt{17}-5)$,   h) $x < -\sqrt{\frac{7}{3}}$ or $x > \sqrt{\frac{7}{3}}$,   i) No solutions,
j) $\frac{1}{2}\left(-a-\sqrt{a^2+4b}\right) < x < \frac{1}{2}\left(-a+\sqrt{a^2+4b}\right)$,   k) $x < -\frac{3}{4}$ or $x > \frac{1}{3}$,   l) $\frac{1}{6}(7-\sqrt{37}) < x < \frac{1}{6}(7+\sqrt{37})$.

4). a) $x < 7$ or $x \ge 11$,   b) $-4 < x < 2$,   c) $\frac{5}{6} < x < \frac{3}{2}$,   d) $x \le \frac{7}{3}$ or $x > \frac{5}{2}$,   e) $x < -\frac{4}{7}$ or $x > -\frac{6}{13}$,
f) $-\frac{5}{6} < x < 0$.

5). $-3 < k < 3$.

6). $3 - \sqrt{8} < k < 3 + \sqrt{8}$.

7). $k < -\frac{2}{\sqrt{7}}$ or $k > \frac{2}{\sqrt{7}}$.

8). a) $x < 0$ or $2 < x < 5$,   b) $x \le \frac{1}{2}$ or $2 \le x < 4$,   c) $\frac{1}{2}(-1-\sqrt{37}) \le x \le 1$ or $\frac{1}{2}(-1+\sqrt{37}) \le x < 3$.

Review Exercises 1 — (page 47)

1). $\frac{5}{7}\sqrt{7}$.

2). 14 cm^2.

3). 18.

4). $\frac{13}{3} + \frac{40}{9}\sqrt{3}$.

5). $x^3 - x^{-3}$

6). $x = 4 + 3\sqrt{2}$, $y = -7 + 5\sqrt{2}$.

7). $\frac{1}{3a^2}$.

8). Two of the sides have gradients $-\frac{2}{3}$ and $\frac{3}{2}$.

9). a) AC, BC have gradients 5, $-\frac{1}{5}$,   b) $(\frac{18}{5}, 0)$.

10). a) $y = 3x - 9$,   b) $B(5,6)$, $D(3,0)$.

11). a) $AB = BC = CD = DA = 5\sqrt{2}$,   b) AB has gradient $\frac{1}{7}$, BC has gradient -1 — not perpendicular.

12). a) $4x - 3y = 13$,   b) $(4,1)$,   c) 5.

13). Two sides have length 13. The area is 78.

14). $3x - 4y = 1$.

15). $(\frac{7}{2}, 4)$, $D(4,3)$.

16). a) $x + 3y = 9$,   b) $(\frac{9}{10}, \frac{27}{10})$,   c) $\frac{3}{10}\sqrt{10}$.

17). Gradient between any two points is $\frac{4}{5}$.

18). $3x + 5y - 4 = 0$, $(\frac{4}{3}, 0)$.

19). $(\frac{7}{2}, -\frac{3}{2})$, -7, $x - 7y - 14 = 0$.

20). a) $A(-3,0)$, $B(0, \frac{3}{2})$,   b) $x - 2y + 3 = 0$,   c) $(\frac{9}{5}, \frac{12}{5})$.

21). $x - 2y - 8 = 0$, $(2,-3)$, $4\sqrt{5}$.

22). 25.

23). a) $x + y = 1$,   b) $B(2,-1)$, $D(0,1)$.

24). A line perpendicular to $y = m_1 x + c_1$ has gradient $-m_1^{-1} = m_2$, and so is parallel to $y = m_2 x + c_2$. Thus the two lines are perpendicular.

25). $x = 8, -1$.

26). $x = \frac{8}{7}$.

27). -2

28). $x = -\frac{5}{6}$.

29). $(x,y) = (3,-1), (-\frac{1}{3}, \frac{7}{3})$.

30). $k = \pm 8$.

31). $3 \le x \le 5$

32). a) $x = 2\sqrt{3}, 4\sqrt{3}$,   b) $x = \pm 1.86, \pm 2.63$. 34). $x^2 = \frac{1}{8}\left(4 \pm (\sqrt{2} + \sqrt{6})\right)$, so $x = \pm 0.991, \pm 0.131$.

35). $-1 < k < 6$

36). a) $\left(\frac{b}{a}, \frac{ac-b^2}{a}\right)$,　b) $c = \frac{b(b+1)}{a}$.

37). $-4 < x < 3$.

38). $-1 < x < 0$ or $x > 1$.

39). $-3 \le x \le 0$ or $x \ge 2$.

40). $x < -2$ or $x > \frac{2}{3}$.

41). $2(p_1 - p_2)x + 2(q_1 - q_2)y = p_1^2 - p_2^2 + q_1^2 - q_2^2$. This condition is the equation of the perpendicular bisector of AB.

42). a) $x = 2$,　b) $x = 2 \pm \sqrt{10}$.

43). $a = 1, b = 1, c = -2, d = -4$. $(x, y) = (1, 0), (-3, -4), (7, 12), (3, 8)$.

Exercise 4A — (page 54)

1).　(a)

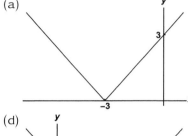

　(b)

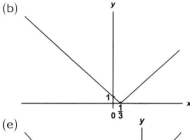

(c)

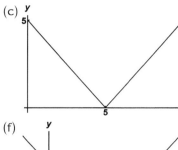

(d)

(e)

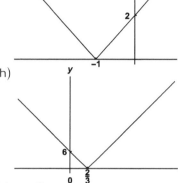

(f)

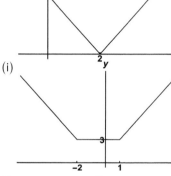

(g)

(h)

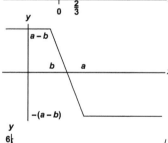

(i)

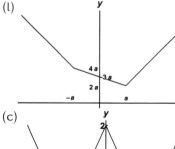

(j)

(k)

(l)

2).　(a)

　(b)

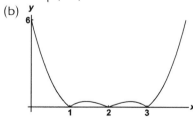

(c)

(d)

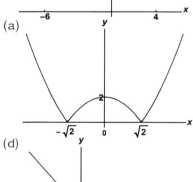

3). a) $2 \le x \le 4$,　b) $x < -\frac{5}{2}$ or $x > -\frac{3}{2}$,　c) $1.45 \le x \le 1.55$,　d) $x \le -\frac{5}{4}$ or $x \ge \frac{11}{4}$. 4). $-1 < x \le 6$.

5). $\left| |a| - |b| \right|$.

Exercise 4B — (page 58)

1). a) $x = -7, 3$, b) $x = -\frac{11}{3}, 3$, c) $x = 0, 3$, d) $x = \frac{2}{3}, 4$, e) $x = -2, \frac{1}{2}$, f) $x = -8, -2$, g) $x = -1$, h) $x = \pm 2$, i) $x = -\frac{1}{2}(1 + \sqrt{41}), 3$. 2). a) $-3 < x < -1$, b) $-5 < x < -2$, c) $x \le -\frac{10}{3}$ or $x \ge 2$, d) $x < -\frac{3}{4}$ or $x > \frac{1}{2}$, e) $x < -3$ or $x > -\frac{7}{3}$, f) $1 < x < 3$, g) $x \le -\frac{5}{3}$ or $x \ge 1$, h) $x > 5$, i) $\frac{1}{2}(1 - \sqrt{33}) < x < 2$. 3). a) $-1 \le x \le 1$, b) $x \ge 1$, c) $x \le -1$. 4). $x = \frac{1}{2}(9 - \sqrt{17}), 4$. 5). $x = -5, -\frac{5}{2}, \frac{5}{3}, \frac{15}{2}$. 6). $\frac{1}{2}\left[\sqrt{b^2 + 4a^2} - b\right] < x < \frac{1}{2}[\sqrt{b^2 + 4a^2} + b]$.

Exercise 5A — (page 63)

1). a) 3, b) 1, c) 4, d) 0, e) 1, f) 0. 2). a) $4x^2 + 7x + 6$, b) $5x^3 + 3x^2 - 6x - 3$, c) $8x^4 - 3x^3 + 7x^2 - 3x + 1$, d) $2x^5 + 2x^4 - 5x^2 + 3$, e) $-x^3 - 2x^2 - 5x + 4$. 3). a) $2x^2 + x - 8$, b) $3x^3 + 7x^2 - 8x + 9$, c) $-2x^4 - x^3 + 7x^2 + 3x - 3$, d) $2x^5 - 2x^4 - 6x^3 + 5x^2 + 1$, e) $-x^3 - 6x^2 + 9x + 2$. 4). a) $2x^3 - 3x^2 + 9x - 2$, b) $3x^3 - 7x^2 + 16x - 13$, c) $x^3 - 4x^2 + 7x - 11$, d) $3x^3 - 8x^2 + 17x - 17$. 5). a) $6x^2 - 7x - 3$, b) $x^3 + x^2 - 7x + 2$, c) $2x^3 + 5x^2 - 3x - 9$, d) $12x^3 - 13x^2 + 9x - 2$, e) $x^4 + 2x^3 - 2x^2 + 2x - 3$, f) $8x^4 - 6x^3 - 15x^2 + 18x - 5$, g) $x^4 + 5x^3 + 5x^2 + 3x + 18$, h) $x^5 - 5x^4 + 3x^3 + 10x^2 - 8x + 5$, i) $3 + 8x - 4x^2 + 13x^3 - 4x^4 + 4x^5$, j) $8 - 22x + 19x^2 - 3x^3 - 3x^4 + x^5$, k) $6x^3 + 29x^2 - 7x - 10$, l) $2x^5 - 7x^4 + 6x^3 - 10x^2 + 4x - 3$. 6). a) $0, 1$, b) $11, 1$, c) $3, 9$, d) $25, 8$, e) $20, 21$, f) $16, 13$, g) $17, 1$, h) $5, 11$, i) $5, 6$, j) $11, 8$. 7). a) $4, 1$, b) $2, 3$, c) $2, 1$, d) $3, 2$, e) $1, 2$, f) $2, 3$, g) $2, 3$, h) $2, 1$.

Exercise 5B — (page 65)

1). a) $1, 5, 22$, b) $1, 8, 11$, c) $3, 4, 0$, d) $3, 1, 4$, e) $4, 1, 4$, f) $7, 1, 8$. 2). a) $1, 3, 5, 2$, b) $1, 2, 4, 22$, c) $1, 1, 1, 3$, d) $4, 1, 3, 11$, e) $2, 7, 1, 0$, f) $3, 0, 5, 10$. 3). a) $2, 3, 4, 1, 2$, b) $4, 1, 0, 2, 3$, c) $3, 1, 1, 2, 0$, d) $1, 2, 5, 3, 2$.

Exercise 5C — (page 68)

1). a) $x - 2, -4$, b) $x + 1, -7$, c) $2x + 7, 13$, d) $x + 2, 3$, e) $2x - 1, -1$, f) $x, 0$. 2). a) $x^2 - 3, 7$, b) $x^2 + 2x + 15, 71$, c) $2x^2 - 6x + 22, -71$, d) $5x^2 + 20x + 77, 315$, e) $x^2 - x - 1, -6$, f) $2x^2 + 7x - 1, 3$. 3). a) $x^2 - 4x + 2, -x + 7$, b) $x^2 - 2x + 3, 2x + 5$, c) $2x - 6, 9x^2 + 4x + 11$, d) $3x^2 + 2x - 5, 30$.

Exercise 5D — (page 70)

1). a) 5, b) 13, c) 50, d) -355, e) $\frac{7}{8}$, f) $7\frac{13}{27}$, g) 0, h) 279. 2). -1. 3). -2. 4). -5. 5). 3. 6). $5, 3$. 7). $4, -3$. 8). $2, 1$. 9). $5, 3$. 10). a) $(x + 1)(x - 2)(x + 3)$, $-3, -1, 2$, b) $(x - 1)(x - 3)(x + 1)$, $-1, 1, 3$, c) $(x - 1)(x - 5)(x + 3)$, $-3, 1, 5$, d) $(x + 1)^2(x - 5)$, $-1, 5$, e) $(x - 2)(x + 2)(x + 3)$, $-3, -2, 2$, f) $(2x + 1)(x - 1)(x + 4)$, $-4, -\frac{1}{2}, 1$, g) $(3x - 1)(x - 2)(x + 2)$, $-2, \frac{1}{3}, 2$, h) $(x + 1)(2x - 1)(3x + 2)$, $-1, -\frac{2}{3}, \frac{1}{2}$, i) $(x - 1)(x^2 + 3x - 1)$, $1, \frac{1}{2}\left(-3 \pm \sqrt{13}\right)$. 11). a) $(x - 3)(x - 1)(x + 1)(x + 2)$, $-2, -1, 1, 3$, b) $(x - 2)(x + 1)(x + 2)(x + 3)$, $-3, -2, -1, 2$, c) $(x - 3)(x - 1)(x + 2)(2x + 1)$, $-2, -\frac{1}{2}, 1, 3$, d) $(x + 1)(x2)(2x + 1)(3x + 2)$, $1, \frac{2}{3}, -\frac{1}{2}, 2$, e) $(x - 1)^2(x + 1)$, $-1, 1$, f) $(x - 2)^2(2x + 1)^2$, $\frac{1}{2}, 2$. 12). a) $(x - 2)(x^2 + 2x + 4)$, b) $(x + 2)(x^2 - 2x + 4)$, c) $(x - a)(x^2 + ax + a^2)$, d) $(x + a)(x^2 - ax + a^2)$, e) $(x - a)(x + a)(x^2 + a^2)$, f) $(x + a)(x^4 - ax^3 + a^2x^2 - a^3x + a^4)$. 13). b) n must be odd, $x^{n-1} - ax^{n-2} + a^2x^{n-3} - + a^{n-1}$. 14). 7. 15). $-\frac{1}{24}$.

Exercise 6A — (page 76)

1). a) $2x - 4$, b) $3x + 2$, c) $x^2 - 3x + 6$, d) $\frac{1}{3x+2}$, e) $(x + 3)(x - 2)$, f) $\frac{1}{x^2+x+1}$. 2). a) 5, b) $\frac{1}{4}$, c) 1, d) -1, e) 1, f) $\frac{2}{3}$. 3). a) $x + 4$, b) $\frac{1}{x+7}$, c) $\frac{3x+2}{2x+1}$, d) $\frac{x+6}{x-3}$, e) $\frac{x+4}{x-4}$, f) $-\frac{2(4x+5)}{3x+1}$. 4). $\frac{5x}{12}$, b) $\frac{25x}{12}$, c) $\frac{1}{12}(7x + 11)$, d) $\frac{1}{15}(x - 7)$, e) $\frac{1}{4}(x^2 + 4x + 2)$, f) $\frac{1}{5}(13x + 14)$. 5). a) $\frac{3x+8}{4x}$, b) $\frac{5}{2x}$, c) $\frac{7}{12x}$, d) $\frac{3x-5}{2x}$, e) $-\frac{x^2-5x+2}{2x}$, f) $\frac{(x+1)^2}{x^2}$. 6). a) $\frac{2(3x+5)}{(x+1)(x+3)}$, b) $\frac{13x-1}{(x-2)(2x+1)}$, c) $\frac{2(x+5)}{(x+3)(x+4)}$, d) $\frac{5x+13}{(x-3)(x+1)}$, e) $\frac{22x+19}{(2x+3)(3x+1)}$, f) $\frac{2(13x-10)}{(5x-3)(2x+1)}$. 7). a) $\frac{4x+7}{(3x-1)(2x+1)}$, b) $-\frac{3}{2x(4x+1)}$, c) $\frac{x(8x+13)}{(x+2)(x+1)}$, d) $\frac{x(6x+17)}{(2x-1)(x+2)}$, e) $\frac{2x^2+6x+5}{(x+1)(x+2)}$, f) $\frac{x^2-2x+18}{(x+4)(x-2)}$. 8). a) $\frac{4x+5}{(x+1)(x+3)}$, b) $\frac{6x-1}{(x-1)(x+2)}$, c) $\frac{2(3x+1)}{x(x-3)}$, d) $-\frac{4x}{(x-2)(x+2)}$, e) $\frac{1}{x-3}$, f) $\frac{5}{2x-1}$. 9). a) 6, b) $3x$, c) $\frac{3(x+5)}{x+3}$, d) $\frac{x+3}{x+1}$, e) $\frac{2(x+1)}{x+3}$, f) $\frac{(2x+3)(3x-2)}{(2x-3)(3x+2)}$. 10). a) 2, b) $-\frac{1}{3}$, c) $\frac{x+4}{x+2}$, d) $\frac{(5x-1)(x+2)}{x-1}$, e) 1, f) -1. 11). $5, 10, 4$. 12). $x^2 - 9$. 13). a) $\frac{2(8x-3)}{(x+4)(x-3)}$, b) $\frac{7(x-11)}{(x+4)(x-3)}$. 14). a) $\frac{3}{x(x-1)(x-3)}$, b) $\frac{1}{(2x+1)(3x-1)}$.

Exercise 6B — (page 83)

1). a) $\frac{1}{x+5}+\frac{1}{x+3}$, b) $\frac{3}{x-1}+\frac{7}{x+5}$, c) $\frac{5}{x-5}-\frac{4}{x-4}$, d) $\frac{8}{2x-1}-\frac{4}{x+3}$. 2). a) $\frac{5}{x+2}+\frac{3}{x-1}$, b) $\frac{5}{x-4}-\frac{5}{x+1}$, c) $\frac{4}{x-3}+\frac{6}{x+3}$, d) $\frac{3}{x}-\frac{6}{2x+1}$. 3). a) $\frac{3}{x+2}-\frac{5}{x-1}+\frac{2}{x-3}$, b) $\frac{9}{x+3}-\frac{2}{x+1}+\frac{1}{x-1}$, c) $\frac{3}{x}+\frac{5}{x-6}+\frac{7}{x+4}$. 4). a) $\frac{3a}{x+2x}+\frac{a}{x-a}$, b) $\frac{1}{x+a}+\frac{1}{x-a}$, $\frac{1}{x+2a}+\frac{1}{x-a}-\frac{2}{x+a}$. 5). a) $\frac{2}{x-\sqrt{5}}-\frac{2}{x+\sqrt{5}}$, b) $\frac{1+\sqrt{3}}{x+2+\sqrt{3}}+\frac{1-\sqrt{3}}{x+2-\sqrt{3}}$, c) $\frac{1}{2\sqrt{10}}\left(\frac{1}{x+3-\sqrt{10}}-\frac{1}{x+3+\sqrt{10}}\right)$. 6). a) $\frac{1}{x-1}-\frac{1}{x-3}+\frac{2}{(x-3)^2}$, b) $\frac{5}{x+2}+\frac{2}{(x+2)^2}+\frac{1}{x-1}$, c) $\frac{3}{2x}-\frac{3}{2(x-2)}+\frac{3}{(x-2)^2}$, d) $\frac{2}{2x-1}-\frac{1}{x+1}-\frac{5}{(x+1)^2}$, e) $\frac{4}{x+1}+\frac{2}{x+2}+\frac{5}{(x+2)^2}$, f) $\frac{2}{2x-3}-\frac{5}{5x+2}+\frac{1}{(5x+2)^2}$. 7). a) $\frac{1}{x-1}+\frac{1}{x^2+1}$, quad b) $\frac{1}{x+1}-\frac{x}{x^2+4}$, c) $\frac{1}{x+3}+\frac{x-2}{x^2+4}$, d) $\frac{4}{2x-3}-\frac{x-4}{x^2+1}$, e) $\frac{1}{3x+2}-\frac{1}{x^2+16}$, f) $\frac{1}{1+4x}-\frac{1-4x}{4+x^2}$, g) $\frac{2}{1+2x}-\frac{2+x}{4+x^2}$, h) $\frac{2}{x}-\frac{x}{x^2+9}$, i) $\frac{3}{x+4}-\frac{6x+1}{2x^2+7}$. 8). $\frac{1}{3}\left(\frac{1}{x-1}-\frac{x+2}{x^2+x+1}\right)$. 9). $\frac{1}{x+1}-\frac{1}{x+2}$. 10). $\frac{1}{7}\left(\frac{1}{x-6}-\frac{1}{x+1}\right)$ and $\frac{1}{7}\left(\frac{6}{x-6}+\frac{1}{x+1}\right)$. 11). $A=1, B=2, C=-1, D=1, E=-1, F=4$.

Exercise 6C — (page 85)

1). a) $1+\frac{1}{x}$, b) $1-\frac{1}{x+1}$, c) $1+\frac{2}{x-1}$, d) $1+\frac{1}{x-1}-\frac{1}{x+1}$, e) $3+\frac{3}{2x-3}-\frac{2}{x-2}$, f) $4+\frac{1}{2x+5}-\frac{2}{3x+1}$. 2). a) $1-\frac{1}{x^2}+\frac{1}{x}-\frac{2}{x+1}$, b) $1+\frac{1}{x}-\frac{2}{x^2+1}$, c) $1-\frac{x-4}{x+4}+\frac{x-1}{x^2+1}$, d) $2+\frac{5}{x-2}-\frac{3}{(x+2)^2}$, e) $3+\frac{5}{x-2}-\frac{2}{x+2}-\frac{3}{2x-1}$, f) $-1+\frac{2}{x}+\frac{1}{2x-5}+\frac{3}{2x+5}$, g) $1+\frac{2}{x-1}-\frac{1}{x}-\frac{1}{x+1}$, h) $1+\frac{3}{x^2}-\frac{4}{x+2}$, i) $3-\frac{2}{x-1}+\frac{4}{4x^2+9}$. 3). $x+\frac{2}{3}\frac{a^2}{x+a}+\frac{1}{3}\frac{a^3-2a^2x}{x^2-ax+a^2}$.

Review Exercises 2 — (page 87)

1). $x<\frac{1}{2}$. 2). $-2\le x\le 3$. 3). The two curves meet at $(-10,8)$ and $(\frac{2}{3},\frac{8}{3})$, so the solution is $-10<x<\frac{2}{3}$. 4). $x<0$. 5). $x<-\frac{1}{3}$ or $x>\frac{1}{5}$. 6). $-a\le x\le a$. 7). a) $(0,3)$, $(-6,9)$, b) $x<-6$ or $x>0$. 8). $a=-3, b=1$. 9). 1. 10). $3x+4, 2x+3$. 11). $a=-1$, $b=-10$. 12). 6. 13). $-1, \frac{1}{2}, -t\frac{3}{2}$. 14). a) 2 b) $2, \sqrt{2}, -\sqrt{2}$. 15). $(x-3)(x^2+x+)$; one root only as the discriminant of the quadratic is negative; one point only, as the equation for the intersections is the given cubic. 16). $x^2+4x+6=(x+2)^2+2$. 17). x^2-3; x^2+x+2. 18). b) $p=-\sqrt{5}, q=\sqrt{5}$. 19). $4x+7$. 20). $x^2+2x+2, 0$. 21). a) $84, 0$; $x-2$ is not a factor of $p(x)$, but $x+2$ is, b) $-2, -\frac{3}{2}, \frac{1}{2}$. 22). a) -15, b) $(x+2)(x-5)(x+\sqrt{5})(x-\sqrt{5})$, c) $x<-\sqrt{5}, -2<x<\sqrt{5}, x>5$. 23). A $(-\sqrt{3},0)$, B $(\sqrt{3},0)$; $(x-2)(x+1)^2$, a) 2, b) They touch at $(-1,-2)$. 24). a) $f(1), f(-1)\ne 0$, b) $6x-4$, d) $1, 1-\sqrt{2}, 1+\sqrt{2}$. 25). $\frac{1}{x-3}-\frac{1}{x+1}$. 26). $\frac{1}{x+1}+\frac{1}{x-1}-\frac{2}{x}$. 27). $\frac{1}{x}+\frac{1}{x-1}+\frac{3}{(x-1)^2}$. 28). $\frac{1}{8}\left[\frac{19}{x+1}+\frac{20}{(x+1)^2}-\frac{49}{3x-1}\right]$. 29). $\frac{1}{x}+\frac{1}{x^2}-\frac{1}{x-3}$. 30). $\frac{3x-1}{4x-3}$. 31). $\frac{2x}{x^2-9}$. 32). $1+\frac{1}{3}\left[\frac{1}{2x-3}-\frac{6}{(2x-3)^2}-\frac{1}{2x+3}\right]$. 33). a) $\frac{1}{x}-\frac{x+1}{2x^2+3}$, b) $\frac{2}{x-1}+\frac{x-1}{3x^2+2}$. 34). $\frac{1}{20}\left[\frac{1}{x+2}-\frac{1}{x-2}\right]+\frac{1}{30}\left[\frac{1}{x-3}-\frac{1}{x+3}\right]$. 35). a) $A=2, B=-3, C=-11, D=6$, b) $a=-14$, c) $\frac{1}{5}\left[\frac{2}{2x-1}-\frac{1}{x+2}\right]$. 36). $\frac{1}{x-1}-\frac{1}{x+2}$ 37). b) $x<-\sqrt{a^2-1}, a-1<x<a$ or $x>a+1$, c) $-\sqrt{a^2-1}<x<a-1$ or $x>a+1$. 38). $|x|<\frac{1}{2}$ or $|x|>2$. 39). a) $x<1$ or $x>\frac{5}{3}$, b) $|x|<1$ or $|x|>\frac{5}{3}$, c) $x<\frac{3}{5}$ or $x>\frac{5}{3}$. 40). a) $a=, b=1, c=1, d=-2$, b) $(y+2)(x-2y+1)(x-3y+5)$. 41). $(k_1-1)(k_2-1)\cdots(k_n-1)=1-a_1+a_2+\cdots+(-1)^n a_n$; $-2, -6, -6, -8$.

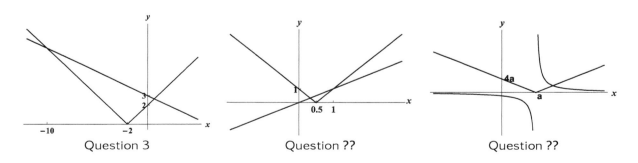

Question 3   Question ??   Question ??

Exercise 7A — (page 94)

1). a) 11, b) 5, c) -3, d) 0. 2). a) 50, b) 5, c) 29, d) 29. 3). a) 15, b) $5\frac{1}{4}$, c) 8, 0, d) 24, 0. 4). a) 17, b) 9, c) $g(5)=h(31)=125$, d) 33. 5). $n=4$. 6). $a=5, b=-3$. 7). a) $x\in\mathbb{R}, x\ge 0$, b) $x\in\mathbb{R}, x\le 0$, c) $x\in\mathbb{R}, x\ge 4$, d) $x\in\mathbb{R}, x\le 4$, e) $x\in\mathbb{R}, x\ge 4$ or $x\le 0$, f) $x\in\mathbb{R}, x\ge 4$ or $x\le 0$, g)

$x \in \mathbb{R}, x \le 3$ or $x \ge 4$, h) $x \in \mathbb{R}, x \ge 2$, i) $x \in \mathbb{R}, x \ne 2$, j) $x \in \mathbb{R}, x > 2$, k) $x \in \mathbb{R}, x \ge 0$, l) $x \in \mathbb{R}, x \ne 1, 2$. 8). a) $f(x) \in \mathbb{R}, f(x) > 7$, b) $f(x) \in \mathbb{R}, f(x) < 0$, c) $f(x) \in \mathbb{R}, f(x) > -1$, d) $f(x) \in \mathbb{R}, f(x) > -1$, e) $f(x) \in \mathbb{R}, f(x) > 3$, f) $f(x) \in \mathbb{R}, f(x) \ge 2$. 9). a) $f(x) \in \mathbb{R}, f(x) \ge 4$, b) $f(x) \in \mathbb{R}, f(x) \ge 10$, c) $f(x) \in \mathbb{R}, f(x) \ge 6$, d) $f(x) \in \mathbb{R}, f(x) \le 7$, e) $f(x) \in \mathbb{R}, f(x) \ge 2$, f) $f(x) \in \mathbb{R}, f(x) \ge -1$. 10). a) $f(x) \in \mathbb{R}, 0 \le f(x) \le 16$, b) $f(x) \in \mathbb{R}, -1 \le f(x) \le 7$, c) $f(x) \in \mathbb{R}, 0 \le f(x) \le 16$, d) $f(x) \in \mathbb{R}, 4 \le f(x) \le 25$. 11). a) $f(x) \in \mathbb{R}, f(x) \ge 0$, b) $\mathbb{R}$, c) $f(x) \in \mathbb{R}, f(x) \ne 0$, d) $f(x) \in \mathbb{R}, f(x) > 0$, e) $f(x) \in \mathbb{R}, f(x) \ge 5$, f) $\mathbb{R}$, g) $f(x) \in \mathbb{R}, 0 \le f(x) \le 2$, h) $f(x) \in \mathbb{R}, f(x) \ge 0$. 12). $A = w(12 - w) = 36 - (6 - w)^2$ for $w \in \mathbb{R}, 0 < w < 12$. 13). $V = x(22 - 2x)(8 - 2x)$ for $x \in \mathbb{R}, 0 < x < 4$.

Exercise 7B — (page 101)

1).

2).

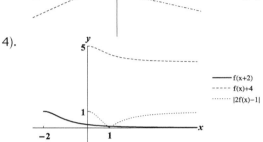

3).

4).

5).

6). a)

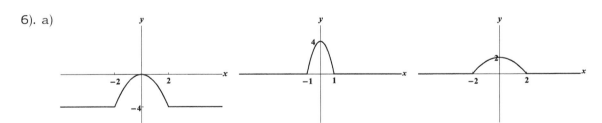

b)

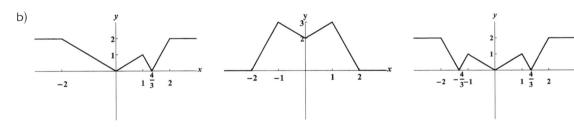

c)

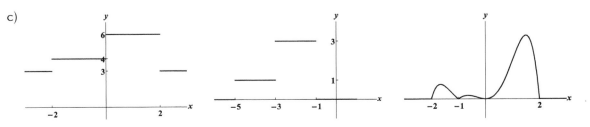

d)

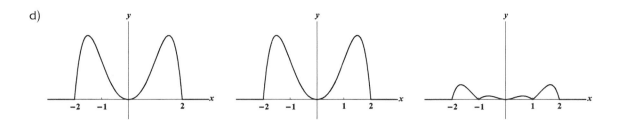

7). a) $y = f\left(\frac{1}{2}x - 1\right)$,   b) $y = f\left(\frac{1}{2}x + \frac{1}{2}\right)$.   8). $y = a\left(x + \frac{b}{2a}\right)^2 + \frac{4ac-b^2}{4a}$: horizontal translation by $-\frac{b}{2a}$, then vertical stretch, factor a, then vertical translation by $\frac{4ac-b^2}{4a}$.   9). First a horizontal stretch, factor $\frac{1}{2}$ ($y = 8x^3 - 6x$), then a horizontal translation by -1 ($y = 8x^3 + 24x^2 + 18x + 2$) then a vertical translation by -2.

Exercise 7C — (page 103)

1). a) $\mathbb{R}$,   b) $y \in \mathbb{R}, 5 \leq y \leq 50$,   c) $y \in \mathbb{R}, 1 \leq y \leq 26$.   2). a) $y \in \mathbb{R}, y \neq 1$,   b) $y \in \mathbb{R}, y < 1$,   c) $y \in \mathbb{R}, 0 \leq y \leq \frac{1}{2}$.   3). $y \in \mathbb{R}, -3 \leq y \leq 1$ or $y = -4$.   4). a) $y \in \mathbb{R}, -2 \leq y \leq 5$,   b) $y \in \mathbb{R}, -6 \leq y \leq 15$,   c) $y \in \mathbb{R}, 0 \leq y \leq 5$,   d) $y \in \mathbb{R}, -2 \leq y \leq 5$.   5). $\{0, 1, 2, 3, 4, 5, 6, 7, 8, 9, 10, 11, 12, 13, 14, 15\}$.   6). $y \in \mathbb{R}, y \leq \frac{1}{4}$.   7). $y \in \mathbb{R}, y \neq \frac{a}{c}$.   8). $y \in \mathbb{R}, y \geq \frac{1}{4a}[4ac - b^2]$.   9). $y \in \mathbb{R}, 0 \leq y \leq 2a$.

Exercise 7D — (page 108)

1). a) 4,   b) -14,   c) -9,   d) 33,   e) 23,   f) -17,   g) 16,   h) 0.   2). a) 49,   b) 59,   c) 35,   d) $\frac{1}{16}$,   e) 9,   f) 899.   3). a) 5,   b) -19,   c) 1,   d) $\frac{1}{2}$,   e) $\frac{1}{2}$,   f) -1,   g) $3\frac{2}{3}$,   h) 2.   4). a) $fg(x) = 2x^2 + 5$,   b) $gf(x) = 4x^2 + 20x + 25$,   c) $fh(x) = \frac{2+5x}{x}$,   d) $hf(x) = \frac{1}{2x+5}$,   e) $ff(x) = 4x + 15$,   f) $hh(x) = x$,   g) $gfh(x) = \left(\frac{2+5x}{x}\right)^2$,   h) $hgf(x) = \frac{1}{4x^2+20x+25}$.   5). a) $hf(x) == \sin x° - 3$,   b) $fh(x) = \sin(x - 3)°$,   c) $fhg(x) = \sin\left(\frac{3}{x} - 3\right)°$,   d) $fg(x) = \sin(x^3)°$,   e) $hhh(x) = x - 9$,   f) $gf(x) = \left(\sin x°\right)^3 = \sin^3 x°$.   6). a) fh,   b) fg,   c) hh,   d) hg,   e) gf,   f) $gffh$,   g) $ffffgg$,   h) hf,   i) $hffg$.   7). a) $a = 4, -\frac{8}{3}$,   b) $b = 7$,   c) $c = 1$.   8). $a = 3, = -7$ or $a = -3, b = 14$.   9). $a = 4, b = 11$ or $a = \frac{9}{2}, b = 10$.   11). $\frac{1}{4}\sqrt{2}$.   12). $f^{(2015)}(x) = \frac{1}{1-x}$.

Exercise 7E — (page 112)

1). a) Yes,   b) No,   c) No,   d) Yes,   e) No,   f) Yes,   g) Yes,   h) No,   i) No,   j) No,   k) Yes,   l) No.   2). a) Yes,   b) No,   c) Yes,   d) No,   e) Yes,   f) Yes,   g) Yes,   h) Yes,   i) No,   j) Yes.   3). a) 0,   b) -1,   c) $\frac{2}{3}$,   d) 4,   e) -5,   f) -1,   g) $\frac{3}{2}$,   h) 1,   i) 4.   4). a): Monotonic: No, 1-1: No,   b) Monotonic: Yes, 1-1: Yes,   c) Monotonic: No, 1-1: Yes,   d) Monotonic: Yes, 1-1: Yes,   e) Monotonic: No, 1-1: Yes,   f) Monotonic: No, 1-1: No,   g) Monotonic: No, 1-1: No,   h) Monotonic: Yes, 1-1: Yes,   i) Monotonic: No, 1-1: No,   j) Monotonic: Yes, 1-1: Yes,   k) Monotonic: No, 1-1: No,   l) ; Monotonic: Yes, 1-1: No.   5). $x_+x_- = 1$. Since $x_+ > 1$ for $0 < y < \frac{1}{2}$, $x_- < 1$.

Exercise 7F — (page 115)

1). a) $f^{-1}(x) = x - 4$,   b) $f^{-1}(x) = x + 5$,   c) $f^{-1}(x) = \frac{1}{2}x$,   d) $f^{-1}(x) = 4x$,   e) $f^{-1}x = \sqrt[3]{x}$,   f) $f^{-1}(x) = x^5$.   2). a) 10,   b) 7,   c) 3,   d) 5,   e) -4.   3). a) 4,   b) 20,   c) $\frac{7}{5}$,   d) 15,   e) -6.   4). a) 8,   b) $\frac{1}{8}$,   c) 512,   d) -27,   e) 5.   5). a) $f^{-1}(x) = \frac{1}{3}(x + 1)$, $x \in \mathbb{R}$,   b) $f^{-1}(x) = 2x - 8$, $x \in \mathbb{R}$,   c) $f^{-1}(x) = \sqrt[3]{x - 5}$,   d) $f^{-1}(x) = (x + 3)^2$, $x \geq -3$,   e) $f^{-1}(x) = \frac{1}{5}(2x + 3)$, $x \in \mathbb{R}$,   f) $f^{-1}(x) = \sqrt{x - 6} + 1$, $x \in \mathbb{R}, x \geq 6$.   6). a) $f^{-1}(x) = \frac{1}{4}x$, $x \in \mathbb{R}$,   b) $f^{-1}(x) = x - 3$, $x \in \mathbb{R}$,   c) $f^{-1}(x) = x^2$, $x \in \mathbb{R}, x \geq 0$,   d) $f^{-1}(x) = \frac{1}{2}(x - 1)$, $x \in \mathbb{R}$,   e) $f^{-1}(x) = 2 + \sqrt{x}$, $x \in \mathbb{R}, x \geq 0$,   f) $f^{-1}(x) = \frac{1}{3}(1 - x)$, $x \in \mathbb{R}$,   g) $f^{-1}(x) = \frac{3}{x}$, $x \in \mathbb{R}, x \neq 0$,   h) $f^{-1}(x) = 7 - x$, $x \in \mathbb{R}$.

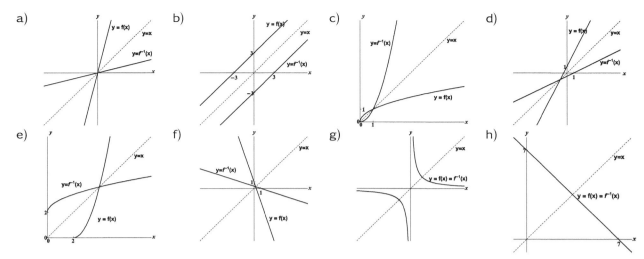

7). a) $f^{-1}(x) = \frac{2x}{x-1}$, $x \in \mathbb{R}, x \neq 1$, b) $f^{-1}(x) = \frac{4x+1}{x-2}$, $x \in \mathbb{R}, x \neq 2$, c) $f^{-1}(x) = \frac{5x+2}{x-1}$, $x \in \mathbb{R}, x \neq 1$, d) $f^{-1}(x) = \frac{3x-11}{4x-3}$, $x \in \mathbb{R}, x \neq \frac{3}{4}$. 8). a) $x \in \mathbb{R}, x > -1$, b) $f^{-1}(x) = 2 + \sqrt{x+1}$, $x \in \mathbb{R}, x > -1$ has range $x \in \mathbb{R}, x > 2$. 9). a) $x \in \mathbb{R}, x > 3$, b) $f^{-1}(x) = (x-3)^2 + 2 = X^2 - 6x + 11$, $x \in \mathbb{R}, x > 3$ has range $x \in \mathbb{R}, x > 2$, c) $x = \frac{1}{2}[7 \pm \sqrt{5}]$. 10). The greatest value of k is -1, a) $x \in \mathbb{R}, x \geq 5$, b) $f^{-1}(x) = -\sqrt{x-5} - 1$, $x \in \mathbb{R}, x \geq 5$ has range $x \in \mathbb{R}, x \leq -1$. 11). $f^{-1}(x) = \frac{1}{2}(x-1), g^{-1}(x) = \frac{1}{4}(x+3), gf(x) = 8x+1, (gf)^{-1}(x) = \frac{1}{8}(x-1)$, $f^{-1}g^{-1}(x) = \frac{1}{8}(x-1)$. 12). $p = 7, q = -15$. 15). a) f is constant. 16). $4p + q^2 < 0$.

9).c):   11)c):

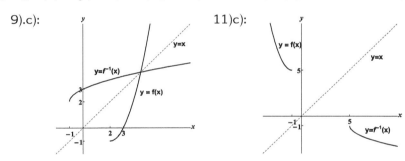

Exercise 8A — (page 123)

1). a) $x^2 + y^2 - 2x + 6y - 90 = 0$, b) $x^2 + y^2 + 4x + 4y + 7 = 0$, c) $x^2 + y^2 - 4y = 0$, d) $x^2 + y^2 + 6x = 0$, e) $x^2 + y^2 - 2ax = 0$, f) $x^2 + y^2 - 2ax - 2by + b^2 = 0$. 2). a) $(3,2)$, 4, b) $(7,0)$, 2, c) $(0,0)$, $\sqrt{10}$, d) $(-10,-10)$, $10\sqrt{2}$, e) $(-4,-1)$, 6, f) $(-\frac{3}{2},\frac{7}{2})$, 3, g) $(-\frac{3}{2},2)$, $\frac{5}{2}$, h) $(1,0)$, 2, i) $(0,-b),b$, j) $(-\frac{1}{2}a,-\frac{1}{2}b)$, $\frac{3}{2}\sqrt{a^2+b^2}$. 3). a) $k < 20$, b) $k > -\frac{5}{4}a^2$, c) $|k| > 1$, d) $k < -\frac{1}{5}$ or $k > 0$. 4). $x^2 + y^2 - 4x + 6y - 52 = 0$. 5). $x^2 + y^2 - 10x - 2y + 1 = 0$. 6). $x^2 + y^2 - 6x - 10y + 25 = 0$. 7). $x^2 + y^2 - 4x - 14y + \frac{81}{2} = 0$. 8). The angle in a semicircle is a right angle. 9). $x^2 + y^2 - 16x - 10y + 39 = 0$. 10). $\left(x - \frac{3}{4}\right)^2 + \left(y - \frac{17}{4}\right)^2 = \frac{25}{8}$. 11). The circles have radii $\sqrt{11}$ and $\sqrt{23}$, and their centres are $\sqrt{34}$ apart. Use Pythagoras' Theorem. 12). $(x-5)^2 + y^2 = 16$. A circle, centre $(5,0)$, radius 4. 13). $x + 3y - 7 = 0$. 14). $-\frac{2}{a}$. Angles on the same arc are equal.

Exercise 8B — (page 127)

1). a) $\frac{1}{2}\pi$, b) $\frac{3}{4}\pi$, c) $\frac{1}{4}\pi$, d) $\frac{1}{6}\pi$, e) $\frac{2}{5}\pi$, f) $\frac{1}{10}\pi$, g) $\frac{2}{3}\pi$, h) $\frac{1}{8}\pi$, i) $\frac{1}{9}\pi$, j) $\frac{5}{12}\pi$, k) $\frac{5}{9}\pi$, l) $\frac{1}{180}\pi$. 2). a) $60°$, b) $9°$, c) $36°$, d) $67.5°$, e) $40°$, f) $144°$, g) $112.5°$, h) $108°$, i) $4°$, j) $270°$, k) $15°$, l) $50°$. 3). a) $\frac{1}{2}\sqrt{3}$, b) $\frac{1}{\sqrt{2}}$, c) $\frac{1}{\sqrt{3}}$, d) $-\frac{1}{2}$, e) $\frac{1}{\sqrt{2}}$, f) $-\frac{1}{2}\sqrt{3}$, g) $\sqrt{3}$, h) $\frac{1}{2}\sqrt{3}$.

Exercise 8C — (page 131)

1). a) $C = 1.32$, b) $C = 2.12$, c) $B = 2.16$, d) $B = C = 1.47$. 2). a) $b = 18.96$ cm, $c = 11.1$ cm, b) $b = 3.04$ cm, $c = 4.28$ cm, c) $a = 29.6$ cm, $c = 26.8$ cm, d) $a = 3.83$ cm, $b = 6.84$ cm.

3). a) 10.2 cm, b); 4.45 cm, c) 19.9 cm. 4). a) 42.5 cm^2, b) 6.16 cm^2, c) 67.1 cm^2, d) 8.84 cm^2. 5). a) $BC = \sqrt{2x^2(1-\cos 2\theta)} = 2x\sin\theta$, b) $\frac{1}{2}x^2 \sin 2\theta = \frac{1}{2} \times 2x\sin\theta \times x\cos\theta$. 6). $\sqrt{440} = 21.0$ cm^2. 7). $81 = AC^2 = AM^2 + 16 - 8AM\cos\theta$, $25 = AB^2 = AM^2 + 16 + 8AM\cos\theta$, $AM = \sqrt{37} = 6.08$ cm. 8). $\frac{7}{4}$. 9). The length of any one side must be less than the sum of the other two sides: otherwise the triangle is not constructible. $a < b + c \Rightarrow \frac{b^2+c^2-a^2}{2bc} > -1$, $a > |b - c| \Rightarrow \frac{b^2+c^2-a^2}{2bc} < 1$. 10). d) The length of any one side is less than the sum of the lengths of the other two sides.

Exercise 8D — (page 133)

1). a) $s = 8.4$, $A = 29.4$, b) $s = 7.35$, $A = 12.8625$, c) $\theta = 1.5$, $A = 48$, d) $r = 20$, $A = 140$, e) $\theta = 2.4$, $s = 12$, f) $r = 8$, $\theta = 2$, g) 8, h) $\frac{5}{3}$. 2). a) 2.26 cm^2, b) 1.47 cm^2, c) 830 cm^2, d) 9.05 cm^2, e) 0.556 cm^2. 3). 6.72 cm^2. 4). 28.2 cm. 5). 25 cm^2. 7). 26.3 cm^2. 8). 15.5 cm, 14.3 cm^2. 9). a) $1.61r$, b) $0.315r$. 10). a) 21.9 cm, b) 16.8 cm^2. 11). a) 15.7 cm, b) 4.03 cm^2. 12). b) $\frac{1}{2}\pi r^2$.

Exercise 9A — (page 139)

1). a) $7, 14, 21, 28, 35$ b) $13, 8, 3, -2, -7$ c) $4, 12, 36, 108, 324$ d) $6, 3, \frac{3}{2}, \frac{3}{4}, \frac{3}{8}$ e) $2, 7, 22, 67, 202$ f) $1, 4, 19, 364, 132499$. 2). a) $u_r = u_{r-1} + 2$, $u_1 = 2$, b) $u_r = u_{r-1} - 2$, $u_1 = 11$, c) $u_r = u_{r-1} + 4$, $u_1 = 2$, d) $u_r = 3u_{r-1}$, $u_1 = 2$, e) $u_r = \frac{1}{3}u_{r-1}$, $u_1 = \frac{1}{3}$, f) $u_r = \frac{1}{2}u_{r-1}$, $u_1 = \frac{1}{2}a$, g) $u_r = u_{r-1} + c$, $u_1 = b - 2c$, h) $u_r = -u_{r-1}$, $u_1 = 1$, i) $u_r = qu_{r-1}$, $u_1 = \frac{p}{q^3}$, j) $u_r = \frac{b}{a}u_{r-1}$, $u_1 = \frac{a^3}{b^2}$, k) $u_r = \frac{5}{x}u_{r-1}$, $u_1 = x^3$, l) $u_r = (1+x)u_{r-1}$, $u_1 = 1$. 3). a) $5, 7, 9, 11, 13$; $u_r = u_{r-1} + 2$, $u_1 = 5$, b) $1, 4, 9, 16, 25$; $u_r = u_{r-1} + 2r - 1$, $u_1 = 1$, c) $1, 3, 6, 10, 15$; $u_r = u_{r-1} + r$, $u_1 = 1$, d) $1, 5, 14, 30, 55$; $u_r = u_{r-1} + r^2$, $u_1 = 1$, e) $6, 18, 54, 162, 486$; $u_r = 3u_{r-1}$, $u_1 = 6$, f) $3, 15, 75, 375, 1875$; $u_r = 5u_{r-1}$, $u_1 = 3$. 4). a) $10 - r$, b) 2×3^r, c) $r^2 + 3$, d) $2r(r+1)$, e) $\frac{2r-1}{r+3}$, f) $\frac{r^2+1}{2^r}$. 5). a) $3, 7, 47, 2207, 4870847$, b) $2, 2, 2, 2, 2$, c) $0, 6, 6, 6, 6$, d) $1, 2, 4, 8, 16$, e) $2, 4, 6, 10, 16$, f) $2, 8, \frac{1}{4}, \frac{1}{32}, \frac{1}{8}$, g) $2, 4, 8, 32, 256$, h) $2, -4, -40, -3280, -21523360$. 6). $1, 3, 3$. 7). $-1, 2, 756$. 8). $4, 4, 0$. 11). a) $2, -1$, b) $5, -3$, c) $2, 0$, d) $0, 1$, e) $-1, 7$, f) $4, -4$. 12). a) $a^2 = 9$, b) $u_r = 3u_{r-1} + u_{r-2}$, $u_r = -3u_{r-1} + 13u_{r-2}$. 15). $2, -3, -\frac{1}{2}, -\frac{1}{2}$; $u_2 = 0$, $u_3 = 1$, u_4 undefined. 16). $(-1)^{r-1}$. 17). b) $4^r - 3^r$.

Exercise 9B — (page 143)

1). a) Divergent, b) Convergent to 0, c) Convergent to 1, d) Divergent, e) Convergent to 2, f) Divergent, g) Convergent to 0, h) Convergent to 0, i) Convergent to 0, j) Convergent to 0, k) Convergent to 1, l) Convergent to 1. 3). a) Divergent, b) Divergent, c) Convergent to 2, d) Divergent, e) Divergent, f) Convergent to 0. 4). a) Not periodic, b) Periodic of period 2, c) Periodic of period 1 (constant), d) Not periodic, e) Periodic of period 3, f) Not periodic. 5). a) The first nine terms are $32, 16, 8, 4, 2, 1, 4, 2, 1, \ldots$, after which the sequence is periodic of period 3, b) The first eleven terms of the sequence are $3, 10, 5, 16, 8, 4, 2, 1, 4, 2, 1, \ldots$, after which the sequence is periodic of period 3, c) The first twenty terms are $7, 22, 11, 34, 17, 52, 26, 13, 40, 20, 10, 5, 16, 8, 4, 2, 1, 4, 2, 1, \ldots$, after which the sequence is periodic of period 3, d) The first twenty four terms are $19, 58, 29, 88, 44, 22, 11, 34, 17, 52, 26, 13, 40, 20, 10, 5, 16, 8, 4, 2, 1, 4, 2, 1, \ldots$ 7). b) Each error is smaller than the square of the previous error, and the first error is less than 1. 8). a) $\alpha = 2 + \alpha^{-1}$ implies $\alpha^2 - 2\alpha - 1 = 0$; $\alpha = 1 + \sqrt{2}$, b) Yes.

Exercise 9C — (page 147)

1). a) 100, b) -28, c) $\frac{363}{140}$, d) 210, e) 1360, f) 40, g) 256, h) $\frac{4}{5}$, i) 112. 2). a) $0 + 3 + 6 + 12 + 20$, b) $4 - 8 + 16 - 32$, c) $\sqrt{1} + \sqrt{2} + \sqrt{3} + \sqrt{4} + \sqrt{5} + \sqrt{6}$, d) $1 + 0 + 1 + 2$, e) $\sin\frac{1}{5}\pi + \sin\frac{2}{5}\pi + \sin\frac{3}{5}\pi + \sin\frac{4}{5}\pi$, f) $\frac{1}{5} + \frac{1}{10} + \frac{1}{17}$. 3). a) $\sum_{r=1}^{5} r^2$, b) $\sum_{r=1}^{6} (-1)^{r-1} r^2$, c) $\sum_{r=7}^{12} r^3$,

d) $\displaystyle\sum_{r=1}^{10} r(r+2)$, e) $\displaystyle\sum_{r=0}^{11} (-1)^r(2r+1)$, f) $\displaystyle\sum_{r=0}^{10} 2^r$, g) $\displaystyle\sum_{r=1}^{100} \frac{r}{r+1}$, h) $\displaystyle\sum_{r=1}^{7} (-1)^{r-1}\frac{r}{2^r}$, i) $\displaystyle\sum_{r=3}^{n} r^2$, j)

$\displaystyle\sum_{r=1}^{n} (r^2-1)$, k) $\displaystyle\sum_{r=1}^{n} \frac{r}{r^2+1}$, l) $\displaystyle\sum_{r=2}^{8} \frac{4r-5}{2^r}$. 4). $r(r+5)$. 5). r^4. 6). a) This follows from adding up the

terms in a different order, b) $\frac{1}{2}n(3n+7)$, d) $(-1)^{2s-1}(2s-1)+(-1)^s(2s)=1$ for each $1\le s\le n$.
7). 0.

Exercise 9D — (page 151)

1). a) Yes, 3, b) No, c) No, d) Yes, -2, e) No, f) Yes, q, g) No, h) Yes, x. 2). a)
$12, 2r$, b) $32, 14+3r$, c) $-10, 8-3r$, d) $3.3, 0.9+0.4r$, e) $\frac{7}{2}, \frac{1}{2}(r+1)$, f) $43, 79-6r$, g)
$x+10, x+2(r-1)$, h) $1+4x, 1+(r-2)x$. 3). a) 14, b) 88, c) 36, d) 11, e) 11, f) 11,
g) 16, h) 28. 4). a) 610, b) 795, c) -102, d) 855.5, e) -1025, f) 998001, g);
$3160a$, h) $-15150p$. 5). a) $54, 3132$, b) $20, 920$, c) $46, 6532$, d) $28, -910$, e) $28, 1120$,
f) $125, 42875$, g) $1000, 50050000$, h) $61, -988.2$. 6). a) $a=3, d=4$, b) $a=2, d=5$, c)
$a=1.4, d=0.3$, d) $a=12, d=-\frac{5}{2}$, e) $a=25, d=-3$, f) $a=-7, d=2$, g) $a=3x, d=-x$,
h) $a=p+1, d=\frac{1}{2}p+3$. 7). a) 20, b) 12, c) 16, d) 40, e) 96, f) 28. 8). a) 62, b)
25th. 9). a) £76, b) £1272. 10). £1626000. 11). $\frac{1}{2}$. 12). 3,4. 13). 1. 14). a) $\frac{1}{2}n(3n+1)$,
b) $(n^2-n+1)(n^2+n+3)$, c) $6n^2-7n+2$. 15). $n=10$. 16). 3 or -3. 17). Either $-2b, b, 4b$ for
$b>0$ or $4b, b, -2b$ for $b<0$.

Exercise 9E — (page 157)

1). a) $2, 24, 48$, b) $4, 128, 512$, c) $\frac{1}{2}, 4, 2$, d) $-3, 162, -486$, e) $1.1, 1.4641.1.61051$, f)
x^{-1}, x^{-1}, x^{-2}. 2). a) $2\times3^{n-1}$, b) $5\times2^{2-n}$, c) $(-2)^{n-1}$, d) 3^{5-n}, e) x^n, f) $p^{2-n}q^{n+1}$. 3). a)
11, b) 13, c) 7, d) 14, e) 6, f) 13. 4). a) $3, \frac{4}{3}$, b) $2, \frac{3}{2}$ or $-2, \frac{3}{2}$, c) $\frac{1}{3}, 531441$,
d) $\sqrt{2}, 4$ or $-\sqrt{2}, 4$, e) $7, 16807\times7^{1-n}$ or $-7, 16807\times(-7)^{1-n}$. 5). a) 59048, b) -29524, c)
1.9922, d) 0.6641, e) 12285, f) 8.9998, g) $\frac{x(1-x^n)}{1-x}$, h) $\frac{x(1-(-x)^n)}{1+x}$, i) $\frac{x^{2n}-1}{x^{2n-3}(x^2-1)}$, j)
$\frac{x^{2n}-(-1)^n}{x^{2n-2}(x^2+1)}$. 6). a) 2047, b) 683, c) 262143, d) $\frac{1023}{512}$, e) $\frac{14762}{19683}$, f) $\frac{635}{32}$, g) $\frac{341}{1024}$, h)
$2-2^{-n}$, i) $\frac{1}{3}(64-4^{-n})$, j) $\frac{1}{4}(243+(-3)^{-n})$. 7). £2684354.55. 9). a) 2, b) 8th. 10). a)
3, b) 14th. 11). $2, 3$ or $-\frac{4}{3}, -2$, 12). $3, 7$ or $-3, -14$. 13). 2. 14). $\sqrt{\frac{3}{2}}$. 15). 2. 16). $8; 24, 12, 6$,
$\frac{1}{2}(3\sqrt2+4); \frac{3}{2}(3\sqrt2+4), \frac{3}{2}\sqrt2, \frac{3}{2}(3\sqrt2-4)$, or $-\frac{1}{2}(3\sqrt2-4); -\frac{3}{2}(3\sqrt2-4), -\frac{3}{2}\sqrt2, -\frac{3}{2}(3\sqrt2+4)$. 17). $\pm2, \pm\frac{1}{2}$.
18). a) $\frac{p}{q}, n$, c)i. n, ii. S_n converges to n as r tends to 1, iii. $-n$.

Exercise 9E — (page 157)

1). a) 2, b) $\frac{3}{2}$, c) $\frac{1}{4}$, d) $\frac{1}{9}$, e) $\frac{3}{4}$, f) $\frac{1}{6}$, g) 3, h) $\frac{1}{3}$, i) $\frac{20}{3}$, j) $62\frac{1}{2}$, k) $\frac{x}{1-x}$, l)
$\frac{1}{1+x^2}$, m) $\frac{x}{x-1}$, n) $\frac{x^3}{x+1}$. 2). a) $\frac{4}{11}$, b) $\frac{41}{333}$, c) $\frac{5}{9}$, d) $\frac{157}{333}$, e) $\frac{1}{7}$, f) $\frac{2}{7}$, g) $\frac{5}{7}$, h) $\frac{13}{70}$.
3). a) $\frac{1}{6}$, b) $-\frac{5}{6}$. 4). a) 3, b) $19\frac{1}{5}$. 5). $\frac{2}{3}$ m east of O, 2 m. 6). 10 seconds. 7). 19 m. 8). 8.

9). $1<a<3, -1$. 10). b equals d when $a=c$. 11). $-\frac{1}{2}, \frac{2}{3}u_1$. 12). $\frac{1}{2}(\sqrt5-1)$, $a\left[1-\left(\frac{\sqrt5-1}{2}\right)^{\frac{1}{m}}\right]^{-1}$, 5.

13). $\frac{x}{(1-x)^2}$.

Review Exercises 3 — (page 165)

1). a) gf, b) ff, c) g^{-1}, d) fhg, e) hfg, f) f^{-1}, g) $g^{-1}fhg$, h) hf^{-1}. 2). $1\pm\sqrt3$.
3). $k=1$, $f^{-1}(x)=1-\sqrt{x+6}$, $x\ge6$. 4). $a=2, b=-13$ or $a=-2, b=11$. 5). a)
$f^{-1}(x)=\frac{1}{4}(x-5)$, $x\in\mathbb{R}$, b) $g^{-1}(x)=\frac{1}{2}(3-x)$, $x\in\mathbb{R}$, c) $f^{-1}g^{-1}(x)=-\frac{1}{8}(x+7)$, $x\in\mathbb{R}$, d)
$gf(x)=-8x-7$, $x\in\mathbb{R}$, e) $(gf)^{-1}(x)=-\frac{1}{8}(x+7)$, $x\in\mathbb{R}$. 6). a) $f^{-1}(x)=\frac{1}{2}(x-7)$, $x\in\mathbb{R}$, b)
$g^{-1}(x)=\sqrt[3]{x+1}$, $x\in\mathbb{R}$, c) $g^{-1}f^{-1}(x)=\sqrt[3]{\frac{1}{2}(x-5)}$, $x\in\mathbb{R}$, d) $f^{-1}g^{-1}(x)=\frac{1}{2}\left(\sqrt[3]{x+1}-7\right)$,
e) $fg(x)=2x^3+5$, $x\in\mathbb{R}$, f) $gf(x)=(2x+7)^3-1$, $x\in\mathbb{R}$, g) $(fg)^{-1}(x)=\sqrt[3]{\frac{1}{2}(x-5)}$, $x\in\mathbb{R}$,

h) $\frac{1}{2}\left(\sqrt[3]{x+1}-7\right)$. 7). a) 3, b) 7, c) 3, d) 7. 8). a) x, $x \neq \frac{1}{2}$, b) $\frac{x+5}{2x-1}$, $x \neq \frac{1}{2}$, c) x, $x \neq \frac{1}{2}$, d) x, $x \neq \frac{1}{2}$, e) $\frac{x+5}{2x-1}$, $x \neq \frac{1}{2}$. 9). a) $\frac{4}{2-x}$, $x \neq 0, 2$, b) $\frac{4}{2-x}$, $x \neq 0, 2$, c) x, $x \neq 0, 2$, d) $\frac{2x-4}{x}$, $x \neq 0, 2$, e) x, $x \neq 0, 2$, f) $\frac{2x-4}{x}$, $x \neq 0, 2$. 11). ± 2 12). a) $x \in \mathbb{R}$, $0 < x \leq \frac{16}{9}$, b) $f^{-1}(x) = \frac{4}{\sqrt{x}} - 3$, $x \in \mathbb{R}$, $0 < x \leq \frac{16}{9}$, c) 1. 13). a) 2, 7, b) 5, c) $\left(-\frac{11}{5}, \frac{2}{5}\right)$. 14). a) $(3, -5), 4$, b) $4\sqrt{5}$, c) 8. 15). a) $(10, 20), \sqrt{10}$, b) $y = 3x, y = \frac{13}{9}x; (7, 21), \left(\frac{63}{5}, \frac{91}{5}\right)$, c) $\frac{14}{5}\sqrt{5}$. 16). a) $x + 3y + 1 = 0$, b) $(5, -2), 5\sqrt{2}$, c) 3.182. 17). a) 5, $(x-3)^2 + (y-1)^2 = 15$, b)i. $(-1, -2), (3, 6)$, ii. 11.1 cm. 18). a) $(\theta + 2)r, \frac{1}{2}r^2\theta$, b) 10, 2. 19). 3.6 cm, 10.8 cm^2. 20). $\frac{1}{4}$. 21). r^2. 22). $\frac{2}{3}\pi, \frac{1}{3}\pi - \frac{1}{4}\sqrt{3}$. 23). 17.1 cm^2. 24). a) $6\sqrt{2} = 8.49$ cm, b) $9\pi - 18 = 10.3$ cm^2. 25). a) (i) $1, 2, 5, 14, 41$, (ii) $2, 5, 14, 41, 122$, (iii) $0, -1, -4, -13, -40$, (iv) $\frac{1}{2}, \frac{1}{2}, \frac{1}{2}, \frac{1}{2}, \frac{1}{2}$, b) (i) $b = \frac{1}{2}$, (ii) $b = \frac{2}{3}$, (iii) $b = -\frac{1}{2}$, (iv) $b = 0$. 26). a) $3, 1, 3$, alternating between 3 and 1, b) All terms after the first are 2, c); 2. 27). a) Alternately -1 and 0; after the first term, alternately -1 and 0; getting increasingly large, b) $\frac{1}{2}(1 \pm \sqrt{5})$, c) $0, -1, \frac{1}{2}(1 \pm \sqrt{5})$. 28). $n(2n+3)$. 29). 168. 30). -750. 31). $2n - \frac{1}{2}$. 32). $167167, 111445$. 33). 40. 34). a) $0, 1, 4, 9, 16; r^2$, b) $0, 1, 2, 3, 4; r$, c) $1, 2, 4, 8, 16, 2^r$. 35). $6\frac{1}{4}$. 36). $a = 3, r = -\frac{1}{4}, 2.4\left[1 - \left(-\frac{1}{4}\right)^n\right]$. 37). $\frac{4}{5}, 18$. 38). $8\left[1 - \left(-\frac{1}{2}\right)^n\right], 8, 13$. 39). $r = 0.917, a = 40$. 40). $r = -\frac{1}{3}$. 42). $r = \frac{k-1}{k+1}$. 43). $\frac{(1-x)(1-x^{3n+3})}{1-x^3}, |x| < 1; \frac{1}{1+x+x^2+x^3+x^4}, |x| < 1$. 44). a) $b = 20a$, b) £250, c) $u_n - b = 1.05^n(5000 - b)$, d) 15 years. 45). Either $p = 3, q = 9$ or $p = -4, q = 16$. 46). $a^3 - 4ab + 8c = 0; 1 \pm \sqrt{\sqrt{5} - 2}$.

Exercise 10A — (page 173)

1). a) $4x^2 + 4xy + y^2$, b) $25x^2 + 30xy + 9y^2$, c) $16 + 56p + 49p^2$, d) $1 - 16t + 64t^2$, e) $1 - 10x^2 + 25x^4$, f) $4 + 4x^3 + x^6$, g) $x^6 + 3x^4y^3 + 3x^2y^6 + y^9$, h) $27x^6 + 54x^4y^3 + 36x^2y^6 + 8y^9$. 2). a) $x^3 + 6x^2 + 12x + 8$, b) $8p^3 + 36p^2q + 54pq^2 + 27q^3$, c) $1 - 12x + 48x^2 - 64x^3$, d) $1 - 3x^3 + 3x^6 - x^9$. 3). a) 42, b) 150. 4). a) 240, b) 54. 5). a) $1 + 10x + 40x^2 + 80x^3 + 80x^4 + 32x^5$, b) $p^6 + 12p^5q + 60p^4q^2 + 160p^3q^3 + 240p^2q^4 + 192pq^5 + 64q^6$, c) $16m^4 - 96m^3n + 216m^2n^2 - 216mn^3 + 81n^4$, d) $1 + 2x + \frac{3}{2}x^2 + \frac{1}{2}x^3 + \frac{1}{16}x^4$. 6). a) 270, b) -1000. 7). $1 + 2x + 5x^2 + 4x^3 + 4x^4$. 8). $x^3 + 12x^2 + 48x + 64, x^4 + 13x^3 + 60x^2 + 112x + 64$. 9). $72x^5 + 420x^4 + 950x^3 + 1035x^2 + 540x + 108$. 10). 7. 11). $a = 5, b = \pm 2$. 12). 1120. 13). $x^{11} + 11x^{10}y + 55x^9y^2 + 165x^8y^3 + 330x^7y^4 + 462x^6y^5 + 462x^5y^6 + 330x^4y^7 + 165x^3y^8 + 55x^2y^9 + 11xy^{10} + y^{11}$. 14). 59136.

Exercise 10B — (page 175)

1). a) 35, b) 28, c) 126, d) 715, e) 15, f) 45, g) 11, h) 1225. 2). a) 220, b) 10, c) 680, d) 190, e) 161700, f) 24040016, g) 15504, h) 155117520. 7). 2^n.

Exercise 10D — (page 184)

1). a) 10, b) -56, c) 165, d) -560. 2). a) 42, b) -448, c) 4032, d) $24\frac{3}{4}$. 3). a) 3003, b) 192192, c) 560431872, d) 48048. 4). a) $1 + 13x + 78x^2 + 286x^3 + \cdots$, b) $1 - 15x + 105x^2 - 455x^3 + \cdots$, c) $1 + 30x + 405x^2 + 3240x^3 + \cdots$, d) $128 - 2240x + 16800x^2 - 70000x^2 + \cdots$. 5). a) $1 + 22x + 231x^2 + \cdots$, b) $1 - 30x + 435x^2 + \cdots$, c) $1 - 72x + 2448x^2 + \cdots$, d) $1 + 114x + 6156x^2 + \cdots$. 6). $1 + 16x + 112x^2 + \cdots$; 1.1712. 7). $4096 + 122880x + 1689600x^2 + \cdots$; 4220.57. 8). $1 + 32x + 480x + 4480x^3 + \cdots$; 5920. 9). $1 - 30x + 405x^2 + \cdots$; 234. 10). 7. 11). $2 + 56x^2 + 140x^4 + 56x^6 + 2x^8$; 2.0056014000560002. 12). $a = 4, n = 9$. 13). $a = -5, n = 7$. 14). c) $218\sqrt{2}$, 308. 15). c) $a = 5, n = 7$. 16). a) 2^n, b) 0, c) $^{2n}C_n$.

Exercise 10D — (page 184)

1). a) $1 - 3x + 6x^2 + \cdots$, b) $1 - 5x + 15x^2 + \cdots$, c) $1 + 4x + 10x^2 + \cdots$, d) $1 + 6x + 21x^2 + \cdots$. 2). a) $1 - 4x + 16x^2 + \cdots$, b) $1 + 6x + 24x^2 + \cdots$, c) $1 + 12x + 90x^2 + \cdots$, d) $1 - x + \frac{3}{4}x^2 + \cdots$. 3). a) 84, b) -8, c) -270, d) 256, e) $\frac{56}{27}$, f) $-20a^3$, g) $20b^23$, h) $\frac{1}{6}n(n+1)(n+2)c^3$. 4). a) $1 + \frac{1}{3}x - \frac{1}{9}x^2 + \cdots$, b) $1 + \frac{3}{4}x - \frac{3}{32}x^2 + \cdots$, c) $1 - \frac{3}{2}x + \frac{3}{8}x^2 + \cdots$, d) $1 + \frac{1}{2}x + \frac{3}{8}x^2 + \cdots$, e) $1 + 2x - 2x^2 + \cdots$, f) $1 - x + 2x^2 + \cdots$, g) $1 - 8x + 8x^2 + \cdots$, h) $1 + \frac{1}{8}x + \frac{5}{128}x^2 + \cdots$. 5). a) $-\frac{1}{2}$, b) $\frac{625}{16}$, c) $\frac{5}{24}$, d) $-\frac{5}{2}$, e) 20, f) $\frac{1}{8}\sqrt{2}$, g) $-\frac{1}{16}a^3$, h) $\frac{1}{48}n(n+2)(n+4)b^3$. 6). a) $1 - \frac{1}{8}x - \frac{1}{128}x^2 + \cdots$, b) $1 + \frac{1}{8}x - \frac{1}{128}x^2 + \cdots$, c) $2 + \frac{1}{4}x - \frac{1}{64}x^2 + \cdots$, d) $6 + \frac{3}{4}x - \frac{3}{64}x^2 + \cdots$. 7). $|x| < \frac{2}{3}$,

a) $4 + 12x + 27x^2 + \frac{27}{8}x^3 + \cdots$,   b) $\frac{1}{4} + \frac{3}{4}x + \frac{27}{16}x^2 + \frac{27}{8}x^3 + \cdots$.   8). a) $1 - 3x - \frac{9}{2}x^2 - \frac{27}{2}x^3 + \cdots$, $|x| < \frac{1}{6}$,   b) $1 - 5x + 25x^2 - 125x^3$, $|x| < \frac{1}{5}$,   c) $1 - 3x + 18x^2 - 126x^3 + \cdots$, $|x| < \frac{1}{9}$,   d) $1 + 8x + 40x^2 + !60x^3 + \cdots$, $|x| < \frac{1}{2}$,   e) $1 + x^2 - \frac{1}{2}x^4 + \frac{1}{2}x^6$, $|x| < \frac{1}{2}\sqrt{2}$,   f) $2 - \frac{4}{3}x - \frac{8}{9}x^2 - \frac{80}{81}x^3 + \cdots$, $|x| < \frac{1}{2}$,   g) $10 - 4x + \frac{6}{5}x^2 - \frac{8}{25}x^3 + \cdots$, $|x| < 5$,   h) $1 + \frac{1}{2}x + \frac{1}{4}x^2 + \frac{1}{8}x^3 + \cdots$, $|x| < 2$,   i) $\frac{1}{8} - \frac{3}{16}x + \frac{3}{16}x^2 - \frac{5}{32}x^3 + \cdots$, $|x| < 2$,   j) $2x - \frac{1}{4}x^4 + \frac{3}{64}x^7 - \frac{[5}{512}x^{10} + \cdots$, $|x| < \sqrt[3]{4}$,   k) $1 + 2x - 6x^2 + 28x^3 + \cdots$, $|x| < \frac{1}{8}$,   l) $\frac{4}{3} - \frac{16}{9}\sqrt{3}x + \frac{40}{9}x^2 + \frac{80}{27}\sqrt{3}x^3 + \cdots$, $|x| < \sqrt{3}$.   9). $1 + 4x - 8x^2 + 32x^3 + \cdots$, 1.039232,   a) 10.39232,   b) 1.73205.   10). $1 + \frac{4}{3}x - \frac{16}{9}x^2 + \cdots$,   a) 5.06578,   b) 9.99667.   11). 6.   12). 15.   13). $1 + 3x + \frac{15}{2}x^2 + \cdots$, $|x| < \frac{1}{4}$, 4.123.   14). $4, 6, -100$.   15). $1 + x + 2x^2 + 3x^3 + 5x^4 + \cdots$, 1.001002003005.   16). a) $2 - 2x + \frac{7}{2}x^2 + \cdots$,   b) $1 + 5x + 6x^2 + \cdots$.   17). $-\frac{56}{27}$.   19). b) $a = \frac{1}{3}, b = -\frac{1}{3}$.

Exercise 11A — (page 193)

1). a) $4.002, 6.003, -2.001$,   b) $3.9998, 5.9997, -1.9999$,   c) $8.004, 12.006, -4.002$,   d) $7.998, 11.997, -3.999$,   e) $12.000002, 18.000003, -6.000001$,   f) $11.99998, 17.99997, -5.99999$.   2). a) $2x$,   b) $2x - 1$,   c) $8x$,   d) $6x - 2$,   e) -3,   f) $1 - 4x$,   g) $4 - 6x$,   h) $\sqrt{2} - 2\sqrt{3}x$.   3). a) 6,   b) 3,   c) -3,   d) 8,   e) -8,   f) -6,   g) 4,   h) -17.   4). a) $\frac{3}{4}$,   b) $\frac{1}{2}$,   c) $-\frac{3}{2}$,   d) -1,   e) $\frac{3}{2}$,   f) $\frac{1}{2}$ 5). a) 3,   b) $-6x$,   c) 0,   d) $2 + 6x$,   e) $-2x$,   f) $6 - 6x$,   g) $2 - 4x$,   h) $4x + 1$.   6). a) $3x^2 + 4x$,   b) $-6x^2 + 6x$,   c) $3x^2 - 12x + 11$,   d) $6x^2 + 6x + 1$,   e) $4x - 24x^3$,   f) $-3x^2$.   7). a) -10,   b) 6,   c) 58,   d) -1,   e) 8,   f) 12.   8). a) ± 2,   b) $2, -\frac{4}{3}$,   c) $7, -5$,   d) 1,   e) $-1, -\frac{1}{3}$,   f) None.   9). a) $\frac{1}{\sqrt{x}}$,   b) $\frac{2}{\sqrt{x}} + 4$,   c) $1 - \frac{1}{4\sqrt{x}}$,   d) $1 - \frac{1}{\sqrt{x}}$,   e) $1 + \frac{1}{x^2}$,   f) $2x + 1 - \frac{1}{x^2}$,   g) $1 - \frac{2}{x^2}$,   h) $\frac{1}{\sqrt{x}} + 1$.   10). a) $-\frac{1}{4x^2}$,   b) $-\frac{6}{x^3}$,   c) 0,   d) $\frac{3}{4\sqrt[4]{x}}$,   e) $\frac{2}{\sqrt[3]{x^2}}$,   f) $-\frac{2}{x\sqrt{x}}$,   g) $-\frac{3}{x^2} - \frac{1}{x^4}$,   h) $10x\sqrt{x}$,   i) $\frac{3}{2}\sqrt{x}$,   j) $-\frac{1}{6x\sqrt[3]{x}}$,   k) $\frac{4-x}{x^3}$,   l) $\frac{3x-1}{4x\sqrt[4]{x}}$.   11). b) $\frac{1}{h}\left[(x+h)^n - x^n\right] = (x+h)^{n-1} + (x+h)^{n-2}x + \cdots + (x+h)x^{n-2} + x^{n-1}$ tends to nx^{n-1} as h tends to 0.   12). a) $-2x^{-3}$,   b) $\frac{x}{\sqrt{1+x^2}}$,   c) $-\frac{4x^3}{(1+x^4)^2}$.

Exercise 11B — (page 195)

1). $12y = -4x + 33$.   2). $4y = 4x + 3$.   3). $\left(-\frac{9}{4}, \frac{81}{4}\right)$.   4). $4y = 4x - 1$.   5). $y = 0$.   6). $y = -2x$.   7). $12y = 12x - 17$.   8). $x = 1$.   9). $7y = -x + 64$.   10). $y = 4x + 2$.   11). $y = x + 2$.   12). $4y = x + 4$.   13). $4y = -x + 4$.   14). $x = 1$.   16). $y = -2x - 6$.   17). $y = -a^2x$, $y = 2a^2x + 2a^3$, $y = 2a^2x - 2a^3$.   18). $\left(\frac{1}{2}, -2\right)$.   19). $3y - x = 4$, $y + 3x = 28$.   20). $\left(\frac{3}{4}, 0\right)$ and $(0, 12)$.   21). $\left(\frac{3}{4}, -\frac{1}{4}\right)$; PR and QR have gradients -1 and 1, so are perpendicular; $\frac{1}{16}$.   22). $\left(-\frac{7}{3}, \frac{37}{9}\right)$.   23). $(-8, -230)$.   24). $(2, 7)$ and $(-1, 4)$.   25). b); Use the Factor Theorem; $f'(a)$,   c) Use The Factor Theorem again,   d) '...$x = a$ as a repeated root'.   26). a) $y = px - ap^2$,   b) Q has coordinates $(ap, 0)$; FQ has gradient $-\frac{1}{p}$,   c) $\frac{1}{p}$,   d) $\alpha = \beta$,   e) A light source at F will produce a parallel beam of light, directed along the y-axis.

Exercise 11C — (page 198)

1). a) $2x + 3, 2, 0, 0$,   b) $6x^2 + 1, 12x, 12, 0$,   c) $4x^3, 12x^2, 24, 24$,   d) $\frac{1}{2}x^{-\frac{1}{2}}, -\frac{1}{4}x^{-\frac{3}{2}}, \frac{3}{8}x^{-\frac{5}{2}}, -\frac{15}{16}x^{-\frac{7}{2}}$,   e) $-\frac{1}{2}x^{-\frac{3}{2}}, \frac{3}{4}x^{-\frac{5}{2}}, -\frac{15}{8}x^{-\frac{7}{2}}, \frac{105}{16}x^{-\frac{9}{2}}$,   f) $\frac{1}{4}x^{-\frac{3}{4}}, -\frac{3}{16}x^{-\frac{7}{4}}, \frac{21}{64}x^{-\frac{11}{4}}, -\frac{231}{256}x^{-\frac{15}{4}}$.   2). a) $2x - 5, 2, 0, 0$,   b) $10x^4 - 6x, 40x^3 - 6, 120x^2, 240x$,   c) $-4x^{-5}, 20x^{-6}, -120x^{-7}, 840x^{-8}$,   d) $6x - 6x^5, 6 - 30x^4, -120x^3, -360x^2$,   e) $\frac{3}{4}x^{-\frac{1}{4}}, -\frac{3}{16}x^{-\frac{5}{4}}, \frac{15}{64}x^{-\frac{9}{4}}, -\frac{135}{256}x^{-\frac{13}{4}}$,   f) $\frac{3}{8}x^{-\frac{5}{8}}, -\frac{15}{64}x^{-\frac{13}{8}}, \frac{195}{512}x^{-\frac{21}{8}}, -\frac{4095}{4096}x^{-\frac{29}{8}}$.   3). a) $n!$,   b) $\frac{1}{2}(n+2)!x^2$,   c) 0.   4). a) $(-1)^n n! x^{-n-1}$,   b) $\frac{(2n)!}{n!}x^n$,   c) $(-1)^{n-1}\frac{(2n-2)!}{2^{2n-1}(n-1)!}x^{\frac{1}{2}-n}$.

Exercise 11D — (page 204)

1). a) $2x - 5, x \geq \frac{5}{2}$,   b) $2x + 6, x \geq -3$,   c) $-3 - 2x, x \leq -\frac{3}{2}$,   d) $6x - 5, x \geq \frac{5}{6}$,   e) $10x + 3, x \geq -\frac{3}{10}$,   f) $-4 - 6x, x \leq -\frac{2}{3}$.   2). a) $2x + 4, x \leq -2$,   b) $2x - 3, x \leq \frac{3}{2}$,   c) $2x - 3, x \leq \frac{3}{2}$,   d) $4x - 8, x \leq 2$,   e) $7 - 4x, x \geq \frac{7}{4}$,   f) $-5 - 14x, x \geq -\frac{5}{14}$.   3). a) $3x^2 - 12, x \geq 2$ and $x \leq -2$,   b) $6x^2 - 18, x \geq \sqrt{3}$ and $x \leq -\sqrt{3}$,   c) $6x^2 - 18x - 24, x \geq 4$ and $x \leq -1$,   d) $3x^2 - 6x + 3$, all x,   e) $4x^3 - 4x, x \geq 1$ and $-1 \leq x \leq 0$,   f) $4x^3 + 12x^2, x \geq -3$,   g) $3 - 3x^2, -1 \leq x \leq 1$,   h) $10x^4 - 20x^3$, $x \leq 0$ and $x \geq 2$,   i) $3 + 3x^2$, all x.   4). a) $0 \leq x \leq 3$,   b) $4x^3 + 8x, x \leq 0$,   c) $3x^2 - 6x + 3$, nowhere, d) $12 - 6x^2$, $x \geq \sqrt{2}$ and $x \leq -\sqrt{2}$, e) $6x^2 + 6x - 36$, $-3 \leq x \leq 2$, f) $12x^3 - 60x^2$, $x \leq 5$, g) $72x - 8x^3$, $-3 \leq x \leq 0$ and $x \geq 3$, h) $5x^4 - 5$, $-1 \leq x \leq 1$, i) $nx^{n-1} - n$, $x \leq 1$ if n is even, and $-1 \leq x \leq 1$ if n is odd. 5). a) $\frac{1}{2}x^{\frac{1}{2}}(5x - 3)$; increasing for $x \geq \frac{3}{5}$, decreasing for $0 \leq x \leq \frac{3}{5}$, b) $\frac{1}{4}x^{-\frac{1}{4}}(3 - 14x)$; increasing for $0 \leq x \leq \frac{3}{14}$, decreasing for $x \geq \frac{3}{14}$, c) $\frac{1}{3}x^{-\frac{1}{3}}(5x + 4)$; increasing for $x \geq 0$ and $x \leq -\frac{4}{5}$, decreasing for $-\frac{4}{5} \leq x \leq 0$, d) $\frac{13}{5}x^{-\frac{2}{5}}(x^2 - 3)$; increasing for $x \leq -\sqrt{3}$ and $x \geq \sqrt{3}$, decreasing for $-\sqrt{3} \leq x \leq \sqrt{3}$, e) $1 - \frac{3}{x^2}$; increasing for $x \leq -\sqrt{3}$ and $x \geq \sqrt{3}$, decreasing for $-\sqrt{3} \leq x < 0$ and $0 < x \leq \sqrt{3}$, f) $\frac{1}{2}x^{-\frac{3}{2}}(x - 1)$; increasing for $x \geq 1$, decreasing for $0 < x \leq 1$. 6). a) $(4, -12)$, minimum, $y \geq -12$, b) $(-2, -7)$, minimum, $y \geq -7$, c) $(-\frac{3}{5}, \frac{1}{5})$, minimum, $y \geq \frac{1}{5}$, d) $(-3, 13)$, maximum, $y \leq 13$, e) $(-3, 0)$, minimum, $y \geq 0$, f) $(-\frac{1}{2}, 2)$, maximum, $y \leq 2$. 7). a) $(-4, 213)$, maximum, $(3, -130)$, minimum, b) $(-3, 88)$, maximum, $(5, -168)$, minimum, c) $(0, 0)$, minimum, $(1, 1)$, positive inflexion, d) $(-2, 65)$, maximum, $(0, 1)$, negative inflexion, $(2, -63)$, minimum, e) $(-\frac{1}{3}, -\frac{11}{27})$, minimum, $(\frac{1}{2}, \frac{3}{4})$, maximum, f) $(-1, 0)$, positive inflexion, g) $(1, 2)$, minimum, $(-1, -2)$, maximum, h) $(3, 27)$, minimum, i) none, j) $(\frac{1}{4}, -\frac{1}{4})$, minimum, k) $(6, \frac{1}{12})$, maximum, l) $(-2, 17)$, minimum, m) $(1, 3)$, maximum, n) $(-1, -5)$, minimum, o) $(0, 0)$, minimum, $(\frac{4}{5}, \frac{256}{3125})$, maximum. 8). a) $y \geq \frac{3}{4}$, b) $y \geq -16$, c) $|y| \geq 2$. 9). a) $(-1, -2)$, minimum, $(1, 2)$, maximum, b) $(0, 0)$, maximum, $(2, -4)$, minimum, c) $(0, 1)$, minimum, d) $(-1, 11)$, maximum, $(2, -16)$, minimum, e) $(2, -\frac{3}{8})$, minimum, f) $(-1, 2)$, minimum, $(1, 2)$, minimum, g) $(2, \frac{1}{4})$, maximum, h) $(2, 22)$, positive inflexion. 10). a) $(-1, -8)$, minimum, $(0, -3)$, maximum, $(2, -35)$, minimum, b) $(1, 6)$, positive inflexion, c) $(-\frac{4}{3}, -14\frac{2}{9})$, minimum, $(\frac{4}{3}, 14\frac{2}{9})$, maximum, d) $(-2, 3)$, minimum, e) $(-2, -4)$, maximum, $(2, 4)$, minimum, f) $(6, \frac{1}{12})$, maximum, g) $(0, -7)$, positive inflexion, h) $(0, 1)$, minimum, $(1, 2)$, positive inflexion. 11). $\frac{1}{h}[f(q + h) - f(q)] > 0$ for all $0 < h < r - q$. 12). $\frac{1}{h}[f(q + h) - f(q)]$ is negative for $h > 0$, but positive for $h < 0$, and so $f'(q) = 0$.

Exercise 11E — (page 208)

1). a) $6t + 7$, b) $1 - \frac{1}{2\sqrt{x}}$, c) $1 - 6y^{-3}$, d) $2t - \frac{1}{2t\sqrt{t}}$, e) $2t + 6$, f) $12s^5 - 6s$, g) 5, h) $-2r^{-3} - 1$. 2). a) Velocity, b) (i) Increasing, (ii) Decreasing, c) 9. 3). a) $\frac{ds}{dt} = k$, b) $\frac{dS}{dt} = kS$, c) $\frac{dx}{dt} = f(T)$. 4). 80 kmh. 5). 20 m. 6). 36. 7). $4\sqrt{5}$. 8). $V = 32\pi$ when $r = 4$, and $V = 0$ when $r = 0$. 9). 25. 10). b) 1800 m^2. 11). $0 < x < 20$, 7.36 cm. 12). 20 cm. 13). b) 38400 cm^3. 14). 2420 cm^3. 15). 15 kmh. 16). $\frac{1}{\sqrt{3}}$. 17). a) $\left(\frac{ma+b}{m}, 0\right)$, $(0, ma + b)$, c) $2ab$.

Exercise 12A — (page 213)

1). a) $x^4 + c$, b) $x^6 + c$, c) $x^2 + c$, d) $x^3 + x^5 + c$, e) $x^{10} - x^8 - x + c$, f) $-x^7 + x^3 + x + c$.
2). a) $3x^3 - 2x^2 - 5x + c$, b) $4x^3 + 3x^2 + 4x + c$, c) $7x + c$, d) $4x^4 - 2x^3 + 5x^2 - 3x + c$, e) $\frac{1}{2}x^4 + \frac{5}{2}x^2 + c$, f) $\frac{1}{2}x^2 + \frac{2}{3}x^3 + c$, g) $\frac{2}{3}x^3 - \frac{3}{2}x^2 - 4x + c$, h) $x - x^2 - x^3 + c$. 3). a) $\frac{1}{5}x^5 + \frac{1}{3}x^3 + x + c$, b) $\frac{7}{2}x^2 - 3x + c$, c) $\frac{2}{3}x^3 + \frac{1}{2}x^2 - 8x + c$, d) $\frac{3}{2}x^4 - \frac{5}{3}x^3 + \frac{3}{2}x^2 + 2x + c$, e) $\frac{1}{6}x^4 + \frac{1}{6}x^3 + \frac{1}{6}x^2 + \frac{1}{6}x + c$, f) $\frac{1}{8}x^4 - \frac{1}{9}x^3 + \frac{1}{2}x^2 - \frac{1}{3}x + c$, g) $\frac{1}{2}x^2 - x^3 + x + c$, h) $\frac{1}{4}x^4 + \frac{1}{3}x^3 + \frac{1}{2}x^2 + x + c$. 4). $4x^2 - 5x$. 5). $2x^3 - x - 19$. 6). $\frac{1}{8}x^4 + \frac{1}{8}x^2 + x + -21$. 7). $5x^3 - 3x^2 + 4x - 6$. 8). a)

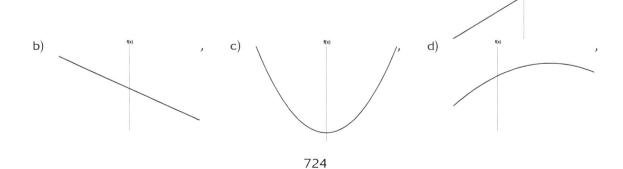

b) , c) , d) ,

e) 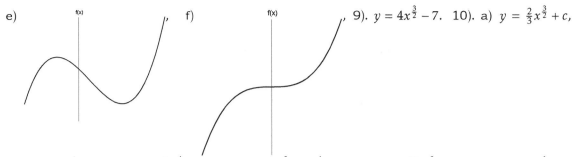 f) , 9). $y = 4x^{\frac{3}{2}} - 7$. 10). a) $y = \frac{2}{3}x^{\frac{3}{2}} + c$,

b) $y = 12x^{\frac{1}{3}} + c$, c) $y = \frac{3}{4}x^{\frac{4}{3}} + c$, d) $y = \frac{4}{3}x^{\frac{3}{2}} - 4x^{\frac{1}{2}} + c$, e) $y = \frac{15}{2}x^{\frac{2}{3}} + c$, f) $y = -6x^{\frac{1}{3}} + c$.
11). a) $f(x) = -x^{-1} + c$, b) $f(x) = -x^{-3} + c$, c) $f(x) = -3x^{-2} + c$, d) $f(x) = 2x^2 + 3x^{-1} + c$,
e) $f(x) = -\frac{1}{2}x^{-2} + \frac{1}{3}x^{-3} + c$, f) $f(x) = -2x^{-1} - \frac{2}{3}x^3 + c$. 12). $y = 13 - 4x^{-1}$. 13). $y = \sqrt{x} - 2$.
14). $y = \frac{3}{4}x^{\frac{4}{3}} + 3x^{-2} + \frac{5}{4}$. 15). a) $y = x^3 - 3x^2 + c$, b) $4x^3 - x^2 - 10x + c$, c) $2x^2 - x^{-1} + c$, d)
$y = \frac{2}{3}x^{\frac{3}{2}} + 8x^{\frac{1}{2}} + c$, e) $y = \frac{1}{2}x^2 + \frac{20}{3}x^{\frac{3}{2}} + 25x + c$, f) $x + 10\sqrt{x} + c$. 16). a) 118.4 cm, b) 27 years.
17). $12\sqrt{2} = 16.97$ months. 18). $f(x) = 3x^3 + 2x^2 - 7x - 4$, $f(4) = 192$. 19). $f(x) = 3 - \frac{3}{2}x^3 + \frac{9}{2}x$ will
do. 20). $y = \frac{7}{4}x^4 + \frac{1}{2}x^6 + \frac{1}{4}x - \frac{7}{4}$.

Exercise 12B — (page 217)

1). a) $2x^2 + c$, b) $5x^3 + c$, c) $\frac{1}{3}x^6 + c$, d) $9x + c$, e) $\frac{1}{18}x^9 + c$, f) $\frac{2}{15}x^5 + c$. 2). a) 7, b)
84, c) 4, d) 4, e) $\frac{1}{16}$, f) 2. 3). a) $3x^2 + 7x + c$, b) $2x^3 - x^2 - 5x + c$, c) $\frac{1}{2}x^4 + \frac{7}{2}x^2 + c$,
d) $\frac{3}{5}x^5 - 2x^4 + 3x^3 - \frac{1}{2}x^2 + 4x + c$, e) $\frac{2}{3}x^3 - \frac{3}{2}x^2 - 20x + c$, f) $\frac{1}{4}x^4 - 2x^2 + c$. 4). a) 22, b) 22,
c) 36, d) $\frac{43}{6}$, e) 210, f) 0. 5). 72. 6). 15. 7). 195. 8). $2a^3$. 9). 80. 10). $10a + \frac{2}{5}a^5$.
11). $\frac{1}{2}(5 + 13) \times 2 = \left[2x^2 + x\right]_1^3 = 18$. 12). $\frac{1}{2} \times 8 \times 4 = \left[\frac{1}{4}x^2 - 3x\right]_6^{14} = 16$. 13). a) 39, b) $\frac{16}{3}$, c)
$\frac{32}{3}$, d) 10, e) 500, f) $\frac{16}{3}$. 14). a) $-\frac{1}{2}x^{-2} + c$, b) $\frac{1}{3}x^3 + \frac{1}{2}x^{-2} + c$, c) $\frac{2}{3}x^{\frac{3}{2}} + c$, d) $\frac{18}{5}x^{\frac{5}{3}} + c$,
e) $2x^3 - 5x^{-1} + c$, f) $2\sqrt{x} + c$. 15). a) 144, b) $\frac{3}{2}$, c) 20, d) $\frac{27}{4}$, e) 16, f) 3. 16). $\frac{7}{4}$.
17). $\frac{3}{4}(b^4 - a^4)$. 18). $\frac{10}{3}$. 19). 7. 20). 5. 21). a) $\frac{68}{3}$, b) $\frac{19}{8}$. 22). 96. 24). $\frac{343}{8}$. 25). a)
$\frac{1}{3}(a^2 + ab + b^2)$, b) $\frac{2}{\sqrt{a} + \sqrt{b}}$. 26). a) $\frac{a}{n}$, The jth rectangle has height $\frac{aj}{n}$ and width $\frac{a}{n}$, c) The
sum is $\frac{n+1}{2n}a^2$.

Exercise 12C — (page 224)

1). 2 ($x^3 - 3/2x^2$ evaluated at 2). 2). a) $\frac{32}{3}$, b) 8, c) $\frac{9}{4}$, d) $\frac{11}{6}$. 3). $\frac{32}{3}$. 4). 32. 5). $\frac{136}{3}$.
6). $\frac{1875}{4}$. 7). 108. 8). $\frac{128}{3}$. 9). $\frac{9}{2}$. 10). 36. 11). a) $\frac{1}{4}$, b) 6, c) 100. 12). $\frac{s^{1-m}-1}{1-m}$, $\frac{1}{m-1}$.
13). $\frac{2152}{15} = 143\frac{7}{15}$.

Exercise 12D — (page 228)

1). a) $\frac{98}{3}\pi$, b) $\frac{3093}{5}\pi$, c) $\frac{279808}{7}\pi$, d) $\frac{3}{4}\pi$. 2). a) 504π, b) $\frac{3498}{5}\pi$, c) $\frac{15}{2}\pi$, d) $\frac{16}{15}\pi$.
3). a); 4π, b) 9π, c) 3355π, d) $\frac{3}{10}\pi$, e) $\frac{648}{5}\pi$, f) $\frac{9}{2}\pi$, g) 156π, h) $\frac{202}{9}\pi$. 4). a)
$\frac{512}{15}\pi$, b) $\frac{16}{15}\pi$, c) $\frac{1}{30}\pi$, d) $\frac{81}{10}\pi$. 5). a) $\frac{2}{15}\pi$, b) $\frac{1}{6}\pi$. 6). a) $\frac{2048}{15}\pi$, b) $\frac{128}{3}\pi$. 7). a) $\frac{3}{10}\pi$,
b) $\frac{3}{10}\pi$. 8). $\frac{1}{10}\pi$. 9). 9π. 10). $\frac{16}{15}\pi$. 11). b) $2\pi^2 ab^2$.

Review Exercises 4 — (page 231)

1). a) $1 + 40x + 720x^2 + \cdots$, b) $1 - 32x + 480x^2 + \cdots$. 2). a) -48384, b) $\frac{875}{4}$.
3). $256 + 256x + 112x^2 + 28x^3 + \cdots$, 258.571. 4). $256 - 3072x + 16128x^2 + \cdots$, 253. 5). $x^6 + 3x^3 + 3 + \frac{1}{x^3}$.
6). $16x^4 - 96x + \frac{216}{x^2} - \frac{216}{x^5} + \frac{81}{x^8}$. 7). $2x^6 + \frac{15}{2}x^2 + \frac{15}{8x^2} + \frac{1}{32x^6}$. 8). 48. 9). 20000. 10). 30.
11). $1024 - \frac{2560}{x^2} + \frac{2880}{x^4} + \cdots$; 999. 12). B, D. 13). $\frac{7}{16}$. 14). $\frac{6435}{128}$. 15). -2024. 16). $1 + 12x + 70x^2 + \cdots$;
1.127. 17). $270x^2 + 250$; $\pm\frac{4}{3}$. 18). a) $1 + 5\alpha t + 10\alpha^2 t^2 + \cdots$, b) $1 - 8\beta t + 28\beta^2 t^2 + \cdots$, c)
$10\alpha^2 - 40\alpha\beta + 28\beta^2$. 20). a) $217 + 88\sqrt{6}$, b) $698\sqrt{2} + 569\sqrt{3}$. 21). a) 568; 567 and 568, b)
969 and 970. 22). $1 + 5x + \frac{15}{2}x^2 + \frac{5}{2}x^3 + \cdots$. 23). $1 - 2x - 2x^2 - 4x^3 + \cdots$. 24). $1 - 6x + 24x^2 - 80x^3 + \cdots$.
25). $1 - 4x^2 + 12x^4 - 32x^6 + \cdots$. 26). $2 + \frac{1}{4}x - \frac{1}{64}x^2 + \cdots$; $|x| < 4$. 27). $1 - \frac{3}{2a^2}x^2 + \frac{15}{8a^4}x^4 + \cdots$.
28). $1 + \frac{1}{2}x - \frac{1}{8}x^2 + \cdots$; $a = 2$, $b = -\frac{3}{4}$. 29). $1 + 2x + 3x^2 + 4x^3 + \cdots$; $a = 5$, $b = 7$. 30). $4 + x - \frac{1}{16}x^2 + \cdots$,
$|x| < \frac{8}{3}$. 31). $1 - \frac{1}{3}x - \frac{1}{9}x^2 - \frac{5}{81}x^3 + \cdots$. 32). $1 + \frac{1}{4}x - \frac{3}{32}x^2 + \cdots$. 33). $\frac{3}{2} - \frac{3}{4}x + 3x^2 + \cdots$. 34). $n = 15$,

$1 - \frac{1}{2}x - \frac{1}{8}x^2 + \cdots, \frac{1351}{780}$.   35). $1 - \frac{1}{4}x + \frac{5}{32}x^2 + \cdots, 1.49535$.   38). Minimum 6, maximum 10.   39). a) $\frac{dk}{dS}$ is initially zero, positive in the subsonic region, initially positive in the transonic region, becoming zero at the speed of sound and then becoming negative, then negative throughout the supersonic region. $\frac{d^2k}{dS^2}$ is positive in the subsonic and supersonic regions, and is negative in the transonic region; it is zero at the boundaries between the three regions,   b); between the subsonic and the transonic regions,   c) k seems to be levelling out, tending to a constant value.

40). $A = 10x - (2 + \frac{1}{2}\pi)x^2, \frac{10}{4+\pi} = 1.40, \frac{d^2A}{dx^2} = -4 - \pi < 0$.   41). a) Maximum 0 when $x = 0$, minimum $-\frac{4}{27}a^3$ when $x = \frac{2}{3}a$,   b) Minimum $-\frac{27}{256}a^4$ when $x = \frac{3}{4}a$,   c) Minimum 0 when $x = 0$, maximum $\frac{1}{16}a^4$ when $x = \frac{1}{2}a$, minimum 0 when $x = a$,   d) Maximum $\frac{108}{3125}a^5$ at $x = \frac{3}{5}a$, minimum 0 at $x = a$. If n is even, there is a turning point at $x = 0$, which is a minimum if m is even, and a maximum if m is odd. There is a turning point at $x = \frac{na}{n+m}$, which is a maximum if m is even, and a minimum if m is odd. If m is even, there is a minimum at $x = a$.   42). a) $f^{(n)}(x) = \frac{1}{2}(-1)^n(n+2)!x^{-n-3}$, b) $f^{(n)}(x) = (-1)^{n-1}\frac{(2n-2)!}{2^{2n-1}(n-1)!x^{\frac{1}{2}(2n-1)}}$.   43). a) $(1,15)$ and $(3,31)$ (positive inflexion),   b) $(1,2)$.

44). Maximum at $(-2,-4)$, minimum at $(2,4)$. The function is increasing for $x \le -2$ and $x \ge 2$. 45). a) $\frac{dn}{dt} = kn$,   b) $\frac{d\theta}{dt} = -k\theta$,   c) $\frac{d\theta}{dt} = -k(\theta - \beta)$.   46). $v = u + 2kt, a = 2k$.   47). $v = 20 - 4t$, $a = -4; 0 \le t \le 5$.   48). a) 20 m,   b) 6 s,   c) 40 ms^{-1}.   49).   50).   50). a) $9\sqrt{2}$ cm,   b) 40.5 cm^2.   51). a) $(-1,-7), (2,20)$,   b) Graph crosses the x-axis three times,   c) $y = -5$ also has three intersections with graph,   d) (i) $-7 < k < 20$, (ii) $k < -7$ or $k > 20$.   52). $(-2,4)$ and $(2,-28)$, $-28 \le k \le 4$.   53). $(0,0)$ and $(-\frac{2}{3}, \frac{4}{27}), 0 < k < \frac{4}{27}$.   54). $(-1,5), (0,10)$ and $(2,-22)$,   a) $5 < k < 10$, b) $k > 10$ or $-22 < k < 5$.   55). $(\frac{1}{3}, \frac{4}{27})$ and $(1,0), |k| > \frac{2}{3\sqrt{3}}$.   56). a) $P = 2x + (2 + \frac{1}{2}\pi)r, A = xr + \frac{1}{4}\pi r^2$, b) $x = \frac{1}{4}r(4 - \pi)$.   57). Maximum at $(2, \frac{1}{4})$,   a) $(2, 5\frac{1}{4})$,   b) $(3, \frac{1}{2})$.   59). a) $20(55 - x)$,   b) £$20x(55 - x)$,   c) £$(24000 - 400x)$; £37.50.   60). a) The gradient at P' is the negative of the gradient at P, so $f'(-p) = -f'(p)$. The derivative of an even function is odd.   61). $4x^{\frac{3}{2}} + c$, 28. 62). $(-2,0), (2,0)$; 32.   63). a) $-\frac{1}{2}x^{-2} + \frac{1}{4}x^4 + c$,   b) 6.   64). $\frac{27}{4}$.   65). $\frac{4}{3}$.   66). a) $\frac{1}{4}x^4 - x^2 + c$, b) 2.   67). ± 2.   69). a) $y = \frac{1}{2}(3 - x)$,   b) $\frac{125}{48}$.   71). a) $y = 2x - 2$,   b) $\frac{27}{4}$.   73). $(0,0), (2,-16)$ and $(-2,-16)$; both areas are $\frac{162}{5}$.   74). $\frac{206}{15}\pi$.   75). $\frac{4}{3}\pi ab^2, \frac{4}{3}\pi a^2 b$.   76). 4π.   77). a) 8,   b) 12. 78). $\left(a^{\frac{2}{3}} + b^{\frac{2}{3}}\right)^{\frac{3}{2}}$.

Exercise 13A — (page 242)

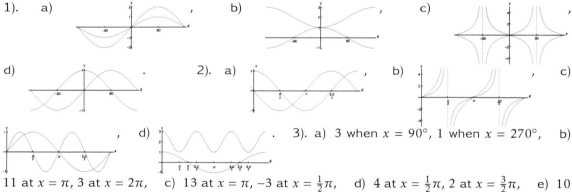

1). a) , b) , c) , d) . 2). a) , b) , c) , d) .   3). a) 3 when $x = 90°$, 1 when $x = 270°$,   b)

11 at $x = \pi$, 3 at $x = 2\pi$,   c) 13 at $x = \pi$, -3 at $x = \frac{1}{2}\pi$,   d) 4 at $x = \frac{1}{2}\pi$, 2 at $x = \frac{3}{2}\pi$,   e) 10 at $x = 27.5°$, 8 at $x = 72.5°$,   f) 5 at $x = 90°$, $\frac{15}{8}$ at $x = 450°$.   4). a) $160°$,   b) $320°$,   c) $240°$, d) $50°$,   e) $220°$,   f) $340°$,   g) $40°, 140°$,   h) $30°, 330°$,   i) $70°, 250°$,   j) $80°, 100°$,   k) $160°, 200°$,   l) $100°, 280°$.   5). a) $160°$,   b) $-40°$,   c) $-120°$,   d) $50°$,   e) $-140°$,   f) $-20°$, g) $40°, 140°$,   h) $30°$,   i) $70°, -110°$,   j) $80°, 100°$,   k) $160°, -160°$,   l) $100°, -80°$.   6). a) $\frac{9}{10}\pi$,   b) $\frac{9}{5}\pi$,   c) $\frac{4}{3}\pi$,   d) $\frac{4}{9}\pi$,   e) $\frac{8}{7}\pi$,   f) $\frac{21}{11}\pi$,   g) $\frac{23}{24}\pi$,   h) $\frac{1}{6}\pi, \frac{11}{6}\pi$,   i) $\frac{1}{5}\pi$,   j) $\frac{1}{3}\pi$, $\frac{2}{3}\pi$,   k) $\frac{2}{5}\pi, \frac{8}{5}\pi$,   l) $0, \pi$.   7). a) $\frac{1}{\sqrt{2}}$,   b) $-\frac{1}{2}$,   c) $-\frac{1}{2}$,   d) $\sqrt{3}$,   e) $-\frac{1}{\sqrt{2}}$,   f) $\frac{1}{\sqrt{3}}$,   g) -1, h) $-\frac{1}{\sqrt{3}}$ i) $-\frac{1}{\sqrt{2}}$,   j) 0,   k) 1,   l) $\frac{1}{\sqrt{2}}$,   m) $-\frac{1}{2}$,   n) -1,   o) $-\frac{1}{2}$,   p) 0.   8). a) $60°$,   b) $240°$,   c) $120°$,   d) $30°$,   e) $30°$,   f) $135°$,   g) $210°$,   h) $90°$.   9). a) $\frac{2}{3}\pi$,   b) $\frac{1}{3}\pi$,   c) $-\frac{1}{2}\pi$,   d) π,   e) $\frac{1}{3}\pi$,   f) $-\frac{1}{6}\pi$,   g) $-\frac{1}{4}\pi$,   h) $\frac{1}{2}\pi$.   10). 5, 2.8; 7.42 m.

Exercise 13B — (page 246)

1). a) $5.7°, 174.3°$, b) $237.1°, 302.9°$, c) $72.0°, 108.0°$, d) $76.0°, 256.0°$, e) $162.3°$, $342.3°$, f) $6.3°, 186.3°$, g) $203.6°, 336.4°$, h) $214.8°, 325.2°$, i) $161.6°, 341.6°$, j) $49.5°$, $160.5°$, k) $240°, 360°$, l) $10°, 70°$. 2). a) $-42.1°, -137.9°$, b) $96.9°, -96.9°$, c) $-36.9°$, $143.1°$, d) $51.3°, -128.7°$, e) $-135°, -45°, 45°, 135°$, f) $-180°, -60°, 0°, 60°, 180°$. 3). a) $0.62, 2.53, 3.76, 5.67$, b) $0.37, 1.42, 2.46, 3.51, 4.56, 5.61$, c) $1.89, 2.82, 5.03, 5.96$, d) 0.46, $1.11, 2.03, 2.69, 3.60, 4.26, 5.17, 5.83$, e) $0.19, 1.76, 3.33, 4.90$, f) $1.19, 1.95, 3.29, 4.04, 5.38$, 6.14. 4). a) $-2.37, -1.81, -0.28, 0.28, 1.81, 2.37$, b) $-2.20, -0.62, 0.95, 2.52$, c) $-3.07, -2.16$, $-0.98, -0.07, 1.11, 2.03$, d) $-2.48, -0.66, 0.66, 2.48$, e) $-3.01, -2.38, -1.75, -1.12, -0.49, 0.13$, $0.76, 1.39, 2.02, 2.65$, f) $-1.27, -0.20, 1.77, 1.94$. 5). a) $-96.4°, 96.4°$, b) $-107.3°, 162.7°$, c) $-57.9°$, d) None, e) $35.4°$, f) $-43.6°$. 6). a) $\frac{1}{6}\pi, \frac{1}{2}\pi, \frac{7}{6}\pi, \frac{3}{2}\pi$, b) $\frac{1}{8}\pi, \frac{5}{8}\pi, \frac{9}{8}\pi, \frac{13}{8}\pi$, c) $\frac{13}{36}\pi, \frac{17}{36}\pi, \frac{37}{36}\pi, \frac{41}{36}\pi, \frac{61}{36}\pi, \frac{65}{36}\pi$, d) $\frac{11}{18}\pi, \frac{23}{18}\pi, \frac{35}{18}\pi$, e) $\frac{17}{36}\pi, \frac{29}{36}\pi, \frac{53}{36}\pi, \frac{65}{36}\pi$, f) $\frac{4}{9}\pi$, g) None, h) $\frac{1}{4}\pi, \frac{7}{12}\pi, \frac{11}{12}\pi, \frac{5}{4}\pi, \frac{19}{12}\pi, \frac{23}{12}\pi$, i) $\frac{2}{9}\pi$. 7). a) $-170.8°, -9.2°$, b) $-270°, -90°, 90°$, $270°$, c) $-180°, -135°, 0°, 45°, 180°$, d) $-173.4°, -96.6°, 6.65°, 83.4°$, e) $11.3°, 78.7°$, f) $-161.1°, -101.1°, -41.1°, 18.9°, 78.9°, 138.9°$. 8). a) $27°, 63°, 207°, 243°$, b) $4°, 68°, 76°$, $140°, 148°, 212°, 220°, 284°, 292°, 356°$, c) $20°, 80°, 140°, 200°, 260°, 320°$. 9). $0, \frac{1}{4}\pi, \frac{3}{4}\pi$, π. 10). a) $\sin 4\theta, \cos 4\theta, \tan 2\theta$, b) $\sin 18\theta, \cos 18\theta, \tan 9\theta$, c) $\sin \frac{15}{2}\theta, \cos \frac{15}{2}\theta, \tan \frac{15}{4}\theta$, d) $\sin 3\theta, \cos 3\theta, \tan \frac{3}{2}\theta$, e) $\sin \frac{1}{2}\theta, \cos \frac{1}{2}\theta, \tan \frac{1}{4}\theta$, f) $\sin \frac{3}{5}\theta, \cos \frac{3}{5}\theta, \tan \frac{3}{10}\theta$. 11). a) 0.986, b) $12, 6$; 6 hours, 6.7 minutes, c) 20 days before, 202 days after Spring equinox.

Exercise 13C — (page 249)

1). a) $c = 11, \frac{4}{5}, \frac{3}{5}, \frac{3}{4}$, b) $a = 37.5, \frac{15}{17}, \frac{8}{17}, \frac{15}{8}$, c) $c = \sqrt{13}, \frac{3}{\sqrt{13}}, \frac{2}{\sqrt{13}}, \frac{3}{2}$, d) $11, \frac{5\sqrt{3}}{14}, \frac{11}{14}, \frac{5\sqrt{3}}{11}$, e) $c = 17\sqrt{5}, \frac{22}{17\sqrt{5}}, \frac{31}{17\sqrt{5}}, \frac{22}{31}$, f) $c = 12\sqrt{2}, \frac{1}{3}, \frac{2\sqrt{2}}{3}, \frac{1}{2\sqrt{2}}$. 2). a) $-\frac{11}{14}$, b) $\frac{20}{29}$, c) $\pm\frac{1}{2}\sqrt{3}$, d) $0°$, $\pm 78.5°$. 4). a) $30°, 150°, 210°, 330°$, b) $0°, 180°, 360°$, c) $36.9°, 143.1°, 199.5°, 340.1°$, d) $0°, 51.0°, 180°, 309.0°, 360°$. 5). $-116.6, -26.6, 63.4, 153.4$. 6). a) $\frac{1}{2}\pi, \frac{7}{6}\pi, \frac{11}{6}\pi$, b) $0, 2.42$, $3.86, 2\pi$, c) $0.88, 1.97, 4.31, 5.41$, d) $1.05, 1.57, 4.71, 5.24$, e) $\frac{1}{4}\pi, \frac{1}{2}\pi, \frac{3}{4}\pi, \frac{5}{4}\pi, \frac{3}{2}\pi, \frac{7}{4}\pi$, f) $\frac{1}{4}\pi, 2.82, \frac{5}{4}\pi, 5.96$, g) $0.43, 2.71, 3.57, 5.86$, h) $0.39, 1.96, 3.53, 5.10$ (N.B. The exact solutions are $\frac{1}{8}\pi, \frac{5}{8}\pi, \frac{9}{8}\pi$ and $\frac{13}{8}\pi$). 7). a) $30°, 150°, 270°$, b) $52.0°, 128.0°, 180°, 232.0°, 308.0°$, c) $0°, 20.4°, 180°, 159.6°, 360°$, d) $57.8°, 77.2°, 135°, 237.8°, 257.2°, 315°$, e) $0°, 90°, 180°$, $270°, 360°$, f) $25.3°, 85.3°, 145.3°, 205.3°, 265.3°, 325.3°$. 8). $-1, \frac{1}{2}, \frac{2}{3}$.

Exercise 13D — (page 252)

1). a) -0.675, b) 1.494, c) 1.323. 2). a) $\operatorname{cosec} x$, b) $\cot x$, c) $\sec x$, d) $\sec^2 x$, e) $\cot x$, f) $-\operatorname{cosec} x$. 3). a) $\sqrt{2}$, b) 1, c) $-\sqrt{3}$, d) $-\sqrt{2}$, e) $-\frac{1}{3}\sqrt{3}$, f) $\frac{2}{3}\sqrt{3}$, g) Undefined, h) $-\frac{2}{3}\sqrt{3}$. 4). a) 1.05, b) 1.05, c) $2 + \sqrt{3} = 3.73$, d) 2, e) -1.08, f) $2 - \sqrt{3} = 0.268$, g) $\sqrt{2} - \sqrt{6} = -1.034$, h) $-\sqrt{3}$. 5). a) $\frac{7}{20}\sqrt{10}$, b) $\frac{2}{3}\sqrt{10}$, c) $-\frac{1}{15}\sqrt{15}$, d) $\frac{4}{15}\sqrt{15}$. 6). a) $-\frac{4}{7}\sqrt{3}$, b) $-4\sqrt{3}$, c) $-\frac{10}{101}\sqrt{101}$, d) $-\sqrt{101}$. 7). a) $\tan\phi$, b) $\sin\phi\cos\phi$, c) $\cot\phi$, d) $\sin\phi$, e) $\tan\phi$, f) $\cot^2\phi$. 8). a) $3\sec^2\theta - \sec\theta - 3$, b) $0.723, \pi, 5.560$. 9). $1.107, 2.820, 4.249, 5.961$. 10). $\frac{1}{4}\pi, \frac{1}{2}\pi, \frac{3}{4}\pi, \frac{5}{4}\pi, \frac{3}{2}\pi, \frac{7}{8}\pi$. 11). a) $81.9°, 261.9°$, b) $24.1°, 155.9°, 204.1°, 335.9°$, c) $100.3°, 180.3°$, d) $71.6°, 251.6°$, e) $72.6°, 114.5°, 252.6°, 294.5°$, f) $75.8°, 284.1°$, g) $0°$, $75.5°, 109.5°, 250.5°, 284.5°, 360°$, h) $18.4°, 116.6°, 153.4°, 198.4°, 296.6°, 333.4°$. 13). $-\sqrt{3}$, $0, \sqrt{3}$.

Exercise 13E — (page 254)

1). a) $\frac{1}{6}\pi$, b) $\frac{1}{4}\pi$, c) $\frac{1}{2}\pi$, d) $\frac{1}{3}\pi$, e) $-\frac{1}{3}\pi$, f) $-\frac{1}{2}\pi$, g) $-\frac{1}{4}\pi$, h) π. 2). a) $\frac{1}{4}\pi$, b) $-\frac{1}{6}\pi$, c) $\frac{2}{3}\pi$, d) $\frac{1}{6}\pi$. 3). a) 0.5, b) -1, c) $\sqrt{3}$, d) 0. 4). a) $\frac{1}{2}\pi$, b) $\frac{1}{6}\pi$, c) $\frac{1}{6}\pi$, d) 0. 5). a) $\frac{1}{2}$, b) $\frac{1}{2}$, c) $\frac{1}{2}\sqrt{3}$, d) 1. 6). $0.739, x = \cos x$. 7). $\frac{1}{2}\pi$

Exercise 13F — (page 257)

1). $\frac{1}{4}(\sqrt{6} + \sqrt{2}), 2 + \sqrt{3}$. 2). a) $-\frac{1}{4}(\sqrt{6} - \sqrt{2})$, b) $\frac{1}{4}(\sqrt{6} + \sqrt{2})$, c) $-\sqrt{3} - 2$. 3). $\frac{1}{2}(\cos - \sqrt{3}\sin x)$. 4). $-\cos\phi, -\sin\phi$. 5). $\frac{\sqrt{3} + \tan\phi}{1 - \sqrt{3}\tan\phi}, -\frac{1 + \sqrt{3}\tan\phi}{\sqrt{3} - \tan\phi}$. 6). a) $\frac{4}{3}$, b) $\frac{7}{25}$, c) $\frac{4}{5}$, d) $\frac{117}{44}$. 7). $-\frac{63}{65}, -\frac{33}{56}$. 8). $\frac{11}{7}$. 9). $\frac{1}{18}$. 10). $\frac{4 - \sqrt{3}}{4\sqrt{3} + 1}$. 11). a) $2 - \sqrt{3}$, b) $\frac{2}{3}$, c) $5\sqrt{3} - 8$, d) $\sqrt{2} + \sqrt{3} - \sqrt{6} - 2$. 12). b) $-\cot x$.

Exercise 13G — (page 260)

1). $-\frac{1}{3}\sqrt{5}, -\frac{4}{9}\sqrt{5}, -4\sqrt{5}$. 2). $\frac{1}{8}, pm\sqrt{\frac{7}{8}}$. 3). $\tan^2\frac{1}{2}x$. 5). $\pm\frac{5}{6}, \pm\frac{1}{6}\sqrt{11}$. 6). $\frac{2}{3}, -\frac{3}{2}$. 7). $\pm\sqrt{2}-1, \sqrt{2}-1$.
8). a) π, b) $\frac{1}{2}\pi, 3.99, 5.44$, c) $0, 0.87, 2.27, \pi, 4.01, 5.41, 2\pi$, d) $0, 0.60, \pi, 5.68, 2\pi$, e) 0,
$1.77, 4.51, 2\pi$, f) $0, 2.50, 3.79, 2\pi$. 9). a) $-180°, 112.9°, 180°, 247.1°$, b) $0°, \pm80.4°, \pm279.6°$,
$\pm360°$. 11). a) $3\sin A - 4\sin^3 A$, b) $\sin\frac{1}{18}\pi, \sin\frac{5}{18}\pi, -\sin\frac{7}{18}\pi$. 12). a) $\frac{5}{12}, \frac{120}{199}, \frac{1}{239}$. 13). a)
$16\cos^5\theta - 20\cos^3\theta + 5\cos\theta$.

Exercise 13H — (page 264)

1). 0.381. 2). $53.1°$. 3). $\sqrt{34}$. 4). $\sqrt{37}, 0.165$. 5). a) $\sqrt{5}, 1.11$, b) $\sqrt{5}, 0.464$, c) $\sqrt{5}, 1.11$,
d) $\sqrt{5}, 0.464$. 6). $\sqrt{61}\cos(\theta - 0.876)$, a) $\sqrt{61}, 0.876$, b) $-\sqrt{61}, 4.018$. 7). $10\sin(x + 36.9°)$,
a) 1, b) 1, 0. 8). a) $0.87, 3.45$, b) $1.36, 5.68$, c) $0.50, 2.89, 3.64, 6.03$, d) 1.08. 9). a)
12 at 5.64, 2 at 2.50, b) $2 + \sqrt{53}$ at 2.86, -5.28 at 6.00, c) 3 at 3.54, $\frac{3}{14}$ at 0.39, d) 53 at
0.28, 0 at 1.85. 10). $\frac{1}{2}(\pm\sqrt{5}-1)$. 11). $26.6°, 45°, 206.6°, 225°$

Exercise 14A — (page 271)

1). a) 800, b) 141, c) 336. 2). a) 1.059, b) 262 Hz, c) Between D and D♯. 3). a)
$45.5°$ C, b) 13.6 minutes. 4). a) 5.4 hours, b) 5.4 hours. 6). a) $8 = 2^3$, b) $81 = 3^4$, c)
$0.04 = 5^{-2}$, d) $x = 7^4$, e) $5 = x^t$, f) $q = p^r$. 7). a) $3 = \log_2 8$, b) $6 = \log_3 729$, c)
$-3 = \log_4 \frac{1}{64}$, d) $8 = \log_a 20$, e) $9 = \log_h g$, f) $n = \log_m p$. 8). a) 4, b) 2, c) -2, d)
0, e) 1, f) $-\frac{1}{3}$, g) $\frac{3}{4}$, h) $\frac{3}{2}$, i) 7. 9). a) 7, b) $\frac{1}{64}$, c) 4, d) $\frac{1}{10}$, e) $4\sqrt{2}$, f) 6,
g) $\frac{1}{256}$, h) -10, i) $\frac{1}{\sqrt{3}}$.

Exercise 14B — (page 273)

1). See the diagram. 2). a) $\log p + \log q + \log r$,
b) $\log p + 2\log q + 3\log r$, c) $2 + \log p + 5\log r$, d)
$\frac{1}{2}\log p - \log q - \frac{1}{2}\log r$, e) $\log p + \log q - 2\log r$,
f) $-\log p - \log q - \log r$, g) $\log p - \frac{1}{2}\log r$,
h) $\log p + \log q + 7\log r - 1$, i)
$\frac{1}{2} + 5\log p - \frac{1}{2}\log q + \frac{1}{2}\log r$. 3). a) 2, b)
-1, c) $\log 30375$, d) 0, e) 3, f) -3, g)
$\log 8$, h) 0. 4). a) $r - q$, b) $2p + q$, c)
$p + \frac{1}{2}r$, d) $-q$, e) $p + 2q + r$, f) $p - q + 2r$,
g) $-p + q - r$, h) $4p + q - 2r$, i) $p + q - 2r$.
5). $x = \frac{1}{4}, y = 2$. 6). $p = 10, q = 30$.

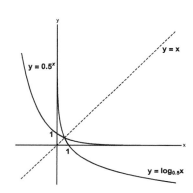

Exercise 14C — (page 275)

1). a) 1.46, b) 1.56, c) 1.14, d) 1.22, e) 3.58, f) 1.71, g) -2.21, h) 3, i) -0.202.
2). a) $x > 1.89$, b) $x < 1.43$, c) $x \le -1.68$, d) $x > 9.97$, e) $x > 8.54$, f) $x < -2$, g)
$x \ge -1$, h) $x \le -5.61$, $x \ge 3.77$. 3). 37. 4). 14. 5). 28. 6). 7. 7). $t > 9.56$ days. 8). 70.
9). a) 0.8909, b) 12 days, c) 19.9 days. 10). $9:49$ am on Tuesday. 11). 389 years. 12). a)
$0, 3$, b) $0, 2$, c) $0.77, 0.86$, d) $-1, 1.58$, e) 0.22, f) 0.74. 13). a) $0 < x < 1.46$, b)
$x > 0.58$, c) $x < 2.92$. 14). $0, 2, 3$. 15). $0.315, 2$. 16). 1.41. 17). a) $0.994, 2.001$, b) $-1, 0, 1$,
c) $-0.389, 1.020$, d) $16, 32$, e) $-3, 2$, f) $\sqrt{2}, 4$, g) $\sqrt{2}, 16$.

Exercise 14D — (page 279)

1). a) $y = 2.52 \times 3.98^x$, b) $y = 10^{12-3x}$, c) $y = 5.01 \times 50.1^x$, d) $y = 5.01x^2$, e) $y = \frac{1}{\sqrt{10x^5}}$.
2). If p is the population in millions, and x the number of years after 1870, then $p = 39.7 \times 1.022^x$
gives $39.7, 49.4, 61.3, 76.3, 94.8$. This model is reasonable, but not very good. 3). $a = 1$,
$n = 1.5$ (that T^2 is proportional to X^3 is one of the laws of planetary motion initially proposed
by Johannes Kepler). 4). Initial investment of £850 at 7.5%. 5). a) $3, 2$, b) 3.15×10^6.
6). $T = 99.2 \times 1.008^{-x}$; No (we would not expect T to tend to 0 as x becomes very large).
7). $y = 2.30 \times 6^{x^2}$ (plot $\log_{10} y$ against x^2).

Exercise 15A — (page 283)

1). a) $30(5x+3)^5$,   b) $\frac{5}{2}(5x+3)^{-\frac{1}{2}}$,   c) $-5(5x+2)^{-2}$. 2). a) $-20(1-4x)^4$,   b) $12(1-4x)^{-4}$,   c) $-\frac{2}{\sqrt{1-4x}}$. 3). a) $15x^2(1+x^3)^4$,   b) $-12x^2(1+x^3)^{-5}$,   c) $x^2(1+x^3)^{-\frac{2}{3}}$. 4). a) $24x(2x^2+3)^5$,   b) $-\frac{4x}{(2x^2+3)^2}$,   c) $-\frac{2x}{(2x^2+3)^{\frac{3}{2}}}$. 5). $24x^3(3x^4+2)$. 6). $18x^2(2x^3+1)^2$ both times. 7). a) $20x^4(x^5+1)^3$, b) $48x^2(2x^3-1)^7$,   c) $\frac{5}{2\sqrt{x}}(\sqrt{x}-1)^4$. 8). a) $8x(x^2+6)^3$,   b) $45x^2(5x^3+4)^2$,   c) $28x^3(x^4-8)^6$,   d) $-45x^8(2-x^9)^4$. 9). a) $\frac{2}{\sqrt{4x+3}}$,   b) $12x(x^2+4)^5$,   c) $-36x^2(6x^3-5)^{-3}$,   d) $3x^2(5-x^3)^{-2}$. 10). a) $-\frac{4}{25}$,   b) 0. 11). $\frac{3}{8}$. 12). a) $6(2x+3)(x^2+3x+1)^5$,   b) $-3(2x+5)(x^2+5x)^{-4}$,   c) $\frac{5x^4-7}{2\sqrt{x^5-7x}}$, d) $-\frac{3}{x^2}\left(\frac{1}{x}+5\right)^2$,   e) $6\left(x+\frac{1}{\sqrt{x}}\right)(4\sqrt{x}+x^2)^2$,   f) $\frac{1}{4}\left(2x-\frac{1}{\sqrt{x}}\right)\left(1-2\sqrt{x}+x^2\right)^{-\frac{3}{4}}$. 13). $y=12x-25$. 14). $x+4y=8$. 15). $x+6y=23$. 16). $\frac{6x}{\sqrt{x^2-1}}\left(\sqrt{x^2-1}+1\right)^5$. 17). $\frac{1}{\sqrt{4x+3+(4x+3)^{3/2}}}$. 18). $(0,3)$, minimum. 19). $-\left(1+\frac{3}{2\sqrt{x}}\right)\left(x+(\sqrt{x}+3)^2\right)^{-\frac{3}{2}}$.

Exercise 15B — (page 285)

1). 4500 per hour. 2). $0.622°$ C min^{-1}. 3). a) 4.8 cm s^{-1},   b) 24 cm^2 s^{-1}. 4). a) 240 mm^2 s^{-1},   b) 2400 mm^3 s^{-1}. 5). $300\pi=942.5$ mm^2 s^{-1}. 6). 0.25 m min^{-1}. 7). 7.64×10^{-3} ms^{-1}. 8). 0.0111 ms^{-1}. 9). 3.98×10^{-3} cm s^{-1}.

Exercise 15C — (page 289)

1). a) $2x$,   b) $x(3x+4)$,   c) $x(5x^3+9x+8)$,   d) $63x^2+100x+39$,   e) $3x^2$,   f) $(m+n)x^{m+n-1}$. 2). a) $x^2(x-3)^3(7x-9)$,   b) $5x^6(x+5)^2(2x+7)$,   c) $(x-1)^2(x+2)(5x+4)$,   d) $2x^3(3x-1)(9x-2)$, e) $32x^2(2x+1)^3(14x+3)$,   f) $7x^4(2x+11)^2(16x+55)$,   g) $x^2(x+1)(3x-1)(21x^2+10x-3)$, h) $10x^3(2x^3-5)^4(19x^3-10)$,   i) $7x^2(x^4+3x^2-x+3)(11x^4+21x^3-5x+9)$. 3). a) $(2x+3)(3x-1)^2(30x+23)$,   b) $-(2-3x)^2(5+2x)(30x+27)$,   c) $-3(1+x+x^2)^2(2-3x)^3(10x^2+3x+2)$, d) $8(3x^2+2)^3(7x^4-8x+1)(42x^5+14x^3-30x^2+3x-4)$,   e) $12x^2(x^4+1)^2(x^3+1)^3(1+x+2x^4)$, f) $(x^2+2x+3)(x^3-5x^2+1)^2(15x^5-60x^4+22x^3-47x^2-90x+4)$. 4). a) $\frac{3x+8}{2\sqrt{4+x}}$,   b) $\frac{2-3x}{\sqrt{5-2x}}$,   c) $\frac{2x^2(10x+9)}{3(1+x^2)^{\frac{2}{3}}}$,   d) $\frac{1+14x+5x^2}{\sqrt{2x+7}}$,   e) $\frac{(3x+2)(9x^2+2x-18)}{\sqrt{x^2-3}}$,   f) $\frac{2x+1}{2\sqrt{(x+2)(x-1)}}$. 5). a) $2(2x+1)(x-2)(4x-3)$, b) $\frac{x+1}{\sqrt{x(x+2)}}$,   c) $\frac{2(x^2+1)}{\sqrt{x^2+2}}$. 7). $(1,-3\sqrt{3})$. 8). $V=51.8$ when $x=\frac{32}{5}$. 9). a) $\frac{1}{(1+5x)^2}$,   b) $\frac{x(3x-4)}{(3x-2)^2}$,   c) $\frac{2x}{(1+2x^2)^2}$,   d) $\frac{1-2x^3}{(1+x^3)^2}$,   e) $\frac{1-x^2}{(1+x^2)^2}$,   f) $\frac{1-2x}{(1+x)^4}$. 10). a) $\frac{x+2}{2(x+1)^{\frac{3}{2}}}$,   b) $\frac{10-x}{2x^2\sqrt{x-5}}$, c) $-\frac{3x+4}{4x^2\sqrt{3x+2}}$,   d) $-\frac{5-12\sqrt{x}+5x}{2(x-5)^4\sqrt{x}}$,   e) $\frac{(x^2+1)^2(11x^2+12x-1)}{2(x+1)^{\frac{3}{2}}}$,   f) $\frac{x}{(x^2+1)^{\frac{1}{2}}(x^2+2)^{\frac{3}{2}}}$. 11). $-\frac{1}{\sqrt{(1-x)(1+x)^3}}$;

$(-2-2\sqrt{2}, 2-2\sqrt{2})$, minimum at $(-2+2\sqrt{2}, 2+2\sqrt{2})$. 15). $\frac{(x-1)(x+3)}{(x+1)^2}$; decreasing for $-3\le x<-1$ and $-1<x\le1$. 16). a) $\frac{2(x+3)(x^2+3x+2)}{(x+2)^2}$,   b) $\frac{3x^3+5x^2-x+1}{2(x+1)^2\sqrt{x}}$,   c) $\frac{3(x^8+4x^6-1)}{(x^6-1)^{\frac{1}{2}}(x^2+3)^{\frac{3}{2}}}$. 17). Rate of change of x: $0.1a$ ms^{-1}, Rate of change of gradient: -0.2 s^{-1}.

(In the list above, item 12). $y=\frac{2}{3}$. 13). $14y=8x-37$. 14). Maximum at)

Exercise 15D — (page 293)

1). Use $\theta=\frac{1}{6}\pi$. 2). $\frac{\pi}{180}$. 3). a) $-\cos x$,   b) $\sin x$,   c) $4\cos 4x$,   d) $-6\sin 3x$,   e) $\frac{1}{2}\pi\cos\frac{1}{2}\pi x$,   f) $-3\pi\sin 3\pi x$,   g) $-2\sin(2x-1)$,   h) $15\cos(3x+\frac{1}{4}\pi)$,   i) $5\sin(\frac{1}{2}\pi-5x)$,   j) $2\cos(\frac{1}{4}\pi-2x)$,   k) $2\sin(\frac{1}{2}\pi+2x)$,   l) $\pi\cos\left(\frac{1}{2}\pi(1+2x)\right)$. 4). a) $2\sin x\cos x$,   b) $-2\cos x\sin x$,   c) $-3\cos^2 x\sin x$,   d) $5\sin\frac{1}{2}x\cos\frac{1}{2}x$,   e) $-8\cos^3 2x\sin 2x$,

f) $2x\cos x^2$, g) $-42x^2\sin 2x^3$, h) $\sin(\frac{1}{2}x - \frac{1}{3}\pi)\cos(\frac{1}{2}x - \frac{1}{3}\pi)$, i) $-6\pi\cos^2 2\pi x\sin 2\pi x$, j) $6x\sin^2 x^2\cos x^2$, k) 0, l) $-\cos\frac{1}{2}x\sin\frac{1}{2}x$. 6). a) $2\sec 2x\tan 2x$, b) $-3\mathrm{cosec}3x\cot 3x$, c) $\sec(x - \frac{1}{2}\pi)\tan(x - \frac{1}{2}\pi) = -\mathrm{cosec}\,x\cot x$, d) $-3\mathrm{cosec}^2(3x - \frac{1}{6}\pi)$, e) $3\sec^2(3x + \frac{1}{5}\pi)$, f) $2\mathrm{cosec}(\frac{1}{4}\pi - 2x)\cot(\frac{1}{4}\pi - 2x)$, g) $6\sec^2(6x - \frac{1}{7}\pi)$, h) $5\mathrm{cosec}^2(\frac{1}{3}\pi - 5x)$. 8). a) $6y = 3x + 3\sqrt{3} - \pi$, b) $x + \sqrt{2}y = 2 + \frac{1}{4}\pi$, c) $y = 0$, d) $y = \pi(\pi - x)$. 9). a) Maximum at $\frac{1}{4}\pi$, minimum at $\frac{5}{4}\pi$, b) Positive inflexion at π, c) Maxima at 0, 2π, minimum at π, d) Maxima at $\frac{1}{12}\pi$, $\frac{13}{12}\pi$, minima at $\frac{5}{12}\pi$, $\frac{17}{12}\pi$, e) Minimum at $\frac{1}{4}\pi$, maximum at $\frac{5}{4}\pi$, f) Maxima at $\frac{7}{6}\pi$, $\frac{11}{6}\pi$, minima at $\frac{1}{2}\pi$, $\frac{3}{2}\pi$. 10). 0, $\sin a$; this proves the formula for $\sin(x + y)$. 11). All three are equal to $-2\sin 2x$. Consider the double angle formulae. 12). $\cos 2x$. 13). The tangent intercepts the y-axis at $y = \frac{5}{12}\pi - \frac{1}{2}\sqrt{3} > 0$. 14). The graph curves down when $y > 0$ and curves up when $y < 0$; $y = \sin(nx + a)$. 15). $2\sec^3 x - \sec x$. 16). a) $x^2(x\cos x + 3\sin x + 3)$, b) $\cos^2 x - \sin^2 x$, c) $\cos x - x\sin x$, d) $x(x\cos x - x\sin x + 2\sin x + 2\cos x)$, e) $\sin x(2x\cos x + \sin x)$, f) $2x\sin^2 2x(3x\cos 2x + \sin 2x)$, g) $\sin^3 2x\cos^2 5x(8\cos 5x\cos 2x - 15\sin 5x\sin 2x)$, h) $x^2\sec^2 x(3 + 2x\tan x)$, i) $\frac{x\cos x - \sin x}{x^2}$, j) $(1 - x\cot x)\mathrm{cosec}\,x$, k) $2x(1 - x\cot x)\mathrm{cosec}^2 x$, l) $-\frac{\cos x + 2x\sin x}{2x^{\frac{3}{2}}}$, m) $-\frac{\sec^2 x}{(1+\tan x)^2}$, n) $-\frac{\sec x}{\sec x + \tan x} = -\frac{1}{1+\sin x}$, o) $\frac{1}{1+\cos x}$, p) $\frac{2x\cos x - x\sec x\tan x + \sin x(2 + x + \tan x)}{(2 + \tan x)^2}$. 17). $\cos y$, $\frac{1}{\sqrt{1-x^2}}$. 18). b) $\frac{2}{27}\pi R^3\sqrt{3}$. 19). b) $3\sqrt{3}r$, an equilateral triangle.

Exercise 15E — (page 298)

1). a) $3e^{3x}$, b) $-e^{-x}$, c) $6e^{2x}$, d) $16e^{-4x}$, e) $3e^{3x+4}$, f) $-2e^{3-2x}$, g) $-e^{1-x}$, h) $12e \times e^{2+4x}$, i) $2xe^{x^2}$, j) $-xe^{-\frac{1}{2}x^2}$, k) $-\frac{1}{x^2}e^{\frac{1}{x}}$, l) $\frac{1}{2\sqrt{x}}e^{\sqrt{x}}$. 2). a) $3e^2$, b) $-2e$, c) -1, d) -2. 3). a) $y = e^{-1}(x + 2)$, b) $y = 3x - 1$, c) $y = 4(1 + e^4)x - 4 - 6e^4$, d) $y = e^{-6}(7 - 2x)$. 4). a) $2(2x + 1)e^{x^2+x+1}$, b) $-15e^{-x}\left(e^{-x} + 1\right)^4$, c) $-\frac{x}{\sqrt{1-x^2}}e^{\sqrt{1-x^2}}$. 5). $-\frac{15}{4}$. 6). a) None, b) Maximum at $x = 2$, c) Maxima at ± 1, minimum at 0. 7).

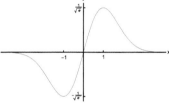

8). a) $(x + 1)e^x$, b) $e^{x^2}\sec x(2x + \tan x)$, c) $e^{2x}(\cos x + 2x\cos x - x\sin x)$, d) $e^{-x}(\cos x - \sin x)$, e) $(x^2 + 2x + 3)e^x$, f) $4x + x(x + 2)e^x$, g) $x^2(2x + 3)e^{2x}$, h) $\frac{2 + e^x(x + 2)}{2\sqrt{e^x + 1}}$, i) $\frac{e^x(2 + 5x + 5x^2)}{\sqrt{2 + 5x^2}}$, j) $e^{ax}\left[a\cos(bx + \frac{1}{2}\pi) - b\sin(bx + \frac{1}{2}\pi)\right]$, k) $\frac{4}{(e^x + e^{-x})^2}$, l) e^{x+e^x}, m) $\frac{e^x(3 - 5x) - 10}{(e^x - 2)^2}$, n) $\frac{e^x(2x - 1)}{(2x + 1)^2}$, o) $2\sec^2 2xe^{\tan 2x}$, p) $-6\sin 3x\cos 3xe^{\cos^2 3x}$. 9). a) $y = 0$, b) $y = (1 - \pi)x + \pi^2$, c) $(e^2 + 1)^2y = e^2x + e^2(e^2 - 1)$. 10). Turning points at $(n - \frac{1}{4})\pi$ for $n \in \mathbb{N}$; a maximum when n is odd, a minimum when n is even. 11). 0 is a positive inflexion when n is odd, and minimum when n is even; n is always a maximum. 12). $y = e^a(x + 1 - a)$; $e^x - e^a(x + 1 - a) = e^a\left[e^{x-a} - (x - a) - 1\right] \geq 0$. 13). a) 0, b) $E(a)$, c) $E(x)E(y) = F_{x+y}(x) = F_{x+y}(0) = E(x + y)$.

Exercise 15F — (page 301)

1). a) x^{-1}, b) $\frac{2}{2x-1}$, c) $-\frac{2}{1-2x}$, d) $2x^{-1}$, e) $\frac{b}{a+bx}$, f) $-x^{-1}$, g) $-\frac{3}{3x+1}$, h) $-\frac{5}{(2x+1)(3x-1)}$, i) $-6x^{-1}$, j) $\frac{2x+1}{x(x+1)}$, k) $\frac{3x-2}{x(x-1)}$, l) $\frac{2x+1}{x^2+x-2}$. 2). a) $y = 2x - 1 - \ln 2$, b) $y = 2x - 1$, c) $y = -3x - 1 - \ln 3$, d) $y = e^{-1}x + \ln 3$. 3). a) Minimum of 1 at $x = 1$, b) Minimum of $\frac{1}{2} - \ln 2$ at $x = 1$, c) Minimum of 1 at $x = 1$, d) Minimum of 1 at $x = 1$. 4). a) $\frac{3x^2}{1+x^3}$, b) $\frac{2x^3}{2+x^4}$, c) $\frac{3x^2+4}{x^3+4x}$. 5). $ey = x$. 6). $y = 1 - \frac{1}{2}x$. 7). a) $x > 6$, $\frac{2(x-4)}{(x-2)(x-6)}$, positive throughout $x > 6$, b) $2 < x < 6$, $\frac{2(4-x)}{(x-2)(6-x)}$, positive for $2 < x < 4$, negative for $4 < x < 6$, c) There is no natural domain! 8). a) $x(2\ln x + 1)$, b) $6x\ln x + 3x + 4x^{-1}$, c) $\cot x$, d) $e^x(\ln x + x^{-1})$, e) $\ln(x^2 + 1) + \frac{2x^2}{x^2+1}$, f) $\frac{1}{x\ln x}$, g) $\frac{1}{2\sqrt{x}}(\ln 2x + 2)$, h) $12(4x + 1)^2\ln 3x + x^{-1}(4x + 1)^3$, i) $\frac{1}{x\ln x}$, j) $\frac{1-\ln x}{x^2}$, k) $\frac{2}{(x^2+4)} - x^{-2}\ln(x^2 + 4)$, l) $\frac{3}{(3x+2)(2x-1)} - \frac{2}{(2x-1)^2}\ln(3x + 2)$.

Review Exercises 5 — (page 303)

1). a) $\cos x$, b) $-\cos x$. 2). a) $21.8°, 201.8°$, b) $11.8°, 78.2°, 191.8°, 258.2°$. 3). $24.1°, 155.9°$.
4). $30°, 270°$. 5). a) $2\sin 2x$, b) $105°, 165°, 285°, 345°$. 6). a) $168.5°$, b) $333.4°$, c) $225°$,
d) $553.1°$. 8). a) 2 at $180°$, 0 at $90°$, b) 9 at $240°$, 1 at $60°$, c) 49 at $105°$, 9 at $45°$, d) 8
at $90°$, 5 at $180°$, e) 6 at $180°$, 3 at $360°$, f) 60 at $7.5°$, 30 at $52.5°$. 9). a) $0°, 180°, 360°$,
b) $0°, 30°, 150°, 180°, 360°$, c) $67.5°, 157.5°, 247.5°, 337.5°$, d) $30°, 120°, 210°, 300°$. 10). a)
$\frac{360}{T}$, b) $\frac{k}{360}$. 11). $\alpha = 1$, $\beta = 12$, $A = 0.2$, $B = 1.8$. 12). $\frac{1}{2}\pi$ when $x > 0$ and $-\frac{1}{2}\pi$ when $x < 0$.
13). a) Domain: $-1 \le x \le 1$, Range: $-\pi - 4 \le y \le \pi - 4$, b) Domain: $3 \le x \le 5$, Range: $-\pi \le y \le \pi$.
14). b) $-\frac{25}{24}$. 15). $60°, 120°, 240°, 300°$. 16). a) 1, b) $\frac{4}{5}$. 17). $73.9°$. 18). $26.6°, 90°, 206.6°$,
$270°$. 20). $2\sin(\theta + 60°)$; $90°, 330°$. 21). a) $2\cos(x + 60°)$, b) $0°, 60°, 180°, 240°, 360°$. 22). a)
$15\cos(x - 0.6435)$, b) 0.276. 23). $\sqrt{5}\cos(x - 26.6°)$; a) $90°, 323.1°$, b) $-\sqrt{5} \le k \le \sqrt{5}$.
24). $-\frac{1}{2}$. 25). a) $13\sin(x + 67.4°)$, b) 7.5 at $202.6°$, 1 at $22.6°$. 26). $5\cos(x + 53.1°)$; a)
$13.3°, 240.4°$, b) $\frac{1}{3}, \frac{1}{13}$. 27). a) $y = \frac{1}{2}(3 - x)$, b) $\sqrt{5}\sin(x + 63.4°)$, c) $(2\sin\theta, 2\cos\theta)$, $74.4°$.
28). a) $(56.8°, 0)$, $(123.2°, 0)$, b) $(53.1°, \frac{3}{5})$, $(120°, -\frac{1}{2})$. 29). a) $\frac{2}{\sqrt{5}}, \frac{2-\sqrt{3}}{2\sqrt{5}}, -\frac{2+\sqrt{3}}{2\sqrt{5}}$, b) $\pm\frac{11}{2}$.
30). a) $x = \frac{1}{\log_{10} a - 2}$, b) $x = \sqrt{\frac{5}{2}a}$. 31). 0.774. 32). $f^{-1}(x) = 10^x - 1$ for $x \in \mathbb{R}$. 33). $\log_{10} 50$.
35). $\log_{10} 3 - \frac{1}{6}$. 39). $\log_2 \frac{x+2}{x}, \frac{2}{7}$. 40). 10000, 451 years. 41). $k = 2.6$, $n = 0.9$, 72%. 42). a)
$a = 2.3$, $b = 0.1$, 3.2 g, b) $k = 2.0$, $c = 1.2$, c) The second model is much more accurate. 43). a)
5, b) 1, 1, 9. 44). $80(4x - 1)^{19}$. 45). $y + 24x = 49$. 46). $3x + 4y = 18$. 47). 0.377 cm^2 s^{-1}.
48). $8x + 5y - 34 = 0$. 49). $\frac{x^2 - 1}{2\sqrt{x^3(x^2+1)}}$. 50). $y = 2x - 3$. 51). a) Minimum, b) 20. 52). 0.0477 cm
s^{-1}. 53). Minima at $(0, -4), (\pm\sqrt{3}, -4)$, maxima at $(\pm 1, 0)$. 54). $\frac{1}{2}$, minimum. 55). $(3, 0)$. 56). a) -1
at $x = 1$, b) 1 at $x = 1$. 57). $(0, 1), (\pm 3, e^{-81})$. 58). $e^{-2a} = 3a$ 60). b) $\frac{1}{2}\pi, \frac{5}{6}\pi$, c) Oscillations
should decay with time, so a decay factor like e^{-kt} would help. 61). a) $\frac{1}{2}\cos\frac{1}{2}x - \frac{1}{3}\sin\frac{1}{2}x$, b) 1,
$\frac{1}{2}$, c) $4\pi. 6\pi$, d) 12π. 62). a) $\frac{2}{3}\pi, \pi, \frac{4}{3}\pi, 2\pi$, c) $\cos x + 2\cos 2x$. 63). a) $x^2(x\cos x + 3\sin x)$,
b) $\frac{x+6}{2(x+3)^{\frac{3}{2}}}$. 64). $(1 - 3x)e^{-3x}$, $(\frac{1}{3}, \frac{1}{3e})$. 65). a) $2\cos 2x \cos 4x - 4\sin 2x \sin 4x$, b) $\frac{3x(2\ln x - 1)}{(\ln x)^2}$, c)
$-2(1 - \frac{1}{5}x)^9$. 66). $(\frac{1}{2}, 4\sqrt{2})$. 67). $\frac{x\cos x - \sin x}{x^2}$. 70). $\frac{n+1}{a}$, $M = \left(\frac{n+1}{a}\right)^{n+1} e^{-n-1}$. 71). When $n = 2$, all
rectangles give the same value. When $n = 3$, the square gives the least value.

Exercise 16A — (page 313)

1). a) $(180, 60)$, b) $(5, -10)$. 2). a) $(\frac{2}{3}, \frac{4}{3})$, b) $(2, 0)$. 3). $\frac{1}{2}\pi$. 4). $\frac{2}{3}\pi$.

5).   6).   7).   8).

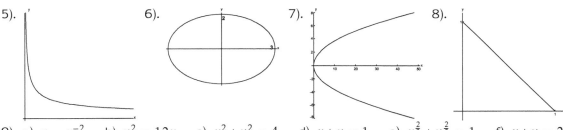

9). a) $y = x^{-2}$, b) $y^2 = 12x$, c) $x^2 + y^2 = 4$, d) $x + y = 1$, e) $x^{\frac{2}{3}} + y^{\frac{2}{3}} = 1$, f) $x + y = 2$,
g) $4x^3 = 27y^2$, h) $5x + 2y = 3$, i) $y = \frac{1+x}{1-2x}$, j) $y^2 = 1 + x^2$, k) $x^5 = y^3$, l) $x = \frac{2y}{1-y^2}$.

Exercise 16B — (page 315)

1). a) $\frac{2}{3t^2}$, b) $-\tan t$, c) $-\frac{3}{2}\cot t$, d) $\frac{2t-1}{3t^2+1}$. 2). a) 2, b) $\frac{1}{3}$, c) $\frac{3}{5}$, d) $-\frac{1}{18}$. 3). a) -3,
b) 1, c) $\sqrt{3}$, d) -8. 5). a) $\frac{1}{3}$, b) $3y = x - 1$. 6). $x + y = \pi + 1$. 7). a) $3y - x = 9$, b)
$5y = 3\sqrt{3}x - 30$. 8). a) $3x + y = 165$, b) $y = -\sqrt{3}x$. 9). a) $y = 4x - 30$, b) $(-\frac{1}{2}, -32)$. 10). a)
$y = 2x - 36$, b) $(27, 18)$. 11). a) $3y = 2\sqrt{3}x + 3$.

Exercise 16C — (page 318)

1). a) t, $\frac{1}{2}$, b) $\frac{1}{3}e^{t-2}$, $\frac{1}{9}e^{t-2}$, c) $\frac{1}{2t}e^t$, $\frac{1}{4t^2}(t-1)e^t$, d) e^{t^2}, e^{t^2}, e) $\frac{t(3t+4)}{3t^2-1}$, $-\frac{2(6t^2+3t+2)}{(3t^2-1)^3}$, f)
$e^{-t}\cos t$, $-e^{-2t}(\cos t - \sin t)$. 2). $-\frac{2(t^2-6t-1)}{9(t^2+1)^3}$; minimum at $(38, -5)$ $(t = 3)$. 3). $\frac{d^2y}{dx^2} = -\frac{1}{4a}\text{cosec}^4\frac{1}{2}t < 0$.

4). $-e^{-t}(\cos t + \sin t)$; maximum at $t = \frac{1}{4}\pi$, minimum at $t = \frac{4}{5}\pi$.   5). $2\cos 2t \sec t$, $-2(\cos 2t + 2)\sec^2 t \tan t$; maxima at $(\pm\frac{1}{\sqrt{2}}, 1)$ ($t = \frac{1}{4}\pi$, $\frac{7}{4}\pi$), and minima at $(\pm\frac{1}{\sqrt{2}}, -1)$ ($t = \frac{3}{4}\pi$, $\frac{5}{4}\pi$).

8). N must lie on the circle with centre 0 and radius $\sqrt{2}$, no matter when P lies on H. This circle is tangent to the hyperbola at the points $(1,1)$ and $(-1,-1)$.

Exercise 16D — (page 322)

1). $-\frac{1}{3}$.   2). $3x - 2y = 8$.   3). $x - 2y = 7$, $-\frac{86}{13}$.

4). a) $-\frac{1}{\sqrt{3}}$,   b) 0,   c) -2,   d) $-\frac{1}{3}\pi$.   5). $3y - x = 5$.   6). $x = 1$.   7). $(3,1)$, $(-3,-1)$.

8). a) $(\pm 1, 0)$, $(0, \pm\frac{1}{2})$,   b) $-1 \le x \le 1$, $-\frac{1}{2} \le y \le 1$,   d) $y' = -\frac{x}{4y}$; the curve crosses the y-axis horizontally,   e) the curve crosses the x-axis vertically.   9). a) $(\pm 1, 0)$ only,   b) $|x| > 1$, $y \in \mathbb{R}$, d) $y' = \frac{x}{y}$; since x cannot be 0, there are no turning points,   e) the curve crosses the x-axis vertically.   10). a) $(1,0)$, $(0,1)$,   b) y cannot be negative,   c) $y' = \frac{2(x-1)}{3y^2}$, $-\frac{2}{3}$,   d) the modulus of the gradient becomes very large,   e) $y^3 = X^2$.   12). b) $y' = -e^{x-y} < 0$,   c) $x, y \le \ln 2$. 13). a) The curve is symmetrical in the y-axis,   b) $y' = -\frac{2x}{3y^2}$ is negative for $x > 0$ and positive for $x < 0$,   c) Maximum.   14). 0 at $(0,0)$, 1 at $(-1,0)$.   15). 1 at $(0,0)$, -2 at $(0,1)$, 1 at $(0,2)$. 16). b) $(\pm\frac{1}{4}\sqrt{6}, \frac{1}{4}\sqrt{2})$, $(\pm\frac{1}{4}\sqrt{6}, -\frac{1}{4}\sqrt{2})$, $(\pm 1, 0)$.

8).f)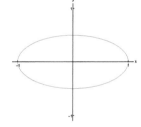

9).f)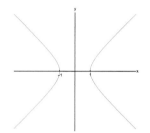

10).f)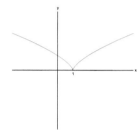

11).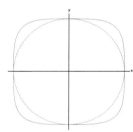

12).c)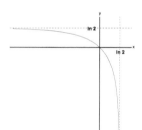

13).d)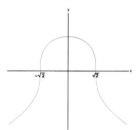

16).d)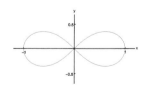

Exercise 16E — (page 324)

1). a) $-\frac{x^2}{y^2}$, $-\frac{2(x^4 + xy^3)}{y^5}$,   b) $-\frac{\cos x}{\cos y}$, $\frac{\cos^2 y \sin x + \cos^2 x \sin y}{\cos^3 y}$,   c) $\frac{3x^2 - 2y^2}{4xy}$, $-\frac{3(3x^4 - 4x^2 y^2 - 4y^4)}{16x^2 y^3}$,   d) $-\frac{y(2x+y)}{x(x+2y)}$, $\frac{6y(x+y)(x^2+xy+y^2)}{x^2(x+2y)^3}$,   e) $\frac{1 - e^{x+y}}{1 + e^{x+y}}$, $-\frac{4e^{x+y}}{(1 + e^{x+y})^3}$,   f) $-\frac{y^2 - 1}{2xy - 1}$, $\frac{2(y^2 - 1)(3xy^2 - 2y + x)}{(2xy - 1)^3}$.   2). a) -10,   b) $\frac{19}{18}$,   c) $\frac{3}{2}$, d) 1.   3). a) Minimum at $(-4, -4)$, maximum at $(-4, 6)$,   b) Minimum at $(-4, -8)$, maximum at $(2, 4)$,   c) Minimum at $(\frac{1}{2}, 1)$,   d) Minimum at $(1, 1)$, maximum at $(\sqrt[3]{3}, -\sqrt{33})$.   4). b) Minimum at $(2, 3)$, maximum at $(-4, 1)$,   c) $(0, 5)$, $(-2, -1)$.

Exercise 17A — (page 327)

1). a) $\frac{1}{14}(2x + 1)^7 + c$,   b) $\frac{1}{15}(3x - 5)^5 + c$,   c) $-\frac{1}{28}(1 - 7x)^4 + c$,   d) $\frac{2}{11}(\frac{1}{2}x + 1)^{11} + c$,   e) $-\frac{1}{10}(5x + 2)^{-2} + c$,   f) $\frac{2}{3}(1 - 3x)^{-1} + c$,   g) $-\frac{1}{4}(x + 1)^{-4} + c$,   h) $-\frac{1}{8}(4x + 1)^{-3} + c$,   i) $\frac{1}{15}(10x + 1)^{\frac{3}{2}} + c$, j) $\sqrt{2x - 1} + c$,   k) $\frac{6}{5}(\frac{1}{2}x + 2)^{\frac{5}{3}} + c$,   l) $\frac{16}{9}(2 + 6c)^{\frac{3}{4}} + c$.   2). a) 820,   b) $\frac{26}{3}$,   c) $\frac{2}{15}$,   d) $\frac{16}{225}$.

3). 2.25.   4). 9.1125.   5). a) 24.3,   b) $\frac{9}{2}$.   6). $\frac{1}{20}$.   7). $\frac{1}{6}$.   8). a) $\frac{1}{36}(x^2+1)^{18}+c$,   b) $\frac{2}{9}(x^3-1)^{\frac{3}{2}}+c$,   c) $\frac{1}{12}(x^2+2x-3)^6+c$,   d) $\frac{4}{3}(x^2+3x+1)^{\frac{3}{2}}+c$,   e) $\frac{1}{4}(\sqrt{x}+1)^8+c$,   f) $\frac{1}{2}(x^{\frac{1}{3}}+1)^6+c$.
9). $\ln[x+\sqrt{x^2+5}]+c$. 10). a) $\frac{1}{3}e^{3x}+c$,   b) $-e^{-x}+c$,   c) $\frac{3}{2}e^{2x}+c$,   d) $e^{-4x}+c$,   e) $\frac{1}{3}e^{3x+4}+c$,   f) $-\frac{1}{2}e^{3-2x}+c$,   g) $-e^{1-x}+c$,   h) $\frac{3}{4}e^{3+4x}+c$. 11). a) $\frac{1}{2}(e^4-4^2)$,   b) $e-e^{-1}$,   c) $\frac{1}{2}(e^5-1)$,   d) $2(e^{10}-e^8)$,   e) 6,   f) $\frac{3}{4}e$,   g) $\frac{1}{\ln 2}$, $\frac{3^{12}-1}{3^3\ln 3}=17900$. 12). $\frac{1}{2}(e^4-1)$. 13). $1-e^{-N}$, 1. 14). a) $\frac{1}{2}\ln x+c, x>0$,   b) $\ln(x-1)+c, x>1$,   c) $-\ln(1-x)+c, x<1$,   d) $\frac{1}{4}\ln(4x+3)+c, x>-\frac{3}{4}$,   e) $-2\ln(1-2x)+c, x<\frac{1}{2}$,   f) $2\ln(1+2x)+c, x>-\frac{1}{2}$,   g) $-2\ln(-1-2x)+c, x<-\frac{1}{2}$,   h) $2\ln(2x-1)+c$, $x>\frac{1}{2}$. 15). a) $\ln 2$,   b) $\frac{1}{2}\ln 3$,   c) $\frac{1}{2}\ln\frac{13}{7}$,   d) $\ln\left(\frac{5e-7}{4e-7}\right)$,   e) $\ln 2$,   f) $8+\ln 5$. 16). $\pi\ln\frac{3}{2}$.
17). $y=1+\frac{3}{2}\ln\left(\frac{2x+1}{3}\right)$. 18). $\frac{1}{2}\pi\ln 2$. 19). a) $\frac{1}{2}\sin 2x+c$,   b) $-\frac{1}{3}\cos 3x+c$,   c) $\frac{1}{2}\sin(2x+1)$,   d) $-\frac{1}{3}\cos(3x-1)$,   e) $\cos(1-x)+c$,   f) $-2\sin(4-\frac{1}{2}x)+c$,   g) $-2\cos(\frac{1}{2}x+\frac{1}{3}\pi)+c$,   h) $2\cos\frac{1}{2}x+c$ i) $\frac{1}{3}\sec 3x+c$,   j) $-\frac{1}{4}\operatorname{cosec}4s+c$,   k) $\frac{1}{5}\tan 5x+c$,   l) $\frac{1}{2}\sec 2x+c$. 20). a) 1,   b) $\frac{1}{\sqrt{2}}$,   c) $\frac{1}{2}$,   d) $-\frac{1}{3\sqrt{2}}$,   e) $\frac{1}{6}(\sqrt{3}-1)$,   f) 0,   g) $\sin 1$,   h) $2\left(\cos 1-\cos\frac{5}{4}\right)$,   i) 4,   j) $\frac{1}{3}(1-\sqrt{2})$,   k) $\frac{1}{2}(\cot\frac{1}{2}-\cot 1)=\frac{1}{2}\operatorname{cosec}1$,   l) $4(\sec 0.075-\sec 0.025)$. 21). a) $\frac{1}{4}$,   b) 0,   c) $\frac{3}{2}$,   d) $\frac{1}{27}\sqrt{3}$.
22). $(0,1),(\frac{3}{4}\pi,0),1+\sqrt{2},\frac{1}{4}\pi(3\pi+2)$.

Exercise 17B — (page 331)

1). a) $-\ln 4$,   b) $-\frac{1}{2}\ln 3$,   c) $-\frac{2}{3}\ln\frac{8}{5}$,   d) $\ln\left(\frac{7-2e}{7-e}\right)$,   e) $-\ln\frac{5}{3}$,   f) $2-\ln 2$.   2). a) $\frac{1}{2}x-\frac{1}{4}\sin 2x+c$,   b) $\frac{1}{2}x+\frac{1}{2}\sin x+c$,   c) $\frac{3}{8}x-\frac{1}{4}\sin 2x+\frac{1}{32}\sin 4x+c$,   d) $\frac{3}{8}x+\frac{1}{4}\sin 2x+\frac{1}{32}\sin 4x+c$,   e) $\tan x+\frac{1}{3}\tan^3 x+c$,   f) $-\frac{1}{3}\cot 3x-\frac{1}{9}\cot^3 3x+c$,   g) $-\cos x+\frac{2}{3}\cos^3 x-\frac{1}{5}\cos^5 x+c$,   h) $\frac{1}{3}\sec^3 x-\sec x+c$,   i) $-\frac{1}{2}\cot 2x-x+c$,   j) $\frac{1}{5}\tan 5x-x+c$,   k) $-\frac{1}{6}\cos^3 2x+\frac{1}{10}\cos^5 2x+c$,   l) $\sin x-\cos x+\frac{2}{3}\sin^3 x-\frac{2}{3}\cos^3 x+c$.   3). They add to x plus an arbitrary constant.
$1\equiv(\cos^2 x+\sin^2 x)\equiv\cos^4 x+\sin^4 x+\frac{1}{2}\sin^2 2x$. 4). $2-\frac{1}{2}\pi$. 5). a) $(\frac{1}{4}\pi,\frac{1}{4}\sqrt{2})$,   b) $\frac{1}{6}(5\sqrt{2}-4)$.
6). a) $\frac{1}{4}\sin 2x-\frac{1}{8}\sin 4x+c$,   b) $\frac{1}{4}\cos 2x-\frac{1}{12}\cos 6x+c$,   c) $\frac{1}{12}\sin 6x-\frac{1}{24}\sin 12x+c$,   d) $\frac{1}{2}\sin x-\frac{1}{14}\sin 7x+c$. 7). $\frac{2}{5}\sqrt{3}-\frac{1}{3}\pi$.

Exercise 17C — (page 337)

1). a) $2\ln(2-\sqrt{x})+c$,   b) $-\frac{1}{3(3x+4)}+c$,   c) $-3\cos(\frac{1}{3}x-\frac{1}{2}\pi)+c$,   d) $\frac{1}{7}(x-1)^7+\frac{1}{6}(x-1)^6+c$,   e) $\ln(e^x+1)+c$,   f) $\frac{1}{2}\ln(3+4\sqrt{x})$,   g) $\frac{6}{5}(x+2)^{\frac{5}{2}}-4(x+2)^{\frac{3}{2}}+c$,   h) $\frac{2}{3}(x+6)\sqrt{x-3}+c$,   i) $\ln(\ln x)+c$,   j) $\sin^{-1}\frac{1}{2}x+c$. 2). a) $\frac{1}{20}(2x+1)^5-\frac{1}{16}(2x+1)^4+c$,   b) $\frac{1}{28}(2x-3)^7+\frac{7}{24}(2x-3)^6+c$,   c) $\frac{1}{10}(2x-1)^{\frac{5}{2}}+\frac{1}{6}(2x-1)^{\frac{3}{2}}+c$,   d) $\frac{2}{3}(x+2)\sqrt{x-4}+c$,   e) $\ln(x+1)+\frac{1}{x+1}+c$,   f) $\frac{1}{4}(2x+3)-\frac{3}{4}\ln(2x+3)+c$.
3). a) $\frac{1}{3}\sin^{-1}3x+c$,   b) $\frac{1}{2}x\sqrt{16-9x^2}+\frac{8}{3}\sin^{-1}\frac{3}{4}x+c$,   c) $\frac{1}{2}\ln(1+2e^x)+c$,   d) $\frac{3}{10}(1+x)^{\frac{2}{3}}(2x-3)+c$,   e) $\frac{x}{\sqrt{1-x^2}}+c$,   f) $-2\sqrt{x}-4\ln|2-\sqrt{x}|+c$. 4). b) $\tan^{-1}e^x+c$. 5). a) $\ln(\frac{1+e}{2})$,   b) $2\ln 2$,   c) $\frac{13}{42}$,   d) $\frac{16}{15}$,   e) $\frac{1}{6}\pi$,   f) $109\frac{1}{15}$,   g) 8π,   h) $\frac{1}{8}\pi$,   i) $\frac{1}{2}$,   j) $\frac{1}{\sqrt{3}}$,   k) $3\ln\frac{3}{2}$. 6). $\frac{1}{4}\pi-\frac{1}{2}$.
7). a) $\frac{1}{4}(x^2+1)^4+c$,   b) $\frac{1}{3}(4+x^2)^{\frac{3}{2}}+c$,   c) $\frac{1}{6}\sin^6 x+c$,   d) $\frac{1}{4}\tan^4 x+c$,   e) $-\sqrt{1-x^4}+c$,   f) $-\frac{1}{8}\cos^4 2x+c$. 8). a) $\ln(e+1)$,   b) $\frac{1}{2}\ln 2$,   c) $\frac{1}{2}\ln\frac{4}{3}$,   d) $\frac{2}{3}$,   e) 78,   f) $\frac{1}{12}(4-\sqrt{2})$,   g) $\frac{860}{3}\sqrt{2}$,   h) $\frac{1}{6}$,   i) $\frac{2}{3}(10\sqrt{10}-1)$,   j) $\frac{1}{3}$,   k) $\frac{1}{n+1}$,   l) $\frac{7}{3}$. 9). a) $\ln|\sec x+\tan x|+c,\ln|\operatorname{cosec}x+\cot x|+c$,   b) $\ln|\tan(\frac{1}{2}x+\frac{1}{4}\pi)|+c,\ln|\tan\frac{1}{2}x|+c$. 10). Try $u=ax+b$ and $u=f(x)$ respectively. 11). $P(7,0)$
at $t=2, Q(0,3)$ at $t=1; \frac{47}{5}$. 12). $\frac{4}{3}\pi ab^2$. 13). $\frac{3}{16}\pi$. 14). π. 15). a) $\frac{1}{4}\pi$,   b) $\frac{1}{2}\pi$,   c); $\frac{1}{6}\pi$,   d) π,   e) 1,   f) $\frac{1}{2}\pi$. 16). $\frac{1}{9}\pi\sqrt{3}$. 18). $\frac{1}{16}$.

Exercise 17D — (page 341)

1). a) $\frac{1}{2}x^2+2x+9\ln|x-2|+c$,   b) $\frac{1}{2}x^2+5\ln|x+3|+c$,   c) $\frac{1}{4}x^2-\frac{1}{4}x+\frac{1}{8}\ln|2x+9|+c$,   d) $\frac{1}{3}x^3-\frac{3}{2}x^2+9x-27\ln|x+3|+c$,   e) $\frac{1}{4}x^4+\frac{1}{3}x^3+\frac{1}{2}x^2+x+2\ln|x-1|+c$,   f) $\frac{3}{4}x^2+\frac{1}{2}x+2\ln|x-2|+c$. 2). a) $\ln\left(\frac{(x+2)^2}{|x+1|}\right)+c$,   b) $\ln\left|\frac{(x+1)^5}{x^3}\right|+c$,   c) $\frac{1}{8}\ln\left|\frac{x-4}{x+4}\right|+c$,   d) $3\ln\left|\frac{x+2}{x+1}\right|-\frac{4}{x+2}+c$,   e) $3\ln|x-3|-\frac{10}{x-3}+c$,   f) $2x^{-1}+\frac{1}{2}\ln\left|\frac{(x-4)^3}{x}\right|+c$,   g) $3\ln\frac{|x|}{\sqrt{x^2+1}}+c$,   h) $\ln|x-2|+\tan^{-1}\frac{1}{2}x+c$,   i) $\frac{2}{3}\tan^{-1}\frac{1}{3}x+\frac{1}{9}\ln\frac{|x|}{\sqrt{x^2+9}}+c$.

3). a) $\ln\frac{5}{3}$, b) $-\frac{5}{3}\ln 5$, c) $\ln\frac{4}{3}$, d) $\frac{2}{15}-\frac{2}{25}\ln\frac{3}{2}$, e) $-\frac{1}{6}+\frac{1}{9}\ln 200$, f) $\frac{3}{2}+\ln\frac{125}{32}$, g) 0, h) $\frac{1}{4}\pi-3\ln\frac{3}{2}$, i) $\frac{1}{6}\pi\sqrt{3}-\frac{1}{2}\ln 3$. 4). $\frac{1}{x+2}-\frac{1}{x+3}$, $\ln\left|\frac{x+3}{x+2}\right|+c$, $-\frac{1}{x+2}-\frac{1}{x+3}+2\ln\left|\frac{x+3}{x+2}\right|+c$. 5). $2x^{\frac{1}{2}}-3x^{\frac{1}{3}}+6x^{\frac{1}{6}}-\ln\left(x^{\frac{1}{6}}+1\right)+c$. 7). $(1,1)$, $2\ln\frac{4}{3}$. 8). $4\ln\frac{32}{27}$. 9). $\frac{1}{72}\pi(9-2\sqrt{3})$. 10). $\frac{1}{3}\ln|x+1|-\frac{1}{6}\ln|x^2-x+1|+\frac{1}{\sqrt{3}}\tan^{-1}\frac{2x-1}{\sqrt{3}}+c$. 11). a) $\frac{1}{2a}\ln 3$, b) $\frac{1}{48a^3}\pi(4+3\ln 3)$.

Exercise 17E — (page 345)

1). a) $-x\cos x+\sin x+c$, b) $3(x-1)e^x+c$, c) $(x+3)e^x+c$, d) $(\frac{1}{2}x-\frac{1}{4})e^{2x}+c$, e) $\frac{1}{4}x\sin 4x+\frac{1}{16}\cos 4x+c$, f) $\frac{1}{2}x^2\ln 2x-\frac{1}{4}x^2+c$, g) $-\frac{1}{2}x^2\cos x^2+\frac{1}{2}\sin x^2+c$, h) $-\frac{1}{2}x(x^2+1)^{-1}+\frac{1}{2}\tan^{-1}x+c$, i) $x\sec x-\ln|\sec x+\tan x|+c$. 2). a) $\frac{1}{6}x^6\ln 3x-\frac{1}{36}x^6+c$, b) $(\frac{1}{2}x-\frac{1}{4})e^{2x+1}+c$, c) $x\ln 2x-x+c$. 3). a) $\frac{1}{4}(1+e^2)$, b) $\frac{1}{2}(4-\pi)\sqrt{2}$, c) $\frac{1}{(n+1)^2}(ne^{n+1}+1)$, d) $\frac{4}{3}$. 4). a) $\frac{1}{4}(2x^2-2x+1)e^{2x}+c$, b) $2x^2\sin\frac{1}{2}x+8x\cos\frac{1}{2}x-16\sin\frac{1}{2}x+c$, c) $\frac{1}{4}x^2\left(2(\ln x)^2-2\ln x+1\right)+c$, d) $\frac{1}{5}e^x(\sin 2x-2\cos 2x)+c$, e) $e^x(x^3-3x^2+6x-6)+c$, f) $\frac{2}{3}x^2(x+1)^{\frac{3}{2}}-\frac{8}{15}x(x+1)^{\frac{5}{2}}+\frac{16}{105}(x+1)^{\frac{7}{2}}+c=\frac{2}{105}(x+1)^{\frac{3}{2}}(15x^2-12x+8)+c$. 5). $\frac{1}{15}(3x-1)(2x+1)^{\frac{3}{2}}+c$. 6). Put $u=v'=\sin x$. 7). $1-3e^{-2}$, $\frac{1}{4}\pi(1-13e^{-4})$. 8). $\frac{1}{9}\pi$, $\frac{1}{324}\pi^2(2\pi^2-3)$. 9). a) $\frac{1}{2}(1+e^{-\pi})$, b) $\frac{1}{10}(e^{4\pi}-e^{-4\pi})$, c) $\frac{1}{a^2+b^2}\left[a+e^{2\pi a}(b\sin 2\pi b-a\cos 2\pi b)\right]$. 10). $\frac{1}{2}-\frac{1}{2}e^{-n}(\cos n+\sin n)$, $\frac{1}{2}$. 12). $\frac{35}{256}\pi$.

Exercise 18A — (page 352)

1). a) $y=x^3-5x^2+3x+c$, b) $x=\frac{1}{2}t-\frac{1}{12}\sin 6t+c$, c) $P=500e^{\frac{1}{10}t}+c$, d) $u=c-50e^{-2t}$, e) $y=\frac{2}{3}x^{\frac{3}{2}}+2x^{\frac{1}{2}}+c$, f) $x=\ln(\sin t)+2\sin t+c$. 2). a) $x=1+5e^{0.4t}$, b) $v=3-3\cos 2t-2\sin 3t$, c) $y=-\ln(1-t^2)$. 3). a) $y=\ln x+x^{-1}-1$, b) $y=2\sqrt{x}-4$, c) $y=x-2\ln(x+1)$. 4). $10\sqrt{2}=14.1$ seconds. 5). 2. 6). $-6-\frac{5}{2}\pi$, $3-\frac{3}{2}\sqrt{3}+(\frac{5}{3}-\frac{5}{8}\sqrt{3})\pi=2.237$. 7). $y=c-\frac{1}{2}x^2$. 8). $\frac{5-6e^{-0.2}}{1-e^{-0.2}}=0.483$ m, $0.0483-0.1h$. 9). a) $A+kt$, b) $A+kt-\frac{k}{4\pi}\sin 2\pi t$, c) $A+kt+\frac{5k}{4\pi}\sin\frac{1}{5}\pi t$, d) $A+kt-\frac{k}{4\pi}\sin 2\pi t+\frac{5k}{4\pi}\sin\frac{1}{5}\pi t-\frac{5k}{176\pi}\sin\frac{11}{5}\pi t-\frac{5k}{144\pi}\sin\frac{9}{5}\pi t$; all four models predict $A+10k$ in 10 years. 10). a) $y=-\frac{1}{x+c}$, b) $y=\sin^{-1}e^{x+c}$, c) $x=Ae^{4t}$, d) $z=\sqrt{2(t+c)}$, e) $x=\cos^{-1}(c-x)$, f) $u=\sqrt[3]{3ax+c}$. 11). a) $x=3e^{-2t}$, b) $u=\frac{1}{\sqrt{1-2t}}$. 12). a) $y=(2e^{-x}-1)^{-1}$, $0\le x<\ln 2$, b) $y=-\ln(3-x)$, $0\le x<3$. 13). $400\ln\frac{8}{3}=392$ seconds. 14). $\frac{3}{2}\ln 11=3.56$ minutes. 15). 443 seconds. 16). a) $\sqrt{25-h}$ must make sense, b) $\frac{dh}{dt}=0.2\sqrt{25-h}$, $t=50-10\sqrt{25-h}$, c) 1.01 years, 10 years, d) $h=t-\frac{1}{100}t^2$ for $0\le t\le 50$. 17). If we fit the values of r for $t=0$ and $t=1$ exactly, the expansion factor at time $t=4$ is $\left[1+4(5^{1-m}-1)\right]^{\frac{1}{1-m}}$; this equals 25.6 for $m=\frac{1}{3}$ and 35.3 for $m=\frac{1}{2}$, so $m=\frac{1}{3}$ is better. 18). a) $\frac{da}{dt}=ka(1-a)$, c) a tends to 1; eventually only chemical A remains.

Exercise 18B — (page 357)

1). a) $y^3-x^3=c$, b) $y^2-x^2=c$, c) $y=Ae^{\frac{1}{2}x^2}$, d) $y=\sqrt{2\ln(Ax)}$. 2). $y=\frac{4x}{x+1}$. 3). $x^2+y^2=c$, circles centred at the origin, $x^2+y^2=25$. 4). $(x+1)^2+(y-2)^2=c$, circles centred at $(-1,2)$. 5). a) $y^2=4x^3$, b) $y^2x^3=128$, c) $\cos x+\sin y=\frac{1}{2}$, d) $\cos y=2\cos x$. 6). $v^2+\omega^2x^2=c$, $v^2+\omega^2x^2=\omega^2a^2$. 7). a) $y^2+1=A(x^2+1)^2$, b) $\cos y=A\cos x$. 8). a) $y=\frac{2}{2-x}$, b) $\sin x\cos y=\frac{1}{2}$, c) $y^2=\frac{2}{x-1}$, d) $y=2\sec x$. 9). a) $\left|\frac{y-2}{y+2}\right|=Ax^4$, b) $e^y=x\ln x+c$, c) $y^2=4\tan\frac{1}{2}x+c$. 10). $y-2=A(x-1)^n$. 11). a) $n=5000e^{0.01(0.05-50\sin 0.02t)}$, b) $50\cos^{-1}0.02=76.04$, 3150. 12). $v^2=V^2-20R+20R^2x^{-1}$; provided that $V^2\ge 20R$, v^2 is always positive, and so the rocket never stops climbing. 13). $x^2+(y\pm 1)^2=c$, $x^2+(y+1)^2=1$ and $x^2+(y-1)^2=1$. 14). $y=\frac{1}{2}x^2+c$, $y=Ae^x$, $y=Ae^{-\frac{1}{2}x^2}$. 15). b) $y=Ae^{2x}-\frac{1}{2}x-\frac{1}{2}x^2+c$. 16). b) $x=e^{\frac{y-x}{2(y+x)}}$.

Review Exercises 6 — (page 361)

1). a) $\frac{1}{4}\pi$, b) $2x+y=2\sqrt{2}$. 2). $6\cos t$. 3). a) $\frac{t^2-1}{t^2+1}$, c) $y^2-x^2=4$. 4). a) $\frac{2t}{3t^2+1}$, b) $2x+y=6$. 5). $\frac{e^t-1}{e^t+1}$, minimum at $(-1,1)$ $(t=0)$. 6). a) $2x+y=9$, b) $y=4x-x^2$.

7).a)   7).b)   7).c)   7).d)

7).e)   7).f)   7).g)   7).h)

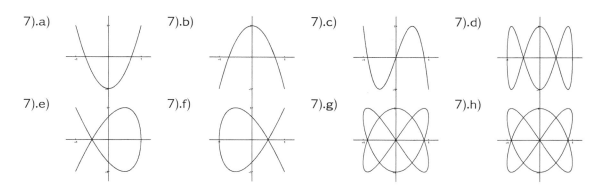

8). $5x - 13y + 3 = 0$.   9). a) $\frac{x-y}{x-4y}$, $(2,2)$, $(-2,-2)$,   b) $2x - y = 3\sqrt{3}$.   10). $3x - 7y = 13$.

11). a) $\frac{2+x-2xy}{2+x^2}$,   b) Maximum at $(2,1)$, minimum at $(-1,-\frac{1}{2})$.   12). a) $\frac{a^2}{x^2} + \frac{b^2}{y^2} = 4$.   13). ± 3.

14). 4.   15). a) $\frac{1}{1-8y^3}$,   c) 1; y'' is zero at O, but positive near O. We have a positive

inflexion at O.   17). $\frac{1}{2}(\ln|2x - 1| - (2x - 1)^{-2}) + c$.   18). $2\ln 2 - \frac{3}{4}$.   19). $\frac{1}{6}\tan^{-1}\frac{2}{3}x + c$.

20). $\frac{1}{110}$.   21). $\frac{1}{12}(3 - e^{\frac{2}{3}})$.   22). a) $x\cos^{-1}x - \sqrt{1-x^2} + c$,   b) $x\tan^{-1}x - \frac{1}{2}\ln(1 + x^2) + c$,

c) $x(\ln x)^2 - 2x\ln x + 2x + c$.   23). $\frac{1}{3}\pi - 1$.   24). $\frac{1}{2}\tan^{-1}(\frac{1}{2}e^x) + c$.   25). $\ln(1 + 3x^2) + c$.

26). $\frac{1}{2}\ln 10$.   27). $\frac{2}{5}\sin^5 x + c$.   28). $2\sqrt{x} - 2\ln(1 + \sqrt{x}) + c$.   29). a) $\frac{1}{60}(6x + 1)(4x - 1)^{\frac{3}{2}}$,   b)

$-\frac{2}{15}(3x + 4)(2 - x)^{\frac{3}{2}}$,   c) $\frac{1}{5}(x - 1)(2x + 3)^{\frac{3}{2}}$.   32). $\frac{1}{54}(3x - 1)^6 + \frac{1}{45}(3x - 1)^5 + c$.   33). $\frac{1}{8}(\pi + 2)$.

34). a) $\frac{1}{56}(1 + x)^7(7x - 1) + c$,   b) $\frac{1}{182a^2}(13ax - b)(ax + b)^{13} + c$.   35). $1 - 2e^{-1}$.   36). 16.

37). $\pi(8\ln 2 - 3)$.   38). $\frac{3}{4}\pi$.   39). $\frac{1}{2} - \frac{1}{2}\ln 2$.   40). $3\pi a^2$, $5\pi^2 a^3$.   41). $\frac{3}{8}\pi a^2$.   42). $2 - \ln\frac{27}{25}$.

44). $x^2 + 7x + 2 + 3\ln x$.   45). $t = \frac{10z}{20-z}$.   46). $y = x^3 - 11x^2 + 15x + 100$, $(\frac{7}{3}, \frac{2371}{27})$, maximum,

$(5,25)$, minimum.   47). a) $\frac{dA}{dr} = 2\pi r$, $\frac{dr}{dA} = \frac{1}{2\pi r}$,   b) $\frac{dr}{dt} = \frac{1}{\pi r(t+1)^3}$,   c) $A = \frac{t(t+2)}{(t+1)^2}$.

48). $\frac{dx}{dt} = -kx$.   49). a) 4 people are served every minute, $x = 0.7t^2 - 4t + 8$.   50). a)

$16x^2 + y^2 = 0.16$,   b) $(\pm 0.1, 0)$, $(0, \pm 0.4)$.   51). $N = 5000 + 3000e^{\frac{1}{50}t}$, $50\ln 2 = 34.7$ days,

$50\frac{dN}{dt} = N - 50F$, $N - 50F < 0$ for $N \leq 11000$, $F > 220$.   52). a) $T = 470 - 6x$, $360°$

C,   b) $\frac{dT}{dx} = -\frac{1}{5}x$, $T = 380 - \frac{1}{10}x^2$.   53). a) $T = T_0(1 + (\lambda - 1)e^{-kt})$,   c) $\frac{\ln(20(\lambda-1))}{2\ln 2}$ minutes.

54). $y^2 + 1 = A(x - 1)^2 e^{2x}$. 55). $\ln y = \frac{1}{2}xe^{2x} - \frac{1}{4}e^{2x} + \frac{1}{4}$. 56). 2 minutes, $\frac{1}{4}\pi$. 57). a) $12, 4.5$, $\frac{dN}{dt}$

approaches 0, population growth stops,   c) $N = \frac{500A}{A + e^{-\frac{1}{10}t}}$, $N = \frac{500}{1 + 4e^{-\frac{1}{10}t}}$, $10\ln 6 = 17.9$ years.

58). $(1-y^2)\sin 2x = c$. 59). $-y^{-1} = \frac{1}{3}\ln\left(\frac{x-2}{x+1}\right)+c$, $3(1-y^{-1}) = \ln\left(\frac{2(x-2)}{x+1}\right)$. 60). $y^3 = \frac{3}{2}x-\frac{3}{4}\sin 2x+1$.

61). $(1 + y)e^{-y} = (1 - x)e^x$.   62). a) £$\frac{1000}{3}\sqrt{5}$ = £745,   b) $\frac{400}{3}\sqrt{5}$ = 298 £per hour.   63). a)

$P = P_0e^{\sin kt}$,   b) e^2.   64). $\sin y = \frac{1}{2}(\ln x)^2$ $0 < x < e^{\sqrt{2}}$.   65). a) $y = x + 1$, a straight line,   b)

$y^2 = \frac{(\ln x)^2 + 1}{x}$.

Exercise 19A — (page 372)

2). a) $(4\mathbf{i} + \mathbf{j}) + (-3\mathbf{i} + 2\mathbf{j}) = \mathbf{i} + 3\mathbf{j}$,   b) $3(\mathbf{i} - 2\mathbf{j}) = 3\mathbf{i} - 6\mathbf{j}$,   c) $4\mathbf{j} + 2(\mathbf{i} - 2\mathbf{j}) = 2\mathbf{i}$,   d) $(3\mathbf{i} + \mathbf{j}) - (5\mathbf{i} + \mathbf{j}) = -2\mathbf{i}$,   e) $3(-\mathbf{i} + 2\mathbf{j}) - (-4\mathbf{i} + 3\mathbf{j}) = \mathbf{i} + 3\mathbf{j}$,   f) $4(2\mathbf{i} + 3\mathbf{j}) - 3(3\mathbf{i} + 2\mathbf{j}) = -\mathbf{i} + 6\mathbf{j}$.
3). a) $\binom{1}{2}$,   b) $\binom{3}{0}$,   c) $\binom{-1}{1}$,   d) $\binom{4}{-3}$.   4). $s = 2$.   5). $s = 4$. $\mathbf{q} = \frac{1}{4}\mathbf{r} - \frac{1}{4}\mathbf{p}$.   6). $s = 2$, $t = 3$.
7). $s = \frac{3}{2}$, $t = -\frac{1}{2}$.   8). $\binom{4}{-2}$ and $\binom{-6}{3}$ are parallel, but $\binom{3}{1}$ is in a different direction; $\binom{-1}{2}$ is not

parallel to $\binom{1}{1} - \binom{3}{4}$. 9). We can have $f = x$, $g = -x$ and $h = 2x$ for any x. 10). a) No, since $\mathbf{p}$ and

$\mathbf{r}$ are parallel, but $\mathbf{q}$ is in a different direction,   b) $u = -2$, $v = 0$.

Exercise 19B — (page 375)

1). a) $(9,3)$,   b) $(-1,-2)$,   c) $(2,-1)$,   d) $(-8,-1)$,   e) $(10,5)$,   f) $(5, 2.5)$. 2). a) $(-13, -23)$,
b) $(-1,1)$. 3). $\mathbf{c} = 2\mathbf{b} - 2\mathbf{a}$, $\mathbf{b} = \frac{1}{2}(\mathbf{a} + \mathbf{c})$. 4). $\mathbf{c} = \frac{3}{7}\mathbf{a} + \frac{4}{7}\mathbf{b}$. 6). $\mathbf{b} - \mathbf{a} = \mathbf{c} - \mathbf{d}$;   a) $\mathbf{a} - \mathbf{d} = \mathbf{b} - \mathbf{c}$,   b)
$\mathbf{e} = \mathbf{a} + \mathbf{c} = \mathbf{b} + \mathbf{d}$. 7). $\frac{1}{2}(\mathbf{b} + \mathbf{c} - 2\mathbf{a})$, $\frac{1}{4}(\mathbf{b} + \mathbf{c} - 2\mathbf{a})$. G is the midpoint of AD. 8). $\mathbf{b} = \mathbf{a} + \mathbf{c}$, $\mathbf{m} = \frac{1}{2}\mathbf{a} + \mathbf{c}$,
$\mathbf{p} = \frac{1}{3}\mathbf{a} + \frac{2}{3}\mathbf{c}$. O, P and M are collinear, and P is a point of trisection of OM. 9). $\mathbf{d} = \frac{1}{2}(\mathbf{b} + \mathbf{c})$,

$\mathbf{e} = \frac{1}{4}(2\mathbf{a}+\mathbf{b}+\mathbf{c}), \mathbf{f} = \frac{2}{3}\mathbf{a}+\frac{1}{3}\mathbf{c}, \mathbf{g} = \frac{1}{4}(2\mathbf{a}+\mathbf{b}+\mathbf{c})$. 10). $\overrightarrow{AP} = \frac{4}{15}\mathbf{b}-\frac{13}{15}\mathbf{a}, k = \frac{15}{13}, \mathbf{r} = \frac{4}{13}, \mathbf{s} = \frac{2}{11}\mathbf{a}$. 11). a) $\mathbf{x} = s\mathbf{a}+(1-s)\mathbf{b}$ for $0 < s < 1$, $\mathbf{p} = t\mathbf{x}$ for $0 < t < 1$, so $\alpha = st$, $\beta = (1-s)t$, b) $\mathbf{x} = \frac{\alpha}{\alpha+\beta}\mathbf{a} + \frac{\beta}{\alpha+\beta}\mathbf{b}$, $\mathbf{y} = \frac{\beta}{1-\alpha}\mathbf{b}, \mathbf{z} = \frac{\alpha}{1-\beta}\mathbf{a}$, c) $\frac{OZ}{ZA} = \frac{\alpha}{1-\alpha-\beta}, \frac{AX}{XB} = \frac{\beta}{\alpha}, \frac{BY}{YO} = \frac{1-\alpha-\beta}{\beta}$.

Exercise 19C — (page 377)

1). $\begin{pmatrix} 3 \\ 0 \\ 2 \end{pmatrix}$. 2). $\begin{pmatrix} 3 \\ -6 \\ -6 \end{pmatrix} = 3\mathbf{i} - 6\mathbf{j} - 6\mathbf{k}$. 3). a) No, b) Yes. 4). a) $\begin{pmatrix} 1 \\ 2 \\ -7 \end{pmatrix}, \begin{pmatrix} -6 \\ 4 \\ -8 \end{pmatrix}, \begin{pmatrix} -2 \\ 0 \\ 1.5 \end{pmatrix}$, b) $(-4, 7, -17.5)$. 5). $\mathbf{i}+\mathbf{j}-6\mathbf{k}, \mathbf{i}+\mathbf{j}-6\mathbf{k}$; $ABCD$ is a parallelogram. 6). a) $-3\mathbf{i}+6\mathbf{j}+\mathbf{k}$, b) $-2\mathbf{i}+4\mathbf{j}+\frac{2}{3}\mathbf{k}$, c) $2\mathbf{i}+3\mathbf{j}+\frac{8}{3}\mathbf{k}$. 7). a) $2\mathbf{i}+2\mathbf{j}+\mathbf{k}$, b) $2\mathbf{i}+2\mathbf{j}+\mathbf{k}$.

Exercise 19D — (page 382)

1). $-8, 11, 3$. 2). $11, -3, 8$. 3). $18, 0, 0$; $\mathbf{r}$ is perpendicular to both $\mathbf{p}$ and $\mathbf{q}$. 4). a) and d) are perpendicular, as are b) and c). 5). $-4, -8, -12$. 6). a) 5, b) $\sqrt{5}$, c) $\sqrt{5}$, d) 1, e) 3, f) 13, g) 5, h) $\sqrt{6}$, i) $\sqrt{5}$, j) $\sqrt{13}$, k) $\sqrt{30}$, l) 2. 7). $5, \begin{pmatrix} 0.8 \\ -0.6 \end{pmatrix}$. 8). $\frac{1}{3}\mathbf{i}-\frac{2}{3}\mathbf{j}+\frac{2}{3}\mathbf{k}$ and $\frac{2}{3}\mathbf{i}-\frac{1}{3}\mathbf{j}+\frac{2}{3}\mathbf{k}$. 9). a) $45°$, b) $167.3°$, c) $180°$, d) $136.7°$, e) $7.0°$, f) $90°$. 10). $\sqrt{(x_1-x_2)^2+(y_1-y_2)^2}$ is the distance between the points with position vectors $\mathbf{r}_1$ and $\mathbf{r}_2$. 11). $7.8°$ or $172.2°$. 12). $80.4°$ or $99.6°$. 13). $70.5°$ or $107.5°$. 14). $76.4°$. 15). $48.2°$. 16). $48.2°$. 17). $\left(\frac{\cos\theta-1}{\sin\theta}\right)\cdot\left(\frac{\cos\theta+1}{\sin\theta}\right) = 0$. 18). $OA^2+OB^2 = 2OC^2+2AC^2$. 19). a) $|\mathbf{a}| = |\mathbf{b}| = |\mathbf{c}| = R$, the radius, d) $\mathbf{h} = \mathbf{a}+\mathbf{b}+\mathbf{c}$, e) O, G and H are collinear. 20). a) $\mathbf{I} = \mathbf{i}\cos\theta + \mathbf{j}\sin\theta, \mathbf{J} = -\mathbf{i}\sin\theta + \mathbf{j}\cos\theta$, b) $a = A\cos\theta - B\sin\theta$, $b = A\sin\theta + B\cos\theta$.

Exercise 19E — (page 386)

1). a) $\mathbf{r} = \begin{pmatrix} 2 \\ -3 \end{pmatrix}+t\begin{pmatrix} 1 \\ 2 \end{pmatrix}, y = 2x-7$, b) $\mathbf{r} = \begin{pmatrix} 4 \\ 1 \end{pmatrix}+t\begin{pmatrix} -3 \\ 2 \end{pmatrix}, 2x+3y = 11$, c) $\mathbf{r} = \begin{pmatrix} 5 \\ 7 \end{pmatrix}+t\begin{pmatrix} 1 \\ 0 \end{pmatrix}, y = 7$, d) $\mathbf{r} = t\begin{pmatrix} 2 \\ -1 \end{pmatrix}, x+2y = 0$, e) $\mathbf{r} = \begin{pmatrix} a \\ b \end{pmatrix}+t\begin{pmatrix} 0 \\ 1 \end{pmatrix}, x = a$, f) $\mathbf{r} = \begin{pmatrix} \cos\alpha \\ \sin\alpha \end{pmatrix}+t\begin{pmatrix} -\sin\alpha \\ \cos\alpha \end{pmatrix}, x\cos\alpha + y\sin\alpha = 1$. 2). a) $\mathbf{r} = \begin{pmatrix} 2 \\ 0 \end{pmatrix}+t\begin{pmatrix} 0 \\ 1 \end{pmatrix}$, b) $\mathbf{r} = \begin{pmatrix} 1 \\ 2 \end{pmatrix}+t\begin{pmatrix} 0 \\ 1 \end{pmatrix}$, c) $\mathbf{r} = \begin{pmatrix} 4 \\ 1 \end{pmatrix}+t\begin{pmatrix} 5 \\ 2 \end{pmatrix}$. 3). a) $(7,3)$, b) $(8,-5)$, c) None, d) $(\frac{119}{25}, \frac{92}{25})$, e) $(7+6s, 1-4s)$ for any s, f) $(-1,1)$. 4). $(2+t, 3t-1), (4,5)$. 5). $(3,1)$. 6). $(8,9), (-6,-12), (3\frac{1}{3}, 2)$. 7). a) $\mathbf{r} = \begin{pmatrix} 3 \\ 7 \end{pmatrix}+t\begin{pmatrix} 2 \\ -3 \end{pmatrix}$, b) $\mathbf{r} = \begin{pmatrix} 2 \\ 3 \end{pmatrix}+t\begin{pmatrix} 0 \\ 1 \end{pmatrix}$, c) $\mathbf{r} = \begin{pmatrix} -1 \\ 2 \end{pmatrix}+t\begin{pmatrix} 2 \\ -1 \end{pmatrix}$, d) $\mathbf{r} = \begin{pmatrix} -3 \\ -4 \end{pmatrix}+t\begin{pmatrix} 2 \\ 3 \end{pmatrix}$, e) $\mathbf{r} = \begin{pmatrix} -2 \\ 7 \end{pmatrix}+t\begin{pmatrix} 1 \\ 0 \end{pmatrix}$, f) $\mathbf{r} = \begin{pmatrix} 1 \\ 3 \end{pmatrix}+t\begin{pmatrix} 1 \\ 1 \end{pmatrix}$. 8). $\mathbf{r} = \begin{pmatrix} 4 \\ -1 \end{pmatrix}+t\begin{pmatrix} 3 \\ 1 \end{pmatrix}, \mathbf{r} = \begin{pmatrix} -3 \\ 2 \end{pmatrix}+t\begin{pmatrix} 1 \\ -1 \end{pmatrix}$, $(1,-2)$, b) $(13\frac{1}{3}, -5), (4, 11\frac{4}{5})$. 9). a) Yes, b) Yes, c) Not a valid question — $\mathbf{0}$ has no direction, $\mathbf{r} = \begin{pmatrix} 1 \\ 2 \end{pmatrix}+t\begin{pmatrix} -4 \\ 3 \end{pmatrix}$. 10). $\begin{pmatrix} 3 \\ 3 \end{pmatrix}, \mathbf{r} = \begin{pmatrix} 1 \\ 5 \end{pmatrix}+t\begin{pmatrix} 3 \\ -1 \end{pmatrix}, (4,4)$. 11). $(2,0)$. 12). $\mathbf{r} = \begin{pmatrix} -1 \\ 1 \end{pmatrix}+t\begin{pmatrix} 1 \\ 2 \end{pmatrix}, (t-1, 2t+1)$, $(-1,1)$ and $(3,9)$. 13). $(1,8)$ and $(-7,-4)$. 14). a) $\overrightarrow{EF} = \frac{1}{2}\overrightarrow{CB}$, b) $\mathbf{r} = \frac{1}{4}(2\mathbf{a}+\mathbf{b}+\mathbf{c})+t(\mathbf{b}+\mathbf{c})$, c) $\mathbf{n} = \frac{1}{2}(\mathbf{a}+\mathbf{b}+\mathbf{c})$, d) $\overrightarrow{OG}, \overrightarrow{ON}$ and $\overrightarrow{OH}$ are all multiples of $\mathbf{a}+\mathbf{b}+\mathbf{c}$, e) The nine-point circle has half the radius of the outcircle.

Exercise 19F — (page 389)

1). a) $\mathbf{r} = \begin{pmatrix} 1 \\ 2 \\ 3 \end{pmatrix}+t\begin{pmatrix} 0 \\ 1 \\ 2 \end{pmatrix}$, b) $\mathbf{r} = t\begin{pmatrix} 0 \\ 0 \\ 1 \end{pmatrix}$, c) $\mathbf{r} = \begin{pmatrix} 2 \\ -1 \\ 1 \end{pmatrix}+t\begin{pmatrix} 3 \\ -1 \\ 1 \end{pmatrix}$, d) $\mathbf{r} = \begin{pmatrix} 3 \\ 0 \\ 2 \end{pmatrix}+t\begin{pmatrix} 4 \\ -2 \\ 3 \end{pmatrix}$. 2). a) $\mathbf{r} = (2\mathbf{i}-\mathbf{j}+2\mathbf{k})+t(\mathbf{i}+2\mathbf{k})$, b) $\mathbf{r} = (\mathbf{i}+2\mathbf{j}+2\mathbf{k})+t(\mathbf{i}-4\mathbf{j})$, c) $\mathbf{r} = (3\mathbf{i}+\mathbf{j}+4\mathbf{k})+t(4\mathbf{i}-\mathbf{j}+\mathbf{k})$. 3). They are all the same. 4). a) Yes, b) No, c) No. 5). a) Yes, b) No. 6). a) $s = 2$, $t = -3$, b) No, c) $s = 3, t = 1$. 7). a) $(3,-1,5)$, b) $(3,-5,4)$. 8). $f = \lambda, g = 2\lambda, h = -3\lambda$; the three translations are all in the same plane. 9). $(4,-3,0)$. 10). All are $\frac{1}{4}(\mathbf{a}+\mathbf{b}+\mathbf{c}+\mathbf{d})$; the lines joining the midpoints of opposite pairs of sides in a tetrahedron are concurrent, bisecting each other. 11). $\frac{1}{4}\mathbf{e}+\frac{3}{4}\mathbf{f}, \frac{1}{3}(\mathbf{a}+\mathbf{b}+\mathbf{c}), \frac{1}{4}(\mathbf{a}+\mathbf{b}+\mathbf{c}+\mathbf{d})$; the four lines joining each vertex to the centroid of the opposite face of a tetrahedron are concurrent. 12). a) Intersect at $(1,-1,0)$, b) Parallel, c) Skew. 13). 0.4 m.

Exercise 19G — (page 392)

1). 5. 2). $\frac{5}{13}$. 3). 3. 4). $\frac{1}{5}\sqrt{17}$. 5). $\mathbf{r} = (\mathbf{i}+3\mathbf{j}+\mathbf{k})+t(3\mathbf{j}+\mathbf{k}), \frac{1}{5}\sqrt{65}$. 6). $\frac{ab}{\sqrt{a^2+b^2}}$. 8). a) $\mathbf{p} = \begin{pmatrix} s \\ s-1 \\ 3s+10 \end{pmatrix}, \mathbf{q} = \begin{pmatrix} 2t-8 \\ 11 \\ 2-t \end{pmatrix}$, b) $11s+t+20 = 0, s+5t-8 = 0$, so $\mathbf{p} = \begin{pmatrix} -2 \\ -3 \\ 4 \end{pmatrix}, \mathbf{q} = \begin{pmatrix} -4 \\ 11 \\ 0 \end{pmatrix}$, c) $6\sqrt{6}$.

Exercise 20A — (page 398)

1). a) 4, b) $6i$, c) 13, d) $24i$, e) $24i$, f) -10, g) 16, h) -36. 2). a) $4-i$, b) $2+3i$, c) 7, d) $5+2i$, e) $5-5i$, f) $8+6i$, g) $\frac{1}{5}+\frac{7}{5}i$, h) $\frac{1}{10}-\frac{7}{10}i$, i) $1-3i$, j) $2+4i$, k) $-\frac{1}{2}-\frac{3}{2}i$, l) $\frac{3}{5}+\frac{1}{5}i$. 3). $2x-y=1$, $x+2y=3$; $x=y=1$. 4). a) 3, b) -3, c) 3, d) -6, e) $\frac{1}{2}$, f) -1. 5). a) Yes, b) Yes, c) No, d) Yes, e) No, f) No. 6). 1. 7). $(a^2+b^2)(c^2+d^2)=(ac-bd)^2+(ad+bc)^2=(ac+bd)^2+(bc-ad)^2$; $1568=31^2+25^2=35^2+19^2$. 8). $\cos(\theta+\phi)+i\sin(\theta+\phi)$.

Exercise 20B — (page 401)

1). a) $-2-5i$, b) $\frac{7}{3}-\frac{2}{3}i$, c) $-\frac{5}{2}+\frac{1}{2}i$, d) $\frac{7}{25}+\frac{24}{25}i$. 2). a) $2, i$, b) $1+i, 2i$. 3). a) $\pm 3i$, b) $-2\pm i$, c) $3\pm 4i$, d) $-\frac{1}{2}\pm\frac{5}{2}i$. 4). a) $1-7i$; $2, 14i, 50, -\frac{24}{25}+\frac{7}{25}i$, b) $2-i$; $4, 2i, 5, \frac{3}{5}+\frac{4}{5}i$, c) 5; 10, 0, 25, 1, d) $-3i$; 0, $6i$, 9, -1. 5). a) $(z+5i)(z-5i)$, b) $(3z-1+2i)(3z-1-2i)$, c) $(2z+3+2i)(2z+3-2i)$, d) $(z-2)(z+2)(z-2i)(z+2i)$, e) $(z-3)(z+3)(z-i)(z+i)$, f) $(z-2)(z+1+2i)(z+1-2i)$, g) $(z+1)(z-2+i)(z-2-i)$, h) $(z-1)^2(z+1+i)(z+1-i)$. 6). $1\pm i$, $-1\pm 2i$. 7). $-2\pm i$, $2\pm i\sqrt{7}$. 9). $\ldots z+z^\star=0$. 10). $a^5-10a^3b+5ab^4$, $5a^4b-10a^2b^3+b^5$ and $a^5-10a^3b+5ab^4$, $-(5a^4b-10a^2b^3+b^5)$. 11). $a=-8$, $b=70$; $-3\pm i$, $\frac{5}{2}\pm\frac{1}{2}i\sqrt{3}$.

Exercise 20C — (page 407)

3). a) $\pm 1, \pm i$, b) $-1, \frac{1}{2}\pm\frac{1}{2}i\sqrt{3}$, c) $-2, 1\pm 3i$, d) $1, -3, -1\pm i\sqrt{2}$, e) $\pm 2i, -\frac{1}{2}\pm\frac{1}{2}i\sqrt{3}$. 4). $1, -1, \frac{1}{2}\pm\frac{1}{2}i\sqrt{3}$; all have modulus 1. 5). a) Circle centre 0, radius 5, b) Line $x=3$, c) Line $x=3$, d) Line $y=1$, e) Circle centre 2 radius 2, f) Line $x=2$, g) Line $y=2x+3$, h) Circle centre $\frac{1}{2}$, radius $\frac{3}{2}$, i) Parabola $y^2=4x$, j) $x=|y|$, l) Hyperbola $xy=1$, l) Half-plane $x>0$. 6). $2+4i$. 7). a) Exterior of circle, centre 0, radius 2, b) Interior (and edge) of circle centre $3i$, radius 1, c) Half-plane $x+y\le 0$, d) Interior of circle centre -1, radius 2. 8). $|z|^n=|z^n|=|-a^n|=a^n$, so $|z|=a$. 11). c) If ABC is a triangle, and M is the midpoint of BC, then $AB^2+AC^2=2(AM^2+BK^2)$. This is Apollonius' Theorem. Alternatively, the sum of the squares of the diagonals of a parallelogram is equal to the sum of the squares of its four sides. 12). Semicircle $x^2+y^2=1$ for $y>0$ (the difference in arguments equals $-\frac{1}{2}\pi$ in the bottom half of the circle). 14). a) Line $x=0$, b) Circle centre $\frac{k^2+1}{k^2-1}a$, radius $\frac{2ka}{|k^2-1|}$; think 'magnets',

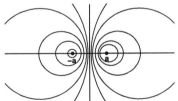

Exercise 20D — (page 409)

1). a) $\pm(1-i)$, b) $\pm(1+2i)$, c) $\pm(3+2i)$, d) $\pm(3-i)$. 2). a) $i, -1-i$, b) $2, -3+i$, c) $-3+i, -1-i$, d) $-1+i, -2i$, e) $-2-i, 1$. 3). a) $\pm 2(1+i), \pm 2(1-i)$, b) $\pm\frac{1}{\sqrt{2}}(3+i), \pm\frac{1}{\sqrt{2}}(1-3i)$. 4). $-2i, \pm\sqrt{3}+i$. 5). $-1-i$, $z^2-(1+i)z+2i=0$, $\frac{1}{2}(1\pm\sqrt{3})+\frac{1}{2}i(1\mp\sqrt{3})$.

Exercise 21A — (page 415)

1). $f(-1.5)=-5.5$, $f(-1)=2$. 2). $f(2)=0.1353$, $f(3)=-0.95$, so $N=2$. 3). $f(3)=1.91$, $f(4)=-29.6$; the sign-change indicates a root of $3x+7=e^x$ for $3<x<4$. 4). $f(-1.086745)=4.10\times 10^{-6}$, $f(-1.086755)=-1.17\times 10^{-4}$, $x^2-4.087x+6.441=0$, $2.04\pm 1.51i$. 5). a) $x=\sqrt[5]{5x-6}$, $x=\frac{1}{5}(x^5+6)$, $x=\frac{6}{x^4-5}$, b) $x=\ln(\frac{5}{x})$, $x=5e^{-x}$, $x=\sqrt{5xe^{-x}}$, c) $x=\sqrt[5]{1999-x^3}$, $x=\frac{1999}{x^4+x^2}$, $x=\sqrt[3]{1999-x^5}$. 6). a) $x^{11}-x^7+6=0$; $0, -1.1769, -1.22266, -1.23379$, $-1.23673, -1.23752$; monotonic decreasing, convergent; yes, b) $x^4-x^3-34x^2+289=0$; 3, 7.11, 22.3, 463.1, 214440, 4.60×10^{10}; monotonic, divergent, c) $x^4-500x-10=0$; 7, 7.94456, 7.94366, 7.94366, 7.94366, 7.94366; monotonic increasing, convergent; yes, d) $x^3+x-40=0$; 4, 3.30193, 3.32313, 3.32249, 3.32252, 3.32251; oscillatory, convergent; yes.

7). $1^5 + 1 - 19 = -17 < 0 < 15 = 2^5 + 2 - 19$; 1.61981, 1.87806, 1.69321, 1.82081, 1.73045, 1.79331; the sequence is oscillatory and convergent, with $1.73045 < \alpha < 1.79331$.   8). a) $f(2) = 0.6109$, $f(3) = -5.085$,   b) $x_{10} = 0.7895$, the sequence is monotonic decreasing and convergent.   9). $e^2 - 2^3 + 2 = 1.389 > 0 > -4.914 = e^3 - 3^3 + 2$; the first iteration scheme gives $x_3 = -1.1637$, and so x_4 is undefined; using $x_0 = 2$ and $x_{n+1} = \sqrt[3]{e^x + 2}$ yields an increasing sequence with (eventually) $x_{12} = 2.26611$, $x_{13} = 2.26642$, $x_{14} = 2.26661$. Since $f(2.665) = 0.0112$ and $f(2.275) = -0.0466$, where $f(x) = e^x - x^3 + 2$, the root is 2.27 to 2 decimal places (the iteration scheme $x_{n+1} = \frac{e^{x_n} + 2}{x_n^2}$ gets there much more quickly).   10). a) 9,   b) $x_4 = x_5 = 9.725$; the sequence is oscillatory, to $\alpha = 9.725$ to 4 significant figures.   11). –   12). 2 roots; using $x_0 = 1$ and $x_{n+1} = \sqrt{\cos x_n}$ yields a convergent oscillatory sequence with $x_8 = 0.8244$, $x_9 = 0.8240$, so the root is 0.824 to 3 decimal places; the alternative iterative scheme yields $x_1 = \frac{1}{2}\pi$, with x_2 undefined.   13). 1, 1; the scheme with F_+ diverges, the scheme with F_- converges (Knowing that $F'(\alpha) = 1$ tells us nothing about the convergence).

Exercise 21B — (page 421)

3). $0.2, 0.188, 0.171, 0.149, 0.123, 0.093, 0.065, 0.041, 0.024, 0.013, 0.007$; $0.2, 0.376, 0.685, 1.195, 1.963, 2.985, 4.151, 5.263, 6.147, 6.744, 7.102$; $A = 8$.   4). a) Unsuitable; $F^{-1}(x) = \frac{3}{x+1}$, 1.303,   b) Unsuitable; $F^{-1}(x) = \frac{1}{3}\ln(5 - x)$, 0.501,   c) Not suitable; $F^{-1}(x) = \tan^{-1}(2x)$, 1.1656,   d) Not suitable; $F^{-1}(x) = -\sqrt[4]{300 - 10x}$, −2.6237,   e) Suitable; 1.8955.   5). a) $k = 5$, 1.179,   b) $k = -13$, 6.730,   c) $k = 10$, −1.896,   d) −3.485, 12.87.

Exercise 21C — (page 425)

3). $0.285714, 0.289167, 0.289169, 0.289169$; 0.289169.   4). 1.2393.   5). 1.867.   6). 2.175 cm.   7). −0.5522, 0.7296, 24.8226.   8). 0.5314, 3.1830.   9). 0.7879.   10). $0.2739 = \frac{1}{5}\cos^{-1} 0.2$.   11). 1.4710, 7.8571 (solve the equation $1.3^x = x$).   12). We get $Au_{n+1} = (Au_n)^2$; we obtain quadratic convergence to 0 if $|au_0| < 1$.

Review Exercises 7 — (page 427)

1). 58.5°.   2). a) 7, 7,   b) −32,   c) 49.2°.   3). $\frac{1}{\sqrt{14}}(\mathbf{i} - 3\mathbf{j} - 2\mathbf{k})$, $\frac{1}{\sqrt{14}}(3\mathbf{i} + \mathbf{j} - 2\mathbf{k})$, 73.4°.   4). a) 8.5°.   5). a) $\frac{1}{2}\mathbf{i} + \frac{1}{2}\mathbf{j} + \frac{1}{\sqrt{2}}\mathbf{k}$,   b) 45°.   6). a) 60°,   b) $\frac{3}{2}\sqrt{3}$.   7). $\overrightarrow{AB} = \begin{pmatrix} 2 \\ -2 \\ -4 \end{pmatrix}$, $\overrightarrow{AC} = \begin{pmatrix} 4 \\ 17 \\ 3 \end{pmatrix}$, $\lambda = \frac{13}{14}$, $\mu = \frac{2}{7}$. A, B, C, O are coplanar.   9). $\begin{pmatrix} 9 \\ -1 \\ 4 \end{pmatrix}$.   10). 0.51 km, 20 s.   11). a) $\begin{pmatrix} -2 \\ 6 \\ 2 \end{pmatrix}$, $m = 1$, $2\sqrt{11}$,   b) 47.9°,   c) $m = 21$.   12). a) $3\mathbf{i} + 3\mathbf{j} + 4\mathbf{k}$, 25°,   b) $5\mathbf{i} + 9\mathbf{j} + 12\mathbf{k}$, $-\frac{15}{13}\mathbf{i} - \frac{123}{13}\mathbf{j} - \frac{164}{13}\mathbf{k}$,   c) $\frac{5}{2}\mathbf{i} + \frac{3}{2}\mathbf{j} + 2\mathbf{k}$.   13). $u > \frac{1}{2}$ or $u < -1$; $\frac{1}{2} < u < 0.753$.   14). $\mu = \lambda^{-1}$, $ABDC$ is a parallelogram.   15). $3 - 4i$.   16). $\frac{5}{3}$, $-3i$.   17). $1 - 3i$, $z^3 - 4z^2 + 14z - 20 = 0$.   18). a) $a = 3, b = 3$,   b) $4i$.   19). $\pm(5 - 2i)$.   20). $3 - i, -3 + 3i$.   21). $-\frac{1}{2} - \frac{1}{2}i\sqrt{3}$, 1. The roots are $w, w^2, 1 + i, 1 - i$.   22). 2.   23). $1 + i$ 24). a) $kz^2 + 2iz - k = 0$, $ikz = 1 \pm \sqrt{1 - k^2}$,   b) $\alpha \le 0$ if $k \le 1$,   c) $\beta = \frac{1}{2}k\left[\frac{2k}{1+k^2} + i\frac{1-k^2}{1+k^2}\right]$.   25). $\frac{5x-6}{(x+2)(x^2+4)} \equiv \frac{2x+1}{x^2+4} - \frac{2}{x+2}$.   27). 2.   28). b) 0.77.   29). 2.13.   30). 1.210.   31). 6.72.   32). a) 1, 1.389; since $f'(0) = -4$, there could be more than one root there,   b) 0.310 or 0.756; $f(0.3095) > 0 > f(0.3105)$ for example,   c) 0.62 or 1.51.   33). a) $f(3) = -1$, $f(4) = 15$,   b) 3.11111, 3.10332, 3.10384, 3.10380, 3.10380; $\alpha = 3.104$ (sequence oscillatory).   34). a) $f(2) < 0 < f(3)$,   b) $x_{n+1} = 4 - \ln x_n = F(x_n)$ is better ($|F'(\alpha)| < \frac{1}{2}$), 2.93.   35). a) $N = 3$,   b) $t = 1 + \frac{\ln(9t)}{\ln 4} = 1 + \log_4(9t)$, $t = \frac{1}{9}4^{t-1}$; $t = 1 + \log_4(9t)$ is better ($|F'(r)| < 1$); $r = 3.486$.   36). a) $(\pm\sqrt{5}, \pm\sqrt{5})$,   b) $x_1 = \frac{5}{2}$, $x_2 = 2$; the series ie periodic of period 2, and does not converge,   c) $g^{-1} = g$,   d) Newton-Raphson gives $r = 2.236068$.   37). The graphs of $y = F(x)$ and $y = F^{-1}(x)$ meet on the line $y = x$,   a) 1.32472,   b) 0.11183, 3.57715.   38). 1.4265.   39). a) $f'(x_0) = 0$, 0,   b) 0.3432.

Exercise 22A — (page 439)

1). 72 km south.   2). 21.2 hours.   3). 25.2 km south.   4). 8.18×10^{13} km.   5). $33\frac{1}{3}$ ms^{-1}.   6). a) $3\sqrt{13} = 10.8$ m,   b) 12 m north.   7). a) 1200 m,   b) $4500\mathbf{i} + 100\mathbf{j} + 1200\mathbf{k}$ m, $100\sqrt{2449} = 4950$ m.   9). 4 ms^{-2}, 125 m.   10). 7.5 ms^{-1}.   11). 1.6 ms^{-2}, 60 ms^{-1}, 15.5 s.   12). 6 s, $1\frac{2}{3}$ ms^{-2}.   13). 30 s, 2 ms^{-2}.   14). 20 ms^{-1}, 1500 m.   15). 25 s, 175 m.   16). 30 ms^{-1}, 675 m, −1.5 ms^{-2}, 20 s.   17). 20 ms^{-1}, 2 ms^{-2}.   18). 22 s, $53\frac{1}{3}$ m.   19). $\frac{1}{36}$ ms^{-2}.   20). 5D.

Exercise 22B — (page 443)

1). a) 11, b) 16, c) −1.5, d) 45, e) 102, f) 1.2m, g) 14, h) 2.5, i) 24, j) $−\frac{80}{3}$, k) 20, l) 2, m) $\frac{4}{3}$, n) 25. 2). 40 seconds, $\frac{8}{9}$ ms^{-2}. 3). $v = \sqrt{0.2s}$. 4). 0.06 ms^{-2}. 5). 1500 m. 6). a) 2700 m, b) 250 seconds. 7). a) $\sqrt{900 - 20s}$ ms^{-1}, b) 10 ms^{-1}, c) 5 m. 8). 60 m. 9). $(5 + 0.8t)$ ms^{-1}, $(5t + 0.4t^2)$ ms^{-2}, 15 seconds, 17 ms^{-1}. 10). 2.5 ms^{-2}, 2 ms^{-2}. 11). 1800 km h^{-2}, 40 km h^{-1}. 12). $(10 - 4t + \frac{1}{2}t^2)$ m, Yes. 13). $\sqrt{5}$ = 2.24 seconds, $10\sqrt{5}$ = 22.4 ms^{-1}. 14). 1.8 seconds. 15). $4 - \sqrt{7}$ = 1.35 seconds. 16). $3 + \sqrt{3}$ seconds, $3(2 + \sqrt{3})g$ metres. 17). 2 seconds, a) 2 seconds, b) The lower ball would hit the ground before the two balls collided. 18). a) $\frac{3s_1 - s_2}{2t}$, b) The train's speed at C is $\frac{3s_2 - s_1}{2t} > 0$, c) $\frac{(3s_1 - s_2)^2}{8(s_1 - s_2)}$.

Exercise 22C — (page 448)

1). a) $\mathbf{i} + 3\mathbf{j}$, b) $-\mathbf{i} + 2\mathbf{j}$, c) $\frac{1}{3}\mathbf{i} - \frac{5}{3}\mathbf{j}$, d) $\frac{1}{2}\mathbf{i} + \frac{1}{2}\mathbf{j}$. 2). a) $2\mathbf{i} + 4\mathbf{j}$, $2\sqrt{5}$, b) $7\mathbf{i} - 5\mathbf{j}$, $\sqrt{74}$, c) $14\mathbf{j}$, 14, d) $2\mathbf{i} + 11\mathbf{j}$, $5\sqrt{5}$. 3). $\frac{5}{4}\mathbf{i} - \frac{19}{4}\mathbf{j}$, $18\mathbf{i} + 30\mathbf{j}$. 4). $\frac{11}{5}\sqrt{5}$, $\frac{95}{2}\mathbf{i} + 20\mathbf{j}$. 5). a) $\mathbf{f} = t(\mathbf{i} + \mathbf{j})$, $\mathbf{g} = t(-2\mathbf{i} + 3\mathbf{j})$, b) 78.7°, c) $\frac{100}{\sqrt{13}}$ = 27.7 seconds. 6). a) $(6t - 0.05t^2)\mathbf{i} + 0.015t^2\mathbf{j} + (1 - 0.01t^2)\mathbf{k}$, b) After 10 seconds, c) 5.01 ms^{-1}, d) 086.6°. 7). No, Yes.

Exercise 22D — (page 450)

1). $3t^2 + 4$, $6t$; 22 m, 16 ms^{-1}, 12 ms^{-2}. 2). $20 - 4t^3$, $-12t^2$; 22 m, 16 ms^{-1}, -12 ms^{-2}; -18 m, -88 ms^{-1}, -108 ms^{-2}. 3). 0 m, 10 ms^{-1}, -14 ms^{-2}. 4). 6 ms^{-1}, $\frac{3}{4}$ ms^{-2}. 5). 2 seconds, -24 ms^{-1}, -24 ms^{-2}. 6). 5 seconds, 20 m. 7). 4 ms^{-1}. 8). $\frac{4}{3}$ ms^{-2}. 9). $\frac{177}{8}$ m, 54 ms^{-2}. 10). a) 18 ms^{-1}, b) 4 ms^{-2}. 11). a) 120 s, 1380 m, b) 0.384 ms^{-2}, c) 1.15 ms^{-2}, d) 80 s, 20.5 ms^{-1}. 12). a) 952 m, 62.4 ms^{-1}, b) -41.0 ms^{-2}, -10 ms^{-2}, -0.328 ms^{-2}, c) 40 ms^{-1}, d) 35 s. 13). $\dot{x} = b + 2ct$, $\ddot{x} = 2c$ is constant. a = initial displacement, b = initial velocity, $2c$ = acceleration. 14). a) The object oscillates back and forth between $x = -a$ and $x = a$, c) $x = \pm a$, d) $a\omega$, e) $\ddot{x} = -\omega^2 \dot{x} = 0$ when $\dot{x} = 0$. 15). a) $\dot{y} = \frac{1}{2}(\dot{s} - u - t\ddot{s})$, b) $y = 0$ implies $\ddot{y} = 0$, which implies $\dddot{s} = 0$, or $\dot{a} = 0$.

Exercise 22E — (page 453)

1). $t^3 + 8t + 4$ m, 28 m, 20 ms^{-1}. 2). $v = -4 + 10t - 2t^3$ ms^{-1}, $x = \frac{23}{2} - 4t + 5t^2 - \frac{1}{2}t^4$ m, 11.5 m, -4 ms^{-1}, 10 ms^{-2}. 3). 20 m. 4). 60 m. 5). 22 m. 6). 10 m. 7). 28.5 m. 8). 1364.8 m. 9). a) 54 m, b) 4 m, c) 4 m; 62 m, 54 m. 10). 4.99 ms^{-1}, 5 ms^{-1}. 11). 7.5 m, $v = 2t^{-2} > 0$, $x = 2 - 2t^{-1} < 2$. 12). $92 = \frac{33^2 - 13^2}{2 \times 5}$ m. 13). a) 9 ms^{-1}, b) 8 ms^{-1}, $\frac{80}{3}$ m. 14). $\frac{3}{4}$, 204.8 m. 15). $\frac{p^{n+1}}{(n+1)q}$. 16). $t^3 - t^2 + 4t - 1$. 17). $x = \frac{1}{2} - \frac{1}{2}e^{-t}(\cos t + \sin t)$, $\ddot{x} = e^{-t}(\cos t - \sin t)$. 18). $(\frac{1}{3}t^3 + 3t)\mathbf{i} + (2t^2 - t)\mathbf{j} + (1 - t^3)\mathbf{k}$ m. 19). a) $t = 5$, b) $\frac{5}{2}\sqrt{10}$. 20). a) The object moves around a circle of radius a in an anticlockwise direction, b) $\dot{\mathbf{x}} = -a\omega \sin \omega t \mathbf{i} + a\omega \cos \omega t \mathbf{j}$, $\ddot{\mathbf{x}} = -a\omega^2 \cos \omega t \mathbf{i} - a\omega^2 \sin \omega t \mathbf{j}$, c) $a\omega$, 0; velocity is tangential to the circle, d) radially inwards.

Exercise 23A — (page 460)

1). a) 0.717 N on bearing 215.3°, b) 3.51 N on bearing 080.3°, c) 35.3 N on bearing 048.6°. 2). a) 30.1 N on bearing 162.4°, b) 24.6° on bearing 180°, c) 42.7° on bearing 261.1°. 4). a) $X = 30$, $Y = 35$, b) $X = 13.3$, $Y = 23.4$, c) $X = 72.5$, $Y = 8.03$, d) $X = 25.2$, $\theta = 73.8°$, e) $X = 29.4$, $\phi = 21.2°$, f) $X = 26.7$, $\theta = 33.6°$. 5). a) 22.8 N on bearing 044.7°, b) 26.0 N on bearing 065.0°, c) 10.9 N on bearing 095.9°, d) 9.10 N on bearing 035.1°. 6). 543.5 N at an angle 0.0288° to the right of straight ahead. 7). a) 24 N vertically up, b) 8 N vertically down, c) 16.5 N at 14.0° below horizontal. 8). a) $P = Q = 13.1$ N, b) $P = 47.0$ N, $Q = 25$ N, c) $P = 42.4$ N, $Q = 58.0$ N, d) $P = 17.8$ N, $Q = 27.2$ N.

Exercise 23C — (page 469)

1). 35.1 N. 2). 350 N, 8350 N. 3). 6 kg. 4). $50 - \frac{1}{2}T$. 5). a) 25.4°, b) 31.6 N. 6). 11.7°, 511 kg. 7). 170 N, 339 N. 8). 8.66 N. 9). 21.8 N, 63.9 N. 10). 35.2 N, 691 N. 11). $mg \sin \theta \sec \alpha$, $mg \sin \theta$. 12). 4.66 N, 28.0°. 13). 559 N, 26.6°. 14). 41.0 N, 113 N. 15). 61.9 N, 82.4 N. 16). 52.4°. 17). a) The ring is smooth, b) $\frac{13}{10}mg$. 18). $2Mg \sin \frac{1}{2}\theta$.

Exercise 23D — (page 474)

1). $\frac{2}{5}$. 2). a) 5900 N, equilibrium, b) 6000 N, limiting equilibrium. 3). a) $P - 50\sin\alpha$ N down the slope, $\mu > \frac{P}{50}\sec\alpha - \tan\alpha$, b) $50\sin\alpha - P$ up the slope, $\mu > \tan\alpha - \frac{P}{50}\sec\alpha$. 4). $8.20 \le P \le 37.7$. 5). $36.5°$. 6). $\frac{3}{7}$. 7). 80 N. 8). 33.3 N. 9). $\tan\theta \le \mu$. 10). $23.1°$. 11). No. 12). $mg\tan(\alpha + \beta)$.

Exercise 24A — (page 479)

1). 1.5 ms^{-2}. 2). 9240 N. 3). 4 s. 4). $\frac{24}{25}m$ N. 5). 18.75 m. 6). 6.4 ms^{-2}, 12.8 N. 7). 0.12 ms^{-2}, 22.4 s. 8). 40500 N each. 9). 125 N. 10). 2120 N. 11). 165 N. 12). 45 N, 2 ms^{-2}. 13). 3125 N. 14). 10.75 N, 2.81 m. 15). 52.2. 16). 7.5 s. 17). 0.4 ms^{-2} in the same direction as the 2 N force. 18). 6.02 ms^{-2}. 19). $F = ma = \frac{1}{2}X, \frac{3}{2}a$. 20). $2\ln 2$ seconds, the velocity v is increasing and tends to 1 as t tends to ∞.

Exercise 24B — (page 482)

1). 2 ms^{-2}. 2). 17920 N. 3). 13000 N, 0.4 ms^{-2}. 4). 7.92 N. 5). $7g = 72.4$ ms^{-2}. 6). 1270 N, 1.5 ms^{-2}. 7). 90 kg, 6.67 ms^{-1}. 8). 1.6 N. 9). 40 N, 16 kg. 10). $s = \dfrac{Mv^2}{2(T - Mg)}$. 11). 33 m, 900 N. 12). 8400 N.

Exercise 24C — (page 487)

1). Forwards, the train is accelerating, 0.4. 2). 0.49. 3). 725 kg, 0.122 ms^{-2}. 4). 9 m. 5). 0.024. 6). 0.2. 7). 0.806. 8). a) 1180 N, 2.44 ms^{-1}, b) 1690 N, 2.44 ms^{-2}. 9). 4.10 m, 1.49 s. 10). 0.734. 11). 0.465 N, 1.55 N. 12). 0.526. 13). 0.374, 1.58 ms^{-2}. 14). 0.186, 3.34 ms^{-2}. 15). $\dfrac{20(3 - 4\mu)g}{4 + 3\mu} \le P \le \dfrac{20g(3 + 4\mu)}{4 - 3\mu}$, $P = \dfrac{120g}{4 - 3\mu}$.

Review Exercises 8 — (page 489)

1). a) 1.5 ms^{-2}, b) $\sqrt{120} = 11.0$ ms^{-1}. 2). a) 40 seconds, b) 24.85 ms^{-1}. 3). $4\sqrt{14} = 15.0$ ms^{-1}. 4). $a = \frac{1}{8}$, $T = 20$. 5). 2 ms^{-2}, 200 m. 6). $\frac{3}{4}t^2$, 2 seconds, 31 m. 7). 0.2 ms^{-2}, 0.338 ms^{-2}. 8). 10.8 m. 9). 0.08 ms^{-2}. 10). a) 0.5 ms^{-2}, 7200 m, b) 460 s, c) No. 12). a) $\sqrt{\frac{d}{5}}$, b) $\sqrt{\frac{d}{5}} + \frac{d}{330}$, c) 29.1 m. 13). 32.7 ms^{-1}, 18.7°. 14). a) $5t^2 - \frac{1}{3}t^3$, b) $10 - 2t$ cm s^{-2}, c) $83\frac{1}{3}$ cm, 25 cm s^{-1}, d) 12 cm s^{-1} is smaller than $12\frac{3}{4}$ cm^{-1}. 15). a) $t = 2$, 6 ms^{-1}, b) 3 m from O in the negative direction, c) 3 times. 16). $\frac{6}{25}$ ms^{-1}, $\frac{2}{5}$ m. 17). a) 18 m, 21 ms^{-1}, -24 ms^{-2}, b) 3 s, -24 ms^{-1}, -6 ms^{-2}, c) 1 s, 28 m, -18 ms^{-2}, d) 4 s, -26 m, -27 ms^{-2}. 18). a) $0 \le t < 2$, b) $\frac{5}{4} < t < 2$ and $4 < t < 5$, c) $0.569 < t < 2$ and $2.931 < t < 5$. 19). b) 3, d) $\frac{16}{9}$ m. 21). $P = 10.3$ N, $Q = 28.2$ N. 22). 31.1 N. 23). a) $\tan^{-1}\frac{12}{5} = 67.4°$, b) 2. 24). $P = 1.46$ N, $Q = 4.26$ N; 'horizontally' to the left. 25). $P = 7.90$ N, $Q = 14.8$ N. 26). $X = 0.761$ N, $Y = 2.20$ N; in the opposite direction to the absent 1.2 N force. 27). a) 8 N, b) 1.7 kg; 13.6 kg. 28). 23.5 N, equilibrium is not limiting ($\mu > \tan 28°$). 29). 137 N. 30). $R = 14500$ N, $F = 1880$ N; 0.268. 32). 0.314. 33). $X = \dfrac{\mu mg}{\cos\theta - \mu\sin\theta}$ if $\mu\tan\theta < 1$, the crate never moves if $\mu\tan\theta \ge 1$; $Y = \dfrac{\mu mg}{\cos\theta + \mu\sin\theta}$ is always less than X. 35). 8 m, 3.96 ms^{-2}. 36). 17500 N. No, gravitational effects are negligible compared with other forces. 37). 10 kg, 60 m. 39). a) 0.84 ms^{-2}, b) 0.482 ms^{-2}, c) 5.92 ms^{-1}. 40). 0.4 s. 41). $g\sin\alpha$, $g\sin\beta$. 42). 26 N, 0.243. 43). 4.90 ms^{-2}. 44). 0.301. 45). 2.25 m, 2.70 ms^{-1}. 46). 20.2 s. 47). 3.17 ms^{-1}, 599 N. 48). 3.05 s. 49). $\frac{1}{2k}\ln\left(1 + \frac{ku^2}{g}\right)$.

Exercise 25A — (page 502)

2). 400 N, 500 N; 800 N, the car is being pushed from behind. 3). 0.2 ms^{-2}, 15300 N. 4). 270 kN and 180 kN. 5). a) 0.48 ms^{-2}, 170 N, b) 0.08 ms^{-2}, 170 N. 6). 50 N, 250 N; a) 0.05 ms^{-2}, 67.5 N, b) 0.05 ms^{-2} deceleration, 37.5 N, c) 0.156 ms^{-2} deceleration, 10.9 N, d) 0.175 ms^{-2}, 6.25 N (tension), e) 0.2 ms^{-2}, 0 N, f) 0.25 ms^{-2}, 12.5 N (thrust). 7). $\dfrac{F - P - Q}{M + m} + g\sin\alpha$. 8). mg, $2mg$, $3mg$, $4mg$ (bottom to top), $\frac{9}{10}g$, a) 0 N (all strings), b) $\frac{1}{20}mg$, $\frac{1}{10}mg$, $\frac{3}{20}mg$, $\frac{1}{5}mg$ (bottom to top).

Exercise 25B — (page 508)

1). $\frac{12}{5}g$ N, $\frac{1}{5}g$ ms^{-2}, 2.2 m.   2). a) Tension 10 N, friction 10 N,   b) Tension 10 N, friction 15 N,   c) Tensions 20 N, 10 N, friction 10 N,   d) Tension 7.5 N, friction 7.5 N,   e) Tension 17.3 N, friction 2.32 N,   f) Tension 35.4 N, friction 55.4 N.   3). a) $\frac{1}{8}g$ ms^{-2},   b) 2.5 ms^{-2},   c) $\frac{1}{13}g$ ms^{-2},   d) 3 ms^{-2},   e) 0.464 ms^{-2},   f) 6.15 ms^{-2}.   4). a) $\frac{1}{12}g$ ms^{-2},   b) 2.14 ms^{-2},   c) $\frac{1}{26}g$ ms^{-2},   d) 2.98 ms^{-2},   e) 0.204 ms^{-2},   f) 5.96 ms^{-2}.   5). 10 kg.   6). Cylinder $\frac{1}{8}g$ ms^{-2} down, mass $\frac{1}{16}g$ ms^{-2} up.   7). 3 : 1.   8). 2.31 ms^{-2}, 30.8 N, 12.3 N.   9). $\frac{1}{5}m \le M \le m$; $\frac{M-m}{M+m}g$ if $M > m$, $\frac{m-5M}{5(m+M)}g$ if $M < \frac{1}{5}m$.

Exercise 26A — (page 514)

1). a) 30 N s,   b) 30 kg m s^{-1},   c) 15 ms^{-1}.   2). 6 N.   3). 2.37 Ns at a angle of 71.6° to line of travel of the ball.   4). 4.24 N s.   5). 50 N s.   6). 2 kg.   7). a) 2 n s,   b) 18 N s,   c) 5.04 N s.   8). a) 40 N s,   b) 200 ms^{-1}; No.   9). $\frac{I}{\mu mg}$.   10). 105 N.   11). 500 N.   12). 11.5 N s.   13). a) $\frac{10}{\pi} = 3.18$ N s, 250,   b) 3.18 ms^{-1} in both cases,   c) the second mass would experience higher acceleration.

Exercise 26B — (page 519)

1). a) $v_2 = 2.5$,   b) $m_2 = 10$,   c) $v_1 = \frac{1}{2}(u-1)$, $v_2 = \frac{1}{2}(u+1)$,   d) $v = 1$,   e) $v = -\frac{99}{101}V$.   2). 2 ms^{-1}.   3). 4.55 ms^{-1}.   4). 30.6 g.   5). 1.25 ms^{-1}, 0.5 ms^{-1}.   6). The 2 kg and 3 kg spheres have velocities -0.1 ms^{-1} and 0.9 ms^{-1} respectively. The spheres keep moving until the string becomes taut, after which both spheres will be travelling with velocity 0.5 ms^{-1}.   7). 1 ms^{-1}.   8). $v_2 - v_1 \le u$.   9). $m_1 m_2 \left[(u_1 - u_2)^2 - (v_2 - v_1)^2\right] = 2(m_1 + m_2)\left[T_{\text{old}} - T_{\text{new}}\right]$, $v_2 - v_1 \le u_1 - u_2$.   10). $v = V \ln\left(\frac{M}{m}\right)$.

Exercise 26C — (page 525)

1). a) $\frac{2}{5}$,   b) $\frac{1}{4}$,   c) $\frac{1}{2}$,   d) 1.   2). a) $v_1 = 0$, $v_2 = 4$,   b) $v_1 = -\frac{2}{3}$, $v_2 = 2$,   c) $v_1 = -\frac{3}{7}u$, $v_2 = \frac{1}{14}u$,   d) $v_2 = \frac{1}{5}u$, $e = \frac{3}{5}$,   e) $m_2 = \frac{3}{4}m$, $e = \frac{3}{4}$.   3). X and Y have speeds $\frac{21}{8}$ ms^{-1} and $\frac{7}{8}$ ms^{-1} away from the wall; 17.3 J.   4). Since $\frac{1}{2}(1-e)u \ge 0$ for all $0 \le e \le 1$, the first particle does not change direction; $\frac{1}{3}$.   5). $e = \frac{1}{3}$.   6). 3 : 2.   7). After three collisions, A, B and C have velocities $\frac{147}{512}u$, $\frac{165}{512}u$ and $\frac{25}{64}u$.   8). $\sqrt{\frac{2h}{g}}\frac{1+e}{1-e}$ seconds, $h\frac{1+e^2}{1-e^2}$ m.   9). a) $\frac{1}{2}$,   b) $\frac{9}{16}u$, $\frac{5}{8}u$, $\frac{25}{32}u$.

Exercise 27A — (page 532)

1). 13 ms^{-1}, -20 ms^{-1}.   2). 72 m, 28.8 m.   3). $\sqrt{30^2 + 24^2} = 38.4$, $\tan^{-1}\frac{24}{30} = 38.6°$.   4). $\binom{30}{-20}$ m.   5). 80.4 m, 22.5 m, 26.8 ms^{-1}, -7.50 ms^{-1}.   6). a) 7 s,   b) -70 ms^{-1},   c) 490 m.   7). a) 0.4 s, quad b) -4 ms^{-1},   c) 14.9 ms^{-1},   d) 5.97 m.   8). 20 ms^{-1}, 15 ms^{-1}, 25 ms^{-1} at an angle of 36.9° above the horizontal.   9). 36.0°.   10). 28.3 ms^{-1}, 24.5 ms^{-1}.   11). 19.5 ms^{-1}.   12). 1.65 s.   13). 14.5 m.   14). a) 16.3 ms^{-1} at 42.5° above horizontal,   b) 2 m,   c) 6.05 m.   15). 53.1°, 35; air resistance.   16). a) $\binom{15}{-3}$ ms^{-1},   b) 4 m, 1.2 m.   17). 24.6 ms^{-1} at 54.3° above the horizontal.   18). $h = 15 - 5t^2$, $\frac{40}{3}$, $\frac{50}{3}$, 36.9°.   19). a) $x = 9.1t\cos 76°$, $y = 9.1t\sin 76° - 5t^2$, so $y = x\tan 76° - \frac{5}{9.1^2\cos^2 76°}x^2 = 4.01x - 1.03x^2 \approx 4x - x^2$,   b) 3.89 m (4 m using the approximation).   20). 3.55 s, 75.5 m.   21). $x = Vt\cos\theta$, $y = Vt\sin\theta - \frac{1}{2}gt^2$.   22). a) i. $d = ut$, $h = vt - \frac{1}{2}gt^2$, $D = uT$, $H = vT - \frac{1}{2}gT^2$,   ii. $h = \frac{u}{v}d - \frac{g}{2u^2}d^2$, $H = \frac{u}{v}d - \frac{g}{2u^2}D^2$,   b) Since $\frac{g}{2u^2} = \frac{Dh-dH}{dD(D-d)}$ and $\frac{v}{u} = \frac{D^2h-d^2H}{dD(D-d)}$, we need $Dh - dH$ and $D^2h - d^2H$ to be positive,   c) $\frac{5}{6}\sqrt{6gd}$.   23). a) $\tan\theta$ must be greater than $\frac{h}{d}$.

Exercise 27B — (page 536)

1). 17.8°, 72.2°.   2). 113 ms^{-1}.   3). 2.57 s, 39.4 m.   4). 11.6 ms^{-1}.   5). 69.0°.   6). 8.14 ms^{-2}.   7). 375 m, 20.2 m, 325 m.   8). 36.9 ms^{-1}.   9). 32.0° or 68.2°.   10). 17.7 ms^{-1}.   11). 35.9°.   12). 31.1 ms^{-1}.   13). 21.8°.   15). $\tan\alpha = \frac{1}{2}(\tan\theta - 1)$; no.   16). $\frac{dr}{d\theta} < 0$ when $\theta = 45°$.   17). a) $\dot{\mathbf{r}} = ue^{-kt}\mathbf{i} + \frac{g}{k}(e^{-kt} - 1)\mathbf{j}$,   b) $\mathbf{r} = \frac{u}{k}(1 - e^{-kt})\mathbf{i} + \frac{g}{k^2}(1 - e^{-kt} - kt)\mathbf{j}$,   c) the particle tends towards the state of moving vertically downwards with constant speed $\frac{g}{k}$, a horizontal displacement of $\frac{u}{k}$ from its starting point.

Review Exercises 9 — (page 489)

1). 558 N. 2). 1 ms^{-2}, speeding up. 3). $\frac{15}{4}g = 37.5$ N. 4). 444 N, 0.2 m. 5). 4.47 ms^{-1}, 3 m, 7.75 ms^{-1}. 6). 1.62 N, 0.176 kg. 8). $\frac{4}{13}g = 3.08$ N, 4 ms^{-1}, 5.11 m. 9). 18.6 N, 0.275, 0.144 m. 10). $a = \frac{X-600}{10000}$, $X < 600$, $X < 60$. 11). a) 3200 N, b) 3330 N. 12). a) 1310 N, b) 3480 N; 15.5 s. 13). b) $a_1 = \sqrt{3}a_2$. 14). a) $\frac{1}{5}U$, b) $\frac{2}{5}MU^2$. 15). $\frac{V}{k+1}$, $\frac{k}{k+1}mV^2$. 16). 1.57 s, 3.92 m.

17). 6.5 N s. 18). $mv\sqrt{2 - \dfrac{2x}{\sqrt{1+x^2}}}$ at an angle of $\tan^{-1}\left(\sqrt{1+x^2} - x\right)$ to the direction of travel

of the particle opposing the motion; $\frac{1}{\sqrt{3}}$ m. 19). $\frac{3}{8}mu^2$. 20). $\frac{1}{2}$. 21). $3mu$. 22). $\frac{1}{5}$, $\frac{9}{5}mV$.

23). a) $\frac{m_1 - m_2 - 2em_2}{m_1 + m_2}u$, $\frac{m_1 - m_2 + 2em_1}{m_1 + m_2}u$ in A's original direction of travel, b) $\frac{m_1 - m_2}{2m_2}$. 24). a) $-\frac{2}{1+\lambda}V$, $\frac{\lambda-1}{\lambda+1}V > 0$ in direction towards R, b) $\lambda > 2 + \sqrt{3}$. 25). a) $-\frac{3}{20}V$, $\frac{7}{20}V$, $-\frac{7}{40}V$ towards the wall, b) $10d$. 26). $\frac{m_1^2}{2(2m_1 - m_3)}v^2$, $\frac{1}{2}m_1v^2$. 27). 10 ms^{-1}, -2.679 ms^{-1}. 28). 41.8°, 22.4 ms^{-1}. 29). 24.6 ms^{-1} at 29.2° below the horizontal. 30). a) 42.7 ms^{-1} at 24.2° below the horizontal, b) 25.3 m; no air resistance. 31). $u = 20$, $v = 24.5$, 27.8° below the horizontal. 32). b) 12 m, c) the size of the ball. 33). b) $\frac{4k^2}{9g}\sqrt{3}$ (angle of release is 35.3°). 34). a) 13.8 ms^{-1}, b) 1.38 s, c) 3.63 ms^{-1}; air resistance. 35). a) No air resistance, b) 150 ms^{-1} at 15.6° above horizontal, 8.08 s. 36). 22.3 ms^{-1}, a) 1.32 s, b) 6.73°, descending, c) No air resistance, and the ball is a point particle. 37). $x = 10.1t\cos\alpha$, $y = 10.1t\sin\alpha - 5t^2$, b) $20.4\sin\alpha\cos\alpha$, c) $2.02\sin\alpha$, d) $y = x\tan\alpha - 0.00490x^2\sec^2\alpha$; 8.93 m.

Exercise 28A — (page 553)

1). 5.4 kg; 5.7 kg. 2). 40. 3). a) 27.5, b) 1.1. 4). 6. 5). 4.5. 6). 78, 63; on average, the men are heavier than the women. 7). 37.9. 8). $502.

9). a)

Time t s	1.0 − 2.4	2.5 − 3.9	4.0 − 5.4	5.5 − 6.9	7.0 − 8.4	8.5 − 9.9	10.0 − 11.4	11.5 − 12.9
Freq.	13	16	18	15	6	8	2	2

4.9, b) 5.0; the data is not evenly spread in the $4.0 - 5.4$ class. 10). 34.4. 11). a) 0, b) None, c) $2 - 3$, d) 2.

Exercise 28B — (page 558)

1). 10.5 2). Men: 181.3 cm, Women: 167.1 cm; students seem to be taller, on average, than the national population. 3). a) 11.3, b) 105.5. 4). 0.319. 5). 3.59. 6). 24.3. 7). 88.8 km/h. 8). a) $0 - 2.5, 2.5 - 5.5, 5.5 - 8.5, 8.5 - 11.5, 11.5 - 15.5$, b) 3.56 (if the first class were assumed to be $-0.5 - 2.5$, then the estimate for the mean would be 3.42. 9). £12.89, £12.39. 10). 503.46 ml. 11). 3, 7. 12). 12, 4. 13). The mean of the dataset. 15). 7, 5.

Exercise 28C — (page 563)

1). a) $17, 14 - 6 = 8$, b) $9.1, 7.6 - 4.8 = 2.8$. 2). $76 - 54 = 22$ cm. 3). $4 - 1 = 3$ times. 4). $30800, $47000. 5). Street 1: 70.1, 4.7; Street 2: 72.6, 4.6; Street 1 has a lower median noise level, but a slightly greater spread; noise levels are more variable. 6). Mondays have median 169.5 and IQR 153, Wednesdays have median 305.1 and IQR 137; audiences on Wednesdays are larger, and more consistent. 7). $Q_1 = 4$, $Q_3 = 8$. 8). $M = 2$, $Q_1 = 1$, $Q_3 = 3$. 9). 3. 10). a) 4.5, b) $11 \le a \le 21$, c) 2.5.

Exercise 28D — (page 568)

1). 0.740, 1.13. 2). $s = 1.58$, Range = 6. 3). 797 mins^2. 4). 251 g, 3.51 g; increase the sample size and decrease the class width. 5). 0.711. 6). $-17.2, 247.36$. 7). 135.7, 176.5. 8). 37.5, 11.9 (the class midpoints are 18.5, 23.5, 28.5, 33.5, 38.5, 46, 56, 66); the second company has a lower average age, and less spread of ages. 9). 0.976, 1.62. 10). 3.6. 12). All values in the dataset are the same (equal to the mean).

Exercise 28E — (page 572)

1). a) Negative skew, no outliers, b) Positive skew, $-25°$ C is an outlier, c) Symmetric, 110 m is an outlier. 2). $93.70, $99.24, $102.83; negative skew. 3). 140 and 10 are outliers. 4). a) 3.76, 1, 7.75, 0, 4, b) 0.5, 1.07, c) Positive.

Exercise 29A — (page 579)

1). -0.218; a slight negative correlation.   2). 0.263.   3). 0.620, but storks do not deliver babies!
4). 0.903; boys get taller as they get older.   5). 0.306.   6). -0.789.   7). 0.641.   8). This data would
imply that $r_{uv} = -1.16 < -1$.   9). -0.840; because the relation between x and y is not linear (albeit
perfect), the correlation coefficient is not -1.   10). 0.431.   12). a) $F(t) = S_{xx}t^2 - 2S_{xy}t + S_{yy}$,   b)
$F(t)$ must have nonnegative discriminant,   c) Consider $G(t) = \sum_i [t(x_i - \overline{x}) - (y_i - \overline{y})]^2$ instead.

Exercise 29B — (page 586)

1). a) $y = 1.423 + 0.464x$,   b) $y = 1.710x - 29.1$,   c) $y = 2.442 + 0.673x$,   d) $y = 77.04 - 1.083x$.
2). a) $y = 92.20 - 5.116x$,   b) $y = 2.158 - 0.298x$,   c) $y = 1.784 + 1.717x$,   d)
$y = 2.281 - 0.3467x$.   3). $y = 2.569 + 1.191x$.   5). $y = 29.648 + 0.9638t$, $y = 29.648 + 192.8x^{-1}$;
31.8; probably not (the range of t given by the data is from 1.70 to 2.61, and we want to use
$t = 1.54$, so we would be extrapolating, but not by much).   6). a) 5,   b) 7.   7). $b = \frac{s_y}{s_x}r_{xy}$,
0.   8). $y = 40.83 + 0.7949x$, 113.8 Zoddybits a gram.   9). $h = 0.9970 + 0.6970t$, 6.22.
10). $y = -0.4037 - 1.4224x$, $y = 1.257x$.   11). $\frac{S_{xx}S_{yy} - S_{xy}^2}{S_{xx}} = S_{yy}[1 - r_{xy}^2] \geq 0$, and so $-1 \leq r_{xy} \leq 1$.

Exercise 29C — (page 590)

1). $y = 9.8 + 0.213x$;   a) 11.96, 0.260,   b) 10.8, 0.213.   2). y on x: $y = 23.58 - 0.637x$, x
on y: $x = 32.63 - 1.171y$,   a) y on x,   b) x on y.   3). $r_{xy} = -0.975$; $x = 167.8 - 1.656y$,
51.9 year olds.   4). $y = 26.85 + 0.814x$; Amanda, 81.4%.   5). a) $y = 39.70 + 1.672x$,   b)
49.7,   c) From the x on y curve: 3.68.   6). $x = 2042.4 - 0.0474y$; 2019, but this is extrapolation.
7). $\alpha + \beta q - s = \overline{v} - \beta \overline{u} + \beta q - s = y\overline{y} - p\beta \overline{x} = ra$.   8). a) $(\overline{x}, \overline{y})$,   b) It must be perfectly correlation
$(r_{xy} = \pm 1)$.   9). $y = 16.15 - 0.1x$ (code $x = 45 + 10u$, $y = 10 + 2v$).

Exercise 30A — (page 598)

1). 5040.   2). 24.   3). 120.   4). 720.   6). 119.   7). 50400.   8). a) 720,   b) 48.
9). $4 + 12 + 24 + 24 = 64$; $18 + 24 = 42$.   10). 5760.   11). 115165670400.   12). 432.   13). 210, 150.
14). 6227020800, 609638400.

Exercise 30B — (page 600)

1). 22100.   2). $\frac{3}{14}$.   3). 215760.   4). a) 24,   b) 256.   5). a) 56,   b) 48.   6). 70, 63.   7). $\frac{1}{4}$.
8). 0.0128.   9). a) 0.222,   b) 0.0703,   c) 0.112,   d) 0.180.   10). a) 330,   b) 60,   c)
65.   11). a) 190, 1140,   b) 170.   12). a) $^nC_2$,   b) $n + {}^nC_4 = \frac{1}{24}n(n^3 - 6n^2 + 11n + 18)$,   c)
$1 + {}^nC_2 + {}^nC_4 = \frac{1}{24}(n^4 - 6n^3 + 23n^2 - 18n + 24)$.   13). b) $\binom{n-k}{k}$.

Exercise 30C — (page 603)

1). a) 3632428800,   b) 259459200,   c) 39916800,   d) 457228800.   2). a) 1024,   b) 210,
c) 0.205.   3). a) 5.35×10^{13},   b) 3.097×10^{12},   c) 0.0579.   4). a) $13! = 6227020800$,   b)
43545600,   c) 609638400.   5). a) 1260,   b) 540,   c) 300,   d) 120.   6). a) 39916800,   b)
20736,   c) 1814400.   7). a) 12,   b) 115.   8). a) $\frac{1}{120}$,   b) $\frac{1}{10}$,   c) 14.   9). Perfect squares.
10). a) $\binom{n+1}{k+1}$,   b) $\binom{m}{k}$ if $k + 1 \leq m + 1 \leq n + 1$, 0 otherwise.   11). 277.

Review Exercises 10 — (page 607)

1). a) $Q_2 = \$0.52$, $\overline{x} = \$0.617$, modes are \$0.4, \$0.42, \$0.49,   b) the median, since it is less af-
fected by a small number of extreme values,   c) \$0.236.   2). a) 2.56, exact,   b) 2, 2.   3). a)
The data has been grouped,   b) 69.4,   c) The estimate of the mean would increase, but the
estimate of the median would not change.   4). 3.48 or 3.36 depending on which order the 12 and
9 appear in the frequency table.   5). a) 20.55 minutes,   b) The data is grouped, and may not be
evenly spread across the classes,   c) 21.1 minutes,   d) Negative skew.   6). Yes $(2 \leq 2 \leq 2.56)$;
$m = 3$, $Q_2 = 4$, $\overline{x} = 3.6$, so Q_2 is not in the middle.   7). a) 453.9, 462.9, 9; yes,   b) 294.5, 266.5,
5; no.   8). Robin: 23.2 cm, 1.32 cm. Sparrow: 22.9 cm, 1.13 cm; the sparrow has a smaller
wingspan, and a smaller spread of wingspans.   9). a) 18.69 m, 36.20 m^2,   b) 18.92 m, 36.20
m^2.   10). a) 0.0598 cm,   b) IQR $= 3.04 - 2.96 = 0.08$; $\frac{IQR}{s} = 1.34$, quite close to 1.3; the distribution is fairly symmetric.   11). a) Sam's standard deviation of weights is 0 kg,   b) Ali landed
12.84 kg, Les landed 12.16 kg, Sam landed 2 kg, so Ali wins,   c) 3.12 kg.   12). a) $Q_1 = 1.809$,
$Q_2 = 1.854$, $Q_3 = 1.885$,   b) $Q_2 - Q_1 > Q_3 - Q_2$, so negative skew,   c) $\overline{x} = 1.85$, $s = 0.0689$,   d)
-0.193 confirms negative skew.   13). a) 26.94, 13.02,   b) 22.3,   c) The median is better with

skewed data. 14). $y = 22.04 + 0.431x; 65.1$ kg (but extrapolation is likely). 15). a) -0.994, b) $y = 4.964 - 1.937x$, c) 1.090. 16). c) $\frac{1}{3}n(n^2 - 1)$. 17). a) $y = 11.474x - 2.804$, b) $r_{xy} = 0.953$, so the model is good, c) 56.86. 18). 0.781. 19). 0.527 some evidence that people like spicy pizzas, and dislike plain ones. 20). b) 0.701, c) $y = 4.330 + 0.564x$. 21). a) $y = 2.191 + 1.949x$, $x = 14.735 + 0.252y$, b) 27.3. 22). $a = 5$. 23). a) $S_{xx} = 2$, $S_{yy} = \frac{2}{3}(a^2 - 7a + 19)$, $S_{xy} = 3$, b) 2 or 5. 24). $3628800, 45$. 25). a) 40320, b) 1152. 26). 630. 27). 360. 28). a) 1440, b) 2880. 29). a) 240, b) 480. 30). 210. 31). 151200. 32). a) 0.112, b) 0.368. 33). a) 360, b) 60. 34). 720. 35). a) 24, b) $120; 2880$. 36). a) 70, b) $\frac{1}{35}$. 37). a) $(1,1,8)$, $(1,2,7), (1,3,6), (1,4,5), (2,2,6), (2,3,5), (2,4,4), (3,3,4)$, b) $\frac{1}{4}$. 38). 1260. 39). a) 60, b) 5. 40). $^{52}C_5 = 2598960$, $^{39}C_5 = 575757; 0.0109$, the deck is rigged. 41). $23! \times 4! = 24!$. 42). 400000, $500000, 2388, 2089.5$. 43). b) 210.

Exercise 31A — (page 620)

1). a) $\frac{1}{2}$, b) $\frac{2}{3}$, c) $\frac{1}{2}$, d) $\frac{1}{2}$, e) $\frac{1}{6}$, f) $\frac{5}{6}$, g) $\frac{2}{3}$. 2). a) $\frac{1}{2}$, b) $\frac{3}{13}$, c) $\frac{5}{13}$, d) $\frac{5}{26}$, e) $\frac{9}{13}$. 3). a) $\frac{1}{6}$, b) $\frac{5}{12}$, c) $\frac{5}{12}$, d) $\frac{25}{36}$, e) $\frac{11}{36}$, f) $\frac{5}{18}$, g) $\frac{1}{6}$, h) $\frac{1}{2}$. 4). The sample space is $\{3, 4, 5, 6, 7, 8, 9, 10, 11\}$, with associated probabilities $\frac{1}{15}, \frac{1}{15}, \frac{2}{15}, \frac{2}{15}, \frac{1}{5}, \frac{2}{15}, \frac{2}{15}, \frac{1}{15}, \frac{1}{15}$. a) $\frac{1}{5}$, b); $\frac{2}{5}$, c) $\frac{1}{3}$, d) $\frac{1}{2}$. 5). a) 0.36, b) 0.16, c) 0.48, d) 0.84, e) 0.6. 6). $\frac{7}{12}$. 7). $\frac{2}{9}$. 8). $\frac{2}{3} \leq \mathbb{P}[A \cap B] \leq \frac{5}{12}$. 9). $\frac{1}{7}$ 10). $\{-8, -6, -4, -2, 0, 2, 4, 6, 8\}$ with probabilities $p(-8) = p(8) = \frac{1}{256}$, $p(-6) = p(6) = \frac{8}{256}$, $p(-4) = p(4) = \frac{28}{256}$, $p(-2) = p(2) = \frac{56}{256}$, $p(0) = \frac{70}{256}$; $\frac{10}{256}$, a little more than $p(8) + p(6)$. 11). a) $\frac{1}{216}$, b) $\frac{6}{216}$, c) $\frac{18}{256}$, d) $\frac{1}{2}$ (consider the map $(a, b, c) \mapsto (7 - a, 7 - b, 7 - c)$ on the sample space). 12). $\frac{27}{100}$. 13). $A' = B$; $\mathbb{P}[A] = \frac{1}{2}$. 14). c) $I_{(A' \cap B')'} = I_A + I_B - I_{A \cap B} = I_{A \cup B}$, d) $\mathbb{P}[A]$. 15). $\mathbb{P}[A] + \mathbb{P}[B] + \mathbb{P}[C] - \mathbb{P}[A \cap B] - \mathbb{P}[A \cap C] - \mathbb{P}[B \cap C] + \mathbb{P}[A \cap B \cap C]$.

Exercise 31B — (page 630)

1). a) $\frac{1}{3}$, b) $\frac{2}{15}$, c) $\frac{8}{15}$, d) $\frac{13}{15}$, e) $\frac{3}{5}$; no. 2). a) $\frac{11}{221}$, b) $\frac{10}{17}$, c) $\frac{7}{17}$, d) $\frac{7}{102}$. 3). a) 0.27, b) 0.35, c) 0.3375. 4). a) $\frac{8}{15}$, b) $\frac{7}{15}$, c) $\frac{3}{5}$, d) $\frac{2}{5}$, e) $\frac{9}{16}$, f) Yes, g) No. 5). a) 0.24, b) 0.42, c) 0.706. 6). a) 0.12, b) 0.44, c) 0.048, d) 0.34, e) 0.03, f) 0.07, g) 0.32. 7). a) $\frac{1}{16}$, b) $\frac{15}{16}$, c) $\frac{671}{1296}$. 8). 0.491. 9). 0.507. 23 is the smallest number of people for which this probability is greater than $\frac{1}{2}$. 10). $0.75, 0.8$. 11). $\frac{1 - (2r - r^2)(1 - p)}{1 - r(1 - p)}$. 12). 97.5%. 13). $\mathbb{P}[A \cap B] = \mathbb{P}[A]\mathbb{P}[B|A]$, $\mathbb{P}[B] = \mathbb{P}[A]\mathbb{P}[B|A] + \mathbb{P}[A']\mathbb{P}[B|A']$. 14). 9.98×10^{-4}. The accused is still extremely unlikely to be guilty. 15). c) $\mathbb{P}[A(3, r)] = \frac{1}{4}$ for $1 \leq r \leq 4$, d) $\mathbb{P}[A(n, r)] = \frac{1}{n+1}$ for $1 \leq r \leq n + 1$, so any possible proportion is equally likely, e) No, it seems as if the proportion of black balls in the urn might stabilise.

Exercise 32A — (page 636)

1).

x	0	1	2	3	4
$\mathbb{P}[X = x]$	$\frac{1}{16}$	$\frac{4}{16}$	$\frac{6}{16}$	$\frac{4}{16}$	$\frac{1}{16}$

2).

d	0	1	2	3	4	5
$\mathbb{P}[D = d]$	$\frac{3}{18}$	$\frac{5}{18}$	$\frac{4}{18}$	$\frac{3}{18}$	$\frac{2}{18}$	$\frac{1}{18}$

3).

x	1	2	3	6	8
$\mathbb{P}[X = x]$	$\frac{1}{6}$	$\frac{1}{3}$	$\frac{1}{6}$	$\frac{1}{6}$	$\frac{1}{6}$

4).

h	1	2	3	4	5	6
$\mathbb{P}[H = h]$	$\frac{23}{36}$	$\frac{7}{36}$	$\frac{3}{36}$	$\frac{1}{36}$	$\frac{1}{36}$	$\frac{1}{36}$

5).

m	1	2	3	4	6	8	9	12	16
$\mathbb{P}[M = m]$	$\frac{1}{16}$	$\frac{2}{16}$	$\frac{2}{16}$	$\frac{3}{16}$	$\frac{2}{16}$	$\frac{2}{16}$	$\frac{1}{16}$	$\frac{2}{16}$	$\frac{1}{16}$

6).

g	0	1	2
$\mathbb{P}[G = g]$	$\frac{5}{12}$	$\frac{6}{12}$	$\frac{1}{12}$

7).

c	1	2	3	4
$\mathbb{P}[C = c]$	$\frac{1}{13}$	$\frac{16}{221}$	$\frac{376}{5525}$	$\frac{4324}{5525}$

8). 3 coins : , 4 coins : ,

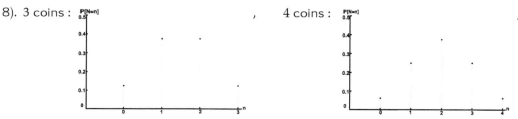

5 coins , 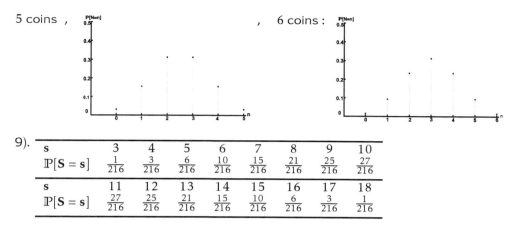 , 6 coins :

9).

s	3	4	5	6	7	8	9	10
$\mathbb{P}[S = s]$	$\frac{1}{216}$	$\frac{3}{216}$	$\frac{6}{216}$	$\frac{10}{216}$	$\frac{15}{216}$	$\frac{21}{216}$	$\frac{25}{216}$	$\frac{27}{216}$

s	11	12	13	14	15	16	17	18
$\mathbb{P}[S = s]$	$\frac{27}{216}$	$\frac{25}{216}$	$\frac{21}{216}$	$\frac{15}{216}$	$\frac{10}{216}$	$\frac{6}{216}$	$\frac{3}{216}$	$\frac{1}{216}$

Exercise 32B — (page 639)

1). $\frac{1}{20}$. 2). 0.3. 3). 0.15. 4). $\frac{1}{8}$. 5). $\mathbb{P}[X = x] = \frac{1}{12}$ for $x = 2, 4, 6$, $\mathbb{P}[X = x] = \frac{1}{4}$ for $x = 1, 3, 5$.
6). $\frac{1}{21}$. 7). $\frac{20}{49}$. 8). 0.2. 9). $\mathbb{P}[X = 5] = 0$. 10). $x < y$. 11). $c = \frac{2}{3}$, $\frac{1}{3} \le d \le \frac{1}{2}$. 12). $k = 2$, $\frac{1}{9}$.
13). $\frac{241}{243}$; $\mathbb{P}[U = u] = 3^{u-1}$ for $u \in \mathbb{Z}$, $u \le 0$, while $\mathbb{P}[U = u] = 3^{-u}$ for $u \in \mathbb{N}$.

Exercise 32C — (page 640)

1). a) 130, b) 40, c) 120, d) 160, e) 360. 2). a) 105, b) 105, c) 245. 3). 12, 31, 34,
18, 5, 0 (rounding the last number down makes the total equal to 100. 4). 0.468, 103 5). 3.52%.
No.

Exercise 32D — (page 645)

1). 5.5. 2). 5. 3). a) $2p - 1$, b) $4p + 1$, c) 1, d) 1, e) $4p(1 - p)$. 4). 0.1, 1.7.
5). $\mathbb{E}[X^2] = 1 \ge (2p - 1)^2 = \mathbb{E}[X]^2$. 6). $\frac{3}{2}$. 7). 2.7, 14.5. 8). $\frac{27}{56}$. 9). a) $a = b = \frac{1}{5}$, b) $a = 0.1$,
$b = 0.6$, c) $a = \frac{1}{6}, b = \frac{1}{3}$. 10). $2.5 \le \mathbb{E}[Y] \le 5$. 11). 0.75, 0.75. 12). $\frac{10}{3}, \frac{23}{3}$. 13). $\frac{16}{9}$. 14). -2.5.
15). $\frac{1}{2}(N + 1)$. 16). $\mathbb{P}[X = 27] = \frac{1}{1326}$, $\mathbb{P}[X = 24] = \frac{5}{1326}$, $\mathbb{P}[X = 2] = \frac{324}{1326}$, $\mathbb{P}[X = -1] = \frac{996}{1326}$;
$\mathbb{E}[X] = -\frac{67}{442} = -0.152$. 17). $M > {}^{50}C_6 = 15890700$. 18). $\mathbb{P}[A]$.

Exercise 32E — (page 649)

1). a) $\frac{15}{8}$, b) 0.05. 2). 4, $\frac{18}{5}$. 3). $\frac{46}{9}, \frac{116}{81}$. 4). a) $\frac{11}{6}, \frac{29}{36}$, b) $\mathbb{P}[Y = 2] = \frac{1}{4}$, $\mathbb{P}[Y = 3] = \frac{1}{6}$,
$\mathbb{P}[Y = 4] = \frac{13}{36}$, $\mathbb{P}[Y = 5] = \frac{1}{9}$, $\mathbb{P}[Y = 6] = \frac{1}{9}$; $\frac{11}{3}, \frac{29}{18}$. 5). B has a greater expected profit. 6). a)
0.3, 0.51, b) 5.7, 0.51, c) The means add to 6, while the variances are the same. 7). $\frac{61}{36}$,
$\frac{1859}{1296} = 1.4344$. 8). $a = 0.2$, $\mu = \frac{14}{5}$, $\sigma = \frac{7}{5}$. 9). $a = b = 0.15$, $\sigma = 1.7$. 10). a) $\mathbb{P}[X = 1] = \frac{1}{6}$,
$\mathbb{P}[X = 2] = \frac{5}{36}$, $\mathbb{P}[X = 3] = \frac{25}{216}$, $\mathbb{P}[X = 4] = \frac{125}{216}$, b) 0.1717; $\frac{91}{216} = 0.5177$; -20.563. 11). b)
$\mathbb{P}[H = 0] = \frac{1}{3}$, $\mathbb{P}[H = 1] = \frac{11}{24}$, $\mathbb{P}[H = 2] = \frac{1}{6}$, $\mathbb{P}[H = 3] = \frac{1}{24}$, c) $\mathbb{E}[H] = \frac{11}{6}$, d) $\frac{95}{144} = 0.6597$.
12). a) $-a + c, a + c - (a - c)^2$, b) $x = -\frac{1}{2}, 0, \frac{1}{2}$ only, c) It must be constant (take a single value
with probability 1), since (a, b, c) must be one of $(1, 0, 0)$, $(0, 1, 0)$ or $(0, 0, 1)$.

Exercise 32F — (page 655)

1). $\frac{1}{2}$. 2). 17, 84; $\frac{1}{2}$. 3). 0.128. 4). 0.270, 0.0225. 5). 0.0593. 6). a) $\mathrm{Geo}(\frac{1}{m})$, b) $U(m)$;
1000, 500.5. 7). 0.798; 72, 5040. 8). a) 0.941, b) $\mathrm{Geo}(0.0585)$; 17.1, 0.485, c) 10^{12}. 9). a)
$q^{j-1}p$, b) $\mathrm{Geo}(p)$, The probability of winning does not improve, no matter what the length of
the losing streak. 10). a) $\frac{9}{64}$, b) 0.822, c) 0.0323. 11). $\frac{1}{7}$. 12). $-\frac{4}{3}$; a) 1, 5, b) $\lambda = 6 - \sqrt{5}$
minimises the expected profit.

Exercise 32G — (page 657)

1). a) 0.0819, b) 0.0154, c) 0.0001. 2). a) 0.2561, b) 0.2048, c) 0.0005. 3). a) 0.2119,
b) 0.4728, c) 0.0498. 4). a) 0.0017, b) 5. 5). a) 0.2461, b) 0.4102, c) 0.0195, d)
0.9102. 6). a) 0.0781, b) 0.0176. 7). This formula enables us to calculate ${}^nC_x$ without
needing to evalue factorials. 8). We get equality when $(n + 1)p$ is an integer.

Exercise 32H — (page 659)

1). a) 0.650, b) The students' ages would not longer be independent. 2). 0.913; no. 3). a) $B(30, \frac{2}{3})$, b) 0.548, 0.153. 4). a) $\mathbb{P}[X = 10] = 0.0157$, $\mathbb{P}[X = -1] = 0.9843$; $\mathbb{E}[X] = -0.827$, b) $\mathbb{P}[X = 10] =$, $\mathbb{P}[X = -1] = 0.9532$; $\mathbb{E}[X] = -0.485$, c) $\mathbb{P}[X = 10] = 0.005$, $\mathbb{P}[X = -1] = 0.995$; $\mathbb{E}[X] = -0.945$. 5). a) $\frac{7}{18}$, b) 0.1395, c) 0.124. 6). 0.1143, 0.223; eggs in the same box will not get broken independently of each other. 7). 0.0652; hurricanes must occur in different months with the same probability, independently of the incidence of hurricanes in other months. Hurricanes are more common in some months than in others. 8). 0.204; any adult must wear jeans with probability 0.35, independently of any other adult. 9). We are not conducting a sequence of identical trials. 10). a) The six boys chosen are likely to have similar heights, which are not independent of each other, b) The probability of reaching 20°C is greater for days in Summer than for days in Winter. 11). The events A, B, C and D are not independent.

Exercise 32I — (page 661)

1). a) 2.8, 2.408, b) 0.455. 2). 0.84, 0.907. 3). 10.5, 6.825. 4). 0.258. 5). 1.6. 6). 0.141.

Exercise 33A — (page 670)

1). a) $0.8907 = 0.891$, b) $0.9933 = 0.993$, c) $0.5624 = 0.562$, d) $0.1082 = 0.108$, e) $0.0087 = 0.009$, f) $0.2783 = 0.278$, g) $0.9664 = 0.966$, h) $0.9801 = 0.980$, i) $0.5267 = 0.5274$, j) $0.0336 = 0.034$, k) $0.0030 = 0.003$, l) $0.4184 = 0.418$, m) $0.9500 = 0.950$, n) $0.0500 = 0.050$, o) $0.9500 = 0.950$, p) $0.0500 = 0.050$. 2). a) $0.0366 = 0.037$, b) $0.1202 = 0.120$, c) $0.3416 = 0.342$, d) $0.4394 = 0.439$, e) $0.9555 = 0.956$, f) $0.7804 = 0.780$. 3). a) $0.8559 = 0.856$, b) $0.2088 = 0.209$, c) $0.0320 = 0.032$, d) $0.1187 = 0.119$, e) $0.4459 = 0.446$, f) $0.9500 = 0.950$, g) $0.9800 = 0.980$, h) $0.8064 = 0.806$, i) $0.0164 = 0.016$. 4). a) $s = 0.44$, b) $t = 1.165$, c) $u = 2.15$, d) 1.017, e) $s = 0.24$, f) $t = 1.178$, g) $u = 2.450$, h) $v = 0.758$, i) $s = -2.83$, j) $t = -1.955$, k) $u = -1.035$, l) $v = 0$, m) $s = -2.74$, n) $t = -2.192$, o) $u = -1.677$, p) $v = -0.056$, q) $s = 1.645$, r) $t = 1.281$, s) $u = 2.576$, t) $v = 0.674$.

Exercise 33B — (page 672)

1). a) $0.9332 = 0.933$, b) $0.0062 = 0.006$, c) $0.7734 = 0.773$, d) $0.0401 = 0.040$. 2). a) $0.9522 = 0.952$, b) $0.0098 = 0.010$, c) $0.7477 = 0.748$, d) $0.0038 = 0.004$. 3). a) $0.1359 = 0.136$, b) $0.0606 = 0.061$, c) $0.7333 = 0.733$, d) $0.7704 = 0.770$, e) $0.8664 = 0.866$. 4). $0.0668 = 0.067$. 5). a) $0.1587 = 0.159$, b) $0.0228 = 0.023$. 6). a) $s = 54.35$, b) $t = 40.30$, c) $u = 52.25$, d) $v = 41.85$. 7). a) $s = 17.73$, b) 14.62, c) 17.52, d) 14.45, e) 3.29. 8). a) 41.6, b) 29.9, c) 37.3, d) 31.7. 9). 10.03. 10). 65.00. 11). 42.0, 8.27. 12). 9.51, 0.303.

Exercise 33C — (page 675)

1). a) $0.037 = 0.04$, b) $0.0062 = 0.006$, c) $0.8209 = 0.821$. 2). a) $0.2094 = 0.209$, b) $0.0086 = 0.009$, c) $0.1788 = 0.179$, d) $0.6405 = 0.641$; 105, 4.3, 89.4, 320. 3). a) 13.4, b) 83.5, c) 121. 4). a) $0.0048 = 0.005$, b) $0.1944 = 0.184$, c) 80, 100. 5). 1970. 6). a) $0.6139 = 0.614$, b) 20.9, 16.3, c) 17. 7). 336 ml. 8). 40.8 g. 9). 47 hours². 10). 49.1, 13.4. 11). a) $0.0026 = 0.003$, b) 0.025; probably. 12). a) $B(n, p)$, b) p, $\frac{pq}{n}$, c) $2\Phi\left(0.03\sqrt{\frac{n}{pq}}\right) - 1$, d) 801, e) 1068.

Review Exercises 11 — (page 679)

1). $\frac{2}{3}$. 2). 0.58, 0.6. 3). $\frac{1}{2} > \frac{5}{11}$. 4). a) 20%, b) 10%. 5). b) $\frac{23}{189}$, $\frac{166}{189}$. 6). $\frac{3}{20}$, $\frac{9}{35}$, $\frac{7}{12}$. 7). a) $1 - \frac{2}{3} \times \frac{1}{3} \times 16 = \frac{26}{27}$, b) $\frac{9}{26}$. 8). a) $\frac{1}{5}$, $\frac{5}{13}$, $\frac{17}{25}$, $\frac{1}{2}$, b) $\frac{21}{25}$. 9). a) 0.5, b) $5p, 4p$, c) $\frac{1}{40}$. 10). a) $\frac{3}{52} = 0.577$, b) $\frac{261}{2470} = 0.1057$, c) $\frac{1649}{2470} = 0.6676$. 11). a) $\frac{3}{253} = 0.0119$, b) $\frac{43}{138} = 0.312$, c) $\frac{11}{138} = 0.0797$, d) $\frac{11}{69} = 0.159$. 12). a) 0.32, b) 0.56; 8. 13). a) $\frac{3}{8}$, $\frac{4}{15}$, b) $\frac{27}{125}$, $\frac{8}{125}$, $\frac{38}{125}$. 14). a) $\frac{1}{8}$, b) $\frac{3}{8}$, c) $\frac{8}{9}$. 15). 0.017, $\frac{2}{3}$. 16). a) 0.030, b) 0.146, c) 0, d) 0.712. 17). a) $\frac{4n-3}{n(n+1)}$, b) $\frac{9}{4n-3}$. 18). a) $\frac{3^3}{^9C_3} = \frac{9}{28}$, $\frac{9}{28}$, b) $\frac{n^3}{^{2n}C_3}$, c) $\frac{(n!)^2 2^n}{(2n)!} \approx 2^{-n}\sqrt{n\pi}$. 19).

x	0	1	2	3
$\mathbb{P}[X = x]$	$\frac{248}{1105}$	$\frac{496}{1105}$	$\frac{304}{1105}$	$\frac{57}{1105}$

20).

x	0	1	2	3	4	6
$\mathbb{P}[X = x]$	$\frac{1}{4}$	$\frac{1}{3}$	$\frac{1}{9}$	$\frac{1}{6}$	$\frac{1}{9}$	$\frac{1}{36}$

, 120.

21). a) $\frac{1}{18}$, b) $\frac{17}{36}$, c) $\frac{11}{17}$. 22). a) $\frac{1}{6} \times 60 = 10$, b) 8.3. 23). $\frac{1}{8}$. 24). a) 1, b) 2.05, c) 3.16, d) 13.4; 20. 25). 0.580. 26). a) $B(20, 0.1)$, b) 0.677. 27). a) $B(8, 0.2)$, b) 0.0563. 28). a) 0.337, b) 0.135. 29). a) 0.286, b) 0.754. 30). a) $\frac{1}{16}, \frac{4}{16}, \frac{6}{16}, \frac{4}{16}, \frac{1}{16}$, b) $\frac{356}{128} = 0.273$, c) $\frac{5}{16}$. 31). When a sequence of identical and independent trials is begin conducted, where each trial is either a success or a failure; a) 0.0246, b) 0.138; 83. 32). a) 0.116, b) 0.386, c) 0.0680. 33). Hens must lay eggs (or not) independently of each other, or of whether they laid an gg the day before, and always with the same probability; $\frac{5}{6}$; 1.07, 4.02, 8.04, 6.70. 34). a) 0.9, b) 0.08, c) 0.14, d) 0.3; 0.747. 35). a) 2.56, 2.25, b) 123. 36). 47.9. 37). 2, 0.8, 0.3456. 38). 1.3, 1.01, 3.8, 0.76;

a)

z	3	4	5	6	7	8
$\mathbb{P}[Z = z]$	0.15	0.16	0.33	0.19	0.14	0.03

b) $\mathbb{E}[Z] = 5.1$, $\text{Var}[Z] = 1.77$.

21). 2 and 15 are outliers; 0.0160, 0.021.

22). a) 0.8704,

x	1	2	3	4
$\mathbb{P}[X = x]$	0.4	0.24	O.144, 0.216	

c) 2.176, 1.377.

23).

w	0	1	2
$\mathbb{P}[W = w]$	$\frac{5}{15}$	$\frac{8}{15}$	$\frac{2}{15}$

; 0.8.

24). a) $b = 0.06$, b) 1.6644.

25). a)

y	0	1	2	3	4
$\mathbb{P}[Y = y]$	0.00672	0.06912	0.24832	0.38912	0.28672

b) 2.88, 0.8576.

27). a) $\frac{6}{(n+2)(n+3)}$, c) $\frac{n+9}{n+3}$. 28). 0.0913 = 0.091. 29). 0.9213 = 0.921. 30). 0.9599 = 0.960. 31). 0.9332 = 0.933. 32). 0.9568 = 0.957. 33). 0.5253 = 0.525. 34). 0.3674 = 0.367. 35). Luxigloss, 0.9361 = 0.936. 36). 19.0. 37). a) 0.8859 = 0.886, b) The distribution is not symmetric. 38). a) 20.2%, b) 81.0 g. 39). a) 70, b) 44.7. 40). 10.3. 41). 6.82, 0.4435 = 0.444. 42). a) 9.7%, b) 28.5%, c) 40. 43). a) 25, b) 0.6730 = 0.673. 44). b) 0.0693 = 0.069. 45). 47, 15. 46). a) 0.4875 = 0.488, b) 281, 5.00. 47). 53.18. 48). 10.15 = 10.2. 49). 0.397. 50). a) 46.49 = 46.5%, b) 0.532 m, c) 1.00 m. 51). a) $a + b - 1$, $\frac{2b-1}{b}$, b)i. $\frac{4a+2b-3}{6a+4b}$, b)ii. $\frac{3}{4}, \frac{2}{3}$.

Solutions to STEP Questions

Review Exercises 1, Question 42 (page 49)

(a) Putting $y = \sqrt{x+2}$, the equation becomes

$$(y+12)(y-2) = y^2 + 10y - 24 = 0$$

and hence $y = -12, 2$. Since $y = \sqrt{x+2}$ must be positive, we deduce that $y = 2$, so that $\sqrt{x+2} = 2$, and hence $x = 2$.

(b) Doubling the equation gives $2x^2 - 8x + 2\sqrt{2x^2 - 8x - 3} - 18 = 0$. Putting $y = \sqrt{2x^2 - 8x - 3}$, the equation becomes
$$(y+5)(y-3) = y^2 + 2y - 15 = 0$$

and hence $y = -5, 3$. Since y must be positive, we deduce that $y = 3$, so that $2x^2 - 8x - 3 = 9$, and so $x^2 - 4x - 6 = 0$, so that $x = 2 \pm \sqrt{10}$.

Review Exercises 1, Question 43 (page 49)

The terms $4x$ and $-4y$ can only come from $a(x-y+2)^2$, since the $(cx+y)^2$ expression contains no linear terms. Thus we must have $a = 1$. It is now easy to show that

$$5x^2 + 2y^2 - 6xy + 4x - 4y = (x-y+2)^2 + (-2x+y)^2 - 4$$

so that $a = 1$, $b = 1$, $c = -2$, $d = -4$.

To be able to make progress with the second half of the question, we shall hope that $6x^2 + 3y^2 - 8xy + 8x - 8y$ can be written in terms of $(x-y+2)^2$ and $(-2x+y)^2$. Considering the $8x$ and $-8y$ terms quickly leads us to

$$6x^2 + 3y^2 - 8xy + 8x - 8y = 2(x-y+2)^2 + (-2x+y)^2 - 8$$

Thus the two simultaneous equations become

$$(x-y+2)^2 + (2x-y)^2 = 13 \qquad 2(x-y+2)^2 + (2x-y)^2 = 22$$

and hence we deduce that $(x-y+2)^2 = 9$ and $(2x-y)^2 = 4$. There are four cases to consider:

- If $x - y + 2 = 3$ and $2x - y = 2$, we obtain $(x,y) = (1,0)$.

- If $x - y + 2 = 3$ and $2x - y = -2$, we obtain $(x,y) = (-3,-4)$.

- If $x - y + 2 = -3$ and $2x - y = 2$, we obtain $(x,y) = (7,12)$.

- If $x - y + 2 = -3$ and $2x - y = -2$, we obtain $(x,y) = (3,8)$.

Review Exercises 2, Question 40 (page 90)

(a) The expression $f = x^3 - 5x^2 + 2x^2y + xy^2 - 8xy - 3y^2 + 6x + 6y$ can either be regarded as a polynomial in x with coefficients involving y, or else as a polynomial in y with coefficients involving x:

$$f(x,y) \equiv x^3 + (2y-5)x^2 + (6-8y+y^2)x + (6y-3y^2) \equiv (x-3)y^2 + (2x^2-8x+6)y + (x^3-5x^2+6x)$$

If $x-3$ is to divide $f(x,y)$, we must have $f(3,y) \equiv 0$, which will only happen if $x-3$, $2x^2-8x+6$ and x^3-5x^2+6x all vanish at $x=3$. This is true, and we divide $f(x,y)$ by $x-3$ to obtain

$$f(x,y) = (x-3)\left(x^2 + (2y-2)x + (y^2-2y)\right) = (x-3)(x+y)(x+y-2)$$

and so $a=1$, $b=0$, $c=1$ and $d=-2$.

(b) This time we write

$$
\begin{aligned}
6y^3 - y^2 &- 21y + 2x^2 + 12x - 4xy + x^2y - 5xy^2 + 10 \\
&= (y+2)x^2 + (12-4y-5y^2)x + (10-21y-y^2+6y^3) \\
&= (y+2)x^2 + (y+2)(6-5y)x + (y+2)(5-13y+6y^2) \\
&= (y+2)\left[x^2 + (6-5y)x + (5-13y+6y^2)\right] \\
&= (y+2)\left[x^2 + (6-5y)x + (1-2y)(5-3y)\right] = (y+2)(x+1-2y)(x+5-3y)
\end{aligned}
$$

Review Exercises 2, Question 41 (page 90)

It is clear that $k_1 k_2 \cdots k_n = f(0) = a_n$. Moreover

$$(1+k_1)(1+k_2)\cdots(1+k_n) = f(1) = 1 + a_1 + a_2 + \cdots + a_n$$

Similarly

$$(-1+k_1)(-1+k_2)\cdots(-1+k_n) = f(-1) = (-1)^n + (-1)^{n-1}a_1 + (-1)^{n-2}a_2 + \cdots + a_n$$

and hence

$$(k_1-1)(k_2-1)\cdots(k_n-1) = 1 - a_1 + a_2 - \cdots + (-1)^n a_n$$

For our quartic we deduce that

$$
\begin{aligned}
k_1 k_2 k_3 k_4 &= 576 = 2^6 \times 3^2 \\
(k_1+1)(k_2+1)(k_3+1)(k_4+1) &= 1323 = 3^3 \times 7^2 \\
(k_1-1)(k_2-1)(k_3-1)(k_4-1) &= 175 = 5^2 \times 7
\end{aligned}
$$

One of k_1-1, k_2-1, k_3-1 and k_4-1 must be divisible by 7. Let us try $k_4=8$ (note that 8 divides 576 and 9 divides 1323, so this choice is at least possible. The equations now become

$$
\begin{aligned}
k_1 k_2 k_3 &= 72 = 2^3 \times 3^2 \\
(k_1+1)(k_2+1)(k_3+1) &= 147 = 3 \times 7^2 \\
(k_1-1)(k_2-1)(k_3-1) &= 25 = 5^2
\end{aligned}
$$

and it is easy to see that these are satisfied by $k_1=2$, $k_2=k_3=6$. The solutions of the quartic equation are thus -2, -6 (twice) and -8.

Review Exercises 3, Question 46 (page 169)

We can write

$$
\begin{aligned}
x^4 + ax^3 + bx^2 + cx + d &\equiv fg(x) \equiv (x^2+rx+s)^2 + p(x^2+rx+s) + q \\
&= x^4 + 2rx^3 + (p+r^2+2s)x^2 + (pr+2rs)x + (ps+q+s^2)
\end{aligned}
$$

precisely when

$$a = 2r \quad b = p+r^2+2s \quad c = pr+2rs \quad d = ps+q+s^2$$

The first three of these equations are the important ones; if we can find p, r and s to satisfy these them, then q can be chosen to satisfy the fourth.

Suppose we can find suitable values of p, r and s. Then

$$8c = 8r(p + 2s) = 4a(p + 2s) = 4a(b - r^2) = 4ab - a^3$$

so that $a^3 - 4ab + 8c = 0$. Conversely, suppose that $a^3 - 4ab + 8c = 0$. Then we choose $r = \frac{1}{2}a$. For any choice of p, choose s so that $b = p + r^2 + 2s$. We have chosen p, r and s to satisfy the first two equations. But then

$$pr + 2rs = \tfrac{1}{2}a(b - r^2) = \tfrac{1}{2}ab - \tfrac{1}{8}a^3 = c$$

and so the third equation is automatically satisfied.

Being able to write the quartic in the form $(x^2 + ux + v)^2 - k$ is just being able to write the quartic as $fg(x)$ where $f(x) = x^2 - k$, in other words being able to perform our initial decomposition with $p = 0$. We have seen above that, when a decomposition of a quartic into the shape $fg(x)$ is possible, it can be done with a free choice of the coefficient p, and so can certainly be done with $p = 0$. Thus the condition $a^3 - 4ab + 8c = 0$ is precisely the condition to enable us to write the quartic in the form $(x^2 + ux + v)^2 - k$.

Applying these ideas to the stated problem, we obtain

$$\begin{aligned}
x^4 - 4x^3 + 10x^2 - 12x + 4 &= 0 \\
(x^2 - 2x + 3)^2 - 5 &= 0 \\
x^2 - 2x + 3 &= \pm\sqrt{5} \\
(x - 1)^2 &= -2 \pm \sqrt{5}
\end{aligned}$$

Since the roots must be real, we deduce that $(x - 1)^2 = \sqrt{5} - 2$, and hence $x = 1 \pm \sqrt{\sqrt{5} - 2}$.

Review Exercises 3, Question 47 (page 170)

(a) The Cartesian equation of P is

$$\begin{aligned}
AP^2 &= 4BP^2 \\
(x - 5)^2 + (y - 16)^2 &= 4(x + 4)^2 + 4(x - 4)^2 \\
x^2 + y^2 - 10x - 32y + 281 &= 4x^2 + 4y^2 + 32x - 32y + 128 \\
3x^2 + 3y^2 + 42x &= 153 \\
x^2 + y^2 + 14x &= 51 \\
(x + 7)^2 + y^2 &= 100.
\end{aligned}$$

(b) The Cartesian equation of Q is

$$\begin{aligned}
QC^2 &= k^2 \times QD^2 \\
(x - a)^2 + y^2 &= k^2(x - b)^2 + k^2 y^2 \\
x^2 - 2ax + a^2 + y^2 &= k^2 x^2 - 2k^2 bx + k^2 b^2 + k^2 y^2 \\
(k^2 - 1)x^2 + (k^2 - 1)y^2 + 2(a - k^2 b)x &= a^2 - k^2 b^2 \\
x^2 + y^2 + \tfrac{2(a - k^2 b)}{k^2 - 1}x &= \tfrac{a^2 - k^2 b^2}{k^2 - 1}
\end{aligned}$$

Since the paths of P and Q are the same, we deduce (comparing the equation for Q with the penultimate form of the equation for P) that

$$\frac{a - k^2 b}{k^2 - 1} = 7 \qquad \frac{a^2 - k^2 b^2}{k^2 - 1} = 51$$

and these equations together imply that

$$\frac{a + 7}{b + 7} = k^2 = \frac{a^2 + 51}{b^2 + 51}$$

Hence

$$(a+7)(b^2+51) = (b+7)(a^2+51)$$
$$ab^2 + 7b^2 + 51a + 357 = a^2b + 7a^2 + 51b + 357$$
$$a^2b - ab^2 + 7a^2 - 7b^2 - 51a + 51b = 0$$
$$(a-b)[ab + 7(a+b) - 51] = 0$$
$$(a-b)[(a+7)(b+7) - 100] = 0$$

Thus, provided that $a \neq b$, we deduce that $(a+7)(b+7) = 100$.

Review Exercises 3, Question 48 (page 170)

(a) Since each $x_j > 0$, each expression $1 + x_j^{-1} > 1$, and hence $x_j > 1$ for all j.

(b) We see that

$$x_1 - x_2 = 1 + x_2^{-1} - 1 - x_3^{-1} = x_2^{-1} - x_3^{-1} = -\frac{x_2 - x_3}{x_2 x_3}$$

(c) Similar arguments will tell us that

$$x_j - x_{j+1} = -\frac{x_{j+1} - x_{j+2}}{x_{j+1} x_{j+2}} \qquad 1 \le j \le n-2$$
$$x_{n-1} - x_n = -\frac{x_n - x_1}{x_n x_1}$$
$$x_n - x_1 = -\frac{x_1 - x_2}{x_1 x_2}$$

and hence

$$x_1 - x_2 = -\frac{1}{x_2 x_3}(x_2 - x_3) = \left(-\frac{1}{x_2 x_3}\right)\left(-\frac{1}{x_3 x_4}\right)(x_3 - x_4) = \cdots$$
$$= \left(-\frac{1}{x_2 x_3}\right)\left(-\frac{1}{x_3 x_4}\right)\cdots\left(-\frac{1}{x_n x_1}\right)\left(-\frac{1}{x_1 x_2}\right)(x_1 - x_2).$$

Each of the factors $-\frac{1}{x_j x_{j+1}}$ and $-\frac{1}{x_n x_1}$ lie between -1 and 0, and so their product certainly has modulus less than 1. We have shown that $x_1 - x_2 = \alpha(x_1 - x_2)$, where $|\alpha| < 1$. This is only possible is $x_1 = x_2$. It is now clear that $x_1 = x_2 = \cdots = x_n$.

Thus x_1 satisfies the equation $x_1 = 1 + x_1^{-1}$, or $x_1^2 - x_1 - 1 = 0$ and hence (since $x_1 > 1$) we deduce that $x_1 = \frac{1}{2}(1 + \sqrt{5})$.

Review Exercises 4, Question 77 (page 238)

We have

$$(1-x)^{-3} = 1 + \frac{(-3)}{1!}(-x) + \frac{(-3)(-4)}{2!}(-x)^2 + \cdots + \frac{(-3)(-4)\cdots(-r-2)}{r!}(-x)^r + \cdots$$
$$= 1 + 3x + 6x^2 + \cdots + \frac{(r+2)!}{2!r!}x^r + \cdots = \sum_{r=0}^{\infty} \frac{1}{2}(r+1)(r+2)x^r$$

for any $|x| < 1$.

(a)
$$f(x) = \frac{1-x+2x^2}{(1-x)^3} = (1-x+2x^2)\sum_{r=0}^{\infty} \frac{1}{2}(r+1)(r+2)x^r$$

$$= \sum_{r=0}^{\infty} \frac{1}{2}(r+1)(r+2)x^r - \sum_{r=0}^{\infty} \frac{1}{2}(r+1)(r+2)x^{r+1} + \sum_{r=0}^{\infty}(r+1)(r+2)x^{r+2}$$

$$= \sum_{r=0}^{\infty} \frac{1}{2}(r+1)(r+2)x^r - \sum_{r=1}^{\infty} \frac{1}{2}r(r+1)x^r + \sum_{r=2}^{\infty} r(r-1)x^r$$

$$= 1 + 3x - x + \sum_{r=2}^{\infty}\left[\frac{1}{2}(r+1)(r+2) - \frac{1}{2}r(r+1) + r(r-1)\right]x^r$$

$$= 1 + 2x + \sum_{r=2}^{\infty}(r^2+1)x^r = \sum_{r=0}^{\infty}(r^2+1)x^r$$

and hence

$$1 + \tfrac{2}{2} + \tfrac{5}{4} + \tfrac{10}{8} + \tfrac{17}{16} + \tfrac{26}{32} + \tfrac{37}{64} + \tfrac{50}{128} + \cdots = \sum_{r=0}^{\infty} \tfrac{r^2+1}{2^r} = f(\tfrac{1}{2}) = 8(1 - \tfrac{1}{2} + \tfrac{1}{2}) = 8$$

(b)
$$1 + 2 + \tfrac{9}{4} + 2 + \tfrac{25}{16} + \tfrac{9}{8} + \tfrac{49}{64} + \cdots = \sum_{r=0}^{\infty} \tfrac{(r+1)^2}{2^r} = \sum_{r=1}^{\infty} \tfrac{r^2}{2^{r-1}} = 2\sum_{r=1}^{\infty} \tfrac{r^2}{2^r} = 2\sum_{r=0}^{\infty} \tfrac{r^2}{2^r}$$

$$= 2\left[\sum_{r=0}^{\infty} \tfrac{r^2+1}{2^r} - \sum_{r=0}^{\infty} \tfrac{1}{2^r} \right] = 2\left[f(\tfrac{1}{2}) - 2 \right] = 12$$

Review Exercises 4, Question 78 (page 238)

Since the line passes through P, Q and R, we deduce that

$$0 = c - mp \qquad q = c \qquad b = c - ma$$

so that $c = ma + b$, $p = a + \frac{b}{m}$, and $q = ma + b$. The sum of the distances of P and Q from the origin is

$$D_1 = p + q = a(m+1) + b(1 + m^{-1})$$

Varying L (while keeping R fixed) involves simply changing the value of m, and so we need to consider

$$\frac{dD_1}{dm} = a - bm^{-2}$$

which vanishes when $m = \sqrt{\frac{b}{a}}$. Thus the minimum value of D_1 is

$$a\left(\sqrt{\tfrac{b}{a}} + 1 \right) + b\left(\sqrt{\tfrac{a}{b}} + 1 \right) = \left(\sqrt{a} + \sqrt{b} \right)^2$$

as required. The distance between P and Q is $D_2 = \sqrt{p^2 + q^2}$ and hence

$$D_2^2 = a^2 m^2 + 2abm + (a^2 + b^2) + 2abm^{-1} + b^2 m^{-2} .$$

Thus

$$\frac{dD_2^2}{dm} = 2a^2 m + 2ab - 2abm^{-2} - 2b^2 m^{-3} = 2a(am + b) - 2bm^{-3}(am + b) = 2(am + b)\left(a - bm^{-3} \right)$$

so the turning point for D_2 occurs when $m = \left(\frac{b}{a} \right)^{\frac{1}{3}}$. Thus the minimum value of D_2 is

$$\sqrt{\left(a + a^{\frac{1}{3}} b^{\frac{2}{3}} \right)^2 + \left(b + a^{\frac{2}{3}} b^{\frac{1}{3}} \right)^2} = \left(a^{\frac{2}{3}} + b^{\frac{2}{3}} \right)^{\frac{3}{2}}$$

Review Exercises 5, Question 29 (page 305)

Using the compound angle formulae for the tangent,

$$\tan 3\theta \equiv \tan(\theta + 2\theta) \equiv \frac{\tan\theta + \tan 2\theta}{1 - \tan\theta \tan 2\theta} \equiv \frac{\tan\theta + \frac{2\tan\theta}{1-\tan^2\theta}}{1 - \tan\theta \frac{2\tan\theta}{1-\tan^2\theta}}$$

$$\equiv \frac{\tan\theta(1 - \tan^2\theta) + 2\tan\theta}{1 - \tan^2\theta - 2\tan^2\theta} \equiv \frac{3\tan\theta - \tan^3\theta}{1 - 3\tan^2\theta} .$$

Now θ is acute and $\cos\theta = \frac{2}{\sqrt{5}}$, then $\sin^2\theta = 1 - \frac{4}{5}$ and so $\sin\theta = \frac{1}{\sqrt{5}}$. Thus $\tan\theta = \frac{1}{2}$, and hence

$$\tan 3\theta = \frac{\frac{3}{2} - \frac{1}{8}}{1 - \frac{3}{4}} = \frac{11}{2} .$$

(a) If $\tan\left(3\cos^{-1}x\right) = \frac{11}{2}$, then $\tan\left(3\cos^{-1}x\right) = \tan 3\theta$, and hence $3\cos^{-1}x = 3\theta + n\pi$ for $n \in \mathbb{Z}$. Thus $\cos^{-1}x = \theta + \frac{1}{3}n\pi$ for $n \in \mathbb{Z}$.

Since $\cos\theta = \frac{2}{\sqrt{5}} > \frac{1}{2}\sqrt{3}$, we deduce that $0 < \theta < \frac{1}{6}\pi$. Since $0 \le \cos^{-1}x \le \pi$, we deduce that $\cos^{-1}x$ must be one of θ, $\theta + \frac{1}{3}\pi$ and $\theta + \frac{2}{3}\pi$. Possible values of x are thus

$$\cos\theta = \frac{2}{\sqrt{5}},$$
$$\cos\left(\theta + \tfrac{1}{3}\pi\right) = \cos\theta\cos\tfrac{1}{3}\pi - \sin\theta\sin\tfrac{1}{3}\pi = \frac{2}{\sqrt{5}}\times\tfrac{1}{2} - \frac{1}{\sqrt{5}}\times\tfrac{1}{2}\sqrt{3} = \frac{2-\sqrt{3}}{2\sqrt{5}},$$
$$\cos\left(\theta + \tfrac{2}{3}\pi\right) = \cos\theta\cos\tfrac{2}{3}\pi - \sin\theta\sin\tfrac{2}{3}\pi = \frac{2}{\sqrt{5}}\times\left(-\tfrac{1}{2}\right) - \frac{1}{\sqrt{5}}\times\tfrac{1}{2}\sqrt{3} = -\frac{2+\sqrt{3}}{2\sqrt{5}}.$$

(b) If $\cos\left(\tfrac{1}{3}\tan^{-1}y\right) = \frac{2}{\sqrt{5}} = \cos\theta$ then, since $-\tfrac{1}{2}\pi < \tan^{-1}y < \tfrac{1}{2}\pi$ and hence $-\tfrac{1}{6}\pi < \tfrac{1}{3}\tan^{-1}y < \tfrac{1}{6}\pi$, we deduce that $\tfrac{1}{3}\tan^{-1}y = \pm\theta$, so that $\tan^{-1}y = \pm 3\theta$, and hence $y = \pm\tan 3\theta = \pm\frac{11}{2}$.

Review Exercises 5, Question 43 (page 306)

(a) We see that

$$\log_{10}5 = \log_{10}10 - \log_{10}2 = 1 - \log_{10}2 = 0.699 \qquad \log_{10}6 = \log_{10}2 + \log_{10}3 = 0.778$$

to 3 decimal places. Thus

$$\log_{10}5 < 0.7121255 < \log_{10}6$$
$$47 + \log_{10}5 < 100\log_{10}3 < 47 + \log_{10}6$$
$$5\times 10^{47} < \quad 3^{100} \quad < 6\times 10^{47}$$

and so the first digit of 3^{100} is 5.

(b) Similarly
$$301 < 1000\log_{10}2 = 301.029996 < 301 + \log_{10}2,$$

and hence $10^{301} < 2^{1000} < 2\times 10^{301}$. The first digit of 2^{1000} is 1. Also

$$3010 < 10000\log_{10}2 = 3010.29996 < 3010 + \log_{10}2,$$

and hence $10^{3010} < 2^{10000} < 2\times 10^{3010}$. The first digit of 2^{10000} is 1. Finally $\log_{10}9 = 2\log_{10}3 = 0.954$ to 3 decimal places, and hence

$$30102 + \log_{10}9 < 100000\log_{10}2 = 30102.9996 < 30103,$$

so that $9\times 10^{30102} < 2^{100000} < 10^{30103}$. The first digit of 2^{100000} is 9.

Review Exercises 5, Question 71 (page 309)

If the circle has radius R, then the rectangle can be defined by the acute angle θ, as shown. Then the sides of the rectangle are $2R\cos\theta$ and $2R\sin\theta$, and so the perimeter is $P = 4R(\cos\theta + \sin\theta)$. Thus

$$\frac{dP}{d\theta} = 4R(\cos\theta - \sin\theta)$$

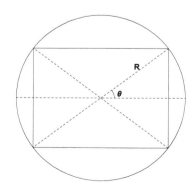

which equals 0 when $\cos\theta = \sin\theta$, so when $\tan\theta = 1$, so when $\theta = \frac{1}{4}\pi$. Since $\frac{d^2P}{d\theta^2} = -4R(\cos\theta + \sin\theta) < 0$ when $\theta = \frac{1}{4}\pi$, this turning point is a maximum.

Thus the perimeter is largest when $\theta = \frac{1}{4}\pi$. For this value the rectangle is a square.

We generalise this problem by trying to maximise

$$P_n(\theta) \;=\; 2\big[(2R\cos\theta)^n + (2R\sin\theta)^n\big] \;=\; 2^{n+1}R^n[\cos^n\theta + \sin^n\theta].$$

When $n = 2$, $P_2(\theta) = 8R^2$ for all θ; no particular rectangle maximises P_2.
When $n = 3$, $P_3(\theta) = 16R^3[\cos^3\theta + \sin^3\theta]$, so that

$$\frac{dP_3}{d\theta} \;=\; 48R^3\big[\sin^2\theta\cos\theta - \cos^2\theta\sin\theta\big] \;=\; 48R^3\sin^2\theta\cos^2\theta(\sin\theta - \cos\theta),$$

so P_3 has turning points when $\theta = 0$, $\tfrac{1}{4}\pi$ and $\tfrac{1}{2}\pi$. Since $\frac{dP_3}{d\theta}$ is negative for $0 < \theta < \tfrac{1}{4}\pi$, and positive for $\tfrac{1}{4}\pi < \theta < \tfrac{1}{2}\pi$, the turning point at $\tfrac{1}{4}\pi$ is a minimum, while the other two turning points are maxima. This time, the square gives the smallest possible value of P_3. The greatest value of P_3 is $16R^3$ is achieved when $\theta = 0$ or $\tfrac{1}{2}\pi$; these values of θ do not give proper rectangles, since the side lengths are $2R$ and 0. However, choosing θ close to 0 provides values of P_3 as close to $16R^3$ as we like.

Review Exercises 6, Question 16 (page 362)
Differentiating implicitly,

$$2x + 2y\frac{dy}{dx} + 2ay + 2ax\frac{dy}{dx} \;=\; 0$$

$$(ax + y)\frac{dy}{dx} \;=\; -(x + ay)$$

$$\frac{dy}{dx} \;=\; -\frac{x+ay}{ax+y}$$

provided that $x + ay \neq 0$. The gradient of the normal at P is thus $\frac{ax+y}{x+ay}$, while the gradient of OP is $\frac{y}{x}$. Hence

$$\tan\theta \;=\; \left|\frac{\frac{ax+y}{x+ay} - \frac{y}{x}}{1 + \frac{ax+y}{x+ay} \times \frac{y}{x}}\right| \;=\; \left|\frac{(ax+y)x - (x+ay)y}{(x+ay)x + (ax+y)y}\right| \;=\; \frac{a|y^2-x^2|}{x^2+y^2+2axy} \;=\; a|y^2 - x^2|$$

Suppose now that $\frac{d\theta}{dx} = 0$ at P. Then $\frac{d}{dx}\tan\theta = 0$, and hence $\frac{d}{dx}(y^2 - x^2) = 0$ at P.

(a) Thus

$$y\frac{dy}{dx} - x \;=\; 0$$

$$-y\frac{x+ay}{ax+y} - x \;=\; 0$$

$$y(x + ay) + x(ax + y) \;=\; 0$$

$$a(x^2 + y^2) + 2xy \;=\; 0.$$

(b) Adding this to the original equation,

$$(1 + a)(x^2 + y^2 + 2xy) \;=\; x^2 + y^2 + 2axy + a(x^2 + y^2) + 2xy \;=\; 1$$

(c) This tells us that $|x + y| = \frac{1}{\sqrt{1+a}}$. Now

$$1 \;=\; x^2 + y^2 + 2axy \;=\; \tfrac{1}{1+a} - 2xy + 2axy \;=\; \tfrac{1}{1+a} - 2(1 - a)xy$$

and so

$$2xy \;=\; -\frac{a}{1-a^2},$$

which in turn implies that

$$(x - y)^2 \;=\; (x + y)^2 - 4xy \;=\; \tfrac{1}{1+a} + \tfrac{2a}{1-a^2} \;=\; \tfrac{1+a}{1-a^2} \;=\; \tfrac{1}{1-a},$$

so that (finally)

$$\tan\theta \;=\; a|y^2 - x^2| \;=\; a|y - x||y + x| \;=\; \frac{a}{\sqrt{1-a^2}}$$

Review Exercises 6, Question 43 (page 364)

Note that $\dfrac{dx}{dt} = -\dfrac{2t}{(t^2-1)^2}$ and $x+1 = \dfrac{t^2}{t^2-1}$, so that $\sqrt{x(x+1)} = \dfrac{t}{t^2-1}$, and hence

$$\int \frac{1}{\sqrt{x(x+1)}}\,dx \;=\; \int \frac{t^2-1}{t} \times \frac{-2t}{(t^2-1)^2}\,dt \;=\; -\int \frac{2}{t^2-1}\,dt$$

$$=\; -\ln\left|\frac{t-1}{t+1}\right| + c \;=\; \ln\left|\frac{t+1}{t-1}\right| + c$$

Now $t = \sqrt{\dfrac{x+1}{x}}$, and hence $t \pm 1 = \dfrac{\sqrt{x+1}\pm\sqrt{x}}{\sqrt{x}}$, so that

$$\frac{t+1}{t-1} \;=\; \frac{\sqrt{x+1}+\sqrt{x}}{\sqrt{x+1}-\sqrt{x}} \;=\; \left(\sqrt{x+1}+\sqrt{x}\right)^2 ;$$

it follows that

$$\int \frac{1}{\sqrt{x(x+1)}}\,dx \;=\; \ln\left(\sqrt{x+1}+\sqrt{x}\right)^2 + c \;=\; 2\ln\left(\sqrt{x+1}+\sqrt{x}\right) + c .$$

The volume of revolution is

$$\pi \int_{\frac{1}{8}}^{\frac{9}{16}} y^2\,dx \;=\; \pi \int_{\frac{1}{8}}^{\frac{9}{16}} \left(\frac{1}{x} - \frac{2}{\sqrt{x(x+1)}} + \frac{1}{x+1}\right) dx$$

$$=\; \pi\left[\ln x - 4\ln\left(\sqrt{x+1}+\sqrt{x}\right) + \ln(x+1)\right]_{\frac{1}{8}}^{\frac{9}{16}}$$

$$=\;=\; \pi\left[\ln\left(\frac{x(x+1)}{(\sqrt{x+1}+\sqrt{x})^4}\right)\right]_{\frac{1}{8}}^{\frac{9}{16}}$$

$$=\; \pi\left[\ln\left(\frac{9\times25}{16^3}\right) - \ln\left(\frac{9}{8^2\times\sqrt{2}^4}\right)\right] \;=\; \pi\ln\frac{25}{16} \;=\; 2\pi\ln\frac{5}{4} .$$

Review Exercises 6, Question 65 (page 367)

If $y^2 = x^k f(x)$, then $2y\dfrac{dy}{dx} = kx^{k-1}f(x) + x^k f'(x)$,
and hence

$$2xy\frac{dy}{dx} \;=\; kx^k f(x) + x^{k+1} f'(x) \;=\; ky^2 + x^{k+1} f'(x)$$

(a) With $k = 1$, so that $y^2 = xf(x)$, the equation becomes

$$y^2 + x^2 f'(x) \;=\; y^2 + x^2 - 1$$
$$f'(x) \;=\; 1 - x^{-2}$$

From this we see that $f(x) = x + x^{-1} + c$, and hence $y^2 = x^2 + 1 + cx$. Since $y = 2$ when $x = 1$, we must have $4 = 1 + 1 + c$, so that $c = 2$, and hence $y^2 = x^2 + 2x + 1 = (x+1)^2$. Again, since $y = 2$ when $x = 1$, it follows that $y = x + 1$. This solution is a straight line.

(b) The trick here is to put $k = -1$. Then $y^2 = x^{-1}f(x)$, and the equation becomes

$$-xy^2 + xf'(x) = x\left[-y^2 + f'(x)\right] \;=\; 2\ln x - xy^2$$
$$f'(x) \;=\; \frac{2\ln x}{x}$$

Since $\dfrac{d}{dx}\ln x = x^{-1}$ we deduce that $f(x) = (\ln x)^2 + c$,

and hence $y^2 = \dfrac{(\ln x)^2 + c}{x}$. Since $y = 1$ when $x = 1$, we deduce that $c = 1$,

and hence
$$y^2 = \frac{(\ln x)^2 + 1}{x}.$$

Review Exercises 7, Question 14 (page 428)

A, B and C form a triangle. P lies inside the line segment AB, while Q lies on the line segment CA extended beyond A. Now

$$\overrightarrow{CQ} = \mu(\mathbf{a} - \mathbf{c}) = \mu\overrightarrow{CA}, \quad \overrightarrow{BP} = \lambda(\mathbf{a} - \mathbf{b}) = \lambda\overrightarrow{BA}$$

and so $CQ \times BP = \lambda\mu \times AB \times AC$. Thus we deduce that $\lambda\mu = 1$, and so $\mu = \lambda^{-1}$
If D is the point with position vector $-\mathbf{a} + \mathbf{b} + \mathbf{c}$, then

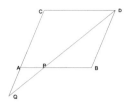

Figure A2.1

$$\overrightarrow{DP} = (\lambda+1)\mathbf{a} - \lambda\mathbf{b} - \mathbf{c}$$
$$\overrightarrow{DQ} = (\mu+1)\mathbf{a} - \mathbf{b} - \mu\mathbf{c} = \mu\left[(\lambda+1)\mathbf{a} - \lambda\mathbf{b} - \mathbf{c}\right]$$

so that $\overrightarrow{DQ} = \mu\overrightarrow{DP}$, and hence the points D, P and Q are collinear.

Finally, since $\overrightarrow{AD} = \mathbf{d} - \mathbf{a} = (\mathbf{b} - \mathbf{a}) + (\mathbf{c} - \mathbf{a}) = \overrightarrow{AB} + \overrightarrow{AC}$, it is clear that $ABDC$ is a parallelogram.

Review Exercises 7, Question 26 (page 429)

If $s = a + bi$ then $|z| = \sqrt{a^2 + b^2}$ is the distance from 0 to z in the Argand diagram. The number $|z_1 - z_2|$ is the distance from z_1 to z_2 in the Argand diagram. The points 0, z_1 and $z_1 + z_2$ form a triangle in the Argand diagram with sides $|z_1|$, $|z_2|$ and $|z_1 + z_2|$, and hence $|z_1 + z_2| \le |z_1| + |z_2|$. Thus

$$|z_1 + z_2 + \cdots + z_n| \le |z_1| + |z_2 + \cdots + z_n| \le \cdots \le |z_1| + |z_2| + \cdots + |z_n|.$$

If $|a_j| \le 3$ for $1 \le j \le n$ and $|z| \le \frac{1}{4}$, then

$$|a_1 z + a_2 z^2 + \cdots a_n z^n| \le |a_1 z| + |a_2 z^2| + \cdots + |a_n z^n| = |a_1||z| + |a_2||z^2| + \cdots + |a_n||z^n|$$
$$\le 3\left(|z| + |z^2| + \cdots + |z^n|\right) = 3\left(|z| + |z|^2 + \cdots + |z|^n\right)$$
$$\le 3\left[\tfrac{1}{4} + \left(\tfrac{1}{4}\right)^2 + \cdots + \left(\tfrac{1}{4}\right)^n\right] = 3\frac{\tfrac{1}{4}\left[1 - \left(\tfrac{1}{4}\right)^n\right]}{1 - \tfrac{1}{4}} = 1 - \left(\tfrac{1}{4}\right)^n < 1$$

and hence $a_1 z + a_2 z^2 + \cdots + a_n z^n$ cannot be equal to 1.

Review Exercises 8, Question 20 (page 491)

(a) Using the SUVAT equations $v^2 = u^2 + 2as$ and $v = u + at$, the first leg of the journey lasts $t_1 = \frac{v-u}{3a}$, and covers a distance $d_1 = \frac{v^2-u^2}{6a}$, while the second leg of the journey lasts $t_2 = \frac{v}{a}$, and covers a distance $d_2 = \frac{v^2}{2a}$. Certainly

$$3d_1 = \frac{v^2 - u^2}{2a} < \frac{v^2}{2a} = d_2.$$

We also note that the average speed during the motion is

$$\frac{d_1 + d_2}{t_1 + t_2} = \frac{\frac{4v^2 - u^2}{6a}}{\frac{4v - u}{3a}} = \frac{4v^2 - u^2}{2(4v - u)}.$$

(b) The first leg of the journey still lasts $t_1 = \frac{v-u}{3a}$; this time the particle first travels a distance of $\frac{u^2}{6a}$ to the left before coming to rest, followed by a distance of $\frac{v^2}{6a}$ to the right before reaching the speed of v, so $d_1 = \frac{v^2+u^2}{6a}$. The second leg of the journey again lasts $t_2 = \frac{v}{a}$ seconds and covers a distance of $d_2 = \frac{v^2}{2a}$. Thus

$$d_2 = \frac{v^2}{2a} < \frac{v^2 + u^2}{2a} = 3d_1 < \frac{2v^2}{2a} = \frac{v^2}{a} = 2d_2.$$

This time the average speed is

$$\frac{d_1 + d_2}{t_1 + t_2} = \frac{\frac{4v^2 + u^2}{6a}}{\frac{4v - u}{3a}} = \frac{4v^2 + u^2}{2(4v - u)}.$$

Since

$$\frac{4v^2 - u^2}{2(4v - |u|)} - \frac{4v^2 + u^2}{2(4v + |u|)} = \frac{(4v^2 - u^2)(4v + |u|) - (4v^2 + u^2)(4v - |u|)}{2(16v^2 - u^2)}$$

$$= \frac{8v^2|u| - 8vu^2}{2(16v^2 - u^2)} = \frac{4v|u|(v - |u|)}{16v^2 - u^2} > 0$$

it follows that the average speed is greater when $u > 0$.

Review Exercises 8, Question 34 (page 493)

Start with some diagrams:

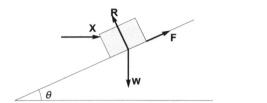 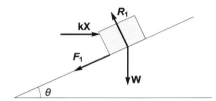

Resolving perpendicular and parallel to the slope in both cases, and using the fact that friction is limiting in both cases, yields

$$R = W\cos\theta + X\sin\theta$$
$$F + X\cos\theta = W\sin\theta$$
$$W\sin\theta - X\cos\theta = \mu(W\cos\theta + X\sin\theta)$$
$$W(\sin\theta - \mu\cos\theta) = X(\cos\theta + \mu\sin\theta)$$

$$R_1 = W\cos\theta + kX\sin\theta$$
$$kX\cos\theta = F_1 + W\sin\theta$$
$$kX\cos\theta - W\sin\theta = \mu(W\cos\theta + kX\sin\theta)$$
$$W(\sin\theta + \mu\cos\theta) = kX(\cos\theta - \mu\sin\theta)$$

and hence

$$\frac{\sin\theta + \mu\cos\theta}{\sin\theta - \mu\cos\theta} = k\frac{\cos\theta - \mu\sin\theta}{\cos\theta + \mu\sin\theta}$$

$$(\sin\theta + \mu\cos\theta)(\cos\theta + \mu\sin\theta) = k(\cos\theta - \mu\sin\theta)(\sin\theta - \mu\cos\theta)$$

$$(1 + \mu^2)\sin\theta\cos\theta + \mu = k\left[(1 + \mu^2)\sin\theta\cos\theta - \mu\right]$$

$$(k-1)(1 + \mu^2)\sin\theta\cos\theta = \mu(k+1)$$

Thus

$$(k-1)(1 + \mu^2) \geq (k-1)(1 + \mu^2)\sin 2\theta = (k-1)(1 + \mu^2)2\sin\theta\cos\theta \geq 2\mu(k+1)$$
$$k(1 + \mu^2 - 2\mu) \geq 1 + \mu^2 + 2\mu$$
$$k(1 - \mu)^2 \geq (1 + \mu)^2$$
$$k \geq \left(\frac{1+\mu}{1-\mu}\right)^2$$

Review Exercises 8, Question 49 (page 495)

The total downwards force on the particle is $-g - kv^2$, and so Newton's second law tells us that the upwards acceleration of the particle is $a = -g - kv^2$. Thus we obtain the differential equation

$$v\frac{dv}{ds} = -g - kv^2.$$

Separating variables, we deduce that

$$\int \frac{v}{g + kv^2}\,dv = -\int ds$$

$$\frac{1}{2k}\ln(g + kv^2) = c - 2ks$$

$$g + kv^2 = kAe^{-2ks}$$

$$v^2 = Ae^{-2ks} - \frac{g}{k}$$

Since $v = u$ when $s = 0$ we deduce that $A = u^2 + \frac{g}{k}$, and hence

$$v^2 = u^2 e^{-2ks} + \frac{g}{k}(e^{-2ks} - 1)$$

The particle reaches its maximum height when $v = 0$, which occurs when

$$\left(u^2 + \frac{g}{k}\right)e^{-2ks} = \frac{g}{k}$$
$$e^{2ks} = 1 + \frac{ku^2}{g}$$
$$s = \frac{1}{2k}\ln\left(1 + \frac{ku^2}{g}\right).$$

On the way down, the resistance of the medium and gravity are pulling in opposite direction, and hence a different differential equation will apply, and so a different formula relating v and s will hold.

Review Exercises 9, Question 14 (page 541)

Suppose that the acceleration of the mass M down the slope is a ms^{-2}. Resolving forces parallel to the two slopes, and applying Newton's Second Law in each case, gives the equations

$$Ma = Mg\sin\alpha - T$$
$$ma = T - mg\cos\alpha$$

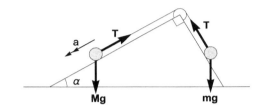

from which we deduce that

$$a = \frac{M\sin\alpha - m\cos\alpha}{M + m}g$$

(a) For the mass M to slide down the slope, we need $a > 0$, and so we must have $M\sin\alpha > m\cos\alpha$, or $\tan\alpha > \frac{m}{M}$.

(b) If $\tan\alpha = \frac{2m}{M}$ the acceleration of the mass M is

$$a = \frac{M\sin\alpha - \frac{1}{2}M\tan\alpha\cos\alpha}{M + \frac{1}{2}M\tan\alpha}g = \frac{g\sin\alpha}{2 + \tan\alpha},$$

as required. Since

$$\begin{aligned}
\frac{da}{d\alpha} &= \frac{g\cos\alpha}{2 + \tan\alpha} - \frac{g\sin\alpha\sec^2\alpha}{(2 + \tan\alpha)^2} = \frac{g\left[\cos\alpha(2 + \tan\alpha) - \sin\alpha\sec^2\alpha\right]}{(2 + \tan\alpha)^2} \\
&= \frac{g\left[2\cos\alpha + \sin\alpha - \sin\alpha\sec^2\alpha\right]}{(2 + \tan\alpha)^2} = \frac{g[2\cos\alpha - \sin\alpha\tan^2\alpha]}{(2 + \tan\alpha)^2} \\
&= \frac{g\cos\alpha(2 - \tan^3\alpha)}{(2 + \tan\alpha)^2}
\end{aligned}$$

we see that a is maximised when $\tan^3\alpha = 2$, so that $\frac{8m^3}{M^3} = 2$, or when $4m^3 = M^3$.

Review Exercises 9, Question 27 (page 543)

If the velocities of the first two particles after the first collision are v_1 and v_2, then

$$m_1 v_1 + m_2 v_2 = m_1 v \qquad -v_1 + v_2 = ev,$$

using Conservation of Momentum and Newton's Law of Restitution. These equations have the solutions

$$v_1 = \frac{m_1 - em_2}{m_1 + m_2}v \quad , \quad v_2 = \frac{m_1(1 + e)}{m_1 + m_2}v.$$

Since the first particle is brought to rest by this collision, it follows that $e = \frac{m_1}{m_2}$.

By symmetry with the first collision, we deduce that the second and third particles have velocities w_2 and w_3 after the second collision, where

$$w_2 = \frac{m_2 - e'm_3}{m_2 + m_3}v_2 = \frac{(1+e)m_1(m_2 - e'm_3)}{(m_1 + m_2)(m_2 + m_3)}v \qquad w_3 = \frac{m_2(1+e')}{m_2 + m_3}v_2 = \frac{(1+e)(1+e')m_1 m_2}{(m_1 + m_2)(m_2 + m_3)}v .$$

Since $w_3 = v$ we deduce that

$$
\begin{aligned}
(1+e)(1+e')m_1 m_2 &= (m_1 + m_2)(m_2 + m_3) \\
(m_1 + m_2)(1+e')m_1 &= (m_1 + m_2)(m_2 + m_3) \\
(1+e')m_1 &= m_2 + m_3 \\
e' &= \frac{m_2 + m_3 - m_1}{m_1}
\end{aligned}
$$

Since $0 \le e' \le 1$, we must have $0 \le m_2 + m_3 - m_1 \le m_1$, and so $m_1 \le m_2 + m_3 \le 2m_1$. The final velocity of the middle particle is

$$
\begin{aligned}
w_2 &= \frac{(1+e)m_1(m_2 - e'm_3)}{(m_1 + m_2)(m_2 + m_3)}v = \frac{m_1(m_2 - e'm_3)}{m_2(m_2 + m_3)}v \\
&= \frac{m_1 m_2 - (m_2 + m_3 - m_1)m_3}{m_2(m_2 + m_3)}v = \frac{m_1 - m_3}{m_2}v
\end{aligned}
$$

and so the kinetic energy of the final system is

$$T = \frac{1}{2}m_2 w_2^2 + \frac{1}{2}m_3 v^2 = \left[\frac{(m_1 - m_3)^2}{2m_2} + \tfrac{1}{2}m_3\right]v^2 .$$

Since $m_1 - m_3 \le m_2 \le 2m_1 - m_3$, we deduce that

$$\left[\frac{(m_1 - m_3)^2}{2(2m_1 - m_3)} + \tfrac{1}{2}m_3\right]v^2 \le T \le \left[\frac{(m_1 - m_3)^2}{2(m_1 - m_3)} + \tfrac{1}{2}m_3\right]v^2$$

$$\frac{m_1^2}{2(2m_1 - m_3)}v^2 \le T \le \tfrac{1}{2}m_2 v^2 .$$

Review Exercises 9, Question 40 (page 545)

If the gunner fires at an angle of α to the perpendicular line from the gun to the road, he must achieve a range of $d\sec\alpha$ if he is to hit the road. If the gun's angle of elevation is θ, this means that

$$\frac{v^2 \sin 2\theta}{g} = d\sec\alpha ,$$

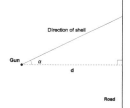

and hence $\sin 2\theta = \frac{gd}{v^2\cos\alpha}$. This implies that $\cos\alpha \ge \frac{gd}{v^2}$, and hence $|\alpha| \le \cos^{-1}\frac{gd}{v^2}$. The requirement of hitting the road limits the possible values of α.

For a suitable value of α, then, the possible values of θ are $\theta_1 = \tfrac{1}{2}\sin^{-1}\left(\frac{gd}{v^2\cos\alpha}\right)$ and $\theta_2 = \tfrac{1}{2}\pi - \theta_1$. Since the length of flight is $\frac{2v\sin\theta}{g}$, the possible flight times are $T_{1,\alpha} = \frac{2v}{g}\sin\theta_1$ and $T_{2,\alpha} = \frac{2v}{g}\sin\theta_1 = \frac{2v}{g}\cos\theta_1$. Since $0 < \theta_1 < \tfrac{1}{4}\pi$, the longer flight time is provided by $T_{2,\alpha}$. Now

$$
\begin{aligned}
g^2 T_{2,\alpha}^2 &= 4v^2\cos^2\theta_1 = 2v^2(1 + \cos 2\theta_1) = 2v^2 + 2v^2\sqrt{1 - \left(\frac{gd}{v^2\cos\alpha}\right)^2} \\
&= 2v^2 + 2\sqrt{v^4 - g^2 d^2\sec^2\alpha}
\end{aligned}
$$

Given the range of possible values of α, the largest value of $T_{2,\alpha}$ is given when $\alpha = 0$. If T is the largest possible flight time, then

$$g^2 T^2 = 2v^2 + 2\sqrt{v^4 - g^2 d^2} .$$

Review Exercises 10, Question 42 (page 612)

There are $\frac{1000000}{2} = 500000$ numbers between 0 and 999999 (inclusive) which are divisible by 2, $\frac{1000000}{5} = 200000$ numbers which are divisible by 5, and $\frac{1000000}{10} = 100000$ numbers which are divisible by 10. Thus there are $500000 + 200000 - 100000 = 600000$ which are divisible by either 2 or 5, and so there are 400000 numbers which are not divisible by either 2 or 5.

To find the average, we could add up these 400000 numbers:

- the sum of all the numbers from 0 to 999999 is $\frac{1}{2} \times 999999 \times 1000000 = 999999 \times 500000$,

- the sum of the even numbers from 0 to 999998 is $2 \times \frac{1}{2} \times 499999 \times 500000 = 499999 \times 500000$,

- the sum of the multiples of 5 from 0 to 999995 is $5 \times \frac{1}{2} \times 199999 \times 200000 = 199999 \times 500000$,

- the sum of the multiples of 10 from 0 to 999990 is $10 \times \frac{1}{2} \times 99999 \times 100000 = 99999 \times 500000$,

and so the sum of the numbers between 0 and 999999 which are not multiples of 2 or 5 is

$$999999 \times 500000 - 499999 \times 500000 - 199999 \times 500000 + 99999 \times 500000 = 400000 \times 500000$$

and hence their average is 500000. More elegantly, we can note that for any number $1 \le m \le 999999$ which is not divisible by either 2 or 5, $1000000 - m$ is another such number. Thus the 400000 numbers of this type come in 200000 pairs of numbers of the form m, $100000 - m$. Since each pair of numbers adds to 1000000, it is clear that the average of all 400000 numbers is 500000.

Similarly, there are 1393 numbers between 0 and 4178 inclusive which are divisible by 3, 597 which are divisible by 7, and 199 which are divisible by 21 (since $4179 = 3 \times 7 \times 199$). Thus there are

$$4179 - 1393 - 597 + 199 = 2388$$

numbers between 0 and 4178 inclusive which are divisible by neither 3 nor 7; these numbers also come in 1194 pairs of the form m, $4179 - m$, and so the average of these numbers is 2089.5.

Review Exercises 10, Question 43 (page 612)

(a) The only combinations of five digits which add to 43 are $9, 9, 9, 9, 7$ and $9, 9, 9, 8, 8$. There are ${}^5C_1 = 5$ five digit numbers comprising four 9s and one 7, and there are ${}^5C_2 = 10$ five digit numbers comprising three 9s and two 8s. Thus there are indeed 15 five digit numbers whose digits sum to 43.

(b) There are more combinations of digits to consider this time. The various combinations, and the number of numbers of each type, are given in the table below:

Digits	Count
$9, 9, 9, 9, 3$	${}^5C_1 = 5$
$9, 9, 9, 8, 4$	${}^5C_3 \times 2 = 20$
$9, 9, 9, 7, 5$	${}^5C_3 \times 2 = 20$
$9, 9, 9, 6, 6$	${}^5C_3 = 10$
$9, 9, 8, 8, 5$	${}^5C_2 \times 3 = 30$
$9, 9, 8, 7, 6$	${}^5C_2 \times 3! = 60$
$9, 9, 7, 7, 7$	${}^5C_2 = 10$
$9, 8, 8, 8, 6$	${}^5C_3 \times 2 = 20$
$9, 8, 8, 7, 7$	$5 \times {}^4C_2 = 30$
$8, 8, 8, 8, 7$	${}^5C_1 = 5$

and hence there are a total of 210 such numbers.

Review Exercises 11, Question 18 (page 681)

(a) With $k = n = 3$, the probability that I pick one tablet of each type on the first day is

$$\frac{3^3}{{}^9C_3} = \frac{27}{84} = \frac{9}{28}$$

This is also the probability that I have one tablet of each type left on the last day (choosing tablets on the other two days is just another way of choosing the tablets on the third day).

(b) With $k = 3$, but general n, the probability that I pick one tablet of each type on the first day is

$$\frac{n^3}{^{2n}C_3}$$

(c) With $k = 2$, the probability that I choose one pill of each type on all n days of an n-day holiday is

$$\frac{n^2}{^{2n}C_2} \times \frac{(n-1)^2}{^{2n-2}C_2} \times \frac{(n-2)^2}{^{2n-4}C_2} \times \cdots \times \frac{1^2}{^2C_2} = \frac{(n!)^2(2n-2)!(2n-4)!(2n-6)!\cdots 2!0!(2!)^n}{(2n)!(2n-2)!(2n-4)!\cdots 4!2!} = \frac{(n!)^2 2^n}{(2n)!}$$

$$\approx \frac{2n\pi\left(\frac{n}{e}\right)^{2n} 2^n}{\sqrt{4n\pi}\left(\frac{2n}{e}\right)^{2n}} = \frac{\sqrt{n\pi}}{2^n}$$

Review Exercises 11, Question 44 (page 685)

We only use the digits 1, 2, 3, 4 or 5, and so there are $5^5 = 3125$ possible numbers, all equally likely. We could have anything between 1 and 5 different digits. Let X be the number of different digits:

$X = 1$: 5 of these numbers contain just 1 digit.

$X = 2$: There are two types of number with 2 distinct digits. We could have 4 of one digit, and 1 of another. There are 5 choices for the 4-fold repeated digit, and then 4 choices for the singleton digit. There are then 5 places where the singleton digit can go. Thus there are $5 \times 4 \times 5 = 100$ numbers of this type.

Alternatively we could have 3 of one digit, and 2 of another. There are 5 choices for the 3-fold repeated digit, and then 4 choices for the other digit. There are then $^5C_3 = 10$ ways of arranging the three identical digits, with the other two digits filling the gaps. Thus there are $5 \times 4 \times 10 = 200$ numbers of this type.

Thus there are $100 + 200 = 300$ numbers with 2 digits.

$X = 4$: Numbers with 4 digits must have 2 digits of one type, and 3 other distinct digits. There are 5 choices for the digit to be omitted, and then 4 choices for the digit to be doubled. There are then $^5C_2 = 10$ ways of arranging the two identical digits, and then $3! = 6$ ways arranging the other digits. Thus there are $5 \times 4 \times 10 \times 6 = 1200$ numbers of this type.

$X = 5$: There are $5! = 120$ numbers containing 5 digits.

$X = 3$: Thus there are $3125 - 5 - 300 - 1200 - 120 = 1500$ numbers containing 3 digits (this number could have been built up, since we could calculate that there are 600 numbers which have one number three times, and two other singleton digits, and also 900 numbers which have two doubleton digits and one singleton digit).

Thus the number X of different digits is a random variable with the following distribution:

x	1	2	3	4	5
$\mathbb{P}[X = x]$	$\frac{5}{3125}$	$\frac{300}{3125}$	$\frac{1500}{3125}$	$\frac{1200}{3125}$	$\frac{120}{3125}$

and hence

$$\mathbb{E}[X] = \frac{1 \times 5 + 2 \times 300 + 3 \times 1500 + 4 \times 1200 + 5 \times 120}{3125} = \frac{10505}{3125} = \frac{2101}{625} = 3.3616$$

Review Exercises 11, Question 45 (page 685)

The simplest approach to this question is to assume that the three girls are indistinguishable and the n boys are indistinguishable. This means there are $^{n+3}C_3 = \frac{1}{6}(n+1)(n+2)(n+3)$ ways of ordering the $n + 3$ children, all equally likely.

(a) To have $K = 3$, the three girls must be all next to each other. We can treat the three girls as a single group, and so we want to know that number of ways of sorting n boys and a triple of girls. There are $n + 1$ ways of doing this, and so

$$\mathbb{P}[K = 3] = \frac{n+1}{\frac{1}{6}(n+1)(n+2)(n+3)} = \frac{6}{(n+2)(n+3)}.$$

(b) If we want $K = 1$, no two girls can be next to each other. Thus the three girls must slot into three of the $n + 1$ 'gaps' between the boys (including the 'gaps' at the ends of the line). There are $^{n+1}C_3 = \frac{1}{6}(n-1)n(n+1)$ ways of doing this. Thus

$$\mathbb{P}[K = 1] = \frac{^{n+3}C_3}{^{n+1}C_3} = \frac{n(n-1)}{(n+2)(n+3)}$$

(c) Since K can only take the values 1, 2 or 3, we see that

$$\mathbb{P}[K = 2] = 1 - \frac{n(n-1)}{(n+2)(n+3)} - \frac{6}{(n+2)(n+3)} = \frac{6n}{(n+2)(n+3)}$$

and hence

$$\mathbb{E}[K] = \frac{1 \times n(n-1) + 2 \times 6n + 3 \times 6}{(n+2)(n+3)} = \frac{n^2 + 11n + 18}{(n+2)(n+3)} = \frac{(n+2)(n+9)}{(n+2)(n+3)} = \frac{n+9}{n+3}$$

Review Exercises 11, Question 69 (page 687)

Although X is not normally distributed, we can handle this question using the same symmetry tricks that we use with the normal distribution.

(a) Thus

$$\begin{aligned}
\mathbb{P}[\mu - \tfrac{1}{2}\sigma \leq X \leq \mu + \sigma] &= \mathbb{P}[X \leq \mu + \sigma] - \mathbb{P}[X \leq \mu - \tfrac{1}{2}\sigma] = a - \mathbb{P}[X \geq \mu + \tfrac{1}{2}\sigma] \\
&= a - (1 - b) = a + b - 1 \\
\mathbb{P}[\mu - \tfrac{1}{2}\sigma \leq X \leq \mu + \tfrac{1}{2}\sigma] &= 2b - 1 \\
\mathbb{P}[X \leq \mu + \tfrac{1}{2}\sigma | X \geq \mu - \tfrac{1}{2}\sigma] &= \frac{2b-1}{\mathbb{P}[X \geq \mu - \tfrac{1}{2}\sigma]} = \frac{2b-1}{\mathbb{P}[X \leq \mu + \tfrac{1}{2}\sigma]} = \frac{2b-1}{b}
\end{aligned}$$

(b) Let F be the event that a carton of milk is full-fat, and S the event that a bottle of milk is skimmed.

a) Then

$$\begin{aligned}
\mathbb{P}[500 < X < 505 | F] &= \mathbb{P}[\mu \leq X \leq \mu + \tfrac{1}{2}\sigma] = b - \tfrac{1}{2} \\
\mathbb{P}[500 < X < 505 | S] &= \mathbb{P}[\mu + \tfrac{1}{2}\sigma < X < \mu + \sigma] = a - b \\
\mathbb{P}[500 < X < 505] &= 0.6(b - \tfrac{1}{2}) + 0.4(a - b) = 0.4a + 0.2b - 0.3
\end{aligned}$$

and, similarly,

$$\begin{aligned}
\mathbb{P}[X < 505 | F] &= \mathbb{P}[X \leq \mu + \sigma] = a \\
\mathbb{P}[X < 505 | S] &= \mathbb{P}[X \leq \mu + \tfrac{1}{2}\sigma] = b \\
\mathbb{P}[X < 505] &= 0.6a + 0.4b
\end{aligned}$$

and hence

$$\mathbb{P}[X > 500 | X < 505] = \frac{0.4a + 0.2b - 0.3}{0.6a + 0.4b} = \frac{4a + 2b - 3}{6a + 4b}$$

b) Since 70% of the cartons bought have contained at most 505 ml of milk, we know that $0.4a + 0.6b = 0.7$, or $4a + 6b = 7$. We also know that

$$\tfrac{1}{3} = \mathbb{P}[F | X > 495] = \frac{\mathbb{P}[X > 495 | F]0.4}{\mathbb{P}[X > 495]} = \frac{\tfrac{1}{2} \times 0.4}{\tfrac{1}{2} \times 0.4 + 0.6b} = \frac{1}{1 + 3b}$$

so we deduce that $b = \tfrac{2}{3}$, and hence $a = \tfrac{3}{4}$.

Mathematical Formulae and Statistical Tables

These formulae are the subcollection of the official Pre-U formula booklet MF20. The formulae and tables included are those appropriate to the Single Mathematics Pre-U examination

PURE MATHEMATICS

MENSURATION

Surface area of sphere $= 4\pi r^2$
Area of curved surface of cone $= \pi r \times$ slant height

TRIGONOMETRY

$$a^2 = b^2 + c^2 - 2bc \sin A$$

ARITHMETIC SERIES

$$u_n = a + (n-1)d \quad S_n = \tfrac{1}{2}n(a+\ell) = \tfrac{1}{2}n\{2a + (n-1)d\}$$

GEOMETRIC SERIES

$$u_n = ar^{n-1}$$
$$S_n = \frac{a(r^n - 1)}{r - 1}$$
$$S_\infty = \frac{a}{1-r}$$

SUMMATIONS

$$\sum_{r=1}^{n} r^2 = \tfrac{1}{6}n(n+1)(2n+1)$$

$$\sum_{r=1}^{n} r^3 = \tfrac{1}{4}n^2(n+1)^2$$

BINOMIAL SERIES

$$\binom{n}{r} = {}^nC_r = \frac{n!}{r!(n-r)!}$$
$$\binom{n}{r} + \binom{n}{r-1} = \binom{n+1}{r+1}$$

$$(a+b)^n = a^n + \binom{n}{1}a^{n-1}b + \binom{n}{2}a^{n-2}b^2 + \cdots + \binom{n}{n-2}a^2b^{n-2} + \binom{n}{n-1}ab^{n-1} + b^n, \, n \in \mathbb{N}$$

$$(1+x)^n = 1 + nx + \frac{n(n-1)}{2!}x^2 + \cdots + \frac{n(n-1)\cdots(n-r+1)}{r!}x^r + \cdots, \, (|x| < 1, \, n \in \mathbb{R})$$

LOGARITHMS AND EXPONENTIALS

$$e^{x \ln a} = a^x$$

COORDINATE GEOMETRY

The perpendicular distance from (h, k) to $ax + by + c = 0$ is $\dfrac{|ah + bk + c|}{\sqrt{a^2 + b^2}}$

The acute angle between lines with gradients m_1 and m_2 is $\tan^{-1}\left|\dfrac{m_1 - m_2}{1 + m_1 m_2}\right|$

TRIGONOMETRIC IDENTITIES

$$\sin(A \pm B) = \sin A \cos B \pm \cos A \sin B$$
$$\cos(A \pm B) = \cos A \cos B \mp \sin A \sin B$$
$$\tan(A \pm B) = \frac{\tan A \pm \tan B}{1 \mp \tan A \tan B} \quad \left(A \pm B \neq (k + \tfrac{1}{2})\pi\right)$$
For $t = \tan \tfrac{1}{2}A$: $\sin A = \frac{2t}{1+t^2}$, $\cos A = \frac{1-t^2}{1+t^2}$
$$\sin A + \sin B = 2\sin\tfrac{1}{2}(A+B)\cos\tfrac{1}{2}(A-B)$$
$$\sin A - \sin B = 2\cos\tfrac{1}{2}(A+B)\sin\tfrac{1}{2}(A-B)$$
$$\cos A + \cos B = 2\cos\tfrac{1}{2}(A+B)\cos\tfrac{1}{2}(A-B)$$
$$\cos A - \cos B = -2\sin\tfrac{1}{2}(A+B)\sin\tfrac{1}{2}(A-B)$$

VECTORS

The resolved part of $\mathbf{a}$ in the direction of $\mathbf{b}$ is $\frac{\mathbf{a} \cdot \mathbf{b}}{|\mathbf{b}|}$

The point dividing AB in the ratio $\lambda : \mu$ is $\frac{\mu\mathbf{a} + \lambda\mathbf{b}}{\lambda + \mu}$

If A is the point with position vector $\mathbf{a} = a_1\mathbf{i} + a_2\mathbf{j} + a_3\mathbf{k}$ and the direction vector $\mathbf{b}$ is given by $\mathbf{b} = b_1\mathbf{i} + b_2\mathbf{j} + b_3\mathbf{k}$, then the straight line through A with direction vector B has equation
$$\frac{x - a_1}{b_1} = \frac{y - a_2}{b_2} = \frac{z - a_3}{b_3} (= \lambda)$$

DIFFERENTIATION

$\mathbf{f(x)}$	$\mathbf{f'(x)}$	$\mathbf{f(x)}$	$\mathbf{f'(x)}$
$\tan kx$	$k\sec^2 kx$	$\sin^{-1} x$	$\dfrac{1}{\sqrt{1-x^2}}$
$\sec x$	$\sec x \tan x$	$\cos^{-1} x$	$-\dfrac{1}{\sqrt{1-x^2}}$
$\operatorname{cosec} x$	$-\operatorname{cosec} x \cot x$	$\tan^{-1} x$	$\dfrac{1}{1+x^2}$

INTEGRATION — $(+c \, ; \, a > 0$ where relevant$)$

$\mathbf{f(x)}$	$\int \mathbf{f(x)\,dx}$	$\mathbf{f(x)}$	$\int \mathbf{f(x)\,dx}$
$\sec^2 kx$	$\frac{1}{k}\tan kx$	$\dfrac{1}{\sqrt{a^2 - x^2}}$	$\sin^{-1}\left(\frac{x}{a}\right)$
$\tan x$	$\ln|\sec x|$	$\dfrac{1}{a^2 + x^2}$	$\frac{1}{a}\tan^{-1}\left(\frac{x}{a}\right)$
$\cot x$	$\ln|\sin x|$	$\dfrac{1}{x^2 - a^2}$	$\frac{1}{2a}\ln\left|\frac{x-a}{x+a}\right|$
$\operatorname{cosec} x$	$-\ln|\operatorname{cosec} x + \cot x| = \ln\left|\tan\left(\frac{1}{2}x\right)\right|$	$\sec x$	$\ln|\sec x + \tan x| = \ln\left|\tan\left(\frac{1}{2}x + \frac{1}{4}\pi\right)\right|$

NUMERICAL SOLUTION OF EQUATIONS

The Newton-Raphson iteration for solving $f(x) = 0$: $\quad x_{n+1} = x_n - \dfrac{f(x_n)}{f'(x_n)}$

PROBABILITY

PROBABILITY

$\mathbb{P}[A \cup B] = \mathbb{P}[A] + \mathbb{P}[B] - \mathbb{P}[A \cap B]$

$\mathbb{P}[A \cap B] = \mathbb{P}[A]\mathbb{P}[B|A]$

$\mathbb{P}[A|B] = \dfrac{\mathbb{P}[B|A]\mathbb{P}[A]}{\mathbb{P}[B|A]\mathbb{P}[A] + \mathbb{P}[B|A']\mathbb{P}[A']}$

Bayes' Theorem: $\mathbb{P}[A_j|B] = \dfrac{\mathbb{P}[A_j]\mathbb{P}[B|A_j]}{\sum_i \mathbb{P}[A_i]\mathbb{P}[B|A_i]}$

DISCRETE DISTRIBUTIONS

For a discrete random variable X taking values x_i with probabilities p_i

$$\begin{aligned} \text{Expectation (mean)}: \quad & \mathbb{E}[X] = \mu = \sum x_i p_i \\ \text{Variance}: \quad & \text{Var}[X] = \sigma^2 = \sum (x_i - \mu)^2 p_i = \sum x_i^2 p_i - \mu^2 \\ \text{For a function } g(X): \quad & \mathbb{E}[g(X)] = \sum g(x_i) p_i \end{aligned}$$

STANDARD DISCRETE DISTRIBUTIONS

Distribution of X	$\mathbb{P}[X = x]$	Mean	Variance
Binomial $B(n, p)$	$\binom{n}{x} p^x (1-p)^{n-x}$	np	$np(1-p)$
Geometric $\text{Geo}(p)$ on $1, 2, \ldots$	$p(1-p)^{x-1}$	$\frac{1}{p}$	$\frac{1-p}{p^2}$

CORRELATION AND REGRESSION

For a set of n pairs of values (x_i, y_i)

$$\begin{aligned} S_{xx} &= \sum (x_i - \overline{x})^2 = \sum x_i^2 - \frac{1}{n}\left(\sum x_i\right)^2 \\ S_{yy} &= \sum (y_i - \overline{y})^2 = \sum y_i^2 - \frac{1}{n}\left(\sum y_i\right)^2 \\ S_{xy} &= \sum (x_i - \overline{x})(y_i - \overline{y}) = \sum x_i y_i - \frac{1}{n}\left(\sum x_i\right)\left(\sum y_i\right) \end{aligned}$$

The product-moment correlation coefficient is

$$ r = \frac{S_{xy}}{\sqrt{S_{xx} S_{yy}}} = \frac{\sum (x_i - \overline{x})(y_i - \overline{y})}{\sqrt{\{\sum (x_i - \overline{x})^2\}\{\sum (y_i - \overline{y})^2\}}} = \frac{\sum x_i y_i - \frac{1}{n}\left(\sum x_i\right)\left(\sum y_i\right)}{\sqrt{\left(\sum x_i^2 - \frac{1}{n}\left(\sum x_i\right)^2\right)\left(\sum y_i^2 - \frac{1}{n}\left(\sum y_i\right)^2\right)}} $$

The regression coefficient of y on x is $b = \dfrac{S_{xy}}{S_{xx}} = \sum (x_i - \overline{x})(y_i - \overline{y}) \sum (x_i - \overline{x})^2$

Least squares regression line of y on x is $y = a + bx$, where $a = \overline{y} - b\overline{x}$.

CUMULATIVE BINOMIAL PROBABILITIES

$n = 5$

p	0.05	0.1	0.15	1/6	0.2	0.25	0.3	1/3	0.35	0.4	0.45	0.5	0.55	0.6	0.65	2/3	0.7	0.75	0.8	5/6	0.85	0.9	0.95
$x=0$	0.7738	0.5905	0.4437	0.4019	0.3277	0.2373	0.1681	0.1317	0.1160	0.0778	0.0503	0.0313	0.0185	0.0102	0.0053	0.0041	0.0024	0.0010	0.0003	0.0001	0.0001	0.0000	0.0000
1	0.9774	0.9185	0.8352	0.8038	0.7373	0.6328	0.5282	0.4609	0.4284	0.3370	0.2562	0.1875	0.1312	0.0870	0.0540	0.0453	0.0308	0.0156	0.0067	0.0033	0.0022	0.0005	0.0000
2	0.9988	0.9914	0.9734	0.9645	0.9421	0.8965	0.8369	0.7901	0.7648	0.6826	0.5931	0.5000	0.4069	0.3174	0.2352	0.2099	0.1631	0.1035	0.0579	0.0355	0.0266	0.0086	0.0012
3	1.0000	0.9995	0.9978	0.9967	0.9933	0.9844	0.9692	0.9547	0.9460	0.9130	0.8688	0.8125	0.7438	0.6630	0.5716	0.5391	0.4718	0.3672	0.2627	0.1962	0.1648	0.0815	0.0226
4	1.0000	1.0000	0.9999	0.9999	0.9997	0.9990	0.9976	0.9959	0.9947	0.9898	0.9815	0.9688	0.9497	0.9222	0.8840	0.8683	0.8319	0.7627	0.6723	0.5981	0.5563	0.4095	0.2262
5	1.0000	1.0000	1.0000	1.0000	1.0000	1.0000	1.0000	1.0000	1.0000	1.0000	1.0000	1.0000	1.0000	1.0000	1.0000	1.0000	1.0000	1.0000	1.0000	1.0000	1.0000	1.0000	1.0000

$n = 6$

p	0.05	0.1	0.15	1/6	0.2	0.25	0.3	1/3	0.35	0.4	0.45	0.5	0.55	0.6	0.65	2/3	0.7	0.75	0.8	5/6	0.85	0.9	0.95
$x=0$	0.7351	0.5314	0.3771	0.3349	0.2621	0.1780	0.1176	0.0878	0.0754	0.0467	0.0277	0.0156	0.0083	0.0041	0.0018	0.0014	0.0007	0.0002	0.0001	0.0000	0.0000	0.0000	0.0000
1	0.9672	0.8857	0.7765	0.7368	0.6554	0.5339	0.4202	0.3512	0.3191	0.2333	0.1636	0.1094	0.0692	0.0410	0.0223	0.0178	0.0109	0.0046	0.0016	0.0007	0.0004	0.0001	0.0000
2	0.9978	0.9842	0.9527	0.9377	0.9011	0.8306	0.7443	0.6804	0.6471	0.5443	0.4415	0.3438	0.2553	0.1792	0.1174	0.1001	0.0705	0.0376	0.0170	0.0087	0.0059	0.0013	0.0001
3	0.9999	0.9987	0.9941	0.9913	0.9830	0.9624	0.9295	0.8999	0.8826	0.8208	0.7447	0.6563	0.5585	0.4557	0.3529	0.3196	0.2557	0.1694	0.0989	0.0623	0.0473	0.0159	0.0022
4	1.0000	0.9999	0.9996	0.9993	0.9984	0.9954	0.9891	0.9822	0.9777	0.9590	0.9308	0.8906	0.8364	0.7667	0.6809	0.6488	0.5798	0.4661	0.3446	0.2632	0.2235	0.1143	0.0328
5	1.0000	1.0000	1.0000	1.0000	0.9999	0.9998	0.9993	0.9986	0.9982	0.9959	0.9917	0.9844	0.9723	0.9533	0.9246	0.9122	0.8824	0.8220	0.7379	0.6651	0.6229	0.4686	0.2649
6	1.0000	1.0000	1.0000	1.0000	1.0000	1.0000	1.0000	1.0000	1.0000	1.0000	1.0000	1.0000	1.0000	1.0000	1.0000	1.0000	1.0000	1.0000	1.0000	1.0000	1.0000	1.0000	1.0000

$n = 7$

p	0.05	0.1	0.15	1/6	0.2	0.25	0.3	1/3	0.35	0.4	0.45	0.5	0.55	0.6	0.65	2/3	0.7	0.75	0.8	5/6	0.85	0.9	0.95
$x=0$	0.6983	0.4783	0.3206	0.2791	0.2097	0.1335	0.0824	0.0585	0.0490	0.0280	0.0152	0.0078	0.0037	0.0016	0.0006	0.0005	0.0002	0.0001	0.0000	0.0000	0.0000	0.0000	0.0000
1	0.9556	0.8503	0.7166	0.6698	0.5767	0.4449	0.3294	0.2634	0.2338	0.1586	0.1024	0.0625	0.0357	0.0188	0.0090	0.0069	0.0038	0.0013	0.0004	0.0001	0.0001	0.0000	0.0000
2	0.9962	0.9743	0.9262	0.9042	0.8520	0.7564	0.6471	0.5706	0.5323	0.4199	0.3164	0.2266	0.1529	0.0963	0.0556	0.0453	0.0288	0.0129	0.0047	0.0020	0.0012	0.0002	0.0000
3	0.9998	0.9973	0.9879	0.9824	0.9667	0.9294	0.8740	0.8267	0.8002	0.7102	0.6083	0.5000	0.3917	0.2898	0.1998	0.1733	0.1260	0.0706	0.0333	0.0176	0.0121	0.0027	0.0002
4	1.0000	0.9998	0.9988	0.9980	0.9953	0.9871	0.9712	0.9547	0.9444	0.9037	0.8471	0.7734	0.6836	0.5801	0.4677	0.4294	0.3529	0.2436	0.1480	0.0958	0.0738	0.0257	0.0038
5	1.0000	1.0000	0.9999	0.9999	0.9996	0.9987	0.9962	0.9931	0.9910	0.9812	0.9643	0.9375	0.8976	0.8414	0.7662	0.7366	0.6706	0.5551	0.4233	0.3302	0.2834	0.1497	0.0444
6	1.0000	1.0000	1.0000	1.0000	1.0000	0.9999	0.9998	0.9995	0.9994	0.9984	0.9963	0.9922	0.9848	0.9720	0.9510	0.9415	0.9176	0.8665	0.7903	0.7209	0.6794	0.5217	0.3017
7	1.0000	1.0000	1.0000	1.0000	1.0000	1.0000	1.0000	1.0000	1.0000	1.0000	1.0000	1.0000	1.0000	1.0000	1.0000	1.0000	1.0000	1.0000	1.0000	1.0000	1.0000	1.0000	1.0000

$n = 8$

p	0.05	0.1	0.15	1/6	0.2	0.25	0.3	1/3	0.35	0.4	0.45	0.5	0.55	0.6	0.65	2/3	0.7	0.75	0.8	5/6	0.85	0.9	0.95
$x=0$	0.6634	0.4305	0.2725	0.2326	0.1678	0.1001	0.0576	0.0390	0.0319	0.0168	0.0084	0.0039	0.0017	0.0007	0.0002	0.0002	0.0001	0.0000	0.0000	0.0000	0.0000	0.0000	0.0000
1	0.9428	0.8131	0.6572	0.6047	0.5033	0.3671	0.2553	0.1951	0.1691	0.1064	0.0632	0.0352	0.0181	0.0085	0.0036	0.0026	0.0013	0.0004	0.0001	0.0000	0.0000	0.0000	0.0000
2	0.9942	0.9619	0.8948	0.8652	0.7969	0.6785	0.5518	0.4682	0.4278	0.3154	0.2201	0.1445	0.0885	0.0498	0.0253	0.0197	0.0113	0.0042	0.0012	0.0004	0.0002	0.0000	0.0000
3	0.9996	0.9950	0.9786	0.9693	0.9437	0.8862	0.8059	0.7414	0.7064	0.5941	0.4770	0.3633	0.2604	0.1737	0.1061	0.0879	0.0580	0.0273	0.0104	0.0046	0.0029	0.0004	0.0000
4	1.0000	0.9996	0.9971	0.9954	0.9896	0.9727	0.9420	0.9121	0.8939	0.8263	0.7396	0.6367	0.5230	0.4059	0.2936	0.2586	0.1941	0.1138	0.0563	0.0307	0.0214	0.0050	0.0004
5	1.0000	1.0000	0.9998	0.9996	0.9988	0.9958	0.9887	0.9803	0.9747	0.9502	0.9115	0.8555	0.7799	0.6846	0.5722	0.5318	0.4482	0.3215	0.2031	0.1348	0.1052	0.0381	0.0058
6	1.0000	1.0000	1.0000	1.0000	0.9999	0.9996	0.9987	0.9974	0.9964	0.9915	0.9819	0.9648	0.9368	0.8936	0.8309	0.8049	0.7447	0.6329	0.4967	0.3953	0.3428	0.1869	0.0572
7	1.0000	1.0000	1.0000	1.0000	1.0000	1.0000	0.9999	0.9998	0.9998	0.9993	0.9983	0.9961	0.9916	0.9832	0.9681	0.9610	0.9424	0.8999	0.8322	0.7674	0.7275	0.5695	0.3366
8	1.0000	1.0000	1.0000	1.0000	1.0000	1.0000	1.0000	1.0000	1.0000	1.0000	1.0000	1.0000	1.0000	1.0000	1.0000	1.0000	1.0000	1.0000	1.0000	1.0000	1.0000	1.0000	1.0000

CUMULATIVE BINOMIAL PROBABILITIES

n = 9

x \ p	0.05	0.1	0.15	1/6	0.2	0.25	0.3	1/3	0.35	0.4	0.45	0.5	0.55	0.6	0.65	2/3	0.7	0.75	0.8	5/6	0.85	0.9	0.95
0	0.6302	0.3874	0.2316	0.1938	0.1342	0.0751	0.0404	0.0260	0.0207	0.0101	0.0046	0.0020	0.0008	0.0003	0.0001	0.0001	0.0000	0.0000	0.0000	0.0000	0.0000	0.0000	0.0000
1	0.9288	0.7748	0.5995	0.5427	0.4362	0.3003	0.1960	0.1431	0.1211	0.0705	0.0385	0.0195	0.0091	0.0038	0.0014	0.0010	0.0004	0.0001	0.0000	0.0000	0.0000	0.0000	0.0000
2	0.9916	0.9470	0.8591	0.8217	0.7382	0.6007	0.4628	0.3772	0.3373	0.2318	0.1495	0.0898	0.0498	0.0250	0.0112	0.0083	0.0043	0.0013	0.0003	0.0001	0.0000	0.0000	0.0000
3	0.9994	0.9917	0.9661	0.9520	0.9144	0.8343	0.7297	0.6503	0.6089	0.4826	0.3614	0.2539	0.1658	0.0994	0.0536	0.0424	0.0253	0.0100	0.0031	0.0011	0.0006	0.0001	0.0000
4	1.0000	0.9991	0.9944	0.9910	0.9804	0.9511	0.9012	0.8552	0.8283	0.7334	0.6214	0.5000	0.3786	0.2666	0.1717	0.1448	0.0988	0.0489	0.0196	0.0090	0.0056	0.0009	0.0000
5	1.0000	0.9999	0.9994	0.9989	0.9969	0.9900	0.9747	0.9576	0.9464	0.9006	0.8342	0.7461	0.6386	0.5174	0.3911	0.3497	0.2703	0.1657	0.0856	0.0480	0.0339	0.0083	0.0006
6	1.0000	1.0000	1.0000	0.9999	0.9997	0.9987	0.9957	0.9917	0.9888	0.9750	0.9502	0.9102	0.8505	0.7682	0.6627	0.6228	0.5372	0.3993	0.2618	0.1783	0.1409	0.0530	0.0084
7	1.0000	1.0000	1.0000	1.0000	1.0000	0.9999	0.9996	0.9990	0.9986	0.9962	0.9909	0.9805	0.9615	0.9295	0.8789	0.8569	0.8040	0.6997	0.5638	0.4573	0.4005	0.2252	0.0712
8	1.0000	1.0000	1.0000	1.0000	1.0000	1.0000	1.0000	0.9999	0.9999	0.9997	0.9992	0.9980	0.9954	0.9899	0.9793	0.9740	0.9596	0.9249	0.8658	0.8062	0.7684	0.6126	0.3698
9	1.0000	1.0000	1.0000	1.0000	1.0000	1.0000	1.0000	1.0000	1.0000	1.0000	1.0000	1.0000	1.0000	1.0000	1.0000	1.0000	1.0000	1.0000	1.0000	1.0000	1.0000	1.0000	1.0000

n = 10

x \ p	0.05	0.1	0.15	1/6	0.2	0.25	0.3	1/3	0.35	0.4	0.45	0.5	0.55	0.6	0.65	2/3	0.7	0.75	0.8	5/6	0.85	0.9	0.95
0	0.5987	0.3487	0.1969	0.1615	0.1074	0.0563	0.0282	0.0173	0.0135	0.0060	0.0025	0.0010	0.0003	0.0001	0.0000	0.0000	0.0000	0.0000	0.0000	0.0000	0.0000	0.0000	0.0000
1	0.9139	0.7361	0.5443	0.4845	0.3758	0.2440	0.1493	0.1040	0.0860	0.0464	0.0233	0.0107	0.0045	0.0017	0.0005	0.0004	0.0001	0.0000	0.0000	0.0000	0.0000	0.0000	0.0000
2	0.9885	0.9298	0.8202	0.7752	0.6778	0.5256	0.3828	0.2991	0.2616	0.1673	0.0996	0.0547	0.0274	0.0123	0.0048	0.0034	0.0016	0.0004	0.0001	0.0000	0.0000	0.0000	0.0000
3	0.9990	0.9872	0.9500	0.9303	0.8791	0.7759	0.6496	0.5593	0.5138	0.3823	0.2660	0.1719	0.1020	0.0548	0.0260	0.0197	0.0106	0.0035	0.0009	0.0003	0.0001	0.0000	0.0000
4	0.9999	0.9984	0.9901	0.9845	0.9672	0.9219	0.8497	0.7869	0.7515	0.6331	0.5044	0.3770	0.2616	0.1662	0.0949	0.0766	0.0473	0.0197	0.0064	0.0024	0.0014	0.0001	0.0000
5	1.0000	0.9999	0.9986	0.9976	0.9936	0.9803	0.9527	0.9234	0.9051	0.8338	0.7384	0.6230	0.4956	0.3669	0.2485	0.2131	0.1503	0.0781	0.0328	0.0155	0.0099	0.0016	0.0001
6	1.0000	1.0000	0.9999	0.9997	0.9991	0.9965	0.9894	0.9803	0.9740	0.9452	0.8980	0.8281	0.7340	0.6177	0.4862	0.4407	0.3504	0.2241	0.1209	0.0697	0.0500	0.0128	0.0010
7	1.0000	1.0000	1.0000	1.0000	0.9999	0.9996	0.9984	0.9966	0.9952	0.9877	0.9726	0.9453	0.9004	0.8327	0.7384	0.7009	0.6172	0.4744	0.3222	0.2248	0.1798	0.0702	0.0115
8	1.0000	1.0000	1.0000	1.0000	1.0000	1.0000	0.9999	0.9996	0.9995	0.9983	0.9955	0.9893	0.9767	0.9536	0.9140	0.8960	0.8507	0.7560	0.6242	0.5155	0.4557	0.2639	0.0861
9	1.0000	1.0000	1.0000	1.0000	1.0000	1.0000	1.0000	1.0000	1.0000	0.9999	0.9997	0.9990	0.9975	0.9940	0.9865	0.9827	0.9718	0.9437	0.8926	0.8385	0.8031	0.6513	0.4013
10	1.0000	1.0000	1.0000	1.0000	1.0000	1.0000	1.0000	1.0000	1.0000	1.0000	1.0000	1.0000	1.0000	1.0000	1.0000	1.0000	1.0000	1.0000	1.0000	1.0000	1.0000	1.0000	1.0000

n = 12

x \ p	0.05	0.1	0.15	1/6	0.2	0.25	0.3	1/3	0.35	0.4	0.45	0.5	0.55	0.6	0.65	2/3	0.7	0.75	0.8	5/6	0.85	0.9	0.95
0	0.5404	0.2824	0.1422	0.1122	0.0687	0.0317	0.0138	0.0077	0.0057	0.0022	0.0008	0.0002	0.0001	0.0000	0.0000	0.0000	0.0000	0.0000	0.0000	0.0000	0.0000	0.0000	0.0000
1	0.8816	0.6590	0.4435	0.3813	0.2749	0.1584	0.0850	0.0540	0.0424	0.0196	0.0083	0.0032	0.0011	0.0003	0.0001	0.0000	0.0000	0.0000	0.0000	0.0000	0.0000	0.0000	0.0000
2	0.9804	0.8891	0.7358	0.6774	0.5583	0.3907	0.2528	0.1811	0.1513	0.0834	0.0421	0.0193	0.0079	0.0028	0.0008	0.0005	0.0002	0.0000	0.0000	0.0000	0.0000	0.0000	0.0000
3	0.9978	0.9744	0.9078	0.8748	0.7946	0.6488	0.4925	0.3931	0.3467	0.2253	0.1345	0.0730	0.0356	0.0153	0.0056	0.0039	0.0017	0.0004	0.0001	0.0000	0.0000	0.0000	0.0000
4	0.9998	0.9957	0.9761	0.9636	0.9274	0.8424	0.7237	0.6315	0.5833	0.4382	0.3044	0.1938	0.1117	0.0573	0.0255	0.0188	0.0095	0.0028	0.0006	0.0002	0.0001	0.0000	0.0000
5	1.0000	0.9995	0.9954	0.9921	0.9806	0.9456	0.8822	0.8223	0.7873	0.6652	0.5269	0.3872	0.2607	0.1582	0.0846	0.0664	0.0386	0.0143	0.0039	0.0013	0.0007	0.0001	0.0000
6	1.0000	0.9999	0.9993	0.9987	0.9961	0.9857	0.9614	0.9336	0.9154	0.8418	0.7393	0.6128	0.4731	0.3348	0.2127	0.1777	0.1178	0.0544	0.0194	0.0079	0.0046	0.0005	0.0000
7	1.0000	1.0000	0.9999	0.9998	0.9994	0.9972	0.9905	0.9812	0.9745	0.9427	0.8883	0.8062	0.6956	0.5618	0.4167	0.3685	0.2763	0.1576	0.0726	0.0364	0.0239	0.0043	0.0002
8	1.0000	1.0000	1.0000	1.0000	0.9999	0.9996	0.9983	0.9961	0.9944	0.9847	0.9644	0.9270	0.8655	0.7747	0.6533	0.6069	0.5075	0.3512	0.2054	0.1252	0.0922	0.0256	0.0022
9	1.0000	1.0000	1.0000	1.0000	1.0000	1.0000	0.9998	0.9995	0.9992	0.9972	0.9921	0.9807	0.9579	0.9166	0.8487	0.8189	0.7472	0.6093	0.4417	0.3226	0.2642	0.1109	0.0196
10	1.0000	1.0000	1.0000	1.0000	1.0000	1.0000	1.0000	1.0000	0.9999	0.9997	0.9989	0.9968	0.9917	0.9804	0.9576	0.9460	0.9150	0.8416	0.7251	0.6187	0.5565	0.3410	0.1184
11	1.0000	1.0000	1.0000	1.0000	1.0000	1.0000	1.0000	1.0000	1.0000	1.0000	0.9999	0.9998	0.9992	0.9978	0.9943	0.9923	0.9862	0.9683	0.9313	0.8878	0.8578	0.7176	0.4596
12	1.0000	1.0000	1.0000	1.0000	1.0000	1.0000	1.0000	1.0000	1.0000	1.0000	1.0000	1.0000	1.0000	1.0000	1.0000	1.0000	1.0000	1.0000	1.0000	1.0000	1.0000	1.0000	1.0000

CUMULATIVE BINOMIAL PROBABILITIES

n = 14

x	0.05	0.1	0.15	1/6	0.2	0.25	0.3	1/3	0.35	0.4	0.45	0.5	0.55	0.6	0.65	2/3	0.7	0.75	0.8	5/6	0.85	0.9	0.95
0	0.4877	0.2288	0.1028	0.0779	0.0440	0.0178	0.0068	0.0034	0.0024	0.0008	0.0002	0.0001	0.0000	0.0000	0.0000	0.0000	0.0000	0.0000	0.0000	0.0000	0.0000	0.0000	0.0000
1	0.8470	0.5846	0.3567	0.2960	0.1979	0.1010	0.0475	0.0274	0.0205	0.0081	0.0029	0.0009	0.0003	0.0001	0.0000	0.0000	0.0000	0.0000	0.0000	0.0000	0.0000	0.0000	0.0000
2	0.9699	0.8416	0.6479	0.5795	0.4481	0.2811	0.1608	0.1053	0.0839	0.0398	0.0170	0.0065	0.0022	0.0006	0.0001	0.0001	0.0000	0.0000	0.0000	0.0000	0.0000	0.0000	0.0000
3	0.9958	0.9559	0.8535	0.8063	0.6982	0.5213	0.3552	0.2612	0.2205	0.1243	0.0632	0.0287	0.0114	0.0039	0.0011	0.0007	0.0002	0.0000	0.0000	0.0000	0.0000	0.0000	0.0000
4	0.9996	0.9908	0.9533	0.9310	0.8702	0.7415	0.5842	0.4755	0.4227	0.2793	0.1672	0.0898	0.0426	0.0175	0.0060	0.0040	0.0017	0.0003	0.0000	0.0000	0.0000	0.0000	0.0000
5	1.0000	0.9985	0.9885	0.9809	0.9561	0.8883	0.7805	0.6898	0.6405	0.4859	0.3373	0.2120	0.1189	0.0583	0.0243	0.0174	0.0083	0.0022	0.0004	0.0001	0.0000	0.0000	0.0000
6	1.0000	0.9998	0.9978	0.9959	0.9884	0.9617	0.9067	0.8505	0.8164	0.6925	0.5461	0.3953	0.2586	0.1501	0.0753	0.0576	0.0315	0.0103	0.0024	0.0007	0.0003	0.0000	0.0000
7	1.0000	1.0000	0.9997	0.9993	0.9976	0.9897	0.9685	0.9424	0.9247	0.8499	0.7414	0.6047	0.4539	0.3075	0.1836	0.1495	0.0933	0.0383	0.0116	0.0041	0.0022	0.0002	0.0000
8	1.0000	1.0000	1.0000	0.9999	0.9996	0.9978	0.9917	0.9826	0.9757	0.9417	0.8811	0.7880	0.6627	0.5141	0.3595	0.3102	0.2195	0.1117	0.0439	0.0191	0.0115	0.0015	0.0000
9	1.0000	1.0000	1.0000	1.0000	1.0000	0.9997	0.9983	0.9960	0.9940	0.9825	0.9574	0.9102	0.8328	0.7207	0.5773	0.5245	0.4158	0.2585	0.1298	0.0690	0.0467	0.0092	0.0004
10	1.0000	1.0000	1.0000	1.0000	1.0000	1.0000	0.9998	0.9993	0.9989	0.9961	0.9886	0.9713	0.9368	0.8757	0.7795	0.7388	0.6448	0.4787	0.3018	0.1937	0.1465	0.0441	0.0042
11	1.0000	1.0000	1.0000	1.0000	1.0000	1.0000	1.0000	0.9999	0.9999	0.9994	0.9978	0.9935	0.9830	0.9602	0.9161	0.8947	0.8392	0.7189	0.5519	0.4205	0.3521	0.1584	0.0301
12	1.0000	1.0000	1.0000	1.0000	1.0000	1.0000	1.0000	1.0000	1.0000	0.9999	0.9997	0.9991	0.9971	0.9919	0.9795	0.9726	0.9525	0.8990	0.8021	0.7040	0.6433	0.4154	0.1530
13	1.0000	1.0000	1.0000	1.0000	1.0000	1.0000	1.0000	1.0000	1.0000	1.0000	1.0000	0.9999	0.9998	0.9992	0.9976	0.9966	0.9932	0.9822	0.9560	0.9221	0.8972	0.7712	0.5123
14	1.0000	1.0000	1.0000	1.0000	1.0000	1.0000	1.0000	1.0000	1.0000	1.0000	1.0000	1.0000	1.0000	1.0000	1.0000	1.0000	1.0000	1.0000	1.0000	1.0000	1.0000	1.0000	1.0000

n = 16

x	0.05	0.1	0.15	1/6	0.2	0.25	0.3	1/3	0.35	0.4	0.45	0.5	0.55	0.6	0.65	2/3	0.7	0.75	0.8	5/6	0.85	0.9	0.95
0	0.4401	0.1853	0.0743	0.0541	0.0281	0.0100	0.0033	0.0015	0.0010	0.0003	0.0001	0.0000	0.0000	0.0000	0.0000	0.0000	0.0000	0.0000	0.0000	0.0000	0.0000	0.0000	0.0000
1	0.8108	0.5147	0.2839	0.2272	0.1407	0.0635	0.0261	0.0137	0.0098	0.0033	0.0010	0.0003	0.0001	0.0000	0.0000	0.0000	0.0000	0.0000	0.0000	0.0000	0.0000	0.0000	0.0000
2	0.9571	0.7892	0.5614	0.4868	0.3518	0.1971	0.0994	0.0594	0.0451	0.0183	0.0066	0.0021	0.0006	0.0001	0.0000	0.0000	0.0000	0.0000	0.0000	0.0000	0.0000	0.0000	0.0000
3	0.9930	0.9316	0.7899	0.7291	0.5981	0.4050	0.2459	0.1659	0.1339	0.0651	0.0281	0.0106	0.0035	0.0009	0.0002	0.0001	0.0000	0.0000	0.0000	0.0000	0.0000	0.0000	0.0000
4	0.9991	0.9830	0.9209	0.8866	0.7982	0.6302	0.4499	0.3391	0.2892	0.1666	0.0853	0.0384	0.0149	0.0049	0.0013	0.0008	0.0003	0.0000	0.0000	0.0000	0.0000	0.0000	0.0000
5	0.9999	0.9967	0.9765	0.9622	0.9183	0.8103	0.6598	0.5469	0.4900	0.3288	0.1976	0.1051	0.0486	0.0191	0.0062	0.0040	0.0016	0.0003	0.0000	0.0000	0.0000	0.0000	0.0000
6	1.0000	0.9995	0.9944	0.9899	0.9733	0.9204	0.8247	0.7374	0.6881	0.5272	0.3660	0.2272	0.1241	0.0583	0.0229	0.0159	0.0071	0.0016	0.0002	0.0000	0.0000	0.0000	0.0000
7	1.0000	0.9999	0.9989	0.9979	0.9930	0.9729	0.9256	0.8735	0.8406	0.7161	0.5629	0.4018	0.2559	0.1423	0.0671	0.0500	0.0257	0.0075	0.0015	0.0004	0.0002	0.0000	0.0000
8	1.0000	1.0000	0.9998	0.9996	0.9985	0.9925	0.9743	0.9500	0.9329	0.8577	0.7441	0.5982	0.4371	0.2839	0.1594	0.1265	0.0744	0.0271	0.0070	0.0021	0.0011	0.0001	0.0000
9	1.0000	1.0000	1.0000	1.0000	0.9998	0.9984	0.9929	0.9841	0.9771	0.9417	0.8759	0.7728	0.6340	0.4728	0.3119	0.2626	0.1753	0.0796	0.0267	0.0101	0.0056	0.0005	0.0000
10	1.0000	1.0000	1.0000	1.0000	1.0000	0.9997	0.9984	0.9960	0.9938	0.9809	0.9514	0.8949	0.8024	0.6712	0.5100	0.4531	0.3402	0.1897	0.0817	0.0378	0.0235	0.0033	0.0001
11	1.0000	1.0000	1.0000	1.0000	1.0000	1.0000	0.9997	0.9992	0.9987	0.9951	0.9851	0.9616	0.9147	0.8334	0.7108	0.6609	0.5501	0.3698	0.2018	0.1134	0.0791	0.0170	0.0009
12	1.0000	1.0000	1.0000	1.0000	1.0000	1.0000	1.0000	0.9999	0.9998	0.9991	0.9965	0.9894	0.9719	0.9349	0.8661	0.8341	0.7541	0.5950	0.4019	0.2709	0.2101	0.0684	0.0070
13	1.0000	1.0000	1.0000	1.0000	1.0000	1.0000	1.0000	1.0000	1.0000	0.9999	0.9994	0.9979	0.9934	0.9817	0.9549	0.9406	0.9006	0.8029	0.6482	0.5132	0.4386	0.2108	0.0429
14	1.0000	1.0000	1.0000	1.0000	1.0000	1.0000	1.0000	1.0000	1.0000	1.0000	0.9999	0.9997	0.9990	0.9967	0.9902	0.9863	0.9739	0.9365	0.8593	0.7728	0.7161	0.4853	0.1892
15	1.0000	1.0000	1.0000	1.0000	1.0000	1.0000	1.0000	1.0000	1.0000	1.0000	1.0000	1.0000	0.9999	0.9997	0.9990	0.9985	0.9967	0.9900	0.9719	0.9459	0.9257	0.8147	0.5599
16	1.0000	1.0000	1.0000	1.0000	1.0000	1.0000	1.0000	1.0000	1.0000	1.0000	1.0000	1.0000	1.0000	1.0000	1.0000	1.0000	1.0000	1.0000	1.0000	1.0000	1.0000	1.0000	1.0000

CUMULATIVE BINOMIAL PROBABILITIES

n = 18

x \ p	0.05	0.1	0.15	1/6	0.2	0.25	0.3	1/3	0.35	0.4	0.45	0.5	0.55	0.6	0.65	2/3	0.7	0.75	0.8	5/6	0.85	0.9	0.95
0	0.3972	0.1501	0.0536	0.0376	0.0180	0.0056	0.0016	0.0007	0.0004	0.0001	0.0000	0.0000	0.0000	0.0000	0.0000	0.0000	0.0000	0.0000	0.0000	0.0000	0.0000	0.0000	0.0000
1	0.7735	0.4503	0.2241	0.1728	0.0991	0.0395	0.0142	0.0068	0.0046	0.0013	0.0003	0.0001	0.0000	0.0000	0.0000	0.0000	0.0000	0.0000	0.0000	0.0000	0.0000	0.0000	0.0000
2	0.9419	0.7338	0.4797	0.4027	0.2713	0.1353	0.0600	0.0326	0.0236	0.0082	0.0025	0.0007	0.0001	0.0000	0.0000	0.0000	0.0000	0.0000	0.0000	0.0000	0.0000	0.0000	0.0000
3	0.9891	0.9018	0.7202	0.6479	0.5010	0.3057	0.1646	0.1017	0.0783	0.0328	0.0120	0.0038	0.0010	0.0002	0.0000	0.0000	0.0000	0.0000	0.0000	0.0000	0.0000	0.0000	0.0000
4	0.9985	0.9718	0.8794	0.8318	0.7164	0.5187	0.3327	0.2311	0.1886	0.0942	0.0411	0.0154	0.0049	0.0013	0.0003	0.0001	0.0000	0.0000	0.0000	0.0000	0.0000	0.0000	0.0000
5	0.9998	0.9936	0.9581	0.9347	0.8671	0.7175	0.5344	0.4122	0.3550	0.2088	0.1077	0.0481	0.0183	0.0058	0.0014	0.0009	0.0003	0.0000	0.0000	0.0000	0.0000	0.0000	0.0000
6	1.0000	0.9988	0.9882	0.9794	0.9487	0.8610	0.7217	0.6085	0.5491	0.3743	0.2258	0.1189	0.0537	0.0203	0.0062	0.0039	0.0014	0.0002	0.0000	0.0000	0.0000	0.0000	0.0000
7	1.0000	0.9998	0.9973	0.9947	0.9837	0.9431	0.8593	0.7767	0.7283	0.5634	0.3915	0.2403	0.1280	0.0576	0.0212	0.0144	0.0061	0.0012	0.0002	0.0000	0.0000	0.0000	0.0000
8	1.0000	1.0000	0.9995	0.9989	0.9957	0.9807	0.9404	0.8924	0.8609	0.7368	0.5778	0.4073	0.2527	0.1347	0.0597	0.0433	0.0210	0.0054	0.0009	0.0002	0.0001	0.0000	0.0000
9	1.0000	1.0000	0.9999	0.9998	0.9991	0.9946	0.9790	0.9567	0.9403	0.8653	0.7473	0.5927	0.4222	0.2632	0.1391	0.1076	0.0596	0.0193	0.0043	0.0011	0.0005	0.0000	0.0000
10	1.0000	1.0000	1.0000	1.0000	0.9998	0.9988	0.9939	0.9856	0.9788	0.9424	0.8720	0.7597	0.6085	0.4366	0.2717	0.2233	0.1407	0.0569	0.0163	0.0053	0.0027	0.0002	0.0000
11	1.0000	1.0000	1.0000	1.0000	1.0000	0.9998	0.9986	0.9961	0.9938	0.9797	0.9463	0.8811	0.7742	0.6257	0.4509	0.3915	0.2783	0.1390	0.0513	0.0206	0.0118	0.0012	0.0000
12	1.0000	1.0000	1.0000	1.0000	1.0000	1.0000	0.9997	0.9991	0.9986	0.9942	0.9817	0.9519	0.8923	0.7912	0.6450	0.5878	0.4656	0.2825	0.1329	0.0653	0.0419	0.0064	0.0002
13	1.0000	1.0000	1.0000	1.0000	1.0000	1.0000	1.0000	0.9999	0.9997	0.9987	0.9951	0.9846	0.9589	0.9058	0.8114	0.7689	0.6673	0.4813	0.2836	0.1682	0.1206	0.0282	0.0015
14	1.0000	1.0000	1.0000	1.0000	1.0000	1.0000	1.0000	1.0000	1.0000	0.9998	0.9990	0.9962	0.9880	0.9672	0.9217	0.8983	0.8354	0.6943	0.4990	0.3521	0.2798	0.0982	0.0109
15	1.0000	1.0000	1.0000	1.0000	1.0000	1.0000	1.0000	1.0000	1.0000	1.0000	0.9999	0.9993	0.9975	0.9918	0.9764	0.9674	0.9400	0.8647	0.7287	0.5973	0.5203	0.2662	0.0581
16	1.0000	1.0000	1.0000	1.0000	1.0000	1.0000	1.0000	1.0000	1.0000	1.0000	1.0000	0.9999	0.9997	0.9987	0.9954	0.9932	0.9858	0.9605	0.9009	0.8272	0.7759	0.5497	0.2265
17	1.0000	1.0000	1.0000	1.0000	1.0000	1.0000	1.0000	1.0000	1.0000	1.0000	1.0000	1.0000	1.0000	0.9999	0.9996	0.9993	0.9984	0.9944	0.9820	0.9624	0.9464	0.8499	0.6028
18	1.0000	1.0000	1.0000	1.0000	1.0000	1.0000	1.0000	1.0000	1.0000	1.0000	1.0000	1.0000	1.0000	1.0000	1.0000	1.0000	1.0000	1.0000	1.0000	1.0000	1.0000	1.0000	1.0000

n = 20

x \ p	0.05	0.1	0.15	1/6	0.2	0.25	0.3	1/3	0.35	0.4	0.45	0.5	0.55	0.6	0.65	2/3	0.7	0.75	0.8	5/6	0.85	0.9	0.95
0	0.3585	0.1216	0.0388	0.0261	0.0115	0.0032	0.0008	0.0003	0.0002	0.0000	0.0000	0.0000	0.0000	0.0000	0.0000	0.0000	0.0000	0.0000	0.0000	0.0000	0.0000	0.0000	0.0000
1	0.7358	0.3917	0.1756	0.1304	0.0692	0.0243	0.0076	0.0033	0.0021	0.0005	0.0001	0.0000	0.0000	0.0000	0.0000	0.0000	0.0000	0.0000	0.0000	0.0000	0.0000	0.0000	0.0000
2	0.9245	0.6769	0.4049	0.3287	0.2061	0.0913	0.0355	0.0176	0.0121	0.0036	0.0009	0.0002	0.0000	0.0000	0.0000	0.0000	0.0000	0.0000	0.0000	0.0000	0.0000	0.0000	0.0000
3	0.9841	0.8670	0.6477	0.5665	0.4114	0.2252	0.1071	0.0604	0.0444	0.0160	0.0049	0.0013	0.0003	0.0000	0.0000	0.0000	0.0000	0.0000	0.0000	0.0000	0.0000	0.0000	0.0000
4	0.9974	0.9568	0.8298	0.7687	0.6296	0.4148	0.2375	0.1515	0.1182	0.0510	0.0189	0.0059	0.0015	0.0003	0.0000	0.0000	0.0000	0.0000	0.0000	0.0000	0.0000	0.0000	0.0000
5	0.9997	0.9887	0.9327	0.8982	0.8042	0.6172	0.4164	0.2972	0.2454	0.1256	0.0553	0.0207	0.0064	0.0016	0.0003	0.0002	0.0000	0.0000	0.0000	0.0000	0.0000	0.0000	0.0000
6	1.0000	0.9976	0.9781	0.9629	0.9133	0.7858	0.6080	0.4793	0.4166	0.2500	0.1299	0.0577	0.0214	0.0065	0.0015	0.0009	0.0003	0.0000	0.0000	0.0000	0.0000	0.0000	0.0000
7	1.0000	0.9996	0.9941	0.9887	0.9679	0.8982	0.7723	0.6615	0.6010	0.4159	0.2520	0.1316	0.0580	0.0210	0.0060	0.0037	0.0013	0.0002	0.0000	0.0000	0.0000	0.0000	0.0000
8	1.0000	0.9999	0.9987	0.9972	0.9900	0.9591	0.8867	0.8095	0.7624	0.5956	0.4143	0.2517	0.1308	0.0565	0.0196	0.0130	0.0051	0.0009	0.0001	0.0000	0.0000	0.0000	0.0000
9	1.0000	1.0000	0.9998	0.9994	0.9974	0.9861	0.9520	0.9081	0.8782	0.7553	0.5914	0.4119	0.2493	0.1275	0.0532	0.0376	0.0171	0.0039	0.0006	0.0001	0.0000	0.0000	0.0000
10	1.0000	1.0000	1.0000	0.9999	0.9994	0.9961	0.9829	0.9624	0.9468	0.8725	0.7507	0.5881	0.4086	0.2447	0.1218	0.0919	0.0480	0.0139	0.0026	0.0006	0.0002	0.0000	0.0000
11	1.0000	1.0000	1.0000	1.0000	0.9999	0.9991	0.9949	0.9870	0.9804	0.9435	0.8692	0.7483	0.5857	0.4044	0.2376	0.1905	0.1133	0.0409	0.0100	0.0028	0.0013	0.0001	0.0000
12	1.0000	1.0000	1.0000	1.0000	1.0000	0.9998	0.9987	0.9963	0.9940	0.9790	0.9420	0.8684	0.7480	0.5841	0.3990	0.3385	0.2277	0.1018	0.0321	0.0113	0.0059	0.0004	0.0000
13	1.0000	1.0000	1.0000	1.0000	1.0000	1.0000	0.9997	0.9991	0.9985	0.9935	0.9786	0.9423	0.8701	0.7500	0.5834	0.5207	0.3920	0.2142	0.0867	0.0371	0.0219	0.0024	0.0000
14	1.0000	1.0000	1.0000	1.0000	1.0000	1.0000	1.0000	0.9998	0.9997	0.9984	0.9936	0.9793	0.9447	0.8744	0.7546	0.7028	0.5836	0.3828	0.1958	0.1018	0.0673	0.0113	0.0003
15	1.0000	1.0000	1.0000	1.0000	1.0000	1.0000	1.0000	1.0000	1.0000	0.9997	0.9985	0.9941	0.9811	0.9490	0.8818	0.8485	0.7625	0.5852	0.3704	0.2313	0.1702	0.0432	0.0026
16	1.0000	1.0000	1.0000	1.0000	1.0000	1.0000	1.0000	1.0000	1.0000	1.0000	0.9997	0.9987	0.9951	0.9840	0.9556	0.9396	0.8929	0.7748	0.5886	0.4335	0.3523	0.1330	0.0159
17	1.0000	1.0000	1.0000	1.0000	1.0000	1.0000	1.0000	1.0000	1.0000	1.0000	1.0000	0.9998	0.9991	0.9964	0.9879	0.9824	0.9645	0.9087	0.7939	0.6713	0.5951	0.3231	0.0755
18	1.0000	1.0000	1.0000	1.0000	1.0000	1.0000	1.0000	1.0000	1.0000	1.0000	1.0000	1.0000	0.9999	0.9995	0.9979	0.9967	0.9924	0.9757	0.9308	0.8696	0.8244	0.6083	0.2642
19	1.0000	1.0000	1.0000	1.0000	1.0000	1.0000	1.0000	1.0000	1.0000	1.0000	1.0000	1.0000	1.0000	1.0000	0.9999	0.9997	0.9992	0.9968	0.9885	0.9739	0.9612	0.8784	0.6415
20	1.0000	1.0000	1.0000	1.0000	1.0000	1.0000	1.0000	1.0000	1.0000	1.0000	1.0000	1.0000	1.0000	1.0000	1.0000	1.0000	1.0000	1.0000	1.0000	1.0000	1.0000	1.0000	1.0000

CUMULATIVE BINOMIAL PROBABILITIES

n = 25 p	0.05	0.1	0.15	1/6	0.2	0.25	0.3	1/3	0.35	0.4	0.45	0.5	0.55	0.6	0.65	2/3	0.7	0.75	0.8	5/6	0.85	0.9	0.95
x = 0	0.2774	0.0718	0.0172	0.0105	0.0038	0.0008	0.0001	0.0000	0.0000	0.0000	0.0000	0.0000	0.0000	0.0000	0.0000	0.0000	0.0000	0.0000	0.0000	0.0000	0.0000	0.0000	0.0000
1	0.6424	0.2712	0.0931	0.0629	0.0274	0.0070	0.0016	0.0005	0.0003	0.0001	0.0000	0.0000	0.0000	0.0000	0.0000	0.0000	0.0000	0.0000	0.0000	0.0000	0.0000	0.0000	0.0000
2	0.8729	0.5371	0.2537	0.1887	0.0982	0.0321	0.0090	0.0035	0.0021	0.0004	0.0001	0.0000	0.0000	0.0000	0.0000	0.0000	0.0000	0.0000	0.0000	0.0000	0.0000	0.0000	0.0000
3	0.9659	0.7636	0.4711	0.3816	0.2340	0.0962	0.0332	0.0149	0.0097	0.0024	0.0005	0.0001	0.0000	0.0000	0.0000	0.0000	0.0000	0.0000	0.0000	0.0000	0.0000	0.0000	0.0000
4	0.9928	0.9020	0.6821	0.5937	0.4207	0.2137	0.0905	0.0462	0.0320	0.0095	0.0023	0.0005	0.0001	0.0000	0.0000	0.0000	0.0000	0.0000	0.0000	0.0000	0.0000	0.0000	0.0000
5	0.9988	0.9666	0.8385	0.7720	0.6167	0.3783	0.1935	0.1120	0.0826	0.0294	0.0086	0.0020	0.0004	0.0001	0.0000	0.0000	0.0000	0.0000	0.0000	0.0000	0.0000	0.0000	0.0000
6	0.9998	0.9905	0.9305	0.8908	0.7800	0.5611	0.3407	0.2215	0.1734	0.0736	0.0258	0.0073	0.0016	0.0003	0.0000	0.0000	0.0000	0.0000	0.0000	0.0000	0.0000	0.0000	0.0000
7	1.0000	0.9977	0.9745	0.9553	0.8909	0.7265	0.5118	0.3703	0.3061	0.1536	0.0639	0.0216	0.0058	0.0012	0.0002	0.0001	0.0000	0.0000	0.0000	0.0000	0.0000	0.0000	0.0000
8	1.0000	0.9995	0.9920	0.9843	0.9532	0.8506	0.6769	0.5376	0.4668	0.2735	0.1340	0.0539	0.0174	0.0043	0.0008	0.0004	0.0001	0.0000	0.0000	0.0000	0.0000	0.0000	0.0000
9	1.0000	0.9999	0.9979	0.9953	0.9827	0.9287	0.8106	0.6956	0.6303	0.4246	0.2424	0.1148	0.0440	0.0132	0.0029	0.0016	0.0005	0.0000	0.0000	0.0000	0.0000	0.0000	0.0000
10	1.0000	1.0000	0.9995	0.9988	0.9944	0.9703	0.9022	0.8220	0.7712	0.5858	0.3843	0.2122	0.0960	0.0344	0.0093	0.0056	0.0018	0.0002	0.0000	0.0000	0.0000	0.0000	0.0000
11	1.0000	1.0000	0.9999	0.9997	0.9985	0.9893	0.9558	0.9082	0.8746	0.7323	0.5426	0.3450	0.1827	0.0778	0.0255	0.0164	0.0060	0.0009	0.0001	0.0000	0.0000	0.0000	0.0000
12	1.0000	1.0000	1.0000	0.9999	0.9996	0.9966	0.9825	0.9585	0.9396	0.8462	0.6937	0.5000	0.3063	0.1538	0.0604	0.0415	0.0175	0.0034	0.0004	0.0001	0.0000	0.0000	0.0000
13	1.0000	1.0000	1.0000	1.0000	0.9999	0.9991	0.9940	0.9836	0.9745	0.9222	0.8173	0.6550	0.4574	0.2677	0.1254	0.0918	0.0442	0.0107	0.0015	0.0003	0.0001	0.0000	0.0000
14	1.0000	1.0000	1.0000	1.0000	1.0000	0.9998	0.9982	0.9944	0.9907	0.9656	0.9040	0.7878	0.6157	0.4142	0.2288	0.1780	0.0978	0.0297	0.0056	0.0012	0.0005	0.0000	0.0000
15	1.0000	1.0000	1.0000	1.0000	1.0000	1.0000	0.9995	0.9984	0.9971	0.9868	0.9560	0.8852	0.7576	0.5754	0.3697	0.3044	0.1894	0.0713	0.0173	0.0047	0.0021	0.0001	0.0000
16	1.0000	1.0000	1.0000	1.0000	1.0000	1.0000	0.9999	0.9996	0.9992	0.9957	0.9826	0.9461	0.8660	0.7265	0.5332	0.4624	0.3231	0.1494	0.0468	0.0157	0.0080	0.0005	0.0000
17	1.0000	1.0000	1.0000	1.0000	1.0000	1.0000	1.0000	0.9999	0.9998	0.9988	0.9942	0.9784	0.9361	0.8464	0.6939	0.6297	0.4882	0.2735	0.1091	0.0447	0.0255	0.0023	0.0000
18	1.0000	1.0000	1.0000	1.0000	1.0000	1.0000	1.0000	1.0000	1.0000	0.9997	0.9984	0.9927	0.9742	0.9264	0.8266	0.7785	0.6593	0.4389	0.2200	0.1092	0.0695	0.0095	0.0002
19	1.0000	1.0000	1.0000	1.0000	1.0000	1.0000	1.0000	1.0000	1.0000	0.9999	0.9996	0.9980	0.9914	0.9706	0.9174	0.8880	0.8065	0.6217	0.3833	0.2280	0.1615	0.0334	0.0012
20	1.0000	1.0000	1.0000	1.0000	1.0000	1.0000	1.0000	1.0000	1.0000	1.0000	0.9999	0.9995	0.9977	0.9905	0.9680	0.9538	0.9095	0.7863	0.5793	0.4063	0.3179	0.0980	0.0072
21	1.0000	1.0000	1.0000	1.0000	1.0000	1.0000	1.0000	1.0000	1.0000	1.0000	1.0000	0.9999	0.9995	0.9976	0.9903	0.9851	0.9668	0.9038	0.7660	0.6184	0.5289	0.2364	0.0341
22	1.0000	1.0000	1.0000	1.0000	1.0000	1.0000	1.0000	1.0000	1.0000	1.0000	1.0000	1.0000	0.9999	0.9996	0.9979	0.9965	0.9910	0.9679	0.9018	0.8113	0.7463	0.4629	0.1271
23	1.0000	1.0000	1.0000	1.0000	1.0000	1.0000	1.0000	1.0000	1.0000	1.0000	1.0000	1.0000	1.0000	0.9999	0.9997	0.9995	0.9984	0.9930	0.9726	0.9371	0.9069	0.7288	0.3576
24	1.0000	1.0000	1.0000	1.0000	1.0000	1.0000	1.0000	1.0000	1.0000	1.0000	1.0000	1.0000	1.0000	1.0000	1.0000	1.0000	0.9999	0.9992	0.9962	0.9895	0.9828	0.9282	0.7226
25	1.0000	1.0000	1.0000	1.0000	1.0000	1.0000	1.0000	1.0000	1.0000	1.0000	1.0000	1.0000	1.0000	1.0000	1.0000	1.0000	1.0000	1.0000	1.0000	1.0000	1.0000	1.0000	1.0000

CUMULATIVE BINOMIAL PROBABILITIES

$n = 30$ p	0.05	0.1	0.15	1/6	0.2	0.25	0.3	1/3	0.35	0.4	0.45	0.5	0.55	0.6	0.65	2/3	0.7	0.75	0.8	5/6	0.85	0.9	0.95
x = 0	0.2146	0.0424	0.0076	0.0042	0.0012	0.0002	0.0000	0.0000	0.0000	0.0000	0.0000	0.0000	0.0000	0.0000	0.0000	0.0000	0.0000	0.0000	0.0000	0.0000	0.0000	0.0000	0.0000
1	0.5535	0.1837	0.0480	0.0295	0.0105	0.0020	0.0003	0.0001	0.0000	0.0000	0.0000	0.0000	0.0000	0.0000	0.0000	0.0000	0.0000	0.0000	0.0000	0.0000	0.0000	0.0000	0.0000
2	0.8122	0.4114	0.1514	0.1028	0.0442	0.0106	0.0021	0.0007	0.0003	0.0000	0.0000	0.0000	0.0000	0.0000	0.0000	0.0000	0.0000	0.0000	0.0000	0.0000	0.0000	0.0000	0.0000
3	0.9392	0.6474	0.3217	0.2396	0.1227	0.0374	0.0093	0.0033	0.0019	0.0003	0.0000	0.0000	0.0000	0.0000	0.0000	0.0000	0.0000	0.0000	0.0000	0.0000	0.0000	0.0000	0.0000
4	0.9844	0.8245	0.5245	0.4243	0.2552	0.0979	0.0302	0.0122	0.0075	0.0015	0.0002	0.0000	0.0000	0.0000	0.0000	0.0000	0.0000	0.0000	0.0000	0.0000	0.0000	0.0000	0.0000
5	0.9967	0.9268	0.7106	0.6164	0.4275	0.2026	0.0766	0.0355	0.0233	0.0057	0.0011	0.0002	0.0000	0.0000	0.0000	0.0000	0.0000	0.0000	0.0000	0.0000	0.0000	0.0000	0.0000
6	0.9994	0.9742	0.8474	0.7765	0.6070	0.3481	0.1595	0.0838	0.0586	0.0172	0.0040	0.0007	0.0001	0.0000	0.0000	0.0000	0.0000	0.0000	0.0000	0.0000	0.0000	0.0000	0.0000
7	0.9999	0.9922	0.9302	0.8863	0.7608	0.5143	0.2814	0.1668	0.1238	0.0435	0.0121	0.0026	0.0004	0.0000	0.0000	0.0000	0.0000	0.0000	0.0000	0.0000	0.0000	0.0000	0.0000
8	1.0000	0.9980	0.9722	0.9494	0.8713	0.6736	0.4315	0.2860	0.2247	0.0940	0.0312	0.0081	0.0016	0.0002	0.0000	0.0000	0.0000	0.0000	0.0000	0.0000	0.0000	0.0000	0.0000
9	1.0000	0.9995	0.9903	0.9803	0.9389	0.8034	0.5888	0.4317	0.3575	0.1763	0.0694	0.0214	0.0050	0.0009	0.0001	0.0000	0.0000	0.0000	0.0000	0.0000	0.0000	0.0000	0.0000
10	1.0000	0.9999	0.9971	0.9933	0.9744	0.8943	0.7304	0.5848	0.5078	0.2915	0.1350	0.0494	0.0138	0.0029	0.0004	0.0002	0.0000	0.0000	0.0000	0.0000	0.0000	0.0000	0.0000
11	1.0000	1.0000	0.9992	0.9980	0.9905	0.9493	0.8407	0.7239	0.6548	0.4311	0.2327	0.1002	0.0334	0.0083	0.0014	0.0007	0.0002	0.0000	0.0000	0.0000	0.0000	0.0000	0.0000
12	1.0000	1.0000	0.9998	0.9995	0.9969	0.9784	0.9155	0.8340	0.7802	0.5785	0.3592	0.1808	0.0714	0.0212	0.0045	0.0025	0.0006	0.0001	0.0000	0.0000	0.0000	0.0000	0.0000
13	1.0000	1.0000	1.0000	0.9999	0.9991	0.9918	0.9599	0.9102	0.8737	0.7145	0.5025	0.2923	0.1356	0.0481	0.0124	0.0072	0.0021	0.0002	0.0000	0.0000	0.0000	0.0000	0.0000
14	1.0000	1.0000	1.0000	1.0000	0.9998	0.9973	0.9831	0.9565	0.9348	0.8246	0.6448	0.4278	0.2309	0.0971	0.0301	0.0188	0.0064	0.0008	0.0001	0.0000	0.0000	0.0000	0.0000
15	1.0000	1.0000	1.0000	1.0000	0.9999	0.9992	0.9936	0.9812	0.9699	0.9029	0.7691	0.5722	0.3552	0.1754	0.0652	0.0435	0.0169	0.0027	0.0002	0.0000	0.0000	0.0000	0.0000
16	1.0000	1.0000	1.0000	1.0000	1.0000	0.9998	0.9979	0.9928	0.9876	0.9519	0.8644	0.7077	0.4975	0.2855	0.1263	0.0898	0.0401	0.0082	0.0009	0.0001	0.0000	0.0000	0.0000
17	1.0000	1.0000	1.0000	1.0000	1.0000	0.9999	0.9994	0.9975	0.9955	0.9788	0.9286	0.8192	0.6408	0.4215	0.2198	0.1660	0.0845	0.0216	0.0031	0.0005	0.0002	0.0000	0.0000
18	1.0000	1.0000	1.0000	1.0000	1.0000	1.0000	0.9998	0.9993	0.9986	0.9917	0.9666	0.8998	0.7673	0.5689	0.3452	0.2761	0.1593	0.0507	0.0095	0.0020	0.0008	0.0000	0.0000
19	1.0000	1.0000	1.0000	1.0000	1.0000	1.0000	1.0000	0.9998	0.9996	0.9971	0.9862	0.9506	0.8650	0.7085	0.4922	0.4152	0.2696	0.1057	0.0256	0.0067	0.0029	0.0001	0.0000
20	1.0000	1.0000	1.0000	1.0000	1.0000	1.0000	1.0000	1.0000	0.9999	0.9991	0.9950	0.9786	0.9306	0.8237	0.6425	0.5683	0.4112	0.1966	0.0611	0.0197	0.0097	0.0005	0.0000
21	1.0000	1.0000	1.0000	1.0000	1.0000	1.0000	1.0000	1.0000	1.0000	0.9998	0.9984	0.9919	0.9688	0.9060	0.7753	0.7140	0.5685	0.3264	0.1287	0.0506	0.0278	0.0020	0.0000
22	1.0000	1.0000	1.0000	1.0000	1.0000	1.0000	1.0000	1.0000	1.0000	1.0000	0.9996	0.9974	0.9879	0.9565	0.8762	0.8332	0.7186	0.4857	0.2392	0.1137	0.0698	0.0078	0.0001
23	1.0000	1.0000	1.0000	1.0000	1.0000	1.0000	1.0000	1.0000	1.0000	1.0000	0.9999	0.9993	0.9960	0.9828	0.9414	0.9162	0.8405	0.6519	0.3930	0.2235	0.1526	0.0258	0.0006
24	1.0000	1.0000	1.0000	1.0000	1.0000	1.0000	1.0000	1.0000	1.0000	1.0000	1.0000	0.9998	0.9989	0.9943	0.9767	0.9645	0.9234	0.7974	0.5725	0.3836	0.2894	0.0732	0.0033
25	1.0000	1.0000	1.0000	1.0000	1.0000	1.0000	1.0000	1.0000	1.0000	1.0000	1.0000	1.0000	0.9998	0.9985	0.9925	0.9878	0.9698	0.9021	0.7448	0.5757	0.4755	0.1755	0.0156
26	1.0000	1.0000	1.0000	1.0000	1.0000	1.0000	1.0000	1.0000	1.0000	1.0000	1.0000	1.0000	1.0000	0.9997	0.9981	0.9967	0.9907	0.9626	0.8773	0.7604	0.6783	0.3526	0.0608
27	1.0000	1.0000	1.0000	1.0000	1.0000	1.0000	1.0000	1.0000	1.0000	1.0000	1.0000	1.0000	1.0000	1.0000	0.9997	0.9993	0.9979	0.9894	0.9558	0.8972	0.8486	0.5886	0.1878
28	1.0000	1.0000	1.0000	1.0000	1.0000	1.0000	1.0000	1.0000	1.0000	1.0000	1.0000	1.0000	1.0000	1.0000	1.0000	0.9999	0.9997	0.9980	0.9895	0.9705	0.9520	0.8163	0.4465
29	1.0000	1.0000	1.0000	1.0000	1.0000	1.0000	1.0000	1.0000	1.0000	1.0000	1.0000	1.0000	1.0000	1.0000	1.0000	1.0000	1.0000	0.9998	0.9988	0.9958	0.9924	0.9576	0.7854
30	1.0000	1.0000	1.0000	1.0000	1.0000	1.0000	1.0000	1.0000	1.0000	1.0000	1.0000	1.0000	1.0000	1.0000	1.0000	1.0000	1.0000	1.0000	1.0000	1.0000	1.0000	1.0000	1.0000

THE NORMAL DISTRIBUTION FUNCTION

If Z has a normal distribution with mean 0 and variance 1 then, for each value of z, the table gives the value of $\Phi(z)$, where

$$\Phi(z) = \mathbb{P}[Z \le z].$$

For negative values of z use $\Phi(-z) = 1 - \Phi(z)$.

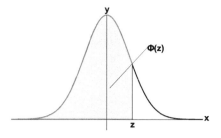

z	0	1	2	3	4	5	6	7	8	9	1	2	3	4	5	6	7	8	9
															ADD				
0.0	0.5000	0.5040	0.5080	0.5120	0.5160	0.5199	0.5239	0.5279	0.5319	0.5359	4	8	12	16	20	24	28	32	36
0.1	0.5398	0.5438	0.5478	0.5517	0.5557	0.5596	0.5636	0.5675	0.5714	0.5753	4	8	12	16	20	24	28	32	36
0.2	0.5793	0.5832	0.5871	0.5910	0.5948	0.5987	0.6026	0.6064	0.6103	0.6141	4	8	12	15	19	23	27	31	35
0.3	0.6179	0.6217	0.6255	0.6293	0.6331	0.6368	0.6406	0.6443	0.6480	0.6517	4	7	11	15	19	22	26	30	34
0.4	0.6554	0.6591	0.6628	0.6664	0.6700	0.6736	0.6772	0.6808	0.6844	0.6879	4	7	11	14	18	22	25	29	32
0.5	0.6915	0.6950	0.6985	0.7019	0.7054	0.7088	0.7123	0.7157	0.7190	0.7224	3	7	10	14	17	20	24	27	31
0.6	0.7257	0.7291	0.7324	0.7357	0.7389	0.7422	0.7454	0.7486	0.7517	0.7549	3	7	10	13	16	19	23	26	29
0.7	0.7580	0.7611	0.7642	0.7673	0.7704	0.7734	0.7764	0.7794	0.7823	0.7852	3	6	9	12	15	18	21	24	27
0.8	0.7881	0.7910	0.7939	0.7967	0.7995	0.8023	0.8051	0.8078	0.8106	0.8133	3	5	8	11	14	16	19	22	25
0.9	0.8159	0.8186	0.8212	0.8238	0.8264	0.8289	0.8315	0.8340	0.8365	0.8389	3	5	8	10	13	15	18	20	23
1.0	0.8413	0.8438	0.8461	0.8485	0.8508	0.8531	0.8554	0.8577	0.8599	0.8621	2	5	7	9	12	14	16	19	21
1.1	0.8643	0.8665	0.8686	0.8708	0.8729	0.8749	0.8770	0.8790	0.8810	0.8830	2	4	6	8	10	12	14	16	18
1.2	0.8849	0.8869	0.8888	0.8907	0.8925	0.8944	0.8962	0.8980	0.8997	0.9015	2	4	6	7	9	11	13	15	17
1.3	0.9032	0.9049	0.9066	0.9082	0.9099	0.9115	0.9131	0.9147	0.9162	0.9177	2	3	5	6	8	10	11	13	14
1.4	0.9192	0.9207	0.9222	0.9236	0.9251	0.9265	0.9279	0.9292	0.9306	0.9319	1	3	4	6	7	8	10	11	13
1.5	0.9332	0.9345	0.9357	0.9370	0.9382	0.9394	0.9406	0.9418	0.9429	0.9441	1	2	4	5	6	7	8	10	11
1.6	0.9452	0.9463	0.9474	0.9484	0.9495	0.9505	0.9515	0.9525	0.9535	0.9545	1	2	3	4	5	6	7	8	9
1.7	0.9554	0.9564	0.9573	0.9582	0.9591	0.9599	0.9608	0.9616	0.9625	0.9633	1	2	3	4	4	5	6	7	8
1.8	0.9641	0.9649	0.9656	0.9664	0.9671	0.9678	0.9686	0.9693	0.9699	0.9706	1	1	2	3	4	4	5	6	6
1.9	0.9713	0.9719	0.9726	0.9732	0.9738	0.9744	0.9750	0.9756	0.9761	0.9767	1	1	2	2	3	4	4	5	5
2.0	0.9772	0.9778	0.9783	0.9788	0.9793	0.9798	0.9803	0.9808	0.9812	0.9817	0	1	1	2	2	3	3	4	4
2.1	0.9821	0.9826	0.9830	0.9834	0.9838	0.9842	0.9846	0.9850	0.9854	0.9857	0	1	1	2	2	2	3	3	4
2.2	0.9861	0.9864	0.9868	0.9871	0.9875	0.9878	0.9881	0.9884	0.9887	0.9890	0	1	1	1	2	2	2	3	3
2.3	0.9893	0.9896	0.9898	0.9901	0.9904	0.9906	0.9909	0.9911	0.9913	0.9916	0	1	1	1	1	2	2	2	2
2.4	0.9918	0.9920	0.9922	0.9925	0.9927	0.9929	0.9931	0.9932	0.9934	0.9936	0	0	1	1	1	1	1	2	2
2.5	0.9938	0.9940	0.9941	0.9943	0.9945	0.9946	0.9948	0.9949	0.9951	0.9952	0	0	0	1	1	1	1	1	1
2.6	0.9953	0.9955	0.9956	0.9957	0.9959	0.9960	0.9961	0.9962	0.9963	0.9964	0	0	0	0	1	1	1	1	1
2.7	0.9965	0.9966	0.9967	0.9968	0.9969	0.9970	0.9971	0.9972	0.9973	0.9974	0	0	0	0	0	1	1	1	1
2.8	0.9974	0.9975	0.9976	0.9977	0.9977	0.9978	0.9979	0.9979	0.9980	0.9981	0	0	0	0	0	0	0	1	1
2.9	0.9981	0.9982	0.9982	0.9983	0.9984	0.9984	0.9985	0.9985	0.9986	0.9986	0	0	0	0	0	0	0	0	0

CRITICAL VALUES FOR THE NORMAL DISTRIBUTION

If Z has normal distribution with mean 0 and variance 1 then, for each value of p, the table gives the value of z such that

$$\mathbb{P}[Z \le z] = p.$$

p	0.75	0.90	0.95	0.975	0.99	0.995	0.9975	0.999	0.9995
z	0.674	1.282	1.645	1.960	2.326	2.576	2.807	3.090	3.291